Praise for *1,000 Foods to Eat Before You Die*

"Mimi Sheraton was one of the few critics or writers on food who, had she expressed displeasure with me, would have caused me to consider quitting the business. As a chef, I feared and respected her. As a writer and observer and enthusiast—as someone who travels largely on his stomach—I can tell you that **what Mimi doesn't know is hardly worth knowing.** This fat, comprehensive guide to the 1,000 foods to eat before dying is just that: 1,000 foods you NEED to try, urgently. Read . . . and seek."

—**ANTHONY BOURDAIN,** AUTHOR, HOST, ENTHUSIAST

. . . .

"There is no one more authoritative than Mimi Sheraton to help you discover *1,000 Foods to Eat Before You Die*. And that's because she has actually eaten each and every one of them with gusto, and with one of the world's most discerning and educated palates. **This book may just become my go-to source for new menu ideas at our restaurants!**"

—**DANNY MEYER,** RESTAURATEUR AND AUTHOR OF
SETTING THE TABLE: THE TRANSFORMING POWER OF HOSPITALITY IN BUSINESS

. . . .

"We are forever grateful to the incomparable Mimi Sheraton for her knowledge and certainty as a journalist and critic."

—**THOMAS KELLER,** CHEF/PROPRIETOR OF THE FRENCH LAUNDRY

. . . .

"Few people in the world have the experience that Mimi Sheraton brings to the subject of food. **I'll be spending the rest of my days knocking off dish by dish** in *1,000 Foods to Eat Before You Die*."

—**BOBBY FLAY,** CHEF, RESTAURATEUR

. . . .

"Informative, evocative, and enterta
**off the foods you've eaten and to
haven't yet enjoyed."**

—**MARCUS SAMUELSSON,** COOKBOOK AUTH

D0440681

"I'm in awe of Mimi's ability to compile such **a beautiful and insightful book,** again proving why she is one of the most important food writers of our time. This book is **a gift to all food lovers,** a thorough, delicious guide to the best dishes and ingredients around the globe."

—DANIEL HUMM, CHEF/OWNER, ELEVEN MADISON PARK AND THE NOMAD

. . . .

"If you love food, this is a book to read before you die! **Mimi Sheraton's knowledge of the world's foods is legendary, as is the sharpness of her opinions.** On nearly every page of *1,000 Foods to Eat Before You Die,* I've learned something new or honed my own judgment on hers. And with its links to sources and resources all over the world, I'll be dining in and out on it for years to come."

—HAROLD MCGEE, AUTHOR OF *ON FOOD AND COOKING: THE SCIENCE AND LORE OF THE KITCHEN* AND *KEYS TO GOOD COOKING: A GUIDE TO MAKING THE BEST OF FOOD AND RECIPES*

. . . .

"Who else would you trust on topics ranging from English jellied eel to hokey pokey ice cream from New Zealand and everything in between? Only the well-seasoned Mimi Sheraton."

—GRANT ACHATZ, CHEF/CO-OWNER OF ALINEA, NEXT, THE AVIARY

. . . .

"Mimi Sheraton has always reminded us that eating is an activity as much of the imagination as of the palate and the tongue. In *1,000 Foods to Eat Before You Die,* she reaps the rich harvest of her prodigious gifts of endless curiosity, lightly worn knowledge, and elegance of style. She has provided us with **a feast to be tasted and savored with the greatest pleasure."**

—MARY GORDON, AUTHOR OF *THE LIAR'S WIFE* AND *FINAL PAYMENTS*

. . . .

"This book reads like **a map to many of the great food experiences the world has to offer.** A valuable addition to any food library."

—ERIC RIPERT, CHEF, LE BERNARDIN, AUTHOR OF *AVEC ERIC: A CULINARY JOURNEY WITH ERIC RIPERT*

"Gargantuan in its appetite and encyclopedic in its scope, this is the most comprehensive book ever written on the great foods of the world. The book every food writer dreams of writing. **A tour de force."**

—STEVEN RAICHLEN, AUTHOR OF THE *BARBECUE! BIBLE* COOKBOOKS
AND HOST OF *PRIMAL GRILL*

. . . .

"Mimi Sheraton has written the definitive international guide for food lovers. Each page is **filled with culinary treasures and surprises,** presented in an engaging and entertaining manner. Reading and dining pleasure awaits you!"

—DREW NIEPORENT, RESTAURATEUR, TRIBECA GRILL, NOBU, BÂTARD

. . . .

"To this non-foodie, *1,000 Foods to Eat Before You Die* was a revelation—**perhaps the most useful travel guide on my shelf.** I'm heading to Marrakesh for tagine right now."

—ANDREW MCCARTHY, TRAVEL WRITER, ACTOR, DIRECTOR

. . . .

"Mimi Sheraton is a national treasure. Her knowledge of food can't be beat—if anyone knows the 1,000 foods of a lifetime, it's Mimi."

—DANIEL BOULUD, CHEF, RESTAURANT DANIEL, NEW YORK CITY

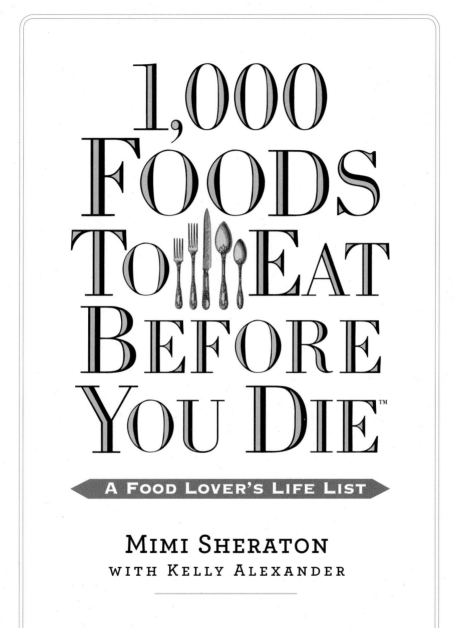

1,000 FOODS TO EAT BEFORE YOU DIE™

A FOOD LOVER'S LIFE LIST

MIMI SHERATON
WITH KELLY ALEXANDER

WORKMAN PUBLISHING, NEW YORK

1,000 . . . BEFORE YOU DIE is a registered trademark of
Workman Publishing Co., Inc.

1,000 FOODS TO EAT BEFORE YOU DIE
is a trademark of Workman Publishing Co., Inc.

Library of Congress Cataloging-in-Publication Data is available.

ISBNs: 978-0-7611-4168-6 (pb); 978-0-7611-8554-3 (hc)

Design by Janet Vicario
and Orlando Adiao

Photo research by Bobby Walsh,
Melissa Lucier, and Jenna Bascom

Photo credits appear on pages 987–990.

Workman books are available at special discounts when
purchased in bulk for premiums and sales promotions
as well as or fund-raising or educational use.
Special editions or book excerpts can also be created to
specification. For details, contact the Special Sales Director
at the address below, or send an email to
specialmarkets@workman.com.

Workman Publishing Company, Inc.
225 Varick Street
New York, NY 10014-4381
workman.com

Printed in South Korea
First printing December 2014

10 9 8 7 6 5 4

"The joys of the table belong equally to all ages, conditions, countries, and times; they mix with all other pleasures, and remain the last to console us for their loss."

—JEAN ANTHELME BRILLAT-SAVARIN

Dedication

To my son, Marc Falcone,
my daughter-in-law, Caitlin Halligan,
and my granddaughter, Anna Falcone,
with love and gratitude for their support,
companionship, and affection,
and for the joys they always bring.

And to the memory of our adored
Richard Falcone, the husband, father,
father-in-law, and grandfather whom we
shall always love and miss.

Acknowledgments

⊘∬∫~

I n a work of this size that took so many years to complete, it should be no surprise that there is a very long of list of wonderful people to whom I am indebted for their insights, expertise, willingness to help, and, perhaps most of all, friendship.

During my sixty years as a food writer, I have worked with many fine publishers, but never with one so patient, dedicated, cooperative, and helpful as Workman Publishing. Primary credit for that goes to the company's founder, Peter Workman, who agreed to do this book and who believed in it enough to never even hint at pulling the plug after one deadline gave way to another. His commitment to quality books and the integrity he brought to publishing permeates the company he left behind. I shall always regret that he did not live to see this come to fruition and I hope he would have thought it all worth the wait.

My first entry into Workman came via its affable executive editor, Suzanne Rafer, who continued to guide, cajole, and encourage as work progressed. Similarly, Suzie Bolotin, editorial director, also never nagged or threatened me but always kept an overall eye as material went through, making valuable suggestions that I sometimes even took. Above all, the most noble work was done by Margot Herrera, the saintly editor in charge of this project. With her unerring eye for detail and her insistence on accuracy, she bore the brunt of outbursts and exasperations from one who loathes details and the nitty-gritty. Margot never once lost her temper, even as I so often lost mine.

I am also forever indebted to Heather Schwedel, who was always at the other end of an email to straighten out my confusions in scheduling, organization, and to guide me safely whenever I was lost in cyberspace, which was often.

I know I was spared much embarrassment by the work of Caitlin McEwan and Kelly Rummel, who did diligence as fact checkers, and Savannah Ashour, who line-edited the book.

I am grateful also to Workman's art department. That so many divergent entries appear so attractively and functionally is due to the efforts of many, beginning with the combined talents of Janet Vicario, the art director, and Orlando Adiao, the book's designer. Bringing it all to a coherent pass was the meticulous work of the production editor, Kate Karol, assisted by Jessica Rozler, as well as the production manager, Doug Wolff, not to forget the intricacies of the typesetting process overseen by Barbara Peragine.

Entries would not appear so clear and intriguing without the photographs ingeniously unearthed by Anne Kerman's expert photo research team, including Bobby Walsh, Melissa Lucier, and Jenna Bascom. I thank Rachael Mt. Pleasant and Caitlin McEwan for their help with the captions.

Also, for getting the word out by publicizing the book, I offer my deepest appreciation to Workman's director of publicity, Selina Meere, and Noreen Herits, executive publicist.

That this work ever was completed at all is due to the dedicated, invaluable help of two friends and colleagues: Kelly Alexander and Megan Peck.

Kelly Alexander of Chapel Hill, NC, is herself an accomplished food writer who, with Cynthia Harris, coauthored *Hometown Appetites: The Story of Clementine Paddleford, the Forgotten*

Food Writer Who Chronicled How America Ate. Working with my selections and guidelines, Kelly painstakingly and reliably researched and reported a third of the entries in this book.

Megan Peck is a young New York food professional who, on her blog, meganpeckcooks .com, serves up modern riffs on recipes from the cookbooks of her late, influential grandmother, Paula Peck, a dear friend of mine during the 1960s. That made working with Megan a pleasant, sentimental journey as she searched out reliable recipes for the dishes in the book, as well as for retail and mail order sources of foods, information on food festivals, and other assorted details.

In addition, many friends and colleagues in various parts of the world generously came through with tips, suggestions, and local sources, and checked out details for me as I asked for them. Among them are Michael Bauer and Miriam Morgan of the *San Francisco Chronicle,* who answered queries on sources in their food-minded city and its surrounding areas. Similarly, Teresa Byrne-Dodge both personally and through her terrific magazine, *My Table,* offered valuable tips on restaurants in and around Houston. Sara Baer-Sinnott of the Oldways Preservation Trust provided information on the Boston area, and Nathalie Dupree did the same with suggestions for her home city, Charleston, and Atlanta.

My dear friend, the engaging novelist Mary Gordon, was always ready with lists of restaurants she had enjoyed in Rome and Naples while doing research for superb novels and short stories set in those cities. Sarah Humphreys of *Real Simple* magazine checked out Capetown for me during her visit to South Africa.

My cousin and very reliable food judge, Dr. William Wortman of Pasadena, CA, led me to some of his favorite eating places, especially for hamburgers, in and around Los Angeles. In New Orleans, Thomas Lemann did the same.

I'm also grateful to Jenny Glasgow for her information on *bicerin* in Turin, and to Nell Waldman for her research on *shritzlach* (as well as for bringing me a sample from her native Toronto).

Dr. Martha Liao—a lapsed geneticist who lives in New York and Beijing when she's not touring with her husband, the opera singer Hao Jiang Tian (and who prepares a Peking duck feast whenever he performs in concert)—checked details for me in Beijing. She also provided insights into the preparations for that magical duck, as well as the recipe for glazed pork belly, Dong Bo Rou, on page 763.

Reliable guidance to Japanese cuisine in Paris and Tokyo came from my dear old friend, Kazuko Masui, herself the author of several stunning food books. From Berlin, food journalist Ursula Heinzelmann, whose recently published *Beyond Bratwurst* is an invaluable and discerning history of German food, was always ready with up-to-date suggestions from her native land. So was Trine Hahnemann in Copenhagen, a successful caterer and author of several lovely books on Nordic cooking, the newest of which is *Scandinavian Baking.*

The incomparable food writer Dalia Lamdani offered prized insights into foods and lore of her Israeli homeland. Peter Grünauer, who with his family operates Grünauer restaurant in Kansas City, MO, looked into all sorts of facts whenever he went home to Vienna. Kurt Gutenbrunner of Wallsé and several other fine New York restaurants also always came through with much Austrian culinary wisdom.

To all, I am forever indebted and to all I send love and kisses.

Much love and many kisses also to my wonderful, adorable family who were patient and supportive as I slogged my way through this: my son, Marc, daughter-in-law, Caitlin, and granddaughter, Anna. I can never thank you enough. I only wish that our darling Dick had lived to see this book come to pass after bearing with me during its long preparation.

Contents

INTRODUCTION

The World on a Platter

Odd as it may seem, this book is my autobiography, or at least a very big part of it. During the six decades I have been writing about food, I have gone in search of the world's most outstanding dishes, ingredients, restaurants, farms,

shops, and markets, and met with more chefs, home cooks, and food craftsmen and producers than I can count. Along the way, I have reaped many rewards by way of life experiences, especially in foreign countries, where I have found food to be a ready introduction to other cultures.

Traveling to gather material for articles or books, I met many strangers who, because we came together on the common ground of an interest in food, often became fast—and, in many cases, lasting—friends. Quests for various ingredients and dishes have taken me to corners of the world that I would not have ventured into otherwise, teaching me much about social customs and attitudes, local celebrations, spiritual and superstitious beliefs, and the richness of human ingenuity that enables so many to make so much out of so little.

All of which should not be surprising, considering that food and the concerns surrounding it are central to life, simple sustenance being an essential aspect of all of our days. Such were the thoughts that guided me in making the selections for this book. I strove for an overall collection that includes not only the pleasurable—though that was my primary purpose—but also the unusual (the uninitiated might even say outlandish and bizarre)—*Hirn mit Ei* (scrambled eggs with brains, see page 295), *Liang Ban Hai Zhe* (Sichuan cold jellyfish salad, see page 772), *Testina* (roasted lamb's or calf's head, see page 244), and more. The aim was to curate a sort of jigsaw puzzle that pieces together a picture of what the world eats.

My mother judged others by their ability to cook chicken soup.

My unshakeable interest in food undoubtedly traces back to my Brooklyn childhood, growing up in a family where passion for the subject was always paramount, if not obsessive. My mother was an outstanding, ambitious cook and hostess who tried recipes clipped from newspapers and who judged all other women by their ability to cook, especially their prowess at chicken soup. My father was in the wholesale fruit and produce business in New York's bygone Washington Market, then located in the now-fashionable neighborhood known as Tribeca.

When we gathered for dinner each evening, not only would we discuss the details of the food before us, but my father would describe the various fruits and vegetables he had handled that day and assess their relative merits. Thus I gathered early that California oranges were more flavorful than those from Florida, but the southern state was the winner when it came to grapefruit. He considered apples from the West Coast inferior (not enough cold nights) to those from New York and Massachusetts, and as for peaches, none held a candle to Georgia's Elberta freestones.

Not surprisingly, those evaluations have stuck with me through the years, but the most important lesson I took away was to practice discernment. Ever since then, I have paid close attention to the qualities of whatever I am tasting and have compared one iteration with another. Wherever possible, I have tried to hold the choices in this book up to the same standards, allowing that much has changed for better and worse over the years in the name of progress.

Coupled with my interest in food was my incurable wanderlust, the seeds of which I believe were first planted in me as I read a poem fittingly titled "Travel" by Robert Louis Stevenson in *A Child's Garden of Verses*. The opening lines tempt me even today: "I should like to rise and go / Where the golden apples grow." I have been rising and going in search of golden apples for many years, and, in the pursuit of food knowledge, have now visited nearly everywhere that I originally longed to see. Indeed, a savvy editor I worked for once accused me of being a person who appears to be doing one thing, but who is really doing something else. He sure had my number, as the food articles I proposed were invariably inspired by the places I wanted to see. (Want to visit southern Spain? Why not suggest an article on the growing, harvesting, and curing of capers? It worked for me and might for you.) That is one reason this book is organized geographically by cuisine, rather than by type of food. It is almost impossible for me to understand an ingredient or a dish without knowing its original context, much of which I tried to impart with each entry.

My problem was not arriving at a thousand entries but whittling down the final tally from twice that number. Almost every single one of the chosen thousand has a special meaning for me, due to my outsize and enduring love for it, fond memories of the circumstances under which it was first experienced, or the ways in which it has permanently influenced my taste.

Many of my thoughts and longings for individual foods and meals have been inspired by oblique or direct references in cultural works, including books, films, and paintings. Fiction such as Jorge Amado's *Gabriela, Clove and Cinnamon* and nonfiction such as Eleanor Clark's *Oysters of Locmariaquer;* films that are all about food, such as *La Grande Bouffe,* and others in which food is just a detail, as in *The Bicycle Thief;* and so many still-life paintings— all these have started me dreaming of the feasts those works planted so firmly in my mind. Still, my reach has always exceeded my grasp, and I know more tastes and textures are in store for me.

||||||||||||||||||||||||||||||||||||||||||||||||||||||||||||

The aim was to curate a sort of jigsaw puzzle that pieces together a picture of what the world eats.

The world of food has never been as exciting as it is now, as I hope the choices for this book indicate. Mass travel and mass communication have hastened fusion, something as old as mankind but never before occurring so rapidly and on so vast a scale. That acceleration sometimes created difficulties in determining which cuisine to categorize a dish in—for example, is *chakchouka* Tunisian or Israeli? But people have been wandering far from home ever since they could walk, and along with military conquests and the resultant colonialism, changing methods and equipment, and simply a hunger for variety, natural fusions were fostered long before intellectual chefs began consciously doing the same. I did my best to properly classify them all here.

So bon voyage and, especially, bon appétit. May your senses and stomach be strong and your pleasures great.

How the Book Is Organized

The geography of flavor and culinary style, rather than strict geographical borders, guided the organization of this book into some seventy cuisines. Along the way, I wrestled with issues such as where Middle Eastern food ends and North African cuisine begins. In the end, such distinctions are somewhat arbitrary, and I did my best to capture and classify the flavor and spirit of each selection. This is also true of traditional dishes that have become international favorites. For example, although we regularly enjoy Italian and Chinese foods in America (the best tirami sù I ever had was in Napa Valley) and even have Americanized versions of some of them, for the most part they have been classified with their root cuisines.

Within each cuisine, entries are in rough alphabetical order based on their most commonly used name in their country of origin. When this name is in another language, if neither the tagline that appears above the entry title nor the first line of that entry make it clear what the food is, a translation is provided.

Because there are some foods that completely transcend geography and are enjoyed the world over, there is a special designation called "Food of the World." Entries with this stamp are peppered throughout the book. For a full list of them, see the index on page 919.

At the end of each entry is information that will help you either obtain or cook the food being described. Here is a rundown of the type of information offered:

WHERE: This tells you where you can find the food in question. Usually that refers to

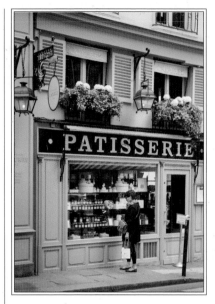

restaurants that serve the dish or the meal or brick-and-mortar shops that offer the ingredients, both in the United States and abroad. Each includes a phone number and Web address when available, and, if the restaurant or market itself is the main subject of the entry, its street address as well.

Caveat: Although I have visited many of the restaurants named, others were included after careful research and consultation with at least three reliable personal or professional sources (not consumer-based ratings on websites). Nonetheless, restaurants change quickly, as do chefs and menus; they also close without notice. The same can be said for stores and online food purveyors. For these reasons, recommendations are necessarily provisional.

A note on phone numbers: All non-U.S. and Canadian phone numbers are listed with their country codes. To call any of them, you have to add on your international access code (011 in the U.S. and Canada) before dialing the listed number. To call the U.S. and Canada from elsewhere, dial 1 between your international access code and the listed number. In some countries, when you are calling locally you have to dial 0 before the number (and of course the country code is not required).

MAIL ORDER: These are online merchants that offer the ingredients and dishes recommended. I have tried many of those named, and the rest have been drawn from long-standing suppliers.

Caveat: I have recommended mail order sources only where the food can be reasonably expected to arrive in good condition. To accomplish this, the shipping fees can be costly, as with anything that has to be delivered within twenty-four hours and thus requires overnight air service. This can add up to an amount more than double that of the food being sent, so check carefully before placing an order.

FURTHER INFORMATION AND RECIPES: What you cannot find in a restaurant, you may well be able to prepare at home, hence a collection of cookbooks and websites that offer further reading and what I consider excellent recipes for a dish or a meal or interesting and suitable use of an ingredient. Some of the best of those books may be out of print but all are available at one or another of the following sources:

- alibris.com
- barnesandnoble.com
- amazon.com
- Powell's, tel 800-878-7323, powells.com
- Bonnie Slotnick Cookbooks, tel 212-989-8962, bonnieslotnickcookbooks.com
- Kitchen Arts & Letters, tel 212-876-5550, kitchenartsandletters.com

In cases where I point you toward a website, to avoid long and cumbersome Web addresses, I have instead frequently provided search terms. When you visit the website in question, simply locate the search bar and type in the terms there—the recipe or page I referenced should pop right up.

TIP: This includes pointers on selecting the best samples of a food and/or on storing or handling it efficiently and safely. Alternatively, a tip may simply offer an extra tidbit of useful information.

SPECIAL EVENTS: There are many festivals, celebrations, and holidays honoring particular dishes or ingredients, and food-minded travelers might want to plan to attend when a favorite is the subject. I provide the name of the festival, where it takes place and during which month, and a website for more information.

SEE ALSO: Many culinary cultures include similar dishes (such as Egypt's Kosheri and India's Biryani, see pages 711 and 868) and if such references have not already been mentioned in the entry, they are added for perspective.

A warning about street eating: A number of street foods are included in this book and all can be enjoyed with the same precautions that I have taken for many years without ever once becoming ill. I eat only very hot meats or fish that are grilled, boiled, fried, or roasted before my very eyes, instead of any that seem to have been lying around. I never street-eat cold meats or seafood, nor any raw vegetable or fruit that cannot be peeled. And I drink only bottled water or soda that is uncapped right in front of me. In questionable situations, I avoid dairy products not taken from refrigeration, especially whipped cream or egg custard pastries or desserts. And because I am likely to eat raw shellfish in restaurants in questionable locales, I make sure that my vaccination against hepatitis A is up to date.

There is always a bit of risk involved with trying something or visiting someplace new, so use your best judgment and keep an eye out for travel advisories or other news that may affect the safety of your food or travels.

BRITISH
and
IRISH

English, Welsh, Scottish

EVERYTHING STOPS FOR TEA

Afternoon Tea

English

O ne of life's pleasantest indulgences is afternoon tea, preferably in London, although as this cosseting meal regains popularity, it can be enjoyed in upscale hotels and romantic tearooms around the world. A custom that originated in the nineteenth century, when life grew busier and the dinner hour grew later, a sustaining afternoon tea is a nibbler's paradise. It begins with delectable crustless sandwiches trimmed into rounds or finger shapes. Spread with sweet or herb-seasoned butter, filled with thin slices of icy cucumber, ham, or smoked salmon, or with spreads of meat or shrimp paste and miniature cress, these dainty sandwiches are mere preludes to currant-studded scones and crumpets (the forerunners of the English muffin) and pound cakes such as the caraway seed classic (see page 23), topped with clotted cream (see page 7) and fruit jams and marmalades.

Overdo it on those temptations and you might have to skip the final display of fruit and cream pastries, set out on silver trays or footed cake stands. There are choices of teas, of course, ranging from the smoky lapsang souchong to the lemony, bergamot-scented Earl Grey, the subtle black Chinese oolong (see page 777), and the complex Darjeeling (see page 873), lusty enough to be considered the coffee-drinker's tea. Milk or lemon? That depends upon the tea. There is even a choice of sugars, all delightful dilemmas presented amid flowers, bone china, and fine linens.

Newcomers take note: While the term *high tea* may seem to designate an even posher version of this afternoon meal, it actually denotes the opposite—a heavier meal that includes meat pies, spreads, and perhaps sausages, traditionally served as a tea-supper for working-class families.

WHERE: *In London*, The Ritz Hotel, tel 44/20-7300-2345, theritzlondon.com; The Connaught, tel 44/20-7499-7070, the-connaught.co.uk; Brown's Hotel, tel 44/20-7518-4155, brownshotel.com; Claridge's, tel 44/20-7409-6307, claridges.co.uk; Hyde Park Hotel, tel 44/20-7243-5000, thehydepark .com; Fortnum & Mason, tel 44/20-7734-8040, fort numandmason.com; Harrods, tel 44/20-7730-1234, harrods.com; *in New York*, Tea & Sympathy, tel 212-989-9735, teaandsympathynewyork.com; *throughout the U.S.*, at most Four Seasons hotels, tel 800-819-5053, fourseasons.com.

COMFORT WITH A BANG

Bangers and Mash

English

B ig, plump pork sausages sputter with savory juices atop a buttery nest of mashed potatoes, with overtones of pepper and a golden brown onion sauce lending a bittersweet burnish . . . This is bangers and mash, a lunch or dinner favorite in English pubs and a satisfying home-made supper to boot. It appears in one of its most refined presentations at London's stylish Green's Restaurant, where Cumberland bangers are enhanced by strips of crisp, smoky bacon. More aromatic pork bangers hinting of sage, nutmeg, and mace are the specialty of Cumberland, while those from Yorkshire and Lancashire are based upon beef.

These sausages were dubbed bangers after World War I, when water added to stretch the scarce meat of the filling caused the frying sausages to burst—with a bang. Usually fried or

The popularity of the dish inspires much variation, from rustic pub fare to luxury renditions.

grilled in their own fat, bangers emerge more plumply moist and golden when brushed with butter and oven roasted, especially if their casings are unbroken. (Ignore the advice of those who say they should be pierced before cooking.) Devotees shun mass-produced bangers, especially if skinless, and lean turkey or chicken bangers in favor of those made by artisanal butchers who use natural casings and a pork mix that includes just enough snowy fat to preserve juices.

Ideally, the boiled, starchy potatoes should not be pureed but rather broken down with an old-fashioned potato masher as butter and milk or cream are worked in. A few lumps add textural contrast, providing the right purchase for the roux-thickened onion gravy.

WHERE: *In London,* Green's Restaurant, tel 44/20-7930-4566, greens.org.uk; *in New York,* Tea & Sympathy, tel 212-989-9735, teaandsympathy newyork.com; *in Austin, TX,* Banger's Sausage House and Beer Garden, tel 512-386-1656, bangers austin.com. **MAIL ORDER:** For bangers, R.J. Balson & Son, tel 321-281-9473, balsonbutchers.com. **FURTHER INFORMATION AND RECIPES:** *How to Cook Everything* by Mark Bittman (2006); theguardian .com (search bangers and mash).

—|||||||||||||||||||||||||||||||||—

"OF ALL NATIONS AND COUNTRIES, ENGLAND IS BEST SERVED OF FISH."
—WRITER AND PHYSICIAN ANDREW BOORDE, 1542

Billingsgate Fish Market

English

Surrounded by the cold salt waters of the North Sea and the Atlantic Ocean, Britain is a treasury of firm and flavorful fish, mollusks, and crustaceans—and there is no better showcase for its wares than a visit to the exciting Billingsgate

Market at daybreak. Operating in the fish trade since the sixteenth century, the market dates back to 1400, when King Henry IV granted the city a charter to collect tolls at several such water gates on the Thames. Today the U.K.'s largest

wholesale fish center, Billingsgate, is spread over thirteen acres near London's Canary Wharf, providing a great adventure for all early risers (or night owls) who love seafood. Tuesday through Saturday, the colorfully boisterous market opens to the clang of a bell that sounds an on-your-mark signal at 4:45 a.m., and fifteen minutes later a second bell vibrates through the fog-filled dawn, indicating that the market is open for business.

The market's gleaming white interior is drippingly wet, hoses keeping floors and counters immaculate until closing time at 8:30 a.m. There is nary a hint of acrid fish odor, but rather a clean and cool, sea-air freshness, reinforced by the sight of the market workers in their spotless white coats; some will conduct training tours for novices in the fish trade and, on advance notice, can accommodate tourists. Buyers from shops and restaurants work the aisles—sniffing, touching, calculating—before placing orders. Members of the public can be found making their way through the market, too, although the really big days for nonprofessionals are Saturdays, when some 4,000 jam the aisles and parking lots.

There are many imports here, but pay closest attention to the delectable local specimens: halibut and salmon from Scottish and Irish waters, flat and snowy Dover sole, red-spotted plaice, huge diamond-shape slabs of turbot, members of the cod family including whiting and haddock, slim green-white pilchards halfway between herring and sardines, miniscule whitebait to be crunchily fried whole. You will find all gradations of squid, octopus, and shrimp; sparklingly briny oysters from Whitstable in Kent, as well as Colchesters and Blackwaters from Essex and Helfords from Cornwall; Dublin Bay prawns; Donegal crab; Scottish langoustines; whelks; cockles, which look like ridged scallops; blue mussels; and periwinkles, which are tiny stone-black sea snails. The variety itself (about 150 daily) is a tip-off to the diversity of London's immigrant population; as seafood favored by each group is added to the larder, so, too, are sales staff speaking a United Nations of languages.

Two coffee shops restore market workers and visitors with hearty breakfasts, and it is said that if you buy a piece of fish at one of the stalls, cooks at the Piscatorial Café will prepare it for you.

WHERE: Trafalgar Way, London, tel 44/20-7987-1118, cityoflondon.gov.uk (search billingsgate).

----⊢|||||||||||||||||||||||||||||||||⊣----

CRACKERS FOR CHEESE LOVERS AND COOKIE MONSTERS

Biscuits

English

S oothing to stomach and spirit, English biscuits provide exactly the right foil for the firm and pungent cheeses of their home country. Technically, the word *biscuit* means twice-cooked, originally referring to rusklike biscotti or

zwieback that were baked, then sliced and toasted, and other long-lasting varieties that were boiled prior to being baked. Today, in its English usage, the term describes all sorts of crisp crackers that are not to be confused with the fluffy, buttery biscuit rolls of the American South (see page 528).

The most authentic English biscuits are made by Carr's, Hovis, Jacobs, and McVitie's, and their offerings range from simple, lean white water biscuits to thicker, creamier varieties and sweet, cookielike, rustic whole wheat or wholemeal types considered digestives in England. (Companies are no longer allowed to make that claim in the U.S.) Most producers also offer the biscuits in pepper, cheese, or herb varieties that do nothing but compromise the flavors of cheese and limit the delightful crackers' versatility.

Charcoal biscuits are an unusual variant—dusky gray, cosseting, chiplike wafers popular in the nineteenth and early twentieth centuries as gastrointestinal purifiers, and still used as such today. Composed of willow charcoal powder, wheat flour, eggs, salt, and the merest hint of sugar, they are teasingly gritty on the tongue yet innocently neutral in flavor, working as palate cleansers after intensely sweet desserts.

Where: *In New York,* Myers of Keswick, tel 212-691-4194, myersofkeswick.com. **Mail order:** British Corner Shop, britishcornershop.com (search digestives); amazon.com (search original digestive biscuits). **Further information and recipes:** *1200 Traditional English Recipes* by Ethel Meyer (2010); food.com (search english digestive biscuits). **Tip:** Look for Carr's, Jacobs, McVitie's, Hovis, or Miller's Damsels brands in upscale supermarkets and gourmet food stores.

MAKING A HASH OUT OF PUDDING

Black Pudding Hash

English

With crisply fried outer edges enveloping a succulently emollient, meaty interior, hash made with the filling of black blood pudding sausages is a delicious first course or breakfast garnish for eggs—no matter how forbidding it may sound. It is a popular dish in Lancashire, where the sausages are made by the Bury Black Pudding Company—one of several local, esteemed producers—and also sold hot and ready to eat from their Bury Market stall.

Black pudding hash isn't just for morning fry-ups anymore. Seasoned with a hint of onion and perhaps a touch of cloves and cinnamon, it often is elegantly served as a dinner appetizer at Roast, the lively modern restaurant above the Borough Market in London. Cool, sour-sweet applesauce cuts the richness of the meat for an intriguing effect.

Where: *In London,* Roast, tel 44/84-5034-7300, roast-restaurant.com; *in Glasgow,* Redstones Hotel, tel 44/16-9881-3774, redstoneshotel.com. **Further information and recipes:** *The Ploughman's Lunch and the Miser's Feast* by Brian Yarvin (2012).

A TASTER'S PARADISE

Borough Market

English

The time-strapped traveling food lover looking to sample local English fare can do no better than a visit to London's Borough Market, said to be the city's oldest. (It has occupied the same site for some 2,500 years, ever since the Romans built the first London Bridge nearby.) Monday and Tuesday, the market is wholesale-only, except for lunch; but Wednesday through Saturday, it opens its gates to the public, welcoming in a rapacious and food-obsessed crowd.

Although the market features an international array of products, visitors would be wise to stick to an all-British tour. Stands are overflowing with temptations and many a hard-to-resist free sample, so focus is of the essence. Under the watery light filtering through a soaring, glass-covered iron framework, one finds the best of British seafood: cockles, mussels, langoustines, and, perhaps tastiest of all, the oysters

of the icy North Sea. (The deliciously steely and salty Colchester oyster in particular is not to be missed.)

In another section you can compare earthily complex farmhouse Cheddars by Keen's and Quicke's alongside myriad jams and preserves, buns and biscuits. Rosy-pink hams and bangers from various parts of the British Isles are yours for the tasting, as are hot and crunchy examples of fish and chips, best made with cod or haddock and excellent at the open stand named "fish! kitchen." For more serious seafood dining, "fish!" has an adjoining restaurant. Also on the market grounds is the stylish Roast, offering a wide range of English food, with a focus on meats.

After a two-year renovation, Borough Market reopened in February 2013, drawing eager shoppers.

Most visitors like to eat and walk, but benches throughout the market offer respite to those who tire. Better yet is a picnic on the benches just five minutes across the road in the garden of the Southwark Cathedral, a graceful and romantic charmer of a church whose mixed architectural styles date back to the thirteenth century.

Where: 8 Southwark Street, London, tel 44/20-7407-1002, boroughmarket.org.uk. **When:** Wed. and Thurs. 10 a.m. to 5 p.m.; Fri. 10 a.m. to 6 p.m.; Sat. 8 a.m. to 5 p.m.

⊢||||||||||||||||||||||||||||||||||⊣

OLD(E) ENGLAND'S OWN

Cheddar

English, Scottish

With its tauntingly sharp yet buttery flavor and its subtly lingering overtones of malty sweetness, a well-made and sufficiently aged Cheddar is one of the world's most satisfying cheeses. Paired with some combination of crackers,

bread, pickled onions or gherkins, walnuts, and apples, it makes a wonderfully sustaining snack; its knack for melting qualifies it for a prime spot

in various grilled sandwiches and as the star in the savory Welsh rarebit sauce (see page 36); and it lends that strong pungency and golden finish to the many cooked and baked dishes in which it appears as an ingredient.

First produced in the Somerset town of Cheddar in South England, it is the most copied cheese in the world—a cheese so common, in fact, that it is rarely regarded as special or distinguished. Too often, it is factory-produced from pasteurized milk, dull-flavored and gummy, and sealed in airtight plastic or coated with thick wax. That is the kind of cheese that is "made to be sold, not eaten," as accurately diagnosed in Osbert Burdett's *The Little Book of Cheese,* published in England in 1935. With its pale ivory to orange color (depending on the use of the coloring annatto, a more popular custom in the U.S. than in Britain), Cheddar was the inspiration for waxy, plasticlike processed American cheese. But such sorry imitations should not dissuade one from seeking out the sublime farmhouse Cheddars made of unpasteurized cow's milk in the British Isles, where varying degrees of aging produce differences in the sharpness. The real stuff derives its firm but gently crumbling texture from the process known as cheddaring, in which the curds are cut several times and then stacked for compression and the draining off of whey. Formed into unwaxed wheels, true farmhouse Cheddars are cloth-wrapped, never sealed in plastic.

Among the most reliable imports are those labeled Keen's, Montgomery's, and the pleasantly earthy Mrs. Quicke's, made in Devon. By far the best and most complex of all, and the rarest in the U.S., is Isle of Mull Cheddar, from the Sgriob-ruadh farm (the Gaelic means "red furrow" and is pronounced "SKEE-brooah") on the Isle of Mull in the Inner Hebrides.

Both the United States and Canada produce some estimable Cheddars, but none really match the subtle complexities of the British product. Four- to six-year-old Grafton Four Star Cheddar from Vermont and the Forfar or Black Diamond Cheddars from Canada are a couple of the top contenders, although finding sufficiently aged (at least six months) versions of the latter can be difficult.

When shopping for Cheddar, look for a smooth, hard, transparent rind and no streakiness in the color of the cheese itself, and buy cheese cut to order, not in prewrapped sections. Try for a clean, full flavor, with a pleasant but not harsh bite.

WHERE: *In London,* Neal's Yard Dairy at three locations, nealsyarddairy.co.uk; Paxton & Whitfield, tel 44/20-7930-0259, paxtonand whitfield.co.uk; *in New York,* Murray's Cheese Shop, tel 888-692-4339, murrayscheese.com. **FURTHER INFORMATION:** farmhousecheesemakers .com; britishcheese.com/cheddar.

"TO SIT ON A CUSHION AND SEW A FINE SEAM . . .
AND FEAST UPON STRAWBERRIES, SUGAR AND CREAM"
—FROM THE NURSERY RHYME "CURLY LOCKS"

Clotted Cream

English

Strawberries, sugar, and cream indeed. As long as that cream is the clotted ivory specialty of Devon and Cornwall, the spread is sure to be a feast. Only cows grazing on the grasses of these two English regions are said to

produce milk rich enough in butterfat and the proper enzymes to result in this sublime dessert cream, much favored for afternoon tea. The dairy delicacy is considered an indispensable component of a Devonshire cream tea, a treasured regional institution that consists of a hot pot of tea and scones or buns called "Devon splits," still warm from the oven, cut in half and spread with clotted cream and dollops of fresh strawberry jam. (Cornwall features a similar cream tea but prides itself on its custom of spooning the clotted cream atop the jam on each scone.) Its luscious ripe flavor and satiny clumps or "clots" make it a delectable treat on scones and

A Devonshire-style scone: jam on top of cream

firm pound cakes, or spooned over ripe berries. It is traditionally prepared with the thick cream that rises to the surface of raw milk left to stand for twelve hours, then scalded. Cornish clotted cream is said to taste more of its scalding than its smoother, firmer rival in Devonshire.

WHERE: *In London,* the Georgian Restaurant at Harrods, tel 44/20-7225-6800, harrods.com; *in New York,* Myers of Keswick, tel 212-691-4194, myersofkeswick.com.

FISH AS COMFORT FOOD

Codfish Cakes

English

A s appreciated in England as they are in New England, crisply fried codfish cakes offer homey sustenance (as well as an excellent use for leftover fish). Moist, mild, and firm, the snowy flesh of the Atlantic cod is mellowed with mashed potatoes and a hint of onion, dredged in flour and fine white bread crumbs, then crisply fried in butter. The cakes are best accented by pungent, mayonnaise-based dressings such as

Watercress adds a light touch to rich fish cakes.

tartar or rémoulade sauce sprightly with lemon, capers, tarragon, and bits of the tiny vinegar pickles known as cornichons or gherkins. Those who prefer lustier flavor and texture make the cakes with salt-preserved codfish or smoked haddock (Finnan Haddie; see page 40). Salmon cakes have a lovely blush of coral pink, but cod wins out for its chewier texture. Freshly made and served hot, this is English food at its most basic and comforting and the inspiration for a New England classic.

WHERE: *In London,* Green's Restaurant tel 44/20-7930-4566, greens.org.uk; *in Boston and environs,* Jasper White's Summer Shack at multiple locations, summershackrestaurant. com. **FURTHER INFORMATION AND RECIPES:** *The Ploughman's Lunch and the Miser's Feast* by Brian Yarvin (2012); bbcgoodfood.com (search crisp crumb fish cakes).

PLEASURES OF THE FLESH

The Cook, the Thief, His Wife, and Her Lover

English

The Cook, the Thief, His Wife, and Her Lover, a deliciously over-the-top 1989 British film written and directed by Peter Greenaway, serves up quite a feast. Its setting, Le Hollandais, is an unimaginably grandiose restaurant whose opulent décor calls to mind a baroque ballroom; it is owned by Albert the Thief (Michael Gambon), a man of ugly appetites, and frequented by Georgina, his diffident slut of a wife (a young and lithe Helen Mirren). There, they gorge on parades of presciently nouvelle-cuisine dishes as well as antiquated set pieces such as game birds *en plumage,* lofty frozen puddings, and *pièces montées* based on crimson shellfish, all prepared by the quintessentially laconic French cook (Alan Howard). Between courses the wife ducks out with her lover (Richard Bohringer), a regular diner there, to heat things up in the meat cooler.

In the enormous kitchen recalling those of Henry VIII's Hampton Court and King Ludwig II's Neuschwanstein Castle, feathers fly as birds are plucked, copper pots are made to gleam, endless foods are chopped and roasted over roaring fires, profiteroles are doused with chocolate, and terrines are glazed with aspic by an exhausted, half-naked kitchen staff suggestive of Dickens's vassal waifs.

It's a movie that has everything, from food to murder and cannibalism to wonderful costumes from various real and imagined periods created by the Paris couturier Jean-Paul Gaultier. (For a fun guessing game, try to predict who winds up as the main course.)

"Don't you realize that a clever cook puts unlikely things together?" Albert asks at one point. To which we all can answer: "We do. We do."

MAIL ORDER: *The Cook, the Thief, His Wife, and Her Lover,* directed by Peter Greenaway (1989), DVD, barnesandnoble.com.

FAST-FOOD LUNCH FOR HUNGRY MINERS

Cornish Pasties

English

Cornwall's crisp, juicy half-moon meat pie, the pasty (sometimes written as *pastie* but always rhyming with *nasty,* although it is anything but), is a first cousin to the Latin-American empanada and the Russian piroshki. Crimped edges of browned pastry enclose a traditional filling of chopped beef, root vegetables, onions, and herbs or, more recently, more inventive forcemeats of fish, poultry, or only vegetables. Before baking, the savory filling is added to a sturdy circle of short-crust or puff pastry, which is then folded in half. Believed to have been developed in Cornwall as a portable fast-food lunch for tin miners who could not leave the mines at mid-day, the pasty's thick crust keeps the savory little pie fillings warm for many hours. And still today, it provides a complete, portable meal for those on-the-go types who need to eat and run.

A portable meal on its own, no brown bag required.

In the nineteenth century, the pasties followed Cornish miners to places such as Wisconsin and Michigan, where the pies are still favored, warm or cold, for lunches and snacks. But despite the pasty's popularity with the hearts and stomachs of the New World, it remains an English dish. Today, the pasty is "the national dish of Cornwall," and no visit to this region would be complete without a stop at one of the many traditional shops selling hot, fresh pasties.

WHERE: *In Cornwall, U.K.,* Proper Cornish Food Company, tel 44/1208-265-830, www.proper cornish.co.uk; *in New York,* Myers of Keswick, tel 212-691-4194, myersofkeswick.com; *in Mineral Point, WI,* Red Rooster Café, tel 608-987-9936; Pointer Café, tel 608-987-3733; *in Tempe, AZ,* Cornish Pasty Co., tel 480-894-6261, cornish pastyco.com. **FURTHER INFORMATION AND RECIPES:** *Jamie Oliver's Great Britain* by Jamie Oliver (2012); saveur.com (search cornish pasties).

THE CONNOISSEUR'S DESSERT APPLE

Cox's Orange Pippin

English

O ne of the most luscious and subtly sweet of all apples, the crisp and meaty Cox's orange pippin has recently become available in the United States at farmers' markets, a cause for celebration. It's a wonderfully crisp English eating apple with a highly perfumed skin, a bronzed matte surface that shows only a melon blush of red with orange overtones, and slightly astringent flavor that accents a caramelized sweetness, almost as though the apple had been baked. Considered one of the finest dessert apples in the world, it derives the first part of its name from Richard Cox, the horticulturalist and retired brewer who developed the fruit in the early nineteenth century in Colnbrook,

near what is now Heathrow Airport; the second, from the Ribston pippin cultivar from which it was bred. November to April is its prime season for flavor, but it keeps fairly well through late spring. Connoisseurs of this hard-to-grow apple prefer those from English soil rather than New Zealand imports, with some kudos beginning to emerge for U.S. specimens.

MAIL ORDER: Orange Pippin Fruit Trees, tel 616-258-2244, orange pippintrees.com. **FURTHER INFORMATION:** orangepippin.com; english applesandpears.co.uk.

Dover Sole

English

No member of the flatfish family is more highly prized by fish fanciers than *Solea solea*: the sole that owes its snowy firmness and elegant, saline overtones to the icy waters of the North Sea and its name to the port that was a prime supplier for London's markets.

Although most soles (Soleidae) can be prepared in the same manner, none are quite so firm as the Dover, with its savoriness and its slight elasticity. None are quite so high in price, either, which is why many fishmongers and chefs are inspired to cheat, offering fillets of lesser soles or even local flounder. (True, fresh Dover sole is flown into the U.S., adding to its cost.)

It is easier to recognize the authentic specimen in fish markets, where one can see the whole fish. Dover sole usually runs about 24 inches in length and has an almost perfect oval shape, with even fringes of fins on both edges. It is smaller and thinner than its cousin, the only slightly less delicious North Sea lemon near-sole (*Microstomus kitt*), also an import. Like most soles, the Dover is right-eyed, with both of its eyes on its right side.

Sole with lemon and parsley

Sole does not spoil as easily as many other seafood varieties, and some believe that the flavor reaches its zenith twenty-four hours after being caught. It is the particular combination of flavor and firmness that makes the Dover sole a chef's favorite; it can be filleted and folded into the roll-ups known as paupiettes.

It does, however, seem a travesty to compromise so superb a fish with complicated sauces and fillings. Dover sole looks and tastes best when prepared whole and on the bone, preferably either grilled and served with a glossing of butter and lemon or a brassy touch of mustard sauce; or, as in the intricately demanding French style, sautéed *à la meunière* (see page 86).

WHERE: *In London,* Wiltons, tel 44/20-7629-9955, wiltons.co.uk; *in New York,* La Grenouille, tel 212-752-1495, la-grenouille.com. **FURTHER INFORMATION:** *North Atlantic Seafood* by Alan Davidson (2003).

Eccles Cakes

English

Squashed Fly Cakes. Dead Fly Pies. Fly's Graveyard. Don't let this pastry's colorful colloquial nicknames, which refer to the black currants that poke through its dough, dissuade you from indulging in what is an excellent teatime treat.

Eccles cakes are small tea cakes with a chewy filling of allspice- and nutmeg-scented dried currants, sugar-frosted and baked into crisp, golden rounds. Their proper name comes from the town of Eccles in the city of Salford in northern England, where baker James Birch is credited with inventing them in the late eighteenth century.

As with any food that has been around for a while, Eccles cakes generate some gentle controversy. Contended points include the use of flaky puff pastry or the firmer short-crust, and the matter of candied fruit peel in the filling, an embellishment some swear by but others scorn. Choose your side secure in the knowledge that whatever you decide, you will hardly go wrong.

Though all the cakes need for company is a cup of strong tea, for a sophisticated contrast they do not suffer from being served with slivers of Lancashire's own snowy, tangy cheese, as they are at St. John Bar & Restaurant in London (see page 26).

WHERE: *In London,* St. John Bar and Restaurant, tel 44/20-7251-0848, stjohngroup.uk .com. **FURTHER INFORMATION AND RECIPES:** *Beyond Nose to Tail* by Fergus Henderson and Justin Piers Gellatly (2007); visitsalford.com (search history of eccles cake); epicurious.com (search eccles cake).

||||||||||||||||||||||||||||||||||||||||||||||||||||||||||||||||||||||||||||||||||||||||||||||||||||||||

DON'T CALL IT A RAISIN

 # Currants

A far cry from the dried impostors used in baking and puddings—in reality, Greek miniraisins—true currants are not dried grapes. Like gooseberries, they are members of the *Ribes* family, and eaten fresh, the tiny droplets bring their alluring sweet-tart flavor to jams, juices, and syrups, or act as sublime flavorings and toppings for ice cream.

Most beloved of all may be the red currants, whose garnet sparkle and deeply rich winey flavor have been highly prized since they were first cultivated in Europe during the sixteenth century.

They are the prime ingredient in "Cumberland sauce," the heady, pungent blend of port, dried mustard, and ground ginger; named after the Duke of Cumberland, the sauce makes a perfect condiment for game. Their white cousins, with a slightly milder, more elusive flavor, are actually albinoid variants, and the fully saturated black currants are too tart to be eaten raw. Cooked, their aggressive character is muted and they become a sharp, titillating delight, deeply rich and teasingly tangy.

Brits have made a specialty of black currant pie for centuries, also adding the fruit to teatime treats like Eccles cakes, tarts, fools, and puddings. The French cherish the black currants, too. They famously appear in the syrupy liqueur crème de cassis, mixed into Champagne for one of the world's classiest cocktails, the kir royale. (When made with white wine, it's just a kir.) In Germany and Austria, red and black currants are crushed into juices, to be blended with chilled soda water for refreshing aperitifs long after the midsummer fresh currant season has ended.

Stateside, red currants are available, but not widely so. During their short growing season (it peaks in early July), they can be found mostly in fancy food and farmers' markets. Black currants, however, are hosts for white blister pine rust, a European disease that spread in the U.S. during the 1800s. Because it destroys white pine trees, the growing of black currants was banned in some states until the mid-1960s, when disease-resistant varieties became available. Growing them remains illegal in a handful of states (including Maine, the so-called Pine Tree State).

Mail order: For fresh black currants in July, and frozen currants and preserved currant products year-round, Queener Fruit Farm, tel 503-769-8965, queenerfruitfarm.com. **Further information and recipes:** *The Pie and Pastry Bible* by Rose Levy Beranbaum (1998); *The Joy of Jams, Jellies, and Other Sweet Preserves* by Linda Ziedrich (2009); cookstr.com (search steamed currant pudding). **Special event:** Sarau (Blackcurrant) Festival, Upper Moutere Village, New Zealand, February, saraufestival.co.nz.

OUT OF THE FRYING PAN

Fish and Chips

English

Think of moist, thick, snowy shards of firm, white-fleshed fish such as haddock, whiting, sole, hake, plaice, or cod, encased in a crackling-hot, crisp batter. Add to that crunchy fried potato slivers, the whole sparked with salt and a refreshing zap of malt vinegar, and you'll understand why this plebeian English specialty is famous the world over. Basically street food, it's a working-class meal sold at fairs and from designated fish-and-chip shops, or "chippies," traditionally served as a walk-away specialty in grease-absorbing paper cones. But for a distinctly perfect upscale version, the hands-down London winner is the cheerfully casual Sea Shell restaurant in Lisson Grove, a short walk from the Marylebone station. This authentic outpost fries everything immaculately in peanut oil that imparts a sweet luster to the very fresh fish, some of which is served in smaller portions as appetizers, including plates of tiny, wispy whitebait and thick, grainy slabs of cod roe.

Where: *In London,* Sea Shell of Lisson Grove, tel 44/20-7224-9000, seashellrestaurant.co.uk; *in New York,* A Salt & Battery, tel 212-691-2713, asaltandbattery.com; *in Seattle,* Chinook's at Salmon Bay, tel 206-283-4665, anthonys.com (click Restaurants, then Casual Dining). **Further information and recipes:** *The Ploughman's Lunch and the Miser's Feast* by Brian Yarvin (2012).

A MATTER OF TASTE

Gentleman's Relish

English

The "gentleman" to blame or celebrate for this example of the perverse strain in the English palate is John Osborn, an Englishman residing in Paris, who devised this gastronomic devilry in 1828. If you're familiar with Thailand's *nam pla* or ancient Roman garum—high-protein condiment sauces based on fermented fish innards—you'll have an idea of what this unctuously sweet, sour, bitter, and salty anchovy paste tastes like. Like that so-called restorative Marmite, or its Australian cousin, Vegemite (see page 907), this relish has lip-curling malt-yeast-fish-oil overtones. No wonder, then, that the Gentleman's Relish is sold in tiny crocks.

This condiment is made exclusively by Elsenham Quality Foods, whose handsome, antique-looking black labels (usually printed onto the lids) promise that even if you hate the relish (also identified there by its Latinate name, Patum Peperium), you'll relish the crock for holding sea salt or paper clips.

Incredibly, though, Gentleman's Relish can become addictive, scraped thinly onto buttered toast, perhaps with slivered cucumber as a foil, and taken with a glass of wine or a cup of tea. Hard-core fans stir a bit into salad dressing or dab it over eggs, boiled, scrambled, poached, or fried. It is also a key component of Scotch woodcock, which consists of soft, creamy scrambled eggs served atop slices of toast spread with Gentleman's Relish.

WHERE: *In London,* Harrods, tel 44/20-7730-1234, harrods.com; Fortnum & Mason, tel 44/20-7734-8040, fortnum andmason.com; *in New York,* Myers of Keswick, tel 212-691-4194, myers ofkeswick.com. **FURTHER INFORMATION:** theguardian.com (search sybil kapoor gentleman's relish).

‖‖‖‖‖‖‖‖‖‖‖‖‖‖‖‖‖‖‖‖‖‖‖‖‖

A NOT-SO-FOOLISH SUMMER DESSERT

Gooseberry Fool

English

D ating back to Tudor times, the fruit fool is a prized English dessert based on a puree of cooked ripe fruit, chilled and swirled through various kinds of cream. Lusciously rich yet restorative, fools are most classically made with berries, or can

also incorporate stone fruits such as cherries, plums, peaches, and apricots. For full flavor and color, any berry or stone fruit to be used for a fool should be at the last opulent stages of ripeness. In earlier times, the pureed fruit was combined with a cooked egg custard, but these days, whipped or clotted cream is turned through the fruit for a streaky, marbleized effect.

Gooseberry bushes thrive in the English climate, and early summer gooseberries, with their green and glassy shimmer and tart, juicy flavor, are justifiable favorites for fools. (The inch-long berries are available throughout the summer season, but the riper, fatter, sweeter berries of late summer are best suited to eating raw.)

Heaped into parfait glasses or sherbet dishes after the stems and spiky bits have been removed and the berries have been cooked, they are as coolly appealing to the eye as they are pleasing to the palate, with the tartness of the fruit pleasantly gentled by the cream. For added sophistication, a few drops of rose or orange flower water or a fruit wine such as elderberry can be stirred through the fruit puree before it is turned through the cream.

FURTHER INFORMATION AND RECIPES: *Food in England* by Dorothy Hartley (2009); *British Cookery* edited by Lizzie Boyd (1989); epicurious .com (search gooseberry fool); theguardian .com (search nigel slater gooseberry fool).

―|||||||||||||||||||||||||||||||||||+―

"IF YOU CAN EAT OR DRINK IT, YOU'LL FIND IT AT HARRODS."

The Food Halls at Harrods

English

The motto of the famed, gleaming Food Halls at London's posh department store Harrods is still close enough to truth. Yet these days, the energetic food scout will surely be able to unearth exotica that even this retailer, long celebrated

for variety, is missing. But it would be churlish to complain, as the luxurious department store near Hyde Park devotes some four and a half acres to designer clothing and one-of-a-kind merchandise of all stripes. No single department is more impressive than the ground-floor food halls, a collection of well-appointed alcoves, niches, and counters (many of antique English beauty) stocked with the finest imported delicacies from around the world: from Spain's *jamón Ibérico* to Caspian Sea caviar from Russia and Iran to *macarons* from Ladurée in Paris. The sheer vastness of the collection is incredibly impressive, but for a traveler with limited time and capacity, it would be wise to concentrate on the purely English provender. This is the place to sample an array of English teas, jams and preserves, farmstead cheeses, and all the cakes, puddings, pastries, breads, and buns that fortify afternoon tea.

Not too surprisingly, Harrods has its roots in food, as a grocery store opened by the miller Charles Henry Harrod in 1849, when Knightsbridge was a slum. Harrods' good fortune followed that of the neighborhood, allowing the store to pioneer the concept of destination department store dining. Now more than 15 million people, many of them tourists, are said to visit Harrods each year. Amid the gleaming antique tiles, they can take a seat at bars offering caviar, dim sum, Champagne, or a stunning array of ice-cold local oysters from various parts of the Isles. Amblers will detect whiffs of freshly ground, brewing coffee, the salt-air tang of seafood, and the warm, enveloping

An employee in the seafood section of Harrods delicatessen proudly exhibits a tray of delicacies.

aroma of chocolate—all teasers that inevitably lead to delectable splurges.

WHERE: 87–135 Brompton Rd., London, tel 44/20-7730-1234, harrods.com. **TIP:** In addition to the Food Halls, Harrods has several inviting, expectedly expensive restaurants—including a Veuve Clicquot Champagne bar and an old-fashioned ice-cream parlor with hot fudge sundaes.

EVEN SLIPPERIER THAN MOST EELS

Jellied Eel

English

Currently enjoying a new wave of popularity that crosses class lines, jellied eels are being featured in various upscale seafood restaurants, but are still mainly consumed as walk-away street food in London's East End.

Sometimes accompanied by mashed potatoes and peas, cool jellied eel makes a tantalizing first course or between-meal snack. In the eighteenth and nineteenth centuries, it was a staple dish for the London poor, and "eel, pie, and mash" houses proliferated. Jellied eels are gaining popularity with a new generation, but concerns about the European eel's endangered status have recently limited the number of them available for consumption.

At its most effete, the dish is prepared with sea eel that is boned, skinned, and boiled,

A staple appetizer at M. Manze

the meaty, nicely oily chunks caught in a green-gold glassy aspic sharpened with white wine, vinegar, onion, and bay leaves and flecked with parsley; but to be at its best, the skinned eel should be cooked in slices, on the bone, however challenging that might make it for diners picking their way through the jelly. Such messy hard work is well rewarded.

WHERE: *In London,* M. Manze at multiple locations, tel 44/20-7277-6181, manze.co.uk. **FURTHER INFORMATION AND RECIPES:** the guardian.com (search joy of jellied eels); recipewise .co.uk (search jellied eels).

A PIE AT CHRISTMAS

Mince Pie

English

"I lay pretty long in bed, and then rose, leaving my wife desirous to sleep, having sat up till four this morning seeing her maid make mince pies. . . ." Samuel Pepys thus described his Christmas Day in 1666, when mince pies were

already long established as a traditional Christmas treat. The origins of this rich dessert lie in the

Middle Ages, and although Oliver Cromwell issued a law banning meat in mince pie at

Christmas (he associated holiday celebrations with paganism and gluttony), this law happily did not survive the end of the English Civil War.

Factory-produced commercial pies with crusts suggesting wet cardboard and cloyingly sweet, soggy fruit fillings have given this pie a bad name. At its Yuletide best, mince pie is rich with chewy, flavorful jewels of dried fruits such as currants, raisins, figs, candied citrus peel, and crunches of walnuts or almonds enriched by brandy, rum, whiskey, sherry, or a heady combination of several spirits. Gently sweetened with molasses and brown sugar and scented with cinnamon, cloves, nutmeg, and allspice, this darkly glistening treat tastes mystically historic.

In the sixteenth century, fillings did indeed include cooked meat—generally beef and suet, sometimes mutton, chicken, or tongue—along with the dried fruits, spices, and spirits that were put up to ripen months before the Christmas season. The most authentic crust is made with flour, lard, and hot water, providing a neutral foil for the lavish filling, although today's tastes tend to run to a lighter, flakier, buttery pastry.

WHERE: *In London,* Harrods, tel 44/20-7730-1234, harrods.com; *in New York,* at Christmas, Myers of Keswick, tel 212-691-4194, myersof keswick.com. **FURTHER INFORMATION AND RECIPES:** *The James Beard Cookbook* by James Beard (2002); foodnetwork.com (search mince pie). **SPECIAL EVENT:** The Mince Pie Project, England, December, themincepieproject.com.

PEASE PUDDING HOT

Mushy Peas

English

D on't be put off by the name. This soothing jade-colored puree of fresh green peas fluffed with butter, salt, pepper, and perhaps a touch of cream or a handful of chopped mint is the traditional side dish served with Fish and Chips

(see page 13). It also provides a cushy accompaniment to boiled beef or ham, or roasted meats and game, and is an essential component of the northern English comfort dish pie and peas. In Tudor times, dried peas were used and were wrapped in pudding cloths to be simmered in

Mushy peas complement a meal of haddock and chips.

stock along with boiling pickled pork, ham, or beef. Many recipes still call for dried marrowfat peas, soaked overnight, but fresh peas provide sweet, luscious flavor. (For purists, canned mushy peas are to be scorned.)

For best results, the cooked fresh peas should be rubbed through a sieve before being beaten smooth with a wooden spoon. That way, they attain a velvety texture that cannot be matched with an electric blender or food processor, which tend to liquefy the mixture. Garnishes of minced fresh chervil or parsley add elegance.

MAIL ORDER: For marrowfat peas, English Tea Store, tel 877-734-2458, englishteastore.com (search peas). **FURTHER INFORMATION AND RECIPES:** getmecooking.com (search mushy peas); bbc .co.uk/food (search mint mushy peas).

||||||||||||||||||||||||||||||||

THE TRUE BREAKFAST OF CHAMPIONS

Oatmeal Porridge

English, Irish, Scottish, Welsh

To those unfortunates who know only of quick-cooking rolled oats, oatmeal is a sad proposition indeed. Minus the rolling, oatmeal is a nourishing, comforting tradition that is lately much in vogue on trendy brunch menus all over the place.

Originally a grain cultivated by Central European Celts, oats made into breakfast porridge in Scotland, Ireland, and Wales are more coarsely milled than those used for bread flour or sausage fillings. Ideally, they are steel-cut rather than rolled, to retain a bit of the bran layer that lends them their nutty flavor and chewy texture. Simmered very slowly in spring water, or steamed in a double boiler, the oats should be seasoned with salt only midway through cooking, lest it toughen the cereal.

Way back when, oatmeal was served in communal hardwood bowls to be eaten with horn spoons that did not draw out heat. Each person would dip each spoonful of porridge into a small bowl of cold milk, cream, or buttermilk. For maximum satisfaction today, serve it in individual heated ceramic bowls, and do dip each spoonful into the milk of your choice or, as many prefer, into hot melted butter—or both. Deserving children were once rewarded with a trickle of honey or treacle on their Sunday porridge, but grown-up palates may mature beyond that state, perhaps even to adding a sprinkle of salt and freshly ground black pepper. Young or old, anyone can reap the benefits of this now-trendy cereal that is high in protein and said to be helpful in lowering cholesterol and blood pressure while soothing the gastrointestinal tract.

Where: *In London,* St. John Bread & Wine Spitalfields, tel 44/20-7251-0848, stjohngroup .uk.com/spitalfields; *in New York,* Tea & Sympathy, tel 212-989-9735, teaandsympathy newyork.com. **Mail order:** bobsredmill.com (search steel cut oats); amazon.com (search mccann's steel cut). **Further information and recipe:** mccanns.ie; epicurious.com (search griddled steel-cut oatcakes).

||||||||||||||||||||||||||||||||

NOT FOR PLANTING

Potted Shrimp

English

What might also be called a shrimp terrine or pâté was a popular English appetizer as far back as the eighteenth century, and no wonder: Tiny shrimp, gently simmered, are stirred through lots of melted butter spiked with mace and

cayenne pepper. The mix may be packed into small, round individual ramekins to be chilled

to a congealed, pâté-like firmness, then turned out onto thin toast or lacy salad greens like frisée or cress; or it might be poached in crocks or jars to be scooped out in portions, as is generally the case in takeout food shops. If the tiniest shrimp are not available, larger ones can be cut into small pieces after being cooked, for an only slightly less delicate result. Either way, the pure, almost naive flavors prove that there is nothing remiss in simplicity.

Potted Shrimp

6 servings

1 pound shrimp, approximately 25
¼ to ½ teaspoon powdered mace,
   or to taste
½ to 1 teaspoon salt, or to taste
Pinch of cayenne pepper, to taste
7 tablespoons unsalted butter
6 small individual ramekins

Any meat or shellfish can be potted; shrimp is a favorite.

1. Rinse the shrimp, then place in a saucepan with cold water to cover. Bring water to a boil, cover pot, and turn off heat. Let stand for 5 minutes or until all shrimp are pink. Drain shrimp and immediately cover with cold water to stop the cooking.

2. Peel and devein shrimp and chop them coarsely. Sprinkle with mace, salt, and cayenne pepper.

3. Melt 4 tablespoons of the butter in an 8-inch skillet over a very low flame and add seasoned chopped shrimp. Stir, still over low heat, until butter is absorbed and evenly distributed throughout shrimp mixture. Taste to correct seasonings. It should be fairly spicy, so add cayenne and mace accordingly.

4. Divide warm shrimp mixture into 6 portions and pack each firmly into a ramekin, leaving about a ¼-inch space at the top. Melt the remaining butter and pour a layer into each ramekin to make a cap about ¼-inch thick. Cover each crock with plastic wrap and chill for at least 6 hours before serving.

5. Just before serving, turn contents of each ramekin out onto a salad plate and garnish with thin toast slices, a wedge of lemon, and greens, too, if you choose.

    WHERE: *In London,* Wiltons, tel 44/20-7629-9955, wiltons.co.uk.

NOTHING TO GROUSE ABOUT

Red Grouse

English, Scottish, Irish, Welsh

The lyrical partridge in a pear tree means far less to lovers of wild game than does richly flavorful red grouse, a small, portion-size bird with dark, gently gamy meat. Native only to the British Isles, the red grouse resists being farm raised or reared in captivity and is the only game bird in Britain that is still considered truly wild. By law it may be killed only by gunshot, and hunters pay steep fees for the privilege ($150–$200 for a brace of birds), especially on the Scottish moors. Some hunt the birds for their own use, but others do so to fill orders from restaurants and game wholesalers. Because the birds may not be unsportingly shot on the ground, beaters are hired to shoo them into the air, where they become fair game.

"To be on a grouse moor with a loaded shotgun at dawn on the 12th of August is to know the true meaning of exclusivity," one writer recently opined in the *Telegraph*. The Glorious Twelfth—August 12—is the much-celebrated opening day of red grouse hunting season, and the period from mid-September through the rest of the autumn season sees the bird featured on many menus. Like other game birds favored by the British—pheasant, quail, partridge—grouse is traditionally roasted and garnished with bread sauce, game chips (thin, crisp potato chips), a gloss of pan juices, and a Cumberland sauce, a combination of red currants, port wine, orange, and mustard.

Where: *In London,* Wiltons, tel 44/20-7629-9955, wiltons.co.uk. **Mail order:** Scottish Gourmet USA, tel 877-814-3663, scottishgourmet usa.com; D'Artagnan, tel 800-327-8246, dartagnan .com. **Further information and recipes:** *Mrs. Bridges' Upstairs, Downstairs Cookery Book* edited by Adrian Bailey (1974); saveur.com (search roast grouse with bread sauce and game crumbs).

⊩||||||||||||||||||||||||||||||⊩

THE ROYAL ROAST

Roast Beef and Yorkshire Pudding

English

Only one cut of the best, fat-enriched beef will do for this most regal of meat dishes—the standing prime rib roast, bones and all. Not for serious carnivores is the boned and rolled version, no matter how easy it is to slice,

nor roasts cut from other parts of the burly Aberdeen Angus steers. Rubbed with dry mustard and black pepper, then lightly dredged with flour (add salt only after slicing) and roasted to a turn, the beef turns a silky American Beauty rose-red, trickling juices at once slightly salty, beefy, and with a mellow edge of flavor, while the outer fat becomes bacon-crisp. Those who like beef cooked beyond rare will endure a loss of texture and flavor; a similar fate befalls those who ask for their roast beef thickly sliced. Technically known as an English cut, the proper slice is supple and thin, easier to cut and chew, and best experienced with enhancements of brassy English mustard and horseradish sauce. As a lagniappe the next day, leftover meaty bones can be deviled—

In many British households, the "Sunday roast" is the most important meal of the week.

brushed with melted butter, mustard, and bread crumbs—and slowly broiled under low heat until crunchy and brown on all sides.

For the perfect roast beef feast, a slab of puffy, eggy Yorkshire pudding is the proper accompaniment, especially if that giant pop-over is made the traditional way: the golden batter poured into a pan, placed in the oven, and then moistened with seasoned drippings from the roasting meat itself. That is about as close as we come these days to the original method of preparation, when the meat was roasted on a spit above the Yorkshire, gilding the pudding's crust with its flavorful drippings.

WHERE: *In London,* Simpsons in the Strand, tel 44/20-7836-9112, simpsonsinthestrand.co.uk; The Goring Restaurant (on Sundays), tel 44/20-7396-9000, thegoring.com; *in New York,* Tea & Sympathy (Sundays), tel 212-989-9735, teaand sympathynewyork.com. **FURTHER INFORMATION AND RECIPES:** *The Ploughman's Lunch and the Miser's Feast* by Brian Yarvin (2012); food network.com (search roast prime rib of beef with yorkshire pudding). **SPECIAL EVENT:** World Yorkshire Pudding Championships, North Yorkshire, June, grassington-festival.org.uk.

─┤||||||||||||||||||||||||||||||├─

"THERE NEVER WAS SUCH A GOOSE."
—BOB CRATCHIT, IN *A CHRISTMAS CAROL* BY CHARLES DICKENS

Roast Goose with Sage-Onion Stuffing

English

Probably no roast in history has tantalized and nourished as many generations as this literary main course. As Bob Cratchit observes in Charles Dickens's *A Christmas Carol,* "Its tenderness and flavour, size and cheapness, were the themes of universal admiration." A fitting centerpiece, indeed, of the meal that inspired an epiphany in the miserly Ebenezer Scrooge as he watched the family of his downtrodden clerk enjoying a hard-won Christmas dinner. Cushioned by a fragrant sage and onion stuffing and "eked out" with a chocolate-dark giblet gravy, mashed potatoes, and nutmeg-scented applesauce by the necessarily frugal Mrs. Cratchit, it is *the* symbol of Christmas dinners past.

The meal's central position in English celebrations stretches back well past the Victorian era: According to legend, Queen Elizabeth I was dining on roasted goose when she learned of the English defeat of the Spanish Armada. The queen then decreed that goose was to be served on this day, which happened to be Michaelmas, a fall holiday, every year thereafter. (Some believe that the American tradition of Thanksgiving turkey evolved from this annual celebratory feast.)

With its golden, crackling-crisp skin and unctuously moist, darkly gamy meat, roast goose will also, we hope, remain a main feature of Christmases yet to come. Although its hegemonic position at the holiday dinner table has in recent decades been usurped by turkey, perhaps due to the high amount of fat on a goose, roast goose rewards diners with a stronger, richer, more interesting flavor.

From the ghost of Christmas dinners past, here's the recipe as the Crachits might have enjoyed it, recommended by Esther Copley in 1838's *The Housekeeper's Guide:*

Roasted Goose
with Sage-Onion Stuffing,
Giblet Gravy

Roast a goose before a brisk fire but at considerable distance at first. It will require basting, for which purpose a little butter should be used at first, but its own fat will soon begin to drip.

Dredge with flour and salt, and see that it is nicely browned all over. A green goose, i.e., one that has not attained its full growth, will take 50 minutes to 1¼ hours; a full-grown goose will require nearly or quite 2 hours.

FURTHER INFORMATION AND RECIPES: *A Christmas Carol* by Charles Dickens (1843); *British Cookery* edited by Lizzie Boyd (1989); bbcgoodfood.com (search classic roast goose with cider gravy).

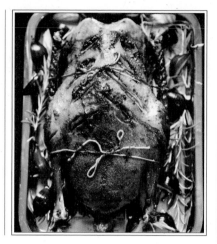

"I WANTED TO LIVE DEEP AND SUCK OUT ALL THE MARROW OF LIFE . . ."
—HENRY DAVID THOREAU, *WALDEN*

Bone Marrow

Thoreau may have been speaking metaphorically, but the instinct to devour the lusciously fatty, seductively satiny marrow at the center of bones is a wise one. Wherever there are long, large leg or shoulder bones of beef, bison, veal, or lamb, the marrow nestled within will be a special prize.

Sometimes used as an ingredient in dishes such as true Milan risotto (see page 233), German dumplings (see page 324), English salad dressings, and French, Chinese, Japanese, and Korean sauces and dressings, marrow is perhaps most delectable on its own: simply cut out of the bones of roasted or grilled meat and spread on toast. Marrow can also be deliciously extracted at the table, as it is with boiled beef or veal osso buco, the unctuously gelatinous treasure gracefully reached with the aid of the slim, elongated silver marrow spoon.

Like so many of life's temptations, bone marrow presents a dilemma in being as good for you as it is bad. High in iron, minerals, and valuable, easily absorbed protein, it is also famously high in cholesterol. But waste not, want not, as the saying goes.

WHERE: *In London,* St. John Bar & Restaurant, tel 44/20-7251-0848, stjohngroup.uk.com; *in New York,* Kin Shop, tel 212-675-4295, kinshopnyc.com; Prune, tel 212-677-6221, prunerestaurant.com; *in Morrison, CO,* The Fort, tel 303-697-4471, thefort.com; *in Los Angeles,* Animal, tel 323-782-9225, animalrestaurant.com. **FURTHER INFORMATION AND RECIPES:** *Bones* by Jennifer McLagan (2005); bonappetit.com (search roast bone marrow); ruhlman.com (search how to prepare and serve bone marrow).

Scotch Eggs, or Nargisi Kofta

English (Anglo-Indian)

Which came first, Scotch eggs or *nargisi kofta*? That is the sort of argument food historians thrive on—while the rest of us indulge in carefree delight. Whether the Scotch egg originated as a spoil of the British empire in India or

an invention of the London provisioners Fortnum & Mason, the appetizer-snack is a savory conceit. It begins with a peeled, half-boiled egg; lightly dredged in egg and flour, it is then enclosed in finely ground meat, either pork sausage or a mixture of ham, anchovies, and herbs. Veneered with bread crumbs and then quickly deep-fried in oil, it emerges scrumptiously hot and golden, ready to be dressed with brown gravy or tomato sauce or enjoyed cold as a nibbler with drinks, especially in pubs.

As might be expected, the Indian version, nargisi kofta, has more exotic scents and flavors, with ground lamb or beef spiked with onions, garlic, and a rainbow of spices. The coated eggs are fried with onions in clarified butter or vegetable oil and are cut in half lengthwise before serving to reveal the yolk, looking

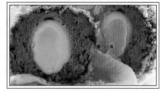

Scotch eggs served cold with salad

like the yellow center of a white flower. Madhur Jaffrey, in her 1973 cookbook *An Invitation to Indian Cooking*, speculates that the appearance of the cut-open kofta accounts for the name *nargisi*, meaning narcissus.

WHERE: *In London,* The Handmade Scotch Egg Company at farmers' markets, hand madescotcheggs.co.uk; *in New York,* The Breslin, tel 212-679-1939, the breslin.com; *in Woodland Hills, CA,* Taste of India, tel 818-999-0600, tasteofindiala.com. **FURTHER INFORMATION AND RECIPES:** *An Invitation to Indian Cooking* by Madhur Jaffrey (1973); *The Ploughman's Lunch and the Miser's Feast* by Brian Yarvin (2012); the guardian.com (search how to cook the perfect scotch egg). **SPECIAL EVENT:** The Scotch Egg Challenge, London, September, theship .co.uk.

Seed Cake

English, Scottish, Irish

The licorice tang of caraway seeds is an enticing accent in a thin, round butter-and-egg cake traditionally popular throughout the British Isles, albeit with some regional variations. Dating back in British food history at least as far as the sixteenth century, seed cake was a Victorian favorite—one apparently also enjoyed by the Bellamy family of television's *Upstairs Downstairs*.

As appealing at teatime as it is with morning coffee, this firm, moist, sunny cake, fragrant with cinnamon and cloves or nutmeg, makes a restorative accompaniment to a glass of port or Madeira, or a decorative dessert when served with soft vanilla ice cream and berries.

Scotland's version includes diced candied fruits and a whiff of brandy or Scotch whisky, while Ireland's seed cake relies on—no surprise—that country's own eye-opening whiskey.

FURTHER INFORMATION AND RECIPES: *Delights and Prejudices* by James Beard (2001); *Mrs. Bridges' Upstairs, Downstairs Cookery Book* edited by Adrian Bailey (1974); food.com (search victorian seed cake); npr.org (search caraway seed is a spice worth meeting).

UNDER A CLOUD OF MASHED POTATO

Shepherd's Pie and Cottage Pie

English

As reassuring as a lullaby, a steaming-hot and savory casserole-like pie of minced meat crowned with lightly glazed mashed potatoes is comfort food of the most elemental order. Forkful after forkful, you break through the thick mashed-potato crust to mine the delicious filling beneath. Soothing flavors come by way of sautéed onions, marjoram, parsley, Worcestershire sauce, and a rich brown gravy boosted by plenty of freshly ground black pepper.

The difference between shepherd's pie and cottage pie is the meat—lamb or mutton is correct for the former, and beef fills the latter. Unsurprisingly, shepherd's pie is believed to have been first prepared by shepherds in England and Scotland sometime in the eighteenth century. Cottage pie has a longer history as an economical farm and country dish.

According to the *Oxford Companion to Food,* both pies became widely popular home dishes in the 1870s, with the advent of mincing machines. As British celebrity chef Hugh Fearnley-Whittingstall observes, while cottage pie is "by its nature an improvised dish, nevertheless it is one to approach with a certain amount of care and respect—because when you make a good one it's one of the most delicious things on the planet."

The pies are often used by home cooks as a clever application for leftover cooked meat, but fresh, raw meat results in a more delicate, fresher flavor and texture. Grated mild Cheddar sprinkled over the potato topping just before baking assures a bright golden finish and adds aromatic zest. A kick often comes by way of the addition of ground nutmeg to the mashed potatoes, an improvement suggested by Alexis Soyer, the French chef who made his reputation in Victorian London. Regardless of these perfecting touches, the hearty, filling, and simple pies are favorites in homes, pubs, and stylish restaurants alike.

WHERE: *In New York*, Tea & Sympathy, tel 212-989-9735, teaandsympathynewyork.com. **FURTHER INFORMATION AND RECIPES:** *The Ploughman's Lunch and the Miser's Feast* by Brian Yarvin (2012); *The Oxford Companion to Food* by Alan Davidson (1999); theguardian.com (search nigel slater classic shepherd's pie).

AN ENGLISH BLUE CHEESE BY WAY OF SCOTLAND

Shropshire Blue

English

A t first glance, with its silvery blue riddles and speckles etched into a marigold orange base, Shropshire blue cheese suggests a Cheddar gone rotten. Yet it is the contrast between the needling-sharp, almost metallic sting of those blue spots and the sunshine-butteriness of its orange base that makes this cheese so alluring.

Shropshire Blue makes for a conspicuous and beguiling addition to any cheese counter. Perhaps not so lofty or complex as centuries-old Stilton, this younger blue does share Stilton's texture—hard and crumbly, yet still creamy. That similarity is no accident, as the two cheeses both originate in Nottinghamshire and Leicestershire, in England's western Midlands. Shropshire Blue's story, however, begins in Inverness, Scotland, with enterprising and food-loving retired Royal Air Force pilot David Hutchinson Smith and his wife, Jill, an agricultural scientist. In the 1970s, they created the unpressed cow's milk cheese as a Scottish imitation of Stilton. To set it apart, Hutchinson Smith colored it orange with annatto, a natural dye derived from the South American achiote tree; the blue mold was the result of the growth of *Penicillin roqueforti* (the same mold used in both Stilton and France's Roquefort; see pages 27 and 127). To market Shropshire, Jill

Hutchinson Smith claimed that it had English roots—and eventually the cheese did settle there. When the Hutchinson Smiths' dairy closed, a spot in the English county of Cheshire took up production of Shropshire Blue, followed not long after by dairies in Nottinghamshire and Leicestershire, now the cheese's biggest producers. The Ludlow Food Centre in Shropshire produces it, too.

Shropshire Blue is an excellent dessert cheese, pairing well with fruit and dessert wines such as port and sherry.

WHERE: *In London,* Paxton and Whitfield, tel 44/20-7930-0259, paxtonandwhitfield.co.uk; *in Shropshire,* Ludlow Food Centre, tel 44/1584-856000, ludlowfoodcentre.co.uk; *in New York and environs,* Fairway Markets, fairwaymarket.com. **FURTHER INFORMATION:** *Cheese Primer* by Steven Jenkins (1996); britishcheese.com. **TIP:** Look for widespread, deep blue mold and a bright orange base. If the orange has faded or the rind is cracked, the cheese is past its prime and will be too dry to be enjoyable.

THE FISH THAT DRANK TOO MUCH

Soused Herring

English

O ne of the oldest methods of preserving fish, sousing or pickling is said to have been taught to the Romans by the Greeks, and thence to the rest of the world—including England, a nation of enthusiastic herring eaters.

For English-style sousing, herring fillets are soaked in a brine, then rolled and baked in the pickling liquid of malt or white wine vinegar, spices and herbs such as mace, pepper, mustard seeds, and bay leaves. After cooling for at least twenty-four hours, the fish emerges firm but tender, aromatic with a palate-tingling edge of saltiness. That edge is gently mitigated by thin slices of buttered dark bread, the whole most vividly enhanced by a complement of icy gin, vodka, or aquavit—a "brine" that ensures that before long, guests will be properly soused, too.

WHERE: *In London,* Harrods, tel 44/20-7730-1234, harrods.com; Fortnum & Mason, tel 44/20-7734-8040, fortnumandmason.com; The Goring Restaurant, tel 44/20-7396-9000, thegoring.com. **FURTHER INFORMATION AND RECIPES:** *British Cookery* edited by Lizzie Boyd (1989); theguardian.com (search nigel slater's soused mackerel); great britishkitchen.co.uk/recipebook (search soused herrings).

A CHEF WITH REAL GUTS

St. John Bar & Restaurant

English

W arm pig's head, anyone? This is only one of the delectable shockers in store for the brave of palate who entrust themselves to the wiles of chef-owner Fergus Henderson. It's an only-in-London experience, unless one is lucky enough to catch the master chef doing a restaurant stint abroad. An architect manqué, Henderson has a way with animal innards, making the succulent best of unexpected menu items like pigeon livers (on toast) as well as more-usual restaurant fare like silky roasted beef marrow (tossed in a parsley-onion salad spread on crunchy bruschetta), both magical dishes that have placed St. John high atop the list of favorite London restaurants.

Cooking whole beasts from nose to tail, Henderson varies his seasonal menu with offal such as deep-fried tripe; beefy, tender grilled ox heart with green beans and shallots; or a thin and golden-crusted pie of ox tongue and chicken. But it is pig parts that really inspire this gutsy chef, who dishes up crisp cheeks or ears with dandelion salad, gelatinous braised trotters, rolled spleen, and crackling tails garnished with bacon-wrapped prunes filled with foie gras. Kinder cuts for the less adventurous include deliciously prepared fish dishes, rabbit simmered with turnips, and moist roasted guinea hen served with celeriac.

The seasonal dessert menu may include the winey red-berry Summer Pudding (see page 29), a sweetly burnished Treacle Tart (see page 31), and Lancashire's crumbly sharp and earthy cheese served as a foil to Ferguson's riff on Eccles Cakes (see page 11).

Fittingly located next to Smithfield Market, the city's wholesale center for meat, St. John's sky-lit and sparklingly white-walled, smart setting was formerly a pork smokehouse. You can also visit Henderson's more casual St. John Bread & Wine in the Spitalfields Market. It's a great place for a hearty breakfast of herring roes, deviled kidneys on toast, or a crunchy smoked-bacon butty—a sandwich on a warm and puffy buttered bun.

WHERE: St. John Bar & Restaurant, 26 St. John Street, Smithfield, London, tel 44/20-7251-0848, stjohngroup.uk.com; St. John Bread & Wine, 94–96 Commercial Street, Spitalfields Market, London, tel 44/20-3301-8069, stjohngroup.uk.com/spitalfields. **FURTHER INFORMATION AND RECIPES:** *The Whole Beast: Nose to Tail Eating* by Fergus Henderson (2004), *Beyond Nose to Tail* by Fergus Henderson and Justin Piers Gellatly (2007).

—|||||||||||||||||||||||||||||—

AS BRITISH AS JOHN BULL

Steak and Kidney Pie

English

A hearty, fragrant pie with a flaky top crust covering a lusty stew of fork-tender beef chunks and bits of beef or lamb kidney gentled with heady brown gravy, this British classic has been a standard of the English kitchen since Shakespeare's time. The teasing acidity of the kidneys is subtly sweetened by plenty of softly cooked onions and, often, earthy black-gilled morel mushrooms, dried or fresh. A variant, steak and oyster pie, is a classic dish of the Ballymaloe Cookery School in County Cork, Ireland.

For nearly 350 years, first-time visitors to London have ordered—however apprehensively—steak and kidney pie for lunch at Ye Olde Cheshire Cheese in Fleet Street, the former newspaper district of The City. The dimly lit seventeenth-century chophouse with flagstone floors, half-timbered walls, and fumed ceiling beams was a regular pit-stop for literary luminaries such as Dr. Samuel Johnson, Charles Dickens, and Sir Arthur Conan Doyle, and has continued to be so for the current generation of writers and tourists. Visitors to Dr. Johnson's house, walking distance from the restaurant, are advised to get there before lunch; given the effects of the golden ale that classically washes down the pie, deciphering the old script of Dr. Johnson's dictionary postprandially may pose far too great a challenge.

WHERE: *In London,* Ye Olde Cheshire Cheese, tel 44/20-7353-6170; *in New York,* Tea & Sympathy, tel 212-989-9735, teaandsympathynewyork.com. **FURTHER INFORMATION AND RECIPES:** foodnetwork .com (search steak and kidney pie); theguardian .com (search steak kidney pie whitingstall).

—|||||||||||||||||||||||||||||—

*"STILTON HAS SURVIVED A PASSING THREAT FROM ROQUEFORT. IT HAS NO FEAR OF GORGONZOLA." —*OSBERT BURDETT IN *THE LITTLE BOOK OF CHEESE,* 1935

Stilton

English

E ngland's noble, heady Stilton is not intimidated, not even by Italy's royal Parmigiano-Reggiano (see page 216), so firm a position does it hold in the world pantheon of cheeses. Never mind its uncertain pedigree. (It was created either by a housekeeper, Elizabeth Scarbrow of Leicestershire, in 1720, or by one Cooper Thornhill of Yorkshire around the same time.)

The pungent, aged triumph is produced in only three counties—Darbyshire, Leicestershire, and Nottinghamshire. The cheese owes its iconic steel-blue veining to the crust of the cheese being pierced with long, stainless steel needles, allowing air into the core. In a fully ripened cheese, aged for a period of six months to a year, the sharpness of that blue veining should be gently mitigated by the crumbly creaminess of the tannish background—but overly ambitious producers and retailers often choose to sell the cheese before its prime.

Although Stilton is often sold in small, wrapped pieces or in attractive crocks, such packages are really intended for souvenir buyers, not connoisseurs. It is far better to purchase it cut to order from a 14- to 16-pound cylinder. That way, you can judge the quality of the cheese by looking for an abundance of blue veining running all the way to the edges of the cylinder, which ought to have a dry, parchment-brown rind. And then, of course, you can taste before you buy, a wise step with so expensive a product.

With its decadent aroma and its complex, sharp-to-mild flavor that varies with age, Stilton fares as well with raw vegetables such as celery, cucumbers, scallions, and radishes as it does with walnuts or fruits such as ripe pears, apples, and muscat grapes. It also provides a sparkling accent to aged ruby or tawny port or a well-burnished Madeira. The best foils for this strong, assertive, easy-to-spread cheese are mild-flavored English water biscuits; thinly cut, firm-textured light wheat bread; or even Scandinavian whole-grain crispbreads (as long as they are not seasoned with caraway).

Where: *In London,* Neal's Yard Dairy at three locations, nealsyarddairy.co.uk; *in New York,* Murray's Cheese Shop, tel 888-692-4339, murrayscheese.com. **Further information:** *Cheese Primer* by Steven Jenkins (1996).

A CHEESE THAT STANDS ALONE—AND NO WONDER

Stinking Bishop

English

Elusively, lavishly runny and fast-ripening, this butter-colored semisoft cheese with a moist orange rind and a malevolent aroma is a must-taste for anyone claiming cheese connoisseurship—a quest with which a bit of trivia never hurt.

In the 2005 animated film *Wallace & Gromit and the Curse of the Were-Rabbit,* the cheese was portrayed as being so pungent it revived Wallace from the dead.

Love it or hate it, but skip it and you are bypassing a mystically seductive flavor with a hint of rich cream and overtones of the bitter, the salty, and the mushroomy. As with similar strong ripening cheeses—French Epoisses, Alsatian Munster, and German handkäse—the Stinking Bishop is best accented by a ripe, tangy pear or ice-cold radishes or celery, along with thin water biscuits and gently sparkling hard cider or light beer.

The evil-smelling cheese, made from pasteurized cow's milk, was developed in 1972 by Charles Martell for the Teddington Cheese Company in Gloucestershire. Its improbable name represents no sacrilege, as it refers not to a prelate, but to the Stinking Bishop pear; the fruit's juice is mildly fermented into an alcoholic cider called perry, in which the cheese rind is washed every four weeks as it ages.

Where: *In London,* Neal's Yard Dairy at three locations, nealsyarddairy.co.uk; *in New York,* Murray's Cheese Shop, tel 888-692-4339, murrayscheese.com.

━━━━━━━━━━━━━━━━━━━━━━━━━━━━━━━┤||||||||||||||||||||||||||||||├━━━━━━━━━━━━━━━━━━━━━━━━━━━━━━━

A BOWLFUL OF SUMMER

Summer Pudding

English

Ripe red raspberries, red currants, blueberries, and blackberries are favorites for this cool and moist dessert with the sparkle of liquid garnets. Although the word *pudding* suggests either a hot and steamy dish in the English vein or

a creamy dessert favored by children, in this case it refers to a cool, fresh press of lightly crushed and sugared berries encased in white bread that turns lusciously crimson as fruit juices seep through. But it is a pudding in form, as it is turned out of a bowl, a soufflé dish, or a charlotte mold to be spooned into individual dishes and topped with a swirl of whipped cream, crème fraîche, or clotted cream, the sweet, thick cream topping hugely popular in Devon and Cornwall (see page 7). This cool

The pudding can be made in a large bowl or individual molds.

enchantment is generally offered in English restaurants and homes in midsummer; these days, however, it can be had year-round if frozen or imported berries are deemed acceptable. For the very best results, use raspberries and red currants and, to avoid having to cook them, select berries that are very ripe and flavorful.

Summer Pudding

Serves 6 to 8

About 3 pounds (2 quarts) of soft, ripe, but unspoiled berries (raspberries, red or black currants, blueberries, blackberries, strawberries), washed and well drained

1 cup plus 2 tablespoons superfine sugar

Grated zest and strained juice of 1 lemon

2 tablespoons unsalted butter, melted

10 to 12 slices of good, dense white bread, trimmed of crusts

2 cups heavy cream, lightly whipped to soft peaks; or 2½ cups crème fraîche

1. In a medium-size saucepan, combine the berries with the sugar and lemon juice and, without adding water, simmer over low heat for 3 or 4 minutes, until the berries just begin to lose their shape and give up their juices. Remove from heat and stir in the lemon zest. (Very ripe, soft berries need not be cooked. Simply combine them with the sugar, lemon juice, and zest and stir somewhat vigorously with a wooden spoon until the berries are slightly mushy.)

2. Brush the melted butter all around the insides of a 2-quart bowl or a soufflé or charlotte mold.

3. Trim all but 2 of the bread slices to fit so they line the bottom and sides of the mold in one layer. Reserve the 2 slices to cover the top.

4. Pour in all the fruit and juices and cover with the reserved 2 slices of bread.

5. Cover with a plate or saucer that fits just inside the bowl or mold and set a 3-pound weight on top, such as a kitchen weight, a few large cans, or a small heavy pan. Chill for 12 to 18 hours, or until the bread is thoroughly reddened with fruit juices.

6. To serve, remove the weight and the plate or saucer and invert a pretty glass or china serving plate onto the top of the mold. Holding plate and mold together, invert the mold so that the pudding slips onto the plate. If it does not do so easily, wipe the sides with a paper towel wrung out in hot water to slightly melt the pudding so it slips out easily. Spoon into individual plates and top with the thickened cream of your choice.

WHERE: *In London,* Wiltons (in summer), tel 44/20-7629-9955, wiltons.co.uk; *in San Francisco,* Greens Restaurant, tel 415-771-6222, greens restaurant.com; *in New York,* Tea & Sympathy (in summer), tel 212-989-9735, teaandsympathynew york.com. **TIP:** Unless you bake your own white bread or live near a bakery offering *pain de mie,* the French sandwich loaf, use something akin to Pepperidge Farm's Original white bread.

|||||||||||||||||||||||||||||||||||||

SAUSAGES IN HIDING, NO TOADS IN SIGHT

Toad-in-the-Hole

English

In his biting *Devil's Dictionary* of 1911, the American satirist Ambrose Bierce includes an advertisement for toad-in-the-hole under his definition of rarebit: "A Welsh rabbit, in the speech of the humorless, who point out that it is not a rabbit.

To whom it may be solemnly explained that the comestible known as toad-in-the-hole is really not a toad, and that *riz-de-veau à la financière* is not the smile of a calf prepared after the recipe of a she banker." Indeed, toad-in-the-hole has nothing to do with amphibious wildlife and everything to do with the working-class Brits who, as early as the 1700s, were taking scraps of meat, frying them in a bit of butter, and then tucking them into simple Yorkshire pudding batters of flour, milk, and eggs before baking them. It was a great way to make inexpensive

Timeless, satisfying fare as humble as its name

ingredients stretch—while still having something delicious for teatime. Now crunchy, pork-filled bangers are blanketed with the same egg-rich batter used for Yorkshire pudding and popovers, and as the sort-of pie bakes and the batter shrinks, the sausages edge up and peek out of their "holes." The result is a hearty combination of crisp, golden crust and sputteringly juicy, peppery meat.

In the earliest days of toad-in-the-hole, recipes were published in such seminal cookbooks as *The Art of Cookery, Made Plain and Easy* by Hannah Glasse (1747) and *The Experienced English Housekeeper* by Elizabeth Raffald (1769). Toad-in-the-hole has survived these many years because it offers homey, comforting pleasure that's never been in fashion—and so has never been out of it either. It is a decidedly old-world dish that is a welcome addition to any modern brunch table. Creative contemporary British chefs offer their own versions: Jamie Oliver says he likes to "go huge," and values a toad-in-the-hole that rises high over the top of the baking dish, while Nigella Lawson prefers to use small cocktail wieners. Either way, the dish goes well with the customary onion gravy and mashed potatoes, but for a lighter, contemporary garnish, try it with a bright, zesty green salad.

WHERE: *In London,* Dirty Dicks, tel 44/20-7283-5888, dirtydicks.co.uk; *in Savannah, GA,* Churchill's Pub & Restaurant, tel 912-232-8501, thebritishpub.com; *in Winnipeg,* Toad in the Hole Pub & Eatery, tel 204-284-7201, toadinthehole.ca. **FURTHER INFORMATION AND RECIPES:** *Happy Days with the Naked Chef* by Jamie Oliver (2001); *Nigella Kitchen* by Nigella Lawson (2010); saveur.com (search toad in the hole).

HARRY POTTER'S FAVORITE DESSERT

Treacle Tart

English

Considering the enormous popularity of J.K. Rowling's fantasy series, it's surprising that a mainstream American baking company hasn't yet introduced packaged versions of the tart so beloved by the boy hero. An unctuously sweet confection with a lattice crust topping, it is filled with a deceptively simple blend of bread crumbs, butter, spices, and evaporated sugarcane syrup. Known in England as light treacle or golden syrup, the sugary liquid is thick, amber-colored, and honeylike; Lyle's Golden Syrup is the traditional choice. Scented with lemon juice, ginger, cinnamon, and perhaps allspice or cloves, the tart develops an appealing aroma as it bakes in its flaky crust. Local variations include Suffolk's treacle tart, which has eggs beaten into the syrup for a custardlike effect, and Yorkshire's, which includes chopped dried fruit and grated apple. Treacle tart is best when just cool enough to allow the filling to gel, but still warm from the oven. Don't forget a cloudlet of whipped cream to modify the sweetness.

WHERE: *In London,* St. John Bar & Restaurant, tel 44/20-7251-0848, stjohngroup.uk.com. **FURTHER INFORMATION AND RECIPES:** *Mrs. Bridges' Upstairs, Downstairs Cookery Book* edited by Adrian Bailey (1974); *Beyond Nose to Tail* by Fergus Henderson and Justin Piers Gellatly (2007); saveur.com (search treacle tart).

THERE'S NOTHING "MERE" ABOUT A TRIFLE

Trifle

English, Scottish

Cool and sparkling in a big cut-crystal bowl, this opulently moist Madeira- or sherry-perfumed layering of custard and/or whipped cream, golden sponge cake, bitter almond macaroons, and zesty raspberry or strawberry jam is an easy-to-love dessert that appeals to the child in all of us—and it's simple to make, with gorgeous layers that make for excellent tabletop decoration. Trifles appear to have evolved from fools (see page 14), and the earliest examples were little more than flavored thick cream that reflected the dessert's insubstantial name. Today, a trifle is a favorite at holiday meals, where it provides a lighter alternative to the dense Christmas pudding. Spiked with Drambuie in Scotland, Scottish trifle is called tipsy laird and provides the perfect dessert for a Burns

A festive and enticing dessert

Supper, the annual celebration marking the January 25 birthday of poet Robert Burns, which frequently features poetry readings, bagpipe music, toasts, and a main course of haggis (see page 40).

WHERE: *In London,* Wiltons, tel 44/20-7629-9955, wiltons.co .uk; St. John Bar & Restaurant, tel 44/20-7251-0848, stjohngroup .uk.com. **FURTHER INFORMATION AND RECIPES:** *The Ploughman's Lunch and the Miser's Feast* by Brian Yarvin (2012); theguard ian.com (search how to make perfect trifle). **SEE ALSO:** Tirami Sù, page 245.

------|||||||||||||||||||||||||||||||------

PUTTING A LITTLE ENGLISH ON IT

Wiltons

English

Set in the midst of London's fashionable men's tailors and haberdasheries, this thoroughgoing and revered classic of a restaurant dates back to 1742 and seems like a time warp, with the formal setting and staff manners to match.

Yet Wiltons has proven to be permanently au courant for those longing to try the best of traditional English seafood, along with a few game specialties, most especially grouse, in season. A series of clublike rooms, done up with ochre-colored walls, green velvet draperies, dark wood trim, and cushy chairs, open one onto the next while providing plenty of quiet, intimate corners. Those choice spots are usually inhabited by movers and shakers from the worlds of business and politics, speaking in assorted languages and puffing on assorted cigars, sipping brandy as they gather to wheel and deal at lunch, by far the most colorful time to be there.

Here is the place to try a variety of superb British Isle oysters (especially Colchesters) at

their iciest, briniest best; sublime lobster cocktails; miraculously large and tender Scottish langoustines; or very English, very seductive Potted Shrimp, a sort of pâté set in butter and redolent of mace and lemon (see page 18). Rarely will you find Dover Sole à la Meunière brought to more golden, dewy perfection (see page 86); or a more ethereal, soufflé-light, and lemony Hollandaise sauce, which tops the restaurant's bright coral Irish salmon, succulent Scottish halibut, or satiny turbot.

Tiny steamed potatoes and childishly delicious mushy peas are traditional side dishes worth trying, as is a strangely satisfying Stilton cream soup in which the pungency of the blue-veined cheese is ameliorated by soothing, neutral overtones of celery. If it is summer, do not miss the winey red berry Summer Pudding for dessert (see page 29); and if it is not, go for the unctuously decadent steamed syrup sponge pudding or the intoxicating, sherry-spiked trifle.

As you might expect, the prices for the food and the awesome French wines list are anything but trifling.

WHERE: 55 Jermyn Street, London, tel 44/20-7629-9955, wiltons.co.uk.

CURED, SMOKED, AGED

York Ham

English

O ne of the world's highly prized hams, the York original is made from the meaty Large White commercial pigs of Yorkshire and dry cured for about three weeks by a method traditional in the York region. (Thanks to this curing

process, York has a distinctively drier and saltier taste than other English hams.) Rubbed with brown sugar and salt, the ham is then smoked over oak and aged for about four months to achieve mellow ripeness. The meat is either boiled and served cold, thinly sliced, or roasted with a sweet glaze or a crisp bread crumb layer. It is equally desirable with breakfast eggs as it is on buttered bread as a teatime snack.

A 1928 magazine ad for Marsh & Baxter's York Ham

The chances of finding a true York ham in the U.S. are slim, so a visit to England is in order. There, it is readily available by the pound in upscale London food shops.

WHERE: *In London,* Fortnum & Mason, tel 44/20-7734-8040, fortnumandmason.com; Paxton & Whitfield, tel 44/20-7930-0259, paxtonandwhitfield.co.uk. **SEE ALSO:** Jabugo Ham, page 262; Schlachtplatter, page 310; Yunnan Ham, page 795.

PLEASE *DO* EAT THE FLOWERS

Nasturtiums

A mong edible flowers such as roses (see page 386), chrysanthemums, and violets, nasturtiums may be the most widely associated with the gourmet plate. Enjoyed in England at least as far back as the seventeenth century, they traveled to the French table in the

eighteenth. The food authority of that era, Brillat-Savarin, credited one Marquis d'Albagnac for what became a veritable French vogue for edible flowers after the French Revolution. (The marquis had made a name and fortune for himself as a "salad designer" in stately English homes.)

As part of the trend toward the fresh and natural, the nasturtium's delicate spring-green leaves and silky red, yellow, and orange blossoms have found renewed popularity these days. The tender leaves have a verdant peppery flavor similar to that of watercress.

The plant's Latin name, *Tropaeolum majus*, translates to "trophy," and was chosen because the plant's leaves resembled shields hung by Romans as trophies after battle. Another one of its names is "Jesuits' cress," reflecting the nasturtium's path as it was introduced from its native South America to Europe by colonizing Spanish Jesuits.

Today the flowers are most likely to be found strewn across salads, the leaves adding a springy texture and a sprightly essence, and the blossoms imparting a bright dash of color and a faintly perfumed bitterness. But old English recipes made a meal out of the nasturtium, stuffing its blossoms with chopped tuna, capers, gherkins, chervil, parsley, and mayonnaise. Its buds and seeds can be pickled as stand-ins for capers, a procedure accomplished by placing them in a jar, and covering them with boiled spiced vinegar, then leaving them in a cool dark spot for several months.

It does come back around to the oh-so-pretty and refreshing nasturtium salad, ever so simply described in the 1922 English cookbook *From a Housewife's Note Book* with the following recipe: "Put a plate of flowers of the nasturtium in a salad bowl with a tablespoonful of chopped chervil, sprinkle over half a teaspoonful of salt, two or three tablespoonfuls of olive oil, and the juice of a lemon; turn the salad in the bowl with a spoon and fork till well mixed, and serve."

FURTHER INFORMATION AND RECIPES: *Cooking with Flowers* by Miche Bacher (2013); food.com (search stuffed nasturtium flowers); splendid table.org (search nasturtium capers); epicurious.com (search nasturtium pizza).

"WOMEN RESPOND DELIGHTEDLY TO ITS BLANDNESS."
—OSBERT BURDETT IN *THE LITTLE BOOK OF CHEESE*, 1935

Caerphilly

Welsh

Named for the Welsh town where it was widely produced and sold in the early nineteenth century, Caerphilly is a white, crumbly, semisoft cheese that was especially satisfying to miners for its restorative saltiness and easy portability.

For the rest of us nonminers—women, men, and children alike—that salty, dairy astringency and softly moist texture make it an easy-to-like snack.

In the early twentieth century, Welsh Caerphilly came to be produced almost exclusively in Somerset, England, where cheesemakers were better able to meet the high public demand. Then, during World War II, strict rationing caused the production of Caerphilly to come to a halt entirely. Eventually, the cheese came to be mass-produced of pasteurized cow's milk, making for an unfortunately drier, less flavorful product.

Now, thankfully, creamier artisan specimens are being turned out in both England and Wales, based on unpasteurized milk and aged one to three months at the longest to develop a dry pewter-gray rind and a butter-colored interior without spoiling or becoming chalky. The result lends itself to eating out of hand with fruit or raw vegetables and crackers, and can be grilled in sandwiches or melted down for rarebits or sauces.

RETAIL AND MAIL ORDER: *in New York,* Murray's Cheese, tel 888-692-4339, murrayscheese.com. **MAIL ORDER:** igourmet.com. **TIP:** The best brands are Duckett's from England and Glynlyon, Caws Cenarth Caerffili, and Gorwydd from Wales.

⊦||||||||||||||||||||||||||||||⊦

THE SOUP THAT SPRANG A LEEK

Leek Broth and Cock-a-Leekie

Welsh, Scottish

To honor the patron saint of Wales, Saint David, on his feast day, every March 1, the Welsh serve dishes made with leeks, the tall, stately member of the onion family that is their national symbol. Although strictly apocryphal, legend has it that Saint David advised ancient Briton soldiers to wear leeks in their hats to distinguish them from the Saxons they battled in the seventh century, thus avoiding casualties from their allies.

Whatever the custom's origins, the story ends well: with an enticing leek broth (or *cawl cennin,* its Cymric/Welsh name) that is a meal in a bowl, based on chicken stock and thickened with oatmeal, and adrift with bacon, potatoes, carrots, cabbage, and plenty of aromatic leeks. Cock-a-leekie, the Scottish leek soup seen in restaurants in England and Scotland, remains more widely available than its Welsh counterpart. The soup combines leeks with fowl, barley, a slight sweet note from prunes, and a spark of cayenne pepper and mace. Although a large chicken is used now, the original was prepared with a cock or rooster, as the dish's name suggests— often the loser of a cockfight. Both soups can easily be prepared at home, preferably with young, slender leeks as opposed to the large, older ones with tough white bases and even tougher leaves.

Cock-a-leekie pie is a stylish variation, much like chicken potpie, made with the same ingredients as the soup, minus some liquid, and baked under a pale golden crust. Try it at The Narrow, in London, one of Chef Gordon Ramsay's celebrated outposts on the banks of the Thames.

WHERE: *In London,* The Narrow, tel 44/20-7592-7950, gordonramsay.com/thenarrow. **FURTHER INFORMATION AND RECIPE:** *The Whole World Loves Chicken Soup* by Mimi Sheraton (1975); *The Ploughman's Lunch and the Miser's Feast* by Brian Yarvin (2012); theguardian.com (search traditional british soup cock-a-leekie fearnley-whittingstall).

Cock-a-leekie is served at Scottish celebrations of St. Andrew's Day, Burns Night, and Hogmanay.

‖‖‖‖‖‖‖‖‖‖‖‖‖‖‖‖‖‖‖‖‖‖‖

THE ORIGINAL GRILLED CHEESE SANDWICH

Welsh Rarebit

Welsh, Scottish, Irish, English

To call it melted cheese on toast would be to miss out on the glamour of this tangy, creamy between-meal snack regarded almost as a savory dessert throughout the British Isles. The Welsh original depends on the use of a Cheddar or Caerphilly (see page 34) produced in Wales, melted and whisked with swirls of butter and cream or ale, and finally poured over hot buttered toast.

Wales has had the credit for this dish since the fourteenth century, and the arguments about rabbit versus rarebit go almost that far back. In the definitive tome *British Cookery,* it is conjectured that the original Welsh word was *rabbit,* but allows that *rarebit* must have some validity, as the dish is indeed a "rare bit." Certainly, by the late nineteenth century, the word *rarebit* had caught on among the best chefs and finest diners, and the name bestowed a greater dignity to the dish (after all, the "rabbit" version of the name is also said to derive from the Welsh being such poor hunters that their forays after rabbits resulted in cheese suppers instead).

As one might suspect, Irish rarebit begins with an Irish Cheddar, while the Scottish is made with Dunlop cheese from East Ayrshire, and is seasoned with a splash of malty stout. Farmhouse Cheddar is the best choice for the English version, which is often seasoned with Worcestershire and most classically poured over wine-soaked toast. For the elaborate brunch variation called buck rabbit, poached eggs top the cheese-laden toast, their rich yolks mingling with the sharp cheese. For the sake of style, some tony restaurants glaze the cheese-topped open sandwich under a grill, while those who want to make a show of it melt and season the cheese in silver chafing dishes and ladle it over the toast tableside, in a British version of fondue.

Where: *In London,* Wiltons, tel 44/20-7629-9955, wiltons.co.uk. **Further information and recipes:** *The Ploughman's Lunch and the Miser's Feast* by Brian Yarvin (2012); theguardian.com (search how to cook perfect welsh rarebit). **See also:** Raclette, Fondue, and Beyond, page 332.

‖‖‖‖‖‖‖‖‖‖‖‖‖‖‖‖‖‖‖‖‖‖‖

"CLOQUET HATED REALITY BUT REALIZED IT WAS STILL THE ONLY PLACE TO GET A GOOD STEAK." —FROM "THE CONDEMNED" BY WOODY ALLEN

Black Angus Beef

Scottish

Steak truly is one of those things that makes this mortal coil bearable—especially when it's a steak made of Black Angus beef. Originating in the rolling hills of Scotland, the breed of stocky, short-legged, full-figured cattle is prized for its excellent marbling and especially for its thick layer of back fat, which not only helps protect the meat from bacteria but also ensures that it will be seductively tender, deliciously beefy, and most succulent when cooked rare to medium rare, the latter being the outer bounds of decency for such superb meat.

The breed, technically called Aberdeen Angus after the geographic region where the cows graze, has roamed Scotland for centuries, but was first recorded in herding books around the time butcher shops started appearing in that country, during the 1770s. An enterprising Scotsman, George Grant, imported four Angus bulls from his homeland to the prairie of Victoria, Kansas, introducing the breed to the United States in 1873. Americans at first considered the steer funny-looking—it was solid black and didn't have horns—so Grant crossbred

Angus with Texas longhorns. The results were very well received, and by 1883 some twelve hundred more Angus had been imported. The Black Angus remains one of the most sought-after breeds, as the basis for the decadent super-hamburgers we so crave. The "brand name" version of Aberdeen Angus cattle, introduced into the U.S. around 1979, is called "certified Angus beef"; to receive that encomium, the meat must be raised according to prescribed standards.

WHERE: *In Linlithgow, Scotland,* The Champany Restaurant, tel 44/15-0683-4532, champany.com/the-restaurant. **MAIL ORDER:** Creekstone Farms, tel 866-273-3578, creekstone farms.com. **FURTHER INFORMATION AND RECIPES:** *Lobel's Prime Time Grilling* by Stanley, Leon, Evan, Mark, and David Lobel (2007); certified angusbeef.com.

A SCORCHED, SCOTCHED DELIGHT

Butterscotch

Scottish, English

A candy so common you might be inclined to take it for granted, truly well-made butterscotch is a golden delight of brassily caramelized brown sugar, lemon juice, salt, butter, and sometimes powdered ginger. Whipped to creamy

richness, then cooled into a taffy that provides long-lasting pleasure, it is an excellent treat to make at home. When going with store-bought, the trick is finding artisanal producers whose talents match those of legendary confectioners like Yorkshire sweetmaker Samuel Parkinson, who began selling his Doncaster Butterscotch (reputedly the first) in 1817.

The name of the candy clearly suggests Scottish origins. (A Dylan Thomas riff on the association in *A Child's Christmas in Wales* refers to the same candy as "Butterwelsh for the Welsh.") But as the word was first recorded in Doncaster, England, *scotch* is likely either a reference to the process of cutting, or "scotching,"

the candy or a derivation of the word *scorch*—the butterscotch-making process being a hot one indeed.

Cooked to a soft, velvety consistency, hot butterscotch becomes a sauce that can be ladled over vanilla ice cream; sprinkle on a few toasted almonds, and you have a top-notch sundae.

FURTHER INFORMATION AND RECIPES: *Butterscotch Lover's Cookbook* by Diana Dalsass (2001); food.com (search traditional scottish butterscotch candy); myrecipes.com (search butterscotch caramels). **TIP:** Look for Callard & Bowser's, Gardiners of Scotland, and Parkinson's brands of butterscotch.

SO WRONG IT'S RIGHT

Deep-Fried Mars Bar

Scottish

I t is the treat that has just about everything wrong with it—except the meltingly cool-hot chocolate and the texture of that crisp coating contrasting with a seductively chewy edge of caramel. It may make you fat and ruin your teeth as well as your gourmet standing, but place such trifling concerns aside, as you shouldn't miss the chance to try a deep-fried Mars bar at least once.

Invented in Scotland in the 1990s, this strange confection is featured mainly at fish-and-chips outposts, and for good reason: The chilled bar, which is similar to a Milky Way, consisting of nougat and caramel coated in milk chocolate, is dipped into much the same milk- or beer-soaked batter that the fish is dipped into and, also like the fish, deep-fried in vegetable oil.

Although the deep-fried Mars bar is believed to have been born in a Glasgow pub, the Champany Restaurant in Linlithgow claims credit for inventing the oozingly sweet dessert. Due to its instant, perverse appeal, the treat spread throughout the U.K., then into both Canada and Australia.

WHERE: *In Stonehaven, Scotland,* The Carron Fish Bar, tel 44/15-6976-5377, carronfishbar.webecomservices.co.uk.; *in New York,* A Salt & Battery, tel 212-691-2713, asaltandbattery.com; *in Jamaica Plain, MA,* The Haven, tel 617-524-2836, thehavenjp.com. *in Santa Barbara, CA,* Mac's Fish & Chip Shop, tel 805-897-1160, macssb.com. **MAIL ORDER:** Mars bars can be ordered at amazon.com. **FURTHER INFORMATION AND RECIPES:** *Nigella Bites* by Nigella Lawson (2002); theguardian.com (search deep fried mars bars are a fine scottish tradition).

FOR CHRISTMAS, FOR WEDDINGS,
AND FOR NO REASON AT ALL

Dundee Cake

Scottish

A ccording to legend, Dundee cake was invented on behalf of Mary, Queen of Scots, a ruler who did *not* like cherries in her fruitcake. A moist and aromatic accompaniment to tea, coffee, or a glass of Madeira or Irish whiskey, the tawny cake is jeweled with candied citrus peel, currants, raisins, and sultanas—hold the cherries—its top typically decorated with concentric rings of blanched or glazed almonds.

The butter-rich cake, a classic from the city of Dundee, was first commercially produced in the nineteenth century by the Keiller's marmalade company. Today, it is especially popular at Christmas. Although not traditionally made with alcohol, Dundee cake improves with a bit of spiking: Lightly moisten the uncut cake with whiskey, rum, or brandy, then wrap in cloth or wax paper for a day or two before cutting. For weddings, it is often baked in layers, each of which is covered with rolled marzipan, and the cake as a whole is enveloped in royal icing.

Where: *In London,* Fortnum & Mason, tel 44/20-7734-8040, fortnumandmason .com. **Further information and recipes:** *The Scots Kitchen* by F. Marian McNeill and Catherine Brown (2010); *A World of Cake* by Krystina Castella (2010); ifood.tv (search christmas dundee cake).

Many cooks make Dundee cake days, weeks, or even months in advance, so that the flavors will mellow.

THE *UR*-MARMALADE

Dundee Orange Marmalade

Scottish

Golden, glassy chips of bitter Seville orange rind distinguish the amber marmalade said to have been first simmered up in Dundee, Scotland, in the eighteenth century, when a Spanish ship carrying oranges sought refuge from a storm in the town's harbor. The fruit preserve is generally believed to have been the creation of one Janet Keiller, whose family name eventually became the best-known brand of orange marmalade. Similar fruit-and-caramelized-sugar gels (minus the rind) were produced in Europe as far back as the sixteenth century; the word *marmalade* comes from the Portuguese *marmelo,* for quince, the fruit used to make a thick and chewy sweet conserve in Portugal.

At its best, the marmalade contains large chips of rind thickly netted through sticky sweet jelly, to be lavishly spread on hot buttered toast or the latter-day crumpets we call English muffins. The bittersweetness of the marmalade is also a fine accent to pungent British cheeses and a delectable spread on waffles or pancakes. A spoonful or two gently stirred into vanilla ice cream or rich yogurt cannot go amiss, and it makes for a sprightly condiment with roasted goose, duck, or pork.

Mail order: amazon.com (search dundee orange marmalade). **Further information and recipe:** marthastewart.com (search classic seville orange marmalade). **Tip:** Look for James Keiller and Mackays brands. **Special events:** Dalemain Marmalade Festival, Penrith, England, February–March, dalemainmarmaladeawards .co.uk; Herefordshire Marmalade Festival, Bromyard, England, February–March, hereford shiremarmaladefestival.org.uk. **See also:** Dulce de Cáscara de Naranja Amarga, page 259.

————————|||||||||||||||||||||||||||||————————

Finnan Haddie with Poached Egg

Scottish

The zesty salt-smoke flavor of this flaky smoked haddock (a member of the cod family), gentled in hot milk and melted butter and topped with a poached egg, is the stuff of elegant weekend breakfasts and sustaining lunches and high teas throughout Scotland and England. Alas, the dish is difficult to find abroad; popular on the American East Coast at the turn of the twentieth century, it later held down a spot on the breakfast menu at the Ritz-Carlton Hotel in Boston for many decades.

Though the name of the dish may itself sound like a song lyric, it refers to a specific fish, and a specific place: Haddie is a fond nickname for haddock, and Finnan is the locals' name for Findon, Scotland, a fishing hamlet just south of Aberdeen where the fishermen's wives developed the method of smoking haddock over peat or seaweed (and later sawdust) fires after salting and drying the fillets. Some try to argue that Finnan actually refers to the village of Findhorn rather than Findon, but either way, the name—and the dish—are Scottish to the core.

A word to the wise: Finnan haddie is also delicious grilled and swathed in unsalted butter, or baked with onions—but its rustic flavor is best complemented by an egg in some form, whether fried, scrambled, or poached.

Mail order: Scottish Gourmet USA, tel 877-814-3663, scottishgourmetusa.com; Mackenzie, Ltd., tel 800-858-7100, mackenzieltd.com; Stonington Seafood, tel 207-348-2730, stonington seafood.com. **Further information and recipes:** *The Country Cooking of Ireland* by Colman Andrews (2009); *Roast Chicken and Other Stories* by Simon Hopkinson with Lindsey Bareham (2007); bbc.co.uk (search smoked haddock with poached egg).

————————|||||||||||||||||||||||||||||————————

"GREAT CHIEFTAIN O' THE PUDDIN' RACE"
—ROBERT BURNS

Haggis

Scottish

Many a food lover would jump at the chance to taste a slice of subtle pâté or a country sausage fragrant with onions, cayenne, parsley, and perhaps a touch of anchovy and red wine. Might they balk if told the meat filling was made of sheep's innards and, even worse, had been steamed inside an animal's stomach? Perhaps, but the more dedicated among them would persevere. Mind over matter!

Haggis is indeed a kind of steamed sausage, and the practical, economical sack used for its steaming should be no more off-putting than the use of intestines as sausage casings.

The name *haggis* is believed to have been derived from the French *haché*, or the Scottish *hag*, both meaning chopped, although meat and/or innards have been chopped and steamed in animal stomachs or wrappers of caul, the lacy fat peeled off the kidneys, at least as far back as Roman times.

Once over that gustatory hurdle, the appeal of the haggis depends on the herbs and seasonings the cook adds to the ground offal, meat, and oatmeal filling. All is readied and enjoyed on Hogmanay (New Year's Eve) and Burns Night, the January 25 birthday celebration for that most Scottish of poets, Robert Burns—forever linked to the dish by his poem "Address to a Haggis" (only a bit less famous than another well-known song and poem of his, "Auld Lang Syne").

Cock-a-leekie soup, made of leeks and chicken stock, begins the feast (see page 35), and the main dish is traditionally served with tatties an' neeps, potatoes and yellow turnips mashed separately or together, which cushion the haggis. So does plenty of good Scotch whisky and the windy whines of bagpipes.

WHERE: *In Edinburgh,* The White Hart Inn, tel 44/131-226-2806, whitehart-edinburgh.co.uk; *in Glasgow,* Ubiquitous Chip, tel 44/141-334-5007, ubiquitouschip.co.uk; *in Indianapolis,* MacNiven's Restaurant and Bar, tel 317-632-7268, macnivens.com. **MAIL ORDER:** Scottish Gourmet USA, tel 877-814-3663, scottishgourmetusa.com; McKean's, scottishhaggis.com. **FURTHER INFORMATION AND RECIPES:** *The Macsween Haggis Bible* by Jo Macsween (2013); macsween.co.uk; foodnetwork.com (search alton brown's haggis); bbc.co.uk (search robert burns address to a haggis). **SPECIAL EVENT:** Haggis Bowl, Newport, OR, June, ncfhg.com/Haggis.html.

IT'S NOT THE BEES, IT'S THE HEATHER

Heather Honey

Scottish

You sense the heather first in the color of the honey—a mauve cast overlaying a deep sunset gold. Then there is the warm, dusty aroma, like a lush, swaying field of full-bloom heather on a summer afternoon. Finally there is the flavor:

a flowery sweetness with a slight brassy tingle, good enough to eat by the spoonful, though more likely to be spread on toast, drizzled over ice cream and summer fruits and berries, or stirred into yogurt, tea, or lemonade.

Writing in 1933, Le Vicomte de Mauduit explained in his book *The Vicomte in the Kitchen* that Scottish honey is the world's best not because the bees do their job better,

but because of "the excellence of the clover and the heather which are fuller in nectar." Whatever the reason, heather honey, according to F. Marian McNeill in her definitive cookbook, *The Scots Kitchen*, should appear on every tradition-respecting Scottish breakfast table, along with orange marmalade.

Honey should be stored in a tightly covered jar or crock in a cool, dry place. An old Greek rule: "Honey keeps where salt stays dry." If it should solidify and become sugary, place the container in hot water until the honey liquefies.

MAIL ORDER: Scottish Gourmet USA, tel 877-814-3663, scottishgourmetusa.com; amazon.com (search mellis heather honey). **FURTHER INFORMATION AND RECIPES:** *The Scots Kitchen* by F. Marian McNeill and Catherine Brown (2010); honeytraveler.com (click Single Flower Honey, then Heather Honey).

⊢||||||||||||||||||||||||||||||⊣

A NEW TREAT FROM SCOTTISH WATERS

Scottish Langoustines

Scottish

D ublin calls them prawns. Italy, scampi. When caught off the icy waters of Scotland's west coast—where, as national pride would tell it, their firm, silken flesh and saline sea-air flavor are unparalleled—these little cousins of the lobster

are called langoustines. Pale orange in color and 7 or 8 inches in length, they wear most of their meat in their tails and in their long, skinny claws.

For the best experience, you should dine upon them in situ—in restaurants in Scotland or England—where the roseate crustaceans can be kept alive until cooking. But for a second best option that is still revealingly delicious, blast-frozen U.S. imports are also available. Steamed briefly, then served hot and dipped into melted butter, or chilled and dabbed with lemony mayonnaise, either method yields delectable flavor. Many prefer these langoustines grilled, but their delicacy is best retained by gentler cooking.

Loch Fyne boasts world-famous langoustines.

WHERE: *In Paris,* Pierre Gagnaire, tel 33/1-5836-1250, pierre-gagnaire.com. **MAIL ORDER:** Scottish Gourmet USA, tel 877-814-3663, scottish gourmetusa.com.

⊢||||||||||||||||||||||||||||||⊣

WHERE THERE'S SMOKE, THERE'S SALMON

Scottish Smoked Salmon, Wild and Tamed

Scottish

O ne of the world's poshest treats, wild salmon smoked in Scotland is the gold standard for this luxurious appetizer. Thinly cut in the long, narrow rectangles known as banquet slices, the firm and satiny rose-coral flesh has almost invisible lacings of fat, with just enough smoke to lend sophistication to the deep-sea flavor of the fish itself.

The wild fish, caught in cold North Atlantic waters, is increasingly scarce and so exorbitantly priced that very little comes to the United States. Lovers of this delicacy who cannot make it to pricey London food shops and do not wish to wait for a mail-order source must consider the next best option; salmon farmed and smoked in Scotland, just slightly oilier and the slightest bit less firm, but elegant nonetheless.

Slices with lemon and capers

It is the Scottish cold-smoking process that distinguishes that country's salmon. Whole fish, lightly cured with salt, are hung high over slow-burning fires of oak mixed with chips from retired whisky casks, imparting smoky, autumn overtones. Irish smoked salmon is second only to Scotland's, based on the same fish from the same waters, but cured to a firmer, dryer texture with a stronger burr of flavor developed by smoking over peat. (These are much the same subtleties that characterize the differences between Irish and Scottish wool tweeds and whiskies as well.)

Such superb smoked salmon requires little enhancement—say, a spray of lemon juice and, if you must, a few salty bronze capers. Thin slices of buttered brown bread and a shot or two of any top-shelf white spirit such as aquavit, vodka, or gin complete the feast. Smoked salmon is also a lavish garnish for scrambled eggs or cool asparagus in a vinaigrette dressing.

WHERE: *In London,* Harrods, tel 44/20-7730-1234, harrods.com; Fortnum & Mason, tel 44/20-7734-8040, fortnumandmason.com. **MAIL ORDER:** Scottish Gourmet USA, tel 877-814-3663, scottish gourmetusa.com.

SHORT AND SWEET

Shortbread

Scottish

The defining feature of shortbread, or short'ning bread, is a high content of butter or other shortening and the meltingly fragile, crumbly crust that results. A finely gritty cookie-cake, Scottish shortbread is redolent of that pure, sweet butter held together with sugar and a combination of wheat and rice flours. It is the latter that imparts a nicely dry, "short," sandy texture to this pleasurable cake.

Shortbread's popularity is such that the rest of the U.K. bakes it, too, and other countries have created their own versions. American bakers boldly dip their shortbread in melted chocolate, spread icing on its top, or toss sweet extras into its batter; these versions are not to be confused with American shortcake, the leavened biscuity concoction typically served or layered with strawberries and cream.

Among shortbreads, Scotland's are the classic originals, "the jewel in the crown" of that nation's proud baking tradition, as Scottish chef John Quigley described it in 2009. Traditional in Scotland for Christmas and New Year's, shortbread is a descendant of the pagan Yule cake called an oat bannock. When baked in the round, shortbread is scored in wedges (also called petticoat tails) radiating from its center as a symbol of the sun's rays. It's also sometimes baked in rectangular wooden molds whose ridges indicate where portions should be broken off. Why such precision? It all stems from the superstition that to cut bannock with a knife is to invite bad fortune.

Mail order: walkersshortbread.com; amazon .com (search scottish shortbread). **Further information and recipes:** *Visions of Sugarplums* by Mimi Sheraton (1981); saveur.com (search real scottish shortbread). **Special event:** Sarasota Shortbread Contest, Sarasota, FL, February, sarasotahigh landgames.com. **Tip:** Unwrap packaged shortbread 20 to 30 minutes before it is to be eaten so any overly intense butter aromas can dissipate. (Do the same for any packaged butter cookie.)

A SURPRISING LITERARY SNACK

Bread Fried in Bacon Grease

Irish

No matter how bizarre or even detested, some tastes of childhood may waft into memory later in life, bringing on the sort of longing that can only be called nostalgia. In his wonderfully rich and moving memoir *Angela's Ashes,* Irish-born writer Frank McCourt describes many childhood meals that consisted merely of bread fried in bacon grease—the only food his dysfunctional mother, Angela, could afford. He doesn't describe that dish with anything like affection, implying instead a distaste that readers immediately share. And yet the author has admitted to an occasional longing for that bread fried in bacon grease, even going so far as to prepare it for himself two or three times a year.

A curious cook of a perhaps perverse nature who tries this doubtful treat can be rewarded with a surprisingly delicious snack. Stack the deck by getting some very good Irish bacon and an acceptable, but not extraordinary, white, fine-textured bread (on the supermarket level, a safe choice would be Pepperidge Farm's Original loaf). Then slowly and carefully fry the bacon strips in a skillet that can hold as many bread slices as you want to fry. Four slices of bacon should give you enough rendered fat for four slices of bread. Remove the cooked bacon from the skillet and reserve it for whatever use you care to make of it, the wisest choice being to consume it at once, while it is still hot and crisp.

Over low heat and with the rendered fat at a low sizzle, add the bread slices. After about two minutes, press lightly with a spatula for a minute or two, or until the first side is a light golden brown. Flip the bread over and repeat on the other side until it, too, is golden brown. Remove the fried bread slices and drain them on paper towels for a minute or two. Then, while the slices are still hot and, hopefully, crisp, sprinkle them with coarse salt—a touch undoubtedly not added by Angela McCourt. Another enhancement would be a fried or poached egg with a runny yolk, especially if the fried bacon strips are crumbled over it all.

Where: *In New York,* Myers of Keswick, tel 212-691-4194, myersofkeswick.com. **Mail order:** The British Food Depot, britishfooddepot.com (search winston irish style bacon). **Further information:** *Angela's Ashes* by Frank McCourt (1996).

Colcannon and Champ

Irish, Welsh

The soul-soothing potato dish colcannon is best described by its simple recipe: Cooked, chopped cabbage and sliced scallions are folded into a pile of softly mashed potatoes, all to be mounded in a bowl with a well of hot,

melted butter and a haze of black pepper in the center. To consume it, work your way slowly around the edges of that well, so butter glosses each forkful of this humble country fare.

Though it brings comfort to any cold night, the dish is traditionally served on All Hallows' Eve (Halloween), with coins or charms hidden in it. In Victorian times, the colcannon itself was the charm: Unmarried girls would hang socks holding a lump of the stuff on their door handles; the first man to enter was said to be their future husband.

Even more elemental, and much loved in both Ireland and Wales, is champ. For this, potatoes are mashed with warm, sharply tangy buttermilk just before butter and chopped scallions are stirred in.

Either way, a sprinkling of minced parsley adds a dose of welcome freshness.

FURTHER INFORMATION AND RECIPES: *The Country Cooking of Ireland* by Colman Andrews (2009);

There is a wistful Irish folk song, "Colcannon."

theguardian.com (search colman andrews colcannon); food52.com (search buttermilk mashed potatoes). **TIP:** For best results, use old, starchy potatoes. Look for russets, aka Idaho baking potatoes. Kale is often substituted for cabbage for a lustier result.

Corned Beef and Cabbage

Irish

Call it fusion or coincidence: Preserved (or corned) beef, slowly simmered then teamed with cabbage cooked in the same broth, is as much a fixture in Ireland as in the Eastern European Jewish kitchen, and for much the same reasons.

Before reliable refrigeration, both areas traditionally relied heavily on salt-preserved meats during the cold months, and cabbage was available throughout the winter. (Ireland produced a significant amount of corned beef from the seventeenth to nineteenth centuries, although beef was considered a luxury for the vast majority of its people.)

It's a meal that is both humble and succulent, at its meltingly tender best when the

Billions of pounds are consumed every March 17.

corned beef is cut from softly fatty brisket; in Ireland, leaner silverside is a good alternative. Onion, bay leaves, peppercorns, and a sprig of thyme season the rose-red meat and the earthy cabbage for a heartwarming combination.

Whether in Ireland or in any large American city, the day to look for corned beef and cabbage is St. Patrick's Day, March 17. Elevated to its current status as an iconic and beloved Irish meal by millions of Irish immigrants to North America, this simple dish has become an essential component of the annual celebration of all things Ireland.

WHERE: *In Dublin,* Oliver St. John Gogarty, tel 353/1-671-1822, gogartys.ie; *in Arlington, VA,* Ireland's Four Courts, tel 703-525-3600, irelands fourcourts.com. **FURTHER INFORMATION AND RECIPES:** *Saveur Cooks Authentic American* by Colman Andrews and Dorothy Kalins (1998); mrfood.com (search classic corned beef and cabbage). **SPECIAL EVENT:** Milwaukee Irish Fest, Milwaukee, WI, August, irishfest.com.

THE MEAL THAT LASTS ALL DAY

Irish Breakfast

Irish

A delectable model for self-destruction, the over-the-top Irish breakfast seems to be gaining popularity outside of its home country as a leisurely weekend brunch. Once a daily meal for farm workers and anyone preparing for the day's

hard labor, today it is more of a weekend indulgence, one worth risking a couple of times a year.

Picture a plate piled with fried eggs, black and white pudding (black pudding is a blood sausage, while white pudding contains oatmeal and leeks), thick and smoky rashers of Irish back bacon or gammon (a cured cut from the pig's hind leg), fried tomato, fried potatoes, bread, and mushrooms—maybe beans, too— and don't forget the jam. A strong cup of breakfast tea is the traditional accompaniment, and

traditional or not, hot whiskey-spiked Irish coffee topped with whipped cream might be just the right finish.

WHERE: *In Dublin,* Slattery's Bar & Early House, tel 353/1-874-6844, slatterysbar.com; *in Arlington, VA,* Ireland's Four Courts, tel 703-525-3600, irelandsfourcourts.com. **MAIL ORDER:** Food Ireland, tel 877-474-7436, foodireland .com (search traditional irish style breakfast). **FURTHER INFORMATION AND RECIPES:** *Irish Traditional Cooking* by Darina Allen (2012).

—||||||||||||||||||||||||||||—

CHEESECAKE TIES ONE ON

Irish Whiskey Cheesecake

Irish

I f creamy, gently sweet cheesecake redolent of lemon and a hint of vanilla isn't enticement enough, imagine the lift a bracing shot of rustic Irish whiskey can impart. Whether it's the sweet, velvety flavor of Bailey's Irish Cream or the

strong smoothness of Jameson's whiskey, both provide a decadent cure for the common cheesecake that goes beautifully with a touch of chocolate, too—whether it's a handful of chocolate chips in the batter, or a chocolate swirl on top. Cheesecake dates back to the ancient Greeks, who pounded cheese into a pan with honey, flour, and wheat, but never has it seemed so spirited as in this modern, inebriated version.

WHERE: *In Lake Mary, FL,* Liam Fitzpatrick's Restaurant and Irish Pub, tel 407-936-3782, liamfitzpatricks.com. **FURTHER INFORMATION AND RECIPES:** tablespoon.com (search irish cream cheesecake); irelandwhiskeytrail.com (click Food & Whiskey, then Desserts, then Jameson Whiskey Cheesecake); for Bailey's Irish cream cheesecake, irish-genealogy-toolkit.com (click Recipes, then search irish cream cheesecake).

—||||||||||||||||||||||||||||—

AS SIMPLE AS BREAD CAN BE . . .

Soda Bread

Irish

N ecessity was the obvious mother of this snowy, satisfying invention, the product of an era when time and cooking fuel were often hard to come by. When baking soda and then baking powder gained widespread usage in the

nineteenth century, Irish bakers invented a bread that didn't require heavy kneading and a long period of waiting for the dough to rise. The nicely chewy result is Irish soda bread, which depends on the acidity of buttermilk or sour milk along with baking powder and baking soda to elevate it into cushiony rounds.

Irish soda bread lends itself well as a foil for dishes with complex flavors, from Corned Beef and Cabbage (see page 45) to a hearty lamb stew, and it is best served the day it is baked. For a dressier result, black currants are often kneaded into the dough. The formed, unbaked loaves are scored in quarters (resembling a four-leaf clover) so portions can be broken off. Warm from the oven, they are delightful spread with sweet or salted butter and a dab of jam or marmalade.

WHERE: *In Castledawson, Northern Ireland,* Ditty's Home Bakery, tel 44/28-7946-8243, dittys bakery.com; *in San Francisco,* Arizmendi Bakery, tel 415-566-3117, arizmendibakery.com; *in Dorchester, MA,* Greenhills Irish Bakery, tel 617-825-8187, greenhillsirishbakery.com. **MAIL ORDER:** Food Ireland, tel 877-474-7436, food ireland.com (search irish soda bread). **FURTHER INFORMATION AND RECIPES:** *The Country Cooking of Ireland* by Colman Andrews (2009); epicurious .com (search noreen kinney's irish soda bread).

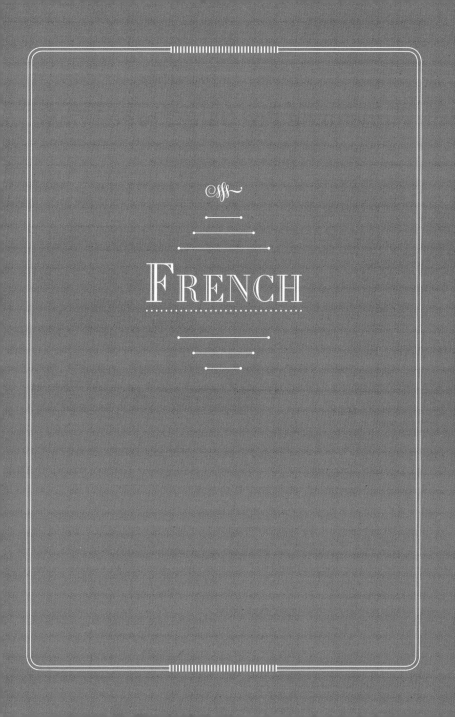

FRENCH

—|IIIIIIIIIIIIIIIIIIIIIIIIIIIIIII|—

SEASONED BY MOTHER NATURE

Agneau de Pré-Salé, Three Ways

Salt Meadow Lamb

French (Breton and Norman)

Serious gourmet cooks consider buying preseasoned meat an unforgivable gaffe, anticipating bland commercial spice mixtures at best. But when the seasoner is Mother Nature herself, who can argue? Cavils end with a taste of the

verdantly saline, lean lamb from France's coastal provinces of Normandy and, especially, Brittany. There, lamb and sheep graze on the reclaimed salt meadows known as *prés-salés*, nibbling random herbs and bits of sprightly green seaweed along the way (or, in the hills around Provence, on the wild lavender that lends sweet overtones to the meat). These *agneaux* (lambs) or *moutons* (mutton) *de pré-salé* are treasured marks of quality on menus and in butcher shops throughout France.

Mont Saint-Michel crowns the largest salt meadow area in France.

Restraint and balance being two of the hallmarks of the best French cuisine, chefs and home cooks respect the elegant natural taste of this meat and are careful not to overpower it, hence the following favorite methods for appreciating this lamb and mutton.

Gigot aux flageolets à la Bretonne—Brittany leg of lamb with beans.

A great classic roast that is fast disappearing from French restaurants in the U.S., this leg of lamb is adorned with only pepper and a few slivers of garlic, inserted close to the bone, before it is roasted to roseate perfection at an inner temperature of 145 to 148 degrees Fahrenheit.

Once cooked, the roasted meat lends its rich juices to beans, preferably the small, dried ivory or jade flageolets, or, almost as good, the creamy white haricots. After a good soak, the beans are simmered with onion, thyme, bay leaf, and garlic until tender, and then are baked to an inviting mellow brown color along with lamb pan juices and perhaps a touch of tomato.

True gigot, cut from a whole leg of lamb, is hard to find in American restaurants these days. Changing eating habits mean that not enough customers order roasted meat, so a whole leg would lead to uneconomical leftovers. Thus, what often passes for gigot is really a lamb steak cut from the leg and grilled or roasted to order— not the same thing by a long shot.

Carré d'agneau persillé—Parsleyed rack of lamb.

A cut that stretches from the loin of the carcass to the first rib, the rack or *carré* of lamb is really a long row of unseparated lamb chops—plump, tender, and attached to riblike bones that in this dish are typically "frenched," the meat and fat stripped away from the bare bones to create a refined and useful set of handles. Roasted to a rare state, the rack is removed from the oven, lightly brushed with spicy Dijon mustard, and encrusted with a heady mix of bread crumbs, garlic, and minced parsley. Then it goes back into the oven until the meat is medium rare and the coating crisp, golden, and fragrant. The rack is carved into chop portions and hopefully laid alongside a square of creamy baked *pommes Dauphinoise* (see page 116).

***Navarin d'agneau printanier*—Spring lamb stew.** Even the cherished salt meadow lamb includes some cuts that are better braised than roasted, among them the neck and shoulder meat. With the coming of spring, two-inch cubes

of these cuts are gently stewed until almost tender with a little dry white wine, a few tomatoes, thyme, garlic, and a bay leaf. The meat is jeweled with new white potatoes, tiny onions, young carrots and turnips, and freshly shelled new peas, and cooked until tender; it's served as a gastronomic celebration of the vernal equinox.

Of course, all of these methods are also applied to less exalted lamb, when it is the chef who seasons to taste.

FURTHER INFORMATION AND RECIPES: *The Food of France* by Waverley Root (1992); *Mastering the Art of French Cooking, Volume 1* by Julia Child, Louisette Bertholle, and Simone Beck (1961); foodnetwork.com (search rack of lamb persillade).

THE WORLD'S BEST MASHED POTATOES

Aligot

French (Auvergnat)

Silken smooth or rustically lumpy, mashed potatoes rank high among the world's comfort foods. But no version is as wickedly rich or sensuously addictive as aligot, a fonduelike specialty of the Auvergne region in south central France.

Preparation begins with starchy potatoes that are cooked and pureed with butter, crème fraîche, and a hint of crushed garlic, and then dramatically finished at the table in a copper saucepan. There, the concoction is whipped and stirred, and whipped and stirred again, along with soft curds of the cow's milk Cantal or Salers cheese or the acidic, nutty Tomme de Laguiole. As a wooden spoon is worked through the mixture, it becomes elastic and stretchy. A skillful practitioner can turn the

Aligot's impressive stretch

process into a veritable floor show, pulling the potato-and-cheese-coated spoon high above the pot before dipping it back again, in an act reminiscent of mozzarella production.

As elegantly as it is presented now, aligot is believed to have originated as a shepherds' dish, and it was much favored by supplicants stopping to rest overnight in the Auvergne en route to the shrine of Santiago de Compostela in Galicia, Spain. This delicious dish often accompanies roasted meats, and it is traditionally topped with darkly pungent, crisp-skinned blood sausage, as it is at L'Ambassade d'Auvergne in Paris.

WHERE: *In Paris,* Ambassade d'Auvergne, tel 33/1-42-72-31-22, ambassade-auvergne.com; *in*

New York, Minetta Tavern, tel 212-475-3850, minettatavernny.com; *in Los Angeles,* Spago, tel 310-385-0880, wolfgangpuck.com. **FURTHER INFORMATION AND RECIPE:** *Cheese Primer* by Steven Jenkins (1996); cookstr.com (search aligote).

A CLASSIC BISTRO

L'Ami Louis

French

At first glance, a newcomer to this venerable bistro might decide he or she had come to the wrong address. Given its justifiable reputation for high prices—*really* high prices—L'Ami Louis looks like a dump. But what a noble

dump it is. Opened in 1930, it is said not to have been painted since—a claim the smoke-and-garlic-glazed wine-dark walls do not refute. If you toss your coat on the rack above your table, realize that it will exude the faint scent of garlic until its next visit to the cleaner. That side effect has not discouraged loyal patrons past or present, including fashion designers such as the elegant Madame Grès, stars of stage and screen such as Helen Mirren, politicians like Bill Clinton, musicians such as Seiji Ozawa, and anybody in jeans or a tux who is passionate about eating well.

Chef Antoine Magnin's spirit lives on at L'Ami Louis.

At least that lingering aroma of garlic reminds all that they have partaken of a truly spectacular meal. For when the original chef, Antoine Magnin, died at the age of eighty-six in 1987, he left behind a well-trained maître d' in Louis Gadby. Wood still fuels the stove and oven, and the same wood burns in the dining room's ancient heater, a unifying touch that the previous chef valued. There have been two recent improvements—replacing the barbaric

Napoleonic toilet and allowing credit cards, meaning that diners no longer have to arrive in armored cars full of cash.

As for the menu, fish lovers had best go elsewhere, as the only sea creatures tolerated here are scallops with roe when in season, roasted on the half-shell as an appetizer. The large, plump snails are also great starters, bathed in green-gold garlic and parsley butter, and so sizzling hot they appear to still be wriggling. Do not overlook the most awesome appetizer of all, the house-prepared signature foie gras—not a pâté but rather a solid, rose-pink block, pure and chilled, like a dream of an indecently rich ice cream. Served with slabs of crusty baguette toasted over the wood fire, the dish would be a meal in itself at any place but Louis's.

Draw breath and consider the main courses, among them what is surely the world's best roasted chicken, the blue-footed Bresse specimen cooked in Normandy butter. If not that, then consider a succulently tender gigot of lamb or a lusciously blood-rare *côte de boeuf,* to which not even the best American or Argentine steak can hold a candle. Heat-burnished roasted veal kidneys, properly ruby-rare at the center, and golden roasted pheasant are also usually on hand. If you order a week ahead, you can have (for two or more) the traditional *salmis* of duck or pheasant, that medieval-tasting stew whose sauce is rich with poultry blood.

Accompanying the meat are delectable potatoes, sliced and roasted in duck fat or finely slivered and crisped. Should you be lucky enough to be at L'Ami Louis in the late spring, order a copper saucepan full of woodsy, earthy wild morels bathed in heavy cream.

Vegetables? Well, maybe the first asparagus of spring, but Magnin didn't like to fool around with such insubstantial fare, and neither does his heir. However, for exotic fruits and nuts—fresh almonds still in their green suedelike husks and tasting more like fruit—there is always a place at the dessert table.

A soothing frozen nougat dessert is about the most anyone can manage after a huge and hearty meal that is best accompanied by one of the house's special Fleurie wines.

Where: 32, rue du Vertbois, Paris, tel 33/1-48-87-77-48. Closed Mondays and Tuesdays and from mid-July to mid-August.

LEAVING IT TO ARTICHOKES

Artichauts à la Barigoule

French (Provençal)

Even in its simplest incarnation—steamed or boiled, served with a dipping sauce of vinaigrette or lemony melted butter—the multipetaled bud of the *Cynara scolymus* thistle plant is a delight. In this Provence specialty, it is slowly

Artichauts violets

simmered to silken tenderness in olive oil and a touch of lemon juice, with seasonings of onion and garlic and slivers of ham or bacon; mushrooms, carrots, and even the slightest trace of tomato may make an appearance as well. What must be present is thyme, or *barigoule* (Provence's bastardized version of the Niçois word *farigoule*), the defining herb.

After having carefully trimmed the leaves and removed the thorny choke, some cooks choose to stuff the opened, raw artichokes with the aforementioned ingredients, then tie the chokes closed and let them simmer in the broth. Either way, small, young artichokes give the most tender results.

Served warm in a bowl that can accommodate a shallow pool of the pan juices, the artichokes make light and palate-priming appetizers. This cooking method, known as *à la grecque*, renders the entire artichoke edible, so no need to tackle yours leaf by leaf; just use a fork and dig in, not forgetting to sop up the last of the savory juices with some bread or a spoon.

Further information and recipes: *Cuisine Niçoise: Recipes from a Mediterranean Kitchen* by Jacques Médecin (1991); *The Lutèce Cookbook* by André Soltner with Seymour Britchky (1995); saveur.com (search artichauts a la barigoule). **See also:** Carciofi Romaneschi, page 174.

—|||||||||||||||||||||||||||||||—

A DESIGNING MAN'S FAVORITE DISH

Aubergine en Caton

Roasted Eggplant

French (Provençal)

Once asked in an interview which food he remembered most fondly from his boyhood in Provence, the celebrated haute couture designer Christian Lacroix answered, "Aubergine en caton." The dish of his memories is a lusciously

silken roasted eggplant served as a luminous, jade-green puree, its smoky bitterness sparked with a piquant sauce of capers, anchovies, garlic, parsley, lemon juice, and olive oil. Crisp baguette crusts or strips of raw vegetables can be used to dip into the mixture.

Although recipes for this dish are hard to locate, the preparation is so simple that an informal description suffices. Use a large eggplant if the dish is to be shared; smaller specimens may be served as stylish individual portions. Pierce small holes all over the eggplant with a skewer or the slim point of a sharp paring knife (to prevent bursting), and then place it on a pan and roast it in a hot oven until the skin wrinkles and takes on a bronze cast.

When it is cool enough to handle, split the eggplant open and serve it warm, its flesh scooped out onto pretty plates. Because the puree is so sheer and elusive, it is best not to bed it down on greens, among which it might disappear. Mix capers, anchovies, garlic, parsley, lemon juice, and olive oil into a sauce, and whisk. Spoon the sauce over the eggplant to taste; you'll see why this very local favorite appetizer deserves a much wider audience.

Tip: Choose eggplant that is unblemished and very ripe, with a deep black-purple skin that needs only be wiped clean with a damp towel. If preparing more than one, be sure they are of equal size for even cooking. **See also:** Baba Ghanoush, page 495; Sichuan Eggplant, page 785.

—|||||||||||||||||||||||||||||||—

MIXED MEATS FROM THE BAKER'S OVEN

Baeckeoffe

French (Alsatian)

Can't decide between lamb, pork, or beef? With this dish, you don't have to; all three are baked together in a large earthenware casserole known as a "baker's oven," a term that applies to both the container and its contents.

Like many other long-cooking, one-pot meals deriving from earlier days when home ovens were uncommon (see *cholent,* page 434), the Baeckeoffe was traditionally taken to the baker to be placed in his big stone oven.

As with choucroute, the dish is a by-product of Alsace's long, sparkling winter season, when hearty meals cooked at a leisurely pace warm kitchens and, eventually, bodies and souls. The ingredients are simple: Wine- and herb-marinated meats—including pigs' feet, which add viscosity to the sauce—are slow-baked with carrots, onions, celery, potatoes, leeks, and goose fat. To retain heat and flavor, the casserole's lid is sealed with a flour-and-water paste and the whole is placed in the oven. Three hours later, when that seal finally is broken and the lid removed, the resultant aroma—heady scents of rich meats, thyme, bay leaf, garlic, and wine—will almost be sustenance enough. Take a few bites anyway, and then see if you can stop. Don't forget to add mustard, and enjoy it with a cold beer or a dry Alsatian white wine, a clean-tasting riesling, or a piquant gewürztraminer. Complete the meal with a green salad and a crusty loaf of bread.

WHERE: *In Strasbourg,* Le Baeckeoffe d'Alsace, tel 33/3-88-23-05-40; baeckeoffe.com. **FURTHER INFORMATION AND RECIPES:** *The Lutèce Cookbook* by André Soltner with Seymour Britchky (1995); *The Cuisine of Alsace* by Pierre Gaertner and Robert Frederick (1981); epicurious .com (search baeckeoffe).

HOW TO FEEL FRENCH IN FIVE MINUTES

Baguette

French

It might be France's most iconic image. That long, slim, gold-crusted baton of bread carried home before each meal, most picturesquely by a small child in a pastel-colored cotton school smock, stands for the best of bourgeois France and its dedication to the things that really count. (Seek out the great Henri Cartier-Bresson's 1959 photo of a young boy carrying armfuls of baguettes, *Village of Piolenc near Orange,* for a visual reference.)

That old-timey apparition has become less frequent as family schedules and lifestyles have changed, and with bread baking for the most part turned industrial, even in France. Yet, when the artisanal baguette can be found, it still resonates with a sense of place—even though it's actually a relative newcomer, dating back only to the nineteenth century.

France's gastronomic history includes many older, more traditional breads, some of which are enjoyed now for their rustic, hard crusts and wheaty textures and flavors. Particularly good are the crackling round peasant loaves turned out by the country's most

French essentials: beret, bike, and baguettes

famous *boulanger,* Poilâne. But the baguette remains a favorite, with a light texture and flavor that make it a perfect nonintrusive foil for food, and its loose, airy crumb works as an efficient sponge for the country's most famous sauces.

There's no better base for a dab of supple foie gras or a garlic- and brandy-scented country pâté, and it's got the stamp of the law on its side: By decree, French baguettes may contain no preservatives. Because their crusts are fairly thin and dry, they become stale rapidly—hence the need for thrice-daily visits to the *boulangerie* in the good old days.

Unlike many lustier breads, the classic baguette is made up of about three times more soft wheat flour than hard wheat flour, and relies on a sourdough starter and a little salt for its subtle flavor. Once the shaped loaves have risen, just before being baked, they are slashed diagonally in several places across the top with a curved knife blade. As the bread bakes in a steam-filled oven, those cuts expand and open to become the typical flower-petal designs on the top crust. Baguette loaves are most often baked (especially when homemade) in a series of six connected long, fluted pans stamped in thin, shiny aluminum or steel, with lightly embossed patterns that make it easy for the cooled loaves to be snapped out.

Like all overly popularized French foods, the baguette can be found in airports the world over in distressingly chewy, stale, and flavorless iterations that would bring a real *boulanger* to tears. But the real thing abides.

Where: *In Paris and environs,* Poilâne, poilane.fr; *in New York,* Sullivan Street Bakery, tel 212-265-5580, sullivanstreetbakery.com; *in San Francisco,* Acme Bread Bakery at multiple locations, acmebread.com. **Further information and recipes:** *The Breads of France* by Bernard Clayton Jr. (2004); *The Food Lover's Guide to Paris* by Patricia Wells (2014); saveur .com (search four hour baguette). **Special event:** La Fête du Pain (Festival of Bread), France, mid-May, lafetedupain.com.

IN A DELECTABLE JAM

Bar-le-Duc Confiture de Groseilles

French (Lorraine)

C onfiture, the French word for jam, sounds so much more exotic—and it's perhaps a more fitting descriptor for one of the world's most expensive preserves, *confiture de groseilles.* A specialty of Bar-le-Duc, the French town near Lorraine's capital city of Metz, the translucent spread is made of red or white currants (*groseilles*) and packed in tiny faceted jars with metal lids topped by the handsome black-white-and-gold labels of Dutriez, the best-known producer.

Gently sweet, with a nice, tingly acid bite and a luxurious softness on the tongue, Bar-le-Duc makes an elegant topping for morning croissants or scones lightly dabbed with cream cheese or clotted cream (but is far too delicate for plain toast, English muffins, or bagels). It can also add luster to desserts when used as a topping for vanilla ice cream, or vanilla cream-filled crêpes.

What makes Bar-le-Duc so expensive? Not only the increasing

Currant preserves

rarity of currants (especially white ones) and the high cost of growing them, but also the painstaking manual work required to produce the confiture. In a method that sounds practically medieval, multiple seeds must be removed from each tiny currant by hand, one by one, by de-seeders using sharpened goose quills. (Try it the next time you come across a currant, if you can find a goose quill, and you'll probably come to the conclusion that store-bought Bar-le-Duc is a bargain.) Only then can the fruit be simmered with sugar into a shimmering, seedless jell.

Mail order: bienmanger.com, tel 33/4-66-32-90-80, (search seedless white currant jam). **Further information:** *Larousse Gastronomique* (2009).

||||||||||||||||||||||||||||||||||||||||||||||||||||||||||||||||||||||||||||||||||||||||||||||||||

A CINDERELLA OF BEEF CUTS

Beef Cheeks

Though once cheap and used largely in frozen hamburger patties, plump and juicy, flavorful and satisfyingly chewy beef cheeks have become a sought-after ingredient in the contemporary kitchen. The formerly humble cut may receive its most elevated American treatment at Thomas Keller's legendary Napa Valley restaurant, the French Laundry, where it is featured as "Tongue in Cheek"—braised beef cheeks and veal tongue cooked with baby leeks and horseradish cream. But the celebrated French chef Joël Robuchon is also an advocate, as is Greek-Sicilian chef Michael Symon; on the menu at Symon's Cleveland restaurant Lola Bistro is a family recipe for beef-cheek pierogies.

Cut from the muscle behind the steer's cheekbone, the meat is well marbled and succulent, the kind of tough cut that yields a bounty of flavor only after it has been intricately cleaned and trimmed and then gently and lengthily braised over low heat. This is how the old-fashioned French bistro standard *joues de boeuf* achieves its irresistibly rich, beefy essence. Beef cheeks can also help create the most luscious of sauces, act as delectable filling for ravioli or pierogies, or star in the best stews of the world, be they daube, stracotto, or goulash.

WHERE: *In New York,* Babbo, tel 212-777-0303, babbonyc.com; *in Cleveland,* Lola Bistro, tel 216-621-5652, lolabistro.com; *in Yountville, CA,* The French Laundry, tel 707-944-2380, frenchlaundry.com. **MAIL ORDER:** Golden Gate Meat Company, tel 415-983-7800, goldengatemeatcompany.com; U.S. Wellness Meats, tel 877-383-0051, grasslandbeef.com. **FURTHER INFORMATION AND RECIPES:** *The French Laundry Cookbook* by Thomas Keller (1999); *The Babbo Cookbook* by Mario Batali (2002); *Live to Cook* by Michael Symon (2009).

---||||||||||||||||||||||||||||||||---

THE FRESH-AIR FLAVOR OF NORMANDY

Beurre d'Isigny

French (Norman)

The ultimate in butter, this golden creamy spread from the herb-laden grazing fields of Normandy almost deserves to be eaten as a cheese. Savor a generous pat as it melts on the tongue, and you will experience soft, nutty overtones and

a sense of the bracing sea air of the Norman coast. Spread it on a piece of bread if you must, but you will sacrifice the pure sensation of the piquant butter-to-cream transition uncompromised by other textures.

The damp, chalky clay soil surrounding Isigny, where the butter has been produced since the sixteenth century, flavors the local water and gives the grazing cows' milk a high concentration of trace elements and an exceptional mineral salt content. The region's lush grass, rich in iodine and carotene, contributes a distinctive flavor. The heavy sweet cream is ripened with the help of several different strains of bacilli (customary in much of Europe, if not in the U.S.). But the crowning touch is a fat content of 82 percent, higher than the typical 80 percent of regular butters. That 2 percent variable doesn't sound like much, but it makes a big difference in taste. The resulting butter retains a certain silky creaminess even when melted, making it the perfect choice for the

Vintage ad for a Norman company's premium butter

satiny sauce known as beurre blanc.

Although the town of Isigny bestows the most prestigious label a butter could wear, runners-up include nearby Cormeilles and Neufchâtel, as well as the neighboring province of Brittany.

WHERE: *In New York and environs,* Fairway Markets, fairway market.com; *in San Francisco,* Mollie Stone's Markets, tel 415-255-8959, molliestones.com. **MAIL ORDER:** gourmetfoodstore.com (search isigny butter). **FURTHER INFORMATION:** *The Food of France* by Waverley Root (1992).

A WELCOMING CHRISTMAS FRUIT BREAD

Bireweche

French (Alsatian)

A mong the world's Christmas breads, this rich, darkly dense Alsatian specialty is one of the least known yet most sustaining and subtle. Although it takes its name from dried pears, it includes prunes, figs, raisins, and nuts, all scented with spices and kirsch for a festive treat best thinly sliced and served with coffee or red wine.

Bireweche

Makes 1 loaf

For the fruit filling

¼ pound (about ⅓ cup) dried pears
¼ pound (about ⅓ cup) pitted prunes
¼ pound (2 tablespoons) dried figs
2 ounces (2 tablespoons) golden raisins
2 ounces (2 tablespoons) black raisins
1 ounce (about ⅓ cup) unblanched
    hazelnuts, coarsely chopped
1 ounce (about ⅓ cup) blanched almonds,
    coarsely chopped
1 ounce (about ⅓ cup) walnuts, coarsely
    chopped

¼ cup sugar
1 cup kirsch
Pinch each of nutmeg, cinnamon, and cloves

For the bread dough

1 envelope instant dry yeast
2 to 3 cups bread flour, plus more for
    dusting the work surface
1 teaspoon salt
Butter, for greasing the bowl and baking sheet
1 large egg yolk beaten with 1 tablespoon
    cold water

1. Prepare the fruit filling: About 12 hours before you plan to bake the bread, place the pears, prunes, and figs in a saucepan and add just enough water to cover. Let the water come to a simmer over moderate heat and cook the fruit until it softens slightly, 8 to 10 minutes. Drain the fruit, let it cool a bit, then cut it into slim strips. Place the strips of fruit in a large mixing bowl.

2. Rinse the golden and black raisins under warm running water. Drain the raisins well, then coarsely chop them. Add the raisins to the fruit strips along with the hazelnuts, almonds, walnuts, sugar, kirsch, nutmeg, cinnamon, and cloves. Mix well, cover the bowl loosely with plastic wrap, and let it stand at room temperature overnight.

3. Make the bread dough: Pour 1½ cups of cool water into a large mixing bowl and sprinkle the yeast on top. Set the bowl in a warm place until the yeast mixture begins to foam, 5 to 8 minutes.

4. Using an electric mixer, beat 2 cups of the flour and the salt into the yeast mixture. Beat in as much of the remaining flour as the batter will take (the dough should be stiff but pliable). Turn the dough out onto a floured work surface and knead it until smooth and slightly blistered, about 10 minutes. Place the dough in a lightly greased bowl, cover it

loosely with a cotton dish towel, and set the bowl in a warm, draft-free corner until it has doubled in bulk, about 1½ hours. Punch the risen dough down and place it on a floured work surface.

5. Turn the fruit mixture out on the dough. Fold the dough over the fruit, using both hands; fold, refold, and knead the fruits into the dough until well distributed. Shape the dough into a loaf about 10 inches long and 3 or 4 inches wide and place it on a buttered baking sheet. Cover with plastic wrap and let rise in a warm place for about 30 minutes.

6. Preheat the oven to 350°F.

7. Brush the top of the loaf with the beaten egg yolk and bake it until the crust is golden brown and the loaf sounds hollow when tapped on the bottom.

8. Transfer the loaf to a wire rack to cool. When cool, wrap in plastic wrap or aluminum foil.

WHERE: *In Colmar, France,* Pâtisserie Jean, 33/3-89-41-24-63, mulhaupt.fr. **TIP:** The flavor develops best if the loaf is not cut for 24 hours.

BEEF WITH STRINGS ATTACHED

Boeuf à la Ficelle

French

This succulent poached beef dish, with its juicy, rosy meat and rich broth, remains one of the cherished specialties of Cartet, a bistro that began in the true French tradition of the *mère* or mother restaurant. Although the original *mère*, the late Madame Cartet, is long gone, the current owner-chef continues with much of her menu.

High on the list of favorites is still *boeuf à la ficelle*. To make it, a length of top sirloin trimmed of all fat is snugly tied with strings attached to the two handles of a pot; this arrangement keeps the meat evenly suspended in a stock strengthened with leeks, onions, celery, carrots, and a bouquet garni. Lightly poached so that the interior remains a glistening rose-pink and the meat emerges fork-tender, it is sliced and sauced with either a pungent blend of olive oil, Dijon mustard, capers, chopped parsley, and

chives; or a creamy froth of freshly grated horseradish folded into whipped crème fraîche. Boiled potatoes and a splash of the beef stock make a perfect foil for meat and sauce.

It's a wonder that this supreme elevation of poached beef has not spawned a revival complete with showmanship: bringing the pot into the dining room and ladling stock at tableside.

WHERE: *In Paris,* Restaurant Cartet, tel 33/1-48-05-17-65. **FURTHER INFORMATION AND RECIPES:** *The New Making of a Cook* by Madeleine Kamman (1997); splendidtable.org (search boeuf a la ficelle); latimes.com (search boeuf a la ficelle).

—||||||||||||||||||||||||||||||||||—

Boeuf à la Mode en Gelée

French

S ay it's a boiling-hot day and you're starved for something solid, yet cannot face the prospect of steaming-hot food. If you have lived right and are lucky, you will be offered a glistening oval of cold, clear bronze aspic encasing a tender, rich slice of chilled braised beef. The aspic will be ornamented with flower designs cut from tarragon leaves; carrots, onions, or perhaps sweet red peppers as petals; and dots of black olives or even truffles.

This triumph of the garde-manger (the chef in charge of cold food) requires lengthy and patient preparation, beginning with the braising of the beef, done in the style of a daube: A whole piece of beef (chuck, rump, first-cut brisket) is marinated and simmered in red wine heightened with thyme, bay leaves, garlic, bacon, a hint of brandy, and, for its gelatinous properties, a veal knuckle bone or a calf's foot. The tedious part begins after the beef has melted to succulent tenderness and is allowed to cool, unsliced. The stock in which the beef was simmered must then be painstakingly clarified—strained and brought to a boil no fewer than three times. Between each boiling, it must be chilled for twelve to twenty-four hours, or until the fat rises to the top and solidifies for ease of removal. When the sauce is nearly crystal clear, it is finally ready to be poured into a mold or pan to be decorated with a tiny flower-like bouquet of vegetables and inlaid with the sliced beef before being sent off for its final chilling session. It's a far cry from the convenience-biased American aspics of the 1950s.

Although *boeuf en gelée* is most elegant when molded in individual forms, the dish can also be made in a large pan and sliced just before serving (but only if the whole dish will be eaten at once—when cut, the gel will leak and the pretty arrangement will melt away like April snow). A cool string bean salad with a tarragon vinaigrette dressing makes for a lovely and traditional accompaniment, as do some good French bread and a glass of chilled rosé.

FURTHER INFORMATION AND RECIPE: *French Provincial Cooking* by Elizabeth David (1999); *Mastering the Art of French Cooking, Volume 1*, by Julia Child, Louisette Bertholle, and Simone Beck (1961).

—||||||||||||||||||||||||||||||||||—

Boeuf Bourguignon

French

I f you think of beef stew as a somewhat mundane dish that is characteristically short on finesse, you have probably never tried the authentic, richly complex creation of France's Burgundy region. It is one of many country dishes that rely on wine (preferably Burgundy's own lusty red) to tenderize tough meat, with a flavor that is further enhanced by such savory additions as onions, garlic, shallots, thyme, and perhaps even carrots, mushrooms, and a sunny strip of dried orange peel "to taste."

All of the above simmer long and gently, developing slowly until the meat is fork-tender and the juices have coalesced into a rich, dark sauce. The cooked stew is further improved if it is allowed to mellow, covered, in the refrigerator for twenty-four hours before being reheated and served. Although the marinating makes this a lengthy process, skip this step at your own peril. The time and care the dish requires are well spent—it's a delectable stew that makes the most of economical cuts of beef, and it can be made in quantity and held for a week in the refrigerator or a month in the freezer.

Boeuf Bourguignon

Serves 4 to 6

2½ pounds lean beef chuck,
*   cut into 1½-inch cubes*
1½ to 2 cups good but not extravagant red
*   Burgundy or Côtes-du-Rhône wine*
4 tablespoons olive oil
1 large onion, coarsely chopped
2 cloves garlic, peeled and lightly crushed
*   with the flat side of a chef's knife*
4 sprigs fresh flat-leaf parsley,
*   plus 2 tablespoons minced parsley,*
*   for sprinkling over the potatoes*
1½ teaspoons thyme
1 large bay leaf
4 or 5 black peppercorns, crushed
2 slices bacon, diced
10 pearl onions, peeled
Salt and freshly ground black pepper
2 tablespoons all-purpose flour
¼ cup brandy
1 cup beef stock
2 shallots, peeled and lightly crushed with
*   the flat side of a chef's knife*
1 strip (about 2 inches long and 1½ inches
*   wide) orange peel, dried in the oven at*
*   325°F for 8 to 10 minutes*

2 tablespoons (¼ stick) unsalted butter
About 10 large white mushroom caps,
*   wiped with a damp paper towel and*
*   thickly sliced*
8 to 12 small new potatoes, boiled and
*   peeled, for serving*

Robust red Burgundy wine is this meal's star.

1. Place the beef in a large glass or ceramic bowl and add enough wine to cover it. Add 2 tablespoons of the olive oil, the chopped onion, garlic, 2 sprigs of parsley, ½ teaspoon of the thyme, the bay leaf, and crushed peppercorns, and cover the bowl with plastic wrap. Let the beef marinate at room temperature for 3 to 4 hours, or in the refrigerator for 6 to 7 hours. If you are marinating the beef in the refrigerator, remove it 30 minutes before proceeding with the recipe.

2. Heat the remaining 2 tablespoons of olive oil over moderate heat in a heavy 2-quart pot or Dutch oven, preferably of enameled cast iron or another nonreactive material. When the oil is hot, add the bacon and cook until lightly browned, about 7 minutes. Using a slotted spoon, transfer the bacon to a paper towel-lined plate to drain.

3. Add the small white onions to the hot fat and cook over low heat until browned on all sides, about 5 minutes, shaking the pot frequently so the onions brown evenly. Transfer the onions to a bowl and set them aside.

4. Remove the marinated beef from the bowl

and pat it dry thoroughly with paper towels. Strain the marinade, discarding the solids, and set the marinade aside. Increase the heat to medium, then add the beef a few pieces at a time to the hot fat, browning them on all sides. Transfer the pieces of beef to a separate bowl as they brown, adding more to the pot until all of the beef is browned. Do not crowd the pot, or the beef will steam and not brown.

5. Return all of the browned beef to the pot and season it with salt and pepper to taste. Stir in the flour. Cook the beef over low heat, stirring gently but constantly with a wooden spoon, until the flour is absorbed, about 5 minutes.

6. Add the brandy to the pot and, as it simmers, use a wooden spoon to scrape up the brown bits from the bottom of the pot. Let the brandy boil briskly until it evaporates. Pour the strained marinade into the pot along with the beef stock, shallots, the remaining 2 sprigs of parsley, 1 teaspoon of thyme, and the dried orange peel. Cover the pot tightly and let simmer gently until the beef is almost tender, about 2 hours.

7. Melt the butter in a saucepan over low heat. Add the mushrooms and cook them until they give up their liquid and turn golden, about 7 minutes. Add the mushrooms to the pot along with the reserved onions and drained bacon pieces.

8. Cover the pot and let the meat simmer over low heat until it is thoroughly fork-tender, 30 to 40 minutes. Turn off the heat and let the stew stand for about 10 minutes, then skim the grease off the surface. Taste for seasoning, adding more salt and/or pepper as necessary. Return the pot to the stove and let the stew come to a boil just before serving.

9. Serve the stew with the boiled new potatoes sprinkled with the minced parsley and, of course, a good red Burgundy wine. Any other kind would be blasphemy.

WHERE: *In Dijon,* Brasserie B9, tel 33/3-80-38-32-02, brasserie-b9.com; *in New York,* La Grenouille, tel 212-752-1495, la-grenouille.com; *in Greenwich, CT,* Versailles, tel 203-661-6634, versaillesgreenwich.com; *in Great Falls, VA,* L'Auberge Chez François, tel 703-759-3800, laubergechezfrancois.com. **FURTHER INFORMATION AND RECIPES:** *Mastering the Art of French Cooking, Volume 1,* by Julia Child, Louisette Bertholle, and Simone Beck (1961); *French Provincial Cooking* by Elizabeth David (1992); foodandwine.com (search beef stew in red wine sauce); epicurious.com (search boeuf bourguignon 2001).

CHOCOLATE CHIC

Bonbons au Chocolat by Hévin

French

Bonbon is a cutesy way to say "good" twice, and an apt name for the mouth-size, chocolate-covered candy that French confectioners do better than any others. Chocolate, preferably midnight-dark and tauntingly bittersweet, enrobes dried or

fresh fruits, flavored creams, crunchy nuts, pralines, liqueurs, or brittles, the surprise inside each one a mystery until the eater bites in. For the most serious chocolate connoisseurs, however, bonbons just don't cut it; only pure bars unadulterated in texture or flavor afford the proper appreciation and evaluation.

But how many of us are that serious all the time? When frivolity is desired, just call a French chocolatier; preferably Jean-Paul Hévin, whose genius is on delectable display in his very first shop, opened on Avenue de la Motte-Picquet in

1988, and now throughout his pretty sweetshops in Paris, Tokyo, and Hong Kong. Among his triumphs are vanilla and crème fraîche truffles and firm, intensely dark ganache-filled chocolate cigars. All of his wares are exquisitely packaged in milk-chocolate-and-royal-blue boxes and tins that match the color scheme of his shops—a combination almost good enough to eat.

In acknowledgment of Hévin's expertise, the prestigious *Guide des Croqueurs de Chocolat* (Chocolate Lovers' Guide) noted that "the chocolates by that cocoa bean aficionado feature a bitterness so excellent that

The Jean-Paul Hévin flagship store boasts a lavish array of bonbons.

even the most finicky of purists will be won over. At the same time, adventurous types will be satisfied with the unexpected flavors."

Members of that first category will be relieved to discover that Hévin does, of course, trade in the simple bars they seek. In fact, this particular chocolatier's true gift may be his ability to understand and blend different chocolates from various parts of the world, a talent most discernible in bars such as the woodsy Java, the more mellow Trinite, and the mild Ecuador, the last of which is sure to appeal to children.

So whether it's bonbons or bars or another form of chocolate, do sample the artistry on display at the very best of French chocolateries.

RETAIL AND MAIL ORDER: *In Paris*, Jean-Paul Hévin at several locations, tel 33/1-55-35-35-96, jphevin.com.

―――――――――|||||||||||||||||||||||||||||||―――――――――

"THIS BOUILLABAISSE A NOBLE DISH IS SORT OF SOUP, OR BROTH, OR BREW, OR HOTCHPOTCH OF ALL SORTS OF FISHES, THAT GREENWICH NEVER COULD OUTDO."
—FROM "THE BALLAD OF BOUILLABAISSE," BY WILLIAM MAKEPEACE THACKERAY

―――――――――

Bouillabaisse

French (Provençal)

It took a full eleven stanzas for Thackeray to express his appreciation of the complex fish stew that he so loved in Paris, a dish he felt could not be equaled in his native England. Oddly, two of the fish that he mentions, roach and dace, swim in

freshwater and are commonly found in the English river Avon. To complicate matters, these *aren't* the fish one typically sees in a bouillabaisse, which today's purists claim should include only saltwater fish and shellfish—though the matter is shrouded in argument. Some allow mollusks but outlaw crustaceans; all agree on the permanent exclusion of shrimp and scallops (but don't ask why). One undisputed point is the necessity of a rascasse in the mix—a scorpion fish with a poisonous spine that must be extracted very carefully. Rascasse adds a slightly viscous tone to the texture, along with a solid, mildly acidic underpinning of flavor.

Whatever the mix, expect an exquisite still life of whole or large chunks of fish, lobster, crab, gleaming ebony mussels, snowy rings of calamari, and perhaps pearly gray ropes of eel—all floating in a magnificent rose-gold broth redolent of tomato, saffron, fennel, perhaps leek and garlic, and, always, white wine. The soup is usually presented first, accompanied by croutons and plenty of rouille (the cayenne-fired sauce that is spooned onto the croutons and into the broth); then comes the fish, with a little broth

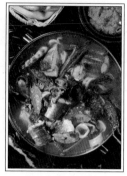

The dish is native to Provence.

spooned over it, and maybe a boiled potato or two to refresh the palate.

"Bouillabaisse was invented by Venus to put her husband Vulcan to sleep when she had a rendezvous with Mars," Waverley Root writes in *The Food of France*—an origin story worthy of such a magnificent dish.

WHERE: *In Paris,* La Méditerranée, tel 33/1-43-26-02-30, la-mediterranee.com; *in Antibes, France,* Bacon, tel 33/4-93-61-50-02, restaurantdebacon.com; *in New York,* Aquagrill, tel 212-274-0505, aquagrill.com. **FURTHER READING AND RECIPES:** *The Food of France* by Waverley Root (1992); *French Provincial Cooking* by Elizabeth David (1960). **SEE ALSO:** Brodetto Vastese, page 170.

BOUILLABAISSE'S KISSING COUSIN

Bourride

French (Provençal)

The rose-gold bouillabaisse of Marseille, with its crackling flavor and diverse combination of snowy fish and firecracker-red shellfish, is undoubtedly the world's most famous fish soup. However, food-loving visitors to the area are often surprised to discover bourride, "the other fish soup," and to many palates the more elegantly subtle of the two. It is a satiny ivory broth adrift with chunks of three types of firm, white-fleshed fish such as porgy, cod, sole, haddock, or striped bass, but no shellfish.

All are cut into serving portions, but are neither boned nor skinned, ensuring that they retain texture and full deep-sea flavor. Wafting from the tureen are heady overtones of white wine and a vibrant fish stock gentled with leeks, musty-sweet bay leaves, bosky wild fennel seeds, and an astringent strip of dried orange peel. Then comes the alluring addition of the evocative sauce aioli, or garlic mayonnaise.

When it is correctly served for maximum heat and flavor, the broth is ladled into a wide soup bowl over poached fish on a butter-toasted croustade. Aioli is passed to be added at will, as though anyone could ever get enough.

WHERE: *In Nice,* L' Ane Rouge, tel 33/4-93-89-49-63, anerougenice.com. **FURTHER INFORMATION AND RECIPES:** *The Food of France* by Waverley Root (1992); *The New Making of a Cook* by Madeleine Kamman (1997); cookstr.com (search bourride with aioli).

Brandade de Morue

French (Provençal)

Few ingredients with gourmet status have origins as humble as those of the dried salt cod known as *morue* in France and *bacalao* (give or take a few letters here and there) in Spain, Portugal, and Italy. Valued for centuries as a reliable winter fish eaten on meatless fast days, this product of Northern Europe was so essential to the Catholic Mediterranean that it fostered close commercial and political ties between the two regions: Along with herring, salt cod was the main cargo that financed the ships of the north's powerful Hanseatic League, formed by merchant associations in 1241.

Over time, salt cod has transformed from basic necessity to connoisseurs' treat, whether in the form of English codfish cakes (see page 8), New England fish cakes, or Portugal's crisp round croquettes, or in its Spanish incarnation, mantled with a silken parsley-and-garlic green sauce (see page 262). In Italy, salt cod may be simmered with tomatoes and spooned over pasta, or used in a Venetian version of *brandade* known as *bacalao mantecato,* meaning "worked by hand."

The luscious appetizer *brandade de morue* is one of salt cod's most elegant presentations.

Well-soaked, carefully poached fish is whipped up with warm milk, splashes of golden olive oil, and plenty of garlic and black pepper. Electric blenders or food processors generally do the whipping these days, but old-timers will tell you the fish should first be worked smooth with a mortar and pestle. (While they are at it, they'll also probably warn against the addition of mashed potatoes to the mix, a common infraction.) The result, a mousselike spread that is creamy yet retains the intriguing underlying chewiness of the fish, is usually served with slim points of toast or toasted baguette and black olives; at its gourmet zenith, shavings of black truffles may be added as well.

FURTHER INFORMATION AND RECIPES: *Roast Chicken and Other Stories* by Simon Hopkinson (2007); *French Provincial Cooking* by Elizabeth David (1960); cookstr.com (search brandade de morue); foodandwine.com (search brandade de morue).

A CLICHÉ, BUT A WORTHY ONE

Brie

French

Made of raw cow's milk (although the highly prized *Brie de Meaux* is sometimes made with pasteurized milk), an authentic brie will hint of nuts, mushrooms, garlic, and, according to some food writers, fried eggs—

a lot of flavors for one simple cheese to deliver.

Perhaps because it is easy for Americans to pronounce, and seems so quintessentially French, it's a name that is thrown around to describe all manner of flat, ivory disks of runny, creamy cheese. Oddly, brie is not among France's name-controlled cheeses (those bearing the Appellation d'Origine Contrôlée mark assuring that their point of origin, ingredients, and processing are protected by French law). But authentic bries from the Île-de-France—*Brie de Meaux* and *Brie de Melun,* which have both been granted A.O.C. status—are far from supermarket fare. In fact, *they* should be considered the standard: They've been setting the bar for flavor since 774, when Charlemagne was reputed to have tasted his first slice. The cheese became a favorite of his, earning it the title *le roi du fromage* (the king of cheese).

There is actually very little resemblance between real bries and their imitators. The latter are generally gooey when cut, whereas whole disks or large wedges of true brie bulge, but do not run. As for flavor, the imitators are largely bland affairs, chewy versions of butter with little to no complexity. Sadly, locating one of the A.O.C. bries stateside is no easy task. U.S. Federal Drug Administration laws require that raw-milk cheeses be aged for a minimum of sixty days; because brie is unaged, only pasteurized Brie de Meaux can be imported. The moral of the story? When a real brie is found, savor every bite, edible rind and all.

Remember that once a brie is cut, its ripening process comes to a halt. When shopping for uncut brie, avoid any cheese that sinks around its edges, and look for an intact bloomy white rind with beige flecks. Serve the brie at room temperature, with simple, traditional accompaniments like a chunk of crusty rustic baguette or water biscuits and a dry sparkling white wine.

FURTHER INFORMATION: *French Cheeses* by Kazuko Masui and Tomoko Yamada (1996); *Cheese Primer* by Steven Jenkins (1996). **TIP:** Look for Rouzaire's pasteurized Brie de Meaux.

MORNING SUNSHINE IN A ROLL

Brioche

French

It's not surprising that two great French painters thought the light and spongy brioche beautiful enough to be the subject of still lifes. The first, Chardin, rested a plump brioche on a white cloth and crowned it with a spray of pale spring blossoms. Years later, Manet made a similar painting, relying on his characteristic chiaroscuro, or black-and-white contrasts, and sticking a white rose in the center of the large round breakfast roll. Both painted the big communal brioche that is divided among many; more usual now are the individual versions called brioche à tête, topped with a knobby head of crusty pastry.

Usually baked in a fluted mold, the airy, eggy, gently sweet bread-cake is a near second to the croissant as a favorite French breakfast. Plain or braided, it's a light and absorbent bread that is perfect for fluffy, sunny French toast or equally good with a dab of butter and a dollop of jam. Happily, the soft brioche dough also lends itself to many other preparations. Without sugar, it makes a crust for sausages or enfolds delicate pâtés. With sugar and baked in a cone or ring form, it is translated into luscious desserts such as juicy rum-soaked babas or cream-filled Savarins.

Communal brioche and diminutive brioche à tête

Because the quality of the butter is so essential to a good brioche, one theory holds that the bread was invented in Normandy, source of the world's best dairy products, sometime before it arrived in Paris during the seventeenth century. Its name is said to derive from *broyer,* or breaking up, referring to the heavy, steady kneading the dough requires to take in air and so rise to the occasion.

WHERE: *In many locations in France and in New York,* Ladurée, laduree.com. **FURTHER INFORMATION AND RECIPES:** *The Oxford Companion to Food* by Alan Davidson (1999); *Mastering the Art of French Cooking, Volume 2,* by Julia Child, Louisette Bertholle, and Simone Beck (1970).

||||||||||||||||||||||||||||||||||

A SWEET LOG FOR CHRISTMAS

Bûche de Noël

French

Young children may wish Christmas came around more often—and the adults who have tasted the *bûche de Noël* will share their sentiments. Surely no one would mind if this wickedly rich and creamy log of a cake showed up at other times, perhaps even at Easter. Why let tradition dictate when we can dig into the tender blond, vanilla-and-rum-scented cake of the lightest, eggiest sponge dough, wrapped jelly roll–style around a thick and delectably oozy buttercream filling of chocolate or mocha?

But honor its origins we must. Like the European log cakes of England, Norway, and Lithuania, the *bûche* dates back to pre-Christian times when huge Yule logs were burned in fireplaces to honor the winter solstice. To replicate that ancient tree-trunk look, the rolled and filled cake is decorated with more buttercream frosting, scored to resemble bark, and adorned with tinted marzipan formed into tiny mushrooms and woody knots. Other garnishes might be candied cherries, sprigs of holly, and toasted almonds or pistachios, with piping spelling out "Joyeux Noël" or the numbers of the New Year.

In France, the bûche de Noël is traditionally eaten at the *réveillon* supper held after midnight mass on Christmas Eve, though it reappears in patisseries and restaurants throughout the holiday season. Soft and rich when served at room temperature, the bûche can be even more subtle and seductive when half frozen so the buttercream sets to almost ice-cream consistency and the cake's sweetness becomes less intense.

WHERE: *In many locations in France and in New York,* Ladurée, laduree.com; *in Colmar, France,* Pâtisserie Jean, tel 33/3-89-41-24-63, mulhaupt.fr; *in Oakland and Berkeley, CA,* La Farine Boulangerie, lafarine.com. **FURTHER INFORMATION AND RECIPES:** *Visions of Sugarplums* by Mimi Sheraton (1986); *The Art of French Pastry* by Jacquy Pfeiffer and Martha Rose Schulman (2013); saveur.com (search a slice of christmas).

━━━━━━━━━━━|||||||||||||||||||||||||||||||||━━━━━━━━━━━

A LITTLE BIRD TOLD ME. . . .

Compote de Caille en Gelée

Quail in Aspic

French

O ne of the delights of Au Crocodile, the celebrated restaurant in the Alsatian capital of Strasbourg, is a stunning appetizer that appears in a small, oval terra-cotta terrine, its top glistening with a rich mahogany-brown aspic.

Breaking through that fragrant covering, dotted with sprigs of tarragon and hard-cooked egg white, yields quite a prize: a tenderly braised, boneless quail or squab that is mouth-wateringly scented with Madeira. Cutting through the layers of tender quail meat holds, amazingly enough, further reward in the form of a richly emollient stuffing of truffled foie gras. All the while, the flavorful aspic—the braising gravy, cooked with a calf's foot for gelatin—slowly melts into a chiffonlike sauce.

With a chunk of bread and a refreshing salad of spiky frisée lettuce, this luxurious compote makes for a sublime lunch or an elegant midnight supper. Though only occasionally available on the menu at Au Crocodile, it is prepared by many graduates of that restaurant's kitchens.

WHERE: In Strasbourg, Au Crocodile, tel 33/3-88-32-13-02, au-crocodile.com. **FURTHER INFORMATION AND RECIPE:** *Mastering the Art of French Cooking, Volume 2,* by Julia Child, Louisette Bertholle, and Simone Beck (1970), see Volailles en Escabèche and substitute quail.

━━━━━━━━━━━|||||||||||||||||||||||||||||||||━━━━━━━━━━━

THE GOLDEN-FLESHED MELON OF PROVENCE

Cavaillon Melon with Wild Strawberries or Raspberries

French (Provençal)

W e're beginning to see them from late spring to early fall in upscale restaurants and greengrocers in large cities throughout the United States: those green-and-cream-striped, small round melons of Provence. Labeled Cavaillons or

Charentais, they are members of the musk-melon family, with netted rinds much like that of the cantaloupe. As with all muskmelons, ripe-ness is signaled by a pink blush on the rind, and general quality by a well-rounded form with no bruises or soft, damp spots. The honey-sweet,

rose-gold flesh is delicious when the slightly chilled melon is cut into boat-shaped wedges and doused with only a little lime juice, or for purists, served straight up.

For a special-event dessert, one small melon per person can be filled with liquor-flavored

Cavaillons at a street market in Aix-en-Provence

berries. To accomplish this, cut a lid from the top of each melon and scoop out the flesh, taking care not to break through the rind. Discard all seeds, but retain as much of the juice as possible.

Cut the flesh into spoon-size cubes, and combine with a little superfine granulated sugar and small strawberries, preferably *fraises des bois*, or raspberries. Add a splash or two of kirsch or Grand Marnier per melon—or go for broke and mix the two. Pack everything back into the melons and replace the lids. Encase each melon in plastic wrap and chill in the refrigerator for about two hours. Unwrap and serve very cold as a sophisticated finale to a warm-weather meal.

MAIL ORDER: In August and September, Melissa's Produce, tel 800-588-0151, melissas .com (search charentais melons). **SPECIAL EVENT:** Fête du Melon, Cavaillon, France, June, melon decavaillon.com

---

"CAMEMBERT, POETRY, BOUQUET OF OUR MEAL,
WHAT WOULD BECOME OF LIFE IF YOU DID NOT EXIST?"
—JEAN ANTHELME BRILLAT-SAVARIN

Camembert de Normandie

French (Norman)

With its sunny ivory hue and unctuously molten texture, authentic camembert cheese is a mushroomy, almost woodsy delight. *Authentic* is the operative word, however, and divining the true *Camembert de Normandie* requires a good

eye and a sensitive nose. Like so many great originals, this cheese has many bland imitators; because the ingredients, processing, and point of origin of camembert are not protected by French law, the cheese is not accorded the Appellation d'Origine Contrôlée (AOC) label. But to establish some sort of quality designation, any camembert produced according to the specific laws of Normandy earns the marking V.C.N., Véritable Camembert de Normandie. Any other camembert will be second-rate at best.

Determining a camembert's ripeness is famously tricky. Cheese mongers advise clients to touch a closed eye with one index finger and the cheese with the other, in the hope of discovering matching textures. Why go to such lengths? Because, as with any cheese, the ripening process ends when your camembert is cut open. The next step is to remove your finger from your eye and make sure that the paste bulges against its wrapper rather than runs, the latter being a sign of overripeness. If the wheel or wedge meets both of these criteria, hurry home with it.

Generously spread onto a crusty chunk of baguette, it becomes a *casse-croûte*, Normandy's favorite pick-me-up sandwich. The most serious aficionados eat the rind as well, for an extra belt of calcium and flavor.

Authentic camembert is unavailable in the United States because FDA laws prohibit the import of unpasteurized cheeses not aged for at least sixty days. The best pasteurized imported brand is Le Châtelain.

Where: *In New York and environs,* Fairway Markets, fairwaymarket.com. **Further information:** *Camembert: A National Myth* by Pierre Boisard (2003); *French Cheeses* by Kazuko Masui and Tomoko Yamada (1996); *Cheese Primer* by Steve Jenkins (1996).

––––––––––|||||||||||||||||||||||||||||||||||||––––––––––

BEANS GET CONTROVERSIAL

Cassoulet

French

A ny traditional dish composed of many ingredients will spark controversy as to its authenticity. Which elements, seasonings, and techniques are essential and which are verboten? France's magnificently soul-warming cassoulet is no exception, with three basic versions assigned to three different cities—allowing for constant crossovers that incite argument and unnecessarily confuse the truly delectable issue.

Cassoulet de Castelnaudary is the simplest, based on white beans such as the American Great Northerns, baked with various pork cuts—smoked ham, fresh pork shoulder, salt pork with its rind, and spicy, firm sausage. For Cassoulet de Carcassonne, the cook also throws in boned chunks of lamb or mutton and, in season, a wild game bird such as partridge or quail. For Cassoulet Toulousain, the cook goes for broke, adding not only most of the above but also duck or goose confit, the chunks of fat-preserved poultry that give the final result an unctuously rich finish.

Inevitably, one will come across a stupendous cassoulet with an ingredient that belies its geographical label—say a chunk of duck confit

Recipes vary, but all start with beans and sausage.

in one called Castelnaudary. As Waverley Root said in his seminal work, *The Food of France,* "Cassoulet is what you find it." Ultimately the best thing to do is eat up and revel in its deeply satisfying deliciousness.

Controversy aside, some features are the same in all cassoulets, beginning with the cooking vessel itself. To produce exactly the right softly blended result, with white beans and meats cooking evenly and a nice crisp crust developing on top, you must have a wide, deep, round casserole made of terra-cotta that is glazed inside. The only possible substitute would be a similar shape in enameled cast iron. When all of the ingredients are in, a thick topping of bread crumbs is added. Authenticity demands that this crust be broken and stirred into the other ingredients three to seven times during cooking, each time allowing it to redevelop until at the end it is very crisp and thick, and layered down into the mix.

A feast for the eyes and nose as it is served, this blend of tender beans and meats, aromatic with garlic, onion, cloves, thyme, bay leaves, white wine, and good strong beef stock, requires only one more element for it to be enjoyed at its zenith: a miserably cold, wet, blustery, gray winter evening.

Where: *In Paris,* Benoit, tel 33/1-42-72-25-76, alain-ducasse.com; *in Toulouse, France,* Le Colombier, tel 33/5-61-62-40-05, resaurant-le colombier.com; *in New York,* Quatorze Bis, tel 212-535-1414. **Further information and recipes:** *Mastering the Art of French Cooking, Volume 1,* by Julia Child, Louisette Bertholle, and Simone Beck (1961); *The Food of France* by Waverley Root (1992); saveur.com (search hearty cassoulet). **Special events:** Fête du Cassoulet, Toulouse, France, August, fete-du-cassoulet.com.

‖‖‖‖‖‖‖‖‖‖‖‖‖‖‖‖‖‖‖‖‖‖‖‖‖‖‖

THE ROOT OF AN ELEGANT SALAD

Céleri Rémoulade

French

Humble celeriac (*Apium graveolens rapaceum,* also known as celery root or knob celery) is a bit like the Cinderella of celery. The bulbous, tangled knob grows underground while its better-known stalk sister is a favorite for salads and seasonings. But with a little attention and the proper dressing—in this case, the mustard seed–based mayonnaise known as rémoulade—celeriac becomes a star. Frugal French cooks long ago figured out that the creamy, soothing rémoulade made a perfect foil for the root, maximizing its clean and earthy flavor and toothsome texture.

To get the best out of celeriac, some work is required: First, its stalk, leaves, and tough darker outer layer must be peeled away with a sharp knife, preferably of stainless steel. When only ivory remains, the root must be julienned into ultrathin bite-size pieces and quickly dropped into water that has been acidulated with lemon juice or white vinegar. Once thoroughly drained, the slivers are tossed with rémoulade, creating a salad that serves as a crunchy, refreshing companion to charcuterie and seafood dishes or stands on its own as an hors d'oeuvre. It also makes a great unorthodox slaw for fish sandwiches or burritos.

Where: *In California and Las Vegas,* Bouchon Bistros, bouchonbistro.com. **Further information and recipes:** *Bouchon* by Thomas Keller (2004); cookstr.com (search celery remoulade). **Tip:** Celeriac is in season between winter and early spring; choose small to medium roots that are firm, and refrigerate in a plastic bag for up to a week.

‖‖‖‖‖‖‖‖‖‖‖‖‖‖‖‖‖‖‖‖‖‖‖‖‖

A BRAINY CHEESE FROM LYON

Cervelle de Canut

French (Lyonnaise)

In these days of political correctness, naming a cheese "brain of the silk worker" might cause sit-ins and other street demonstrations. Yet such is the literal translation for the addictive Lyonnais cheese spread composed of *fromage blanc*

A spread, or a meal in itself

mixed with garlic, shallots, chives, and the fresh herbs that give the spread its tiny, dark pinpoint markings. The odd name dates back to the cheese's origins in the seventeenth and eighteenth centuries, the peak of Lyon's silk industry. The preparation was a favorite among local housewives, who likened its mushy and splotchy appearance to the brains of the silk workers, who were also great fans of the treat. Despite the obvious slight, and although the laborers and looms of the past are now long gone, *cervelle de canut* remains.

Predictably, every family believes theirs to be the very best version. Although variations abound, all must begin with fromage blanc: the utterly fresh, slightly fermented cheese with a teasingly sour edge. (Lacking true fromage blanc, many an inventive cook has substituted fresh ricotta and proceeded from there.) Most recipes then call for chopped garlic, shallots, and chives, followed by a combination of herbs such as chervil, parsley, tarragon, and thyme; salt and pepper; and olive oil. Gently mixed, the spread is served as a snack or an appetizer, usually on buttered toasts, though many prefer to eat it straight, by the spoonful. Chilled, cervelle de canut can be an ideal cheese course and a marvelously rich end to a meal.

WHERE: *In Lyon*, at the market Les Halles de Lyon, tel 33/4-78-62-39-33, halledelyon.free.fr; *in Miami*, DB Bistro Moderne, tel 305-421-8800, dbbistro.com/miami. **FURTHER INFORMATION AND RECIPES:** *French Cheeses* by Kazuko Masui and Tomoko Yamada (1996); *The Complete Encyclopedia of French Cheese* by Pierre Androuet (1973).

‖‖‖‖‖‖‖‖‖‖‖‖‖‖‖‖‖‖‖‖‖‖‖‖‖

TAKE YOUR BRAINS AND FRY THEM

Cervelles au Beurre Noir

French

Is there something slightly evil about eating brains? From a rational point of view, no; but our rational minds rarely govern our attitudes toward food, and that subconscious frisson may actually contribute to our enjoyment of this classic delicacy. Who knows?

This luscious appetizer or main course begins with the soft, pearl-gray brain of a young calf or lamb. Soaked in ice water, skinned, and blanched lightly to attain a solid but still-soft form, the brain is lightly dusted with flour and sautéed in clarified sweet butter that is allowed to turn a deep coffee-black, just this side of being truly burned. Into that butter go a few shots of fresh lemon juice and a handful of minced parsley, all to be spooned over the finished dish.

If *beurre noir* seems too *noir* and acidic, try the brains *au beurre noisette*—in nut-brown butter also finished with lemon juice and parsley.

Noir or *noisette*, a few chopped rinsed capers provide a saline finishing touch. The dish is best served on warm toast slices that become unctuously delicious as they absorb the flavorful cooking juices.

A note for the health-conscious: Diners wary of cholesterol content should know that brains pack megadoses of B vitamins and iron. Hopefully that knowledge can help tip the balance.

Further information and recipes: *Larousse Gastronomique* (2009); *Mastering the Art of French Cooking, Volume 1*, by Julia Child, Louisette Bertholle, and Simone Beck (1961). **See also:** Cervello Arreganata, page 179.

TRUMPETING THE GOLD

Chanterelles

French

Prized by the French as *girolles* and by the Germans as *pfifferlinge*, the tiny golden *Cantharellus cibarius* are one of several types of wild mushrooms broadly known to us as chanterelles. Growing in tiny clumps in the conifer forests

of Europe, Japan, North Africa, Australia, and the United States, they have an intense orange-gold color that gives them the look of flat, unfurled apricots. These cute and cheery mushrooms keep well, and so can be found fresh in markets long after their autumn season. Although they are available both dried and canned, only fresh chanterelles are worth the price and bother, as in their preserved forms they generally become unpleasantly metallic.

The simplest quick sauté in butter or olive oil, perhaps with a hint of garlic or shallots, results in a faintly sweet but slightly earthy garnish. Prepared that way, chanterelles lend a fruity apricot-peach flavor accent to omelets or scrambled eggs and to meats. In Germany's Black Forest region and in Alsace, in France, they're often served as an aromatic accompaniment to fall game dishes.

Mail order: Oregon Mushrooms, tel 800-682-0036, oregonmushrooms.com. **Further information:** *Chanterelle Dreams, Amanita Nightmares* by Greg Marley (2010); *The Oxford Companion to Food* by Alan Davidson (1999).

Foragers can strike gold in any temperate forest.

|||||||||||||||||||||||||||||||||

Chaource

French

Although the supremacy of its bubbly wines is widely acknowledged, the Champagne region's rich and creamy cow's milk cheese is too often overlooked. Superb at almost any age, with its silky ripened body and fragrantly bloomy, edible rind, Chaource is an exceptional culinary pleasure. When very young—around two weeks old—its flaky white interior tastes extremely mild and milky. As the cheese ages, its body darkens in color and its flavor intensifies. At its prime (no more than two months old), it becomes runny, sharp, and earthy, with more complexity and depth than brie, to which it is quite similar and is often compared. Chaource is one of France's elite name-controlled cheeses (Appellation d'Origine Contrôlée), meaning that French law strictly regulates its ingredients, processing, and point of origin. Because the cheese is aged for only a short time, only the pasteurized version is allowed entry to the U.S. Look for the Lincet brand.

FURTHER INFORMATION: *Cheese Primer* by Steven Jenkins (1996); *French Cheeses* by Kazuko Masui and Tomoko Yamada (1996). **TIP:** The Musée du Fromage à Chaource offers exhibits, information, and cheese tasting, tel 33/3-25-40-10-67.

|||||||||||||||||||||||||||||||||

Assiette de Charcuterie

French

Care for a plate of assorted cold cuts or a deli platter? Although its American incarnations sound mundane indeed, lucky is the diner who happens into a traditional bistro that offers an *assiette de charcuterie* as a first course. Accompanying a basket of assorted sausages will be several glazed terrines packed with both firm and softly spreading pâtés, along with a cutting board, a sharp knife, a little crock of Dijon mustard, and crusty chunks of firm-textured baguette and slices of toast. Of course, the only problem with an eat-all-you-want first course is forgetting when to stop. Which is why those most passionate about charcuterie might prefer to make a meal of it, washing it down with plenty of strong red wine before retiring for a nice, long nap.

Charcuterie shops can be an even more enticing means of delivery, for like all super-delis, they exude nose-tweaking aromas bound to drive serious eaters crazy. Such temptations were celebrated in Émile Zola's novel *The Belly of Paris*. Florent, the protagonist, starts work at a charcuterie in the old Les Halles, where he is dazzled by the "vast quantities of rich, succulent things . . .

jars of rillettes, boned hams, stuffed Strasbourg tongues . . . great cuts of veal and pork, whose jelly was as limpid as crystallized sugar."

Most charcuterie offerings are ready to eat, no cooking needed, and shops display other prepared and semiprepared dishes as complements to the meats. Among the most traditional are refreshing, mustard-zapped *céleri rémoulade,* slim haricots verts, or French potato salad with wine vinegar and nut-oil dressings.

Also on offer are snails, prepacked into shells and capped with parsley-garlic butter, and *coquilles St-Jacques,* scallops in oven-proof seashell-shaped dishes topped with béchamel and grated Gruyère. Both dishes are ready to be popped into the oven. A few soups and cooked stews of the day—*coq au vin,* veal Marengo, *boeuf Bourguignon*—join whipped potatoes, perhaps ratatouille, slow-simmered white beans, and a few cheeses and fruits to round out a quick meal at home.

A market stall in France offers abundant choices.

The roots of the term *charcuterie* mean cooked (*cuit*) meat (*chair*), a designation wide enough to encompass a beautiful host of variations. Usually the meat is pork, alone or mixed with others and in varied forms and textures, but there are a number of charcuteries made solely of game birds and meats, rabbit, poultry, innards, and even horsemeat, controversial in the States but beloved elsewhere for its rich, somewhat gamy flavor.

To quickly assess the quality of a charcuterie's products, choose a *pâté de campagne.* Once excellent wherever it was found, this country pâté has spawned mass-produced versions that are often bland and stiffly compact, oversalted, and zapped with preservatives. The good ones are heady with brandy and bay leaves, and can be nibbled on their own with a touch of mustard, plated with a garnish of céleri rémoulade, or slipped into a baguette sandwich. The meat mixture usually includes pork with some veal and/or ham, fat in the form of lard or fatback, and flavorings of onions, garlic, wine, Calvados or another brandy, and a heady haze of spices such as juniper, thyme, mace, and the beloved French mix *quatre-épices,* of pepper, ginger, nutmeg, and cloves.

More elegant, upscale pâtés, often enriched with truffles, pistachios, and Madeira, are the creamy, silken result of a concentration of ground livers: pork, veal, chicken, or the foie gras of ducks and geese. *Pâté Bourguignon* is worth looking for, too; it is a subtle blend of guinea hen meat, red wine, onions, bacon, and chanterelle mushrooms.

Some of the softest and most unctuously irresistible pâtés are the rillettes based on pork, duck, goose, or rabbit, the meat simmered for hours in its own fat until it disintegrates into threads (*rillettes*) to be packed in crocks, chilled, and then spread onto rounds of toasted bread.

The best charcuteries also display a glittering array of aspic-captured meats that may include the wonderful *jambon persillé,* softly cooked ham that simmers in stock and white wine along with herbs, garlic, and a pig or calf foot to add the desired glassy gel. Scooped out of big bowls, the sunny parsley-flecked aspic and tender pink ham combine for an ethereal effect, almost as lovely to see as to taste. The jellied meat and cartilage of animal heads, feet, and tails—pig, lamb, calf, and ox—are equally seductive and generally pretty well perfumed with garlic.

Sausages hang everywhere, among them the classic dried versions—*saucissons secs*—we call salami or cervelat. Perhaps the best and finest of these is the *rosette de Lyon,* from the city considered the mecca for charcuterie: a dark red, medium-size pork, garlic, and pepper-spiced winner. Like all nicely chewy dried sausages, it should be very thinly sliced. Wild boar sausage is similar in size and texture, but with a more vibrant flavor. There is one type of rose-pink *saucisson à l'ail* that is meant to be poached, and another that is dried and ready for slicing. The tripe sausage andouille is also ready to eat, with a strong, almost feral appeal.

Among the sausages meant to be cooked and served hot is a smaller tripe-filled cousin of andouille—*andouillette*—that is grilled or fried with a sauce. (Neither should be confused with the Cajun andouille, which has nothing to do with tripe.) The chubby little *boudin noir* is a black sausage, also known as black pudding, prepared most traditionally with pigs' blood, but for which beef blood is now used in the U.S. due to health restrictions. Either way, it is a dark, velvety, and spicy treat most delicious when grilled and served with mashed potatoes. *Boudins blancs,* looking like little white frankfurters, are a much milder affair made with poultry and perhaps also veal and pork.

Jésus de Morteau is filled with roughly chopped pork and closed at one end of its casing with a wooden peg. The mild sausage, often poached in a red wine such as Beaujolais, is a specialty of Alsace, the Jura, and Switzerland.

As you might guess, there are also many types of cooked and cured raw hams on view in charcuteries, none more highly prized than the *jambon de Bayonne,* a lightly smoked and salted beauty that is a specialty of the southwest Basque country around its namesake city.

Let us not forget the cute little bread-crumb–coated, ham-shaped mounds called *jambonneau,* made of the shoulder or hip knuckles of pork. A bone left sticking out on top suggests a whole mini-ham that needs only to be sliced to be enjoyed.

Traveling food lovers who'd like to try these many delights can gather a meal at a charcuterie and take it out to a park bench—or, more comfortably, sneak it up to their hotel room. It's a very good idea to travel with a fork, knife, and spoon, and maybe even a few paper plates, just in case the shop does not offer utensils and hotel management is not willing to comply.

WHERE: *In Biarritz,* for superb Bayonne ham: Didier Carrère, a stall in Les Halles, tel 33/5-59-22-13-01, halles-biarritz.fr; *in New York,* for rosette de Lyon, Salumeria Biellese, tel 212-736-7376, salumeriabiellese.com. **MAIL ORDER:** Olympic Provisions, tel 503-894-8275, olympic provisions.com (search french sausage); D'Artagnan, tel 800-327-8246, dartagnan.com (search charcuterie). **FURTHER INFORMATION:** *The Art of Charcuterie* by Jane Grigson (1991); *The Oxford Companion to Food* by Alan Davidson (1999). **SEE ALSO:** Italian *salumi,* page 230, and Wursts to Walk With, page 317.

CABBAGE HEAD OF THE CLASS

Chou Farci à la Grassoise

French

In almost every one of the many countries where stuffed cabbage is a favored dish, whatever the ingredients and seasonings, it is comprised of various fillings placed in individual cabbage leaves that are then rolled and steamed or baked. In

Provence, especially around the town of Grasse, traditional cooks have another take altogether. Known in the local dialect as *sou fassum,* the dish involves a high-wire act that is beautifully demonstrated in the 2013 French film *Haute Cuisine*— stuffing and cooking a whole head of cabbage.

The favored cabbage for this is the bright green, crinkly Savoy, whose soft leaves can more easily be spread apart to be stuffed. Blanched first if it seems stiff, the cabbage is gently opened, and the innermost core of small, pale leaves is eased out. The core is finely chopped, to be added to a stuffing that includes ground meats such as pork, ham, veal, or crumbled pork sausage, alone or in combination, along with onion, garlic, tomatoes, and dark green leaves of Swiss chard. The stuffing is seasoned with nutmeg, mace, hot pepper flakes, thyme, savory, rosemary, and oregano.

A ball of the savory mixture is placed in the hollowed-out heart of the cabbage, and the remaining stuffing is carefully, neatly pressed between all the other leaves, working from the center out. The stuffed cabbage is then gathered up in a ball and firmly wrapped in cheesecloth.

(Around Grasse, a string bag is kept on hand purely for this purpose; it's known as a *fassumier,* hence the name *sou fassum,* meaning "under the string bag.") The next step is a gentle, almost imperceptible simmer in strong, beefy stock on the stove for several hours, or, for an even richer result, a braise in the oven with bacon or a pig's foot, root vegetables, and herbs.

Once cooked, the cabbage is unwrapped, briefly drained, and then presented whole. Cut into thick wedges and typically anointed with a light tomato sauce, it releases its mouthwatering aroma of meat and herbs and is best complemented by a glass of the delicate local Bandol rosé wine.

FURTHER INFORMATION AND RECIPES: *Simple French Food* by Richard Olney (1992); *Elizabeth David Classics: French Country Cooking* (1980); nytimes.com (search chou vert farci).

||||||||||||||||||||||||||||||||||||||||||||||||||||||||||||||||||||||||||||||||||||||||||||||||||||||||||||||||||||||||||||||||

NO STOMPIN' AT THIS SAVOY

Savoy Cabbage

With its lavishly ruffled, silky puckered leaves, the dark silver-green savoy cabbage is the most delicate member of the diverse *Brassica oleracea* family; the stiffer and more common green, white, and red cabbages are well suited to many preparations but lack the refined gentleness and pliability of those exuberant heads of savoy.

More fragile and requiring less cooking time, Savoy has a nutty flavor that is less overpoweringly cabbagey. Once lightly blanched, its soft leaves easily absorb the pan juices of braised meats and game. In Germany, *wirsingkohl* is a fall favorite when cooked with pheasant or quail, sometimes with the addition of kohlrabi, a first cousin in the brassica family (see page 387). In France, where the cabbages originated in the Savoie region of the Western Alps, the florid heads are stuffed with ground pork and seasonings (see opposite page). Around Milan, Italy, *verza* is a necessary addition to the authentic winter hot pot dinner that is *cassoeula* (see page 176). Because it has a soft leaf, savoy cabbage does not hold up too well once cooked, and so should be served as soon as possible. Raw and salted until wilted, it makes an especially ethereal coleslaw.

TIP: When selecting savoy cabbages, look for firm, dark-green outer leaves; avoid any heads that have been too closely trimmed down to white leaves or that show any rust-spotting or brownish areas of dampness.

———————————|||||||||||||||||||||||||||||———————————

TURNIPS IN A PICKLE

Choucroute de Navets

French (Alsatian)

While Alsace is widely known for the pungent cabbage-based sauerkraut that is choucroute, the region is also home to the beloved turnip-based variation, *choucroute de navets*. Known in the local dialect as *Süra Rüawa* (sour turnips), the dish is the subject of its own festivals in and around the town of Krautergersheim.

The autumn specialty begins in mid-September, when long white turnips are harvested and finely slivered to resemble vegetable spaghetti—think slivered cabbage. Scented with bay leaves and piney juniper berries and layered into barrels with lots of coarse salt, the turnips are weighted down and left to cure for about five weeks. When a veritable confit, the mixture is rinsed and cooked in the style of sauerkraut; it is enriched with pork fat, white wine, onions, perhaps garlic, and the sprightly accents of juniper and black peppercorns. The pungently pickled result is earthy, temptingly chewy, and a perfect foil for *schifela*, the Alsatian roast smoked pork shoulder—or as the basis of the classic *choucroute garni*, mantled with garlands of sausages and cuts of pork.

To prove that everything old can indeed seem new again, some of the most creative Alsatian chefs working in the U.S. intermittently feature *choucroute de navets* on their menus, inevitably to be congratulated by critics on their inventiveness.

FURTHER INFORMATION AND RECIPE: home preservingbible.com (search sauerkraut turnip). **SPECIAL EVENT:** Fête de la Choucroute, Krautergersheim, France, September, tel 33/3 -88-95-78-78.

———————————|||||||||||||||||||||||||||||———————————

SAUERKRAUT TAKES FLIGHT

Choucroute Garnie

French (Alsatian)

An iconic winter dish, Alsace's *choucroute garnie* takes its name from the silky, teasingly pungent sauerkraut that is its base—but that base is hardly the whole story. First, those fragrant mounds of salt-pickled cabbage are infused with flavors of duck or goose fat, onion, garlic, caraway, juniper, bay, and the region's dry white riesling, plus a final shot of kirsch. Then comes a stupendous slew of "garnishes": smoked and fresh pork and beef sausages, smoked pork loin and shoulder, and meaty slabs of bacon. The ultimate version also requires slices of smoked or pickled beef tongue; pigs' knuckles, ears, and tails; and airy calf or pork liver dumplings. Poached and then briefly sautéed with onions, these dumplings are the crowning glory of the Choucroute Royale that is served every Saturday at lunch in the folksy Chez Hansi in Colmar.

A standard on the menus of French brasseries (originally brewery-owned taverns featuring foods especially complementary to beer), the same lusty array is known as a *Schlactplatte,* or butcher's plate, across the border, in the German province of Swabia. In Switzerland it is a *Bernerplatte,* named for the city of Berne, just next door to Alsace. Or there's *choucroute à la Juif,* the version prepared by the kashruth-observing Jews of Alsace, who substitute fresh and pickled cuts of beef and beef sausages for pork. Last but not least is *choucroute des navets,* another much-loved Alsatian version made with turnips (see page 78).

The Alsatian soil and climate are well suited to producing the right kind of cabbage for pickling, and the abundant supply means there are still many homes, shops, and restaurants where sauerkraut is cured on the premises. Finely shredded fresh cabbage is layered with rock salt and juniper berries in a wooden barrel or stoneware crock, covered with a cloth, and weighted down by a lid made of nonreactive material.

Hearty fare for a cold winter day

Within three weeks, the cabbage cures itself as it releases its own brine. To try this, choose an outdoor or basement location, lest the rising aroma of the pickling cabbage turn you off long before it is ready to be eaten.

Whether you're self-curing or hiring out the job, please pass the sharp Dijon mustard or the sweeter, grainier *moutarde ancienne,* along with floury boiled potatoes and a glass of golden beer or an Alsatian sylvaner or riesling.

WHERE: *In Paris,* Chez Jenny, tel 33/1-44-54-39-00, chezjenny.com; *in Colmar, France,* Chez Hansi, tel 33/3-89-41-37-84; *in New York,* Quatorze Bis, tel 212-535-1414; *in Great Falls, VA,* L'Auberge Chez François, tel 703-759-3800, laubergechezfrancois.com. **FURTHER INFORMATION AND RECIPES:** *The Lutèce Cookbook* by André Soltner with Seymour Britchky (1995); foodnetwork.com (search choucroute garnie). **SPECIAL EVENTS:** Sauerkraut festivals: Waynesville, OH, October, sauerkrautfestival .com; Phelps, NY, August, phelpsny.com/sauerkraut-festival; Scappoose, OR, September, scappoosecommunity.org.

---||||||||||||||||||||||||||||||||||---

A BAKED CUSTARD DESSERT FOR NON-BAKERS

Clafoutis Limousin

French (Limousin)

Cherry bread pudding might be the easiest way to describe this simple but seductive dessert, at its best when the juiciest cherries are in season. Lovely and light and perfumed with vanilla, it is as cheerful looking as it is novel (at least in the world beyond France), a crustless custard pie dimpled with whole cherries. The cherries should not be too large, and, if you and your guests are brave, should remain unpitted to prevent their juices from running out. A batter much like that used for crêpes—eggs, milk, flour, vanilla, and perhaps a touch of brandy—should be poured over the whole cherries, and the top then liberally sprinkled with sugar to impart a crystalline glaze.

Clafoutis is best served warm. Its center will relax and sink a bit after it is pulled out of the oven. Never mind—just give it a snowfall of confectioners' sugar right before cutting it.

Clafoutis can be made with many other fruits—plums, pears, apples, and blueberries, for example—but winey cherries deliver the best color and flavor.

FURTHER INFORMATION AND RECIPE: *Mastering the Art of French Cooking, Volume 1,* by Julia Child, Louisette Bertholle, and Simone Beck (1961); saveur.com (search cherry clafoutis).

LET THEM EAT . . . COOKIES

The French Cookie Jar

French

Need proof that France occupies the geographic heart of gastronomy? Consider the humble cookie, which is approached with the same delicacy and intricacy the French apply to haute cuisine. The results are as gorgeous as

they are delicious. Cookies in France are not kid stuff, and they are as likely to be found in high-end bakeries as in grocery stores. Though variations abound, seven classic types abide:

Langue de chat. The slender slip of a cat's tongue is an accurate descriptor for these fragile, paper-thin butter cookies. Extremely delicate, the langue de chat has a pure, subtle flavor evocative of fresh, sweet heavy cream. A few regional variations exist, including an excellent chocolate candy version, but in general the plain butter version predominates. Historians date the cookies to the seventeenth century, when white sugar and piping bags (necessary for turning out the precise amount of dough that begets the langue de chat) simultaneously became commonplace. The gently sweet, snappingly thin treat makes a wonderful accompaniment to ice creams and chilled desserts, and is welcome with tea.

Macarons. Perhaps history's first official cookie, the macaron is traced by food historians to Cormery, the commune in central France where it was first made at a monastery in 791. Local legend says the cookies were created in the shape of monks' navels, but their name comes from the Venetian word *macarone,* which means fine paste and refers to the ground-up almonds from which they are made. Traditionally, the diminutive cookie involved little more than those almonds and/or coconut, along with sugar and egg whites, but in the name of high fashion, macarons became lighter and more like meringues, sandwiched together with crème, chocolate,

Stacks of colorful macarons have timeless French allure.

ganache, and fruit jam or honey. The original stands unequivocally above the rest. Macarons have the distinction of having been adopted as a Passover seder dessert alongside traditional macaroons. No one is quite sure how this came to be, beyond the cookie's lack of flour. Several regions in France are famous for macarons, most particularly Saint-Émilion, the small medieval village near Bordeaux in the southwest. In Paris, many fine patisseries specialize in the dessert; the two most famous are Ladurée, which has been baking the treats since 1862 and prides itself on its variety of flavors, and Pierre Hermé, a former head pastry chef at Ladurée who has set up his own shop, which has arguably become even more famous than its forerunner.

Calissons d'Aix. Soft, flat, narrow ovals with pointed ends, the traditional sweetmeats of Aix-en-Provence are shaped like almonds. Made of almonds, sugar, candied melon, and fruit syrup or orange-flower water or rosewater, the marzipanlike delights are in fact so prized that they are protected by the French government: The sweets are historic, having been made for centuries in Aix. (The exact moment of origin is the subject of controversy; some pinpoint a wedding breakfast in the 1400s, while others vouch for the commemoration of the end of the plague in the 1600s.) Regardless, the makers of these emblematic cookies (the *calissoniers*) form the Union des Fabricants de Calissons d'Aix, a group whose aim is to protect the integrity of the product and provide a guarantee of quality to the consumer. Government regulations spearheaded by the *calissoniers* stipulate that in order for the cookies to receive the label *calissons d'Aix*, the almonds must be from the Mediterranean and the cookies cannot include preservatives or artificial coloring and must be made only in Aix. Eaten with coffee, tea, Champagne, and the musky-sweet Beaumes-de-Venise dessert wine, they often come in keepsake metal boxes; particularly lovely is the circular version, in which the cookies are arranged like flower petals, said to be a special gift for those in love. This isn't one to try at home: According to Elizabeth David in *A Book of Mediterranean Food,* "these delicacies belong rather to the province of the professional pastry-cook or confectioner than to that of the amateur cook."

Crêpes dentelles. The classic cookie of Brittany, the crêpe dentelle starts as a very thin, lacy pancake that is rolled into a cigarlike cylinder and then cooled to a beautiful brown, buttery crisp. The indulgence was invented in the late nineteenth century in the town of Quimper, where the superbly crunchy cookies are still made today by the very same method: Crêpe batter is thinly spread on a flat griddle; when it has cooked to the right temperature and consistency, the "pancake" is folded around a long, sharp knife, then cooled until crisp. Some canny home cooks roll thin pancakes into layers and bake them, but there's no need to bother: The crêpes dentelles made by Brittany's Gavottes brand are delicious and fanciful fun in their distinctive foil wrappers. They are available in good gourmet food shops around the world.

Tuiles. Considered by many connoisseurs to be France's best and most iconic cookie, the tuile is named for the beloved old Roman-style terracotta tiles atop Venetian villas. A whisper-thin, crisp curved disk made of ground almonds, the tuile achieves its characteristic shape by being taken straight out of the oven and instantly slid over a rolling pin or wine bottle to cool.

Palmiers. The name *palmier* may translate to "palm leaf," but most Americans know these caramelized sugar and puff pastry cookies as elephant ears, for their double-lobed shape. Flaky, buttery, and marvelously, shatteringly crackling, palmiers are made by folding the pastry several times and then coiling it into its much-loved heart shape.

Where: *In many locations in France and in New York,* Ladurée, laduree.com; *in France,* Pierre Hermé at various locations, pierreherme .com; La Cure Gourmande, la-cure-gourmande .fr; *in Aix-en-Provence,* Calissons du Roy René, tel 33/4-42-26-67-86, calisson.com. **Mail order:** The Frenchy Bee, thefrenchybee.com (search gavottes crepe dentelle; macarons; calissons de provence). **Further information and recipes:** *Macarons* by Pierre Hermé (2009); for a tuile recipe, *Butter Sugar Flour Eggs* by Gale Gand (1999); for palmier recipes, *Martha Stewart's Cookies* by Martha Stewart (2008) and *The Fearless Baker* by Emily Luchetti (2011); for a langue de chat recipe, *The French Cookie Book* by Bruce Healy (1994); caramelizedblog.com (search saint emilion old-fashioned macarons).

⊢||||||||||||||||||||||||||||||⊣

DRUNKEN CHICKEN

Coq au Vin

French

Here is a frugal answer to the quandary of owning a rooster past his mating prime: the classic French peasant stew that showcases a brilliant collaboration between wine and poultry, traditionally a *coq*—that is, a rooster, not a *poulet* or a *poussin* or a *poularde*—and *vin*, something as red, rustic, and feisty as the old bird himself. Stewed long and slowly, the tough meat becomes soft and toothsome.

The old boy is cut up, put in a pot, and bedded down with onions, shallots, carrots, garlic, parsley, thyme, bay leaf, plenty of salt and pepper, a little salt pork, small white mushrooms, and a quantity of red wine, most suitably from Burgundy. From this humble start comes a magnificently mellow blend of

Savor this classic in a rustic setting.

homey flavors, the bird's juices commingling with the wine in a wintry, saucy tribute to good old-fashioned French home cooking.

One of the first published accounts of coq au vin appeared in 1913, when the French zoologist and natural philosopher Mathurin Jacques Brisson discovered the dish while traveling in the south-central Chaîne des Puys region and recorded his pleasure at learning that a tough old rooster could morph to such benignly mellow goodness. It traveled stateside via Julia Child, who popularized the rustic preparation through her 1960s PBS television program *The French Chef.*

As Julia demonstrated, coq au vin really does make a great home-cooked meal, especially now that ordering a rooster from a specialty butcher shop is becoming ever more possible. Failing that, choose a nice, plump chicken weighing four to five pounds. The classic accompaniment is steamed new potatoes sprinkled with parsley, but it's sometimes fun to take a flyer and serve it with buttered fresh noodles.

Where: *In Nuits-Saint-Georges, France,* Au Bois de Charmois, tel 33/3-80-61-04-79, aubois decharmois.com; *in New York,* La Mangeoire, tel 212-759-7086, lamangeoire.com; the Breslin, tel 212-679-1939, thebreslin.com; *in Miami,* DB Bistro Moderne, tel 305-421-8800, dbbistro.com/miami; *in Orlando,* Le Coq au Vin Restaurant, tel 407-851-6980, lecoqauvinrestaurant.com; *in Washington, D.C.,* Et Voila, tel 202-237-2300, etvoiladc.com. **Further information and recipes:** *The New Making* of a Cook by Madeleine Kamman (1997); Mastering the Art of French Cooking, Volume 1, by Julia Child, Louisette Bertholle, and Simone Beck (1961); *The Food of France* by Waverley Root (1992); hubertkeller.com (click Recipes, then Poultry).

Crème Renversée

French

Vanilla-scented crème caramel and Spanish flan, with their bittersweet burnt sugar sauce and their uniformly voluptuous texture, are entitled to their popularity, but the same ingredients reach their true apotheosis in this ultimate French variation.

The easy part is preparing the sauce that will become custard—a cooked, frothy blend of eggs, sugar, milk, vanilla, or pungent orange rind. The hard part begins with caramelizing the sugar, watching like a hawk so that it doesn't in one blinding instant go from pale gold to burnt black. When it turns just the right bronzy golden brown, it must be poured into a chilled mold (a porcelain soufflé dish or, preferably, the fez-shaped metal mold called a charlotte). Very quickly, that mold must be tipped (*renversé*) and rotated so the caramel evenly coats its bottom and sides.

The custard is then poured in and the mold is set in the oven. Cooled and unmolded, the silken custard will be encrusted with a shiny sugar glaze that provides a crackling contrast in texture and flavor. A few strawberries or raspberries and a knob of whipped cream make for worthy, if unnecessary, garnishes.

The popular crème brûlée is a variation that combines the same rich custard and burnt sugar glaze. The well-chilled custard, set in wide, flat dishes, is topped with brown sugar and glazed under the broiler, the salamander or, in many restaurants, with a white-hot blowtorch, a trick best skipped in homes lacking an experienced welder.

FURTHER INFORMATION AND RECIPES: *Roast Chicken and Other Stories* by Simon Hopkinson (2007); *The New Making of a Cook* by Madeleine Kamman (1997); recipekey.com (search creme renversee).

Croissants

French

These flaky golden pastry crescents are among the most iconic foods of France, found on standard *petit dejeuner* trays in even the dreariest of hotels and cafés—which means they are not always perfect.

To achieve that vaunted state, the croissants must be made with pure butter—never mind those adulterers who claim margarine produces a more reliable effect. The slightly sweet yeast dough must be turned in the manner of puff pastry in order to be what is technically known as yeast puff pastry—the same dough that distinguishes Danish and Viennese pastries at their best. Properly done, the results will be quintessentially buttery and messily flaky, with a yellow-white interior that is just the least bit elastic as it is pulled from the center to be spread with dabs of butter and perhaps some fresh fruit jam.

Those who like their croissants served warm are entitled to their choice, but heating results in a much softer crust and an interior that can be greasy. Customers with a sweet tooth will be well acquainted with the pain au chocolat based on the same yeast puff pastry, wrapped around a rod or two of bittersweet chocolate for an extra morning lift.

There was a time when all croissants in France were made in one reliable, authentic way. But these days, even some authentic patisseries will have two batches, one marked butter, the other margarine—so pay attention as you choose. In America, most croissants have become much too huge, on the theory that the customer will pay a higher price for a larger crescent, thereby covering the high cost of hand labor. Yet small croissants are preferable, yielding the right proportion of outer crisp crust and crunchy horn tips to a softer interior.

Although now universally synonymous with the home country of the baguette (see page 55), the croissant is another of the gastronomic treasures western Europe supposedly won following the seventeenth-century siege of Vienna. To celebrate the defeat of the Turks by the Polish King John Sobieski, the story goes, the Viennese bakers formed this roll in the shape of the crescent on the Turkish flag. According to legend, coffee was introduced to Vienna at the same time, as the Viennese went into the deserted battlefields and scooped up the beans they had noticed the Turks brewing. The bagel, too, is considered by some to be a product of the same battle. What would breakfast be like if the Turks had won?

Where: *In Paris,* Pâtisserie Jean Millet, tel 33/1-45-51-49-80, patisserie-jean-millet.com; *in New York,* Bakehouse, tel 646-559-9871, bakehousenyc.com. **Further information and recipes:** *The Art of French Pastry* by Jacquy Pfeiffer and Martha Rose Shulman (2013); cookstr.com (search croissants).

NOT YOUR AVERAGE GRILLED CHEESE SANDWICH

Croques, Monsieur and Madame

French

Though pizza may be a favorite worldwide snack—hot and bubbling on short notice—*croques monsieur* and *madame* are its worthy rivals. The grilled ham and cheese sandwiches par excellence are as likely to be served at chic cafés, bistros,

and tearooms as in the anonymous *tabacs* that line the sidewalks of Paris. They are simple, yet subject to interpretation: sometimes broiled, sometimes grilled, other times fried; sometimes graced by a cheese-flavored béchamel sauce on top. In their worst incarnation, they are preformed, heated in the microwave, and based on cheeses far more mundane than the authentic Gruyère.

There are differences, of course, between

monsieur and madame. Both begin, one hopes, with good-quality, finely knit white sandwich bread—ideally, the French *pain de mie*—liberally buttered. The male of the species boasts a layer of ham between its slices. Broiled or pan-grilled until golden, the sandwich is topped with a generous sprinkling of grated Gruyère and slid under

An egg atop a croque madame

the broiler until the cheese melts to an unctuous bronze ooze. Madame, as one might expect, lays an egg—a bit of sandwich personification that is one part French wit, one part culinary sexism. That egg is either fried and placed atop the finished sandwich or slipped into a round well cut into the top slice, sprinkled with cheese, and cooked under the broiler. To many minds, the male is preferred, the soft egg yolk presenting a lush but awkward distraction.

Pan-grilled or broiled, with cheese on top or in the middle, or even French-toasted—the entire sandwich dipped into an egg-milk batter and pan-fried—the result is a seething mass of pleasure. Firm, smoky ham and hot buttery bread, piquant overtones of melting cheese, and perhaps the lavish accent of béchamel sauce . . .

Less interesting, if a bit lower in cholesterol, is a third version of this sandwich, the interloper known as croque mademoiselle, with bland white turkey meat standing in for the ham. Whichever you end up trying, know that the sandwich goes equally well with a cold light beer, a chilled white wine, or a very good cup of coffee.

WHERE: *In Paris,* Angelina, tel 33/1-42-60-82-00, angelina-paris.fr; Café Marly, tel 33/1-49-26-06-60, beaumarly.com; *in New York,* Maison Kayser at three locations, maisonkayser usa.com. **FURTHER INFORMATION AND RECIPES:** *Bouchon* by Thomas Keller (2004); cookstr.com (search croque monsieur silverton); epicurious .com (search croque monsieur).

DON'T PASS ON THE DIJON

Dijon Mustard

French (Dijonnais)

There are as many different styles of mustard to choose from as there are songbirds, but none has quite the status of Dijon. One of nature's happy accidents, the sharp, brassy spread came into being when a gaggle of grapevines

and yellow-specked mustard plants tangled up together in the hills of Dijon, the capital of Burgundy, in the Côte d'Or region. There, in the Middle Ages, local brown and black mustard seeds were crushed and mixed with wine, thereby inspiring the condiment's name, from the Latin *must,* meaning the remnants of pressed wine.

Mustard actually dates back at least as far as the Roman Empire, but it wasn't until Dijon's product introduced its characteristic and appealing tartness that mustard manufacturing really took off. By the fourteenth century, laws regulating Dijon's production were put into effect in France, and by the seventeenth, an alliance to oversee the role of the individual mustard creator, or *moutardier,* was officially created.

Today, in keeping with many of France's most special and classic wines and cheeses, the mustard holds a protective Appellation d'Origine Contrôlée status that mandates a set of requirements necessary for a condiment to officially rank as Dijon. But the law, written in 1937, was relatively loose, failing to specify a site for its production or the sourcing of its mustard seeds. The result is that most modern Dijon is still made in its namesake city, but from seeds imported primarily from Canada.

Were it not for the work of Maurice Grey, one of the most well-known Dijon-based mustard men, folks outside of Europe might never have become acquainted with the spread. A nineteenth-century character who invented a steam-powered device that efficiently ground mustard seeds into powder, he launched the Grey Poupon mustard label with fellow *moutardier* Auguste Poupon. It wasn't until the 1980s, though, that Dijon mustard became truly popular in the United States. Those Grey Poupon commercials might have had something to do with it.

WHERE: *In Dijon,* La Boutique Maille, tel 33/1-80-30-41-02, maille.com. **TIP:** In addition to Grey Poupon, look for Maille or Amora brands from Dijon.

A MILLER'S WIFE WITH SOLE

Dover Sole à la Meunière

French

Whatever else may prompt controversy in the French kitchen, most French cooks would agree that the only way to treat a delicately flavored Dover sole is in the classic preparation, *à la meunière*—in the style of the miller's wife.

What the good woman brings to her *poisson* is a fine dusting of flour that protects the fish, which gilds in an oval meunière pan large enough to hold the entire sole. Leaving skin and bones intact ensures that no juices are lost and uncompromised texture and flavor remain.

The result is a firm, pearly fish as enticing as a fresh sea breeze, enhanced only by hot, nut-brown butter, a dash of lemon juice, and a sprinkling of bright green parsley. Ideally, the fish should be opened at the table, the fillets deftly lifted off the bone with surgical skill by trained restaurant captains, who seem to belong to an endangered species.

So simple a preparation requires the utmost attention to detail on the part of the chef. In addition to the fresh, authentic Dover sole caught in the North Sea waters around the British Isles (see page 11), a proper result demands that the copper sauté pan be lined with tin, which imparts just the right golden-brown finish; the only alternative is stainless steel—a bit trickier to handle, as it can develop hot spots that scorch the fish. The butter must be unsalted, and clarified prior to cooking to remove the milk solids—basically sugars—that might blacken under the high heat required for quick sautéing. All of which might explain why this specialty, not to be mistaken for the layman's filet of sole meunière, fetches between $50 and $75 a portion in New York City restaurants.

Steamed white rice or dry, floury boiled new potatoes are about the only acceptable sides, although a little creamed spinach might not go amiss, nor would a glass or two of a dry white or light French red wine. This meal is a rite of passage for anyone with pretentions of gastronomic connoisseurship.

WHERE: *In Paris,* Le Divellec, tel 33/1-45-51-91-96, le-divellec.com. **FURTHER INFORMATION AND RECIPES:** epicurious.com (search sole meuniere); bonappetit.com (search classic sole meuniere).

Époisses de Bourgogne

French (Burgundian)

To taste an authentic and properly ripened Époisses de Bourgogne is to cross over to the other side. But getting there may take some work, as this cow's-milk cheese is not for the faint of palate. Washed with *marc de Bourgogne,* the Burgundian spirit of distilled grape remnants, its rind takes on an ocher-orange hue and a distinctive barnyard smell so strong that the cheese has been rumored—incorrectly—to have been barred from public transportation in France.

Dating back to the Cistercian monks in the sixteenth century, Époisses nearly became extinct when local men left their farms and dairies to fight the two world wars. It wasn't until the mid-1950s that a couple of dedicated cheese makers, Robert and Simone Berthaut, almost singlehandedly revitalized its production. Their company still makes Époisses de Bourgogne that has a complex pungency and a sweet-saltiness to it. Alas, it exports only pasteurized versions of its cheeses to the States, where raw-milk cheese must be aged a minimum of sixty days; the flavor of pasteurized cheeses generally pales beside the flavor of raw-milk varieties.

The short of it is that you really have to be there, in Burgundy, France, where the Époisses is always unpasteurized and where the real deal bears the handy Appellation d'Origine Contrôlée stamp, assuring that point of origin, processing, and ingredients meet requirements set by nothing less than French law. Like many ripening cheeses, it is best served at room temperature, when its thick texture has softened and become elegantly spreadable. The intense flavor of Époisses de Bourgogne dictates that it be served at the end of a meal, never at its start.

RETAIL AND MAIL ORDER: *In New York,* Murray's Cheese, tel 888-692-4339, murrayscheese.com. **FURTHER INFORMATION:** *French Cheeses* by Kazuko Masui and Tomoko Yamada (1996); *Cheese Primer* by Steven Jenkins (1996). **TIP:** Look for a Berthaut cheese that fills up its entire box, an indication of supreme ripeness.

Escargots à la Bourguignonne

French

A classic French bistro meal with *steak frites* as the main course (see page 136) allows for only one choice as a starter: *escargots à la bourguignonne.* These plump snails are nestled in their shells and bathed in an aromatic sauce of garlic, shallots, parsley, and lots of hot butter. Eaten scalding hot between sips of red wine and nibbles of little crusts of bread soaked in their tantalizing juices, six of these slow-moving wonders make a fine appetizer, although a dozen is more than twice as good.

There are many other ways to prepare snails, and many riffs on this classic, a delicacy since ancient Roman times; but none shows them off to such great advantage as escargots à la bourguignonne. One allowable deviation: ditching the shells, from which the snails have to be removed and cleaned (tediously) and then replaced (laboriously).

Butter is a key element of this dish.

In fact, there is so much handwork involved in this presentation that many restaurant owners, mindful of labor costs, eliminate the dish from their menus entirely. Function would suggest that, once out of the shells, snails are more conveniently nestled in the indentations of the special small casseroles made for the purpose.

Still, there is a certain amount of fun in the challenge of grasping the hot and buttery shells in the appropriate clamps and wresting the snails from the winding interior with the typical two-tined fork.

For the record, escargots à la bourguignonne are not to be confused with *escargots de Bourgogne*. The first refers to snails served in their highly perfumed butter; the second defines snails raised in Burgundy, where they feed on grape leaves to become what are considered France's best. Any of France's snails, however, are better than the canned variety imported from China that are often fishy and bitter—so whether fresh or canned, try to discover the source.

Where: *In Paris,* L'Ami Louis, tel 33/1-48-87-77-48; *in New York,* Bar Boulud, tel 212-595-0303, barboulud.com/nyc. **Further information and recipes:** *The Food of France* by Waverley Root (1992); saveur.com (search snails in garlic herb butter).

A ONCE-IN-A-LIFETIME CLASSIC

Faisan à la Souvaroff

Pheasant Souvaroff

French

In both victory and defeat, the French have a penchant for naming dishes after military battles. Consider veal Marengo, mayonnaise, and lobster Thermidor, each marking a campaign in the Napoleonic wars. One of the most luxuriously

spectacular—and an endangered species among culinary classics—is pheasant Souvaroff, named for the Russian general who turned back the French army in a battle the French were fighting with the Italians near Milan in 1799.

It may be hard to understand how so dire an outcome (for the French) provoked so succulent a main course, but we'll leave that to the historians. Much better to spend time mastering this fantastic dish yourself, or to find a serious

French chef who is happy to recall his haute-cuisine training.

The essentials are a fine, fresh pheasant, black truffles, duck or goose foie gras, good strong game or beef stock, Madeira wine, and plenty of patience. The buttered pheasant is browned in the oven, then filled with slivers of truffles and foie gras and placed in an oven-proof casserole, preferably of copper or enameled cast iron. More truffles and foie gras are added to the casserole, along with brown stock and Madeira. The lid is then placed on and sealed with a stiff flour-and-water paste. As a variation, the casserole with all ingredients in it is sealed with a covering of puff pastry. All is baked in a very hot oven for about 20 minutes, then should be presented at the table, where the wondrous experience begins with the aroma.

For as the seal is cracked open and the lid removed, the air becomes heady with the perfume of slightly sweet wine, earthy truffles, ripe foie gras, and the buttery roasted bird.

As you might imagine, the flavor justifies the effort. The experience of biting into the tender game meat mellowed with the velvety flavors of liver, truffles, and winey sauce—offset, one would hope, by perfectly steamed potatoes or a nutty wild rice pilaf—makes this a dish that anyone serious about food should experience at least once in a lifetime. Maybe twice.

Where: *In Paris,* Lasserre, tel 33/1-43-59-02-13, restaurant-lasserre.com. **Further information and recipes:** *Classic French Cooking* by Craig Claiborne and Pierre Franey (1970); *Modern French Culinary Art* by Henri-Paul Pellaprat (1962); ifood.tv (search pheasant souvaroff).

THE SUBLIME DECADENCE OF LIVER

Foie Gras

French

Unctuously seductive and tantalizingly decadent, foie gras has been one of mankind's incurable weaknesses since ancient Roman days. One of the world's priciest delicacies, the "fatty liver" is produced by the controversial practice

of force-feeding corn to ducks and geese; their livers become engorged with butter-sweet fat, taking on the sublime texture and ripe overtones that are the hallmarks of foie gras.

Dedicated connoisseurs avoid the mixtures dubbed pâté, opting for slices of whole, unadulterated livers that have been slowly melted in their own juices with only a dash of salt. As flavorful and supple as warm foie gras can be, whether sautéed alone or used in smaller proportions as an enhancement to other ingredients, only its chilled state can offer the full foie gras experience: the slow-melting, ice-cream-like texture and the rich aroma that is released as the fat gentles onto the palate. The best foie

Try serving a chilled slice with figs on toast.

gras is creamy in color, with a tinge of pink toward the center. Edged in a golden rim of its own pure renderings, the delicacy requires only a slice of toast or, better yet, a slab of baguette toasted over a wood fire. The latter is the way L'Ami Louis, in Paris, serves the best foie gras in the world (see page 52).

At Morimoto, New York's lavish Japanese fusion restaurant, Iron Chef Masaharu Morimoto adds foie gras to the steamed egg custard, *chawan mushi,* to ethereally silky effect.

Though fine foie gras is produced in several countries—primarily in France's Alsace and Périgord regions; in the Czech Republic, Hungary, and Israel; and, increasingly, in the U.S.—its legal fate currently hangs in the balance. It is now illegal to create or serve foie gras in California.

Where: *In Paris,* L'Ami Louis, tel 33/1-48-87-77-48. **Mail order:** D'Artagnan, tel 800-327-8246, dartagnan.com. **Further information and recipe:** saveur.com (search terrine de foie gras).

—|||||||||||||||||||||||||||||||||||||||—

IN CELEBRATION OF WHOLE LIVERS

Foie de Veau à la Bourgeoise

Whole Braised Calf's Liver

French

Think calf's liver and you probably summon up visions of satiny slices, thick or thin, grilled or sautéed and enhanced with crisp bacon. Some prefer them Venetian-style, smothered in onions, or in the French manner known as *beurre noisette,* with parsley, lemon, and caper butter.

As enticing as the liver is when cooked in slices, it ascends to even greater gastronomic heights when it is braised whole and sliced at the table, the meat giving off fragant juices and glowing rose-pink. However, as the organ is not universally adored, restaurateurs are reluctant to prepare whole livers, lest too much go to waste. But once upon a time in the small town of Wheeling, Illinois, in his great restaurant Le Français, chef-proprietor Jean Banchet served whole liver baked *en croûte,* the flaky crust lined with a veneer of foie gras—making this much-loved specialty liver *avec* liver.

That's hardly the only way the French serve whole livers, and any one of them is well worth a try. The *à la bourgeoise* style is simply the whole liver larded with bacon strips for moisture and simmered with spices, parsley, and root vegetables, after which all is flambéed with brandy. *Foie de veau piqué des pousterles* is spiked with bacon and braised in goose fat along with chopped Bayonne ham, crushed garlic, onion rings, parsley, bread crumbs, Armagnac, and dry white wine. For *foie de veau Médéric,* the liver is wrapped in a caul of fat and braised with veal bones and root vegetables, resulting in an especially sublime sauce that Americans would consider a gravy.

An order of whole calf's liver needs to be placed ahead of time with the butcher, and should satisfy an average of four to six happy eaters, depending on what goes before and along with. Mashed potatoes, perhaps with pureed celery root, seem the right accompaniment to any of these succulent pot-roasted livers.

Further information and recipes: *Larousse Traditional French Cooking* by Curnonsky (1987); *The German Cookbook* by Mimi Sheraton (2014). **See also:** Fegato alla Veneziana, page 187; Lamb's Liver, page 497.

┤||||||||||||||||||||||||||||||├

A CHALLENGER TO ROQUEFORT'S THRONE

Fourme d'Ambert

France

With its silvery-blue veins and warm ivory pâte, Fourme d'Ambert is considered by many connoisseurs to be the best of the French blues. That title bears tribute to its sharp, smooth, and salty complexities, and to a more subtle tasting experience than that offered by the stronger, less nuanced, and better known Roquefort.

Amazingly enough, historians posit that Fourme's origins predate the Roman Empire, and that it has been made for centuries just the way it is today.

The ancient cheese is based on raw milk from cows in the Auvergne region, southeast of central France. Traditionally, these cows roamed the pastures nearest Ambert, from which we get the second half of the cheese's name. *Fourme* refers to the mold—not a fungus, in this instance, but a form—which shapes the cheese into tallish, narrow cylinders. Standing about eight inches high, Fourme d'Ambert is

One cylinder requires 6.5 gallons of milk.

something of the tall, blonde bombshell of cheeses. Its beige-to-straw-colored paste is beautifully marbled with blue-gray mold, visually striking against its dark brown rind. The pâte should be firm but supple, making Fourme a more than suitable companion for bread, fruit, and salads. When shopping for this cheese, try to have it freshly cut, and avoid any that has a green tinge to the blue veins, that has a cracked rind, or that show soft, tannish edging between the pâte and the rind.

FURTHER INFORMATION:
French Cheeses by Kazuko Masui and Tomoko Yamada (1996); *Cheese Primer* by Steven Jenkins (1996); cheesesoffrance.com.

┤||||||||||||||||||||||||||||||├

WILD ABOUT STRAWBERRIES

Fraises des Bois

French

For food lovers, neither blooming crocuses nor cherry blossoms are as welcome a sign of spring's arrival as the tiny, wild woodland strawberries known as *fraises des bois*. Of course, "wild" has not been quite accurate for at least seven centuries.

But even when cultivated, as they are in France or in terra-cotta planters in any sunny garden, the diminutive oval berries are still memorably flavorful.

No larger than shelled almonds, they have just enough acidity to add interest to their juicy, sweet, slightly almondy essence. Pinpoint seeds add crunch to rosy berries that need nothing more than a light splash of heavy sweet cream or a dab of crème fraîche. In Italy—where they are known as *fragole di bosco*—they are sprinkled with a few drops of aged, sharply sweet balsamic vinegar, or tossed with a pinch of sugar and a dash of freshly squeezed lemon juice.

Although fraises des bois are sometimes simmered into a luxurious jam, cooking them should be considered a culinary felony. But placing them atop vanilla-scented pastry cream in a pre-baked tart shell is a fine idea, and one not at all compromised by a dab of whipped cream.

MAIL ORDER: For info, plants, and seeds, fraisesdesbois.com. **FURTHER INFORMATION AND RECIPE:** food.com (search barquette de fraises des bois).

|||||||||||||||||||||||||||||||||||

HOW TO DRESS A BERRY

Fraises au Jus Glacé or Strawberries Ali-Bab

French

A well-traveled mining engineer by profession and an obsessive cook and gourmand by preference, Henri Babinsky, known as Ali-Bab, was a Frenchman of Polish descent who lived from 1855 to 1931 and used his spare time to put together a 1,281-page compendium of French cuisine. His *Gastronomie Pratique: Études Culinaires* was published in 1907 and is to this day considered a classic reference.

Most of the recipes are too complex for the average cook, but the lovely springtime ode to strawberries remains a tempting exception. Few desserts are simpler to prepare or more delightful at the end of an early-summer's meal. For best results, it should be made with small, perfect berries, ripely red and fragrantly juicy all the way through. (Our usual gigantic California strawberries, with their pale and hollow insides, should be a last resort.) Although Ali-Bab did not suggest any liqueur as a finishing touch, the orange flavor here adds a certain sophistication, as do the bright green color and pleasing aroma of a mint leaf or two.

Strawberries Ali-Bab
Serves 4

1 quart best strawberries available,
*   preferably from a local farmers' market*
2 to 3 teaspoons fine sugar
A few drops of lemon juice
1 to 2 teaspoons Grand Marnier (optional)
Mint leaves (optional), for garnish

1. Rinse the strawberries under cold running water. Trim and drain the berries, then set aside about one quarter of them, choosing the least attractive ones. Leave the remaining berries whole if they are small. If large, cut them lengthwise in half or quarters. Refrigerate the berries until serving time.

2. Using a blender or a food processor, puree the reserved one quarter of the berries with 2 teaspoons of sugar, the lemon juice, and the

Grand Marnier, if using. Taste for sweetness, adding more sugar as necessary. Place the strawberry puree in the freezer for 1 hour before serving.

3. Just before serving, divide the whole or cut berries among 4 individual serving bowls, preferably glass, and

Fresh wild strawberries, a simple pleasure

spoon some of the semifrozen puree on each portion, stirring gently to mix. Garnish each serving with a mint leaf or two, if desired. Serve at once.

FURTHER INFORMATION AND RECIPE: *Encyclopedia of Practical Gastronomy*, by Ali-Bab, translated by Elizabeth Benson (1974).

⊣||||||||||||||||||||||||||||||⊢

AN EPIC BOILED FISH DINNER

Grand Aïoli

French (Provençal)

To be worthy of its name, a *grand aïoli* requires so many types of fish and vegetables that it would be difficult to serve for only a few guests. A Christmas Eve specialty along the Côte d'Azur, it can be ordered a few days ahead from many of the seafood restaurants in that region. On Christmas Day, the same combination of garnishes might be gathered, either with seafood or a moistly tender poached capon, for another stupendous meal.

The centerpiece of this enormous dish is fluffy chunks of well-soaked, gently poached salt cod. Around the fish are amassed steamed new potatoes in their earthy jackets, hard-boiled eggs, steamed baby artichokes, chickpeas, silvergray sea snails called periwinkles, cooked squid, green beans, and pearly onions or green leeks. The main event, however, is the magical aioli, the garlicky mayonnaise that may be blushed with saffron or spiked with cayenne pepper.

Once a favorite on Fridays, this beloved monster of a dish was also served at communal affairs during the summer in Provençal villages. The culinary still life would be set out in public squares for all to share, probably to be washed down with a local rosé.

Less ambitious cooks present more limited versions of the grand aïoli, offering perhaps only snails or poached vegetables with the garlicky mayonnaise. The aioli sauce has so many food-enhancing uses (as a dip for cold seafood and raw vegetables, or as a spread on chicken or turkey sandwiches) that the following recipe is worth mastering.

Sauce Aïoli

Makes about 2½ cups

2 cloves garlic, peeled
3 or 4 extra-large egg yolks (see Note)
Salt and freshly ground white pepper
2 cups extra-virgin olive oil
1 tablespoon freshly squeezed lemon juice
Cayenne pepper (optional)

1. Place the garlic in a mortar and crush it using a pestle. Or crush the garlic in a garlic press. Place the crushed garlic in a medium-size mixing bowl and add 3 of the egg yolks and a pinch each of salt and white pepper. Begin to blend the egg yolk mixture gently with a wire whisk.

2. When the yolks are runny, very slowly trickle in a thin stream of olive oil, whisking constantly until the mixture begins to thicken.

3. When 1 cup of the oil has been beaten in, stir in the lemon juice along with 1 teaspoon of warm water to prevent the yolks from curdling. Keep adding olive oil a bit more quickly, again beating constantly, until all of it is absorbed and you have a thick mass that is about the consistency of soft pureed potatoes.

4. If the aioli curdles, remove it from the mixing bowl and set it aside. Beat an additional egg yolk in the mixing bowl; then, using the whisk, gradually add the curdled mixture with a spoonful or two of warm water and slowly beat it into the egg. Taste for seasoning, adding a pinch of cayenne, white pepper, and salt as needed. The aioli can be refrigerated, covered, for 1 week, and will require only a brief stir before serving.

Note: Anyone worried about eating raw egg yolks, or who finds the process of making aioli from scratch too complex, can arrive at a passable substitute by starting with 2 cups of a good commercial mayonnaise and stirring in 2 cloves of crushed garlic, then slowly trickling in a thin stream of olive oil, all the while beating with a wooden spoon. The 2 cups of prepared

Grand aïoli is an essential taste of Mediterranean France.

mayonnaise should absorb about 1 cup of olive oil. Stir in 2 to 3 teaspoons of lemon juice at the end and taste for seasoning, adding salt, white pepper, and cayenne as desired. If the mixture curdles, beat in warm water, 1 teaspoon at a time, until smoothly blended.

FURTHER INFORMATION AND ADDITIONAL RECIPES: *Roast Chicken and Other Stories* by Simon Hopkinson with Lindsey Bareham (2007); *Simple French Food* by Richard Olney (1974); saveur.com (search grand aioli).

IN PURSUIT OF A CINEMATIC FEAST

La Grande Bouffe Lamb with Pissaladière

French

One of the cinematic hits of 1973, *La Grande Bouffe* featured three wealthy, handsome, and bored bachelors determined to eat themselves to death over a long weekend in a villa outside of Paris. One by one they succeed, and the film is remembered for the stellar performances of Marcello Mastroianni, Philippe Noiret, and Hugo Tognazzi as the suicidal gourmands. But to many serious eaters, its real star is the sumptuous, nonstop avalanche of dishes prepared by the chef, played by Michel Piccoli.

One of the most memorable "snacks" of that found-and-lost weekend was a garlic-infused gigot of lamb spit-roasted over a wood fire, kept moist by intermittent brushings with olive oil–soaked branches of herbs. The meat was sliced down blood-rare and placed alongside slabs of golden, soothingly piquant *pissaladière* (see page 114), with its crisp yeast bread crust and a piquant topping of silky onions, salty anchovies, and black Niçoise olives—a perfect complement to the gentle flavor of the young lamb. The director may have failed to add a glass of Provence's chilled, rose-ate Bandol wine, but you should not.

Mail order: *La Grande Bouffe*, directed by Marco Ferreri (1973), DVD, barnesandnoble.com.

||||||||||||||||||||||||||||||||||||||||||||||||||||||||||||||||||||||||||||||||||||||||||||||||||||||||||||||||||||||||||||||||||||

A FISH ON THE WING

Skate or Ray

T he strangely anthropomorphic "face" and wide, gray-white flapping side wings of the large, diamond-shaped fish known as *skate* or *ray*—terms generally used interchangeably—might discourage potential gourmands from its pleasures. That would be their great loss, because the meat of this snowy, mild-flavored fish is seductively silky. The wings are the only edible portions of the fish; constructed much like fans, they are held together by riblike slivers of cartilage which, when removed, leave a flat fillet that cooks quickly.

If the skate is to be poached and doused with melted butter or a cream sauce, it's best to leave the cartilage in place, lest the fragile meat disintegrate. But for sautéing or frying—the cooking methods that bring the fish to its best, most delicate flavor—the cartilage should be removed first for even cooking.

Although mild, skate's flavor may seem unpleasant to those who detect a faint hint of ammonia, which dissipates if it is held (under refrigeration) for twenty-four to forty-eight hours after being caught, before it is cooked. (Cooking also helps evaporate most remaining overtones.) Yet it is that lingering antiseptic hint, modified by seasonings and other ingredients, plus the smooth texture of the pearly flesh, that delight the most devout skate lovers.

Beyond doubt, the single most luscious preparation for skate is the French specialty *raie au beurre noir*, in which the boned wing is first dusted with flour and then sautéed in clarified butter, *meunière* style, to be finished with the "black" butter—browned in the pan with lemon juice, brassy capers, and a sprinkling of freshly minced parsley. Second place among skate preparations goes to a quick deep-frying that renders the fillets gold-leaf crisp and as delectable on a plate with chips as on a toasted bun slathered with tartar sauce. Fried skate is also delicious as crunchy strips layered over a vinaigrette-dressed green salad. A side of lemon wedges is nonnegotiable.

Where: *In New York,* Barchetta, tel 212-255-7400, barchettanyc.com; Pearl Oyster Bar, tel 212-691-8211, pearloysterbar.com; *in Los Angeles,* Cliff's Edge, tel 323-666-6116, cliffsedgecafe.com; *in San Francisco,* Rue Lepic, tel 415-474-6070, ruelepicsf.com; *in Yountville, CA,* Redd, tel 707-944-2222, reddnapavalley.com. **Further information and recipes:** *North Atlantic Seafood* by Alan Davidson (1979); marthastewart.com (search skate au beurre noir); bbc.co.uk/food (search skate wing with caper butter sauce).

+||||||||||||||||||||||||||||||+

WHEN SOUR IS SWEET

Griottes

French

The delicious morello sour cherry, called the *griotte* in France, is one of the world's best known. Small and juicy, the dark red and tender-fleshed fruit is a jewel to behold—but its intense acidity means that it must be cooked or somehow preserved. The French have come up with the loveliest applications for its charms, which make it the perfect sour-sweet ingredient in pies, jams, cordials, and, in Belgium, beer. To the French, griotte means more than just the cherry itself; it also refers to any preparation in which the cherries are preserved, preferably in sugared brandy. The ruby-red, meaty, sweet-tart treat serves as a garnish for many classic French dishes, from desserts such as chocolate mousse and crème brûlée to platters of roasted duck and servings of foie gras. Canned cranberry sauces are well advised to run for cover.

Mail order: Dean & Deluca, tel 800-221-7714, deananddeluca.com (search morello cherry fruit spread); amazon.com (in Grocery and Gourmet Food, search griottes). **Further information and recipes:** *Professional Baking* by Wayne Gisselin (2004); *The Oxford Companion to Food* by Alan Davidson (1999).

+||||||||||||||||||||||||||||||+

THE LOBSTER GETS DRESSED

Homard à l'Américaine

French

Lobster *à l'Américaine* and lobster *à l'Armorique* form another of those "You say potatoes, I say po-tah-toes"–style debates in the food world: The two names describe a single preparation that dresses the crimson crustacean in a sublimely rich and velvety sauce. The dish itself is a miracle of complementary textures and flavors—the gently firm, saline white meat of the crustacean contrasting with the satiny cream and tomato-blushed sauce heady with tarragon, leeks or shallots, and Cognac, white wine, or both.

But the dispute has nothing to do with the dish's ingredients, beginning instead with its point of origin—some say it was Brittany (formerly known as Armorique) while others swear it was Paris where the dish was supposedly created in 1867 at the Noël Peters restaurant for a group of late-night American diners. But the debate doesn't end there—preparation also plays a part. If the story of its Parisian origin is true, then the lobster should be steamed before it is arrayed in the succulent sauce; other recipes, including that of Prosper Montagne, who penned the first edition of the historic French food primer *Larousse Gastronomique*, require that a live lobster be submerged directly in the hot cooked sauce. Only in a nation so food-centric could such distinctions wreak so much havoc. As the late gourmand James Beard put it, ". . . no dish in French cuisine has been more controversial."

The dish pairs well with Chenin blanc.

WHERE: *In Carqueiranne, France,* Auberge Lou Petoulet, tel 33/4-94-58-50-07, loupetoulet .eu; *in New York,* La Grenouille, tel 212-752-1495, la-grenouille.com; *in Philadelphia,* Parc Restaurant, Bistro & Cafe, tel 215-545-2262, parc-restaurant.com. **FURTHER INFORMATION AND RECIPES:** *Mastering the Art of French Cooking, Volume 1,* by Julia Child, Louisette Bertholle, and Simone Beck (1961); for Julia Child demonstrating this recipe on her TV show *The French Chef,* youtube.com (search Julia Child lobster); *The Country Cooking of France* by Anne Willan (2007); foodreference.com (search lobster l'americaine vogel).

━━━━━━━━━━━━━|||||||||||||||||||||||||||||||||━━━━━━━━━━━━━

HAMMING IT UP

Jambon de Canard

French

*J*ambon de canard is one of the triumphs of Michel Guérard's elegant hotel-spa and restaurant, Les Prés d'Eugénie, in southwest France. The literal translation: duck ham. Thinly sliced, with a polished gold-garnet glow, the supple, subtle meat is layered onto firm-textured French bread veneered with sweet butter and sprinklings of freshly ground black pepper. The combination creates ethereally delicious open sandwiches to devour as snacks or appetizers.

The term *ham* refers, of course, to the curing of the duck. Ideally, that should begin with the thick, fat-marbled breast, or *magret,* of the plump, long-bodied moulard duck of the Bordeaux region. Boneless, but with skin and a thin lining of tenderizing fat still in place, the raw duck breast is seasoned with bay leaves, thyme, coriander, and other spices before being placed in the refrigerator for about thirty-six hours.

After it is wiped clean, the spice-infused meat is tied up like a fat sausage, enveloped in cheesecloth, and hung in a cool room or cellar for about two weeks. (At home, the ripening can take place in the refrigerator over a period of about three weeks; the process results in a somewhat less intense texture and flavor.)

As the duck juices evaporate, the meat firms up and develops a tantalizing patina of ripe flavor. The roseate breast meat is sliced in long, almost transparent ribbons to be furled onto platters garnished with curlicues of butter and mounds of pickled pearl onions and cornichons. The skin and thin edge of fat can be included in the slicing, or the skin can be removed and rendered into crunchy cracklings for salads or mashed potatoes.

WHERE: *In Eugénie-les-Bains, France,* Les Prés d'Eugénie tel 33/5–58-05-06-07, michel guerard.com. **MAIL ORDER:** D'Artagnan, tel 800-327-8246, dartagnan.com. **FURTHER INFORMATION AND RECIPES:** *Michel Guérard's Cuisine Gourmande* by Michel Guérard (1979); epicurious.com (search duck prosciutto).

A HIGH CROWN OF A CAKE

Kugelhopf

French (Alsatian)

A subtly sweet coffee cake, the tall, turban-shaped *kugelhopf* is a raisin- and almond-studded wonder scented with orange and lemon rind and dusted with snowy confectioners' sugar. Toasted, it makes a delicious base for ice cream or poached fruit; past its prime, it can become transcendent French toast.

Dust the cooled cake lightly or lavishly with powdered sugar.

One of the prides of the Alsatian pastry kitchen, kugelhopf is also a staple of German and Austrian bakers, who generally call it *gugelhupf.* Austrians claim it was invented in Vienna—shaped to mock the sultan's turban in commemoration of the Turks' defeat at the gates of the city in 1683. For Alsatians, the fluted cake harkens to the time when the three magi were walking from Bethlehem to Colmar (don't ask why) and enjoyed a night's rest in the inn of one Herr Kugel. By way of thanks, they baked the first kugelhopf and presented it to their generous host. That inaugural kugelhopf begat the slice of kugelhopf and glass of wine that are traditionally served to Alsatian wedding guests on their arrival to sustain them during the lengthy ceremony, as well as the customary gift of a whole kugelhopf made by the bride's mother for the officiating priest, minister, or rabbi.

The kugelhopf's ingredients vary according to region: Some bakers use very few eggs, to make it more of a white sweet bread than a golden cake, while others add many yolks and walnuts for a richer mix. Either way, kugelhopf is most traditionally baked in a Turk's-head ceramic ring mold, glazed only on the inside to impart an especially tender brown outer crust while ensuring thorough inner cooking. Economics being what they are, unbreakable metal pans tend to replace the ceramic. In either case, the mold's center tube, or funnel, confers the ring shape, which is not merely decorative. As with many breads and cakes with a dense dough, it would be difficult to thoroughly cook the inside of a solid block of kugelhopf without burning its outside. Eliminating the center dispenses with that danger, in coffee cakes and doughnuts alike.

WHERE: *In Colmar, France,* Pâtisserie Jean, tel 33/3-89-41-24-63. **FURTHER INFORMATION AND RECIPES:** *The Lutèce Cookbook* by André Soltner with Seymour Britchky (1995); epicurious.com (search kugelhopf).

Lentilles de Puy

French

High in fiber and protein, good-for-you lentils come in a variety of hues—red, yellow, black, and brown—but for good looks, health, *and* elegance, none surpass the dark bluish-green *lentilles de Puy*. Nutty in flavor and firm in texture,

these satisfyingly starchy delights most often come from Le Puy-en-Velay in the Haute-Loire region of the South of France, a sunny, dry place of volcanic soil, surrounded by mountains. These conditions are essential to growing hardy lentils with a deep, rich flavor.

So different are lentilles de Puy from the usual flat brown varieties that the French government protects them with an Appellation d'Origine Contrôlée label, so buyers can be sure they're getting the genuine article. Another key to these smaller lentils involves their preparation: They take longer to cook, but are better at retaining their shape and texture.

These lentils are luxury legumes that are embraced by top chefs and often listed on menus by name, whether as the main ingredient in salads and stews or as a garnish for lamb or game. At any price, the tiny disks offer a big nutritional bonus—they're rich in minerals and B vitamins and, unlike many other legumes, lentils do not contain sulfur, the gas-producing element found in most beans. Prior to cooking, lentils should be picked over thoroughly and any little bits of stone removed. Store uncooked lentils in an airtight container in a cool, dry place for up to twelve months.

MAIL ORDER: touchofeurope.net (search lentilles de puy). **FURTHER INFORMATION AND RECIPE:** saveur.com (search lentil salad).

Madeleines

French

"Those squat, plump little cakes called 'petites madeleines,' which look as though they had been molded in the fluted valve of a scallop shell." Who better to describe the spongy, fragrant blond tea cakes than Marcel Proust,

who immortalized them as a touchstone for memory in *Swann's Way,* the first book in his seven-volume *Remembrance of Things Past.* Biting into one as an adult, Proust began to recall the Sunday mornings as a child when his aunt shared the delicate pastries with him;

suddenly his entire life flashed before him, and an epic was born.

Remarking on the literary mileage Proust eked out of that one small pastry, A. J. Liebling noted in *Between Meals,* "In light of what Proust wrote with so mild a stimulus, it is the world's loss that he did not have a heartier appetite." The formidable journalist and trencherman speculated that an even greater masterpiece might have resulted had Proust dined on a dozen oysters, a big bowl of clam chowder, steamer clams, scallops, soft-shelled crabs, a few ears of corn, two lobsters, and a duck.

To eat this little cake may be to indulge in cliché, but madeleines have considerable charms; the moist and buttery morsels are soft and light on the inside but satisfyingly crisp at the edges, with a simple flavor that makes them a favorite of children everywhere.

The origin of the madeleine is the subject of hot dispute. Commercial madeleine makers in the town of Commercy say that in 1755, King Stanislas of Lorraine was hosting a luncheon. When his mercurial chef stormed out of the kitchen during the meal, a young assistant saved the day by preparing a little cake similar to one her grandmother made. The king and his guests were so delighted that they named the cake after the girl, Madeleine. Another version suggests that madeleines were invented by Avice, Talleyrand's pastry chef, while he was seeking to create a pound cake in miniature form. Still another tale insists that Marie Leczynska, the wife of Louis XV, perfected them with the advice of her own cook, Madeleine.

Although they are baked throughout France, the town of Commercy in Lorraine is considered the epicenter of their production. Proust fans flock there to buy the biscuits, traditionally packed in quaintly designed oval boxes.

The madeleine's sweetly innocent flavor begins with a blend of egg yolks beaten with sugar and seasoned with grated lemon zest. Folded into flour and combined with snowy beaten egg whites and golden melted butter, the mixture is poured into pretty shell-shaped baking molds. Some recipes call for brandy, but in a quantity that, as Liebling put it, "would not

Traditional blue steel pans can be hard to find, but they produce cakes with the crispest edges.

furnish a gnat with an alcohol rubdown." With or without it, the cakes exude a heavenly scent as they bake. The special metal baking pans with scalloped indentations produce equally charming results when filled with cornbread or gingerbread batter.

WHERE: *In Paris,* Blé Sucré, tel 33/1-43-40-77-73, blesucre.fr; *in New York,* La Maison du Macaron, tel 212-243-2757, nymacaron.com. **MAIL ORDER:** histoiresucree.com (search madeleines de commercy). **FURTHER INFORMATION AND RECIPES:** *Swann's Way* by Marcel Proust (1913); *Between Meals* by A. J. Liebling (1962); *Maida Heatter's Book of Great Desserts* by Maida Heatter (1999); smittenkitchen.com (search classic madeleines).

Maquereaux au Vin Blanc

French

One of the oiliest and fishiest of all fish, mackerel will have little appeal to those who prefer their seafood white, firm, and mildly flavored. But even timid palates have been known to develop an appreciation for these shiny silver-blue

fish when they are prepared as in the following recipe.

After being boned, skinned, and filleted, they are suspended in an astringent aspic based on white wine, onion, garlic, bay leaf, coriander seeds, and a good dose of lemon juice and grated lemon peel. Those aromatics clean up the fish's excessively oily overtones, while the wine and lemon work in tandem to do the job of firming and pickling. Delicious as a cold appetizer, or as a light lunch with bread and a salad, these *maquereaux* are especially welcome in hot weather.

Maquereaux au Vin Blanc
Serves 6

6 medium-size mackerel, gutted but whole (about 1 pound each)
1 cup dry white wine
1 small onion, thinly sliced
1 large clove garlic, peeled and lightly crushed with the flat side of a chef's knife
1 bay leaf
6 to 8 coriander seeds
6 to 8 mustard seeds
2 teaspoons salt
8 to 10 black peppercorns, lightly crushed
Grated rind of ½ medium-size lemon
Juice of ½ medium-size lemon
2 tablespoons minced fresh flat-leaf parsley, for garnish
Hot toast or warm baguette slices, for serving

1. Thoroughly rinse the mackerel under cold running water.

2. Place the white wine, onion, garlic, bay leaf, coriander and mustard seeds, salt, peppercorns, lemon rind and juice, and 1 cup of water in a large saucepan. Bring to a simmer over medium heat, and let simmer until the mixture develops into a court bouillon and becomes flavorful, about 10 minutes. Let the court bouillon cool to room temperature in the saucepan.

3. Place the mackerel in the cooled court bouillon over low heat and let simmer until cooked through, 10 to 15 minutes. Let the fish cool in the broth.

4. Lift the cooled fish gently out of the saucepan, reserving the broth. Remove and discard the heads, bones, and skin of the fish. Cut each fish half into fillets that are about 2 inches long.

5. Place the mackerel fillets in a glass or ceramic serving dish. Boil the broth rapidly over high heat until it is reduced by half, to about ⅔ of a cup. Strain the broth, discarding the solids. Pour the broth over the mackerel and sprinkle the parsley on top.

6. Cover the serving dish with plastic wrap and place it in the refrigerator until the broth sets to a light aspic, 7 to 8 hours. The mackerel will taste even better if it is refrigerated for 12 hours before it is served. Serve the mackerel with the hot toast or warm baguette slices.

FURTHER INFORMATION AND ADDITIONAL RECIPES: *Simple French Food* by Richard Olney (1992); *Daniel Boulud's Café Boulud Cookbook* by Daniel Boulud (1999).

THE MORELS OF THIS STORY

Morilles à la Crème

French

Morels, even when called *morilles,* are not exclusively French. The highly prized luxuries also grow wild on the edges of forests and in mountains elsewhere in Europe, in China, and in the midwestern United States, around Michigan. What *is* French is their best and simplest preparation, the three-ingredient dish called *morilles à la crème:* After their cellular conical caps are brushed clean, the mushrooms are lightly simmered in unsalted butter for about seven minutes, then bathed in hot, heavy sweet cream that bubbles down to an enveloping satiny sauce. Preferably served as a garnish for chicken or game birds, morels also shine when simply sautéed in butter with a hint of shallot and a dash of red wine.

Strictly speaking, from a botanical point of view, morels are closer to truffles than to other members of the edible fungi family, due to their distribution of spores. The most delicious varieties are the ocher-colored *Morchella esculenta* and the chocolate-brown *Morchella deliciosa.* With their peaked honeycombed caps, fat, floppy stems, and generally

Morels usually range in size from 2 to 6 inches.

earthy colorations, they might look a bit ominous to the uninitiated. And, in fact, with good reason: The helvellic acid present in raw morels can be toxic. Amateur foragers had also best beware of highly poisonous look-alike fungi known as false morels. Better to trust your local farmers' market or fancy food stores and live to tell the tale.

Harvested in midspring, morels flourish following a forest fire. They are best eaten fresh; the dried variety, while useful as a flavoring for sauces and stews, can be unpleasantly fibrous, even when soaked and simmered.

WHERE: *In Paris,* L'Ami Louis, tel 33/1-48-87-77-48. **MAIL ORDER:** Melissa's Produce, tel 800-588-0151, melissas.com. **FURTHER INFORMATION AND RECIPES:** *Vegetables from Amaranth to Zucchini* by Elizabeth Schneider (2001); thegreatmorel .com.

ETHEREAL CHOCOLATE DECADENCE

Mousse au Chocolat

French

Chocolate mousse really does live up to all the clichés it engenders: Light, airy, rich, and quintessentially chocolate, it's an iconic symbol of indulgence and of the sensuous pleasures of French food. In the bargain, it is also almost embarrassingly easy to make. Essentially, it consists of chocolate, melted with butter and combined with egg yolk (for a creamy texture), enfolded with sweetened whipped cream and/or beaten egg whites (for an airy touch), and then chilled. The term *mousse* simply means foam. The chocolate version had already achieved its global significance by the eighteenth century, when mousses both sweet and savory were popularized.

In these diet-conscious days, chocolate may be moussed with or without egg yolks, with or without egg whites, and with or without both cream and butter. You may see a mousse frozen, molded, tucked into pie, layered into cake,

and flavored with coffee or any number of fruit liqueurs. All such iterations may have their charms, but the absolute simplest formula remains the purists' favorite, for the best of reasons. The key to making a pure version of chocolate mousse delicious is to use very high-quality bittersweet chocolate with a high percentage of cacao. The chocolate is no supporting actor here, after all—it's the whole show.

FURTHER INFORMATION AND RECIPES: *Jean-Georges: Cooking at Home with a Four-Star Chef* by Jean-Georges Vongerichten and Mark Bittman (1998); *The James Beard Cookbook* by James Beard (2002); bonappetit.com (search classic chocolate mousse).

⊢||||||||||||||||||||||||||||||||⊣

THIS IS WHY THE FRENCH WERE CALLED FROGS

Mousseline de Grenouilles, Paul Haeberlin

French (Alsatian)

American doughboys deployed in France during World War I were so shocked and amused to see the French eating frogs' legs, they couldn't get over it. Thus was bestowed the nickname that seems to have stuck, although it isn't

exactly PC these days. The French have had the last laugh, however, considering how delectable, tender, and sweet those succulent limbs can be. Do they taste like chicken? Well, not exactly. Perhaps a bit gamier, and with just the slightest saline suggestion of their amphibian nature.

Although the most famous French version is *cuisses de grenouilles provençal*, in which the cute little legs are sautéed to crunchy golden bliss in a haze of garlic butter and aromatic *herbes de Provence*, the Alsatian version has to be accorded first place for sophistication and elegance. Created by Paul Haeberlin, the second-generation chef in his family's exquisite garden of a restaurant, L'Auberge de L'Ill, the

preparation starts with a mousseline—a light and creamy mousse, actually a pike puree, whipped to an airy snow with cream and egg whites as it would be for quenelles—which is heaped into small individual ramekins. A well in the center of the mousseline is filled with the boned, silken ivory meat of frogs' legs poached in riesling wine. Baked under a fluff of creamy béchamel sauce, the mousseline is unmolded and nestled onto verdant sautéed spinach and sprinkled with minced chives.

This dish is reason enough for the graceful Auberge's three Michelin stars, which it has impressively held since 1967.

If you're lucky enough to visit the restaurant, also be prepared to try the typically

Alsatian frogs' legs in a cream soup, the quail stuffed with sweetbreads, and the light and mouthwatering local *knepfle* dumplings.

To make the experience complete, it's a good idea to spend at least one night on the same beautifully planted grounds in the charming Hôtel des Berges, the Haeberlins' guest house . . . and to have the whole meal over again the next day.

Where: *In Illhaeusern, France,* L'Auberge de L'Ill, tel 39/3-89-71-89-00, auberge-de-l-ill.com; *in New York,* La Grenouille, 212-752-1495, la-grenouille.com. **Further information and recipe:** latabledeschefs.fr (click Marc Haeberlin).

"WATER-WHITE" SWEETNESS

Narbonne Honey

French

The bees of France's southwestern Languedoc province produce one of the world's most highly prized and long-sought-after honeys. The delicacy was historically prized by ancient Greeks and Egyptians, who traveled far and paid dearly for it.

Collected at the time of the summer solstice—between June 21 and June 24—before blossoms dry and wither, Narbonne honey is valued for a piney, burnished, salty-sweet flavor imparted by nectar drawn from rosemary blossoms, thyme, and a few other wild herbs.

Bees gathering nectar in a field of thyme

Its most distinguishing feature is a crystal-clear sparkle described as "water white," considered the premium color (or absence thereof) for honey.

Its intriguing flavor and lack of color grant the honey a place of pride in many of the region's confections, among them a chewy, snowy nougat studded with almonds, and Languedoc biscuits crunchy with almonds and pine nuts.

As with all honeys, this one should be stored in a tightly closed jar or crock in a very warm, dry area to prevent it from absorbing moisture and expanding. If it crystallizes over time, reconstitute it by placing the jar in a bowl of hot water. (Although still completely edible, honey older than a few years is best used as an ingredient in candies, cakes, cookies, and spice breads; its flavor will be riper and less airy.)

Where: *In Narbonne,* confections made with that honey are at Pâtisserie Combot, tel 33/4-68-65-00-89. **Further information:** cooksinfo .com (search narbonne honey). **See also:** Tasmanian Leatherwood Honey, page 905; Heather Honey, page 41.

Oeufs à la Neige and Île Flottante

French

S nowy cloudlets of sweet egg-white meringue drift across sunny seas of the vanilla-scented custard sauce crème anglaise in two different versions of this fanciful, irresistible dessert. For the snow eggs—*oeufs à la neige*—high oval

spoonfuls of poached, beaten whites are placed around the crème anglaise, each topped with a crackling, diaphanous net of caramelized sugar. One or two of these oval mounds becomes an individual serving.

For the more plebeian version better known in American households, Floating Island—*Île Flottante*—the meringue is baked in a soufflé mold, then turned out onto the custard sauce. A standard in American kitchens during the Fanny Farmer era, this method results in a slightly chewier, less fragile, but no less delicious alternative to its snowy relative. Austrians have their own take on this combination of meringues and custard sauce; see Salzburger nöckerln, page 326.

WHERE: *In New York,* La Grenouille, tel 212-752-1495, la-grenouille.com. **FURTHER INFOR-**

Dress up Île Flottante with a caramel lattice.

MATION AND RECIPES: *The New Making of a Cook* by Madeleine Kamman (1997); cookstr .com (search floating islands).

Oeufs en Gelée

French

T hey may be pretty enough to be used as decorative paperweights, but these shimmering eggs caught in clear golden aspic are of course far too fragile for such a purpose. Instead, adorned with tarragon leaves and dots of tomato or pimiento, the eggs become a classy and palate-enticing first course.

As is so typical of French cuisine, the intricate preparation involved in making them requires more time than skill, along with a large helping of patience. In the beginning, there is a cooked egg. That egg must have a completely set white and a completely runny yolk. That trick can be best accomplished by simmering an egg in the shell to the *mollet*, or soft, stage. This method requires careful timing and handling so that the white does not break as the egg is peeled.

For a rich amber aspic, a strong and savory clarified beef or veal stock should be simmered with a calf or pig foot or some powdered gelatin. A little stock is poured into each egg-shaped mold, slightly chilled to set soft, and then topped with tarragon leaves and whatever other decoration will be used. The cooled egg is laid in and more stock is poured over it until the mold is filled, and then the dish is chilled until set.

Unmolded tarragon side down just before serving, the pretty combination looks its best nested on a bed of crinkly frisée lettuce.

FURTHER INFORMATION AND RECIPES: *Mastering the Art of French Cooking, Volume 1,* by Julia Child, Louisette Bertholle, and Simone Beck (1961); saveur.com (search eggs in aspic).

A cool and elegant addition to a summer picnic

EGGS ON THE SAUCE

Oeufs en Meurette

French (Burgundian)

They are basically poached eggs, but with a twist one might expect not only of the French but also of the wine-informed chefs of Burgundy: a poaching liquid of beef stock and red Burgundy wine. Enriched with matchsticks of bacon, wilted shallots, thyme, garlic, bay leaf, and black and cayenne pepper, the stock is reduced to a satiny shimmer after the eggs have been poached. Placed on freshly browned-in-butter toast, the eggs are mantled with their sublime sauce, after which they may be garnished with sautéed onions or mushrooms. The result is a seductive, multiflavored dish that is generally served as an appetizer, although with two eggs per portion, it's substantial enough to be a lunch main course, perhaps with a green salad and some crisp-crusted bread. Enjoy it with a red Burgundy or lighter Beaujolais wine.

FURTHER INFORMATION AND RECIPES: *Mastering the Art of French Cooking, Volume 1,* by Julia Child, Louisette Bertholle, and Simone Beck (1961); foodnetwork.com (search oeufs en meurette).

‖‖‖‖‖‖‖‖‖‖‖‖‖‖‖‖‖‖‖‖‖‖‖‖‖

"A TASTE OLDER THAN MEAT, OLDER THAN WINE. A TASTE AS OLD AS COLD WATER."
—LAWRENCE DURRELL IN PROSPERO'S CELL

Olives Niçoise

French (Provençal)

Although Lawrence Durrell was romantically describing Mediterranean black olives in general, had he thought about it a bit more carefully—and gastronomically—he might have singled out the tiny, mildly saline black-brown olive Niçoise. Named for the method of curing typical of the region of Nice, the tiny oval black olives offer a rich and intense ripe flavor and are pressed to make what is arguably the world's best olive oil. Like all olives, green or black, large or small, they must be cured to be palatable, which means leaching out the mouth-puckering bitterness present in their natural state. That leaching can be done by drying the freshly picked fruit in the sun, by salting, or by marinating them in plain water, olive oil, or, as, is the case with these, in a salt brine, until they achieve a dewy, silky texture that remains reassuringly meaty.

True, the petite ovals are difficult to pit, an issue should one want to add their pungent gleam to a *salade Niçoise*, ratatouille (see page 124), or tapenade relish without having guests choke or break their teeth. Purists wishing to preserve a firm texture skip the pitting and warn guests of those risks.

To fully understand these olives' charms, eat them au naturel, nibbling around the pits and now and then biting into a piece of bread or a slightly dry cheese.

MAIL ORDER: delallo.com (search nicoise olives). **FURTHER INFORMATION AND RECIPES:** cooksinfo.com (search nicoise olives).

‖‖‖‖‖‖‖‖‖‖‖‖‖‖‖‖‖‖‖‖‖‖‖‖‖

GREEN EGGS FOR SAM-I-AM

Omelette aux Fines Herbes

French

Of all the possible garnishes for an authentic French *omelette*—cheese, mushrooms, caviar, tomato, bacon, ham, spinach, potatoes—none shows off this delicate egg classic better than a verdant blend of minced fines herbes, that classic combination of parsley, chives, tarragon, and chervil. The fresh herbs lend the sprightly flavors of springtime and a lovely emerald speckling to the sun-golden pancake that is a test for so many young chefs.

If they had to pick just one dish, many haute cuisine chefs would judge their young charges by their ability to prepare an omelet. This simple dish—whose name derives from the Latin *lamella,* meaning a thin, round plate—is a perennial reminder that the pursuit of perfection involves more than meets the eye (and palate).

Making a perfect French *omelette* requires just the right number of eggs (usually three large eggs per portion) of consummate freshness. The unbroken egg should feel heavy relative to its volume, and when the egg is cracked onto a plate, its yolk should stand high and round amid a thick ring of white. Although many recipes call for a vigorous beating of the eggs, in fact they should be stirred gently and lightly broken up with a fork. Half of the fines herbes, along with salt and freshly ground black pepper, are stirred into the broken eggs. Then, the mixture is poured into a 10-inch omelet pan already glossed with hot, but not sizzling, butter. The remaining herbs are sprinkled over the top as the cook begins to pull the edges in toward the center, simultaneously tipping the pan so the uncooked portions run to its bottom.

When only a little liquid shimmer remains on its surface, the omelet is ready to be folded in thirds with a fork or a spatula and turned out onto a slightly warmed plate. The final result gives evidence of a craftsmanship that involves the hand, the eye, and even the nose in assessing the freshness of the herbs and the readiness of the melted butter just as it begins to smell nutty.

As one might guess, the technique's apparent simplicity provokes a great deal of argument: Should the eggs be gently stirred or rapidly beaten to take in air and volume? Is a touch of cream or water desirable in the egg mixture, or is a purer result more appropriate? Should the finished omelet have a slight lacy browning on the bottom, or should it be completely yellow? And perhaps most of all in these modern times, can one prepare a proper omelet in a nonstick pan? As convenient as that may be, and as much as it decreases the need for butter, purists contend that the outsides of such omelets are slickly smooth and slightly tough. Better, they feel, to rely on the classic never-to-be-washed omelet pan, and to master the technique that makes for a more tender, slightly porous, bubbly texture.

WHERE: *In New York,* Benoit Bistro, tel 646-943-7373, benoitny.com; *in Yountville, CA,* Bouchon Bistro, tel 707-944-8037, bouchon bistro.com. **FURTHER INFORMATION AND RECIPES:** *On Food and Cooking* by Harold McGee (2004); *French Provincial Cooking* by Elizabeth David (1999); *An Omelette and a Glass of Wine* by Elizabeth David (1985); nytimes.com (search fines herbes omelet); cookstr.com (search fines herbes omelet).

A TASTE OF THE SEA

The Oysters of Locmariaquer

French

Anyone passionate about oysters should consider the fully immersive experience of a visit to the coast of Brittany for a sampling of the seductively salty and silky specimens known as belons or Armoricaines. Such intrepid food travelers may learn to better appreciate the flavor of the extraordinary *Ostrea edulis,* but they will probably never be able to accurately describe it. Even the brilliant novelist Eleanor Clark, author of an intriguing book on the history and cultivation of these mollusks and their native habitat, admitted defeat on that score: "It is briny first of all, and not in the sense of brine in a barrel. . . .There is the shock of freshness to it. . . . Some piercing intuition of the sea and all its weeds and breezes shiver you a split second. You are eating the sea, that's it . . . something connected with the flavor of life itself."

First published in 1959, *The Oysters of*

Locmariaquer is rightfully considered one of the great works of food literature. So for the maximum experience, get the book and set aside a vacation week in January or February when the ocean is coldest and the oysters are at their best. Then consult your *Guide Michelin* to find the hotels in Brittany that remain open during that off-season, ideally around the Gulf of Morbihan in towns such as Quiberon, Auray, Vannes, or La Trinité-sur-Mer. Pack some warm clothes and head for the charming half-deserted coast, where each day you can walk on the beach watching dark waves break against the shore, then warm up indoors with a coffee or a brandy and read a chapter or two of Clark's wonderful book. At least twice each day, go into a snack bar, café, or restaurant to sample her beloved "plates," with their flat, rounded, stone-gray ruffled shells. Needless to say, you will eat them neat—straight from the shell, without even a drop of lemon juice to adulterate the taste sensation.

Eleanor Clark immortalized oysters in her writing.

Not only will you have tasted oysters in their peak season but you will have become part of history. Oysters have been cultivated off the Brittany coast since Roman times, and modern methods have not changed much. The larval form of the oysters, or "spat," need support to survive and grow, so they are put into banks of hollow tiles that are planted in the sea in late May or early June, a colorful sight in itself. After about eight months, the young oysters are stripped off the tiles and moved to protected sea parks, or *claires.* There, they mature unharmed by predatory sea life for three or four years, whereupon they are transferred to even more perfect conditions for their *affinage,* or refinement.

The belons flourish when cultivated in Maine, but they are products as much of geography as of genetics. As good as our naturalized belons are, they bear hardly any similarity to their lusty Breton ancestors.

Further information: *The Oysters of Locmariaquer* by Eleanor Clark (1959); *North Atlantic Seafood* by Alan Davidson (2012).

——————|||||||||||||||||||||||||||||||—————

A SALAD IN A SANDWICH

Pan Bagnat

French (Provençal)

Nothing goes to waste in any frugal kitchen, least of all stale bread, which is cleverly worked into some of the Western world's most beloved dishes. Of course, we're all aware of French toast, known as *pain perdu,* or lost bread, but there are bread puddings (see pages 534 and 711); soup (see page 267); and the cool and lovely Italian summer salad *panzanella* (see page 215), among many others.

Along the Côte d'Azur, the desire to make use of stale bread led to the creation of this sustaining and remarkably healthful summer sandwich that is essentially a *salade Niçoise* heaped into a crusty loaf of French bread. Sliced in half lengthwise, the cut sides of the baguette are liberally rubbed with garlic and doused with olive oil, hence the name *pan bagnat*—bathed or wet bread. The fixings are layered in: thinly sliced tomatoes, onions, green peppers; always hard-boiled eggs; and either the soft, salty accents of anchovy fillets or dark tuna cured in olive oil. The final touch is tiny black olives Niçoise (see page 107), authentically unpitted, though the hazards are obvious. Once composed, the sandwich is wrapped firmly in wax paper, covered with foil, and then pressed down with some kind of weight for about an hour. Thus all the ingredients meld together, and olive oil oozes out until it is a downright threat to pristine shirt fronts. A bib might well be in order.

So might a glass of cool white wine, or an astringent, licorice-tasting pastis. In his classic work on French Mediterranean food, Jacques Médecin recommends this sandwich as a

Pan bagnat is a classic Provençal sandwich.

mérenda or midmorning snack, or as "a wonderful summer hors-d'oeuvre, an excellent and practical component of the picnic basket, or even a complete meal if you are out fishing or if the weather is hot and your appetite is flagging." Who could ask for anything more?

Where: *In Nice,* at stalls and cafés in the open market on the Cours Saleya. **Further information and recipes:** *Cuisine Niçoise* by Jacques Médecin (1991); *Flavors of the Riviera* by Colman Andrews (1996); saveur.com (search pan bagnat).

THE COOK'S PASTRY

Pâte à Choux

French

U sually, those who love to cook are not equally fond of baking, and the other way around—a fact well acknowledged in professional kitchens, where chefs and pâtissiers hurl jibes and insults at one another with legendary abandon.

Word is that the operations require different temperaments and skills—the bakers are more disciplined and scientific, while the cooks are more improvisational and freewheeling.

Be that as it may, one basic dough appeals to both: *pâte à choux,* or what Americans know as cream puff pastry. To make pâte à choux, flour, butter, salt, and pepper (or sugar, for a dessert pastry) are heated together until they form a mass, then the dough is polished with beaten eggs. The result is spooned or squeezed from a pastry bag onto a baking sheet and popped into the oven. If all goes well, the rounds or lengths puff up to become hollow, tender-crisp, and lightly eggy in flavor, making them perfect casings for a battery of much-loved pastries, sweet and savory.

Cream puffs and éclairs, two classic uses of this dough, can be made in full or miniature sizes and filled with vanilla-scented pastry cream or lightly flavored whipped cream. True devotees shun more highly flavored fillings, such as chocolate or coffee cream, although some do allow their round puffs or long éclairs to be brushed with chocolate or mocha icing. Others, preferring their shells to have an unmarred crispness, opt for a dusting of confectioners' sugar.

Gâteau St. Honoré, named for the patron saint of pastry chefs, is a lush combination of tiny custard-filled cream puffs bedded down on a round sheet of buttery pie crust. The center is filled with an extravagant lake of custard cream adrift with cloudlets of meringue and dottings of crystallized cherries and candied violets.

Paris-Brest is a showy riff on gâteau St. Honoré. For this luscious charmer, pâte à choux is set in an 8- to 10-inch ring on a baking sheet. Once baked and cooled, it is split horizontally and filled with smooth praline cream and the smoky-sweet burnish of crushed, caramelized almonds. If the arrangement suggests a bicycle wheel, it's because this delectable pastry was created to mark the first Paris-to-Brest bicycle race in the late nineteenth century. Not that it retains its shape very long before it is gleefully cut . . .

Profiteroles are recurrent favorites on dessert menus throughout the Western world, and small wonder, as they're essentially grown-up ice-cream sundaes. The airy puffs are filled with ice cream—traditionally vanilla, but chocolate or coffee aren't bad, either—and mantled with warm, dark chocolate fudge sauce and a dollop or two of unsweetened whipped cream.

A strawberry shortcake cream puff may not be part of the French pâtissier's pantheon, but the high-style version of an American favorite is an innocent and worthy interloper. Fill the puffs with vanilla ice cream and top with sweetened sliced strawberries. Or fill with strawberries and top with whipped cream. Or . . . take your pick, but do add a few drops of rosewater to the berries for a real breath of springtime. A sprig of fresh mint doesn't hurt, either.

Croquembouche is the wedding cake among wedding cakes—a pyramidal mound of tiny custard-filled cream puffs stuck together and then crowned with lacings of glasslike spun sugar. The cake's bottom is decorated with whipped cream and candied fruits. It's a trick that bakers are loath to guarantee, lest the wedding day be rainy and the cream puffs slide out of place. Order at your own risk—though perhaps only a minor risk, compared to the main one you will take on the big day.

Gougères are cheese puffs based on the same pastry as the previously mentioned desserts, but seasoned with salt, pepper, and grated nutmeg, sans sugar. They are a lovely nibble with aperitifs or as a garnish for a main-course salad. For a mild, subtle result, grated Gruyère or Emmental cheese is melted into the hot cooked dough before it is formed. For the sprightliest flavor, Parmesan is the cheese of choice.

WHERE: *In Paris,* L'Atelier de L'Éclair, tel 33/1-42-36-40-54, latelierdeleclair.fr; Popelini, tel 33/1-44-61-31-44, popelini.com. FURTHER INFORMATION AND RECIPES: *Mastering the Art of French Cooking, Volume 1,* by Julia Child, Louisette Bertholle, and Simone Beck (1961); foodand wine.com (search pate a choux).

———————|||||||||||||||||||||||||||||||||||————————

———————————————

Pâte Feuilletée

French

We call it puff pastry—the buttery, flaky miracle that deliciously defines many of France's most famous dessert temptations. Never mind that the form is believed to have originated in Szeged, Hungary, sometime before the eighteenth century. A minimalist creation of crisp, paper-thin golden leaves layered just thick enough to hold their eventual fillings, *pâte feuilletée* provides a teasing, toothsome crunch en route to the lavish custards, flavored whipped creams, or nut pastes within. Shaped into pastry casings that are known as vol-au-vents if they are large and communal, or *bouchées* if meant as individual portions, they are showy servers for sauced fillings of poultry, sweetbreads, or shellfish.

Raspberry mille-feuille mixes cream and crunch.

Puff pastry is a standard lesson in any serious French cookery class and an art worth mastering. It allows one to create elegant-looking dishes, sweet or savory, that may be based on the simplest preparations and ingredients. Ideally, the *pâte* is a mix of ordinary and strong durum wheat flours for elasticity, water, a little salt, and a lot of the best unsalted butter—although some maintain that combining butter with another shortening makes for a more stable, hot-weather-resistant result.

The mixed dough is put through a series of rollings and foldings, each capturing bits of butter, and then is chilled and rerolled until the final turn is completed. Rolled out flat and baked, the dough flakes into parchment-thin leaves as the butter melts between the layers, resulting in 1,458 to 3,645 leaves, the final count depending upon the number of turns made. Whatever the exact count, there are always more than enough gilded leaves to astound and entice.

And that's where the magic begins, as the puff pastry is turned into classics that beckon to us from the cases of every patisserie worthy of that name.

***Mille-feuille* or Napoleon.** Perhaps the best-known use of the golden pastry, these high rectangles sandwich three layers of puff pastry with fillings of whipped cream or eggy vanilla custard; their outsides are usually glazed with burnt sugar and are sometimes topped with a thin layer of icing. The most ethereal version of all combines the two fillings—whipped cream folded into pastry cream—for the sumptuous mixture known as St. Honoré Chantilly. The Napoleon, as the resulting pastry is most often called in the U.S., is equally popular in Italian and French pastry shops; its name is believed to have been derived by the French from Napolitano, honoring the city of Naples for its plethora of cream-filled pastries.

Gâteau mille-feuilles. In the gâteau mille-feuilles, we see the Napoleon transformed into a cake with three round layers of crunchy puff pastry parchment. Between them are sandwiched vanilla pastry cream and lushly red raspberry jam; the top is frosted with rum fondant and a showering of chopped toasted almonds or pistachios, and sometimes finished with candied violets. The Napoleon's combination of crisp and creamy, and the taste of that pure, innocent vanilla sweetness, is here writ large.

Gâteau Pithiviers. Claimed by the French town of Pithiviers, this crackling, shiny-topped, bronze-gold cake also echoes the Napoleon, but in a completely different form. The big difference is a center filling of almond-accented pastry cream sandwiched between two round layers of puff pastry. Swirls carved into the top not only add a merry look but also indicate where wedge-shaped portions should be cut.

Of *palmiers* and *papillons*. Call them pigs' or elephants ears, which some think they resemble, or more accurately palms, as in palmiers, these flat crunchy scrolled cookies are favorites on after-dinner petits-fours trays. When splayed out in the form of butterflies, they are called papillons. In whatever form, crunches of crystal sugar iced between the pastry's crisp, buttery edges and folds provide an alluring contrast of taste and texture.

WHERE: *In Paris,* Pâtisserie Jean Millet, tel 33/1-45-51-49-80. **FURTHER INFORMATION AND RECIPES:** *Baking and Pastry: Mastering the Art and Craft* by the Culinary Institute of America (2009). **SEE ALSO:** Rétes, page 397; Sfogliatelle, page 239.

||||||||||||||||||||||||||||||||

JUMPING IN WITH BOTH FEET

Pieds de Porc Sainte-Ménehould

Grilled Pigs' Feet

French

A classic late-night snack in the days when the French food market, Les Halles, was located in the middle of Paris, these crunchy garlic- and bread-crumb–encrusted pigs' feet are still served (at all hours) in many old-style French bistros, and are a gift from the town of Sainte-Ménehould, where they were created. The gently simmered trotters, coated with buttered bread crumbs and grilled until crackling and fragrant, are treats for the serious nibblers who know that the meat is sweetest closest to the bones—though the pork's rich flavor and gelatinous finish still come through when the cooked meat is *désossé,* or boned, prior to being grilled, as is more common these days.

Even when it comes to more elegant variations, wherein black truffles are slid into pouchy packets of pork skin, the best accompaniment is mustard—either smooth, brassy Dijon or the grainy, bitter-sharp *à l'ancienne.* Add some tiny pickled cucumbers, or cornichons, for a well-rounded appetizer, or, if the meat is the *plat de résistance,* a helping of buttery mashed potatoes.

Such preparations can also be applied to sheep's feet—softer, stronger in flavor, and earthier, and generally even more richly endowed with fat than their porcine equivalents.

WHERE: *In Paris,* Au Pied de Cochon, tel 33/1-40-13-77-00, pieddecochon.com; Le Pied Rare, tel 33/8-99-02-13-89; *in Sainte-Ménehould, France,* Le Cheval Rouge, tel 33/3-26-60-81-04, lechevalrouge.com. **FURTHER INFORMATION AND RECIPES:** *The Escoffier Cookbook* by Auguste Escoffier, H. L. Cracknell, and R. J. Kaufmann (2011); bonjourparis.com (search pieds de porc).

———┤||||||||||||||||||||||||||||├———

Pigeons en Crapaudine

French

Many gourmands who claim to love squabs balk when told they are eating pigeons. True, no responsible cook targets the street-smart pigeons of city parks, but the birds are essentially the same. The real difference is between those farm-raised on corn or other feed, and those captured in the wild, that forage for anything they can find. Since selling the latter is usually illegal, you're unlikely to find them on menus or in markets.

Old-timey French bistros have wonderful ways with these tiny, fine-boned birds and their dark, moist, and tantalizingly gamy meat. One such preparation, *pigeons en crapaudine*, begins with butterflying or spatchcocking—different words for the same technique, in which the tender birds are split and fanned out, their wings tucked behind their shoulder bones in a final form that suggests a toad, or *crapaud*. Brushed with butter and sprinkled with salt and pepper, they are then grilled or pan-grilled under a weight.

A variation with squabs in green pea puree

For a richer, homier rendition, whole squabs or the younger *pigeonneaux* are braised golden brown in a cocotte of copper or earthenware, along with the matchsticks of smoky bacon called *lardons*, white pearl onions, sweet lettuce to add moisture, and a handful of the tiny garden peas known as *petits pois*. The knowing palate will detect inklings of white wine and good, strong chicken stock, thyme, and garlic. Boiled new potatoes make the most of the sublime juices; or for textural contrast, a side of the straw-slim fried *pommes pailles* works well, too.

Where: *In New York,* North End Grill, tel 646-747-1600, northendgrillnyc.com. **Further information and recipes:** *Larousse Gastronomique* (2009); celtnet.org.uk (search pigeons with petit pois).

———┤||||||||||||||||||||||||||||├———

Pissaladière

French (Provençal)

One of the most basic and tempting of Nice's exquisitely light and lovely street foods, *pissaladière* suggests a pizza, but one that took off in its own savory, sophisticated way. It's a slower sort of pizza, its basic yeast bread dough rising fragrantly while slivers of onion in olive oil mellow on the stove for close to an hour, emerging deeply, richly sun-gold in color. Seasoned with salt and pepper, the onions are spread onto the flattened dough; locals say the onion layer should be fully half as thick as the crust. The silky mantle of onion is dotted with tiny, black Niçoise olives (most authentically unpitted, so watch out), and salty anchovy fillets are sometimes added in the form of the fermented anchovy sauce *pissala,* the origin of the name of this savory pie. (Although innovators might add tomatoes and/or cheese, either would compromise the purer, leaner contrast of sweet onions, salty olives, and anchovies with crisp, yeasty bread.) The pissaladière is finished with a sprinkling of sweet-scented thyme and oregano or marjoram, and then baked on a rectangular tray in a very hot oven, preferably made of stone and wood-fired for an extra-smoky burnish.

Sold in markets and bakeries by the slice, pissaladière is best enjoyed on the go, as part of a scenic stroll through the Cours Saleya in the heart of Vieux Nice—though dawdlers may find

Toppings may be scattered or arranged in patterns.

it just as pleasant to enjoy a slice and a glass of the local rosé, Bandol, at one of the cafés.

Where: *In Nice,* at the open-air market on the Cours Saleya. **Further information and recipes:** *Flavors of the Riviera* by Colman Andrews (1996); *French Provincial Cooking* by Elizabeth David (1999); saveur.com (search pissaladiere). **See also:** *La Grand Bouffe* Lamb with Pissaladière, page 94.

STRICTLY A WOMAN'S WAY WITH FISH

Poisson au Beurre Blanc

French

The fish should be snowy, mild-flavored, carefully steamed so it is pearly and moist, and, needless to say, sea-breeze fresh. It should be adrift in a heavenly, satiny sauce that, convention dictates, can be made properly only by a female

cook holding forth in what is known as a *cuisine de mère* or mother restaurant—a traditional keeper of the flame with the eye, wrist, nose, and patience necessary to produce this seemingly simple sauce that can so easily go wrong.

The preparation begins with finely minced shallots, sending forth their onion-garlic essence as they are sweated in a combination of red wine vinegar, white wine, and sometimes a few

drops of fish stock. Meanwhile, unsalted butter is constantly whisked to its foamy melting point in the top of a double boiler set over water that is smilingly hot, but not bubbling, lest the sauce curdle.

Slowly, gradually, the fragrant shallot mass is whisked into the butter, one spoonful at a time, until all is absorbed and the sauce has the smooth consistency of hollandaise. Then the rush is on, as the sauce must be served at once, spooned over the hot, steamed fish (most classically it is bass, pike, or turbot) graced with a few small, steamed white potatoes. And, fair warning, asking for a piece of lemon might have you ejected from the restaurant.

FURTHER INFORMATION AND RECIPES: *French Country Cooking* by Elizabeth David (2011); for beurre blanc sauce, *Mastering the Art of French Cooking, Volume 1,* by Julia Child, Louisette Bertholle, and Simone Beck (1961); cookstr .com (search beurre blanc).

--------⊣||||||||||||||||||||||||||||||⊢--------

ONE POTATO, TWO POTATO, THREE POTATO, FOUR

Pommes de Terre, Four Ways

French

Potatoes, of course, are great in the simplest of ways: boiled, baked, mashed, whipped, or crisped up as fries. But by playing on their textural adaptability and their knack for absorbing rich flavors, the French have come up with elegant refinements that raise the humble tubers to haute levels.

The success of all of the following dishes depends heavily on uniform slicing on a mandoline, as well as the selection and use of the right *kind* of potatoes. They should be on the order of our Idaho russets, and relatively old, so they are starchy and dry enough to retain their shape and not turn mushy during the cooking process. As delicious as new potatoes or golden Yukons are for other uses, they will not stand up in these preparations.

Pommes Dauphinoises. Few potato dishes go as well with roast beef as does this gratin, in which uniformly thin slices of potatoes are layered into a wide baking dish with butter, garlic, salt, pepper, grated Gruyère cheese, a pinch of nutmeg, and milk. All is baked until the potatoes tenderize as they absorb the other ingredients, emerging from the oven with a golden-brown top glaze and a flavor so rich and buttery you'd swear they were made with heavy cream. Two equally mouthwatering variations are *pommes Savoyard,* in which beef stock replaces the milk for a leaner dish, and *pommes Jurassienne,* in

Pommes gaufrettes alone make a satisfying snack.

which heavy sweet cream does substitute for the milk.

Pommes Anna. A neat trick if you can carry it off, this one requires a special baking dish that is usually made of copper and is, unsurprisingly, known as a pommes Anna casserole. The preparation again begins with uniformly thin slices of potato. Layered into the 2- to 3-inch-deep round casserole with salt and pepper, they are tucked in with almost their weight in dots of sweet butter. Another dish or lid that fits inside the casserole is added as a cover and weight, and the whole is simmered very slowly until the butter has tenderized the potatoes and a golden crust forms on the bottom and sides. The crust will be in tantalizing view when the potato "cake" is inverted onto a serving dish.

Pommes Soufflés. If these look like swollen French fries, it's because that's sort of what they are. Thin, long slices of potatoes are chilled in ice water then blanched quickly in very hot, deep fat and removed as soon as they rise to the surface and begin to swell. Drained and held until just before they are to be served, the potatoes are then treated to another dip in scalding fat, which prompts them to balloon up and become very crisp. All it takes to reach perfection is a quick draining and a liberal sprinkle of good coarse sea salt. For rich, meaty flavor, use rendered suet for the frying fat; if vegetable oil is substituted for health's sake, add a small piece of suet for flavor.

Pommes Gaufrettes. Think waffled potato chips. With the ruffled blade of a mandoline, slices are cut and scored into a waffle grid, then deep-fried (again, ideally in rendered suet) to emerge with several levels of crackling crispness. These *pommes* are the perfect companions to grilled meats such as blood-rare steaks and seared, roseate lamb chops. Add a big clump of watercress and a glass of a bold red wine, and you have a feast.

FURTHER INFORMATION AND RECIPES: *The Escoffier Cookbook* by Auguste Escoffier, H. L. Cracknell, and R. J. Kaufmann (2011).

||||||||||||||||||||||||||||||

IN THE CUPS

Pots de Crème au Chocolat

French

When it comes to the outrageously rich French dessert known as *pots de crème au chocolat,* not much is lost in translation. The name refers to both the baked French custard and the small, lidded cups in which it's steamed, and the dessert adds up to little pots of utterly thick, rich, creamy chocolate (and little else). Make no mistake—this is no chocolate mousse, and "airy" is not a property that applies to pots de crème. What is prized in this game is substance, which is why the acid test of a pot de crème is that a spoon dipped into its petite cup should stand upright unassisted. And yet, the dessert consists merely of cream, milk, eggs, sugar, and chocolate, which makes it a cousin to such canonical French dessert classics as crème brûlée and crème caramel. The key to its exceptional richness is the high proportion of egg yolks to whites; it is the abundance of yolks that creates its distinctively silky, smooth texture. The treat is also coddled a bit: While baking, the small pots are partially submerged in a bain-marie (water bath) and are steamed slowly at a low temperature until the just-right dense and seductive texture is achieved.

FURTHER INFORMATION AND RECIPES: *Maida Heatter's Book of Great Chocolate Desserts* by Maida Heatter (1995); *Bouchon* by Thomas Keller (2004); epicurious.com (search pots de creme).

Poularde en Demi-Deuil

Poached Chicken with Black Truffles

French (Lyonnais)

Alas, poor chicken. But hooray for us. Whatever loss this tender, fat hen may have suffered, her mourning attire makes for great eating. Or rather, her state of half-mourning, in which the skin over her breast is loosened and lined with thin slices of black truffles. (The bird's thigh and leg quarters receive no such treatment, hence the designation "half-mourning.") After this dressing, the bird is wrapped in cheesecloth and slowly, lusciously poached in a stock fragrant with thyme, bay leaves, parsley, leeks, and root vegetables.

Truffles intact, the sliced meat is served with a silken ivory sauce based on the poaching stock, give or take a little white wine, some heavy cream, and some extra slices of truffle. Snowy steamed rice and a soft, buttery puree of green beans or new spring peas make the most felicitous garnishes. The dish may be based on the authentic, plump poularde or the elegant, younger *poulets,* but

Elegant truffle-lined bird nestled in vegetables

the best mourners are of the highly prized blue-footed variety known as *poulets de Bresse.*

What a few truffles can do for a dish as simple as boiled chicken . . . As the architect Mies van der Rohe once noted, "God is in the details." But for the less detail-oriented, there's a variation that's just as enticing: Line the breast meat of a poularde with truffles. Roast the whole bird. Finish the mourner with a sauce of golden pan juices and more diced truffles, and send her to the table with creamy *pommes dauphinoises* (see page 116).

Further information and recipes: For an involved but inspired modern rendition, *Grand Livre de Cuisine* by Alain Ducasse (2009); food network.ca (search poularde demi-deuil).

Poulet à l'Estragon

Tarragon Chicken

French

Enhanced by the licoricey dragon's herb, tarragon, and roasted or sautéed to a bewitching nut-brown in a healthy dose of butter, this chicken became a classic for the best of reasons. The dish entered the American pantheon in the early

1970s, due primarily to the praise of author and cooking school guru James Beard. It grew so popular, in fact, that it attained the cliché status that's a hallmark of menu saturation, even making regular appearances in the White House kitchens during John F. Kennedy's tenure. Happily, *estragon* fatigue has ebbed, and *poulet à l'estragon* remains one of the easiest, most fragrant and flavorful chicken dishes a home cook (or a professional chef, for that matter) can make, just as fitting for an elaborate dinner party as it is for a family meal. The preparation could hardly be simpler: browning chicken in a skillet of hot butter and oil before adding shallots and green onions, then lowering the heat to allow the chicken to simmer for twenty minutes; the dish is then finished over high heat with white wine and tarragon.

Other cooks, including the legendary *New York Herald Tribune*'s food reporter, Clementine Paddleford, proposed slow-roasting a whole buttered chicken stuffed with fresh tarragon and drizzled with lemon juice, regularly basting the bird with its own juices to produce that crisp, golden-brown skin. When roasting, do not miss out on the chance to brown diced potatoes in the chicken's drippings. The bistro staple shines alongside potatoes in any form, whether they're simply mashed with plenty of butter or steamed and sprinkled with parsley.

Where: *In Baltimore,* Petit Louis Bistro, tel 410-366-9393, petitlouis.com; *in Toronto;* Café Boulud Toronto, tel 416-963-6000, cafeboulud .com/toronto. **Further information and recipes:** *Mastering the Art of French Cooking, Volume 1,* by Julia Child, Louisette Bertholle, and Simone Beck (1961); *The Country Cooking of France* by Anne Willan (2007); saveur.com (search roast chicken with tarragon sauce).

Tarragon accents a whole butter-roasted chicken.

⊦||||||||||||||||||||||||||||||⊦

A SECOND ACT FOR A BYGONE DISH

Poulet Farnèse

Roast Chicken with Hazelnut Sauce

French (Provençal)

A longtime favorite in the graceful little Provence town of Vence, the charming Auberge des Seigneurs was once a famed haunt of Impressionist painters like Renoir and Modigliani. A seventeenth-century inn with a restaurant on its ground

floor, it was formerly presided over by chef-owner Pierre Rodi, who did most of his cooking in a huge, brick wood-fired oven—really a

fireplace—at one end of the rustic, romantically lit dining room. Fortunately, his successor continues the same practice along with the serving of savory roast-meat specialties, none more memorable than *poulet Farnèse,* a small, plump chicken, rotisserie-turned to moist perfection over the low, white-hot fire. Scented with bay leaves and garlic, and sauced with toasted hazelnuts, butter, and a quick flambé of brandy, it is a supreme triumph. Fortunately, a close approximation can be achieved in a home oven or rotisserie. (Alas, the same cannot be said for the buttery apple tart that also emerged from Rodi's magic fireplace. *C'est dommage.*)

Mashed or roasted potatoes do right by the chicken and its sauce, as do slim haricots verts in shallot butter, or steamed asparagus in season.

Poulet Farnèse

Serves 4 to 6

½ pound shelled hazelnuts
*   (about 1⅔ cups)*
2 broiler chickens
*   (2½ to 3 pounds each)*
Salt and freshly ground black pepper
12 bay leaves
4 large cloves garlic, peeled and
*   lightly crushed with the flat side*
*   of a chef's knife*
12 tablespoons (1½ sticks) unsalted butter
Chicken stock, if necessary
⅓ cup Cognac or other brandy

1. Preheat the oven to 400°F.

2. Place the hazelnuts in a single layer in a pie pan and bake them until the skins begin to flake off the nuts, about 20 minutes. Leave the oven on.

3. Transfer the hazelnuts to a clean dish towel and fold the towel over to cover them. Vigorously rub the nuts through the towel to remove the skins. Chop the nuts moderately fine and set them aside.

4. Sprinkle the inside of each chicken with salt and pepper. Place 4 or 5 bay leaves inside each chicken along with 2 cloves of garlic and 2 tablespoons of butter. Break the remaining bay leaves in half or quarters and slip 1 piece under the skin of each chicken breast half and thigh. Season the outside of the chickens with salt and pepper and rub them with the remaining 8 tablespoons of butter, dividing it evenly between them.

5. Truss the chickens and place them on a rack set in a roasting pan and bake until the drumsticks can be moved easily in their sockets and the juices run clear when the thighs are pierced with a fork or skewer, about 1 hour and 15 minutes or until the temperature reaches 175–180°F. Baste the chickens frequently with the pan drippings. If the pan drippings begin to turn brown and burn, add a little water or chicken stock to the pan.

6. Untruss the chickens and cut them into quarters, setting aside the bay leaves and garlic cloves from inside the chickens. Cut out and discard the backbones (being sure to nibble the meat off them; it's a cook's treat). Place all of the chicken quarters skin side up in a large, heavy skillet, add the pan drippings along with the reserved bay leaves and garlic; cook over medium heat until the juices reduce and turn slightly sticky, about 5 minutes, shaking the skillet vigorously. Carefully remove and discard all of the bay leaves and garlic.

7. Add the brandy or Cognac to the skillet and heat it until warmed through, about 2 minutes. Standing back from the pan, ignite the brandy with a match and let it burn until the flames die down.

8. Add the hazelnuts to the skillet and cook over high heat, shaking the skillet, until the sauce is reduced and takes on an almost syrupy sheen, 2 to 3 minutes.

9. Place the chicken on individual heated serving plates or a warmed serving platter, making sure that all of the bits of bay leaf have been removed, and spoon the sauce over all.

Variation: If using a rotisserie, fasten the chickens onto it and place a pan beneath to catch the drippings, which should be used for frequent bastings.

Where: *In Vence, France,* Auberge des Seigneurs, tel 33/4-93-58-04-24, auberge-seigneurs.com.

|||||||||||||||||||||||||||||||||||||

A SALAD FROM THE SEA

Pousse-Pierre

French

Known by various names—*Salicornia europaea, salicorne,* St. Peter's cress, marsh samphire, sea beans, sea asparagus, *passe-pierre*—this emerald-green, delicate, and exquisitely salty seaside plant is a late spring and early summer

favorite in France, and elsewhere when imported or harvested locally for upscale greengrocers and restaurateurs. (Due to its mineral content, it once was used in glass production, hence yet another name, glasswort.)

The leafless, fleshy plant grows in salt marshes along the North Sea coast of France and England and in some regions of the U.S. Its strings of tiny berries, best appreciated raw and freshly gathered, need only be trimmed of a few brownish, dried tip ends. The berries may be nibbled; if very tender, the entire stalk can be eaten, but tough stalks are best blanched, chilled, and dressed. In salad, *pousse-pierre* should be glossed with a bit of wine vinegar and olive or walnut oil.

Although it seems a pity to destroy its bright

By any name, a fine salty treat

green color and crackling texture, pousse-pierre is sometimes lightly sautéed in butter or pickled with capers, vinegar, or lemon. For an unusual treat, the greens are rubbed through a sieve and stirred into a hot cream soup garnished with mussels lightly poached in white wine—a refreshing taste of the sea. In fact, because of its natural affinity with seafood, pousse-pierre often is sold in fish markets in France.

Pousse-pierre was in style in U.S. salads during the 1990s; it could be due for a nicely saline comeback.

MAIL ORDER: Melissa's Produce, tel 800-588-0151, melissas.com (search sea bean). **FURTHER INFORMATION:** *The Oxford Companion to Food* by Alan Davidson (1999); inlandseafood.com (search pousse-pierre).

||||||||||||||||||||||||||||||||||||||||||||||||||||||||||||||||||||||||||||||||||||||||||||||||||||||||||||||||||

AN ELEVATED CONDIMENT

Salts of the Earth

One of the world's most essential ingredients is neither plant nor animal but chemical compound—our beloved salt being the product of the reaction between sodium and chlorine (NaCl). The ancient Greek mathematician Pythagoras put it a little more poetically when he proclaimed the stuff to be "born of the purest of parents: the sun and the sea," and indeed it is just as ancient and elemental as that lineage suggests.

Used as purifier and preserver of food since before the written word existed, salt has been considered sacred by nearly every culture. It makes frequent appearances in the Bible—"Can anything which is unsavory be eaten without salt?" Moses asks in the Book of Job; and who could forget Lot's wife, who was turned into a pillar of salt as she fled Sodom and turned to look back. The Egyptians used it to make mummies, the Romans paid their soldiers in salt, and in traditional Japanese theater, it was sprinkled on the stage to protect actors from evil spirits.

In the modern world, salt has become a buzzword. "Salt is the new olive oil," chef Thomas Keller of The French Laundry and Per Se (see page 562) has said, and like olive oil, it has spawned a varied subculture of gourmet, exotic salts. Frequently, these are not meant for cooking but are considered "finishing salts," meant to be sprinkled over dishes just before serving; heating them reduces their intensity and downplays their unique characteristics.

There are Mediterranean sea salts, rich in natural curing agents, the finest of which is the French *fleur de sel* ("flower of salt") from the marshes of Brittany, hand-harvested from the surface of salt ponds in order to retain its natural shape—not compact and solid but instead flaky and hollow, rather like a miniature and very delicate snowflake. There is Murray Darling salt from the Murray River in southeastern Australia, a pink crystal with a soft aroma. And Himalayan rock salt, which is noted for its umami, or mouthwatering savoriness.

(This last in particular should never be added to food before cooking, as high heat destroys its delicate aromas and the organic materials that cling to the crystals, tinting them pink and gray and giving the salt its character.)

Grand Reserve Hawaiian sea salt from Kauai obtains its red hue via the natural process of being mixed with a ruddy volcanic clay; it is then dried by slow baking in ovens made from the same clay, which imparts a sweetly earthy hint to its flavor. Among Hawaii's other salts are the Molokai red, with a full, almost buttery flavor; and black lava salt, naturally harvested and then purified with the lava and charcoal that lend it distinctively earthy and mineral notes.

The English Maldon salt is a coarse, natural sea salt with a fresh, briny taste produced by panning the salt beds in Essex's coastal marshes near the town of Maldon. From India, there are edible black rock salts and pink rock salts, essentially large pieces of crystallized salt resembling unpolished jewels. These can be found in Indian groceries; ground using a mortar and pestle, they add a marvelous crunchy texture to any dish. Pink Peruvian salt from the Andes is harvested from the remains of ancient ocean beds for a faintly sweet and subtle flavor, and smoked Danish sea salt is incredibly strong, with an effect rather like adding a dash of fire to your food. A little goes a long way.

MAIL ORDER: Zingerman's, tel 888-636-8162, zingermans.com; the Meadow, tel 888-388-4633, atthemeadow.com; SaltWorks, tel 800-353-7258, saltworks.us.

---||||||||||||||||||||||||||||||||---

THE FISH THAT WENT TO HEAVEN

Quenelles de Brochet

Pike Dumplings

French (Lyonnais)

E thereally cloudlike in texture but substantial in rich flavor, these elegant oval dumplings, most traditionally made with pike, owe a debt to the artistry of the French kitchen. Lightly flavored with no more than salt and white pepper and a pinch of nutmeg, the boneless fish is beaten with heavy sweet cream into a silky-smooth mousseline. For substance, the mousse is blended into an eggy pâte à choux dough (see page 110), also known as a *panade,* before it is shaped with a tablespoon into supple dumplings.

Into the poaching water or fish stock these go. Added richness comes from the sauce, classically the satiny Lyon version, cream-colored and heady with strong stock and white wine; an alternative is called *sauce Nantua,* featuring a roseate base sparked with essences of shellfish. The first is far more subtle, while the second appeals to those who need a bigger taste bang for their buck. Either way, steamed rice is the correct accompaniment.

With so much going on already in this dish, balance is essential. In this case, gilding the lily means stirring a bit of Swiss cheese into the sauce and/or browning the finished dish under the broiler or salamander, thereby destroying its purity, simplicity, and texture. An even sadder, and unfortunately common, state of affairs: quenelles made of different fish or crustaceans—salmon, other firm-fleshed saltwater fish, scallops, crabmeat—or even chicken. Imposters all.

WHERE: *In Lyon,* Daniel et Denise, tel 33/4-78-60-66-53, daniel-et-denise.fr; *in New York,* La Grenouille, tel 212-752-1495, la-grenouille.com. **FURTHER INFORMATION AND RECIPE:** *Mastering the Art of French Cooking, Volume 1,* by Julia Child, Louisette Bertholle, and Simone Beck (1961).

‖‖‖‖‖‖‖‖‖‖‖‖‖‖‖‖‖‖‖‖‖‖‖‖‖‖‖

REAL MEN EAT IT, TOO

Quiche Lorraine

French (Lorrainoise)

I n these days of culinary one-upmanship, the savory baked custard tart known as quiche might include bits of almost anything: seafood, meats, vegetables, herbs, cheeses, and perhaps even fruit. But the one, the only, and still the most delectable

is the original quiche Lorraine, which to be truly authentic may include only bacon, eggs, cream, nutmeg, salt, and pepper.

Although the incident may have faded from memory, quiche became something of an American joke in 1982. The publication of Bruce Feirstein's bestselling book *Real Men Don't Eat Quiche,* a send-up of modern macho culture, succeeded for a while in branding the tart as sissy food—an undeserved slight for a delicious dish that has been around since the sixteenth century, when the French invented it in the northeastern city of Nancy, then the capital of the Lorraine region. (In an etymological twist that may only add fuel to the sissy-food fire, the word *quiche* is said to have been adapted from the German *küchen,* or cake; possibly because, though its pastry crust has long been

standard, quiche Lorraine was originally made with bread dough.)

Now a gender-neutral staple of brunch menus across America, it is usually accompanied by a green salad. More substantially and dramatically, in Lorraine it is traditionally served on May Day along with roast suckling pig in aspic.

WHERE: *In Paris,* Angelina, tel 33/1-42-60-82-00, angelina-paris.fr; *in New York,* François Payard Bakery, tel 212-956-1775, fpbnyc.com; *in Sonoma,* The Girl & The Fig, tel 707-938-3634, thegirlandthefig.com. **FURTHER INFORMATION AND RECIPES:** *Mastering the Art of French Cooking, Volume 1,* by Julia Child, Louisette Bertholle, and Simone Beck (1961); *The Country Cooking of France* by Anne Willan (2007); saveur.com (search quiche lorraine julia child).

THE LUXURY OF RADICAL SIMPLICITY

Radis au Beurre

Red Radishes with Butter

French

Although you'll find far more complex appetite awakeners in the pantheon of French hors d'oeuvres, few are as refreshing or as surprising as this one to the uninitiated. It is comprised merely of three simple ingredients: sharply pungent, ice-cold ruby-red radishes, a hearty sliver of smooth and creamy sweet butter; and a sprinkling of coarse sea salt.

To put it all together, cut off a small piece of butter, keeping it on the knife blade. Draw that blade right through a whole radish, leaving the butter behind. Sprinkle with salt, and bite in. That's all there is to it. The ingredients may be ordinary, but the mix—crunchy and smooth, radish-peppery, and butter-creamy—is pure sensory pleasure.

The only trick lies in getting the butter to stay put on the radish as you draw the knife through. For his NoMad restaurant, the inventive chef Daniel Humm cleverly molds the radishes in thimblelike cups of sweet butter, so all a diner has to do is dip into a tiny mound of sea salt. When you're making *radis au beurre* at

Fresh radishes are enhanced by salt and butter.

home, look for the long, tender, white-tipped French variety at farmers' markets in large cities or create an absolutely acceptable proxy with the ultra-common red American radish.

WHERE: *In New York,* NoMad, tel 347-472-5660, thenomadhotel.com.

A DISH TO ENGAGE THE FIVE SENSES

Ratatouille

French (Provençal)

This softly succulent vegetable stew has grown so common on restaurant menus we well might consider it a cliché, too often underappreciating its aesthetic appeal. Yet to anyone who delights in the sensual aspects of cookery, ratatouille offers irresistible rewards, not least of which is the fun of pronouncing its name. It begins with the ingredients, all candidates for a Dutch painter's still life—the shiny, black-purple eggplant contrasted with small gray-green zucchini, deep emerald peppers, scarlet-hued tomatoes, amber-skinned onions, paper-white slices of garlic, and flurries of forest-green parsley.

Next come the tactile elements, as one washes, cuts, slices, and dices each vegetable into its proper form. Once all is in the stew pot, sprinkled with coarse salt and freshly ground black pepper and anointed with good olive oil, the simmering begins. That's when the olfactory sense kicks in, as the garlic, oil, and vibrant freshness of the vegetables begin to blend and waft up the very essence of summer in Provence.

To know if the stew is cooking at the right speed, one need only listen for the *pil-pil* of burbling juices. Too strong a sound, and the flame is turned down; too faint, and the heat gets turned up. Finally, the sense of taste takes over. More salt? A few leaves of fresh basil? A drizzle of oil to smooth out flavor and texture? A dab of tomato paste to bind the whole, in case the vegetables are watery.

Now for improvisation and possibilities. Serve the fragrant ratatouille hot, warm, or cool, but never refrigerator-cold. Steaming hot, it provides a harmonious contrast to grilled or roasted lamb; add whole capers, chopped anchovy fillets, or pitted Niçoise olives for meaty texture and a zesty tingle. Combine room-temperature ratatouille with clumps of the best Mediterranean olive oil–packed tuna for a sustaining salad or as part of an hors d'oeuvre assortment. If the mix is juicy and hot, toss it into any cooked short pasta, such as penne, rigatoni, or fusilli, for a richly satisfying sauce. Or consider the Italian variation known as *cianfotta*, in which potatoes and celery add sustenance.

FURTHER INFORMATION AND RECIPES: *Mastering the Art of French Cooking, Volume 1,* by Julia Child, Louisette Bertholle, and Simone Beck (1961); saveur.com (search ratatouille provence).

A SECOND-MILKING CHEESE

Reblochon de Savoie

French

A fresh and airy flavor with a gentle pungency accounts for the widespread popularity of reblochon, an orange cheese with a pink blush, a slightly fluffy rind, and an unctuously supple pâte, developed in the mountains of Savoie.

Although today it's one of France's best-known cheeses, it wasn't always so.

Locals in its region of origin tell an age-old story about the days when farmers were taxed on the amount of milk they sold. Under the watch of the taxman, they'd pretend to drain their herd's supply, paying dues on their stock. Once the law enforcers departed, a second, secret milking was conducted, drawing milk that was higher in butterfat—and the farmers' wives used this richer milk to make the delightfully toothsome, creamy cheese that was eventually dubbed reblochon, from the verb

reblocher, literally, "to milk again."

Intended for consumption at home rather than for sale, the cheese was aged quickly and washed with brine, which accounts for its light piquancy and nutty overtones. Today, the proper aging period for A.O.C. Reblochon is between fifty and fifty-five days, which makes export tricky; U. S. Federal Drug Administration laws require that raw-milk cheeses age a minimum of sixty days. Some importers, drawing on the improvisatory thinking to which we owe the mountain cheese, have been known to ask producers to age reblochon just a few days longer to enable legal stateside import. If some of the resulting products make their way to you, look for a dry, light-brown rind and a creamy, ivory paste when making your selection, then allow the cheese to soften and ripen at room temperature for about two hours before serving.

WHERE: *In France*, visit the farms where reblochon is produced: reblochon.fr (click le Reblochon Fermier, Carte des Producteurs). **FURTHER INFORMATION:** *French Cheeses* by Kazuko Masui and Tomoko Yamada (1996); *Cheese Primer* by Steven Jenkins (1996).

A CRUSTY CASE FOR SWEETBREADS

Croustade de Ris de Veau à la Financière

French

This classic Belle Epoque dish, a savory blend of sweetbreads in a crisp pastry-shell mold, is as delectable today as it was in the heyday of Maxim's in Paris and Delmonico's in New York, and is often available on advance order from the most serious and traditional-minded French chefs. Though most of its ingredients are relatively easy to come by, it does contain a couple of surprises. Among its fixings are calf or lamb sweetbreads (the tender white thymus glands are blanched, sautéed in butter, then cut into supple nuggets), chicken or veal (to be shaped into tiny, light quenelle dumplings), fluted button mushroom caps and slivers of truffle, sautéed chicken livers, the makings of the puff pastry *bouchée* that houses it all, and as the finishing touch, cockscombs, the orangey, fleshy crests that crown roosters' heads (blanched and skinned to tender toothsomeness). That last component may sound exotic, if not downright lurid, but cockscombs are beginning to appear again at a few tapas-style restaurants around the U.S.

Bound with a rich brown Madeira sauce and dotted with minced black truffles, it does indeed make for a dish worthy of a financier.

FURTHER INFORMATION AND RECIPES: *Larousse Gastronomique* (2009); *A Guide to Modern Cookery* by Auguste Escoffier, H. L. Cracknell, and R. J. Kaufmann (2011).

THE BLESSING OF THE GOATS

Rocamadour

French

Just about two inches in diameter and a mere quarter inch thick, with an earthy, nutty flavor and a luxurious, dry yet spreadable interior, the tiny cakes of Rocamadour cheese deserve to be eaten crust and all for maximum appreciation.

Rocamadour clings to cliffs above the Alzou River.

These are the goats whose rich milk is the basis of about a dozen raw-milk cheeses that have distinguished the region of Quercy since the fifteenth century. There and in surrounding areas, these cheeses are known as *cabécou* (dialect for "a little goat"), and they are popular throughout south and southwest France. Rocamadour is the only *cabécou* to bear the Appellation d'Origine Contrôlée label that gives the cheese and its production techniques the serious imprimatur of French law.

When aged a mere two to three weeks, the soft, bite-size cheese develops a distinctly chestnutlike flavor; the longer it ages, the chewier it becomes and the more its exterior comes to resemble an actual chestnut shell, transforming from light beige to golden brown. Unfortunately, because rocamadour is aged for less than sixty days, it is unavailable in the U.S. When you're lucky enough to sample it in France, allow it to soften and ripen at room temperature for at least one hour before serving.

FURTHER INFORMATION: *French Cheeses* by Kazuko Masui and Tomoko Yamada (1996); *Cheese Primer* by Steven Jenkins (1996). **SPECIAL EVENT:** Fête des Fromages, Rocamadour, France, May or June, tel 33/5-65-33-22-00, fromages.rocamadour.free.fr.

Each Pentecost season in Rocamadour, a medieval town in the South of France, a distinctive sound rings out: the clip-clop of hooves clattering on stone streets as herds of small goats file in to receive their blessing, an event that signals the start of the annual Fête des Fromages, the region's largest cheese festival.

⊢||||||||||||||||||||||||||||||||⊣

"THE REASON GOD MADE CAVES."—STEVEN JENKINS, *CHEESE PRIMER*

Roquefort

French

The contrast of its teasingly sharp, salty blue-green mold with its firmly mellow white mass makes Roquefort one of the world's most sophisticated cheeses—and one that is oftentimes much too strong for novice palates. The mold also imparts a look of evil that, as is said about the oyster, makes one salute the brave man who first took a taste.

That act of bravery might have happened eons ago. According to a local legend, Roquefort was born of a happy accident in medieval times, when a smitten shepherd abandoned his lunch in a Combalou cave to search for a shepherdess. No one knows whether he found the lady, but when he returned to his cave some time later, he found his cheese covered in a blue-green mold—the distinctive *Penicillium roqueforti* fungus that gives Roquefort its hue. Amazingly enough, these caves are still the sole incubation point for the cheese's requisite mold. Today, all of the world's Roquefort emerges from the mythical shepherd's spot, a mile-and-a-half-long section of limestone caves near Roquefort-sur-Soulzon in southern France; that tiny stretch of caves also houses an intricate, modern network of offices, cellars, and ripening rooms occupied by seven cheese makers.

Roquefort's production is never left to chance. In preparation for cheese making, the native Lacaune sheep are strategically mated. Special loaves of rye are baked, left in the caves to rot, and broken in order to capture the necessary *Penicillium roqueforti*. As a product with Appellation d'Origine Contrôlée status—France's first cheese to receive the prestigious designation—Roquefort's point of origin, ingredients, and processing are also tightly regulated by French law. It's a complicated system for a complex cheese with a flavor that is at once spicy, tart, and salty. But not everything about Roquefort is difficult. Serving it is easy. When ripe, Roquefort deserves to be appreciated as a main event, at the end of a meal, when it can

Roquefort is aged for a minimum of three months.

deepen the flavor of anything with which it's paired, most successfully pears, grapes, walnuts, and Sauternes. When selecting Roquefort, look for copious blue-green streaks running to the edge of the bone-white, crumbly cheese.

Where: *In France,* sample Roquefort at its point of origin. Three cheese companies offer tours of their Combalou caves: Roquefort Papillon, tel 33/5-65-58-50-08, roquefort-papillon .com; Roquefort Gabriel Coulet, tel 33/5-65-59-90-21, gabriel-coulet.fr; Roquefort Société, tel 33/5-65-58-58-58, roquefort-societe.com. **Further information:** *French Cheeses* by Kazuko Masui and Tomoko Yamada (1996); *Cheese Primer* by Steven Jenkins (1996).

—|||||||||||||||||||||||||||||||||||—

TWIN PLEASURES FOR CHEESE LOVERS

Saint-Marcellin and Banon

French

Dipped in brandy or wine, enfolded in chestnut leaves, and tied with a raffia ribbon, this gently crumbly cheese has a piquancy that's reminiscent of damp autumn leaves and the crisp astringency of an early fall evening. Based on cow's

milk and virtually rindless, Saint-Marcellin was said to have been a favorite of the young King Louis XI. According to legend, the Dauphin's affection for the cheese stemmed

from the memorable experience of finding himself lost in the forest and at the mercy of a bear. Luckily, wandering woodsmen in the Dauphiné region of northern Provence spirited him to safety and served him bread and a local cheese—Saint-Marcellin.

Stateside and elsewhere today, you won't find the soft cow's milk cheese in its traditional leafy wrapping, but rather in small crocks, which, contrary to popular belief, in no way diminish the flavor. But if it's a leafy cheese that's desired, Saint-Marcellin's first cousin, Banon, may fit the bill. Artisans in Haute-Provence, Comtat, and Tricastin continue to wrap this raw goat's milk cheese in chestnut or grape leaves that have been soaked in eau-de-vie, imparting fruity, earthen flavors to the exterior that subtly filter within. Unfortunately, U.S. FDA laws require that raw-milk cheeses be aged a minimum of sixty days, a stipulation the exquisite Banons fail to meet. But in the U.S., excellent options do exist: Judy Schad of Indiana's Capriole Farms makes an outstanding variety called O'Banon, which is a noteworthy approximation of the real thing.

Both are crumbly and tart until ripe, when they become liquidy, golden, and appealingly fruity-woodsy in flavor.

WHERE: *In New York and environs,* Fairway markets, fairwaymarket.com. **MAIL ORDER:** Capriole Farms's O'Banon cheese, capriolegoat cheese.com. **FURTHER INFORMATION:** *French Cheeses* by Kazuko Masui and Tomoko Yamada (1996); *Cheese Primer* by Steven Jenkins (1996).

⊢||||||||||||||||||||||||||||||||⊣

A DAINTY CHEESE TO SET BEFORE A KING

Saint-Nectaire

French

This unctuous, semisoft, aromatic cow's milk cheese is said to have been a favorite of Louis XIV, although surely he was not the last *fine gueule* to prefer it. Traditionally, the earthy, woodsy cheese was produced on the high ridges of

France's central Auvergne region, where the cows feed on thick, rich, volcanic soil–lined pastures. A hearty cheese with a smooth, melting, velvet texture, it has a haunting mushroom-like flavor and reveals a creamy, straw-colored interior when cut. After it is made, the cheese is formed into three-and-a-half-pound rounds and then aged on rye mats in Auvergne's caves. There, the flavor of Saint-Nectaire is further developed by several strands of bacteria that also impart a distinctive reddish tint to its rind. (The noted cheese authority Mother Noella Marcellino, whose dissertation on French cheeses eventually led to the PBS documentary *The Cheese Nun,* located fourteen different strands of bacteria among the seven caves in which Saint-Nectaire ages.)

In 1955, the legendary cheese became the first farm-style cheese to receive the government's Appellation d'Origine Contrôlée (A.O.C.) designation protecting its point of origin, ingredients, and processing by law. As with many of Europe's greatest cheeses, U.S. FDA laws mean that Saint-Nectaire's most flavorful varieties aren't available in the U.S. Yet even the pasteurized versions sold in America hint at the complex flavors that make it the perfect companion for Auvergne's spicy red wine, Chanturgue.

WHERE: *In Farges, near Saint-Nectaire, France,* La Ferme Bellonte provides tours, tel 33/4-73-88-52-25. **FURTHER INFORMATION:** *French Cheeses* by Kazuko Masui and Tomoko Yamada (1996); *Cheese Primer* by Steven Jenkins (1996). **TIP:** When choosing Saint-Nectaire, look for a smooth, uncracked rind.

Salade Lyonnaise or Frisée aux Lardons

French (Lyonnaise)

"After all, it's only a salad," a naïve dieter might proclaim, presuming any dish bearing that name to be beneficently light and nonfattening. Just as long as there is plenty of greenery in view, never mind what is tucked beneath.

Let's hope the naïfs *do* go ahead and order this sumptuous salad from Lyon, the city famous for its lusty charcuterie and lavish cream-enhanced fare. More of a lunch main course than an appetizer, this salad combines springy frisée lettuce with a gently poached or boiled egg, the yolk still runny, and *lardons*. Chunks of sautéed chicken liver hidden under the greens add an even more velvety heft, and the whole is tossed with a red wine vinaigrette brightened by a hint of mustard and garlic.

In springtime, another version of this salad is made with the sprightly dandelion greens known as *pissenlits*—a play on wetting the bed that derives from the plant's alleged diuretic effect. Considering how much the runny egg yolks, the wilting fat of the fried lardons, and the red-wine-vinegar-and-olive-oil dressing do to relax and enhance the piquantly bitter greens, it's worth taking the risk.

Where: *In Lyon,* Daniel et Denise, tel 33/4-78-60-66-53, daniel-et-denise.fr; *in Paris,* Aux Lyonnais, tell 33/1-42-96-65-04, auxlyonnais .com; *in New York,* Bar Boulud, tel 212-595-0303, barboulud.com/nyc. **Further information and recipes:** *Daniel Boulud's Café Boulud Cookbook* by Daniel Boulud (1999); gourmet.com (search frisee salad with lardons and poached eggs).

Salsify, White and Black

The sweetly burnished earthiness of white salsify makes it a favorite winter root vegetable in many parts of Europe. Although popular in the U.S. in the early Colonial days, over time it practically disappeared. But the newly vegetable-conscious locavore movement has granted salsify a comeback, and it's become a favorite on menus and at farmers' market stands.

Tragopogan porrifolius, as the root is scientifically known, looks like a skinny white carrot or parsnip covered in long, hairy filaments, which account for its first name, *Tragopogan,* or goat's beard. Above ground, it sprouts the slender, green, leeklike leaves that are increasingly and delightfully finding their way into salads. Another name, oyster plant, indicates the saline essence that is a hallmark of salsify's flavor;

its German name, *schwarzwurzel,* or black root, refers both to its dark color (before its skin is scraped off) and to the way its cut flesh can quickly turn black due to oxidation. To prevent discoloration, keep the flesh acidulated with lemon juice or vinegar, or put it into a flour and water bath, just as you would with cardoons, artichokes, celery root, and parsnips.

Originating in the Near East, salsify began to be grown in central Europe in the sixteenth century and is now most popular in France, Germany, and other parts of northern Europe. Its root is delicious as a base for cream soups. In Germany, it is tossed with butter and toasted bread crumbs or baked au gratin under a cheese-glazed cream sauce.

A close first cousin is *Scorzonera hispanica,* or black salsify, a thicker, rounder, less tapered root also with a rough black-brown skin. Most popular in Spain and Italy, scorzonera distinguishes itself from its relative with an almost dairylike sweetness, but it lends its subtle earth overtones to the same preparations and requires identical precautions against discoloration of the flesh (including yours as you handle it).

As when shopping for any root vegetable, look for specimens that are full and firm, with no damp softness indicating rot, and avoid any that look dry or withered. Use a stainless-steel blade to scrape these roots, and, because the peeled and cut salsify should be cooked with a little lemon juice or vinegar, choose a cooking vessel made of a nonreactive material such as enameled cast iron, stainless steel, or glass.

Mail order: specialtyproduce.com (search salsify). **Further information and recipes:** *Vegetables from Amaranth to Zucchini* by Elizabeth Schneider (2001); saveur.com (search rarefied root chicken with salsify).

NICE'S ANSWER TO THE PIZZA

Socca

French (Provençal)

The tantalizingly crisp and peppery *socca* is a favorite in Nice toward the end of the day, when working people in need of sustenance unwind with a glass of the local light rosé wine or a beer. Similar to focaccia but thinner and crisper,

the warm pancakelike flatbread is based on a chickpea flour that lends an inviting grittiness to a dough made sprightly with salt, pungent with generous grindings of black pepper, and aromatic with olive oil and leaves of fresh rosemary. Here, as in Liguria, where the same flatbread is known as *farinata,* a piece is torn off the whole huge round and eaten out of hand.

Although socca is best when baked in a thin, round copper pan in a blazing wood-fired oven, as at the more traditional taverns (and is especially enticing when one has worked up an

At Chez Pipo, socca is baked in a huge copper pan.

appetite shopping at the festive outdoor food market along Nice's Cours Saleya), one can turn out fairly convincing substitutes at home. Because it is based on chickpea flour, socca is a treat for those on gluten-free diets. Just don't forget the glass of Provençal rosé.

WHERE: *In Nice,* Chez Pipo, tel 33/4-93-55-88-82, chezpipo.fr. **MAIL ORDER:** For chickpea flour, amazon.com (search bobs mill garbanzo flour). **FURTHER INFORMATION AND RECIPE:** *Flavors of the Riviera* by Colman Andrews (1996); saveur.com (search socca).

--||||||||||||||||||||||||||||||||||--

NOTHING BUT HOT AIR

Soufflés of All Sorts

French

I t's amazing what some hot air will do for a few simple eggs. Leave it to the frugal French to stretch the humblest of ingredients into a gourmet dish (generally with a gourmet price point attached). It's all a matter of physics, of course, the air beaten into egg whites that expand with heat, lifting the flavored egg yolk mix and causing the whole to take on an ethereal, cloudlike elegance.

As in the realm of physics, every little thing matters: the proportion of aerating egg whites to liquid egg-yolk flavoring; the amount of air beaten into the stiff, shiny whites; the oven temperature; the application of sugar (or bread crumbs, for a savory soufflé) to the inside of the mold so that the mass can gain purchase on the sides and rise; and the careful removal from the oven so that a sudden gust of cold air does not cause collapse.

While most soufflés take on the guise of sweet dessert, savory soufflés can make enticing first or main courses that are zesty with cheeses such as Gruyère, Parmesan, and even one of the pungently spicy blues if mollified with some heavy sweet cream and chives. Crumbles of salmon (smoked or fresh), crustaceans such as crab or lobster, finely puréed asparagus, spinach, or even game meats, poultry, or calf's brains with black truffles—all can be worked into airy triumphs, each properly herb-seasoned.

But it is as desserts that soufflés most often enchant. Think dark, bittersweet chocolate, just a bit molten at the center; the more sophisticated overtones of coffee, or orangey Grand Marnier, or kirsch-spiked strawberries; sun-gold apricots; autumn chestnuts with their woodsy tang; even the sweet plainness of vanilla. Some like their soufflés cooked through until they are

Lemon soufflé is delicately inviting.

slightly spongy at the center, while others maintain they should be a bit unset and runny. All agree that, when sprinkled with sugar for a crystalline finish, and served with appropriate sauces or just softly whipped cream on the side, a soufflé dessert is what lies at the end of the gustatory rainbow.

Years ago, the New York restaurant La Grenouille found a way to make it easy to sample multiple soufflé iterations in one go. Its kitchen still turns out so-called harlequin soufflés, half-and-half flavor combinations achieved with the placement of a piece of parchment or wax paper down the center of the mold. The two flavors of mix can then be poured in, one on each side. Halfway through the baking, when the mix has set, the paper is pulled out, to magical effect. Here's to a dream of infinite soufflés.

Where: *In New York,* La Grenouille, tel 212-752-1495, la-grenouille.com. **Further information and recipes:** *Mastering the Art of French Cooking, Volume 1,* by Julia Child, Louisette Bertholle, and Simone Beck (1961).

"THE BEST KIND OF ONION SOUP IS THE SIMPLEST KIND."—AMBROSE BIERCE

Soupe à l'Oignon

French

Once upon a very long time ago in fine French restaurants, onion soup was served without the gratinéed cheese and bread topping that is now ubiquitous; as appealing as that gooey topping may be, it renders the soup much too heavy as

a precursor to a substantial main course. The now-prevalent version gained popularity in the bistros of the Parisian wholesale vegetable market, Les Halles, where in the wee hours it was a single course, believed to be an antidote to a night of heavy drinking. But in formal restaurants, onion soup used to be ladled out into wide soup plates, with bowls of grated Gruyère or Emmental, or French Comté cheese and some toasty croutons on the side. Special care in preparation gave the soup a richness and shimmer of its own.

As with so many dishes, its popularization led to an overall decline in its quality. Renditions became either too bland and devoid of onions, or so intensely dark brown and matted with onions that they seemed more like gravy. Even worse were the onion soups based on metallic-tasting canned or dehydrated bases.

Like all seemingly simple dishes, perfect onion soup allows little margin for error. For

There's no need to coat onion soup with cheese.

starters, the onions should be deep yellow in color, meaning that they have aged and lost much of their water; this is how they gain a high concentration of the sugar that, when caramelized, imparts a rich golden brown color and deep, multilayered flavor to the broth. Thinly sliced, the onions are slowly sweated in butter in a heavy saucepan or soup pot, for about

35 minutes. The pot should be closely watched and frequently stirred until the onions turn a bright, deep gold with just a hint of brown, but never black—although the exact shade may vary with the cook's palate. Some add a pinch of sugar to the browning step to speed the coloring, but usually the onions need no such help.

Next, they are sprinkled with a little flour to bind the final result, and then they are doused with hearty beef stock, alone or in a half-and-half blend with water and a splash of dry white wine. The mixture is simmered, half-covered, for 30 to 45 minutes. If not served immediately it gets a final reheating, and the flavor is adjusted with salt, freshly ground pepper, and a shot of Cognac, Calvados, or kirsch—or, for milder tastes, sherry or Madeira. These days the preferred cheese may be Parmesan, but Gruyère, Comté, and Emmental are far more subtle, allowing the other flavors to be more discernible.

Those who prefer onion soup gratinéed should pour each portion into fireproof crocks made especially for this purpose, and place a crouton of bread browned in olive oil or butter and a blanket of grated cheese on top. The crocks then go under the broiler until the topping is a molten golden brown.

Further information and recipes: *Mastering the Art of French Cooking, Volume 1,* by Julia Child, Louisette Bertholle, and Simone Beck (1961); smittenkitchen.com (search french onion soup).

⊣||||||||||||||||||||||||||||⊢

PROVENCE BY THE BOWLFUL

Soupe au Pistou

French (Provençal)

If summer doesn't sound like soup season, you've probably never sampled Provence's colorful and fragrant *soupe au pistou,* the classic country vegetable-and-bean stew enhanced with a *pistou* sauce of basil, garlic, and olive oil.

In the Provençal dialect, *pistou* also stands for the pestle that, along with a mortar, mashes that basil, garlic, and olive oil into a velvety, verdant seasoning. The paste, of course, is similar to a sauce made famous by the neighboring Italians of Liguria—pesto (see page 223). In fact, this summer favorite is a first cousin to Italy's minestrone, no coincidence given that all of this region once belonged to the House of Savoy and these lands share the same Mediterranean climate.

Soupe au pistou is at once homey and chic.

As with any beloved local specialty, soupe au pistou has many variations. At its most basic, it begins with the creamy local white beans known as *coco blanc* and the tan beans called *coco rouge.* The beans are sautéed with onions (some cooks add bacon, pancetta, or even a pig's foot at this stage for flavoring), and then the vegetables are slowly added to the pot—while nonnegotiables are green beans, potatoes, and tomatoes, other favorites include leeks, squash, zucchini, and carrots. (The only no-nos are vegetables that would bleed and overpower the base, such as spinach.) Depending on the cook, water or chicken stock goes in, and then it's time for the pasta—most traditionally, the thinnest angel-hair strands at the end of the cooking process, but some prefer elbow macaroni or small shells.

The cook can choose to make a version that's almost fancy by trimming the vegetables to uniform sizes, or utterly rustic by throwing in the ingredients in various shapes. Either way, the final texture should be thick enough to allow a spoon to stand tall, and the single most important moment is the addition of the pistou: It must be added as late in the process as possible, after the soup has been removed from the stove, and preferably at the table. (A sprinkling of Parmesan may be added at this time, too.) This timing ensures that none of the garlic's bite or the basil's intense sweetness can cook off, lending the soup a marvelous brightness of flavor. Something magical happens when the raw sauce hits the hot liquid and the tender beans

and vegetables—and it's this moment that turns the soup from a winter warmer into a warm-weather delight. Indeed, this soup is an ideal evocation of the lushness of late summer when it is served at room temperature, or even a little cooler, as is minestrone in Milan.

WHERE: *In Mougins, France,* Le Bistrot de Mougins, tel 33/4-93-75-78-34, lebistrotdemougins .com; *in New York,* Café Boulud, tel 212-772-2600, cafeboulud.com/nyc; *in New Orleans,* La Provence, tel 985-626-7662, laprovencerestaurant .com; *in Roseville, CA,* La Provence Restaurant & Terrace, tel 916-789-2002, laprovenceroseville .com. **FURTHER INFORMATION AND RECIPES:** *Daniel Boulud's Café Boulud Cookbook* by Daniel Boulud (1999); *Glorious French Food: A Fresh Approach to the Classics* by James Peterson (2002); gourmet.com (search soupe au pistou).

‖‖‖‖‖‖‖‖‖‖‖‖‖‖‖‖‖‖‖‖‖‖‖‖‖‖‖

A SOUP FIT FOR A PALACE

Soupe aux Truffes Noires V.G.E.

French

To celebrate being awarded the French Legion of Honor in 1975 by France's then president, Valéry Giscard d'Estaing, Paul Bocuse was invited to prepare a meal at the presidential residence, the Elysée Palace. Rising to the occasion,

the famed chef created an almost indecently tantalizing soup that has since become a classic at his three-star restaurant in Collonges-au-Mont-d'Or, just outside of Lyon.

Bocuse took the big, round, ovenproof footed bowl known as a *gratinée lyonnaise* and filled it with a heady chicken stock bolstered by sautéed mushrooms, carrots, and onions—and then added thick slices of Périgord's black winter truffles and lumps of goose foie gras. He capped the whole with a dome of puff pastry and baked it all together until the soup was fuming with fragrance and the dome emerged as a flaky, golden crust. When that crust was opened, the dizzying, ecstatic aroma made the act of

A lofty pastry crown on a fragrant soup

sniffing almost as fulfilling as that of eating. It still does.

WHERE: *In Collonges-au-Mont-d'Or, France,* L'Auberge du Pont de Collonges, tel 39/4-72-42-90-90, bocuse.fr. **FURTHER INFORMATION AND RECIPE:** theworldwidegourmet.com (search black truffle soup elysee). **SEE ALSO:** Truffe Noires de Périgord, page 140; Tartufi de Alba, page 243.

THE CLASSIC BISTRO MAIN COURSE

Steak Frites

French

Asked what dishes they favor when eating at home, innumerable and diverse chefs cite four choices: omelets, roast chicken, thinly sliced rare roast beef, and steak frites. The last is a classic on the menus of just about every French bistro anywhere in the world.

What of the steak itself? If the bistro is upscale, in France, and warrants healthy prices, the beef should be identified as Charolais, a white, grass-fed steer bred around the Burgundian town for which it is named. It is France's best breed of beef cattle and, according to some, is a more flavorful choice than even Argentina's much-vaunted specimens. Succulently marbled, the glorious beef may lack that unctuous tenderness Americans prize so highly, but it more than makes up for it with a rich and quintessential beefy essence. A little extra chewing never hurt anyone.

The kindest cut is also a deviation from the American standards of porterhouse, sirloin, and filet mignon, which are all hindquarter cuts. While upscale restaurants might present the luxurious chateaubriand, the classic French bistro cut is the delicately marbled entrecôte, or rib steak, carved from the four quarters, generally from just between the shoulders. Left on the bone to ensure a tantalizing ripe aroma and flavor, the meat is grilled in the French manner, on a hot iron skillet with a raised grid pattern that produces crisscross sear marks—there is no charcoal overwhelming the beef with acrid charring.

As for the degree of doneness, you have a choice: *bleu,* meaning it will be blue, cold, and raw inside; *saignant* for blood-rare and slightly warm at the center; *à point* for medium rare; or *bien cuit,* so well-done you might as well have ordered pot roast. Neither a generous dab of the parsley- and lemon juice–accented butter known as maître d'hôtel, nor the more elaborate warm, pungent tarragon-and-shallot-spiked béarnaise will hurt a bit. Then all that is needed is a mound of the crisp thin *pommes frites* we call French fries and a glass or two of a strong red wine.

FURTHER INFORMATION AND RECIPES: *Roast Chicken and Other Stories* by Simon Hopkinson (2007); foodandwine.com (search raichlen steak friles). **SEE ALSO:** Hanger Steak, Flank Steak, and Skirt Steak, page 578.

An indisputable classic, steak frites appear on countless bistro menus.

||||||||||||||||||||||||||||||||||

CHEF, YOUR PIZZA IS ON FIRE!

Tarte Flambée Alsacienne

French (Alsatian)

A s flatbread pies go, Italian pizza is far more ubiquitous, but Alsace's flaming cheese-and-bacon tart is rapidly gaining ground in the U.S. And no wonder—it's a luscious, palate-intriguing combination that melds thin, free-form dough,

charred crisp, with melting *fromage blanc* (a slightly ripe pot-cheese), crème fraîche, slivers of crisp bacon, and shreds of lightly roasted onion. A sprinkling of aromatic peanut oil, nutmeg, salt, and freshly ground pepper ties it all together into a salty and addictive snack.

Tarte flambée alsacienne, also known as *flammeküche*, gained early popularity in the United States at the landmark French restaurant Lutèce, now closed. André Soltner, the Alsatian-born chef who reigned over its kitchen from the 1960s to the mid-'90s, intermittently offered the tart as an appetizer or an amuse-bouche. (For the latter, he prepared it with a delicate puff pastry crust rather than the more traditional bread dough.)

A late-night favorite at brasseries throughout Alsace, the flaming tart is so named because it is

Intense heat ensures a crisp edge and soft center.

(or should be) baked close to very hot, burning embers in a brick oven. It presents only one dilemma: whether to wash it down with a crystalline white such as a riesling or sylvaner, or with the foamy, golden local beer for which Alsace is equally famous.

WHERE: *In New York,* The Bar at MoMA, tel 212-333-1220, the modernnyc.com; *in Chicago and Boston,* Brasserie Jo, brasseriejo .com; *in Costa Mesa, CA*, Marché Moderne, 714-434-7900, marche moderne.net. **FURTHER INFORMATION AND RECIPES:** *The Cuisine of Alsace* by Pierre Gaertner and Robert Frederick (1981); *The Lutèce Cookbook* by André Soltner with Seymour Britchky (1995); saveur.com (search tarte flambee). **SPECIAL EVENT:** Tarte Flambée Festival, Munster, Alsace, July and August, tourisme-alsace.com.

||||||||||||||||||||||||||||||||||

BY ANY NAME, A SAVORY SNACK

Tarte à l'Oignon

French (Alsatian)

Y ou say onion, I say *oignon*. No matter which way it's ordered—as *tarte à l'oignon*, as *zwiebelkuchen,* or as *zewelwai,* depending on the region—this sweetly fragrant, savory tart is well worth the potential pronunciation challenge.

An aromatic kissing cousin to the quiche Lorraine (see page 123), this onion tart is actually a silky, open-face pie filled with a rich egg-bacon-and-onion custard.

The preparation of the onions is essential to the success of this restorative and homey dish. Alsatian cooks say those onions must be very thinly sliced and then slowly, slowly sweated in goose fat (although butter will do) until they melt into lacy filaments. "There should be a lot of creamy filling on very little pastry," wrote Elizabeth David in her classic *French Provincial Cooking*. And indeed there is, although the Alsatian onion tart is not as deep as a traditional quiche. The custard itself is gently set, a texture that's the result of more onions than cream in the mix. That ratio also defines the tart's flavor, the sweetness of the onions contrasting with the salty smokiness of the bacon, the whole spiked with thyme and sometimes anchovy.

WHERE: *In Bergheim, France,* Wistub du Sommelier, 33/3-89-73-69-99, wistub-du-somme lier.com; *in Paris,* Angelina, tel 33/1-42-60-82-00, angelina-paris.fr; *in New York,* The Modern at MoMA, tel 212-333-1220, themodernnyc.com; *in Las Vegas,* Fleur, tel 702-632-9400, hubertkeller .com. **FURTHER INFORMATION AND RECIPES:** *The Lutèce Cookbook* by André Soltner with Seymour Britchky (1995); *French Provincial Cooking* by Elizabeth David (1999); foodandwine.com (search alsatian onion tart); epicurious.com (search alsatian onion and bacon tartlets).

⊢||||||||||||||||||||||||||||||⊣

THE OTHER APPLE PIE

Tarte Tatin

French

An elegantly royal take on apple pie, the exquisite *tarte Tatin* deserves a place in dessert paradise. The name honors the sisters Tatin, the proprietors of a restaurant near Orléans who devised the dessert in the early 1900s. The recipe

begins simply enough, with flavorful apples of the not-too-juicy variety, sliced and seasoned with melted butter, sugar, and cinnamon and laid in a heavy butter-and-sugar-lined skillet. Topped with a round of buttery pie-crust pastry, the whole is baked until the crust has crisped and the apples turn golden and sweetly syrupy.

Then comes the moment of drama. The whole tart-filled pan—hot and heavy—is inverted onto a serving platter. What emerges, hopefully, are silken, golden-caramelized apples atop an unbroken bronze crust. Those in search of the cleanest, roundest form should stick with the dry golden delicious apples, while those willing to take a risk on shape for the sake of flavor should opt for Northern Spies or Cortlands, both at their best in Fall.

Use either large chunks of fruit or thin slices.

Most delicious and aromatic when warm, the tarte Tatin needs only a cool splash of crème fraîche or half-whipped, unsweetened cream as a topping, although a small scoop of slightly softened vanilla ice cream can't hurt. A nice thick wedge of the tart and a cup of coffee makes a decadent special-occasion breakfast.

FURTHER INFORMATION AND RECIPES: *Mastering the Art of French Cooking, Volume 1,* by Julia Child, Louisette Bertholle, and Simone Beck (1961); *Larousse Gastronomique* (2009); tarte tatin.org; jamesbeard.org (search tarte tatin).

A GREEN VEGETABLE FOR DESSERT

Tourte de Blettes Sucrée

French (Provençal)

M any a modern chef would be celebrated for having invented such an unexpected application for Swiss chard, served as a dessert in this mildly sweet and seductive pastry. Sound strange? It's divine. The flaky dough wrapping

contrasts with softly wilted leaves of the bittersweet chard, enhanced by dottings of pine nuts and golden raisins. A bit of brown sugar, brandy or rum, butter and olive oil, and a binding of eggs and grated Parmesan cheese work their magic. The thin dessert is served sprinkled with confectioners' sugar and cut into squares at many bistros and street stands in Provence. It is particularly evident at outdoor food markets along the Cours Saleya in Nice, where it shines among the other tempting street foods.

Tourte de blettes in official French becomes *la tourta de blea* in the dialect of Provence, which claims this verdant creation as its own. It can also be made in a *salée,* or savory, version that omits the sugar, liquor, and raisins and incorporates rice and Parmesan cheese. Eaten as an appetizer, a main dish, or en plein air as a picnic item, the dish is usually served at room temperature.

Tourte de blettes *sucrée* may seem like a cutting-edge dessert, now that parents are trying to get their children to eat more healthfully and following the advice of cookbooks that tell them to sneak in the veggies using culinary subterfuge (contaminating brownies with the addition of spinach, for instance). But parents may be so

Greens and sweet pastry prove a delectable pair.

carried away with this enticing pastry that there will be little left for the kids.

FURTHER INFORMATION AND RECIPES: *Flavors of the Riviera* by Colman Andrews (1996); epicurious.com (search swiss chard raisin pine nut tart).

"IF I CANNOT HAVE TOO MANY TRUFFLES, I WILL DO WITHOUT TRUFFLES."—COLETTE

Truffes Noires de Périgord

French

There probably is no flavor more difficult to describe than that of the whole, fresh winter black truffle—*Tuber melanosporum*—associated with France's Périgord region. For what a great black truffle tastes like is a great black truffle. Dug up from the ground between November and January in damp, leafy forests by trained pigs and, more often now, by dogs, this costly fungus looks like a mottled lump of coal and has a somewhat wet and earthy flavor. Its mysterious, sweet but musty essence and firm but yielding texture link it to its mushroom relatives, but it has a nose-twitching aroma all its own.

Because of the black truffle's high price, one often sees pâtés and sauces, pastas, salads, and even ice cream flavored with the tiniest of its shavings or peelings (or, unfortunately, with a synthetic truffle oil with an overpowering, nauseatingly larger-than-life scent)—contributing perhaps less, in these cases, to flavor than to a perception of value that allows restaurateurs and chefs to charge more for their truffle-infused offerings.

Practically, of course, it makes sense to use whatever one can to impart the truffle's exquisite flavor—even its aroma can be harnessed to the cook's advantage. Place a truffle or any part of one in a closed container with whole raw eggs for two or three days and the scent will permeate the shells and deliciously perfume the eggs; try them softly scrambled with a touch of cream, or fried in butter. Similarly, a truffle buried in raw rice and kept in a tightly closed jar seasons the grains, which can then be worked into a savory risotto. The truffle itself remains available for other uses, protected by the rice so that it stays dry, its precious fragrance intact.

But practicality has its critics. Expounding on the scourge of scrimpy truffle tactics, the inimitable Colette had this to say: "You pay its weight in gold, then in most cases you put it to paltry use. You smear it with foie gras, you bury it in poultry overloaded with fat, you chop it up and drown it in brown sauce, you mix it with vegetables covered in mayonnaise. . . . To hell with thin slices, strips, trimmings, and peelings of truffles! Is it not possible to like them for themselves?"

Not only possible, but essential. The only way to really understand the truffle's magic and firmly fix it in your mind's palate is to have one whole, perfect specimen all to yourself. It should be brushed or peeled of its rough outer surface, then coated with a bit of goose or duck fat and wrapped in cooking parchment to be roasted under white-hot ashes—*sous cindres*. Or simmer the cleaned whole truffle in butter, goose fat, and Madeira. Taste that once, and you will surely make plans to taste it twice.

Tuber melanosporum is not the only variety of truffle, but it is by all accounts the finest. Italy's white truffles of Alba—*Tuber magnatum* (see page 243)—have their own vibrantly dazzling attributes, but cannot approach their French cousins when it comes to elegant complexity and a gloriously decadent richness. And as for the so-called summer truffle—*Tuber aestivum*—the name is a euphemism for bland impostors dug up between May and September, and very short on flavor and aroma. As romantic as they sound, summer truffles are usually the ones you find for sale in jars at airport gift shops.

Though not all of the so-called Périgord truffles are actually dug up in that southwestern region of France (most come from surrounding areas but are processed and marketed at the big truffle fair held in Périgord every December), that regional stamp still holds sway. Anything simply called a "black winter truffle" is probably the product of another region or country altogether; these days, truffles are being cultivated "in the wild"—close to the trees that best nurture them—in places as far away as Oregon and China.

Where: *In Paris,* La Maison de la Truffe, tel 33/1-42-65-53-22, maison-de-la-truffe.com. **Mail order:** urbani.com (search fresh black winter truffles). **Further information:** *The Oxford Companion to Food* by Alan Davidson (1999); thenibble.com (search types of truffles: a glossary, black truffles). **Tip:** Explore truffle lore, cultivation, and cookery at two truffle museums in France—Maison de la Truffe et du Tricastin in Saint-Paul-Trois-Châteaux, tel 33/4-75-96-61-29, maisondelatruffe .com; Écomusée de la Truffe in Sorges, tel 33/5-53-05-90-11, ecomusee-truffe-sorges.com.

CATCHING A LIVE ONE

Truite au Bleu

French, German

Timing is all, in the preparation of this striking dish, which translates to "blue trout." In order for the trout to turn the proper shade of brilliant sapphire, it must be alive until it is eviscerated, and then sent to the *poissonnière* within ten

minutes at the most. The chemical reaction between the traditional vinegar bath and substances on the fish's skin creates the azure tone—proof that the fish indeed was alive moments before it was cooked. Another piece of proof: The trout's body forms a circle,

The trout must be handled briefly and skillfully.

indicating the final response of its still-vibrant nervous system to contact with the simmering water.

What may seem like gratuitous ghoulishness is really a necessary path to the sweet-flavored tenderness that this most delicate of freshwater fish deserves. Lightly poached, then doused with a little lemon juice, melted butter, and flakes of freshly grated horseradish, blue trout is an elegant dish. At the Mönchs Posthotel in the little Bavarian spa town of Bad Herrenalb, a net full of live trout is held in a stream that runs by the premises so the fish can be caught as they are ordered as Blaugekochte Forelle. In a city or restaurant, the trout must swim in a tank in the kitchen.

Connoisseurs of this dish are on to pseudo blue trout, presented with its tail tightly clamped in its mouth—a sign that the long-dead fish was thus arrayed by a cunning chef prior to cooking. To say nothing of the fact that the impostor fish's skin is more silvery than blue.

WHERE: *In Bad Herrenalb, Germany,* Mönchs Posthotel, tel 49-7083-7440; *in Strasbourg, France,* Maison des Tanneurs, tel 33/3-88-32-79-70, maison-des-tanneurs.com; *in Queens, NY,* M. Wells Steakhouse, tel 718-786-9060, magasinwells.com. **FURTHER INFORMATION AND RECIPE:** *The German Cookbook* by Mimi Sheraton (2014); cookitsimply.com (search truite au bleu).

THE FRENCH LOST A BATTLE, THE WORLD GAINED A STEW

Sauté de Veau Marengo

French

Call it snatching a culinary victory from the jaws of defeat. The apocryphal story has it that Napoleon's Swiss cook, flustered as the French army was losing the Battle of Marengo to the Italians in 1800, searched for ingredients he could combine to take the general's mind off his troubles. Some say he came up with veal, others say it was chicken, but all seem to agree that he magically also found tomatoes, small white onions, and mushrooms, and threw them into the sauté pan, adding white wine so the whole could braise into what we now consider a stew.

No matter which meat is used, much of this dish's deep, rich flavor comes from the slow sautéeing of individual ingredients. Thus onions and mushrooms are gilded in hot butter and then set aside while the browned meat simmers for a while with tomatoes, thyme, garlic, parsley, bay leaf, and crushed shallots. The browned mushrooms and onions are added for a final heating before the stew is served with thin slices of bread that have been skillet-browned in olive oil, a finishing touch highly recommended in *The Alice B. Toklas Cookbook,* a delicious collection of recipes that Toklas prepared for her life partner, Gertrude Stein, and their famous guests.

According to *Larousse Gastronomique,* the chicken version requires garnishes of crayfish, deep-fried eggs, truffles, and croutons. One wonders where even the wiliest cook would find all of those amid post-battle disarray—but then, of course, they were in Italy. Origin stories aside, we prize this dish not for its colorful history, but rather for its temptingly aromatic appeal and the soothing sustenance it provides, to say nothing of its convenience as a main course that can be prepared well ahead of time, if desired.

FURTHER INFORMATION AND RECIPES: *The Alice B. Toklas Cookbook* by Alice B. Toklas (2010); *Mastering the Art of French Cooking, Volume 1,* by Julia Child, Louisette Bertholle, and Simone Beck (1961); cuisine-france.com (search veal marengo); epicurious.com (search chicken marengo).

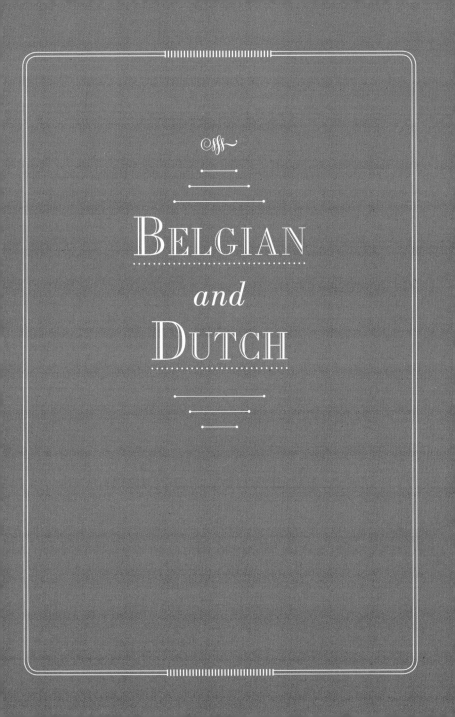

BELGIAN

and

DUTCH

|||||||||||||||||||||||||||||||||

Café Liégeois

Belgian

A longside such lush coffee-dessert drinks as the Italian *affogato* (see page 163) and the Viennese *einspanner* (see page 320), this Belgian counterpart holds its own. Its requirements are good, strong, slightly bitter coffee syrup, mocha ice cream, and a cloud of freshly whipped heavy sweet cream. The ice cream goes into a tall parfait glass, with syrup poured over and whipped cream crowning the effort. As the ice cream melts and mingles with the coffee syrup, additional reward comes by way of an excruciatingly delicious sauce. Although it's not traditional, a shot of dark rum or aged brandy adds sophisticated overtones, and a thin, crisp *gaufrette* wafer adds textural contrast.

Contrary to its name, the *café liégeois* was not created in Liège. In fact, it was originally known in France as a *café viennois* (Viennese coffee). However, during World War I, with the Battle of Liège in full swing and Vienna representing the enemy, Parisian cafés started renaming the dessert café liégeois in honor of Belgium's embattled forts. Curiously, for a while at least, in Liège itself it continued to be known as café viennois.

WHERE: *In La Quinta, CA,* for Barcelona Liégeois, Figue, tel 760-698-9040, eatfigue.com. **FURTHER INFORMATION AND RECIPES:** diplomatic kitchen.com (search cafe liegeois); chefde melogue.com (click April Archive, find April 2013 post).

|||||||||||||||||||||||||||||||||

Callebaut Chocolate

Belgian

F amous for his extraordinary prowess as a detective, Hercule Poirot is also known for his fondness for hot chocolate, which he takes with brioche at breakfast. Given how finicky Agatha Christie's Belgian hero is about food, one can only assume that, although he lives in London, he has remained loyal to the exquisite Callebaut chocolate from his homeland—made for more than 150 years in a country long noted for that elegant treat.

A favorite of pastry chefs and confectioners, Callebaut owes its deep, rich overtones to the finest grinding of selected roasted cocoa beans. The superfine grind releases layers of subtle flavors, with pure cocoa butter and a hint of natural vanilla adding harmonious undertones.

Whether you're cooking with chocolate or just eating it, for best results you'll want to buy it in the large professional bittersweet blocks and knock off chunks as effectively as you can (the blocks can be hard to break). (Connoisseurs will shun Callebaut's milk and white chocolates as the depressing interlopers they are.) Nibble away and you will be rewarded: The chocolate will begin to melt upon hitting your tongue, one of the marks of a good-quality product that has been well tempered with the right amount of cocoa butter. Lesser specimens, over-tempered to prolong shelf life, take longer to melt and one can feel a sort of skin developing on the tongue before the chocolate finally dissolves.

For the fullest and most direct experience of Callebaut's excellence, take a cue from Poirot, whose hot chocolate is surely made from a bittersweet block melted in a double boiler with a couple of splashes of heavy sweet cream, then whisked into simmering-hot whole milk. Hold the marshmallow, but please do add the brioche.

MAIL ORDER: World Wide Chocolate, tel 603-942-6032, worldwidechocolate.com (click Callebaut). **FURTHER INFORMATION AND RECIPES:** For an almost endless array of delectable chocolate preparations, callebaut.com (click Recipes). **SEE ALSO:** Lindt Chocolate (page 331).

---------||||||||||||||||||||||||||||||||---------

A BREWER'S STEW OF BEEF OR BOAR

Carbonnade à la Flamande, or Vlaamse Karbonaden

Belgian

Carbonnade à la flamande in French-speaking Belgium, *vlaamse karbonaden* in Flemish . . . Whichever language you're speaking, beer is of the essence in this succulent, darkly rich and malty stew that joins meat, vegetables, and a hunk of gingerbread for a dish that is a satisfying multicourse meal in a pot.

Belgium produces an array of complex wheat- and barley-based beers, many of them sweet and some flavored with fruit, such as Kriek, with its winey overtones of sour cherries. For this stew, the wisest choice would be the dry and complex Duvel; its deeply smoky flavors mellow the meaty essence of tender beef chuck (or, for more exotic tastes, wild boar, a

game meat that is much loved and well prepared in Belgium, as well as in Holland).

Many chefs favor dark Belgian abbey beers for beef carbonnade.

Cut into 2-inch cubes and dredged in flour, the meat is lightly seared in butter among softening onions and garlic, with bay leaf, thyme, and peppercorns, before simmering gently in a bath of beer and beef stock. When the meat is falling-apart soft, the stew is thickened and mellowed with a crust of spicy brown gingerbread that disintegrates in the sauce. Balancing doses of brown sugar and red wine vinegar are gradually stirred in.

Although *pommes frites* are usually served alongside the dish, mashed or boiled potatoes are more useful sops for the luscious gravy; red cabbage cooked with sour apples would also not go amiss. Obviously, beer is the thing to drink, preferably the same one used in cooking.

So beloved is this dish in the Flemish kitchen that it is difficult to imagine any so-called Belgian restaurant, anywhere in the world, *not* offering beef carbonnade on its menu. Economical and restorative—especially in winter—the stew is also a boon to the home cook as an easy-to-serve, easy-to-time company dish that lends itself especially well to advance preparation.

WHERE: *In Brussels*, Aux Armes de Bruxelles, tel 32/2-511-5598, auxarmesdebruxelles.com/en; *in the U.K.* at several locations, Belgo, belgo-restaurants.co.uk; *in New York*, Petite Abeille at several locations, petiteabeille.com; Markt, tel 212-727-3314, marktrestaurant.com; *in Washington, D.C.*, Belga Café, tel 202-544-0100, belgacafe.com. **FURTHER INFORMATION AND RECIPES:** *Everybody Eats Well in Belgium Cookbook* by Ruth Van Waerebeek and Maria Robbins (1996); saveur.com (search carbonnade flemish beef and beer stew).

THIS IS HOW THE COOKIE CRUMBLES

Destrooper's Gemberkoekjes

Ginger Thins

Belgian

S ay it in Flemish (*gemberkoekjes*) or say it in French (*biscuits de gingembre*). By any name, these rectangular, crackling-thin, peppery cookies are teasingly addictive—and they're among the very few packaged cookies that really retain

crispness and freshness and seem convincingly homemade.

The pungent cookies' high quality speaks to the company behind them: Jules Destrooper NV, also bakers of other *klein koekjes*—small cakes, some waffled, others mellowed with almonds or cinnamon, but none quite as special as these gingery, parchment-thin wafers. Spices were apparently an obsession of the company's founder, who traveled to Africa and the Far East gathering exotic spices to enhance his baking hobby before opening his first biscuiterie in 1886. Among ingredients such as

flour, butter, sugar, cinnamon, salt, and ginger extract, these fragile cookies develop their nicely stinging, peppery essence from high-quality powdered ginger zapped with flecks of jewellike, pale golden candied ginger root.

As difficult as it is to keep from eating every ginger thin in sight once that fetching blue-and-white box has been opened (encouraged, no doubt, by the skinny cookies' attractively low calorie count), it's a good idea to reserve a few. It would be a shame not to have any left for nibbling with a cup of hot tea, or to crumble over vanilla ice cream. Those given to cookie construction might consider carefully spreading the thins with the merest veneer of whipped cream cheese or soft lemon curd. Or, the experimentally inclined could serve a few alongside a bowl of thick and creamy pea soup that just might profit from a spark of ginger and a subtly sweet crispness.

Mail order: amazon.com (search jules destrooper ginger thins). **Tip:** Like all packaged butter cookies, gemberkoekjes taste best after being unwrapped and left to sit on a plate for about ten minutes before they are eaten.

------||||||||||||||||||||||||||||||||||||------

HIDDEN FROM THE SUN

Endive au Jambon Sauce Mornay

Endive with Ham and Mornay Sauce

Belgian

Americans call it endive, Europeans say chicory. In French it's *chicorée de Bruxelles,* and in Flanders it is *witloof,* or "white leaf." Whatever it is called, the ivory stalk is generally thought of as Belgian, although it's now grown in many other places using a technique that's been in practice since Roman times, when white was considered a premium color for food.

To this day, to enhance the endive's pale hue and satiny sheen, farmers plant its young roots in cellar-caves, or under coverings of sand, soil, or cardboard. The idea, as with white asparagus (see page 159), is to prevent light from reaching the leaves, lest they turn green as chlorophyll develops. Apparently, the trick was rediscovered by accident in 1830 in Belgium, when the director of a botanical garden uncovered forgotten roots that had sprouted yellow-tipped leaves.

Endives baked with ham and cheese

Some of us know endive leaves, with their gently bitter flavor and mildly crisp texture, mainly as a raw component in our salad bowls, but in many parts of Europe they are braised, sautéed, or baked. Among the most elegant preparations may be the French-Belgian dish *endive au jambon sauce Mornay.* Dabbed with butter and baked under parchment until they begin to soften, the split endive sheaves are then wrapped in ham—preferably the mildly salty, meaty product from Ardennes in Belgium. Laid out in a gratin dish, the wrapped endives are topped with a rich Mornay sauce, which combines cream, egg yolks, and Gruyère and Parmesan cheeses, then all is glazed to molten gold under the broiler.

FURTHER INFORMATION AND RECIPES: *The French Chef Cookbook* by Julia Child (2002); memorie diangelina.com (search chicons au gratin). **TIP:** When purchasing endives, look for firm, solid sheaves with bottoms that are white and firm, not damp, soft, or brown. Trim the leaves close to serving time, as the edges will brown where they have been cut.

MUSSELING IN FOR A MEAL

Moules Frites

Belgian

To anyone unfamiliar with Belgium's elegant French-informed cuisine, the phrase *moules frites* might raise expectations of fried mussels. But the *frites* here refers to the accompanying slender, crunchy, golden-brown *pommes frites*—the true French fries for which Belgium is famed. As for the mussels, the shiny, purple-black, oblong bivalves with a toothsome, chewy meat and a salty-sea flavor are simmered up in a bath of white wine or one of the distinctive Belgian wheat beers, seasoned with shallots, garlic, and parsley in the style of the French *moules marinières*.

Some consider moules frites to be Belgium's national dish.

Long a mainstay of French cuisine—mussels have been gathered on the French bay of l'Aiguillon since at least 1235—in France they are employed in countless ways both homey and haute. But it is the neighboring Belgians who have elevated mussel-eating to an art form. Their access to a corner of the ice-cold North Sea means a harvest of the freshest, most flavorful mussels, and their unparalled frites are thrice-fried to a state of crunchy perfection in fresh vegetable oil. Traditionally served in grease-absorbing paper cones, they are dipped into a pungent, lemon-and-mustard-zapped mayonnaise (a big surprise to ketchup lovers) for a dripping, slurping, utterly delicious affair.

Possibilities abound here, and the original moules marinières is only the beginning. Now mussels are steamed in broths that are curried, tomato based, or even infused with Southeast Asian flavors of lemongrass, cilantro, and Thai basil. Despite many successful creative efforts, the original truly remains the best.

WHERE: *In Brussels,* Aux Armes de Bruxelles, tel 32/2-511-5598, auxarmesdebruxelles.com/en; *in the U.K.,* Belgo at several locations, belgo-restaurants.co.uk; *in New York,* Petite Abeille at several locations, petiteabeille.com; *in Washington D.C.,* Belga Café, tel 202-544-0100, belgacafe.com; *in Seattle*, Marché, tel 206-728-2800, marcheseattle.com; *in Minneapolis*, Vincent A Restaurant, tel 612-630-1189, vincentarestaurant.com. **Further information and**

recipes: *Haute Potato* by Jacqueline Pham (2012); saveur.com (search steamed mussels and fries); emerils.com (search mussels meuniere with frites).

⊣|||||||||||||||||||||||||||||||⊢

DON'T DRIVE IF YOU EAT THE GRAVY

Rognons à la Liégeoise

Veal Kidneys, Liège-Style

Belgian

The most fervent lovers of veal kidneys might recoil at the notion of having those rose-pink morsels cooked any way other than plainly roasted, and they do have a point. But before shutting the door on possibility, try out these Belgian triumphs,

a specialty of the city of Liège. Sautéed in butter to crisp, ruby-red perfection, fork-size pieces of fresh veal kidney are then simmered with crushed juniper berries and a generous dousing of aged gin. These provide a cleansing accent to the tender kidneys, resulting in a gravy that cries out for softly cooked potatoes and a cool cucumber salad.

Veal Kidneys, Liège-Style

Serves 4 to 6

4 fresh young veal kidneys
3 tablespoons unsalted butter
2 small shallots, finely chopped
6 to 8 juniper berries, crushed
Salt and freshly ground black pepper
2 teaspoons flour
⅔ to ¾ cup dry gin
Chopped fresh flat-leaf parsley, for garnish
Toast points or mashed or boiled potatoes,
for serving

1. Rinse the kidneys under cold running water and pat them dry with paper towels. Trim the kidneys, removing most of the fat and all tubes

or sinews. Cut the kidneys into ½-inch slices.

2. Heat the butter in a large skillet over low heat. When bubbling, add the kidneys and cook, turning once or twice, until all sides are a light golden brown, 7 to 8 minutes.

3. Increase the heat to medium-high, add the shallots and juniper berries, and cook for 8 to 10 minutes, shaking the pan so the shallots soften but do not brown. Season the kidney mixture with salt and pepper to taste. Sprinkle the flour on top and stir to distribute it evenly.

4. Add the gin, let it heat for a second or two, then carefully light it with a match. When the flames die down, reduce the heat to low, partially cover the pan, and let the kidneys finish cooking, 5 to 7 minutes, or until they are a bright rose color in the center. Sprinkle parsley over the kidneys and serve at once on toast points or with mashed or boiled potatoes. Spoon pan gravy over all.

Where: *In Brussels*, Le Bugatti, tel 32/2-646-1417, lebugatti.eu. **Tip:** Kidneys must be very fresh. Look for a bright blood color and never buy them frozen.

‖‖‖‖‖‖‖‖‖‖‖‖‖‖‖‖‖‖‖‖‖‖‖‖‖‖

HOT OFF THE IRON PRESS

Waffles

Belgian

We tend to think of waffles as an all-American breakfast food, but the stateside taste for those crisp, golden-brown honeycomb grids is negligible in comparison to Belgium's. In fact, it is believed that waffles, with their two levels of crispness and tiny wells that catch melted butter, maple syrup, honey, whipped cream, or ice cream, traveled to the New World with Pilgrims who had come through Holland or Flanders, now part of Belgium.

Waffles come from the tradition of *gaufres* or *gaufrettes*, batter cakes cooked on long-handled iron griddles with patterned surfaces on two hinged sides, which were originally held over wood fires and date back to medieval times. (Many of these antique irons, with their fanciful patterns and dynastic coats of arms, are now in museum collections; some of the best are held in the Musée de Cluny, in Paris.) Thinner than our contemporary waffles, the gaufres are also the forerunners of our ice cream cones: When hot, the very thin, waffled brown pancakes are flexible enough to be folded into cone shapes.

Practically a street food in their native country, as well as a standard in many cafés, today's modern, thick waffles are generally based on yeast batters. American waffles tend to rely on baking powder for their leavening, and the resulting differences are vast. Yeast not only imparts a richer, more pungent flavor, but it nudges these haute pancakes to rise higher and airier than their plebian counterparts, with a crunchier outer texture that results in an unbeatable contrast.

Like the Belgian crêpes that gained popularity overseas after being featured at the 1964 New York World's Fair, Belgian waffles developed so strong a following that they became standard—at least by name—in cafés and coffee shops across the country. The genuine article is, of course, a far cry from convenience waffles made with packaged mixes or from travesties that are frozen or "toaster-ready."

On native ground, the most serious aficionados take their waffles hot, with just a fluff of butter and a snowfall of confectioners' sugar. Which is not to say they cannot be more elaborately topped with crushed, lightly sugared berries and a dollop of ice cream or whipped cream.

Like crêpes, waffles also live a dual life on the savory side. Think tarragon-scented creamed chicken and mushrooms, or softly scrambled eggs combined with flecks of smoked salmon, creamed spinach, or aromatic Cheddar or Parmesan cheese. Not to forget sideliners such as bacon, frizzled ham, or grilled sausages. No toasters in sight.

Where: *In Brussels*, Aux Armes de Bruxelles, tel 32/2-511-5598, auxarmesdebruxelles.com/en; *in Antwerp*, Van Hecke Waffle House, tel 32/3-233-1972, hof.be/english.html; *in New York*, Markt, tel 212-727-3314, marktrestaurant.com; Petite Abeille at several locations, petiteabeille.com; *in San Francisco* at several locations, Golden Waffle, goldenwaffle.net. **Mail order:** For Belgian waffle iron, surlatable.com (search cuisinart belgian waffle maker). **Further information and recipes:** *Everybody Eats Well in Belgium Cookbook* by Ruth Van Waerebeek and Maria Robbins (1996); allrecipes.com (search belgian waffles).

||||||||||||||||||||||||||||||||||||

FIRST BOIL SOME WATER, THEN CATCH YOUR CHICKEN

Waterzooi à la Gantoise

Chicken Stew

Belgian

Waterzooi is Flemish for boiling water, but that's only the starting point for this exquisitely luxurious Belgian soup-stew, rarely seen outside its home country. Chicken waterzooi—*waterzooi à la gantoise*—is lush, a rich and satiny

egg-, lemon-, and cream-glossed soup scented with celery and leeks and based on a flavorful stewing fowl enriched with generous chunks of veal marrow bone. More subtle is *waterzooi de poissons,* which depends on a lean, clear broth that reveals the delicate flavor of freshwater fish—eel, carp, pike, and perch—laced with the astringent overtones of leeks, celery, bay leaf, white wine, and thyme.

Chicken Waterzooi
Serves 6 as a main course

1 chicken (about 5 pounds),
    quartered, with all giblets
    except the liver
6 tablespoons (¾ stick) unsalted butter
2 large onions, coarsely chopped
3 medium-size leeks, white portions only,
    well rinsed and chopped
1 small parsley root, or ½ parsnip,
    scraped and diced
3 ribs celery, chopped
1 cup dry white wine
3 or 4 sprigs fresh flat-leaf parsley, plus
    finely chopped parsley for garnish
1 bay leaf
½ teaspoon dried thyme
8 to 10 white peppercorns
1 teaspoon salt
4 extra-large egg yolks
1 cup heavy (whipping) cream
2 to 3 tablespoons freshly
    squeezed lemon juice

Freshly ground white pepper
6 to 12 small boiled, peeled
    white potatoes, for serving

1. Place the chicken quarters and giblets in a 7- or 8-quart soup pot and add water to cover. Let the water come to a boil over high heat, then reduce the heat to medium. Partially cover the pot, and let the chicken simmer gently but steadily for 30 minutes, skimming off the foam as it forms on the surface.

2. Melt the butter in a saucepan over low heat. Add the onions, leeks, parsley root or parsnip, and celery and cook until they soften and just begin to turn light golden, 7 to 8 minutes. Add the vegetables to the soup pot along with the white wine, parsley sprigs, bay leaf, thyme, peppercorns, and salt. Let simmer, partially covered, until the chicken begins to fall away from the bone, 1½ to 2 hours.

A variation features peas and mushrooms.

3. Remove the chicken from the broth and trim off and discard all bones and skin. Set aside the drumsticks and wings for snacks. Cut the chicken meat from the thighs and breast into long strips and set aside.

4. Strain the broth into a clean 5-quart pot. Discard all of the vegetables and giblets, unless you are in the mood for some delicious nibbling. Let the broth cool, without stirring, for 20 to 30 minutes. Then, skim off as much fat as possible. There should be 9 to 10 cups of broth. If there is much more, boil the broth rapidly, uncovered, until it is reduced to about 10 cups. The broth can be prepared up to this point, then cooled and refrigerated, covered, for up to 24 hours. After that it will be easy to remove any remaining fat from the top. Refrigerate the chicken meat, covered, separately.

5. Reheat the broth over medium heat until it is barely simmering. Place the egg yolks in a wide bowl and beat them with a whisk or a fork until light in color. Slowly beat in the cream, then gradually dribble in 2 cups of the hot broth, beating constantly. Pour the egg mixture into the pot of barely simmering broth, stirring constantly.

6. Add the reserved strips of chicken and cook for about 10 minutes until heated through, but do not let the soup boil. Season the soup with lemon juice, salt, and white pepper to taste. Serve the soup in heated bowls. Add 1 or 2 boiled potatoes to each portion and sprinkle liberally with chopped parsley.

WHERE: *In Brussels,* Aux Armes de Bruxelles, tel 32/2-511-5598, auxarmesdebruxelles.com/en; *in New York,* Markt, tel 212-727-3314, markt restaurant.com; for seafood waterzooi, Petite Abeille at several locations, petiteabeille.com. **ADDITIONAL RECIPE:** For waterzooi with fish, food52.com (search waterzooi of whitefish).

⊢||||||||||||||||||||||||||||||||⊣

AN ALPHABETICAL DECEMBER TREAT

Banketletters

Dutch

I n the realm of food, form should never be valued over content; yet when the two are of equal excellence, it's a very special thing indeed. Such a concurrence will be on view during a visit to Holland, or to any Dutch-inhabited neighborhood,

on December 5, St. Nicholas's Eve.

To honor the patron saint of children, Dutch confectioners shape delectable alphabet letters out of either rich, dark, bittersweet chocolate or puff pastry filled with almond paste. Each good child is rewarded with his or her initials, a treat supposedly delivered by St. Nicholas (or Sinterklaas), who rides a white stallion over rooftops and slides his gifts down the chimney—never mind what happens to the fragile treats if there's a fire on the hearth. With him is a less generous companion called Zwarte Piet, or Black Peter, who gives naughty children only a birch stick or a lump of coal.

Known as *banketletters,* or bakery letters, the sizeable sweets are about eight inches high. "Q," "X," and "Y" need not apply, probably because none works as the first letter of any Dutch name.

Although not as personalized, two other enticements are available to the well behaved on St. Nicholas's Eve and Day: deep-fried dumplings called *oliebollen*, studded with raisins and candied fruit peel and sprinkled with cinnamon sugar; and the crisp, savory, ring-shaped apple fritters called *appelbeignet.*

RETAIL AND MAIL ORDER: *In New York,* for chocolate letters, Li-Lac Chocolates, tel 212-924-2280, li-lacchocolates.com; *in Pella, Iowa,* for pastry banketletters, Jaarsma Bakery, tel 641-628-2940, jaarsmabakery.com. FURTHER INFORMATION AND RECIPE: For pastry letters, *Visions of Sugarplums* by Mimi Sheraton (1981).

||||||||||||||||||||||||||||||||||

THE COMFORTING SPOILS OF WAR

Hutspot met Klapstuk, or Hochepot

One-Pot Winter Stew

Dutch, Belgian

A defeated army flees without stopping to rinse out its pots and pans, and from this understandable instance of poor housekeeping a brand-new dish is born. This is the origin of *hutspot met klapstuk,* one of Holland's most comforting winter

dishes, a soft, peppery stew of beef, potatoes, onions, and carrots, slow-simmered in a pot until it melds into an almost fully disintegrated, cozy mash.

The story has it that when occupying Spanish soldiers were driven out of the northern Dutch town of Leiden in 1574, they left behind unwashed pots in which the Dutch found remains of a meat and vegetable stew. History has not recorded who was the first intrepid taster of those leftovers, but suffice it to say that soon after, local cooks approximated what they thought to be the original. What is said to be the original cauldron—hopefully washed—is on view in Leiden's Museum De Lakenhal.

Hochepot morsels cook until soft but not mushy.

Hutspot falls into the category of sustaining one-pot winter stews that the Dutch call *stamppots*—all sneakily addictive and, when prepared in large quantities, great at hanging around and improving through several reheatings. *Hutspot met witte bonen en spek* combines bacon and salt pork with onions and white beans. *Stampot van zuurkool met spek en worst* is a more piquant version in which sauerkraut underlies potatoes, bacon, and smoky frankfurters. *Stammpot van boerenkool met worst* is the heartiest version, based on dark-green winter kale, potatoes, and sausages enriched with bacon or lard. That kale, incidentally, is at its most tender when it has been allowed to freeze in the cold winter air before being cooked.

Typically, the Belgians heat up a more soigné version of hutspot for the dish they call *hochepot*, simmering the carrots, onions, potatoes, and meat into small, fork-tender chunks rather than total mush. Thyme, cloves, and bay leaves add sprightly touches to intrigue the more demanding Belgian palate.

Despite their slight differences, both hutspot and hochepot call for some of the cold, sunny beer both countries are famous for and, after that, a nice long nap through the winter afternoon twilight.

Further information and recipes: foodnetwork.com (search hutspot mit klapstuk); the dutchtable.com (search hutspot met klapstuk).

GREAT BALLS OF FIRE

Kroketten and Bitterballen

Croquettes

Dutch

To spend any part of a winter's day outdoors under Holland's quicksilver skies is to know what it feels like to be damp-chilled to the bone, almost as if you were wearing no clothes at all. What a blissful wonder, then, to come upon a vending machine, street stand, or snack shop offering crusty golden spheres of *bitterballen,* bite-sized treats fashioned from chopped, cooked meat, parsley, and bread crumbs bound with white sauce and deep-fried. Or you might choose one of the log-shaped *kroketten* made with either cheese, meat, potatoes, or bits of seafood. Among the tastiest of these is a hotly spiced, plump, and crunchy round of curry-flavored rice inspired by the fried rice dish *nasi goreng,* which the Dutch came to love in Indonesia, known in colonial days as the Dutch East Indies.

Kroketten and bitterballen warm a wintry day.

The savory curried rice snack is handwarmingly hot, with further warmth coming from seasonings such as cayenne, dry mustard, golden curry powder, and black pepper, joined by occasional fine mincings of ham. Lucky is the traveler who finds it in a train station's vending machine—the more improbable the location, the more satisfying the snack.

Where: *In Amsterdam,* Kwekkeboom Patisserie, tel 31/20-673-7114, kwekkeboom.nl; Van Dobben, tel 31/20-621-4200, vandobben.nl; *in Ouderkerk de Amstel,* Café Loetje, tel 31/20-662-8173, amsterdam.loetje.com; **Further information and recipes:** *The Art of Dutch Cooking* by C. Countess van Limburg Stirum (1962); allrecipes.com (search dutch croquetten); coquinaria.nl/english (click Recipes, Dutch Cuisine, then Kroketten and Bitterballs); expatica.com (search how to make traditional dutch croquettes).

⊢||||||||||||||||||||||||||||||⊣

SPEAKING IN LAMBS' TONGUES

Lamstongetjes in Madeira Saus

Dutch

Slim, pink, and tender lamb tongues each make a single portion in this traditional Dutch dish. They add up to subtle, wondrous morsels, particularly when they come from the breed of Texel lambs that feed on Holland's North Sea salt marshes. Just as the French prize their *agneau de pré-salé* (see page 50), so the Dutch appreciate the gentle saline accent the meat acquires.

The tender tongues are briefly simmered with bay leaf, mace, a few crushed juniper berries, onion, parsley, and celery, and are then trimmed. Just before being served, they are sliced and sautéed in butter with a hint of garlic, then finished with a Madeira sauce. Fluffy steamed white rice is the traditional foil for all of this richness.

Lambs' tongues are not easily come by in most food markets, save those catering to Greek and Middle Eastern customers. Calves' tongues work as well, as do small, fresh beef tongues, neither pickled nor smoked.

FURTHER INFORMATION AND RECIPES: *The Art of Dutch Cooking* by C. Countess van Limburg Stirum (1962); recipehound.com (search lamb tongues in madeira sauce); emomrecipes.com (search tongue in madeira sauce a la julia child).

⊢||||||||||||||||||||||||||||||⊣

HERRING TAKES TO THE STREETS

Nieuwe Haring

Dutch

A holiday for herring may seem an odd sort of celebration. Unless, of course, you are Dutch and it is May 31. On that day, and through most of June, all of Holland turns out to eat the season's *maagdekensharing*. These so-called maiden herring (also known as green herring) have not yet spawned, so are considered virgins, whatever status that imparts. What it undeniably grants the silky raw fillets is a gently saline, sea-fresh flavor that gets a sprightly enhancement of minced onion and hard-cooked egg. ("Fresh" is a technicality here, because by law the fish must be

Traditional Dutch herring eating method

brined and frozen solid in oak barrels for a minimum of twenty-four hours—a process that kills parasites without diminishing gustatory pleasure, and that in fact adds additional layers of saltiness.)

Although you can find this first green herring in restaurants and homes, it is best enjoyed from street carts, with the damp North Sea breezes adding a seasoning of their own. The Dutch book of etiquette permits the fillets to be eaten out of hand: intermittently dabbed with onion and egg, and then held up by the tail and lowered into the mouth in the style of a sword swallower.

Officially, the first seasonal catch of these luscious little fish belongs to the queen, but wisely she shares it with the country's commoners and their guests. There is no evidence that she ever has pronounced, "Let them eat herring."

So generous is the queen with this very local treat that each year a portion of the brined catch is even exported for sale in restaurants and fancy food stores, some of which affect a cart to approximate the true Dutch experience.

WHERE: *In New York,* Grand Central Oyster Bar, tel 212-490-6650, oysterbarny.com; *in Brooklyn,* Grand Central Oyster Bar Brooklyn, tel 347-294-0596, oysterbarbrooklyn.com. **RETAIL AND MAIL ORDER:** Russ & Daughters, tel 212-475-4880, russanddaughters.com. **SPECIAL EVENT:** The Vlaardingen Herring Festival, Vlaardingen, Holland, June, goeurope.about.com (search netherlands herring festival).

THE QUALITY OF LIGHT

The Fine Art of Oysters

Dutch, Belgian

C ountries bordering on the frigid waters of the North Sea are rightfully proud of the silky, saline oyster varieties available to them, but few have raised them to such artistic heights as the celebrated, bygone painters of the Dutch and

Belgian-Flemish schools of the sixteenth and seventeenth centuries. Challenged by the rough, rocky gray outside shells, the shimmering, pearly interiors, and the limpid, translucent oyster itself, these painters regarded their challenging subject as an exercise in technique. They attempted to match texture and color, yet to keep the eating of these oysters in mind, arranged them in suggestive, elegant still lifes that often included a lemon cut into quarters, with the peel partially pared

Still Life *by Osias Beert the Elder (1580–1624)*

into sunny coils, as well as a loaf of bread and cheese. (There wasn't a school dedicated to painting oysters au gratin—baked under rich and puffy coverings of cream, butter, and cheese—but the preparation is much favored in both Holland and Belgium.)

The unparalleled Dutch way with light is on full display in *Still Life with a Glass and Oysters* (c.1683) by Jan Davidsz. de Heem, with its refreshing green grapes, curled lemon peel, and sparkling green goblet filled with white wine. An even more elaborate spread is offered in *Still Life*, by the Antwerp painter Osias Beert the Elder (1580–1624): white wine in a clear goblet, a chunk of crusty bread, and ten shimmering, open oysters.

Where: *Still Life with a Glass and Oysters* is in the Metropolitan Museum of Art, New York, NY, tel 212-535-7710, metmuseum.org; *Still Life* by Osias Beert the Elder is in the Museo Nacional del Prado, Madrid, Spain, tel 34/913-30-28-00, museodelprado.es/en.

Paling in 't Groen

Dutch, Belgian

The deliciously plump, firm-textured eels that slither and writhe off the North Sea coast of Holland and Belgium lend themselves to a host of richly succulent dishes. Although the Dutch love eels any way they can have them, the rich oiliness of these tasty, snakelike fish makes them perfect for smoking. The lubricating, subtly flavored oil under their skin adds much to the eel's meaty, salt-tinged appeal, and if it results in high calories, there's consolation in the fact that it also brings a healthful dose of the beneficial omega-3 fatty acids and vitamin E.

The traditional smoked preparation results in skin that takes on a golden, savory crackle, while the long fillets of meat lifted off the bone achieve a woodsy, deep-sea flavor that vies even with that of other luxury smoked fish, such as sturgeon, trout, and salmon.

Served with buttered dark bread or toast and dabs of creamy horseradish, or alongside scrambled eggs, smoked eel—*gerookte paling*—is one of Holland's most elegant appetizers, especially washed down with a few shots of old genever gin (also known as Dutch gin and Holland gin).

Flemish cooks in Belgium prefer their eels "greened" in the style they call *paling in 't groen,* or in French, *anguilles au vert.* The most critical herb in the bright green sauce is sorrel (*oseille* in French), its distinctly needling, elegantly sour edge joining other herbaceous greenery such as chervil, parsley, tarragon, and chives. The minced herbs are whipped into egg yolks and further acidulated with lemon juice, before being slightly warmed on the top of a double boiler. The warm sauce is spooned over fork-size cuts of eel that have been braised in white wine. Most people like the verdant dish served fragrantly hot, but some like it cold, when the eel's bones form a silky gelatin—a related preparation, if far more elegant, to the British favorite, jellied eel (see page 16).

Where: *In Brussels,* Le Bugatti, tel 32/2-646-1417, lebugatti.eu. **Further information and recipe:** erecipe.com (search anguilles au vert).

HOLLAND'S NATIONAL CANDY

Rademaker's Haagsche Hopjes

Dutch

About 215 years ago, there lived in the Dutch city of The Hague one Baron Hendrik Hop. The good baron was much depressed, as his physician had ordered him to stop drinking the coffee he so loved. Fortunately he had a friend in the baker Theodorus van Haaren, whom he urged to create a confection to sate his urges. Playing around with coffee, sugar, butter, and good sweet cream, van Haaren devised *Rademaker's Haagsche Hopjes* (named after Baron Hop and The Hague), a resounding success that is considered Holland's national candy.

The sweets were packed in the red, black, white, and gold silk-screened tins that are still used today, and the square hard candies known as *hopjes* are as soul-soothing as ever, notable for dissolving in the mouth without becoming sticky or soft. They exude hints of all the good, fresh ingredients they are made with:

Candies on a classic tin

coffee enhanced by overtones of butter and cream, all mellowed by caramelized sugar. It's a combination that does as much to soothe the throat as to enliven the spirit and, even more practically, its doses of caffeine and sugar are doubly energizing. Fans can borrow an idea from the Russians, who hold a lump of sugar in their mouths to sweeten tea as they sip; learn to do the same with a hopje while drinking unsweetened black coffee. It's easy to do without dribbling, once you get the knack.

MAIL ORDER: amazon.com (search rademaker hopjes coffee candies); hollandamericanbakery.com (search rademaker hopjes).

SANDWICHING IN SOME SNACKS

Uitsmijters and Broodjes

Dutch

"Winter eggs are very poor eating," warns Mynheer Kleef, the innkeeper in the children's classic *Hans Brinker, or, The Silver Skates*. Be that as it may, when featured in Holland's ubiquitous and homey open sandwich, the *uitsmijter* (AUTZ-may-ter, meaning bouncer), those lesser winter eggs can warm and delight even the coldest of ice skaters.

The sandwich begins with a slice or two of

white bread spread with unsalted butter and sometimes fried on one side. Over that goes a generous layering of sliced roast beef, veal, or ham, and two sizzling-hot, sunny-side-up fried eggs sprinkled with black pepper. A final topping of cool, crisp, and astringent slivers of pickled dill cucumber adds zest as teeth sink through the deliciously complex layers. Those eating abstemiously might have only one fried egg, in which case the sandwich is deemed a *halve uitsmijter*. Either way, it is a snack easily realized in an American kitchen for those unfortunates who cannot make it to Amsterdam.

Most difficult for the uninitiated to get used to is the glass of milk that accompanies the uitsmijter. Good Dutch beer or a cup of hot coffee might be more felicitous, if untraditional, in the Netherlands.

As popular as the uitsmijter is, it is not the only favored Dutch sandwich by a long shot. A wide variety of eat-and-run *broodjes* (BREWT-chahs) are offered in *broodjeswinkels*—informal spots (not to be missed by any visitor to Amsterdam) serving quick and relatively inexpensive sustenance by way of sandwiches on warm, freshly baked, buttered rolls. Fillings include beef tartare, all kinds of sausages, liver spread, and sliced pickled or roasted meats, salads, and Dutch cheeses such as Edam, Gouda, and the lesser known but more interesting smoky Kernhem and caraway- or cumin-flecked Leyden.

Where: *In Amsterdam,* Café Waterloo, tel 31/20-624-9831, cafewaterloo.nl; Broodje Bert, tel 31/20-623-0382. **Further information and recipes:** theguardian.com (search broodje kroket sandwich); design-your-travel.com (search uitsmijter); thedutchtable.com (search uitsmijter).

————————————|||||||||||||||||||||||||||||||||||————————————

DON'T LET THE SUNSHINE IN
———————————

White Asparagus, Dressed to Kill

Dutch

Thick, white asparagus, with their silken ivory sheen, have been highly prized in Europe for many years, while in the U.S. and Britain they have only relatively recently come into favor, vying with green asparagus for gourmet status. Perhaps the

reason for white asparagus's lack of favor stateside was that the only type familiar in the United States was the watery, bitter, canned variety.

Actually, green or white, it is the same vegetable *(Asparagus officinalis)*. A member of the lily family, asparagus raised to be white are kept covered with soil as they grow so that light does not cause the development of chlorophyll (that said, some white varieties are allowed to develop pale, amethyst-tinged tips for visual appeal). White asparagus have a milder flavor and are somewhat more fibrous than their verdant cousins, and so require more peeling and slightly longer cooking.

Because they are among the first edible harbingers of spring, asparagus are celebrated throughout Europe, especially in the colder, northern countries such as Belgium, Holland, Germany, Austria, and Switzerland, where special asparagus menus (called *spargelkarte* in Germany and Austria) are featured in restaurants at almost all levels. Each country has its own special way of preparing them—hot, cold, in soups, and in salads. In Italy they are served cold with a dressing of lemon juice and olive oil. In France, after being peeled and washed, the stalks are braised in butter, a little chicken stock, and with a bay leaf until tender. Once chilled, they are dressed with a mustardy mayonnaise—a pungent sauce called *gribiche*—or the simplest vinaigrette enhanced with hazelnut oil and chervil.

However delicious the various preparations of white asparagus may be, the best of all is a standard in Holland and Belgium, prepared in a style the French have named *à la flamande*. If lucky, one can experience the full ritual of having the asparagus dressed at the table

White asparagus with Hollandaise

just before they are served, a practice still found in a few traditional, upscale restaurants in Holland. The hot, cooked asparagus are brought to the table folded into a snowy napkin and laid out on a *gueridon* (a rolling serving cart complete with burner and chafing dish), along with garnishes of melted butter, chopped whites and yolks of hard-cooked eggs, and whole nutmegs beside a silvery grater. The long, white spears are portioned onto individual warmed plates, doused with butter, sprinkled first with the egg whites, then with the yolks, and finally with a grating of the nutmeg for an unusual and sweetly aromatic touch. In a simpler, homier service, diners form their own paste from the garnishes, the asparagus stalks to be dipped into it before each bite, a practice that also has made its way to England.

For more elaborate tastes, asparagus in Holland are mantled with a rich, sunny Hollandaise sauce based primarily on egg yolks, lemon juice, and butter, not to forget nutmeg. Although the sauce's name implies it was created in Holland, its origin is open to dispute, one theory being that it was created in northern France to honor a visiting Dutch nobleman.

WHERE: *In Amsterdam,* Die Port Van Cleve, tel 31/02-714-2000, dieportvancleve.com; *in Brussels,* Aux Armes de Bruxelles, tel 32/2-511-5598, auxarmesdebruxelles.com/en; *in Berlin,* Lutter & Wegner, tel 49/30-2029-5415, l-w-berlin.de.; *in New York,* Wallse, tel 212-352-2300, kg-ny.com; Markt, tel 212-727-3314, marktrestaurant.com; *in Kansas City, MO,* Grünauer, tel 816-283-3234, grunauerkc.com; *in Santa Monica, Venice, and Culver City/Mar Vista, CA,* Röckenwagner, rockenwagner.com. **MAIL ORDER:** Melissa's Produce, tel 800-588-0151, melissas.com. **FURTHER INFORMATION AND RECIPES:** *Vegetables from Amaranth to Zucchini* by Elizabeth Schneider (2001); for white asparagus soup, *Neue Cuisine* by Kurt Gutenbrunner (2011); recipegoldmine .com (search asparagus a la flamande); saveur .com (search white asparagus with olive oil sabayon; white asparagus with sorrel hollandaise). **SPECIAL EVENTS:** For asparagus festivals in various locations, asparagus-lover.com (click Fun Facts and Health, then Festivals).

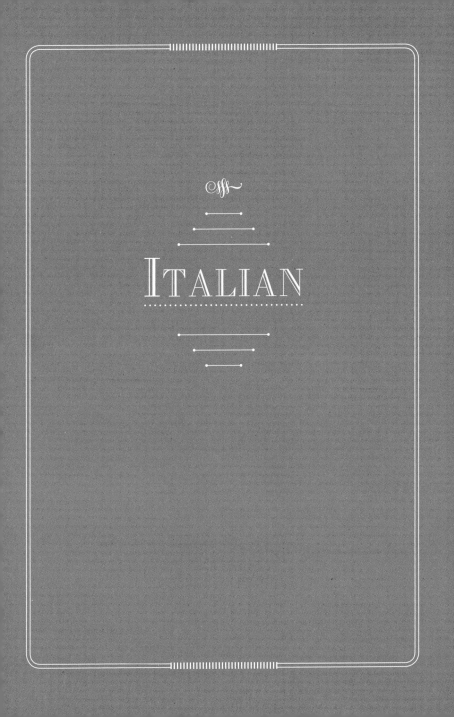

ITALIAN

⊣||||||||||||||||||||||||||||||||||⊢

A SUNNY EASTER MIRACLE

Abbacchio Brodettato

Braised Lamb in Egg and Lemon Sauce

Italian

The pungently bright lemon-egg sauce that enlivens so many Greek specialties is less expected (though no less appreciated) in the Italian lamb dish *abbacchio brodettato*. And given the symbolic importance of both lamb and eggs, it's no wonder abbacchio brodettato is an Easter favorite in Rome and in the Adriatic regions of Abruzzo and Apulia. Also known as *agnello all'uovo e agro di limone* (lamb with egg and the bitterness of lemon), the dish begins with the tenderest milk-fed lamb, cut into bite-size pieces and gently stewed along with prosciutto, onions, white wine, and stock.

The magic happens when the meltingly tender lamb is about to be served. Over low heat, it is doused with a sunny blend of egg yolk, lemon juice and grated zest, marjoram, and pepper, all beaten lightly and quickly with a fork. The result is a creamy sauce that remains a satiny liquid without any scrambled egg coagulation, a neat trick that is the mark of a skillful cook. The astringent acidity of the lemon provides just the right contrast to the strong, earthy flavor of the meat.

In both Abruzzo and the neighboring region of Apulia, the dish is sometimes made with baby goat (kid), or *capretto*. The sauce can also be prepared with freshly grated nutmeg instead of marjoram, for a warmer, more exotic touch.

Given that the typical Easter meal would begin with a few antipasti and a pasta, abbacchio brodettato would be a sufficient and delicious main course.

WHERE: *In Rome,* Ristorante Matricianella, tel 39/06-683-2100, matricianella.it. **FURTHER INFORMATION AND RECIPES:** *Italian Cuisine* by Tony May (2005); *Naples at Table* by Arthur Schwartz (1998), see Agnello Cacio e Vova; for the Apulia and Abruzzi versions, *Flavors of Puglia* by Nancy Harmon Jenkins (1997); italianfood.about.com (search abbacchio brodettato).

⊣||||||||||||||||||||||||||||||||||⊢

THE KING OF VINEGARS

Aceto Balsamico

Italian (Emilian-Romagnan)

Have you ever had deeply bronzed, syrupy garnet vinegar drizzled sparingly over a small chunk of Parmesan cheese or a spring bowlful of the wild woodland strawberries *fraises des bois* (see page 91)? If not, you may never have encountered a genuine *balsamico* at all. Winey, top-dollar balsamics have become enormously popular, but the category is almost always misrepresented by thin, cheap, watery impostors bestowing undesired sweetness to all sorts of salads, main courses, and sauces that should be savory.

The real balsamic vinegar that is the specialty of Emilia-Romagna, and in particular of the region around the towns of Modena and Reggio, can cost as much as $150 for a tiny bottle—which is why it is portioned out as carefully as caviar. Its flavor should hint of Madeira wine with a brassy candied sweetness, a winey acidity, and undertones of oak. By contrast, cheap balsamic tastes like artificially sweetened wine vinegar.

To be sure that you're getting the real McCoy, look for regional authentication via a Denominazione di Origine Controllata (D.O.C.) label indicating that the vinegar has been produced and aged a minimum of twelve years (with the best and most expensive going to twenty-five) in and around the areas of Modena and Reggio, according to Italian law. Regional consortiums send representatives annually to check the progress of these vinegars as they age, determining which are ready to bottle, which need more time, and which are never going to make it due to imperfections detected during their development.

Mecca for balsamic lovers is the Osteria di Rubbiara in Nonantola, just outside of Modena, a sprawling, lively wine tavern where a single meal is served each night, all dishes having been prepared with *balsamico*. The real revelation is a visit to the back of house, where the management maintains its balsamico "cave" (albeit on a second floor). Here one can see the rows of small oak barrels filled with the aging vinegar, and hear them all described.

It is the custom of the owners' family to put up a barrel of vinegar for each new baby born to the family, to be given as a sort of inheritance twenty-five years later. And a valuable inheritance it is. According to Lynne Rossetto Kasper's excellent book *The Splendid Table*, the name *balsamic* refers to a balm or cure. And this vinegar has been considered a balm since as far back as the seventeenth century—some still swear by a few drops as a remedy for sore throats. (Others use it as a cure for blandness on a grilled veal chop, and it makes an elegant touch when a droplet or two tops a dessert portion of Parmesan cheese.)

WHERE: *In Nonantola, Italy,* Osteria di Rubbiara, tel 39/59-549019. **FURTHER INFORMATION AND RECIPES:** *The Splendid Table: Recipes from Emilia-Romagna, the Heartland of Northern Italian Food* by Lynne Rossetto Kasper (1992).

------||||||||||||||||||||||||||||||||||------

A PICK-ME-UP FOR DESSERT

Affogato

Italian

An *affogato*—vanilla ice cream that is "suffocated" in a bath of hot espresso—is pure simplicity. It consists of only those two ingredients and is as easy to prepare as it is appealing as a light dessert. There is majesty in its combination of hot and cold, liquid and (melting) solid, bitter and sweet as well as in the way the espresso washes over the ice cream—lovely to behold and even better to sip or delicately slurp from a long-handled spoon. And the affogato only gets better as the ice cream dissolves. Technically called *gelato affogato al caffè*, affogato—as it's commonly shortened to on restaurant menus—the invention is generally credited to Turin, where it is served in nearly every bar. It became popular stateside sometime in the late 1990s, and is now a staple on chic Italian dessert menus across the U.S. But it is dead easy to prepare at home: All you need in order to make the world's most urbane sundae is good cold ice cream, preferably vanilla; a narrow juice-size glass; and very fresh, very hot espresso. Skip the sugar and, of course, the milk or cream. . . .

WHERE: *In New York,* Sandro's, tel 212-288-7374, sandrosnyc.com; Marea, tel 212-582-5100, marea-nyc.com; *in Los Angeles,* Angelini Osteria, tel 323-297-0070, angeliniosteria.com. **FURTHER INFORMATION AND RECIPE:** foodnetwork .com (search affogato ina garten).

THE ARISTOCRAT OF PORK

Arista alla Fiorentina

Rosemary-Scented Roast Pork Loin

Italian (Tuscan)

According to the authoritative 1967 cookbook *Le Ricette Regionali Italiane,* this roasted, rosemary-scented pork loin has an antique past: A specialty of the Florentine kitchen, the dish owes its name to the visiting Greek clergy who, attending the ecumenical council of 1430, declared it *árista* (Greek for "the best").

One might expect a more complex recipe for such a heralded dish, but simplicity seems to have prevailed through the ages: Studded with slivers of garlic, rubbed down with salt and pepper, firmly bound with string, and tucked with sprigs of rosemary, the loin is ideally threaded onto a skewer and cooked on a rotisserie in front of an open fire, where it turns slowly, fragrantly, and succulently. (More likely these days—and only a bit less tantalizingly—the arista is slowly oven-roasted in an open pan.)

It is so simple, yet is distinguished by the inclusion of rosemary, the herb that differentiates the Florentine arista from pork loins roasted in other parts of Italy. A most traditional accompaniment would be pearly white beans, done either *all'uccelletto* (stewed with tomato, garlic, fresh sage leaves, and olive oil) or *al forno fiorentina* (baked in an earthenware casserole with tomatoes, pancetta, leeks, garlic, and olive oil), for a rich, thick nest for the sliced pork.

WHERE: *In Florence,* Coco Lezzone, tel 39/055-287-178, cocolezzone.it. **FURTHER INFORMATION AND RECIPES:** For a braised version, *Marcella's Italian Kitchen* by Marcella Hazan (1986), see Lombata di Maiale al Forno; saveur.com (search roasted herb-stuffed pork loin).

This impeccably simple dish is equally delicious hot or cold.

⊢||||||||||||||||||||||||||||||⊣

A REAL (OR PAINTED) FEAST

A Basket of Summer Fruit

Italian

As far as virtual feasts go, *Basket of Fruit,* painted in 1599 by the Renaissance master Michelangelo Merisi da Caravaggio (1571–1610), is a masterpiece of the genre. For Italy-bound food tourists, it may also serve as an inspirational prelude to a tasting of the country's incomparable summer fruits, most of which are available in open-air produce markets such as Rome's Campo dei Fiori between late spring and early autumn.

It should be no surprise that the country that is home to arguably the most exquisite fruit still-life painting ever created also produces the world's most fragrant and delectable pears, peaches, apricots, grapes, and figs. Fortunately, it is not necessary to go to Milan's Pinacoteca Ambrosiana to have a glimpse of the painting (although that's not a bad idea). Widely available for viewing in art books and online, the painting celebrates Italy's most luscious fruits not only in their succulent prime, but also as some sadly and inevitably age toward decay, making them prey for a few of the most beguiling little worms and bugs ever drawn and colored.

Caravaggio achieved intense realism with his Basket of Fruit.

A masterpiece of trompe l'oeil, *Basket of Fruit* ignites the salivary glands and invites the viewer to reach out for a red-gold peach, a sunny pear, plump and honeyed black and green figs, a perfect tart quince, a few luscious berries, and juicy red and green grapes. Try not to disturb the pretty grasshopper as you reach in.

Where: *In Milan,* Pinacoteca Ambrosiana, tel 39/02-806921, ambrosiana.eu.

⊢||||||||||||||||||||||||||||||⊣

A DESSERT DRINK FOR COFFEE AND CHOCOLATE LOVERS

Bicerin

Italian (Piedmontese)

In 1852, the French writer and gourmand Alexandre Dumas asserted: "Among the many good and beautiful things that I have found in Torino, I will never forget the *bicerin,* the best drink made with coffee, milk, and chocolate, served in all the cafés at a relatively low price." Dumas was not the only intellectual to hold this beguiling beverage in such high regard. The creamy, steamy blend of dark chocolate, espresso, and milk also captivated Ernest Hemingway, Italo Calvino, and Pablo Picasso, among others. Lest we ascribe too much merit to its powers, however, let us remember that although Friedrich Nietzsche was also a fan of bicerin (pronounced bee-cha-REEN), its rich mocha essence did little to cure his bleak melancholia.

Served in small, stemmed glasses at many cafés in its native Turin, the elegant city long celebrated for fine chocolates, this soul-warming confectionery drink is best experienced at Caffè al Bicerin—a fixture on this Piedmont city's antique Piazza della Consolata, close to the colorfully gentrified quarter of Quadrilatero Romano, since 1763.

Some credit this café with the invention of the beverage (whose name derives from *bicchierino,* referring to the small glass that is so very far removed from the oversize monstrosities used for mochas in the U.S.), while others believe it was created at the extant and even older Caffè Florio. In any case, as far back as the seventeenth century, Turin and its province of Piedmont were already known for the Bavareisa, a similar drink in which the same luscious ingredients were stirred together. (In the bicerin they are layered in the glass.)

To prepare an authentic bicerin, you need a steady hand and a 4- or 5-ounce stemmed glass, slightly warmed. Fill it about a quarter of the way with strong, freshly brewed espresso, then another quarter or so with melted bittersweet chocolate, and finally crown it all with rich frothed whole milk or half-and-half. Sit back and take a sip. As coffee, chocolate, and creamy topping mingle into a blissful mocha haze, do not be surprised if Nietzsche, Hemingway, Picasso, or Calvino should happen to come by for a visit.

WHERE: *In Turin,* Caffè al Bicerin, tel 39/011-436-9325, bicerin.it/eng; *in New York and Chicago,* Eataly, eataly.com. **FURTHER INFORMATION AND RECIPE:** newyorktimes.com (search bicerin recipe).

A CLAIM TO STEAK

Bistecca alla Fiorentina

Italian (Tuscan)

Americans may be the world's most famous devourers of steak, but the Tuscans, too, deserve some credit for their fervor—as well as for the perfection of their great specialty, *bistecca alla fiorentina.* A large and lovely slab of the cut Americans call porterhouse, it is the pride of Florence, and of all Italy as well.

Its preparation is simple enough, but leaves no room for carelessness. The slightly aged meat is brushed with olive oil via a branch of rosemary. Sprinkled with salt, pepper, and sometimes fresh lemon juice, it is then grilled over wood charcoal that lends an aromatic autumnal patina to the meat. That's it as far as cooking goes —so the steak must truly speak for itself.

Thankfully it does not disappoint. Florentine steaks come from Chianina, the local white-coated grass-fed cattle, which are leaner than their typical American counterparts; their careful feeding results in just enough fat to impart a lusciously rich and tender beefiness to the steak. Believed to be one of the oldest breeds in the world, Chianina originated in Val di Chiana, in Tuscany's Maremma district, a region famous for its Italian-style cowboys.

Preferred blood-rare by the cognoscenti, the big, thick slabs of bistecca are served family style, with knives that allow hungry diners to do the portioning themselves. Fried potatoes are optional, but a must is a good spongy bread to absorb the pungent drippings that collect on plate and platter, not to mention glasses of one of Tuscany's big red wines.

Although the import of Chianina beef is prohibited in the United States, some Chianina cattle are domestically raised for a few very upscale restaurants; you'll also find many restaurants serving prime American beef in the style of Florence's bistecca.

WHERE: *In Florence,* Sostanza, tel 39/055-212691; *in Chianti,* Officina della Bistecca, tel 39/055-852176, dariocecchini.com; *in New York,* Costata, tel 212-334-3320, costatanyc.com; *in Boston,* Toscano, tel 617-723-4090, toscano boston.com. **FURTHER INFORMATION AND RECIPES:** American Chianina Association, chicattle.org; *The Food of Italy* by Waverley Root (1992); *Giuliano Bugialli's Foods of Italy* by Giuliano Bugialli (1984); foodnetwork.com (search bistecca alla fiorentina).

THE MOST SANGUINE OF CITRUS FRUITS

Blood Oranges

Italian

Beneath its unremarkable rind, the Sicilian blood orange—*arancia rossa*—exposes a crimson flesh that is equally awesome for its visual drama and for its tart, sweet, and pungent flavor. Blood oranges grow in Spain, throughout

the Mediterranean, and in California, but the lustiest fruits are the product of southern Italy's balmy climate. The winter's warm days and cool nights foster its particular anthocyanins—the pigments responsible for the fruit's bright reddish-blue coloring—and the summer heat develops its sweetness.

Sicilian farmers weren't trying for an exotic fruit. Sometime after the 1400s, they reported that the fruits began developing in the groves on their own, the unplanned offspring of blond sour oranges and sweet oranges. Today, the flushed fruit makes up a huge portion of Italy's citrus production, and its point of origin and quality are protected by the European Union's venerable Indicazione Geografica Protetta (I.G.P.) regulations. When it comes to flavor, the torocco variety, grown between January and May, is hailed as the sweetest. Aesthetically, the moro, ripe between December and February, is favored for its striking reddish rind and rich interior hues, which produce beautiful juices and sorbets.

Care should be taken when handling the fruits, as their juice tends to stain. The extra bit of caution is more than worthwhile when you consider all the sublime sorbets, granitas, and ice creams in store.

MAIL ORDER: Melissa's Produce, tel 800-588-0151, melissas.com. **FURTHER INFORMATION AND RECIPES:** *The Perfect Scoop* by David Lebovitz (2011); bloodorange.com. **TIP:** Ciao Bella makes an intense and delicious Sicilian Blood Orange Sorbet, ciaobella.com.

─┤||||||||||||||||||||||||||||├─

POOR MAN'S CAVIAR

Bottarga

Italian

The dried, pressed, and salted roe that is also known as poor man's caviar, *bottarga* is an addictively salty, gently chewy fish-egg specialty usually harvested from tuna or mullet. With a hue that mimics a rosy Mediterranean sunset, it is especially prized in southern Italy, including Sicily and Sardinia.

A product of sun, sea, and air, bottarga begins with the gentle massaging of the pouch of roe, which compresses the pouch's contents while reducing air pockets. Then it is time for a spot of alfresco air-drying, before two to three weeks of curing in salt. Thus handled, the roe firms up into a dry, hard slab, often a burnished red-orange-gold color, with the exact hue depending on the type of fish.

At its best, bottarga has a very intense fishy flavor that packs a serious savory punch. *Bottarga di muggine*, from the mullet, is more amber in hue and more subtle in flavor; *bottarga di tonno*, from the tuna, is both redder and more assertive. Usually thinly sliced or grated, most often over pasta—*spaghetti alla bottarga* being a specialty of Sardinian cuisine—the roe is equally delicious atop scrambled eggs or crème fraîche–dolloped canapés, in salads (as in a Caesar, taking the place of anchovies), or sliced atop ripe tomatoes as they prefer it in Sicily. Despite its nickname, bottarga fetches relatively high prices in upscale Italian food shops.

WHERE: *In Florence,* for *spaghetti alla bottarga,* Trattoria Cammillo, tel 39/055-212-427; *in New York,* Sandro's, tel 212-288-7374, sandros nyc.com. **RETAIL AND MAIL ORDER:** *In New York and Chicago,* Eataly, eataly.com. **FURTHER INFORMATION AND RECIPES:** *The Young Man and the Sea: Recipes and Crispy Fish Tales from Esca* by David Pasternack (2007); *Molto Italiano* by Mario Batali (2005); foodnetwork.com (search batali spaghetti alla bottarga); bottargaclub .com (click Bottarga Recipes).

─┤||||||||||||||||||||||||||||├─

SLOW COOKING FROM THE LAND OF SLOW FOOD

Brasato and Stracotto

Braised Meats

Italian

Slowly, slowly simmered with aromatic vegetables and herbs, the braised meats broadly known as pot roasts are as satisfying to prepare as they are to eat. For the cook, there is the satisfaction of transforming large, relatively tough cuts into melting tenderness while filling the home with comforting, mouthwatering aromas that ripen and change over the course of the braising. For the diner, these dishes offer nurturing tenderness and heady gravies that soak into soul-soothing carbs such as boiled potatoes, rice, polenta, silky fresh egg noodles, or airy dumplings.

In this homey and fragrant realm, Italy has two wonderful specialties well worth preparing and eating. *Brasato al Barolo* is much loved in Piedmont, where the region's deeply red and complex Barolo wine is the basis of the marinade. Larded with strips of pork fat, a meaty rump of beef is given a six- to twelve-hour bath in wine flavored with carrots, onions, and aromatic herbs such as thyme, rosemary, sage, and parsley. Once dried and flambéed with Cognac, the meat is seared in a combination of olive oil and butter, then simmered in the strained marinade until it falls apart at the touch of a fork. In Lombardy, the braising wine will also include garlic, as well as a dash of tomato puree to boost the color and flavor of the sauce.

Emilia-Romagna and Tuscany call their braised beef dish *stracotto*. It begins with a firm

Red wine complements brasato with mushrooms.

cut of round, rump, or chuck studded with garlic and simmered for six or seven hours in a terra-cotta casserole with red wine, parsley, carrots, celery, onions, and a haze of tomato puree. By the time the long-cooked beef is done, it is delectably falling apart, joining the gravy in a glorious meld. In Tuscany, in the place of potatoes or polenta, white beans cooked with bay leaves, onion, and a touch of tomato are preferred as an accompaniment.

Take heed: Resisting these aromatic braises is a tremendous feat of willpower, but the cooked meat develops maximum flavor and tenderness if it is kept in the refrigerator for twenty-four hours before being reheated and served.

WHERE: *In Florence,* Alla Vecchia Bettola, tel 39/055-224-158, florence.ala.it/bettola **FURTHER INFORMATION AND RECIPES:** *The Italian Country Table* by Lynne Rossetto Kasper (1999); italianfood.about.com (search brasato al barolo).

A BITTER, AND BETTER, BROCCOLI

Broccoli di Rapa

Italian

Twenty years ago, food writers might have laughed at the idea that a vegetable as bitter as the dark green *broccoli di rapa* (broccoli rabe) would one day become the height of fashion in the U.S. Yet this is the rags-to-riches tale of this

member-in-good-standing of the cabbage family, rich in iron, potassium, and antioxidants such as vitamin C. Credit its success to impeccable cooking, word of mouth and of the press, and the increasing sophistication of the American palate.

First cousin to the more common "American" broccoli, with its closely packed flowers, broccoli di rapa, which translates to the rather humble-sounding "turnip broccoli," is a more florid bouquet, with large, lively, dark green leaves and a few tiny florets ranging from yellow to green. Its seductive bitterness is almost always mitigated by plenty of garlic and a light coating of olive oil, and sometimes with a sprinkling of the dried hot red chile flakes called *peperoncini.*

The warm, enveloping flavor of broccoli di rapa is best suited to cold weather, when the vegetable might serve as a bed for the steamed garlicky pork sausage *cotechino* or a pan-grilled pork chop. It is also served as a *minestre,* a soup in which the leaves and florets are cooked *affogato* style, meaning suffocated: The vegetable is tossed in olive oil with sliced garlic and then slowly steamed with a little water in a tightly covered pot. The result is served in a deep

A side of broccoli rabe with olive oil and Parmesan

dish—pot liquor and all—with some coarse sourdough bread. Followed by chunks of Parmesan cheese and a ripe pear, it acts as the centerpiece of a satisfying light lunch.

When served as a vegetable side dish, the broccoli di rapa is first blanched, which reduces its bitterness somewhat and also its water. Drained and chopped, it is sautéed in garlic-flavored olive oil just before being brought to the table. (Leftovers can be enjoyed at room temperature as a side dish or as part of an antipasto.)

In the southern Adriatic region of Apulia, where the combination of pasta with vegetables is especially popular, sautéed broccoli di rapa—with or without crumbles of pork sausage—is tossed through the region's favorite pasta, the orecchiette or little ears. No cheese, please, but feel free to add lots of black pepper, peperoncini, or both.

FURTHER INFORMATION AND RECIPES: *Flavors of Puglia* by Nancy Harmon Jenkins (1997); cook str.com (search broccoli rabe and sausage bastianich; sautéed broccoli di rapa marchetto; orecchiette with rapini).

WHEN SOMETHING FISHY IS WELCOME

Brodetto Vastese

Italian (Abruzzese)

Along the Mediterranean coast of Italy, a hearty fish soup is called *zuppa di pesce.* Travel east to the edge of the Adriatic, to the provinces of Marche and Abruzzo, and *zuppa* becomes *brodetto*—each variation subject to intense

competition from town to town. In one place, exactly thirteen kinds of fish may be required; in another, ten or fourteen. Some versions include shellfish but not mollusks, and may use hot fresh or dried peppers, while in others only saffron or vinegar will do. The soup may be portioned out of a tureen or prepared as individual servings.

The gold standard is *brodetto Vastese,* credited to the lively clifftop town of Vasto, which overlooks its own *spiaggia,* or beach, and the clear, blue Adriatic. Almost every *ristorante* and trattoria in the region boasts a brodetto Vastese, but for the cognoscenti, all roads lead to the tiny Abruzzi village of Rocca San Giovanni and its Ristorante Il Cavaluccio, the seahorse. This big resortlike restaurant, with outdoor tables and a family-friendly beach in summer, sits at the edge of the sea, where its own nets and traps are fished out before every meal. (Actual seahorses are perhaps the only denizens of the deep not on its menu.)

Each portion of its legendary brodetto is individually prepared in a terra-cotta *tiello*, much like a pie pan in shape, and filled with rows of fish from roseate *triglie* (red mullet) to silvery *merluzzo*, or cod, plus local pink crustaceans and stony mussels and clams. A tomato broth is fired with incendiary dried red peppers and milder fresh green ones, all still at the boil when served, so that the fish seem to be jumping

to escape. They'd best give up, as no one who tastes this supple blend of seafood, spices, garlic, and sprightly parsley would ever stop while there was a single morsel left, nor before every drop of the aromatic broth had been sopped up with coarse, yeasty bread.

WHERE: *In Rocca San Giovanni,* Il Cavalluccio, tel 39/087-260-196, lidocavalluccio .it; *in New York,* Marea, tel 212-582-5100, mareanyc.com. **FURTHER INFORMATION AND RECIPES:** *Italian Regional Cooking* by Ada Boni (1994); foodnetwork.com (search brodetto fish soup). **SPECIAL EVENT:** Festivale Internazionale del Brodetto e delle Zuppa de Pesce, Fano, Italy, September, festivalbrodetto.it.

AN ANCIENT ANISE BREAD

Buccellato

Italian (Luccan)

R ich and fragrant, satisfying yet light, the anise-flavored sweet bread *buccellato* has been a specialty of the Tuscan town of Lucca since almost Roman times— its exquisite balance no doubt the result of years of cumulative practice in an

ancient town that is the proud birthplace of Giacomo Puccini and home to the elegant San Michele in Foro church, built between 1100 and 1300.

Lucca's bakers, particularly those at the Pasticceria Taddeucci, family owned and operated since 1881, have had plenty of time to get the formula straight. The long, narrow shop sells all manner of traditional Italian sweets and drinks, including bracing espresso and fennel-scented biscotti, along with its excellent loaves (*filoni*) and rings (*ciambelle*) of buccellato Lucchese. The bread itself is chewy, with a texture reminiscent of coffee cake, and perfumed heavily with yeast and anise. Its venerable recipe derives from

buccellatum, the bread of the Roman legions who took over the formerly Etruscan region in 180 B.C. (It's been sweetened since those days.)

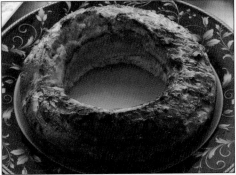

If you visit Lucca without eating buccellato, you'll miss out.

Classic buccellato is made with only flour, sugar, anise, egg, and yeast, but variations have sprung up; *treccia,* also on offer at Taddeucci, includes gratings of chocolate, raisins, bitter orange peel, and candied fruit. At the little tables outside overlooking the piazza, visitors can enjoy either one with their espresso. The rings, traditionally baked on feast days and holidays, keep well for several days and thus make great gifts—assuming you don't devour them on the plane home. In Italy they are typically purchased by grandparents in honor of their grandchildren's religious confirmations. As an extra reward, leftover slices make delicious French toast.

Where: *In Lucca,* Pasticceria Taddeucci, tel 39/0583-494-933; *in New York,* Pasticceria Bruno, tel 212-982-5854, pasticceriabruno.com. **Further information and recipes:** *The Italian Country Table* by Lynne Rossetto Kasper (1999); italianfood.about.com (search buccellato di lucca).

A CREAMY SURPRISE WITHIN

Burrata

Italian (Apulian)

The ultimate in creamy luxury, fresh burrata cheese is a specialty of the southern Adriatic province of Apulia. It is a fragile, fleeting pleasure best consumed within about twelve hours of its handcrafting, and therefore preferably on home ground. (Many cheesemakers, however, will tell you that, refrigerated and uncut, it can last up to two weeks.)

Suggesting a plump pouch of mozzarella made of Italy's richest milk, *fior di latte,* or with buffalo milk, and filled with pure, heavy sweet cream, burrata oozes with a satiny richness that puts whipped cream to shame. Wrapped in wild asphodel leaves that impart a subtly green flavor, it is the essence of springtime.

Although burrata is made in various towns of Apulia (including Foggia, Martina Franca, and Torremaggiore) and beyond, in the province of Basilicata, the benchmark product comes from Andría, halfway between Bari and the legendary tenth-century octagonal castle of Federico I. But because not even air travel brings the imported cheese to grocers' shelves soon enough to satisfy the dictates of its consumption, if you cannot sample it in Italy, opting for a local domestic variety is your best bet. Either way, it makes for a delicious dessert when served with ripe peaches, white muscat

Peaches and prosciutto accent the cheese.

grapes, or wild strawberries; or a sublime antipasto when plated with olives, prosciutto, and crusty bread or handmade breadsticks.

Where: *In New York and Chicago,* Eataly, eataly.com; *in El Monte, CA,* Gioia Cheese Co., tel 626-444-6015, gioiacheeseinc.com. **Further information:** *Cheese Primer* by Steven Jenkins (1996); *Flavors of Puglia* by Nancy Harmon Jenkins (1997); thenibble.com (search burrata cheese).

"LEAVE THE GUN. TAKE THE CANNOLI."—THE GODFATHER

Cannoli

Italian (Sicilian)

Probably the most widely known and beloved of all Italian pastries is the cannoli, whose name means "pipes." The pipes in question, crisply fried pastry tubes, come with a heavenly filling of sweetened ricotta cheese that is scented with rose-water and perhaps a whiff of cinnamon (sometimes in the form of cinnamon oil, to avoid the dusty flecks). Depending upon the pastry chef, the filling may be enlivened with crunchy chocolate bits and/or candied fruits and toasted pignoli nuts, or the open creamy ends dipped into bright green chopped pistachios for a modern touch of eye-grabbing color—that last being overkill for some.

For cannolis to be at their best, the crisp shells should be filled just before they are served, or not long before they leave the *pasticceria*. Pre-filled cannoli left standing around on shelves are inclined to become soggy, thereby losing one of the main appeals: the textural contrast of the crackling shells against the cool and silky softness of the filling. At some of the most impeccable Italian bakeries, the shells are sold empty and a container of the filling is provided. (A pastry tube comes in handy.)

In this time of gastronomic excess, chocolate-dipped cannoli shells filled with ricotta flavored in all manner of ways are not uncommon. Such embellishments are to be avoided, as all they do is override the pastry's innate subtlety.

WHERE: *In Rome,* La Cannoleria Siciliana, tel 39/06-6880-6874, lacannoleriasiciliana.it; *in New York,* Veniero's, tel 212-674-7070, venieros pastry.com; *in Boston,* Mike's Pastry Shop, tel 617-742-3050, mikespastry.com; *in New Orleans,* Angelo Brocato, tel 504-486-1465, angelobrocato icecream.com; *in San Francisco,* Stella Pastry Café, tel 415-986-2914, stellapastry.com. **FURTHER INFORMATION AND RECIPES:** *Pomp and Sustenance: Twenty-Five Centuries of Sicilian Food* by Mary Taylor Simeti (1989); epicurious.com (search sicilian cannoli). **SPECIAL EVENT:** Annual Cannoli Eating Competition, San Gennaro Festival, New York, September, sangennaro.org.

THE MOST MEDITERRANEAN OF BLENDS

Caponata

Italian

Taking its name from the salt-cured capers—*capperi*—that are its main ingredient, caponata is a silky vegetable salad with plenty of bite. The zesty Sicilian relish owes its sunshiny richness to an all-Mediterranean blend of eggplants, celery, olives, tomatoes, onions, those capers, and drizzlings of good red wine vinegar and olive oil, with a pinch of sugar to smooth things out; but its many recipes and variations sometimes call for artichoke bottoms, peppers, and anchovies as well. Italian scholars guess that the dish likely came to Sicily via the Spanish Catalonians; they have a similar cold vegetable salad called *caponada,* from the Spanish word for capers, *alcaparras.*

Served at room temperature, and especially restorative on a summer day, caponata is delicious as a topping for *crostini* (see page 185) or bruschetta, a filling for crisp celery stalks, or spooned onto cucumber slices or hard-cooked eggs. Though traditionally an antipasto, the spread can also be warmed slightly and tossed into short pasta such as rigatoni, ziti, or penne. (Cheese would be unnecessary, but chopped parsley adds a fresh kick.)

In a fastidious Sicilian kitchen, its preparation can be a leisurely affair. First, unpeeled, cut eggplants are lightly steamed and then fried. Celery is sautéed until just al dente so as not to become mushy. Tomatoes are simmered separately as well. Salt-dried capers are thoroughly rinsed and chopped. Once mixed, the caponata is often refrigerated for up to twenty-four hours to develop a rich, ripe flavor. Then, the mix must warm to room temperature. It's a taste of summer that's ripe for the picking—but not without a little bit of finessing.

WHERE: *In New York and Chicago,* Eataly, eataly.com. **FURTHER INFORMATION AND RECIPES:** *Coming Home to Sicily: Seasonal Harvests and Cooking from Casa Vecchie* by Fabrizia Lanza and Kate Winslow (2012); *Pomp and Sustenance: Twenty-Five Centuries of Sicilian Food* by Mary Taylor Simeti (1989); epicurious .com (search classic caponata); saveur.com (search eggplant caponata). **SEE ALSO:** Aubergine en Caton, page 54.

EDIBLE THISTLE, ROMAN VARIETY

Carciofi Romaneschi

Italian

There are artichokes and there are artichokes. None can match the dark green *carciofi Romaneschi,* the delectable thistle whose meaty leaves and tender heart are celebrated in Roman markets like the Campo dei Fiori from

late February through March. The artichoke-loving Romans certainly do embrace other varieties in other seasons, but this flat-topped globe specimen is best suited to that city's most famous preparations for the vegetable. There's *carciofi alla Romano,* in which the chokes are gently simmered in olive oil with parsley, mint, and lemon.

Also known as mammola *or* cimarolo, *Roman artichokes are exceptionally tender.*

And *carciofi alla Giudea,* a gift to the local cuisine from the Jewish ghetto, where the raw chokes are flattened and then deep-fried, to emerge looking like dried sunflowers. (Crisp, chiplike outer petals hint at the velvety, slightly bittersweet flavor of the tender heart that is the final reward.)

Highly prized since ancient Roman times, the

artichoke even inspired a legend. It seems there was a beautiful nymph, Cynara, who, after displeasing an irascible god, was metamorphosed into an artichoke. Thus, *Cynara scolymus* is the botanical name for the globe artichoke that contains the compound cynarin, said to ignite the taste buds. And thus, Italians may toast that nymph with the artichoke-based liqueur Cynar, a bitter, medicinal brew. Better to eat the artichoke, leaf by delectable leaf.

WHERE: *In Rome,* Campo dei Fiori market, Piazza Campo dei Fiori, tel 39/06-0606; Ristorante Matricianella, tel 39/06-683-2100, matricianella.it; Ristorante Piperno, tel 39/06-6880-6629, ristorantepiperno.com. **FURTHER INFORMATION AND RECIPES:** *Italian Food* by Elizabeth David (2001); *Marcella's Italian Kitchen* by Marcella Hazan (1986); saveur.com (search roman-style artichokes hazan).

LOOKS LIKE CELERY, TASTES LIKE ARTICHOKES

Cardoon

Italian

Where artichoke, celery, and fennel meet, the alluring flavor of the cardoon begins. And with giant, prickly, silver-green stalks that can grow to three feet, the look of the cardoon says nothing so much as celery with an overactive pituitary gland.

This Mediterranean favorite, a particular specialty in Italy that is best enjoyed in season, between November and January, takes its name from *charduus,* Latin for thistle—and thereby hangs a clue as to its challenging nature. "Our countrymen are fools to serve vegetables which asses and other beasts refuse for fear of pricking their lips," Pliny the Elder declared of the cardoon in the first century. But cardoons aren't just prickly. Like artichokes, which belong to the same thistle family, the vegetables blacken quickly when cut or peeled, tainting the hands that prepare them; an immediate soaking in water acidulated with lemon juice solves the first problem, and, if you can stand working with them, latex gloves negate the second.

Despite drawbacks that include high prices, cardoons have remained popular with the cognoscenti. To anyone who has sampled them, the reason for this popularity is obvious. Beneath each stalk's thorny, suedelike coating, the cardoon flesh is tender yet crisp, with a bittersweet flavor.

The finicky thistle grows well in the temperate climate that has benefited the plant since its first cultivation, in the fifteenth century. Known there as *cardone,* the vegetable is served raw in an old-fashioned Piedmontese preparation, cut up into pieces and submerged in a *bagna cauda*—a "warm bath" of olive oil, anchovies, and garlic. Alternatively, the cardoon pieces may be dipped in egg and flour and fried in olive oil, or blanched and baked under a mantle of butter and grated Parmesan. All are delectable options that reward the patient cook.

WHERE: *In New York and Chicago,* Eataly, eataly.com; *in Berkeley, CA,* Chez Panisse, tel 510-548-5525, chezpanisse.com. **FURTHER INFORMATION AND RECIPES:** *Vegetables from Amaranth to Zucchini* by Elizabeth Schneider (2001); *Chez Panisse Café Cookbook* by Alice Waters (1999); *Chez Panisse Vegetables* by Alice Waters (1996); Ocean Mist Farms, oceanmist.com (click Products, then Cardone); cookstr.com (search cardoons a la greque); epicurious.com (search fried cardoons).

‖||||||||||||||||||||||||||||||||‖

RAW, RED, AND DRESSED TO THE NINES

Carpaccio

Italian

Delicately silky, thinly sliced raw beef is the base of carpaccio, a dish invented in 1950 at Harry's Bar in Venice by Giuseppe Cipriani, who opened that famed restaurant in 1931. His creation stemmed from a desire to accommodate Contessa Amalia Nani Mocenigo, whose doctor had advised her to eat only raw meat.

The resourceful Cipriani sliced some garnet-red sirloin shell steak and drizzled it with a piquant ivory sauce based on mayonnaise, sunny-yellow dry mustard powder, an amber dash of Worcestershire sauce, lemon juice, olive oil, and the merest dribble of milk. He named the dish for the fifteenth-century Venetian painter Vittore Carpaccio, who favored the same deep-red and ivory-white hues, and whose work was on exhibition in Rome that year. Nowadays, we might name it after Jackson Pollack, as the sauce is artfully streamed in ribbons over the vibrant meat.

Still served throughout what has become a Cipriani empire, carpaccio has also traveled the world, turning up in all manner of guises as a seductive appetizer or light main course, sometimes enhanced with shavings of Parmesan cheese and a few leaves of arugula, and often sauced with only a drizzle of olive oil and some lemon juice. But its success has fostered copycat confusion, so that now almost anything served cold and thinly sliced is dubbed carpaccio. Restaurateurs, take heed: While the name might be acceptable when applied to raw tuna or lamb (but never, of course, to raw pork or chicken), it becomes absurd when used to describe sliced zucchini, beets, or cucumber.

To prepare it for its thinnest possible slicing, the beef used for carpaccio should be half-frozen —firm enough for a very sharp, thin-bladed but rigid knife to cut through evenly. After slicing, a very light pounding relaxes the texture. The slices are arranged on individual plates so the artistry of the streamed sauce remains intact when the dish is served, preferably with freshly made melba toast and a glass of light red wine.

WHERE: Harry's Bars and Cipriani restaurants around the globe, cipriani.com. **FURTHER INFORMATION AND RECIPES:** *Harry's Bar: The Life and Times of the Legendary Venice Landmark* by Arrigo Cipriani (1996); saveur.com (search carpaccio harry).

‖||||||||||||||||||||||||||||||||‖

A POT THAT WASTES NONE OF THE PIG

Cassoeula

Italian (Lombardian)

Theoretically, the stew called *cassoeula* could be enjoyed wherever one finds the right cuts of cured and fresh pork and sausages, the properly rippled savoy cabbage, and the carrots, celery, and onions. So much for the easy part. What is actually required for maximum appreciation—to truly grasp the beauty of this steaming dish—is the gray, businesslike city of Milan in late fall and winter, when its many-spired fifteenth-century Gothic cathedral is wrapped in the penetrating damp fog called the *nebbia*. It is this bone-chilling setting that gives this Lombardian specialty true meaning.

The rich casserole is filled with a scalding, slightly viscous broth verdant with wisps of the crinkly savoy cabbage the Italians call *verza,* plus root vegetables that impart an earthy sweetness. Broth and vegetables provide the base for a butcher's array of pork cuts both fresh and cured: Two pigs' feet and one ear lend a sensuously gelatinous body to the broth, and the firm and aromatic pork sausage *luganega da Monzo* is joined by fresh cuts of pork rump, smoked rib chops, and a chunk or two of bacon for diversity and heartiness.

This simmering-hot main course, so welcome in the foggy Milanese winter chill, is served in and eaten from individual earthenware casseroles, with broth typically spooned up before the meats and vegetables are tackled. The meats are often dabbed with hot mustard or horseradish as they are eaten.

Just like so many other robust culinary extravaganzas, cassoeula is traditionally a weekend lunchtime dish, often accompanied by soft, golden cornmeal polenta that provides soothing contrast and added assurance that no one leaves the table hungry. A light red wine or a frothy beer further ensures that the only dessert following this opulent and hearty main course will be a long afternoon nap.

Now most often served in homes, cassoeula remains one of the favorite winter specialties at the more than one-hundred-year-old Antica Trattoria della Pesa, a former weigh station with the telltale scales still outside the door. Its wood paneling, comfortable booths, pretty flowers, and impressive displays of antipasti and desserts (save room for the wine-baked pears) lie about twenty minutes outside Milan's center, close to the Cimiterio Monumentale, where many celebrity graves are marked with important sculptures. Visit the Cimiterio and its sculptures before the cassoeula; it is doubtful anyone will be up to the walk afterward.

WHERE: *In Milan,* Antica Trattoria della Pesa, tel 39/02-655-5741, anticatrattoriadella pesa.com. **FURTHER INFORMATION AND RECIPES:** *Italian Regional Cooking* by Ada Boni (1994); food52.com (search cassoeula).

WHAT LUCKY BABIES CUT THEIR TEETH ON

Castagnaccio

Italian (Tuscan and Ligurian)

About as subtle as a dessert can be, the *castagnaccio* is a cake so spare and simple it used to be served as a first solid food to the lucky babies of Liguria, where it remains a beloved tradition on both All Souls' Day and Easter.

Much appreciated in fall and winter, though it's available year-round, the thin, single-layer cake is based on a fine tawny flour milled of chestnuts, or *castagne*. A tweedy, grainy, plain-looking round that's more savory than sweet, it is gently accented with olive oil, rosemary, toasted pignoli nuts, and currants or white sultana raisins.

At first taste, the castagnaccio might prove a disappointment to those used to really sweet sweets. But after several tries, its understated aromas and flavors begin to emerge and beguile, most especially if downed with a good red Tuscan wine or a heady grappa. For a frivolous touch, a slice can be topped with cinnamon- or rum-flavored ice cream—but best to keep such transgressions out of sight of any Tuscans, although none seem too upset by the cloudlet of ricotta added at Cantinetta Antinori in Florence.

In Liguria, a similar version includes fragrant, lightly crushed fennel seeds that add an aniselike aroma. A cool, light white wine that is slightly sparkling, or *frizzante,* is the favored accompaniment.

This smooth cake features raisins, pine nuts, and rosemary.

Where: *In Florence,* Cantinetta Antinori, tel 39/55-292-234, cantinetta-antinori.com; *in New York,* Il Ristorante Rosi, tel 212-517-7700, salume riarosi.com. **Further information and recipe:** food52.com (search castagnaccio).

||||||||||||||||||||||||||||||

FIT FARE FOR BRAINIACS

Cervello Arreganata

Baked Calves' Brains with Seasoned Bread Crumbs

Italian

Ever since the mad cow scare of the early 2000s, it has been difficult to find brains on restaurant menus. And in this age of nose-to-tail eating, that's a pity. Properly prepared brains have a luxuriously creamy texture and a subtly

seductive flavor akin to but more delicate than that of sweetbreads. In addition, brains (like sweetbreads) are good for you, as they are extremely high in the B vitamins and rich in protein if also, alas, in cholesterol.

While delicious brain specialties are enjoyed in many areas of the world, Italy's ultimate version of the heady meat is one of a kind—surpassing even the breaded and golden-fried brains popular in many countries.

Where you are lucky enough to find it, *cervello arreganata* (or oreganata) will be a star attraction. The dish should arrive at the

table sizzling hot and creamy under a mantle of crisp golden crumbs, perfumed with garlic, oregano, parsley, olive oil, and the slight salty needling of capers. The result is a mouthwatering main course defined by the contrast of crisp crumbs and pungent garlic with the brains' satiny softness and slightly acidic pinch of flavor. Only a small, sprightly green salad and a glass of light red wine are needed to complete the feast.

Calves' brains are the standard for most Italian cooks, but the smaller lambs' brains, with an even more interestingly complex flavor, lend themselves beautifully to this preparation in Italy's Abruzzo region. Whatever the animal of origin, the elimination of brains from menus can hardly be counted as gastronomic progress—let's hope for at least small signs of their resurgence before too long.

Cervello Arreganata

Serves 2 as main course,
4 as appetizer

For the most attractive presentation, bake and serve the brains in individual copper or enameled cast-iron gratin pans or shallow ovenproof baking dishes like small pie pans. For two main course servings, each dish should be 6 to 7 inches in diameter and 1 1/2 to 2 inches deep. For an appetizer, the brains can be baked in a 9-inch gratin or pie pan.

2 pounds fresh whole calves' brains
Ice
½ cup distilled white vinegar
Salt
8 whole black peppercorns
6 tablespoons (¾ stick) unsalted butter
2 medium-size cloves garlic, peeled
1 cup fine unseasoned bread crumbs
1 tablespoon dried oregano leaves
Freshly ground black pepper
2 to 4 lemon wedges sliced lengthwise

1. Place the brains in a large bowl of ice water with ¼ cup of the vinegar and a pinch of salt to remove the blood. Let the brains soak in the refrigerator until they look white to very pale pink and the water has turned deep pink, about 3 hours. Drain the brains.

2. Bring water to boil in a 2- to 3-quart pot with a pinch of salt, the peppercorns, and the remaining ¼ cup of vinegar. Turn off the heat, add the brains, and cover the pot. Let the brains stand for about 20 minutes.

3. Remove the brains from the pot and rinse them under cold running water until they are cool enough to be comfortably handled. Discard the cooking water.

4. Using your fingers, gently pull off bits of the thin, filmy membranes and the thickest white tubes that are visible around the brain mass. Try not to break up the lobes any more than necessary but clumps can be massed together when the brains are placed in the baking dish(es). The brains can be prepared in advance up to this point and refrigerated for about 4 hours. Let them come to room temperature, about 30 minutes, before continuing.

5. About 30 minutes before serving time, place a rack in the middle of the oven and preheat the oven to 400°F.

6. Melt the butter in a 7- to 8-inch sauté pan over very low heat. Using a garlic press, crush the garlic into the melted butter. Stir and let the garlic simmer over very low heat until it loses its raw smell but does not turn darker than a pale yellow, about 3 minutes.

7. Stir in the bread crumbs, adding about 2 tablespoons at a time. Cook over low heat, stirring gently but constantly, until the butter is absorbed. Continue adding bread crumbs until the overall texture looks like slightly damp sand but is a bit fluffy. Stir in the oregano, crushing it slightly between your fingers as you do so. Taste for seasoning, adding salt and ground black pepper to taste (see Note).

8. Butter the inside of the baking dish(es). Place half of the brains in each dish for individual portions or all of them in a single baking dish. Push together any clumps of brains that have separated so there is a solid mass filling the dish.

9. Cover the brains completely with a sprinkling of the seasoned bread crumbs. Do not tamp the crumbs down or they will absorb moisture and become mushy.

10. Bake the brains until the bread crumbs become a bright golden brown, 15 to 20 minutes. Serve the brains at once with the lemon wedges on the side.

Note: The seasoned arreganata bread crumbs can be prepared 4 or 5 hours ahead and kept covered at room temperature.

Tip: Order calves' brains from a butcher several days in advance, preferably fresh, not frozen. **See also:** Hirn mit Ei, page 295; Cervelles au Beurre Noir, page 72.

|||||||||||||||||||||||||||||||||||||||||||||||||||||||||||||||||||||||||||||||||||||||||||||||||||||||||||||||||||||||||||

A VERSATILE AND FESTIVE NUT

Chestnuts

Chestnuts really do roast on open fires, as an autumnal street food that warms hands and hearts and brings teasing twitches to noses inhaling the scents of hot charcoal and toasting shells. Among the most quintessential of seasonal harbingers wherever they are enjoyed (a connection so entrenched in Italy that fall there is known as *la tempa de castagne,* the season of chestnuts), chestnuts are velvety soft inside with a light outer glazing of smoke.

The word *chestnut* refers primarily to the fruit of the European sweet castanea or Spanish chestnut tree, wonderful when foraged wild but also prized when cultivated. Called *marron* in French, the nut is mainly grown around Lyon, where it is also candied to become the famed *marron glacé.* As *kuri,* chestnuts are also considered autumn treats in Japan.

Though it's a luxury food today, the chestnut's distinctive rich starchiness made it a staple food of European peasants for centuries. Chestnuts were also frequently used as feed for swine, fattening and enriching the pork with hints of chestnutty sweetness, but these days the roasted nuts can be seen elevating all sorts of dishes, from creamy soups based on game stock to stuffings, cabbage, risottos, and innumerable desserts, in particular the one called *Monte Bianco* (*Mont Blanc* to the French). This is served as a holiday treat, a rich puree of cooked chestnut meat savory with wine or brandy, sugar, and spices that is piped out in a mountain (*monte*) of squiggles and topped with snowy whipped cream (*bianco*).

But the very best way to experience a chestnut is freshly roasted. To roast chestnuts at home, preheat the oven to 375°F. Use a sharp knife to cut a small cross into the round side of each chestnut. Roast them on a parchment-lined baking sheet for about 40 minutes, or until the cut crosses pop open when lightly pressed to split the skins. Or roast them over a fire, using a special perforated chestnut-roasting pan.

Where: Roasted chestnuts are sold by outdoor vendors in New York City and throughout much of southern Europe, particularly in Rome, Corsica, southern France, and Spain, and particularly from October to January. **Mail order:** For chestnuts and long-handled chestnut roasting pans, Melissa's Produce, tel 800-588-0151, melissas.com. **Further information and recipes:** *Italian Holiday Cooking: A Collection of 150 Treasured Recipes* by Michele Scicolone (2001); cookstr.com (search chestnuts bittman); ehow .com (search about roasting chestnuts). **Tip:** Chestnuts are generally in season from October through December. When buying fresh chestnuts from green grocers, look for shells that are dark brown and without significant blemishes. If the nuts rattle in the shell, they are too dried out. **Special events:** Kalorama Chestnut Festival, Kalorama, Victoria, Australia, first Sunday in May, chestnutfestival.com.au; West Virginia Chestnut Festival, Rowlesburg, WV, October, wvchestnutfestival.com.

———————||||||||||||||||||||||||||||||||||||||———————

Christmas Eve Fish Dinner

Italian

Christmas Eve—*La Vigilia* in Italy—is indeed a night of vigilance, if not for the eastern star that guided the Wise Men, then perhaps for the odd bone hiding in that plate of fish. In Italy, at least, this would be a wise vigil, for the traditional feast on that mystical evening is a multifish dinner, with the required number of specimens ranging from seven to thirteen. Leave it to the food-wise Italians to end the traditional Catholic day of fasting with a feast highlighting the delectable variety of fish and shellfish that abound in Italian waters.

Now fashionable enough to be featured as a Christmas Eve special in some of the more ambitious Italian restaurants around the United States, the multicourse extravaganza is better realized in homes, where one can eat in relaxed, informal surroundings and take time to gossip and reminisce between courses.

To many, including the celebrated chef Mario Batali, seven is the magic number of fish to be served on this night. But as he notes, no one is truly sure of the proper number: "Some families do seven for the sacraments. Some do ten for the stations of the Cross. And some even do thirteen for the twelve apostles plus Jesus."

Festa, Helen Barolini's book of Italian holiday foods, tells us that seven is variously thought to represent the sacraments, Christ's seven utterances from the cross, the seven gifts of the Holy Spirit, or seven heroes of Christianity—saints Andrew of Scotland, Anthony of Italy, David of Wales, Denis of France, George of England, James of Spain, and Patrick of Ireland.

Whatever the target number, one might assume one could fulfill the numerical requirement with a single opulent dish such as, say, a seafood salad, or the mixed fry that is *fritto misto de pesce* (see page 190), or *brodetto* fish soup (see page 170). But that would be cheating, for tradition dictates that each fish be served as a separate course or, if combined, be counted only as one, with other dishes added to make up the required total.

The meal might begin with seafood salad or baked clams and mussels *arreganata,* followed by two pastas, each with a different fish sauce, then by a series of individually prepared fish such as bass, mullet, flounder, and certainly eel, that last being a mandatory symbol of good fortune on Christmas Eve.

Batali's menu begins with the baked clams in garlic bread crumbs, then moves on to marinated anchovies, linguine with clams, spaghetti with mussels, salt cod (*baccalà,* in Spanish *bacalao*) simmered with tomatoes and capers, jumbo shrimp Marsala, and eel braised with olives, chiles, and capers.

Barolini suggests mussels in white wine sauce, an anchovy-dressed salad, a sardine pâté on crostini, two bowls of spaghettini—one with red clam sauce, the other with white—then broiled shrimp and poached whiting. Neither mentions octopus or calamari, but these cephalopods often join the party.

WHERE: *In New York,* Ai Fiori, tel 212-613-8660, aifiorinyc.com; Greenwich Grille, tel 646-609-3615, greenwichgrille.com. **FURTHER INFORMATION AND RECIPES:** *Festa* by Helen Barolini (1988); for Christmas Eve seafood pasta, *Rao's Recipes from the Neighborhood* by Frank Pellegrino (2004); thedailymeal.com (search my italian-american christmas eve); epicurious.com (click Video, then search Mario Batali's feast of the seven fishes).

A SAUSAGE FOR SPREADING

Ciauscolo

Italian (Marchigian)

A particular favorite in the Marche, the bountiful bourgeois province set between the Adriatic Sea and the Apennine mountains, *ciauscolo* (chee-AHS-cole-oh) is an unctuously seductive pork spread disguised as a sausage, much

in the style of German tea-wursts and French rillettes (see page 75). One theory has it that the velvety spread, with its spicing of pepper, garlic, wine, and (variously) grated orange rind, cloves, and mace, was created by French settlers living in the Macerata area of the Marche, where the town of Visso is now the center of ciauscolo worship. Difference was, the French did not pack the spread into sausage casings made of intestines, but rather into earthenware terrines; nor did they gently smoke it over fragrant juniper wood before aging it for a couple of months—these are purely Italian innovations.

With its mild flavor and seductive aroma, ciauscolo

Slice or slather on bread.

may be habit-forming. It can be eaten sliced or spread onto bread or toast. Its name (sometimes *ciavuscolo* or *ciabuscolo*) is believed to have been derived from the medieval Latin *ciabusculum*, meaning small or little food, or what we might call a snack today—and a pretty good one at that.

WHERE: *In New York*, Babbo, tel 212-777-0303, babbo nyc.com; Salumeria Rosi, tel 212-877-4800, salumeriarosi .com. **RETAIL AND MAIL ORDER:** *In Senigallia, Italy*, Enoteca Galli, tel 39/071-63811, gallienoteca .it; *in Chicago*, West Loop Salumi, tel 312-255-7004, west loopsalumi.com. **FURTHER INFORMATION AND RECIPE:** lpoli.50webs .com (click Formulations, then Ciauscolo).

KEEPING ABREAST OF THINGS

Cima Ripiena alla Genovese

Italian (Ligurian)

Tender veal breast meat with a lavish, savory stuffing, Genoa's delectable and elegant *cima* offers great reward for its complex preparation. Although ingredients vary from one cook to another, at its most classic and best, the carefully boned breast of veal is filled with a colorful pâtélike mix of ground veal enriched with the calf's own silky sweetbreads and brains—a mix that is studded with tiny green peas, diced artichokes, grated lemon rind, ivory pignoli nuts, minced parsley, hard-cooked eggs, and tiny dicings of roasted red peppers or cooked carrots, forming a sparkling mosaic when the meat is sliced. Lush seasonings of grated Parmesan cheese, salt, pepper, marjoram, garlic, and, for some, a grating of nutmeg add to the appeal.

Slices reveal the colorfully elaborate stuffing.

The stuffed loaf is wrapped in cheese-cloth and poached in a rich vegetable broth, then cooled and pressed lightly between two platters to firm up; for full flavor and the right texture for slicing, the cima is thus weighted and chilled overnight.

It's a dish that is especially suited to buffet service, pretty enough to be a centerpiece when bedecked with some frilly green garnishes. A rice salad is an especially welcome accompaniment, as are roasted red peppers (if none appear in the stuffing). A dab of Liguria's signature fragrant basil pesto adds a final bit of flourish to each slice. If it is to be served warm, which is less common, the whole pressed and chilled cima is reheated very slowly in vegetable broth. It is sliced and served with either pesto or spicy mustard.

FURTHER INFORMATION AND RECIPES: *Giuliano Bugialli's Foods of Italy* by Giuliano Bugialli (1984); *A Mediterranean Feast* by Clifford A. Wright (1999); italianfood.about.com (search cima alla genovese). **TIP:** It is best to have a butcher do the boning so the meat will not be badly torn.

—|IIIIIIIIIIIIIIIIIIIIIIIIIIIIIII|—

A PALATE-COOLER FROM THE MEDICIS

Cinnamon Granita

Italian

Considered an aid to digestion as well as to sexual prowess, cinnamon was a favorite in ancient Rome, where overindulgence in the gustatory and carnal pleasures would have accounted for its popularity.

We tend to think of fruit when we think of flavored ices. But in Renaissance Italy, especially around Florence and other Tuscan cities where trade with Asia was in full swing, lavishly used spices were extravagant status symbols—so it's no surprise to see them taking center stage in this simplest of desserts. The exotic, warm, and woodsy-sweet overtones of cinnamon are a teasingly seductive foil for the cool, clear, fine-grained ices that, in the tradition of a true granita, contain no milk or cream. To avoid specks of cinnamon that might be mistaken for dust, cinnamon oil was used to flavor these refreshing treats.

Cinnamon Granita

Makes about 1½ quarts, serves 8 to 10

2¼ cups sugar
10 cups water
¼ teaspoon cinnamon oil
4 or 5 drops red food coloring (optional,
  see Note)

1. Combine the sugar and water in a heavy saucepan and boil gently until a light syrup forms, about 7 minutes. Refrigerate the sugar water until it is completely cool, about 20 minutes.

2. Stir in the cinnamon oil and pour the mixture into a bowl or a shallow dish. Cover with a piece of heavy-duty aluminum foil and place in the freezer.

3. As the mixture begins to turn slushy, beat it with a wire whisk or rotary beater to break down the ice particles, then smooth the mixture back into place. Re-cover with the foil and return to the freezer. Repeat every 30 minutes until the granita is firm, without liquid but still icily granular, about 4 hours. Serve the granita in small chilled glasses or ceramic dishes.

Note: If you would like the cinnamon granita to have an appealing red color, add the food coloring with the final beating. However, be prepared for some wag to identify the final result as granita de Lavoris.

Tip: Cinnamon oil can be obtained at many specialty food shops as well as from Internet sources and some pharmacies. **See also:** Italian Ices, page 199.

AN ITALIAN APPROACH TO SAUERKRAUT

Crauti, Italian-Style

Italian

O n first consideration, no food appears more antithetical to the Italian palate than sauerkraut, that totally Germanic salt-preserved cabbage—its assertive, pungent sourness seems hopelessly at odds with typical Italian seasonings.

But there are many Italys, of course, and in the northern regions, a strong Austro-German influence is a holdover from the sixth to eighth centuries, when the Langobards (hence, Lombardy) held sway. A taste for sauerkraut—*crauti*—remains a minor relic of that period in regions stretching from Lombardy to Emilia-Romagna, Trentino–Alto Adige, and Friuli–Venezia Giulia, which includes the city of Trieste.

How does sauerkraut translate into irresistible and irresistibly Italian specialties? Let us count the ways. In Lombardian Milan, as well as in the Emilian city of Modena, you can bite into scrumptiously juicy sandwiches of warm sauerkraut topped with thick slices of the coarse cooked pork sausage known as *cotechino* (when enclosed in a traditional sausage casing) or as *zampone* (when encased in a pig's foot). The soft, mild meat and sprightly crauti glossed with mustard or horseradish on a soft-but-crusty bun make for a very particular taste treat.

In the beautifully alpine Dolomite region of Trentino–Alto Adige, restaurants offer ravioli on sauerkraut—but these are not ravioli as we know them. Here, the thin dough pouches enfold richly meaty, earthy bloodwurst, the dark velvety Austrian sausage of pig's blood that gets a light spicing of clove, nutmeg, and pepper.

In Emilia-Romagna, home cooks simmer a lusty soup of beans, pork, and sauerkraut. In areas around the piney spa town of Merano, you'll find the local bread dumplings known as *canederli* (their word and form suggestive of the Jewish matzoh balls called *knaidel*). Tyrolesi canederli include specks of bacon, onions, and parsley; canederli neri, or black canederli, are based on gritty brown buckwheat groats; and

yet another variety, *canederli di fegato*, is made with liver. Nestled on crauti fragrant with garlic, bay leaves, and olive oil, all make for a hearty and delicious repast.

WHERE: *In Naturno, near Merano, Italy,* Ristorante Wiedenplatzerkeller, tel 39/04-7367-3280, restaurant-naturns.com. **FURTHER INFORMATION AND RECIPES:** *Italian Regional Cooking* by Ada Boni (1994); *Essentials of Classic Italian Cooking* by Marcella Hazan (1992), see Beans and Sauerkraut Soup.

TOAST, RENDERED SUBLIME

Crostini

Italian (Tuscan)

One of the most justly celebrated appetizers in Florence has got to be *crostini di fegato*—the canapés of crisply pan-toasted bread topped with an irresistible velvety mash of chicken livers that have been slowly simmered in olive oil and are fragrant with sage leaves.

A particularly well-executed version has delighted at least four generations of diners at the authentically rustic favorite Trattoria Sostanza, a no-frills restaurant founded in 1869 and known for its Florentine steaks, these crostini, and little else worth ordering. Here, the liver and sage are simmered with piney crushed juniper berries, a hint of garlic, salt and black pepper, and red wine; for textural contrast, some of the livers are cut in small chunks and added toward the end of cooking. Just before they arrive at your table, the crostini are spread with a thick layer of the room-temperature liver puree and topped with whole sage leaves.

Another classic of the Tuscan kitchen, *crostini di fagioli*, is an iteration topped with little white cannellini beans. Sautéed with heady additions of hot red *peperoncini* flakes, garlic, tomato paste, rosemary, olive oil, and lemon

juice, the beans are mashed into a rich puree, sprinkled with emerald-green minced leaves of Italian parsley, and spread on those crispy bread slices as a delectable accompaniment to predinner aperitifs. (Chickpeas can be substituted for the cannellini for a slightly earthier effect.)

One currently popular riff on crostini is bruschetta, based on thicker slices of lightly toasted bread. Often served with chopped tomatoes, basil, and garlic, it's especially delicious topped with sautéed chunks of chicken livers.

WHERE: *In Florence,* Trattoria Sostanza, tel 39/055-212691; *in New York,* for bruschetta with chicken livers, ABC Kitchen, tel 212-475-5829, abckitchennyc.com. **FURTHER INFORMATION AND RECIPES:** *Giuliano Bugialli's Foods of Italy* by Giuliano Bugialli (1984); epicurious.com (search chicken liver sage crostini).

⊣||||||||||||||||||||||||||||||⊢

THE FILET MIGNON OF PORK

Culatello

Italian (Emilian-Romagnan)

To connoisseurs of Italian cured meats, the real prize is *culatello,* the delicately aged chunk of tender, meaty pork leg. Never mind those who accord first-place honors to prosciutto: The culatello is the most prime part of the pig's hind legs—the cheeks, or *culo*—whereas regular prosciutto is cut from the whole leg.

Believed to have been created in the mid-fourteenth century, the ham has been a matter of written record in Parma since 1735. (It was the avowed favorite of the poet Gabriele D'Annunzio, who in 1891 specified that it be aged "where the air of the Po is often humid and good for the mold that preserves this fatless cut of meat.") The meat's texture is at once supple and firm enough to titillate the palate, with wisps of snowy fat bringing out its luxuriously earthy, nutty flavor.

Culatello di Zibello

The best culatello comes from Emilia-Romagna, the province so justly celebrated for its proficiency with many types of hams and sausages. Historically, strict American food regulations meant that very little genuine culatello made it stateside; thankfully, 2013 saw the lifting of the USDA's constraints on Italian cured meats, with a flourishing of import activity sure to follow.

Within Emilia-Romagna, the ultimate product is *culatello di Zibello,* produced artisanally in a specific area around Parma, centered in the town of Zibello—a product so distinctive that its name is protected by the territorial Denominazione di Origine Protetta (D.O.P.) label. The label assures not only that the meat was cured within the area, but that the pig resided there while alive, and that all steps of the slaughter, butchering, and curing were performed within the region's boundaries.

The cut for culatello is the bundle of muscles from the upper hind leg of the native pig. After being skinned and boned (another way in which culatello differs from prosciutto, which is cured on the bone), the cut is salted down; enmeshed in a net of twine that imparts a pear shape, it is then encased in a pig's bladder for a year-long hanging in a cold curing room, where it dehydrates to a weight of six to ten pounds.

When it has cured to perfection, the snowy mold-covered chunk must be trimmed of twine and washed in warm water, then left to soften in dry white wine for a few days. For the tenderest results and most felicitous mouthfeel, the meat should be hand-sliced into thin, silky folds that follow its grain and form.

WHERE: *In Bologna,* Tamburini, tel 39/051-234726, tamburini.com. **FURTHER INFORMATION:** *The Splendid Table* by Lynne Rossetto Kasper (1992). **SPECIAL EVENT:** November Porc, tastings of culatello di Zibello, Emilia-Romagna, November, novemberporc.com.

Espresso

Italian

Sure, you can get espresso everywhere these days—but will it be made with just the right amount of the right coffee, and with perfect water at a precise temperature, by a trained barista? For a benchmark espresso, stroll around the Pantheon in Rome (the most complete ancient Roman building in town) to Piazza Sant'Eustachio and knock one back at the bar of Caffè Sant'Eustachio, famous for the mellow strength of its espresso and the quality of its telltale spuma. This foam topping is considered perfect when it is tinted a creamy tan, never black (an indication of brewing with overheated water), and can hold a sprinkling of sugar for several seconds before it sinks. Lightly sweetened unless requested otherwise, Sant'Eustachio's espresso is designed for the Roman palate—prepared with less-acidic coffee than is preferred in northern Italy (Rome being the dividing line between Italy's north and south).

It's easy to get into arguments about Rome's best espresso, but Tazza d'Oro seems to be the top challenger to Sant'Eustachio. The chain has several locations, but the outpost aficionados prefer is also near the Pantheon.

Amble back and forth between Tazza d'Oro and Sant'Eustachio and decide for yourself, but beware of catching a case of the jitters while you're at it. In summer, at either café, try the restorative icy *granita di caffè*—what we know as Italian ice, made of this lusty caffeinated drink. For a real indulgence, order it *con panna*, with a cloudlet of softly whipped cream.

WHERE: *In Rome,* Il Caffè Sant'Eustachio, tel 39/06-686-1309, santeustachioilcaffe.it; La Casa del Caffè del Tazza d'Oro, tel 39/06-67-89-792, tazzadorocoffeeshop.com. **TIP:** Do it yourself with imported espresso coffee from Illy or Danesi, both widely available in the U.S.

Fegato alla Veneziana

Venetian-Style Calf's Liver

Italian (Venetian)

It has been said that liver is often both underrated and overcooked—and this statement is all too true. Lightly and delicately sautéed in butter, the tender meat *should* emerge with just a faint golden glow and a blush-pink interior.

It should also be calf's liver, with its smooth, unctuous texture and mild, delicate flavor—or pig's or lamb's liver, the latter of which is typically seen around the Mediterranean. Coarse, strong beef liver is usually what gives all liver a bad name.

Nowhere is calf's liver more exalted than in the Veneto region of Italy, where *fegato alla veneziana* began its reign: Thin slices of tender, sage-seasoned calf's liver were sautéed with satiny soft onions, a splash of vinegar (or sometimes white wine) ending it all with a tang. The dish was elevated to new and fashionable heights when the Cipriani family opened Harry's Bar in Venice in 1931 and took the then-daring step of putting the offal on the menu. The move kicked off a new feeling about rustic Italian food and put calf's liver with onions on the culinary map. (A sunny helping of softly cooked polenta didn't hurt the cause.)

Lightly sautéed, the dish is delicate but satisfying.

Where: *In Venice,* Harry's Bar, tel 39/ 041-528-5777, harrysbarvenezia.com; *in New York,* Harry Cipriani, tel 212-308-5653, cipriani .com; *in Scottsdale, AZ,* Veneto Trattoria, tel 480-948-9928, venetotrattoria.com. **Further**

Information and recipes: *The Harry's Bar Cookbook* by Harry Cipriani (1991); *Saveur Cooks Authentic Italian* edited by *Saveur* magazine (2008); foodnetwork.com (search calves liver venetian style).

A CHRISTMAS TREAT FROM CAMPAGNA

Fichi Ripieni al Forno

Baked Figs with Almonds

Italian (Neapolitan and Calabrian)

Come November, most serious, upscale Italian delis or groceries begin to stock little square straw baskets holding tightly compressed, golden-brown figs, each stuffed with a whole toasted almond. In a treat that is traditional to the

Naples area, the figs are baked with a topping of fragrant bay leaves, some redolent of wine or brandy, and all with a sweet, chewy succulence that contrasts with the sudden snap-crunch of the almond within.

The Calabrian version has a richer stuffing: Powdered cocoa is added to slivered almonds, along with the diced peels of oranges, lemons, and citrons. While hot, the baked, stuffed figs are dipped in red wine and layered into a terrine, along with sprinklings of powdered cinnamon, cloves, and sugar. They're then left to cool and their flavors to ripen. They remain

delectably fresh, chewy, and moist for months, their exotic blend of flavors intact; if they do dry out, a brief simmering in clove-scented red wine (in which they can be left to marinate for a day or two) will return them to a lusciously viable state once again.

Whether of the Neapolitan or the Calabrian persuasion, baked stuffed figs are delicious with glasses of wine, grappa, or strong tea, and make an elegant and satisfying small dessert after a large meal.

Where: *In New York and Chicago,* seasonally, Eataly, eataly.com.

—||||||||||||||||||||||||||||||—

CHEESE FOR TRUFFLE LOVERS

Fontina d'Aosta

Italian

The parallels in flavor between a ripe, pungent white truffle and this cheese from the same Piedmont region of northern Italy are examples of the power of *terroir*. Fontina d'Aosta's earthy essence is not really so surprising. But welcome it is, enhancing a firm ivory cheese that is soft enough for nibbling but more alluring when cooked.

Made for centuries from unpasteurized cow's milk, Fontina d'Aosta is a classic semi-hard cheese. It comes in sunny twenty-pound wheels that sport official emblems attesting to its authenticity. Thankfully we can import high-quality Fontina d'Aosta to our shores because it is ripened for nearly four months, satisfying U.S. import laws, which require raw-milk cheeses to be aged a minimum of sixty days. Look for Fontina marked Denominazione di Origine Protetta (D.O.P.), assuring its point of origin, ingredients, and methods of processing, all overseen by a consortium authorized by the Italian ministry.

Fontina graces all manner of pressed sandwiches and pizzas, but it makes its most authentic appearance in the dish *fonduta*. A first cousin to the Swiss fondue, the hearty mountain specialty involves a heated, whipped combination of cheese, milk, butter, and eggs, spooned atop rice, polenta, or vegetables. (Urbane city-folk seeking kingly meals would be well advised to top homemade *fonduta* with grated white truffles and serve it with a Piedmont red wine such as Barbaresco.)

RETAIL AND MAIL ORDER: *In New York,* Murray's Cheese, tel 888-692-4339, murrays cheese.com. **FURTHER INFORMATION AND RECIPES:** *Lidia Cooks from the Heart of Italy* by Lidia Bastianich (2009); *Cheese Primer* by Steven Jenkins (1996). **TIP:** When shopping for fontina, avoid old rounds, detectable by their off, some-what foul odor or cracked appearance.

—||||||||||||||||||||||||||||||—

THE LOOK OF FRIED LACE

Frico

Italian

It's hard to believe that the lacy-edged and crisp *frico*—literally "little trifle"— is simply a bit of grated hard cheese fried in olive oil or baked in a hot oven. The quintessentially cheesy and utterly habit-forming appetizer, traditionally made with a sweet and milky cow's cheese called Montasio, has a marvelous simplicity that belies a long and fascinating history: A specialty of Italy's northeastern Friuli–Venezia Giulia region, it was a snack that the wives of vineyard workers made for their spouses at lunchtime as early as the fifteenth century.

Inventive cooks eventually figured out that hot-off-the-griddle frico can be molded before it cools, perhaps formed into little baskets to be filled with polenta, green salad, or a sautéed potato and onion concoction. (But bite-size is by far the more commonplace, popular primarily with an aperitif or as a premeal nibble.)

Where: *In Denver,* Panzano, tel 303-296-3525, panzano-denver.com; *in Kansas City, MO,* Lidia's Kansas City, tel 816-221-3722, lidias-kc.com; *in Pittsburgh,* Lidia's Pittsburgh, tel 412-552-0150, lidias-pittsburgh .com. **Mail order:** igourmet.com (search montasio). **Further information and recipes:** *Lidia's Italian Table* by Lidia Bastianich (1998);

Gently curved cheese crisps are delicious solo or with dip.

saveur.com (search montasio cheese crisps). **Tip:** When baking frico, use a nonstick Silpat sheet. If frying, use a nonstick pan. If you can't find Montasio, Parmigiano-Reggiano, grana padana, or asiago are workable alternatives.

||||||||||||||||||||||||||||||||

OTHER FISH TO FRY

Fritto Misto di Pesce

Italian (Southern)

While Tuscany's meaty mixed fry (see facing page) is largely unknown outside of its homeland, Southern Italy's popular fish and shellfish version has traveled the world. No matter where it is prepared, its highly anticipated arrival

Pair with crisp white wine for a summer meal.

is heralded by the warm scent of fresh and sunny vegetable oil (never olive, but preferably corn or sunflower) and the tangy salt-air aroma of the sea. A pre-fry dusting of flour on the seafood is all the preparation that is needed, and in very hot cooking oil the frying will take only a few minutes. Some seafood types must cook longer than others. Tiny, lacy tentacles of squid need more time than slim fingers of flounder or cut lengths of eel. Whiting (*merluzzo*) should be fried whole, as should temptingly tiny new spring crabs. Traditionalists will insist that if shrimp are included, they should be left unshelled, with heads on, as they would be in

Italy. De rigueur, no matter the mix, are shelled clams and mussels.

Most important of all is the fact that *fritto misto di pesce* should be eaten no more than five minutes after it is fried and drained on paper towels so that it remains deliciously crisp and light. Some insist on a dipping sauce—a light marinara or a mayonnaise-based sauce akin to rémoulade—but for true cognoscenti, nothing more than a squirt of lemon juice is needed.

Where: *In Venice,* Corte Sconta, tel 39/041-522-7024, cortescontavenezia.it; *in New York,* Il Mulino, tel 212-673-3783, ilmulino.com. **Further information and recipe:** epicurious.com (search fritto misto).

A MIXED FRY OF INNARDS

Fritto Misto Toscana

Italian (Tuscan)

Order *fritto misto* in an Italian restaurant, and nine out of ten times you will receive a wonderfully crisp and golden mixed fry of various fish and shellfish. Nothing to be sneered at, of course; see the previous entry for proof. It is, however, quite apart from what the Tuscans will serve when you request the dish of the same name.

The more lavish and sophisticated Tuscan fritto misto consists of veal innards: calves' sweetbreads, perhaps cuts of the heart and spinal cord, and always ribbons of tender, pink liver. With those meats comes a tempura-like array of fried vegetables: quartered hunks of young artichoke, pencil sticks of zucchini, friendly little mushroom caps, and slices of eggplant, yellow squash, and fresh, mild onion. The most impeccable frying is done in a combination of butter (for flavor) and vegetable oil (to prevent the fat from burning and becoming acrid), thus producing the desired *dorato e croccante* (golden and crisp) perfection Italian recipes prescribe. And no matter where it is served or what it includes, a fritto misto always cries out for generous wedges of lemon to be sprayed over all for a touch of sunshiny freshness.

Further information and recipes: *Italian Cuisine* by Tony May (2005); *Italian Regional Cooking* by Ada Boni (1994).

DADA'S IN THE KITCHEN

A Futuristic Feast

Italian

In 1932, the Italian artist and futurist Filippo Tommaso Marinetti (1876–1944) published a cheekily avant-garde cookbook addressing what he considered a pressing problem: an Italian diet too heavy for the coming modern age. The main enemy, in the artist's view, was pasta—primarily because he believed that, unlike other starches such as rice and bread, it did not have to be chewed. Marinetti felt that pasta was clumping up digestive systems across the land and contributing to a population that was lethargic, unproductive, and dumbed down. Such a population, he believed, would not be as light-footed as necessary in the coming age of aluminum vehicles, air travel, and imminent war.

In *La Cucina Futurista* (*The Futurist Cookbook*), the artist set forth his theories—which started with pasta avoidance but ranged to color-coding your food and sensory experiments like tasting olives and kumquats while alternately fondling swatches of velvet, silk, and sandpaper—including recipes and even diagrams on how to serve the strange dishes he envisioned. To prove the recipes were more than a high-concept ruse, the artist took his art and message on the road, putting on elaborate futurist dinners in various parts of Europe.

In the place of Italian hero sandwiches, Marinetti and his artist colleagues gave us the *Traidue* ("Between Two"): one slice of bread spread with anchovy paste, another topped with finely minced apple skins, and two thin slices of salami sandwiched in between. *La Truta Immortale* (Immortal Trout) becomes the fish course, in which a whole cleaned and gutted trout is stuffed with chopped nuts and fried in olive oil. Each fish is then wrapped in a paper-thin slice of calf's liver—raw or cooked, who knows? Futurists curious about the taste of metal should fill a small chicken with steel ball bearings, truss the bird, and roast it in a slow oven "until the steel imparts its flavor to the chicken" (by which point the chicken is likely to have dried out to the texture of that sandpaper).

For dessert, *Mammalle de Fragola* (Strawberry Breasts): Two upright female breasts are formed out of drained, pressed ricotta cheese dyed pink with Campari. With strawberry nipples properly in place, it should be possible "to bite into an ideal multiplication of imaginary breasts." Past, present, or future, that's Italian!

MAIL ORDER: *The Futurist Cookbook* by F. P. Marinetti, English language edition translated by Suzanne Brill (1991), is available at barnesandnoble.com.

THE FINE ITALIAN WAY WITH ICE CREAM

Gelato

Italian

Among the many treasures bequeathed to us by Sicily, few are more precious than gelato—the inspired Italian ice cream said to have originated on that Mediterranean island around 1650, with snow from Mount Etna providing abundant natural cooling. The unique Italian version of ice cream (the word comes from *gelare,* meaning "to freeze") is notable for being denser in texture and far richer in flavor than any of its relations. Traditionally made with milk blended with egg yolks, it is also cooked, rather like a pudding or custard, before it is frozen— the eggs contribute richness and the cooking contributes density. Because it is made in a machine that churns relatively slowly, gelato also has less air whipped into it than standard American or French ice cream.

Key to the early popularity of gelato was a young Sicilian cook named Francesco Procopio dei Coltelli, a fisherman's son who moved to Paris and opened the Café Procope in 1686, across from the Comédie-Française. The café would go down in history as the place that introduced gelato to the masses; it also holds the honor of being the oldest restaurant in Paris still open today.

Popularizers aside, many gelato aficionados argue that Sicily is still home to the very best in the world. There's only one way to find out.

Display cases keep gelato barely frozen, for a silky texture.

WHERE: *In Palermo,* Al Gelato 2, tel 39/091-52-8299; *in Rome,* Gelateria Giolitti, tel 39/066-991243, giolitti.it; *in Florence,* Gelateria Vivoli, 39/055-292334, vivoli.it; *in Paris,* Café Procope, tel 33/1-40-46-79-00, procope.com; *in New York,* Il Laboratorio del Gelato, tel 212-343-9922, laboratoriodelgelato.com; *in New Orleans,* Angelo Brocato Ice Cream and Confectionery, tel 504-486-0078, angelobrocatoicecream.com. **FURTHER INFORMATION AND RECIPES:** *Making Artisan Gelato* by Torrance Kopfers (2009); *Pomp and Sustenance: Twenty-Five Centuries of Sicilian Food* by Mary Taylor Simeti (1989); ciaobellagelato.com; whygelato.com. **SPECIAL EVENT:** Gelato Festival, Florence, Italy, May, italiagelatotour.it.

HOW TO EAT DESSERT FIRST

Gelato en Briocha

Italian (Sicilian)

A perplexing sight to first-timers in Sicily is that of the locals walking around on hot summer mornings, taking bites out of what look like hamburgers—judging by the big, round, golden-brown buns. But retrace the burger-eaters' steps

and you will find yourself at a *pasticceria,* or pastry shop. The pasticceria will offer not only pastries but also the delicately creamy, eggy gelati for which Sicily is famous. What the wall signs advertise, and what the morning and mid-afternoon customers feast on, is this incomparable ice cream sandwiched inside a gently sweet and spongy brioche. *Ecco! Gelato en briocha.* For breakfast!

Although it has caught on as a between-meal snack or a dessert in a few places in the United States, given the American sweet tooth it's a wonder the chic treat has not attained breakfast status. But there's still hope. . . .

To make your own gelato en briocha, make sure you use real gelato-style ice cream; because it is based on egg-enriched cooked custards, it will melt less rapidly and have more body than American ice cream. For a delectable brioche with a gentle but firm texture and a mild hint of sweetness that will not obscure the ice cream's flavor, seek out a quality Italian bakery. (If you have a choice, go Sicilian—Sicilians are Italy's most accomplished and inspired bakers, with a talent for sweets that reflects Arabic influences from North Africa.)

All it takes to complete this sublime start to the day is coffee strong and black enough to stain the cup. Summer or winter, in Sicily that coffee will be steaming hot. Hold the milk.

WHERE: *In Palermo,* Gelateria Ciccio Adelfio, tel 39/091-616-1537, gelateriadaciccio.it; *in New York and Chicago,* Eataly, eataly.com. **FURTHER INFORMATION AND RECIPE:** epicurious.com (search brioche gelato sandwiches); cookingchanneltv.com (search brioche gelato sandwich).

A LITTLE BIT OF ORGAN MUSIC

Gniummerieddi

Grilled Organ-Meat Brochettes

Italian (Southern)

A favorite at Saints' Day fairs in Italy and in the U.S., this meaty street food poses an obvious challenge of the phonetic variety. Try "new," as the treat may be to you; "murr," to rhyme with a cat's satisfied purr; and "yedi," to signal your readiness to try new things. (To complicate matters, *gniummerieddi* is also known as *gnemeriedde* and *turciniedde.)*

Now that you can pronounce the word, here's what you'll be asking for: tender, well-cleaned organ meats of lamb (and sometimes of pig or goat), cut into small pieces, seasoned with salt and pepper, and wrapped in lacy sheets of caul fat (*rete,* or net, in Italian). These meaty packets, threaded along with fresh bay leaves onto small metal skewers, are grilled over a wood charcoal fire. As the caul fat melts, it keeps the meat well basted and moist; reduced to nothing but crisp strands, it provides textural contrast to the sputtering hot, fragrant, juicy meat.

As the bay leaves char and the caul fat sizzles over tiny portable braziers, the succulent gniummerieddi lure customers with their nose-twitching aroma. They must be served immediately, garnished only with extra dashes of salt and black pepper. (If you choose them at a street fair, accept them only hot off the grill—they have no shelf life at all.)

WHERE: Street fairs in the U.S. and in Italy, especially at the Feast of San Gennaro in September. **FURTHER INFORMATION AND RECIPE:** *Italian Regional Cooking* by Ada Boni (1994), see Fegatelli alla Petroniana.

Festa di San Paolo at Palazzolo Acreide in Sicily

━━━━━━━━━━━━|||||||||||||||||||||||||||||||||━━━━━━━━━━━━

THE BEST WAY TO TAKE YOUR PENICILLIN

Gorgonzola

Italian

At once acidly tangy, sweet, and creamy, the blue-veined Gorgonzola is justifiably one of Italy's most celebrated cheeses—and it has been since before Italy even was Italy, as far back as the fifteenth century, in the town of Gorgonzola in Lombardy.

Gorgonzola is colored by blue-green veins that are strands of mold grown from the bacteria *Penicillium,* which is present in the drafty, damp caves in which the cheese is aged. Before it reaches the cave stage, however, the cheese is already distinguished by being made from two different milk curds.

Cheese and pears bring out the best in each other.

Because, historically, the town of Gorgonzola was situated between cattle pastures, ranchers would often stop there to spend the night and milk their cows. The old-fashioned cheese makers began to use the excess milk to make cheese. The curd from the evening's milk was wrapped in cloth and then suspended so that the whey would drip out and the curd could ripen overnight. In the morning, the curd was transferred into a wooden mold and covered with the fresh morning milk. The mixture was then placed inside damp, drafty caves to age, and the rest is history.

Modern demand for the cheese has necessitated faster production, and technology has obliged. Most cheese makers today pierce the cheese with copper and stainless-steel needles, permitting the bacteria-laden air to enter and shortening the cave-aging period to three months.

There are two general types of Gorgonzola.

Gorgonzola *dolce* is the soft, mild, fragrant young cheese, while the longer-aged Gorgonzola *naturale* is firmer in texture, with a more intense flavor. Gorgonzola is often confused with its French cousin, Roquefort (see page 127), a sheep's milk blue. Although the two bear the same characteristic blue-green veins and were developed around the same time, Roquefort is crumblier, saltier, and more subtly complex, whereas Gorgonzola's flavor is stronger, more rustic, and earthier.

The strongly flavored cheese stands on its own merits, but to take the cheese to the next level, Peck, Milan's famous gourmet shop, prepares a specialty that showcases Gorgonzola in the most decadent of ways. In *zola crèma,* a wheel of Gorgonzola naturale is split horizontally, then reassembled with layers of fresh, soft, sweet mascarpone in between. The palate-seducing result is irresistible, especially when accompanied by some of Italy's summer-ripe muscat grapes or winey pears.

RETAIL AND MAIL ORDER: *In New York,* Murray's Cheese, tel 888-692-4339, murrays cheese.com. **FURTHER INFORMATION AND RECIPES:** *Cheese Primer* by Steven Jenkins (1996); *Giuliano Bugialli's Foods of Italy* by Giuliano Bugialli (1984). **TIP:** Notable brands include Galbani, Klin, Lodigiani, and Mauri.

SUNSHINE ON A PLATE

Insalata de Finocchio e Arancie

Fennel and Orange Salad

Italian (Sicilian)

Given the quality of the sublime oranges grown in Sicily, it's no wonder they tend to find their way to center stage. In this tantalizing salad, as delicious as it is colorful, pale jade-green fennel with subtle hints of licorice is tossed with slices of sun-gold oranges. A teasing appetizer or a restorative follow-up to the main course—particularly refreshing after a fish meal—the combination of juicy orange and firm fennel bulb gets a pretty touch from the feathery fronds of the fennel, a delicate herb that acts as a final grace note. Black olives, arugula, and/or endives are sometimes added to the salad as diverting accents.

The best extra-virgin olive oil is glossed over all, along with freshly ground black pepper and—for an extra bit of zing, by way of both flavor and color—almost invisibly sheer slivers of ruby-red onion.

Because fennel can be tough and so resistant to a salad dressing, it is a good idea to sliver the tenderest inner stalks and relax them in ice water for two or three hours before drying and adding them to the salad bowl.

WHERE: *In New York,* Patsy's, tel 212-247-3491, patsys.com. **FURTHER INFORMATION AND RECIPES:** *Patsy's Cookbook* by Salvatore Scognamillo (2002); saveur.com (search sicilian fennel salad).

"FOR THE SOPHISTICATED TASTE OF LICORICE . . .
THERE IS NO VEGETABLE [THAT] EQUALS IT IN FLAVOUR."
—THOMAS APPLETON TO THOMAS JEFFERSON, 1824

Fennel

A bulbous stalk with wispy green fronds, fennel has a flavor suggesting a cross between celery, dill, and licorice and a crunch that is all its own. Long regarded for its health benefits, this vegetable is also especially high in Vitamin C.

Raw fennel is sweet and refreshing, with a snappy texture that makes it a welcome and bracing addition

to salads. Its bulb and stalks soften as they are cooked into side dishes like creamy gratins, and its frilly fronds work herbaceous wonders in seafood, poultry, and rice, providing one of the essential flavors of bouillabaisse. It also adds crunch and interest to the Sicilian salad in which it is combined with oranges (see above), and fusion-minded Japanese chefs add paper-thin slices of fennel to their tempura menu.

The versatile vegetable grows in California and throughout the Mediterranean, particularly in Italy and France, where the stalks can reach upward of five feet. During the Middle Ages, the tall stalks were supposedly wielded as weapons by the *bernandanti,* an agrarian group in Northern Italy whose members claimed to fight evil at night. (Despite the seemingly benign aim of their night watch—ensuring a season of healthy crops—they were tried as witches by the Roman Inquisition.)

Further information and recipes: *A Mediterranean Feast* by Clifford A. Wright (1999); *Vegetarian Cooking for Everyone* by Deborah Madison (2007); *The Barefoot Contessa Cookbook* by Ina Garten (1999); cookstr.com (search shaved fennel salad; braised fennel malouf; fennel soup with pernod cream). **Tip:** When selecting fennel, look for bright green fronds and a small, intact white bulb. If you can find only large bulbs, remove one or two tough and fibrous layers until you reach the more tender, whiter ones. Reserve the removed tough portions for flavoring soups and stews.

THE SEA PROVIDES THE SALAD

Insalata di Frutti di Mare

Italian (Neapolitan)

An edible still life in shellfish, the classic Neapolitan seafood salad presents a shimmering rainbow of whites, silver-grays, rose-pinks, and deep purples, with flutterings of emerald parsley. Silky, barely steamed, recently shelled mollusks

(including the mandatory clams and coral-tipped mussels) are combined with the ivory rings and lacy tentacles of baby squid. Rosy shrimp nestle between amethyst puckerings of boiled and sliced octopus. To that basic combination may be added a more expensive array of shellfish such as scallops, crab, or lobster—delicious, of course, even if each supplement makes for a more costly dish.

After each variety is cooked separately, and ever so lightly to avoid toughness, the seafood is combined while still warm in a sunny bath of olive oil, lemon juice, lots of black pepper, and minced Italian parsley leaves. A lustier, more colorful version of the dish includes hot red flakes of *peperoncini,* finely diced roasted sweet red peppers, and slivers of raw garlic; for

Bring the colorful bounty of the ocean to your table.

the faint-of-palate, the garlic can be stuck onto toothpicks for easy removal (though it does lose its sting after the salad has been marinating for a few hours).

Served just a bit below room temperature, *insalata di frutti di mare* can be part of an assorted antipasto, but it deserves to be appreciated on its own—hopefully without a superfluous, bourgeois nest of bottom-dwelling lettuce leaves.

The elegant way to serve insalata di frutti di mare is to arrange it on a salad plate in a little of its own juice, garnished with only a wedge of fresh lemon. Mop up the sauce with generous hunks of crusty bread and wash it all down with a light and flowery white wine.

WHERE: *In Venice,* Corte Sconta, tel 39/041-522-7024, cortescontavenezia.it; *in New York,* Rao's, tel 212-722-6709. **RETAIL AND MAIL ORDER:** *In New York and Chicago,* Eataly, eataly.com. **FURTHER INFORMATION AND RECIPES:** *Rao's Cookbook* by Frank Pellegrino (1998); *The Classic Italian Cook Book* by Marcella Hazan (1976); saveur.com (search seafood salad rao's); the foodmaven.com (search neapolitan seafood salad).

A LUXURIOUS AUTUMN SALAD

Insalata de Ovoli e Tartufi

Ovoli Mushroom and White Truffle Salad

Italian (Northern)

With Italian food so thoroughly assimilated into global food culture, one might think it would have few surprises left to reveal. But food lovers visiting the northern provinces of Lombardy and Piedmont in autumn still have a sublime salad to discover—the enjoyment of which is likely to dispel any resentment over what will surely be an exorbitant price.

Elegantly prepared to order at the table, the salad bewitches by way of its luxurious simplicity. It boasts only two main ingredients: white truffles, the aromatic treasures with a rabid fan base (see page 243), and the lesser-known but no less ecstatically delicious ovoli (pronounced OH-voe-lee), an orange mushroom that is egg shaped (hence its name, which means egg).

Ancient Romans cherished the ovoli and nicknamed it Caesar, because it was favored by the emperors. Germans know the mushroom as the *kaiserling,* another reference to royalty, and even the French declare it *impériale.*

The smooth, coral-red, half-round cap of the young ovoli turns convex and striated as the mushroom ages. Thriving in dark, dank broadleaf conifer forests and starting in midsummer, the mushroom is ready for harvesting in mid-October. (Better not to do the foraging yourself, lest you mistake the benign *Amenita caesarea* for its wicked, highly poisonous doppelgangers, *Amenita muscaria* and *Amenita phalloides.*)

Almost always served in thin raw shavings, the ovoli reaches its gastronomic apotheosis in this gold-and-ivory-colored Italian *insalata.* The moist, faintly earthy yet airy flavor of the ovoli, as well as its tender, gentle texture, make it a perfect foil for the heady richness of the shaved white truffle. The fungi are enhanced by tiny crunches of celery, gratings of fragrant Parmesan cheese, and a light dousing of lemon juice and olive oil, resulting in a salad that is undeniably fit for royalty—or for an Italian food lover who thought there was nothing left to discover under the Italian sun.

FURTHER INFORMATION AND RECIPES: rossa-di-sera.com (search ovoli e tartufo).

‖‖‖‖‖‖‖‖‖‖‖‖‖‖‖‖‖‖‖‖‖‖‖‖‖‖‖‖‖

FROZEN WATER NEVER TASTED THIS GOOD

Italian Ices

Italian

A wonderous restorative on hot days, frosty "Italian ices" are a staple of summer street fairs and most Italian pastry shops. Festively floral-colored and flavored with sugary syrup, they are easy-to-like, childish treats, but that seeming simplicity belies the history and pure intensity of an authentic Italian ice.

The tradition of sweet ices is at least as old as ancient Rome. In those days long before refrigeration, slaves would climb the foothills of the Alps and return with barrels and flasks of "drinking snow," to which various flavorings were added. (The most traditional was fresh lemon juice and zest.) Somewhere along the line, milk or cream was added, resulting in what is technically known as sherbet—*sorbetti* in Italian—a smoother and richer affair. But the simple, pure-water version is still the favorite of true cognoscenti.

Because authentic ices are shaved and flavored as they're served, they are further distinguished by a texture that lies halfway between grainy and slushy, not as smooth or creamy as sherbet. That's why *granita* is the official name for the Italian ice—the word means granular or grainy.

By 1686, Italian ices had spread from Italy—first to Paris, courtesy of the enterprising Palermo native Francesco Procopio dei Coltelli, whose Café Procope is still chilling out Paris today. By the time the granita got to the United States around 1900 (along with a wave of Italian immigrants through Ellis Island), it was being sold by Italian pushcart vendors peddling their ices in little paper cups in heavily trafficked Manhattan neighborhoods. But the Italian ice would travel even farther, going on to become a staple at beach resorts and children's parks nationwide. It remains an enduring symbol of summer and sunshine wherever it is found.

WHERE: *In Florence,* Gelateria Carabè, tel 39-055-289476, gelatocarabe.com; *in Chicago,* Anthony's Homemade Italian Ice, tel 773-868-4237, anthonysice.com; *in New York and environs,* Sant Ambroeus at five locations, sant ambroeus.com; Ralph's Famous Ices at many locations, ralphsices.com; *in New Orleans,* Angelo Brocato, tel 504-486-0078, angelobrocato icecream.com. **FURTHER INFORMATION AND RECIPES:** *The Perfect Scoop* by David Lebovitz (2010); saveur.com (search Italian ice; coffee and lemon granita; tart red cherry granita). **SEE ALSO:** Cinnamon Granita, page 184.

Scoop out orange halves and fill with Italian ice for an appealing summertime presentation.

WALKS LIKE AN ONION

Lampascioni

Grape Hyacinth Bulbs

Italian (Apulian)

L ooking for all the world like small onions or shallots sculpted in amethyst, *lampascioni* are a favorite of the southern Italian Adriatic province of Apulia. But despite their appearance and their monikers—*cipollini amaro* (bitter little onions) or *cipollotti selvatici* (wild onions)—lampascioni are not onions at all; they are the bulbs of the grape or tassel hyacinth, the latter so called because of its early-spring-blooming purple sprays.

The bracingly pungent purple-rose bulbs are celebrated as fashionable members of Italy's *cucina povera*—"the cuisine of the poor." Searingly bitter when raw, they retain only a hint of this when gentled by the sugars that develop as they cook. To leach out additional bitterness, the little bulbs are first peeled, and a cross is cut along their root ends to create more surface area for the bitterness to escape from. Generally boiled in salted water or simmered in olive oil, they also can be roasted under the ashes of a wood fire. Once cooked, they are dressed with red wine vinegar and olive oil, to be eaten with appetizers or as a garnish for meat and poultry.

Flavorful little bulbs

In Apulia, they are often served as sprightly accents to *fave,* the regional staple of pureed fava beans. The bulbs are also popular in Greece, where they are known as *volvi,* pickled in brine or packed in olive oil and sold in jars.

Raw lampascioni can be found in markets in Italian and Greek neighborhoods and are easily grown in gardens. As with all edible bitter vegetables, they come with all sorts of alleged nutritional benefits, from probably specious claims of blood purification to touts of diuretic or appetite-improving qualities. Oddly, they have yet to find their way into the Gibson, the ultradry martini usually enhanced with a pickled pearl onion or two.

MAIL ORDER: goitalygourmet.com (search lampascioni in brine). **FURTHER INFORMATION AND RECIPE:** *Flavors of Puglia* by Nancy Harmon Jenkins (1997).

THE FAT OF THE LAND

Lardo

Italian (Tuscan)

O f all the unlikely delicacies that beguile the epicurian, this cured white pork fat is perhaps the least likely to appeal to the uninitiated, at least until first taste. But to simply describe the ancient Tuscan delight as white pork fat would be as insensitive as calling caviar fish eggs. Thinly sliced into cool, satiny ripples and layered over narrow slabs of lightly toasted bruschetta sprinkled with sea salt—and, if you are lucky, shavings of white truffles—*lardo* is an inimitably sensuous experience for nose, palate, soul, and psyche.

Although relatively new as a food fashion in the United States, having been introduced at New York restaurants in the early 1990s, lardo was cured by the ancient Romans who worked the marble quarries around the Tuscan cities of Colonnata and Carrara. The pork's excellent flavor was the result of the pigs' opulent diet of chestnuts, acorns, and herbs foraged from local woodlands and fields.

To cure this richly flavored pork, white fatback is cut in bricklike slabs from the freshly slaughtered pigs. Vast, porous marble tubs are rubbed down with garlic, and the pork—cleaned and coated with sea salt—is layered in. Rosemary, pepper, and fennel are sprinkled on

Lardo is best sliced thin.

in profusion before heavy marble slabs are pressed on top of the fatback, all to be stored in cool caves for at least six months. The salt draws water out of the fat to create a bacteria-killing brine, preparing the fat to absorb a light glossing of olive oil when it becomes firm.

A growing interest in artisanal cured meats has seen quite a few examples of American-made lardo appear in upscale Italian delicatessens and restaurants. But none match the depth of flavor of the authentic Lardo di Colonnata, which bears an Indicazione Geografica Protetto (I.G.P.) label protecting it from impostors. Trendiness has left lardo open to much misuse, most especially as a topping for pizzas, on which it melts to gooey liquid in the oven heat. Have it cool atop an only slightly warm bruschetta—and then don't go in for a cholesterol reading for at least a week.

WHERE: *In New York and Chicago,* Eataly, eataly.com. **FURTHER INFORMATION AND RECIPE:** johndellavecchia.com (search lardo).

⊢||||||||||||||||||||||||||||||||||⊣

BETWEEN THE (EDIBLE) SHEETS

Lasagne

Italian

The baked pasta dish known as lasagne may be a red-sauce-Italian-restaurant cliché, but it can also be utterly delectable, and to try one of its many authentic regional variations is to cease taking it for granted once and for all.

As with most riffs on the dish, the lush and eminently recognizable version made in Naples begins with wide, silky dried pasta noodles layered with two or three tiers of sliced meatballs or crumbled meat (beef, pork, sausage, or prosciutto), enhanced with a basil- and garlic-scented tomato sauce and luxuriously

oozy with ricotta, mozzarella, and Parmesan cheeses.

For a more elegant interpretation, in Emilia-Romagna the lasagne noodle is generally tinted a pretty spring green with spinach, its mild, seductive filling of assorted meats, sausage, and chicken livers lushly moistened with a rosy cream-and-tomato-tinged Bolognese sauce. Parmesan is the only cheese.

Similarly, Abruzzo, the Adriatic province famous for its culinary prowess, prefers lasagne made with whole, olive-size meatballs that combine beef, veal, and prosciutto and are sautéed in butter before being layered in a light white-wine-flavored tomato sauce. The cheeses in this version are the dried mozzarella called *scamorze* and a showering of grated pecorino.

For something quite different, you must go to the Marche, that peacefully bourgeois Adriatic region set between sea and mountains, to sample *vincisgrassi*. The lasagne was created in 1799 by the chef to the Austrian prince and general Windish Graetz, who was stationed in Ancona with his troops during the Napoleonic wars. The general's name was assigned to the dish, eventually morphing into the Italianized vincisgrassi. (Say Windish Graetz a few times fast and you'll get it.) For his creation, the ambitious chef had combined tender nuggets of organ meat, such as sweetbreads and minced chicken giblets, and seasoned the mixture with carrots, onion, white wine, a touch of tomato sauce, chicken broth, and a light drizzle of milk.

Layered with noodles and spread on a nutmeg-scented béchamel sauce, the end result is a thinner, crunchier pasta dish with a teasing bite from the unusual meats and a light Parmesan topping, all glazed with a final brushing of melted butter as it comes bubbling hot from the oven.

Where: *In Macerata, Italy,* Da Secondo, tel 39/0733-260-912, dasecondo.com. **Further information and recipes:** *Naples at Table* by Arthur Schwartz (1998); *The Splendid Table* by Lynne Rossetto Kasper (1992); saveur.com (search lasagne layers of history). **See also:** Pastitsio, page 477.

There is no better fate for fresh tomatoes and basil.

——————|||||||||||||||||||||||||||||||||——————

THE DEVIL'S MAGIC

———————————

Lobster Fra Diavolo

Italian American

I n the kitchen, the *diavolo,* or devil's, work generally consists of adding fire—in this case by way of the pungent dried red chiles called *peperoncini.* And to the devil thanks be due, for with a garlic- and chile-zapped tomato sauce imparting a

red-hued kick to its snowy, tender meat, lobster achieves a special kind of splendor.

An invention of the good old red-sauce Italian-American kitchen, lobster *fra diavolo* represents an early form of fusion: Food scholars suggest that lobster fra diavolo was never actually prepared in Italy, but was instead a

concoction created by southern Italian immigrants. (Though it is remarkably similar to many dishes in the Neapolitan and southern Italian tomato-sauced-seafood pantheon.)

Records show that it was served in the early part of the twentieth century at a Greenwich Village restaurant called Enrico & Paglieri, founded in 1908. (Fifty-five cents bought you a serving *and* a bottle of wine.) Long a specialty of Angelo's, in New York's Little Italy, the dish also has a long-standing spot on the menu at Patsy's, opened in 1944—in fact, Patsy's current chef-owner, Sal Scognamillo, credits his grandfather, Pasquale, who emigrated from Naples in the 1920s, with bringing the recipe with him. Such claims are impossible to substantiate, but whatever its origins, by the 1940s lobster fra diavolo was part of the standard repertoire at Italian American restaurants throughout New York City.

At its best, lobster fra diavolo is nothing short of luxurious, with chunks of unshelled lobster glistening in a bright red sauce that is palate-stinging yet not hot enough to overpower the delicacy of the lobster. It is not served with a distracting, sauce-absorbing heap of pasta, which is a telltale sign of a tourist trap. The best way to enjoy lobster fra diavolo is with some good crusty bread and an astringent, sprightly, and bold Italian red wine that can stand up to its audacious flavors.

WHERE: *In New York,* Rao's, tel 212-722-6709; Patsy's, tel 212-247-3491, patsys.com; *in Las Vegas,* Rao's in Caesar's Palace, tel 877-346-4642; *in Baltimore,* La Scala, tel 410-783-9209, lascaladining.com; *in Boston,* The Daily Catch, tel 617-523-8567, dailycatch.com. **FURTHER INFORMATION AND RECIPES:** *Rao's Cookbook* by Frank Pellegrino (1998); *Lidia's Italy in America* by Lidia Bastianich (2011); lidiasitaly.com (search lobster fra diavolo). **SEE ALSO:** Homard à l'Américaine, page 96 and Lobster Savannah, page 593.

PALERMO'S NOT-SO-MEAN STREETS

The Markets of Palermo

Italian (Sicilian)

Even in Italy, where almost every city has its share of dazzling outdoor food markets, Palermo shines. By all means, allow time to explore Sicily's most graceful of cities, to wander among its romantic cathedral and chapels and take in

its luscious blue tile work and palmy squares and gardens. But any food-loving traveler should set aside several mornings simply for its three stunning street markets, which wind through alleys in the center of the city.

The oldest and once the noisiest is the Mercato della Vucciria. Many take its name to mean "vociferous," thereby explaining the vendors' shouts and yells, but another theory has the name deriving from *bucceria*, after the many meat vendors once in attendance. The shouts may be

Ballarò Market is over 1,000 years old, and as feisty as ever.

quieting these days, and the market not quite what it once was, but the Vucceria still has enough colorful stalls to make a visit more than worthwhile. Vegetables, olives, oils, spices, cheeses, and rugged, bloody Soutine-style displays of meat are all in abundance. Here, as in all markets in Italy, great chunks of swordfish are sold next to their disembodied heads, sabres pointing skyward, while nearby, huge rounds of tuna glow freshly bloody.

The largest and most sprawling Palermo *mercato* is Il Capo, which runs right through the city's heart, making it hard to miss when in transit. It is a long river of a street, with small tributary alleys lined by shops and stalls selling not only food but household goods, clothing, and utensils.

For a glimpse of Palermo's demographic changes, there is no better or more exciting market to visit than the Ballarò, where, in addition to all the Sicilian vendors, recent immigrants from North and sub-Saharan Africa and the Middle East add their own languages, foods,

spices, colors, textures, and wares to the mix.

In each of these markets there is much to sustain nibblers, most typically slabs of thick chewy bread that distinguishes Sicilian pizza when spread with oregano-scented crushed tomatoes; or *sfincione*, the local foccacia that may enclose a creamy filling of spleen or be topped by tomato and herbs. There are also *panelle*, crunchy sandwiches made with fried chickpea pancakes and slices of eggplant; and crisply cozy rounds of the mozzarella-filled rice balls that look like tiny oranges and so are called *arancine*. And as always in Sicily, one is never very far away from a vendor of cool, jewel-bright gelati or a chewy slab of the nut-studded nougat called *torrone*, to be followed by the darkest, stain-the-cup-black espresso in all of Italy.

WHERE: palermo.com (search outdoor markets). **WHEN:** Monday through Saturday, best before noon. **FURTHER INFORMATION:** *Pomp and Sustenance: Twenty-Five Centuries of Sicilian Food* by Mary Taylor Simeti (1989).

A TOPPING THAT PUTS WHIPPED CREAM TO SHAME

Mascarpone

Italian

Made in northern Italy's Lombardy region since the sixteenth century, creamy mascarpone cheese is a confusing delight. Somewhere between a crème fraîche or Devonshire cream and a superfine ricotta, from a taste and textural point of view it hardly seems to qualify as a cheese at all. Like those spreadable, soft-textured treats, the exquisitely rich dairy product generally adorns sweet or savory dishes as a topping—thereby earning its name, from the Italian verb *maschere*, to dress up. What it dresses

A versatile topping, smooth and buttery

up most elegantly are fruits like strawberries, raspberries, peaches, and green figs; it's also an indispensable ingredient in many classic Italian desserts, including *tirami sù* (see page 245).

To achieve what is in fact a sublime cream cheese, cow's milk is acidified with lemon juice or another citric acid; when it begins to set, it is drained through a cloth. Because no starter (rennet or otherwise) is used to solidify mascarpone's texture, what is left is a satiny concoction blissfully high in butterfat and pleasantly sweet from all the lactose, with just enough sting to appeal to sophisticated palates.

Where: *In New York and Chicago,* Eataly, eataly.com. **Further information:** *Cheese Primer* by Steven Jenkins (1996). **Tip:** The best way to select good mascarpone is to taste it, if possible. Avoid any variety that is lumpy or intensely salty, and carefully check the expiration date if buying it prepackaged—mascarpone is highly perishable and good for only a few days. In the U.S., look for the Vermont Creamery brand.

THE SUBTLE APPEAL OF WHITE ON WHITE

Merluzzo in Bianco

Poached Whiting

Italian

The fish called *merluzzo* refers to hake in Spain and to cod in Italy, but to Italian Americans it generally means whiting. The main difference is in size, as cod can run from four to ten pounds, while it is difficult to find whiting any larger than two pounds, if that, in domestic fishmarkets. And size matters, because the best version of the luscious dish known as *merluzzo in bianco* is made with large, thicker-fleshed whiting or, as a substitute, baby cod or haddock.

A main course in summer and a pleasing appetizer year-round, its preparation begins with poaching, the skin and bones left on for flavor, in water salted and perhaps seasoned with a few peppercorns. Lightly cooked, the fish is gently lifted out of the cooking liquid and boned and skinned, with the fillets kept as large as possible. These are laid out in a single layer in a rimmed serving dish and sprinkled with salt, pepper, and a dash of fresh lemon juice, then covered with paper-thin slices of raw garlic, which may or may not be skewered on toothpicks to allow for easy removal if desired. Over all goes a glossing of good olive oil and a blanket of chopped Italian parsley. The dish then sits at room temperature or in the refrigerator (depending upon how long until

The fish are poached with skin intact to seal in flavor.

the meal) and is served with lots of crusty Italian bread.

For the best flavor, the finished dish should mellow for about five hours in the refrigerator or two to three at room temperature. If chilled, it should be allowed to come to room temperature before being served.

Further information and recipe: starchefs .com (search merluzzo in bianco).

—|||||||||||||||||||||||||||||||||||—

Minestrone

Italian

I f ever there was a main course slyly posturing as a soup, it is the authentic minestrone, a lush vegetable and pasta or rice soupy stew that takes several savory forms throughout Italy. In the U.S., minestrone is merely vegetable soup—but in Genoa, where it originated, or in Milan, where it's also beloved, it is nothing less than an elixir meant to warm heart and soul.

Minestrone, or "big soup" in Italian, is part of a tradition of thick soups that are served all over Italy. It grew up in Genoa, a port city and the capital of Liguria, as a hearty respite for sailors returning to shore. It was always thick, richly brown-red, and packed with vegetables meant to nourish the seagoing men. And so it goes that the secret to great minestrone is a variety of really fresh vegetables—chard, zucchini, potatoes, white beans, tomatoes, celery, and onions are standard, but cauliflower, turnips, and carrots may be added to the mix. Also common are short pasta forms like the little tubes known as *ditali*, added to the long-simmered soup in the last few minutes of cooking.

Served hot, the fragrant potage gets a final grating of Parmesan for an extra belt of flavor. In Genoa, minestrone is finished with a spoonful or two of the bracing basil pesto that graces many other dishes. Regional variations abound, of which the Milanese boast a number: Their hot minestrone often includes pancetta and rice, while a cool version served in summer is made with greens only. No surprise that the word *minestrone* is also used euphemistically, to describe a complicated mishmash of a situation, as in: "Don't make a whole minestrone out of this wedding!"

WHERE: *In Milan,* Trattoria Milanese, tel 39/02-8645-1991; *in New York,* Trattoria Spaghetto, tel 212-255-6752, trattoriaspaghetto.com; *in Auburn Hills, MI,* Lellis of Auburn Hills, tel 248-373-4440, lellisrestaurant.com; *in San Francisco,* Kuleto's, tel 415-397-7720, kuletos.com. **FURTHER INFORMATION AND RECIPES:** *Flavors of the Riviera* by Colman Andrews (1996); *Lidia's Favorite Recipes* by Lidia Bastianich and Tanya Bastianich Manuali (2012); *The Food of Italy* by Waverley Root (1992); epicurious.com (search minestrone); saveur.com (search minestrone).

—|||||||||||||||||||||||||||||||||||—

Mortadella

Italian (Bolognese)

P ossibly the world's largest sausage (it can weigh up to 220 pounds), mortadella offers quintessential Italian flavor. A finely ground, densely packed, pale-pink pork number in a smoke-darkened red casing, it is redolent of garlic, pepper, and coriander, and studded with dicings of pork fat and bright green pistachios (although these last are not favored by traditionalists on home turf).

The sausage, probably named for the *mortaio*, or mortar, in which the meat used to be pounded—though you might also know its filling as bologna, named after the city in Emilia-Romagna—has a long and storied history. The ancient Romans enjoyed a sausage of the same name, and a liver-filled version called *mortadella de fegato* appeared in the sixteenth-century cookbook of Cristoforo da Messisbugo.

Today it is often served in cubes, speared on toothpicks as an hors d'oeuvre; but the meat is even more subtly succulent when thinly sliced and rolled, so the teeth can sink through several silky layers. It makes satisfying sandwiches in little panini rolls, either cold or pressed and toasted with cheese. Chopped, it adds savor to fillings for stuffed pastas such as tortellini, and nestled in creamy ricotta it brings

Formidable blocks of mortadella from Bologna

substance to the crunchy deep-fried "pants leg" (which is what *calzone* translates to), a specialty at street fairs and pizzerias.

For an apotheosis of mortadella, travel to the Friulian town of Gradisca D'Isonzo and visit the convivial wine and snack tavern Molin Vecio. There, laid out across a counter, is a 171-pound mortadella, easily 18 inches in diameter and heady with proper aging. Enjoy a few slices as part of an antipasto to accompany drinks at lunch or aperitif time. In Bologna, the best source is the irresistible haute deli Tamburini, which opened in 1932 and whose mortadella remains exemplary. Have sandwiches prepared for picnics or relax over a sustaining, casual lunch of sausages and local pasta specialties in the adjoining café.

For years, Americans had to be satisfied with pallid domestic imposters, but thanks to the inevitable triumph of culinary enlightenment, more intensely flavored imported mortadella is now available in upscale food stores and Italian *salumerias*.

WHERE: *In Bologna,* Tamburini, tel 39/051-234-726, tamburini.com; *in Gradisca D'Isonzo, Italy,* Molin Vecio, tel 39/44-481-99783, molin vecio.it. **SPECIAL EVENT:** Mortadella Festival, Bologna, October, mortadellabo.it. **TIP:** The best imported brand is Parmacotta, available at Eataly markets in New York and Chicago, eataly.com. Salumeria Biellese in New York makes the best domestic mortadella, salumeria biellese.com.

||||||||||||||||||||||||||||||

EDIBLE JEWELS

Mostarda di Cremona

Mustardy Fruit Relish

Italian

If gemstones were edible, they might well taste like the rainbow preserve that is *mostarda di Cremona*—the mustardy fruit relish of the ancient northern Italian city most widely known for its violins. The vibrant-looking and piquant-tasting spread is most often served as an accompaniment to cold meat platters or to *bollito misto,* the classic northern specialty of mixed boiled meats in a heady, restorative broth.

Traditionally made with an assortment that includes cherries, tiny oranges, figs, plums, and apricots—with the occasional slices of melon, pumpkin, pineapple, and pear thrown in—mostarda di Cremona is at once sticky-sweet and bitingly tart. Boiled and then preserved in white wine, honey, and mustard oil, the jarred fruits take on a stained-glass glow and make for elegant displays in the windows of the finest gourmet shops; at their most spectacular, the fruits are preserved whole and served on stunning platters at the most

Snack elegantly on relish and salami.

upscale restaurants in Italy.

The mustard oil school of preserving is believed to have existed since the days of the Roman Empire. Mostarda di Cremona was certainly a favorite of Catherine de' Medici, who allegedly placed a jar of it in her dowry when she married the son of the king of France in 1533.

MAIL ORDER: Formaggio Kitchen, tel 617-354-4750, formaggiokitchen.com; amazon .com (search fieschi mixed fruit mostarda). **FURTHER INFORMATION AND RECIPES:** *The Heritage of Italian Cooking* by Lorenza de' Medici (1995); *The Food of Italy* by Waverley Root (1992); *Pomp and Sustenance: Twenty-Five Centuries of Sicilian Food* by Mary Taylor Simeti (1989); food.com (search italian fruit mustard).

||||||||||||||||||||||||||||||||||

MOZZARELLA AT ITS BEST

Mozzarella di Bufala

Italian

L ayered with slices of tomatoes, leaves of fresh basil, and a sprinkling of olive oil, it's a sublime lunch or first course. Melted atop pizza or capping that great Italian American creation, veal parmigiana, mozzarella is an irreplaceable

superstar—springy and supple, it takes its spherical shape, name, and distinctive pull-apart character from the process of stretching, kneading, and tearing called *mozzare.* Delicious when based on cow's milk, it reaches even greater heights when made of milk from water buffalo.

The areas south and west of Naples are particularly known for marvelously supple, sweet, buttery *mozzarella di bufala,* made from the pasteurized milk of the water buffalo that have

roamed the region for more than a millennium. Dating back to at least the 1400s, hand-worked mozzarella di bufala has a depth of flavor and a soft texture that sets it apart from cow's milk or machine-made mozzarellas, and its processing, ingredients, and point of origin are protected by Italy's Denominazione di Origine Contrallata (D.O.C.) designation. In and around Naples, mozzarella mavens prefer their local product so fresh that they claim it's past its prime by the time it reaches Rome, just one province away.

Fortunately, much artisanal mozzarella is now being made farther afield, making it more accessible for all.

WHERE: *In New York,* Di Palo's Dairy, tel 212-226-1033, dipaloselects.com; *in New York and Chicago,* Eataly, eataly.com. **FURTHER**

INFORMATION: *Cheese Primer* by Steven Jenkins (1996). **TIP:** Salted mozzarella will last longer than its unsalted counterpart: about a week compared to a day or two. Buffalo mozzarella should always be packed in whey- or brine-filled containers and held on ice in the store.

AND THE OSCAR GOES TO . . . THE CHEESE SANDWICH

Mozzarella in Carrozza

Italian (Neapolitan)

Inarguably the world's most sumptuous grilled cheese sandwich, mozzarella *in carrozza* (meaning "in a carriage") did a star turn in the classic 1948 Italian film *The Bicycle Thief,* the Vittorio De Sica masterpiece that would win a special award at the following year's Academy Awards.

The sandwich deserves its own accolade for being one of the humblest, most dependable snacks in an Italian mother's repertoire, the standard she can rely on to appease her family's random hunger on the shortest notice. Anyone who has ever been tantalized by this fried sandwich, with its slightly crisp and eggy "carriage" of white bread enfolding an intoxicatingly rich and melting ooze of mozzarella, had to empathize with the hungry boy in the movie, whose father orders that treat for him in a restaurant, knowing he does not have the money to pay for it. It would be hard to forget the poignant close-up of the boy's face as he savors each mouthful of the warm, melting

Serve with salad for a little extra crunch.

cheese, or the anguish on the father's as he awaits the humiliating denouement.

The best bread for mozzarella in carrozza is a dense white sandwich loaf—although most white Italian bread will do. With crusts removed, slices are cut into triangles and fitted out with a slice of fresh mozzarella; the sandwich is dipped into egg and then flour and, by some cooks, into fine bread crumbs. Naturally, methods vary: Milk can be added to the beaten egg for a lighter coating, and some dip the sandwich in flour first and then in the egg. Most do the pan-frying in olive oil; for a more delicate result, combine the oil with unsalted butter. Lemon wedges are usually enough of a garnish, but for elegant appetizers or light-lunch main courses, restaurants will add a warm, buttery meld of anchovies, capers, minced parsley, and lemon juice or a side of hot marinara sauce. A few greens as well wouldn't be amiss.

A variation on this delectable theme is *fritto di mozzarella,* fried mozzarella—the same idea, minus the bread: A half-inch-thick slice of the cheese is dusted with flour, bathed in beaten egg, dredged in fine bread crumbs, and fried to golden perfection in olive oil.

WHERE: Rao's; *in New York,* tel 212-722-6709;

in Las Vegas, tel 877-346-4642; *in Los Angeles*, tel 323-962-7267, raosrestaurants.com. **FURTHER INFORMATION AND RECIPES:** *Rao's Cookbook* by Frank Pellegrino (1998); cookstr.com (search mozzarella carrozza). **SEE ALSO:** Croques, Monsieur and Madame, page 84.

———————————————||||||||||||||||||||||||||||||||———————————————

FOR COOKS WITH TIME ON THEIR HANDS

———————

Olive all'Ascolana

Fried Stuffed Olives

Italian

Café-sitting in the medieval square of Ascoli-Piceno, in Italy's Marche region, is an activity that offers up a multitude of delights. . . . Watching the evening *passaggiata*. Sipping the local anisette. And nibbling on miniature fried conceits like tiny meatballs, bits of vegetables, and *olive all'Ascolana*—fried stuffed olives, particularly the large green ones for which this region is famous.

Making these at home takes a generous helping of patience. Easier to like than to prepare, the green olives are pitted and carefully split diagonally before they are wrapped around

These bite-size treats make a satisfying portable snack.

a peppery ground-pork filling. Breaded with flour, eggs, and bread crumbs, they are then quickly deep-fried in olive oil. The teasingly salty result serves up, in just one little bite, a true expression of the pleasures of contrasting textures: a crunchy outside with a soft, tangy, chewy center. Given this painstaking preparation, home cooks generally make the olives only for holidays like Christmas and Easter. But the snacks are staples on restaurant and bar menus, where labor costs make them a relatively expensive all too delicious treat.

WHERE: *In Ascoli-Piceno, Italy*, Migliori, tel 39/0-736-25-0042, miglioriolive.it. **FURTHER INFORMATION AND RECIPE:** *Enoteca: Simple, Delicious Recipes in the Italian Wine Bar Tradition* by Joyce Goldstein (2001).

———————————————||||||||||||||||||||||||||||||||———————————————

AN OPEN PURSE THAT BEGS TO BE DEVOURED

———————

Open Ravioli

Italian (Milanese)

The ravioli we know and love are little square pasta turnovers, tightly pinched closed and usually filled with meat and/or spinach and cheese. But one day in the 1980s, the gifted Milanese chef Gualtiero Marchesi looked down at some failed

Wild mushrooms, no longer shyly tucked away in pasta

ravioli on his plate and had an idea. Not properly pinched, these ravioli had unfolded, leaving their disks of meaty filling sliding around on the plate.

The next thing the culinary world knew, Maestro Marchesi had invented the open raviolo: a large, silky "kerchief" of a pasta sheet that he folded loosely around some lightly steamed scallops, glossing all with melted butter and a sprinkle of grated Parmesan. Not long after, his ultramodern, *nuova cucina* restaurant, Ristorante Gualtiero Marchesi, became the first in Italy to receive three stars from the Michelin Guide.

Now ravioli are opening everywhere—or at least in the most luxurious Italian restaurants in and outside of Italy. The most delicious treasures coyly offered up by these delicate, floppy squares of fresh egg pasta are lightly poached eggs, whose oozy yolks are topped with shavings of earthy white truffle; or bits of shellfish such as lobster or scallops; or exotic wild morel mushrooms under a mantle of black caviar.

Once the raviolo opened, it would never be closed again—at least not in places catering to the wealthy chic.

WHERE: *In Milan,* Ristorante Gualtiero Marchesi, tel 39/03-0776-0562, gualtieromarchesi .it. **FURTHER INFORMATION AND RECIPE:** bbcgood food.com (search open ravioli with squash and porcini).

AGAINST THE TYPICAL GRAIN

Orzotto

Barley Risotto

Italian (Friulian)

The luscious Italian specialty risotto takes its name from *riso*—rice—the grain with which it is traditionally prepared. But in the Veneto region of Friuli–Venezia Giulia, bordering what was Yugoslavia (now Slovenia) and with its own historic Austro-Hungarian Hapsburg influences, *orzo*—the Italian word for barley (as well as for the small rice-shaped pasta)—is a much favored grain. Inspired by barley's silky viscosity and gentle bite, savvy cooks in this region simmer up *orzotto,* following the risotto method of preparation but substituting this seductively rich and delicately chewy alternative. The result is a dream of succulent creaminess, as the washed and briefly soaked barley is sautéed in butter, perhaps with a bit of pancetta and finely minced shallots or onion. It is then stirred and steamed, risotto-style, with a combination of veal or chicken broth and one of the sprightly white Friulian wines. Other minced vegetables, such as carrots, zucchini, onions, mushrooms, or tiny peas, are also stirred in to add a rainbow of color, texture, and flavor. Although most often served as a separate first or second course, in place of soup or pasta, orzotto is also favored as a side dish with game birds such as quail, pheasant, or guinea hen.

Orzotto may have evolved from an even more popular Friulian specialty, a soup, or *minestre*, known as *orzo con fagioli*. Combining barley with small white beans and an array of colorful, aromatic root vegetables, the substantial, restorative stew is much appreciated in winter. The removal of the barley's outer husk helps the shiny white beads of grain absorb more flavor.

WHERE: *In Andreis, Italy,* Al Vecje For, tel 39/0427-764437; *in Casarsa della Delizia, Italy,* Novecento, tel 39/0434-86203; *in New York,* Narcissa, tel 212-228-3344, narcissarestaurant .com. **FURTHER INFORMATION AND RECIPES:** *Lidia's Favorite Recipes* by Lidia Bastianich and Tanya Bastianich Manuali (2012); foodandwine.com (search mushroom orzotto batali). **SEE ALSO:** Risotto, page 233; Bulgur Pilavi, page 481.

⊢|||||||||||||||||||||||||||||||||⊣

MILAN'S MARROW-FILLED MARVEL

Osso Buco

Italian (Milanese)

Milan's greatest export may be its osso buco, the memorable dish in which meltingly tender domes of meaty, gelatinous veal glimmer under a deeply bronzed sauce of dry white wine, tomatoes, onions, garlic, thyme, and bay leaves.

These so-called hollow bones are not quite so hollow—the cross-sections of veal shank are filled with unctuously creamy and earthy marrow, the efficient extraction of which is best accomplished via long, slender spoons created specifically for the purpose. As if that weren't gift enough, a luscious lagniappe arrives in the form of the traditional *gremolata*—a mix of finely grated lemon rind, garlic, anchovies, and parsley minced together and spread over each portion as it is served.

In the true Lombardian spirit, the proper accompaniment to osso buco is risotto Milanese (see page 233), the slowly stirred and simmered rice dish that here is flavored with saffron—which happens to be this city's favorite color for food. Softly cooked golden cornmeal polenta also makes a proper bed for the meat and its heady gravy. (Mashed potatoes, somehow, do not do the trick.)

A variation on the theme, also popular throughout Lombardy, is *stinco di vitello*. It begins with the same veal shank, braised whole rather than sliced, with the marrow withdrawn all at once and spread over the rounds of crostini that are served with each portion. Risotto Milanese remains the accompaniment of choice.

When buying osso buco at the butcher's, be sure to look at both sides of each slice and to avoid pieces with so wide a bone that they leave very little meat. Each sawed (not chopped) slice should be about two and a half inches long, and should be tied up with string to keep the meat and fragrant juices intact during braising.

For the cook, timing is of the essence; if the meat is braised for too long, the precious marrow will melt away. As to the rest, argument abounds. In his seminal book *The Food of Italy,* Waverley Root reported finding seven different recipes in seven authentic cookbooks, some advising that the meat be browned in butter, others calling for lard or olive oil. Some insisted on flouring the meat or adding tomatoes; others eschewed both. Anchovies were called for in a few recipes for the gremolata and were ignored elsewhere. But all quarrels are but a precursor to the final and most important decision of all: Who gets the last bone?

WHERE: *In Milan,* Antica Trattoria della Pesa, tel 39/02-655-5741, anticatrattoriadellapesa.com; *in New York,* Sandro's, tel 212-288-7374, sandros nyc.com. **FURTHER INFORMATION AND RECIPES:** *The Classic Italian Cook Book* by Marcella Hazan (1976); cookstr.com (search veal shanks milan style).

THE MANY STAFFS OF LIFE

Pane

Italian

W hen the Italian writer Ignazio Silone titled his most famous book *Bread and Wine,* he was invoking those two staples of the table as symbols of the earthly and the spiritual in the lives of the downtrodden peasants he portrayed. The connection is not merely symbolic, however, as bread does in fact occupy a central place in rustic Italian cuisine. In more affluent northern Italy, far less bread is eaten than in the poorer Mezzogiorno region south of Rome; and the best-quality breads tend to be found in the south (affluence apparently being the enemy of great bread).

A growing appreciation for good artisanal breads means you can now locate excellent versions of many Italian loaves without making the trip. There are the flat, tender-crusted, slipper-shaped ciabatta that make for much-appreciated, lusty sandwiches; the long *integrale,* or whole wheat loaves; the small, chewy panini, or "little breads," that make excellent sandwich rolls; and even the crisp little rings called *taralli* that go so well with cheese and wine. We can also find *pane pepato*—coarse-crusted rings dotted with crisped bacon, lard, or prosciutto and crushed black peppercorns. And then there are breadsticks, always best when handmade, be they delicately slim or stout and crunchy, and often deliciously scented with rosemary.

Still other great regional Italian breads are best sampled on native soil. In that category, traveling food lovers would do well to seek out some of the following.

Sicilian breads are by far the most beautiful in Italy. Rather dry and light, most typically with pale, sand-colored crusts dotted with sesame seeds, Sicilian breads are often formed into fanciful shapes (flowers, starfish, snails, and more) or into rings and long, slim loaves. Designed to stay fresh in a hot, humid climate, they are baked rather dry to retard spoilage, much in the manner of the famed bread of Louisiana, a style established there by bakers who emigrated from Sicily.

Carta da musica—sheet music—is Sardinia's claim to bread fame. These most unusual "leaves," looking somewhat aged and worn, are often described as having a crisp flavor. Though the question of whether texture can double as a flavor is debatable, the bread's toasty neutrality makes it a superb vehicle for olive oil or soft appetizer spreads.

Pane sciocco, or "silly" bread, is the signature loaf of Tuscany—considered foolish by some for its lack of salt. But as cooking teacher and cookbook author Giuliano Bugialli insists, that is the point: The hard-crusted, moist, and yeasty bread must remain absolutely neutral in flavor in order to work as a foil for the richly herbaceous Tuscan cuisine, with its lusty wild mushrooms, game, and incomparable beefsteaks.

Pan de patata, potato bread, is much loved in Apulia and is especially delectable toasted. As the name suggests, it includes potatoes, which are mashed and worked into the yeast-raised wheat flour dough. The resulting loaves have pale-golden, parchment-crisp crusts and a snowy, tender crumb seasoned only with sea salt.

Schüttelbrot, "shaken-up" bread, is the dark, moist, and malty specialty of the Austro-Italian towns of Trento and Merano. The long, plump cylinders are baked of dark wheat and barley flours for a mix that is spongy enough to sop up the rich gravies and sauces typical of this Alpine region.

FURTHER INFORMATION AND RECIPES: *Flavors of Puglia* by Nancy Harmon Jenkins (1997); *The Food of Italy* by Waverley Root (1992); *Giuliano Bugialli's Foods of Tuscany* by Giuliano Bugialli (1992); saveur.com (search italian breads); south-tirol.com (search schuttelbrot).

TONI'S BREAD

Panettone

Italian

O ne of Italy's fabled celebratory sweet breads, the sunny, cakelike panettone is eaten throughout the year but is a vital part of the Christmas and Easter tables. Based on a rich and buttery yeast dough, golden with egg yolks and dotted

with raisins and bits of candied fruit, the panettone is a festive, fragrant delight. Known for its cylindrical form topped with a big brown-gold dome, the bread is a specialty of Milan, its origins shrouded in apocrypha.

Supposedly, around the fifteenth century, a Milanese baker named Toni had a daughter whose aristocratic suitor worked alongside them in the bakery (who knows why—perhaps to get closer to his beloved?) where he created the cake that eventually became known as *pan di Toni.* Another version of the tale suggests that the daughter was to marry the aristocrat, and that the baker created this golden edible because he could not afford to give her gold as a dowry.

The sweet bread is sold everywhere in Italy and in Italian markets around the globe, often beautifully packaged in a ribbon-wrapped box. It's delicious fresh or toasted, spread with butter or (more decadently) mascarpone. It can also be served as toasted fingers that diners dip into zabaglione. For festive occasions, it is often accompanied by a light sparkling wine like Moscato d'Asti or the still, sweet Vin Santo.

WHERE: *In Milan,* Peck, tel 39/2-87-6774, peck.it; *in Seattle,* Gelatiamo, tel 206-467-9563, gelatiamo.com; *in Larkspur, CA,* Emporio Rulli, in the bakery and by mail order, tel 415-924-7478, rulli.com. **FURTHER INFORMATION AND RECIPES:** *The Art of Fine Baking* by Paula Peck (1961); *The Italian Baker, Revised: The Classic Tastes of the Italian Countryside* by Carol Field (2011); *The Food of Italy* by Waverley Root (1992); epicurious.com (search panettone batali). **SPECIAL EVENT:** Panettone and Pandoro Festival, Rome, November, panettonepandoro .com. **TIP:** Panettone keeps very well, but it should be sliced only just before it is to be eaten.

||||||||||||||||||||||||||||||||||

Panforte di Siena

Italian

S weet and chewy, crunchy with nuts and fruits candied in a gentle, honeylike gel, *panforte*—strong bread—is the medieval holiday specialty of the colorful city of Siena. Revered for its art and culture, its museums, and a spirited

biannual horse race called the *palio*, the ancient city also wins international acclaim for its flat rounds of panforte, papered with a sugary white coating reminiscent of communion wafers.

With a history that dates back to the thirteenth century, the dessert is almost a cross between cake and candy. Loaded with dried fruits (figs, prunes, plums, apples), nuts (hazelnuts and almonds), orange zest, citron, and spices such as cinnamon, anise, clove, and nutmeg, the round, flat cake is most likely a direct descendant of medieval honey cake. With its rich caramel overtones and warming spices and flavors, panforte is typically baked only from October to December and is traditionally associated with Christmas.

Specially wrapped in bakery paper folded into a precise octagonal shape, panforte di Siena makes for a long-lasting treat. There are several versions, one made with chocolate, but the most popular is the panforte Margherita, named for the queen credited with uniting Italy, who preferred a light, delicate version with an abundance of honey and almonds. Panforte is best cut into tiny pieces and savored with a glass of the sweet wine Vin Santo or, for greater punch, meady grappa brandy, preferably in full view of the magnificent Gothic cathedral, the Duomo di Siena.

MAIL ORDER: Chef Shop, tel 800-596-0885, chefshop.com; pastacheese.com, tel 800-386-9198. **FURTHER INFORMATION AND RECIPES:** *The Italian Baker* by Carol Field (1985); *Visions of Sugarplums* by Mimi Sheraton (1981); tuscan recipes.com (click Recipes, then, under Desserts, Panforte di Siena).

||||||||||||||||||||||||||||||||||

Panzanella

Italian

A mong the many wonderful dishes that can be realized from stale bread, none is more soigné or coolly satisfying than the Italian summer salad *panzanella*. Chunks of bread that have become stale, or have been laid out at room temperature

to dry slowly (but are never toasted), are tossed with pieces of ruby-ripe tomato, slivers of sweet red onion, icy jade cuts of cucumber, and

crushed basil leaves. A bath of olive oil, red wine vinegar, salt, and pepper serves as the binding agent and flavoring. Once mixed, the salad chills for several hours and, after a light retossing, is served as an appetizer.

Basically a Tuscan dish, panzanella (sometimes called *pan molle*) is also favored in the

Leftover bread was never so stylish.

provinces of Lazio, where chopped parsley stands in for basil. Feel free to add both if the idea appeals, or toss in some celery and capers as they do in Umbria. The erstwhile smart celebrity magnet Da Silvano, in New York's Greenwich Village, prepared its inspired panzanella not with bread but with cooked kernels of the nutty whole wheat known as farro. Some of the more creative iterations have incorporated touches like anchovies mashed with capers, garlic, and a few dried flakes of hot *peperoncino* chiles—but these additions tend to be heavy-handed detractors from the pristine simplicity of this dish.

Where: *In New York,* Peasant, tel 212-965-9511, peasantnyc.com. **Further information and recipe:** food.com (search biba's panzanella).

‖‖‖‖‖‖‖‖‖‖‖‖‖‖‖‖‖‖‖‖‖‖‖‖‖‖‖

TO MANY, THE KING OF CHEESES

Parmigiano-Reggiano

Italian

The singularly salty-sweet, nutty bite. The unmistakable aroma. The addictively crystalline, crumbly texture that lends itself so well to grating and melting in a variety of well-loved dishes, but also stands up to the most minimalist of treatments.

Parmigiano-Reggiano's incredible versatility and singular flavor have made the noble cheese a cornerstone of Italian cuisine—one that has won its way into the hearts of cooks and nibblers around the world. The hard, aged cheese, which takes its name from its birthplace city of Parma in the province of Reggio-Emilia, is a *grana* (grainy) style variety, so called because its texture includes those delectably crunchy crystal proteins. The authentic product is protected by Italian law and must be made in Parma, Reggio-Emilia, or Modena, as well as select parts of Bologna and Mantua—the cheese's *zona-tipica*.

Parmigiano-Reggiano is created using partially skimmed raw cow's milk from those regions only, between mid-April and mid-November each year, a timeline that ensures the cattle have grazed on the freshest grasses possible. The cheese is made with two batches of milk: One is delivered in the evening, laid out in great troughs, and skimmed. The second batch arrives at dawn on the day of the cheese making and is used whole. Both are combined in gigantic heated copper vats until curd forms. The curd is then placed within large wooden molds (*fascera*) that hold a minimum of sixty-six pounds of cheese. The rinds of the cheese are proudly imprinted all around with the name Parmigiano-Reggiano, along with information about the location and season in which each cheese was made. The large wheels are then repeatedly brushed with sea salt over a period of multiple weeks and left to age for a minimum of fourteen months. Most Parmigiano ages from eighteen months to three years, two years being the average. (*Stravecchio* refers to Parmigiano-Reggiano that has aged for three years, and *stravecchione*, four.) The older the cheese, the more golden its yellow-white interior becomes and the grainier the crunch.

It takes three to five specially made tools to crack open and portion a sixty-six-pound (or heavier) round of cheese, and most of the people who know how to wield these tools come from families who have been schooled in them for centuries. Parmigiano's popularity, of course, means that there are plenty of imitators: The insulting, clumpy, powdered stuff sold as Parmesan (the French term for the cheese,

which has been adopted in America and elsewhere) in most U.S. supermarkets bears no resemblance to the distinct and intense pleasure of the real thing.

For full appreciation, try chunks of Parmigiano with sliced pears and shelled walnut meats as an elegant dessert or even a light lunch. For an extra-special belt of complex flavor and a softly appealing winey edge, look for Vacche Rosse (red cow) Parmigiano, a premium version made from the milk of red cows.

WHERE: *In New York and Chicago,* Eataly, eataly.com. **FURTHER INFORMATION AND RECIPES:** *Cheese Primer* by Steven Jenkins (1996); *The Splendid Table* by Lynne Rossetto Kasper (1992). **TIP:** Avoid buying even the best quality Parmigiano-Reggiano already grated. The cheese undergoes a drastic loss of flavor when cut. Ideally, it should be freshly grated over whatever food it is to grace.

"THE ANGELS IN PARADISE EAT NOTHING BUT VERMICELLI AL POMODORO...."
—DUKE OF BOVINO, MAYOR OF NAPLES, 1930

Pasta

Italian

" **P**asta is such a brilliant invention that it would be nice to set up a monument to the man responsible, but the origins of all flour and water combinations are as remote as prehistoric man himself." That perceptive and sensible opening

to *Pasta*, by the much-respected Italian food journalist Vincenzo Buonassisi, should help supplant the oft-told story about Marco Polo bringing the first pasta over from China. And the *real* first pasta? Who knows? Even more, who cares?

What we do know is that no food matches it in popularity. A few years ago, Oxfam, the international antipoverty organization based in Oxford, England, conducted a survey that asked respondents in seventeen countries to name their single favorite food. The hands-down winner? Pasta. (To be clear, Italian pasta was

differentiated from all other noodles, including those of Germany, Eastern Europe, and Asia.)

What makes pasta so widely preferred over almost all other comfort foods is a fortunate confluence of science and aesthetics. All starches supply the carbohydrates that encourage the brain's production of serotonin, the feel-good substance that soothes us and lulls us to sleep. Added to that is the seductive texture of pasta, or what sensory scientists call its organoleptic qualities—what is more commonly known as "mouthfeel." Properly cooked pasta has a satisfyingly chewy yet gently soft consistency that varies depending on its shape, yet is always delightfully toothsome. That correct consistency is a matter of minor dispute; one man's al dente (meaning "to the tooth") is another's underdone. But within the appropriate range, and whatever the herbs, garlic, vegetables, meats, or seafood that make up its sauce, pasta just has a way of sliding down easily and reassuringly.

The Rules

Joining the almost infinite variety of shapes in the pasta arsenal is a set of traditional rules related to both etiquette and serving. These rules may be broken, but they should be broken consciously.

First, there are rules concerning the way pasta is meant to be eaten: The long forms, with a hole or without—spaghetti, linguine, bucatini, perciatelli, cappellini, fettuccine, and so forth—should not be twirled on a fork against a spoon. At least not in northern Italy. Spoon-assisted twirling may still be countenanced in the South, especially around Naples, where, long ago, eating pasta by the handful was considered good form and remains a special-occasion pleasure. The "correct" method is to twirl strands of long pasta against the side of the plate, a technique that requires much greater skill and may result in much messier shirt fronts, especially if the sauce is abundant with tomatoes and the pasta is thick. Above all, long pasta should never be cut with a knife; to do so would be declared as gauche as audibly slurping from a soup spoon anywhere in the Western world.

Another increasingly ignored rule is

that short pastas, or what are generally considered *maccheroni* (the tubular rigatoni or slimmer penne, the little corkscrewlike fusilli, the butterfly-like farfalle, and the little "ears," orecchiette) should never be served with seafood, the texture of the pasta being too close to that of the shellfish. But as parvenu pasta fans often find the longer pasta too difficult to negotiate gracefully, the shorter forms are now found sauced with seafood—mostly in the United States, but also in some touristic *trattorie* in Italy. In any case, grated cheese should never be used with any fish or seafood sauce. (The justifications as to why are both legion and passionate.)

Finally, pasta should always be served steaming hot. Cold pasta, however welcome it may be in summer salads, is anathema to the true cognoscenti, and for the best of reasons—it loses its light, melting chewiness, turning into a leaden approximation of its former self. (In case it comes to mind, Japanese buckwheat soba—see page 815—is another matter entirely.)

Fresh Versus Dried

Its myriad shapes aside, on the most basic level pasta is divided into two groups: fresh and dried. The term *fresh* tends to have a halo effect, to some instantly denoting superiority over the dried and generally packaged version. But each has its purpose. Fresh pasta usually includes egg, which lends its dough a supple, delicate touch; because it is not dried out, it contains water as well, which also contributes to its silky texture. Best served with fairly light sauces, it spoils easily and melts down quickly in the cooking water if even slightly overdone.

Because of its delicacy, fresh pasta is more expensive than dried. Dried pasta is usually made with only flour and water and is less fragile and perishable than fresh varieties. At its best, it is formed with the old bronze dies that impart sharper, more toothsome edges to the noodle; such pasta is always imported from Italy, which will be indicated on the package. Pastas colored pink with tomato or beets, green with spinach, or black with squid ink are always better fresh, as their flavors go stale quickly. When buying dried pasta, select brands you can examine through the box, so you can avoid any that looks dull and vaguely dusty or webby, indicating staleness.

Matching Pasta and Sauce
In general the oily sauces, such as the simple olive oil and garlic gloss (the restorative *aglio e olio*), as well as the similar white clam sauce, do not pair well with fresh pasta, which tends to absorb the oil. Sauces that go either way are marinara, meaty Bolognese, and the Roman *amatriciana*, to name just a few—though the meat sauces would not be suited to the thin fragility of angelhair pasta, *capelli d'angelo*. (Whether you choose long or short pasta depends upon whether you want the sauces wrapped around the pasta or enclosed in it, the latter requiring the short tubular and curled types.)

The Fillings
Because they almost always contain perishable fillings such as meat and cheese, the small stuffed pastas, such as ravioli, agnolotti, tortellini, and cappelletti, are generally made with fresh egg-enriched dough—still considered fresh even if it is allowed to partially dry so it can be held in the refrigerator for a day or two, then cooked without falling apart. The names of such filled pastas vary with the region, as they do with the merest difference in shape.

The Pastas of Rome
The Eternal City's half-dozen or so noodle specialties are worthy of attention in and of themselves. *Cacio e pepe*, most traditionally made with silky, easily wound spaghetti, is true to its name. Adorned only with a pungent cheese like grated sheeps' milk pecorino, it makes an eloquent showcase for a liberal tossing of coarsely ground black pepper. As soon as the hot spaghetti is cooked and drained, the cheese is tossed in to melt slightly as it traps the gritty grains of pepper.

Carbonara is one of the most misrepresented pasta dishes. In the U.S., it often appears with an inexplicable cream sauce, and sometimes with sautéed onions as well. Run far away from such abominations. The true carbonara is said to have been named for the coals over which woodsmen in the Apennines prepared the sauce for boiled pasta on their iron shovels. Authentically, it consists of spaghetti hot out of the colander, quickly tossed with bits of panbrowned guanciale, the Roman bacon made of meat from pigs' cheeks, along with beaten eggs and a mix of grated pecorino and Parmesan. Add generous sprinklings of salt and pepper, and you have a satiny, slightly fluid, sunny pasta accented with crisp nuggets of the guanciale.

Spaghetti gricia is "carbonara light"—about as spare as pasta can get, aside from the simplest olive oil and garlic. Carbonara minus the eggs, gricia has the hot pasta mingling only with the browned diced guanciale and cheese.

Pasta pagliata is a favorite in this offal-loving city, but the dish is not a fit for the squeamish. Usually made with short, wide, ridged rigatoni or spaghetti, it is defined by a slightly creamy, meaty sauce that suggests a combination of minced veal and ricotta. In fact, pagliata is the chopped intestines of milk-fed calves or lambs in which some of that milk remains undigested, lending a cheeselike creaminess to the meat when heated.

Bucatini all'amatriciana features the long, wide tubes unequivocally beloved in Rome, but the origin of its delicate yet satisfying sauce of tomato, onion, and bacon is a matter of territorial dispute. The sauce's birthplace, the small town of Amatrice in the Sabian Hills, was once part of the Marche region of Italy; later, the town was folded into the Roman province of Lazio. So who owns the origin story? Twirl some pasta around your fork, take a bacon-and-onion-laced bite enhanced with grated pecorino or Parmesan and some minced parsley, and you'll be too content to argue.

WHERE: *In Rome,* Ristorante Matricianella, tel 39/06-683-2100, matricianella.it; Al Moro, tel 39/06-678-3495, ristorantealmororoma.com; *in New York,* Sandro's, tel 212-288-7374, sandros nyc.com. **RETAIL AND MAIL ORDER:** *In New York and Chicago,* Eataly, eataly.com. **FURTHER INFORMATION AND RECIPES:** *Pasta* by Vincenzo Buonassisi (1973); *Bugialli on Pasta* by Giuliano Bugialli (2000); *Sauces & Shapes: Pasta the Italian Way* by Oretta Zanini De Vita and Maureen B. Fant (2013).

|||||||||||||||||||||||||||||||||||||||||||||||||||||||||||||||||||||||||||||||||||||||||||||||||||||||||||||

"A MAN TAKING BASIL FROM A WOMAN WILL LOVE HER ALWAYS."
—SIR THOMAS MORE

Basil

But could a woman ever love a man who snatched her basil? Certainly not in summer, when great handfuls of the herb are required for bowls of pasta al pesto (see page 223) or salads of heirloom tomatoes, lightly glossed with olive oil and sea salt.

Indeed, the fragrant, licorice-lemon-scented herb with its pleasantly mild, minty flavor is one to cherish. Growing in several species and varieties, basil actually *is* a member of the mint family (genus *Ocimum*), originating in India, Southeast Asia, and Northeast Africa but now so closely associated with Italy as to be something of a culinary trademark. A fast grower and lover of warm climates, the plant reaches full glory in summer, making it a culinary soul mate for tomatoes. The two are well matched for reasons beyond seasonal compatibility: Basil's pungent essence lends zest and balance to tomato sauces and offers contrast to the tomato's sweet-tart nature. In the form of pesto, basil enlivens the French Provençal *soupe aux pistou,* it perfumes the classic Thai stir-fry *gai pad krapow,* and nouvelle cuisine chefs use it to flavor ice creams and sorbets as refreshing palate soothers.

Of basil varieties available to cooks, the small-leaved *Ocimum basilicum,* which grows throughout the Mediterranean, is the most familiar. The *Nano verde* variety (or green dwarf basil) is the most heavily scented, while the so-called lemon basil (*O. basilicum citriodorum*) is named for its mild astringency. Purple-leaved basil, or Thai purple basil, is heavier on the notes of clove and anise. *Ocimum sanctum,* sometimes called tulsi, is the "holy basil" of India, used by Hindus to treat digestive disorders but perhaps more felicitously to enhance many of their complex sauces.

FURTHER INFORMATION AND RECIPES: For basil frittata and other basil recipes, *Marcella Cucina* by Marcella Hazan (1997); *Cracking the Coconut: Classic Thai Home Cooking* by Su-mei Yu (2000); saveur.com (search many shades of green basil; laab; basil gelato). **TIP:** To judge freshness when buying basil, look for whole, undamaged leaves that are smooth and bright green, with no black spots. To store the herb, trim the bottoms of the stems and place the stalks in a few inches of water in a glass. Cover the glass with a plastic bag and store it out of sunlight. Or wrap the herb, stems and all, in several layers of wet newspaper or paper towels and store it in the refrigerator vegetable bin.

||||||||||||||||||||||||||||||||

Pecorino Toscano

Italian (Tuscan)

Various parts of Italy boast various versions of pecorino, the pungent cheese made from the milk of sheep, *pecore* in Italian. Pecorino from Sardinia, Sicily, and Apulia tends to be the sharpest. Abruzzo's is somewhat milder, and Rome's seems higher in acidity and is usually drier than the others. But of them all, the most sophisticated and elegant is the pecorino of Tuscany. Aged to a mellow complexity, it is generally considered among the world's best cheeses for eating or grating. No less of an expert than Steven Jenkins calls this cheese his second favorite. (He awards top honors to Reblochon, see page 125—among three dozen others.)

Pecorino Toscana earns such praise because the sheep's milk on which it is based is especially high in the butterfat that lends such a distinctly rich and utterly nutty flavor. But even within Tuscany, you'll see dozens of variations on the pressed cheese. The milk may be raw or pasteurized. Some rinds are plain while others are washed in olive oil or rubbed in tomato paste to enhance color and flavor.

The choice is personal, but as pecorino Toscano ages, the cheese becomes firmer and its rind darkens even as the flavor becomes more complex. Some prefer a younger, fresher version with less bite, which lends itself to a salad of spring fava beans heightened by nothing more than a few drizzles of golden Tuscan olive oil.

RETAIL AND MAIL ORDER: *In New York,* Murray's Cheese, tel 888-692-4339, murrays cheese.com; *in New York and Chicago,* Eataly, eataly.com. **FURTHER INFORMATION AND RECIPES:** *Giuliano Bugialli's Foods of Italy* by Giuliano Bugialli (1984); *Cheese Primer* by Steven Jenkins (1996).

||||||||||||||||||||||||||||||||

Peperoni Arrostiti

Roasted Red Peppers

Italian

Delectably cool and moist, sweet with just a slight tease of bitterness, *peperoni arrostiti*—roasted red peppers—are among Italy's favorite vegetable side dishes and garnishes. Embodying the quintessential warm taste of summer, they also taste quintessentially red, if color can be said to suggest a flavor. Green, yellow, and orange peppers are also frequently roasted, but they lack the velvety richness of the deeply red, ripe, sweet capsicums and are less reliable to work with; the yellow and orange versions can contain too much water, and the green is inclined to excess bitterness when charred.

Although Italian-style roasted peppers are widely available in jars, many of the commercial renditions are only minimally acceptable—they cannot match homemade specimens that, as a bonus, impart a mouthwatering aroma to the house in which they are roasting.

Vibrant and summery to the eye as well as the palate

To roast peppers successfully, choose specimens that are a dark, almost bluish red; they'll be riper and easier to peel. But perhaps more important is uniformity in color and size, which allows for even cooking. Oven-roasting is the most common method. Each pepper should be washed, dried, and, if possible, stood on end on a baking sheet, with one holding the next erect (but not crowded in). Depending upon the size and ripeness of the peppers, 20 to 25 minutes in a 400°F oven, with occasional rotations of the peppers, should result in skins that are wrinkling off the flesh and charred (but not burned) on all sides.

An alternative road to a nicely charred flavor and a firmer flesh is to roast the peppers over an open flame. They can be handled one or two at a time, held over the flame with a set of tongs or a long, wood-handled fork that does not transmit heat (or use a heavily insulated pot holder). They must be turned constantly until charred on all sides.

The roasted peppers must be peeled to gain their supple, soigné appeal. While still very hot,

they should be placed in a paper bag, or enfolded all together in a big sheet of aluminum foil, and then sealed off and left to stand for 5 to 8 minutes. In their hothouse packets, the rising steam loosens the papery skin for efficient removal with fingers or a paring knife. Each pepper should be split and cooled just enough to be handled before it is seeded and trimmed of any soft, yellowish rib edges.

Place sections of peeled peppers on paper towels to dry, salt them lightly, and layer them into a jar or bowl before covering them with the best available olive oil. Although most adaptable when simply seasoned with salt and olive oil, the peppers can be flavored with a crushed clove of garlic or a sprig of fresh thyme or oregano added to the jar. In southern Italy, raisins and pignolis are often included.

Delicious warm, especially with grilled meats, roasted peppers are most often served slightly chilled or at room temperature as inspired accompaniments to sliced mozzarella cheese, good oily Mediterranean canned or jarred tuna, or in an antipasto assortment along with cold sliced meats and sausages.

If resorting to jarred peppers, rinse them under cold running water until all of their packing liquid is removed and they lose their slippery feel. To serve, dry them on paper towels, salt lightly, and stack them in a jar or serving bowl before covering them with oil. Although jarred peppers seem extra oily, it is their own natural viscosity that accounts for the slippery effect.

WHERE: *In New York and Chicago,* Eataly, eataly.com. **MAIL ORDER:** Rao's, raos.com (search roasted peppers with pine nuts); delallo.com (search roasted red peppers). **FURTHER INFORMATION AND RECIPE:** *Rao's Recipes from the Neighborhood* by Frank Pellegrino (2004). **TIP:** At the supermarket, look for DeLallo and Mancini brands.

———||||||||||||||||||||||||||||||———

THE GREEN-SCENTED BREEZES OF SUMMER

Pesto

Italian (Ligurian)

G reen, aromatic pesto has a way of evoking the most indolent, bosky summer days. A first cousin of Provençal *pistou* by way of Genoa, the sauce is composed of fresh basil (with luck, just picked), garlic, pignoli nuts, Liguria's sunny, sweet olive oil, and Parmesan, the latter often combined with an earthy sheep's milk cheese such as sardo or pecorino. Only parsley and walnuts are traditionally permitted as substitutions, and the pesto must be mixed by hand in a stone or ceramic mortar with a wooden pestle. The more convenient blenders or food processors may render the basil bitter. Skip overworked inventions laden with arugula, cilantro, cream, or who knows what, in favor of the spare, basil-pure original.

The paste is best appreciated folded into Liguria's tiny handmade corkscrew dumplings, *trofie*, stirred into slender strands of the local, linguine-like pasta called *trenette*, or spooned into bowls of steaming minestrone. It can also add elegance to baked or boiled new potatoes. In Genoa, tender green beans and chunks of potato, cooked right in the pasta water, are tossed with the pasta and sauce in the classic preparation known as pesto Genovese. Sprinkle lightly with additional cheese and twirl in.

Fresh ingredients mixed by hand yield the best results.

Pesto Perfetto

Makes enough for 1 pound of pasta; serves 6

½ teaspoon coarse salt, such as kosher
  or sea salt, or more to taste

3 cups loosely packed basil leaves,
  preferably direct from the garden

2 large cloves garlic, peeled and lightly
  crushed with the side of a chef's knife
  or chopped

2 tablespoons pine nuts (pignoli),
  or to taste

¾ cup freshly grated Parmesan, or ½ cup
  Parmesan plus ¼ cup grated pecorino
  Romano cheese, plus more Parmesan
  for serving

⅓ cup extra-virgin olive oil, preferably
  Ligurian

4 tablespoons (½ stick) unsalted butter,
  melted

Place the salt and basil leaves in a large ceramic or marble mortar and, using a pestle, gently crush the basil against the salt. Add the garlic and pine nuts and grind the mixture to a fine paste, working in the cheese at the end. Slowly trickle in the olive oil, beating with a wooden spoon to incorporate the oil into the basil puree. When all of the olive oil has been added, stir in the melted butter. Taste for seasoning, adding more salt as necessary. The pesto can be stored, tightly covered, in the refrigerator for a week and can be frozen for a month after ½ inch of olive oil is poured over the surface of the pesto. Before serving, let it come to room temperature.

Variation: Pesto Presto (if you must). Place the salt, basil leaves, garlic, and pine nuts in a blender or food processor and gradually trickle in olive oil as the mixture thickens. Then, puree at top speed. Add the cheese and process for 1 second. Transfer the pesto into a serving bowl and stir in the melted butter. Don't invite a purist to dinner.

FURTHER INFORMATION AND RECIPES: *Italian Food* by Elizabeth David (1999); *Flavors of the Riviera* by Colman Andrews (1996); bonappetit .com (search classic pesto).

THE PERFECT PIE

Pizza

Italian

I t's hard to believe that before World War II, pizza was virtually unheard of in the U.S. outside of the Italian communities, where it was known to many as *a'beetz*, as in "a pizz'." Prepared in pizzerias belonging mostly to Neapolitan immigrants who spoke a soft, casual dialect and tended to drop their final syllables, the pie zoomed to worldwide prominence as soon as once-parochial American eaters took a chance on it. (They even learned to negotiate the scalding-hot cheese and sauce by folding big handheld wedge-shaped slices in half before biting into them.)

While its origins are somewhat hazy (some credit the Greeks), it's generally thought that the practice of spreading tomatoes over flat bread was a quick snack prepared by wives of Neapolitan fisherman as they

Italian bakers take great pride in their lovingly crafted pizza.

returned from sea. But the pizza we know as the basic classic—the Margherita topped with tomatoes, mozzarella cheese, and basil—was created by Raffaele Esposito. He was a baker in a *panificio* or bread shop on the side of the Vomero—the mountain perched over the Bay of Naples with a clear view of the volcano, Vesuvius, a scene that has inspired many a pizzeria mural. He presented the combination in 1889 and named it after Queen Margherita of Savoy, honoring her state visit to Naples by dishing up the colors of the Italian flag: red, white, and green. The city remains the world capital of pizzas, their crisp, wood-fire-charred dough topped by succulently melting mozzarella and a glossing of oregano-scented tomato sauce.

To the most serious cognoscenti, the Margherita is still the only pizza worthy of the name. But even for nonpurists, things may have gone too far: Toppings like fried eggs, pineapple, shrimp, clams, and many more crowd our pies, making them modern-day trenchers, the plates cut from stale loaves of bread on which food was served in medieval times. Not that there's anything wrong with pizza topped with moderately apportioned crumbles of garlicky, grainy pork sausage, slices of meatballs, seared green peppers and onions, or mushrooms. (The popular pepperoni salami slices are intrinsically flawed as a topping as they dry out and harden while the pizza bakes.)

As with any popular food item, pizza begets opposing tastes. Some people favor the New York style, with a crisp crust and a drier topping achieved via the aged mozzarella cheese known as *scamorze*; others go for the Neapolitan way, with thinner, wetter crusts and juicier toppings resulting from the use of fresh, cream-oozing mozzarella or the even creamier buffalo milk mozzarella. Both iterations will hopefully be baked in a wood- or coal-fired oven, directly on the stone oven floor.

And then there is the calzone, in which pizza dough is stuffed with ricotta cheese and dicings of mozzarella, possibly along with mortadella or salami, and folded into a semicircle, which conceivably looks like a trouser leg, which is what *calzone* means. Whether baked, as in pizzerias, or deep-fried, as at street festivals, the sandwich-pizza compromise wins its fair share of devout followers.

Where: *In Naples,* Pizzeria Trianon da Ciro, tel 39/081-553-9426, pizzeriatrianon.it; Pizzeria La Notizia, tel 39/081-714-2155, pizzerialanotizia .com; Pizzeria da Michele, tel 39/081-553-9204, damichele.net; *in New York,* Numero 28 at three locations, numero28.com; John's Pizzeria at three locations, johnspizzerianyc.com; *in Morton Grove, IL,* Burt's Place, 847-965-7997. **Further information and recipes:** *Pizza: Easy Recipes for Great Homemade Pizzas, Focaccia, and Calzones* by Michele Scicolone (2007); saveur.com (search pizza margherita; pasta da pizza; gold of naples).

BUCKWHEAT FOR NOODLE LOVERS

Pizzoccheri

Italian (Lombardian)

Somehow, the toasty, grainy specialty of the high Alpine regions of Valtellina remained a well-kept secret. *Pizzoccheri,* the name for both the rustic, sand-beige pasta and the luxuriously creamy, colorful dish made with it, is based on flour ground from buckwheat—in Italian, *grano de Saraceno,* or Saracen grain.

Technically not a grain, buckwheat is a grass (and the basis of Eastern European kasha, see page 442). It boasts a nicely gritty texture and a delicious nutty flavor, along with a high content of the essential amino acid lysine. Because it is heavy and absorbent, it is combined in this case with the lighter wheat flour to make a pasta dough more suitable for saucing.

Rolled out and cut into narrow fettuccine-like strands, the pizzoccheri is briefly cooked while still fresh with diced potatoes and shredded Swiss chard or savoy cabbage. (If the pasta has been purchased dried and packaged, it must cook a bit longer to achieve the same relaxed silkiness.)

Well drained, pasta and vegetables are put into a casserole that has been rubbed with a cut clove of garlic, then layered with ruby dicings of red onion, silver-green leaves of sage, butter, the region's special, white, soft-melting *bitto* cheese (somewhat like a dry fontina), and sprinklings of grated Parmesan. Heated for a few minutes, the pizzoccheri emerges in a luscious steaming mass given a crackling contrast by the fruity, bright Sassella wine of this region.

Where: *In Forcola, Italy,* La Brace, tel 39/0342-660-408, labrace.it; *in Queens, NY,* Ornella Trattoria, tel 718-777-9477, ornellatrattoria.com. **Retail and mail order:** *In New York and Chicago,* Eataly, eataly.com. **Further information and recipes:** *More Classic Italian Cooking* by Marcella Hazan (1982); *Italian Regional Cooking* by Ada Boni (1994); foodnetwork.com (search how to make pizzoccheri).

Pizzoccheri is traditionally cut by hand.

GRITS BY ANOTHER NAME

Polenta

Italian (Northern)

Polenta, Italy's creamy yet rustic way with cornmeal, really means porridge, and could thus be applied to any grain cooked as morning cereal. But the word characteristically belongs to the popular cornmeal dish typical of northern Italy, especially Lombardy and parts of the Veneto.

Properly stone-ground to a fine grain that still maintains texture and bite, the cornmeal is slowly cooked in water to a very soft, mashed-potato consistency. Always nurturing and restorative, it can be served as a simple meal on its own—with a lump of butter or a grating of Parmesan for breakfast—or as a luxurious bedding for sauce-enriched dishes such as osso buco, braised oxtail, beefy stews, and calf's liver *alla veneziana* (see page 187).

Given polenta's ubiquity throughout Italy, it's hard to believe cornmeal was a New World food before it found its way to Europe—in this case in the mid-seventeenth century, when maize was first introduced to the Venetians by the Americans. The Italians knew just what to do with the stone-ground grain, boiling it in water and stirring constantly until the meal became thick enough to support a freestanding spoon.

Some prefer it just this way, spooned into a bowl and topped with butter and cheese (Gorgonzola and Parmesan being favorites), sometimes enhanced by a soft poached egg. But an equally traditional way to prepare polenta is to pour the cooked meal into a baking dish and allow it to cool into a firm layer before cutting it into squares to be baked, grilled, or fried.

Although similar to the cornmeal or grits of the American South, polenta is based on a different variety of corn. In the U.S., dent corn is by far the most common, known for the soft center of its kernels. In Italy, the much grittier flint corn is the kernel of choice, most authentically cooked in an unlined copper pot called a *paiolo* that hangs suspended over a family's hearth when not in use.

Where: *In New York and Chicago,* Eataly, eataly.com. **Mail order:** amazon.com (search de la estancia polenta; valsugana polenta); for authentic polenta pots, Creative Cookware, creativecookware.com; Williams-Sonoma, tel

877-812-6235, williams-sonoma.com. **Further information and recipes:** *Essentials of Classic Italian Cooking* by Marcella Hazan (1992); *The Food of Italy* by Waverley Root (1992); lacucina italianamagazine.com (search grilled polenta; polenta and game bird; polenta with salt cod and onions; polenta taragna with stewed pork);

food52.com (search Carlo Middione's polenta facile). **Tip:** Avoid instant or quick-cooking varieties of polenta. To prevent lumping, let the meal trickle through your fingers as you pour it into the simmering water or whisk the polenta into a little bit of cold water, bring that to a boil, then whisk in boiling water.

—||||||||||||||||||||||||||||||||||—

A POUND CAKE WORTH ITS WEIGHT IN GOLD

Polenta Pound Cake

Italian American

Although better known for its rich and creamy pastries, Italy also deserves kudos for this nicely gritty, fragrant golden pound cake, a much-lauded specialty of the bygone Manhattan restaurant Coco Pazzo. Firm but moist, perfumed with

essences of vanilla and almond, the cake relies on polenta, Italy's cornmeal, for its golden glow and its palate-engaging texture. Non-instant American cornmeal can be used, but the Italian meal is slightly coarser (though not as coarse as Southern grits), with an earthier, cornier flavor.

Like all pound cakes, this one is delicious lightly toasted and buttered for breakfast or topped with ice cream and fresh berries as a dessert.

Polenta Pound Cake

Makes 1 loaf, about 10 slices

1½ cups cake flour, plus a little for dusting the pan
¾ cup Italian polenta (not instant)
1 teaspoon baking powder
Pinch of salt
¾ cup (1½ sticks) unsalted butter, at room temperature, plus a little for greasing the pan
½ cup almond paste
1¼ cups sugar
1 teaspoon pure vanilla extract
½ teaspoon pure almond extract
6 extra-large eggs, separated
1 cup heavy (whipping) cream

1. Position a rack in the center of the oven and preheat the oven to 375°F. Butter and lightly flour a 9½- by 5½- by 3-inch loaf pan, preferably metal. Invert the pan and tap out any excess flour.

2. In a medium-size bowl, sift together the cake flour, polenta, baking powder, and salt. Set the dry ingredients aside.

3. Place the butter in a large mixing bowl and, using an electric mixer, beat it until it is smooth and creamy. Add the almond paste and beat until the mixture is fluffy. Add 1 cup of the sugar and beat until the butter mixture is very pale and light. Beat in the vanilla and almond extracts. Beat the egg yolks into the batter one at a time, mixing thoroughly before adding the next. Add the dry ingredients and the cream in small amounts, beginning and ending with the dry ingredients and beating each addition until combined.

4. Place the egg whites in a separate, medium-size bowl and, using an electric mixer, beat them until foamy. Add the remaining ¼ cup of sugar and beat until the whites form soft, shiny peaks. Using a spatula, fold the egg whites into the batter gently but thoroughly. Spoon the batter into the prepared loaf pan; it should be about ⅞ full.

Top with berries for dessert.

5. Bake the cake until a cake tester or toothpick inserted in the center comes out clean, about 1 hour. Do not test or move this cake before it has baked for

45 minutes, as it will be fragile and might fall.

6. Transfer the cake to a wire rack to cool before removing it from the loaf pan. The cake will keep for a week wrapped well in plastic wrap and stored in a cool place.

Where: *In New York,* Freds at Barneys, tel 212-833-2200, barneys.com. **Mail order:** amazon.com (search de la estancia polenta; valsugana polenta).

━━━

CHICKEN MEETS BRICK

Pollo al Mattone

Italian (Tuscan)

Although when we think "Italian" and "flat-pressed," paninis may spring to mind, the flattened and pan-grilled *pollo al mattone*—chicken under a brick—deserves that honor. The dish is a Tuscan triumph, producing a chicken that is

peppery and crusty on the outside but succulently juicy within. (The concept of flattening a chicken so all parts cook evenly and the skin takes on a parchment crispness is not Italy's alone; for a pungent and more rustic version, see the Georgian Chicken Tabaka, page 391; for a spicier version, see Pigeons en Crapaudine, page 114.)

In this case, the flattening is most traditionally accomplished with the aid of a cooking utensil made of red terra-cotta and known as a *mattone,* or brick. Ideally the small chicken (broiler size) should be butterflied—split at the backbone but not separated into pieces—before being pounded flatter with a mallet or heavy skillet, then sprinkled with olive oil, coarse sea salt, plenty of crushed black peppercorns, and fresh rosemary leaves. Placed on a thick terra-cotta plate on a stovetop burner, it is covered with a heavy matching round lid that keeps the chicken

flat as it fries. The bird is turned several times during the 40 to 45 minutes of cooking, and the pan juices are drizzled over all.

A similar version was devised by food writer Mark Bittman in *The New York Times.* Using two skillets—one inside the other, to do the flattening—he sears the chicken on the stovetop, then finishes it in the oven, still sandwiched between the two pans.

Either way, the resulting dish cries out for a sprinkle of fresh lemon juice, a healthy heap of crisply fried shoestring potatoes, and a nice big clump of watercress or baby arugula, for which the chicken's rich juices will provide a savory dressing.

Where: *In New York,* Sandro's, tel 212-288-7374, sandrosnyc.com. **Further information and recipes:** *Giuliano Bugialli's Foods of Tuscany* by Giuliano Bugialli (1992); nytimes.com (search bittman chicken under a brick).

Prosciutto

Italian (Northern)

Some contend that the world's finest preserved ham is Spain's Jabugo Ham (see page 262). Others grant that honor to Italian prosciutto, though further contention can be aroused by weighing the choice specimens from Parma or San Daniele.

It would be difficult to imagine a more thoroughly delicious project than a comparative taste-off. Sampling one superbly rich, complex, silky, and gently saline air-cured product after another, knowing that even the least of these will be superb . . . There are worse comparisons.

Preserving pork, and especially the hind legs, is a craft that dates back some two thousand years. Early on, Romans became skilled at preserving ham, or what Italians named prosciutto. Gradually they devised the craft of packing each leg heavily with sea salt and hanging it to air-dry anywhere from six months to two years—the longer it dried, the more exquisitely intense the flavor and the higher the price. The result is firm but supple meat, teasingly salty but with buttery overtones and without any smokiness to compromise the flavor.

In the town of Parma, in Italy's Emilia-Romagna region, the process is an art form. Butchers take raw hams, dry-salt them with sea salt, and leave them to cure for as long as a month. Then they hang the hams and air-dry them for at least eight months and sometimes, depending on weather and temperature conditions, as long as eighteen months. This process yields *prosciutto di Parma*, the elegant, thinly sliced ham that is prized the world over for its exquisite combination of richness of flavor and lightness of texture.

Its biggest competition comes from the town of San Daniele, in the Friuli–Venezia Giulia region equally famed for its prosciutto: Although it is otherwise treated quite similarly, this ham's center bone is removed before it is cured and pressed into a fairly even, flat shape. It is aged for about a year, resulting in a richer, parchmentlike patina and a more even and intense flavor. As with the Parma method, no preservatives of any kind, other than salt, are permitted.

No matter its provenance, the prosciutto produced by small artisanal manufacturers is far superior to the big factory versions. The latter standardize production and do not take into account the subtle effects of proper climate and drying time on the meat. Aging is a subjective and inexact science, as well as a costly process that ties up much capital in inventory, requires space for the aging rooms, and entails a loss of weight through dehydration, meaning that the producer buys more meat than he ultimately has left to sell.

Well-aged prosciutto should be sliced very, very thin—a $\frac{1}{16}$-inch thickness being the preference of cognoscenti. Traditionally offered as a salty accent to sweet, ripe fruits such as figs, honeydew, or cantaloupe, it pairs excellently with ripe pears as well. It can also replace more plebeian hams as the centerpiece of a simple sandwich on a butter-dabbed baguette or dress up a crunchy snack when wrapped around really good *grissini* (the distinctive thin breadsticks served in many Italian cafés and bakeries).

When buying prosciutto, always ask for a sample slice so that you can judge the color of the meat (you want light, rosy reddish-pink, not brownish or dark), the degree of saltiness, and the texture (ideally tender but with a satisfying, meaty bite). Avoid presliced versions, which dry out quickly and are not worth the high price. Cooking prosciutto is a mistake, as exposure to heat makes it leathery. However, the big, unsliceably thick ends or chunks of bone can be added to stewing beans or lusty soups for an extra belt of flavor.

Retail and mail order: *In New York and Chicago,* Eataly, eataly.com. **Further information and recipes:** *The Splendid Table* by Lynne Rossetto Kasper (1992); prosciuttosandaniele .it; www.prosciuttodiparma.com. **Special event:** Aria di Festa: La Festa del Prosciutto, San Daniele, Italy, July, ariadifesta.it. **See also:** York Ham, page 33; Yunnan Ham, page 795.

|||||||||||||||||||||||||||||||||

A WINDING DRIVE FOR WILD PROSCIUTTO

Prosciutto di Cinghiale

Wild Boar Prosciutto

Italian (Abruzzese)

High up in the ominously beautiful, misty Apennine mountains of Italy's Abruzzo region sits a rustic inn and restaurant called Il Rifugio del Cinghiale, meaning the refuge of the boar. It is a fitting name, as one of the house's most prized specialties is its *salumi*—preserved meats and sausages—made of the meat of the semiwild boars that inhabit the surrounding woodlands. Of those products, the most sophisticated and delectable is the mahogany-dark, firm but still silky, air-dried prosciutto.

With an earthier, meatier, and understandably gamier flavor than the usual prosciutto (from the legs of domestic pigs), this is just one of the irresistible game dishes offered in the simplest preparation in these unadorned but charming surroundings.

The legs of the boar are much smaller than those of domestic pigs, and when air-cured, pressed, and somewhat shrunken, resemble small, polished violins. Lean and firm-textured, they make ethereal treats when thinly sliced and served with dabs of unsalted butter and hearty local bread—treats well worth the harrowing drive

up hairpin cliffside roads that wind to the mountaintop, just across from the forbidding wall of mountains that is the famed Maiale.

Where: *In Marino, Italy,* Il Rifugio del Cinghiale, tel 39/0873-975044, rifugiodelcinghiale.it; *in Baltimore,* intermittently, Cinghiale, tel 410-547-8282, cgeno.com. **Retail and mail order:** *In New York and Chicago,* Eataly, eataly .com.

Dried meats on display at a shop in Orvieto

IT'S NOT ALWAYS EASY BEING GREEN

Puntarelle

Catalonian Chicory

Italian

A particular favorite in Rome, spiky, bittersweet *puntarelle* (also known as Catalogna de Galatina) is perhaps the most sophisticated of all salad greens. At first glance it suggests the dandelion green, but its flavor is more upper-crust—

at once teasing and satisfying, like a combination of dandelion, arugula, and licorice-scented fennel. Lacy and pretty, with its variegated jades and whites, puntarelle's complex texture combines the refreshing crunch of its delicate stems with the nurturing softness of its serrated leaves. And like many of the dark green chicories, puntarelle delivers valuable nutrients such as iron, potassium, and antioxidants.

Were it more widely available and less time-consuming to prepare, it might well have displaced arugula as the Italian salad green of choice. But the season for this wild-looking member of the chicory family is limited to November through January, and because its stems are tougher than its leaves, the most careful cooks like to strip its stalks apart and sliver the stems to make them more easily edible. It is an annoying process, but happily many Italian markets, Rome's beautiful Campo dei Fiori among them, offer the green ready-stripped. It is also sometimes presoaked in an ice-water bath that relaxes the stems and leaves so they can absorb a dressing instead of resisting it. Such limitations make puntarelle less attractive to American home cooks and a costly proposition for restaurants, so it is sold only in the most upscale markets.

Serious Italian restaurants in the U.S. often offer it in season, and nowhere is it more meticulously and deliciously realized than at Sandro's in New York, where the Roman chef-*patrone* Sandro Fioriti soaks the greens for twelve to eighteen hours. He also glosses them with the most traditional and efficacious dressing, a combination of olive oil, red wine vinegar, and a tangy pounded puree of garlic and anchovies, the sweet saltiness of which cushions the bitter bite of the greens.

WHERE: *In Rome,* Ristorante Matricianella, tel 39/06-683-2100, matricianella.it; *in New York,* Sandro's, tel 212-288-7374, sandrosnyc.com. **FURTHER INFORMATION AND RECIPE:** saveur.com (search puntarelle in salsa di alici).

WHEN LIFE GIVES YOU LEMONS

Rao's Famous Lemon Chicken

Italian American

The small, unprepossessing trattoria that is the original Rao's, in New York's Spanish Harlem, is quite possibly more difficult to get into than any other restaurant in the United States. Not only has its somewhat rakish reputation made it inordinately popular, but it amplifies the longing diner's challenge by having only ten tables and being closed on Saturdays and Sundays. Add to that the fact that a handful of local movers and shakers virtually own time shares on those tables and you begin to understand the long wait for reservations.

What makes all this understandable is the very special food that is strictly Rao's style: a kind of American red-sauce Italian, but done with finesse and a distinctly robust character. It's a winning formula that was established by founders Vincent Rao and his wife, Anna, who presided over the kitchen until their deaths. It is currently carefully guarded by two nephews. (There are now also Rao's restaurants in Los Angeles and Las Vegas.)

In addition to all of the classic pastas, Rao's serves a dynamite shellfish salad, tender meatballs, juicy pork chops, and sausages zapped with vinegar and chile-fired peppers. But perhaps the most iconic dish is the seductive lemon chicken. This culinary marvel is achieved by heating a broiler to volcanic intensity and introducing a small, halved chicken to its flames. Once it has cooked through and acquired a lightly charred, brassy patina, the bird is chopped into serving pieces and basted with a pungent sauce of fresh lemon juice, winey red vinegar, olive oil, garlic, oregano, and salt and pepper before being returned to the seething broiler to be recharred on all sides.

It is the contrast of the glazed skin, the succulent meat, and the sunshine sparkle of the sauce—reduced and brightened with chopped parsley—that makes this chicken incomparable. Devout Rao's fans know to have chunks of bread at the ready to sop up any leftover sauce, and the smartest of the bunch order crisp fried potatoes and chopped broccoli rabe on the side.

WHERE: Rao's, *in New York*, tel 212-722-6709; *in Las Vegas*, tel 877-346-4642; *in Los Angeles*, tel 323-962-7267, raosrestaurants.com. **FURTHER INFORMATION AND RECIPE:** *Rao's Cookbook* by Frank Pellegrino (1998); saveur.com (search raos famous lemon chicken).

A FRESH CHEESE THAT GOES SWEET OR SAVORY

Ricotta

Italian

Creamy yet enticingly grainy, sweet but with an alluring tang, ricotta is Italy's elegant version of cottage cheese—though it's so luxurious and delightful that the comparison seems inapt. Mixed with cut raw cucumbers and radishes

or, better yet, with ripe pears, berries, or peaches, ricotta can begin or end a meal. It can also be found adding a soothing richness to pasta dishes and lending a firm but airy texture to the Italian cheesecake Torta di Ricotta (see page 249).

To get technical, ricotta is not actually a cheese but rather a cheese by-product made from whey that is left over from other cheese making. Once this whey is collected, it is reheated (giving the word *ricotta* its Italian meaning, recooked) until curds form and a soft white mass emerges. The original ricotta was made by Roman cheese makers, who used the whey left after making Romano cheese.

In Italy, ricotta is usually made with sheep whey or water buffalo whey, whereas in the United States it is almost always made from cow's milk, resulting in a finished product that is both smoother and blander than its Italian counterpart. A dried, salty, and distinctly Sicilian version of the cheese is ricotta salata, made from sheep's milk that is pressed and dried before being aged for at least three months; the result is a hard cheese with a mild, milky flavor that's just right for grating and excellent shaved atop pastas and salads.

Good-quality ricotta is moist and snowy white, and emits a clean dairy aroma. As with any irresistibly tempting, ready-to-eat ingredient, buy more than you think you'll need, knowing you will be dipping in as you go.

FURTHER INFORMATION AND RECIPES: *Home Cheese Making* by Ricki Carroll (2002); *The Cheese Lover's Cookbook and Guide* by Paula Lambert (2000); *More Classic Italian Cooking* by Marcella Hazan (1982); saveur.com (search one ingredient many ways ricotta).

RICE THAT'S WORTH THE WAIT

Risotto

Italian (Northern)

The most richly luxurious of all rice dishes, a perfectly made risotto may surpass even the sparkling allure of gold-leaf-flecked Indian *biryanis* (see page 868), the Turkish pilafs that beguiled the harem hour, or the soothing Japanese stewed rice called *kamameshi* (see page 804).

To qualify as perfectly made, the risotto must start with Arborio rice imported from the Po Valley. The comparatively short, wide grain contains a visible white inner kernel that should remain a bit firm when cooked; in order to absorb the liquid that enables it to swell up softly and gently, it requires longer, slower cooking than American long-grain rice.

Prior to cooking, the raw, unrinsed rice grains should be rubbed between two layers of clean cotton towel so that any loose starch is removed. Briefly sautéed in butter or olive oil until glassily parched and translucent, they are then gradually moistened with boiling stock— vegetable, meat, poultry, or seafood—added in increments while the rice is continuously stirred. The finished stage leaves the rice looking somewhat like a liquid, at the consistency known as *all'onda,* or moving in subtle waves when the pot is gently shaken. A swath of butter and possibly cheese and herbs is the final anointment.

The most tradition-bound Milanesi eat their risotti with spoons, emphasizing its liquidy appeal. Anyone preparing this dish must commit to anywhere from 25 to 30 minutes at the stove, stirring constantly and adding the boiling liquid in small quantities. And the last rule of thumb? Guests wait for the risotto; the risotto waits for no one.

Risotto Milanese. The golden classic: The grains are sautéed in butter with bits of onion or shallots and bone marrow, then doused with white wine and saffron-infused chicken stock. The oldest recipes for this dish call for crumbles of the firm sausage *cervellato*, which is no longer available; marrow is the stand-in of choice.

Risotto Piemontese. Piedmont's favorite risotto is a creamy white affair, based on white wine, butter, chicken stock, Parmesan, and a lavish layering of shaved white truffles from Alba (see page 243).

Risotto verde. This green risotto is a springtime favorite, verdant with parsley and tiny new peas or spears of young green asparagus added during the last ten minutes of cooking, and perhaps dotted with bits of pancetta.

Risotto bianco. As simple as it gets, this risotto relies only on butter, white wine, stock, and grated Parmesan.

Risotto Certosina. Probably the most complex risotto, this seafood triumph incorporates frogs' legs, shrimp, bits of fish fillets, tomatoes, peas, mushrooms, carrots, onions, celery, olive oil, white wine, and fish stock. (No cheese, please!)

Risotto ai Frutti di Mare. Finely chopped mollusks and crustaceans—clams, mussels, squid, shrimp, prawns, and so on—season this tomato-based risotto, lightly flavored with onion, garlic, and a liberal sprinkling of parsley, but again, never cheese.

Risotto nero. One of the richest, most dramatic of risotti and a great specialty in Venice, the nero comes by its name and color from the midnight-dark squid ink that adds a velvety depth of flavor reminiscent of both caviar and the deep blue sea. Again, no cheese, but a few flecks of red-hot *peperoncini* would be a nice accent.

Risotto saltato (or *al salto*). In the unlikely event that your risotto pan is not scraped clean, this spin-off of the Milanese specialty presents an inspired use for leftovers. Any remaining risotto is chilled overnight, then pressed into a very thin layer on a hot, generously buttered frying pan. When the first side has browned, the rice pancake is flipped (or "jumped," the meaning of *saltato*) so both sides emerge crisp and golden.

Where: *In Imola, Italy,* Ristorante San Domenico, tel 39/0542-29000, sandomenico.it; *in Venice,* Ristorante da Fiore, tel 39/041-721308, dafiore.net. **Retail and mail order:** For arborio rice, *in New York and Chicago,* Eataly, eataly .com. **Mail order:** amazon.com (search molinella arborio rice; fondo di toscana arborio rice). **Further information and recipes:** *The Splendid Table* by Lynne Rossetto Kasper (1992); *The Classic Italian Cook Book* by Marcella Hazan (1976); *Italian Cuisine* by Tony May (2005); *The Da Fiore Cookbook* by Damiano Martin (2003); foodnetwork.com (search easy risotto nero); cookstr.com (search risotto verde); starchefs.com (search frog legs risotto); epicurious.com (search seafood risotto); lidias italy.com (search truffle risotto). **Special events:** Fiera del Riso, Verona, Italy, September through October, tel 39/045-7300089, fieradelriso.it; Risotto Festival, Houston, November, risotto festival.com.

ALMOST TOO PRETTY TO EAT

Romanesco

Italian

Broccoli haters may not want to take a chance when it comes to the stunning vegetable *Brassica oleracese* (in Latin) or *broccolo romano* (in Italian), looking as it does like a cross between its broccoli and cauliflower relatives. Their loss.

The only problem romanesco poses for the rest of us might be our reluctance to cut into its breathtaking spring-green pyramid, with its craggy peaked buds spiraling up into a single turreted fractal. So ease your aesthetic conscience by rimming it with pink roses and using it as an ornamental centerpiece for a day before you cook it.

The existence of this venerable vegetable was documented as far back as sixteenth-century Europe, and Thomas Jefferson unsuccessfully planted its seeds at Monticello in the eighteenth century. But romanesco is a vegetable-come-lately to our markets, having become fashionable only in the latter part of the twentieth century. Generally considered a Roman specialty, partly because it grows best between Lazio and Campagna and also because that city's cooks have developed its best-known preparations, the vegetable's main season is from mid-autumn through midwinter. The Marche region of Italy, especially around the town of Jesí, has its own version—of a sunlit ivory instead of the more typical brilliant green.

Green or ivory, the vegetable's cut sections should be gently simmered until their last trace of crispness gives way to a just-yielding tenderness. It's at that point that romanesco will develop the ethereal, almost chewy flavor that combines the zestiness of broccoli with the buttery, cabbagy overtones of cauliflower. Like its cousins, romanesco delivers generous amounts of vitamins C and K, along with fiber and antioxidants.

Although it can be prepared using any of the methods suited to broccoli and cauliflower, Roman cooks usually stick to one of three ways. It may open the meal as a soup, given a zesty start with a blend of minced garlic, parsley, and guanciale sautéed to mellowness in olive oil, then submerged in a tomato-laced stock that is finished off with thin strands of angel-hair pasta and gratings of pungent pecorino.

The now-closed Da Silvano trattoria in Manhattan served the lightly cooked flowerets warm with a sprightly sauce of mashed anchovies, garlic, lemon, mint, and olive oil— much like a bagna cauda dip for raw vegetables.

Last but not least, there is romanesco with pasta, as a first or main course. The aesthetically correct choices would be the flat, ear-shaped orecchiette, little shell-like cavatelli, or the butterfly-winged (or bowtied) farfalle, and the dish can be served with or without crumbles of sweet or hot pork sausage. No cheese is required, but a sprinkling of dried hot chile peppers—*peperoncini*— would not go amiss.

WHERE: *In New York,* available at city greenmarkets from mid-autumn to mid-winter. **FURTHER INFORMATION AND RECIPES:** cookstr.com (search spaghetti romanesco); epicurious.com (search charred romanesco with anchovies and mint).

PERPETUALLY SEASONAL

San Marzano Tomatoes

Italian (Campagnan)

Grown around Naples, in the village of San Marzano sul Sarno, at the foot of Mount Vesuvius near Pompeii, these tomatoes are considered by cognoscenti to be the best on earth. Rather scrawny, pointy, and wiggly, they are not especially beautiful fruits, though they are a deep blood red. But what they lack in physical beauty they more than make up for in deeply concentrated, perfectly balanced acid-sweet flavor. Their thin skins and yielding yet unmushy flesh join the flavor party to create a near-perfect tomato for which there are several factors to credit. One is weather: Summers are long in this part of Italy, which gets almost ten months of sunshine every year. Another is the soil: Enriched by Vesuvius over the years to extreme fertility, it is also loaded with reflective minerals that redirect sunlight to bathe the tomato plants from every angle.

Though it's hard to envision the Italian kitchen without them, tomatoes were a New World food. And in fact, although they were imported to Europe, they didn't really take off in Italy until the beginning of the canned tomato industry in the 1800s.

Especially suited for preserving, San Marzanos are known far and wide not just as excellent tomatoes but as the very best *canned* tomatoes. Their skins slip off easily (a boon to cooks) and they retain their distinctive flavor on the shelf; they have less juice than most American tomatoes, and so cook down more quickly. In fact, their quality is so high that, except perhaps in the very peak of summer, it's often better to have San Marzanos canned than most other varieties fresh.

Not all Italian canned tomatoes are San Marzanos, so make sure you see those words on the label. (Strict government rules regulate the nomenclature.) Also look for a Denominazione di Origine Protetta label (D.O.P.), or protected designation of origin, to ensure authenticity.

FURTHER INFORMATION AND RECIPES: *The Food of Italy* by Waverley Root (1992). **TIP:** Quality brands include La Valle, San Marzano, DeLallo, Carmelina, and Asti.

┤||||||||||||||||||||||||||||||├

A BLOODY GOOD DESSERT

Sanguinaccio

Sweet Blood Pudding

Italian (Southern)

Not everything that looks and even tastes like chocolate pudding is in fact that deep, dark, and silken sweet treat. At first glance, the uninitiated might mistake the aromatically spiced winter dessert *sanguinaccio* for an Italian version of

My-T-Fine. They would be advised to study their Latin, as the dessert's name derives from the word *sanguinarius* . . . for blood.

The use of pig's blood in this rich Italian pudding harks back to the days when animals were slaughtered without a morsel going to waste—a practice once again fashionable among chefs who advocate the more responsible "nose-to-tail" consumption.

In the rich Neapolitan version of sanguinaccio, the blood (which can be purchased from

butchers by city dwellers lacking access to freshly killed pigs) is cooked and folded into a sunny, golden, vanilla-perfumed custard seasoned with molten bittersweet chocolate, cinnamon, cloves, pignolis, and bright bits of candied fruits. It is served well chilled in round glass dessert cups or as a filling for pastry; it can also appear as a dip for plain, crisp biscotti or the tender blond Savoy biscuits called ladyfingers.

Farther south in Calabria, *sanguinaccio con*

riso is much beloved. In this iteration, the blood is cooked with rice, then stirred through with raisins, cinnamon, cocoa powder, and grated lemon rind and chilled to a seductively solid consistency. (A simpler regional variation omits the rice and raisins but includes toasted almonds.)

Always served cold, blood pudding is generally associated with the celebration of St. Joseph's Day on March 19—largely due to its proximity to the midwinter slaughtering season. (Pigs are usually slaughtered in cold weather, often in February, and the blood—highly perishable when raw—must be cooked to a thick and stable state as quickly as possible, whether for these puddings or for savory dark sausages.) Where the sale of pig's blood is prohibited for health reasons, the dessert can pose a problem. In the United States, beef blood is often substituted, with slightly less lusty results, although sanguinaccio is so generously spiced that the differences are virtually obscured.

As an added bonus, sanguinaccio offers nutritional benefits: Rich in protein and iron, it is the perfect dessert not only for connoisseurs but also for anemics.

Where: *In Queens, NY,* in winter, Ornella Trattoria, tel 718-777-9477, ornellatrattoria.com. **Further reading and recipe:** deliciousitaly.com (search sanguinaccio).

THE IMPORTANCE OF NOT BREAKING THE MOLD

Sartù di Riso

Fez-Shaped Rice Mold with Savory Filling

Italian (Neapolitan)

One of Naples's most operatic dishes, the fez-shaped *sartù* is a molded dish of risotto-like rice concealing goodies such as tiny beef meatballs, green peas, bits of cooked chicken livers and pork sausage, flecks of molten mozzarella, dried earthy porcini, and sliced hard-cooked eggs. All is moistened with broth, lard, and olive oil and flavored with savory additions such as Parmesan, tomato, grated lemon peel, nutmeg, and basil; packed carefully into a mold and baked, it is ceremoniously unmolded as expectant diners and cooks await with anticipation.

Complex and artistic

Much like the bowl-shaped *timpano* (a riff on the more common name, *timballo*) made famous in the film *Big Night,* sartù is a culinary high-wire act, the trick being to keep it all together until it is unmolded and cut to reveal a rainbow of flavors and fragrances. Believed to have been created in the seventeenth century by French cooks serving the Bourbon court in Naples, its name developed from *sûrtout,* meaning "above all else."

Perhaps not too surprisingly, this labor-intensive dish is generally not available on Italian menus, even in Naples, but at certain restaurants it can be ordered in advance for a specified number of diners.

Where: *In Naples,* O Murzillo, tel 39/081-593-7706; *in Brooklyn,* for special occasions such as pre-Lenten Carnevale, Tommaso's Restaurant, tel 718-236-9883, tommasoinbrooklyn .com. **Further information and recipes:** *Naples at Table* by Arthur Schwartz (1998); ifood.tv (search sartu di riso).

‖‖‖‖‖‖‖‖‖‖‖‖‖‖‖‖‖‖‖‖‖‖‖‖‖

A SHRIMP OF A LOBSTER

Scampi Adriatic-Style

Italian

Most Americans hear the word *scampi* and immediately conjure up the garlic-doused shrimp that's been a favorite on Italian American menus for decades. To start, a far more accurate way of describing that dish would be "shrimp, scampi-style." True scampi is actually the Norway lobster (*Nephrops norvegicus*), a prawnlike crustacean abundant in the Mediterranean and Adriatic.

Technically small lobsters, scampi dwell in the muddy soil at the bottom of the ocean, only coming up to feed at night. Mostly caught by trawling, they are meaty, succulent, and sweet. Because they thrive in the waters near Venice, they are forever associated with that city and its legendary fish market, La Pescaria. There, the lobsterettes, as they're sometimes called, are prepared very simply: Butterflied and packed tightly on skewers, they are brushed with olive oil, lemon juice, and garlic, and then grilled or roasted. Frequent bastings with yet more garlic-spiked butter ensure a result that is wildly delicious. Alternatively, they are sautéed with olive oil and lemon juice.

Although not made with true scampi, American shrimp scampi is an obvious homage with a charm of its own—especially when you're a long way from Venice.

WHERE: *In Venice,* Corte Sconta, tel 39/041-522-7024, cortescontavenezia.it; Rao's, *in New York, Los Angeles, and Las Vegas,* raosrestaurant.com; *in New York,* Patsy's, tel 212-247-3491, patsys.com; **FURTHER INFORMATION AND RECIPES:** *Lidia's Italian-American Kitchen* by Lidia Bastianich (2001); *The Classic Italian Cookbook* by Marcella Hazan (1976); foodandwine.com (search classic shrimp scampi).

‖‖‖‖‖‖‖‖‖‖‖‖‖‖‖‖‖‖‖‖‖‖‖‖‖

SEE YOUR FISH AND EAT IT TOO

Seafood in Venice

Italian (Venetian)

"The rationalist mind has always had its doubts about Venice," wrote Mary McCarthy in her classic book *Venice Observed.* Considering all of the opulent wonders of that mythical floating city, it's no wonder visitors sometimes have a hard time believing even as they see. With its elaborate, confectionery architecture, its dazzling museums of classical and modern art, its operatic street life, its winding bridge-laced alleyways, and its real-life gondoliers in traditional costume, Venice is a place that does defy rationality.

Much the same can be said of one of its main gastronomic specialties: the impeccable fish and seafood drawn fresh daily from the surrounding waters. Deposited in the morning at the Rialto fish market at the foot of the famed bridge that crosses the Grand Canal, today's catch might include creamy, saline *calamari;* tomorrow's, the true, seasonal scampi to be grilled on skewers in a haze of garlic butter; or the giant, hard-shelled *granceole* crabs, which Venetians love to eat chilled under a light glossing of olive-oil-scented mayonnaise.

Rialto Market buzzes with activity at daybreak.

In this market, neatly arrayed from one stall to another, lies a virtual menu of the city's best offerings: the tiny pink mullet known as *triglie;* silvery bass (*dentice*); ivory chunks of monkfish (*coda de rospo*); and prized swimmers such as *spigola* and orata. Most breathtaking, however, is the assortment of mollusks and

crustaceans, each with its own moniker, from standard mussels named *cozze* to the clamlike varieties that suggest straight-edged razors (*dateri*).

It's a place where to believe what one sees, one must eat it. And for ultimate satisfaction in this realm, one must make a lunch reservation at Corte Sconta. Casually chic in a typically Italian way, this "hidden court" can produce a meal that incorporates just about everything on display in the fish market, from the squid sperm to the lightly fried squid rings and tentacles to the squid ink that is not to be missed on either linguine or risotto. There are some raw starters of mollusks, more seafood-informed pastas, and, for the main course, various fish broiled, fried, or poached in the way that makes the most of their natural texture and flavor. Corte Sconta serves a dinner that is equally delightful, but nothing beats lunch as a follow-up to a morning stroll through that fabled market.

WHERE: *In Venice,* Corte Sconta, tel 39/04-1522-7024, cortescontavenezia .it; Ristorante da Fiore, tel 39/041-721308, dafiore.net; Rialto Fish Market, daily 7 a.m. to 2 p.m., veniceconnected.com (search rialto market). **FURTHER INFORMATION AND RECIPES:** *The Da Fiore Cookbook* by Damiano Martin (2003); *Venetian Cooking* by H. F. Bruning, Jr. and Cav. Umberto Bullo (1973).

||||||||||||||||||||||||||||||||||||||

FROM LEAF TO CLAW (BY WAY OF PASTRY)

Sfogliatelle

Italian (Neapolitan)

This puffy golden pastry, shaped like a rounded triangle or clamshell, derives its name from *una sfoglia,* a leaf—a reference to the dozens of thinly translucent pastry leaves (or sheets) that enfold its custardy cheese filling. As in its French puff-pastry counterpart, the mille-feuille, in this Neapolitan dessert the sheets of dough are layered, brushed with butter, and baked into a crust that takes on a buttery, palate-teasing crackle. With their filling flavored with candied peels of orange, lemon, and citron, cherries, cinnamon, and, in the most elegant examples, whiffs of rosewater, *sfogliatelle* are classics of the traditional Neapolitan *pasticceria,* much loved for the contrast of crisp pastry and succulently cool, soft filling.

Most traditionally a croissant-size delight, sfogliatelle are now often turned out as one-bite miniatures that may be consumed by the halfdozen. Both versions are generally sprinkled with confectioners' sugar just before they're served. Beware: On rainy or otherwise humid days, the pastry can become tough and soggy.

On the other end of the spectrum, mirroring the propensity of so many foods to reconfiguration in monster portions these days, the sfogliatelle, too, has morphed into the obscene extravaganza known as the lobster claw—with the same layerings of puff pastry formed into a giant tapering cone, more or less shaped like said claw and usually filled with whipped cream, sometimes chocolate-flecked, or pastry cream flavored with vanilla or chocolate. This exaggerated *dolce* is surely enough for two, if not three; a single diner may find out just how deadly a lobster's claw really can be.

WHERE: *In Naples,* La Sfogliatella Mary, tel 081-402218; *in New York,* Veniero's, tel 212-674-7070, venierospastry.com; *in Boston,* Mike's Pastry Shop, tel 617-742-3050, mikespastry.com; *in San Francisco,* Stella Pastry Café, tel 415-986-2914, stellapastry.com. **FURTHER INFORMATION AND RECIPES:** *Naples at Table* by Arthur Schwartz (1998); epicurious.com (search sfogliatelle).

Sweet-flavored ricotta spills from crisp pastry.

THE MAGIC OF OREGANO, BREAD CRUMBS, AND GARLIC

Shellfish Arreganata

Italian American

Never underestimate the power of oregano (*Origanum vulgare*), the herb so inextricably associated with Italian American cooking. A wild perennial of the mint family, it is beloved for its versatility and for its deeply woodsy, earthy flavor.

While it can be overused to deleterious and palate-numbing effect, in shellfish *arreganata* (often dubbed *oreganata*) it is employed as the deliciously comforting base note in a fragrant, garlicky harmony.

One of the oregano-laced preparations most associated with Italian American restaurants, the dish has managed to retain its status as a classic without becoming dated. And it's no wonder. With fresh lobster, shrimp, or clams heady with garlic and oregano and sprinkled liberally with toasty bread crumbs, what's not to like about this crunchy and downright addictive dish? Baked, the topping forms a delectably crusty contrast to the tender, olive-oil-laced seafood still nested in its shells.

When made with shrimp or clams, it's usually served as an appetizer—and these wonderfully salty morsels of seafood that happen to pair so perfectly with drinks do make for a great way to begin a meal. Based on lobster, it's a substantial (and pretty expensive) main course.

The key to delicious shellfish arreganata is to apply the bread crumbs to the still-raw seafood. Clams should be on the half-shell, freshly opened. Shrimp should be peeled and deveined. More challengingly, lobster should be split live.

Where: Rao's, *in New York,* tel 212-722-6709; *in Las Vegas,* tel 877-346-4642, *in Los Angeles,* tel 323-962-7267, raosrestaurants.com. **Further information and recipes:** *Rao's Cookbook* by Frank Pellegrino (1998); *Lidia's Italian-American Kitchen* by Lidia Bastianich (2001); foodnetwork.com (search baked clams oreganata). **Tip:** The best oregano is either Italian or Greek and is sold dried and still on the branch.

ELECTRIC SUNSHINE HAS A RIND

Sorrento Lemons

Italian (Southern)

In 1985, the German artist Joseph Beuys exhibited a new minimalist work called *Capri Batterie.* It was a yellow lightbulb plugged into a big lemon. The caption explained that the sun's energy, absorbed by the lemon, gave it enough power to light the bulb. The work was billed as an *ommagio* to Capri, which is the site of the lemon grove, or *limoneto,* where the exquisitely yellow citrus grows. Sorrento, which gives its name to the variety of lemon, is nearby.

Gastronomes would have made the connection via the elongated oval lemon's beguiling liquid-sunshine flavor—cool and sweetly fresh, with that teasing sour sting. Sorrento lemons have a sweeter, cleaner, brighter flavor than other varieties. They would know the juice of this knobby, thick-skinned fruit, recalling its animating presence in salads, risotto, fettuccine, and frosty granita ices; its perfumed leaves adding interest to the cheeses they enfold as well as to the snowy custard that is *panna cotta*—cooked milk. They would know the preciousness of its grated rind, wasted at the diner's own peril, lest it fail to enliven meatballs and pasta or live out its usefulness as the basis for the liqueur Limoncello.

One sublime Italian salad that shows off this lemon at its best is prepared by peeling off the rind, then cutting the inner flesh into almost invisibly sheer round slices and arranging them on individual salad plates, to be topped with chopped pistachios, a few grains of granulated sugar, and a spritz of olive oil. One lemon makes a portion that is best prepared about fifteen minutes before serving time, as a vibrantly astringent refresher between courses or as a side dish to roast pork, duck, or goose.

Native to the area around Sorrento, these lemons are now also grown in limited quantities around Jamul, California, although the different terrain leads to slightly less exquisite fruit.

Mail order and recipes: specialtyproduce.com (search italian sorrento lemons).

||||||||||||||||||||||||||||||||

ALWAYS AT CHRISTMAS, SOMETIMES FOR EASTER

Struffoli

Italian

Held together in merry mounds by a cinnamon-and-lemon-flavored honey glaze, these tiny golden-brown nuggets of lightly fried dough make for one of the sweetest and most delightful treats in the holiday canon. Like popcorn or salted nuts, the Neapolitan specialty is habit-forming—it's hard to know when to stop pinching off bites of these chewy mini-crullers. Sprinklings of multicolored confetti candy and, often, pastel-iced Jordan almonds create the visual enticement that makes them favorites not just for Christmas and Easter celebrations but also as birthday cakes throughout the year.

Other delightful versions abound. In what's known as a *pignolata,* the mound of tiny crullers is masked with a creamy chocolate icing. In Sicily, the nuggets are turned through cooked honey and studded with toasted blanched almonds, pignolis, and mixed candied fruits, which set like jewels and add crunch and interest to the finished confection. In the Portuguese city of Evora, long strips of dough are fried, glazed with honey, and arranged in Christmas logs called *nogados.*

Bet you can't eat just one.

The honeyed mass invites festive adornment.

WHERE: *In New York,* Veniero's, tel 212-674-7070, venierospastry.com; *in Boston,* Mike's Pastry Shop, tel 617-742-3050, mikespastry.com; *in San Francisco,* Stella Pastry Café, tel 415-986-2914, stellapastry.com. **FURTHER INFORMATION AND RECIPES:** *Naples at Table* by Arthur Schwartz (1998); foodnetwork.com (search struffoli batali).

||||||||||||||||||||||||||||||||

THE HEALING POWER OF NEW GRAPES

Sugo di Uva, or Traubensaft

Freshly Pressed Grape Juice

Italian (Tyrolean)

Learn to order it in Italian as *sugo di uva.* Then learn to order it in German as *Traubensaft,* because you don't want to pass up a chance to quaff this liquid jewel of cool, clear, freshly pressed grape juice. Gently sweet, with a teasing hint of grapey tartness, it is the centerpiece of the Merano Grape Festival in the northern Alpine province of Alto Adige, most colorfully experienced in the charming garden of the Merano resort spa.

Still remembered as the South Tyrol, this stunning mountain area belonged to Austria before World War I and has struggled with its Austro-Italian dual identity ever since. Both languages are still in evidence, hence the dual names for the refreshing drink squeezed from newly harvested grapes.

Come late September, and all through October, big glass pitchers of the unfermented, nonalcoholic juice are offered to guests in hotel breakfast rooms and cafés, and at corner street stands decorated with vines and branches. One pitcher holds the winey-looking garnet juice of red grapes, the other the sparkling citrine liquid of pale green ones. Lightly chilled but not iced, both are thought to restore prime health to those who drink three glasses a day during the six- to eight-week season—equivalent to downing two pounds of whole grapes daily. Those with lustier palates and a preference for red wine will choose the red-grape elixir, while those who like life on the crystalline light side can opt for the green. Or, better yet, have one type at breakfast, another at lunch, and the one you prefer in midafternoon.

Assuming you do not faint from the sharply lowered blood pressure a large quantity of grape juice can induce, you will be in for a bracing, head-clearing experience.

Celebrated each afternoon with a parade through the pretty center of Merano as part of a companion music festival, the season also means marchers in lederhosen, oom-pah-pah brass bands, and fair young maidens decked out with vine leaves in their hair. Yet another reason to laud this coolly seductive cure.

WHERE: *In Merano, Italy,* many cafés, restaurants, and street stands from late September through October. **SPECIAL EVENT:** Merano Grape Festival, Merano, October, meran.eu/en (search grape festival).

⊣||||||||||||||||||||||||||||||||⊢

THE UNDERGROUND SENSATION

Tartufi de Alba

Italian (Piemontese)

The fungi known as truffles are easily among the most subtly flavored, elusive, expensive, and mysterious foods of the world, not least because they grow entirely underground. Although there are some seventy species, two are most prized by connoisseurs: the black truffle (*Tuber melanosporum*), found in various parts of France, especially in Périgord and Provence, and in Italy's Umbria region (see page 140); and the white truffle (*Tuber magnatum*), a pale yellowish-beige mushroom found at its best in northwest Italy's Piedmont region, near Alba. A lesser variety is found in the Marche.

White truffles are diabolically alluring, with a powerful fragrance that verges on the obscene, much in the way of a ripe and almost embarrassingly odoriferous cheese. But their aroma is merely a teaser for a profound and complex flavor so precious it is not to be tampered with—which is why truffles are almost never cooked, but are instead blissfully shaved raw into creamy risottos or fresh, delicate pastas such as fettuccine. White truffles also elevate a number of egg dishes—scrambled, poached, or fried—and shine, as part of a classic salad, with ovoli mushrooms (see page 198). Restaurants in Piedmont serve truffles simply grated over just about everything: taglierini (thin egg noodles traditionally dressed with butter and sage), risotto (see page 233), *fonduta* (fontina cheese melted into creaminess; see page 189), veal carpaccio, and even buttered bread.

A highly specialized treasure with a short season that runs from September to December, white truffles will grow only beneath certain trees (usually oaks, but also lindens, willows, hazelnuts, and poplars), but not with any consistency: Neither farmers nor scientists have been able to predict which trees will grow truffles, but they do know that the soil must be chalky and that the most efficacious weather conditions include a rainy spring, a hot summer, and a stormy August.

Because of this lack of predictability, truffles are hunted rather than harvested—and traditionally, the best truffle hunters were sows. No coincidence, then, that German scientists have found truffles to contain a natural chemical similar to the pheromone secreted in male pig saliva. The helpful swine tend to eat the truffles, so now dogs are more often deployed.

Difficult to find, truffles can be worth more than their weight in gold.

MAIL ORDER: Urbani Truffles, tel 212-247-8800, urbani.com; D'Artagnan, tel 800-327-8246, dartagnan.com. **FURTHER INFORMATION AND RECIPES:** *The Food of Italy* by Waverley Root (1992); *More Classic Italian Cooking* by Marcella Hazan (1982). **SPECIAL EVENT:** White Truffle Festival, Alba, Italy, December, fieradeltartufo.org. **TIP:** A good truffle should be intensely pungent and firm to the touch, not spongy when pressed with the finger. The most prized specimens are uniformly round in shape, but a truffle is good as long as it isn't broken and has no holes.

THE TRUE MEANING OF *MEATHEAD*

Testina, or Capuzzelle

Italian (Southern)

Nose-to-tail cookery has been in vogue over the past few years, presenting undaunted chefs with the worthy challenge of leaving no part of the animal unused. It's an idea whose time has come—once again. Down on the farm, especially

in olden days, very few parts of any slaughtered animals were wasted. Blood became a filling for sausages; cleaned intestines morphed into sausage casings; and scalded stomachs were handy sacks in which to poach chickens and steam or roast ground meat mixtures.

Since everything old is new again, it should

be no surprise to see today's succulently moist, luxuriously rich cheeks, tongues, and creamy brains of lambs, goats (kids), or calves served right in the heads to which they belong. Yet many diners are shocked when first served this *testina,* meaning head, or *capuzzelle* in the dialect of southern Italy.

Those heads, one might argue, are nature's own tureens for this poor man's treat and gourmand's delight. To prepare this rustic feast (often served at weddings in southern Italy), the cleaned and scraped craniums are split down the middle, right through the bones (with eyes intact, as the most authentic Italian recipes demand), and then roasted. Splitting assures that the brains can easily be dipped into and that the tender, pink, and gamy tongue can be slipped out and shared, as can the juiciest, plump cheek meat.

Sheep's or lamb's heads are favored in southern Italy, where the testina is prepared in several regional variations—the most delicious being in the Marche, Apulia, and Abruzzo, where the meat is aromatic with rosemary, prosciutto, garlic, salt, and pepper. Basilicata cooks add a nice touch with a coating of bread crumbs and grated sharp pecorino cheese that crisps up in the oven, and in Sicily the split head is gently stewed in a pungent tomato sauce sparked with grated lemon peel, sage, and cloves. The least embellishment is preferred in Calabria, with only olive oil, parsley, salt, and pepper added before the head is roasted along with unpeeled new potatoes that absorb the elegant pan juices.

Calf's heads are more generally served in northern Italy, but they often are boned and cooked as terrines or soft, gelatinous stews in the manner of calves' or pigs' feet.

As for the eyeballs, passionate aficionados claim them as the best parts of all.

Further information and recipes: *Italian Cuisine* by Tony May (2005); gourmet.com (search a brain is a terrible thing to waste).

⊢||||||||||||||||||||||||||||||⊣

DRAW ME CLOSE

Tirami Sù

Italian

Delectable squishes of spongy ladyfingers or eggy genoise layered with chocolate, coffee, and cloudlets of creamy mascarpone cheese, all heady with the scent of rum, brandy, or bittersweet Marsala wine, indeed explain the

name of the irresistible dessert *tirami sù,* translated as "draw me close." Basically a modern riff on Naples's *zuppa inglese,* tirami sù is also set in a big bowl, preferably of glass, to attain the texture of a pudding-cake. The English trifle (see page 31) was the inspiration for that Neapolitan derivation.

Now a much overworked menu item, the Italian dessert takes on a luscious new meaning in its best-ever version, surprisingly found in the charming Napa Valley restaurant Terra,

Creamy layers on display

where it is presented in individually made portions. Five-layered, featherlight, it's the perfect balance of textures and flavors.

Where: *In St. Helena, CA,* Terra Restaurant, tel 707-963-8931, terrarestaurant.com; *in New York,* Da Umberto, tel 212-989-0303, daumbertonyc.com; Patsy's, tel 212-247-3491, patsys .com. **Further information and recipes:** *Patsy's Cookbook* by Salvatore Scognamillo (2002); foodnetwork.com (search tiramisu mario batali; tiramisu italiano tyler florence).

A DENTIST'S DREAM

Torrone

Italian

Torrone isn't just one thing; it's a world of its own. A chewy blond confection with a firm taffy texture and crunches of toasted nuts, it's an Italianate version of French nougat, equally ubiquitous as street fair snack and elegantly wrapped Christmas gift.

So integral to the winter holidays that Marcella Hazan declared it "an inseparable part of any well-stuffed Christmas basket," torrone is also surrounded by lore. One legend has it that a court confectioner created the candy for the marriage of Bianca Maria Visconti to Francesco Sforza in 1441, modeling it on the landmark tower (*torre*) in Cremona. Historians, however, suggest that the nougat is made in the style of *turrón*, a sweet that Islamic immigrants introduced in Spain. Still made there today, as it has been since medieval times—primarily as a Christmas specialty in the cities of Alicante and Jijona—the Spanish version of the treat is garnished with the region's disk-shaped Marcona almonds.

In general, there are two types of Italian torrone, though they spawn many iterations. One is soft, white-blond in color, and made with honey, egg whites, and nuts (most often almonds). The other is a hard, peanut-brittle-like praline the color of dark caramel, made of sugar, water, and nuts.

White torrone with hazelnuts

The soft candy is usually left to the professionals, given the laboriousness of a process in which egg whites and honey are whipped together over a warm water bath for at least seven hours, until the mixture becomes just thickly fluffy. It is then flattened onto work surfaces (while still burning hot) before being rolled out and cut into the traditional log shape.

From here, confectioners adhere a thin sheet of edible rice or potato starch paper to keep the candy from sticking to its wrapper. Torrone made in this way is a particular specialty of Bagnara, on Calabria's coast, and has been made there for hundreds of years by small, family-owned artisanal producers.

Home cooks tend to tackle the crunchier version made of just sugar, water, and nuts, but there are many variations even of this simpler sweet. Torrone may be enhanced with orange or rosewater essence, studded mosaic-style with candied fruits, made with hazelnuts or pistachios instead of the almonds, or covered with white or dark chocolate (horrors). In almost any incarnation, it's a textural delight: a candy that can be soft but that gains character as it hardens and complexity as it is enjoyed, so that as you chew you discern more intense, multifaceted, and honeyed flavors in every bite.

WHERE: *In Bagnara, Italy,* Cundari Confectioners, tel 39/ 0966-372505, cundarivincenzo.it. **MAIL ORDER:** eataly.com; zingermans.com; dipaloselects.com. **FURTHER INFORMATION AND RECIPES:** *Visions of Sugarplums* by Mimi Sheraton (1981); *Pomp and Sustenance: Twenty-Five Centuries of Sicilian Food* by Mary Taylor Simeti (1989). **SPECIAL EVENT:** Festa del Torrone, Cremona, Italy, October, festadeltorronecremona.it. **TIP:** Look for Tiu Boele, Sorelle Nurzia, D. Barbero, and Maria Grammatico brands.

Hazelnuts

Almonds, pistachios, and macadamia nuts may have their fans, but the most sophisticated nut of all is the tender yet crunchy, lusciously subtle little round hazelnut that is *Corylus avellana* or *C. maxima. Noisette* to the French and *nocciola* to the Italians and to the Germans, *Haselnuss,* the toothsome hazelnut provides gently sweet, almost smoky undertones beneath its polished shell.

In France, hazelnuts are crushed into hot, golden-brown butter for *beurre noisette,* a butter sauce that enhances sautéed fish or chicken. Its satiny, fragrant oil is also much in demand there for salad dressings. In Italy, hazelnuts are studded into the nougat candy called *torrone,* or pounded to a paste and combined with chocolate to make *gianduja,* the luxuriously soft filling for pastries and bonbons that is the inspiration for the mass-market success, Nutella (which is popular as a creamy filling for crepes). In their purest and perhaps most tempting form, hazelnuts are simply roasted and served warm with aperitifs.

Although favored by some in their unripe green state, the creamy nuts, which grow hidden in leafy pouches, attain their best flavor when harvested fully ripe before being toasted. Their loose brown inner skins are easily rubbed off between two cloths for a more refined result when the nuts are used in baking and candy making. Ground with their skins, crushed hazelnuts substitute for flour in true (i.e., flourless) tortes. And wherever the hazelnut tree flourishes, its twigs are valued as water-divining rods—used in an ancient, Ouija-board-like ritual in which farmers and other prospectors seek out groundwater via the twitches of the twig.

In the U.S., the term "hazelnut" is technically applied only to the wild variety of this cheerful, roundish nut. Though the terms tend to be used interchangeably in Great Britain, its cultivated twin is called a filbert, a handle that may have its origins in Normandy. There, a seventh-century monk later canonized as St. Philibert is honored on August 22—just about the time hazelnuts ripen and drop from their trees into the huge nets suspended like hammocks to catch them.

Grown in many parts of Europe, the best still come from Italy, although some very good examples are grown in Oregon and Washington State. Italy's Piedmont region is the home of the round, so-called Roman filbert, prized for its delicate flavor and its high yield. Some prefer the more bracing, elongated *nocciola* grown around the Campagna town of Avellino.

MAIL ORDER: nuts.com, tel 800-558-6887. **FURTHER INFORMATION AND RECIPES:** *The Oxford Companion to Food* by Alan Davidson (1999); *Oregon Hazelnut Country: The Food, the Drink, the Spirit* by Jan Roberts-Dominguez (2010); saveur.com (search chocolate-dipped hazelnut cookies). **TIP:** To be sure of freshness, try shaking a few of the unshelled nuts. If the kernels do not rattle, the nuts are too tight in their shells and have not aged enough to allow moisture to evaporate. Unless you can taste for freshness and will use them immediately, do not buy shelled hazelnuts, as they can become rancid quickly.

||||||||||||||||||||||||||||||

HOW TO GO NUTS FOR CHOCOLATE

Torta Caprese

Italian (Campagnan)

The stylishness of the Mediterranean isle of Capri (when it's not in the throes of peak tourist season) is lusciously transmuted into this elegantly thin but intense chocolate cake, a true torte that substitutes finely ground, blanched almonds

for flour. The almonds contribute fragrance, flavor, and a firm but gently moist texture, granting a teasingly crisp finish to the cake's top and sides. A favorite in nearby Naples and throughout the region of Campagna, the torte is easy to make and keeps nicely if well wrapped and stored in a cool place.

Torta Caprese

Serves 6 to 8

⅔ cup (11 tablespoons) unsalted butter,
*   plus some for greasing the pan*
Flour for dusting the pan
1¼ cups blanched almonds
6 ounces semisweet chocolate
1 cup sugar
6 extra-large eggs, separated
Pinch of salt
Confectioners' sugar, for serving
Whipped cream
*   (optional), for serving*

1. Position a rack in the center of the oven and preheat the oven to 350°F. Butter and lightly flour a 10-inch round cake pan; tap out any excess flour.

2. Grind the almonds to a fine meal in a food processor or blender. Combine the butter and chocolate in the top of a double boiler over simmering water and stir until melted. Set aside to cool.

3. Beat the sugar and egg yolks together in a large bowl until thick and pale yellow. Stir in the ground almonds and the cooled chocolate mixture.

4. Add a pinch of salt to the egg whites and beat them in a large bowl until stiff but not dry. Using a spatula, fold the egg whites gently but thoroughly into the chocolate mixture until no whites are visible. Spoon the batter into the prepared baking pan and smooth the top with the spatula.

5. Bake the cake until a cake tester or toothpick inserted in the center comes out clean, about 1 hour.

6. Transfer the cake in the pan to a wire rack to cool. When the cake has cooled completely, remove it from the pan and place it on a serving dish. Sprinkle the cake generously with confectioners' sugar. Serve it plain or with a topping of whipped cream or a dab of vanilla ice cream.

WHERE: *In Naples,* Pasticceria Scaturcchio, tel 39/081-551-6944; *in New York,* Vico, tel 212-876-2222. **TIP:** Cinnamon is not a traditional flavoring for this cake, but it is a delectable one. Consider adding ½ teaspoon when you stir in the almonds. The result will be perhaps more Mexican than Italian, but why quibble with something so delicious?

Almonds add nutrition and flavor to this treat.

‖‖‖‖‖‖‖‖‖‖‖‖‖‖‖‖‖‖‖‖‖

A RIVAL TO NEW YORK'S CHEESECAKE

Torta di Ricotta

Italian

Grainier than the classic American cheesecake, and more aromatic thanks to rose or orange flower water and a hint of vanilla, the typical Italian *torta di ricotta* (also known as *pizza di ricotta*, when it appears in pie form) is an invitingly rich delight. Unlike New York and eastern European cheesecakes based on creamier cream cheese and cottage cheese, this one owes its teasingly acidic tang to ricotta. A lighter and more artisanal version of the traditional confection, it traditionally bears a high crust and lattice top made from the intensely rich and buttery dough known as *pasta frolla*. Some cooks exploit the dessert's slightly coarse texture, giving it even more body by including two or three different kinds of ricotta.

Especially favored at Christmas and Easter, the cake is subjected to an extra-special dose of celebratory treatment during the latter holiday—a week after Lent's fasting period. Neapolitan bakers make an especially eggy version called *pastiera Napoletana*, in which farro's whole wheat kernels are added to the cake. The torta may also be studded with any number of traditional enhancements, from candied fruit peels to rum-soaked raisins or currants and toasted pignolis.

WHERE: *In New York,* Pasticceria Bruno, tel 212-982-5854, pasticceriabruno.com; *in Baltimore,* Piedigrotta Bakery of Baltimore, tel 410-522-6900, piedigrottabakery.com; *in Portland, OR,* Nostrana, tel 503-234-2427, nostrana.com. **FURTHER INFORMATION AND RECIPES:** *Dolce Italiano: Desserts from the Babbo Kitchen* by Gina DePalma (2007); *More Classic Italian Cooking* by Marcella Hazan (1982); bonappetit.com (search ricotta cheesecake).

‖‖‖‖‖‖‖‖‖‖‖‖‖‖‖‖‖‖‖‖‖

EVERYTHING OLD IS NEW AGAIN

Veal Parmigiana

Italian American

Rare is the modern-day gourmet who would be caught praising veal parmigiana. That's too bad, as this easy-to-love dish has been emerging from its cloud of gastronomic disrepute and moving toward foodie it-list status, albeit in loftier stylings and at higher prices. A case in point: The restaurant Carbone in New York's Greenwich Village now offers a gigantic portion of the dish for upwards of $50, a comparatively gigantic price.

A creation of the Italian American red-sauce kitchen, in its original heyday veal parmigiana was often served (to the horror of Italian food purists) right alongside a portion of spaghetti, providing a satisfying meal at a moderate price.

Basically a thin, carefully pounded, breaded, and fried veal scallop, it is topped with thin slices or dicings of mozzarella and an oregano- and garlic-scented tomato sauce and then baked to succulent, melting glory. While the name of the dish suggests veal that is cooked "Parma-style," there's really nothing in Parma that resembles it; instead, food scholars believe the name refers to Parma's most significant product, Parmigiano-Reggiano cheese.

Though poorly prepared versions of this classic have abounded, when prepared correctly it is utterly addictive, especially to children. Because veal is a delicately flavored and soft-textured meat, not overcooking it is key. So is using the right cut—a boneless chop or "scallop" (or, to be fair, *scaloppine* in Italian or *paillard* in French) cut from the leg—which must be treated as carefully as if it were being prepared for an elegant, stylish meal. The veal should be pounded between sheets of wax paper to a uniform thickness of about ½ inch, dredged in an egg and very good breading, then fried in olive oil until crisp and lacy-edged. It should be covered lightly with a marinara sauce and thin slices or dicings of mozzarella and a sprinkling of grated Parmesan (so it doesn't devolve into a watery mess), baked until bubbly, and then served immediately before the sauce cools and the cheese hardens. Obviously, real imported Parmigiano-Reggiano rather than overly salty pregrated jarred Parmesan is key.

Instead of that sad heap of plain spaghetti alongside the dish, try an accompaniment of chopped broccoli, either regular or rabe, sautéed in garlic and olive oil. As a bonus, room-temperature leftovers make luscious sandwiches the next day.

WHERE: *Throughout the U.S.,* The Palm Restaurant, thepalm.com; *in New York,* Carbone, tel 212-933-0707, carbonenewyork.com. **FURTHER INFORMATION AND RECIPES:** *The James Beard Cookbook* by James Beard (2002); *Rao's Cookbook* by Frank Pellegrino (1998); saveur .com (search veal parmesan); parmesan.com (search veal parmesan).

—————————————|||||||||||||||||||||||||||||||—————————————

A CLASSIC WAY WITH SURF 'N' TURF

Vitello Tonnato

Veal with Tuna Sauce

Italian

One of the most sumptuous of Italy's cold summertime dishes, and a creation worthy of the most demanding cognoscenti, *vitello tonnato* can be served as an appetizer or as a light luncheon or late-supper main course.

Unsurprisingly, the preparation of those paper-thin slices of rose-pink veal and that tangy, silky sauce is subject to the differences of opinion that surround so many revered dishes. Many agree that the veal rump or loin should be poached with bay leaves, vegetables, and garlic prior to being chilled and very thinly sliced. The veal is then napped with a sauce based on tuna, a little anchovy, and capers—and here is where roads most commonly diverge.

Traditionalists insist that the sauce should contain no mayonnaise; instead, the tuna must be worked with olive oil and trickles of the poaching stock until it becomes a mayonnaise-like emulsion. Of course, whipping the tuna into mayonnaise with some olive oil added as a thinner is an easier way to achieve that silky consistency, so this method has become increasingly common among cooks. In either case, the tuna must be of the oil-packed, jarred variety, so as to be intensely salty and mashingly soft. Fresh tuna simply doesn't cut it.

Another variation, this one a smart innovation recommended by the English food writer Elizabeth David, is to roast the veal to a medium-rare state, rather than poaching it, so the meat remains firm and does not become waterlogged.

The flavors of veal and smooth tuna sauce blend harmoniously.

A look at the dish's origins, by way of the Livornese cookbook *Il Cuciniere Italiano Moderno* (1842), sheds some light on the reasoning behind its unusual flavor dichotomy. At the time, veal was much less expensive than tuna, and was often seasoned to taste like a substitute, such as mock tuna. Tuna itself never touched the dish. Rather, cuts of veal were boiled with anchovies to impart a fishy flavor to the meat, and the simmered-down stock—anchovies and all—was beaten with olive oil into a thickened sauce. Fishy veal was the result.

Surely modern versions are more sublime, especially when served with some good hearty bread and a glass of dry white wine.

WHERE: *In New York,* Sistina, tel 212-861-7660, sistinany.com. **FURTHER INFORMATION AND RECIPE:** *Italian Food* by Elizabeth David (1999).

+|||||||||||||||||||||||||||||||||||||+

THERE'S SAUSAGE AFOOT . . .

Zampone

Italian (Emilian-Romagnan)

If you're a bit startled to see a pig's foot hanging from a hook in your local Italian delicatessen, rest easy. That foot is merely the casing for *zampone*—one of the most dramatic and rustically satisfying specialties of the pork-savvy city of Modena.

Made of a mixture of head, neck, and shoulder meat, zampone derives its teasingly sensuous stickiness, also common in head cheeses, from the gelatin imparted by those boney, cartilaginous cuts. Fragrant nutmeg, a spice popular in Emilia-Romagna, is joined by pepper, cinnamon, and cloves, along with the requisite salt (still copious but used in smaller quantities today than it once was). Poaching the sausage is a lengthy process because it must be done gently, lest the casing split.

Filled with its aromatic, coarsely ground

blend of pink pork, spices, and just enough fat to keep things succulently moist, zampone is a winter favorite. Modenese purists elect potatoes or spinach as top-choice accompaniments, but gastronomic rebels are free to stray to their palate's content. Zampone is delicious served hot, carved into thick slices nested on stewed lentils or laid atop a golden cloud of polenta, chopped spinach, or *broccoli di rapa*. (see page 169). Zampone also makes an appearance in the province's famed mixed boil of meats, *bollito misto*. Less dramatically, but no less deliciously, the same pork mixture can be used to fill the smaller, more conventionally shaped *cotechino* sausage, always served hot.

A striking presentation

A well-known product around Modena since the seventeenth century, zampone is generally believed to have existed a hundred years earlier, harking back to the time when the sixteenth-century Italian poet Ortensio Lando dubbed the city of Modena "the fecund mother of sausages."

WHERE: *In New York,* by advance order, Faicco's Pork Store, tel 212-243-1794; Salumeria Biellese, tel 212-736-7376, salumeriabiellese.com. **FURTHER INFORMATION AND RECIPES:** *The Food of Italy* by Waverley Root (1992); *The Splendid Table* by Lynne Rossetto Kasper (1992); foodnetwork.com (search zampone fagioli; zampone with potatoes and balsamic mustard). **SEE ALSO:** Ciauscolo, page 182.

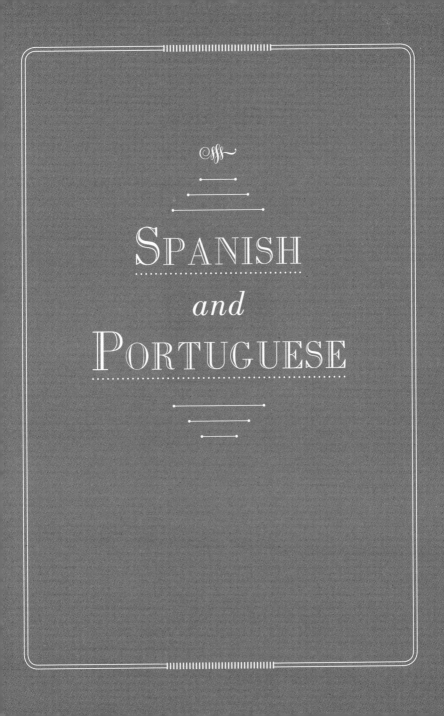

SPANISH

and

PORTUGUESE

—|||||||||||||||||||||||||||||||—

FOOLING THE EYE BUT NOT THE PALATE

Angulas

Glass Eels, Elvers

Spanish, Mediterranean

Pasta with eyes only for you? That might be your impression after a first look at the silky, ivory-white layer of teeny baby eels, or elvers, whose glowing translucence inspires their other name, glass eels. Served in small, individual, round earthenware or iron cocottes, seething in a bath of hot olive oil fragrant with lightly browned garlic and spicy red pepper flakes, they suggest a thread-slim Italian pasta such as *capelli d'angelo* (angel's hair) in the classic *aglio-olio* sauce. But look closer and you will note the tiny pinpoints of gray-black eyes staring up at you (accusingly?). And when you twirl a few of those tempting specimens onto a special miniature two-pronged fork made of wood,

A tiny, slippery Basque treat

you find they are no more than four inches long, with a tenderly meaty texture and a subtle deep-sea flavor akin to that of delicate shellfish.

The eels are rare and expensive, netted during a short season that runs from early November to mid-February. They're popular in France and Italy—but the most enthusiastic elver lovers of all are found in Spain. The price of this delicacy can reach $200 a pound, which puts these infant swimmers among the world's luxury foods. Favorites in Spain's Basque region, they are known in the local language as *txitxardin,* meaning worms (much like the thin Italian pasta called vermicelli, for "little worms").

For all of their fragile appearance, these fish are prodigious travelers, a trait inherited from their mothers who, after being impregnated along the European coasts, swim four thousand miles to the wide Sargasso Sea in the treacherous Bermuda Triangle. Once there, the females lay their eggs and die. The newly hatched glassy offspring, each less than a half-inch long, begin to swim, float, and drift with tides that, in about three years, carry them back to their ancestral home. Nestling in the rocky waters of rivers and inlets along the Atlantic and Mediterranean coasts, they grow to be baby eels that are good enough to eat.

First quickly blanched in either water or vinegar, the silky white eels are then given a scant minute to cook in sizzling garlic- and hot pepper–flavored olive oil. All you have to do to indulge is find a restaurant that serves them, learn to manipulate the miniature wooden fork designed to keep them from slipping off, and have some chunky bread on hand to absorb what is left of the irresistible pan juices. Although some inventive Spanish chefs get creative with *angulas,* it is doubtful that any can surpass the classic preparation.

Where: *In Madrid,* La Trainera, tel 34/91-576-0575, latrainera.es; *in Bilbao,* Guria, tel 34/944-415-780, restauranteguria.com; *in New York,* Sandro's, tel 212-288-7374, sandrosnyc.com; *in San Francisco,* Piperade, tel 415-391-2555, piperade.com. **Further information and recipes:** *The Basque Kitchen* by Gerald Hirigoyen (1999); *The Foods & Wines of Spain* by Penelope Casas (1982); *Gastronomy of Spain and Portugal* by Maite Manjón (1990); spanishfood.about.com (search angulas bilbaina).

—||||||||||||||||||||||||||||||||—

Caldo Gallego

Spanish

Caldo gallego, Galician soup-stew, is a hearty peasant comfort food meant to ease the cold winter days of the mountains of northwestern Spain. Its traditional key ingredients are humble foods that stretch tight budgets: potatoes, *grelos*

(a variety of broccoli rabe, although stateside kale, cabbage, Swiss chard, or turnip greens are often substituted), and small, chewy nuggets of salted smoked pork, plus zesty chorizo sausage, with the meat traditionally coming from pigs raised in many of the Galician villages.

Each ingredient plays a critical role. The greens lend the brew its signature satiny dark-green glow and earthy depth of flavor. The potatoes add an agreeably viscous finish, and the smoky pork and spicy sausage lend bite. Onions and white beans cushion the combination. The whole is marvelously restorative, pleasingly

thick, pungent, and bracing. A meal in a pot, caldo gallego has become famous around the world for its homey charm. It has also been enthusiastically co-opted by Cuban cooks, who celebrate the dish in their home cooking as well.

WHERE: *In Santiago, Spain,* Restaurante Sexto II, tel 34/981-56-05-24, restaurantesexto .com; *in New York,* El Quijote, tel 212-929-1855, elquijoterestaurant.com; *in Chicago,* Café Iberco, tel 312-573-1510, cafeiberico.com. **FURTHER INFORMATION AND RECIPES:** *The Foods & Wines of Spain* by Penelope Casas (1982); cook str.com (search caldo gallego batali).

—||||||||||||||||||||||||||||||||—

Capers

Spanish, Mediterranean

Considering their minuscule size, moist and teasingly bitter-sharp bronze capers offer outsize wallops of flavor and equally astounding amounts of botanical and cultural lore—a lot of baggage indeed for what is merely a piquant condiment.

These tiny buds of the *Capparis spinosa* plant have been prized since ancient Greece and flourish in stony, dry-as-dust landscapes, most notably in southern Spain; on a small island 85 kilometers from Sicily, called Pantelleria; and on the Greek island of Cyprus. Because they thrive in such adverse conditions—they even bloom in airborne bushes in Roman ruins and

the Western Wall in Jerusalem!—the frilly, mauve-white caper flowers were made the symbol of Neot Kedumim, a sprawling biblical heritage botanical park close to Ben Gurion Airport in Israel.

Capers may be hardy, but they are near hell to harvest. The bushes grow low to the ground, with long, splayed branches. On each is a progression of the caper buds, the largest (and most prized) at the tip, and smaller ones growing nearer the center. They must be picked one by one, with ungloved hands, for if the branch is broken, or if its silver-green leaves are stripped, the plant will not produce the following year. And here is Mother Nature's little joke: Behind each and every caper bud lurks a long, needle-sharp thorn. Even so, practiced pickers work quickly because they are paid by the kilo.

Capers, like olives, cannot be eaten in their natural, raw state. The searingly bitter fluid inside them must be leached out, either by soaking them in brine (as in Spain) or by salting them and drying them in the sun (as on

Pantelleria). Also, they must be picked before their flowers bloom. If blooms appear, a stemmed, olive-shaped caper-berry develops; this is the larger, fruitier garnish used in martinis and in tapas selections.

The tiny round bud of the caper,

Capers grow on the ends of the plants' thorns.

once cured, dots salads and sauces to add a ripe and complex, metallic saltiness that some love and others hate (the latter crowd usually detesting anchovies as well). Opposing views on the use of capers also abound. In some countries, they reinforce other salty and piquant ingredients, as in tapenade (*tapeno* being the Provençal word for the bud called *capre* in French). In Italy, where they are known as *capperi*, they spike up pungent Sicilian pasta sauces and the vegetable relish caponata. But in Germany (*kapre*) and England, capers punch up otherwise bland cream sauces.

When buying capers, whether jarred in brine or sold dry, look for uniform size and a good, even green-bronze color that has not faded to yellow. Whether dry or brine-cured, all capers should be rinsed before being used; the dried variety should be soaked for about ten minutes in warm water or olive oil.

MAIL ORDER: amazon.com (search mario camacho nonpareille capers; pantelleria capers in sea salt). **FURTHER INFORMATION AND RECIPES:** *The Foods & Wines of Spain* by Penelope Casas (1982); nytimes.com (search caper chase sheraton). **SPECIAL EVENT:** Festa del Cappero (Caper Festival), Salina, Italy, June, siciliainfesta.com (search festa del cappero).

SAY *QUESO* AND SMILE

The Great Cheeses of Spain

Spanish

Cheese is sacred to Spaniards. Their shepherds have been making it for thousands of years, and for a few hundred, the rest of the populace has been nibbling away at it in great quantities while sipping aperitifs at tapas bars.

Among the wide variety of cheeses that have emerged from the country over the ages, the following four—all protected under Denominación de Origen (D.O.) legislation—are the best-known of the old guard, and were

the first to become widely available outside their homeland.

Manchego is easily Spain's most popular cheese, and became well known for reasons likely to do with its famous place of origin. It is made in La Mancha (Cervantes even refers to it in *Don Quixote*) in the interior of Spain, a dry highland known for its blustering winds. In winter, the region becomes so windy that the long-haired sheep are the only living creatures who don't seem to mind. Made from the milk of these hardy animals, manchego can be served both very young (aged only two months) and very old (aged two years or more). Beloved for its mild flavor, with hints of brine and nutty accents, it's a cheese that is easy to like and plays well with others, particularly Andalusian olives for a bar snack, or *membrillo* (quince paste) for dessert. A sturdy, salty, simple pleasure.

Cabrales and **Picón Bejes-Tresviso** are blue cheeses made from the combined milks of cows, sheep, and goats. They are crafted in the Asturia-Cantabria region just east of Galicia, inland from the coast, where the highlands are wild and rugged and the animals graze in perfect pastures. An incredibly strong, intense affair, Cabrales is shot through with amethyst-colored veins. It bears a deep, complex flavor and a scent you can detect from miles away—not one for the faint of heart, but a reward for the stalwart. Fragile and crumbly without being sticky, it leaves an impression on the palate that makes one long for another bite. Picón Bejes-Tresviso (often referred to as picón) is buttery and slightly

oily, marbled with bluish-green veins, and also quite assertive. Both cheeses are often triple-wrapped in large maple leaves, foil, and plastic before being sold. They are excellent choices for after-dinner cheeses, with sherry.

Idiazábal, a nutty, raw sheep's milk number that is usually smoked, is an ancient cheese from the Basque country. (It used to be stored in the chimneys of shepherds' huts.) With a rust-brown exterior hiding a pale yellow, dense, and firm interior, it's perfect for grating or melting over just about anything—and, with accompaniments of bread and perhaps some lusty, thinly sliced salami, durable enough to withstand a picnic.

Equally excellent are the many other Spanish cheeses that have been made for centuries: tetilla, Mahón, Izbores, and Roncal, along with Garrotxa, the goat's milk cheese from Catalonia, and torta del Casar, the almost-liquid sheep's milk cheese that many consider the very top of the bunch.

RETAIL AND MAIL ORDER: *In Manhattan, Queens, and Princeton, NJ,* Despaña, despana brandfoods.com. MAIL ORDER: La Tienda, tel 800-710-4304, tienda.com. FURTHER INFORMATION: *Cheese Primer* by Steven Jenkins (1996); *The Foods & Wines of Spain* by Penelope Casas (1982).

—|||||||||||||||||||||||||||||||—

ALL THE WORLD LOVES A CRULLER

Churros

Spanish and Hispanic

The good-health police can rant and rave against the deleterious effects of fat and sugar, but the worldwide popularity of deep-fried yeast dough encrusted with sugar persists. Nowhere is this truer than in Spain and Latin American

countries, where churros are the treats that satisfy that primal doughnut urge. Long, fluted,

crunchy, and fragrant with cinnamon sugar, the twists are eaten hot as morning pick-me-ups and then again as late-night soothers, either with strong coffee or (even better) with thick, rich hot chocolate.

Churros are formed by pressing yeast dough through tubes so it emerges as slim ridged ropes, which are then deep-fried in vegetable oil and showered with sugar and sometimes cinnamon while still hot. Served all over Spain, they are the particular specialty of Madrid, most

The origins of the churro are still a mystery.

famously at the funky Chocolatería San Ginés. Operating since 1894 on a quiet backstreet close to the Church of San Ginés and the Teatro Eslava, the popular post-theater destination has an old-time décor of wood paneling, weathered antique mirrors, and green velvet upholstery. There, dunking may continue into the early morning, when Ginés closes for the day.

Not to be outdone by the Spanish capital, Seville is celebrated for the lighter, more delicate churros sold by its street vendors. Churros are also on the menu at the venerable Café Tortoni in Buenos Aires, where intellectuals and tourists alike have been enjoying them since 1858.

Where: *In Madrid,* Chocolatería San Ginés, tel 34/913-656-546, chocolateriasangines.com; *in Buenos Aires,* Café Tortoni, tel 54/11-4342-4328, cafe-tortoni.com.ar. **Further information and recipes:** *Cooking in Spain* by Janet Mendel Searl (1987); saveur.com (search churros ortega).

WHAT DOES A MOLECULE TASTE LIKE?

A Dream of Dinner at El Bulli

Spanish

It's too late to sit down to one of the much-celebrated dinners created by Chef Ferran Adrià at El Bulli, the Costa Brava restaurant that was declared the most influential in the world. It closed in July 2011, supposedly forever, although it will

reportedly reopen as a research foundation.

But if the palate must be denied, the eyes and mind need not be: All of the master chef's intricately scientific culinary magic is revealed clearly, mouthwateringly, and mind-bogglingly in the documentary *El Bulli: Cooking in Progress.* The film exposes the wizardry of molecular cookery with such realism that one can almost smell and taste the glorious, intellectually wrought outcomes. Essences of herbs and fats and fruits and meats and shellfish are reduced to mere filmy gels and dreamy foams, carefully

carved or re-formed into morsels. Colorful edible mosaics adorn Adrià's plates, looking as though nature had always intended them to take their current form.

Molecular cuisine's naysayers miss the point: No ultramodern deviation, its techniques are in fact an evolution of classic French methods for concentrating flavors by the use of reduction. The scientific methods and equipment now available to curious-minded chefs are actually being put to quite a traditional purpose.

Feeling frustrated by the enticements

revealed in the film and wanting to try your hand at the techniques? There are books that explain Adrià's thoughts and methods and even include a recipe or two. Or, depending on your finances and patience, you could visit restaurants that feature similar examples of this futuristic gastronomic genre, such as Alinea in Chicago (see page 518) and the Bazaar in Los Angeles.

One of Ferran Adrià's extraordinary, edible creations

WHERE: *In Chicago,* Alinea, tel 312-867-0110, alinearestaurant.com; *in Washington, DC,* Minibar by José Andrés, tel 202-393-0812, minibarby joseandres.com; *in Los Angeles,* The Bazaar by José Andrés, tel 310-246-5555, sbe.com/restaurants/brands/thebazaar. **MAIL ORDER:** For a DVD of the documentary *El Bulli: Cooking in Progress* directed by Gereon Wetzel (2011), barnesandnoble.com. **FURTHER INFORMATION AND RECIPES:** *Modernist Cuisine at Home* by Nathan Myhrvold and Maxime Bilet (2013); *The Family Meal* by Ferran Adrià (2011).

TAKING THE BITTER WITH THE SWEET

Dulce de Cáscara de Naranja Amarga

Seville Bitter Orange Marmalade

Spanish

With its glistening amber overtones and luxuriously rich texture, this extraordinary confiture made with Seville's famous bitter bigarade oranges (the same fruit used to prepare the French classic *canard à l'orange*) is perhaps the most sophisticated of marmalades. It's especially delicious as prepared by the sisters of the Monasterio de Santa Paula, about a half-hour's drive from Seville, in Andalusia.

These gentle nuns, who have taken vows of silence, gather many of the oranges they need from their own orchard within the compound, then simmer them into burnished, bittersweet perfection in this gold-brown confection, rendering it more intense than the sweeter, lighter Dundee orange marmalade (see page 39). It is sold only at the monastery by young acolyte trainees or older, retired sisters released from their vow of silence. Other fine marmalades made at this monastery include fig, chestnut, and more, but the *dulce de cáscara de naranja amarga* is the way to go.

WHERE: Monasterio de Santa Paula, Calle Santa Paula 11, Santa Paula, Spain, tel 34/954-540-022, santapaula.es.

|||||||||||||||||||||||||||||||||

Gazpacho, Red and White

Spanish

The ideal antidote to summer's heat is a cold soup of crushed ripe tomatoes with finely diced cucumber, peppers, and onions, tossed with croutons, olive oil, and vinegar. Cool, biting, and acidic, it is the very definition of refreshment and one of Spain's top contributions to gastronomy, second only to paella in its familiarity to eaters all over the world.

No newcomer to the global stage, it is even referenced as "gaspacha" in *The Virginia Housewife* by Mary Randolph, the 1824 cookbook thought to be the first published in America. (Though that dish isn't much like the real thing.) The more authentic gazpacho's route to America, like that of many now common, once "foreign" foods (including pizza, originally known as "pizza pie"), occurred in the wake of World War II.

The tomato-based version Americans are most familiar with is the definitive Andalusian dish. Now one of summer's premier appetizers, it used to be served at the end of a meal. Farther back, the dish began its life as a lunch salad for farmworkers, brought to them in the fields by their wives on summer's hottest days.

In Spain there are a number of variations on the theme, chiefly *gazpacho blanco,* or *ajo blanco,* a specialty of Málaga. The white soup is a blend of garlic, bread, and almonds, garnished with green grapes. All gazpachos, though, seem to have at least three elements in common: bread, oil, and vinegar.

WHERE: *In Seville, Spain,* for white gazpacho, Bar Ajoblanco, tel 34/954-22-93-20, bar ajoblanco.net. **FURTHER INFORMATION AND RECIPES:** *The Foods & Wines of Spain* by Penelope Casas (1982); saveur.com (search gazpacho andaluz); epicurious.com (search ajo blanco). **TIP:** Gazpacho is essentially a summer dish, best when made with juicy, vine-ripe tomatoes. It may be prepared in other seasons, with good-quality canned tomatoes that are improvements over mushy fresh specimens. To keep the soup very cold when serving it in summer, freeze some of it in ice cube trays, to be popped out and added to the soup so it will be chilled but not diluted.

|||||||||||||||||||||||||||||||||

YOU CAN'T MAKE THESE *HUEVOS* WITHOUT BREAKING A FEW EGGS

Huevos Estrellados

Spanish

Among the many diverting aspects of the sophisticated Madrid restaurant Casa Lucio is the clientele, a set of smartly dressed and self-assured movers and shakers from the world of politics and high society. Gathered in the trim, handsome setting, these fortunate diners sample such dishes as sizzling baby eels in garlic and oil (see page 254) and the massive *churrasco*, a well-marbled chateaubriand steak that weighs about a pound and is blood-rare under its crusty charring. The restaurant's service is of the ultraprofessional sort found at world-renowned establishments. But one attraction not to be ignored, as humble as it sounds, is the stunning appetizer known as *huevos estrellados*: broken eggs.

The dish arrives at the table heaped high on a huge platter, a mountain of golden brown sliced potatoes topped with broken fried eggs. (Straight out of the pan, the eggs are transferred to the potatoes and then encouraged to break, so the yellow yolks slide over the hot potatoes.)

When you know it is about to be followed by a gargantuan steak, watching this hearty appetizer get wolfed down for the first time can be a little shocking. But the dish's appeal becomes all too easy to understand once you have a taste. Egg yolks become a supple sauce for the olive oil–glossed, well-peppered potatoes, and as a bonus, the cooked whites add a satiny softness, for an earthy, satisfying experience. Cured Spanish ham or chorizo often joins the mix as well.

A similar dish, credited to Don Quixote's beloved La Mancha, is known as *huevos estrellados mojete*. In this version, eggs and potatoes are slowly cooked together in a heatproof casserole. If it seems a bit heavy as a first course, try it for brunch or a simple supper.

Huevos Estrellados Mojete

Serves 6

*6 large starchy potatoes, such as russets,
    peeled and thinly sliced*
*2 teaspoons coarse kosher or sea salt,
    plus more to taste*
⅓ cup olive oil, preferably Spanish
2 cloves garlic, peeled and lightly crushed
½ teaspoon Spanish sweet paprika
*½ teaspoon Spanish hot or smoked paprika
    (see Note)*
8 extra-large eggs
Freshly ground black pepper

A hearty appetizer made of simple ingredients

1. Toss the potato slices with the salt and place them in a heatproof 2-quart casserole, preferably earthenware or cast iron. Add the olive oil, garlic, and paprikas.

2. Cook the potatoes slowly over low heat, shaking the casserole back and forth once in a while so the potatoes soften evenly and turn a bright golden color, about 30 minutes. If the potatoes tend to stick to the casserole, place a heat diffuser underneath and continue cooking, adding very little more olive oil only if needed.

3. When the potatoes are tender, break the eggs over them and sprinkle a little salt and a lot of black pepper on top. Cover the casserole and continue cooking the eggs until set, about 5 minutes.

4. Gently slide the potatoes and eggs onto a heated platter or cut them in portions and slide them onto individual heated plates. If the egg yolks break, well, so they should to be truly *estrellados*.

Note: For a milder result, eliminate the hot or smoked paprika and use a total of 1 teaspoon of sweet paprika.

Where: *In Madrid,* Casa Lucio, tel 34/913-65-32-52, casalucio.es. **Further information and additional recipe:** for a variation with chorizo, tastingtable.com (search huevos estrellados).

---‖‖‖‖‖‖‖‖‖‖‖‖‖‖‖‖‖‖‖‖‖‖‖---

FED BY CHESTNUTS AND MOUNTAIN AIR

Jabugo Ham

Spanish

G iven that ham is simply a hind leg of pig, cut above its hock, or knee joint, and cured and preserved by salting, drying, and sometimes smoking, the number of its possible variations is impressive. A classic mentioned in the records of the

ancient Gauls and Romans, it was brined and smoked even then. In medieval days, hams of many types were made all over Europe, differing according to the breed of pig, what the pigs were fed, and how the hams were cured and stored.

No ham has a more noble heritage than Spain's; it is perhaps the best of the lot. Based on the Jabugo black-footed pigs, acorn-fed natives of the mountain town of that name, the ham is earthy, meaty, and substantial while still remaining lean. Its distinctive sweet-salty, toothsome quality begins with the pig itself, an Iberian variety known for its black or dark gray trotters (and so dubbed *pata negra*). Curing is done by dry-salting—the hams are hung in the air for one

year without any smoking—and the delectable result bears a characteristic unctuousness, with soft yellowish-gray fat surrounding the meat and adding a luxurious note to the ham's flavor.

Jabugo ham used to be unavailable in the U.S. Fortunately, the import bans were lifted, but the price rremains sky-high.

WHERE: *In Madrid,* El Museo de Jamón, a museum-delicatessen that offers tastings, tel 34/915-41-20-23, museodeljamon.es. **RETAIL AND MAIL ORDER:** *In Manhattan, Queens, and Princeton, NJ,* Despaña, despanabrandfoods.com. **MAIL ORDER:** La Tienda, tel 800-710-4304, tienda.com. **FURTHER INFORMATION:** jabugo.com. **SEE ALSO:** York Ham, page 33, Yunnan Ham, page 795.

---‖‖‖‖‖‖‖‖‖‖‖‖‖‖‖‖‖‖‖‖‖‖‖---

SURF AND TURF (THE GREEN KIND)

Mariscada en Salsa Verde

Shellfish Sauté in Green Sauce

Spanish

G listening and alive, fresh from the sea, mollusks and shellfish such as mussels, clams, shrimp, and squid get an aromatic transformation in this Spanish specialty from the earthy, flavorsome duo of garlic and parsley. The mingling of

these two ingredients lends character to a basic steaming liquid of white wine and strong seafood stock. The result is gently cooked shellfish in a satiny green sauce with a tantalizing and intense scent.

Many proteins-in-green-sauce dishes are found throughout the Mediterranean, and they have become especially popular on menus in the States, where the formula seems to be replicated in nearly every Spanish-themed restaurant. *Salsa verde* itself is a typical accoutrement of the Basque and Galician regions, often gracing *merluza* (the fish known as hake in Spain, as cod in Italy, and as whiting in the U.S.). No matter which fish is used, it's complemented by the sauce—add some good crusty bread and a chilled white wine for complete enjoyment.

Where: *In New York,* Café Español, tel 212-505-0657, cafeespanol.com; *in Cleveland, OH,* Mallorca, tel 216-687-9494, clevelandmallorca .com. **Further information and recipes:** *The Gastronomy of Spain and Portugal* by Maite Manjón (1990); cookstr.com (search twenty minute shellfish sauté). **Tip:** Be careful to scrub all sand from any seafood to be cooked and served in the shell, such as clams and mussels.

‒‖‖‖‖‖‖‖‖‖‖‖‖‖‖‖‖‖‖‖‖‖‖‖‖‖‖‖‖‖‖‖‖‖‒

"'THAT BIG DISH THAT I SEE SMOKING DOWN THERE," SAID SANCHO, "IT LOOKS TO ME LIKE AN OLLA-PODRIDA.'*"*—FROM *DON QUIXOTE* BY MIGUEL DE CERVANTES

Olla Podrida

Stinking Pot

Spanish

Sancho Panza's excitement could hardly have been misplaced: The wide array of tempting ingredients that go into this lush Spanish everything-in-one-pot dish is indeed cause for celebration. But like so many other multi-ingredient stews,

olla podrida has become a metaphor for hodge-podges of all sorts. A Spaniard might say, "Let's not make it an olla podrida"—meaning a big, complicated to-do. In Louisiana, the same sort of event might be labeled a big gumbo, and in France, a bouillabaisse. Yiddish speakers might refer to a tzimmes, to mean an unnecessarily mixed-up event.

The dish itself, with its savory, deeply satisfying complexity, has a long history in Spain. Believed to be derived from the *adafina*, a slow-cooking pre-Sabbath casserole introduced to Spain by the Jews, it is also considered the forerunner of the very similar *cocido madrileño*, one of the country's many regional *cocidos* (stews). Because the Spanish adaptation included pork, a meat forbidden to Jews, olla podrida was eaten in plain sight by Jews during the Inquisition as proof of their conversion to Christianity.

As Cervantes's hero, Don Quixote, observed, *olla podrida* translates to "stinking pot." In olden times, the earthenware crock (*olla*) was rarely washed, and so developed a putrid aroma (*podrida* meanmeans "rotten"). Nevertheless, by the

Cervantes referenced the stew in Don Quixote, *a scene from which is pictured here.*

sixteenth century the stew had become a favorite of commoners and royalty alike, and by 1660, Marie Thérèse of Austria had it served at her wedding to Louis XIV of France.

Despite its evocative name, it is a royal feast indeed. The most lavish versions include a vast array of meats: beef, marrow bones, both cured ham and fresh pork, chicken, a chunk of veal shoulder, and chorizo and blood sausages are all in the mix. For extra nourishment, cuts of fresh and salted ivory pork fat might make an appearance. Such meaty richness is mitigated by vegetables, of course, among them cabbage, leeks, carrots, turnips, and tomatoes (along with chickpeas for a little extra protein). All is mellowed with seasonings of caraway seeds and sometimes cinnamon and a gilding of saffron.

Variations according to individual cooks and regions are bound to be legion. Elinor Burt's *Olla Podrida: Piquant Spanish Dishes from the Old Clay Pot* includes several Latin American

versions, among them one based on fish. But at its most traditional, olla podrida is served as a three-course meal. The opulent stew provides an opener of golden, aromatic broth, plain or with rice or noodles. A platter of flavor-infused vegetables arrives, and finally the meats, sometimes graced with sauces of green herbs and capers in olive oil, garlicky potato-based aioli, or a light blend of olive oil, tomatoes, and cumin.

Protocol suggests a white wine with the soup and a red with the vegetables and meat, to say nothing of a long nap for dessert.

Mail order: For classic olla pots, La Tienda, tel 800-710-4304, tienda.com. **Further information and recipes:** *The Foods & Wines of Spain* by Penelope Casas (1982); *The Cuisines of Spain* by Teresa Barrenechea (2009); *Olla Podrida* by Elinor Burt (2009); spanish-food.org (click Meat Stews, then Olla Podrida); finedining lovers.com (search olla podrida).

||||||||||||||||||||||||||||||||||||||||||||||||||||||||||||||||||||||||||||||||||||||||||||||||||||||||||||||||||||||||||||

THE MOST EXPENSIVE SPICE

Saffron

One of the world's costliest food products and certainly its most expensive spice, saffron is the 24-carat gold of the culinary world. Warmly sunny, mildly medicinal, and profoundly complex, it is valued for the memorably rich and earthy flavor and golden hue that it imparts to a multitude of beloved foods.

Indeed, saffron's color was the inspiration for its Arabic name, *za'fran* (meaning "yellow"), which was transmuted to the Spanish *azafran* as the spice traveled the world between the eighth and fifteenth centuries.

Saffron actually begins with the color purple, in the mauve to amethyst tones of the

narrow blossoms of the crocus bulb *Crocus sativus L.* Within those blossoms lie wispy inner stamens that divide into fragile slim threads. These are saffron, the golden threads that must be painstakingly extricated by hand, and only in early morning, during a brief harvest that runs from mid-October to about mid-November. Quite a daunting task, considering it takes some 75,000 blossoms to realize a single pound of saffron threads. And therein lies the reason the spice fetches such an extraordinary price, especially when it is of the highest quality. Fortunately, a little saffron goes a long way; a half-teaspoonful of crumpled threads adds enough color and flavor for eight to ten servings of *paella Valenciana* (see next entry).

Lesser-quality saffron is usually sold in the less-expensive powdered form, but the best saffron comes in threads and is generally grown in La Mancha in Spain, and in even more limited amounts in India and the Abruzzi region of Italy. Once dried by roasting, the brittle threads turn deep brick-red in color, releasing their yellow-gold hue only after being soaked in water, wine, or broth just before being added to recipes.

Almost all the world has loved saffron at one time or another. Cleopatra is said to have taken baths in water suffused with the spice, then believed to smooth complexions and increase sex appeal. And centuries ago, the Chinese and Japanese brewed medicinal tisanes from its threads, still valued as a good source of vitamin B_2 and riboflavin. During the Medieval and Renaissance periods, saffron was used as a dye for fabrics as well as for painters' pigments, and even today, it appears as a coloring agent in many cosmetics.

In the realm of the gustatory, saffron is much favored in rice dishes such as Indian *biryani* (see page 868), Iranian *kuku*, and the sweet Tibetan rice pudding *dresi* that commonly makes appearances during Losar, the Tibetan New Year. At any time of year, the Milanese rely on it for the golden glow it adds to their native *risotto* (see page 233). The French insist upon it for authentic *bouillabaisse* (see page 63), and some Italians consider it essential in the similar fish soup-stew *brodetto* (see page 170). The Swedish gild their St. Lucia yeast buns with the spice (see page 373) just as some Milanese bakers add it to *panettone* (see page 214). The English county of Cornwall is as well known for its golden sunsets as it is for the many versions of Cornish saffron cakes, breads, and buns that light up its bakery windows.

Because saffron is so expensive, many cooks are driven to substitutes such as turmeric or the annatto seeds commonly used in Latin America's yellow rice dishes. With milder, somewhat less complex flavors, these substitutes may fool the eye, but rarely the nose or the palate.

MAIL ORDER: spicehouse.com (search spanish saffron, annato seeds, turmeric). **FURTHER INFORMATION AND RECIPES:** For an intriguing history of saffron as a coloring agent, *Color: A Natural History of the Palette* by Victoria Finlay (2002). See also *The Essential Saffron* by John Humphries (1998); *The Foods & Wines of Spain* by Penelope Casas (1982); *Spice: Arabic Flavors of the Mediterranean* by Ana Sortun (2000); saveur.com (search saffron for a multitude of good recipes); festivals.iloveindia.com (search Tibetan dresi sweet saffron rice). **TIP:** Exposure to light and air weakens saffron's color, aroma, and flavor, and moisture causes spoilage—so saffron should be stored in opaque containers of the smallest possible size in a cool, dry closet. Assuming it was fresh when purchased, it should keep for between eighteen months and two years.

WHEN SCRAPING THE BOTTOM PAYS OFF

Paella

Spanish

From their posts halfway down the Mediterranean coast of Spain, Valencians are justifiably proud of their delicate short-grain rice and of the famous dish based on it. For paella is more than just a dish: It is a grand passion, a subject of controversy, and an exercise in culinary proficiency that has tied with gazpacho as Spain's best-known restaurant dish.

The key to a classic preparation lies in the paella pan—a giant, flat vessel into whose slightly concave center the ingredients are placed, most authentically to simmer outdoors over a wood fire. That fire is integral as well, lending a smoky patina that adds interest, whether the paella is made with seafood, poultry, or game. In properly made paella, a crust of caramelized rice forms on the bottom of the pan: This is the prized *socarrat*, from the Spanish verb for toasting.

Named for the pan—the term comes from the Latin *patella*, which the Castilians adapted to *paella*, meaning simply a pan or cauldron for frying—the original paella Valencia was a celebratory dish cooked in the open air of the rice field and eaten straight from the pan with wooden spoons. The saffron-flavored rice would be combined with rabbit and chicken, broad green beans, white beans such as lima or butter beans, tomatoes, paprika, and snails in their shells. Seafood paella (*paella de marisco*), which is often confused with the original, was a later invention; typically it is not made with meat or fowl, although sometimes pungent *morcilla* sausage gets added to the mix.

One of the most unctuously rich and flavorful of paellas is made with black squid ink, decked out with the tiniest flecks of the squid itself—called *arròs negre*, it's a charcoal-gray enticement that suggests caviar and fresh ocean breezes.

Paella's composition sparks a competitive streak among its cooks, and the etiquette surrounding its service follows suit. Some insist it is best as a midday meal, while others argue that it must be eaten for supper. Some cooks finish it in the oven after it's simmered over an open flame, while others consider that an act of blasphemy. No one disagrees that the key to the dish is the Valencia-grown rice, most especially the variety known as *bomba especial*, and that the smell of wood smoke is essential.

Where: *In Valencia,* Restaurante La Pepica, tel 34/963-71-03-66, lapepica.com; *in Beverly Hills,* La Paella Restaurant, tel 323-951-0745, usalapaella.com; *in Miami,* Casa Juancho, tel 305-642-2452, casajuancho.com; *in Washington, DC,* Taberna del Alabardero, tel 202-429-2200, alabardero.com. **Mail order:** For paella pans, amazon.com (search for stainless steel or carbon steel paella pans by Garcima or Paderno). **Further information and recipes:** *La Paella: Deliciously Authentic Rice Dishes from Spain's Mediterranean Coast* by Jeff Koehler (2006); *Made in Spain* by José Andrés (2008); cookstr.com (search spring paella). **Special events:** International Paella Competition, Sueca, Spain, September, foodsfromspain.com (click Shop, Travel & Dine, then Festivals); Pinot and Paella, Temple, CA, June, pinotandpaella.com; Paella Lovers United Annual Get-Together, Austin, TX, November, paellaloversunited.com/wordpress; the noted Spanish chef José Andrés, who operates three Jaleo restaurants in Washington, DC, hosts paella festivals sporadically, jaleo.com.

A chef participates in a paella-cooking competition in Spain.

―||||||||||||||||||||||||||||||||||||||||―

RED-HOT SMOKE

Pimentón

Spanish

Say paprika and everyone thinks of Hungary, but in fact Spain currently holds the aesthetic high ground with its version of the beautiful brick-red spice known there as *pimentón*. That glowing seasoning begins as fiery Spanish *pimientos*, slowly smoke-dried over wood before being pulverized. The smoking burnishes the chile heat of the pepper to play up its fruity overtones, and the result is a pungent flavor and a fiery sting. Small wonder that high-profile chefs of all stripes have embraced the seasoning in their various cuisines, especially for use in barbecue glazes and sauces.

One of the dishes that profits most from this smoky Spanish paprika is *pollo al pimentón*—a small chicken cut into eight parts and lightly fried in olive oil until it attains a bright, golden brown patina. Onions, garlic, and diced sweet green peppers are added and sautéed until soft, along with a little flour, some pimentón, and, for good fiery measure, a hit of cayenne pepper. Some water or stock and crushed tomatoes are stirred in, and the whole

The peppers are dried and ground.

is covered and baked. Upon serving, the chicken is tossed with dollops of sour cream, gently turned through the steaming sauce to create a pink-white moiré pattern as pretty as it is delicious. It's not a far cry from Hungarian chicken *paprikash*—and given that Spain was once a part of the Austro-Hungarian empire, this should come as no surprise.

RETAIL AND MAIL ORDER: *In Manhattan, Queens, and Princeton, NJ,* Despaña, despanabrandfoods .com. **MAIL ORDER:** amazon.com (search santo domingo pimenton de la vera). **FURTHER INFORMATION AND RECIPES:** *The Gastronomy of Spain and Portugal* by Maite Manjón (1990); *The Basque Kitchen* by Gerald Hirigoyen (1999); recetasamericanas.com (search receta pollo al pimento—you may need to translate the page.)

―||||||||||||||||||||||||||||||||||||||||―

WATER'S LEAP TO IMMORTALITY

Sopa de Ajo Castellana

Spanish

If garlic soup sounds like slim fare, consider the belt of protein provided by the sunny poached egg adrift in this heady, translucent bronze soup. Admittedly light, it is one of the simplest dishes imaginable—and indeed, it is Spain's quintessential "poverty dish."

Credited primarily to the Castilla y León region, the potent potable has comforted generations in a country with a long-held custom of hearty peasant soups meant to warm and temporarily fill body and soul. Clearly devised for economic reasons, the soup consists of nothing more than water, dried-out leftover bread, garlic, olive oil, and egg.

Traditionally nourishing as a mid-morning restorative after three or four hours of farm work, the garlic-water-and-egg combination is now ubiquitous throughout the Mediterranean. In Portugal's Alentejo province, cilantro paste is added to the brew. For a more luxurious touch, heavy cream and a shot of dry sherry are added at Casa Irene, a hotel-cum-restaurant on the banks of the Garona river in the Pyrenees.

Utterly homey and comforting in any setting, the soup is said to be a cure-all for all kinds of common ailments—not least because it makes you break a sweat.

Sopa de Ajo Castellana

Serves 4

½ cup good Spanish olive oil
5 cloves garlic, peeled and thinly sliced
5 thin slices white bread, crusts removed
*   and bread cubed*
2 teaspoons sweet Spanish paprika
Salt
4 extra-large eggs

1. Heat the oil in a deep, wide, heavy saucepan or soup pot over moderate heat until it is shimmering. Add the garlic and cook until it is a light golden brown, 3 or 4 minutes. Do not let the garlic burn.

2. Stir in the bread cubes and paprika and cook until the paprika loses its raw smell and the bread begins to toast, about 3 minutes.

3. Add at least 1 quart of water to the saucepan; the water should cover the bread cubes. Add a couple of pinches of salt. Cover the pan and let the soup simmer gently until the bread softens, about 7 minutes. Taste for seasoning, adding

more salt as necessary. Increase the heat to high and let the soup come to a rolling boil.

4. Break an egg into each of 4 well-heated soup bowls and ladle the boiling soup into each bowl. The eggs will cook when they are broken with a spoon at the table, but only if the broth is boiling hot.

Notes: Individual heatproof casseroles are preferable to bowls, as they can be filled with soup and heated, and the egg broken into each as it is removed from the heat.

Water is the traditional liquid for this poor man's dish, but using a light beef broth instead wouldn't hurt a bit, both for flavor and sustenance.

Where: *In Artiés, Spain,* Casa Irene, tel 34/973-64-43-64, hotelcasairene.com; *in Madrid,* La Bola Taberna, tel 34/915-47-69-30, labola.es; *in Newark, NJ,* Spain Restaurant, tel 973-344-0994, spainrestaurant.com; *in Cleveland, OH,* Mallorca, tel 216-687-9494, clevelandmallorca .com. **Further information and recipes:** *The Foods & Wines of Spain* by Penelope Casas (1982); *Cooking in Spain* by Janet Mendel Searl (1987); foodnetwork.com (search sopa de ajo garlic soup).

A "poor-folks' dish" that pleases all kinds

Squid and Its Ink

Spanish, Mediterranean

What does squid have that its fellow mollusk, the octopus, lacks? The midnight-dark, silken ink that graces rice and pasta dishes wherever squid are eaten, but most temptingly in Spain and Italy. Best and most delicate when drawn from the small calamari—slightly larger squid produce a stronger, saltier ink—the liquid need only be cooked slightly to become a velvety, seductive sauce that strongly suggests an essence of caviar.

Enticingly earthy, excitingly saline, quintessentially rich, and a bit dangerously lurid, the ink may be simmered with the whole small squid, or prepared on its own as the base for a crystal gray paella in which bits of squid tentacle are the only solids other than the rice. In Spain, squid might be stuffed with minced ham, onions, garlic, and bread crumbs and bathed with an ink sauce enlivened with onion, brandy, and a touch of hot chiles. In Italy, squid ink makes a wonderful sauce for slim pasta and also blackens the broth for the risotto dubbed *nero*.

In some markets, especially those catering to chefs, you can purchase squid ink that has been extracted from the calamari for you—easy to acquire, but highly perishable. Unless frozen, the ink should be cooked within a day or two of extraction. Pre-inked commercial products such as pasta are easier to handle, but less exciting to taste.

Anything this thick and dark seems like a great candidate for nutritional benefits, but there are arguments on that score. Some cite the minerals and protein, others see only calories and high cholesterol. Fortunately, squid ink is eaten in small enough amounts to render the discussion moot.

WHERE: *In Venice,* Corte Sconta, tel 39/041-522-70-24, cortescontavenezia.it; *in New York,* Osteria Morini, tel 212-965-8777, osteriamorini.com. **MAIL ORDER:** La Tienda, tel 800-710-4304, tienda.com (search squid ink nortindal; tinta de calamar). **FURTHER INFORMATION AND RECIPES:** *The Basque Kitchen* by Gerald Hirigoyen (1999); *The Foods & Wines of Spain* by Penelope Casas (1982); saveur.com (search rice with squid ink).

A SIREN CALL FOR NIBBLERS AND NOSHERS

Tapas

Spanish

Boquerones (fresh whitebait fish served in vinegar). *Tortillas de camarones* (tiny batter-fried shrimp). *Papas aliña* ("dressed" potatoes, or potatoes fried in olive oil with vinegar, onions, tuna, and parsley). *Patatas bravas* (chunks of fried potatoes coated in a spicy sauce made from tomatoes and peppers). *Tortilla española* (wedges of potato omelet, see page 271.) Small slices of the rosy, nutty Jabugo ham from free-range, acorn-fed

Iberian pigs. *Puntillitas* (tiny squid cooked in olive oil with garlic, parsley, and lots of salt). *Montados de lomo* (small pieces of bread with a slice of meat on top, such as marinated loin of pork fillets). *Chorizo a la plancha* (slices of grilled spicy pork sausage). Fresh anchovies. Various locally cured olives and native cheeses.

Sound like a pre-dinner snack?

Welcome to the world of tapas, a term that describes an array of small dishes offered in progression. Authentic tapas—bar food served in small portions—is a culture unto itself. In Spain, tapas bars (*tapeos*) reflect a local approach to life in which at-home entertaining is relatively uncommon. After the day's work, people

An appetizing display of tapas in Madrid, Spain

show up at the *tapeo* not just to eat and drink but also to relax, meet friends, chat with the owners, and get ready for the post–10 p.m. dinner hour. In regions such as the Basque country of northern Spain, the tapeo tends to be one stop of many, a bar-hopping experience in which one typically orders a few tapas at each juncture. By contrast, Andalusians linger in one place, sitting at tables and making meals of their tapas.

Throughout Spain, arguments about the origins of tapas are common. Some say they came into existence when the thirteenth-century Castilian Alfonso X El Sabio (The Learned) was instructed by his doctor to eat several meals a day with wine. Cervantes, in his seventeenth-century classic *Don Quixote*, refers to *llamativos*, or "lures"—tidbits of food designed to arouse hunger or thirst. The most accepted theory is that tapas appeared in Andalusia in the nineteenth century, when tiny morsels on small saucers were set over wineglasses to keep the wine aroma in and the flies out. Lore has it that a savvy entrepreneur figured out that complementary salty morsels would increase thirst and, thereby, bar revenues. Apparently it worked—though today tapas are rarely free—and there are more than a thousand varieties of these small bites.

Every Spanish region, city, and bar has specialties of its own, from baked scallops in Galicia to stuffed peppers in San Sebastián, to cod with bitter-orange juice in Sanlúcar de Barrameda. Traditional *tapeos* do share a similar serving system, however: Very few have printed menus, and dishes are displayed on the bar. *Tapeadors* (*tapeo*-goers) indicate choice *banderillas* (morsels), and small plates are handed around. The libation of choice is sherry; the two types that tend to pair best with most tapas are fino (pale dry sherry from Jerez, served chilled and good with fried seafood) and manzanilla (very dry, delicate, faintly salty sherry produced only in Sanlúcar de Barrameda). *Caña* (draft beer, never served bottled or canned) and *vino* (usually interpreted as house red wine) are other acceptable accompaniments.

WHERE: *In Barcelona,* Cal Pep, tel 34/93-310-79-61, calpep.com; *in Jerez, Spain,* Bar Juanito, tel 34/956-33-48-38, bar-juanito.com; *in Galicia, Spain,* Café Cervantes, tel 34/881-98-46-79; *in New York,* Tertulia, tel 646-559-9909, tertulianyc.com; El Quinto Pino, tel 212-206-6900, elquintopinonyc.com; *in Washington, DC,* Jaleo, tel 202-628-7949, jaleo.com; *in Miami,* Casa Juancho, tel 305-642-2452, casajuancho.com; *in Los Angeles,* The Bazaar by José Andrés, tel 310-246-5555, sbe.com/restaurants/brands/thebazaar. **FURTHER INFORMATION AND RECIPES:** *Tapas: The Little Dishes of Spain* by Penelope Casas (2007); *Tapas: A Taste of Spain in America* by José Andrés and Richard Wolffe (2005); saveur.com (search spanish tapas).

FLIPPING OUT OVER POTATOES AND EGGS

Tortilla Española

Spanish

To say Spanish omelet to the average American is to summon up the image of a thin, coffee-shop egg omelet folded over and perhaps topped with a mushy sauce of tomato, green pepper, and onion. But to Spaniards and those familiar with their cuisine, *tortilla española* refers to the iconic pancake omelet—thick, round, golden brown, and bolstered with sautéed sliced or diced potatoes. Also know as *truita de patata*, this is Spain's go-to comfort food, as much loved in thin wedges or squares as part of the tapas ritual (see page 269), as it is as an appetizer or light main course, especially at brunch and lunch.

The combination of sautéed potatoes and eggs, lightly salted and peppered and redolent of the best olive oil, results in a soul-warming dish with an almost innocent flavor based on its simple, homey, high-quality ingredients. Those who find it too simple sauté finely diced or sliced onion with the potatoes or add flecks of Spain's incomparable cured hams (see page 262). And many a frugal cook tosses in leftover cooked vegetables such as peas or dicings of roasted piquillo peppers. Apparently, Spaniards have a particular love of potato and egg pairings, not only in this tortilla but in *huevos estrellados* (see page 260).

WHERE: *In Barcelona,* Cal Pep, tel 34/93-310-7961, calpep.com; *in Miami,* Casa Juancho, tel 305-642-2452, casajuancho.com; *in Washington, DC,* Taberna Del Alabardero, tel 202-429-2200, alabardero.com. **RETAIL AND MAIL ORDER:** *In Manhattan, Queens, and Princeton, NJ,* Despaña, despanabrandfoods.com. **FURTHER INFORMATION AND RECIPES:** *Catalan Cuisine* by Colman Andrews (1988); saveur.com (search tortilla espanola) **TIP:** If flipping the omelet proves difficult, try this: When the underside is cooked and the top is still a bit runny, slide the pan under the broiler for about five minutes, until the top is set solid and a light golden brown. The flavors are best appreciated when the tortilla is served at room temperature, about thirty minutes after it has been cooked.

MAY VISIONS OF SUGARPLUMS DANCE IN YOUR HEAD

Bombos de Figo

Sugarplums

Portuguese

Sometimes we eat for history or tradition as well as for pleasure or health. But if we're lucky, all of these attributes can be contained in a single food. A case in point can be found in fresh, authentically crafted Portuguese sugarplums, the lovely-sounding Christmas confections many of us would struggle to define. Originally created in Portugal as *bombos de figo* (fig bombes, or rounds) and first recorded in the sixteenth or seventeenth century, these brightly wrapped sweets (also much loved in England as comfits) are formed of dried figs or prunes.(In England sugarplums, also known as comfits, are made from fruits, nuts, or seeds coated and preserved with sugar.) Slowly steamed to luscious, syrupy softness, the dried fruit is ground and seasoned with cinnamon, cloves, and red wine or brandy, then formed into balls with a roasted almond pressed into the center. Finally, they are rolled in white sugar and wrapped in bright, colorful paper.

The Byzantine variety of sugarplum is chunkier—a fragrant, chewy blend of chopped, dried, and softened dates, figs, raisins, currants, walnuts, and pistachios. Accented with the nice, astringent sting of crystallized ginger, orange zest, brandy, or red wine (or lemon juice, for the abstemious), the confections are sprinkled with powdered cloves and cinnamon before being snowballed in confectioners' sugar and wrapped in paper. The result are sweetmeats with a flavor similar to that of plum pudding.

The Portuguese love of both chocolate and almonds manifests in an especially rich version of sugarplums: dried figs steamed open and stuffed with a paste of dark, semisweet chocolate and pounded roasted almonds. These can either be served at room temperature or warmed by a brief baking that melts the chocolate to silky richness.

But for sheer opulence, Portugal takes a backseat to nineteenth-century Czarist Russia. There, so-called sugarplums were very large, whole walnuts with intact shells, brushed with beaten egg whites and then veneered with gold or silver leaf. Matching metallic threads were tied on to permit hanging on Christmas trees. There's no record of anyone having eaten one, but why would you? A golden walnut is forever.

MAIL ORDER: For candied greengage plums, Zingermans, tel 888-636-8162, zingermans.com. **FURTHER INFORMATION AND RECIPES:** *Visions of Sugarplums* by Mimi Sheraton (1981); *Sugar-Plums and Sherbet: The Prehistory of Sweets* by Laura Mason (2004); foodtimeline.org/christmas food.html (click Sugarplums); saveur.com (search sugarplums).

THREADS AMONG THE SYRUP

Fios de Ovos

Sweet Golden Egg Threads

Portuguese, Spanish

Take a hint from the Portuguese and satisfy your lust for gold by way of dessert. The national penchant for the luxurious color is said to have been acquired from the Moors, when they held sway from the eighth to the fifteenth centuries on the Iberian Peninsula. In desserts, the hue is generally arrived at by a combination of egg yolks and sugar, a concoction usually used as a starting point for cake icing and sun-gold custards. But for Christmas, the egg yolk is turned into slim, shiny threads in a dish that bears similarities to the delicacies of many Asian countries, most especially Thailand—part of a Portuguese culinary legacy left by trade and colonization. Boiled into angel hair in a silky, sweet syrup scented with rose or orange flower water, the eggy strands are cooled to a gently chewy state. With its sweetness and its intense egg flavor, the dessert requires a follow-up of unsweetened black coffee or a sharp liqueur.

Fios de ovos is also popular in Brazil, as well as in Spain, where it is known as *huevo hilado*. And this same tantalizingly gooey egg yolk and sugar mixture is transformed by nuns in a Seville convent into individual peaked cones called *yemas de San Leandro*. The mixture is also the basis for the cinnamon- and lemon-accented *yemas de Santa Teresa,* which are shaped into yolklike circles.

Fairly complicated to prepare, golden threads, whether as fios de ovos or yemas, are usually purchased in pastry shops or from convents. But if you're handy at candy making, they are worth a try.

Sweet Golden Egg Threads

Serves 6

16 extra-large egg yolks, the freshest you can find
2 extra-large eggs
8 cups sugar
1 teaspoon rose water or orange flower water
Big bowl of ice water, as a water bath

1. Combine the egg yolks and eggs in a medium bowl and stir gently with a wooden spoon. Do not beat. Strain the eggs through a sieve to remove any white threads and "eyes."
2. Combine the sugar and flower water with 2 cups of water in a deep, heavy 2-quart saucepan over medium-low heat and let simmer gently until the sugar syrup forms threads when dropped into cold water or reaches 220°F on a candy thermometer.
3. Remove 1 cup of the sugar syrup from the saucepan and stir it into the bowl of ice water. Bring the remaining syrup to a low boil.
4. Working in batches, pour the egg yolk mixture through a funnel, holding your finger over most of the spout to let a very thin, threadlike stream flow slowly into the boiling syrup. Pour only enough to form a thin, single layer of yolk.
5. Using a slotted spoon, remove cooked threads of yolk as they float to the surface, after 2 to 3 minutes, and place them directly in the sugared ice water for about 5 minutes. Drain the cooled yolk threads in a colander. Repeat until all of the yolk mixture has been cooked and drained.
6. Lightly pack the yolk threads into 6 individual 1-cup custard cups or small ramekins, or into one 6-cup soufflé dish, and cover and refrigerate overnight. They should be served within 24 hours.
7. Just before serving, invert and unmold the yolk threads onto individual dessert plates, or onto a serving platter if the threads were placed in a soufflé dish.

Where: *In Newark, NJ,* Suissa Bakery & Coffee Shop, tel 973-589-1927; A&J Seabra Supermarket (bakery section; order in advance), tel 973-589-8606. **Further information and additional recipe:** *The Foods & Wines of Spain* by Penelope Casas (1982).

HOW MANY WAYS CAN YOU SAY DOUGHNUT?

Malasadas

Portuguese

Hotly crisp on the outside, nurturingly eggy and spongy within, cinnamon- and sugar-flavored *malasadas* are yet further proof that all the world loves a doughnut (even one without a hole). The origin of these yeasty round puffs, whether smooth or free-formed and knobby, is credited to the Portuguese islands of Madeira and the Azores, where they are a featured treat on the day known as Terça-Feira Gorda—the American Fat Tuesday or Mardi Gras. As with other crullers made in celebration of that rowdy day, they are meant to use up leftover frying fat or oil and sugar before the abstemious days of Lent set in.

But anything that tastes so irresistibly delicious cannot be relegated to a single day, or even a season, so malasadas (also spelled malassadas, meaning lightly roasted) are year-round treats wherever Portuguese émigrés have settled. That includes Hawaii, where workers from Madeira and the Azores went to harvest the sugarcane fields in the late nineteenth century—and where Fat Tuesday is officially called Malasada Day. Other Portuguese immigrants,

Fresh malasadas served on a ti leaf in Hawaii

most notably fishermen, settled in Rhode Island, southeastern Massachusetts, and New Jersey. In Freetown, Massachusetts, malasadas are one of the biggest attractions of the annual Lakeside Family Festival.

Retail bakeries in Hawaii known for their malasadas often sprout lines of not-so-patient devotees waiting for crullers just emerged from the fryer. Glazed with cinnamon-sugar, they are eaten out of hand, a feat true cognoscenti can accomplish without burning fingers or lips. But they are also elegantly served at breakfast at some of Hawaii's most luxurious hotels: The lovely Mauna Lani Bay Hotel on the Big Island serves them accompanied by cups of rich and lusty Kona coffee laced with bubbling hot milk.

Malasadas may be filled with custard, fruit preserves, or chocolate cream, but they are most traditionally (and most delectably) unfilled, allowing the texture of the sunny, airy interior sponge to be fully appreciated without danger of sogginess.

WHERE: *In Honolulu, HI,* Leonard's Bakery, tel 808-737-5591, leonardshawaii.com; *in Kohala Coast, HI,* Mauna Lani Resort, tel 808-885-6622, maunalani.com; *in Kailua, HI,* Agnes' Portuguese Bake Shop, tel 808-262-5367, agnes bakeshop.com; *in Providence, RI,* Silver Star Bakery, tel 401-421-8013, silverstarbakery.com. **FURTHER INFORMATION AND RECIPES:** *The New Portuguese Table* by David Leite (2009); saveur .com (search leonard's bakery malasadas).

GERMAN, AUSTRIAN, and SWISS

⊣||||||||||||||||||||||||||||||||⊢

JUST TRY AND BEAT THIS CREAM

Abgeschlagene Creme

German

Beaten-up cream seems a violent designation for a dessert so ethereally rich, cool, and airy as this chilled, gelatin-set custard, yet that is what *abgeschlagene* means. More elegantly described as Bavarian cream or even as a cold soufflé, it begins with air beaten into egg whites and heavy sweet cream, which inflates a sunny, sweet custard sauce of egg yolks, sugar, and white wine. Flavorings might run to fruit juices or purees, melted dark chocolate, double-brewed espresso, or pure vanilla extract, and the cloudlike dessert is invariably topped off with puffs of whipped cream, and perhaps berries or toasted almonds.

Though seemingly named for the southern German region of Bavaria, where it is indeed a favorite, the dessert is said to have made its mark as a specialty of the popular Café Procope in Paris in the early 1700s. There, it was frequently ordered by visiting Bavarian royalty—hence its French name, *crème Bavaroise*.

There are two kinds of Bavarian cream, distinguished by the method of beating up on the cream. *Feine abgeschlagene creme*, the more opulent variation, has the melted gelatin stirred into a satiny cooked custard of egg yolks and sugar. *Kaltgerührt creme*, or "cold-stirred cream," requires no cooking and depends on a lengthy beating of egg yolks and sugar until the mixture turns thick and almost white and can hold the melted gelatin and liquid seasonings. With a leaner, less creamy finish, it allows any flavoring a more marked presence; it is the preferred method when flavoring with fruit, as opposed to coffee, vanilla, or chocolate, all of which profit from a richer base, and is especially good with lemon juice and grated rind. The latter flavorings result in the dessert called *zitronencreme* in Germany and *citronfromage,* or lemon cheese, in Denmark. With either method, the almost-set mixture can be poured into a baked and cooled piecrust and topped with whipped cream, to be served as a cold chiffon pie. But generally it is presented in a big, round crystal bowl, to be lushly spooned out into individual dishes.

FURTHER INFORMATION AND RECIPES: *The Cuisines of Germany* by Horst Scharfenberg (1989); *The German Cookbook* by Mimi Sheraton (2014); epicurious.com (search bavarian cream with raspberry coulis); foodnetwork.com (search bavarian cream).

⊣||||||||||||||||||||||||||||||||⊢

AN APPLE PANCAKE A DAY . . .

Apfel Pfannkuchen

German, Austrian

Despite its Germanic origins, for New Yorkers of a certain age, the apple pancake—big, golden, and redolent of hot butter, rum, cherry brandy, and cinnamon—will always recall the magnificent restaurant Lüchow's, just off

Union Square. With dark wood paneling, stained-glass windows, and what was said to be the world's largest indoor Christmas tree, this art-filled monument to sophisticated *gemütlichkeit* was a meeting place for celebrities from the worlds of theater, literature, music, sports, and politics. Among its elaborate dishes, many of which were prepared tableside with graceful flamboyance, none was more frequently evident than the apple pancake. Alas, the restaurant closed in 1986. Fortunately, the pancake outlived Lüchow's and remains as delectable as ever.

Always served for two, but with a foot-and-a-half diameter easily amounting to dessert for four, the pancake was cooked up by a deft captain on a traveling cooking trolley called a gueridon. Eggs beaten with a little flour, salt, sugar, and milk attained the consistency of heavy cream to form a batter that was poured into hot butter in a big, thin, long-handled iron skillet. Bubbling and brown, the pancake was topped with thinly sliced peeled and cored apples, and then another layer of batter was spooned over the top. Once brown on the first side, it was flipped over with nary a fold nor a tear.

The top of the pancake was dashed with cinnamon sugar and a few splashes of dark rum

The Christmas tree in Lüchow's

and/or the clear, fiery cherry brandy called *kirschwasser,* the prelude to the theatrical if anticipated moment when the dessert would be set aflame for a few seconds. The sublime appeal of caramelized cinnamon sugar and the enticing scent of burning alcohol emanated from the pancake.

The late Jan Mitchell, the urbane, highly cultured owner who raised Lüchow's to its second great incarnation, always advised a glass of cool, sweet Château d'Yquem with this dessert. He cared so much about getting it right that he often sent one over on the house.

Popular as it was, the apple pancake was not the official Lüchow's German Pancake. Strangely, that was the same omelet-like pancake, but minus the apples. Doused with lemon juice after being cooked, that *pfannkuchen* was rolled around *preiselbeeren* (preserved lingonberries) or hot bittersweet chocolate sauce. Not too bad an ending, either.

WHERE: *In Milwaukee,* Karl Ratzsch's, tel 414-276-2720, karlratzsch.com; *in Venice, CA,* Röckenwagner 3 Square Café, tel 310-399-6504, 3squarecafe.com. **FURTHER INFORMATION AND RECIPES:** *Lüchow's German Cookbook* by Jan Mitchell (1996); food.com (search luchows german pancake).

A TREE TAKES THE CAKE

Baumkuchen

German

I t takes only a glance at a *baumkuchen* to understand where this "tree cake" gets its name. And after a taste of the gently sweet, almondy, moist, dense, pound cake–like pastry, you'll also know why Germans consider it the king of cakes.

Standing from two to three feet in height, and even taller for exhibition pieces, the narrow cylindrical cake of stacked, undulating, ridged rings is hollow at the center. Sliced horizontally into rounds or arcs, it reveals concentric layers of golden brown rings, much like the rings in a tree trunk.

Those rings are the result of a most unusual baking method. Although the baumkuchen is said to have originated in nineteenth-century Germany, it belongs to a much older food category known as "spit cakes," a term that might give pause. Fortunately, *spit* refers to a horizontal rotisserie, now powered by gas or electricity, that turns in front of or over a wood or gas fire. As the spit rotates, the baker ladles over it anywhere from ten to forty-five layers of sunny batter with the consistency of a foamy liquid custard. The batter of eggs, sugar, and either flour or cornstarch is most traditionally flavored with marzipan, although vanilla, brandy, and spices are often added—the latter remaining the closely guarded secret of the individual pastry chef.

The tradition of spit cakes goes back centuries.

To hold and shape the cake, the spit is fitted with a wood or metal cone wrapped in layers of parchment or aluminum foil, and preheated in the vertical baumkuchen oven that suggests a big outdoor grill. As each layer bakes, it takes on the toasty finish that defines the rings. Once all the layers are baked on, the spit is removed and hung on a rack, where the cake can take from ten to twenty-four hours to cool. It is then slipped off the spit, stood on end, and glazed with a thin white icing. Nowadays it may be coated with chocolate, which helps preserve the cake and appeals to popular tastes but does compromise the cake's delicate flavor.

Although German bakers keep the edges of the cake smooth by holding a wooden plank against it as it turns to remove drips, in other countries the drips are allowed to bake on and form a crunchy, brambly finish. Such is the case with the Polish *sękacz*, the Lithuanian *šakotis*, and especially the Swedish *spettekaka,* so resplendent with lacy baked-on drips that it resembles a cylinder of golden spun glass.

Oddly enough, baumkuchen is a well-known confection in Japan, where it's been widely available ever since it was introduced there by a German baker in 1919. Known for centuries in France as *gâteau à la broche,* it is still baked by a few artisans there, as well as in England, where it is called trayne roste. At times, it is part of a Tudor-period cooking demonstration in the enormous kitchen of Henry VIII's Hampton Court.

Delicious with coffee and tea, baumkuchen also pairs beautifully with semisweet white dessert wine.

WHERE: *In Berlin,* Café Buchwald, tel 49/30-391-5931, konditorei-buchwald.de; *in Cologne,* Café Reichard, tel 0221/2-57-85-42, cafe-reichard .de; *in Munich,* Konditorei Kreutzkamm, tel 49/89-993-557-0, kreutzkamm.de; *in New York and Tokyo,* Minamoto Kitchoan, kitchoan.com; *in Denver,* Glaze, tel 720-387-7890, glazebau cakes.com; *in Huntington Beach, CA,* The Cake Box, tel 714-842-9132, cakeboxpastries.com. **RETAIL AND MAIL ORDER:** *In Chicago,* Lutz Café and Pastry Shop, tel 877-350-7785, chicago-bakery .com. **FURTHER INFORMATION AND RECIPES:** For a home-baked variation, *The German Cookbook* by Mimi Sheraton (2014); germanculture.com.ua (search baumkuchen).

Beef Tongue

Cooks in Provence prepare it in a slightly sweet, sour, and salty tomato sauce dotted with raisins and capers. In Normandy, it is sliced paper-thin in the elegant specialty Langue Lucullis, a terrine layered with foie gras. In Alsace, it may be found in the savoriest of choucroutes garnies (see page 78), and in Italy it graces the best *bollito misto*. London chef Fergus Henderson tucks it into pie, along with chicken and silky white sauce. Throughout Great Britain, Germany, and Eastern Europe, it is smoked or pickled and served hot along with cabbage and boiled potatoes, or made into the classic Jewish-deli sandwiches on rye with mustard in the same way as corned beef might be. In Korea, it is eaten as *hemmit gui* (see Bulgogi, page 829), grilled over red-hot coals at the table.

In almost every meat-eating culture, tongue is prized. This goes for smaller tongues of lamb, calves, and pigs, delicious in braised preparations, as well as for the thin, bony slivers of ducks' tongues favored by the Chinese. But the meatiest and most versatile tongues are those of beef cattle, often preserved via smoking or pickling: The first method imparts a hamlike flavor, while the second leaves the meat garlicky, with hints of clove, coriander, chiles, and bay leaves. These delicatessen essentials are generally served cold and thinly sliced, piled to towering heights in super-sandwiches on mustard-glossed rye bread.

MAIL ORDER: For smoked tongue, freirich.com (click Products, then Smoked Meats). **FURTHER INFORMATION AND RECIPES:** *Heart of the Artichoke* by David Tanis (2010); *Cooking Without Borders* by Anita Lo and Charlotte Druckman (2011); *Rick Bayless's Mexican Kitchen* by Rick Bayless (1996); *The Norman Table* by Claude Guermont and Paul Frumkin (1985); epicurious.com (search tongue with mustard-horseradish sauce); saveur.com (search tongue in tomatillo; epi's beef tongue); for an article by Fergus Henderson, nosetotailathome.com (search tongue). **TIP:** Fresh uncooked tongue is the preference in France and Italy, and must be ordered in advance from a full-service butcher. Uncooked pickled tongues usually can be ordered from kosher-style delicatessens if requested in advance. Lamb tongues are most common at butchers in Greek neighborhoods and pork tongues in Italian sections.

WE ARE ALL JELLY DOUGHNUTS

Berliner Pfannkuchen

German

Although Americans tend to think of jelly doughnuts as our own invention, in fact, they are one more delectable gift to our pastry kitchens from Germany. The fist-size jelly doughnuts known as Berliners inspired the sweet, yeasty, fried, jelly-filled pastry so beloved here with morning coffee.

The German term *Berliner* can denote either a citizen of Berlin or a jelly doughnut. Berliners—the people—claim to have invented the treats of the same name (though fried pastries date back to the Roman era), which have been found in Berlin for quite some time. As early as the fifteenth century, bakers sold a yeasty, unfilled, and unfried cakelike version in carts in the city streets. In the sixteenth and seventeenth centuries, Berlin's population flourished, and so did its bakery culture. To meet demand, the bakers began frying the pastries (which by this time were filled with apricot or raspberry jam) on the spot, in pans set over an open flame. It was this preparation that gave the pastries the name *Berliner pfannkuchen* (the latter being the word for pancake). Over time, it also became traditional to dust the entire production with fine granulated sugar, making for a messy if completely addictive treat.

Berliners go by many names in Germany: In Bavaria and other parts of southern and central Germany (as well as in much of Austria) they're called *krapfen*; in the Palatinate region they're called *fastnachtsküchelchen*; in Aachen, *puffel*; in and around the Ruhrgebiet, *Berliner ballen*; and in Franken, *faschingskrapfen*.

Around the world, there are even more variations on the theme. In Israel they're *sufganiyot* (jelly doughnuts traditional for Hanukkah, see page 469); in Slovenia they're called *krofi*; in Serbia and Bosnia they're *krofne*; in Poland they're *pączki*; and in Hungary, *fánk*. No matter the name, the treats are essentially identical, jelly doughnuts one and all.

Back on German soil, they can be enjoyed at any time, but are particularly prevalent during the carnival days around Christmas and the New Year. Most of all, they are featured on Shrove Tuesday, the day before Lent begins. As with most fried foods, Berliners are best enjoyed fresh, the day they are made.

WHERE: *In Berlin,* Weichardt-Brot, tel 49/30-873-8099, weichardt.de; Bäckerei & Konditorei Siebert, tel 49/30-445-7576; *in New York,* Orwasher's, tel 212-288-6569, orwashers.com; *in Chicago,* Weber's, tel 773-586-1234, webersbakery .com; *in Santa Monica, Venice, and Culver City/ Mar Vista, CA,* Röckenwagner, rockenwagner .com. **FURTHER INFORMATION AND RECIPES:** *Neue Cuisine: The Elegant Tastes of Vienna* by Kurt Gutenbrunner (2011); *The German Cookbook* by Mimi Sheraton (2014); meganpeckcooks .com (search jelly doughnuts).

SOUP WITH A HEAD ON IT

Biersuppe and Bierkaltschale

Beer Soup

German, Austrian

Given the superb ales and lagers that Germany and Austria produce, it should be no surprise that beer is a malty, enriching ingredient in many of those countries' recipes—including these two uplifting and intriguing soups, one a hot

brew that warms from the inside out in winter, and the other a cool version that refreshes on a summer's day.

Lusty dark beer (*dunkels*) is preferable for

the hot winter brew *biersuppe,* in which the beer is bolstered with a light roux, then flavored with sugar, lemon juice, and either a stick of cinnamon and some cloves or crushed caraway seeds and slivers of fresh ginger. Egg yolks beaten into the hot soup just as it finishes cooking create a creamy froth much like that of a heady glogg. Austrians generally skip the lemon juice and the roux, instead beating milk with the egg yolks for a blond and creamy final touch. Either way, the result is poured into heated mugs or bowls for an especially welcome restorative after an afternoon on snowy ski slopes or even a walk through city streets in the penetrating

German beers add exciting flavor to classic recipes.

cold—especially if the drink can be followed by a lovely nap.

The sunny, golden light beer (*helles*) is better for a *bierkaltschale*—a "beer cold bowl." Grated dry, dark pumpernickel adds malty, grainy richness as it dissolves into a brew seasoned with dark currants and thin, clove-studded lemon slices. All steep together in the refrigerator for about two hours. By that time, the beer will still retain a slight, needling sparkle and will be infused with a delicately cool aroma and flavor. The grated pumpernickel lends body to the soup, which is ladled into small glass bowls or punch cups.

The endearing traditional garnish is one and the same for both beer soups: snowballs—*schneeballen*—tiny cloudlets of poached egg white dumpling seasoned with hints of sugar and cinnamon.

WHERE: *In Munich*, Nürnberger Bratwurst Glöckl am Dom, tel 49/089-2919-450, bratwurst-gloeckl.de. **FURTHER INFORMATION AND RECIPES:** *The German Cookbook* by Mimi Sheraton (2014); *The Cuisines of Germany* by Horst Scharfenberg (1989); justapinch.com (search biersuppe).

||||||||||||||||||||||||||||||||||

THE BAKER'S SIGN, WITH A TWIST

Brezeln

German (Baden-Württembergian)

A big yeasty, soft pretzel that is crisp on the outside, soft on the inside, and encrusted with sparkling grains of coarse salt usually begs only for a dab of mustard. But try it with a dab of butter instead, and you're in for a deceptively simple thrill.

A popular traditional snack in Germany, freshly baked soft pretzels—much like the "bagel pretzels" sold on the street corners of large American cities—are especially beloved around the city of Stuttgart. For the best experience, the pretzel must be fresh. (If the quality is not optimal, the pretzel should be warmed slightly, but not toasted, in an oven on low heat, then allowed to cool a bit so the butter doesn't melt.) Split bagel-style, it should be spread with slightly softened sweet butter, pressed together again, and joyfully devoured along with a cup of good strong coffee, a mug of hot chocolate, or, more ethereally, a glass of rose-hip wine—if you can find it.

Like bagels, these pretzels owe their soft interior and crisp crust to a spell in boiling water before they are sprinkled with coarse salt and baked in the oven. Twisting the dough into ropes is a surprisingly simple and rewarding operation that is great fun for children.

The pretzel shape has a long history, and naturally invites much speculation as to its origin. In Scandinavia, Germany, and Austria, it is the sign of the baker. In medieval Europe, the form was said to suggest arms crossed in prayer; a popular story is that a monk devised pretzels as a reward for catechism students who learned their prayers. In addition to salty treats,

A bakery's historic sign

the pretzel has also always been the shape of countless sweet cookies and cakes, especially at Christmas. Soft, savory classic pretzels were brought to the U.S. by German immigrants from the Palatinate region in the early nineteenth century; the U.S. headquarters for the best handmade originals remains Pennsylvania Dutch country.

WHERE: *In New York,* Sigmund's Bar, tel 646-410-0333, sigmundnyc.com; *in Santa Monica, Venice, and Culver City/Mar Vista, CA,* Röckenwagner, rockenwagner.com. **MAIL ORDER:** Tom Sturgis Pretzels, tel 800-817-3834, tom sturgispretzels.com; amazon .com (search pretzelhaus).

FURTHER INFORMATION AND RECIPES: *The Cooking of Germany* by Nika Standen Hazelton (1969); foodandwine.com (search german soft pretzel sticks). **SPECIAL EVENT:** Germantown Pretzel Festival, Germantown, OH, September, pretzel festival.com.

⊣||||||||||||||||||||||||||||||||⊢

KNOW WHICH SIDE YOUR BREAD IS BUTTERED ON

Brot and Brötchen

German

Given the vast array of cakes, cookies, and pastries produced and consumed in Germany, it's a wonder there's still a demand, much less a hearty one, for bread. But that most elemental of German foods appears in great and varied abundance.

Westphalian pumpernickel is perhaps the most internationally famous of the lot, a dark, grainy rye usually seen in thinly sliced square loaves that are rich with malty, nutty, healthy-tasting overtones. Well wrapped, it keeps for weeks in the refrigerator or freezer. (Because it is steamed, Westphalian pumpernickel retains

its moisture.) The bread almost demands a thin coating of butter, whether it is to be served with smoked salmon, herring, ham, or cheese. Because its own flavor is so pronounced, pumpernickel overpowers more delicate toppings such as crabmeat, caviar, chicken, or fresh, unsmoked meats. Under no circumstances should this firm, rich bread be warmed before it is served—or, even worse, toasted—lest it soften and lose its tightly knit texture.

Bauernbrot (also known as *roggenbrot,* or rye bread) or farmer's bread is huge and rugged, a slightly gray, round loaf of sourdough-based rye; among Ashkenazic Jews and Eastern Europeans, it is known as corn bread, meaning that the dough has been corned, or soured. Its crust is dark, crackly, and certain to give jawbones a good workout, and its moist, yeast-heavy body proves a tantalizing revelation on the palate. The huge oval slices should be cut in half or quarters for serving. Delicious spread with butter, they reach their apotheosis when topped with some of the rendered fat, or schmaltz, of ducks, chickens, or geese, and a sprinkling of coarse salt. Bauernbrot is a bit too heavy for closed sandwiches unless sliced very thin, which is a challenge.

Salzstangen, salt sticks, are the first pieces of bread to be eaten out of any bread basket, and small wonder. The golden brown crusts of these long, thin, crisply curled rolls are crunchy with sprinklings of coarse salt and caraway seeds, an addictive contrast to the soft white bread inside. Broken off in pieces and buttered for the most soul-satisfying results, salzstangen have probably spoiled more appetites than any other bread. Hungry diners innocently snacking on them, beware! They are particularly good with strong cheeses and crisp, cold appetizer vegetables such as cucumbers or black, red, or white radishes.

Mauerlöwerlei, or bricklayer's loaves, are small, neat white-flour rolls whose rounded tops and oblong shape do indeed give them a somewhat bricklike aspect. A specialty of Bavaria, they are particularly good when used for lusty sandwiches, spread with both butter and mustard and filled with cured or cooked ham, liverwurst, rare roast beef, roast pork, or ripe cheeses and thin slices of pungent radishes. Coarse salt and a grinding of black pepper are all that's needed for optimum sandwich enjoyment.

WHERE: *In Berlin,* Weichardt-Brot, tel 49/30-873-8099, weichardt.de; *in New York,* Schaller and Weber, tel 212-879-3047, schallerweber .com; *in Las Vegas,* German Bread Bakery, tel 702-233-2733, germanbreadbakerylasvegas .com; *in Santa Monica, Venice, and Culver City/ Mar Vista, CA,* Röckenwagner, rockenwagner .com. **RETAIL AND MAIL ORDER:** *In Portland, OR,* German Bakery Inc., tel 503-252-1881, the-german-bakery.com; *in Helen, GA,* Hofer's of Helen, tel 706-878-8200, hofers.com. **FURTHER INFORMATION AND RECIPES:** *The Cooking of Germany* by Nika Standen Hazelton (1969); h2g2.com (search german bread); german food.about.com (search buying german bread outside of germany; 10 german bread recipes).

A MECCA FOR *FEINSCHMECKERS*

Dallmayr

German (Bavarian)

What Fauchon is to the French and Harrods or Fortnum & Mason to the English, this sprawling, gorgeous *feinkost*—fine food—shop in Munich is to the Bavarians, and to the rest of Germany as well. Dallmayr, in the center of Munich may just be the most beautiful of the bunch. Giant coffee bean dispensers of Nymphenburg porcelain, hand-painted with birds and flowers in soft pastels, hold the shop's impeccable blends. Live crayfish swim in marble fountains, and the accommodating staff wears shirts and aprons in the blue and white of the Bavarian flag. Everywhere a glowing neatness reassures as it tempts shoppers toward delicacies that can only be described as the best, the most luxurious, and, unsurprisingly, the most expensive.

Opened in 1700 by Christian Reitter, since 1870 the shop has borne the name of its second owner (but not its last proprietor), Alois Dallmayr. Destroyed by fire in 1940 during World War II, the shop rose again between the city's lively Marienplatz and Odeonsplatz squares in an even more lavish iteration—and the owners haven't looked back since.

Which department is the most overwhelming? Hard to say. It might be the caviar section, where the best customers for triple-zero beluga are allowed to taste before making their selections. Or it could be the counter for smoked fish and fish salads, resplendent with golden-skinned smoked pike and carp; roseate salmon; silvery herring in at least a dozen sauces and marinades; and tiny ribbons of smoked fish

known as *Schillerlocken* because they imitate the long curls worn by the poet Schiller. Also on offer are pâtés in jewel-like aspics, wursts, and all of the smoked or air-cured hams Germany is famous for.

In a sweeter corner, shelves are stocked with nosegays made of colorfully wrapped hard candies, Cartier-like chocolate bijous, and pretty jars of every sort of jam and confiture imaginable. Here, too, you'll find the rich, winey bottled berry juices—black currant, raspberry, blackberry—that Germans so love in winter, whether lightened with a spritz of cold sparkling water or mixed with spirits for a holiday punch.

The pride of the house is its own coffee: rich, complex blends that can be packed in lovely and reliably airtight canisters repeating the Nymphenburg motifs, or enjoyed in the shop, along with some of the equally beguiling pastries. If browsing in this shopful of temptations leaves you hungry, consider tea at the in-store Lukullus Bar, or a lovely meal in the Restaurant Dallmayr.

WHERE: Dienerstrasse 14–15, Munich, tel 49/89-213-5100, dallmayr.com. **MAIL ORDER:** For ground and whole bean coffee, Enjoy Better Coffee, tel 800-582-6617, enjoybettercoffee.com; amazon.com (search dallmayr coffee).

MAKING THE MOST OF A GOOSE

Der Ganze Gans

German, Austrian

A goose, it is said, is a bird that is either too big or too small—the determining factor being the amount of fat that melts away as it cooks, leaving what is generally considered to be either too much or too little meat on its bones.

Hence, roasting a goose requires close attention, the goal being to eliminate the heavy golden layer of fat between skin and flesh, keeping the latter moist and luxuriously flavorful while leaving the former tantalizingly crisp.

Pouring boiling water over the skin of the slow-roasting bird and piercing it intermittently to allow fat to drain off are standard practices, but these techniques are just the start.

First, there is the matter of timing. In many

Every piece of the bird can be used for a variety of delicacies.

European countries, especially in the north, geese are slaughtered on St. Martin's Day (Martinmas in England), November 11. They are the unlucky symbol of one Saint Martin of Tours, who hid from adversaries in a barn until the birds' cackling betrayed him. In early November, young geese are just right. Large enough to have depth of flavor, yet still young enough to have a good proportion of meat to fat, they cook up golden brown and crackling crisp, mouthwateringly fragrant and rich with savory juices.

In Germany, the goose is prized not only for its flesh and skin but also as a vehicle for marvelously complex stuffings that become delectable sops for the meat's juices. Fresh apples accent sauerkraut, while dried apple slices combine with raisins, prunes, and brandy in chestnut or grated pumpernickel stuffings. On the savory side, popular stuffings are based on mashed potatoes flecked with diced grilled goose liver, or perhaps nuggets of crumbled bratwurst along with golden brown onions. The result is so delicious, one might almost forget to eat the goose itself.

And indeed, in Germany the goose is only the beginning. There's also *gänseklein schwarzauer,* sour black giblets—a dish that tastes a lot better than it sounds. A small sweet-and-sour soup-stew served as an intimate between-courses treat at family meals, it mellows the gaminess of chopped giblets with dried apples and prunes, onions, celery, cloves, marjoram, and a dash of vinegar. Goose blood, if on hand, binds the rich combination, accented by a garnish of potato dumplings.

Even loose, tubular neck skin is prized as *gefüllter gänsehals,* for which the skin is stuffed with diced goose liver, bacon, drippings, bread, lemon zest, and onion for a sausagelike creation that is gilded in its own unctuous fat. Remaining livers will be pan-browned and topped with sautéed apple and onion rings served beside mashed potatoes.

Although a roast is the usual form in which this noisy bird is enjoyed, its breast meat may be commandeered for other uses. Delicately cold-smoked over hardwood while still protected by a layer of skin, the firm, mahogany-colored meat is thinly sliced. The result, with its silky, supple texture and antique flavor, rivals the best prosciutto.

All of which leaves only the feathers that go into pillows as a traditional, prized filling—and the cackle that betrayed Saint Martin.

WHERE: *In Salzburg,* during the Christmas season, Goldener Hirsch, tel 43/662-80-84-861, goldenerhirsch.com; *in New York,* at Christmas and on advance order for 4 to 6 guests, Wallsé, tel 212-352-2300, kg-ny.com/wallse; Blaue Gans, tel 212-571-8880, kg-ny.com/blaue-gans; *in Milwaukee,* Karl Ratzsch's, tel 414-276-2720, karlratzsch.com. **MAIL ORDER:** D'Artagnan, tel 800-327-8246, dartagnan.com (search goose). **FURTHER INFORMATION AND RECIPES:** *The Cuisines of Germany* by Horst Scharfenberg (1989); *Neue Cuisine: The Elegant Tastes of Vienna* by Kurt Gutenbrunner (2011); germanfood.about.com (search christmas goose). **SEE ALSO:** Roast Goose with Sage-Onion Stuffing, page 21.

—||||||||||||||||||||||||||||||—

Fischereihafen Restaurant

German (Hamburg)

Great local seafood, traditionally and impeccably prepared. A dramatic view of a lively working harbor. Nearby, an operatic fish market in a historically raffish part of town. These are the hallmarks of the Fischereihafen Restaurant, situated in Hamburg's bustling harbor on the Elbe river. En route, you'll pass by the fish market, just off the infamous nighttime red-light district called the Reeperbahn.

The menu changes according to what's fresh in the morning fish market.

While the menu offers many well-made international seafood specialties, serious travelers out to maximize their local experiences will stick with the classic fare of Hamburg, as well as the Hamburg province of Schleswig-Holstein, which once belonged to Denmark. This historical note accounts for some similarities in taste, most especially those for dill, eel, and sailors' hash. The latter is called *labskaus,* a term that literally translates as "scow refreshment" or "hash for sailors," and is common to the cities that were once part of the Hanseatic League, a once-dominant trade alliance: Hamburg, Bremen, Lübeck, Bergen, Oslo, Copenhagen, Amsterdam, and London. A stewed hash, it is composed of finely chopped herring, anchovies, corned beef or pickled pork, potatoes, onions, and pickled beets, and topped with one fried egg per portion and a slice or two of sour pickle.

The hitch? Almost all of the ingredients are preserved—salted or pickled—as they once needed to be so they would keep for months aboard ship.

Before the hash, you'll want to stop at the Fischereihafen oyster bar to sample the big, plump Sylt Royals, one of which can weigh as much as a quarter pound. Farmed in clear, icy North Sea waters off the North Frisian island of Sylt, they are satiny in texture and only mildly salty, allowing warmly nutty, coppery undertones to emerge. Perhaps if you ask, you can follow an old Hamburg custom and have a slice of Cheshire cheese alongside, as well as a glass of red wine or a sunny white Riesling or Moselle.

Among the local specialties are silky, saline fillets of rosy *maatjes* herring with several sauces; and eel, fresh in a dill sauce, jellied in aspic, or smoked and served with apple-horseradish relish and toasted whole grain rye bread. Zander, or pike perch, from the Elbe is firm and meaty, classically served with a caper sauce, spinach, and boiled potatoes. More delicate little perch—*goldbarsch*—are sautéed and topped with a perky rémoulade; the pearly North Atlantic turbot—*steinbutt*—is delicious fried and garnished with hot golden mustard. The menu does have a few meat dishes as well, and these are helpfully grouped under the label *Nicht-Fischesser:* For Non-Fish Eaters.

For dessert, what else but *rote grütze?* Served cold, it's a ruby-red gelled pudding based on the fresh juice of red currants and raspberries or strawberries, each portion crowned with vanilla whipped cream and slivered almonds. This summer dessert is equally popular in Denmark, where it is known as Rødgrød med Fløde (see page 357). If you can say it, you can have it!

WHERE: Grosse Elbstrasse 143, Hamburg, tel 49/40-38-18-16, fischereihafenrestaurant.de.

ALL STEAMED UP

Frankfurter Pudding

German

A first cousin to both the chocolate soufflé and those trendy warm cakes with runny chocolate insides, this special dessert from Frankfurt is an exquisitely dark, bittersweet chocolate pudding. Enhanced with rum or coffee and almonds,

it is steamed in an oblong ridged mold that suggests the look of a half cantaloupe. The pudding must be served hot, emerging from its mold with a light, moist, spongy texture that is optimally contrasted by a cool topping of vanilla-flavored whipped cream and, if one likes, a spoonful of chocolate sauce. Although the steaming process is simple, careful timing is required for the dessert to be ready at the meal's end; the pudding should not sit for more than about fifteen minutes before being unmolded and served.

Frankfurter Pudding

Serves 8

Equipment: 1 melon mold, 6-to-7 cup capacity

3 ounces semisweet chocolate
½ cup (1 stick) unsalted butter
⅔ cup sugar, plus more for the mold
Pinch of salt
5 large eggs, separated
2 tablespoons rum, or 2 tablespoons double-strength brewed black coffee
1½ cups ground unblanched almonds
3 tablespoons dry pumpernickel or zwieback crumbs
Boiling water
2 cups vanilla-flavored whipped cream (optional), for serving
2 cups cold semisweet chocolate sauce (optional), for serving

1. Butter the melon mold and its cover, then sugar it. Tap out any excess sugar. Set the mold aside. Also have ready a lidded pot or casserole large enough to hold the melon mold.

2. Melt the chocolate in the top of a double boiler set over simmering water. Let the chocolate cool for about 10 minutes at room temperature.

3. Combine the butter, sugar, and salt in a mixing bowl and use an electric mixer to cream them until light and fluffy. Beat in the egg yolks, one at a time, waiting until each is fully blended before adding the next. Stir in the melted chocolate. Add the rum or coffee, the almonds, and the bread crumbs.

4. In a separate bowl, beat the egg whites until they are stiff but not dry. Using a rubber spatula, fold the beaten egg whites gently but thoroughly into the chocolate mixture. Spoon the pudding batter into the prepared mold; it should be about two-thirds full. Snap the cover onto the mold.

5. Place the mold, rounded side down, in the pot. Add enough boiling water to come two thirds of the way up the side of the mold. Cover the pot, and place it over high heat. Let the water return to a boil, then reduce the heat and simmer the pudding until it is completely set, about 1 hour and 15 minutes.

6. Remove the mold from the water bath and place on a wire rack, flat side down. Let it stand for 10 to 15 minutes before unmolding. Uncover the pudding and invert it onto a serving platter. Serve the pudding hot, topped with the whipped cream, if desired.

MAIL ORDER: For melon-shaped pudding molds, amazon.com (search scandicrafts melon mold 6.5 cup). **SEE ALSO:** Soufflés of All Sorts, page 132.

A BOWLFUL OF WINTER COMFORT

Fränkischer Grünkern

German (Baden-Württembergian)

Nicely gritty grains of *fränkischer grünkern*—green spelt of the scientific name *Triticum spelta*—are the basis of one of Germany's more obscure winter favorites, prepared as a velvety stew. In this rib-sticking one-bowl meal, the grain's fresh and grassy flavor is enhanced with meat, usually beef or pork, and vegetables such as onions, carrots, and celery.

Sold most widely under the Zimmermann Mühle label in Germany, the grünkern in this dish can be flavored in a variety of ways, starting with the choice of fat (butter or bacon), and continuing on to the cooking liquid (water or any meat or poultry broth) and the choice of vegetables, which may be browned first or added raw.

An ancient grain, spelt has more protein and crude fiber than wheat, with a high concentration of vitamin B17, which is said to ward off cancer. But this deliciously comforting dish isn't eaten for its health benefits.

Fränkischer Grünkern
Serves 4 to 6

1 package (8½ ounces) grünkern
3 tablespoons unsalted butter
3 slices lean bacon (optional),
    diced
1 medium-size onion, chopped
1 medium-size carrot, peeled and diced
1 large rib celery, diced, plus 1 sprig
    celery leaves
1 small piece parsnip, peeled and diced
    (optional)
1 small piece celeriac, peeled and diced
    (optional)
1 small leek (optional), white portion only,
    sliced
½ pound beef or pork in ½-inch cubes,
    preferably a soft cut such as chuck
Pinch of thyme
4 cups chicken, beef, or veal broth
    or water
½ teaspoon salt
¼ teaspoon freshly ground black pepper
Chopped fresh flat-leaf parsley
    or chives (optional), for garnish

1. Rinse the grünkern in a sieve under cold running water. Place it in a large bowl, add 4 cups of water, and let it soak overnight in the refrigerator or at cool room temperature.

2. Melt the butter in a heavy soup pot over moderate heat. Add the bacon, if using, and the onion, carrot, and diced celery and cook until the vegetables begin to turn a light golden brown, 8 to 10 minutes.

3. Add the grünkern with its soaking liquid and stir to mix. Add the celery leaves, the parsnip, celeriac, and leek, if using, and the meat and thyme, followed by the broth or water. Add the salt and pepper and bring to a boil. Reduce the heat to low and let simmer, partially covered, until the grünkern is entirely soft, about 1 hour and 15 minutes, stirring occasionally and

adding water if the mixture becomes too thick or sticks to the bottom of the pot.

4. Taste for seasoning, adding more salt and pepper as necessary. Serve the grünkern in warmed bowls, garnished with the parsley or chives, if desired.

Variation: For a richer flavor, brown the meat for a few minutes along with the onion, carrot, and celery. Potatoes are often a part of this stew, but they make it very starchy and a bit stodgy.

MAIL ORDER: amazon.com (search frankischer grunkern). **FURTHER INFORMATION AND ADDITIONAL RECIPES:** gruenkern.de/recipes. **TIP:** Although not traditional, a teaspoonful or two of crushed caraway seeds added during cooking lends a fresh, airy note to the stew.

SPOON UP YOUR GREENS

Frühlingssuppe

Seven Herb Soup

German

Known as Gründonnerstag, or green Thursday, in Germany and Austria, Holy Thursday is a solemn day between Ash Wednesday and Good Friday during the meatless Lenten season. But there is cause for celebration in the

form of a soup that honors the spring season during the pre-Easter week.

Spinach, watercress, lettuce, chervil, parsley, chives, and the sour grass sorrel, or some variation thereof—a minimum of seven fresh leafy herbs and vegetables—are simmered together in vegetable stock and then pureed to chiffon lightness to create a soup that is full of the promise of spring. A rich and creamy béchamel sauce is stirred into the hot mixture, then a beaten egg yolk is whipped in to brighten and bind.

Each portion gets a final garnish of hard-cooked egg, peeled and cut in half lengthwise to add a sunny bull's-eye to the verdant brew.

The soup is served during Holy Week.

Some sprinkle on grated Parmesan for extra zest.

Lovely as the soup is when it's made of mixed herbs, it becomes even more ethereal as *kerbelsuppe*, made only with chervil; but the fragile and exotic-tasting herb is scarce, and thus more suited for occasional use in home kitchens than as a regular offering in restaurants. As for the flagship green soup, it remains popular after Lent but might be bolstered by a base of chicken or veal stock and the addition of tiny veal or chicken meatballs.

Eating greens—wild or tamed—is still a spring ritual in Pennsylvania Dutch country, where German roots are reflected in many of the region's cooked and baked dishes. But springtime greens-bingeing is common to many cultures, as is the belief that greens, especially bitter greens, have the cathartic effect of purifying the blood.

FURTHER INFORMATION AND RECIPES: *The German Cookbook* by Mimi Sheraton (2014); germanfood.org (search herb soup, then click German Easter Recipes).

JUST HOW GEMÜTLICH CAN IT GET?

Gaststätte Weichandhof

German (Bavarian)

Rarely do travel poster–style local color and high-quality food go together, but anyone out to experience maximum Bavarian *gemütlichkeit* (cozy congeniality) would do well to visit Weichandhof, the guest house in the small, charming suburb of Obermenzing, in Munich.

Die Traditionsgaststätte met Herz—the traditional guest house with heart—was once a farmhouse and was transformed into an inn by a star of folk theater named Philipp Weichand in 1755. Low wood-beamed ceilings, fireplaces, checkered tablecloths, and handsome kitsch such as gray stoneware Bavarian pottery, copper vessels, and paintings adorn the intimate dining rooms. The menu offers echt tradition, and in the most delicious ways.

Classic German specialties are the way to go here—skip the international items on the menu in favor of appetizers and starters such as the homemade headcheeses (*hausegemachter pressack*), bratwurst dumplings (*bratnockerl*), or soups like the mock turtle, the broth adrift with semolina dumplings (*griessnockerl*), and *zandersuppe,* made with the flavorful pike-perch that swim through Bavaria's freshwater lakes and streams.

Then, on to the delectable *spanferkel,* or roast suckling pig, with its bacon-crisp skin and moist flesh nestled against potato dumplings. Or perhaps to the juicy boiled beef, *tafelspitz* (see page 328), served with salsify (*schwarzwurzel*), buttered potatoes, and horseradish-spiked cream sauce. Local game, sauerbraten (see page 306), and the crisp onion-mantled beefsteak *zwiebelrostbraten* (see page 318) are also on the menu, as are pigs' knuckles and shanks. If you can, follow these with wonderful desserts such as light, golden *palatschinken* crêpes (see page 328) filled with various ice creams and fruits, and homemade apple or apricot strudel.

As for drink, nothing but a footed, embossed green-glass *schoppen* of the dry white wines of Württemberg, Baden, Franken or the more flowery Mosel will do.

WHERE: Weichandhof, Betzenweg 81, Munich-Obermenzing, tel 49/89-891-1600, weichandhof .de.

〰〰〰〰〰〰〰〰〰〰

MIDNIGHT SOUP IN MUNICH

Gulyassuppe

German, Austrian, Hungarian

A legacy of the Austro-Hungarian empire, rich and beefy paprika-spiced goulash soup has a special place on the Bavarian menu, most especially in Munich, where it is a late-night antidote to an evening of drinking and reveling.

A feature of beer halls and casual cafés, it is especially popular in the feisty student section of Schwabing. But it can also be had in the many quick snack places, or *schnell imbiss,* all over that graceful, museum-rich city.

Though it's basically a more liquid version of goulash stew, there are some important differences. The spoonable soup is based on tender cuts of beef like chuck, neck, or shin meat, well marbled but free of sinew and gristle. The small cubes of beef are briefly braised with minced onions and finely diced green pepper in lard, bacon, or butter-bacon combination. Salt, pepper, and a half-and-half mix of sweet and hot paprika are stirred in and sautéed over low heat until the paprika loses its raw smell.

The mix is half-covered and simmered over very low heat for about ten minutes before some white vinegar is poured in and allowed to cook off; for a sophisticated touch, heated brandy is poured over the mixture and set aflame.

Then come water and enriching tomato paste, crushed caraway seeds, a pinch of marjoram, a split clove of garlic, and peeled and diced potato. All simmer for an hour or so to a meltingly tender amalgam with a succulent and heady broth. Inevitably, a good goulash soup calls for hair of the dog in the form of just one more beer before the last *guten Abend.*

WHERE: *In Munich,* Weisses Bräuhaus, tel 49/89-290-1380, weisses-brauhaus.de; Ratskeller München, tel 49/89-219-9890, ratskeller.com; *in Houston,* Rudi Lechner's, tel 713-782-1180, rudi lechners.com. **FURTHER INFORMATION AND RECIPES:** *The German Cookbook* by Mimi Sheraton (2014); *Neue Cuisine: The Elegant Tastes of Vienna* by Kurt Gutenbrunner (2011). **SEE ALSO:** Gulyás of All Sorts, page 392.

〰〰〰〰〰〰〰〰〰〰

COOL AS A CUCUMBER SALAD

Gurkensalat

German, Austrian

A gainst the richness and complexity of so many of the classic German and Austrian dishes, the coolly refreshing cucumber salad *gurkensalat* provides a welcome foil. A staple with many variations, at its most basic the salad begins with

thinly sliced rounds of peeled cucumber. Fresh from the garden if possible, they are layered with salt and left to sit for about an hour—a crispness-enhancing process that draws out some of the water that makes up more than 95 percent of their bulk. Drained and rinsed of any remaining salt, the cucumbers are then tossed gently with slivers of fresh onion, a zap of distilled white vinegar, a slosh of sour cream, salt, pepper, and a sprinkling of fresh dill or chives. The result is a creamy, pleasantly tart, crunchy, and brightly flavorful garnish that provides a sharp and welcome contrast to meaty dishes such as wintry stews, braised game, Wiener schnitzel, fried chicken, and roast goose and duck. But a good, fresh gurkensalat need not be limited to just the European table. It would be equally welcome at an American Southern barbecue, a

church supper, or a Fourth of July picnic.

Where: *In New York,* Wallsé, tel 212-352-2300, kg-ny.com/wallse; *in Kansas City, MO,* Grünauer, tel 816-283-3234, grunauerkc.com; *in Santa Monica, Venice, and Culver City/Mar Vista, CA,* Röckenwagner, rockenwagner.com. **Further information and recipes:** *The German Cookbook* by Mimi Sheraton (2014); *Neue Cuisine: The Elegant Tastes of Vienna* by Kurt Gutenbrunner (2011); allrecipes.com (search gurkensalat). **Tip:** This salad is best prepared with young, firm cucumbers. Look for the small Kirby pickling variety or the long, slim, plastic-wrapped European-style cucumbers.

⊢||||||||||||||||||||||||||||||||⊣

EVERYTHING BUT THE KITCHEN SINK

Hamburger Aalsuppe

Hamburg Eel Soup

German

I t's hard to imagine a more improbable-sounding list of ingredients than those that appear in Hamburg's most singular soup, a festive specialty that is far more appealing than it sounds. Actually more of a stew than a soup, this one-dish main course comes from northern Germany's "Free and Hanseatic City." It combines ham and (usually) meats such as chicken and beef with lengths of the firm, rich eels that swim in the rivers of Schleswig-Holstein. Also tossed into the pot are golden chunks of dried apricots and midnight-dark pitted prunes to simmer away with pot vegetables such as leeks, parsnips, celery root, parsley leaves and roots, onions, and carrots. Some cooks have even been known to add cauliflower, string beans, and who knows what else. Aromatic herbs like bay leaf, marjoram, thyme, and savory, as well as plenty of black peppercorns, combine

Hamburg's classic soup

with white wine as finishing touches, along with a dash of vinegar and—wait for it—a spoonful or two of raspberry jam.

The result is a sweet-sour broth that is both meaty and teasingly saline, darkly rich and full of spoonable delicacies, including tiny puffs of nutmeg-scented flour dumplings. Each ingredient gives up something of itself to the benefit of the complex and intriguing whole. Perhaps Hamburg's eel soup should be served daily to United Nations delegates for spiritual inspiration.

Because its authentic versions necessitate so many ingredients, it is virtually impossible not to prepare large quantities of this soup, which is why it is reserved by home cooks for special celebrations. Several traditional Hamburg restaurants, however, feature it as a standard. Because of its rib-sticking heft, it generally is relegated to this handsome port city's cold, gray, and rainy winter months.

Where: *In Hamburg,* Fischerhaus Restaurant, tel 49/40-314-053, restaurant-fischerhaus.de; Alt Hamburger Aalspeicher, tel 49/40-362-990, aalspeicher.de. **Further information and recipes:** *The Cuisines of Germany* by Horst Scharfenberg (1989); for other versions of German eel soup, *Lüchow's German Cookbook* by Jan Mitchell (1996); germanfood.about.com (search hamburg aalsuppe).

⊢||||||||||||||||||||||||||||||⊣

FIRST CATCH A HARE, OR EVEN A RABBIT

Hasenpfeffer

German

H*asen* is the word for hare, the traditional game in this fragrant dish with a dark red wine sauce so rich and complex it tastes like medieval history. But because rabbit (*kaninchen*) is easier to come by for modern cooks, it's often

substituted, for a more delicate if less heady result. Of course, hunters can procure their own hares, saving some of the blood to thicken a sauce similar to that used by the French in pressed duck or in the braised game dishes known as *civets.* When the hare is purchased from a butcher, the sauce may be thickened by scooping some spicy, raw bloodwurst out of its casing and liquefying it in a food processor with a little bit of stock, as suggested by Horst Scharfenberg in *The Cuisines of Germany.*

If fresh-killed, the hare or rabbit must be hung for several days and then skinned, cleaned, and cut into serving portions, the best of which are the legs and the saddle. It is also a good idea to marinate the cuts for about twenty-four hours in buttermilk to tenderize the meat and mellow the gaminess. Along with the giblets, the meat is sautéed with bacon, diced pork, and onions until brown, then placed in a casserole with the blood or bloodwurst puree, bay leaves, juniper berries, lots of black peppercorns, red wine vinegar, and, for bright color and a hint of sweetness, a little red currant jelly. The casserole is sealed closed with a stiff flour-and-water paste, and the whole is baked in the oven for a couple of hours, or until the meat is meltingly tender and the sauce has taken on a velvety texture. For a really tantalizing effect, the unopened casserole is carried to the table so diners can inhale the exquisite aroma when the flour-paste seal is broken.

Alternatively, the braising can be done in a heavy casserole on the stovetop, in which case the blood and seasonings are simmered in to finish the sauce after it has been skimmed of fat. Traditional garnishes are red cabbage with apple, and big, porous bread dumplings or boiled potatoes to soak up the succulent sauce. Just be sure the most highly prized front legs of a hare go to the hunter as a reward for making the treat possible.

Mail order: D'Artagnan, tel 800-327-8246, dartagnan.com (search scottish hare; also whole rabbit fryer). **Further information and recipes:** *The Cuisines of Germany* by Horst Scharfenberg (1989); *Lüchow's German Cookbook* by Jan Mitchell (1996); allrecipes .com (search hasenpfeffer).

⊣||||||||||||||||||||||||||||||||⊢

Haxen

German, Austrian

Veal, pork, and lamb shanks may be fashionable as comfort foods these days, but that's no news to Germans and Austrians. Such lusty, softly fatty, savory cuts are virtually taken for granted as budget dishes in these climes, especially in the casual restaurants and rathskellers devoted primarily to their preparation.

Always presented in enormous whole portions—not in the round cross-cuts the Italians know as osso buco—these haxen may be braised, roasted, and sometimes finished on a grill to give the skin a tantalizing, crackling crispness. In Vienna, pork shanks—*schweinsstelze*—are grilled over a wood fire until their rinds achieve crunchy perfection.

The braised shanks are seasoned with salt and pepper, lightly dredged in flour, and browned in bacon drippings, lard, or butter. Then comes a flurry of minced pot vegetables— carrots, celery, onions, parsnips—and a rosy glow of paprika, along with good beefy stock and dried basil and thyme. The mix is left to simmer almost imperceptibly for a good two to three nose-twitching hours (depending upon the size and number of shanks), after which the sauce is skimmed of fat and simmered with some elevating white wine. That abundant, unctuously enticing gravy demands an absorbent vehicle. Enter boiled potatoes or big, spongy bread dumplings, and just enough cool, fresh cucumber salad (see page 291) to keep the palate interested.

More ambitious cooks (or eaters) like the finished braised shanks to be breaded and fried, and more delicate eaters like the meat sliced off for them—a measure that would

Veal shank with pearl barley and spinach

doubtless have offended the English monarch Henry VIII, who was known for tackling his meat with bare hands.

WHERE: *In Vienna,* Schweizerhaus, tel 43/1-72-80-1520, schweizerhaus.at; *in Munich,* Haxnbauer-im-Scholastikahaus, tel 49/89-216-654-0, kuffler.de/en/muenchen/haxnbauer; *in New York,* Wallsé, tel 212-352-2300, kg-ny.com/wallse; *in Milwaukee,* Mader's, tel 414-271-3377, madersrestaurant.com; Karl Ratzsch's, tel 414-276-2720, karlratzsch.com. **FURTHER INFORMATION AND RECIPES:** *Neue Cuisine: The Elegant Tastes of Vienna* by Kurt Gutenbrunner (2011).

AN EGGHEAD SCRAMBLE

Hirn mit Ei

Scrambled Eggs with Brains

German, Austrian

A lusciously rich late breakfast, lunch, or midnight supper, scrambled eggs enfolding lightly sautéed onions and nuggets of silken, gently flavored brains are getting harder to find on German menus these days—but they definitely deserve to be swept up in the growing trend for organ meats.

Calves' brains are traditional, as are the even more delicate lambs' brains, but the larger steers' brains are often used in this dish as well. Soaked in ice water with a little lemon juice or vinegar for about six hours in the refrigerator (to extract blood), they are then parboiled until just firm, so that the membranes and tubes can be clipped or pulled out before the brain is cut into fork-size bits.

Minced onion and parsley are sautéed in hot butter until soft but not brown, and the pieces of brain are tossed in and fried until lightly golden. Beaten salted eggs are poured over and scrambled until set. Served with or over hot buttered toast and a glass of Alsatian Pinot Gris or Austrian Gewürztraminer, or a tankard of light beer, this is a meal that starts or ends the day right.

For another elegant addition to plain old scrambled eggs, the above preparation can also be applied to sweetbreads. Both, as it happens, are popular with Eastern European Jews, who use vegetable oil instead of butter for the sautéeing if they observe kashruth.

FURTHER INFORMATION AND RECIPES: *The German Cookbook* by Mimi Sheraton (2014); ifood.tv (search scrambled eggs and veal brains). **TIP:** To prepare this dish at home, order the brains from a butcher several days in advance. They will probably arrive frozen, and can be thawed in the first soaking water. Once thawed, they should be cooked and consumed within twenty-four hours, as they are highly perishable.

THE ELEGANT SURF AND TURF

Hummer- und Hühnersalat

Lobster and Chicken Salad

German (Northern)

I n a funny gastronomic coincidence, the delicate combination of lobster and chicken is one that is favored by both the northern Germans and the Chinese from the southern region of Canton. In Germany's misty-gray North Sea city of Hamburg, the fine old Atlantic Hotel used to feature the pairing in a luxurious salad. (The Chinese version is known as Lung Hai Gai Kew.)

At the Atlantic, tender pink nuggets of lightly chilled cooked lobster were combined with pieces of gently poached chicken breast that were torn (rather than diced) for a softer, more tender result that was more receptive to the dressing. Tossed with a chiffon-light, Dijon-accented mayonnaise, the salad was finished with either tiny green peas or the emerald-green tips of asparagus.

Given the northern European penchant for flavors that run to the tropical, the pinch of golden curry powder that was sometimes mixed into the dressing should come as no surprise. Nestled on frilly lettuce leaves and served with hot buttered toast and a glass of sparkling white *sekt,* this salad makes for an elegantly satisfying lunch.

Lobster and Chicken Salad

Serves 4 to 6

2 cups cooked lobster tail and claw meat, cut into bite-size chunks and lightly chilled (see Note)

2 cups cooked chicken breast meat, cut or torn into bite-size chunks and lightly chilled (see Note)

½ teaspoon salt

Pinch of freshly ground black pepper

1 teaspoon freshly squeezed lemon juice

½ to ⅔ cup (depending on dryness of meat) real egg mayonnaise, preferably homemade

1 teaspoon Dijon mustard

Pinch of curry powder (optional)

1 cup cooked fresh or lightly blanched frozen tiny green peas, chilled, or 1 cup cooked 1-inch fresh asparagus tips, chilled

Tender lettuce leaves, such as Boston or Bibb, rinsed and dried, for serving

Minced fresh dill or flat-leaf parsley (optional), for garnish

Slices of hot buttered toast, for serving

1. Place the lobster and chicken breast in a large mixing bowl and sprinkle them with the salt, pepper, and lemon juice.

2. Combine the mayonnaise, mustard, and curry powder, if using, in a small bowl and mix. Fold the mayonnaise mixture into the lobster and chicken. Taste for seasoning, adding more salt, pepper, lemon juice, mustard, and/or curry powder as necessary. Using a fork, gently toss in the peas or asparagus.

3. Refrigerate the salad, covered, for about 20 minutes but no longer, lest the vegetables leak into the dressing, before serving.

4. To serve, arrange lettuce leaves on individual plates and nestle the salad in them. Sprinkle the salad with dill or parsley, if desired. Serve the salad with slices of hot buttered toast, if desired.

Note: The lobster and chicken should be slightly cooler than room temperature. If warm, they will dilute the dressing; if very cold, they will not absorb enough of it.

FURTHER INFORMATION AND ADDITIONAL RECIPE: *The German Cookbook* by Mimi Sheraton (2014). **TIP:** The salad is especially impressively presented when individual portions are heaped in avocado halves.

+|||||||||||||||||||||||||||||||||+

NEVER STOP CARPING

Karpfen, or Carp in Many Ways

German, Austrian

Probably because of its golden color, the carp is considered a lucky fish not only in China and Japan but also throughout much of Eastern Europe. On New Year's Eve, also known in Europe as Sylvester's Eve, it is customary to obtain one

Carp swim in the fresh waters of the Danube River, which meets the Regen River in medieval Regensberg.

golden carp scale and hold onto it for the whole year as a token of good luck; the fish makes an appearance at European Christmas dinners as well.

Gourmands consider it even luckier to eat the extravagantly fatty, meaty *Cyprinus carpio* so abundant in freshwater lakes and rivers like the Danube—but the wisest know to avoid carp caught during the summer. In those hotter months, the fish tend to swim down to the lake or river floor where the water is colder, taking in the mud that produces the same moldy flavor that turns so many people off of catfish. (The most particular old-time cooks let the live carp swim in a home bathtub for a day or two before cooking it, letting the fish take in fresh water to eliminate musty overtones.) Winter carp is firmer, fresher-tasting, and much preferred, even now when much of the fish is farmed.

Beloved in many intriguing preparations, in *blau gekochte karpfen* the carp is prepared "blue," like the trout dish on page 141. It, too, must be gutted live just before being lowered into simmering, vinegar-spiked water. The delicacy is served with melted butter and freshly grated horseradish.

As its name indicates, *karpfen in bier* is braised in dark, malty beer that cuts the fatty texture of its flesh and creates a sauce enlivened by crushed gingersnaps (*lebkuchen*), bay leaves, lemon, and cloves for an aromatically hot, pickled effect. In *rotweinkarpfen*, its red-wine-braised brother, the rich fish meat is mollified by allspice, cloves, thyme, and onions, with wine vinegar and crusts of rye bread adding a yeasty sourness.

Böhmischer karpfen is the Bohemian way of simmering carp with pot vegetables, then finishing it with a sauce of bay leaves, molasses, gingersnaps, almonds, prunes, walnuts, and raisins.

Gebratene karpfen, the Alsatian favorite, which has been readily adopted in the neighboring Schwarzwalder, or Black Forest, is made with a whole fish neatly gutted, rolled in flour, and deep-fried in vegetable oil.

And the list goes on, stretching out to such Eastern European favorites as pickled carp in aspic, with or without ground walnuts, and the gefilte fish mix that includes the ground flesh of carp. In any form, carp proves lucky to the appreciative diner.

FURTHER INFORMATION AND RECIPES: *Gourmet's Old Vienna Cookbook* by Lillian Langseth-Christensen (1959); *The German Cookbook* by Mimi Sheraton (2014); *The Oxford Companion to Food* by Alan Davidson (1999); germanfoodguide.com (search carp blue; pan fried carp). **TIP:** Never taste carp raw to judge the seasonings; like all freshwater fish, it can contain dangerous parasites. **SEE ALSO:** Gefilte Fish, page 436; Quenelles de Brochet, page 122.

—||||||||||||||||||||||||||||||—

WHEN SALAD DAYS RUN HOT AND COLD

Kartoffelsalat

German, Austrian

Formulas for a good potato salad can vary considerably. Diced apples, hard-cooked eggs, and even sweet-and-sour pickle relish may be involved, as they are at church suppers throughout the American South. Mayonnaise may be present, or not, and for some, celery is indispensable. Tastes tend to run to childhood favorites, so what you like in your potato salad probably depends largely on what version you grew up with. But no matter your origins, don't rule out a conversion until you try a German *kartoffelsalat*, hot or cold, especially if it's sidling up to the meaty wursts of Germany, Austria, or American Pennsylvania Dutch country.

For its soothingly warm preparation, kartoffelsalat depends on a tangy dressing of cooked bacon zapped with white vinegar for its distinctive savoriness. So that the insides remain firm and dry, new potatoes are boiled in salted water with the skins on. While they are cooking, diced bacon and onions are sautéed and then combined with oil, vinegar, and mustard seeds. The potatoes are drained, peeled, and returned to the hot but empty pot to be rolled around for a few seconds until floury on the surface, then they are cut into chunks or slices. Tossed with the hot bacon dressing, they are garnished with scallions or parsley or both. The combination of the salty bacon with the bite of vinegar and the creamy, waxy texture of the potatoes is what makes this warm salad so special. In its cold version, the potatoes are cooked the same way but are doused with onion-flavored beef broth and a dash of vinegar. After marinating for about thirty minutes, they are drained and tossed with a little mustard and light vegetable oil, to be finished with a glossing of mayonnaise, sour cream, or both. After a dash of salt and white pepper, the salad is chilled for two to three hours.

FURTHER INFORMATION AND RECIPES: *Neue Cuisine: The Elegant Taste of Vienna* by Kurt Gutenbrunner (2011); allrecipes.com (search authentic german potato salad). **TIP:** Floury potatoes like russets crumble when boiled, so stick to red potatoes, new white potatoes, or Yukon Golds. To make authentic German potato salad, use German-style double-smoked bacon. **SEE ALSO:** Southern Potato Salad, page 624.

—||||||||||||||||||||||||||||||—

HOW ABOUT SOME REALLY CHEESY MUSIC?

Käse mit Musik

Handcheese

German (Frankfurter)

A felicitous nighttime custom in the bustling metropolis of Frankfurt is a brief trip across the river to one of the many antique apple wine inns in Sachsenhausen, the city's medieval quarter. The oldest and most colorful (if also the most touristic) example of these is Zum Gemalten Haus. In rollicking, gemütlich tavern surroundings, revelers sing ever louder as they develop a pleasant buzz from traditional hard apple cider—*apfelwein*, or in dialect, *ebbelwoi*—poured from handsome blue and gray stoneware pitchers. With that cool, mildly bittersweet drink (or beer for those who prefer it), they lustily consume the menu's expected array of sausages and braised meats. But the two most popular specialties are beef tartare, ground to order, and the essential cheap, light, and savory snack *handkäse mit musik* (literally "handcheese with music").

Pouring apple wine at Zum Gemalten Haus

In settings of dark wood, stained-glass windows, and communal tables known as *stammtische,* this small, palm-size cheese is practically a requirement, whether as appetizer or dessert. Before enjoying some, one must first get past the aroma, for this is a creamy, fast-ripening number whose thick, unctuously putrefied scent is much like that of Alsatian Munster, German Limburger, or the American Liederkranz. Like those odoriferous cousins, handcheese has a rich patina of complex flavors, in its case best enjoyed after it has marinated for an hour or two in a combination of olive oil and white vinegar. Spread on a thick slice of buttered, caraway-flecked sour rye bread, it is garnished with minced onion and eaten as an open sandwich—washed down, of course, with apfelwein.

Why the music in the cheese's name? The polite explanation is that the aroma sings a song all its own; less polite is the assertion that the combination is certain to induce flatulence.

Where: *In Frankfurt,* Apfelwein Wagner, tel 49/69-6125-65, apfelwein-wagner.com; Zum Gemalten Haus, tel 49/69-6145-59, zum gemaltenhaus.de. **Further information and recipe:** *The German Cookbook* by Mimi Sheraton (2014).

HAVE A PIECE OF CAKE

The Konditorei Experience

German, Austrian

"Young people these days do not sit in Konditoreien and order several pieces of cake, as we used to. They go to Starbucks for a quick cup of coffee and a biscuit. When young women do come into Kreutzkamm's, they ask,

'Should I have a salad or a piece of cake?' Such a question!"

Such a question, indeed! The answer is that you should rush to have your *konditorei* experience while you still can, for its sumptuous, fattening, pastry-based feast is an endangered

custom even in Germany and Austria, its two most dedicated strongholds. The word comes down from devotee and expert Elisabeth Kreutzkamm-Aumüller, a fifth-generation owner of Café Kreutzkamm outposts in Munich and Dresden.

For those who haven't indulged in konditorei, think of a French patisserie or a bakery shop cum café, and you're on the right track. Fronted by retail bakeries with a kaleidoscopic array of small and large cakes lined up in gleaming glass cases, the cafés offer a variation on table service for patrons in search of instant gratification. Customers make their selections at the counter and are given a table number. Once seated, they are served by waitresses carrying beverages on little silver trays set with white doilies. Of course, those who really know their *kuchen* can sit down and order from the menu, or from memory.

So much for the form—the thrill is in the content. A konditorei menu is a narrow booklet, anywhere from eight to twenty pages in length, that reads like an index to a German baking and dessert manual. Cakes and pastries are classified by types: *Hefegebäck* are the yeast coffee cakes we call Danish pastry; *obstkuchen* are made with fruit; *kuchen* contain cheese, or are nicely gritty pound cakes; *torten* are true tortes made without flour or with very little; *blätter-teig* are puff pastries; *kleingebäck* are cookies and small cakes; *sahnedesserts* are filled with whipped cream, custard, or both; "Für Diabetiker" indicates choices for diabetics. There are nonbaked desserts, such as the ice cream dishes *eisspeissen*. And there are dozens of drinks, alcoholic or not, hot or cold, and milk, soda, or fruit juice–based.

A konditorei in Cochem

One of the most-loved pastries on such menus is the *bienenstich*, a double-layered yeast sponge cake filled with sweet custard cream and topped with a mottled glaze of sugar and slivered blanched almonds that caramelize to resemble a honeycomb—hence the name, which means bee sting. Coiled tubes of the most fragile, irresistibly crisp puff pastry holding thick whipped cream and dusted with confectioners' sugar are called *Schillerlocken* (see page 309), because they imitate the long curls sported by that good poet. The Bavarian *Mohr im hemd,* or "Moor in a

shirt," is a chocolate-iced cream puff filled with vanilla whipped cream. However, in Bremen that name might also land you a parfait of liqueured cherries topped with dark pumpernickel crumbs flavored with cinnamon sugar, and a top swirl of whipped cream. Various *waffeln* are small, open-work *gaufrette* wafers sandwiching a maraschino-spiked whipped cream. *Falscher rehrücken*—mock venison—is a long tunnel of a chocolate cake with indented ridges, a thin, dark chocolate icing, and spiky almonds sticking up at intervals to suggest larding—all in imitation of a saddle of venison, as the name implies.

Beguiling as the sweets are, they comprise only part of the story. To dedicated konditorei fans, the savory portion of the menu holds equal appeal. Served all day long are various egg dishes, cereals, and *belegte brotchen,* or open sandwiches, including the Toast "Hawaii," which combines pineapple, grilled ham, and cheese. Later in the day, two delectable stand-bys are the strong and heady *kraftbrühe,* a double chicken consommé that sometimes has a raw yolk coddled into it, and the *königin-pastetchen,* which Americans might call chicken à la king in a pastry shell. This royal dish arrives as a flaky puff pastry *bouchée,* or cup, holding white wine and lemon-flavored creamed chicken, button mushrooms, peas, and sometimes diced calf's tongue or sweetbreads.

After such a lunch, do not plan an early dinner.

Where: *In Munich and Dresden,* Kreutzkamm, tel 49/89-993-5570, kreutzkamm.de; *in Baden-Baden,* Café König, tel 49/7221-23573, chocolatier .de/kh_koenig.php; *in Berlin,* Café Buchwald, tel 49/30-391-5931, konditorei-buchwald.de; *in Vienna,* Demel, tel 43/1-535-17-17-0, demel.at; *in Chicago,* Lutz Café and Pastry Shop, tel 877-350-7785, chicago-bakery.com; *in Santa Monica, Venice, and Culver City/Mar Vista, CA,* Röckenwagner, rockenwagner.com.

GO POACH A MEATBALL

Königsberger Klopse

German

An airy lightness accented by the sudden, salty piquancy of anchovies, sprightly capers, and a satiny, lemony sauce accounts for the enduring popularity of the *klopse* (meatballs) of Königsberg. These sizable meatballs, much appreciated by the late *New York Times* food writer Craig Claiborne, offer a surprisingly subtle reward.

Very fine thrice-ground pork is mandatory to the mixture, as is at least one other meat—beef, veal, or, even better, both. Also on deck are milk-soaked white bread, golden sautéed onions, eggs, grated lemon rind, and finely minced anchovies or anchovy paste, all combined with the meat into lemon-size balls. The meatballs' puffy delicacy is the result of a poaching in richly flavored beef or veal broth, with no browning to speak of. That broth then becomes the basis for a smooth velouté sauce, bulked up with a flour-and-butter roux and finished with a dash of lemon juice, a sprinkle of capers, and a dollop of whipped sour cream. (Cooks with richer tastes beat egg yolks into the sauce as a final thickening before the sour cream.)

Though they're often served with mashed potatoes, the klopse are more traditionally bedded down on a mound of hot sauerkraut. At the risk of committing heresy, try slicing chilled leftover klopse and eating them on toast as a sort of pâté. (Just don't tell any purists you read it here.)

Where: *In Berlin,* Restaurant Haus Berlin, tel 49/30-242-5608, haus-berlin.net; *in Milwaukee,* Karl Ratzsch's, tel 414-276-2720, karlratzsch .com. **Further information and recipes:** *The Cooking of Germany* by Nika Standen Hazelton (1969); *The German Cookbook* by Mimi Sheraton (2014); nytimes.com (search konigsberger klopse claiborne); food.com (search konigsberger klopse in creamy caper sauce).

A dish that packs a punch of many flavors

WHO PUT THE CHEESE IN THE LIVER?

Leberkäse

German (Bavarian)

Get over the name as quickly as you can. This so-called liver cheese—*leberkäse,* an off-putting term for what is essentially a loaf of hot pâté—is worth it. A specialty of Bavaria that is much loved all over Germany, the baked and steamed loaf is made with a combination of very finely ground lean pork and pork liver mixed with diced bacon and sometimes other meats. Gently fragrant with garlic, onion, and nutmeg, the meat is kneaded with ice water into a satiny-smooth amalgam.

Once baked in a water bath, the loaf takes on the satisfyingly toothsome, slightly porous texture of bologna, although it is much more tender served when hot. A bit complicated and messy to prepare at home, leberkäse is usually purchased from a favorite butcher or delicatessen and sliced and resteamed at home just before it is to be served. Sold at the fast-food stands and cafés known as *schnell imbiss* and in rathskellers and outdoor market stalls, leberkäse is most traditionally eaten as a lunch or snack along with a good crusty roll and dabs of sweet Bavarian mustard. (Though many prefer the brassy hot Dusseldorf mustard *senf.*)

Not nearly so fine—or quite so expensive— is *fleischkäse,* or meat cheese. Composed of a slightly coarser grind of pork, minus the liver, it makes up for what it lacks in silkiness or refinement with a rustic deliciousness of its own.

WHERE: *In Munich,* Zum Franziskaner, tel 49/89-231-8120, zum-franziskaner.de; Viktualienmarkt, tel 49/89-8906-8205, viktualienmarkt.de; *in Frankfurt,* Zum Gemalten Haus, tel 49/69-6145-59, zumgemaltenhaus.de; *in New York,* Schaller and Weber, tel 212-879-3047, schallerweber.com. **FURTHER INFORMATION AND RECIPES:** *The German Cookbook* by Mimi Sheraton (2014); familycook bookproject.com (search leberkaese).

HIGH LIVERS

Leberwurst

German

To love smooth, unctuously rich and smoky liverwurst is to be on a delightfully endless search for various types and degrees of refinement. In this pursuit, there is no better place to start than Germany—for within the seemingly unbounded

world of German sausages, the liverwurst family deserves special recognition (especially when contrasted to the bitter, stiff, and chemical-tasting examples common in the average supermarket). In fact, the fillings in good liverwursts, scooped out of their casings and packed into crocks, could easily pass for pâtés and fool even the most astute *feinschmecker.*

The plainest and least expensive *leberwurst* will contain a familiar fine grind of smoked pink-tan pork liver with varying amounts of starch filler, depending upon price. Salt, pepper, and flavorings like nutmeg and garlic will be in evidence to varying degrees.

But that's only the beginning of an illustrious roundup that begins with *gänseleberwurst,* a lusciously fat, short, stubby sausage filled with goose liver and packed with a golden coating of rendered goose fat between filling and casing. Or *Hildesheimer streichleberwurst,* creamy with easily spread calf's liver, very finely ground and subtly seasoned. Or *Kasseler leberwurst,* an enticingly coarse grind of pork liver with garlic and herbs that is superb when spread on lightly toasted slices of sour rye bread.

Braunschweiger is an even softer, looser, coarse and chewy grind of pork liver, but otherwise much like the Kasseler. A meaty, coarse version is *Grobe* (coarse) liverwurst.

Closing up the ranks are *zwiebelwurst,* pork liverwurst seasoned with flecks of browned onions; *sardellenwurst,* with anchovies mixed through to spike its pork filling; and truffle wurst, with diced black truffles nestled in its filling of calf's liver.

Alas, there's one liverwurst that is nothing but a bygone dream. A specialty of the also-bygone Michelson *feinkost* (delicatessen) in Hamburg, it was labeled *gänseleberwurst*, but featured one magnificent difference: The three-inch-thick sausage was centered around a whole goose liver surrounded by a luscious goose liver pâté. It's hard to say why this miracle disappeared. Perhaps one day it will return.

Farmhouse bread topped with leberwurst makes a perfect German dinner.

Where: *In Munich,* Viktualienmarkt, tel 49/89-8906-8205, viktualienmarkt.de; *in Vienna,* Naschmarkt, naschmarkt-vienna.com. **Retail and mail order:** *In New York,* Schaller and Weber, tel 212-879-3047, schallerweber.com; *in Milwaukee,* Usinger's, tel 800-558-9998, usinger .com; *in Tulsa, OK,* Siegi's Sausage Factory, Deli, Meat Market & Restaurant, tel 877-492-8988, siegis.com (search grobe liverwurst). **Tip:** Liver is very perishable (the reason all liverwursts are preserved by smoking), so purchase the sausages fresh, store them in the refrigerator, and consume them within two weeks.

——|||||||||||||||||||||||||||||||||||——

THE CHEESE THAT DOESN'T STAND ALONE

Liptauer Käse

German, Austrian, Hungarian

The pungent cheese spread that goes by many names (among them Obatzter and Gervais Angemacht) is an appetizer favorite in Germany and Eastern Europe alike, sometimes also standing in as a savory dessert. Named for a region of what is now Slovakia, Liptauer Käse can be made many ways, starting with a base of a soft, fresh cheese such as cottage, quark, or farmer's. Additions of grated Gruyère or strong blue cheese add doses of pungency, as does a fork-mashing with sour cream, grated onion, chopped capers, mustard, Worcestershire, caraway seeds, chopped anchovy fillets, and cayenne. Brandy or beer are sometimes drizzled in for a heady good measure. When prepared with Camembert or the similar Gervais cheese as a base, the mixture is usually served for dessert.

Almost all ingredients are optional, and seasoning to taste is highly encouraged. Whatever the mix, the spread will develop more flavor after ripening in the refrigerator for eight to twenty-four hours. Before being served, it should soften at room temperature for an hour or so, for easy spreading on small rye rounds or squares of Westphalian pumpernickel, or even over slices of cucumber or as a filling for celery sticks.

Further information and recipes: *The Cuisines of Germany* by Horst Scharfenberg (1989); *Neue Cuisine: The Elegant Tastes of Vienna* by Kurt Gutenbrunner (2011); food.com (search liptauer austria); youtube.com (search KCI grunauer).

—————————|IIIIIIIIIIIIIIIIIIIIIIIIIIIIIIII|—————————

FOOLING THE EYE—BUT NOT THE PALATE

Marzipan

German, Danish

Germany has two centers for the production of the addictively unctuous, sweet almond paste marzipan: Königsberg and Lübeck. Each has its advocates: Lübeck, the medieval Hanseatic port on the Baltic Sea, with its turreted, half-timbered brick guild houses, is favored for its intensely almondy, teasingly bitter rendition. When baked, as is the custom in Königsberg, the firm, smooth almond paste achieves true sophistication, with a burnishing of caramelized sugar modifying what some might consider a cloying sweetness, and with a haunting flavor of roasted bittersweet almonds emerging as one chews. (The excellent marzipan made in Hans Christian Andersen's Danish hometown of Odense deserves an honorable mention as well.)

A gift from Persia that arrived in Europe in the Middle Ages, marzipan is an instant favorite of almost all young children.

It's perhaps most familiar in the forms of fruits, vegetables, miniature toys, animals, and holiday ornaments—and quite astonishing in those most convincing life-size, fool-the-eye fruits created and displayed in Catania, Sicily.

Molded marzipan is fairly wet and sticky. But mixed with egg white and then formed into thin ropes, it can be twisted into pretzel shapes or rolled out between sheets of wax paper. The latter versions, cut with cookie cutters and brushed with egg yolk, are baked until the tops turn a toasty golden brown and the treats take on the firm, satisfying texture of crisp cookies.

There is some debate surrounding marzipan's makeup. To some, a pure, smooth blend of almonds and sugar is the only true marzipan; to others, such a concoction is merely almond paste. The latter group insists on egg white blended into the mix. Choose for yourself, but know that store-bought marzipan rarely includes perishable egg white.

Marzipan candies frequently masquerade as fruit.

Where: *In Berlin,* Wald Königsberger Marzipan, tel 49/30-323-8254, wald-koenigsberger-marzipan.de. **Mail order:** For Lubech marzipan, amazon.com; for niederegger marzipan, igourmet.com (search niederegger marzipan). **Further information and recipes:** *The Oxford Companion to Food* by Alan Davidson (1999); *Visions of Sugarplums* by Mimi Sheraton (1981); *The Cuisines of Germany* by Horst Scharfenberg (1989).

Munich Beer Radishes and Easter Egg Radishes

German

Wander into any German beer hall or rathskeller in fall—especially during Oktoberfest—and you will see many happy imbibers nibbling from plates full of what may at first glance look like uncooked noodles. Closer examination will prove them to be the graceful spiral curls of peppery white radishes known, in fact, as Munich beer radishes. The icicle-like winter radishes taper from thin roots to about 2 inches in diameter, with a shape suggestive of daikon, and are carved on a special cutter that creates the slim curls. Served with dark, coarse pumpernickel and sweet butter to mollify their stinging bite, they provide a wonderfully peppery crunch as the grainy bread adds its own malty overtones to the beer.

Springtime brings the small, round white Easter Egg radish to the German table, its almost sweet accent contrasting a mild, earthy bitterness. This radish is often grated into *rettichsalat*, a salad dressed with a mix of lemon juice or mild vinegar and sour cream, plus gentle hints of onion or scallions and spring herbs such as chervil, parsley, or tarragon. More impulsively, the crisp little Easter Egg radish is eaten out of hand with a mere dip into coarse sea salt.

The arrival of both varieties is cause for celebration in colorful outdoor markets such as the Viktualienmarkt in Munich, but fortunately radishes are easy to grow in home gardens. Seeds for both radishes are readily available, as are the somewhat expensive spiral cutters that work on many other long, firm vegetables such as zucchini, cucumbers, potatoes, and carrots.

WHERE: *In Munich,* Zum Franziskaner, tel 49/89-231-8120, zum-franziskaner.de. **MAIL ORDER:** For seeds, reimerseeds.com (search german beer radishes; giant white round radishes); for spiral slicer, amazon.com (search benriner cook help vegetable slicer). **FURTHER INFORMATION AND RECIPES:** *The Cuisines of Germany* by Horst Scharfenberg (1989); todaysgardenideas.com (search how to grow radishes).

Rehrücken Baden-Baden

Saddle of Venison with Red Wine

German (Bavarian)

If Germany is home to some of the world's best game preparations, then within the country's boundaries, Bavarian cooks are generally acknowledged to be the maestros. With hunting in the piney Black Forest still a most popular sport, the handling of the catch is no small matter. Boar, hare, and venison, wild or farmed, are among the best-loved meats, while game birds are equally popular. But if a single specialty stands out, it is this succulent, exotic, and tender saddle of venison.

Baden-Baden is the Bavarian spa town that attracted European nobility in its Edwardian heyday. In the context of this dish, it refers to the classic garnish of halved pears poached in white wine and filled with garnet-red currant jelly, and to the local garnish of spätzle (see page 312). Alternatively, these garnishes may be known as *Schwarzwalder ärt* (in the style of the Black Forest) or *Bayerisches ärt* (in the style of Bavaria).

The full, long, narrow saddle (double rack) of venison—the *rehrücken*—is the real point, of course. The meat is rendered mellow by a marinade based on a robust red wine, preferably a Burgundy, along with onions, juniper berries, sliced carrots, peppercorns, a bay leaf, and often a stick of cinnamon, which is popular for use with boar as well. Larded with matchstick strips of pork fat, which add a dewy softness, the saddle is then oven-braised with bacon and the strained marinade's onions and carrots. (Skimmed of grease and mixed with sour cream, that marinade is eventually bolstered with roasted meat juices to become an opulent gravy.)

The Germans like their saddle of venison so much, they have devised a reminder of it in the dessert they call *falscher* (mock) *rehrücken*: a moist, dark-chocolate Quonset hut–shaped iced

A succulent saddle of venison with spätzle noodles and berries

cake with rows of almonds stuck in the top, standing in for the larding.

WHERE: *In New York*, Wallsé, tel 212-352-2300, kg-ny.com/wallse. **MAIL ORDER:** For venison, D'Artagnan, tel 800-327-8246, dartagnan.com; for lingonberry preserves, igourmet.com (search lingonberry). **FURTHER INFORMATION AND RECIPES:** *The Cuisines of Germany* by Horst Scharfenberg (1989); *The Cooking of Germany* by Nika Standen Hazelton (1969); alleasy recipes.com (search roast saddle of venison with red wine); nytimes.com (search roast saddle of venison with red wine); uktv.co.uk/food (search saddle of venison with poached pear).

NOSH ON THE RHINE

Rheinischer Sauerbraten

German (Rhenish)

An operatic dish worthy of Wagner's Rhine-centered Ring Cycle, sauerbraten is rarely prepared as it should be. Usually, impatience or economy allows insufficient time for the marinating process; the big cut of beef (preferably a five-pound rump, but bottom round will do) really requires three to five days in which to tenderize and be infused with overtones of peppercorns, onion, and a rainbow of pickling spices such as coriander, bay leaves, chiles, cloves, and mustard seeds. Sometimes the roast sits for too long after being cooked, so that the meat becomes stringy and the sauce turns thin and greasy.

Regional differences abound, but the Rhineland's sauerbrauten is the echt, characterized by the sweet-and-sour contrast of vinegar, lemon juice, sugar, raisins, and *lebkuchen*, the piquant gingersnaps crushed and added to flavor and bind the sauce.

That dark mahogany sauce . . . therein lies a secret one can ferret out only along the Rhine—say, in the kitchen of a very traditional restaurant in Cologne. The trick is to begin the roux, or *einbrennen*, with sugar, and to stir that into the hot fat—bacon, beef drippings, butter—before the flour, thereby allowing the sugar to begin to caramelize and brown and add that authentic, golden-black patina that spreads through the finished sauce. Plump, absorbent dumplings of potato, semolina, or bread—*kartoffelklösse, griessknödel,* or *semmelknödel*—do justice to this wondrous sauce, but tiny droplets of spätzle are popular alternatives.

Around Munich, a version of sauerbraten is prepared with beer, much like the Belgian carbonnade. In the western part of Bavaria, in the Black Forest bordering French Alsace, sauerbraten is marinated in red wine and spices absent even an intimation of sweetness. And at the bygone, elegant Lüchow's in New York, sauerbraten in summer was served cold, encased in a silken Madeira aspic.

WHERE: *In Cologne,* Früh am Dom, tel 49/ 022-1261-3211, frueh.de; *in Milwaukee,* Mader's, tel 414-271-3377, madersrestaurant.com; Karl Ratzsch's, tel 414-276-2720, karlratzsch.com. **FURTHER INFORMATION AND RECIPES:** *The German Cookbook* by Mimi Sheraton (2014); *Lüchow's German Cookbook* by Jan Mitchell (1996); food network.com (search rhineland-style sauerbraten); saveur.com (search sauerbraten sheraton).

⊣‖‖‖‖‖‖‖‖‖‖‖‖‖‖‖‖‖‖‖‖‖‖‖‖‖‖‖‖‖‖‖⊢

ONE HOT *KARTOFFEL*

Salzkartoffeln

German

They call them salt potatoes, but really they're just potatoes boiled in very well salted water. Such a description, however, hardly does justice to their important place in German cuisine. Potatoes in general are pervasive throughout the Germanic food landscape. Prepared in dozens of ways on their own, they also appear in the dough for noodles and for sweet or savory dumplings, as well as in the famously moist and rich *schokoladen kartoffeltorte* (chocolate potato torte). But nowhere is the importance of the common spud made plainer than in the careful method by which boiled potatoes are prepared. Usually peeled only after being boiled (unless they are the tiniest new potatoes, which are eaten skins and all), they are cooked at a rolling rate in abundant water with handfuls of salt—the reasoning being that, just as with pasta, whole boiled potatoes cannot be satisfactorily salted once they are cooked.

When they are tender but not quite falling apart, they are well drained and peeled (or not), then returned to the empty pot and dried over low heat for a minute or two. The pot is gently jostled until all potato surfaces take on a floury snow-white finish—a step that renders them immune to sogginess, even if they sit for fifteen or twenty minutes. A few of the smallest might break apart, and that's a good thing: Perfectly boiled potatoes will shatter at the slightest touch of a fork, and the German rule of etiquette forbids cutting them with a knife. To do so is to be labeled a boor and a cultural illiterate, as Italians regard anyone who cuts pasta with a knife. Breaking the potatoes has a functional advantage too, as the uneven edges allow the pieces to better absorb butter—which is, after all, their reason for being.

Herbs garnish the spuds.

In addition to melted butter, possible dressings for these paragons of simple perfection might include freshly ground black pepper, crushed bits of bacon, sautéed onions, sprinklings of caraway seeds, minced herbs, such as parsley, chives, or dill, and dried fine bread crumbs.

All this is a fine treatment for a food that got such a slow start in Germany, one of the last countries in Europe to grow and eat the earthy tubers—Germans shied away from them for almost two centuries after potatoes emigrated from South America. Like other Europeans, they feared health results of eating unknown foods, especially those in the botanical nightshade family that also included tomatoes and eggplants. That potatoes eventually made it onto the menu at all was due to the wisdom and power of Frederick the Great, who in the mid-eighteenth century recognized their value as a food crop and handed out potato seed tubers to farmers, even putting a militia in place to ensure they would be planted. (How he made sure they would be eaten remains a mystery.)

WHERE: *In New York,* Blaue Gans, tel 212-571-8880, kg-ny.com/blaue-gans; Café Sabarsky, tel 212-288-0665, kg-ny.com/cafe-sabarsky. **FURTHER INFORMATION AND RECIPE:** *The German Cookbook* by Mimi Sheraton (2014). **TIP:** Small California white potatoes or small red bliss are best for boiling. Yukon Gold and russets do not work as well.

"YOU GREETED ME, MY SAUERKRAUT, WITH YOUR MOST CHARMING SAVOR."
—FROM "ODE TO SAUERKRAUT" BY HEINRICH HEINE

Sauerkraut

German, Austrian

So synonymous is sauerkraut with Germany that during World War I its citizens were themselves maligned by American doughboys as "krauts." It's a pity the moniker isn't taken as a compliment, for the eye-opening pickled cabbage hits

the palate with a bitter-sour-salty essence that is nothing short of delectable. A showcase for seasonings of piney juniper, caraway, pepper, onion, apple, wine, and bacon, it is adaptable to many more lusty dishes than can be easily counted. Among such are steaming soups, savory strudels, stuffings for roast duck and goose, and even baked apples.

Often acting as the centerpiece for various assortments of fresh and cured meat, sauerkraut defines *choucroute garnie* in French Alsace (see page 78). In Germany and Austria, it anchors the similar butcher's plate known as a *schlachtplatter* (see page 310), featuring, among other meats, the tender smoked pork chops *Kasseler rippchen.* In many Russian, Polish, and Ashkenazic Jewish homes, cold uncooked sauerkraut is served with pickled cucumbers and green tomatoes as a sort of salad accompanying meats, especially in winter.

Strictly speaking, *kraut* means cabbage, and the souring comes via salt, in a simple fresh pickling method designed to give a cold country the gift of vegetables in wintertime. Classified as "fresh pickled" because the cabbage is uncooked, sauerkraut can spoil, especially if it isn't completely covered by the liquid in the pickling vat or jar.

In many Eastern European neighborhoods, you will be able to buy this pale blond delicacy from wooden barrels. Barring that sure sign of authenticity, experiment until you find a brand that is not soft or gray. There should be no vinegar and little or no sugar. Jarred kraut is preferable to that sold in plastic sacks, and the mild, newly pickled cabbage of August is a special favorite among kraut experts in Bavaria and neighboring French Alsace, where the cabbage is slivered into much finer threads.

Sauerkraut should always be rinsed twice: first in cold water, then in warm, with an extra wash if it still tastes too sour. As much water as possible should be squeezed out, handful by handful. The kraut is fluffed up with a fork as it is put into a nonreactive pot made of terra-cotta, glass, or enameled cast iron. Some recipes call for braising sauerkraut with chopped onion in fat—butter, bacon, lard, or the rendered schmalz of chicken, duck, or goose—before adding liquid in the form of water, stock, or wine. Others bind it after cooking, using the fat and a flour roux known as an *einbrennen.* Whatever the technique, the desirable texture for cooked sauerkraut is "dry but juicy." Shun the steam table travesties of overcooked, mushy, gray kraut that give this good dish a bad name (and an equally unpleasant smell).

Although sauerkraut is generally served with meat, the royal chef Theodor Hierneis recounts in his book *The Monarch Dines* that his patron, King Ludwig II of Bavaria, nicknamed Ludwig der Verrückte (The Mad), liked his with fish. The favored dish was *hechtenkraut,* sauerkraut baked with pike, browned onions, crayfish tails, and plenty of butter under a crisp bread crumb crust—sheer madness to more conventional German palates.

WHERE: *In Berlin,* Kurpfalz-Weinstuben, tel 49/30-883-6664, kurpfalz-weinstuben.de; *in New York,* Blaue Gans, tel 212-571-8880, kg-ny.com/blaue-gans; *in Kansas City, MO,* Grünauer, tel 816-283-3234, grunauerkc.com. **RETAIL AND MAIL ORDER:** *In New York,* Schaller and Weber, tel 212-879-3047, schallerweber.com; *in Chicago and Des Plaines, IL,* Kuhn's Delicatessen, tel 800-522-9019, kuhnsdeli.com; *in North Waldoboro, ME,* Morse's Sauerkraut, tel 866-832-5569, morses sauerkraut.com. **FURTHER INFORMATION AND RECIPES:** *Neue Cuisine: The Elegant Tastes of Vienna* by Kurt Gutenbrunner (2011); *The Lutèce Cookbook* by André Soltner and Seymour Britchky (1995); cookstr.com (search home cured sauerkraut); germanfoodguide.com (search sauerkraut).

CREAM-FILLED PASTRY WORTHY OF A POET

Schillerlocken

German

The Marbach-born Jewish poet Friedrich Schiller (1759–1805), whose poems were banned by the Nazi regime, was previously honored by way of two food specialties, both called *Schillerlocken,* after the long, twisted curls that adorned his head. One was a strip of smoked dried herring and the other an extraordinarily sumptuous pastry. Flaky and fragile, its crunchy coiled horn uses a very special dough known as *hefeblätterteig,* a puff pastry made with yeast that Americans recognize as Danish.

Formed and baked on individual metal tubes, the horns must cool completely before being generously—very generously—filled with the thickest, richest imaginable whipped cream, often enhanced with a whisper of vanilla or combined with a light custard, and then dusted

The man (and curls) behind the pastry

with a snowfall of confectioners' sugar. In the best *konditorei,* a Schillerlocken pastry will be filled just before it is served, so the crust remains crisp—much the way cannoli are handled in the best Italian *pasticcerias* (see page 173).

Like cannoli, the Schillerlocken has come in for some needlessly complicating enhancements. Chocolate, nuts, or candied fruits have been folded in with the whipped cream, or even added to the dough—all gilded-lily travesties upon the elegantly simple original. But for all-around vulgarity, none rivals the dinner plate–size version of Schillerlocken known as the lobster claw. Better to opt for the normal size, just a bit larger than cannoli.

WHERE: *In Munich and Dresden,* Kreutzkamm, tel 49/89-993-5570, kreutzkamm .de. **MAIL ORDER:** For cone forms, amazon.com (search fox run cream horn molds; norpro 6 piece cream horn case set). **FURTHER INFORMATION AND RECIPES:** *The German Cookbook* by Mimi Sheraton (2014); carolynnsrecipebox.blogspot. com (search cream horns).

EATING HIGHEST ON THE HOG

Schlachtplatter

German

How many different ways are there to preserve ham? Let us not count them, for the variables include the type of pig, what the pig was fed, whether the meat was cured or smoked, how it was seasoned, whether it was boned, and whether it

was pressed flat or left in the round. Each has a special color, flavor, and texture all its own.

Germany may take the prize for greatest number of subtly different hams produced within a single country—and a visit to any one of its good *feinkost,* or gourmet shops, or to a high-class *schlächter* (butcher) should result in a tantalizing embarrassment of choices. You

will find a great many cooked ham dishes, but just as the Italians have their prosciutto and the Spanish their jamón Ibérico, it is the raw cured hams that are considered delicacies by serious *feinschmeckers* (gourmets). Like their Eastern European counterparts, German hams tend to be lustier and stronger flavored than the air-dried hams of France, Spain, and Italy; most are smoked, adding a woodsy burnish and darker, dryer finish to the meat.

If you happen by a German or Austrian restaurant or *bierstube* (beer hall) offering a *schlachtplatter,* or butcher's platter, of hams, try it. Usually thin-sliced and splayed on wooden plates or boards, the array of meats will be accompanied by rye bread, hot or sweet mustard, pickled pearl onions, and gherkins. In some places, varieties of sausage are added to the lusty mix for good measure. Liquid accompaniments might be shot glasses filled with a clear, fiery, fruit-based schnapps such as *kirschwasser,* steins of beer, or the rounded, footed green goblets known as *schoppen,* holding fruity local white wines.

Westfälische schinken (Westphalian ham) is Germany's finest and most highly prized raw smoked ham. Taken from pigs fed on acorns in the oak forests of Westphalia, the meat is a delicate rose color, fine-grained and supple in texture, and gently flavored with the woodsy overtones of the beech and juniper it is smoked over. Dark, moist, thinly sliced Westphalian pumpernickel is the complementary bread of choice.

Schwarzwälder schinken (Black Forest ham) is a name bandied about outside Germany as a supposedly high-quality filler in sandwiches. The true Black Forest ham, freshly sliced from a bone-in leg, is far more rustic than these mass-produced versions. Slow-smoked over pine, it has a flavor hinting at autumnal fires of burning leaves.

Nuss schinken (nut ham) has a nutty flavor, as its name implies, but the moniker actually refers to the cut of meat—a small, boneless, rather lean oval from the larger leg.

Lachsschinken (salmon ham) is a delicately pink and silky ham, only mildly smoked and lean, which looks much like sliced smoked salmon.

The ***Schwarzwälder rauchfleisch*** or *schinken-speck* (Black Forest smoked meat or ham-bacon) traditional in Bavaria as a *gabel frühstück*—a mid-morning "fork breakfast"—is lightly smoked and close to raw, with silky streaks of ivory fat running through bright and rosy meat. The moist, dense sourdough bread that is *bauernbrot*—farmer's bread—is the right foil for the delectably fatty meat, as is the icy cold cherry schnapps *kirschwasser,* or the sharper, raspberry-based *himbeergeist.*

Where: *In New York,* Blaue Gans, tel 212-571-8880, kg-ny.com/blaue-gans; Café Sabarsky, tel 212-288-0665, kg-ny.com/cafe-sabarsky. **Retail and mail order:** *In New York,* Schaller and Weber, tel 212-879-3047, schallerweber.com.

⊦||||||||||||||||||||||||||||||||⊦

DESSERT GOES BAROQUE

Schwarzwälderkirschtorte

Black Forest Cherry Cake

German

A native of the southwestern German province of Swabia that is known for its *kirschwasser*—the icy-clear firewater that is cherry brandy—the *Schwarzwälderkirschtorte* rose to prominence during the 1930s in Berlin's pastry shops and became a favorite in bakeries and restaurants across Britain, America, Austria, and Switzerland in the late twentieth century.

Whatever variations this miraculously rich

and subtle sweet may inspire, know that all authentic versions include layers of moist, bittersweet chocolate cake sprinkled with fiery kirsch brandy and interspersed with drifts of whipped cream. The finishing touches, dottings of brandied cherries and chocolate shavings, result in a dessert that tastes every bit as good as it looks. Although aerated cream, poor-quality cooking chocolate, and canned cherries can conspire to give the spectacular-looking creation a bad name, the real thing is utterly, decadently irresistible.

Where: *In Baden-Baden,* Café König, tel 49/72-21-23573, chocolatier.de/kh_koenig.php; *in Munich and Dresden,* Kreutzkamm, tel 49/89-993-5570, kreutzkamm.de; *in Chicago,* Lutz Café and Pastry Shop, tel 877-350-7785, chicago-bakery.com; *in Houston,* Rudi Lechner's, tel 713-782-1180, rudilechners.com. **Further information and recipes:** *The German Cookbook* by Mimi Sheraton (2014); *Neue Cuisine: The Elegant Tastes of Vienna* by Kurt Gutenbrunner (2011); *The Cake Bible* by Rose Levy Beranbaum (1988); saveur.com (search black forest cherry cake anderson würz). **Tip:** The German Museum of Confectionery, in Kitzingen, Bavaria, Germany, has a small but thorough history of the Schwarzwälderkirschtorte; tel 49/93-21-92-94-35, conditorei-museum.de.

HEROES TO GRAVY

Spätzle

German, Austrian

The chewy nuggets of dough called spätzle are made with nothing more than flour, eggs, and water, or sometimes milk. But form is everything where German noodles are concerned, and well-made spätzle must be tiny and ethereally light if they are to serve as vehicles for the rich gravies and drippings of the northern European kitchen. Mostly served as a side dish, the diminutive savories are perfect foils for the juices of roasted meats and game.

Their simple dough requires no kneading, tossing, resting, or rolling, but it must be pressed through a sieve or colander, or better yet through a dedicated spätzle press, directly into salted boiling water—an acquired skill. When sufficiently cooked, after only a few minutes, the adorable little dumplings float to the top, ready to be drained. Then the noodles may be sautéed in hot butter until golden, or tossed in butter with herbs such as dill, chives, or parsley and spices like nutmeg and mace.

A centuries-old staple in Germany and Austria, spätzle are believed to have taken their name from one of two origins: the word *spatzen* in the southern German dialect, meaning sparrow; or the Italian *spezzare,* "to cut into pieces." Whatever their etymological origin, the heart of spätzle land indisputably lies in southern Germany's Black Forest. Fortunately the chewy mini-dumplings appear on fashionable menus

Stirring in rye flour brings out a nutty flavor.

wherever there is good gravy to be sopped up.

WHERE: *In Berlin,* Weinschenke Weinstein, tel 49/30-441-1842, weinstein.eu; *in New York,* at the restaurants of Kurt Gutenbrunner, including Wallsé, tel 212-352-2300, Blaue Gans, tel 212-571-8880, and Café Sabarsky, tel 212-288-0665, all at kg-ny.com; *in Kansas City, MO,* Grünauer, tel 816-283-3234, grunauerkc.com; *in Milwaukee,* Mader's, tel 414-271-3377, madersrestaurant.com; Karl Ratzsch's, tel 414-276-2720, karlratzsch .com; *in Seattle,* Lecosho, tel 206-623-2101, lecosho.com; *in San Francisco,* Suppenküche, tel 415-252-9289, suppenkuche.com; *in Santa Monica, Venice, and Culver City/Mar Vista, CA,* Röckenwagner, rockenwagner.com. **MAIL ORDER:** For spätzle presses, germandeli.com (search spaetzle press); deutscheshaus.cc (search spaetzle press); amazon.com (search westmark classic round noodle maker; danesco stainless spaetzle maker). **FURTHER INFORMATION AND RECIPES:** *Neue Cuisine: The Elegant Tastes of Vienna* by Kurt Gutenbrunner (2011); cookstr. com (search spaetzle dumplings hensperger); smittenkitchen.com (search spaetzle).

A CAKE THAT'S DOWNRIGHT CRUMMY

Streuselkuchen

German

Named for the streusel, or crumbs, that make up its crisp and buttery, cinnamon-scented topping, *streuselkuchen* is the ultimate in comforting coffee cakes. A heavenly match for a cup of hot coffee, it also goes well with

strong tea or hot chocolate for a felicitous breakfast or an afternoon lift. Baked in individual portions called crumb buns, it is ubiquitous in Germany's coffee stands and shops, as it once was in U.S. diners.

Pastry indulgences are generally devised for richness and complexity, the gooier and creamier and sweeter the better. By comparison, this subtly addictive cake looks basically harmless and almost dull, like a flat sponge or pound cake with a golden brown crumb topping. At its best and most authentic, it will be a yeast cake, developing ripe and winey overtones as it rises modestly. Butter and the grated zest of lemons and oranges bestow a sunniness that's a pleasing match to the cake's fine, spongy texture, to which the butter, flour, and cinnamon-sugar crumbs add a satisfying crunch.

The crumb cakes and buns available commercially outside of Germany are rarely made of a yeast dough, which takes time to be proofed.

An easy, fast, and fairly convincing substitute for the home baker is *blitzkuchen,* or lightning cake, for which baking powder produces the rise.

WHERE: *In Berlin,* Weichardt-Brot, tel 49/ 30-873-8099, weichardt.de; Café Buchwald, tel 49/30-391-5931, konditorei-buchwald.de; *in Munich and Dresden,* Kreutzkamm, tel 49/89-993-5570, kreutzkamm.de; *in Baden-Baden,* Café König, tel 49/7221-23573, chocolatier.de/kh _koenig.php; *in Vienna,* Demel, tel 43/1-535-17-17-0, demel.at; *in New York,* Café Sabarsky, tel 212-288-0665, kg-ny.com/cafe-sabarsky; *in Chicago,* Lutz Café and Pastry Shop, tel 877-350-7785, chicago-bakery.com; *in Santa Monica, Venice, and Culver City/Mar Vista, CA,* Röckenwagner, rockenwagner.com. **FURTHER INFORMATION AND RECIPES:** *The German Cookbook* by Mimi Sheraton (2014); germanfood.about .com (search streuselkuchen sheet cake); epicurious.com (search streusel kuchen).

—|||||||||||||||||||||||||||||||||—

WHEN EVERYTHING GELS JUST RIGHT

Sülze

German, Austrian

Succulently moist pork captured in white-diamond aspic is the basis for three delicious Austro-German specialties that are especially popular in Berlin. Most authentically the gel is a result of boiling pig's feet into a stock.

Sülzkotelette, or pork chops in aspic, is by far the most elegant of the three, a refreshing main course in warm weather or a stylish course for a late supper. Tender loin chops are set in their gelatin-rich stock, which hints of onion, root vegetables, bay leaves, and peppercorns. Turned out of cutlet molds onto frizzy greens, they are garnished with cooked carrots, hard-cooked eggs, and freshly grated horseradish.

Sülze, or headcheese, is a luminous gel capturing boneless bits of mostly tender and flavorful pork's head meat—tongue, cheeks, and all—much like French *tête de veau* and *jambon persillé.* Sülze is usually sliced from gelled loaves, and is verdant with parsley and perky with onions and garlic. Gherkins and tiny pickled white onions complement the amber gel, as does a touch of hot mustard.

Saure sülze, jellied or pickled pigs' feet, tend to be favorites of hearty beer drinkers. If meat is usually sweetest closest to the bone, this meat must be a confection—plenty of bones here. Also sometimes made with calves' feet, these bay leaf–, black pepper–, and white vinegar–accented snacks are often found at bars in traditional beer halls.

RETAIL AND MAIL ORDER: *In New York,* Schaller and Weber, tel 212-879-3047, schallerweber .com (search headcheese; click Find & Buy for sources in the U.S.); *in Wheeling, IL,* Stiglmeier Sausage Co., tel 800-451-8199, stiglmeier.com (search sulze; head cheese). FURTHER INFORMATION AND RECIPES: *The German Cookbook* by Mimi Sheraton (2014); *Lüchow's German Cookbook* by Jan Mitchell (1996); *Gourmet's Old Vienna Cookbook* by Lillian Langseth-Christensen (1959); ifood.tv (search schwein sulze).

—|||||||||||||||||||||||||||||||||—

SWEET DREAMS OF SPRING

Waldmeister

Woodruff

German

Along with asparagus, new peas, and woodland strawberries, woodruff (also known as *Galium odoratum* or *waldmeister*) is a favorite harbinger of springtime in Germany, where it is enjoyed in a cooling ice or punch throughout the summer. The herb, bedecked with starry white flowers and elegantly long, slim green leaves, grows wild in forests and does well as a ground cover in shaded gardens. With a flavor suggesting newly mown hay and dewy fresh air, it is highly prized as a flavoring for white wine punches, or *bowle*, drinks based on Mosel and Champagne (most typically the *Maibowle*, a May Day specialty). You'll also see it stuffed into sachets to perfume linens; in a pillowcase, woodruff is said to ensure sweet dreams.

The word waldmeister *translates to "master of the wood."*

The dried woodruff available in herb shops is an ethereal ingredient for sophisticated diamond-yellow ices that renew the palate between courses or provide a refreshing finish to a heavy meal. To prepare the ices, woodruff sprigs are steeped in a combination of sugar syrup and fruity white apple or grape wine, or a prepared woodruff syrup is used. Brightened with orange and lemon juice and strained before being frozen, the mixture is garnished with strawberries for a roseate finish.

MAIL ORDER: For woodruff plants, whiteflower farm.com (search sweet woodruff); amazon .com (search dried woodruff; for seeds, search 20 sweet woodruff asperula; for syrup, search tri top sirup waldmeister). **FURTHER INFORMATION AND RECIPES:** *Gourmet's Old Vienna Cookbook* by Lillian Langseth-Christensen (1959); youtube .com (search waldmeistereis woodruff ice).

BETTER THAN AN ANIMAL SACRIFICE

Weihnachtsgebäck

Christmas Cookies

German, Austrian

The baking begins about a month before Christmas. In professional *konditoreien* and the homes of ambitious cooks alike, scents of butter and hot sugar combine with exotic wafts of ginger, cardamom, cloves, nutmeg, allspice, and

gentle hints of lemon, almonds, and vanilla. This enticing assault on the nostrils continues right up until Christmas, for it takes that long to amass a sufficient number and variety of all the cookies (to say nothing of the breads, cakes such as stollen, and candies) with which

Germans, Austrians, and other northern Europeans celebrate the holiday.

The results, crisp, buttery little conceits that are delicious to nibble with tea, coffee, milk, or the spicy hot red punch called *glühwein*, often have symbolic significance in pagan or Christian lore. Stars are obvious icons, evoking the famous speck of light that guided the Three Wise Men (one of whom, the dark-skinned Balthazar, is honored with an eponymous fudgy chocolate and nut confection of his own). Marzipan and many other doughs will be cut into star shapes during the Christmas season—baked into the simple butter cookies called *mailanderli,* iced or decorated with colored sprinkles, or doused with cinnamon and nuts as *zimtsterne.*

Symbols of the light that guided the Three Wise Men

Then there are cookies printed with animals or monklike religious figures, like the almond- and rosewater-flavored *Frankfurter bettelmännchen* (Frankfurt beggar men) and the egg white–glazed *spekulatius.* The story behind these animal cookies goes that in pagan times, a midwinter festival demanded the sacrifice of a farm animal. Since the poor could not afford such a sacrifice, they were permitted to substitute cookies in the form of animals.

Some Christmas cookies celebrate the romantic, expensive spices from the East that brighten midwinter darkness with a touch of luxury. Among those are the toothsome, hard little "pepper nuts," or *pfeffernüsse,* and the crisply white, anise-scented drops called *anislaibchen.* Dozens more vary in name and form from one region to another, but all are kept fresh and tempting stored in airtight cookie tins in a cool place. But not in the refrigerator, where they lose their snap.

Then there are various kinds of the sweet yeast bread, stollen, including one with a roll of marzipan in the middle and *quarkstollen* which is made with a yogurtlike cream that is quark,

halfway between sour cream and cheese. All stollens, because of their oblong folded forms, represent the swaddled newborn Christ child.

Zimtsterne (Cinnamon Stars)

Makes about 6 dozen cookies

> 3 extra-large egg whites
> 1¼ cups superfine sugar, plus sugar for
>   rolling out the cookies (optional)
> 1½ pounds (about 5 cups) unblanched
>   almonds, finely ground, plus ground
>   almonds for rolling out the cookies
>   (optional)
> 3 teaspoons ground cinnamon
> ½ teaspoon pure almond extract, or
>   1 teaspoon brandy

1. Preheat the oven to 300°F. Butter 1 or more large baking sheets.

2. In a large bowl, beat the egg whites with an electric mixer. As they begin to foam and stiffen, gradually beat in the sugar. Continue beating until the whites form stiff peaks that retain the mark of a knife blade. Set aside ½ cup of the beaten egg whites.

3. Sprinkle 3½ cups of the almonds and the cinnamon and almond extract or brandy over the remaining whites and stir together gently but thoroughly. The mixture should be thick and fairly dense. Add more almonds if the dough is too sticky to roll out.

4. Sprinkle ground almonds or sugar over a work surface. Roll out the dough to ¼-inch thickness. Using a 1½-inch star cookie cutter, cut the dough into star shapes, gathering up the scraps and rolling them out again. Arrange the cookies on the prepared baking sheet(s), leaving about ½ inch between the cookies. Brush the top of each cookie with a little of the reserved beaten egg whites.

5. Bake the cookies until they are pale golden brown on top, about 20 minutes. Transfer the cookies from the baking sheet(s) to wire racks to cool thoroughly. Stored in airtight containers, the cookies will keep for several weeks.

Where: *In Munich and Dresden,* Kreutzkamm, tel 49/89-993-5570, kreutzkamm.de; *in*

Baden-Baden, Café König, tel 49/7221-23573, chocolatier.de/kh_koenig.php; *in Berlin,* Café Buchwald, tel 49/30-391-5931, konditorei-buchwald.de; Bäckerei & Konditorei Siebert, tel 49/30-445-7576; *in Vienna,* Demel, tel 43/1-535-17-17-0, demel.at; *in Chicago,* Lutz Café and Pastry Shop, tel 877-350-7785, chicago-bakery .com; *in Santa Monica, Venice, and Culver City/ Mar Vista, CA,* Röckenwagner, rockenwagner .com. **MAIL ORDER:** During the Christmas season, shop.rockenwagner.com. **FURTHER INFORMATION AND RECIPES:** *Visions of Sugarplums* by Mimi Sheraton (1969); *The 20 Best German Christmas Cookies* by Liane Guterhof (2013).

—||||||||||||||||||||||||||||||||||||—

THE BEST OF THE WURST

Wursts to Walk With

German, Austrian

An expected but still welcome perk of a visit to Germany or Austria is the variety of luscious street wursts of all kinds that abound throughout the cities almost always served alongside—but not *in*—various sorts of bread. Suitable garnishes such as sauerkraut (see page 308), braised red cabbage, and potato salad (see page 628) will be on offer, along with smooth and hot or grainy and sweet mustard. The array of ingredients may be a bit hard for the novice to juggle, but new challenges are one reward of travel.

The Bavarian city of Munich weighs in with delectable walk-away wursts sold at many street stands, most temptingly in the Viktualienmarkt, the huge, abundant outdoor food market just a few squares away from the landmark Frauenkirche cathedral with its romantic glockenspiel. Wurst action begins before breakfast when the market opens, and continues until mid-afternoon. The Munich morning ritual for *frühstück*—fork breakfast—is the delicate, steamed veal and pork *weisswurst,* a snowy sustainer to be eaten out of hand, with sour rye *bauembrot* on the side and Bavaria's typical sweet-and-sour mustard. (Local protocol dictates that eating *weisswurst* is never acceptable after 11 a.m., but it seems to be available a lot later than that.) Heartier choices are grilled, gray pork bratwurst nestled against sautéed onions or sweet-and-sour red cabbage; and Hungarian-style Debreziner, named for the Hungarian city of Debrecen, famous for the hot paprika that flavors and colors this wurst. Kielbasa-style *polnischer*—coarse, peppery, and heady with garlic—is sliced in big hot chunks, and goes especially well with vinegary potato salad. If you have no plans for the rest of the day, try Munich's traditional, sleep-inducing *weissbier,* a powerful, sunny brew brightened with a slice of fresh lemon. If not that, then malty, *dunkel* (dark) Löwenbräu *en fass*—on tap.

For a late-night supper after a round of heavy drinking, Berlin streets and subway stands offer currywurst, an exotic combination of lightly smoked pork wiener and an improbable topping of curry-spiked tomato sauce. Ketchup sometimes substitutes for or is combined with tomato sauce, but the sauce alone is preferable. Currywurst is most traditionally served on a paper plate, cut into chunks to be pierced with a small skewer; it can now also be had in a bun, but bread muffles the full flavor and texture of meat and sauce. (Side note: Although Berlin is credited as the home of currywurst, and a museum there supports this view, an intriguing book, *The Invention of Curried Sausage,* insists it originated in Hamburg.)

The medieval city of Nuremberg, famous for its cathedral and its Christmas gift market—the Christkindlmarkt (see page 319) —is not the only place to get Nurnberger bratwurst, but it's the obvious choice. There, the finger-slim mini-bratwursts of pork, grilled on skewers or wire racks over a wood fire, are served with sauerkraut and potato salad; they may also come with *erbsenpuree*, a soft jade puree of green split peas topped with sautéed onions. Whether at indoor tables or from stands, customers order the bratwurst by the pair, six being the local minimum. Bavarian mustard and *mauerlöwerlei*—bricklayer's rolls—are standards with these charred, woodsy treats.

Vienna's morning food market, aptly named the Naschmarkt—noshing market—displays a similar panoply of wurst temptations as Munich's.

WHERE: *In Munich,* Viktualienmarkt, every day except Sunday, tel 49/89-8906-8205, viktualienmarkt.de; Zum Franziskaner, tel 49/89-231-8120, zum-franziskaner.de; *in Berlin,* for currywurst, Bier's Kudamm 195, tel 49/30-881-8942; Curry 36 at the Zoo station, tel 49/30-3199-2922, curry36.de; Konnopke's Imbiss, tel 49/30-442-7765, konnopke-imbiss.de; *in Vienna,* Naschmarkt, naschmarkt-vienna.com; *in New York,* The Standard's Biergarten, tel 212-645-4100, standardhotels.com/high-line/food-drink/biergarten; *in Milwaukee,* Usinger's, tel 800-558-9998, usinger.com. **RETAIL AND MAIL ORDER:** *In New York,* Schaller and Weber, tel 212-879-3047, schallerweber.com. **FURTHER INFORMATION:** *The Invention of Curried Sausage* by Uwe Timm, translated by Leila Vennewitz (1995). **TIP:** At the German Currywurst Museum in Berlin, you can learn all about the snack as well as sample it; tel 49/30-8871-8647, currywurstmuseum.de.

—|||||||||||||||||||||||||||||||||||—

STEAK WITH ALL THE TRIMMINGS

Zwiebelrostbraten

German, Austrian

The best Austro-German-Tyrolean hybrid on the market may be *zwiebel-rostbraten*—not a car but an arguably equally powerful pan-seared rib steak topped with a mound of fine, golden, and glassily crisp onion filaments.

Some may argue that the correct cut for this specialty is the sirloin or strip steak, but true *feinschmeckers* know that the rib produces the juiciest, beefiest contrast to the burnished sweetness of the onions.

The one- to one-and-a-half-inch-thick steak is traditionally pan-seared in lard, but these days vegetable oil is substituted in the more effete places. The thinly slivered onions, very lightly floured, are turned into the pan when the steak has been removed. Once crisp and golden, the onions are set aside and a little pan sauce is created: The remaining lard is poured off and a bit of butter and a splash of beef stock are swirled into the pan to be spooned over the steak before it is crowned with the onions. Creamy potatoes, either scalloped or pureed, and a lettuce or watercress salad are the finishing touches.

There are other *rostbraten,* although none as stunning as this onion-topped favorite. *Esterházy rostbraten* is Hungarian in feel, with its sauce of chopped onions, carrots, and celery, lightly browned and seasoned with paprika, vinegar, and sour cream. *Schwäbischer,* or Swabian, *rostbraten* is a club steak pounded thin, fried in butter, and garnished with browned onions, bacon-topped sauerkraut, tiny fried bratwursts, and spätzle (see page 312). With all of those garnishes, who needs the steak?

WHERE: *In Vienna,* Beim Novak, tel 43/1-523-3244, beimnovak.at; *in Salzburg,* Goldener Hirsch, tel 43/662-80-84-861, goldenerhirsch .com; *in Washington, DC,* Café Berlin, tel 202-543-7656, cafeberlindc.com; *in Kansas City, MO,* Grünauer, tel 816-283-3234, grunauerkc .com. **FURTHER INFORMATION AND RECIPES:** *The Cuisines of Germany* by Horst Scharfenberg (1989); foodnetwork.com (search zwiebelrost-braten puck).

THE TASTE OF CHRISTMAS, FOR SALE

Christkindlmarkt

Austrian, German, Northern European

In what's officially become a global phenomenon, the European Christmas shopping season begins on the first Sunday of Advent, often coinciding with our Thanksgiving Day weekend. That's the day when Christkindlmarkts, or Christ Child markets, open in Germany, Austria, parts of Switzerland, and even in the French province of Alsace. These paroxysms of holiday glitter, gifts, and foods sparkle and tempt shoppers in just about every town until a trumpet sounds at 1 p.m. on December 24.

While Nuremberg's is the largest and Salzburg's possibly the most charming, the oldest and one of the most colorful of these markets is in Munich, where the custom originated more than six hundred years ago. Open from mid-morning onward, these markets take on a special magic

Once called "Nicholaus Markets," the fairs began in the 1300s.

at night, when their glowing garlands of colored lights mark the way through wintry frost. Open stalls trimmed with green boughs and pine wreaths offer all sorts of gifts: toys, handcrafted housewares, sweaters, mittens, jewelry, wood carvings, and *krippen,* or nativity scene crèches.

A joy for pleasure-seekers of all sorts, Christkindlmarkts are especially enticing to food lovers. Drawn by the aroma of the clove- and cinnamon-scented mulled wine *glühwein,* they discover a dazzling array of *weihnachtsgebäck* or Christmas cookies (see page 315); wursts and *leberkäse* (see page 301); candies of nuts and honey, rum, and chocolate; and cherry- and citron-studded marzipan baked in heart and floral shapes (see page 304).

Not all of the food products are meant to be eaten. In the decorative realm are whole, dried spices wired into small kitchen wreaths or piled into decorated sachets. *Zwetschgen menschen* (prune people) are small figures of men and women formed of wired prunes and nuts, usually signifying two storybook Christmas characters: Krampus, who brings coal to bad children, and

Nicolo, who has lovely things for good children. Best to get several of each for good measure.

WHERE: In Munich, Nuremberg, Vienna, Salzburg, and almost all towns and cities in Germany, Austria, Alsace, and the German regions of Switzerland. **FURTHER INFORMATION:** germanfoodguide.com (search christmas markets); germanculture.com.ua (search christkindlmarkt); nytimes.com (search the marzipan heart of munich by mimi sheraton).

⊢||||||||||||||||||||||||||||||⊣

FILL UP YOUR LOYALTY CARDS

Coffee in Vienna

Austrian

No one who hasn't spent at least a week cultivating a serious caffeine high in Vienna can claim true coffee connoisseurship—not just for having sampled the various luscious presentations of the rich, soul-satisfying drink, but also for having experienced the culture of the city's storied coffeehouses.

Neither the black espresso of Italy nor the sugary, thick brew of the Middle East, Viennese coffee is at once more complex and more mellow, with a caramelized finish and a mocha patina similar to that preferred in Germany, Switzerland, Denmark, and Sweden. Viennese importers pay high prices for the world's best beans, and the medium-dark roast they favor reveals a host of subtle flavors. By contrast, the very dark roasts known as "French," "espresso," or "West Coast" obscure the innate character of the beans, heightening acidity and rendering bean quality less important, which is why professional coffee tasters rely on a uniform degree of roasting that leaves beans a cinnamon-cocoa color.

Coffee first came to Europe through Vienna, a result of the defeat of the Turks by the Poles in 1683. The armies of the victorious Polish king, John Sobieski, who led the Austrian-Hapsburg troops, noticed the Turks brewing up something special while they were camped outside Vienna. Taking a sack of the beans that were left behind when the Turks fled, they brewed them up—and the rest is delectable history.

One of the best examples of Viennese-style coffee is produced by Julius Meinl, a company that began in 1862 as a small shop selling pre-roasted beans, a convenient innovation at the time; previously, green beans had to be roasted at home. These days the company uses Arabica beans grown in the highlands of South America, Ethiopia, India, and New Guinea; roasted medium-dark; and sealed in airtight packages.

To fully understand Viennese coffee drink menus, a grasp of the word *schlagobers* is in order—*schlag* for cream and *ober* meaning over, sometimes adding up to an indulgent topping of whipped cream. Among the most seductive offerings are the *einspanner* (literally, a one-horse coach) and the *fiaker* (a two-horse coach). The *fiaker* comes as a tall, footed glass of coffee with hot milk. The *einspanner* adds a snowfall of whipped cream, offering a titillating contrast of cold and hot. Most sublime, if perhaps not the best idea for breakfast, is a shot of brandy added to the *einspanner.*

A *kapuziner* is a small cup of dark coffee with a dollop of whipped cream. *Kaisermelange* includes milk and a beaten egg yolk as a morning-after cure. A *melange* combines espresso, a froth of milk, and a dusting of cinnamon or cocoa, much like a cappuccino. And perhaps the ultimate is the *Wiencaffe,* or *Eiskaffe,* which is hot coffee in a glass with a scoop of vanilla ice cream and a dome of schlagobers. No harm in adding a splash of rum, Cognac, or coffee liqueur to the concoction.

As for the choice of cafés, Café Hawelka has offered a late-night student scene since 1938; the elegant Café Landtmann has been a mid-morning choice for solid burghers gathering to read newspapers in its elegant, clublike setting since 1873; and the spare Café Central, which appeals most to fans of its Jugendstil décor, has stood the test of time since 1860.

WHERE: *In Vienna*, Café Hawelka, tel 43/1-5128230, hawelka.at; Café Landtmann, tel 43/1-24-100-100, landtmann.at; Café Central, tel 43/1-533-37-63, palaisevents.at/cafecentral; *in New York*, Café Sabarsky and Café Fledermaus in Neue Galerie, neuegalerie.org (click Cafés); *in Chicago*, Julius Meinl Coffee Houses, northamerica.meinl.com. **MAIL ORDER:** Julius Meinl coffees, meinl.com. **FURTHER INFORMATION:** *Neue Cuisine: The Elegant Tastes of Vienna* by Kurt Gutenbrunner (2011).

A DELICIOUS CLOUD OF SCHLAG

Whipped Cream

I f the Austro-German term *schlag* doesn't sound romantic enough, try calling whipped cream by its French name, *crème Chantilly*. Or say it in Italian: *panna montata*, and lots of it, please!

Usually appearing as a cool and creamy grace note atop desserts, whipped cream should be allowed to shine on its own. Why not? Imagine the sublime indulgence of sitting down where no one can see you and spooning your way through a bowlful, the size depending on your capacity and your conscience . . . the vaguely obscene bliss of slowly savoring its thickly whipped, gently sweet creamy clouds perhaps enhanced with just a virtuous whiff of vanilla and, for textural contrast, dry, nut-filled biscotti.

That most perfect of whipped creams starts with the very heaviest, butterfat-rich sweet cream you can find, sometimes labeled "whipping cream." Obviously the cream should be as fresh as possible, so search the refrigerator case for a container marked with the latest expiration date. (Quite often in supermarkets,

the containers in the front of the case, even if not expired, can be as much as a week older than those loaded later in back, a fact worth remembering with all dairy products, eggs included.)

The trick to whipping is to achieve the largest, airiest peaks before the cream separates and solidifies into butter. To avoid that, the cream and all whipping utensils should be chilled in the refrigerator until quite cold. The cream should also be whipped patiently; the slower the whipping process, the longer the finished cream will hold its air. Using the whisk attachment on a handheld electric mixer, begin on low speed, increasing the speed as the cream foams. Use one of the faster speeds only when the end is in sight. If whipped cream is to be held longer than two hours before being served, it's a good idea to gradually beat in some confectioners' sugar; the cornstarch it contains will hold the cream intact and prevent leakage. For sweetening alone, fine granulated sugar is best, as it dissolves quickly in the cold cream.

Vanilla lends a lovely airy note to whipped cream and can be added in the form of liquid extract or as scrapings from a fresh bean. For real subtlety, try vanilla-flavored sugar: Bury a strip of split vanilla bean in a tightly closed jar of granulated or confectioners' sugar. Just a week or so does the trick, and the perfumed sweetener will be at the ready for months.

So much for the sweet side of whipped cream. Far less known or appreciated in our country is salted whipped cream, a finishing touch much loved in Northern Europe. With salt added just as the creamy foam begins to thicken, the unsweetened cream becomes an opulent garnish to hot and cold soups, including seafood bisques and jade-green soups made with asparagus, spinach, or spring-green peas. Salt and freshly grated horseradish can be folded into whipped cream to adorn poached Rhine salmon, blue-cooked trout (see page 141), many hot-meat dishes such as boiled beef, and, in Denmark, frozen corned duckling (see page 355). Gently beaten into lemony and eggy mayonnaises or hollandaise sauces, salted whipped cream transforms these into the classic sauce *mousseline,* cold or hot.

WHERE: *In* Vienna, Demel, tel 43/1-535-17-17-0, demel.at; Café Sacher, tel 43/1-514-560, sacher.com. **FURTHER INFORMATION AND RECIPES:** *Joy of Cooking* by Irma S. Rombauer, Marion Rombauer Becker, and Ethan Becker (2006); joyofbaking.com (search whipped cream frosting); saveur.com (search flavored whipped creams). **SEE ALSO:** Charlotte Russe, page 541; Chocolate Cream Pie, page 544; Coffee in Vienna, page 320; Krämmerhüse med Flødesküm, page 354; Pavlova, page 902).

┤|||||||||||||||||||||||||||||├

A GIFT FROM A FOOLISH KING

Kaiserschmarren

Austrian, German

Credit Hapsburg pastry chefs with the invention of this light, eggy, scrappy pancake redolent of brandy and cinnamon sugar. Generally served as a dessert, it can also be eaten as a simple lunch or supper.

Typically a dessert, it also doubles as a meal.

Created to delight an emperor and appeal to his vanity, Kaiser Franz Joseph I's *schmarren* —"nonsense"—can be realized in either of two ways. The grander version begins as an airy baked soufflé, vanilla-scented and rich with cream. The second and more typical version is made up of many thin crêpes, melded together and flipped to become lacy golden brown on both sides. Just before being served, the soufflé or crêpes are torn into jagged 1- to 2-inch pieces with two forks and tossed in a skillet with hot melted butter, a handful of brandy-soaked dark raisins or currants, and a liberal shower of cinnamon sugar. The sugar melts and caramelizes, coating the golden pieces with a luscious glaze, and chopped walnuts add an optional but toothsome crunch. Each hot, aromatic portion gets a final snowfall of confectioners' sugar.

WHERE: *In Salzburg*, Goldener Hirsch Restaurant, tel 43/662-80-84-861, goldenerhirsch .com; *in Vienna*, Hotel Sacher, tel 43/1-514-560, sacher.com; Meierei im Stadtpark, 43/1-713-3168-10, steirereck.at; *in New York*, Wallsé, tel 212-352-2300, kg-ny.com/wallse; *in Queens*, Zumstammtisch, tel 718-386-3014, zumstammtisch .com; *in San Francisco*, Suppenküche, tel 415-252-9289, suppenkuche.com. **FURTHER INFORMA-TION AND RECIPES:** *Neue Cuisine: The Elegant Tastes of Vienna* by Kurt Gutenbrunner (2011); wolfgangpuck.com (click Recipes, then search kaiserschmarren); allrecipes.com (search kaiserschmarrn).

WELL OILED IN STYRIA

Kürbiskernöl

Pumpkin Seed Oil

Austrian, Styrian

With a glow that suggests liquid amethysts and a flavor at once nutty and pungent, pumpkin seed oil—a specialty of Austria's region of Styria—is gaining wide popularity for the best of reasons. Taken to the old world from the new by Christopher Columbus, the pumpkin, with its orange flesh, provides welcome inspiration for pies, chips, breads, soups, and puddings of all kinds, but may find its most sophisticated culinary expression via its seeds. When pressed, the seeds of the so-called oil pumpkin variety (*Cucurbita pepo*) exude a thick, viscous, dark bronze-purple oil. The oil lends a warm nuttiness to many dishes, simultaneously tinting them with an inky sheen that may discourage the uninitiated.

The oil has anti-inflammatory properties.

Resembling honeydews, these greenish pumpkins are a particular specialty of the Styrian town of Graz (also celebrated as the birthplace of Arnold Schwarzenegger). There, nearly every home keeps a pumpkin patch, and nearly every table is graced with a bottle of the oil locally known as *kürbiskernöl*. The condiment is made quite simply, by roasting the seeds and then cold-pressing them to extract the oil.

Prized for its uniquely strong, robust, warm, and almost strawlike flavor, pumpkin seed oil has such a low burning point that it is rarely cooked. Instead, it is drizzled over all sorts of dishes, especially salads of greens or roasted potatoes, ladled into soups, and used as a dip for crusty breads. It lends an especially luxurious note to the traditional Styrian appetizer salad of raw beef and slivered onion as served at Steirereck and Beim Novak restaurants in Vienna.

As Mr. Schwarzenegger is no doubt already aware, pumpkin seed oil is also good for you—high in omega-3 fatty acids, vitamin E, and the phytosterols thought to help reduce cholesterol levels.

WHERE: *In Vienna,* beef salad at Restaurant Steirereck, tel 43/1-713-31-68, steirereck.at; Beim Novak, tel 43/1-523-3244, beimnovak.at; *across the U.S.,* Whole Foods Markets, wholefoodsmarket .com. **MAIL ORDER:** amazon.com (search styrian

pumpkinseed oil; chefs warehouse pumpkin seed oil). **FURTHER INFORMATION:** styriangold.com. **TIP:** Because of its very intense flavor, a little pumpkin seed oil goes a long way. Some chefs add a small amount as a flavor boost to another kind of oil, such as peanut or corn, that is better for frying. Pumpkin seed oil can be stored in the refrigerator for about nine months.

WHAT'S PLUMP AND ROUND AND FULL OF HOT AIR?

Nur Knödel

Austrian, German

Nur Knödel (*Only Dumplings*) is the title of a charming Austrian cookbook written in both English and German. As promised, it deals exclusively with a vast array of dumplings—a subject of wide culinary interest in its home country

as well as in Germany and Bohemia. The true dumplings common to these parts are filled with meat, cheese, or—for dessert —cooked prunes or apricots and are raised by being boiled or steamed, as opposed to filled dough-wrapped types like the Italian ravioli or even the German *maultaschen* (mouth pockets) that are boiled but do not rise. And if the category of true dumplings includes Jewish *knaidlach* (matzo balls) and Italian gnocchi, it's no accident, as both of these derive from the German word *knödel.*

The king of all dumplings may be the *leberknödel,* filled with pork or beef liver and often gracing clear and heady meat broths; the golf ball–size wonder is mildly seasoned with onion, marjoram, and grated lemon zest. *Fleischknödel* is a similar, if less refined and silky, choice made with beef, veal, and/or pork. *Markklösschen* are little juicy dumplings based on succulent veal bone marrow. *Mehlklösse* are flour dumplings raised with baking

powder and served atop stews and braised meats as sops for the gravy. *Griessklösschen* are the gently nutmeg-scented semolina dumplings that garnish broths or meats.

Bayrische Semmelknödel are Bavarian bread or, more literally, roll dumplings. They are big and spongy, enriched with bacon, onion, and parsley to go with meats and gravy.

Kartoffelklösse are potato dumplings. Made with raw or cooked potatoes, and savory with rendered goose or duck fat, they are topped with melted butter and toasted bread crumbs and served as a side dish.

Serviettenkloss, literally a napkin dumpling, is made with bread dough that is wrapped in a big cloth (napkin) and then hung over boiling water to steam into one huge globe. Once cooked, it is spoon-broken into portions that thirstily absorb rich gravies.

Last but not least are the sweet varieties that make it possible to subscribe to a dumpling-only philosophy and still enjoy dessert. Enter *zwetschgenknödel* or *marillenknödel*, made of potatoes or bread and filled with blue plums (the former) or apricots (the latter). They are served either sprinkled with cinnamon sugar or strewn with poppy seeds in melted butter. There is also *Topfenknödel*, a puffy quark or cottage cheese dumpling topped with melted butter and cinnamon sugar, or for variety, a little warm chocolate sauce. Dumplings forever!

FURTHER INFORMATION AND RECIPES: *Nur Knödel: The Ultimate Dumpling Book from Austria, Bavaria & Bohemia* by Franziska Helmreich and Anton Staudinger (1995); *The German Cookbook* by Mimi Sheraton (2014); *Neue Cuisine: The Elegant Tastes of Vienna* by Kurt Gutenbrunner (2011); *The Cuisines of Germany* by Horst Scharfenberg (1989); germanfoodguide.com (search dumplings); food.com (search topfenknodel).

THE DEFINITION OF TORTE

Pischinger Torte

Austrian

In technical baking terms, a true torte includes no flour (ground nuts, blanched or not, usually substitute), shortening (egg yolks being the sole source of fat), or chemical leavening (beaten egg whites do the light lifting). But in the panoply of German-Austrian-Hungarian pastries, *torte* is the word used for many of the cakes you'll find beckoning from the shelves of pastry shops, particularly if the cakes are round.

Though the Sachertorte—with light, deeply chocolate layers, apricot jam lining, and dark chocolate icing—and the Dobosctorte, sponge cake layered with buttercream and topped with caramel, are the most famous of the lot, the Pischinger torte may be the very best: a delicious adventure with a glossy chocolate icing covering eight, ten, or twelve paper-thin crunchy layers of the brown *gaufrette* wafers known as *Karlsbader oblaten*. These "leaves" are sandwiched together with thin layers of smooth chocolate buttercream, perhaps seasoned with finely ground hazelnuts and rum. (Milk chocolate is most traditional, but dark bittersweet chocolate lends a richer and more sophisticated effect.)

The oblaten on which the torte is based are the specialty of the spa town formerly called Karlsbad and now returned to the Czech Republic as Karlovy Vary. On weekends and holidays, the town's parks host hordes of pedestrians holding the spouts of elongated teapots up to their lips as they drink in the famed sulfurous spring waters that make the place smell like the world capital of rotten eggs. Odd that it should also be famous for the sweet, toasty oblaten sold in big, stiff, round packages, or in prepared wedges for home pastry cooks. Those who wish to prepare their own Pischinger tortes buy the fragile wafers plain, taking care not to crack them in handling.

WHERE: *In Vienna,* Demel, tel 43/1-535-17-17-0, demel.at; *in Munich and Dresden,* Kreutzkamm, tel 49/89-993-5570, kreutzkamm .de. **MAIL ORDER:** For oblaten wafers, austrian shop.com (search oblaten). **FURTHER INFORMATION AND RECIPES:** *The Cooking of Vienna's Empire* by Joseph Wechsberg (1968); *Gourmet's Old Vienna Cookbook* by Lillian Langseth-Christensen (1959); recipelink.com (search pischinger torte); hungrybrowser.com (search pischinger torte); pischinger.at.

———————|||||||||||||||||||||||||||||||||||||—————————

BAROQUE IS AS BAROQUE DOES

Salzburger Nockerln

Austrian, German

I n a dish that's as baroque as the romantic Austrian city for which it is named, snowy islands of meringues are reimagined as the hot, sweet, and airy dumplings called *nockerln*. Soufflés really, they are baked in milk and finished with a vanilla sauce or vanilla sugar.

The birthplace of Wolfgang Amadeus Mozart, Salzburg is a romantically pastel city with antique proportions, stunningly florid churches, and a nonstop program of operas, symphonies, festivals, and chamber music. It seems exactly the right setting for this luscious

Sugar-dusted nockerln resemble snow-capped peaks.

dessert. No place in that city is more adept at its execution than the justly famous old Hotel Goldener Hirsch, which has been in operation since 1407. Along with *kaiserschmarren* (see page 322), *apfel pfannkuchen* (see page 276), and soufflés, this lavishly sweet ending is classified in Austria and Germany as *mehlspeisen*— literally, flour food, but designating the category of desserts that are not cakes. For most of us, it need be classified only as heavenly.

WHERE: *In Salzburg,* Goldener Hirsch Restaurant, tel 43/662-80-84-861, goldenerhirsch .com; *in New York,* Wallsé, tel 212-352-2300, kg-ny.com/wallse; *in Kansas City, MO,* Grünauer, tel 816-283-3234, grunauerkc.com. **FURTHER INFORMATION AND RECIPES:** *Gourmet's Old Vienna Cookbook* by Lillian Langseth-Christensen (1959); *Neue Cuisine: The Elegant Tastes of Vienna* by Kurt Gutenbrunner (2011); food network.com (search salzburger nockerln); epicurious.com (search salzburger nockerl).

———————|||||||||||||||||||||||||||||||||||||—————————

THE KINDEST CUTLETS

Schnitzel, Wiener, et al

Austrian, German

N o one seems to be lukewarm about Wiener schnitzel. Some regard it as a tasteless, bland cliché, while ardent connoisseurs entirely disagree. Those who adore it study details such as the type of meat and how it was cut and pounded;

the proper thickness; the correct ingredients for breading; and the right oil or fat in which to fry it. Satisfying, savory, and subtle in its simplicity, schnitzel remains de rigueur on almost any traditional Austrian or German menu. Because it is quick to prepare and comforting to eat, it is also a favorite of home cooks.

The dish goes by many names internationally, from the American breaded veal cutlet to the French *côtelette de veau Viennoise* to the Italian *cotoletta de vitello Milanese*. But arguments as to its origin tend to be restricted to Austrians and Italians, the latter claiming to have invented their

The entrance of the Figlmüller restaurant in Vienna, Austria

version in the twelfth century, after which it was adopted by the ruling Hapsburgs. There *are* differences between the two, mostly as concerns the style of breading. Italians like it very thin, and smoothly, tightly veneered to the meat's surface. Although the Italians prepare it with *scalloppine*, the real McCoy is a pounded rib chop with a piece of bone left in. Austrians and Germans always use scalloppine, and prefer a fluffy breading that ruffles up over the meat.

When the name Wiener schnitzel is used in Austria, law dictates that the meat must be veal, but pork is far more flavorful and juicy, and less expensive. In fact, the best schnitzel in the world, and certainly the largest, may be the huge slab of breaded pork that overhangs its plate at Figlmüller in Vienna, where it is served with the traditional cucumber salad and warm potato salad.

As with all simple dishes, every detail matters. So that the meat for schnitzel will not come apart when pounded, it should be cut from the leg, slightly on the diagonal. It must be salted and peppered, dipped into flour, coated in beaten egg, and then with fresh, dry, fine bread crumbs (never the preseasoned packaged travesties), after which it should rest at room temperature for about twenty minutes. The schnitzel should be fried in unsalted butter with a few drops of mild salad oil—corn or sunflower—to keep the butter from blackening. Fried to a bright golden brown

without any hint of black, it must be served at once, ideally with a wedge of lemon. Cold leftover schnitzel makes a delicious sandwich on toast, especially as a hair-of-the-dog breakfast.

Variations on the plain schnitzel include Holsteiner schnitzel—topped with a fried egg, capers, and anchovy fillets; cheese schnitzel, with grated Parmesan mixed with the bread crumbs; and *natur* schnitzel, which is dusted only with flour and topped with a pan gravy. Hunter's schnitzel—*jägerschnitzel*—gets a topping of vegetables sautéed in the same frying pan, whereas cream or paprika schnitzel is rosy with a paprika-flavored cream sauce. Chicken or turkey schnitzels? The less said about those typically bland, dry impostors, the better.

WHERE: *In Vienna,* Figlmüller, tel 43/1-512-6177, figlmueller.at; Schweizerhaus, tel 43/1-72-80-1520, schweizerhaus.at; *in New York,* Wallsé, tel 212-352-2300, kg-ny.com/wallse; *in Kansas City, MO,* Grünauer, tel 816-283-3234, grunauerkc.com; *in Houston,* Charivari, tel 713-521-7231, charivarirest.com; *in Palm Springs, CA,* Johannes, tel 760-778-0017, johannesrestaurants.com. **FURTHER INFORMATION AND RECIPES:** *Neue Cuisine: The Elegant Tastes of Vienna* by Kurt Gutenbrunner (2011); *Lüchow's German Cookbook* by Jan Mitchell (1996); germanfoodguide.com (search schnitzel); saveur.com (search schnitzel a la holstein; wiener schnitzel).

‖‖‖‖‖‖‖‖‖‖‖‖‖‖‖‖‖‖‖

A MOUTHFUL, IN MORE WAYS THAN ONE

Schokoladen Topfenpalatschinken

Cheese-Filled Crêpes in Chocolate Sauce

Austrian, German

A warm, silky, vanilla-scented chocolate sauce glosses hot-baked, tender crêpes enveloping a creamy cheese filling. Behold the *schokoladen topfenpalatschinken,* best accompanied by either a cup of strong mocha coffee or a glass of chilled Champagne. Although it is found in other parts of Austria as well as in Germany and the United States, this luscious mouthful is a traditional post-concert late-night treat in Vienna's old-style supper clubs and restaurants.

The base of the dessert is the most gossamer version of a classic crêpe: an airy mix of flour, sugar, cream, milk, and eggs, gently gilded in butter until both sides achieve a pale golden, lacy pattern. *Topfen*—fine-grained pot cheese—is rubbed through a sieve and then folded into sour cream that has been whipped until frothy, joined by egg yolk, sugar, and, at the cook's pleasure, raisins, chopped nuts, or nothing but grated lemon zest or cinnamon. Filled with this enhanced cheese mixture, the crêpes—*palatschinken*—are rolled and placed side-by-side in a buttered dish that goes into a hot oven for about ten minutes, or until the filling melts to a satiny richness. Once plated, the hot crêpes are sauced with a warm, bittersweet, vanilla-accented chocolate custard. In simpler versions, the cheese-filled crêpes may be dressed only with a spritz of lemon and a sprinkling of sugar, or garnished with fruit compote, apricots (*marillen*) being a special favorite.

The versatile *palatschinken* are almost as delectable in savory guises, made without sugar and paired with creamed fillings of spinach, mushrooms, and cooked or diced chicken, alone or in combination. Brushed with melted butter and a light sprinkling of finely grated Parmesan or Switzerland's Sap Sago cheese, they are briefly baked to succulent perfection.

WHERE: *In Vienna,* Drei Husaren, tel 43/1-512-1092; *in New York,* Blaue Gans, tel 212-571-8880, kg-ny.com/blaue-gans; *in Kansas City, MO,* Grünauer, tel 816-283-3234, grunauerkc.com. **FURTHER INFORMATION AND RECIPES:** *The German Cookbook* by Mimi Sheraton (2014).

‖‖‖‖‖‖‖‖‖‖‖‖‖‖‖‖‖‖‖

THE BIG BEEF IN AUSTRIA

Tafelspitz

Austrian

While outsiders consider Wiener schnitzel to be Austria's national dish, inside the country, and especially in Vienna, that honor goes to the supple boiled beef called *tafelspitz.* It was the preferred lunch of the emperor Franz Joseph I, and the populace apparently followed suit.

The name means "table point," a cut of steer taken from a point just below the sirloin. Some opt for top round or chuck, and there the arguments begin. The food writer and journalist Joseph Wechsberg claimed that no guest who simply asked for boiled beef could be taken seriously in pre–World War II Vienna. At the then-famous restaurant Meissl & Schadn, one had to name the particular cut desired—and there were twenty-four to choose from. The juiciest, most unctuously rich is known as *beinfleisch*, or bone flesh, coming from the leg.

Whatever the cut—and it must be large—it is slowly simmered with fragrant pot vegetables like carrots, leeks, parsnips, the parsley root called *petrouchka*, onions, celery root, and in some instances an unpeeled clove of garlic. Some chicken parts and a marrow bone may join the mix. Constant skimming ensures that the broth emerges as a sparkling clear and heady consommé that will be the meal's only first course, served steaming hot in bouillon cups.

The dewily moist, tender, and savory beef is thinly sliced and sprinkled with gritty coarse salt, and placed alongside a few boiled potatoes and perhaps some carrots. Other sides include leeks or small white onions that were freshly cooked in a little of the broth; or alternatively, just the potatoes and some ruby pickled beets. Pungent grated horseradish, sometimes folded into whipped cream with grated apples or chives, is a luxurious sauce that brings out the pristine meat flavor; those with more rugged palates opt for the simplest condiment of grated horseradish in vinegar.

Leftovers, if any, go into piquant cold salads—usually as an appetizer with sprightly additions of chives, capers, gherkins, oil, and vinegar.

WHERE: *In Vienna,* Rote Bar at Hotel Sacher, tel 43/1-5145-6841, sacher.com; Beim Novak, tel 43/1-523-3244, beimnovak.at; *in New York,* Wallsé, tel 212-352-2300, kg-ny.com/wallse; *in Kansas City, MO,* Grünauer, tel 816-283-3234, grunauerkc.com. **FURTHER INFORMATION AND RECIPES:** *The Cooking of Vienna's Empire* by Joseph Wechsberg (1968); *Lüchow's German Cookbook* by Jan Mitchell (1996); nytimes.com (search tafelspitz gutenbrunner).

UN-AMERICAN FRIED CHICKEN

Wiener Backhendl

Austrian

Throughout Austria and Bavaria, local fast-food chains like Wienerwald offered this beloved, thin-crusted, crunchy fried chicken long before the advent of Colonel Sanders. In fact, when Kentucky Fried Chicken outposts opened in those areas, the colonel's recipe had to be adjusted to appeal to more sophisticated local palates.

The story begins with chickens that are ideally super-fresh, organic fryers or broilers, absolutely no larger than two pounds each. Most traditionally, they are cut into quarters, but for convenience's sake they are often cut into eighths, a practice that results in a less felicitous presentation and a higher ratio of breading to meat. The room-temperature cuts are given a light bath in sunny lemon juice and then patted dry, sprinkled with salt, and given successive dippings in flour and beaten egg and then the lightest coating of very fine, sieved bread crumbs. Then they are set on racks to dry for about fifteen minutes.

Next, they are fried in a deep iron skillet, with either lard (for true flavor) or a more healthful version of shortening such as vegetable oil, although it will not achieve the desired degree of crispness. When all of the pieces are golden brown and cooked through, they are doused with melted butter, set on racks in baking pans, and placed in a low (200°F) oven for fifteen minutes or less. The unsalted butter imparts a fresh sweetness as the breading benefits from a final crisping.

Lemon wedges, sprigs of fried curly parsley, cucumbers or green salad in a light sour cream dressing, and boiled new potatoes are the go-withs. With a dish so irresistible, one chicken is one portion, and a cool, fruity white wine is a better accompaniment than beer. Iced tea or cola need not apply.

Where: *In New York,* Blaue Gans, tel 212-571-8880, kg-ny.com/blaue-gans; *in Kansas City, MO,* Grünauer, tel 816-283-3234, grunauerkc .com. **Further information and recipes:** *Gourmet's Old Vienna Cookbook* by Lillian Langseth-Christensen (1959); *Lüchow's German Cookbook* by Jan Mitchell (1996); wein.info (search backhendl fried breaded chicken); bigoven.com (search wiener backhendl viennese fried chicken).

AIRING YOUR BEEF

Bündnerfleisch

Swiss

Whether as *bündnerfleisch* or *bindenfleisch* in German, or *viande des grisons* in French, this supple and silky mahogany-red dried beef is among the world's most highly prized cured meats. A product of the alpine area of eastern Switzerland known as the Grisons or Graubünden, the boneless top round cut of locally raised, naturally fed beef is brined in white wine with allspice, coriander, cloves, black pepper, and garlic. Hung out to dry for several winter months in the pure, icy mountain air, out of the sun's reach, its quintessentially beefy flavor intensifies as the moisture in the brick-shaped loaf evaporates.

The most purely Swiss among the country's many cured meat specialties—high-quality interpretations of the sausages and hams of its French, German, and Italian neighbors—bündnerfleisch is akin to the Italian dried beef *bresaola,* but with a more intense flavor and a firmer texture. Once cured, the lean, dark-red meat is sliced tissue thin. Seasoned with a few drops of red wine vinegar and a spoonful or two of olive oil and accompanied by a piece of *burebrot,* the region's sourdough country bread, it makes for an enticing appetizer or snack, especially when served with a glass of red wine. Alas, it is very difficult to find Swiss bündnerfleisch outside of its home

Fluffy bread topped with the famous air-dried beef and mushrooms

country, as very little is exported. The best substitutes are the Italian Parmacotto bresaola and Bernina bresaola from Uruguay.

Where: *In New York,* Mont Blanc, tel 212-582-9648, montblancrestaurant.com. **Retail and mail order:** *In New York and Chicago,* Eataly, eataly.com. **Mail order:** amazon.com (search bresaola bernina).

CANDY FOR ADULTS

Lindt Chocolate

Swiss

To the most obsessed chocolate lovers, bonbons filled with nuts, fruits, flavored creams, and what have you are mere novelties. For true, intense chocolate appreciation, nothing but plain, thin bars will do. Chipped-off chunks of heavy-duty bars from Callebaut (see page 144) and Valrhona may have their charms, but it is the flat, crackling thinness of Lindt's smartly wrapped bars that makes them so beloved.

Needless to say (one hopes), the only bars that matter are the dark chocolate, also known as bittersweet, varying in cocoa content and degree of bitterness. True chocolate fans shun puerile milk chocolate, a devilish invention of the Swiss confectioner Daniel Peter, whose savvy use of surplus milk in 1876 was quickly latched onto by the firm of Henri Nestlé.

The "intense dark" chocolates that Lindt & Sprüngli produce for their "Excellence" line allow for easy taste comparisons, with versions containing cocoa percentages of 70, 85, 90, and 99. The last two really separate the men from the boys and the women from the girls. Those who can tolerate the bitterness, also perceived as dryness on the tongue, will find reward in an afterhaze of exotically complex, velvety chocolate essence. Although Lindt also adds flavors to some of its bars (orange, mint, caramel, and so on), the only one worth sampling is spiked with sea salt that etches a delightful tingle into rich, warm chocolateness. Outside of the large, flat bars, Lindt's individual square wafers make lovely mini desserts when served alongside cups of espresso.

One delectable exception to the superiority of plain chocolate bars are Lindt's Bâtons. Filled with either pear brandy or the cherry-based kirsch, the little paper-wrapped cylindrical sticks have been produced by Lindt & Sprüngli's *maître chocolatiers* since 1931. The mystery is in the glassy, leak-proof edible lining between liquid and chocolate; it seems to hold forever—or for at least six months, if the candies are stored in a cool, dry place, such as the upper shelf of a refrigerator.

Somewhat confusingly for an alcohol-filled treat, the confection can also take the form of little dwarfs or Santas, or barrels and similar "toys." But the batons are no child's play—due to their alcohol content, the candies may not be sold in confectionery stores in the U.S. (And, alas, liquor stores don't seem to consider them worthwhile.) When they are brought into the country by savvy tourists, at customs their liquor content is subtracted from the quota allowed for import. Intrepid travelers will accept that restriction and stock up on boxes of the stuff.

Where: For Bâtons, Lindt & Sprüngli shops throughout Europe and especially in Switzerland; also at airport gift shops; for Excellence bars, many Lindt shops and food stores throughout the U.S. **Further information and mail order:** lindt.com. **Tip:** Thin chocolate tastes best when just slightly, snappingly cool (not frozen), and it takes on special sensual appeal when eaten outdoors on a winter day. Chocolate sandwiches were standard pick-me-ups on alpine ski slopes; to prepare one, place a slab of thin dark chocolate between two slices of sourdough rye and nibble away in fresh, cold, snowy air.

||||||||||||||||||||||||||||||||

Raclette, Fondue, and Beyond

Swiss

I f it sometimes seems as though the whole world—at least the American fast-food world—were covered with melted cheese, we can probably lay part of the blame on Johanna Spyri, author of the Swiss children's book *Heidi*. In the book, a fictional

goat-herding grandfather who lives high in the Swiss Alps restores the health of his city-weary granddaughter with suppers of melted goat's cheese and good crusty bread. And ever since its publication in 1880, imaginative children have begged their mothers for the same menu.

Before goat cheese saturated the supermarket aisles, many American mothers came as close as they could with grilled sandwiches of bright orange, processed American cheese. Not exactly what Grandfather had in mind.

Smooth, creamy, finely crafted cheese does lend itself to some delectable melting, delicious examples of which include pizza, the *croque monsieur* (see page 84), mozzarella in carrozza (see page 209), gratiné onion

Raclette trays with toppings

soup—and Heidi's meals as well: "The old man held a large piece of cheese on a long iron fork over the fire, turning it round and round till it was toasted a nice golden yellow on each side. . . ." The description reads like a recipe for raclette, the après-ski snack born in Switzerland but now a popular party dish even on flat land.

Although we refer to the cheese used in this dish as raclette, it is actually a quick-melting, mild-flavored gomser from Conches or Bagnes. Sliced into long cuts that may be held over a wood fire on long forks or melted in a special rack that stands over an electric grill, the softened cheese is scraped onto individual plates alongside tiny boiled new potatoes, pickled white onions, and dark green gherkins. (It is the scraping, *racler*, in French, that gives the cheese, and the dish, its name.) For variety, the raclette is sometimes scraped onto an opened, hot baked potato.

For another variation on the theme, a flameproof earthenware casserole (*caquelon*) full of melted Swiss fondue makes for party merriment and good eating, too. Varying by region, fondue Neuchatel starts with Gruyère and Emmental cheese, while fondue in Fribourg is heady with ripe vacherin; garlic scents the fondue of the Vandois. To all, kirsch brandy, white wine, and touches of nutmeg add subtle depths of flavor. (As guests holding long-handled fondue forks dip bread into the hot cheese, they try not to lose the bread in the swirling, lest they have to buy the next round of drinks.)

A final melted cheese classic begging for adoption beyond its native country is the voluptuously rich soup, Urner Chäässuppä of William Tell's hometown, Altdorf, in the Uri canton. Caraway seeds lend exotic zest to a creamy froth of milk, butter, and grated Emmental cheese, accented with hints of nutmeg, black pepper, and garlic, for a soup that is as restorative for breakfast as it is for a winter supper.

Where: *In New York,* Mont Blanc, tel 212-582-9648, montblancrestaurant.com; *in Foster City, CA,* Chalet Ticino, tel 650-571-0507, chaletticino.com. **Retail and mail order:** *In New York,* Murray's Cheese, tel 888-692-4339, murrays cheese.com; Fairway, at multiple locations, fair waymarket.com; *across the U.S.,* for fondue and raclette grills, Sur La Table, tel 800-243-0852, surlatable.com. **Further information and recipes:** *Swiss Cooking* by Anne Mason (1984); *Bouchon* by Thomas Keller (2004); justhungry.com (search proper swiss cheese fondue); epicurious .com (search raclette cheese toast).

NO PROBLEM WITH THIS HOT POTATO

Rösti

Swiss

One of Switzerland's simplest dishes, the golden-crisp potato pancake known as *rösti* is also among its most justly famous. Buttery and fragrant, with a crackling crust covering soft ribbons of potato, it's a terrific accompaniment to roasted meat and poultry dishes, among them such classic Swiss specialties as Zurich's *leber-spiesschen* (bacon- and sage-wrapped calves' livers grilled on skewers) or the ubiquitous *émincé de veau*. To some serious eaters, the latter seems an insipid mass of veal scraps in sauce, but even for naysayers it may be saved by bites of the accompanying fried potato pancake. Of course, with a salad and perhaps a piece of a soft, ripe cheese, rösti makes a main course all by itself.

The best potatoes for rösti are dry, starchy russets or baking potatoes. Parboiled for about ten minutes, then peeled and chilled for an hour or two, they are grated into long julienne strips on the coarse side of a four-sided box grater. Tossed with salt, the potatoes are formed into a single, plate-size pancake that is turned into a frying pan bubbling with butter, vegetable oil, and perhaps a little rendered bacon fat for extra flavor. Once fried on both sides to a golden-brown crisp, the rösti must be cut in wedges and served at once.

Untraditional but delicious additions to the grated potatoes include minced herbs or flecks of scallion—even jalapeños, for a bit of fusion and heat. Bits of ham and grated Gruyère or Emmental cheese are other candidates for inclusion. When using cheese, the pancake would be baked rather than fried, and flipped when the top has browned.

Where: *In Zurich,* Kronenhalle, tel 41/44-262-9900, kronenhalle.ch; *in Geneva,* Café du Bourg-de-Four, tel 41/22-311-9076, cafedubourgdefour .ch; *in Bern,* Restaurant Anker Bern, tel 41/31-311-1113, roesti.ch/en; *in New York,* Trestle on Tenth, tel 212-645-5659, trestleontenth.com; *in Mahopac, NY,* Dish, tel 845-621-3474, dishmahopac.com; *in Foster City, CA,* Chalet Ticino, tel 650-571-0507, chaletticino.com. **Further information and recipes:** epicurious.com (search roestis); saveur .com (search rosti).

Schenkele, or Cuisses des Dames

Ladies' Thighs Cookies

Swiss

L ike all the northern European countries, Switzerland churns out a dazzling panoply of Christmas cakes, breads, and especially cookies. But the suggestive favorites known as *schenkele* to the German-speaking Swiss and *cuisses des dames*

in French are more unusual than most. Fried rather than baked, crunchy with chopped walnuts, and redolent of vanilla, almond, lemon, and orange, these buttery "thighs" have a long shelf life and are handy nibblers to accompany a glass of wine or brandy, a cup of espresso or tea, ice cream, or fruit desserts.

Ladies' Thighs

Makes 6 to 7 dozen cookies

8 tablespoons (1 stick) unsalted butter
1 cup sugar
3 extra-large eggs
1 tablespoon kirsch
1½ teaspoons pure almond extract
1½ teaspoons pure vanilla extract
Grated zest of 1 lemon
Grated zest of ½ medium-size orange
1 cup finely chopped walnuts
½ teaspoon baking powder
½ teaspoon salt
3½ to 4½ cups all-purpose flour, as needed
Vegetable shortening or oil, for deep frying
Confectioners' sugar, for serving

1. Place the butter and sugar in a large mixing bowl and cream until light and fluffy. Beat in the eggs, one at a time, beating well between additions. Beat in the kirsch, almond and vanilla extracts, lemon and orange zest, walnuts, baking powder, and salt. Mix well between additions.
2. Gradually sift in the flour, beating between additions, until the batter is too stiff to stir.

Transfer the batter to a work surface and knead in as much additional flour as necessary to make a dough that is smooth and not sticky but still pliable.
3. Pinch off pieces of the dough, each about the size of a small walnut. Flour your hands and roll each ball of dough into a long, thin, cigar-shaped shank, about 3 inches long and ½ inch at the midpoint, tapering toward each end.
4. Cover a cutting board or platter with wax paper, sprinkle it with flour, and place the shaped "thighs" on top. Let them dry uncovered overnight in a cool place, but not in the refrigerator.
5. Pour oil to a depth of 3 inches into a deep fryer or deep saucepan. Attach a deep-fry thermometer to the side of the pan and heat the fat or oil over moderate heat until the thermometer registers 365°F. Working in batches and being careful not to overcrowd the pan, fry a few cookies at a time until golden brown, about 8 minutes per batch. Using a slotted spoon, transfer the fried cookies to paper towels to cool.
6. When all cookies are fried and cooled, store them in a tightly covered canister into which you have punched a few holes. Sprinkle the cookies with confectioners' sugar just before serving.

Tip: The flavor of the cookies improves enormously after 24 hours, and those with unusual willpower consider 1 week the proper maturing time. They will keep for 2 weeks in a cool spot. **See also:** Weihnachtsgebäck, page 315; The French Cookie Jar, page 80.

‖‖‖‖‖‖‖‖‖‖‖‖‖‖‖‖‖‖‖‖‖‖‖‖‖‖‖‖‖

THE APOTHEOSIS OF MILK

Vacherin du Mont d'Or

Swiss

A large, flat white disk, very thick, often slightly askew, with a sunken, patinaed rind. Within, a heavy, slowly runny liquid satin cream. This is Vacherin du Mont d'Or, the cow's milk cheese with an incomparably salty-sweet, nutty flavor.

Its ascendance to the state of cheese perfection has been the subject of some discord between the countries of Switzerland and France. For most of its more than two-hundred-year history, the name Vacherin du Mont d'Or designated several cheeses made in the Jura mountains just north of the Alps, in both Switzerland's Vaud canton and the neighboring Franche-Comté region of France. Relations between cheese makers were reportedly quite amicable, even though many experts cited the Swiss creation as slightly superior. The Swiss apparently agreed, and in 1981 they acquired the exclusive legal right to the name; the French product now has to be referred to as Vacherin du Haut-Doubs. Both have been awarded the Appellation d'Origine Contrôlée, the prestigious certification that lends official geographical designation status to certain precious wines, cheeses, and other foods.

A circular spruce box adds flavor and keeps the cheese's shape.

In both regions, the remarkable cheeses are made according to strict, time-honored standards. The raw milk can come only from the cows of the Montbéliard and Simmentaler breeds. The cheese must be shaped into a round within a ring of spruce bark and be ripened on a spruce wood board. The process takes at least three weeks, and the cheeses must be rotated several times before being placed in the characteristic paper-thin bandbox of spruce.

Vacherin du Mont D'Or is produced only between September and the end of March, and the ivory-hued wonder is runniest and richest when perfectly, luxuriously ripe. To try it at its best, serve it at room temperature straight from the wooden box, with a spoon. You will need a cut of crusty bread and if you can find one, a ripe winter pear.

RETAIL AND MAIL ORDER: *In New York,* Murray's Cheese, tel 888-692-4339, murrayscheese.com; Fairway, at multiple locations, fairwaymarket s.com. **FURTHER INFORMATION:** *Cheese Primer* by Steven Jenkins (1996); vacherin-montdor.ch. **SPECIAL EVENT:** Fête du Vacherin, Les Charbonnières, Switzerland, September, vacherin-montdor.ch/en/news/fete-du-vacherin. **TIP:** Because the original cheese must be made from raw milk and is aged for less than sixty days, the version available on American shores is pasteurized and often referred to as Vacherin du Jura.

Zuger Kirschtorte

Swiss

P astry chefs in Switzerland practice a fine art, and a sweet and creamy example of their skills lies in the Zuger kirschtorte. The lusciously rich layer cake is the specialty of Zug, the Swiss canton known for its kirsch—a clear and fiery cherry brandy distilled from the fruit grown in its orchards.

Many old recipes describe this torte as a simple sponge cake devoid of any hint of cherries, leaving the origin of the kirsch in its name a mystery. Other recipes call for kirsch in the batter as a flavoring, with a final anointing to moisten the finished cake while it is still warm. The most delectably elaborate is the version prepared by the talented Swiss pastry chef Albert Kumin, a delight created for the original menu of the Four Seasons restaurant in New York.

Layers of nut-meringue, sponge cake, and buttercream

The seductively complex masterpiece begins with rounds of crisp and snowy hazelnut-crunchy Swiss meringue alternating with soft, fluffy layers of the lightest, sunniest génoise (the gentle sponge cake so beloved in Europe). The layers are bound by a vanilla- and kirsch-perfumed, pink-tinted buttercream that also is spread over the top and sides of the fully assembled cake. The cake is then sprinkled liberally with chopped hazelnuts and chilled for two to three hours so that hints of kirsch and vanilla seep through its layers. Just before being served, it is showered with confectioners' sugar. As you might imagine, there's reward to be found here not only in the flavor but also in the intriguing contrast of crisp, soft, and chewy layers, and the crackle of hazelnuts in every bite.

The snowy meringue defined as Swiss, by the way, differs from a standard French meringue in that the egg whites and sugar are gently beaten in a double boiler until the sugar is dissolved, then are removed from the heat and beaten vigorously to attain full volume. (In French meringue, sugar is added to egg whites and beaten until they form soft peaks.)

WHERE: *In Zurich,* Kronenhalle, tel 41/44-262-9900, kronenhalle.ch; *in Zug, Switzerland,* Confiserie Albert Meier, tel 41/41-711-1049; *in Springfield and Burke, VA,* The Swiss Bakery and Pastry Shop, theswissbakeryonline.com. **FURTHER INFORMATION AND RECIPES:** *A Quintet of Cuisines* by Michael and Frances Field (1970); nickmalgieri.com (search zuger kirschtorte); food.com (search swiss zug cherry torte).

SCANDINAVIAN

Danish, Finnish,
Norwegian, Swedish

—||||||||||||||||||||||||||||||—

PANNING FOR GOLD AROUND THE ARCTIC CIRCLE

Cloudberries

Scandinavian

Imagine raspberries with the oozy soft richness and golden color of honey, and you'll have an idea of what cloudberries are all about. A summer favorite in many countries neighboring Nordic regions, as well as Canada, Alaska, and the

An elusive treasure

northernmost states in the lower forty-eight, *Rubus chamaemorus* is most common in Norway and Finland, where it is known as *hilla, lakka,* and *suomuurain.* (Neighboring Swedes call it *hjortron.*)

The teasingly tart, very soft berries do not keep well, so they are rarely exported fresh. But they do lend themselves to luscious jams and syrups, giving a year-round lift to pies, liqueurs, toasted bread, cream-filled crêpes, waffles, and ice creams. Cloudberries also serve as an elegant garnish for roast pork and duck, and as a coolly astringent accent to the lusty Finnish cheese *leipäjuusto.*

Though cherished for their color and for uniquely sweet-sharp, winey flavor, cloudberries are also valued in northern climes for their exceptional vitamin C content. So valued, in fact, that in 2005 a bumper crop ten times larger than usual prompted thousands of Finns and Estonians to travel to Lapland's swamps, defying black flies to harvest their share, whether to eat it themselves or to sell it.

MAIL ORDER: igourmet.com (search cloudberry preserves); scandinavianbutik.com (click Food, then search cloudberry). **FURTHER INFORMATION AND RECIPES:** *The Scandinavian Kitchen* by Camilla Plum (2011); swedishfood.com (search hjortronglass). **SPECIAL EVENT:** Cloudberry Festival, Vuollerim, Sweden, August, laplandvuollerim.se/en (click Events, then Cloudberry Festival).

—||||||||||||||||||||||||||||||—

THE FRESH AIR FLAVORS OF THE NORTH

Dill and Caraway

Scandinavian

To experience the clean, fresh flavors of Scandinavian cuisine, all you need to do is taste a few wisps of feathery dill. Follow that delicate starter by gnawing on some silvery caraway seeds. An exaggeration, to be sure, but one that's not so

far afield. While these seasonings appear in other European and Middle Eastern cuisines, nowhere are they more central to the taste paradigm as in Scandinavia.

Dill, with its silky, feathery fronds, tiny flowers, and slim yellow-green seeds, is a multipurpose wonder used as a seasoning and in all manner of curing and pickling. It may well have palliative effects, to boot—its name derives from the Norse word *dilla*, to lull, and in some cultures it was steeped in water and used to calm crying babies and adult cramps. Its botanical alias, *Anethum graveolens*, lends both etymological roots and a clean, bright flavor to gravad lax or gravlax (see page 349), the fresh-cured salmon preserved with salt, sugar, and pepper in addition to the leaves and dried seeds of dill.

Fresh air and spring green might be the best descriptions of the slightly sweet, grassy taste of dill's fronds—pleasing, if elusive—while its seeds, used for pickling, have more pungency.

When buying dill, look for sprays that are sprightly and light green, and bypass those that are wilting or have any trace of the dark green, wet look that is an indicator of rotting. Keep them well wrapped in the salad compartment of the refrigerator, and discard them if they darken, or when their aroma becomes overpowering. When possible, buy freshly grown local dill, available in many farmers' markets. It will be more tender and delicate than the tougher, stronger-flavored commercial product. You can also grow your own from seeds; it will flourish outdoors in a temperate climate.

Dill seed sold for seasoning appears in two forms. In midsummer—around late July and August—when the herb goes to seed, it flowers into big sprays tipped by the tiny yellow seeds and is sold in bunches. The seed is also available dried, for year-round use and in instances where greater flavor intensity is desired. As with all dried seeds, be on the lookout for rancidity—difficult if you buy it untried in bottles, but simple if it's sold in bulk at a spice store. Just bite into a few seeds, and if the taste is musty and bitter, move along. Store dried dill seeds in the refrigerator.

Caraway seeds, or *Carum carvi*, have a pleasantly clean taste with a subtle hint of anise, a combination prized in foods and beverages like the classic Scandinavian schnapps aquavit. The seeds lend flavor to crispbreads, cheeses, Christmas cookies, cabbage and potato dishes, pickles, and lamb stews. Caraway seeds contain carvone, an essential oil that will spoil at warm temperatures—so here, too, rancidity can be a problem. Like dill seed, caraway seeds are best stored in the refrigerator. And to work as a really efficient seasoning in cooked or marinated dishes, they should be crushed in a spice grinder, under a knife blade, or with a mortar and pestle.

MAIL ORDER: For whole dried dill and caraway seeds, Penzeys Spices, tel 800-741-7787, penzeys.com. **FURTHER INFORMATION AND RECIPES:** *World-Class Swedish Cooking* by Björn Frantzén and Daniel Lindeberg (2013); *The Complete Scandinavian Cookbook* by Alice B. Johnson (1964); *Scandinavian Christmas* by Trine Hahnemann (2012); saveur.com (search swedish pickled crudites; red cabbage with caraway seeds). **TIP:** Dill is an easy and rewarding herb to grow in a garden or window box; seeds are available at burpee.com.

A BLACK MAGIC TREAT

Läkeröl

Black Licorice

Scandinavian

Humans, it is said by scientists, are the only animals that can learn to like a food they hated on the first try. Other species forever shun a disliked food unless (possibly) they are starving. Which brings us to the lovable bittersweet vetch and so-called confection we know as black licorice. Children often have their first taste of licorice in the form of long, twisted "shoelaces," dome-shaped drops, or little gummy animals, all sweet licorice candies. These have little resemblance to the more adult, lustier Scandinavian versions that replace most of the sugar with salt in the form of ammonium chloride (as opposed to salt's more common form, sodium chloride) for an extra belt of chemical bite and aroma.

Licorice is drawn from the root of the leguminous licorice tree (Glycyrrhiza glabra), a watery plant with delicate leaves much like those of the mimosa tree, native to the Mediterranean. It contains the powerfully sweet compound glycyrrhizin, said to be fifty times sweeter than sucrose yet still not quite sweet enough to compensate for the alluring natural bitterness of the root material. To be shaped into the forms we know, the extract is mixed with gelatin, sugar, salt, water, and flour to form a paste that can be extruded and molded into pipes, drops, ropes, and animals.

Holland and England make fine licorice, but salty licorice reaches an apotheosis in Scandinavia, where it has long been believed to have medicinal properties as a laxative, a throat soother, and a blood purifier, the latter apparently a trait credited to almost anything that is bitter.

Most of all, Scandinavian licorice is enticingly good fun—addictive to many palates, repellent to some, but a worthwhile experience nonetheless. True licorice lovers can also seek out the flavoring in spirits such as the Greek ouzo, Middle Eastern arak, and French pastis, or, on a less felicitous palliative note, that oldtime stomach remedy, paregoric.

MAIL ORDER: scandinavianbutik.com (click Candy, then search halva finnish sweet licorice); allthingsliquorice.co.uk (search lakrids); licoriceinternational.com (search lakerol; heksen drop); epicurious.com (search black licorice ice cream; licorice pudding). **FURTHER INFORMATION:** The Oxford Companion to Food by Alan Davidson (1999). **SPECIAL EVENT:** The Swedish Annual Liquorice Festival, Stockholm, April, lakritsfestivalen.se.

THE BERRIES WITH A CULT FOLLOWING

Lingonberries

Scandinavian

Close relatives of cranberries, lingonberries (*tytteboer* in Norwegian) are tiny, garnet-red berries botanically known as *Vaccinium vitis-idaea* with a sophisticated, winey flavor and a serious tartness that means they cannot be eaten

raw without sugar. Highly prized in Scandinavia, they are also beloved in Russia, Scotland, and in Germany, where they are called *Preiselbeeren*. In England, the berries grow in heather-covered bogs, a circumstance that may account for their name—*ling* being the word for certain types of English heather.

Variously preserved, they are the favored garnish for Swedish meatballs, Danish *frikadeller*, and almost any roasted goose, duck, game, or pork dish in the Scandinavian lexicon. Like a side of glowing red cabbage, they lend a festive touch to the holiday table, whether simmered and pureed as jam or cooked whole as conserves. Their juices flavor and color cold soups and whipped desserts such as the Finnish *kiisseli*, a cornstarch-thickened pudding related to the Russian *kissel*, and the berries are also simmered into *vatkattu marjapuuro*, a Finnish farina-based fluff of a pudding that takes on the rosy pink tint of dawn.

Despite the rich dishes with which they often appear, lingonberries are good for us—full of vitamin C, fiber, and antioxidants. To boot, they have two ripening seasons, the first in mid-summer and the second in early autumn.

RETAIL AND MAIL ORDER: *In Minneapolis,* Ingebretsen's, tel 800-279-9333, ingebretsens .com (search lingonberry preserves). **MAIL ORDER:** scandinavianbutik.com (click Food, then search frozen lingonberries or lingonberry preserve). **FURTHER INFORMATION AND RECIPES:** *Scandinavian Christmas* by Trine Hahnemann (2012); allrecipes.com (search lingonberry jam).

Wild lingonberries, ripe for the picking in late summer

A WORLD OF RUSTIC BROWN BREADS

The Nordic Bread Basket

Scandinavian

Perhaps because in cold climates it takes a long time for yeast doughs to rise, the Scandinavians have developed almost endless variations on what may broadly be categorized as rusks and crispbreads, and in Swedish are called *knäckebröd*.

An especially apt example of onomatopoeia, the word recalls the crackling snap you'll hear inside your head while chewing these rough, palate-scrubbing, whole-grain breads. Leavened with yeast or sourdough starters, some are baked on iron griddles or in wood-fired stone ovens until very dry, a practice left over from olden days, when the breads had to keep through long winters without developing mold. Made from whole grain, and therefore high in fiber and relatively low in calories, the breads are especially suited to today's fluffy-white-bread-averse health food culture. (Even Dr. Atkins would approve.) They also are addictively delicious, with rye flour lending a sophisticated sourish touch that makes them especially harmonious with strong cheeses, supple high-fat butter, and rich spreads.

Some, such as the Finn Crisp and Kavli brands, are well known outside of Scandinavian climes. These wafers, sold in many supermarkets, vary in thickness from about a quarter of an inch to a paperlike thinness. Lesser known are the toughest Swedish knäckebröds, big, round, dimpled wheels meant to be broken into portions as needed. Center holes once allowed them to be strung up on poles so air circulation could help them stay fresh; that practice is no longer necessary, but the holes remain, and rounds of the bread are traditionally presented on tables, stacked onto wooden pegs that are mounted on flat wooden disks.

In addition to these flat crispbreads, each Scandinavian country has a softer, richer, iconic bread of its own. Among the best is the Danish *rugbrød,* or rye bread, that comes packaged in thin, square slices the color of toasted wheat. Firm-textured and somehow always cool and pleasantly moist (toasting ruins its prime qualities), this fragrant bread spread with sweet butter calls to mind the very flavor of Denmark.

Scented with cardamom, anise, and burnishings of molasses, the soft and grainy brown Swedish limpa bread is especially important during the Christmas season, although it is enjoyed all year long.

Ruis bread, the Finnish sourdough rye, is formed into flat rounds, again with a hole in the center, distinguished by a crackled hard crust that gives the loaves an antique look. Cut into thick slices and served with butter and cheese, it traditionally accompanies strong morning coffee lightened with a froth of hot milk.

Norway's main contributions to the Scandinavian bread board are *lefse* and *lompe.* Thin, round pancakes, lefse are soft and subtly salty, usually made from a batter of wheat and rye flours, egg, and soured milk or cream and seared on an ungreased hot stone or iron griddle. A bit thicker and slightly more flexible, lompe pancakes are made with mashed potatoes mixed only with flour and salt. Both can be filled with butter and jam and folded handkerchief-style, or wrapped around ham or hot dogs (*wienerpølser*) for a sandwich known as a *tunnbrödsrulle,* "a thin bread roll."

Scandinavian crispbreads on a wooden pole

WHERE: *In New York,* for Danish rye breads, Breads Bakery, tel 212-633-2253, breadsbakery .com. **MAIL ORDER:** For Finnish Ruis breads, nordic breads.com; scandinavianbutik.com (click Food, then search danish rugbrød; cardamom bread); kuhsdeli.com (search norwegian potato lefse). **FURTHER INFORMATION AND RECIPES:** *Scandinavian Baking* by Trine Hahnemann (2014); *The Great Scandinavian Baking Book* by Beatrice Ojakangas (1999); *Home Baked* by Hanne Risgaard, translated by Marie-Louise Risgaard (2012); cookadvice.com (search lompe potato pancake bread); saveur.com (search cardamom bread); breadexperience.com (search finnish rye bread).

—|||||||||||||||||||||||||||||||||—

NOT ALL HERRING ARE RED

Sild

Scandinavian

Although herring lovers are not confined to Scandinavia, the Nordic countries celebrate those silvery, saline fish like no other part of the world—with more than twenty spectacular variations on the theme. Anyone who hasn't tried a good percentage of these cannot be considered a true herring maven.

Differences lie first in the fish: whether they are the rosy, satiny, salty-sweet reddish fillets of *maatjes* (technically maiden fish that have not yet spawned); the firmer, meatier salt herring; the unctuously rich, supple, and juicy schmaltz or fat herring; or the smallish, intensely flavored Baltic herring *böckling*. From those come a kaleidoscopic array of cuts, cures, and sauces, and a buffet table with fewer than ten specimens is not considered worthy of the title *smörgåsbord* (see page 375).

Rose-red maatjes fillets—cut into *gaffelbiter* or "fork pieces"—are most appreciated raw and plain, laid out on big, bricklike blocks of ice under sprigs of dill, to be picked up in pieces as diners circle the cold table. Cooked, the fillets are sometimes presented as *currysill*, in a curry sauce with bits of potato, onion, and hard-cooked egg; or in a green sauce of spinach, capers, parsley, eggs, and mustard.

Salt herring may be fried (*stekt*) or pickled into the most beautiful of Swedish creations, *glasmästersill*—glassblower's herring, so named because the silver-blue herring pieces are pickled in tall, straight-sided glass jars in a clear brine along with slices of carrots, red onion, and bay leaves, all suggesting an edible stained-glass window. (Schmaltz or *fett* herring are also often pickled, but are favored in creamy mustard sauce, as a dish called *senapssill*.) For a garnet-colored salad of beets, apples, potatoes, and red onion, or for roasting in parchment with dill, parsley, chives, and plenty of sweet butter, salt herring is the choice.

One type of herring you will never find on a smorgasbord is the Swedish *surströmming*, or sour Baltic herring. Sour is an understatement: Cleaned, brined, and cellar-fermented in barrels for a year prior to being canned, the fish attains the crumbling, pasty texture and intense aroma of Roman *garum* or the Vietnamese fish sauce *nam pla*. A can of surströmming is opened out of doors for the best of reasons—assuming the festering gases inside haven't already caused that bulging can to explode, the smell is enough

to cause retching. But believe it or not, a taste for its salty, bitterly fishy flavor can be acquired, if one lives long enough. Almost needless to say, it takes lots of crispbread, aquavit, and beer to get the job done.

And then there are the anchovies—tiny sprats or near-herring that go into such specialties as the Swedish *Janssons frestelse*, or Jansson's temptation: a luscious, layered gratin of julienned potato strips, onions, anchovies, butter, and heavy cream favored not only on the smorgasbord but as a late-night restorative as well.

Another festive favorite, the following herring salad lends color to a smorgasbord and is also common at Christmastime in Sweden.

Sildesalat or Sillsalad (Beet and Herring Salad)

Makes 10 to 20 portions;
serves 6 to 8 as an appetizer

3 large salt herring, ¾ to 1 pound each,
*   soaked and trimmed to make 6 fillets*
3 cups finely diced canned cooked beets,
*   juice reserved*
2 medium-size potatoes, boiled, peeled,
*   and diced*
2 medium-size tart green apples,
*   preferably Granny Smith, peeled,*
*   cored, and finely chopped*
1 small red onion, finely chopped
1 tablespoon distilled white vinegar
About 1½ cups sour cream, beaten
*   until thin*
1 tablespoon Dijon mustard
Salt and freshly ground white pepper
Sugar
2 hard-cooked eggs, for garnish
Fresh dill sprigs, for garnish
Scandinavian crispbread, for serving

1. The herring are best soaked whole for 24 hours in a change of water, but if your store will not do that, have the herring filleted and soak them at home. Place the fillets in a bowl and add cold water to cover. Cover the bowl and let the herring soak in the refrigerator for 24 hours, changing the water several times. Drain the herring fillets and pat them dry with paper towels, making sure all of the fine, hairlike bones are removed. Dice the fillets.

2. Place the diced herring in a large glass or ceramic bowl. Add half each of the beets, potatoes, apples, and red onion, and toss to mix. It is a good idea to add each of these ingredients to the herring gradually so you do not overdo the onion or apple. After adding the first half, taste to see how much more of each ingredient you need for a balanced distribution, setting any leftovers aside for

Beet and herring salad

another use. Add the vinegar and toss to mix.

3. Place 1 cup of the sour cream in a small bowl and blend the mustard into it. Fold the mustard and sour cream mixture into the herring salad. Stir in just enough of the reserved beet juice to add a slight pinkish blush of color, up to ½ cup. Add up to ½ cup more sour cream, if needed, to bind the salad so that it is moist but not runny.

4. Taste the salad for seasoning, adding salt, white pepper, and sugar to taste, and more vinegar and/or mustard as necessary. Refrigerate the salad, covered, for 8 to 24 hours before serving, tossing it very gently with a fork every 5 or 6 hours to distribute the juices.

5. When ready to serve, toss the salad with a fork thoroughly but gently and place it in a glass or ceramic serving bowl. Separate the whites and yolks of the hard-cooked eggs and rub each through a coarse sieve. Sprinkle the grated whites over the salad, then top it with the grated yolks. Arrange a few sprigs of dill around the edge of the salad and pass the crispbread at the table.

WHERE: *In Stockholm,* Den Gyldene Freden, tel 46/8-249-760, gyldenefreden.se; *in New York,* Aquavit, tel 212-307-7311, aquavit.org; *in Elk Horn, IA,* Danish Inn, tel 712-764-4251, danishinnrestaurant.com; *in Santa Barbara, CA,* Andersen's Danish Restaurant and Bakery, tel 805-962-5085, andersenssantabarbara.com. **RETAIL AND MAIL ORDER:** *In New York,* Russ & Daughters, tel 212-475-4880, russanddaughters.com. **FURTHER INFORMATION AND RECIPES:** *Scandinavian Christmas* by Trine Hahnemann (2012); *The Scandinavian Cookbook* by Trine Hahnemann (2009); food.com (search scandinavian pickled herring); saveur.com (search sildesalat).

A SPRINGTIME SOUP IN NEED OF RESURRECTION

Aspargessuppe

Asparagus Soup with Veal Dumplings

Danish

A luscious surprise for those expecting all Danish food to be wintry, this pale jade-colored cream soup is redolent of the season's first asparagus and enriched with airy veal dumplings. Once a standard in Copenhagen's upscale traditional restaurants, it seems to have been relegated to the history books—but it well deserves resurrection, even if only by home cooks.

Asparagus Soup with Veal Dumplings

Serves 6 to 8

For the soup
3 pounds thin, young asparagus stalks
2 cups light cream or half-and-half
1½ cups veal broth or chicken broth
½ cup (1 stick) unsalted butter
5 tablespoons all-purpose flour

For the dumplings
1 pound ground veal shoulder
¼ cup all-purpose flour
2 large eggs
¼ teaspoon freshly ground white pepper
Pinch of ground nutmeg
½ teaspoon salt

For finishing the soup
8 extra-large egg yolks
Salt and freshly ground white pepper
Minced fresh chives or fresh chervil leaves,
*   for garnish*

1. Prepare the soup: Rinse the asparagus well under cold running water. Snap the tough woody part off the bottom of each stalk, setting the tops of the stalks aside. Rinse the bottom ends again to remove any sand, place them in a large saucepan, and add 1 cup of water. Let simmer over moderate heat for about 15 minutes. Strain through a sieve and set the broth aside, discarding the stalk bottoms.
2. Cut the tips off the asparagus tops, about ¾ inch from the end, and set aside the center pieces. Place the asparagus tips in the saucepan, add 1½ cups of water and a pinch of salt, and simmer over moderate heat until tender, about 4 minutes. Drain the asparagus tips, setting them aside. Add the cooking water to the broth already reserved.

3. Cut the remaining, center pieces of asparagus into 1-inch lengths, place them in the saucepan, and add 4½ cups of water and a generous pinch of salt. Simmer the asparagus over moderate heat until tender, about 10 minutes. Transfer the asparagus center pieces and their cooking water to a food processor or blender and puree them. Return the pureed asparagus to the saucepan, adding the reserved asparagus broth, and bring to a simmer.
4. While the pureed asparagus simmers, place the cream in a small saucepan and heat over low heat until tiny bubbles form around the sides of the pan, about 3 minutes. Remove from the heat and cover the pan to keep the cream hot. Place the veal broth or chicken broth in another small saucepan and bring to a simmer.
5. Melt the butter in a saucepan over low heat. When the butter bubbles, stir in the flour, and simmer until well blended and pale blond in color, stirring gently, about 5 minutes. Stir in the hot cream and hot broth all at once and whisk over low heat until thick and smooth, 6 to 7 minutes. Beat the cream mixture into the simmering asparagus puree and simmer until smoothly blended, about 4 minutes. Set the asparagus soup aside.
6. Make the dumplings: Bring a large saucepan of salted water to a boil. Place the veal, flour, eggs, pepper, nutmeg, and ½ teaspoon salt in a mixing bowl and, using a fork, gently combine. Do not pack the veal mixture down. Shape the mixture into tiny balls, about ¾ inch in diameter.

A rite of spring worth rediscovering

7. Drop the veal dumplings gently into the boiling water. When they are done, they will puff up and float to the surface, 7 to 8 minutes. Using a slotted spoon, transfer the cooked dumplings to a bowl and keep them warm in a little of the cooking water.

8. Finish the soup: Just before serving, bring the soup to a simmer. In a medium-size bowl, beat the egg yolks with 3 tablespoons of cold water and then slowly pour 2 cups of the hot asparagus soup into the yolk mixture, beating constantly. Remove the soup from the heat and add the yolk mixture, beating constantly. Taste for seasoning, adding salt and white pepper as necessary. Gently reheat the soup, but do not let it boil or the egg yolks will coagulate.

9. To serve the soup, place 3 or 4 veal dumplings and 4 or 5 asparagus tips in each warmed serving bowl, then ladle in the soup. Garnish each portion with minced chives or chervil.

WHERE: *In Odense, Denmark,* Carlslund, tel 45/65-91-11-25, restaurant-carlslund.dk. **TIP:** The soup can be prepared up to 30 minutes before dumplings are made, but then add egg yolks just before finishing so the soup will not curdle as it is reheated.

A RED, WHITE, AND BLUE (CHEESE) DESSERT

Blue Cheese with Cherry Heering

Danish

With a tingly salt-sharp bite and a fresher, simpler flavor than the more complex blue cheeses of England, France, and Italy, the Danish blue is consistently appealing. Made of fresh cow's milk and almost entirely mass-produced, it features a creamy texture that makes it easy to spread, slice, or crumble. A traditional dessert after a fish dinner, it also forms a delectable open sandwich when topped with a raw egg yolk and some shaved radishes.

But Danish blue reaches its true apotheosis in a preparation invented by the late Peter Heering, the owner of the Cherry Heering brand of deeply winey, sweet-tart cherry liqueur. To intrigue dinner guests, he would begin a meal by presenting a large, five-pound cylinder of Danish blue cheese. With a silver tablespoon, he would scoop out a core four or five inches deep into the top of the cheese. Setting aside the extracted cheese, he poured some ruby-red Cherry Heering into the well and crumbled the reserved cheese back into it. There it sat during the two-hour meal, after which portions of the tangy, cherry-soaked cheese were served as dessert.

Naturally, an extra helping of the liqueur Heering was poured into iced, fluted glasses to help guests better appreciate the mollifying effects of cherries on the sharp sting of the cheese.

MAIL ORDER: For whole wheels of Danish blue, amazon.com (search danablu); for Cherry Heering, internetwines.com (search cherry heering). **FURTHER INFORMATION:** danablu.dk; cherry-heering.com. **TIP:** The Flora Danica brand of Danish blue cheese is that country's finest. It is best to buy the cheese in a shop where it is cut to order in a large piece. But if a large piece is not available, drizzle some Cherry Heering over each portion one hour before serving. A few English-style wafer biscuits would be a good flavor foil.

┤||||||||||||||||||||||||||||├

Flaeskeaeggekage

Bacon and Egg Pancake

Danish

This wonderfully hearty, homey dish used to be a standard in Danish restaurants, especially for lunch. It has become increasingly difficult to find, although exceptions may be spotted in country restaurants or home kitchens doling out traditional comfort foods. But it just might be the poster child for Denmark's best (and best known) food products: sweet, healthy pork; eggs individually stamped with a dated code to ensure freshness; cream-rich unsalted butter, considered by many to be Europe's best; and milk from the contented cows that graze on bright green pastures in this rain-blessed land.

An all-in-one breakfast special

To prepare this lusty brunch or luncheon dish, crisp-fry slices of mellow, lean bacon. Set them aside to drain, leaving their rendered fat behind in the skillet. Whip up a sunny batter of eggs, potato flour, salt, white pepper, and rich Danish milk, and pour it into the hot fat, slowly cooking the mixture omelet-style over a low flame. When the top of the pancake is still somewhat creamy, lay the slices of bacon over it in a star pattern. Sprinkle on minced chives as the batter sets completely (a lid placed over the pan will help with setting). Cut the finished pancake into wedges with the edge of a spatula and serve it directly from the pan, along with buttered slices of rye bread.

Where: *In Copenhagen,* Slotskaelderen hos Gitte Kik, tel 45/33-11-15-37, slotskaelderen .dk; *in Odense, Denmark,* Carlslund, tel 45/65-91-11-25, restaurant-carlslund.dk. **Mail order:** For Danish-style bacon, amazon.com (search boczek dunski bacon). **Further information and recipes:** *The Everything Nordic Cookbook* by Kari Schoening Diehl (2012); food.com (search flaeskeaeggekage).

┤||||||||||||||||||||||||||||├

Franskbøf

Danish

The inspiration for this succulent beef dish is obviously the French filet mignon maître d'hôtel, a rare beefsteak enhanced with a soft spread of lemon- and parsley-brightened butter. For years the Danes offered their more elaborate version: an inch-and-a-half-thick filet mignon cooked rare and topped with almost invisibly thin slices of lemon (seeds and rind removed), and a fat finger of butter rolled in heaps of finely minced curly parsley and placed as a crown on the lemon slices. As one cut down through the enticing meat, rich beef juices mingled with the mildly acidic sunny lemon; the cool, softening, sweet butter; and the chlorophyll-fresh accent of parsley.

Though these days the dish, which is also sometimes called *Pariserbøf,* is not often seen in Danish restaurants, fortunately it is easy enough to prepare at home. Filet mignon is the standard cut, but there's no reason an even more flavorful sirloin strip steak could not be substituted. Whatever the cut, the steak should be pan-grilled in a little butter; the sort of heavy searing or charring that results from broiling under a flame or on the charcoal grill would throw the dish's delicate flavors out of balance. The meat should be rosily

rare and barely warm at its center, neither a near-raw blue nor a drab well-done—you want the juices to flow into the sublime mix.

Have the parsleyed fingers of butter and the trimmed and seeded lemon slices ready in advance and keep them chilled in the refrigerator, removing them just as you begin to prepare the steaks. Don't forget a mound of slim fries (preferably as crisp as spun glass) and a sprightly clump of watercress.

WHERE: *In Copenhagen,* Sankt Annæ, tel 45/33-12-54-97, restaurantsanktannae.dk. **FURTHER INFORMATION AND RECIPES:** *Mastering the Art of French Cooking, Volume 1* by Julia Child, Louisette Bertholle, and Simone Beck (1961); frenchfood.about.com (search maitre d'hotel butter). **TIP:** Be sure the fillets are at room temperature before searing. If a thick finger of butter (unsalted, please) seems too heavy, follow the recipe for maître d'hôtel butter referenced above as sparingly or generously as you wish.

A MEATBALL OF A HAMBURGER

Frikadeller

Danish

Savory and family-friendly, these fried meat cakes are the nurturing comfort food the Danes used to rely on as Americans do hamburgers—never mind that the hamburger may well have displaced *frikadeller* in Denmark. The gently "fried"

(though actually sautéed) cakes are a light, puffy combination of ground veal and pork, made tender with a little flour and airy with a dash of soda water. Some egg, finely minced or ground onion, and salt and pepper are also incorporated into the ground meat mixture, and the whole is allowed to bind and ripen in the refrigerator for a couple of hours. Shaped into meaty ovals, the frikadeller are then slowly and carefully

Veal frikadeller with red onions and horseradish on toast

sautéed in hot butter, the low heat ensuring that the meat remains juicy and tender as it is cooked through.

Whether they're plated or heaped onto sliced bread for open sandwiches, the frikadeller are typically garnished with pickled beets and red cabbage. Mashed potatoes finish the dinner plate, while the sandwich may be decorated with a shimmering sliver of veal aspic.

WHERE: *In Copenhagen,* Kanal Caféen, tel 45/33-11-57-70, kanalcafeen.dk; Sankt Annæ, tel 45/33-12-54-97, restaurantsanktannae.dk; *in Elk Horn, IA,* Danish Inn, tel 712-764-4251, danishinnrestaurant.com; *in Santa Barbara, CA,* Andersen's Danish Restaurant and Bakery, tel 805-962-5085, andersenssantabarbara.com. **FURTHER INFORMATION AND RECIPES:** *Scandinavian Christmas* by Trine Hahnemann (2012); allrecipes .com (search frikadeller).

||||||||||||||||||||||||||||||||||

THE SALT-AND-SUGAR CURE

Gravlax

Danish, Swedish

G ravlax (aka gravad lax), the cured raw salmon with a silky texture and a sunset-coral hue, combines overtones of dill with the contrasting accents of its sugar, salt, and pepper cure. Named after an ancient curing process in which

fishermen preserved their catch by burying it in sand with sugar and salt—the *grav* means "buried" and the *lax* means "salmon"—it is surely one of Scandinavia's greatest contributions to gourmandise.

Delectable when thinly sliced onto lightly buttered, thin whole-grain brown rye bread such as the Danish *rugbrød* or the cracklingly crisp caraway-flavored flatbread *knäckebröd,* and delicious alongside chive-sprinkled scrambled eggs, it also makes an enticing main course when cut into inch-thick slabs and lightly glazed under the grill, a step that imparts briny-sweet overtones as the salt and sugar in the cure caramelize. In all cases, lemon and freshly snipped dill are the typical garnishes, as is a tangy sauce of blended sweet and hot mustards thickened with minced dill. (Iced aquavit or vodka are standard accompaniments.)

As so often happens to very popular foods, gravlax's reputation has at times suffered because of its success, with purveyors who are inept or greedy (or both) taking shortcuts in its

processing, using inferior ingredients, or keeping them around so long that the fish turns waxy and the dill bitter. Other damaging shortcuts: using salmon that are farmed for quick fattening or that come from warm waters, both sure to result in a bland and overly fatty product.

Fortunately, it is easy enough to take matters into one's own hands—and, when shopping for salmon to cure at home, to tell the wild from the farmed. The latter bears numerous white stripes of fat in a sort of moiré pattern, while wild salmon has a finer grain and shows much less white fat. Farmed salmon may also have a deeper red-orange color than wild, usually because a coloring agent was added to the feed. Still, because wild salmon is extremely expensive as well as scarce, substituting relatively lean high-quality farmed salmon is permissible.

No compromise can be broached in the cure, which should be prepared with fresh dill and worked into the fish flesh by hand. A new faction of cooks promotes a very quick cure—often no more than a few hours long—but for a more traditional richness and a firm texture, anywhere from forty-eight to seventy-two hours is the norm, depending on personal taste and the thickness of the fish. A longer cure ensures that any lurking parasites, possible in raw salmon, will be killed, as both salt and sugar draw water out of anything that lives, parasites and bacteria included. (Salt being, after all, the reason the Dead Sea remains dead.)

Dill-Cured Salmon

Serves 10 to 12 as an appetizer

For the salmon

About 5 pounds center-cut skin-on salmon
   fillet, cut into 2 equal-size fillets
2 to 3 tablespoons aquavit or vodka
1 cup sugar
1 cup kosher salt
2 teaspoons white peppercorns, crushed
1 large bunch of fresh dill
About 2 tablespoons dried dill seed

For the mustard sauce

1 cup German or Swedish sweet mustard
   or prepared honey mustard
1 cup hot Dijon mustard
1½ teaspoons sugar
2 tablespoons distilled white vinegar
⅓ cup olive oil or mild vegetable oil
⅔ cup minced fresh dill
Salt and freshly ground black pepper
Thinly sliced squares of Danish whole-
   grain rye bread, rugbrød, *or dark*
   Westphalian pumpernickel, for serving
Minced fresh dill for garnish

1. Prepare the salmon: Work your fingers over the flesh side of each salmon fillet and, using tweezers or your fingertips, carefully pull out any fine bones. Pour one generous tablespoon of aquavit or vodka over the flesh side of each fillet and let stand for about 15 minutes.
2. Combine the sugar, kosher salt, and peppercorns in a bowl. Rinse the fresh dill under cold running water and pat it dry with paper towels.

3. Sprinkle a thin layer of the sugar mixture in the bottom of a large glass or ceramic baking dish that is about 2½ inches deep (a baking dish used for lasagna is perfect; see Note). Arrange 5 or 6 sprigs of dill, stems and all, on top.
4. Pat the flesh side of the salmon fillets dry with paper towels. Gradually work about one third of the remaining sugar mixture into the flesh side of a salmon fillet, packing it on until no more can be absorbed. Repeat with the remaining fillet. Place 1 fillet, skin side down, in the baking dish on top of the dill sprigs. Sprinkle half of the dill seeds over the fillet. Cover the fish thoroughly with a very thick layer of 15 to 20 dill sprigs.
5. Sprinkle the layer of dill sprigs with the remaining dill seeds. Place the remaining salmon fillet, flesh side down, over the dill to make a sort of sandwich. Sprinkle the remaining sugar mixture over the skin of the top fillet. Add a few sprigs of dill to the baking dish, placing them around the fillets.
6. Top the salmon with a double layer of wax paper. Choose another, smaller baking dish with some depth that will fit snugly inside the baking dish holding the salmon. Place this dish on top of the salmon inside the baking dish and weight the top dish down as evenly as possible using cans of food, jars of water, or anything that will press down on the dish firmly and evenly.
7. Marinate the salmon in the refrigerator for 2 to 3 days. About every 12 hours, remove the top dish along with the weights and wax paper. Completely invert the entire fish "sandwich" in the baking dish so that the bottom fillet is on top, skin side up. Do not pour off the liquid that accumulates in the bottom of the dish. Replace the wax paper, top dish, and weights, and continue marinating the salmon.
8. Prepare the mustard sauce: About 12 hours before you plan to serve the salmon, place the sweet mustard and Dijon mustard in a nonreactive bowl and whisk them together, beating in the sugar and 1 tablespoon of the vinegar. When the sugar has dissolved, beat in the remaining

Scandinavia's famous salt-and-sugar-cured salmon

tablespoon of vinegar. Add the oil in a thin, steady stream, beating the sauce constantly. When it is smooth and emulsified, stir in the minced dill. Taste, season with salt and pepper, and add more sugar, vinegar, sweet mustard, and/or Dijon mustard as desired. You might also want to beat in a little more oil to smooth out the texture or flavor. Refrigerate the mustard sauce, covered, until about an hour before serving time.

9. Remove the salmon from the dish 3 to 4 hours before serving time, discarding the marinade and dill sprigs. Carefully scrape all of the sugar, salt, and dill seeds and any mushy residue from the flesh side of each fillet. Do this gently with the blade of a knife, then give the fillets a final wipe with a dampened paper towel.

10. Rinse and dry the baking dish. Return the salmon to the dish without weighting it down, and place in the refrigerator to firm up. Just before serving, slice the salmon thinly on the diagonal. Hold the knife (preferably a salmon slicer or a ham knife) parallel to the work surface and cut long, wide slices, skimming each slice off the salmon skin beneath.

11. Transfer the sliced salmon to a platter and serve the bread squares alongside so guests can make their own canapés, or place slices of salmon on top of the squares of bread. Either way, generously sprinkle the salmon with minced dill. Serve the mustard sauce on the side. Once cleaned of its marinade, unsliced gravlax can be refrigerated, covered, for 3 to 4 days.

Note: Marinating salmon should not come in contact with metal or aluminum. Although stainless steel is nonreactive, connoisseurs swear it makes a difference in flavor. Use wax paper, not aluminum foil, for covering the salmon (plastic wrap is also acceptable but more difficult to handle in this process).

RETAIL AND MAIL ORDER: *In New York,* Russ & Daughters, tel 212-475-4880, russanddaughters .com (search gravlax). **TIP:** The gravlax mustard sauce is also good with *maatjes* (salt herring).

COLD BUTTERMILK SOUP FOR A HOT DAY

Kærnemælkskoldskål

Danish

F unny how citizens of cold countries react to a bit of heat. One might think that given Denmark's long, cold, and damp winters, summer could not be long enough or hot enough. But let Midsummer's Eve arrive in late June, and those

Danes who are at least middle-aged begin to think of *kærnemælkskoldskål*—cold buttermilk soup. Though not unlike the Indian drink *lassi,* based on nicely tangy, thinned-down, spiced yogurt, this addictively piquant Danish version is consumed with a spoon. Luxurious and teasingly flavorful thanks to a zap of lemon juice and some mellow, fresh vanilla bean, it makes a light lunch and a remarkably restorative cooler. This being Denmark, whipped cream and a few crunchy rusks are the finishing touches that turn the simplest dish into an opulent indulgence.

Cold Buttermilk Soup

Serves 4

2 large egg yolks
3 tablespoons sugar
1 vanilla bean, or 1 teaspoon pure
    vanilla extract
Grated zest and strained juice of ½ lemon
1 quart very cold buttermilk
1 cup heavy (whipping) cream
8 to 12 rusks or zwieback biscuits,
    for serving

1. In a large bowl, beat the egg yolks and sugar together until the sugar dissolves and the mixture is thick and light in color.

2. If you are using a vanilla bean, cut the bean in half crosswise and set one half aside for another use. Split the remaining half lengthwise and, using the tip of the knife, scrape the seeds into the yolk mixture (set the empty pod aside for another use) and stir to mix. Or, stir in the vanilla extract, if using.

3. Stir in the lemon zest, lemon juice, and buttermilk and refrigerate the soup, covered, to let the flavors develop, 1 to 2 hours.

4. Just before serving, whip the cream to soft peaks and gently fold it into the cold soup, saving a few dabs to top each portion. Serve the soup in chilled bowls with the rusks on the side.

FURTHER INFORMATION AND RECIPES: *The Scandinavian Cookbook* by Trine Hahnemann (2009); tastingtable.com (search buttermilk soup with biscuits). **TIP:** Organic buttermilk will produce better results than the thinner variety generally available in supermarkets.

A LIGHT TOUCH WITH MEATBALLS

Kødboller i Selleri

Celery Root Balls

Danish

Scandinavians seem to like their meatballs on the light and airy side, and in Denmark, these lovely sage-scented beef balls get an extra touch of sophistication from celery root. The big, round, knobby root (also known as celeriac) is used here in the subtlest of ways: Peeled and cut into chunks, it is not incorporated with the meat but is instead cooked to tenderness in salted, acidulated water. The ground beef, blended with grated onion, salt, pepper, lots of earthy sage, and beaten egg, is then shaped into walnut-size balls that are gently poached in the celery-root cooking water—a simple though worldly sounding step that infuses the meat with bright, faintly sweet vegetable overtones. Once cooked and drained, the meatballs are served in a ring centered around the cooked chunks of celery root. A liberal sprinkle of minced parsley and/or dill and a sauce of the thickened cooking liquid completes the picture.

No pasta, please. Mashed potatoes are the thing, and some pickled beets on the side wouldn't be a bad idea, either.

FURTHER INFORMATION AND RECIPES: *Danish Cooking and Baking Traditions* by Arthur L. Meyer (2011); kitchenfears.blogspot.com (search boller i selleri).

‖‖‖‖‖‖‖‖‖‖‖‖‖‖‖‖‖‖‖‖‖‖‖‖‖

BIG FISH, LARGE POND

Kokt Torsk

Boiled Cod

Danish

A list of must-do's for a visitor to Copenhagen includes the following: Rosenborg castle, the Ny Carlsberg Glyptotek museum, St. Peter's church, countless cutting-edge design shops, the whimsical delights of Tivoli Gardens, and boiled

cod. Boiled cod? Yes. One of this country's great national treats, the banal-sounding dish owes its extraordinary reputation first and foremost to the firm, snowy-fleshed Baltic cod that swim in these ice-cold Nordic waters. The fish played an outsize role in Denmark's commercial history, as it did for all of Scandinavia—an intriguing tale well told by Mark Kurlansky in his bestselling book *Cod*. Now becoming scarce and thus protected against overfishing, this large, lovely fish with gold-spotted silvery skin is the most succulently flavorful of cods, its tender flesh giving way with just the right amount of resistance.

A Baltic delicacy, simply and elegantly prepared

A Christmas and New Year's Eve tradition, boiled cod is most popular in winter months, as the cold renders the fish very flavorful. At its best when its natural elegance and richness is allowed to shine through, the dish is prepared with stunningly simple perfection in Danish homes and at the best of Copenhagen's fish restaurants.

In the more traditional dining rooms, presentation is epic, the whole codfish arriving on a large platter with choice morsels of liver, roe, shoulder and neck meat, and the head complete with tongue, cheeks, and brains—all cherished by the most serious connoisseurs. Gently simmered (not actually boiled) in water with salt, peppercorns, bay leaves, and perhaps a little vinegar, the fish is accompanied by dill, boiled potatoes, chopped hard-cooked eggs, pickled beets, capers, freshly grated horseradish, and mild mustard sauce or a small lake of hot melted butter.

The traditional dessert after this fishy feast is a chunk of Danish blue cheese, usually served with a few slices of cold raw vegetables such as celery, cucumber, and red radishes, plus a few grapes. Naturally you'll be toasting the *torsk* (Danish for cod) with aquavit at the start of the meal, and sustaining yourself through it with a sunny beer or a light red wine. And just as naturally, you'll do as the Danes do and plan for a nap afterward—a necessity due to the meal's high phosphorous content.

WHERE: *In Copenhagen*, in winter, Lumskebugten, tel 45/33-15-60-29. lumskebugten .dk. **FURTHER INFORMATION AND RECIPES:** *Danish Cooking and Baking Traditions* by Arthur L. Meyer (2011); food.com (search boiled cod); scandinaviancooking.com (search spicing up the humble cod).

‖‖‖‖‖‖‖‖‖‖‖‖‖‖‖‖‖‖‖‖‖‖‖‖‖‖

Krämmerhüse med Flødeskům

Danish

Perhaps a forerunner of ice cream cones, this dessert is far simpler to realize, as there is no time-out for freezing. One of the prettiest and most seductive Scandinavian treats, this primarily Danish triumph consists of a crisp, thin, gaufrette-like cone filled with whipped heavy cream, lightly sugared and perhaps dotted with colorful preserves of strawberries, lingonberries, cloudberries, or red currants. The crackling pancake-cookies that act as receptacles for the snowy delight—*krämmerhüse* (*kremmerhuset* in Norwegian) literally translates to "cream houses"—are formed by spreading batter onto baking sheets in long ovals. Once baked, the ovals must be turned into cones immediately, as they become crisp and brittle once cool.

Filled with freshly whipped cream and garnished with fruit just before being served, the cones are most attractive when gathered, bouquetlike, in a footed glass vase or large, wide goblet, anchored in a base of glass marbles.

There they will not stay for long.

WHERE: *In Santa Barbara, CA,* Andersen's Danish Restaurant and Bakery, tel 805-962-5085, andersenssantabarbara.com. **FURTHER INFORMATION AND RECIPES:** *Danish Cooking and Baking Traditions* by Arthur L. Meyer (2011); bigoven.com (search danish cones). **SEE ALSO:** Whipped Cream, page 321.

‖‖‖‖‖‖‖‖‖‖‖‖‖‖‖‖‖‖‖‖‖‖‖‖‖‖

Kransekager

Wreath Cakes

Danish, Norwegian

If the Danish town of Odense, on the island of Fyn, isn't destination enough by virtue of being Hans Christian Andersen's hometown, food tourists take note: It also happens to be an excellent place to sample expertly prepared wreath cakes, *kransekager,* as well as the most respected source of the Danish marzipan much loved in various chocolate-coated forms.

Likely to appear on special occasions with coffee or tea, the kransekage is virtually a trademark among Danish desserts. One taste of the subtly bittersweet pastry, tenderly moist, with toasted, nutty overtones, and you'll understand why. Based on marzipan, the classic confectionery paste of ground almonds, sugar, and egg white, kransekage is distinguished by a blend of bitter and sweet almonds that creates a subtle flavor counterpoint.

Though the *kranse* means wreath, these *kager*—cakes—are most often found in the long finger shapes known as *stykker,* drizzled with lacy zigzags of white sugar frosting. Widely available throughout Denmark and in some U.S. cities, they may be freshly baked,

A festive cake made of almonds, sugar, and egg whites

prepackaged and frozen, or even canned. Not surprisingly, the fresher the better. For special occasions such as birthdays, weddings, and holidays, kransekager are ring-shaped—baked in a series of graduated rings (hence the wreaths), stacked to form tall, tapering towers, and decorated with tiny red-and-white paper Danish flags or red-white-and-blue Norwegian flags. For weddings with a patriotic touch, the baked cakes are iced white before being stacked.

RETAIL AND MAIL ORDER: *In Solvang, CA,* Solvang Bakery, tel 805-688-4939, solvang bakery.com (click Products, then search kransekage); *in Seattle,* Nielsen's Pastries, tel 206-282-3004, nielsenspastries.com (click Dessert Pastry); Larsens Danish Bakery, tel 800-626-8631, larsensbakery.com (search kransekage). **MAIL ORDER:** For Odense marzipan, amazon.com. **FURTHER INFORMATION AND RECIPES:** *Scandinavian Baking* by Trine Hahnemann (2014); scandina vianfood.about.com (search kransekake). **SEE ALSO:** Marzipan, page 304. **TIP:** A cool, flowery white dessert wine adds to your pleasure.

‖‖‖‖‖‖‖‖‖‖‖‖‖‖‖‖‖‖‖‖‖

DUCK DUE FOR A RENAISSANCE

Krydret And med Flødepeberrodssauce

Corned Duck with Frozen Horseradish Cream

Danish

The recipe for this old-fashioned Danish specialty, a blush-pink salt-pickled duck, ought to be revived by some ambitious chef seeking a reputation for ingenuity; it has all the makings of the kind of showy winner that appeals to ordinary diners and food critics alike.

The dish calls for a whole, trimmed, lean bird of about five pounds—a mallard or a wild duck would do nicely. Heavily salted inside and out, and placed in a glass or ceramic bowl with bay leaves and crushed peppercorns, the duck ripens for two days in the refrigerator before being very slowly poached with a large onion, a carrot, a parsnip, a few sprigs of parsley, and a knob of celeriac. It is done after about two hours, or when the meat is falling off the bone tender.

Boned and carved into serving pieces overlaid with strips of skin, the duck is topped with *flødepeberrodssauce,* a frozen combination of whipped cream and grated fresh horseradish. That topping—also popular with boiled beef or poached chicken—melts down and lends its sweet-hot elegance to the luscious meat. Mashed potatoes make the best side,

along with creamed, nutmeg-scented spinach.

WHERE: *In Copenhagen,* Schønnemann, tel 45/33-12-07-85, restaurantschonnemann.dk. **MAIL ORDER:** For whole duck, D'Artagnan, tel 800-327-8246, dartagnan.com (search rohan duck). **FURTHER INFORMATION AND RECIPES:** *The Scandinavian Kitchen* by Camilla Plum (2011); allrecipes.com (search frozen horseradish sauce).

STILL LIFE WITH PIG AND FRUIT

Mørbrad med Svedsker og Æbler

Roast Pork Loin with Prune and Apple Stuffing

Danish

A lthough their lean, sweet pork stands on its own, when the Danes pair the loin with dried prunes and fresh apples, the results are memorable. The fruit adds richness, keeping the meat moist as it roasts to succulent perfection for a dish that

is a favorite throughout the winter, and especially at Christmas.

Trimmed off the rack of bones, the loin is wrapped in thin sheets of pork fat. A hole is punched lengthwise through the center of the meat with a wide-bladed knife and the inside is rubbed with salt, pepper, dry mustard, and a bit of powdered ginger before being packed with pitted prunes (soaked in a rich red wine such as port and seasoned with a few cloves) and chunks of tart apples sprinkled with lemon juice.

Spiced, spiked, and stuffed for the holiday table

Tied and rubbed on all sides with the same spice mixture, the loin is then ready for roasting.

The perfect roasting rack is the intact rack of bones trimmed from the meat, set inside a casserole dish. Roasted slowly in a moderate oven, the pork picks up the sweet and tart overtones of the fruit. As they cook, the meat and bones develop a kind of demi-glace concentration in the pan. This becomes the basis of a robust gravy, bound with flour and thinned with a little Madeira wine and a slight shimmer of sweet cream. All is tinted a festive pink by the final addition of some red currant jelly, which melts into the sauce to gloss the thinly sliced meat surrounding prune and apple. Sides of roasted potatoes and red cabbage are essential to this feast.

WHERE: *In Elk Horn, IA,* Danish Inn, tel 712-764-4251, danishinnrestaurant.com. **FURTHER INFORMATION AND RECIPES:** *Aquavit* by Marcus Samuelsson (2003); food.com (search danish fruit stuffed pork roast).

┤||||||||||||||||||||||||||||├

THE SHRIMPIEST SHRIMP

Rejer

Danish

Summer in Denmark is the time for one of that country's most famous and irresistible treats: the tiny shrimp called *rejer*, innocently sweet and no bigger than a toddler's pinkie finger. To get an idea of just how small these shrimpy shrimp

are, consider that one of the more spectacular open-faced rejer sandwiches, fittingly called "shrimps in a crowd," features a pyramid-pile of two hundred of these mini-crustaceans. Thickly buttered French-style white bread and a thin lettuce leaf should be these tiny beauties' only companions, with permissible additions being a sprig of dill and a slim wedge of lemon. Often the shrimp are served on a plate with bread on the side, but that is about the only variation.

Anything so deliciously salty-sweet and succulently tender comes at a high price—not only because of the law of supply and demand, but also because of the cost of peeling the shrimp, a delicate job that can only be done by hand.

Where: *In Copenhagen,* Kanal Caféen, tel 45/33-11-57-70, kanalcafeen.dk; Sankt Annæ, tel 45/33-12-54-97, restaurantsanktannae.dk; Ida Davidsen, tel 45/33-91-36-55, idadavidsen.dk.

┤||||||||||||||||||||||||||||├

JELL-O FOR GROWN-UPS

Rødgrød med Fløde

Red Berry Pudding with Cream

Danish

In cold countries, summer fruits are highly prized and preserved in countless ways—frozen, jarred, cooked into lush jams and preserves, or bottled up as flavorful juice. It is to red berry juice that the wonderful garnet-red dessert the

Danes call *rødgrød* owes its hue.

The Danes are probably the only people in the world who can pronounce its name, requiring as it does the back-of-the-throat glottal stop typical of the Danish language. Some claim—good-naturedly—the resulting sound to be the consequence of a pervasive throat disease. In Germany, the same dessert is known, a bit more pronounceably, as *rote grütze.*

The height of red pudding season is in fact

summer, when berry juice can be freshly pressed at home—the most desirable berries being red currants, alone or combined with raspberries and black currants, and sometimes with sour cherries. The fruit is simmered for just a few minutes, until it begins to give up its juices. Strained, seasoned with sugar, and mixed with cornstarch, the juices are then cooked again until they thicken to about the consistency of well-stirred yogurt. Poured into individual glass dishes, the bright red substance is chilled until set.

Though rødgrød is most often compared to Jell-O, which owes its clarity to the gelatin with which it is set, here the use of cornstarch makes for an opaque, creamy gel in the style of an English flummery pudding. So popular is the dessert that its ingredients are sold powdered in packages, much like Jell-O or junket—actually quite pleasant, but no match for the freshly pressed version.

Rødgrød, of course, is only the first half of this treat's name. What of the fløde, to say nothing of flødeskum? The former means cream (sweet and heavy), and the latter means whipped cream. In either form, that extra dollop of richness is the classic topping for this cool, sweet, and very red-tasting dessert.

WHERE: *In Santa Barbara, CA,* Andersen's Danish Restaurant and Bakery, tel 805-962-5085, andersenssantabarbara.com. **MAIL ORDER:** scandinavianbutik.com (click Food, then Desserts, then search junket). **FURTHER INFORMATION AND RECIPES:** *Danish Cooking and Baking Traditions* by Arthur L. Meyer (2011); food.com (search rodgrod med flode).

RED CABBAGE GETS THE BLUES

Rødkål

Danish

With its shiny slivers of ruby-red cabbage and its piquant flavor, this festive Danish specialty takes on a jewel-like sheen and sweet-tart overtones as a few dollops of red currant jelly are stirred in for the last minutes of cooking.

As in most northern European countries where red cabbage, *rødkål,* is favored alongside roasted meats and game, in Denmark cooks take pains to preserve the vegetable's color and prevent it from fading to a pale, washed-out state. First, they cut the cabbage with a stainless-steel knife, as opposed to a carbon-steel blade, to help prevent blackening. Then, to further prevent discoloration, they toss the raw slivered cabbage with vinegar and allow it to sit for about fifteen minutes, at which point the mass actually takes on a distinct blue-purple tint (the reason for the dish's German name, *Blaukraut*).

A dish that turns red cabbage into a precious gem

Once these measures are in place, it's time to cook the rødkål in seasoned water, often with diced bacon or duck fat and sliced, peeled apples (first sautéed in butter) stirred in. Gradually seasoned with brown sugar as it softens, the cabbage develops a subtle sweet-and-sour tang. The water should be absorbed by the time the cabbage is soft, resulting in the desired dry-but-juicy state. Then, for the last fifteen minutes or so, it simmers under that color-enhancing glossing of red currant jelly.

The apples may be omitted, or grated raw and added toward the end of the cooking process; sautéed onions may also join the fray at this point. A scant sprinkling of lightly crushed caraway seeds can add an exotic touch to the mix, and the plain, sharp distilled vinegar used as the initial soaking liquid may be replaced by cider or red wine vinegar or the brine of pickled beets. But one thing all cooks agree on is that the dish should be prepared twenty-four hours in advance of serving, so it can develop a rich winey flavor as it ripens in the refrigerator.

Six to eight times higher in vitamin C than green cabbage, red cabbage is most often cooked with a little sugar in Northern Europe, thereby adding calories but also the luxurious flavor that makes it a winter favorite. No Scandinavian Christmas goose, duck, or pork roast would be complete without it. Slightly warm, red cabbage is a favorite topping on open sandwiches of sliced roasted duck breast or pork, or alongside the fried meat cakes called *frikadeller* (see page 348).

MAIL ORDER: For red current jelly, scandina vianbutik.com (click Food, then Preserves, then search red currant jelly). **FURTHER INFORMATION AND RECIPES:** *Scandinavian Christmas* by Trine Hahnemann (2012); epicurious.com (search danish red cabbage). **TIP:** When choosing a red cabbage, look for bright, shiny leaves. Avoid heads with blackened, cracked leaves. For the richest flavor, cook twenty-four hours in advance, chill, and reheat at serving time.

---------||||||||||||||||||||||||||||||----------

A SENSE OF PLAICE

Rødspætte

Plaice

Danish

Dover sole may be considered the world's prime flatfish, but those who have tasted its Danish cousin *rødspætte*, or plaice (*Pleuronectes platessa*), may go to the mat over the distinction. The closest comparison may be summer fluke, the flounderlike fish caught off Long Island, New York.

Taking its Danish name from the tiny, golden-red spots (*rødspætte*) that sparkle on its bronze skin, the plaice develops a remarkably fresh, deep-sea flavor as it swims in the icy salt waters of the North Sea. Firm-textured, the wide flat fish lends itself to many preparations.

Although it is sometimes marinated or smoked, like all great foods plaice deserves to be prepared in respectfully simple ways: sautéed whole, *meunière*-style, and then filleted. It may be topped with a garland of tiny shrimp, a dousing of hot melted butter, and a sprinkling of crisp bread crumbs. Or it can be filleted, quickly fried to a crisp, and accented with a sprightly rémoulade sauce, as it would be in an open sandwich.

Another preparation, "Dry Jutlanders"— named after the peninsula that forms the bulk of Denmark's mainland—is a notable treat in summer. A specialty in Frederikshavn, where the best plaice is caught, the smallest fish are cleaned, trimmed, and tied together in pairs to be salted down for two to three hours. Dried outdoors in the breezy shade until their skin can be stripped off, the fillets can be floured and fried in butter, and are typically served with Danish rye bread.

WHERE: *In Copenhagen,* Schønnemann, tel 45/33-12-07-85, restaurantschonnemann.dk. **FURTHER INFORMATION AND RECIPE:** *The River Cottage Fish Book* by Hugh Fearnley-Whittingstall and Nick Fisher (2012). **TIP:** Along with summer fluke, grey sole is also a fair substitute.

————————————|||||||||||||||||||||||||||||||————————————

Rullepølse

Rolled sausage

Danish

Rullepølse is the sort of creation that makes you wonder who thought of it first. The detailed work involved in making the enticingly spicy rolled-up "sausage" is a tribute to ingenuity, turning undesirable cuts of meat into a delicacy

that one cannot live without. The meat involved is usually one of the tougher cuts of pork, beef, veal, or lamb, the last being the most tender and earthily flavorful.

Boned, split, and flattened, the meat of choice is spread with minced onion or shallots, parsley, crushed black peppercorns, cloves, and allspice—and, commercially, with a bit of salt peter, the curing agent sodium nitrate. Rolled up jelly-roll style and firmly tied, the meat is brined for a few days. Then it's off to a poaching session, after which it is fitted into a wooden box with a screw-down lid and compressed into a small, flat-topped roll.

Several days later, it is finally sliced

paper-thin, the creamy rings of fat entwining with the bright pink meat and the green glints of parsley. Most often rullepølse is served in an open sandwich, atop Danish rye bread spread with pork drippings or fresh lard, and garnished with glistening amber meat aspic—a treat similar to the peppery, garlicky rolled beef fast disappearing from Jewish delicatessens because it is costly to produce.

WHERE: *In Minneapolis,* Ingebretsen's, tel 800-279-9333, ingebretsens.com; *in Solvang, CA,* Nielsen's Market, tel 805-688-3236, nielsensmarket .com. **FURTHER INFORMATION AND RECIPES:** *Danish Cooking and Baking Traditions* by Arthur L. Meyer (2011); cooks.com (search rullepolse).

————————————|||||||||||||||||||||||||||||||————————————

Smørrebrød

Danish

Buttered bread (*smørrebrød*) is the modest name for what are surely the world's most beautiful sandwiches—they are served open, the better to display the handiwork of the artful chefs who painstakingly prepare their *paalaeg,* or toppings.

A Danish mainstay, especially for lunch and between-meal snacks, open sandwiches are said to have come into their own in the eighteenth century, presaging two trends we now consider cutting-edge: meals made up of small

dishes, and the fashion for foods piled high in towering Pisa-like arrangements.

To attain impressive heights of sandwich verticality, open-sandwich chefs master the art of cutting, folding, and splaying cucumbers, tomatoes, sausage slices, and roasted meats into the flower petals and butterfly wings they use to crown their creations. Added to the mix might be spirals of slim fried onions or little hills of sunny, custardy scrambled eggs soft-cooked with cream. Sprigs of dill and parsley and sprinklings of chives and tarragon lend color and aroma.

The sandwiches are customarily ordered in courses—two, three, or four to a meal, depending on one's capacity and the size of the smørrebrød. Fish comes out first: ruby-red slivers of *maatjes* herring (see page 343) topped with curls of red onion and tomato. Glazed flat bronze fillets of smoked eel with cloudlets of horseradish-spiked whipped cream. Coral slices of smoked salmon mantled with scrambled eggs.

An exquisite array of Denmark's famous sandwiches

Then come the meats. Rare roast beef with browned onions and perhaps a raw egg yolk. The same garnish on the popular beef tartare, here scraped to order with a razorlike knife rather than ground. Slices of soft, creamy liver pâté trimmed with bacon strips, a shiny slice of meaty aspic, and a few sautéed wild mushrooms. Cool sausages decked out with Italian salad (a red, white, and green combination of

peas or tiny cuts of green beans, carrots or pimiento, and cauliflower) and accompanied by tarragon-perfumed mayonnaise lightened with whipped cream. As a novel "dessert," a raw egg yolk and a ring or two of onion might soften the bite of Denmark's tangy blue cheese.

Spread thick to act as a buffer between bread and dangerously juicy toppings, Denmark's justly famous butter is extremely important to the success of any open sandwich. So is its bread, generally the moist and grainy *rugbrød*, or rye bread, though a few paalaeg require other varieties. Crisp-crusted, soft white French bread is de rigueur for the meat of crustaceans—lobster, crab, and the tiny Danish shrimp, *rejer*, the latter mounded and garnished with only a twist of lemon and a sprig of dill; for strong cheeses, crisp *knäkebrød* or tangy sourdoughs are just the thing. No matter what the bread or the filling, the sandwiches are best washed down with a glass of the country's yeasty golden beer.

Variety is the spice of life, which is why some restaurants feature open sandwiches in abundance, with certain menus listing up to 250 choices. Such is the volume at Ida Davidsen's celebrated Copenhagen mecca, where the tradition begun in 1883 by Ida's great-grandfather, Oskar Davidsen, lives on. Her restaurant is a must-stop for any newcomer to the smørrebrød custom, although an honest open-sandwich exploration should follow up at lower-key, more quietly traditional local favorites such as the Kanal Caféen and Sankt Annæ, also in the Danish capital.

WHERE: *In Copenhagen*, Ida Davidsen, tel 45/33-91-36-55, idadavidsen.dk; Kanal Caféen, tel 45/33-11-57-70, kanalcafeen.dk; Sankt Annæ, tel 45/33-12-54-97, restaurantsanktannae.dk; *in Santa Barbara, CA*, Andersen's Danish Restaurant and Bakery, tel 805-962-5085, anderssonsantabarbara.com. **FURTHER INFORMATION AND RECIPES:** *Scandinavian Baking* by Trine Hahnemann (2014); *Open Your Heart to the Danish Open . . .* by Ida Davidsen and Mia Davidsen (1999); *The Oskar Davidsen Book of Open Sandwiches* by James R. White (1962).

Wienerbrød

Danish

Visitors looking for authentic pastries in Denmark are usually surprised to discover that the wonderfully buttery treats they seek are known as "Vienna breads," or *wienerbrød*. A second surprise comes when they taste these delectable pastries in any of their traditional forms—especially if the sentence "I'll have a Danish" brings to mind a series of heavy, greasy coffee shop disasters that call diplomatic relations between Denmark and the U.S. into question.

The real thing is based on yeast puff pastry, the yeast adding moisture and a particular nose-twitching pungency to the flavor, and butter folded in between many layers of dough creating that optimum flakiness. (Some insist that margarine makes for a more desirable and workable dough, but pay no heed.)

Once the basic dough is ready, wienerbrød takes on many forms and ingests many fillings. In the snail-like swirls known as *snegle*, it entwines walnuts, currants, cinnamon, and sugar. Strips filled with almond paste fan out into the much-loved cockscombs, or *kamme*. Big square puffs are filled with custard and dabbed with red currant jelly for substantial envelopes, or *spandau*. Apricot jam defines the large double twists known as apricot slips or *abrikossnitte*, and a big, round ring of connected buns flavored only with butter, sugar, and drizzlings of white icing is known simply as butter cake, or *smørkage*. The list of wienerbrød goes on. Some are miniature; some enriched with apples, prunes, or lemon cream; all are intended to take morning or afternoon coffee to a whole new, delectable level.

Traditional Danish pastries on display

Lest you be left wondering: To the Austrians this danish is known as a *plunder*.

WHERE: *In Copenhagen,* Conditori & Cafe H.C. Andersen, tel 45/33-32-80-98, h-c-andersen .dk; Lagkagehuset, tel 45/72-14-47-00, lagkagehuset .dk; *in Santa Barbara, CA,* Andersen's Danish Restaurant and Bakery, tel 805-962-5085, andersens santabarbara.com; *in Glendale, CA,* Berolina Bakery, tel 818-249-6506, berolinabakery.com; *in Seattle,* Larsens Danish Bakery, tel 800-626-8631, larsensbakery.com. **FURTHER INFORMATION AND RECIPES:** *Scandinavian Baking* by Trine Hahnemann (2014); mydanishkitchen.com (search kanel-snegle); taste.com.au (search spandau).

Hirvensarvet

Stags' Antlers

Finnish

E at your reindeer this holiday season, by way of these traditional Nordic Christmas cookies. (Fittingly enough, they come from Finland, where reindeer meat is more common than in any other Scandinavian country.) Crisp, buttery, and aromatic with cardamom, these memorably shaped Stags' Antlers are easy to bake and keep well, stored in an airtight container, preferably a metal cookie tin.

Stags' Antlers

Makes about 4 dozen cookies

¼ cup (½ stick) unsalted butter
¾ cup sugar
1 extra large egg, plus 2 egg yolks
¼ cup heavy (whipping) cream
1 teaspoon cardamom
½ teaspoon salt
2 cups all-purpose flour
1 teaspoon baking soda
¾ cup cornstarch

1. Position a rack in the center of the oven and preheat to 350°F. Lightly butter a baking sheet.
2. Cream the butter and sugar until light and fluffy. Beat in the egg and egg yolks. Stir in the cream, cardamom, and salt.

3. In a medium-size bowl, sift the flour together with the baking soda and cornstarch, then sift the flour mixture into the butter mixture. Blend thoroughly, kneading the dough slightly until it is firm enough to roll out.
4. Flour a work surface and a rolling pin and roll out the dough to a ¼-inch thickness. Cut the dough into strips that are 2 inches long by 1 inch wide. Make 2 slits on 1 edge of each strip, about ¾ inch from each end, cutting down a little more than half the width of the strip. Curve the strips gently to open the slits slightly. Place the strips of dough 1 inch apart on the prepared baking sheet.
5. Bake the cookies until pale golden brown, about 15 minutes. Transfer the baked cookies to a wire rack to cool completely. Repeat with the remaining dough.

FURTHER INFORMATION AND ADDITIONAL RECIPE: ifood.tv (search stags antlers). TIP: Full flavor will develop if the antlers are stored for twenty-four hours before being eaten.

Sauna Sausage

Finnish, Swedish

W hat you will need for this memorable experience, a traditional and unabashedly festive custom in Finland and Sweden: a few of the thick, ring-shaped sausages known as *falukorv,* and access to a sauna. If possible, that sauna should be in a rustic hut at the edge of an ice-cold, clear lake—handy for jumping into when things get too hot inside.

Although a sauna, heated by hot stones, is basically a dry "bath," occasional moisture is needed to induce sweating and keep participants from shriveling like raisins. Hence, intermittent dousings of the occupants and rocks with pails of cold water, or more picturesquely, light beatings with birch branches of sweet-smelling leaves soaked in cold water.

Where do the sausages come into the equation? As one is not supposed to eat for a couple of hours before sauna-ing, hunger builds up. The solution: As guests steam and roast, so does this meaty, ginger-spiced sausage made of fat-edged pork in Sweden and of a pork and mutton mixture in Finland. If placed directly on the hot stones, the sausage sizzles and sputters, annoying those who long to roast in complete silence. For those participants, the sausage is wrapped in aluminum foil, in which it can steam to maximum plumpness in relative silence before being spiked with sharp mustard. (Perverse types who scoff at sausage can take respite in a spread of herring, tomatoes, cucumbers, bread, and cheese.)

Whether the feast is consumed right in the sauna room, in an adjoining dressing room, or outdoors in the long summer evenings, utensils are generally not in attendance. It's fingers all the way.

One works up a thirst quickly in a sauna. The beverage of choice for the post-bath meal is cold beer swigged directly from the bottle. Also on offer in Finland is *sima*, a special cider-like mead fermented with yeast and sweetly soured with a mix of lemon, white and brown sugars, and a molasses-like syrup.

FURTHER INFORMATION AND RECIPES: *The Sauna Cookbook* by Tuula Kaitila and Edey Saarinen (2004); saunascape.com. **TIP:** In lieu of Finnish sauna sausage, Polish kielbasa (see page 401) works almost as well.

A LAMB OF A HAM

Fenalår

Salted Lamb

Norwegian

While salt-cured beef and pork are hardly unusual in many countries, cured lamb is something else again—except for use in sausages, lamb meat is generally eaten young and fresh. But in Norway, where grazing grounds are sparse and so are best suited to sheep, and where harsh winters have long made preserved foods a necessity, lamb and mutton are salt-cured in the style of ham.

The category of dried meats known as *spekemat* may have begun as an ancient necessity, but over time it's become a preferred choice. Whether prepared with young lamb or older mutton, *fenalår*—salted, brined, dried, and smoked to a rich mahogany brown—has a unique flavor not to be missed by anyone who has the chance to try it. As with ham, the cured leg is wrapped in cloth and hung in a cool, well-ventilated room. As with all cured meat, it must hang free. Any part that touches a wall or other surface will rot.

After four to six months, the firm but supple meat is trimmed, thinly sliced, and eaten cold and uncooked just like the Italian prosciutto. Possible accompaniments range from crispbreads (see The Nordic Bread Basket, page 341) or the Norwegian *lefse* or *lompe* breads to boiled buttered potatoes, creamed spinach, or scrambled eggs. The scraps and bone of fenalår are saved to enrich soups.

Where: *In Oslo,* Fenaknoken, tel 47/22-42-34-57, fenaknoken.no. **Mail order:** scandinavian foodstore.com (search willy's fenalaar).

⊣||||||||||||||||||||||||||||||||⊢

A DEEP-SEA BREAKFAST WORTH RISING FOR

Morning Shrimp in Oslo

Norwegian

I f you've never had shrimp for breakfast, you have probably never been to Oslo. It is almost unimaginable that anyone visiting that mountain-rimmed seaside capital would not hurry down to the harbor, just across from the stately town hall square, to buy breakfast from the shrimp boats before the day's supply gives out.

From 7 a.m. to 1 p.m. every day except Sunday, the dock is jammed with boats whose crews have caught shrimp during the night and then boiled them as they sailed toward the harbor. Crowds of waiting gourmands buy paper bags full of these small, sweet, rosy specimens. Then they loll around the docks shelling the shrimp one after the other, sucking the rich fat from their heads and devouring the supple tail meat just as compulsively as one might down salted peanuts. Shells are tossed back into the harbor, where gulls swoop down for their own breakfast, instantly cleaning up the mess. The larger the crowds, of course, the sooner the shrimp supplies give out. (Keep this in mind if there during the summer high tourist season.)

These delicate little creatures, which run about thirty-five to a pound—not as tiny as the Danish *rejer* (see page 357)—offer a revelation in flavor. And because they have not been chilled, they retain the delightful, gentle sweetness of the sea air. Nobody but a latter-day Jacques Cousteau could hope to enjoy a fresher catch.

The early-bird special, harborside

Where: Oslo harbor, Rådhusbrygge 3 (Pier 3). **When:** Monday through Saturday from 7 a.m. to 1 p.m. **Further information:** visitoslo.com (search fishing boats with fresh shrimp and fish).

————————|||||||||||||||||||||||||||||||||||—————————

THE THURSDAY NIGHT SPECIAL

Ärter med Fläsk, Plätter

Yellow Pea Soup with Pork, Swedish Pancakes with Lingonberries

Swedish

If you are lucky enough to be in Sweden on a Thursday night and to be invited to an old-fashioned dinner in a home or at a very traditional restaurant, expect to find a main course of *ärter med fläsk*: a volcanically hot yellow pea soup that is as thick as a stew, soothingly scented with onion, marjoram, ginger, and perhaps a hint of cloves. At the bottom of each substantial portion will lie thin slices of tenderly pink salt pork glistening with edges of nicely saline fat. If the golden pea soup is served on its own, the pork may appear as a second course, along with boiled potatoes and a dab of good Swedish mustard.

It's a custom that dates back to 1577. On a certain Thursday night sometime during that year, King Eric XIV was poisoned by his brother—yellow pea soup being the murderous vehicle.

Does the continuing custom celebrate his death or mourn it? The answer is unclear, and the same uncertainty applies to the course that follows. Hard to say how the tiny, thin Swedish pancakes known as *plätter* (see page 371) came to be the traditional Thursday night dessert, but we can be thankful nonetheless. Our gratitude goes out to the light egg, milk, salt, and flour batter that is fried golden brown in the circular indentations of the classic iron plätter pan, and to the lacy, crisp-edged pancakes that emerge. (Thanks are due as well for the dab of unsalted butter, the sprinkle of confectioners' sugar, and the topping of fresh, stewed, or lusciously preserved lingonberries that adorn this beloved Thursday night treat.)

WHERE: *In Stockholm,* on special days, Den Gyldene Freden, tel 46/8-249-760, gyldene freden.se; *in New York,* Aquavit, tel 212-307-7311, aquavit.org. **MAIL ORDER:** For Swedish split peas, scandinavianbutik.com (click Food, then Vegetables, then search lars own yellow peas); amazon.com (search yellow split peas). **FURTHER INFORMATION AND RECIPES:** *Aquavit* by Marcus Samuelsson (2003); epicurious.com (search scandinavian yellow pea soup). **SEE ALSO:** Lingonberries, page 340.

————————|||||||||||||||||||||||||||||||||||—————————

THE SWEET AND SOUR OF BAKED BEANS

Bruna Bönor

Swedish

When it comes to the humble brown bean—in France, the United States, Italy, and Latin America alike—every cook has his or her own secret recipe. For Sweden's tiny baked brown beans, or *bruna bönor,* four elements are essential before improvisation can even be considered. First, the exactly right, tiny brown kidney beans available in many Scandinavian food shops; then, a precise kind of Swedish corn syrup with molasses-like overtones; next, plain distilled vinegar to add bite; and finally brown sugar.

Some cooks insist on powdered mustard, pepper, an onion buried in the center, and perhaps even some diced salt pork scattered into the soaked beans as they are transferred into the crock; the meat contributes a silky texture and an extra dimension of robust flavor. The beans can be simmered on top of the stove or baked in the oven, the latter making for a more intense, richer result in which the soft but still-intact beans absorb the sweet-tart-spicy overtones of the sauce.

Standard accompaniments include fried slices of salt pork, ham, or meatballs, along with red cabbage and lingonberry preserves. (Of course, if the beans are being served as part of one of Sweden's infamous smorgasbords, the list of accompaniments goes on and on.)

WHERE: *In New York,* Aquavit, tel 212-307-7311, aquavit.org; Smörgås Chef at Scandinavia House, tel 212-686-4230, smorgas.com (click Scandinavia House); *in Chicago,* Ann Sather at multiple locations, annsather.com. **MAIL ORDER:** scandinavianbutik.com (click Food, then Vegetables, then search brown beans). **FURTHER INFORMATION AND RECIPES:** *The Everything Nordic Cookbook* by Kari Schoening Diehl (2012); scan dinavianfood.about.com (search swedish brown beans). **SEE ALSO:** Boston Baked Beans, page 531.

A FEW CUTS ABOVE MOST ROASTED POTATOES

Hasselbackspotatis

Swedish

Roasted to buttery softness with a golden brown crust of bread crumbs and Parmesan, these potatoes are luscious favorites in Sweden, where they often accompany grilled or roasted meats and poultry. What makes them so special

is the scoring, which allows the little oval potatoes to fan out slightly, absorbing the butter and also developing rows of crisp edges as they bake.

Hasselback Potatoes

Serves 4 to 8 as a side dish

8 small oval potatoes, about 3½ inches long and 2 inches wide, such as California whites or russet baking potatoes
½ cup (1 stick) unsalted butter, melted
Salt
Freshly ground black pepper
½ cup fine dry bread crumbs
¼ to ⅓ cup freshly grated Parmesan

1. Peel the potatoes. Each will have to stand level, so if necessary, trim a thin slice from the flattest side. Using a sharp knife with a thin blade, score each potato, making parallel vertical cuts crosswise, a little less than ¼ inch apart and cutting about two thirds of the way down through the potato. Do not cut through the bottom. If this proves difficult, place a potato in the bowl of a wooden spoon and then slice downward; the edge of the spoon will prevent the knife from going all the way down to the bottom of the potato. The potatoes can be prepared to this point up to 2 hours before baking. Place the potatoes in a bowl and add enough water to cover them completely.

2. Preheat the oven to 400°F.

The humble potato meets a very clever knife trick.

them into the dish. Arrange the potatoes in the pan, scored side up, and baste them with the melted butter. Sprinkle the potatoes with salt and pepper to taste.

4. Bake the potatoes until you can slide a skewer almost all the way through a potato, about 30 minutes. Baste the potatoes again with the butter in the baking dish and sprinkle each with bread crumbs and Parmesan. Bake the potatoes until a skewer easily slips all the way through, 15 to 20 minutes longer. Serve the potatoes at once.

3. Pat each potato very dry with paper towels. Select a baking dish just large enough to hold the potatoes close together without cramming

Further information and recipes: scandinavianfood.about.com (search hasselback potatoes); epicurious.com (search hasselback potatoes). **See also:** Pommes de Terre, Four Ways, page 116.

————————|||||||||||||||||||||||||||||||||||—————————

THE WORLD'S SECOND MOST FAMOUS MEATBALLS

Köttbullar

Swedish

Say the word *meatballs* and almost everyone thinks Italian. Everyone, that is, but those who have known the gustatory pleasure of the Swedish mini-meatballs that make regular appearances on smorgasbord tables far and wide.

That's not the only place you'll find them in Sweden, however—in a slightly larger size, they become a main course for lunch or dinner.

Crispy brown on the outside, airy and light within, the meatballs combine beef with pork or veal, all finely ground together with hints of onion, salt, pepper, and an aromatic dash of allspice.

Uniquely, mashed potatoes are added to the mix for lightness, although some cooks prefer fine bread crumbs soaked in cream, perhaps with a little potato starch added for flavor. Whatever the individual tweak, the net result is quite the sticky mass. Meatball makers will find it necessary to use wet hands or two wet spoons to shape the meat into tiny rounds not much bigger than hazelnuts (or walnuts, for a

main-course serving) before quickly browning the meatballs in hot butter.

Those who prefer crispness end the cooking there, while those craving a richer, more luxurious finish pour heavy sweet cream into the empty but still-hot frying pan. Then they scrape up bits and pieces of browned meat and juices, allowing all to reduce to a satiny shimmer while adding a pinch of powdered clove—a festive touch that seems right around Christmastime.

Cushiony, creamy mashed potatoes and garnet-red lingonberry preserves are the natural accompaniments to the *köttbullar*, which also benefit from the addition of lighter sides like red cabbage or cucumber salad.

Where: *In Stockholm,* Den Gyldene Freden, tel 46/8-249-760, gyldenefreden.se; *in New York,* Aquavit, tel 212-307-7311, aquavit.org; Smörgås Chef at Scandinavia House, tel 212-686-4230, smorgas.com (click Scandinavia House); *in Chicago,* Tre Kronor Restaurant, tel 773-267-9888, trekronorrestaurant.com. **Further information and recipes:** *Aquavit* by Marcus Samuelsson (2003); cookstr.com (search swedish meatballs); sweden.se (search meatballs).

—||||||||||||||||||||||||||||||||||||—

FIRST A SAUNA, THEN A FEAST

Kräfter or Rapu

Crayfish

Swedish, Finnish

To the Swedes it's known as *kräftskiva* and to the Finns as *rapujuhlat,* but by any name it's a crayfish party and feast well worth planning a trip around. The feasts take place from late July to mid-September, but if you have the luxury of being particular, opt for early August—peak season for crayfish in Scandinavia, whether the tiny crustaceans have been farmed in its cold, clear freshwater streams or imported from Louisiana ponds (see Crawfish, page 552).

The tender, rosy crayfish, first cousins to the French *écrevisses* and to American crawdads or mudbugs, prompt all-night parties that have crowds of guests gathered around paper-covered tables. Fastidious diners wear decorated bibs as they work their way through massive mounds of cold, succulent shellfish heaped on sprigs of dill.

To partake in this 500-year-old Swedish tradition, place the crayfish in a large pot, cover with cold water, and add some salt and a little sugar. Plunge in some great bouquets of dill, including the flowers gone to seed. When the water comes to a boil, turn off the heat and leave the cover on the pot as the crayfish finish cooking—this should take about eight minutes, depending on their size. Greenish-black when alive, the crayfish turn lobster-red as the water heats. Replace the cooked herb with bunches of fresh dill and let the crayfish cool in the broth before being chilled.

Though many recipes allot only a dozen to

Well-dressed crayfish beget epic late-night revelry.

a portion, hosts in the know plan for as many as thirty to fifty per guest. This may seem like a lot, especially given the fact that each crayfish must be cracked open with fingers or a special knife so the fat can be sucked out of the head and the pearly, sweet-salty meat can be pulled from the tail. A lot, too, when you consider that diners will likely be *sköl*-ing down a shot of schnapps or a quaff or two of beer with each *kräfter*. But a kräftskiva is an energetic affair, requiring much in the way of fuel. Slurping, singing, and speeches extolling the crayfish will grow louder as the evening progresses. Intermittently, guests rinse their fingers in bowls of lemon juice and destroy countless paper napkins.

The most devout traditionalists precede the feast with a sauna, but that hot steam bath might well be more practical as a hangover cure the following day.

Where: *In New York,* in August, Aquavit, tel 212-307-7311, aquavit.org. **Mail order:** scandinavianbutik.com (click Food, then search swedish crawfish). **Further information and recipes:** *The Scandinavian Kitchen* by Camilla Plum (2011); newscancook.com (search boiled crayfish with dill); sweden.se (search crayfish party).

⊢||||||||||||||||||||||||||||||⊣

HOW DO YOU TAKE YOUR COFFEE?

Lammstek

Roast Leg of Lamb with Coffee and Cream

Swedish

Improbable as it may sound, combine some good, strong coffee with a bit of sugar and a touch of heavy sweet cream and you have not only a cup of morning joe but also the perfect baste for a rose-pink leg of lamb. Leave it to the

coffee-loving Swedes to apply their favorite bean to one of their favorite meats. The coffee mollifies the lamb's muttony overtones, while sugar and cream add a lovely flavor and satiny texture to its gravy. If you're dubious, ask any Swede—or, for that matter, any Southerner who uses coffee as a standard ingredient in red-eye gravy (see page 574). Better yet, try this very traditional method at home.

Ideally the dish starts with a leg of young (but not baby) lamb, somewhere around five pounds. Lamb legs that small can be difficult to find unless one lives close to a Greek neighborhood, where butchers will be likely to stock them. Failing that, or ordering from a custom butcher, half a leg will do. In any case, the bone should be left in for maximum flavor and juiciness.

After removing the fell, or thin outer tissue, while leaving a good layer of fat on, insert a few slivers of garlic into the meat, then rub the leg all over with salt, pepper, and a little powdered mustard and ginger. Roast the meat in a 350° oven, allowing about fifteen minutes to the pound for medium-rare, if you're starting with room-temperature meat; if the lamb is cold, allow eighteen to twenty minutes per pound. About halfway through the cooking time, pour on two cups of coffee, brewed double strength and mixed with two teaspoons of sugar and half a cup of cream. Continue roasting the meat with frequent bastings. A proper medium-rare is achieved when a meat thermometer registers 150°. Thicken the strained pan juices with a light blend of cream and flour, and melt in a teaspoonful or two of red currant jelly. Roasted potatoes, braised small white onions, and green salad are classic accompaniments. Once you taste the combination, you'll know why.

Further information and recipes: *Swedish Cooking at Its Best* by Marianne Grönwall van der Tuuk (1962); nytimes.com (search roast leg of lamb swedish style).

Löjrom

Swedish

How depressing the English translation—bleak roe—for so luscious and festive a fish roe as *löjrom*, Sweden's supple, chiffonlike caviar. Although at first glance these tiny, glistening, rose-gold beads look like the less expensive Japanese flying fish roe, tobiko, bleak roe's much softer membrane gives it a more luxurious feel. Its flavor suggests sunlight on water, at once gently salty and faintly sweet.

The eggs are produced by a freshwater fish, the vendace or *Coregonus albula,* that is caught and processed in the town of Kalix, close to the shores of the Gulf of Bothnia.

Almost as pricey as the classic Russian caviar, löjrom is ever more difficult to come by, with its parent fish now protected by preservation efforts. When it is on hand, the roe is much loved atop baked potatoes garnished with thick sour cream and thinly sliced rings of red onion, and also decorates servings of smoked salmon alongside scrambled eggs with minced chives. It makes its most elegant

A fragile, luscious Nordic roe

appearance as the topping for delicately lacy blini enriched with drizzlings of crème fraîche and a few sprigs of dill.

Undoubtedly fresh bleak roe is best, and some fresh, iced löjrom has become available here. But it is fragile to export, and in the States the roe is mostly available only in frozen or jarred forms. The frozen import—slowly thawed and refreshed with a bit of lemon juice—gives a fair idea of how subtly delicious the fresh product can be.

WHERE: *In New York,* Aquavit, tel 212-307-7311, aquavit.org. **MAIL ORDER:** scandinavian foodstore.com (search bleak roe); scandinavian butik.com (click Food, then Seafood, then search bleak roe). **FURTHER INFORMATION AND RECIPE:** swedishfood.com (search löjrom).

Plätter

Swedish

Among the world's most enticing pancakes, be they French crêpes, Italian *crespelle,* or American flapjacks, by far the lightest and most delicate are the tiny round *plätter* of Sweden. The airy, silver dollar–size cakes dabbed with ruby-red lingonberry preserves are as enticing for breakfast as they are for dessert.

There are two secrets to making the tiny treats, the first having to do with flavor and texture. Plätter owe their characteristic richness to a batter that contains more eggs, butter, and sugar—and thus less flour—than that of American flapjacks. As they are not inflated by baking powder, they are thinner as well. The second essential trick is the pan. Leave it to the design-minded Swedes to invent a special device that ensures the exact size and shape of each pancake. Cooks using a *plett*, a special cast-iron plätter griddle into which perfect circles are depressed, cannot possibly err on the size of the finished product. The resulting tiny pancakes are that rare combination of delicate and rich—far too precious to drown in syrup, but great with a fine dusting of confectioners' sugar, perhaps a glossing of butter, and the aforementioned traditional topping of lingonberry preserves.

Sweden's delicate pancakes

The diminutive size means, of course, that a great number of these silky disks can be consumed at a single seating. The homey tearoom-restaurant Sears Fine Food in San Francisco—a plätter landmark since 1938, when it was opened by a retired circus clown whose Swedish wife had inherited a family recipe—claims to serve around 77,000 of the tiny pancakes each week, eighteen to an order, whether for breakfast, lunch, or dinner. What a way to start or end the day!

Where: *In New York,* Aquavit, tel 212-307-7311, aquavit.org; Smörgås Chef at multiple locations, smorgas.com; *in Rockford, IL,* Stockholm Inn, tel 815-397-3534, stockholminn.com; *in North Oaks, Little Canada, and Loomington, MN,* Taste of Scandinavia Bakery & Café, tasteofscandinavia.com; *in San Francisco,* Sears Fine Food, tel 415-986-0700, searsfinefood.com; *in Seattle,* Swedish Cultural Center, tel 206-283-1090, swedishclubnw.org/events/pancake.htm. **Mail order:** For pancake mix, searsfinefood.com; for cast-iron plett pans, La Belle Cuisine, cooksite.com. **Further information and recipes:** *Aquavit* by Marcus Samuelsson (2003); *The Everything Nordic Cookbook* by Kari Schoening Diehl (2012); *The Cooking of Scandinavia* by Dale Brown (1974); foodnetwork.com (search swedish pancakes); nytimes.com (search recipe of the day swedish pancakes). **Special events:** Scanfest, a huge outdoor celebration of culture, Budd Lake, NJ, end of summer, scanfest.org; Scandinavian Day Festival, South Elgin, IL, September, scandinaviandayil.com. **See also:** Lingonberries, page 340.

HOLD THE SLEIGH BELLS

Ren, Poron

Reindeer

Swedish, Finnish, Norwegian

Strange though it may seem to outsiders, reindeer is a meat much loved in all the Nordic zones, and most especially in Lapland, where some of the best specimens are farm-raised. Because reindeer nibble away on lichens, wild plants and grasses in summer, their meat is mild, sweet, and lean—and growing in popularity. In Norway, Sweden, and Finland, reindeer meat is smoked, dried, eaten fresh, or even frozen, so it can be sliced paper-thin and seared quickly on a hot pan. In thicker cuts, it can also be grilled as steak, or marinated and roasted or braised with a larding of bacon and a Madeira-accented sauce.

Also popular are innards such as liver and bone marrow, which are seasoned with sage and rolled into the thin, grilled Norwegian-style crêpes called *lefse* or *tonnbrödsrulle*. But the real prize is smoked reindeer tongue—subtle, supple, and delicately meaty, delicious garnished with soft scrambled eggs.

Where: *In Helsinki*, Restaurant Torni, tel 358/9-4336-6320, ravintolatorni.fi/en. **Mail order:** americanpridefoods.com (search reindeer meat). **Further information and recipes:** *Finnish Cookbook* by Beatrice Ojakangas (1964); food.com (search roast reindeer).

NOT YOUR AVERAGE ROOM SERVICE

Saffransbröd till Luciakaffet

Saffron Buns with Morning Coffee

Swedish

Lucky is the visitor who awakes on December 13 in almost any Swedish home or halfway-decent hotel. For even the grumpiest sleepyheads will be greeted at dawn by a fair maiden (the youngest available) wearing a long white robe and a crown of burning candles on her head to light the winter-dark morning. She will be serving softly pudgy yeast rolls, golden with saffron, studded with raisins, and sparkling with coarse sugar crystals. Along with the rolls will be cups of good, strong Swedish coffee laced with hot milk.

That wake-up ceremony on St. Lucia's Day commemorates the fourth-century Sicilian girl who gave her dowry to impoverished Christians—thus angering her fiancé, who denounced her as a Christian and caused her to be burned as a martyr. A modern reminder of her largesse, these fragrant buns are made in exquisite baroque shapes that vary from one part of Sweden to another.

A St. Lucia's Day celebration

Each form has a name of its own. Those shaped like cats' whiskers are called *lussekatter*; a triple coil of curled "hair" suggesting an English judge's wig is a *prästens hår*; a twist much like a bent horseshoe is *pojke;* a simple S-curve with two raisins in the coils is a *Julgalt;* and a double-S with four raisins is *gullvagn.* A crown-shaped bun is a *Luciakrona;* a whole swirl of a round cake that breaks into seven buns is a *Julkaka;* a sort of bone-shaped bun is a *Julkus;* and a simple long braid is just simply *Julbrod.*

Whatever the shape, the dough is the same: butter, egg, rich milk or half-and-half, yeast, and sugar, with decorations of currants, raisins, crystal sugar, and ground blanched almonds.

Where: *In New York*, at Christmas, Aquavit, tel 212-307-7311, aquavit.org; *in Glendale, CA*, at Christmas, Berolina Bakery, tel 818-249-6506, berolinabakery.com. **Further information**

and recipes: *Scandinavian Baking* by Trine Hahnemann (2014); *Recipes of Sweden* by Inga Norberg (2010); saveur.com (search saffron buns).

——————————|||||||||||||||||||||||||||||||||||—————————

MAKING LENT EASY TO TAKE

Semlor, or Fastelavnsboller

Shrove Tuesday Buns

Swedish, Finnish, Danish

The lead-up to Lenten observances is marked by various doughnuts and crullers, the English-inspired hot cross buns being an obvious example. But by far the most lushly luxurious are these light, airy, and creamy Swedish buns known as

A spin on doughnuts that's positively aristocratic

semlor (or *fastelavnsboller* in Denmark and Norway, *laskaiaspulla* in Finland). The treats begin to appear in bakeries, coffee shops, and restaurants in Scandinavian communities on Shrove Tuesday, or Fastelavn, the day before Lent begins, and then continue to ameliorate any notion of deprivation throughout the Lenten season.

Though many Lenten crullers are deep-fried—the German *Berliner pfannkuchen* (see page 279), or jelly doughnuts, come to mind—

the delicate Swedish clouds are baked to sunny, puffed-up splendor. Once high and golden, the buns are filled with rich, velvety almond paste and a good dollop of whipped cream before being sprinkled with crystals of coarse sugar. For good measure, just before they are served, the buns are set adrift in a wide bowl on a sea of warm milk flavored with cinnamon or vanilla.

As sweet-scented milk seeps into the spongy buns, it melds with the almond paste and whipped cream to form a delightfully saucy filling, for an unctuous indulgence that seems more reward than penance. With luck, the Shrove Tuesday bun will be accompanied by a cup of good, strong coffee that just may be Europe's best: Sweden is said to pay the world's highest price for the highest quality beans,.

Where: *In Glendale, CA*, Berolina Bakery, tel 818-249-6506, berolinabakery.com; *in Santa Barbara, CA,* Andersen's Danish Restaurant and Bakery, tel 805-962-5085, andersenssanta barbara.com. **Further information and recipes:** *The Great Scandinavian Baking Book* by Beatrice Ojakangas (1999); *Scandinavian Baking* by Trine Hahnemann (2014); saveur.com (search semlor). **See also:** Koeksisters, page 741; Sufganiyot, page 469.

THE EPIC BUFFET

Smörgåsbord

Swedish, Scandinavian

In the 1950s and 1960s, *smörgåsbords* were attractions at Scandinavian restaurants in many large cities across the U.S., but the appeal of this exuberant meal has waned. (Thus does fickle fashion deprive us of many pleasures.) At the peak of its popularity, the term—which is actually a combination of the Swedish words for "open-faced sandwich" (*smörgås*) and "table" (*bord*)—was applied to any eat-all-you-want, self-service buffet meal, whether it featured Italian or Jewish food or included a pan-global mix.

Although very few authentic smörgåsbords exist in the States today, the eye-pleasing and palate-enticing groaning board remains popular in Nordic lands, especially Sweden, where it has been beloved since the eighteenth century. The most lavish and authentic example appears at lunch at Operakällaren, the elegant traditional restaurant in Stockholm's opera house.

To get an idea of just how spectacular a smörgåsbords table can be, watch Ingmar Bergman's epic film *Fanny and Alexander*, and feast your eyes on the Christmas buffet those two children enjoy. It's hard to believe that any display of food has ever been as colorful, lavish, or complex.

Rules of etiquette dictate a minimum of four visits to the buffet, though it is doubtful that a guest was ever ejected for making fewer or more rounds. For the first foray, one chooses from cool, silvery herring, roseate smoked or dill-cured salmon, coral shellfish, and cold poached fish. Alongside those you might add a few cold vegetable sides such as cucumber salad, and sauces such as the green-gold dilled mustard or sour cream blushed with beet juice.

Next protocol dictates cold meats such as plump, pink pork sausages, liver pâtés, or tender hams, adding dabs of golden mustard and a warm side dish or two. A few of the milder

A smörgåsbord experience is not complete without at least four visits to the buffet.

cheeses, such as those flecked with caraway seeds, go especially well with meats. The third round focuses on hot dishes that might include the delectable little Swedish meatballs, *köttbullar* (see page 368), along with some *bruna bönor,* the tiny, brown beans baked with pork and molasses (see page 366). Also offered will be various hashes, vegetable dishes, and relishes, none more beloved than pickled beets, ruby-red stewed cabbage, and sparkling preserved lingonberries. One of the most prized offerings is Jansson's temptation, *Janssons frestelse,* or a layered composition of sliced potatoes baked with anchovies, cream, and onion under a crunchy crust of bread crumbs.

For the last visit to the table, choose stronger cheeses streaked with blue mold or aged to nose-twitching aromas. Accompanied by a few ice-cold raw vegetables—radishes, celery, scallions, or cucumber—and jewel-like fruit salad, they are all the dessert needed.

Throughout, diners must be prepared for constant temptation by cream-rich Scandinavian butters and grainy breads and crispbreads and an array of variously flavored aquavits. Several tours around the bread-and-butter table are highly recommended.

WHERE: *In Stockholm,* Veranda Restaurant in the Grand Hotel, tel 46/8-679-3586, grandhotel.se/en; for lunch, Operakällaren, tel 46/8-676-5800, eng.operakallaren.se; *in Ronks, PA,* Miller's Smorgasbord Restaurant, tel 800-669-3568, millerssmorgasbord.com; *in Minneapolis,* on select Sundays at the American Swedish Institute, tel 612-871-4907, asimn.org. **MAIL ORDER:** For a DVD of *Fanny and Alexander* written and directed by Ingmar Bergman (1982), barnesandnoble.com. **FURTHER INFORMATION AND RECIPES:** *The Scandinavian Kitchen* by Camilla Plum (2011); *The Smorgasbord Cookbook* by Anna Olsson Coombs (1949); saveur.com (search smorgasbord).

Eastern European

Balkan, Bulgarian, Georgian,
Hungarian, Polish, Romanian, Russian,
Serbian, Ukrainian

—||||||||||||||||||||||||||||||||||||—

SAVORY AND SUCCULENT

Ćevapčići

Eastern European

Smart grillers the world over ought to consider adding *ćevapčići* to their repertoire. Virtually ubiquitous in their native lands (and understandably so), the skinless homemade sausage-like treats are economical, quick-cooking, and delicious. Enhanced with garlic, black pepper, and hot, dried red chiles, they are most often grilled over charcoal but are sometimes seared on well-oiled iron griddles. To gentle their hefty flavor, thyme or rosemary may be added before the ground meat is formed into chubby sausage shapes and allowed to mellow for an hour or two prior to cooking. As the meat sizzles away, it acquires a lusty patina, juices mingling with spices for succulent results.

Meats vary depending on country and cook. The Jewish-Romanian version called *karnatzlach* will always be made of beef from the forequarters of the steer for reasons of kashruth. In Slovenia, it might be a combination of mutton and beef, while in Romania some suet is considered desirable for the moisture and flavor it adds to the *mititei,* made solely of beef. Lamb might be the meat of choice in Greece, and in Serbia a hunter's version uses venison and rabbit.

Regardless of where the ćevapčići is made, accompaniments tend to follow a pattern: crispy fried potatoes, sauerkraut, cooked red or green cabbage, the eggplant-sweet pepper spread *ajvar,* and a rainbow of pickled vegetables such as red peppers, green tomatoes, and small bronze cucumbers, all piled high on what's traditionally a wooden plate. Not easy to navigate, but well worth the trouble.

Where: *In Sarajevo,* Cevabdzinica Zeljo, tel 387/33-538-426; *in New York,* for karnatzlach, Sammy's Roumanian Steakhouse, tel 212-673-0330, sammysromanian .com; *in Queens, NY,* Bucharest Restaurant, tel 718-389-2300, bucharestrestaurant.com; *in Chicago,* Restaurant Sarajevo, tel 773-275-5310, restaurantsarajevo.com. **Retail and mail order:** *In Queens,* for mititei, Parrot Coffee at three locations, parrotcoffee.com (search mititei). **Further information and recipes:** *Planet Barbecue* by Steven Raichlen (2012), see Balkan Grilled Veal and Pork "Burgers"; for Albanian and Romanian versions, *The Balkan Cookbook* by Vladimir Mirodan (1989); *The Balkan Cookbook* edited by Snezana Pejakovic and Jelka Venisnik-Eror (1987); *Yugoslav Cookbook* by Spasenija-Pata Markovic (1963); for karnatzlach, *From My Mother's Kitchen* by Mimi Sheraton (1979); findbgfood.com; food.com (search yugoslavian cevapcici; cevapcici with paprika lecho; balkan country sausage). **See also:** Wursts to Walk With, page 317; Sauna Sausage, page 363.

The rustic sausage-like meat, with an array of fixings

Poppy Seeds

Eastern European

I t always seems a lucky break to find a mass of poppy seeds encrusted on a bagel, a bialy, a Jewish Sabbath challah, a cookie, or a braided yeasty coffee cake. The tiny, dark seeds of *Papaver somniferum* add a playful needley crunch and a pleasantly smoky, earthy, and mysteriously nutty flavor that enhances every food they grace.

From the Sumerians to the Egyptians to the Greeks and Romans, the ancients knew the charms and the powers of these tiny seeds, relying on them as a cure for insomnia, pain, and assorted stomach troubles. Now, of course, we know why. Poppies and their seeds contain the opium that can be transformed into morphine and heroin. If opiates are desired, the seeds are harvested when they are green and their pods contain liquid; when kitchen-bound, they are harvested fully ripe, after the seed pods have dried. Even so, just a small sprinkling of these merry seeds on a bagel can result in a positive drug test, so be warned—if you expect to be tested, opt for a croissant.

Poppy seeds grow in various parts of the world and come in a few colors. In India, white seeds are prized for their oil. Although jet-black seeds are generally preferred throughout Europe for their dramatic appearance, blue-gray Dutch seeds have the best flavor.

In eastern Europe, Germany, and Austria, black poppy seeds are specially prepped to fill airy dumplings, rolled yeast cakes, the inspired Austro-Hungarian strudel, or the triangular pastries called hamantaschen with which Jews celebrate Purim. Cooked or soaked in milk or water and then ground to near paste, either with special grinders or mortar and pestle, they are then mixed with honey or sugar, cinnamon, and cloves to add a mystical richness to baked goods of all sorts. Unadulterated and whole, they are equally tantalizing tossed into buttered

A cake with a secret jolt of calcium and magnesium

wide noodles or mixed with melted butter as a topping for hot Czech prune dumplings.

RETAIL AND MAIL ORDER: *In Chicago, Milwaukee, and two other locations,* The Spice House, thespicehouse.com. **MAIL ORDER:** Penzeys Spices, tel 800-741-7787, penzeys.com. **FURTHER INFORMATION AND RECIPES:** *The New York Times Jewish Cookbook* edited by Linda Amster (2003); *George Lang's Cuisine of Hungary* by George Lang (1994); *Spice* by Ana Sortun (2006); east europeanfood.about.com (search top eastern european poppy seed recipes). **TIP:** Because poppy seeds contain oil, they turn rancid if they are not stored in a dark, cool place. Purchase seeds from markets frequented by eastern Europeans who know their poppy seeds and buy them in bulk. Ask to taste a few—these very expensive seeds should be bright and sharp in color without any traces of webby dustiness, and they should taste nutty and sweet. Avoid those sold bottled on market shelves. **SEE ALSO:** Hamantaschen, page 439; Mohn Kichel, page 470.

---‖‖‖‖‖‖‖‖‖‖‖‖‖‖‖‖‖‖‖‖‖‖‖‖‖---

A LITTLE MORE NEVER HURTS

Sour Cream

Eastern European

How did Bedřich Smetana, the composer considered the father of Czech opera, feel about his last name? In a country that shares the rest of eastern Europe's passion for that thick and ethereally creamy dairy product, sour cream,

or *smetana,* one can only imagine that it was a badge of pride.

Surely the eastern Europeans—as well as the Germans, the Austrians, and the Ashkenazic Jews who emigrated from those countries—are onto something. "Sour cream with everything" might well be their motto, by which is meant the thickest, richest, most piquant cream soured and thickened by its own *Lactobacillus,* sometimes with the help of other bacteria such as *Streptococcus* and *Leuconostoc.* Rich in protein and calcium, and delicious enough to be a dessert all by itself, sour cream works magic on all sorts of berries, bananas, and peaches, perhaps enhanced with a sprinkle of brown sugar or a drizzle of golden honey.

Rich, creamy, and useful

Best when it is made with full-fat milk, sour cream also enhances countless savory courses. On native ground it is combined with hot boiled potatoes, herring, pot cheese, or a colorful mix of chopped scallions, cucumbers, and red radishes for a light lunch or summer supper. Such a meal might be followed by a plateful of blintzes (see page 433) or *palatschinken* (see Schokoladen Topfenpalatschinken, page 328), decked out with sour cream. The stuff is also whisked into sauces as a thickening and refining agent. The canny cook who plans to use it buys twice as much as the recipe calls for, allowing for irresistible tastes as the preparations progress.

Stores' refrigerator shelves now abound with versions of sour cream containing less butterfat, many resorting to thickeners, such as guar gum and the natural seaweed carrageen, to make up for its loss. By law in the United States, full sour cream must contain 18 to 20 percent butterfat, an amount that accounts for creamy drifts and a luxurious mouthfeel as the subtle, sour-salty, and quintessentially dairy flavors register on the palate. There is good souring and bad, and sour cream is not beyond spoiling. Once a container is opened it ripens quickly, and if kept for several days the sour cream should be thoroughly stirred so that any liquid that has separated out is recombined.

FURTHER INFORMATION AND RECIPES: *The New York Times Jewish Cookbook* edited by Linda Amster (2003); *George Lang's Cuisine of Hungary* by George Lang (1994); saveur.com (search romanian polenta with sour cream; sour cream ice cream with strawberries and brown sugar; old-fashioned sour cream donuts). TIP: Most reliable brands in the U.S. include Daisy, Hood, and Breakstone. When buying sour cream, be sure to check the expiration date. If cooking with sour cream, know that it curdles at the boiling point. To avoid that, blend it with a little flour—about 2 teaspoons per cup of cream—before heating, unless the sauce it will go into already contains some flour. SEE ALSO: Schav, page 464; Pickled Herring, page 457; Transylvanian Baked Sauerkraut with Sausages, page 398; Pelmeni, page 419; Pierogi, page 419.

Walnuts, Three Ways

Balkan

Roses are not the only edible treasures of Bulgaria's Valley of the Roses (see page 386). The walnuts grown in the region's forests are almost as highly prized throughout the Balkan countries for their woodsy flavor and crackling texture, and they find their buttery, crunchy way into dishes generally not seen elsewhere.

Sumptuous nut tortes layered with walnut buttercream and flaky, crisp, phyllo-wrapped pastries may be expected, but a walnut and egg salad is more unusual. *Aselila* is a supple blend of finely crushed walnuts, chopped onions sautéed in butter to a soft, golden puree, and finely chopped hard-cooked eggs. Seasoned with only salt, white pepper, and a drop or two of lemon juice, and served at room temperature, this amplified egg salad is especially good on slices of cucumbers, endive leaves, or thin toast.

Tarator can be a traditional Balkan soup or, in thicker form, a sauce, both of which beg to be rediscovered as cutting edge. A restorative, cold elixir, it combines whipped yogurt with diced or grated cucumbers, minced dill, garlic crushed with coarse salt, lacings of sunflower oil, and a topping of crisp chopped walnuts, with an ice cube or two added to each serving.

Scordolea is the surprise dressing you might find enhancing cold shellfish or chicken breasts. Here, the walnuts have been pounded or blended into a paste and then stirred into a little milk-soaked white bread seasoned with crushed garlic and lemon juice. Walnut oil, sometimes blushed with a pinch of sweet or hot paprika, is whisked in to form the mayonnaise-like emulsion similar to the Turkish sauce prepared for Circassian chicken (see Çerkez Tavuğu, page 481).

Where: *In Sarajevo,* for walnut pastries, Rahat Look, tel 387/33-921-461, rahatlook.ba; *in Chicago,* Restaurant Sarajevo, tel 773-275-5310, restaurantsarajevo.com. **Further information and recipes:** *The Balkan Cookbook* by Vladimir Mirodan (1989); epicurious.com (search tarator sauce); food.com (search tarator soup); ilibili.blogspot.com (search scordolea); food52 .com (search egg walnut salad).

Bulgarian Yogurt

Bulgarian

Cool, snowy, and custard-rich, the soured milk called yogurt lends its elegant piquancy to sweet and savory foods alike, as good combined with honey and ripe strawberries, raspberries, and peaches as it is with chopped cucumbers, radishes, and scallions seasoned with dill and pepper. It's also welcome as a topping for a hot baked potato, stirred into a bowl of steaming borscht, or crowning a juicy, spice-scented fruit pie.

But not all yogurts are created equal, and it's not for nothing that the Latin name for one of the two yogurt-forming microbes is *Bacillus bulgaricus*. Discovered by the Nobel prize–winning Russian microbiologist Ilya Metchnikoff, it was so named because, while traveling in Bulgaria at the end of the nineteenth century, the good professor became intrigued with the eighty-seven-year average life span of the country people, many of whom were centenarians. Researching a connection between that longevity and the local dietary staple—the fermented milk called by its Turkish name, *yoghurt*—he isolated the microbe in yogurt that warded off the growth of a detrimental bacteria in the alimentary canal, which caused illness and a shortened life span.

Whether made of sheep's, goat's, or cow's milk, classic Bulgarian yogurt is based on whole milk. A thick ivory layer of cream gathers on its surface and must be stirred into the whiter custardlike cream below, a step rarely necessary in countries where yogurt is made from skim milk and marketed to dieters.

Well-made domestic and imported whole-milk yogurts have a piquant flavor and pleasingly creamy texture, as well as valuable amounts of B-vitamins, calcium, and protein. But for the most sublime example of a distinguished farmhouse yogurt, you'll have to go to Bulgaria. In addition to the special quality of the country's milk, certain essential microbes naturally present in Bulgarian farmyards cannot be replicated elsewhere.

WHERE: Whole Foods Markets, whole foodsmarket.com, look for White Mountain Foods brand, whitemountainfoods.com. **MAIL ORDER:** For lactobacillus bulgaricus culture, bacillusbulgaricus.com; findbgfood.com (click Marketplace, then Lactobacillus Bulgaricus or Bulgarian Yogurt Kiselo Mlyako). **FURTHER INFORMATION AND RECIPES:** *The Yogurt Cookbook* by Arto Der Haroutunian (2010); *The Oxford Companion to Food* by Alan Davidson (1999); cookstr.com (search yogurt sauce with black salt; zingerman's bulgarian cucumber soup; turkish eggplant puree with yogurt dressing and walnuts); gourmet.com (search yogurt and the bulgarian colonel).

CHEESE THAT GETS YOUR GOAT—OR SHEEP

Feta

Bulgarian

If you think feta is feta, you haven't tried the prized Bulgarian interpretation—regarded by many connoisseurs as the best of the teasingly pungent, snow-white cheeses that are firm yet subtly creamy. Made with the milk of goats, sheep, or cows (the last being the blandest and least interesting) and cured and packed in a pickling brine, blocks of the cheese emerge nicely salty with a sophisticated hint of earthiness.

Feta is at once moist and yet chewy; when drained and allowed to dry a bit, it can be grated for various toppings or broken into chunks to add texture and interest to salads (see Shopska Salata, page 386). Because the cheese is salty, it generally appears as an appetizer (it's especially good cubed and tossed with black, oil-cured olives and a little thyme) or an ingredient in main courses, especially those made with cornmeal (see Mamaliga and Kachamak, page 385), but it also makes an unusual and satisfying dessert when its brininess is complemented by the sweetness of ripe pears or figs, a drizzle of amber honey, and crunchy accents of toasted, unsalted walnuts or almonds.

A creamy, crumbly wonder

Feta is widely available, but the smaller cuts often sold pre-packaged in supermarket refrigerator cases do not show it off to its best advantage. Far better to shop for large blocks of the cheese sunk deep in barrels of brine, if you can find it—for these, you'll probably have to look in markets in Greek and Balkan neighborhoods, or in specialty cheese stores. Although imports mainly come from Romania, Greece, Israel, and France, Bulgarian feta—whether of sheep or goat milk (or a combination)—is less salty and bears an especially soigné burnish of winey acidity and supple texture. Pay your money and take your choice. An international feta tasting might be in order.

Where: *In New York City and environs,* Fairway Market at multiple locations, fairway market.com; Muncan, tel 718-278-8847, muncanfoodcorp.com; *in Queens,* Parrot Coffee at three locations, parrotcoffee.com; *in Chicago,* Elea Mediterranean Food Market, tel 312-207-1655, eleafoodmarket.com. **Mail order:** malincho.com (search bulgarian sheep feta). **Further information and recipes:** *The Balkan Cookbook* by Vladimir Mirodan (1989); *The Balkan Cookbook* edited by Snezana Pejakovic and Jelka Venisnik-Eror (1987); *Yugoslav Cookbook* by Spasenija-Pata Markovic (1963); *The Food and Wine of Greece* by Diane Kochilas (1990); saveur.com (search greek egg feta and herb tart alevropita); easteuropeanfood.about .com (search kachamak).

—⊢|||||||||||||||||||||||||||||||⊣—

A VEGETABLE MARKET IN A POT

Ghivetch

Bulgarian, Romanian

Among the world's great vegetable stews, the savory, sweet, sour, and herbaceous *ghivetch* has to reign supreme—a culinary triumph of rich colors, textures, and aromas imparted by a combination of many vegetables and herbs,

each giving up something of itself to enhance the whole. Taking its name from the deep round or oval earthenware casserole or enameled cast-iron Dutch oven in which it cooks, ghivetch by this or any number of other spellings (*ghiveciu* or *djuvetch*, to cite only a couple) is often made with chunks of meat, poultry, and even fish, but the all-vegetable version is the summer classic that is equally delectable hot, cold, or at room temperature.

Ideally a good ghivetch will have no fewer than twenty vegetables and, for a frisson of sourness, some tart fruit, fresh grape leaves, lemon juice, or the citric acid known as sour salt. With so many vegetables to choose from, no single one is essential, and some substitutions are welcome. For the true spirit of the dish, you will want to include summer or winter squashes, fresh beans, sweet and hot peppers, root vegetables, and some members of the cabbage and nightshade families—tomatoes, eggplant, potatoes. To be excluded are broccoli, kale, collards, spinach, and Swiss chard, or any leafy intruders that soften too quickly and bleed into the stew, unbalancing its color or flavor.

Ghivetch

Serves about 12 as a side dish

8 tablespoons (1 stick) unsalted butter
1 cup sunflower or corn oil
4 medium-size onions, sliced to ⅛-inch
  thickness
1 pound acorn squash, peeled, seeded,
  and cubed
2 medium-size zucchini, sliced
5 medium-size potatoes, peeled and cubed
4 medium-size carrots, scraped and sliced
2 pounds eggplant, cubed
¼ pound string beans, trimmed and
  cut into 2-inch pieces
1 large green bell pepper, seeded and
  cut into strips
1 large red bell pepper, seeded and cut
  into strips
1 small head white or green cabbage,
  shredded
1 small cauliflower, broken into florets
1 pound fresh lima beans, shelled
1 medium-size parsnip, or 1 small parsnip
  and 1 small parsley root, scraped
  and diced
1 medium-size celery root, peeled and
  cubed
1 medium-size white turnip, cubed
3 leeks, white and light green portions,
  rinsed well and sliced
½ pound okra, thickly sliced
5 large tomatoes, peeled, seeded, and
  coarsely chopped
½ cup minced fresh flat-leaf parsley leaves
1 tablespoon coarsely chopped garlic
1 cup sour grapes (see Note)
1 tablespoon chopped fresh dill
2 teaspoons salt
½ teaspoon ground black pepper

1 teaspoon sweet paprika
¼ teaspoon hot paprika (optional)
1 to 2 cups hot beef stock or water, if needed
Sour cream or yogurt (optional), for serving

1. Preheat the oven to 350°F.

2. Place 4 tablespoons of the butter and ½ cup of the oil in a flameproof 5-quart unglazed earthenware casserole or enameled cast-iron Dutch oven and heat over a moderate flame until the butter has melted and the mixture is hot, about 3 minutes. Add the onions and cook over low heat until they are faintly golden brown, about 7 minutes.

3. Add all of the vegetables, the parsley, garlic, sour grapes, dill, black pepper, sweet paprika, and hot paprika, if using, and 1 teaspoon of salt and stir until all of the ingredients are evenly distributed.

4. Heat the remaining 4 tablespoons of butter and ½ cup of oil together in a small saucepan over low heat until the butter melts. Stir the butter and oil into the vegetable mixture. Add the other teaspoon salt and a dash of pepper. Cover the casserole or Dutch oven tightly, let the mixture come to a boil over high heat, and boil gently until liquid begins to accumulate at the bottom of the casserole, about 10 minutes.

5. Transfer the casserole or Dutch oven to the oven and bake the vegetables until they are all tender, but not mushy, and most of the liquid has evaporated, 1 to 1½ hours. Stir the vegetables several times as they bake, adding a little stock or water if necessary to keep the vegetables from scorching. The final texture should be juicy but not runny. Remove the casserole or Dutch oven from the oven and let the vegetables stand for about 20 minutes before serving.

6. Taste for seasoning, adding more salt and/or black pepper as necessary. Serve the vegetables hot, chilled, or at room temperature, with or without a topping of sour cream or yogurt. If you're lucky you'll have leftovers, which will ripen in flavor and are best served at room temperature. Stored tightly covered in the refrigerator, this will keep for 5 to 6 days. If you choose to reheat, allow to come to room temperature, then heat over a low flame.

Note: You can substitute 2 greengage or other sour plums, pitted and chopped, or 5 fresh grape leaves, or the juice of ½ lemon, or 1 generous pinch of sour salt (citric acid) for the sour grapes.

Variation: To make ghivetch with meat, cut 2 pounds of lamb, beef, or pork into 1½-inch cubes and brown them lightly with the onions before adding the other ingredients.

WHERE: *In Chicago,* Little Bucharest Bistro, tel 773-604-8500, littlebucharestbistro.com.

POLENTA BY ANOTHER NAME

Mamaliga and Kachamak

Bulgarian, Romanian

What Italians call polenta (see page 226), the Balkans know as *mamaliga*, a sunny cornmeal porridge that can be served soft and creamy or allowed to set until firm. Best when made from stone-ground cornmeal so it takes on a tantalizing grittiness, mamaliga dates back to Roman times in these parts—and it's still a dietary staple, whether it is served as breakfast porridge doused with melted butter or as a supportive base for meat and poultry at other meals. When it is turned out of the pot onto a wooden board and allowed to set, the result is cut with a taut string into portions that may be glazed under the grill or lightly fried in butter.

For an extra bit of zing, mamaliga may be topped with one of the piquant cow's, goat's, or sheep's milk cheeses produced in the Balkans— bryndza, halloumi, stringy hoop cheese, or tangy feta. The ultimate combination is Bulgaria's deliciously oozy *kachamak,* which is soft mamaliga stirred through with butter and then layered in a baking pan with either shredded bryndza or crumbled feta. The final layer is topped with cheese and dots of butter and the whole thing is baked into a sort of Balkan lasagne. Although it is often served as a side dish with nothing more than a salad, kachamak adds up to a hearty lunch or supper.

WHERE: *In Queens, NY,* Bucharest Restaurant, tel 718-389-2300, bucharestrestaurant.com; *in Anaheim, CA,* Dunarea Restaurant, tel 714-772-7233, dunarea.us. **MAIL ORDER:** parrotcoffee.com (search corn flour malai); amazon.com (search moretti bramata polenta coarse); malincho .com (search bulgarian feta); igourmet.com (search hoop cheese; halloumi). **FURTHER INFORMATION AND RECIPES:** *The New York Times Jewish Cookbook* edited by Linda Amster (2003), see Romanian Mamaliga; *Yugoslav Cookbook* by Spasenija-Pata Markovic (1963), see Polenta with Cheese; easteuropeanfood.about.com (search bulgarian polenta with cheese); saveur .com (search romanian polenta with sour cream). **SEE ALSO:** Polenta, page 226; Feta, page 382.

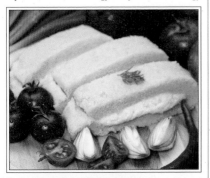

Kachamak—a sort of Balkan lasagne

Rose Petals

Bulgarian

D awn-pink rose petals, fragrant and beaded with early morning dew, have been a legendary specialty of Bulgaria for centuries. Though the petals are famed for the essential oils they lend to perfumes and palliative cosmetic lotions, they also provide luxurious, sensuous, dry, sweet flavoring to condiments and desserts.

Rose water or rose syrup scents confections throughout the Middle East and the Mediterranean, from *pastiera* (the Easter torta of Naples), to marzipans, chocolate bonbons, and cool fruit sherbets. Candied rose petals adorn and sweeten frozen desserts from Paris to Provence; on their own, the petals can be nibbled as breath fresheners. Most romantic of all may be the silken rose petal jam, a gently sweet, prettily pink, and glamorous topping for whipped cream or strawberry ice cream, or to crown scones at teatime.

The origin of the world's most famous and abundant edible roses is the aptly named Valley of the Roses, at the foot of Bulgaria's Rhodope mountains near the town of Kazanlak. There, the month-long picking ritual is a travel-worthy sight—particularly if you heed the advice of Lesley Blanch, who wrote of the event in her 1963 travelogue *Under a Lilac-Bleeding Star:* "It

seems there are only a few weeks, in June, when the roses reach their apotheosis. Rose culture demands not only the precise moment of the year, but the exact moment of the day—sunrise. The flowers must be gathered while the dew is still on them, before the heat of the sun has drawn out all their perfume."

Invited to dinner at a nearby convent, Blanch was welcomed with "a glass of pure water and little saucers of translucent rose-leaf jam; this is the Balkan version of an aperitif. The jam induces a fierce thirst, which, it is inferred, can only be slaked by the host's finest wine."

RETAIL AND MAIL ORDER: *In New York,* Murray's Cheese, tel 888-692-4339, murrays cheese.com (search harvest song rose petal preserves). **MAIL ORDER:** amazon.com (search rose petal jam; candied rose petals; bulgarian rose water). **FURTHER INFORMATION:** *Under a Lilac-Bleeding Star* by Lesley Blanch (1963). **SPECIAL EVENT:** Rose Festival, Kazanlak, Bulgaria, June, rose-festival.com.

Shopska Salata

Bulgarian

W hether in a home or a restaurant, a traditional Bulgarian meal that doesn't start with a pretty nosegay called *shopska salata* is a hard thing to find. Named after the farm village Shopi, near the Bulgarian capital of Sofia, the salad is a pointillistic and sprightly mix of red, white, and green: diced tomato, cucumber, scallions or new white onions, and sweet and/or hot green peppers, the last most typically roasted and peeled (although the sweet green peppers are often diced raw for maximum crunchiness). Final aromatic fillips include salt rubbed through with garlic, along with black pepper, a touch of wine vinegar, and olive or sunflower oil. The essential identifying seasoning is *chubritsa*, a strongly aromatic, dusky gray-green spice blend that takes its name from an herb that has an elusive sage-tarragon flavor.

The predinner dish also known as Bulgarian salad

The crowning glory of shopska salata is a snowfall of feta cheese, copiously grated into the salad for piquancy and creaminess. On special occasions, that feta snowcap might be decorated with a tiny rosette of tomato decked out with pointed leaves cut from green pepper. Although a large, communal shopska salad is made for convenience, it is most appealing in individual portions heaped into colorful bowls, preferably one of the high-glazed, boldly colored types made by Bulgarian artisans.

WHERE: In Pittsburgh, PA, Sarajevo Family Restaurant, tel 412-766-3287, startw.com/sarajevo. **MAIL ORDER:** findbgfood.com (click Marketplace, then Chubritsa); malincho.com (search bulgarian feta). **FURTHER INFORMATION AND RECIPES:** *The Balkan Cookbook* by Vladimir Mirodan (1989); *The Balkan Cookbook* edited by Snezana Pejakovic and Jelka Venisnik-Eror (1987); food52.com (search classic shopska salata); easteuropean food.about.com (search shopska salata).

||||||||||||||||||||||||||||||||||||||||||||||||||||||||||||||||||||||||||||||||||||||||||||||||||||||||||||||||||||||||||||||||||||||

A STAR OF A VEGETABLE, WAITING FOR ITS CLOSE-UP

Kohlrabi

Seductive to those who know and love its charms, kohlrabi remains relatively unknown. Although generally on view in small quantities on greengrocers' shelves and at farmers' markets, it goes untried by many unfamiliar with its uses.

Kohlrabi's most edible portion is its bulblike base, which looks much like a jade-green hand grenade. Yet the knob is not a bulb, but rather a thick, rounded stem that grows just above ground, with stringy roots reaching down into the earth and silvery green, cabbage-like leaves rising from long, thin stems.

The magic of this *Brassica oleracea*, a member of the Gongylodes group, lies in the remarkable if subtle flavor to which the vegetable's Germanic name provides a clue: *kohl* for cabbage, *rabi* for turnip. And with its gently bittersweet overtones, the vegetable is indeed faintly reminiscent of cabbage, along with radishes, mustard, and the white inner portion of broccoli stems. Peeled of its tough, fibrous outer skin, the green-tinged white interior has a texture similar to that of a water chestnut. Although many advise eating kohlrabi raw for its crunch, it really requires thorough cooking to release its mild, intriguing flavor. Its leaves are not nearly as interesting as its bulbous base, but they can be chopped into soups or stews as a much milder stand-in for collard greens.

Kohlrabi's bulbous base is actually a stem.

Although it was present in eighteenth- and nineteenth-century England, kohlrabi has become most popular throughout eastern Europe, Austria, Germany, and Israel, as well as being a favorite latecomer to the Chinese kitchen. Chinese chefs stir-fry thin slices with black mushrooms in ginger and garlic sauces,

and also stuff it with ground pork and garlic, or steam it with ginger and scallions. Eastern Europeans stuff kohlrabi, too, using either chopped vegetables or ground veal or pork, then braising the construction and sometimes topping it with a verdant parsley cream sauce. In Germany, kohlrabi stars in the mixed vegetable stew *Leipziger allerlei* ("Leipzig all together"), a combination that always includes carrots, onions, and green beans, and sometimes peas and mushrooms as well. Diced artichoke hearts may be added, and the cooking liquid may be thickened to make a dill sauce.

WHERE: *In New York,* Donguri, tel 212-737-5656, dongurinyc.com. **MAIL ORDER:** Melissa's Produce, tel 800-588-0151, melissas.com. **FURTHER INFORMATION AND RECIPES:** *Beyond Bok Choy* by Rosa Lo San Ross (1996); *Vegetables from Amaranth to Zucchini* by Elizabeth Schneider (2001); *George Lang's Cuisine of Hungary* by George Lang (1994); *Neue Cuisine* by Kurt Gutenbrunner (2011); saveur.com (search kohlrabi salad slaw); epicurious.com (search kohlrabi slivers and pea shoots with sesame dressing); foodrepublic.com (search tamarind beef and kohlrabi salad). **TIP:** For most purposes, small kohlrabi that are less fibrous are more desirable, although the larger type is useful for stuffing. To peel the bulbs (a necessary step), slip a slim knife point under the woody strings beneath the outer green skin.

THE COFFEE LOVER'S TEA

Georgian Black Tea

Georgian

Known as a coffee drinker's tea, the intense, deeply flavorful, rich black tea grown in the foothills and on the steep hillsides of the Caucasus mountains in Georgia is prized for its earthy qualities and for its distinctive body. Tea was

only introduced from northern China to Georgia in the late nineteenth century, but the region now

produces what is considered by many to be among the most interesting teas in the world, comparable to the Darjeeling it strongly resembles. Its land is ideal for tea growing—a citrus-, grape-, and hazelnut-farming haven with fertile soil, clean air, and an abundance of rain.

Strongly brewed, the tea is customarily served with cherry jam—specifically a variety made from Cornelian cherries, an exceedingly floral-tasting fruit also grown in the area. A spoonful of the jam is stirred into the tea to enliven and sweeten its flavor, and the result is potently soothing and delicious.

The Georgian tea industry faltered during the Soviet regime, but it was revived in the mid-1990s by foreign investors, mainly Germans and Danes, who bought up a number of tea processing plants. Now there are growers devoted to old-fashioned tea production methods, who farm the tea on a small scale—rolling, bruising, twisting, withering, oxidizing, and drying the leaves by hand—making it an exclusive and highly in-demand gourmet food product once again.

RETAIL AND MAIL ORDER: *In New York,* McNulty's Tea and Coffee Co., tel 800-356-5200, mcnultys.com. **MAIL ORDER:** Tea Embassy, tel 512-330-9991, teaembassy.com (search georgian); amazon.com (search granny's secret cornelian cherry jam). **SEE ALSO:** Oolong Tea, page 777; Darjeeling, page 873.

----||||||||||||||||||||||||||||||----

WHAT WELL-DRESSED BEANS WEAR

Lobio Satsivi

Georgian

Green beans in and of themselves may offer few if any taste thrills, but they make wonderful vehicles for many an intriguing sauce or dressing. (Perhaps that is what nature had in mind for them in the first place.) No sauce adds more distinction or interest than the one favored in the Caucasian Republic of Georgia: a crunchy walnut dressing enlivened with garlic, onion, sweet and hot paprika, cilantro, and parsley. In fact, it might well make a perfect, sophisticated garnish for beans served as a side to southern fried chicken or barbecued beef and pork in the *other* Georgia.

Lobio Satsivi

Serves about 6 as a side dish

*1 pound young, tender green beans,
    preferably haricots verts, trimmed*
⅔ cup very finely ground walnuts
1 large clove garlic, crushed in a press
*2 tablespoons finely minced sweet
    onion, such as red, Vidalia, or
    Bermuda onion*
2 to 3 tablespoons red wine vinegar
*3 to 4 tablespoons light vegetable oil,
    such as sunflower or walnut oil*
1½ teaspoons sweet paprika
¼ teaspoon hot paprika
2 tablespoons finely minced fresh cilantro
*1 tablespoon finely minced fresh flat-leaf
    parsley leaves*
Salt
Freshly ground black pepper

1. If the beans are large, cut them into 2-inch pieces. If the beans are small haricots verts, leave them whole.

2. Place the green beans and 2 quarts of lightly salted water in a saucepan and cook them over medium heat until they are just tender but still firm, 8 to 10 minutes. Drain the beans thoroughly on paper towels and set them aside to come to room temperature.

3. Combine the walnuts, garlic, and onion in a large, nonreactive serving bowl made of glass, enamel, or ceramic, add 2 tablespoons of the wine vinegar, 3 tablespoons of the oil, and the sweet and hot paprikas, and toss to mix. Add the cilantro and parsley to the dressing and toss again. Taste for seasoning, adding salt and pepper and more vinegar and/or oil as necessary.

4. Add the green beans to the bowl with the dressing and toss until well coated. The beans can be served at once but will develop more flavor and become mellower if left to sit, lightly covered, at room temperature for 2 to 3 hours.

The beans can also be refrigerated, covered, for 5 or 6 hours; let them return to room temperature before serving.

Where: *In New York,* Oda House, tel 212-353-3838, odahouse.com; *in Brooklyn,* Primorski Restaurant, tel 718-891-3111, primorski ny.com. **Further information and additional recipes:** *Please to the Table* by Anya von Bremzen and John Welchman (1990); *The Georgian Feast* by Darra Goldstein (1999). **Tip:** Look for green beans that are young and tender, avoiding any on which you can see the outlines of the inner beans—a sign that they are overgrown and will be tough and fibrous.

A SAUCE TO PAIR WITH ALMOST ANYTHING

Tkemali

Sour Plum Sauce

Georgian

Newcomers to the savory cuisine of the mountainous Republic of Georgia are frequently amazed—and then beguiled—by the delicate counterpoints of spices and herbs, pepper, chiles, and garlic that lend earthy energy to so many

of its dishes. Noted for its healthfulness and for the longevity it seems to promote, it's a cuisine based on fruits, vegetables, and herbs, many foraged in the wild, with lots of yogurt in between.

The national sauce of the Republic of Georgia

All of these aromatic attributes are combined in the national sauce called *tkemali* (tek-MAHLY), named for the winey dark plums that make up its purply red, fruity, somewhat sour base. Added to the cooked and pureed plums are crushed coriander and fennel seeds, garlic, a good belt of cayenne (Georgians like things hot), and mincings of fresh spearmint and cilantro.

The finished sauce is perhaps most delectably used to grace cooked green beans in the satisfying, intriguing salad known as *lobio* (the name for beans), which also features enhancements of ground walnuts, cinnamon, cloves, and pomegranate juice (see page 389).

Tkemali lends color, aroma, and flavor to soups and stews, and it's almost always a garnish for grilled lamb kebabs and flattened, fried chicken *tabaka* (see below). It plays well with barbecue and even makes for a delightful spread on hearty toasted breads. Virtually ubiquitous as a complement to many of the country's grilled meats, fish, and vegetables, the sauce is always kept on hand in the refrigerator, a sort of Georgian ketchup; often made at home, it is also sold commercially.

WHERE: *In New York*, Oda House, tel 212-353-3838, odahouse.com; Old Tbilisi Garden, tel 212-470-6064; *in Glendale, CA*, Old Village Restaurant, tel 818-551-2000, oldvillrestaurant .com; *in Portland, OR*, Kargi Gogo food cart, tel 503-489-8432, kargigogo.com; *in Toronto*, Suliko, tel 905-760-1989, suliko.ca. **MAIL ORDER:** RussianTable, tel 800-761-2460, russiantable .com. **FURTHER INFORMATION AND RECIPES:** *The New York Times Grilling Cookbook*, edited by Peter Kaminsky (2014); *Please to the Table* by Anya von Bremzen and John Welchman (1990); nytimes.com (search tkemali); georgianrecipes .net (search green tkemali; red tkemali).

┤|||||||||||||||||||||||||||||||||├

FLAT-OUT PERFECTION

Tsyplionok Tabaka

Chicken Tabaka

Georgian

Flattening seems to be an especially effective way to achieve both golden crunchiness and mellow juiciness at once in small chickens. There's an Italian version, *pollo al mattone* (see page 228) and there's a French version, *pigeons en crapaudine* (see page 114). And then there's this lusty specialty of the Caucasian Republic of Georgia, an eloquent showcase for all of the subtle complexities this cooking method makes possible. In chicken tabaka, the same sort of flattened, pan-fried chicken takes on far more vibrant, pungent overtones of garlic and fiery paprika to become a true adventure for the palate.

Small chickens, squabs, or poussins (or, in a pinch or for economy's sake, Cornish hens), each weighing about 1¼ pounds, are split down the back. With spines removed, each gets a firm pounding with a mallet, meat tenderizer, or heavy skillet, until the breast bone is flattened and the tiny bones are cracked. Drumstick ends are pulled through slits in the top skin and wings are folded back under the breasts.

That may be the signature move, but now comes the important part: Each bird is generously rubbed with salt, ground black pepper, crushed garlic, and paprika, preferably the fiery kind (though for milder tastes, a mix of the sweet and hot will do). A brushing of beaten sour cream on the skin side readies the bird to fry skin side down, in clarified butter in a heavy skillet. Pressed down under a slightly smaller but still quite heavy skillet called a *tapa*, and further weighted with cans of food or a brick, the chicken is left to its own devices for about ten minutes, until the skin develops a light golden glow. Once flipped, its other side receives the same treatment, and the meat emerges cooked but still dewy within.

The mellowing, supple finishing touch is either the plummy, garlic- and chile-zapped *tkemali* sauce (see page 390), or a thick, verdant mix of minced parsley, cilantro, and garlic with a light moistening of vegetable oil or melted butter. A refreshing side-dish salad would be *lobio satsivi* (see page 389), green beans in a walnut sauce fragrant with garlic and cilantro.

WHERE: *In Brooklyn,* Primorski Restaurant, tel 718-891-3111, primorskiny.com; *in Glendale, CA,* Old Village Restaurant, tel 818-551-2000, oldvillrestaurant.com; *in Toronto,* Suliko, tel 905-760-1989, suliko.ca. **FURTHER INFORMATION AND RECIPES:** *The Art of Russian Cuisine* by Anne Volokh with Mavis Manus (1989); *Please to the Table* by Anya von Bremzen and John Welchman (1990); food.com (search chicken tabaka); whats4eats.com (search tabaka).

||||||||||||||||||||||||||||||||

PAPRIKA WORKS ITS ROSY MAGIC

Gulyás of All Sorts

Hungarian

S ynonymous with Hungarian cuisine the world over, and for the best of reasons, *gulyás,* or goulash, actually refers to a variety of rich, meaty stews. Spice-laden and aromatic with sweet and/or hot paprika (an essential ingredient), the hearty stews can be made with pork, beef, or a combination of several meats.

Goulash has been around a long time. The rustic stew originated with the shepherds from whom it takes its name—in Hungarian, *gulyás* means shepherd. As early as the ninth century, shepherds carried cuts of dried meat with them on the road; it could easily be reconstituted with water to create a kind of instant soup. Refinements were eventually added to those humble beginnings, most notably the native paprika, the spice most closely associated with Hungarian cooking after Columbus took the special chile peppers back from the New World to Europe.

The stews originated with shepherds.

The most highly prized paprika comes from the southern Hungarian city of Szeged, where the spice became the signature of the local gulyás, with caraway and sage adding subtlety. Pork is usually the meat in Szeged gulyás— browned in its own fat and then stewed for hours with onions, tomatoes, sauerkraut, potatoes, and sometimes grated apple. The resulting dish is at once sour, sweet, hot, and mellow, and incredibly fragrant. In a more liquid form, sans sauerkraut, goulash is the basis of a favorite German antidote to a night of hard partying (see Gulyassuppe, page 291). No matter what the occasion, it's hearty, warming fare for shepherds and city dwellers alike.

WHERE: *In Budapest,* Gundel, tel 36/1-889-8100, gundel.hu/en; Firkász, tel 36/1-450-1118, firkaszetterem.hu; Bagolyvár, tel 36/1-468-3110, bagolyvar.com; *in New York,* Andre's Café, tel 212-327-1105, andrescafeny.com. **FURTHER INFORMATION AND RECIPES:** *George Lang's Cuisine of Hungary* by George Lang (1994); cookstr.com (search hungarian goulash); foodandwine.com (search goulash with sausage and sauerkraut).

—||||||||||||||||||||||||||||||—

HOW TO SAY BOUILLABAISSE IN HUNGARIAN

Halászlé

Hungarian

A clear and subtle fish soup-stew, *halászlé* (HAHL-ash-zlee) deserves its place among the bouillabaisses, bourrides, *brodetti*, and *zuppe de pesce* of the world. Based on the freshwater fish that abound in the lakes of Hungary and other eastern European countries, the soup exudes a milder, more delicate essence than those made with lustier saltwater fish.

The most essential player here is the golden carp, its opulently fatty, meaty texture bolstered by a stock made with its skin, head, and bones, and plenty of sweet onions. Walleye pike, whitefish, sturgeon, perch, and wide-mouth bass also join the fray, and a mix of sweet and hot paprikas sets the heady broth aglow with color and savory flavor.

The fish for this soup is purchased whole—to be gutted by either the fishmonger or the cook—which means that the coral roe of females and the white milt of males may be included as well. These prized additions add hefty overtones to a broth that often contains no vegetables save for a finishing touch of lightly cooked green pepper strips; cooks in some regions do simmer the stock with some sweet and earthy root vegetables such as parsnips, parsley root, carrots, celery root, and a few cloves of unpeeled garlic. In either cases, the strained, clear, paprika-blushed broth is sprinkled with minced dill and served as a first course, while chunks of the fish make up a second course, garnished with boiled potatoes for substance.

WHERE: *In Budapest,* Gundel, 36/1-889-8100, gundel.hu/en. **MAIL ORDER:** For paprika, amazon .com (search szeged paprika). **FURTHER INFORMATION AND RECIPES:** *George Lang's Cuisine of Hungary* by George Lang (1994); food.com (search halaszle); festival.si.edu (search hungarian recipe halaszle). **SEE ALSO:** Brodetto Vastese, page 170; Bouillabaisse, page 63; Bourride, page 64.

—||||||||||||||||||||||||||||||—

LIFE IS JUST A BOWL OF CHERRIES

Hideg Meggyleves

Cold Sour Cherry Soup

Hungarian

A special treat during summer in eastern Europe and the Balkans are cold soups made tangy by hints of lemon juice, acidic fruit, or gritty sour salt. One of the most enticing of the hot-weather soups is a chilled sour cherry version, traditionally enhanced with whipped sour cream, sugar, cinnamon, and perhaps cloves. A splash of white wine and fresh (or jarred, in a pinch) cooked sour cherries contribute to its essential winey flavor and deep blushing beauty. The soup's success depends on the ripeness of its star ingredient—the sour cherries that are one of nature's oldest triumphs and in season early to mid-summer.

On a hot summer's day, cold cherry soup for lunch

Cherries, like other stone fruits, are thought by scholars to have originated in Asia Minor, as well as in the ancient Greek city Kerasounta. There are two main types, sweet (*Prunus avium*) and sour (*Prunus cerasus*), and it is easy to tell the difference: The sour fruits tend to be heart-shaped, slightly soft, and an orange-kissed flame-red color, while ripe sweet cherries are rounder, fleshier, and firmer, a dark burgundy-black. The tart and tangy flavor of the sour fruit carries strong appeal to eastern Europeans and Hungarians in particular, perhaps because trees bearing the sour morello variety grow there in abundance.

How sour is sour? Very sour indeed. As Waverley Root wrote in his authoritative dictionary and visual history *Food*, when it comes to sour cherries, "what the word means in this case is really *acid*."

Where: *In Budapest,* Gundel, tel 36/1-889-8100, gundel.hu/en. **Mail order:** For preserved sour cherries, amazon.com (search american spoon fruit sour cherries). **Further information and recipes:** *George Lang's Cuisine of Hungary* by George Lang (1994); *The German Cookbook* by Mimi Sheraton (2014); saveur.com (search hungarian chilled cherry soup).

ONE OF EUROPE'S GREATEST FOOD MARKETS

Központi Vásárcsarnok

Hungarian

Great—whether applied to size or quality—hardly is an adequate description of the Great Market Hall, a stupendous rose-brick building that is full to the brim with tantalizing aromas and flavors. On the Pest side of teeming Budapest,

the turreted nineteenth-century Gothic complex offers a luscious, three-level nosh that in the span of only a couple of hours can give visitors a fair sampling of the length and breadth of savory Hungarian cuisine.

Opened in 1897 after a design by the local

architect Samu Petz, the market's soaring main hall is reminiscent of Paris's original Les Halles, with its glass paneling set into high-flying steel girders. A wash of light illuminates the brilliant colors of assorted paprikas, necklacelike strings and hanging garlands of smoky dark sausages and burnished country hams, shelves filled with the intricate, butter-crunched pastries Hungarian bakers are famous for, and snowy, rustic country cheeses, most of considerable pungency.

Strolling up and down the wide aisles on this main floor nets visitors a slew of restorative nibbles. Among them are the midnight-dark sausage called black pudding, fried sausages, a variety of filled crêpes and pancakes, and *lángos,* a descendant of Turkish pita that evolved into a crisp, deep-fried pastry moon rubbed with salt and garlic and topped with pungent sour cream and a sheep's or goat's milk cheese. Intermittent theme days honor various national and regional foodways, including those of Croatia, Tunisia, Hungary, and Macedonia, to name only a few.

At some stalls, you'll encounter more substantial dishes, such as stuffed cabbage or red peppers, the beloved *gulyás* (alternatively spelled goulash), or meat prepared *lecso*-style—with a sauce of green peppers, white onions, red tomatoes, and of course paprika. As for that glowing Hungarian spice, there are at least twenty varieties brilliantly on view.

Escalate down to the lower level and you'll find yourself in a sort of supermarket filled with fishmongers, butchers, and stands. Among the offerings here are the pickled vegetables so loved by Hungarians (reminders of the days before fresh vegetables were available in winter), along with local beers, wines such as the famed Tokaji aszú, and teas and coffees. On the uppermost level, colorful Hungarian craftsmanship shines through in carved wood pieces and the sparkling, intricate embroidery that adorns various household linens, shirts, skirts, and scarves.

Where: *In Budapest,* Vámház körut 1-3, Fövám tér, Pest end of Liberty Bridge. **Further information:** piaconline.hu.

"FIERY, SPICY, TEMPERAMENTAL—ALL THESE ADJECTIVES SUGGEST BOTH PAPRIKA AND THE HUNGARIAN NATIONAL CHARACTER."
—FROM *GEORGE LANG'S CUISINE OF HUNGARY*

Paprika

Hungarian

The New World's contributions to the cuisines of old Europe are surprisingly numerous—consider Italy without tomatoes, Ireland without potatoes, or indeed Hungary without its paprika, the fiery-bright powder that adds its crimson

glow and seductive, earthy pungency (along with plenty of vitamin C) to so many of that country's savory cooked dishes and cured meats.

The sweet and hot red chile peppers that are the basis of paprika were introduced to Europe from Mexico via Spain and Morocco, then

Heat releases paprika's full flavor.

rapidly traveled via Turkey to Hungary.

Spanish cooks latched onto the spice in the form of *pimentón* (see page 267); the particular pepper they use is almost heart-shaped, and is more golden in color than the rounded, vermillion *Capsicum annuum* that flourishes around

Szeged and Kalocsa in southern Hungary. The Spanish paprika is also based on peppers that are smoked, giving the powdered spice a sophisticated woodsy flavor. Air-dried Hungarian peppers produce a smoother, more densely earthy paprika that can be found in varying degrees of spiciness; the most finicky cooks have theirs blended to order.

Sweet or hot, paprika has an underlying fruity sweetness that is best displayed in Hungary's goulash (the national dish), in its chicken paprikash, in the fiery freshwater fish soup-stew that is *halászlé* (see page 393), and in roseate pork belly bacon dusted with paprika to spark each lusciously fatty piece.

Because paprika is extremely perishable—its color and flavor fade rapidly and it may attract tiny bugs if kept in a warm place for more than a month—it should be bought in small quantities and stored in the refrigerator in a dark glass or metal container.

RETAIL AND MAIL ORDER: *In Burbank, CA,* Otto's, tel 818-845-0433, hungariandeli.com (search hungarian paprika). MAIL ORDER: Penzeys Spices, tel 800-741-7777, penzeys.com (search hungarian paprika; sharp paprika). FURTHER INFORMATION AND RECIPES: *George Lang's Cuisine of Hungary* by George Lang (1994); *The Oxford Companion to Food* by Alan Davidson (1999); saveur.com (search chicken paprikash); cookstr.com (search goulash james beard). TIP: For the richest results, paprika should be sautéed in some kind of fat for two or three minutes until it loses its raw aroma and its flavor mellows. Only then should other ingredients be introduced.

||||||||||||||||||||||||||||||||

HUNGARY'S ANSWER TO BISCOTTI

Pogácsa

Hungarian

U biquitous in pastry shops and coffeehouses throughout the country, the salty-sweet *pogácsa* (POH-gothcha) are to Hungary what biscotti are to Italy—no less delicious, and just about as diverse in their various incarnations.

Everything about these small, round biscuits is unprepossessing, from their looks to their mild, elusive flavor. But they are reassuring snacks, welcome when one feels peckish or unappreciated. Pleasantly flaky, with an abundance of eggs, butter or lard, and sour cream, the biscuits are delicately enhanced by salt or black pepper, sometimes grated cheese, or even bits of ham or bacon; or they might be sweetened ever so slightly and enriched by finely crushed walnuts.

Whichever end of the spectrum they grace, pogácsa go well with cheese, morning jam, wine, tea, and coffee. Although this recipe relies on baking powder to lighten their texture, yeast is often used as an alternative leavener.

Pogácsa

Makes 1 dozen biscuits

2¾ cups all-purpose flour

1 scant teaspoon baking powder

¼ teaspoon salt

⅔ cup sugar

1 cup (2 sticks) unsalted butter,
  at room temperature

1 extra-large egg

1 extra-large egg yolk

⅓ cup whole-milk sour cream

2 teaspoons crushed black peppercorns
  (optional)
2 tablespoons grated Gruyère-type cheese
  (optional)
2 tablespoons finely chopped ham or
  crumbled cooked bacon
  (optional)

1. Sift the flour, baking powder, salt, and sugar together in a medium-size bowl. Cut in the butter, rubbing with your fingertips or using a pastry blender (or a food processor) until a coarse meal forms.

2. Blend in the egg, egg yolk, and sour cream, working until the dough is smooth. Work in 2 teaspoons crushed black peppercorns, or 2 tablespoons grated Gruyère-type cheese, or 2 tablespoons finely chopped or crumbled cooked bacon. Form the dough into a thick round and wrap it in wax paper or plastic wrap. Refrigerate the dough for 2 hours.

3. Position a rack in the center of the oven and preheat the oven to 350°F. Lightly butter a large baking sheet.

4. Lightly flour a work surface. Using a lightly floured rolling pin, roll out the dough to a thickness of ½ inch. Using a glass or a cookie cutter, cut the dough into 2-inch rounds. Combine and reroll scraps. Place the rounds about 1 inch apart on the prepared baking sheet and prick each 3 or 4 times with the tines of a fork.

5. Bake the cookies until they are a very pale golden brown, about 20 minutes. Let them cool on the baking sheet. They will keep for 1 week stored in an airtight metal container in a cool place.

WHERE: *In Budapest,* Café Gerbeaud, tel 36/1-429-9000, gerbeaud.hu; *in New York,* Andre's Café, tel 212-327-1105, andrescafeny.com. **RETAIL AND MAIL ORDER:** *In Burbank, CA,* Otto's, tel 818-845-0433, hungariandeli.com (search pogacsa). **FURTHER INFORMATION AND ADDITIONAL RECIPES:** *George Lang's Cuisine of Hungary* by George Lang (1994); saveur.com (search pogacsa).

—||||||||||||||||||||||||||||||||||—

HAND-ROLLED FOR OPTIMAL FLAKINESS

Rétes

Hungarian, Austrian, Eastern European

The buttery, flaky pastry we call by its Austro-Germanic name, strudel, is known as *rétes* (RAY-tesh) in Hungary, where bakers brought the dessert to its greatest heights and still turn out the most delectable, gently sweet, and crisp examples.

By either name, the long, flat loaf of golden pastry leaves enfolding cinnamon- or vanilla-scented fillings is one of the world's most delectable pastries.

These luscious, golden, log-shaped rolls with their crisp, gossamer layers and interstices of melting butter began with the Turks and their phyllo-wrapped pastries. When they were introduced in Hungary, local bakers made refinements, gradually adding more butter and using a different blend of flour for the dough in order to achieve a thinner texture. In strudel, dough is everything, and the Hungarians' native flour is made from the particularly hard and hardy Hungarian wheat, high in gluten and protein and considered one of the finest varieties. The ideal, tissue-thin dough was historically created by gentle-handed women who stretched balls of dough quickly and repeatedly, fist over fist, until each sheet was so thin that one could read a newspaper through it. It was an operation so delicate it required that all rings and rough fingernails be removed lest the dough be torn in the stretching.

As it was in the old days, so it is now. The very best rétes still cannot quite be achieved by machine stretching or by using frozen dough, which unfailingly cracks or sloughs off in the baking.

The dough is the thing, but of course the magic comes with fillings, as multiple leaves of parchmentlike pastry are rolled around mellow combinations such as slightly firm sour-sweet apples, vanilla-and-clove-scented poppy seeds, lemony sour cream fluffed with cheese, crushed roasted walnuts and raisins, or savory main-course stuffings such as sautéed mushrooms and onions, peppery cabbage, or mashed potatoes. And each filling demands its own set of traditional spices, easily identifiable by any real strudel maven.

As the true mavens also know, rétes should be served either slightly warm or at room temperature—overheating the dough makes it soggy. But a cold slice of purloined strudel, enjoyed after everyone else has gone to bed, is one of life's more enticing rewards.

WHERE: *In Budapest,* Café Gerbeaud, tel 36/1-429-9000, gerbeaud.hu; Gundel, tel 36/1-889-8100, gundel.hu/en; Café Ruszwurm, tel 36/1-3755-284, ruszwurm.hu; *in Vienna,* Demel, tel 43/1-535-17-17-0, demel.at; *in New York,* Wallsé, tel 212-352-2300, kg-ny.com/wallse; Café Sabarsky, tel 212-288-0665, kg-ny.com/cafe

sabarsky; Hungarian Pastry Shop, tel 212-866-4230; *in San Pedro, CA,* Mishi's Strudel Bakery and Café, tel 310-832-6474, mishisstrudel.com; *in Shaker Heights, OH,* Lucy's Sweet Surrender, tel 216-752-0828, lucyssweetsurrender.com. **FURTHER INFORMATION AND RECIPES:** *George Lang's Cuisine of Hungary* by George Lang (1994); *The Art of Fine Baking* by Paula Peck (1961); cookstr.com (search viennese apple strudel); bonappetit.com (search autumn apple strudel). **SPECIAL EVENT:** Original Apple Strudel Show, Café Residenz, Vienna, March to October, cafe-residenz.at.

Authentic strudel dough is lovingly hand-stretched.

―――――――||||||||||||||||||||||||||||||||||―――――――

DINNER WITH DRACULA

Transylvanian Baked Sauerkraut with Sausages

Hungarian

Bright sauerkraut, preferably fresh from a barrel, layered about three inches deep with meaty slices of garlicky and peppery kielbasa (pork sausage), diced smoky bacon, ground pork shoulder, and chopped onion . . . Baked with lacings of thick sour cream and hot or sweet vermillion paprika, this rich and fragrant main course is usually rounded out with a buttery puree of split peas and plenty of foamy golden beer. Had Count Dracula come upon one of these succulent, rib-sticking casseroles, he might have been inspired toward more benign pursuits.

Transylvanian Sauerkraut and Sausage Casserole

Serves 6 to 8

⅔ cup long-grain rice
2 pounds sauerkraut, preferably fresh
    from a barrel, otherwise packaged
7 ¼-inch-thick slices lean bacon
1½ pounds ground lean pork shoulder
1 large onion, chopped
2 cloves garlic, minced
1 teaspoon paprika, hot or sweet,
    to taste, plus paprika for topping
    the casserole
Salt and freshly ground black pepper
1½ cups chicken stock
4 ½-inch-thick slices slab bacon, diced
1 pound smoked kielbasa,
    sliced ¼ inch thick
3½ cups whole-milk sour cream
½ cup milk

1. Preheat the oven to 350°F.

2. Blanch the rice by placing it in a potful of salted boiling water for 5 minutes. Drain the rice and set it aside.

3. If the sauerkraut is very acidic, rinse it once or twice under cold running water. Squeeze out as much water as possible. Place the sauerkraut in a large saucepan, add water to cover, and cook over moderate heat until it absorbs the liquid, about 20 minutes. Drain the sauerkraut well, squeezing out any excess water. Set the sauerkraut aside.

4. Cook the bacon slices in a 10-inch skillet over low heat until crisp, about 7 minutes. Using a slotted spoon, transfer the bacon slices to paper towels to drain. Set aside 4 tablespoons of the rendered bacon fat; there should be about 3 tablespoons left in the skillet.

5. Heat the bacon fat over moderate heat. Add the ground pork and cook until golden brown, about 8 minutes. Using a slotted spoon, transfer the browned pork to a bowl.

6. Add the onion and garlic to the bacon fat remaining in the skillet and cook over moderate heat until soft and faintly golden brown, about 7 minutes. Add the browned pork, the paprika, 1 teaspoon of salt, and several grindings of black pepper, and cook over high heat until the paprika loses its raw smell, 1 to 2 minutes. Add the chicken stock, reduce the heat to low, and let simmer gently, uncovered, until slightly reduced, 7 to 8 minutes. Set the pork and onion mixture aside.

7. Place the diced slab bacon in a clean 10-inch skillet and cook slowly over low heat until the pieces are golden brown, about 7 minutes. Using a slotted spoon, transfer the slab bacon to a bowl, leaving the bacon fat in the skillet. Add the sliced kielbasa to the skillet and cook over moderate heat until browned, about 10 minutes. Add the browned kielbasa to the bowl with the diced bacon.

8. Stir 2 cups of the sour cream into the kielbasa and diced bacon. Stir in the milk until smoothly blended. Set the kielbasa and sour cream mixture aside.

9. Spread 2 to 3 tablespoons of the reserved bacon fat on the bottom of an approximately 7½- by 10- by 3-inch baking dish, preferably enameled cast iron and not glass.

Bran Castle—also known as Dracula's Castle

10. Pull the sauerkraut apart into shreds and layer one third of it in the prepared baking dish. Top the layer of sauerkraut with half of the kielbasa mixture, spreading it out evenly. Layer half of the remaining sauerkraut on top of the kielbasa and spoon the remaining kielbasa mixture over it, spreading it out evenly.

11. Strain the pork and onion mixture, setting aside the paprika broth. Add all of the rice and then the drained pork and onion mixture to the baking dish. Top the pork mixture with the remaining sauerkraut and pour ¾ cup of the paprika broth drained from the ground pork on top. Using your hands, gently press down on the sauerkraut until the liquid in the baking dish seeps up to the top.

12. Lightly beat the remaining sour cream and spread it over the sauerkraut. Crumble the drained slices of bacon and sprinkle them and some paprika on top. Drizzle the remaining reserved bacon fat over the top.

13. Place the baking dish on the stove and let the liquid come to a simmer over moderate heat, then cover the baking dish loosely with aluminum foil and put it in the oven. Bake the casserole until juices are bubbling to the top and the top is pale golden, about 1½ hours, removing the aluminum foil after 30 minutes. Let the casserole sit for 15 to 20 minutes before serving.

MAIL ORDER: Babcia Foods, tel 888-520-7784, babciafoods.com (search hungarian style bacon; fresh polish kielbasa); Morse's, tel 866-832-5569, morsessauerkraut.com.

|||||||||||||||||||||||||||||||||

A LUSTY HUNTER'S STEW

Bigos

Polish

The avowed national dish of Poland, *bigos* (pronounced BEE-goesh and meaning mish-mash or jumble) is a long-simmered hunter's stew of pork and sauerkraut. A classic in Poland for hundreds of years, it was at one time consumed exclusively by the aristocracy—the only people who could afford to have so much meat in one dish.

These days almost every Polish family has its own variation on the lusty concoction. Most often, it is loaded with chunks of kielbasa and other sausages, plus one or more of any number of additional meats, including smoked pork shoulder, wild boar leg, bacon, pigs' knuckles, ham hocks, or even cocktail franks. Prunes, apples, and sauerkraut join a mix that is enlivened by lots of onion, garlic, and juniper berries.

Some cooks douse the stew with red wine while others swear by vodka. Some, no doubt, use both. Cooked slowly and lovingly until the flavors marry, the meat is meltingly tender, and the kitchen is redolent of onion. Bigos is served up in big bowls with boiled potatoes, hunks of crusty bread, and pots of coarse-grain mustard on the side.

WHERE: *In Cracow,* W Starej Kuchni, tel 48/12-428-00-22, wstarejkuchni.pl/english/index .html; *in Brooklyn,* Łomżynianka, tel 718-389-0439, lomzynianka.com; *in Chicago,* Bobak's, tel 773-735-5334, bobak.com; *in Milwaukee,* Crocus Restaurant, tel 414-643-6383, crocusrestaurant .com. **FURTHER INFORMATION AND RECIPES:** *The Art of Polish Cooking* by Alina Żerańska (1989); easteuropeanfood.about.com (search bigos); saveur.com (search bigos). **SEE ALSO:** Gulyás, page 392; Cassoulet, page 70; Cholent, page 434; Baeckeoffe, page 54.

‖‖‖‖‖‖‖‖‖‖‖‖‖‖‖‖‖‖‖‖‖‖‖‖‖‖‖‖

PORKY, PEPPERY, AND PERFUMED

Kielbasa

Polish, Ukrainian

Meaty, garlicky, peppery, and robust, the smoked sausage ring kielbasa is a mainstay of the long, cold Polish and Ukrainian winters. Historically, sausages rose to prominence in the region as an ideal match for a thriving hunting culture. They provided both an excellent way for hunters to preserve their extra meats and an easy, portable snack to enjoy mid-hunt. And kielbasa is a reigning star of the lot, one of the lustiest sausages of all.

Usually made entirely of pork, but occasionally mixed with a little beef, the smoked brown-red sausage is traditionally distinguished by coarsely ground meat, heavy seasonings of garlic and black pepper, and its stiff, ringed shape. Often simmered just before being served, preferably hot, kielbasa (also known as kielbasy) is satisfyingly salty, greasy, juicy, chewy—and perfect with a strong, cold pilsner. It's a versatile treat, delicious roasted, grilled, or baked atop sauerkraut or cabbage, diced into potato salad, or tossed into cassoulet. And it can also be dressed up: Thinly sliced, it's not out of place at cocktail hour with other nibbles.

RETAIL AND MAIL ORDER: *In Brooklyn,* Sikorski Meats, tel 718-389-6181, sikorskimeats.com; *in Plymouth, PA,* Fetch's Food Store, tel 570-779-9864; *in Philadelphia,* Krakus Market, tel 215-426-4336, krakusmarket.com; *in Rockville, MD,* Kielbasa Factory, tel 240-453-9090, kielbasa factory.com; *in Chicago,* Bobak's, tel 773-735-5334, bobak.com; *in Minneapolis,* Kramarczuk's, tel 612-379-3018, kramarczuks.com. FURTHER INFORMATION AND RECIPES: *The Art of Polish Cooking* by Alina Żerańska (1989); *Please to the Table* by Anya von Bremzen and John Welchman (1990); foodandwine.com (search braised lentils with kielbasa; kielbasa sausage pierogi with caramelized onions). SPECIAL EVENTS: Kielbasa Alive Festival, Plymouth, IN, August, plymouthalive.com; Kramarczuk's Kielbasa Festival, Minneapolis, MN, September, kramarczuks.com/entertainment/events.

‖‖‖‖‖‖‖‖‖‖‖‖‖‖‖‖‖‖‖‖‖‖‖‖‖‖‖‖

PUDDING FOR A CHRISTMAS EVE

Kutya

Wheat Berry Pudding

Polish, Ukrainian

At various times, we choose our foods for different reasons from pure pleasure to health to convenience or economy. But there are foods we delight in because they link us to a long chain of history and meaning: lamb and eggs at

Easter, a *bûche de Noël* at Christmas (see page 67), hamanstaschen for Purim (see page 439), carp for New Year's, and many more.

Joining the list of such treasured dishes is *kutya*, a sweet and healthful dessert pudding that is traditional on Christmas Eve in the wheat-growing regions of Poland and Ukraine. Cooked, drained, and cooled, shiny, sun-gold whole wheat berries much like the Italian farro are stirred through with honey, chopped almonds or walnuts, and ground poppy seeds, the poppy seeds sometimes softened with a splash of heavy sweet cream. The result is a seductively sweet, silky, nutty, and crunchy preparation much like *mote con huesillo* in Chile, the *kamhie* of Lebanon and Syria, and Armenian *anoush abour* (see page 507), give or take some rose water, raisins, and dried or candied fruits here and there.

The difference lies in the ceremony, one in which parents and children might enjoy taking part. Before guests eat their fill, a small bowl of kutya is placed outdoors to bribe Father Frost as insurance on the next season's crops. An additional spoonful or two is set on a dish to feed departed spirits who may return home on that festive night. Finally (and best of all), a cupful or so of the kutya is tossed up to the ceiling. The number of grains that stick predict how many bees a farmer will have in his hive in the year ahead, and is also considered an all-around indication of agricultural prosperity. If nothing else, it is said that this practice keeps wall painters busy around year-end.

RETAIL AND MAIL ORDER: *In New York,* Moscow on the Hudson, tel 212-740-7397, moscowonhudson.com (search wheat groats uvelka). **MAIL ORDER:** amazon.com (search jovial organic einkorn wheat berries; rustichella d'abruzzo whole grain farro). **FURTHER INFORMATION AND RECIPES:** *Visions of Sugarplums* by Mimi Sheraton (1968); *Traditional Ukrainian Cookery* by Savella Stechishin (1991); *Please to the Table* by Anya von Bremzen and John Welchman (1990); foodnetwork.com (search kutya).

A DANCE OF AN EASTER CAKE

Mazurek

Polish

The Polish have a great tradition of sweets, particularly cakes, and the *mazurek* (mazurka in English) is one of the best known, and best loved, of all. Sweet, airy, and crunchy, like a very buttery meringue with a texture reminiscent of

a short crust or a sweet wafer, the mazurek is cut into small squares from a larger piece. It may be topped with jam, vanilla cream, or any type of fruit gel, and then decorated—a crucial step, as mazureks are always elaborately decorated with all manner of lavish patterns and inscriptions—with nuts, candied fruits (especially orange peel and cherries), marzipan, and icings. In bakery windows, mazureks are easy to spot because they're so lovely and colorful—and there are so many types, from

A surprisingly crunchy cake, beloved around Easter

raspberry-walnut to fig to chocolate cream, from which to choose. The special treats are included in almost every holiday celebration, but most especially Easter, when they are decorated with tiny iced lambs and inscribed *Wesołego Alleluja* (Happy Easter).

The origins of the dessert are unclear, but historians guess that mazurek has been made for centuries and was most likely inspired by the sweet pastries of Turkey. The name supposedly comes from the famous Polish folk dance of the same name—Chopin wrote many mazurkas,

and the theory goes that the cake was served at the fashionable parties where they were danced. (Not, one assumes, simultaneously.)

Where: *In Warsaw,* A. Blikle, tel 48/22-826-6619, blikle.pl; *in Brooklyn,* Old Poland Bakery, tel 800-467-6526. **Further information and recipes:** *Polish Heritage Cookery* by Robert Strybel (2005); *The Art of Fine Baking* by Paula Peck (1961); *The Art of Polish Cooking* by Alina Żerańska (1989); easteuropeanfood.about.com (search polish royal mazurek); foodnetwork .com (search mazurkas).

JELLY MEETS DOUGHNUT, IN POLAND

Pączki

Polish

When Lee Radziwill wanted to surprise her Polish-born husband, Prince Stanislaw Albrecht Radziwill (known as Stash), for his birthday, she contacted the famous bakery of A. Blikle in Warsaw. The dessert she had flown to

their London home was not a birthday cake, but rather hundreds of the small, sweet-smelling, yeasty pastries called *pączki* (PAN-tshki), for which the Warsaw patisserie had been known since 1869.

Among other celebrity fans of the puffy wonders was General Charles de Gaulle. A young lieutenant serving in France's military mission to Poland from 1919 and 1921, he was billeted in a room above the Blikle bakery. And as the president of France after World War II, he demonstrated his fond memories of those pastries by downing more than a few.

What's all the fuss about? Pączki are jelly doughnuts with a difference. Made from a firm-textured, slightly sweet, rum-scented yeast dough, they are quickly deep-fried in hot vegetable oil (or, even more flavorfully in the old days, lard) to develop richly brown and crusty tops. Within each crunchy cruller are delectable globs of silky jam—darkly purple prune, golden

apricot, bright cherry or, in the spring, rose petal preserves—providing luxurious contrast to the gently crisp pastry.

Dusted with lemon- or vanilla-perfumed confectioners' sugar, pączki make wonderful companions to tea or coffee at any time of day. Poles everywhere seek out these delectable pastries on New Year's and Shrove Tuesday and then all through Lent. In Warsaw at these times, Blikle bakery is mobbed.

Where: *In Warsaw,* A. Blikle, tel 48/22-826-6619, blikle.pl; *in Buffalo, NY,* on weekends, Muzurek's Bakery, tel 716-768-2157, muzureks bakery.com; *in Chicago,* Racine Bakery, tel 773-581-8500, racinebakery.com. **Further information and recipes:** *The Art of Polish Cooking* by Alina Żerańska (1989); *Polish Cookery* by Marja Ochorowicz-Monatowa (1958); seriouseats.com (click Recipes, then search paczki). **See also:** Sufganiyot, page 469; Berliner Pfannkuchen, page 279.

────────────||||||||||||||||||||||||||||||||||||||────────────

Ciorba

Romanian, Bulgarian

R omanians and Bulgarians, among other Balkan people, share a distinct and unusual preference for a winey sourness in many of their dishes—in fact, they have a special category of sour soups known as *ciorbas* (chee-OR-bahs).

The souring comes by way of dill, sauerkraut juice, sour cream, buttermilk, yogurt, lemon juice, or vinegar, as well as the citric acid crystals known as sour salt. Cooks also rely on tart fruit such as green plums or grapes to provide the sought-after taste.

Many home cooks throughout the region make a sour soup based on smoked pork, broad beans, and sauerkraut. But that's just the tip of the ciorba iceberg. Among the most favored is a Romanian specialty that combines meatballs, rice, pot vegetables, and the chopped cucumberlike herb lovage in a warming and filling soup. In one of Bulgaria's beloved soups, meat-stuffed zucchini go into a marrow-enriched stock along with dill, parsley, cilantro, lovage, and pot vegetables. The soup is thickened with an ivory blend of egg yolk beaten through sour cream.

When a fish soup-stew is on the menu in Romania, look for a thick and chunky *ciorba de peste* redolent of bay leaves, garlic, and a last-minute drizzle of vinegar. Finally, a cold and creamy soup based on pungent sorrel sates the urge for sourness in summer. Variations don't end there, of course—this very local penchant gives rise to endless possibilities.

WHERE: *In Sarajevo,* Restaurant Kibe, tel 387/33-441-936, restaurantkibe.com; *in Queens, NY,* Bucharest Restaurant, tel 718-389-2300, bucharestrestaurant.com; Romanian Garden, tel 718-786-7894. **FURTHER INFORMATION AND RECIPES:** *The Balkan Cookbook* by Vladimir Mirodan (1989); easteuropeanfood.about.com (search romanian sour meatball soup; romanian sour cabbage soup).

────────────||||||||||||||||||||||||||||||||||||||────────────

Blini with Caviar

Russian

T hough caviar doesn't require enhancements, the Russians truly have found a way to render the dark, glowing fish eggs even more magnificent. The extra bit of magic comes via blini, the light and airy buckwheat mini-crêpes leavened

with yeast and raised with beaten egg whites and, perhaps, whipped cream. The tender, delicate pancakes are served hot, lightly glossed

with soft, unsalted butter just before they are topped with the caviar—red, white, or black—and sometimes with sour cream or crème fraîche (in which case it's best to eliminate further top-pings like chopped egg, lemon, or the onions that always overpower the delicate roe). The combination of warm, soft, thin buttered crêpe and saline, chilled roe is at once subtle and rich (almost obscenely so), velvety and satisfying.

Served as an hors d'oeuvre, the duo of caviar and blini has long been a staple of Russian high society—but it gained popularity in the grand hotel dining rooms of western Europe in the nineteenth century, and came from there to America. Wherever it is served, the caviar-blini service is always accompanied by shots of ice-cold vodka or elegant flutes of champagne.

WHERE: *In New York,* Russian Tea Room, tel 212-581-7100, russiantearoomnyc.com; Moscow57, tel 212-260-5775, moscow57.com; *in Paris and London,* Caviar Kaspia at multiple locations, caviarkaspia.com. **DINE-IN, RETAIL, AND MAIL ORDER:** *In multiple locations around the world,* Petrossian, tel 800-828-9241, petrossian .com; *in New York,* Russ & Daughters, tel 212-475-4880, russanddaughters.com. **FURTHER INFORMATION AND RECIPES:** *À La Russe* by Darra Goldstein (1983); *Please to the Table* by Anya von Bremzen and John Welchman (1990); epi curious.com (search blini with sour cream). **SEE ALSO:** Caspian "000" Beluga Caviar, page 407.

A TREASURE FROM THE FORESTS

Borovik Ceps

Russian, Polish

Together with truffles and Caesar's mushrooms, ceps (*Boletus edulis* and *B. aereus*) are unquestionably the world's most highly prized fungi, even allowing for Japan's matsutakes and Italy's porcini. With their puffy, cushionlike

cream and brown caps and tender, fat stems, these boletus were favorites of the ancient Greeks and Romans.

Although the mushrooms grow wild in Australia, North Africa, and North America, the very best examples are found in the coniferous and broadleaf forests of Poland and Russia, where they are called *borovik.* They reach their harvest peaks between September and late November, and come fall, anyone driving outside of large Polish and Russian cities will be met by roadside vendors offering the borovik they have foraged (much as Americans might find corn or tomatoes or watermelon

Dried borovik pack the most punch.

being hawked along country roads in summer).

The delicately earthy, fresh mushrooms are enhanced by a quick sauté in butter and perhaps a sauce of sour cream and beef stock, with a grating of pepper and nutmeg. But the real magic begins when the borovik are dried, as they are for export to all parts of Europe and the United States. For that is when they take on an intensely smoky, woodsy essence that tastes like ancient history, along with a form that is extremely useful: Looking like antiques, or some sort of brown-gray, handcrafted jewelry, the dried borovik are sold on long, looped strings or crushed into culinary sachets that scent soups, stews, kasha, sauerkraut, and cabbage, as well as sauces for meat and autumn game birds.

As might be expected, such gastronomic treasure comes at very high prices—these days dried borovik can fetch about $250 a pound in the U.S. That's not quite as bad as it sounds, as the mushrooms don't weigh much; a pound would be an enormous bagful that might spoil (by dampness or by fading) if not used within six months to a year. So powerful is their perfume and flavor that just three or four caps add noticeable strength to a four-quart pot of soup. Even the water in which they are soaked before being cooked can be strained of sand and added to stews or soup, for a valuable belt of richness.

Where: *In Pittsburgh,* S&D Polish Deli, tel 412-281-2906, sdpolishdeli.com. **Retail and mail order:** *In New York,* Russ & Daughters, tel 212-475-4480, russanddaughters.com. **Further information and recipes:** *Please to the Table* by Anya von Bremzen and John Welchman (1990); *À La Russe* by Darra Goldstein (1983); *The Oxford Companion to Food* by Alan Davidson (1999); marthastewart .com (search polish mushroom soup); east europeanfood.about.com (search creamed mushroom sauce); polishwildmushrooms.com.

—||||||||||||||||||||||||||||||||—

THE WORLD'S MOST SERIOUS SOUP

Borshch

Russian, Ukrainian, Eastern European

Time to set the record straight: Whatever other elements are included in this steaming cabbage- and beet-laden Russian-Ukrainian soup, the letter *T* should not be among them. Never mind the spelling that is standard in the States,

where this immigrant legacy of the eastern European Jews is pronounced and spelled as "borscht."

On native ground, the word is pronounced BORE-sh-ch, with the *sh* as in *shush* and the *ch* as in *cheek* run together almost but not quite imperceptibly—a common sound denoted by the special Cyrillic letter Щ. The name itself derives from the old Slavic word *brsh,* meaning beets, and the earthy rose-red roots are indeed an essential component of any borshch. The exception is a so-called white or green borshch made with cream and leafy greens such as spinach and sour sorrel, much like the Jewish *schav* on page 464.

To give credit where it is due, the borshch we loosely identify as Russian reaches its apogee in Ukraine, which boasts more than a hundred versions. There are still other regional versions, most notably in Moldava and in other Slavic countries such as Poland, where the meat, beet, and cabbage *barszcz* take the chill off icy winters.

As with other complex soups like gumbo and minestrone, one might come to believe that there's no such thing as "authentic" borshch. Every cook has a different interpretation. The cold beet soup that we think of in the United States is just one among them. In fact, outside of the United States, one consistent feature of borshch served in the cooler months is a serving temperature best described as volcanic. Designed for the coldest of winters in the coldest of lands, properly presented borshch will be a scalding brew, much too hot to eat until finally one masters the technique of careful slurping, sipping, or inhaling, perhaps with a piece of bread or a dumpling as an aid, before attempting whole spoonfuls. This much heat presents a challenge, but it enables one to experience the most sublime aromas of leeks, onions, and garlic, the slightly sour edge of shredded cabbage, slivered beets, and the earthy, muffled sweetness of root vegetables such as carrots, celeriac, parsnips, and the white parsley root called *petrushka*.

Generally borshch is blushed with tomatoes and buffered with plenty of meat, most lavishly so in Ukraine. There, it might be beef brisket, lamb, or ham, or more likely a combination of meats including garlicky, peppery slices of smoked kielbasa sausage. Potatoes may be added for heft, and bay leaves and dill for their perfume. Those with a marked taste for a winey, sour soup stir in a few drops of the fermented, ciderlike *kvass* (see page 413). Wine vinegar, lemon juice, citric acid (in the form of sour salt), or even a cut-up unripe pear or apple will also do.

A dish that tastes better twenty-four hours after it is prepared, a good borshch kept cold will improve for as long as a week. A whole boiled potato may be added at serving. Moscovites like theirs garnished with meat-filled *piroshki* pastries while Ukrainians prefer *ushki*, tiny dough-wrapped dumplings much like Italian *cappelletti*. What all agree on is a nice, snowy dollop of cold sour cream right in the

In its home countries, cabbage- and beet-laden borshch is usually served piping hot.

middle of the bowl, a cooling counterpart that unifies all of this glorious soup's diverse flavors into a sublimely satisfying meal.

WHERE: *In Kiev,* Tsarske Selo, tel 380/44-288-9775, tsarske.kiev.ua/en; *in New York,* Mari Vanna, tel 212-777-1955, marivanna.ru/ny; *in Brooklyn,* Tatiana Restaurant, tel 718-891-5151, tatianarestaurant.com; *in Chicago,* Russian Tea Time, tel 312-360-0000, russianteatime.com; *in Toronto,* Suliko, tel 905-760-1989, suliko.ca. **FURTHER INFORMATION AND RECIPES:** *À La Russe* by Darra Goldstein (1983); *Please to the Table* by Anya von Bremzen and John Welchman (1990); epicurious.com (search russian borscht); saveur.com (search polish white borscht); easteuropeanfood.about.com (search schav borscht); for a cold version, foodnetwork.com (search summer borscht).

MANKIND'S MOST EXPENSIVE EGGS

Caspian "000" Beluga Caviar

Russian, Iranian

D islike capers, anchovies, and canned tuna packed in oil? You can probably stop reading right here—because you're likely to feel the same about caviar. And you may be better off, as loving caviar means spending small fortunes each

time you want to indulge in those tiny, glistening, black-diamond beads that lie silky soft on the tongue, exuding a mysterious essence of

deep, dark salt sea with a vague patina of fishiness and the merest hint of earthiness.

In truth, what caviar tastes like is caviar.

And to aficionados, it is unquestionably the single best food in the world.

But even if one is willing to pay top price, the best caviar has become increasingly difficult to find. That distinction belongs to the roe of sturgeon that swim in the Caspian Sea—and unhappily for caviar lovers, Caspian sturgeon is endangered, its fishing virtually banned. There's an added political twist brought about by the current boycott of imports from Iran, the country that, along with Russia, has exclusive access to and the most experience in processing this top product. All of which means that for the moment, the highest-grade caviar is barely available on the global market, at least not legitimately. (Whether Iranian or Russian caviar can come through other countries as a legal import is an open question.)

Still life with caviar, toast, and lemon

It is still possible to locate good-quality caviar, however, and in the wider realm of roe there are three basic types, each with its devotees and price range. The most highly prized is beluga, the roe of giant beluga sturgeon. These are the largest, roundest, and most succulent eggs, and they are graded for color, the top choice being the crystal-gray eggs in the two-kilo tins with the triple-zero symbol. Double and single zeros mark darker shades, which are generally considered a cut below the gray. The smaller sevruga sturgeon produces suitably smaller eggs that fetch lower prices and are also graded for color. Osetra caviar is usually smaller than

beluga and larger than sevruga, its distinguishing feature being its golden brown color and a slightly softer texture.

Nature being what it is, it is entirely possible for the flavor of a particular batch of sevruga or osetra to be better than beluga, depending on the individual fish, the season, the processing, and the salting. It is wise, therefore, to insist upon tasting when buying the world's most expensive eggs. Caviar imported to the States tends to be saltier than that sold in Europe, primarily because in European caviar borax replaces some of the salt as a preservative. (Borax is prohibited for use in food by the USDA.)

No top-grade product is packed in vacuum jars or even in jars with near vaccum-tight lids. In almost all cases, such caviar has been pasteurized for extended shelf life and is more heavily salted than the fresh kind. The best caviar comes in unsealed but covered tins. At the very least, you should see the caviar before buying it to ascertain that the eggs are whole, shiny, and not wrinkled; that there is no free liquid or milky film in the tin; and that the aroma is not stale or musty but rather a reminder of fresh sea air. Once you have opened a tin or jar, the contents should be eaten within a day or two, as oil will run out of the leftover eggs to fill spaces left when some of the roe is removed.

Caviar that needs no refrigeration is not fresh at all, and thus not even a contender. Pasteurization is a cooking process and caviar is a mass of fish roe or eggs. As with all cooked eggs, caviar will develop a tough outer membrane when heated, rendering it chewy and leaving a skinlike residue on the tongue.

Although most caviar is sold during the fall holiday season, the best caviar becomes available in spring and summer. The egg-laying fish are caught about six months before their roe reaches the market, and fish caught in cold winter waters have more flavor than those caught in the warm summer months.

Serving the most sublime caviar with anything other than blini (see page 404) or unbuttered, wafer-thin, freshly made toasts and a squeeze of lemon juice would be profligate. Save the hard-cooked eggs, onions, and sour cream for the lesser impostors, of which there is a growing number as eager entrepreneurs around the world attempt to emulate the Caspian prize. Some have had more success than others, but you can never know without tasting.

Where: *In New York,* Russian Tea Room, tel 212-581-7100, russiantearoomnyc.com; Caviar Russe, tel 212-980-5908, caviarrusse.com; *in Paris and London,* Caviar Kaspia at multiple locations, caviarkaspia.com. **Dine-in, retail, and mail order:** *In multiple locations around the world,* Petrossian, tel 800-828-9241, petrossian.com; *in New York,* Russ & Daughters, tel 212-475-4880, russanddaughters.com. **Further information:** *Caviar! Caviar! Caviar!* by Gerald M. Stein with Donald Bain (1981); *Caviar* by Susan Friedland (1986). **Tip:** Caviar's flavor can be compromised by the touch of silver and most other metals, gold being the single exception; traditional serving implements are made with blades of bone, horn, or gold-plated silver.

SAVORY TO SWEET CREAM OF WHEAT

Guriev Kasha

Russian

Among the sweet and winning dishes invented to commemorate victory in battle, a champion is surely this creamy fruit-and-nut-layered pudding, much loved throughout Russia and a longtime favorite at the original Russian Tea Room restaurant in Manhattan. Its inventor is said to have been one Count Dmitry Guriev, finance minister to Czar Alexander II for more than a decade. It's hard to imagine what made the good count look at some snowy white semolina grains (similar to Cream of Wheat) and decide that they had the makings of a really great dessert, but the impetus was the Russian defeat of Napoleon's armies in 1812.

Served hot or cold or anywhere in between, Guriev Kasha (sometimes known as Gurievskaya Kasha) begins with silky semolina grains simmered with sugar and whole milk or cream until tender. The mixture is layered in a baking pan with alternate slatherings of pulverized walnuts and almonds, jewel-like candied fruits, and glossings of a thick fruit preserve, usually apricot or raspberry. (Originally a complicated requirement held that the milk should be simmered and resimmered to produce a series of skins, each of which was placed between the layers, but the practice was eventually abandoned.) Flavored with vanilla or almond extract and topped either with crumbled vanilla wafers or a veneer of brown sugar, the dessert is baked until the top caramelizes to a rich golden brown and its layers meld into an enticing mix of textures and flavors. A splash or two of cold cream over each serving does not go amiss.

Mail order: For semolina, russianfooddirect.com (search semolina extra; semolina). **Further information and recipes:** *The Horizon Cookbook* by William Harlan Hale (1968); *À La Russe* by Darra Goldstein (1983); foodarts.com (search guriev kasha). **Tip:** Don't let the term *kasha* confuse you. In the U.S., it usually refers to buckwheat groats, but Russians also use the term for porridges made from any variety of grain—much in the way that the most traditional use of the word *polenta* in Italy means not only cornmeal but also any kind of porridge.

THE PROPER WAY TO DO A CUTLET

Kotlety Pozharskie

Russian

The notion of a chicken croquette might seem singularly unexciting, given the bland examples usually served at banquet lunches. But give the dish a romantic name and a history, prepare it with the snowiest of chicken breast meat, glistening with streams of melted butter and aromatic with nutmeg, and you have the beginnings of something special.

Beloved by Russians as a basic staple, much the way the Viennese dote and depend upon the schnitzel, the *kotlety Pozharskie* has such a history. It is said to be named for one Pozharskie, a tavern owner whose business was in the town of Torjok, a popular stopover for travelers halfway between Moscow and St. Petersburg. He made this sort of croquette out of beef, combining it with game meats and poultry and, fittingly enough, naming it after himself.

Although most often made of chicken now, the cutlet has even more body and flavor when ground raw veal is added to the mix. Formed into a slightly flattened oval (that is, a cutlet)

from the smoothly blended mixture, it is veneered with a coating of only the freshest fine bread crumbs and fried in butter. It emerges crisp, golden, and ready to accommodate a rose-pink paprika sauce along with some noodles and creamed mushrooms or spinach.

Given how many fast-food chains offer chicken nuggets, one might almost credit the good tavern owner Pozharskie with being ahead of his time.

WHERE: *In New York,* Mari Vanna, tell 212-777-1955, marivanna.ru/ny; *in Chicago,* Russian Tea Time, tel 312-360-0000, russianteatime.com. **FURTHER INFORMATION AND RECIPES:** *À La Russe* by Darra Goldstein (1983); *Please to the Table* by Anya von Bremzen and John Welchman (1990); nytimes.com (search veal pojarski); gourmet.com (search pojarski).

A MAIN COURSE FIT FOR A CZAR

Kulebyaka

Russian

The French may claim *coulibiac de saumon* (they certainly named it), but historians know that the epic fish pie was created in czarist St. Petersburg, by palace chefs seeking to please the royal Romanovs and their noble guests.

The dish was co-opted by the great French chef Auguste Escoffier, who served coulibiacs for very special parties.

It's no wonder the French wanted to own

this haute-cuisine fish pie. *Kulebyaka* (KOOL-ya-bya-ka), as it was originally known, is by any measure one of the world's most opulent and succulent dishes. A stupendous centerpiece of a main course—a long fish wrapped in a golden crust of sunny brioche dough—it is made by lining the dough with crêpes and then layering it with cooked rice, onions, sliced hard-cooked eggs, and (usually) mushrooms. Finally, a coral slab of fresh, wild salmon is set in place before a second round of the ingredients is layered on in reverse. The dough is folded closed and then adorned with additional dough cut out in the shapes of leaves and flowers. Scented with white wine, hot butter, and dill mixed into the rice, the kulebyaka exudes an irresistibly mouthwatering aroma when it is cut into thick slices, which are further gilded with rivulets of hot melted butter.

A culinary tour de force, celebrated and rare

The preparation is intricate, to say the least, and posing an additional challenge is the necessity of finding *visega*, the sticky dried spinal cord of a sturgeon. It's added to the rice mixture and is the most authentic ingredient in the dish. Although it may be available outside Russia at a few luxury food shops catering to wealthy expatriates, the less fortunate might have to take the

suggestion of food writer Darra Goldstein and substitute well-soaked Chinese bean thread noodles. These provide a similarly silky texture if not quite the same mysteriously ripe, sea-breeze taste. Daniel Boulud suggests soaked and mashed tapioca pearls or tapioca powder or agar-agar for the same sticky effect. Neither recommends gelatin.

For an idea of kulebyaka's complexity, consider a 1973 recipe that took up two pages of *The New York Times*. Wisely—and teasingly—the legendary food editor Craig Claiborne suggested this might be a once-in-a-lifetime effort. Given its specialness, it is understandable that kulebyaka has been celebrated several times in Russian literature, most notably by Anton Chekhov, in a scene from his 1887 short story "The Siren." As judges retired to their chambers for the day, a secretary speculated on what would be most desirable for their dinner: "The *kulebyaka* must be appetizing, shameless in its nakedness, voluptuous so to say in all its glory. . . . As you cut yourself a piece of it, you wink at it, and, your heart overflowing with delight, you make passes with your fingers over it. . . . Then you start eating it and the butter drips like large tears, and the stuffing is succulent, luscious; there are eggs in it and giblets and onions." What he meant by *nakedness* was an absence of heavy sauce, excepting only the melted butter poured over the thick-cut slices of the fish- and rice-filled pastry and so dripping like tears, surely tears of joy.

In his novel *Dead Souls*, Nikolai Gogol expresses a preference for kulebyaka baked in a square shape and made not with salmon and rice but with sturgeon cheeks and kasha (buckwheat groats). There are also mushrooms, onions, eggs, and, for good measure, calves' brains and milts (spleen). He specifies that kulebyaka should be baked so it's browner on one side than on the other, and that it must "melt in the mouth like snow . . . and that one should not even feel it melting."

In a simpler vein, there's always Polish kulebyaka, made without any fish or meat at all. It combines cabbage sautéed with onions, cooked dried mushrooms, and chopped hard-cooked eggs, enfolded in a long, crisp loaf of yeast and sour cream dough.

Where: *In New York,* DB Bistro Moderne, tel 212-391-2400, dbbistro.com/nyc. **Further information and recipes:** *The Best of Craig Claiborne* by Craig Claiborne with Pierre Franey (1999);

Please to the Table by Anya von Bremzen and John Welchman (1990); *À La Russe* by Darra Goldstein (1983); *The Art of Polish Cooking* by Alina Żerańska (1989); jamesbeard.org (search coulibiac); nytimes.com (search coulibiac world's greatest dish); easteuropeanfood.about .com (search kulebiac).

⊢||||||||||||||||||||||||||||||⊣

EASTER BREAKFAST TREATS

Kulich and Paskha

Russian

T he Russian Orthodox celebration of Easter would not be complete without these twin treats, one a sweet yeast bread-cake shaped as a stately domed cylinder, the other a sunny pyramid formed of sweet cheese gilded with eggs

and saffron and jeweled with candied fruits and nuts. The shapes of these treats are so iconic that the famous Troitskaya church in Saint Petersburg, Russia, is known as "Kulich and Paskha" because the rotunda of the church resembles kulich and the pyramidal form of its adjacent belfry suggests a paskha.

A paskha decorated with candied fruits

Kulich is the name of the yeast cake, similar in texture and flavor to the Italian panettone. To achieve its unique shape, bakers pour the batter into large coffee or fruit juice cans. Once cooled, the cake is glazed with frosty white icing that is allowed to drizzle down its sides before being decorated with colorful icing flowers and the letters XB, short for the traditional Orthodox Easter greeting Христос воскресе, "Christ is risen."

Paskha, meaning Easter, is made from *tvorog*—a soft, white cheese resembling farmer's or cottage cheese—blended with egg yolks, butter, sour cream or heavy sweet cream, and sugar. The mixture may be boiled, for longer keeping, or molded uncooked into a truncated pyramid symbolizing Christ's tomb and imprinted with the letters XB. Either way, it has the texture and flavor of cheesecake and may be decorated with red fruit jam or festooned with various candied fruits.

The paskha and kulich are placed in an Easter basket with other festival foods and dyed eggs and then taken to the church for a blessing from the priest. Once back home, the blessed kulich's impressive dome is delicately removed and placed in the center of a serving plate before the remaining loaf is sliced horizontally and arranged around the crown. Slices are spread with creamy paskha for a double breakfast treat. This combination is enjoyed from Easter until Pentecost, fifty days later.

WHERE: *In San Francisco,* at Easter, Cinderella Russian Bakery & Café, tel 415-751-9690, cinderellabakery.com. **RETAIL AND MAIL ORDER:** *In New York,* for kulich, Moscow on the Hudson, tel 212-740-7397, moscowonhudson .com. **FURTHER INFORMATION AND RECIPES:** *The Bread Bible* by Beth Hensperger (2004); *Please to the Table* by Anya von Bremzen and John Welchman (1990); cookstr.com; (search kulich); foodnet work.com (search pashka). **SEE ALSO:** Panettone, page 214; Castagnaccio, page 177; Torta di Ricotta, page 249; Mazurek, page 402.

A FRUITY, YEASTY FERMENTATION

Kvass

Russian

With its amber glow and fruity, ciderlike essence, the delicate and mildly alcoholic drink known as *kvass* is fermented with yeast, either alone or more traditionally along with a big cut of yeasty rye bread. Together with some

flavorful apples, pears, prunes, or fresh stone fruits, the yeast lends a slight fizziness to the results, and the fermentation process produces a naturally sweet-and-sour flavor that is sometimes enhanced by caraway, mint, or blackcurrant leaves, all much improved by a good chilling.

In days when mead was the drink of nobility, kvass was the choice for commoners, easy enough (and cheap enough) to make from leftover black or rye bread. While it is still best made at home, it has long been sold from street stands and trucks in many Russian cities, including Moscow; a commercial kvass can also be purchased in many Russian food stores.

The fruity, mildly fizzy drink has an ABV of less than 1 percent.

WHERE: *In New York,* Mari Vanna, tel 212-777-1955, marivanna.ru/ny; *in Brooklyn,* Café Volna, tel 718-332-0341; *in Indianapolis,* Babushka's Deli, tel 317-843-1920, babushka deli.com. **RETAIL AND MAIL ORDER:** *In New York,* Moscow on the Hudson, tel 212-740-7397, moscowonhudson.com. **MAIL ORDER:** amazon .com (search kvas ochakovsky; kvas monastyrs-kiy). **FURTHER INFORMATION AND RECIPES:** *A Taste of Russia* by Darra Goldstein (1999); *Kvass* by Dan Woodske (2012); kvas.lv/en (click All About Kvass); cooksinfo.com/kvass; natashaskitchen .com (search angelina's easy bread kvas recipe).

‖‖‖‖‖‖‖‖‖‖‖‖‖‖‖‖‖‖‖‖‖‖‖‖‖‖‖‖‖‖

MUSHROOMS WITH EVERYTHING

Marinovannye Griby

Pickled Mushrooms

Russian

For Russians, there is no fungi that can't be made satisfyingly edible, but there's certainly a hierarchy at play. To whit, in his memoir, *Speak, Memory*, Vladimir Nabokov writes of his mother's summer searches for wild, earthily complex *Boletus* mushrooms and her disdain for the small, white field or button mushrooms we know as champignons, classified as *Agaricus* or *Psalliota campestris*. Nevertheless, even the smallest of these snowy, second-rate button mushrooms can be pickled in an enticingly spicy and herbaceous marinade that preserves them for three or four weeks in the refrigerator, where they are readily at hand to spark an appetizer or *zakuski* (hors d'oeuvre) assortment. As

A preparation that exalts the humblest of fungi

the firm mushrooms soften in a dousing of red wine vinegar, they absorb the fragrance and flavors of lemon, garlic, dill, bay leaves, coriander seeds, and, for some tastes, a slight sting of dried hot red chile flakes, for a juicy, tingling palate awakener.

Pickled Mushrooms

Makes 1 quart; serves 6 to 8 as an appetizer or side dish

1 pound uniformly small, very fresh white button mushrooms (see Note)
¾ cup red wine vinegar
2 cloves garlic, peeled and lightly crushed with the side of a chef's knife
6 to 8 black peppercorns
4 whole coriander seeds
1 small bay leaf
1 teaspoon dried dill seed, or 8 to 10 sprigs fresh dill with stems
2 teaspoons salt
1 small, dried hot red chile, or ½ teaspoon dried hot chile flakes (optional)
2 thin, round lemon slices
1 to 2 tablespoons vegetable oil, preferably sunflower, but olive oil will do

1. Clean the mushrooms with damp paper towels and, if the bottoms of the stems look bruised, trim them but leave the mushrooms whole. Set the mushrooms aside.
2. Place the wine vinegar and ⅔ cup of water in a 2-quart enamel or stainless-steel saucepan and bring to a boil over high heat. Add the garlic, peppercorns, coriander seeds, bay leaf, dill seed or sprigs, salt, and dried chile or chile flakes, if using.
3. Add the mushrooms and let simmer, partially covered, over low heat, stirring frequently until the mushrooms are a bit darkened and softened

but have not wrinkled, 8 to 10 minutes. Using a slotted spoon, transfer the mushrooms to a bowl, setting aside the cooking liquid, and let both cool to room temperature.

4. Place the mushrooms in a 1-quart glass or ceramic jar that has a tight-fitting lid. Add the lemon slices and pour in the cooking liquid with its herbs and spices. Gently spoon a ½-inch layer of oil over the top of the marinade and close the lid. If the lid has a metal lining, place a piece of wax paper or plastic wrap over the mouth of the jar before screwing on the lid to prevent corrosion.

5. Let the mushrooms marinate in the refrigerator for at least 2 weeks before serving. If you are not using all of the mushrooms at once, try to leave all the seasonings in the jar with the remaining mushrooms. Always add a fresh layer of oil to cover the remaining mushrooms. The preparation can be refrigerated for 3 to 4 weeks.

Note: Be sure the mushrooms you buy have tightly closed caps, indicating that they are fresh.

WHERE: *In Brooklyn,* Primorski Restaurant, tel 718-891-3111, primorskiny.com. **MAIL ORDER:** Russian Table, tel 800-761-2460, russiantable .com (search pickled mushrooms "maslyata"). **FURTHER INFORMATION AND ADDITIONAL RECIPES:** *The Food & Cooking of Russia* by Lesley Chamberlain (2006); *Please to the Table* by Anya von Bremzen and John Welchman (1990); *À La Russe* by Darra Goldstein (1983); easteuropean food.about.com (search russian pickled mushrooms); natashaskitchen.com (search marinated mushrooms).

||||||||||||||||||||||||||||||||||||||||||||||||||||||||||||||||||||||||||||||||||||||||||||||||||||||||||||||||||||||||||||

PARSLEY'S REFINED COUSIN

Chervil

At first glance, feathery, fernlike chervil may be loved for its delicate lacy leaves, but its flavor is what really enchants. Think of it as parsley with a college degree—which is to say, more subtly complex, with whispery, verdant undertones of anise and springtime.

Highly perishable and fragile, chervil is expensive, so it is not often found in American markets. Fortunately, with careful nurturing it can grow well in window herb gardens or outdoors, in a spot that isn't too bright, and in soil with decent drainage.

French chefs are wise enough to pluck its petite leaves or fine sprays for garnishes, and chervil is an essential player in the traditional French herb mix *fines herbes,* combined with fresh parsley, chives, and tarragon for a subtle blend that's tossed liberally into omelets (see Omelette aux Fines Herbes, page 107) and salads and slipped underneath the skin of roasting chickens. In Germany, it is an essential ingredient in the green herb cream soup served on Holy Thursday and Good Friday (see Frühlingssuppe, page 289), and it lends itself especially to recipes based on eggs, cold shellfish, and poultry. Chervil adds a verdant touch to tea sandwiches in England and in Denmark provides a frilly, festive topping for many open sandwiches, especially those that include egg.

Native to southern Russia and the Caucasus, chervil is still prized there, especially for cold soups. A word of caution: Chervil (*Anthriscus cerefolium*) should never be cooked, as heat will almost surely turn it bitter. Best to use it to add flourish to a food after it has been portioned or is in the serving bowl. Nevertheless, chervil steeped for a minute or two in boiling water is considered by herbalists to be a cure for everything from hiccups to high blood pressure.

MAIL ORDER: To buy seeds for home gardens, Burpee, tel 800-888-1447, burpee.com (search chervil); localharvest.org (click Shop, then Seeds, then Herbs, then Chervil). **FURTHER INFORMATION AND RECIPES:** *The Encyclopedia of Herbs, Spices & Flavorings* by Elisabeth Lambert Ortiz (1992); *Handbook of Herbs and Spices,* Vol. 2, by K. V. Peter (2012); *The Herbal Kitchen,* by Jerry Traunfeld and John Granen (2005); *The German Cookbook* by Mimi Sheraton (2014); epicurious.com (search chicken in horseradish and chervil sauce; spring vegetable ragout with fresh chervil); saveur.com (search kerbelsuppe).

DON'T LET THE SOUP GET WARM

Okróshka, Kholodnyk, and Botvinia

Three Cold Soups

Russian, Ukrainian, Eastern European

I n regions where winters are long, hard, and unrelentingly frozen, soups are understandably served steaming hot. But come summer in those same climes, even a mild heat wave seems torrid to those whose most typical season is

winter—and demand for soups turns to the icily chilled. Just as cold, in fact, as the hot soups were hot, for palates and perhaps temperaments seem to dote on extremes.

A few such chilled soups are well known abroad, most especially cold beet borshch (see page 406), available in jars and quite decent, especially if fresh lemon juice and some sour cream are stirred in before serving. Cold sorrel soup called *schav* (see page 464) and eastern Europe's much-loved sour cherry soup (see page 393) are other beloved cold soups.

But that's only the beginning around the Ural and Caucasus mountains and the Volga river. One of the best-loved cold soups is *okróshka,* a salad-in-a-soup-pot based on the yeast-fermented beverage *kvass* (see page 413). That pungent, tingling liquid is combined with sour cream or buttermilk, diced cucumber pickles, cooked potatoes, chives or scallions, minced boiled beef, chicken or tongue, and slivered radishes, all garnished with a hint of mustard, hard-cooked eggs, and verdant sprinklings of aromatic dill, tarragon, and parsley.

Russia's *kholodnyk* is a leaner chilled soup, based on similar vegetables plus beetroot and its greens, veal, radishes, and cucumbers, both fresh and pickled; its chicken stock base is enriched with a light stirring of sour

Move over, gazpacho. . . .

cream just before serving. The Ukrainian version is uncooked and vegetarian, based on buttermilk, sour cream, and raw vegetables, garnished with dill and chopped hard-cooked eggs, a distant cousin perhaps of Denmark's Kærnemælkskoldskål (see page 351).

For *botvinia,* freshwater fish, such as cooked salmon or sturgeon, is added to a vegetable mix that colorfully combines beets, sorrel, spinach, cucumbers, and scallions, along with smoked whitefish and a few shelled shrimp or crayfish. Ciderlike *kvass,* the basic liquid, lends a pleasant sting to a restorative chilled soup that

is further enlivened by grated horseradish, sprightly mustard, and dashes of lemon juice, with aromatic bay leaves, onions, and dill providing a gentling touch.

FURTHER INFORMATION AND RECIPES: *The Art of Russian Cuisine* by Anne Volokh and Mavis Manus (1989); *À La Russe* by Darra Goldstein (1983); *Please to the Table* by Anya von Bremzen and John Welchman (1990); *The New York Times Jewish Cookbook* edited by Linda Amster (2003); cookstr.com (search cold beet borscht sheraton); natashaskitchen.com (search holodnik; okroshka).

CAVIAR FROM TURF, NOT SURF

Ovoshchi Ikra

Vegetable Caviar

Russian, Eastern European

Despite many scattered attempts to legally require that the term *caviar* be applied only to sturgeon roe, efforts have been in vain. It's not only that all fish roes are billed as caviar. Throughout eastern Europe, and

especially in Russia, various chopped vegetable combinations have also been so designated. Whatever their base, the so-called "poor man's caviars" tend to be slightly salty, and pungent enough with onion and garlic to render them appealing only in small, appetizer quantities. Most often served as cool and silky spreads on thin slices of moist, dark pumpernickel, these caviars are presented much as the real McCoy would be, perhaps even garnished with minced raw onions and chopped hard-cooked eggs.

A favorite member of the group is eggplant caviar—*baklazhanaya ikra*—a heady spread of baked eggplant folded into sautéed chopped onions, garlic, and drained diced tomatoes, well salted, peppered, and sparked with either fresh lemon juice or a little wine vinegar, with a few drops of olive oil whipped in if the mix runs

dry. Some cooks add green pepper, others a finely diced, seeded hot green chile. The dish is close to the Middle Eastern *baba ghanoush* (see page 495), but is slightly coarser in texture and without the smoky overtones of flame-broiled eggplants.

"Mushrooms with everything" could be a Russian motto, and the fragrant fungi, wild or tame, are worked into *gribnaya ikra* to great success. They may be chopped raw with garlic, salt, pepper, grated onion, olive oil, and lemon and left to marinate for an hour or two before being served with a garnish of chopped minced parsley or tarragon; or they may be chopped and sautéed along with onion, garlic, hot chile flakes or cayenne pepper, and dill, then glossed with sour cream.

Beets get the caviar treatment in the appetizer called *svyokla ikra,* cooked and chopped with scallions, fresh dill, light drizzles of sunflower or safflower oil, and a splash or two of lemon juice. In the Republic of Georgia, finely chopped walnuts and prunes join the fray, along with a touch of yogurt or mayonnaise for a spreadable consistency.

Ensuring that no vegetable feels left out, there's the caviar extravaganza called *ghivetch ikra,* for which all of the colorful ingredients of that Balkan and eastern European vegetable stew (see page 383) are cooked until very soft and then lightly stirred to the right consistency with a wooden spoon. After several hours of chilling, the veggies are served garnished with minced scallions and chopped fresh dill.

WHERE: *In Brooklyn,* Nargis Cafe, tel 718-872-7888, nargiscafe.com; *in Chicago,* Russian Tea Time, tel 312-360-0000, russianteatime.com; **FURTHER INFORMATION AND OTHER RECIPES:** *À La Russe* by Darra Goldstein (1983); *The Balkan Cookbook* by Vladimir Mirodan (1989); *Please to the Table* by Anya von Bremzen and John Welchman (1990); *The Food and Cooking of Russia* by Lesley Chamberlain (2006); food.com (search ikra eggplant caviar); easteuropean food.about.com (search ajvar).

————————————|||||||||||||||||||||||||||||||————————————

BROKEN-DOWN PERFECTION

Payusnaya

Pressed Caviar

Russian, Iranian

The best and most staggeringly expensive caviar is the perfect, shiny pinpoint grains of gray-black eggs produced by large beluga or sevruga sturgeons. But, believe it or not, some caviar lovers—notably the late Aristotle

Onassis—are left cold by those perfect premium eggs. The tins and jars that they prize hold caviar that looks like a mass of black tar or softened, melted black licorice. It is *payusnaya*—sturgeon roe that was damaged in handling and is thus comprised of broken eggs stuck together in a midnight-black, compressed mass. What it offers is an intense caviar experience, with the mysteriously seductive texture melting in the mouth, gradually revealing its sensuous saline wonders to tongue and palate.

Scarcer even than the best caviar, fresh, unpreserved, and unpasteurized payusnaya may sell for a fraction of the price of beluga and sevruga—but that fraction still does not amount to small change.

Because the caviar oil congeals when cold, payusnaya should be taken out of the refrigerator about thirty minutes before it is to be served, lest it be too stiff to spread. Like the best undamaged caviar, it should be served only with thin toast and, at most, a squeeze of lemon juice. Nothing should accompany this caviar; not onions, eggs, sour cream, or anything else. Of course, a little iced vodka or chilled Champagne would not be amiss.

WHERE: *In New York,* Russian Tea Room, tel 212-581-7100, russiantearoomnyc.com; Caviar Russe, tel 212-980-5908, caviarrusse.com; *in Paris and London,* Caviar Kaspia at multiple locations, caviarkaspia.com. **DINE-IN, RETAIL, AND MAIL ORDER:** *In multiple locations around the world,* Petrossian, tel 800-828-9241, petrossian .com. **MAIL ORDER:** Marky's Gourmet, markys gourmet.com, tel 800-522-8427 (search paiusnaya). **FURTHER INFORMATION:** *Caviar! Caviar! Caviar!* by Gerald M. Stein with Donald Bain (1981); *Caviar* by Susan Friedland (1986).

A TOUCH OF CHEER FROM SIBERIA

Pelmeni

Russian (Siberian)

"Russian ravioli" is the nickname for these little ear-shaped dumplings, signatures of Siberian cuisine. Chubby pockets most traditionally plumped with lamb (if not beef, pork, or elk meat), they are served adrift in a strong, clear lamb or chicken broth with fragrant featherings of minced dill. Hot, aromatic, and sustaining, it's a luxurious meal in a bowl, though the little dumplings are almost as satisfying glossed with butter and dill and served as a pasta course.

In keeping with most gastronomic history, there are competing theories as to the origins of *pelmeni*. One draws on geographic proximity to suggest that they are derived from the Chinese dumplings called *jiaozi*, likely introduced to Siberia by Mongol invaders. Or could they have originated with the Persians, whose word *pel'men* means ear, and been adopted by the Russians by way of the Udmurts, a Finnish sect based in Siberia?

Whatever the truth, pelmeni now qualify as Siberian comfort food, the kind of dish that sees one through the rigors of a cold winter or just a bad day. They used to almost always be homemade in huge batches, frozen so there would always be some around; but these days frozen versions can be found in some Russian supermarkets and ethnic groceries. When not served in soup, they may be boiled and topped with butter, sour cream, and a dash of lemon juice, or coated with sour cream and herbs and baked in the oven, casserole-style.

WHERE: *In New York*, Mari Vanna, tel 212-777-1955, marivanna.ru/ny; *in Brooklyn*, Café Glechik at two locations, glechik.com; Tatiana Restaurant, tel 718-891-5151, tatianarestaurant.com; *in Winter Park, FL*, Lacomka Bakery & Deli, tel 407-677-1101, lacomka-orlando.com; *in Austin, TX*, Russian House, tel 512-428-5442, russianhouseofaustin.com. **RETAIL AND MAIL ORDER:** *In New York*, Moscow on the Hudson, tel 212-740-7397, moscowonhudson.com. **FURTHER INFORMATION AND RECIPES:** *Please to the Table* by Anya von Bremzen and John Welchman (1990); ruscuisine.com (search pelmeni); grouprecipes.com (search pelmeni).

THE SLAVIC WAY WITH DUMPLING DOUGH

Pierogi

Russian, Polish, Lithuanian

Most every country boasts a dumpling, and for very similar reasons. Dumplings allow the use of tough cuts of meat or leftovers, or transform otherwise humble ingredients into glamourous bites. The sustaining pockets of dough may be small or large, sweet or savory, shaped in a multitude of ways, and boiled, baked, or fried. Whatever the size, filling, and cooking technique, they are guaranteed to emerge sputtering-hot and juicy, providing satisfaction out of all proportion to their size and cost.

One of the lustiest of dumplings is surely the pierogi, a half-moon-shaped turnover of basic egg-and-flour dough that may be stuffed with an incredible variety of fillings, from the buckwheat groats known as kasha to meat to potatoes, prunes, or apricots. Although pierogi are most often associated with Poland, the word itself comes from the Russian for pie: *pirog*. And in fact, in Russia, pierogi are often large square or rectangular baked pies, much unlike the diminutive Polish version most Americans recognize. Very similar dumplings also exist in Lithuania, where they are known as *kolduny*. In Ukraine they are called *pyrohy* by anyone who can pronounce the word.

While the most popular fillings at any size are minced cooked meat (often pork, lamb, and beef, for pierogi destined to become the main course), pierogi can also be found filled with minced mushrooms (plain sauerkraut or a sauerkraut-mushroom mix also being a popular choice), farmer's cheese or cottage cheese (often scented with vanilla for a more delicate pierogi that's best for brunch or a snack), blueberries (a summer dessert favorite), lentils (a specialty of the Podlasie region of northeastern Poland), and mashed potatoes with or without onions.

Post-filling, most pierogi are first boiled and then baked, or preferably fried golden-brown so there's some crispness contrasting the mellow filling. Often, they are served simply boiled—they may be garnished with fried bacon bits, sautéed onions, sour cream, and melted brown butter; the savory ones are sometimes served alongside hearty soups like *borshch*, while the sweet ones are reserved for snacks and dessert.

WHERE: *In Warsaw,* U Hopfera, tel 48/22-828-7352; *in Cracow,* Pierozki u Vincenta, tel 48/501-747-407, pierozkiuvincenta.pl; *in New York,* Veselka, tel 212-387-7000, veselka.com; Little Poland, tel 212-777-9728; *in Chicago,* Kasia's Deli at two locations, kasiasdeli.com; *in Seattle,* Piroshki at two locations, piroshki restaurant.com. **FURTHER INFORMATION AND RECIPES:** *Polish Holiday Cookery* by Robert Strybel (2003); *The Art of Polish Cooking* by Alina Żerańska (1989); epicurious.com (search wild mushroom pierogies and potato pierogi with cabbage and bacon); cookstr.com (search potato and mushroom pierogi; kasha and mushroom pierogi). **SPECIAL EVENT:** Pierogi Festival, Whiting, IN, July, pierogifest.net.

WHO PUT PICKLES IN THE SOUP?

Solyanka

Russian

It's logical that in a country where it gets so cold in winter, soup should play so vital a role. Enter *solyanka,* a thick, rich, gently soured soup usually made with fish, although there are meat variations, and proudly piquant thanks to the

inclusion of bay leaves, capers, plenty of lemon, and chopped dill pickles.

Enticingly aromatic, whether based on strong fish stock or beef stock, solyanka's flavor is distinctly briny, yet at once pleasantly mild. The fish it is made with—often freshwater fish such as salmon, whitefish, or pike, or sometimes deep-sea swordfish—offers enough bite and body to stand up to the seasonings and provide a good (though light) foil for the icy vodka shots that may accompany the proceedings.

Where: *In Brooklyn,* Tatiana Restaurant, tel 718-891-5151, tatianarestaurant.com; Primorski Restaurant, tel 718-891-3111, primorskiny.com;

in Austin, TX, Russian House, tel 512-428-5442, russianhouseofaustin.com; *in San Francisco,* Red Tavern, tel 415-750-9090, redtavernsf.com. **Further information and recipes:** *North Atlantic Seafood* by Alan Davidson (2003); *À La Russe* by Darra Goldstein (1983); easteuropeanfood .about.com (search solyanka); saveur.com (search solyanka).

—||||||||||||||||||||||||||||||||||||||—

A NUT JOB OF A CAKE

Torta od Oraha

Walnut Torte

Serbian, Yugoslavian, Balkan

Thin, crunchy, true tortes, made without flour or fat other than egg yolks, are much favored throughout eastern Europe. This one, distinguished by the fresh, fruity overtones of walnuts finely ground to substitute for flour, is most highly prized

in Serbia, once a part of Yugoslavia. The walnuts impart a toasty aroma and a woodsy, sweet essence that is enhanced by a filling of coffee buttercream.

Walnut Torte

Makes one 10-inch, 2-layer torte

For the torte
1 cup finely ground, lightly toasted walnuts
¼ cup unseasoned dry bread crumbs
⅓ cup plus 2 teaspoons sugar
6 extra-large eggs, separated
1 piece (2 inches) vanilla bean, or 1 teaspoon pure vanilla extract

For the filling
4 tablespoons (½ stick) unsalted butter, at room temperature
¼ cup sugar
⅔ cup cold double-strength brewed black coffee
Coarsely chopped walnuts, for garnish

1. Make the torte: Position a rack in the center of the oven and preheat the oven to 375°F. Butter and lightly flour a 10-inch round or square cake pan. Invert the pan and tap out any excess flour.

2. Combine the walnuts and bread crumbs in a small bowl and set the mixture aside.

3. Place the ⅓ cup of sugar and the egg yolks in a large mixing bowl and beat until the mixture is thick and pale. If you are using a piece of vanilla bean, cut it in half lengthwise and, using the tip of the knife, scrape the seeds out into the yolk mixture. Or stir in the vanilla extract, if using.

4. Beat the egg whites with the 2 teaspoons of sugar until they form firm, shiny peaks. Gently but thoroughly fold the beaten egg whites and the bread crumb and walnut mixture into the yolk mixture.

5. Spoon the batter into the prepared cake pan and bake the torte until a cake tester or toothpick inserted in the center comes out clean, about 25 minutes. Let the torte cool in the pan, then turn it out and split it horizontally into 2 even layers.

6. While the torte cools, prepare the filling: Place the butter and sugar in a bowl and beat them until smoothly blended and the sugar has dissolved, 3 to 5 minutes. Blend in the coffee until it is evenly distributed.

7. Spread half of the filling on top of one torte layer. Place the second torte layer on top and spread the remaining filling over it. Garnish the top of the torte with a generous sprinkling of coarsely chopped walnuts. Let the cake set in a cool place (but not in the refrigerator) for 1 to 2 hours before serving. Covered, the torte will keep for 5 to 7 days.

WHERE: *In Chicago,* City Fresh Market, tel 773-681-8600, cityfreshmarket.com; *in Milwaukee,* Three Brothers Restaurant, tel 414-481-7530. **FURTHER INFORMATION AND ADDITIONAL RECIPES:** *The Balkan Cookbook* edited by Snezana Pejakovic and Jelka Venisnik-Eror (1987); easteuropean food.about.com (search serbian reform torte).

┤||||||||||||||||||||||||||||├

BREAD FIT FOR CELEBRATIONS

Korovai

Wedding Bread-Cake

Ukrainian

G iven the veritable bread basket that is Ukraine, with its vast landscape of wheat fields, it is easy to understand why that grain, and the breads and cakes made from it, are held sacred in the region. They inspire all sorts of prayers and celebratory folk customs, somewhat more numerous for bread than for cake.

The most revered Ukrainian bread is the carefully made *kalach* or *koloch,* with its gluten-strong wheat, granular winey yeast, milk, and small amounts of salt and sugar, all braided into a gold-crusted ring. The word *kolo* means circle, and the bread's shape signifies eternity.

For Christmas and New Year's Eve, three graduated rounds of this bread are stacked, and a candle is placed in their center.

The form known as *korovai,* a wedding bread-cake made of the same dough as koloch, offers a stupendous feast for the eyes. A high-domed, honeyed, golden bread covered with roses intricately sculpted in bread dough, the cake may also boast sculpted pine-cones, often added as a good luck symbol.

To carry out the theme with an old

tradition, invitations to the wedding were (and in some places still are) delivered in the form of bread pinecones and roses. They are much appreciated for the following day's breakfast, when butter moistens the creamy, softly chewy bread interior with its thin veneer of a crust.

Hallmark, take note! Who could say no to such an invitation?

WHERE: *In New York,* with advance order, Larysa Zielyk, 212-677-1551; *in Brooklyn,* with advance order, Bohdana Slyz, 718-457-3517; *in Chicago,* with advance order, Ann's Bakery, tel 773-384-5562. **FURTHER INFORMATION AND RECIPES:** *Traditional Ukrainian Cookery* by Savella Stechishin (1991); kingarthurflour.com (search ukrainian wedding bread); foodgeeks.com (search korovai); ukrainemarriageguide.com/ ?item=korovai.

‖‖‖‖‖‖‖‖‖‖‖‖‖‖‖‖‖‖‖‖‖‖‖‖‖

THE UKRAINIAN WAY WITH FRIED CHICKEN

Kotlety Po-Kievski

Chicken Kiev

Ukrainian

The decadent and quaintly antique entrée takes its names from the capital city of Ukraine—and it's one of those dishes that led a humble life in its homeland and gained cachet upon reaching the United States. The crispy fried, rolled breast of chicken hides a happy surprise for first-timers: a well of hot melted butter that can spurt up and ruin a necktie the minute a knife is stuck into the plump, golden morsel.

The ingredients for chicken Kiev are simple, but its preparation is something of a high-wire act. A boned and skinned chicken breast, pounded thin and wrapped around a chilled pencil-shaped slice of sweet butter, is dipped into flour and then into beaten egg, and finally coated with bread crumbs and fried. When properly pulled off, the technique results in butter that melts but doesn't leak, and chicken whose flesh is incredibly moist and rich, an excellent counterpoint to its crunchy exterior.

Several theories exist as to the dish's invention. One origin story has it created by the French inventor Nicolas Appert in the eighteenth century. Another holds that it was first made at a private club in Moscow in 1912. The most logical theory is the one Ukrainian historians hold, about an unheralded Ukrainian hotel chef who introduced the dish to Moscow in 1819.

A real chicken Kiev is worth seeking out.

Whichever explanation is accurate, the chicken breast originally was served with the first wing joint still attached, which is how some restaurants in Kiev still prepare it. It is customarily served atop buttered toast, with fried shoestring potatoes. An instant classic in that big city, the bird made its first documented appearance in the United States in the 1930s at Chicago's Yar restaurant, a celebrity hotspot whose owner was a Russian immigrant named Wladimir W.

Yaschenko. Since then it has been seen in America with any manner of side dish, most deliciously rice, but also kasha or egg noodles.

Unfortunately, popularity has compromised the labor-intensive chicken Kiev, and it is now available in frozen, ready-to-fry versions. For a time, the airline industry seemed to specialize in bastardized versions of the dish, which has also been co-opted by the low-fat prepared food industry, whose practitioners borrow the term *chicken Kiev* for any number of unbreaded, unbuttered concoctions that bear little resemblance to the original.

The real thing, when you find it, is still about as excitingly extravagant as chicken can be.

WHERE: *In Kiev,* Dnipro Hotel & Restaurant, tel 380/44-254-67-77, dniprohotel.ua/en; Tsarske Selo, tel 380/44-288-9775, tsarske.kiev.ua/en; *in New York,* Mari Vanna, tel 212-777-1955, marivanna.ru/ny; *in Washington, DC,* Russia House Lounge, tel 202-234-9433, russiahouse lounge.com; *in Las Vegas,* Red Square, tel 702-632-7407, redsquarelasvegas.com; *in San Francisco,* Red Tavern, tel 415-750-9090, red tavernsf.com. **FURTHER INFORMATION AND RECIPES:** *À La Russe* by Darra Goldstein (1983); *Please to the Table* by Anya von Bremzen and John Welchman (1990); saveur.com (search chicken kiev); cookstr.com (search chicken kiev blashford-snell).

JEWISH

——————————|||||||||||||||||||||||||||||||||||||||——————————

Appetizing Stores

Jewish (Ashkenazic)

Along with a host of iconic delicatessens and dairy restaurants, one of the Jewish immigrant legacies to large American cities (most notably New York) are the tantalizing food meccas traditionally called "appetizing stores"—their offerings are meant to awaken sleepy palates and to form the basic menu for non-meat meals.

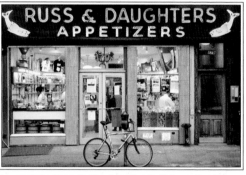

An essential culinary landmark on New York's Lower East Side

Kosher food rules regarding dairy do not prohibit the mixing of dairy and fish, which is why the gastronomic core of these stores is preserved fish—salted and smoked salmon, whitefish, carp, sturgeon, and sable, and all kinds of herring in all kinds of sauces. Prepared salads (egg, fish, potato, eggplant, and coleslaw) join the fray as well, and shoppers can also find appetizer-platter staples like vinegar-accented roasted red peppers; pungently salty, wrinkly, sun-dried black olives; and cheeses such as cream cheese, Swiss, pot, and Munster. There are necklaces of dried Polish or Russian mushrooms (see borovik ceps, page 405), sweets such as halvah, sesame and honey candies, and a jewel-like array of dried apricots, prunes, apples, and pears. Some of these stores carry bagels, onion rolls, and other breads that enhance all of the above; but in days gone by, local rabbis discouraged the shops from carrying breads so that neighboring bakers could make a living.

Although some of the original appetizing stores were strictly kosher, most were not. They never carried any kind of meat (no chopped liver or even chicken soup), but they did offer smoked sturgeon and its prized by-product, caviar, despite the fact that sturgeon has never been strictly kosher. The most observant were limited to the roe of permissible fish, such as salmon, that have not only gills but also recognizable scales.

Several of these classic stores still flourish in New York, largely because they have expanded their wares to draw in a wider range of customers. And because Scandinavians rely on such stores for herring, their special crispbreads are now stocked as well.

With their distinctive, teasingly fresh whiffs of fish, salt, pickling, and sunlit air, the shops live up to their names. At peak hours and on weekends, they're full of fierce activity: long lines forming and customers schmoozing and jostling as they gather the makings of the typical New York Sunday-morning breakfast. Countermen deftly slice thin slivers for tastes here and there so buyers can make informed, if not quick, choices.

Many of the traditional stores have expanded to other gourmet products and even appliances, the famed Zabar's in New York being a prime example. The Lower East Side's Russ & Daughters and Murray's Sturgeon Shop and Barney Greengrass on the Upper West Side have stuck with more traditional fare, although they have added some meat-based products to the mix. Barney Greengrass also features a well-regarded café-restaurant, as does Russ & Daughters.

Where: *In New York,* Zabar's, tel 212-787-2000, zabars.com; Russ & Daughters, tel 212-475-4880, russanddaughters.com; Murray's Sturgeon Shop, tel 212-724-2650, murrayssturgeon .com; Barney Greengrass, tel 212-724-4707, barney greengrass.com; *in Hallandale Beach, FL,* Sage Bagel & Appetizer Shop, tel 954-456-7499, sage bageldeliordering.com; *in Toronto,* Mendel's Creamery N' Appetizer, tel 416-597-1784, kensing tonmarketbia.com/cheese; *in Florida,* Epicure Gourmet Market at three locations, epicuremarket .com. **Further information and recipes:** *Russ & Daughters* by Mark Russ Federman (2013).

LIKE REVENGE, BEST SERVED COLD

Bagels

Jewish (Ashkenazic)

Heat your bagels if you wish, but know that you are flaunting tradition and masking what should be the identifying characteristics of the classic ring-shaped roll. The best bagels of yore had thin, golden crusts and firmly chewy, gray-white interiors, and they measured no more than three-and-a-half inches in diameter. Edible only for about five hours after baking, they soon turned to stone. Even fresh, authentically chewy bagels gave jaws a Sunday morning workout that left facial muscles tingling for a good hour or two. And they were always served at room temperature, whether simply buttered or spread with cream cheese and layered with smoked salmon—or even more authentically, with the unsmoked, very salty brine-cured salmon known as lox.

These days the bagel has morphed into a shadow of its former self. Although still boiled in a lye solution before being baked (ensuring its trademark high gloss and chewy interior), today's bagel incorporates dough conditioners like bromated flour (which keep it fresh and soft for at least two or three days). Most detrimental, perhaps, is the enormous size of the modern bagel; some look more like spare tires than inviting, individual portions with the correct proportion of crust to interior. Such size may be an attempt to justify the high cost occasioned by the handiwork still required for even mildly convincing bagels. (Although they're cheaper, machine-shaped, frozen supermarket bagels rarely attract any cognizant bagel lover.) Under these conditions, toasting may be necessary to impart any texture at all.

New York and possibly London are the last bastions of bagel authenticity, and even in those cities sources are few and generally obscure. In New York, it is possible to pre-order "mini" bagels (two or three dozen at a time) from several bakeries, and these approach the standard size of old-time bagels. Every once in a while, some misguided maven announces that the world's best bagels are to be found in Montreal. Anyone who prefers those thin, tough Canadian rings, flavored with lots of sugar but nary a grain of salt, and glassily encrusted with all sorts of seeds, is not to be trusted—even if the Canadian impostors come from the much-heralded Montreal bakeries St-Viateur or Fairmont.

There has been much speculation on the origins of the bagel. A favorite yarn has it that the rolls were first baked along the Silk Road in Roman times, adopted there by the Jewish traders who took the recipe to eastern Europe. Another holds that bagels were created by Jewish bakers in Austria or Poland after the Siege of Vienna in 1683, to celebrate the victory of Polish general John Sobieski over the Turks; according to this theory, the dough was shaped to emulate the *beugel,* or stirrup, of the horseback-riding general. Whatever their beginnings, bagels have continued to be shaped by their travels. Back in the old days, anyone who pronounced the word BAIG-el would be marked as a Litvak from northern Poland, Lithuania, or Russia. Say BUY-gul and you were kidded for

The original breakfast sandwich

your Galitziana ancestors from southern Poland, Austria, or parts of Ukraine.

Finally, an exception to the no-toasting rule must be noted: one that was formerly prepared in the Fountain Coffee Room of the Beverly Hills Hotel by a counterman named Red. The soft insides of a sliced bagel were pulled out, leaving a quarter-inch shell that was briefly toasted under the broiler. Piled high with hot, softly scrambled eggs, then covered with the toasted top shell, the irresistible morning sandwich could be gently pressed down for convenient noshing by lucky patrons.

WHERE: *In New York,* Freds at Barneys (for Sunday brunch or retail), tel 212-833-2200, barneys.com; *in Brooklyn,* Bagel Hole, tel 718-788-4014, bagelhole.net; *in Los Angeles,* Freds at Barneys, tel 310-777-5877; *in London,* Brick Lane Beigel Bake, 44/20-7729-0616. **DINE-IN, RETAIL, AND MAIL ORDER:** *In New York,* Russ & Daughters, tel 212-475-4880, russanddaughters.com; Eli Zabar, tel 866-354-3547, elizabar.com; *in Ann Arbor, MI,* Zingerman's, tel 888-636-8162, zingermans.com. **FURTHER INFORMATION AND RECIPES:** *Inside the Jewish Bakery* by Stanley Ginsberg and Norman Berg (2011); *The New York Times Jewish Cookbook* edited by Linda Amster (2003); epicurious.com (search bagels); cookstr.com (search bagels roden).

VEGETABLES FOR DESSERT

Berengena Frita

Candied Eggplant

Jewish (Sephardic), Spanish

There's no arguing the fact that frying is a favored method in Jewish cooking. Take the Ashkenazic taste for fried fish like carp, flounder, and herring. Or the veal cutlet and all of the various mixed vegetable fries one can sample in Trastevere, the old Jewish ghetto section of Rome.

Eggplant, much loved and readily available in most of the Mediterranean and Balkan

countries where Jews have lived, is no exception. Brought to Spain by the Moors in the eighth century, the vegetable is the star of the

Spanish-Sephardic dish *berengena frita*, in which it is not only fried but turned into an unusual and enticing dessert.

Just as for savory preparations, for this delicacy, thin, round slices of eggplant must be properly salted as a first step. Patted dry, they are dredged with flour and lightly fried in olive oil until pale sunny gold on both sides. Drained, slightly cooled, and placed on serving plates, they are then sometimes brushed with roseate, winey pomegranate juice before being anointed with honey and showered with toasted sesame seeds.

The result is a beguilingly nutty crunchiness and a warm sweetness that mollifies the eggplant's acidity. It's an unusual combination, but not unique to Jewish cuisine. The same bittersweet balance is also a specialty at the French restaurant Galatoire's in New Orleans, where sticks of fried eggplant are served sprinkled with confectioners' sugar.

Where: *In New Orleans,* Galatoire's, tel 504-525-2021, galatoires.com. **Further information and recipes:** *The Book of Jewish Food* by Claudia Roden (1996); food.com (search fried eggplant with powdered sugar).

THE BAGEL ALTERNATIVE

Bialys

Jewish

Could any photographer or food stylist make this homely, chewy bread roll, with its amorphous, ash-brown crust, indented center, and (nicely) burned onions, look appealing? It's doubtful, but flavor is another matter altogether. To true aficionados of Jewish breads, the toasty yeast roll with a crisp crust and a crackling center is where it's at. Accented with titillating bits of charred onion, at its most authentic the bialy will also be sprinkled with a dusting of crunchy gray-black poppy seeds. Because they used different doughs and different production methods, historically the true bialys and bagels were never turned out in the same bakeries.

But beyond that, bialys engender controversy. Mention them in a crowd and be prepared for a pedantic lecture on bialy origins that will claim the following: The bialy is really a *pletzel* (a flatbread) and is unknown in the northern Polish city of Białystok, but was in fact nicknamed in New York.

Wrong on both counts, though there is some truth to the first allegation. The bialy did morph from the pletzel, that flat, round board of bread sprinkled with poppy seeds and onions.

But the bialy is generally much smaller than a pletzel—about three and a half inches across, although in its native city (more on that in a moment) it is still baked to the size of a salad plate. While the pletzel is level, the bialy is identified by its depressed center, which should be very crisp in contrast to its softer rim.

The bialy was invented in Białystok by Jewish bakers and was called *Białystoker kuchen,* its fans known throughout Poland as *Białystoker kuchen fressers,* or "prodigious eaters" of the fragrant, freshly baked, all-day treats. Sometime around the early 1900s in New York, the shortened name *bialy* came to be, but how the bialy evolved from the pletzel is open to conjecture. One assertion is that a baker dropped an unbaked pletzel on the floor and accidentally stepped on it with his heel. Not wanting to waste the dough, he baked it and the impressed mark formed the first crisp interior round.

Back in old Białystok, those who could afford it ate halvah along with a *Białystoker kuchen*, a chokingly dry experience that is not recommended. Cream cheese is a better fit, but not as it is applied to a bagel. True bialy connoisseurs warm the tight little roll in the oven (no toasting!) unsliced, and schmear spreads on top.

Where: *In New York,* Hot Bread Kitchen, hotbreadkitchen.org; Freds at Barneys (for Sunday brunch or retail), tel 212-833-2200, barneys.com; *in Los Angeles,* Freds at Barneys, tel 310-777-5877; *in Asheville, NC,* Farm & Sparrow, tel 828-633-0584, farmandsparrow.com; *in Montreal,* Hof Kelsten, hofkelsten.com. **Further information and recipes:** *Inside the Jewish Bakery* by Stanley Ginsberg and Norman Berg (2011); *The Bialy Eaters* by Mimi Sheraton (2002); saveur.com (search onion and poppy seed bialys).

THE CARP WHO CARPED

Carpe à la Juive, or Jedisch Fisch

Jewish, Alsatian

B ack in 2003, in the town of New Square, in New York State's Rockland County (home to a large Hasidic community of the Skver sect), an observant fishmonger and his assistant both claimed to have heard a live carp speak—

prophetically, and in Hebrew, no less. The fish they were about to kill had pessimistically predicted the end of the world.

Powers of divination aside, from a linguistic point of view the story does make some kind of sense. If carp could speak, perhaps they *would* speak Hebrew. It was the Jews, after all, who introduced carp to eastern Europe and then to Germany and France. They had sampled the fish in Asia, and—so goes the incredible sounding story—carried *live* specimens with them as they traveled the Silk Road purveying textiles and other treasures of the East. Yes, it has been said that the ancient Romans appreciated a species of local carp. But where's the carp spouting Latin prophesies?

Whatever its lineage, this freshwater fish's golden scales have turned it into a sign of good luck and wealth everywhere it is known, from China and Japan to Europe. In Austria and Poland, a carp scale is placed in wallets on New Year's Eve or Saint Sylvester's Eve, promising twelve months of prosperity. There and elsewhere, the fish is part of elaborate Christmas Eve dinners.

It is also one of the many specialties Jewish cooks added to the Alsatian menu. *Carpe à la Juive,* also known throughout Alsace as *Jedisch* (Yiddish) *fisch,* is a delectably cool, jellied carp covered in a silky, spring-green aspic redolent of parsley and garlic. The fish's sometimes strong, earthy flavor is mitigated with an overnight salting before it is rinsed and poached in a court bouillon of onions, garlic, vegetable (not olive) oil, lemon juice or vinegar or white wine, ginger, bay leaf, parsley, and water; the stock reduces as the fish cooks. Sliced—bones, skin, head, tail, and all—then reshaped on a deep platter and topped with the strained stock, it goes into the refrigerator overnight until a sparkling gel has formed.

Although the dish is most typically served chilled, according to the celebrated Alsatian chef André Soltner of New York's much-missed Lutèce, it is sometimes served hot, with the court bouillon playing the role of a still-liquid sauce instead of a semi-set jelly.

Further information and recipes: *The World of Jewish Cooking* by Gil Marks (1999);

Quiches, Kugels, and Couscous by Joan Nathan (2009); *La Cuisine Juive en Alsace* (in French) edited by Freddy Raphaël (2005); *From My Mother's Kitchen* by Mimi Sheraton (1979). **TIP:** It is not a good idea to buy carp in warm months, from May to October; when water is warm, carp swim to the bottom for cool water, taking in a quantity of mud that shows up in a muddy flavor, much like that which catfish can take on.

GIVE A CHALLAH IF YOU'RE HUNGRY

Challah

Jewish (Ashkenazic)

The gracefully braided, golden-brown challah of the eastern European Jews is surely one of the world's most beautiful breads. And with its creamy-white, soft-textured interior and shiny, golden crust, it is also one of the most elegantly delicious, a briochelike confection that falls just this side of cake.

Challah is the Hebrew word for "priest's portion," and to be considered kosher, a small portion of its dough must be sacrificially burned in a hot oven. Most traditionally, it is the bread of the Sabbath and other special religious holidays, for which it may be baked into various symbolic forms. During Rosh Hashanah and Yom Kippur, the autumn High Holy Days of the Jewish new year, and also for weddings, the dough is shaped in a rising spiral that suggests a huge turban or a coliseum fashioned from bread; the spiraling, round form signifies the eternal cycle of life. For Hanukkah, the festival of lights observed with candles that are lit for eight days, loaves may be baked in the shape of a menorah candelabra. For still other holidays, the bread might be shaped as a ladder (the better to climb to heaven) or a sheaf of wheat (to signify hopes for a plentiful harvest).

Such celebratory breads tend to be a bit sweeter than those served for ordinary sabbaths, due to the addition of golden honey to the dough and its use as a glaze for the crust. Most

An elegant leavened bread

delectably, the soft but reassuringly substantial bread has its soothing, salty-sweet flavor and its very thin, golden crust accented only by the crunch of poppy or sesame seeds.

Leavened with yeast and absent of dairy products, challah is pareve, which means that under kosher laws it may be eaten with both meat and dairy meals. But if meat isn't being served, a luxurious spread of butter (slightly softened so as not to tear the tender crumb) is delicious on a thick (never thin) slice of challah, especially if sprinkled with coarse salt. That enticingly gritty finishing touch is just as welcome if the butter is replaced by the rendered chicken fat called schmaltz (see page 464)—these days undoubtedly served with a side of Lipitor.

Sephardic and Mizrachic Jews honor their versions of challah, generally dotted with dried fruits and aromatic spices, and closer to sweet coffee cake—though it may be somewhat less magical to those raised on the simple, more pervasive Ashkenazic bread.

While fresh challah is in a class of its own, the bread is almost equally cherished in its semistale, leftover state. Then it can be thickly sliced and used for what has to be the world's best French toast, the spongy bread absorbing plenty of the beaten egg and milk mixture (preferably vanilla-scented), all to be slowly fried in sweet butter until golden brown. Leftover chunks of challah can also be the basis for inspired bread puddings, especially good when they include tart apple slices and dark currants. A spritz of schnapps applied halfway through baking couldn't hurt either, whether for the pudding or the baker.

Where: *In Jaffa, Israel,* Abulafia Bakery, tel 972/3-683-4958; *in Brooklyn,* Lilly's Bakery Shop, tel 718-491-2904, lillysbakeryshop.com; *in New York,* Hot Bread Kitchen, hotbreadkitchen.org; Breads Bakery, tel 212-633-2253, breadsbakery .com; *in Montreal,* Hof Kelsten, hofkelsten.com. **Dine-in, retail, and Mail order:** *In New York,* Eli Zabar, tel 866-354-3547, elizabar.com; *in Ann Arbor, MI,* Zingerman's, tel 888-636-8162, zinger mans.com. **Further information and recipes:** *The Book of Jewish Food* by Claudia Roden (1996); *Joan Nathan's Jewish Holiday Cookbook* by Joan Nathan (2004); foodandwine.com (search sephardic challah); cookstr.com (search traditional challah; rosh hashanah challah); epicurious .com (search chernowitzer challah).

||||||||||||||||||||||||||||||

A PASSOVER SPREAD GOES SECULAR

Charoset

Jewish (Ashkenazic and Sephardic)

Although it stands as a symbolic reminder of the mortar used by the Jewish slaves who built the pyramids in Egypt, the fragrant spread called *charoset* deserves more than a once-a-year ritual appearance at the Passover seder table.

The sweet spread that completes the seder table

The rich fruit spread is made in two lovely versions, delectable either for breakfast or teatime on toasted English muffins, matzos, or firm, lightly sweetened, toasted pound cake. The Ashkenazic standard is a chopped blend of tart, juicy apples, walnuts, red kosher-style sweet wine, sugar, cinnamon, and powdered ginger;

Macintosh apples are the perfect choice with Macouns as good stand-ins. Sephardic Jews prepare a richer, midnight-dark mix, chopping dried fruits such as dates, raisins, and figs with walnuts or pistachios, and simmering the lot in wine and spices such as cinnamon and cloves. Both types ripen to maximum flavor when prepared in advance and chilled for twenty-four hours before serving. The Ashkenazic version, if refrigerated, will keep for three days, while the Sephardic will keep for several weeks.

Further information: *The New York Times Passover Cookbook* edited by Linda Amster (2010); *Jewish Cooking in America* by Joan Nathan (1994); epicurious.com (search sephardic charoset; traditional apple-walnut charoset). **Tip:** For Ashkenazic charoset, the fortified red aperitif wine Dubonnet is a good substitute for kosher sweet wine.

〰〰〰〰〰〰〰〰〰〰〰〰〰〰〰〰〰〰

DON'T FORGET THE SOUR CREAM

Cheese Blintzes

Jewish

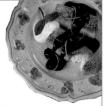

C risp, golden, and buttery, these puffy packets of creamy, vanilla- and cinnamon-scented cheese are among the Jewish Ashkenazic staples that have gone mainstream, and small wonder. Topped with a cooling drift of sour cream and

perhaps a few ripe berries on the side, cheese blintzes are as welcome for dessert as they are for breakfast, lunch, and dinner main courses. And though cheese is by far the best filling for these sheer crêpes that are lightly fried on only one side, sweet or savory ingredients such as apples, berries, or even ground meat or mashed potatoes are also favored by many.

Texture and delectable flavor trump any origin story here, but for what it is worth, blintzes most likely surfaced in the nineteenth century in the Austro-Hungarian Empire. (The word *blintz* is Yiddish, but probably came from *blin*, the Russian word for crêpe or pancake.) Soft, comforting, and addictive, they are often associated with the Jewish holiday of Shavuot.

WHERE: *In Tel Aviv,* Hungarian Blintzes, tel 9723-605-0674, hungarianblintzes.rest-e.co.il; *in New York,* Veselka, tel 212-228-9682, veselka.com; *in Brooklyn,* Junior's, juniorcheesecake .com; *in Chicago,* Manny's, tel 312-939-2855,

mannysdeli.com; *in Boynton Beach, FL,* Flakowitz, tel 561-742-4144, flakowitzofboynton.com; *in Houston,* Kenny & Ziggy's, tel 713-871-8883, kenny andziggys.com; *in Bellevue, WA,* Goldbergs' Famous Delicatessen, tel 425-641-6622, goldbergs deli.com; *in Montreal,* Beautys, tel 514-849-8883, beautys.ca. **DINE-IN, RETAIL, AND MAIL ORDER:** *In New York,* Russ & Daughters, tel 212-475-4880, russanddaughters.com; Barney Greengrass, tel 212-724-4707, barneygreengrass.com; *in Ann Arbor, MI,* Zingerman's, tel 888-636-8162, zinger mans.com. **FURTHER INFORMATION AND RECIPES:** *The Book of Jewish Food* by Claudia Roden (1996); *The New York Times Jewish Cookbook* edited by Linda Amster (2003); cookstr.com (search cheese blintzes). **TIP:** Once blintzes are filled and formed, they can be frozen before the final frying. Do not thaw before cooking, but fry slowly over low flame so that the fillings heat up before the crêpes become overly brown.

〰〰〰〰〰〰〰〰〰〰〰〰〰〰〰〰〰〰

THE KOSHER WAY WITH CHICKEN PAPRIKASH

Chicken Fricassee with Meatballs

Jewish (Ashkenazic)

W ith its aromatic, paprika-bright sauce and its soothing flavor of softly, sweetly simmered onions and garlic, chicken fricassee with meatballs is a quintessential home-style dish almost every Jewish mother used to make, assuming she had roots in eastern Europe. Undoubtedly a riff on the traditional Hungarian chicken paprikash, it differs based on rules of kashruth. Where Hungarians would use butter or lard and finish the sauce with sour cream, kosher cooks avoid pork products and the mixing of meat and dairy. The result is a leaner, more pungent dish with a clear, fiery red sauce rather than a rosily creamy one.

The dish also strays in its inclusion of meatballs, and often of chicken giblets (excepting the liver). Sometimes it's even made in a meatballs-and-giblets–only version, without chicken.

Whatever the protein, the flavor begins with those onions and garlic, very slowly simmered in schmaltz, corn oil, or margarine. Sections of chicken cut into eighths (skin on, bones in) are braised in this mixture for a bit, and then the paprika—sweet, with or without a pinch of the hot—and a good pinch of thyme are added. After a couple of minutes (once the paprika has lost its raw smell), chicken broth or tomato juice is poured in, and, if needed to prevent scorching, a little water.

After about twenty minutes, the formed meatballs are carefully laid in the simmering sauce, the pan shaken gently to help them settle in. They are fragile while raw, but become sturdier after being poached for about ten minutes.

It's a good idea to prepare chicken fricassee several hours, or even a day, before it is to be served, so that any grease that coagulates on top can be removed. Sides of fluffy white rice or grainy, nicely gritty kasha are recommended for their powers of absorption.

WHERE: *In New York,* 2nd Ave Deli at two locations, 2ndavedeli.com; *in Houston,* Kenny & Ziggy's New York Delicatessen, tel 713-871-8883, kennyandziggys.com. **FURTHER INFORMATION AND RECIPES:** *From My Mother's Kitchen* by Mimi Sheraton (1979); *The Book of Jewish Food* by Claudia Roden (1996); *The 2nd Ave Deli Cookbook* by Sharon Lebewohl and Rena Bulkin (1999); cookstr.com (search fricassee sheraton).

"THE SMELL EXHALED WHEN THE LID IS LIFTED IS THE ONE THAT FILLED THE WOODEN HOUSES IN THE SHTETL."—FROM *THE BOOK OF JEWISH FOOD* BY CLAUDIA RODEN

Cholent

Sabbath Stew

Jewish

Mother Necessity, that dear old instigator of invention, surely had her hand in the Jewish cassoulet called *cholent.* Forbidden from lighting fires or activating any energy source between sundown Friday and sundown Saturday—

the beginning and ending of the Sabbath, or Shabbat—Jewish cooks thought ahead and devised this complex potful of meats, vegetables, and savory seasonings. Put in the oven before the Sabbath set in, it could be left to simmer away slowly until Saturday night dinner.

In olden times—actually only three or four generations back—not all home kitchens were outfitted with ovens. And so began the custom of carrying stew-filled pots to the local kosher bread baker; his ovens would have been turned off for the Sabbath, but remained hot enough to slow-cook all the neighborhood's cholents.

The most basic cholents contain white beans and beef cuts such as brisket, flanken, or boneless chuck, and the list might extend to such nurturing substantials as barley, potatoes, and dried lima beans. A dash of powdered ginger or paprika may lend spice to a standard base of onions, garlic, and black pepper, and variations on the theme include the addition of celery, onions, carrots, and schmaltz, hard-boiled eggs that mellow in the rich juices, or the use of a sprinkling of flour or matzo meal as a thickening agent. Not even beef is a given—Jews around the world also make cholent with chicken, lamb, veal, turkey, duck, or goose, or nowadays in vegetarian versions as well.

Although the exact origins of the dish are difficult to pin down, Jewish cooks have been preparing it in some form for centuries, at least since the fourteenth. Its name most probably derives from a combination of the French *chaud*, meaning hot, and *lent*, meaning slow. In the Middle East, especially in Morocco, the dish is called *dfina* (or *adafina*), which is also the Sephardic name for a similar lamb-based casserole.

No matter what cholent contains or what it is called, it's a complex casserole that emits a heady fragrance when its lid is lifted after the twenty-four-hour cooking time. To those who know the scent from childhood, it is the very perfume of home, family, and warm security.

WHERE: *In Las Vegas,* Haifa Restaurant, tel 702-940-8000, haifarestaurant.com. **FURTHER INFORMATION AND RECIPES:** *The Literary Gourmet* by Linda Wolfe (1962); *Sephardic Israeli Cuisine* by Sheilah Kaufman (2013); *The New York Times Jewish Cookbook* by Linda Amster (2003); epicurious.com (search cholent); chabad.org (search cholent); saveur.com (search cholent). **TIP:** The long-held adage of Jewish cooks is that the longer the cholent cooks, the better it will be.

|||||||||||||||||||||||||||||||

FRUIT-ENRICHED, WITHOUT THE DAIRY

Dried Fruit Compote

Jewish

*C*ompote, meaning mixture, is one thing to the French—fresh fruit flavored with wines, brandy, and cream—and quite another to Jewish cooks, who make theirs out of a colorful array of dried fruits. Heavily associated with Passover, the classic seder dessert consists of dried fruits resuscitated by a simmering in a little spiced wine or fruit juice. With its homey charm and deep, warming flavors, the compote is also a year-round favorite as a conclusion to kosher dinners that include meat. Because all ingredients in it are pareve, meaning neutral, it is allowed after both dairy and meat-based meals.

What fruit? Prunes, apricots, apples, pears, cherries, golden raisins, or some combination thereof, simmered slowly with ginger, cinnamon, and perhaps cloves, in a combination of half water, half white or red wine until the fruits are softened and the liquid becomes a smooth,

Dried fruit turns luscious when stewed in spiced wine or fruit juice.

dense syrup. Some Jewish grandmothers add honey for an amber richness, or brown sugar for a caramelized effect, while others squeeze in a bit of the fresh juice from lemons or oranges for a tart finish.

After it is cooked, the compote should be refrigerated for twenty-four hours so the flavors meld and the texture solidifies. The dessert may be served warm or cold; dressed up by spooning it into crystal goblets; or poured into a pan, topped with crushed macaroons or almonds, and baked like a cobbler. In any guise, it has a wonderfully aromatic quality that evokes nothing so much as family dinner and holiday china. It makes an excellent topping for yogurt or ice cream, and a great side dish for roasted poultry or meat. The compote can be stored in a jar or covered bowl in the refrigerator for up to two

weeks. One final bonus: Dried fruit is high in potassium, which is said to relieve hypertension—a welcome attribute, perhaps, after the trials of a big family holiday meal.

RETAIL AND MAIL ORDER: *In New York,* Russ & Daughters, tel 212-475-4880, russanddaughters .com; Zabar's, tel 800-697-6301, zabars.com. **FURTHER INFORMATION AND RECIPES:** *The Veselka Cookbook* by Tom Birchard with Natalie Danford (2009); *The New York Times Passover Cookbook* edited by Linda Amster (2010); kosherfood.about.com (search dried fruit compote); epicurious.com (search fruit compote with port). **TIP:** When buying dried fruits, opt for sundried varieties and/or look for the term "unsulfured" on the packaging. Be sure the fruits are moist and shiny as opposed to leathery and dried out.

⊣||||||||||||||||||||||||||||||⊢

YOU SAY GEFULTE, AND I SAY GEFILTE

Gefilte Fish

Jewish (Ashkenazic)

Gefilte may be the most ubiquitous fish dish in the Jewish culinary lexicon, whether we're talking about the mass-produced, jarred versions available at supermarkets or the ready-made kind from kosher-style delis and dairy

appetizer stores. But it is also the most celebratory fish dish, closely related to the haute-cuisine triumph *quenelles de brochet* (see page 122). Essentially a kind of fish dumpling, it consists of fillets that are ground—or more desirably, chopped, and thus left with bite and texture—and poached in a flavorful broth.

One trick in preparing gefilte fish is to strike the right balance with the different types of freshwater fish. The most successful and traditional inclusions will be pike and whitefish, and maybe meaty red carp, if one can be sure the carp has not ingested mud. Freshwater fish are essential for true gefilte, never mind such fashionable interlopers as the overly soft, sweet

salmon, fibrous cod, and others. But the eastern European Jews who created the dish had easy access to freshwater fish, while many species have become scarce in North America, and therein lies one challenge.

The raw, ground or chopped fish is mixed with eggs, plenty of ground onion, a small amount of matzo meal as a binder, and generous amounts of salt and pepper. To test the seasoning, housewives sometimes taste the raw mix, but they do so at great risk: Freshwater fish can carry a dangerous parasite, and during the High Holy Days when much fish is being "gefilted," the Centers for Disease Control reports many calls about parasite cases. Far better to make a small test ball, poach it, and then taste.

The poaching takes place in a broth flavored with the heads, bones, and skin of the fish, along with many more sliced onions, a sliver of parsnip or the Italian parsley root known as *petrouchka,* a piece of celery root, disks of carrots, and a handful of lightly crushed black peppercorns. After a

The airy wonder of true gefilte

long, very slow simmer, the fish balls are laid out in deep glass or ceramic trays or platters, with the strained broth and reserved carrot slices poured over. Left to set into an aspic as it chills in the refrigerator, the dish tastes best after eight hours and should always be served well chilled, never mind those few renegades who like their gefilte fish hot (and smelly, and cloyingly intense).

You might think all of these steps would assure gefilte perfection, but there's one more: horseradish—a garnet beet version if tastes run to the sweet, or the sparer, sharper white kind that attains utmost pungency when grated at home. And don't forget the matzo, the go-with of choice of serious mavens.

Things used to be even more complicated. The term *gefilte* (Yiddish) or *gefülte* (German) actually means stuffed, harkening back to the dish's original preparation. In the olden days,

prior to being poached, balls of the raw fish mix were wrapped in bands of black-gray fish skin. In a few kosher restaurants in the Marais, Paris's Jewish quarter, the stuffing process was even more ambitious: Whole fish skins were filled with the fish farce, wrapped in cheesecloth, and poached, emerging as "whole" pike or whitefish from which portions were sliced crosswise. These were beautifully garnished with a shimmering aspic and rosettes of carrot. (Leave it to the French.)

WHERE: *In New York,* Barney Greengrass, tel 212-724-4707, barneygreengrass.com; Citarella at multiple locations, citarella.com; *in Houston,* Kenny & Ziggy's New York Delicatessen, tel 713-871-8883, kennyandziggys.com. **DINE-IN, RETAIL, AND MAIL ORDER:** *In New York,* Russ & Daughters, tel 212-475-4880, russanddaughters.com; Eli Zabar, tel 866-354-3547, elizabar.com; *in Ann Arbor, MI,* Zingerman's, tel 888-636-8162, zinger mans.com. **FURTHER INFORMATION AND RECIPES:** *Joan Nathan's Jewish Holiday Cookbook* by Joan Nathan (2004); *The Book of Jewish Food* by Claudia Roden (1996); *The New York Times Jewish Cookbook* edited by Linda Amster (2003); cookstr.com (search gefilte fish lebewohl); epicurious.com (search classic gefilte fish).

UNJUSTLY AN INSULT

Gehakte Leber

Chopped Chicken Livers

Jewish (Ashkenazic)

A must as an appetizer for the traditional Friday-night Sabbath dinner, chopped chicken livers are rarely well prepared in kosher-style delicatessens and restaurants—and that's unfair ammunition for the vocal contingent of liver haters.

Billed simply as chopped liver, it will invariably be made with beef liver, overly strong and bitter and simply wrong from the start. To make matters worse, instead of being truly chopped, it will be ground, for a mushy, if more conveniently realized, result.

A happier outcome follows from broiled or sautéed chicken livers that must be hand chopped with a *hachoir* (a half-moon chopper) or a French chef's knife, along with hard-cooked eggs, onions, salt, black pepper, and a moistening of the rendered chicken fat known as schmaltz (see page 464). For good and savory measure, the leftover cracklings from the rendering, lovingly known as *gribenes,* are also added to the mix. The chopped livers are best spread on unflavored matzo or, better yet, on wafer-thin slices of peeled, sliced, and iced black radish lightly sprinkled with coarse salt.

Chopped Chicken Livers

Makes about 1 pound;
serves 4 to 6 as an appetizer

1 pound chicken livers, well trimmed
(see Notes)
2 extra-large eggs, hard-cooked, peeled,
and chopped
1 medium-size onion, coarsely chopped
⅓ to ½ cup gribenes (optional but
sensational) (see Notes)
2 teaspoons kosher salt
¼ teaspoon freshly ground black pepper
3 to 4 tablespoons chicken schmaltz
(see Notes)

1. To prepare this dish according to kosher laws, preheat the broiler. Line a broiler pan with aluminum foil and place the trimmed chicken livers on top. Sprinkle the livers with kosher salt and place them under the broiler. Broil the livers until light brown, about 10 minutes, turning them once. (If you are not observing kashruth, sauté the livers in a little schmaltz, butter, or margarine until thoroughly cooked but not hard or scorched, about 10 minutes.)

2. Place the cooked livers in a wooden chopping bowl or on a cutting board and chop them,

along with the eggs, onion, gribenes, salt, and pepper until fine-textured but not pasty. Stir in just enough schmaltz to hold the mixture together. Taste for seasoning, adding more salt and/or pepper as necessary.

3. Pack the chopped livers into a crock or bowl. Cover and chill for 8 to 24 hours for maximum flavor. Remove the chopped livers from the refrigerator 15 to 30 minutes before serving. Stored in the refrigerator, chopped liver will keep for 3 days.

Notes: Buy only fresh, bright chicken livers that show no brown dry spots. Clean the livers carefully, trimming off any greenish yellow gall spots. For instructions on how to make schmaltz with gribenes, see page 465.

Where: *In New York,* E.A.T., tel 212-772-0022, elizabar.com/EAT-C25.aspx; *in Miami,* Goldstein's Prime, tel 305-865-4981, goldsteins prime.com; *in Atlanta,* The General Muir, tel 678-927-9131, thegeneralmuir.com; *in Houston,* Kenny & Ziggy's New York Delicatessen, tel 713-871-8883, kennyandziggys.com; *in Los Angeles,* Langer's Deli, tel 213-483-8050, langersdeli.com; *in Montreal,* Hof Kelsten, hofkelsten.com. **Dine-in, retail, and mail order:** *In New York,* Russ & Daughters, tel 212-475-4880, russanddaughters .com (search chopped liver).

Liver topped with hard-cooked egg, onion, and parsley

‖‖‖‖‖‖‖‖‖‖‖‖‖‖‖‖‖‖‖‖‖‖‖‖

GOOD FOR ANYTHING THAT AILS YOU, AND SOME THINGS THAT DON'T

Golden Yoich

Chicken Soup

Jewish (Ashkenazic)

Unrivaled as a panacea for all illnesses of the body and spirit, the soup known as "Jewish penicillin" should be pale and lemony yellow, with tiny globules of fat winking on its surface. Correctly prepared only when it uses a large old fowl

weighing at least seven pounds (tough but flavorful), the soup simmers slowly to extract maximum flavor and aroma from root vegetables and herbs—leeks, onions, parsnips, carrots, the white root of Italian parsley known as *petrouchka*, knob celery and stalk celery with leaves, and sprigs of parsley and dill. Some cooks add a nugget of dried ginger, a chunk of turnip, or even a tomato for additional flavor, but the results are less delicate.

Served steaming hot, spoonful by restorative spoonful, this shimmering, golden soup assures one that all's right with the world—or will be soon. For added heft and interest, there are garnishes such as wide, silky egg noodles, rice, wontonlike beef-filled kreplach, or, for special occasions and always at the Passover seder, matzo balls, aka knaidlach dumplings.

WHERE: *In New York,* 2nd Ave Deli at two locations, 2ndavedeli.com; *in Houston,* Kenny & Ziggy's New York Delicatessen, tel 713-871-8883, kennyandziggys.com; *in Chicago,* Manny's, tel 312-939-2855, mannysdeli.com; *in Los Angeles,* Langer's Deli, tel 213-483-8050, langersdeli.com; *in Los Angeles and Miami,* Jerry's Famous Deli at multiple locations, jerrys famousdeli.com. **FURTHER INFORMATION AND RECIPES:** *Joan Nathan's Jewish Holiday Cookbook* by Joan Nathan (2004); *The New York Times Passover Cookbook* edited by Linda Amster (2010); cookstr.com (search sabbath soup); epicurious.com (search chicken soup lebewohl). **SPECIAL EVENTS:** Chicken Soup Cookoff, Houston, February, chickensoupcookoff.com; Chicken Soup Cookoff, Cincinnati, January, chickensoupcookoff.org.

‖‖‖‖‖‖‖‖‖‖‖‖‖‖‖‖‖‖‖‖‖‖‖‖

WHEN REVENGE IS SWEET

Hamantaschen and Orejas de Haman

Jewish (Ashkenazic and Sephardic)

The most common explanation for the name of *hamantaschen,* those tri-cornered puffs of crisp pastry enfolding oozingly rich and dark, sour-sweet fillings, is that they represent the three-cornered hat worn by the anti-Semitic tyrant

Haman before he was vanquished by the wiles of the beautiful Queen Esther. It is the story recounted in the Megillah, the scroll that tells the tale of the spring holiday Purim.

In German (from which Yiddish is derived) *taschen* means pockets, so the linguistic switch to hats is something of a mystery. Still other conjectures hold that the name comes from the Hebrew, *Hama tash kocho,* for "May Haman become weak." No matter, as eating these seasonal treats is more fulfilling than worrying about their etymology.

Most delicious when formed of parchment-crisp yeast dough, the treats have a close second in flakier,

A densely rich treat

short pastry variations; these are made with butter and cream cheese or neutral (pareve) dairy substitutes such as margarine. Rolled paper thin and cut into circles, the dough is pinched closed around a filling, the most popular being *mohn*: crackly little poppy seeds fragrant with grated orange and lemon zest. Varietal fillings of apricot or raspberry jam and even chocolate are mere gimmicks, cloying and texturally incorrect.

While hamantaschen are the symbolic Purim treat of the Ashkenazim, Sephardic Jews (particularly in the Middle East) prefer to taste revenge by devouring Haman's ears, *orejas de*

Haman. Like hamantaschen, these may be filled with the beloved prune *lekvar,* a tantalizing midnight-dark fruit butter made with lightly cooked pureed prunes, a dash of lemon juice or brandy, pinches of powdered cloves or cinnamon, and perhaps some finely chopped walnuts. In these syrupy-sweet confections, a simple dough based on flour and almonds is rolled into circles, filled, pinched into half circles to resemble tiny ears, and quickly fried in vegetable oil. When cool and crisp, the ears are doused in a syrup made from orange-seasoned honey that cools to a shimmery glaze. Hot tea is the best accompaniment to this Megillah.

Where: *In New York,* Breads Bakery, tel 212-633-2253, breadsbakery.com; Sarabeth's at multiple locations, sarabeth.com; *in Los Angeles,* Eilat Bakery at two locations, eilatbakery.com. **Mail order:** For prune lekvar, amazon.com (search simon fischer lekvar). **Further information and recipes:** *Jewish Holiday Cookbook* by Joan Nathan (2004); *The Book of Jewish Food* by Claudia Roden (1996); *The Sephardic Kitchen* by Rabbi Robert Sternberg (1996); tabletmag .com (search how to make the ultimate hamantaschen); cookstr.com (search hamantaschen); food52.com (search lekvar classic prune filling).

CABBAGE ON A ROLL

Holishkes
Sweet-and-Sour Stuffed Cabbage

Jewish (Ashkenazic)

They arrive at the table looking like little morsels of bronzed jade, silken roll-ups glossed with a shiny, golden-brown sauce dotted with raisins and redolent of lemon juice, sugar, ginger, and cloves. Gently cut with a fork, each wilted cabbage

leaf packet reveals a meaty interior flecked with rice and heady with black pepper. Known as

golubtsi in Russia and *holubtsi* in Ukraine, this deeply traditional main course makes admirable use of a humble, hearty vegetable that isn't inhibited by cold climes or by lengthy periods of storage through long, frosty winters.

First stewed gently with tomatoes, the cooked cabbage rolls are laid out in a baking pan. Their sauce, thickened with crushed gingersnaps and balanced to sweet-sour perfection, is poured over the top to become thick and satiny as the dish bakes. In the most style-conscious households, paper-thin slices of lemon are placed over the top of the arranged rolls as they go into the oven, emerging virtually candied to lend a sunny brightness to the dish. All that's needed to complete the picture are crisp, hot potato latkes (see page 445), home-made applesauce, and perhaps a glass of cold light beer.

Where: *In Kiev, Ukraine,* Tsarske Selo, tel 380/44-288-9775, tsarske.kiev.ua/en; *in New York,* Carnegie Deli, tel 212-757-2245, carnegiedeli .com; *in Miami,* Goldstein's Prime, tel 305-865-4981, goldsteinsprime.com; *in Houston,* Kenny & Ziggy's, tel 713-871-8883, kennyandziggys .com; *in Los Angeles,* Canters Deli, tel 323-651-2030, cantersdeli.com. **Further information and recipes:** *The Book of Jewish Food* by Claudia Roden (1996); *Arthur Schwartz's Jewish Home Cooking* by Arthur Schwartz (2008); *The New York Times Jewish Cookbook* edited by Linda Amster (2003); *How to Feed Friends and Influence People* by Milton Parker and Allyn Freeman (2004); epicurious.com (search holishkes); tasteofhome.com (search sweet-and-sour stuffed cabbage).

SHED A TEAR FOR FLAVOR

Horseradish

Jewish (Ashkenazic), Eastern European

Stingingly peppery and powerfully aromatic, horseradish is a valued condiment in many cuisines, most especially those of northern and eastern Europe, and of the Jews who inhabited those areas. Botanically known as *Armoracia rusticana,*

the ancient herbal root yields a sinus-clearing hot and spicy essence when cut open or grated.

Its fiery fumes enliven many foods otherwise considered bland—raw shellfish such as clams and oysters (heresy to those who prefer their sea-breeze flavor undiluted), and meat- and poultry-bound sauces based on tomato, cream, or butter. It's an important player at Passover as well. At the first Passover seder, the root is cut into small sticks or slices to represent *maror,* the "bitter herb" that symbolizes the harshness Jewish slaves endured at the hands of the Egyptians. Symbols aside, it separates the bold palate from the timid, as seder guests down the *maror* in a contest to see who can withstand its heat. Later in the meal, grated horseradish

serves as a garnish for the oniony gefilte fish; tinted red and slightly sweet with grated beets, it may also be served as an accompaniment to boiled beef.

The biggest problem with preparing this fiery root at home is the tear-producing job of grating it, as the fumes it releases are powerful indeed: The cutting, grinding, or grating process for horseradish crushes its root cells and releases the fiery volatile oils (called isothiocyanates) they contain. The prepared horseradish sold in food markets includes white vinegar, added to stop this chemical reaction and stabilize the horseradish's flavor and color.

Valued for its medicinal properties as well as its taste, horseradish is considered a cholagogue, an agent that stimulates the release of bile from the gallbladder and thus aids in healthy digestion; it also contains a highly useful infection-fighting enzyme called peroxidase. On a more hedonistic note, horseradish adds zip and zest to anything you mix it with, from dips and sauces to pickling vegetables to roast beef sandwiches.

Sixty percent of the horseradish in America grows in Collinsville, Illinois, where the soil is rich in potash, a key nutrient in its growth, and every June since 1988 the town has hosted an International Horseradish Festival that includes parades and lots of Bloody Marys—a drink that would amount to little more than spiced, spiked tomato juice without the inclusion of this memorably rousing root.

When choosing horseradish, look for a root that has green tops and is not too dry and woody. Buy only the amount of the root you plan to use, and store it in a tightly-covered jar in the refrigerator to help it retain freshness. Grate it in a food processor, and stand back when you open the lid—the emanating gases will have a powerful kick. (If possible, open the processor bowl out-of-doors or through an open window.)

Add salt to taste and pack the grated root in a nonreactive, narrow bottle made of glass or ceramic. Pour in just enough distilled white vinegar to cover. Store the bottle, covered, in the refrigerator. If it darkens, throw it out—and never cook prepared horseradish, as heat destroys its flavor.

MAIL ORDER: For prepared horseradish, Zabar's, tel 800-697-6301, zabars.com; Brede Foods, bredefoods.com. For fresh horseradish, Melissa's Produce, tel 800-588-0151, melissas .com. **FURTHER INFORMATION AND RECIPES:** *From My Mother's Kitchen* by Mimi Sheraton (1979); *The Book of Jewish Food* by Claudia Roden (1996); *The New York Times Jewish Cookbook* edited by Linda Amster (2003); foodnetwork.com (search preparing fresh horseradish); bon appetit.com (search prepared horseradish). **TIP:** For a good supermarket brand of prepared horseradish—both white and reddened with beets—try Gold's. **SPECIAL EVENTS:** International Horseradish Festival, Collinsville, IL, June, horseradishfestival.net; National Horseradish Month, July, horseradish.org.

LEAVE THE *VARNISHKES*, TAKE THE KASHA

Kasha

Jewish (Ashkenazic), Eastern European, Russian

Generally featured in kosher-style restaurants, tossed with the butterfly-shaped pasta known as *varnishkes*, nicely gritty, brown kasha often gets a bad rap, suffering from heavy doses of butter, oil, or margarine and way too much time on

a steam table. But when properly cooked, kasha is a nutty, richly flavored accompaniment to all sorts of braised or roasted meats and poultry. It cushions meaty textures, absorbs pan juices and velvety gravies, and is beloved not only by Jewish cooks but also throughout eastern Europe and Russia, where it is the standard enhancement for duck and goose, and a fluffy, sprightly stuffing for roast suckling pig. More interesting than rice, high in fiber and rich in B vitamins, kasha is gluten free, and so a boon to celiac sufferers, providing them with the elemental satisfaction that grains bring to a diet.

Technically, kasha is buckwheat groats—a grass, not a grain, which in the United States grows most prolifically near Buffalo, in upstate

New York. Once milled, it can be ground into three grain sizes: coarse, medium, and fine. The first two are the more interesting as main-course garnishes, while the fine grain lends itself to being cooked as a breakfast porridge.

The best way to cook kasha is as directed on packages of Wolff's, the brand most commonly available in American supermarkets. (Kasha is also sold in bulk in many health and natural foods stores.) The raw grains are coated with beaten raw eggs and parched in a hot, dry skillet until each grain stands separate. Boiling broth or water are stirred in, along with seasonings, resulting in grains that are firm outside but tender within and that retain their texture even when reheated. Added interest might come by way of minced fresh chives and sliced, sautéed mushrooms stirred in just before the kasha has finished cooking.

MAIL ORDER: thebirkettmills.com (search pocono organic kasha; wolff's kasha); amazon .com (search wolff's kasha whole; wolff's kasha medium). **FURTHER INFORMATION AND RECIPES:** *The New York Times Jewish Cookbook* edited by Linda Amster (2003); *The Book of Jewish Food* by Claudia Roden (1996); epicurious.com (search wild mushroom and onion kasha; kasha varnishkes).

||||||||||||||||||||||||||||||

YOU MUST REMEMBER THIS, A KNISH IS STILL A KNISH . . .

Knishes

Jewish (Ashkenazic), Ukrainian

Today's puffy, hot, and fragrant knishes (ka-NISH-es) would have been downright insults to the Jewish and southern Ukrainian home cooks of yore. In these versions, individual pielike portions of this meal-in-a-crust are kept warm

under cover, their rather simplistic flour, water, and oil crusts becoming steamy and soggy—a failure we generally overlook, beguiled as we are by savory fillings of nutty kasha, earthy mushrooms, soothing cabbage or sauerkraut, or an unctuous fluff of mashed potatoes.

But at its most ethereal, a knish is wrapped in a yeasty bread dough, rolled very thin so it turns deep golden brown and truly crusty, thus providing contrast to those soft fillings. It will not be an individual portion but rather will be made in a big, fat ring (Ukrainian style) or a robust horseshoe (Jewish style) to be sliced into portions and served while still steaming hot.

One of the Jewish knish's most succulent, traditional fillings is a mix of lightly sautéed and chopped chicken livers tossed with sautéed onions, cooked kasha, and cracklings of the rendered chicken fat known as schmaltz (see

Fresh out of the oven at New York's Yonah Schimmel Knish Bakery

page 464), along with plenty of ground black pepper. The combination produces such mouthwatering aromas during baking that it's a wonder the knish isn't pulled from the oven before it is half done. For Ukrainians and Russians, the ring-shaped Easter knishes named *piroshky* are near bursting with a pungent mix of onions and garlic and juicy sauerkraut, or sometimes with peppery and garlicky ground beef.

The proper ambiance for the best knish experience in the U.S. is Brooklyn's Coney Island boardwalk in winter, when a hot knish in the hand is worth two pairs of woolen gloves as protection from the damp seaside chill. Just watch out for hungry seagulls.

WHERE: *In New York,* Yonah Schimmel Knish Bakery, tel 212-477-2859, knishery.com. **FURTHER INFORMATION AND RECIPES:** *Knish: In Search of the Jewish Soul Food* by Laura Silver (2014); *The Book of Jewish Food* by Claudia Roden (1996); cookstr.com (search knish schwartz); thedailymeal.com/best-recipes/knish.

IN A FINE PICKLE

Kosher Dill Pickles

Jewish, Eastern European

What gives a kosher-style delicatessen its incomparable aroma? A telltale barrel of cool, bronze-green dill and garlic pickles made from unwaxed Kirby cucumbers. With their snappy texture and juicy interiors, classic kosher

pickles taste only of salt, garlic, dill (both fronds and seeds), and a pickling spice mix of coriander and mustard seed, bay leaves, black peppercorns, and tiny, hot red chile peppers. No sweet spices such as nutmeg, cloves, or allspice need apply, and a pickle brine at its best and most authentic is made without the inclusion of vinegar or alum as aids for crispness and shelf life. The degree of pickling is determined by the amount of time the cucumbers are left in the brine—but to true connoisseurs, nothing less than full sour is worth considering. Although lovers of "new" pickles would argue the contrary, in kosher-style pickles any hint of bright green on the skin is a sign of an under-pickled cucumber.

Kosher-Style Garlic Dill Pickles

Makes 24 to 30 pickles

24 to 30 small, very firm Kirby cucumbers, uniform in size and free of bruises or brown spots
7 or 8 cloves garlic, unpeeled but lightly crushed

1 teaspoon coriander seed
1 teaspoon mustard seed
1 teaspoon black peppercorns
4 or 5 tiny dried red chiles, or
   ½ teaspoon dried hot
   red pepper flakes
3 bay leaves
12 to 14 sprigs fresh dill, preferably with
   seed heads (crown dill), well rinsed, plus
   1 teaspoon dried dill seed, if seed heads
   are not available
¾ cup kosher salt

1. Thoroughly wash a wide-mouthed 3-quart crock, glass jar, or bean pot. Carefully rinse each cucumber, rubbing it gently with a cloth or soft brush to remove all traces of sand. Do not break the skin.

2. Stand the cucumbers on end, filling the crock or jar. A second vertical layer of cucumbers can be added if the vessel is tall enough. The cucumbers should hold each other in place but should not be crammed together. Add the garlic, coriander and mustard seed, peppercorns, chiles or hot red pepper flakes, bay leaves, and dill sprigs and seed.

3. Mix 3 quarts of water with the salt and stir until the salt is completely dissolved. Pour the salt water into the crock so that it completely covers the pickles. The brine should overflow so you are sure that there are no air pockets. If there is not enough brine to do this, place the crock under slowly running water and fill it until overflowing.

4. Dry the outside of the crock and place it on a stainproof surface in a dark, cool corner, but not in the refrigerator. A temperature of between 65°F and 70°F is just right. Fit a small dish or wooden disk directly over the pickles inside the mouth of the crock. It must rest directly on the pickles and should not be made of metal.

5. Weigh down the dish or wooden disk with a jar or glass filled with water. Cover the crock and weight loosely but completely with a double thickness of cheesecloth or a clean dish towel.

6. Every 24 hours, remove the cover and weight and check the pickles. Skim off any white or gray foam that has risen to the surface. Jiggle the crock slightly to distribute the spices and always return the weight to the top. After about 5 days, taste the brine for seasoning, adding more salt or other seasonings if the brine seems bland.

7. The pickled cucumbers will be half sour in 4 to 5 days and fully sour in 10 days. The pickling time depends in part on the room temperature— the warmer the room, the faster the cucumbers will pickle. When the pickles have reached the degree of sourness you like, they can be stored in their brine in tightly closed jars in the refrigerator, where they will stop souring and become nicely firm in about 24 hours. If the jar lids have a metal lining, to prevent corrosion, place a piece of wax paper or plastic wrap over the mouth of the jars before screwing on the lids. Covered in brine, the pickles will keep for about 5 weeks, if they are not eaten long before that.

Variation: Pickled green tomatoes are as enticing as the cucumbers, although harder to find well prepared. You can follow the same recipe as for the cucumbers, but the pickling will require a bit more time. Begin with small, totally green, very firm tomatoes of a uniform size, and prick the surface all over with a needle, making tiny holes. Then follow the instructions for brining the cucumbers and allow to ripen for 10 to 12 days.

RETAIL AND MAIL ORDER: *In New York,* The Pickle Guys, tel 888-474-2553, pickleguys.com. **MAIL ORDER:** Guss' Pickles, tel 718-933-6060, gusspickle.com; for cucumbers, Rising River Farm, tel 360-273-5368, risingriverfarm.com; for pickling cucumbers and crown dill, Melissa's Produce, tel 800-588-0151, melissas.com; for dried dill seed, Penzey's Spices, tel 800-741-7787, penzeys.com. **TIP:** The perfect time for pickling is midsummer, when Kirby cucumbers are at their peak and dill has gone to seed.

—————————————|||||||||||||||||||||||||||||||||||||————————————

THE IMPORTANCE OF BEING CRISP

————————————

Latkes

Potato Pancakes

Jewish

G olden and crunchy on the outside, soft, tender, and oniony on the inside, fried potato pancakes—or *latkes,* as they're called in Yiddish—are the highlight of the Ashkenazic Jewish holiday of Hanukkah. Also known as the Festival of Lights, the holiday has its roots in the second century B.C., when the Romans besieged a group of Jews known as the Maccabees. Determined to die in rebellion rather than be captured, they faced the problem of repairing their desecrated temple without enough oil to light the lamps during rebuilding. Enter a miracle: a tiny jar of oil that lasted eight days and nights, long enough to obtain more oil and restore order.

On Hanukkah, Jews commemorate that remarkable event by frying foods in oil—chiefly latkes for Ashkenazic Jews, and the crullers known as *sufganiyot* (see page 469) for the Sephardim.

Potato latkes are distinctive for their oniony, salty goodness. There are several secrets to turning out an ideal one, which will taste something like hashbrowns, French fries, and potato chips, all rolled into a single addictive disk. First, the potatoes should be grated on a traditional box grater (a food processor is only a fair substitute, turning out watery shreds), alternating with onions; this keeps the grated potato from darkening and ensures that the onion and potato are thoroughly combined. Second, this is one time to throw precaution to the wind and opt for Crisco shortening, the very best fat for crisp and clean, flavorless frying. If you can't muster up the courage, rely on corn oil, the next best frying medium. Once fried, latkes should be drained on paper towels, and they may be held uncovered on a rack in a 375°F oven for about 20 minutes.

Naturally, latkes engender arguments among proprietary cooks and their offspring. Thick, with a lovely, pulpy and savory interior, or thin and all crackle, with virtually no soft insides? And what garnish?

Fresh, homemade applesauce seasoned with cinnamon and served at room temperature is the best answer, although many opt for sour cream, a cold and overpowering mistake. If mini-latkes are to be passed at cocktail hour, a dab of red or black caviar, or minced smoked salmon and a tip of sour cream are excellent amendments.

WHERE: *In New York,* Sammy's Roumanian Steakhouse, tel 212-673-0330, sammysroman ian.com; Russ & Daughters, tel 212-475-4880, russanddaughters.com; *in Houston,* Kenny & Ziggy's New York Delicatessen, tel 713-871-8883, kennyandziggys.com; *in Boynton Beach, FL,* Flakowitz, tel 561-742-4144, flakowitzofboynton .com; *in San Francisco,* Suppenküche, tel 415-252-9289, suppenkuche.com. **FURTHER INFORMATION AND RECIPES:** *From My Mother's Kitchen* by Mimi Sheraton (1979); *The Book of Jewish Food* by Claudia Roden (1996); cookstr.com (search classic potato latkes levy); foodand wine.com (search killer potato latkes). **SPECIAL EVENT:** Annual Latke Festival, Brooklyn Academy of Music, Brooklyn, NY, December, greatperfor mances.com.

TO ENSURE A SWEET YEAR

Lekach

Honey Cake

Jewish, Eastern European

An essential component of the Jewish holiday of Rosh Hashanah, known generally as the Jewish New Year, a honey cake (*lekach* in Yiddish, derived from the German *lecke,* for lick) is meant to symbolize a sweet year ahead. Slices of apples dipped in honey, the other food tradition most associated with Rosh Hashanah, are served for this same reason.

Dark, moist, and mysteriously haunting, made with burnished honey, aromatic spicings of cinnamon and cloves, grated orange rind, and strongly brewed black coffee, honey cake is also eaten the year round. It's a dessert with a history—honey cakes were baked by Jewish slaves in Egypt (they were among the sacrifices sealed in the pharaohs' tombs), and biblical references in Exodus liken the taste of manna to that of honey cake.

Reminiscent of *lebkuchen*, the German-style gingerbread first popularized around the thirteenth century, the cake is simple and delicious. If left to sit for a couple of days after baking, its flavors will intensify; well wrapped in foil and stored in a cool spot, it can keep for weeks. Enjoy it thickly sliced and spread with fresh cream cheese. No need to wait for Rosh Hashanah.

Lekach

Makes one 9½ x 5½-inch loaf

2 cups dark honey
¾ cup black coffee, brewed
    double strength
3 tablespoons mild vegetable oil,
    preferably peanut
4 extra-large eggs
¾ cup sugar
3½ cups sifted all-purpose flour
Pinch of salt
1 teaspoon baking soda
1½ teaspoons baking powder
1 teaspoon cinnamon
1 teaspoon ginger
Grated zest of 1 orange
Grated zest of 1 lemon
10 or 12 whole blanched almonds
    (optional)

1. Preheat the oven to 325°F. Butter a 9½- by 5½- by 3-inch loaf pan. Cut clean brown paper, wax paper, or parchment to fit the bottom and sides of the pan and butter one side. Place the unbuttered side of the paper against the pan.

2. Put the honey in a heavy 3-quart saucepan and slowly bring to a boil over low heat. Set the honey aside and allow it to cool, then stir in the coffee and oil.

A celebratory cake symbolic of a sweet year ahead

3. Beat the eggs with the sugar in a large bowl until light and thick and the mixture forms a ribbon when drizzled into the bowl. Stir in the honey-coffee mixture. Resift the flour, along with the salt, baking soda and powder, cinnamon, and ginger, into the batter. Add the citrus zests and fold the flour and zests in gently.

4. Pour the batter into the lined pan. If you like, make a pattern on top with the almonds.

5. Bake until the top is golden brown and a tester inserted in the center comes out clean, 1¼ to 1½ hours. Let the cake cool in the pan, then invert it with the paper intact (peel off just what is necessary each time you slice the cake). This cake will develop more flavor if it is left uncut for 24 hours. It keeps well in an airtight container at a cool room temperature for 2 weeks.

WHERE: *In New York,* E.A.T., tel 212-772-0022, elizabar.com/EAT-C25.aspx; Citarella at multiple locations, citarella.com; Breads Bakery, tel 212-633-2253, breadsbakery.com. **RETAIL AND MAIL ORDER:** *In New York,* in fall during the High Holy Days, Eli Zabar, tel 866-354-3547, elizabar.com; *in Ann Arbor, MI,* Zingerman's, tel 888-636-8162, zingermans.com.

‖‖‖‖‖‖‖‖‖‖‖‖‖‖‖‖‖‖‖‖‖‖‖‖‖‖

THE BREAD OF AFFLICTION

Matzo, Observed and Unobserved

Jewish

It looks like cardboard, and to some it tastes . . . not so different. But matzo is probably the most elemental, simple bread the world has ever known. In its truest, most authentic form it consists only of flour and water. No salt. No yeast. No fat. No flavorings.

Forget modern, merchandised matzo seasoned with garlic, poppy seeds, or salt. Matzo stands for neutrality, affording comfort to tired palates in need of refreshment between samplings of cheese or caviar, wine or chocolate, and soothing agitated stomachs the world over. To devotees, the crackers are year-round staples, fine substitutes for pricey English water biscuits, and most welcome for the various spreads—butter, or schmaltz sprinkled with coarse kosher salt—and cheeses they accommodate. Matzos are also the essential accompaniment to gefilte fish (see page 436) or, prepared as *matzo brei* (see page 449), are breakfast staples in and of themselves. A flour-like cracker meal or finer cake meal that is made from ground matzos becomes matzo balls, delicate Passover sponge cakes, pseudo-bagels, or the golden, puffy pancakes known as *chremsel,* so lovely sprinkled with sugar and cinnamon.

The plainness of matzo, of course, harks back to its biblical origins, a story that is celebrated every Passover. When the Jews were freed from slavery by the pharaoh in Egypt, they left so quickly that they did not have the time to make leavened bread. As a reminder of that long suffering, during the symbolic eight days of Passover, Jews may not eat anything that is leavened—hence matzos, arguably the one food common to Jews of all backgrounds, be they Ashkenazic, Sephardic, Italian, or Mizrachic.

Although most Passover matzos are nationally branded (for example, Horowitz Margareten or Streit's) and mass-produced according to religious law, the most special holiday matzos are known as *schmura* (watched) matzo. A rabbi observes wheat growing in the field in order to ensure that it is harvested as soon as it is ripe, before rain dampens it and begins the process of fermentation. The harvested grain is taken to Hasidic communities to be ground into flour in special bakeries where it is baked by volunteers from the congregation. The flour is mixed with water just before it is to be rolled out, and the dough is distributed to rows of bakers who, with long, slim rolling pins, form circles that are

Holiday matzo, "watched" by a rabbi and baked by his congregation

pin-pricked so they will not rise and crack when baked.

To avoid fermentation of any part of the dough—believed to begin after nineteen minutes—every seventeen minutes all action stops, rolling pins and boards are sanded or replaced, and the rolled matzos are slid into vast wood-fired ovens that operate only from January until a few days before the beginning of Passover. Baked to parchment crispness, with beautifully seared edges that suggest the antique patina of the Dead Sea Scrolls, the flat, round matzos have a rich, brown, wheaty look and a flavor and crackling texture very close to that of Scandinavian crispbreads.

As might be expected, such a labor-intensive product fetches a special price, somewhere around $20 a pound, which nets about eight boards. Many people buy only two or three of these rounds for use in the seder ceremony. Sadly, packaged schmura matzo, even imported from Israel, is never as crisp or as brightly savory as the type freshly made by local communities.

WHERE: For the best schmura matzos, check local synagogues and Hasidic headquarters in Brooklyn, Miami, Los Angeles, and other cities with large Jewish communities. **MAIL ORDER:** streitsmatzos.elsstore.com. **FURTHER INFORMATION AND RECIPES:** *From My Mother's Kitchen* by Mimi Sheraton (1979); *The New York Times Jewish Cookbook* edited by Linda Amster (2003); *The Book of Jewish Food* by Claudia Roden (1996).

⊣||||||||||||||||||||||||||||||⊢

HOW THE MATZO SCRAMBLES

Matzo Brei

Jewish

T hou shalt make lemonade out of lemon, and out of matzo, *matzo brei*. So the commandment *should* go, for in this eggy, peppery, and buttery dish, the crisp-edged cracker is softened into a deliciously nurturing breakfast. Matzo brei may

have attained gourmet heights in the mid-1990s, when Manhattan's bygone Lobster Club served it with sautéed earthy mushrooms for brunch, but for the most part, it is a homey, plain, and very simple pleasure.

Treated similarly to French toast, the traditional Passover bread is first broken into pieces (making it *brei* in German-derived Yiddish) and then moistened, glossed with beaten eggs and salt and black pepper, and slowly fried in butter.

Variations include using milk for moistening, and frying in a vegetable oil such as corn, sunflower, or safflower oil, or (if the milk isn't being used) in the rendered chicken fat called schmaltz. Should the dish be broken up as it fries, to encourage a non-uniform texture, or cooked as a solid, one-piece pancake to be cut into wedges for serving? The answer depends on the family, but fickle deviations such as garnishes of peanut butter, jelly, cinnamon sugar, or maple syrup are best ignored.

Matzo Brei

Serves 2 to 4

5 matzos
3 cups boiling water
4 extra-large eggs, lightly beaten
1 teaspoon salt, or more to taste
¼ to ½ teaspoon black pepper, or more to taste
8 tablespoons (1 stick) unsalted butter
Cottage cheese, for serving (optional)

1. Break the matzos into 1½- to 2-inch squares. Place the matzos in a large heatproof bowl, preferably with a handle so draining will be easy.

2. Pour the boiling water over the matzos, then drain them immediately and very thoroughly in a sieve or colander. Do not stir the matzo pieces or let them stand. They should be only slightly moistened, not soggy, so they will absorb the egg but not be mushy.

3. Return them to the bowl and add the eggs, salt, and pepper. Matzos have a bland flavor, so plenty of salt and pepper will be needed. Toss the matzos lightly with a fork until all of the pieces are well coated with egg and the seasonings are distributed evenly.

4. Heat the butter in a heavy 10- to 12-inch skillet, preferably cast iron, over medium heat until hot and bubbling but not brown. Add the matzo mixture to the skillet and cook until the bottom begins to brown, about 8 to 10 minutes. Using a spatula, turn pieces of the matzo brei over (it is not necessary to keep it in a pancake shape).

5. Keep turning the matzo brei until all sides are a light golden brown, about 10 minutes. A jumble of golden brown and slightly golden and tender pieces is the ideal. Taste for seasoning once as the matzo brei cooks, adding more salt and pepper as needed. Serve the matzo brei on a heated platter or individual plates, with cottage cheese on the side, if you like.

WHERE: *In New York,* Barney Greengrass, tel 212-724-4707, barneygreengrass.com; *in Atlanta,* Goldberg's at multiple locations, goldbergbagel .com; *in Boynton Beach, FL,* Flakowitz, tel 561-742-4144, flakowitzofboynton.com; *in Chicago,* Manny's, tel 312-939-2855, mannysdeli.com; *in Los Angeles,* Factor's Famous Deli, tel 310-278-9175, factorsdeli.com; *in San Francisco,* Wise Sons Deli, tel 415-787-3354; *in San Francisco and San Rafael, CA,* Miller's East Coast Deli, millerseastcoastdeli.com; *in Bellevue, WA,* Goldbergs' Famous Delicatessen, tel 425-641-6622, goldbergsdeli.com. **MAIL ORDER:** streits matzos.elsstore.com. **FURTHER INFORMATION AND ADDITIONAL RECIPES:** *The New York Times Passover Cookbook* by Linda Amster (2010); *Arthur Schwartz's Jewish Home Cooking* by Arthur Schwartz (2008); cookstr.com (search classic matzo brei); kosherfood.about.com (search matzo brei).

RX FOR A WINTER NIGHT

Mushroom and Barley Soup

Jewish (Askenazic), Polish, Russian

Dotted with cheery bits of carrots, feathery dill, and tender chunks of boiled beef, a thick and silky mushroom and barley soup is a restorative winter classic. Fresh mushrooms sometimes make an appearance, but the important fungi here are the powerfully fragrant and flavored dried *schwammen,* or *borovik* (page 405), the heady ceps found in Poland and Russia (where this soup is known as *krupnik*). Just two or three can flavor a large pot of a soup that includes pearled (polished) barley and iron-rich root vegetables such as parsnips, the parsley root *petrouchka,* and celery root, along with onions, leeks, celery with its leaves, a clove or two of unpeeled garlic, and fresh dill. Chunks of first-cut beef flanken provide sustenance and an additional depth of flavor. Although the beef is most succulent served right in the broth, large pieces are sometimes served as a separate main course, ringed with bits of the cooked vegetables and mantled with beet-reddened or ivory-white horseradish.

Because barley expands and thickens quickly, it should not be added until about halfway through cooking. Pearled barley, its outer husk polished off, is the kind to use—it is subtler and less absorbent than the whole, unpolished barley, which can become overpowering in this soup.

WHERE: *In New York,* 2nd Ave Deli at two locations, 2ndavedeli.com; Sammy's Roumanian Steakhouse, tel 212-763-0330, sammysromanian .com; *in Chicago,* Manny's, tel 312-939-2855, mannysdeli.com; *in Los Angeles,* Nate 'n Al, tel 310-274-0101, natenal.com; *in Los Angeles and Miami,* Jerry's Famous Deli at multiple locations, jerrysfamousdeli.com. **MAIL ORDER:** For dried mushrooms, igourmet.com (search dried porcini); for pearled barley, amazon.com). **FURTHER INFORMATION AND RECIPES:** *The 2nd Ave Deli Cookbook* by Sharon Lebewohl and Rena Bulkin (1999); *From My Mother's Kitchen* by Mimi Sheraton (1979); *The Book of Jewish Food* by Claudia Roden (1996). **TIP:** Because barley tends to absorb liquid when leftover soup is reheated, it may be advisable to add some broth.

THE DARK SEED

Nigella Sativa

N igella sativa has a mysterious sound to its name, and the taste of this rare and intriguing seasoning does not disappoint. The tiny, granular, jet black seeds of a plant in the Ranunculaceae family appear in foods of many ethnic origins, lending their snappy, bitter, licorice-and-oregano flavor to braided challah or to the long, flat, scored, Afghani, Mughlai, and Peshawari bread naan. They're found on Turkish *çörek* (black) buns and bring smoky subtlety to Persian and Mediterranean yogurt sauces and salads.

Finely ground, they play a role in the fragrant Indian spice mixture *panch phoran,* a heady blend that also includes mustard, fenugreek, cumin, and fennel seeds.

Often mistaken for onion seed, black caraway, or black cumin, these brittle and exotic seeds always seem to come as a surprise. They are rarely referred to, even in cookbooks native to the lands in which they are used, and in most languages are named for their ebony hue. Their botanical name, *Nigella,* comes from the Latin *niger;* in Russian and Yiddish they are *chornaya* or *chornushka,* and in Hindi they are *kalonji* or *kalaunji,* all signifying their color.

The shiny seeds have a long history going back to the Old Testament, in which they are referred to as *ketash,* and they were reportedly found in the tomb of Egypt's King Tutankhamen. Once believed to be a cure for many respiratory, digestive, and circulatory ailments and to offer protection against cancer and inflammation of the joints, they are even touted in an old Arabic saying as remedies for all diseases but death.

Modern chefs looking to outdo one another with exotic seasonings could search out these sprightly palate-teasers and use them in unexpected ways. Crushing some into ice cream might be a news-making start.

MAIL ORDER: The Spice House, thespicehouse .com; Penzey's Spices, tel

800-741-7787, penzeys.com. **Further informa-tion and recipes:** *Inside the Jewish Bakery* by Stanley Ginsberg and Norman Berg (2011); *The Artisan Jewish Deli at Home* by Nick Zukin and Michael Zusman (2013); ejozi.co.za (search

nigella). **Tip:** As with all seeds rich in oil, rancidity becomes a danger when the seeds grow stale. If possible, a nibble before purchasing is a good idea, as is checking to see that the seeds look shiny-bright and free of any dusty film.

A SWEET FOR A VERY SPECIAL WEEK

Noant

Jewish (Ashkenazic)

With so many dietary restrictions in place during the Passover week—injunctions against flour, leavening, corn-based products, and more—you might think an observant Jew with a sweet tooth would experience withdrawal. But

ingenuity thrives on constraint, and in this case has given us the gift of *noant*, a chewy Passover indulgence based on dark honey and walnuts enlivened by lemon juice, spicy ginger, sugar, and tangy grated orange rind.

Allowed to set for several hours, the mixture becomes a gloriously chewy, tooth-pulling taffy.

Noant

Makes about 4 dozen candies

1 cup honey, preferably dark and unfiltered
2 cups sugar
1 tablespoon freshly squeezed lemon juice
½ teaspoon ground ginger
Grated rind of ½ medium-size orange
1½ cups coarsely chopped walnuts

1. Have on hand a platter or cutting board that is 12 to 14 inches long and 6 inches wide. When the candy is poured onto a board it is easier to cut, but candy poured onto a platter with a small rim becomes a little thicker.

2. Combine the honey, sugar, lemon juice, and ginger in a heavy, 2-quart saucepan and stir very gently until blended. Place the pan over low

heat and cook, stirring constantly until the sugar completely dissolves, about 8 minutes. Increase the heat to medium-low and cook the honey mixture, stirring frequently, until it turns a deep golden brown and forms a soft ball when a few drops are added to a little ice-cold water, about 15 minutes. Be careful that the honey mixture does not boil up and overflow the pan. Remove the pan from the heat immediately and stir in the orange rind and walnuts. Let the honey mixture cool slightly, about 5 minutes.

3. Meanwhile wet the cutting board or platter with cold water. Pour the honey mixture onto the board or platter. Using a wetted spatula, spread the honey mixture evenly on the cutting board or platter. Let it harden to a stiff, taffy-like consistency, 2 to 3 hours. Cut the candy into 1-inch squares to serve. Stored well wrapped in plastic or wax paper in an airtight metal container, the candy will keep for several weeks.

Mail order: For unfiltered honey, billsbees .com; naturenates.com; carusohoney.com. **Tip:** Do not make noant on a rainy or very humid day, as it will not harden.

┤||||||||||||||||||||||||||├

Passover Seder: Persian Version

Jewish (Mizrachic)

From the menu, you'd hardly know it was a seder—assuming, of course, that you're used to the Ashkenazic version of the meal. With its exotic spicing, verdant, leafy vegetables, and colorfully herbaceous sauces and stews, the Persian (Iranian) seder that is traditional for the eastern or Mizrachic Jews is a connoisseur's delight all the way.

Charoset, the fruity spread that symbolizes the mortar used by the Jewish slaves who were builders in Egypt (see page 432), is represented in this culture by a lusciously dark, sweet jam. A blend of hazelnuts, almonds, raisins, dates, apples, and jewel-like pomegranate seeds sparked with a little wine vinegar and cinnamon, it is traditionally concocted by the father of the house, its formula presumably a well-kept secret.

Being a spring holiday, Passover requires new green herbs and vegetables. And in this, the subtly soft stew *choresh qormeh sabzi* fits the bill, its cuts of tender beef sparked by a combination of parsley, spinach, green onions, fresh dill, and cilantro, with a spurt of lemon juice for freshness. So too does the meatless *kookoo sabzi*, a quichelike spinach and green herb pie fragrant with leeks and scallions. For good measure, there might also be *choresh bademjon*, a kind of goulash of fork-tender beef chunks swathed in satiny simmered-down eggplant, onions, and tomatoes, served with *chelo*, a rice pilaf. (While the Ashkenazic Jews must avoid rice during Passover, it is permitted to Mizrachic Jews.)

Pale-golden and crisp on the outside and meltingly chewy within, dessert macaroons are as common in Iranian Jewish food as they are to all Jews during this holiday, primarily because they require no flour or leavening, depending only on beaten egg whites to provide lightness to their mixture of shredded coconut or ground almonds and sugar.

WHERE: *In Los Angeles,* Shaherzad, tel 310-470-3242, shaherzadrestaurant.com; *in New York,* Parmys Persian Fusion, tel 212-335-0207, parmyspersianfusion.com; *in New York and environs,* Colbeh at multiple locations, colbeh .com; Ravagh Persian Grill at multiple locations, ravaghpersiangrill.com. **FURTHER INFORMATION AND RECIPES:** nytimes.com (search two passover feasts in unusual styles).

┤||||||||||||||||||||||||||├

Passover Seder: Sephardic Edition

Jewish (Sephardic)

So fragrant and tantalizingly exotic are the dishes of the Sephardic seder that they, too, are hardly recognizable as related to their Ashkenazic counterparts, comforting dishes beloved more for their coziness than for the boldness of their flavors. *Sephard* is the Hebrew name for Spain, and the term came to identify the Jews who settled in countries all around the Mediterranean after being expelled from Spain in 1492. As with all other Jews of the Diaspora, their food took on the characteristics of those countries into which they dispersed, the recipes altered to satisfy kosher laws.

The Sephardic seder, a meal rich in ritual

Delicious cases in point are the seder dishes that reflect the influences of Greece and Turkey, starting with the conservelike *charoset* spread, which combines ingredients such as hazelnuts, almonds, and walnuts, raisins, dates, apples, orange juice, and pomegranate seeds, sparked with a little wine vinegar and cinnamon, and at times wine or brandy (see page

432). There is the fish course, either a delicately beautiful coral-and-ruby combination of fresh, supple spring salmon and an astringently tart sauce of spring rhubarb and tomatoes or perhaps a version of sweet and sour salmon (see page 470). *Frittata de espinaca* is a savory spinach pudding bound with eggs and crushed, soaked matzos, equally delightful hot or cold. If the pudding is to be served at a dairy meal, it may benefit from the added creaminess of cottage cheese, which is stirred into the mix before it is baked.

Keftes de prasa, golden, crisp croquettes of matzo meal, eggs, and chopped leeks, provide crunch and another reminder of verdant springtime. *Megina* is an ingenious and diverting riff on lasagna, with moistened sheets of matzo substituting for pasta: A fluffy beef sauce seasoned with onion, parsley, Passover-approved dried thyme, and oregano or cinnamon is layered between the matzos and baked for a soothingly soft yet sustaining result.

Finally, a dessert confection very close to the Ashkenazic nut and honey bon-bons called *noant* (see page 452) is *ahashoo,* a dentistry-defying brittle of walnuts, honey, cinnamon, and ginger.

FURTHER INFORMATION AND RECIPES: *The Book of Jewish Food* by Claudia Roden (1996); *The Sephardic Kitchen* by Rabbi Robert Sternberg (1996); *The New York Times Passover Cookbook* edited by Linda Amster (2010); nytimes.com (search special food of the sephardim).

––––––––––|||||||||||||||||||||||||||||||||||––––––––––

RISING TO THE OCCASION

Passover Sponge Cake

Jewish

A fragrant, light, and satisfying cake created out of matzo-based cake meal? Difficult to believe, but true. The eight days of Passover, when both leavening and ordinary wheat flour are prohibited and only the carefully grown and "watched" flour used for matzos is permitted, have in this case fostered an excellent innovation. That matzo-based cake meal, almost as fine as flour, joins potato starch to become the enabler in a puffy, sunny cake. Redolent of orange and lemon zests and flecked with ground walnuts, it uses beaten egg whites as its sole leavening.

Believed to have come from the English tea-and-cake tradition, sponge cakes were popularized in the eighteenth century. (Jane Austen referred to one in a letter she wrote in 1808.) Today, Jewish bakers pride themselves on making theirs light as air and tall as can be, and on achieving a thinly layered and feathery soufflé-like texture—but so popular and beloved has this sponge cake become that it is made by home bakers the year round. Sliced horizontally into two layers, it becomes a shortcake of sorts, a delicious vehicle for whipped cream and berries or bananas.

Passover Sponge Cake

Makes 8 to 10 servings

12 extra-large eggs, separated
1½ cups sugar
Grated zest of 1 large lemon
Grated zest of 1 large orange
¼ cup orange juice
Pinch of salt
1 cup cake meal (see Note)
¼ cup potato starch
½ cup finely ground walnuts

1. Preheat the oven to 325°F.

2. Using a large, clean piece of brown wrapping paper or parchment, cut a circle to fit the bottom of an 11- or 12-inch springform pan. Then cut a band to fit around the sides. This can be about ½ inch deeper than the pan. Run both pieces of cut paper under cold water very quickly, slightly dampening both sides. Place the circle on the bottom, then fit the band around the inner sides. Set aside.

3. Beat the egg yolks with 1 cup sugar in a medium bowl until they are thick, almost white, and form a ribbon when a little of the mixture is allowed to drip from a spoon, about 7 to 8 minutes. Stir in the grated zests and orange juice.

4. Beat the egg whites with a pinch of salt in a large bowl. As the whites begin to thicken, gradually beat in the remaining ½ cup sugar. The whites should stand in stiff, glossy peaks.

5. Sprinkle the cake meal, potato starch, and ground nuts over the whites. Add the yolk mixture and fold all together gently but thoroughly with a rubber spatula. No egg whites should be showing. Turn the mixture into the pan.

6. Bake until a tester inserted in the center of the cake comes out clean, and the top of the cake, when pressed with your fingertip, springs back to shape, 1 to 1¼ hours.

7. Let the cake cool in the pan. After about 2 hours, or just before serving, remove the sides of the springform and peel off the paper. If you are using only part of the cake, remove the paper only from the section to be cut, as the rest of the cake will keep better with the paper on it. Wrapped in wax paper or parchment and stored in the refrigerator, leftover sponge cake can be kept in good condition for 7 to 10 days, and can even be wrapped in foil and frozen for up to 3 months.

Note: Cake meal should not be confused with matzo meal. Both are made of crushed matzos; however, cake meal is fine and floury, while matzo meal is coarser and more like fine cracker crumbs. They are not interchangeable.

RETAIL AND MAIL ORDER: All of the following sell sponge cake only at Passover: *In New York,* Eli Zabar, tel 866-354-3547, elizabar.com; *in Chicago,* Manny's, tel 312-939-2855, mannysdeli .com; *in Ann Arbor, MI,* Zingerman's Bakehouse, tel 888-636-8162, zingermansbakehouse.com. **MAIL ORDER:** For springform pan, surlatable.com (search platinum professional springform pan); amazon.com (search cuisinart nonstick springform pan). **FURTHER INFORMATION AND ADDITIONAL RECIPES:** *From My Mother's Kitchen* by Mimi Sheraton (1979); *Inside the Jewish Bakery* by Stanley Ginsberg and Norman Berg (2011); *Cooking Jewish* by Judy Bart Kancigor (2007); cookstr.com (search passover sponge cake); epicurious.com (search passover spongecake).

‖‖‖‖‖‖‖‖‖‖‖‖‖‖‖‖‖‖‖‖‖‖‖‖‖‖‖‖

"IF YOU WANT LEAN, ORDER TURKEY . . ."
—THE LATE LEO STEINER, GUIDING SPIRIT OF NEW YORK'S CARNEGIE DELI

Pastrami and Corned Beef

Jewish

The twin meats of the classic New York Jewish deli, corned beef and pastrami are lushly moist, pungently pickled treats that begin their lives as similar cuts of meat—first-cut brisket being ideal for corned beef while beef "plate" is better for pastrami. Both are pickled in brine with spices like bay leaves, coriander, hot chile flakes, black pepper, and garlic. After the pickling, pastrami is coated with crushed peppercorns and smoked—a technique said to have been brought over by Jews from Romania—becoming a drier, deep red meat. Both are steam cooked and served hot.

The meats are available throughout the U.S., but they rarely achieve authentic flavor and texture outside New York City. Good corned beef and pastrami will be firm but laced with enough fat for juiciness (lean pastrami and corned beef are oxymorons), and graced with the right amount of smoke, salt, pepper, and pickling spices.

Although the method is virtually extinct, the best process for making these seductive slabs of meat is a dry cure in which they are layered with salt and spices until the pickling causes juices to run out. Because time is money, the modern method has been sped up with variations like soaking or injecting the beef with brine.

For the best sandwiches, the meat should be hot, richly etched with fat, and thinly hand sliced before it is heaped in mountainous folds between caraway-flecked slices of Jewish sour rye bread. Cheap yellow deli mustard is the condiment of choice, along with kosher-style pickles, pickled green tomatoes, and cold, uncooked sauerkraut—hold the coleslaw, please. While the meats are usually served as sandwiches, both are also delicious in pancake omelets.

Quaff it all down with beer, celery tonic, or hot tea with sugar and lemon. In New York, the highest-quality pastrami and corned beef can still be found at Pastrami Queen, where they will hand slice (but only if you ask). At Katz's, on the Lower East Side, and at Langer's, in downtown Los Angeles, hand slicing happens by default.

WHERE: *In New York,* Pastrami Queen, tel 212-734-1500, pastramiqueen.com; Katz's Delicatessen, tel 212-254-2246, katzsdelicatessen.com; *in Atlanta,* The General Muir, tel 678-927-9131, thegeneralmuir.com; *in Miami,* Goldstein's Prime, tel 305-865-4981, goldsteinsprime.com; *in Chicago,* Manny's, tel 312-939-2855, mannysdeli.com; *in Los Angeles,* Art's Delicatessen, tel 818-762-1221, artsdeli.com; Langer's, tel 213-483-8050, langersdeli.com; *in San Francisco,* Wise Sons Deli, tel 415-787-3354, wisesonsdeli.com; *in Houston,* Kenny & Ziggy's, tel 713-871-8883, kennyandziggys.com. **FURTHER INFORMATION AND RECIPE:** *From My Mother's Kitchen* by Mimi Sheraton (1979).

Juicy pastrami piled high on seeded rye bread

Pickled Green Peppers

Jewish

How can a humble, inexpensive, ubiquitous, and bland green bell pepper (*Capsicum annuum*) attain gastronomic glory? Judging by the enduring popularity of this pungent, head-clearing, garlicky pickle, an icon of the Jewish delicatessen menu, it doesn't take much at all.

The flavor injection begins with either grilling the whole green peppers over an open flame or oven-roasting them until they blister. For best flavor, they should not be peeled (although they often are). Split open and seeded, they are packed in jars and doused with astringent white vinegar and a flock of unpeeled, crushed cloves of garlic. The pickling makes the most of the green pepper's naturally sweet and grassy flavor, creating a refreshing and incredibly garlicky garnish that complements steak in particular, but also any grilled meat or fowl, or simply a slice of Jewish rye bread.

Along with pickled cucumbers (see page 444), green tomatoes, and sauerkraut (see page 308), the peppers are staples throughout eastern Europe, where long winters have historically meant few fresh vegetables. The tradition was carried on in the New World by eastern European peddlers in neighborhoods like the Lower East Side of Manhattan, where the pickled vegetables were produced in neighborhood tenements and sold from pushcarts. A lot has changed on New York's Lower East Side since the pushcart pickle days, but a few streetside purveyors still hold their ground—and a renaissance in pickling among so-called "artisanal" sorts has created a renewed appreciation for briny vegetables of all kinds.

WHERE: *In New York,* Sammy's Roumanian Steakhouse, tel 212-673-0330, sammysroumanian.com; *in Los Angeles,* Langer's Delicatessen, tel 213-483-8050, langersdeli.com. **FURTHER INFORMATION AND RECIPES:** *Arthur Schwartz's Jewish Home Cooking* by Arthur Schwartz (2008); *From My Mother's Kitchen* by Mimi Sheraton (1979).

Pickled Herring

Jewish (Ashkenazic)

Of all the ways Jews and eastern Europeans like their herring—raw, smoked, fried, baked, or in salads—the pickled version may reach supreme heights. Subtly spiced by a pickling mix that includes bay leaves, peppercorns, coriander, mustard seed, and dried red chile peppers, this lightly vinegared, onion-crunched fish is a coolly satisfying treat, especially served with dark pumpernickel or sour rye bread.

Almost always part of the post Yom Kippur fast—a light, dairy-related meal—pickled herring is also considered a good omen for Rosh Hashanah. (As it is in many cultures, herring is a lucky harbinger for the new year.)

Although some swear by the so-called schmaltz or fatty herring as the starting point for pickling, the leaner, firmer salt herring are far more receptive to the flavors and aromas of a curing brine. In any case, the fish should be gutted and soaked whole for twenty-four hours in running cold water—or, if a constant trickle of water is not possible, in frequent changes of cold water—as a first step. After soaking, it should be cut into 1- to 2-inch slices, with skin and bones intact to keep the meat firm and juicy. Fillets may be easier to eat, but they offer blander rewards.

It's a good idea to beat the *A barrel-pickled delicacy* miltz, or spleen, of the fish into the sauce for a tantalizing, sea-bright creaminess that remains pareve, or dietarily neutral. Sour cream should be beaten in just before serving, or not at all—adding sour cream to a whole batch of pickled herring is a mistake on two counts: Sturdy leftovers may become sour, and for those observing kashruth, cream renders the herring inedible before a meat meal.

WHERE: *In New York,* Freds at Barneys, tel 212-833-2200, barneys.com; Barney Greengrass, tel 212-724-4707, barneygreengrass.com; *in Houston,* Kenny & Ziggy's New York Delicatessen, tel 713-871-8883, kennyandziggys.com; *in Los Angeles,* Langer's Deli, tel 213-483-8050, langers deli.com; Art's Delicatessen, tel 818-762-1221, artsdeli.com; Canters Deli, tel 323-651-2030, cantersdeli.com; *in Los Angeles and Miami,* Jerry's Famous Deli at multiple locations, jerrysfamousdeli.com. **RETAIL AND MAIL ORDER:** *In New York,* Zabar's, tel 800-697-6301, zabars.com; Russ & Daughters, tel 212-475-4880, russanddaugh ters.com. **FURTHER INFORMATION AND RECIPES:** *The Book of Jewish Food* by Claudia Roden (1996); *The New York Times Jewish Cookbook* edited by Linda Amster (2003); *The Artisan Jewish Deli at Home* by Nick Zukin and Michael Zusman (2013); epicurious .com (search pickling your own herring).

SWEET AND KOSHER "PIZZA"

Pizza Ebraica

Jewish, Italian

In an obscurely marked shop on a corner of Via del Portico d'Ottavia, the main stem of Rome's old Jewish ghetto, in a building replete with the exquisitely aged, faded apricot-colored walls so typical of that city, lies Pasticceria "Boccione"

Limentani—home of the delectably chewy yet requisitely crisp and firm sweet bread that is somewhat misleadingly known as *pizza ebraica,* or Hebrew pizza.

Also known as pizza Romana, the pizza is actually a complex coffee cake with jewel-like studs of raisins, almonds, pignoli nuts, and candied fruits. A specialty of the Limentani family for about two hundred years, Hebrew pizza is believed to have been brought to Italy by Jews who were expelled from Spain; before working their way to northern Italy, they spent some time in Moroccan-influenced Sicily, and anyone familiar with the richly sticky confections much loved by Arabs will perceive a melding of influences herein.

With its gentle whiffs of cinnamon and sweet wine, pizza ebraica is particularly good with a glass of red wine, or the strong, astringent Italian brandy that is grappa. It is almost as satisfying when eaten with a cup of coffee or tea.

Now run by Graziella Limentani with her three granddaughters, the bakery, also known as Il Forno del Ghetto (the oven of the Ghetto), draws a loyal clientele for other delectables as well. There's the *torta de ricotta e visciole,* a creamy, gentle cheesecake whose sweetness is accented by chunks of winey sour cherries. Another house favorite is the *mezzaluna,* a half-moon-shaped, almond-paste biscuit made only for Yom Kippur, the autumn High Holiday of atonement. Unique to this last of the Jewish ghetto bakeries is *pasticcioli dura,* a very firm, weighty bread rich with honey and crunchy with toasted almonds. It, too, is the right foil for a cup of coffee or a glass of red wine or grappa.

All baking at this *pasticceria* is strictly kosher, and the Limentani family is Sabbath observant (shomer shabbat)—meaning the shop is closed from Friday afternoon to Sunday morning and on all Jewish holidays.

WHERE: *In Rome,* Pasticceria "Boccione" Limentani (Il Forno del Ghetto Boccione), tel 39/6-687-8637. **FURTHER INFORMATION AND RECIPES:** *Cucina Ebraica* by Joyce Goldstein (1998); *The Classic Cuisine of the Italian Jews II* by Edda Servi Machlin (1992); saveur.com (search pizza boccione).

FEET FIRST

P'tcha

Jellied Calf's Foot

Jewish (Ashkenazic)

There's no such thing as a lukewarm reaction to the sticky, meaty, and garlic-scented aspic known as *p'tcha,* or *petchah.* Usually served cold and gelled, the kosher riff on an eastern European pig's-foot favorite is also

sometimes served hot—at which point its heady fragrance of garlic and bones may send p'tcha haters right out of the room. But to its fans, this true Jewish soul food is a deeply satisfying, homey treat. When old-timey kosher butchers abounded, p'tcha could readily be purchased, but today it is nearly impossible to find outside of dedicated and time-honored Jewish enclaves.

A very old-fashioned staple of the Ashkenazic Jewish table, thought to have come to eastern Europe by way of the Ottoman Empire (incidentally, both the Turks and the Greeks have similar dishes made with lamb's feet), p'tcha is humble stuff, made from the cheapest cut of meat: a cleaned and split calf's foot boiled in water for hours, with lots of salt and pepper, until the meat falls from the bone. As it cooks, it emits a pungent aroma, awful to some and merely authentic to others.

In its most elegant and classic preparation, the foot is removed from the liquid and the meltingly tender meat is picked clean from the bones, then chopped and returned to the liquid along with lots of fresh, thinly sliced garlic. Only then is the entire concoction allowed to congeal overnight, so that the meat sets in its own aspic. Sometimes cut into squares like a kind of pâté, the aspic may be garnished with chopped hard-cooked egg and served with mustard. The delicate flavor of the meat and aspic hints at none of the acrid aroma let off during cooking, and the garlic and pepper add pungent interest.

Another version calls for larger pieces of meat on the bone, serving them hot in a garlicky paprika sauce. Any leftovers are then prepared according to the usual method and served again the next day, cold and complete with their congealed gel.

WHERE: *In New York,* Sammy's Roumanian Steakhouse, tel 212-673-0330, sammysroumanian .com; *in Los Angeles,* Simon's La Glatt, tel 323-658-7730. **FURTHER INFORMATION AND RECIPES:** *From My Mother's Kitchen* by Mimi Sheraton (1979); *Jewish Cooking in America* by Joan Nathan (1994); *Encyclopedia of Jewish Food* by Gil Marks (2010); food.com (search petchah). **TIP:** P'tcha has its own community fan page on Facebook, so you can "like" it even if you actually don't.

THE KINDEST KOSHER CUT

Romanian Tenderloin

Jewish

Also known as skirt steak, the lusciously juicy tenderloin cut is popular in many of the world's cuisines, as likely to be found on a well-dressed French plate as on a Mexican fajita platter. Because it comes from the steer's forequarters

and is thus considered kosher (meat from the hindquarters is not), the flavorful and relatively economical cut has also become a staple of Jewish cuisine.

Basically a belt of meat cut from around the animal's middle, tenderloin is narrow and flat, and is only really good served rare—longer cooking renders it tough and dry. Especially associated with Jews of Romanian origin, the cut is popular throughout that country, where the grilling of meat is a special talent. The iconic mantle of mashed, lightly browned garlic that accompanies Romanian-style tenderloin in kosher-style steak restaurants may shock faint palates, but the garlic's mellow heat mingles delectably with the bloody, salt-accented juices of the meat. An

accompaniment of cottage-fried potato slices or crisp French fries completes the meal, with perhaps a pickled green tomato or two adding a cool but pungent accent.

WHERE: *In New York,* Sammy's Roumanian Steakhouse, tel 212-673-0330, sammysroumanian .com; *in Houston,* Kenny & Ziggy's, tel 713-871-8883, kennyandziggys.com; *in Los Angeles,* Langer's Delicatessen, tel 213-483-8050, langers deli.com. **FURTHER INFORMATION AND RECIPES:** *Ten: All the Foods We Love and Ten Perfect Recipes for Each* by Sheila Lukins (2008); *The Mile End Cookbook* by Noah Bernamoff and Rae Bernamoff (2012); *From My Mother's Kitchen* by Mimi Sheraton (1979); food.com (search romanian skirt steak). **SEE ALSO:** Hanger Steak, Flank Steak, and Skirt Steak, page 578.

Sable

Jewish

Though often dubbed "poor man's sturgeon," satiny smoke- and salt-cured sablefish is considered far superior by many connoisseurs of the genre. The sablefish (*Anoplopoma fimbria*) is a long, slender swimmer, with black skin and the silky, oily, and firm pearly-white flesh to which it owes its success. A particularly moist and meaty fish, it can be handled and cooked in myriad ways. But the fish is put to best use when cured in salt and sugar and then smoked over hardwood, with a finishing sprinkle of paprika for a burnished red glow.

Along with smoked salmon and pickled lox and sturgeon, sable is present at almost every function at which Jewish people gather to eat—it is a staple at bar mitzvahs, Yom Kippur fast-breaking, shiva buffets, and Jewish delis alike. It has been sold in New York City since the early twentieth century, but it's also treated as a delicacy in Japan, where it is cured in miso, sake, or green tea.

When buying sable, ask for a taste before choosing. Although sablefish is sometimes referred to as black cod, which it strongly resembles, they are not the same thing. Sable should be firm-fleshed yet silky, flaky but not falling apart, and sweet-salty but not overpoweringly so. It is an obvious choice as a substitute for smoked salmon on a bagel with cream cheese, but becomes far more elegant when served in slices, sprinkled with freshly ground pepper, with a wedge of lemon and a buttered slice of thin Westphalian-style pumpernickel.

DINE-IN, RETAIL, AND MAIL ORDER: *In New York,* Russ & Daughters, tel 212-475-4880, russanddaughters.com; Zabar's, tel 800-697-6301, zabars.com; Murray's Sturgeon Shop, tel 212-724-2650, murrayssturgeon.com; Barney Greengrass, tel 212-724-4707, barneygreengrass.com; *in Toronto,* Mendel's Creamery N' Appetizer, tel 416-597-1784, kensingtonmarket.to/mendels-creamery-n-appetizer.

Salami and Eggs

Jewish (Ashkenazic)

A staple of Ashkenazic Jewish home kitchens and delicatessens, this golden-brown pancake omelet set with garlic- and pepper-scented rounds of firmly chewy beef salami makes for a serious homestyle breakfast. If you gild it with dabs of cheap, brassy deli mustard and flesh it out with French fries and slices of caraway-flecked rye bread (a pickle couldn't hurt either), it suffices as a hearty meal for any time of day.

The key here is the salami itself, which, whether kosher or kosher-style, should be a gently firm beef sausage with heady bursts of garlic, pepper, and enough dots of white fat to render it lusciously chewable. You needn't look far to find the gold standard—Hebrew National's version, virtually ubiquitous, is it.

Further clarification: "Salami and eggs" does not mean slices of salami thrown in with fluffy scrambled eggs. In its proper preparation, Jewish grandmothers and grandfathers (the dish is considered a mom's-night-out specialty) cut tiny notches all around each salami slice so it will not buckle as it fries. Those slices are first browned in a little butter or, if the kitchen is kosher, in Mazola brand corn oil or margarine. Once some fat has rendered from the meat, the beaten, lightly salted eggs are poured over the sausage slices, their edges gingerly lifted to let the uncooked egg flow underneath. When the first side has turned golden brown, the pancake is flipped. The resulting concoction is a warm, salty, deeply satisfying delight.

WHERE: *In New York,* Katz's Delicatessen, tel 212-254-2246, katzsdelicatessen.com; 2nd Ave Deli, tel 212-689-9000, 2ndavedeli.com; *in Chicago,* Manny's, tel 312-939-2855; *in Houston,* Kenny & Ziggy's New York Delicatessen, tel 713-871-8883, kennyandziggys.com; *in Los Angeles,* Langer's Deli, tel 213-483-8050, langersdeli.com; *in San Francisco,* Wise Sons Deli, tel 415-787-3354; *in Toronto,* Caplansky's Deli, tel 416-500-3852, caplanskys.com. **FURTHER INFORMATION AND RECIPES:** *Is Salami and Eggs Better Than Sex?* by Alan King and Mimi Sheraton (1985); *Zingerman's Guide to Good Eating* by Ari Weinzweig (2003); kosherfood.about.com (search salami and eggs).

―――――――――――――||||||||||||||||||||||||||||||――――――――――――

FOR CELEBRATING OR JUST PLAIN SNACKING

Salted Chickpeas

Jewish

Called *arbes* in Yiddish and *nahit* in Hebrew, sunny little golden-brown chickpeas play important and delicious roles in several Jewish celebrations; as with all beans, they are seeds, and thus regarded as symbols of plenty

Hot, nourishing chickpeas as street food in Baghdad

and regeneration. Simply boiled, drained, and tossed with a good sting of salt and lots of black pepper—and in the Middle East, with aromatic zaps of cumin and paprika—chickpeas are ritual snacks in springtime Purim festivities, at welcoming Sabbaths for week-old babies, and even at the *bris milah,* the circumcision and naming ceremony for newborn boys.

The rest of the time, their nutty, satisfying flavor and chewy texture makes them delectable snacks rich in proteins, B-vitamins, and fiber, and as addictive as salted peanuts or popcorn. (And similarly sold on the streets of many Middle Eastern cities.)

The easiest preparation starts with canned, cooked chickpeas, rinsed in a sieve under running cold water to remove all traces of canning liquid and then drained on paper towels before being spiced and salted. A somewhat better, if more time-consuming, method is to soak and boil dried chickpeas. Served on plates as part of an appetizer course, the seasoned legumes profit from a very light drizzle of olive oil, although this step should be skipped if they are to be eaten out of hand. Especially nurturing when eaten slightly warm, they can also be served slightly chilled.

FURTHER INFORMATION AND RECIPES: *The Oxford Companion to Food* by Alan Davidson (2006); *The New York Times Jewish Cookbook* edited by Linda Amster (2003); myjewishlearning.com (search chickpeas for purim). **TIP:** The best brand of canned chickpeas is Goya. If you're using dried, look for Bob's Red Mill garbanzos.

THE SOUR PROMISE OF SPRING

Sorrel

Much like nettles and burdock, sorrel is a decidedly Old World, woodsy herb. A spinachlike, spring-blooming green member of the genus *Rumex*, it is known for its sunny sourness and delicate texture—qualities the French have embraced since the seventeenth century, when chefs relied on *oseille* to infuse the drippings of their meat roasts with a bright acidity. It was also known as a natural fit for shad, as the acid in the herb helps to dissolve the many fine bones of that freshwater river fish. "The shad reclines on its bed of sorrel like a beauty on the ottoman of her boudoir," wrote the French author Grimod de La Reynière in his *Almanach des Gourmands*, an annual essay collection he published between 1803 and 1812. Fortunately, both shad and sorrel become available in spring.

In England, sorrel was historically combined with vinegar and sugar to make a verdant mayonnaise used as a garnish for meat. Eastern Europeans, and most especially Jews, love their sorrel in the refreshingly sour cold soup, *schav*, sometimes dubbed "green borscht" (see page 464). Scandinavians forage for it in the wild and also pair it with fish, especially their native salmon.

When the wave of nouvelle cuisine from France hit American shores in the 1970s, newfound uses for sorrel came along with it. But the still somewhat underappreciated herb deserves more attention for its versatility. Beyond its uses in traditional meat and fish recipes, it's also a great all-purpose fresh herb. Shredded, its leaves make an outstanding garnish for many soups and sauces, and a few of its roughly torn leaves brighten up salads, roasted potatoes, and bean dishes to great effect.

MAIL ORDER: In spring and summer, Melissa's Produce, tel 800-588-0151, melissas.com; for seeds, richters.com; for planting information, growing taste.com/vegetables/sorrel.shtml. **FURTHER INFORMATION AND RECIPES:** *Simple French Food* by Richard Olney (1974); *From My Mother's Kitchen* by Mimi Sheraton (1979); *Vegetables from Amaranth to Zucchini* by Elizabeth Schneider (2001); cookstr.com (search sorrel soup; shad roe idone; baked shad fillets; slow-roasted salmon with spring herb sauce; herbed green mayonnaise). **TIP:** Like spinach, sorrel tends to be sandy and requires several gentle but thorough washings to be rid of grit; it is also best to trim off its stems along with some of the hairy filaments on its leaves.

—||||||||||||||||||||||||||||||||—

COLD SORREL SOUP FOR HOT DAYS

Schav

Jewish (Ashkenazic)

Lightly creamy and green, *schav* (pronounced shahv) is a chilly soup that will be instantly loved by some and perhaps only gradually embraced by others. Based on the long, slender spinachlike herb-vegetable we know as sour grass or sorrel, it is thickened with beaten egg yolk, its tingling sour edge mellowed by a few exquisitely aromatic Polish or Russian dried mushrooms. Those with a strong love of sour add a few drops of lemon juice or sour salt to the broth, while cooks with milder tastes opt for a pinch or two of sugar. A final glossing of sour cream just as the soup is served adds an extra luxurious touch, and garnishes of minced hard-cooked egg, cucumber, and scallions may be on hand for added interest. The verdant gazpacho is especially satisfying when eaten with dark, moist Russian or German pumpernickel—a combination that works as a refreshing lunch or light supper on a scorching midsummer day, when sorrel, botanically known as *Rumex acetosa,* is especially abundant.

MAIL ORDER: For sorrel, in spring and summer, Melissa's Produce, tel 800-588-0151, melissas.com. **FURTHER INFORMATION AND RECIPES:** *The New York Times Jewish Cookbook* edited by Linda Amster (2003); nytimes.com (search schav hodgson).

A chilled sour soup made with sorrel

—||||||||||||||||||||||||||||||||—

THE FAT OF THE LAND

Schmaltz

Rendered Poultry Fat

Jewish (Ashkenazic), German

How did this flavorful, richly emollient, and savory cooking fat get so awful a reputation? Several unfortunate circumstances may have been at play—overuse, an oftentimes poor preparation, and a dynamite amount of cholesterol. But the rendered (melted and clarified) poultry fat known in both German and Yiddish as schmaltz is considered an authentic, desirable ingredient throughout eastern Europe and in Alsace, where chicken, duck, and goose fats go into many pâtés and cassoulets. (An etymological aside: In German, *schmaltz* actually refers to any animal fat that has been rendered and clarified, including pork fat and even butter.)

If the recent pork belly trend is any indication (see page 763), surely there is room in this fat-conscious but all-too-apparently fat-loving world for an occasional spread of freshly made, solidified schmaltz on a piece of matzo or challah bread, sprinkled with kosher salt, as a time-honored nosh.

Certain conditions apply. The schmaltz must be fresh and properly refrigerated. It must contain salt and should never be made with onions or garlic, as it so often is when purchased ready-made, a common error that limits its use and adds a stale taste. As further inducement, making schmaltz at home results in the additional treat of crunchy cracklings (*gribenes* in Yiddish) that family members fight over and eat like salted peanuts. Any that survive the snackers' melee can be added to chopped chicken livers (page 437) or crumbled over potatoes, boiled or baked, or steamed kasha (page 442).

Schmaltz un Gribenes

Makes about ⅓ cup of schmaltz
plus 1 to 2 tablespoons of gribenes

2 cups diced chicken, duck, or goose fat and skin
¾ cup cold water
Salt (optional)

1. Place the diced skin and fat in a heavy-bottomed 1-quart saucepan, add the water, and let simmer very, very slowly over low heat. When all of the water has evaporated and pure yellow fat begins to collect in the pan, about 12 minutes, pour the fat off and set it aside. The fat should be a bright butter yellow without any tint of brown. Continue cooking the pieces of skin until they form crisp, brown cracklings. Transfer the cracklings to paper towels to drain.

2. You can use the cracklings in recipes that call for them or just sprinkle them with salt and eat them before someone else does. The schmaltz will keep tightly covered in the refrigerator for about 1 week. The cracklings should be used or eaten as soon as possible after they are made or they will become soggy.

TIP: Save bits of fat and skin until you have a cupful and then render it all together into a home-made schmaltz that is far superior to any purchased ready-made. Store scraps in the freezer, well wrapped in foil, but do not keep more than a month, as fat never freezes completely.

AN APPETIZER WITH STAYING POWER

Shvartze Retach mit Schmaltz

Black Radish and Onion Conserve

Jewish, Eastern European

Although a radish can shine when adorned with nothing more than a curl of fresh, sweet butter (see page 124), it also lends itself to this hefty, earthy appetizer: a lusciously fatty blend of vibrant black radish and sweet onion gentled with rendered chicken fat (see schmaltz, page 464) and sprightly with salt and black pepper.

Especially popular in Europe as a winter treat, it's a delectable spread on moist, dark pumpernickel or crisp matzo, or served as a garnish for chopped chicken livers. It starts with a muddy-looking, earth-dug black radish that is scrubbed and peeled of its tough, fibrous skin to reveal a snowy-white interior.

Black Radish and Onion Conserve

Makes about 2 cups

2 large black radishes
3 tablespoons kosher salt
1 small Spanish, Bermuda, or Vidalia onion
½ cup schmaltz, refrigerated
Black pepper

1. Scrub and peel the radishes. Grate the radishes on the coarse side of a box grater; you should have about 4 cups. Toss the radishes with the salt and place them, loosely covered, in the refrigerator for about 4 hours.
2. Transfer the radishes to a strainer and rinse them under very cold running water. Pick up handfuls of the radishes and squeeze out as much water as possible; you should have about 2 cups of compacted radishes. Peel and grate the

onion and toss it with the radishes, along with the schmaltz. Season with pepper to taste.

Although the mixture can be served fresh as a salad, it attains more character when allowed to age and ripen. Packed in a glass jar or ceramic crock and stored tightly covered in the refrigerator for four days, it achieves its fully ripened promise, becoming a heady mix that lets the strong of palate triumph over the weak.

The conserve can be refrigerated for weeks.

Mail order: For black radishes in December and January, Melissa's Produce, tel 800-588-0151, melissas.com.

The humble black radish becomes a tasty spread.

━━━━━━━━━━━━━━━━━━|||||||||||||||||||||||||||||||━━━━━━━━━━━━━━━━━

BEES NEED NOT APPLY

Silan

Date Honey

Jewish, Israeli, Middle Eastern

The bees may not have heard the buzz, but it turns out that they aren't the only source of highly prized honey. Among other mind-opening experiences, a visit to Neot Kedumim—the inspiring biblical landscape preserve near Tel Aviv's

Ben Gurion Airport—offers the chance to taste and buy *silan*. The velvety date "honey"—really a syrup—is either pressed directly from very ripe dates or extracted by cooking dates with water until a thick and viscous sauce is released.

Distinguished by a dark mahogany color and a smoky, earthy flavor, date honey is less elegantly nuanced than bee honey. Bees, of course, diversify their wares by flitting around to various deliciously scented blossoms, whereas dates simply grow. But date honey's heftier, almost molasses-like richness certainly has its merits, not least of which is staying power. In Deuteronomy 8:7–10, the abundance of the Holy Land is described by the presence of seven plant varieties: wheat, barley, vines, fig and olive trees, pomegranates, and honey. Bee honey is an animal by-product, so the Talmudic sages decreed that the honey in question was most likely derived from dates.

Wild bees did exist in the land of milk and honey, but none were cultivated until centuries later, making honey gathering a chancy endeavor; dates represented a far more reliable source. Although these days date honey is identified mostly with Israel, it is also favored in the Middle East and North Africa; in Libya it is known as *dibs*.

Rich in minerals, date honey is an especially delectable stand-in for maple syrup on pancakes, French toast, and waffles. It also begs to be used as an addition to barbecue sauce, for earthy flavor and a golden brown glaze, or as a subtle topping for yogurt and vanilla ice cream.

Mail order: israeliproducts.com, tel 877-289-4772 (search galil silan). **Further information**

Date syrup drizzled over a yogurt parfait

and recipes: *Nature in Our Biblical Heritage* by Nogah Hareuveni (1980); cookstr.com (search date honey morse). **Tip:** Date honey acts similarly to bee honey. It should be stored in a cool, dry place; if it solidifies, stand the jar in hot water to liquefy it.

———————————|||||||||||||||||||||||||||||||———————————

THE OTHER (OTHER) JEWISH FISH

Smoked Whitefish

Jewish

A freshwater cousin of salmon (of the genus *Coregonus*), whitefish is a cold-water-loving swimmer with a silvery-greenish skin and a meaty, snowy interior. Its gentle flavor is much loved in northern and eastern Europe, in whose many

lakes it thrives, and where the need for food that keeps through long winters gave birth to the ancient techniques of salt-curing and then cold-smoking fish.

Not really cooked but rather infused with long, slow-burning wood flavor accumulated at a low temperature over many hours, the fish

emerges with an incredibly dewy and tender flesh and a sophisticatedly smoky patina. Whitefish prepared this way is a favorite of Jews around the world, and is consumed at nearly any occasion they can find for eating—from bar mitzvah buffets to shiva spreads.

Interestingly, whitefish also swim in the

waters of the Upper Peninsula of Michigan, where they are equally beloved but are cooked differently. Caught in the waters of the Great Lakes (generally Lake Superior), the fish are hot-smoked, skin on, over a hardwood fire at a much higher temperature. The result is drier, smokier fish that, unlike its more elegant, cold-smoked counterpart, can take stronger condiments.

In their quest not to waste a speck, frugal cooks take leftover bits and crumbles of smoked whitefish and turn them into a seductively creamy salad, ingredients for which include lemon juice, finely diced fresh onion or celery (or both), minced dill, a hard-boiled egg, and either mayonnaise or sour cream, or a combination. It's an excellent topping on light toast or a paper-thin slice of dark pumpernickel, or as the filling for a bagel sandwich. When choosing smoked whitefish, remember that bigger really is better—a larger whitefish will have a higher proportion of edible fish to bones and skin. Choose a whole fish that is plump and fatty, or ask for a cut from a large fish if you'd like a smaller portion. Avoid any fish that has dry,

crackly skin. An excellent fishmonger will fillet the fish for you, removing the small bones but leaving the skin intact to prevent drying.

Where: *In Cambridge, MA,* S&S Restaurant, tel 617-354-0777, sandsrestaurant.com; *in Boynton Beach, FL,* Flakowitz, tel 561-742-4144, flakowitzofboynton.com; *in Miami and Los Angeles,* Jerry's Famous Deli at multiple locations, jerrysfamousdeli.com; *in Chicago,* NYC Bagel Deli at various locations, nycbd.com; *in Moran, MI,* Gustafson's Smoked Fish, tel 906-292-5424; *in Ellison Bay, WI,* Charlie's Smokehouse, tel 920-854-2972, charliessmokehouse.com; *in Houston,* Kenny & Ziggy's New York Delicatessen, tel 713-871-8883, kennyandziggys .com. **Dine-in, retail, and mail order:** *In New York,* Russ & Daughters, tel 212-475-4880, russ anddaughters.com; Zabar's, tel 212-496-1234, zabars.com. **Further information and recipes:** *Russ & Daughters* by Mark Russ Federman (2013); *Arthur Schwartz's Jewish Home Cooking* by Arthur Schwartz (2008); *The Artisan Jewish Deli at Home* by Nick Zukin and Michael Zusman (2013); saveur.com (search whitefish salad).

MAKING THE CASE FOR STUFFING

Stuffed Derma, or Kishke, or Helzel

Jewish

It is basically a form of sausage—a spicy, aromatic mix of chicken schmaltz (see page 464), flour, garlic, onion, and plenty of paprika stuffed into a natural casing such as steer intestines (for stuffed *derma,* also called *kishke*) or the long, thin,

tubular skin from a chicken or turkey neck (for *helzel,* from the German *hals,* for throat or neck). So much for the facts. This waste-not-want-not Jewish specialty is a fragrant and flavorful appetizer or delicatessen nosh. As a main course, in any form, it might be lightly poached, then roasted and set upon a bed of kasha, the golden-brown buckwheat groats best enhanced with sautéed mushrooms and onions.

True farm peasant food that uses otherwise wasted parts, derma, kishke, and helzel are the Jewish equivalents of Scottish haggis (see page 40) or German *saumagen.* Like those, they are heavy, heady, and rich, soul-satisfying and stomach-filling—a marvelous example of traditional stick-to-your-ribs-waist-and-hips food. A presence in ancient Jewish texts, kishke has been a staple of Jewish holidays for at least seven hundred years and counting. Even today, when such a dish is considered hopelessly outdated by many, there are Jews who believe that no *simcha* (party or festive occasion) is complete without it. Good stuffed derma is laborious to prepare. So many commercial delis and restaurants feature mass-produced convenience kishke so dry and dreary it might discourage even the most loyal mavens. Better to opt for those that are delicately homemade.

WHERE: *In New York,* Sammy's Roumanian Steakhouse, tel 212-673-0330, sammysromanian .com; *in Houston,* Kenny & Ziggy's New York Delicatessen, tel 713-871-8883, kennyandziggys .com; *in Los Angeles,* Langer's Deli, tel 213-483-8050, langersdeli.com; *in San Francisco and San Rafael, CA,* Miller's East Coast Deli, millerseastcoastdeli.com; *in Toronto,* Caplansky's, tel 416-500-3852, caplanskys.com. **FURTHER INFORMATION AND RECIPES:** *From My Mother's Kitchen* by Mimi Sheraton (1979); *Arthur Schwartz's Jewish Home Cooking* by Arthur Schwartz (2008); nytimes.com (search kishke recipe); joyofkosher.com.recipes/ kishka; cookeatshare.com (search stuffed helzel recipe); food.com (search stuffed kishka kosher).

"THERE ARE ONLY THREE THINGS IN THIS WORLD THAT GIVE YOU UNQUESTIONED LOYALTY: DOGS, DOUGHNUTS, AND MONEY."
—FROM THE PLAY *OTHER PEOPLE'S MONEY* BY JERRY STERNER

Sufganiyot
Jelly-filled Doughnuts

Jewish (Sephardic)

The Ashkenazic Jews have their potato latkes. For the Sephardic Jews of Mediterranean and Near Eastern roots, *sufganiyot* are sweets for celebrating the winter holiday of Hanukkah.

A *sufganiyah* is a sponge, and the plump and cheery, jelly-filled doughnuts are spongy indeed, fried (just like latkes) to golden-brown perfection in the hot vegetable oil that brings symbolic significance to these two holiday specialties—harkening back to the unexpected supply of olive oil that kept lamps lit and saved the Maccabees from annihilation at the hands of ancient enemies.

Sufganiyot are so popular in Israel that during the weeks leading up to the eight nights of Hanukkah, the city's largest commercial supplier bakes more than a quarter of a million a day. They're traditionally filled with apricot or raspberry jam, but modern bakeries stuff them with all sorts of fillings—among them the currently popular Latin-inspired *dulce de leche.*

WHERE: *In Israel,* Angel Bakeries at various locations, angel.org.il/branches_en.aspx; *in New York,* Breads Bakery, tel 212-633-2253; breads bakery.com; *in Los Angeles,* Eilat Bakery at two locations, eilatbakery.com; *in Lenox and Great Barrington, MA,* Haven Café, tel 413-637-8948, havencafebakery.com; *in Teaneck, NJ* (and by mail order), Butterflake Kosher Bakery of Teaneck, tel 201-836-3516, butterflake.com. **FURTHER INFORMATION AND RECIPES:** *Jewish Holiday Cookbook* by Joan Nathan (2004); *The Book of Jewish Food* by Claudia Roden (1996); epi curious.com (search hanukkah doughnuts). **SEE ALSO:** Berliner Pfannkuchen, page 279, Semlor, or Fastelavnsboller, page 374.

━━━━━━━━━━━━━━━━━━━━━━━━|||||||||||||||||||||||||||||━━━━━━━━━━━━━━━━━━

A HOLIDAY FISH DISH

Sweet-and-Sour Salmon

Jewish

Sweet-and-sour salmon is a homey thing, something a Jewish grandmother might make for a family dinner. Particularly delicious on hot summer days, its cool, tender cuts of rose-gold salmon profit from a gentle simmering in a lightly salted bath flavored with brown sugar, lemon juice, and perhaps a splash of white vinegar, onions, golden raisins, bay leaves, cracked dried ginger, and cloves. The onions supply a magical sweetness, and the cooking liquid becomes a marvelously thick, almost gel-like glaze that is at once tart, tangy, and sweet.

Typical of eastern Europe, where freshwater fish abound, the dish is especially prevalent on Jewish holidays, when cooking must be done in advance. Developed as a preservation technique before modern refrigeration, it echoes similar preparations used for carp and other freshwater fish that are also associated with the Sephardic Jews of Mediterranean countries—most notably Italy, where these dishes were said to have originated in the Jewish ghettos of Rome and Venice.

The strikingly similar Venetian specialty *pesce in saor* can be found on the menu at nearly any restaurant in that watery city where, as in Rome, it is sometimes served hot. It, too, is an ancient specialty that consists of fish first fried and then marinated, no doubt originally to preserve it, in a blend of vinegar and onions.

Where: For pesce in saor, *in Venice*, Da Fiore, tel 39/041-721-308, dafiore.net. **Further information and recipes:** *Cucina Ebraica* by Joyce Goldstein (2005); *From My Mother's Kitchen* by Mimi Sheraton (1979); *The Jewish Festival Cookbook* by Fannie Engle and Gertrude Blair (1988); *The Da Fiore Cookbook* by Damiano Martin (2003); nytimes.com (search almost aunt sandy's sweet and sour salmon).

━━━━━━━━━━━━━━━━━━━━━━|||||||||||||||||||||||||||||━━━━━━━━━━━━━━━━━━

GREAT BISCUITS FOR ASTRONAUTS

Tzibele Kichel and Mohn Kichel

Jewish (Ashkenazic)

Homely, rustic, and pale golden brown, the biscuits called *kichel* are redolent of both onions and poppy seeds. Which of their alternate names they are known by depends on the ingredient the baker chooses to emphasize— *tzibele kichel* for the onion devotees and *mohn kichel* for poppy seed lovers.

Based on yeast dough mixed with poppy seeds and grated onions and allowed to rise outdoors or in a very airy corner overnight so the onion fumes mellow, the biscuits are rolled out and cut into either rounds or diamond shapes before they are baked into a jaw-exercising sort of hardtack. Completely cooled and stored in airtight metal containers, the kichel keep for many weeks, their wonderful flavors enhanced by a good measure of salt and fresh peanut oil and continuing to ripen. These savory nibbles are especially good with drinks such as beer, whiskey, or young red wine; go well with cheeses such as Swiss, Cheddar, or muenster; and are also irresistible simply as noshes by themselves.

Mohn Kichel

Makes about 50 kichel

2 envelopes active dry yeast
Pinch of sugar
3½ cups flour, or more as needed
3 extra-large eggs, lightly beaten
½ pound very fresh poppy seeds
* (about 1½ cups)*
2½ tablespoons salt
1½ teaspoons finely ground black pepper
5 very large or 7 medium-size onions,
* coarsely grated*
¾ cup peanut oil, plus oil for the
* mixing bowl and baking sheets*

1. Sprinkle the yeast into ½ cup of warm water and add a pinch of sugar. Let stand until the mixture begins to foam, 5 to 10 minutes.

2. Place the flour in a large, wide mixing bowl or mound it on a pastry board or wood countertop. Make a well in the center of the flour and add the yeast mixture, eggs, poppy seeds, 2½ tablespoons of salt, and the pepper, grated onions, and peanut oil. Using a fork, beat these ingredients together, then gradually stir the flour into the liquid mixture until thoroughly incorporated. If the dough is too stiff and crumbly, add a little more water. If it is too soft and sticky to knead, which is more likely to be the case, work more flour into the dough until it is light, smooth, and very elastic but not at all sticky.

3. Lightly flour a work surface, then knead the dough very well until it is shiny and blisters form on the surface, 15 to 20 minutes, depending upon the temperature in the room and the vigor with which you knead. You can also knead the

A homemade onion and poppy seed cracker in progress

dough in a stand mixer with a dough hook, but it will be better if it is kneaded by hand for at least 5 minutes at the end.

4. Lightly oil a mixing bowl. Place the dough in it, cover it with a towel, and place the bowl in a warm, draft-free corner to rise until it has doubled in bulk, 1½ to 2 hours.

5. Preheat the oven to 350°F. Brush 2 or 3 large baking sheets with peanut oil.

6. Punch the dough down, divide it into convenient-size batches, and using a lightly floured rolling pin on a lightly floured work surface, roll the dough out ¼ inch thick. Using a sharp knife, cut the dough in squares, diamonds, or circles; the squares and diamonds should be about 3 by 3 inches, the circles about 2 inches in diameter. (You may also use cookie cutters for other shapes and sizes.)

7. Arrange the kichel on the prepared baking sheets about 1 inch apart. Prick the surface of each kichel with a fork and brush the top lightly with peanut oil. Bake the kichel until golden brown, about 45 minutes.

8. Transfer the kichel from the baking sheet to a wire rack to cool thoroughly as soon as they come out of the oven. Packed in an airtight container they will keep for weeks. Their flavor deepens after 24 hours.

MAIL ORDER: For poppy seeds, The Spice House, thespicehouse.com; Penzey's Spices, tel 800-741-7787, penzeys.com. **FURTHER INFORMATION AND ADDITIONAL RECIPES:** *Inside the Jewish Bakery* by Stanley Ginsberg and Norman Berg (2011).

‑‑‑‑‑‑‑‑‑|||||||||||||||||||||||||||||||||‑‑‑‑‑‑‑‑‑

A MEGILLAH IN A POT

Tzimmes

Jewish

Because it contains so many ingredients, tzimmes has become a classic Jewish metaphor denoting a big fuss or mess—as in, "Why are you making such a tzimmes over this?!" In the kitchen, the term refers to a lushly rich, aromatic, and colorful special-occasion stew of vegetables, fruits, and meat. There are as many variations on tzimmes as there are cooks, but in general it always contains onions, garlic, and fork-tender chunks of beef brisket, along with an orange-gold rainbow of carrots, sometimes sweet potatoes, and always one or two dried fruits such as prunes, apples, or apricots.

A long-cooked brisket stew perfumed with dried fruit

Unsurprisingly, tzimmes is the cause of heated arguments among Jewish communities and family members around the world. What is the one and only "right" way to make tzimmes? Some include pumpkin, others oranges or honey. Some throw in chickpeas, or even knaidlach dumplings on top and vegetarians include everything except meat. Whatever the ingredients, the result is decidedly homey and rustic.

An authentic Rosh Hashanah (New Year's) dinner without a tzimmes cannot exist, in part because, like many foods on the Jewish table, its ingredients are highly symbolic: The Hebrew word for carrot is *gezra,* which also means judgment, so it is said that carrots are served to help ensure sweet judgment in the New Year. (The Yiddish word for carrot, *meren,* means to multiply—another possible New Year's wish.)

Tzimmes is equally welcome on any Passover or Shabbat table, provided that the family cook has the time it takes to prepare it.

Where: *In Chicago and Skokie, IL,* The Bagel Restaurant & Deli, bagelrestaurant.com. **Further information and recipes:** *It's Not Worth Making a Tzimmes Over* (for children) by Betsy R. Rosenthal (2006); *The Book of Jewish Food* by Claudia Roden (1996); *Arthur Schwartz's Jewish Home Cooking* by Arthur R. Schwartz (2008); cookstr.com (search basic tzimmes; carrot tzimmes); food52.com/recipes (search big tzimmes for passover). **Special events:** Tzimmes is often served at big Jewish festivals around the country: Jewish Food Festival, Little Rock, AR, April, jewisharkansas.org (search food festival); San Diego Jewish Food Festival, San Diego, CA, April, sdjewishfoodfest.com; Tallahassee Jewish Food & Cultural Festival, Tallahassee, FL, April, tallahasseejewishfood festival.com; Richmond Jewish Food Festival, Richmond, VA, January, richmondjewishfood festival.com.

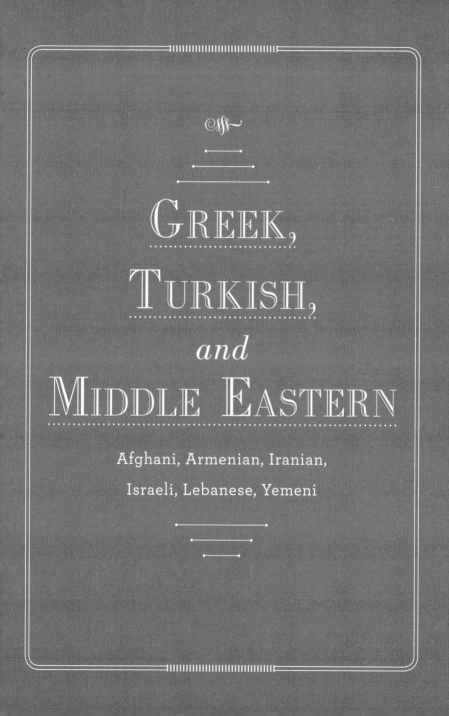

GREEK, TURKISH, and MIDDLE EASTERN

Afghani, Armenian, Iranian,
Israeli, Lebanese, Yemeni

WHERE THE DRIPPINGS ARE DIVINE

Arnaki me Patates

Roast Lamb and Potatoes

Greek

Despite sophisticated culinary technology, rustic and primitive methods often produce the most succulent results. A case in point is barbecued meat, these days done by gearheads who rely on complex and sophisticated automated grills and rotisseries. But on Greece's ancient island of Crete, site of the vast and ingenious Minoan palaces and sculptures, small tavernas roast whole baby lambs on slowly spinning hooks above smoldering wood or charcoal fires. Seasoned with garlic and brushed with rosemary- and thyme-flavored olive oil, lemon juice, and white wine, the Greek meat of choice emerges in luscious chunks edged with crisp, bacony fat.

As good as that meat is, it's only half of the tantalizing story. For under each spinning, roasting lamb will be a large, deep metal pan filled with thinly sliced, sea-salted potatoes that are constantly basted by melting fat dripping from above—much the way traditional Yorkshire pudding is baked under a standing rib roast on a grid. As they become gilt-edged and meltingly tender, the potatoes absorb the flavors and fragrances of meat, oil, and herbs. To many, the spuds are what this culinary creation is all about.

WHERE: *In Chicago,* The Parthenon, tel 312-546-3751, theparthenon.reachlocal.net; *in Montreal,* Milos, tel 514-272-3522, milos.ca. **FURTHER INFORMATION AND RECIPES:** *The Foods of the Greek Islands* by Aglaia Kremezi (2000); *The Parthenon Cookbook* by Camille Stagg (2008); saveur.com (search traditional greek roast lamb with potatoes).

A FUNNY THING HAPPENED ON THE WAY TO THE AGORA

Athens Central Market

Greek

History buffs will be gratified to find the concept of the ancient agora still very much alive in Athens, where the sprawling and colorful Central Market is a bustling and delectably tempting series of streets, alleys, and buildings in the center of town, about a fifteen-minute walk from Syntagma Square, or Constitution Square.

Morning is the best time for a visit through winding streets displaying barrels of green, black, amethyst, and mahogany olives, sacks of dried ivory and green beans, jugs of golden oils and rosy vinegars. Throughout waft the bewitching scents of thyme, oregano, and mint, of roasting coffee beans and the yeasty hot-sugar accents of sesame-coated bread rings, of sweet almond cookies and chewy honeyed pastries. Chunks of snow-white feta cheese swimming in vats filled with whey and yogurt can be ladled out to order.

The spectacular centerpieces of the market are two soaring, enormous halls, one offering fish and seafood, the other meat. The first is rife with water-dwelling creatures, like gnarled purple octopuses, starchy slabs of dried cod, piles of black mussels, and myriad varieties of bright-eyed, silvery fish. But the real stunner may be the meat hall. The painters Rembrandt and Soutine, both known for depicting giant, hanging beef carcasses, would have had a field day here. Aisles and stalls are curtained by bony sides of lamb, goat, pig, and steer, whole rabbits, ducks, and chickens, with glistening organ meats strewn about like bizarre baroque ornaments. The whole place vibrates with cacophonous hawking and haggling and a palpable, bloody freshness that borders on the primitive. Intrepid visitors tempted by the spongy chunks of tripe can head back to the steamy cafeteria, Papandreou, where tripe, or *patsa*, simmers in stews with tomatoes and potatoes, or in the egg-and-lemon-thickened avgolemono.

An appetite worked up on the market tour can also be pleasantly satisfied nearby, in the modest cantina of Diporto, where one peers into pots simmering in the kitchen to choose a meal that might include a stew of white beans with onions, tiny fresh sardines, a Greek salad, and a half-pitcher of the cool, piney wine retsina.

Where: Just off Athinas Street, between Euripidou and Sofokleous Streets; Diporto, 9 Sokratous Street, tel 30/21-0321-1463. **When:** Monday–Saturday, 8:00 a.m.–3:00 p.m. **Further information:** smithsonianmag.com (search athens central market).

A market overflowing with bounty from land and sea

‖‖‖‖‖‖‖‖‖‖‖‖‖‖‖‖‖‖‖‖‖‖‖‖‖‖‖‖‖

EATING THE SHOOTS *AND* THE LEAVES

Celery-Leaf Salad

Greek

A*pium graveolens*, or celery, is one of the humblest of vegetables, valued primarily for the refreshing, icy crunch it lends to appetizers and salads, and as an herbaceous flavoring in soups and stews. A hardworking staple of the vegetable drawer, it becomes ever more useful when its leaves, so often discarded, are incorporated into a refreshing and flavorful salad that's a standard of the Greek kitchen.

Celery exists in three forms: the original plant, a hedgerow-grower with thin, hollow, pale green stalks and an edible leafy top; celeriac, which has an enlarged base that resembles a turnip; and wild celery, also known as *selino*, a parsleylike marshland plant common in the Mediterranean and parts of Asia (especially China), with a stronger flavor than the original variety. Although the leaves from the common celery plant may certainly be employed in an interesting salad, wild celery yields especially pungent results, and has been used since ancient times in Egypt and Greece for various medicinal and religious purposes. The ancient Greeks used the leaves in their funeral garlands, which didn't stop their cooks from also including them in a variety of recipes—there's evidence that they ate celery leaves dressed with oil and pepper even back then. If you can't find selino, Chinese celery is an acceptable substitute.

To make the salad, simply clean the leaves and, if they are large, gently tear them into bite-size pieces; just before serving, dress them with olive oil and lemon juice, or a few drops of white wine vinegar and a little salt and pepper. With an herbaceous, astringent flavor, the leaves also make a delightful garnish for fish dishes or roasts.

Where: *In Athens,* Varoulko, tel 30/21-0522-8400, varoulko.gr; *in Beijing,* Family Li Imperial Cuisine, tel 86/10-6618-0107; *in New York,* Alder, tel 212-539-1900, aldernyc.com. **Mail order:** For Chinese celery, Melissa's Produce, tel 800-588-0151, melissas.com. **Further information and recipes:** *The Greek Vegetarian* by Diane Kochilas (1999); *Beyond Bok Choy* by Rosa Lo San Ross (1996); *Vegetables from Amaranth to Zucchini* by Elizabeth Schneider (2001); *The Foods of the Greek Islands* by Aglaia Kremezi (2000); epicurious.com (search bibb lettuce and celery leaf salad; crispy celery salad). **Tip:** Celery leaves are more perishable than the stalks, and should be rinsed and wrapped in damp paper towels before being stored in the refrigerator's vegetable drawer.

A SECRET INGREDIENT

Mastiha

Mastic, or Wild Pistachio Tree Sap

Greek

With its smoky spiciness and musky warmth, *mastiha,* or mastic, lends a subtle, piney, pleasantly tobacco-ish aroma to whatever foods it enhances, providing the identifying flavor to many of Greece's pastries and breads, the most

traditional of which is *tsoureki*—Greek Easter bread. It also flavors chewing gum, ice cream, liqueurs, and stews, and has been valued since at least the classical era for its supposed healing qualities. It is used for the relief of stomach ulcers, and (today) as an aid for high cholesterol.

The mystery substance is the crystallized sap of the *Pistacia lentiscus* tree, a species of pistachio, though not the nut-producing kind. Only in the southern region of the Greek island Chios does this tree exude resin and each June in Chios, the bark of the mastic tree is ceremoniously slashed in order to draw forth the hazy, amber-golden substance. The resulting sap—referred to in Chios as "tears of the wounded tree"—hardens and falls to the ground before it is harvested as mastic and ground into a fine, crystalline powder. Unground mastic is chewed as a natural breath-sweetening gum, hence its relationship to the word *masticate.*

Retail and mail order: *In New York,* Mastiha Shop, tel 212-253-0895, mastihashopny.com. **Mail order:** parthenonfoods.com (search mastic); greekinternetmarket.com. **Further information and recipes:** *The Foods of the Greek Islands* by Aglaia Kremezi (2000); *The Food and Wine of*

Greece by Diane Kochilas (1993); epicurious
.com (search mamool walnut cookies; cheese
and honey tart santorini); saveur.com (search
evergreen mastic ice cream); greekfood.about.
com (search mastic). **TIP:** Whole mastic should
be ground with a mortar and pestle. To prevent
the spice from sticking to them, add a small
pinch of salt if it is being used for savory foods,
or a small amount of sugar if its destiny is
sweet.

———————————|||||||||||||||||||||||||||||||||—————————————

MAC 'N' CHEESE WITH A DIFFERENCE

———

Pastitsio

Greek

What baked macaroni and cheese is to Americans and lasagne to the Italians,
pastitsio is to the Greeks. A rich, fragrant, and oozy baked layering of short,
tubular, cooked pasta in a spice-scented sauce of tomatoes and ground lamb, it is

topped with a creamy béchamel sauce and a
sprinkling of grated kasseri or kefalotyri cheese.
The bubbling, custardlike overlay puffs up and
browns in the oven, creating an ideal foil for the
zesty bites of pasta, meat, and sauce within—
just the sort of appeal delivered by that other
baked Greek specialty, moussaka. Any of the
short, tubular types of pasta can be used in this
dish, often prepared in its homeland with elbow
macaroni, but more sophisticated when made
with ziti or penne.

Greeks may not have invented pasta, but
they have been enjoying noodlelike foods since
ancient times. In fact, many of the terms we now
associate with Italian food—*lasagna* and *macaroni* being just a couple—are believed by some to
be of Greek origin. Whatever the surely complex
truth, the wheels of culinary influence continue to
spin, and pastitsio is said to have
inspired Cincinnati's famed red
chili, that fragrant, cinnamon-
spiked soup-stew of ground beef
(no beans!) traditionally spooned
over spaghetti and served with
sides of grated American cheese
and beans (if you must). In 1922,
the story goes, a Macedonian
immigrant to that Ohioan city,

named Tom Kiradjieff, was inspired to decon-
struct pastitsio. His chili remains a classic regional
American favorite to this day, however local the
taste for it may be.

With its sustaining flavors and a heady perfume that blends cinnamon, allspice, nutmeg,
and cloves, the dish that inspired him is perfect
for a cold winter's night. In Greece it is particularly popular in February, during the weeks preceding Lent, and especially on the Sunday of
Apokreos, the last day on which the observant
can eat meat. Because it's large and luxurious-
tasting without being expensive, it lends itself to
any dinner for a crowd.

WHERE: *In New York*, Pylos, tel 212-473-0220,
pylosrestaurant.com; *in Chicago*, Greek Islands
Restaurant, tel 312-782-9855, greekislands.net;
in Houston, Yia Yia Mary's, tel 713-840-8665, yia
yiamarys.com; *in Sherman Oaks,
CA*, The Great Greek Restaurant,
tel 818-905-5250, greatgreekcom.
FURTHER INFORMATION AND RECIPES:
The Art of Good Cooking by
Paula Peck (1961); *Greek Islands
Cooking* by Theonie Mark (1974);
The Foods of the Greek Islands
by Aglaia Kremezi (2000);
Remembrance of Repasts by

A spiced, lamb-based lasagna

David E. Sutton (2001); cookstr.com (search pastitsio for a party); epicurious.com (search pasta and lamb casserole pastitsio). **TIP:** Some Greek cooks suggest replacing the béchamel with phyllo dough to provide a buttery, crunchy topping.

⊢||||||||||||||||||||||||||||||⊣

AN ADDICTIVE RICE PUDDING

Rizogalo

Greek

Not all addictions need to be treated. The delicious dessert the Greeks call *rizogalo* (rice milk) is the epitome of comfort food, without the guilt. Cool and creamy, emanating sweet aromas of cinnamon and vanilla, it is based on nothing more alarming than rice and milk. Sure, quantities of sugar and butter are present as well, but why quibble? Inexpensive and easy to love, rizogalo is pure and simple, good for young and old, and not difficult to understand, pronounce, or chew. No wonder almost every Greek restaurant and diner serves it, in more or less elegant forms.

To achieve its transformation, the rice is simmered slowly, long enough to lose its starch and absorb plenty of milk, sugar, and butter, about 20 to 30 minutes. Some cooks prefer their rice pudding ever so slightly tart, and sprinkle on a little grated lemon zest, along with some extra cinnamon and sugar, at the last minute.

Topping your rizogalo with whipped cream is optional but a great idea.

WHERE: *In New York,* Periyali, tel 212-463-7890, periyali.com; *in Chicago,* Athena Restaurant, tel 312-655-0000, athenarestaurant chicago.com; *in Sherman Oaks, CA,* The Great Greek Restaurant, tel 818-905-5250, greatgreek .com. **FURTHER INFORMATION AND RECIPES:** *The Foods of Greece* by Aglaia Kremezi (1999); *The Food and Wine of Greece* by Diane Kochilas (1993); *The Parthenon Cookbook* by Camille Stagg (2008); nytimes.com (search greek rizogalo); greekfood.about.com (search rice pudding rizogalo).

⊢||||||||||||||||||||||||||||||⊣

THERE'S NO SUCH THING AS TOO MUCH CHEESE

Saganáki

Greek

A flaming dish of fried cheese, *saganáki* is one of the most exciting pit stops in the array of Greek appetizers—an unctuously rich and seductive melted cheese extravaganza enlivened by a splash of ouzo, the anise-flavored traditional Greek spirit.

The term *saganáki* refers to the small frying pan in which the cheese is simply and quickly cooked. Rectangles of cheese (either the sheep's milk cheeses kasseri or kefalotyri, or halloumi) are dipped quickly in water, rolled in flour, and fried until the mandatory pale golden crust forms. Then the drama begins, when the goods are placed on a warm plate and a couple of tablespoons of ouzo are poured over the fried cheese. Out comes a match or a lighter and "Opa!" . . . the Greek expression for joy is shouted as soon as the flame rises, a special ritual at the Parthenon restaurant in Chicago.

After the cheer, the flame is doused with fresh lemon juice and the dish is served at once—hot, runny, and ready to be scooped up with triangles of soft pita bread, and with luck, a small glass of the milky, anise-flavored ouzo.

WHERE: *In New York,* Pylos, tel 212-473-0220, pylosrestaurant.com; *in Chicago,* The Parthenon, tel 312-726-2407, theparthenon.com; *in Indianapolis,* The Greek Islands Restaurant, tel 317-636-0700, greekislandsrestaurant.com; *in Houston,* Yia Yia Mary's, tel 713-840-8665, yia yiamarys.com. **FURTHER INFORMATION AND RECIPES:** *The Parthenon Cookbook* by Camille Stagg (2008); cookstr.com (search saganaki); bon appetit.com (search saganaki); foodnetwork .com (search greek saganaki lagasse).

THE BEST WAY TO HIDE THE SPINACH

Spanakopita

Greek

Butter-gilded, flaky phyllo pastry enclosing a dreamy green layer of gently cooked spinach accented with sprightly overtones of lemon and feta cheese . . . This is spanakopita, the Greek spinach pie that makes a delectable snack, appetizer, or light main course. Originating from a farming tradition of handheld foods, spanakopita were meant for the field workers and shepherds who would carry the restorative fare in their pockets and munch while on the job. From such humble beginnings, the little pies rose to loftier gastronomic heights.

Despite practicality, they are anything but simple to prepare. The fragile phyllo sheets must be individually buttered before being layered. Thus prepped, the dough becomes a luscious envelope for a melting filling of salty feta cheese mixed into blanched, earthy spinach spiked with parsley and dill, lemon juice, and softly sautéed chopped onions. The pastry is then baked into large rounds or rectangles, to be cut into portions. For special parties, the phyllo can be formed into individual triangles to be passed as elegant hors d'oeuvres.

Virtually ubiquitous in Greek diners,

downscale or upscale, and in tavernas and restaurants, the treat has traveled abroad to become a staple on catering menus and even in supermarket freezers. If spanakopita has become "as American as pizza," as the Greek food writer Diane Kochilas once said, it's none the worse for wear.

WHERE: *In New York,* Periyali, tel 212-463-7890, periyali.com; Molyvos, tel 212-582-7500, molyvos.com; *in Chicago,* Pan Hellenic Pastry

Enfolded in buttery layers of phyllo, spinach turns decadent.

Shop, tel 312-454-1886, panhellenicpastryshop .com; *in Houston,* Niko Niko's Greek & American Café at two locations, nikonikos.com; *in Sherman Oaks, CA,* The Great Greek Restaurant, tel 818-905-5250, greatgreek.com. **FURTHER INFORMATION**

AND RECIPES: *The Food and Wine of Greece* by Diane Kochilas (1993); *The New Book of Middle Eastern Food* by Claudia Roden (2000); epicurious.com (search spanakopita); foodnet work.com (search spanakopita).

⊣||||||||||||||||||||||||||||||||⊢

PASTRIES TO SATISFY A SULTAN

Baklava

Turkish, Greek, Middle Eastern

E thereally light and crispy layerings of flaky phyllo dough brushed with melted butter and decked out with chopped nuts and oozing, honeyed syrup make baklava one of the world's most seductive pastries. Baked in shallow rectangular

or round metal pans, the still-warm treat is doused—and thus crisped—with ice-cold sugar syrup or honey. Cut into diamond-shaped portions, it is to be nibbled alongside Turkish tea or coffee, in this case preferably unsugared.

Already a popular dessert in the Topkapi Palace in the sixteenth-century days of the Ottoman sultans, baklava was reported to be one of the favorite treats in the harem known as the House of Felicity (a title perhaps due only in part to the presence of pastries). The dessert evolved over the years, baked in varying forms and with fillings of walnuts, almonds, or pistachios, though always fragrant with cinnamon, lemon rind, and orange blossom water.

An ephemeral delight, baklava doesn't keep for long.

One of the most popular riffs on the theme is *bourma,* known as shredded wheat, a dizzyingly sweet and chewy delight in which shredded phyllo is wrapped around nut fillings before it is baked and drowned in syrup.

Finding fresh baklava is no easy matter, but it's crucial. Kept too long, the pastry becomes limp and tough and the nuts turn rancid. If not in a reliable restaurant, find good baklava in busy Greek, Turkish, or other Middle Eastern bakeries where turnover is high. Avoid any that is precut and wrapped, boxed, or canned.

WHERE: *In Gaziantep, Turkey,* Koçak Baklava, tel 90/342-321-0519, kocakbaklava.com.tr; *in Brooklyn,* Sahadi's, tel 718-624-4550, sahadis.com; *in Watertown, MA,* Armenian Market & Bakery, tel 857-228-3014, armenianmarketbakery.com; *in Montreal,* Barbounya, tel 514-439-8858, barbou nya.com. **RETAIL AND MAIL ORDER:** *In Brooklyn,* Mansoura Pastries, tel 718-645-7977, mansoura .com (search baklava); *in New York,* Kalustyan's, tel 800-352-3451, kalustyans.com (search baklava). **FURTHER INFORMATION AND RECIPES:** *The Foods of the Greek Islands* by Aglaia Kremezi (2000); *Secrets of Cooking: Armenian, Lebanese, Persian* by Linda Chirinian (1986); *Spice* by Ana Sortun (2006); epicurious.com (search turkish baklava; walnut and pistachio baklava).

|||||||||||||||||||||||||||||||||||||

RICE PILAF'S EARTHIER TWIN

Bulgur Pilavi

Turkish, Armenian

R ice pilaf is undoubtedly a more familiar and celebrated Turkish specialty, but the fragrantly rustic bulgur pilaf has a nuttier, fuller flavor as well as a heartier and more interesting texture. It's also better for you: Its crushed grains of

whole wheat are higher in fiber than polished rice, and somewhat richer in B vitamins, to boot.

In order to become bulgur, the golden wheat kernels are boiled, dried, and cracked into fine, medium, or coarse textures. Parched in hot butter with finely diced onion and broken strands of vermicelli that turn golden brown, the grain is then simmered in lamb or chicken stock. As with rice pilaf, the bulgur is not stirred during cooking. Imbued with buttery, oniony flavors, it becomes a rich and delectable accompaniment to the many grilled and roasted meats of Turkey and Armenia, where the much-loved dish is known as *tzavari yeghintz*.

WHERE: *In Brooklyn*, Tanoreen, tel 718-748-5600, tanoreen.com. **MAIL ORDER:** For bulgur, Kalustyan's, tel 800-352-3451, kalustyans.com; Sahadi's, tel 718-624-4550, sahadis.com. **FURTHER INFORMATION AND RECIPES:** *Secrets of Cooking: Armenian, Lebanese, Persian* by Linda Chirinian (1986); *The Cuisine of Armenia* by Sonia Uvezian (2004); turkishfood.about.com (search bulgur and vegetable pilaf); epicurious.com (search bulgur pilaf). **TIP:** Bulgur can be purchased in Middle Eastern food stores and also in many supermarkets. If you get it packaged with pre-mixed seasonings for tabbouleh or pilaf, discard them and season it from scratch. **SEE ALSO:** Biryani, page 868.

|||||||||||||||||||||||||||||||||||||

GOING NUTS OVER CHICKEN

Çerkez Tavuğu

Chicken in Walnut Sauce

Turkish

R arely does poultry seem so exotic as it does in this sensuous dish of cold, shredded breast of chicken sauced with a creamy, thick paste of crushed walnuts and paprika. Called *çerkez tavuğu*, it is a specialty of Circassia in Anatolia,

a region whose women were allegedly prized as harem slaves because their thick, arched eyebrows spanned the bridges of their noses, a mark of beauty in those long-gone harem days.

The chicken breast on the bone is cooked

quite simply: poached with pot vegetables and cooled before being skinned and slivered. Its dressing requires more intricate preparation, similar to that of the Balkan *scordolea* (see page 381). Walnuts, milk-softened white bread or fresh bread crumbs, salt, pepper, hot paprika, and sometimes a small piece of onion are ground or pureed until they form a soft, creamy paste that is incorporated with the chicken. As a fragrant and extra-lustrous finish, additional walnuts are ground with paprika until they emit a red-tinted oil. Once the chicken is mounded on plates, this fragrant oil is drizzled over all for a lusciously nutty, creamy, and paprika-spiked first course.

FURTHER INFORMATION AND RECIPES: *A Mediterranean Feast* by Clifford A. Wright (1999); *The Balkan Cookbook* by Vladimir Mirodan (1989); foodandwine.com (search circassian chicken zoutendijk); nytimes.com (search circassian chicken in walnut sauce).

STUFFED VEGETABLES TAKE CENTER STAGE

Dolmas

Turkish, Greek, Middle Eastern

Oil-glossed and slowly simmered to satiny elegance, the Middle Eastern stuffed vegetables generally called dolmas (the word actually means "stuffed") may be part of the enticing appetizer spread known as mezes (see page 498)—but they are important enough to be served in larger portions as a main course in their own right.

To whet appetites, they are usually filled with a savory rice pilaf that is enhanced with cinnamon and allspice and dotted with pine nuts and raisins; these are best served at room temperature. As a main course, they may be plumped with meat and rice fillings of all sorts and served hot. In Iran, the old-time Persian spe-

A pilaf-stuffed legend

cialty is *dolmeh 'ye beh*, a whole quince filled with lamb and saffron rice flavored with onion, pepper, and lime juice.

Ordering à la carte, you usually get just one type of vegetable in your portion, but the really stunning presentation is a gigantic platter of assorted dolmas: shiny, softly collapsed red tomatoes alongside sweet green peppers, silvery-green zucchini, dense orange acorn squash, large snowy onions and potatoes, boat-shaped cuts of small purple-brown eggplant, and ruffled rolls of chartreuse cabbage—what fifteenth-century sculptor Luca Della Robbia might have fashioned had he favored vegetables over fruit.

WHERE: *In New York,* Ali Baba at two locations, tel 212-683-9209, alibabaturkish cuisine.com; Turkish Kitchen, tel 212-679-6633, turkish kitchen.com; *In Houston,* Mary'z Lebanese Cuisine, tel 832-251-1955, maryzcuisine .com. **FURTHER INFORMATION AND RECIPES:** *A Taste of Persia* by Najmieh Batmanglij (2006); *Arabesque* by Claudia Roden (2006); *The Foods of the Greek Islands* by Aglaia Kremezi (2000); *The Arabian Delights Cookbook* by Anne Marie Weiss-Armush (1993); cookstr.com (search dolmas hoffman); greekfood.about.com (search dolmathakia).

||||||||||||||||||||||||||||||||||

SWEET BY THE SLICE

Halvah

Turkish

The word itself—*halvah*, or sometimes *helvah*—means sweetmeats, and in some form or another has existed since 3000 B.C. There are many versions of this confection, most especially in India, where sweetmeats are called *halva* or *halwa* and are made of carrots, semolina, or fruits, yielding a somewhat mushy, overly sweet result.

But none can begin to compete with Turkish halvah, a firm, almost buttery loaf formed of crushed sesame seeds and their gentle oil, most classically enhanced with sugar and vanilla—honey and a touch of rosewater are the only other additions purists permit. Modern variations include additions of chocolate, whether marbleized, fully incorporated into the mix, or coating the loaf, but halvah is most satisfying savored plain or dotted with pistachios and a hint of salt.

Those who dislike halvah describe it as a mouthful of wet sand. Those who love it live for its slowly melting, burnished sweetness and nutty sesame accents, and for its quietly crunchy texture. Still, it's not a bad idea to have a glass of ice water or some hot tea on hand as you negotiate this luscious treat, if only to enable you to eat even more of it.

Every country must have its halvah hero, and for the United States it was Nathan Radutzky, an ambitious confectioner who came from Ukraine with what he claimed was the recipe for a special treat beloved by Turkish sultans and their harems. In 1907, he produced the first batch on Manhattan's Lower East Side, and it rapidly became a favorite of the eastern European Jews who had settled nearby. His company, Joyva, still exists in Brooklyn and makes some of the best mass-produced sesame and pistachio halvah, found mostly in Jewish appetizing stores and Middle Eastern markets.

Whole loaves of halvah—sliced to order—on display

Retail and mail order: *In Istanbul,* Hacı Bekir, tel 90/216-336-1519, hacibekir.com (search halva); *in New York,* Economy Candy, tel 212-254-1531, economycandy.com; Russ & Daughters, tel 212-475-4880, russanddaughters .com (try their terrific halvah ice cream at the cafe). **Mail order:** alibaba.com (search haci bekir halvah). **Further information and recipes:** *The Balkan Cookbook* edited by Snezana Pejakovic and Jelka Venisnik-Eror (1987); saveur.com (search almond halvah); denver post.com (search pistachio honey halva); joyva .com. **Tip:** For halvah at its best, buy it where it is sold in bulk and cut to order from large loaves. Its flavor and perfume are better preserved than when the halvah is precut into small pieces and wrapped individually. Avoid canned halvah, which is musty-tasting and overly oily.

—|||||||||||||||||||||||||||||||||||—

SIZZLING AND JUICY

Kebabs

Turkish, Middle Eastern

Sauced with yogurt for added richness and tang, best and most often made with lamb, meat kebabs come in many ingenious forms in these parts. The most spectacular of these may be the *doner,* or ever-turning, kebab, best known outside Turkey as the Greek gyro or the Arab and Israeli shawarma. An enormous barrel-shaped column of meat upended on a turning spit as it sears in front of a vertical grill, the doner looks like a big, solid tree trunk of meat. But this kebab reality is far more complicated than it seems. For the best traditional doner kebab, the meat will be composed of three different cuts of fresh-killed lamb: scaloppine-like slices, small cubes, and ground meat complete with considerable fat for maximum juiciness and flavor. Marinated briefly with onion juice and various seasonings, the meat is slid onto the long, vertical spit in layers—slices, cubes, ground—all tightly packed so that when cooked and sliced, the meat ripples into almost solid ribbons. In this as in all other kebab preparations, beef can be nearly as good as lamb, but turkey or chicken simply do not make the cut.

The familiar shish kebab (*souvlaki* in Greek), made of cubes of lamb or beef, often gets much the same marinade as the doner kebab. But its meat is threaded onto individual skewers, alternating with cuts of tomato, green pepper, and onion.

Named for Adana, the city of its origin in southeastern Turkey, the Adana kebab is shish kebab's elusive, less famous cousin. More subtly complex and with fiery overtones, the meat is preferably lamb shoulder, sometimes combined with beef. Finely minced, it is thoroughly, richly seasoned with the famed red Aleppo chile flakes, parsley, paprika, and salt and coarsely ground black pepper. Redolent with the red chile's incendiary heat, the meat is shaped into thick, flattish, fingerlike ribbons or belts that are threaded onto extra-long, flat-bladed skewers. Grilled on an open flame, from which they emerge sizzling hot and juicy, the kebabs are eased off their skewers and either served with an assortment of salads and sauces or sold as street foods in pita pockets.

When any of the above kebabs are served *au yaourt,* they come with thin slabs of pita bread that absorb the meat juices and become the base for the dish. (In the case of the doner kebab, the pita is even sometimes placed beneath the grilling meat to catch some of its flavorful drippings.) The yogurt is served at room temperature and sometimes flavored with salt-crushed garlic, its slightly sharp creaminess mingling with the seasoned meat juices—and, for the brave of palate, with a sprinkling of thinly sliced, fiery green chiles.

WHERE: *In Istanbul,* Pandeli, tel 90/212-527-3909, pandeli.com.tr; *in Seyhan, Adana,* Yüzevler Kebap, tel 90/322-454-7513, yuzevler.com.tr; *in New York,* Ali Baba's Terrace, tel 212-888-8622, alibabasterrace.com; *in Brooklyn,* Tanoreen, tel 718-748-5600, tanoreen.com; *in San Francisco,* Tuba Restaurant, tel 415-826-8822, tubarestaurant.com; *in Montreal,* Barbounya, tel 514-439-8858, barbounya.com. **FURTHER INFORMATION AND RECIPES:** *Planet Barbecue!* by Steven Raichlen (2010); *Arabesque* by Claudia Roden (2005); *The Cuisine of Armenia* by Sonia Uvezian (2004); *Greek Islands Cooking* by Theonie Mark (1974); turkishcookbook.com (click Kebabs, then Yogurtlu Kebab); saveur.com (search shish kebab); food.com (search adana kebab).

A SWORDFUL OF SWORDFISH

Kiliç Şiş

Turkish, Greek

Various types of meat and poultry are expected choices for skewered, charcoal-grilled kebabs, but the pairing of swordfish and bay leaves—*kiliç şiş* (KILL-ich shish)—isn't widely known outside of Turkey and Greece, where they're known as *xifias souvlaki*. In these countries, it is a seasonal treat from late June until mid-September, prime months for catching the deep-water fish.

Because swordfish has so little fat, it's a tricky candidate for a successful kebab. To impart succulent moistness and a sunny, fresh-air flavor, one-inch cubes of lean and snowy swordfish are marinated for three or four hours in a combination of lemon juice, olive oil, salt, and pepper. Meanwhile, brittle, dried bay leaves soak in boiling water for about 30 minutes, or until soft and pliable—unless (and preferably) fresh bay leaves are available.

Lightly drained, the fish and bay leaves are threaded onto skewers and brushed with melted butter or leftover marinade as the kebabs grill or broil. The bay leaves lend a piney, dry haze of flavor to the supple and substantial fish, which is slid off the skewers onto a nest of rice or bulgur pilaf. Oil-brushed chunks of tomatoes and green peppers, grilled on separate skewers, are often added to the plate as garnish.

WHERE: *In Chicago,* Athena Restaurant, tel 312-655-0000, athenarestaurantchicago.com. **MAIL ORDER:** for Turkish bay leaves, Penzeys Spices, tel 800-741-7787, penzeys.com. **FURTHER INFORMATION AND RECIPES:** *A Mediterranean Feast* by Clifford A. Wright (1999); *Egyptian Cuisine* by Nagwa E. Khalil (1980); foodandwine.com (search swordfish kebabs with lemon and bay leaves). **TIP:** In order to avoid further depleting the endangered swordfish population, home grillers can substitute mahimahi.

PIZZA BY ANOTHER NAME

Lahmajoun

Turkish, Armenian

As snackable as the more familiar Italian pizza, *lahmajoun* begins with crisp, yeasty rounds or squares of what is essentially pita dough—*pide* in Turkish—topped with a richly thick sauce of ground meat, preferably lamb, that has been simmered with a rich blend of onions, parsley, crushed hot chiles, mint, garlic, green peppers, tomatoes, and perhaps a breath of cumin and allspice. Freshly baked and served hot, it is traditionally garnished with lemon wedges.

Just like pizza, cuts of lahmajoun range from slightly limp and tepid street-fair food to gourmet treats, the entire round or square baked to order and the sauce carefully prepared. And much in the way New Yorkers take their slices—folded up into a sort of pizza sandwich—lahmajoun can be rolled up for snacking convenience. Cut into small squares or wedges, it works equally well as a refined cocktail canapé. As a quicker, crisper alternative to the freshly made dough, the sauce may be spread over the thin bread known as *lavash* and then glossed with melted butter and briefly heated in the oven.

WHERE: *In Los Angeles,* Lamajoon, tel 323-727-7102, lamajoon.com; *in Fresno, CA,* Lahmajoon Kitchen, tel

559-264-5454; Nina's Bakery, tel 559-449-9999. **FURTHER INFORMATION AND RECIPES:** *The Cuisine of Armenia* by Sonia Uvezian (2004); *Spice* by Ana Sortun (2006); saveur.com (search lahmacun).

The pizza of the Middle East—hold the cheese.

ANCIENT RAVIOLI

Manti

Turkish, Greek, Central Asian

Luscious and petite dumplings filled with finely ground, seasoned lamb, hand-formed *manti* are a signature dish of Central Asian countries from Uzbekistan to Greece. Although particularly associated with Turkey, they are thought to have originated in Tibet, and from there to have been carried into Turkey (via China) by the Tartars. Since their migration, their time-consuming, laborious preparation has been adapted by generations of Turkish home cooks—though it's no less work-intensive for their efforts.

Once the dumpling dough is made, it is pinched around a savory lamb filling that usually includes onion, parsley, salt, and pepper. Often compared to ravioli because of their size and shape, the little dumplings are either boiled or steamed. Coated with chile-spiked butter, they are then topped with a traditional piquant Turkish sauce of garlic-enhanced goat's or sheep's milk yogurt. With their soft, velvety texture, they are some of the silkiest, most savory, and most marvelously salty dumplings on

earth—understandably, the craving for manti is often described in the most intense of terms.

WHERE: *In Turkey at several locations,* Bodrum Manti & Café, bodrummanti.com.tr; *in San Francisco,* Tuba Restaurant, tel 415-826-8822, tubarestaurant.com; *in New York,* Turkish Kitchen, tel 212-679-6633, turkishkitchen.com; *in Brooklyn,* Deniz Restaurant & Bar, tel 718-852-6503, deniznyc.com. **FURTHER INFORMATION AND RECIPES:** *Classical Turkish Cooking* by Ayla Algar (1991); *The New Book of Middle Eastern Food* by Claudia Roden (2000); *Turkey: More than 100 Recipes, with Tales from the Road* by Leanne Kitchen (2012); *A Mediterranean Feast* by Clifford A. Wright (1999); cookstr.com (search manti in yogurt); turkishfoodandrecipes.com (search turkish dumpling manti).

||||||||||||||||||||||||||||||||||||||||||||||||||||||||||||||||||||||||||||||||||||||||||||||||||||||||||||

SWEETLY COOL

Mint

Among gum chewers and mint lovers, the world is frequently divided along peppermint or spearmint lines. These two aren't the only members of the cool green *Labiatae* or *Mentha* families, but they are by far the most deliciously visible and edible. *Mentha piperita,* or peppermint, is the stronger and punchiest of the two, and the more likely to be used for its oil, both as a flavoring and medicinally; it's also often featured in liqueurs and cordials and in confections such as crystallized candies and chocolates.

Spearmint, *M. viridis,* is the more graceful and gentler tasting mint, its flavor and scent summoning up memories of the classic Wrigley chewing gum or the Moroccan tea brewed with its soft, pointed and engagingly sweet leaves (see page 704); braised with new peas and shallots in springtime or added to boiled potatoes, spearmint is often used as a beloved garnish for lamb, though all too often in overly cloying jams rather than in more savory and pungent relishes or chutneys. It also adds zest to many Southeast Asian soups and salads.

Outside of the reigning duo, more romantic varieties include the slightly acidic Asian mint, *M. arvensis,* and red or applemint, *M. × gentilis,* the latter an Americana plant whose oils are present in many spearmint flavorings.

Named after the mythical nymph, Minthe, who was turned into a plant after vying with Proserpina (Persephone in the Greek version of the myth) for the affections of Pluto (god of the underworld), mint has been the focus of all sorts of myths and superstitions. A known stimulant, it is believed to invigorate the mind, ensure loyalty, keep milk from curdling, and settle the stomach—and even to banish stomach worms, among other talents.

Once picked, one quality it lacks is hardiness. Like its close cousin basil, mint is hard to keep in good condition. It does best wrapped in wet newspapers or paper towels and stored in the vegetable compartment of the refrigerator; or, if it still has roots, plopped into a glass of cold water in a cool, sunless corner.

A palate-cleansing, stomach-soothing herb

MAIL ORDER: For fresh mint, Melissa's Produce, tel 800-588-0151, melissas.com; for seeds and plants, burpee.com (search spearmint; peppermint). **FURTHER INFORMATION AND RECIPES:** *The Foods of the Greek Islands* by Aglaia Kremezi (2000); *Vegetables from Amaranth to Zucchini* by Elizabeth Schneider (2001); *Arabesque* by Claudia Roden (2005); *A Mediterranean Feast* by Clifford A. Wright (1999); epicurious.com (search mint soup; mint granita; mint raita; crabmeat risotto with peas and mint; savory mint lamb chops; thai ground pork salad with mint and cilantro). **TIP:** When buying mint, look for fresh leaves that don't show spotting or limpness and look crisp and alive. Though mint is also sold dried, in that state it tends to take on an overpowering metallic edge.

—||||||||||||||||||||||||||||||||||||||—

A STREET FOOD SHELL GAME

Midye Dolmasi and Midye Tava

Mussels, Stuffed or Fried

Turkish, Middle Eastern

While mussels are much appreciated wherever they are found, only the Turks have been passionate enough to turn them into a standard street food. Hawked by vendors mainly around the busy Galata Bridge that spans

Istanbul's Golden Horn, the bivalves offer delectable nourishment for visitors taking in the action.

Two mussel specialties are readily available in this quarter bustling with pedestrians, hawkers, and automobiles. One is made by stuffing the nicely salty, tender mussels with a rice pilaf studded with pine nuts and raisins. Called *midye dolmasi*, these may be served hot or at room temperature as part of the meze course throughout the Middle East, but on these street corners they are sold chilled.

The second dish, *midye tava*, is piping hot: mussels deep-fried until crispy in a light and bubbly golden batter right before your eyes. They are

usually dipped into an aromatic *tarator* sauce, a blend of walnuts, garlic, milk-soaked bread, and olive oil, brightened with lemon juice.

WHERE: *In Istanbul,* from street vendors around the Galata Bridge. **FURTHER INFORMATION AND RECIPES:** *The Cuisine of Armenia* by Sonia Uvezian (2004); *A Mediterranean Feast* by Clifford A. Wright (1999); *Secrets of Cooking: Armenian, Lebanese, Persian* by Linda Chirinian (1986); sbs.com.au (search stuffed mussels istanbul street style); turkishcookbook.com (click Seafood, then Deep Fried Mussels; Stuffed Mussels). **SEE ALSO:** Thai Mussels, page 845; Green-Lipped Mussels, page 910; Moules Frites, page 148.

—||||||||||||||||||||||||||||||||||||||—

THE MOST FRAGRANT MARKET

Mısır Çarşısı

Istanbul's Spice Bazaar

Turkish

Of all the sights in Istanbul, none means more to food lovers than the romantic and opulent Spice Bazaar, or Mısır Çarşısı, as it is called in Turkish. The market is also referred to as the Egyptian Market, probably because in

the earliest days of the spice trade, most merchandise passed through Egypt on its way from the Far East to Turkey.

These days the convivial market is alive

with sights, sounds, aromas, and alluring tastes unmatched by even the lavish treasures of the Topkapı Palace or the delights of the seraglio. Lodged in the bustling Eminönü section of

Istanbul, it is attached to a mosque that lies close to the Galata Bridge and the ancient inlet called the Golden Horn.

Commissioned by Sultan Mehmed IV, the Ottoman-style building was completed between 1660 and 1664. Designed by the architect Kasım Ağa, it features soaring, vaulted arches that divide the space into eighty-eight stalls. These display not only food but also magical carpets, gleaming brass and copperware, richly decorated fabrics, leather, perfume essences, and jewelry.

Between the stalls, visitors stroll past pyramids of spices in rainbows of hotly burnished colors ranging from pale yellow (mustard) to hot orange (turmeric), glowing pink (paprika), and the mellow browns of cinnamon, cumin, and cloves. Then, on to garlands of sausages and slabs of cured meat, wreaths of fiery-red, dried chiles, and bins and burlap sacks of rice and other grains, seeds, and nuts. In dizzying view are seeded and braided flatbreads, cuts of snowy cheeses, jewel-like displays of oozingly sweet confections, and myriad variations on honeyed baklava-style pastries.

Every Turkish food worth its sugar (or salt) is available for sampling here, whether at the walkway stalls or on nearby streets. A rite of passage for first-time visitors may be a meal at the pricey restaurant Pandeli, on the upper level of the bazaar, but the real action lies in the rowdier halls and stalls from which no one comes back without mentioning the sound. Not to be confused with noise, it's a musical cacophony of hawking and haggling. Joining in is highly recommended.

Vivid mounds of spices abound in a giant market spanning 384 blocks.

WHERE: Eminönü section of Istanbul. Every day except Sunday. Walking tours can be arranged at misircarsisi .org. Pandeli Restaurant, tel 90/212-527-3909, pandeli .com.tr.

PASTRAMI'S GREAT, GREAT, GREAT GRANDFATHER

Pastirma

Turkish

Although pastrami (see page 456) is generally thought of as an eastern European Jewish delicatessen specialty, its origins go back at least to the sixteenth century. Turkey's Suleiman the Magnificent would have known it as *pastromani,* or

pastramach, or *pasdirma,* a smoked or salt-dried meat specialty thought to be at its best if the meat came from cows in calf, because their flesh was more savory and salty.

Now, as then, the meat is rubbed with a spice mix that might include saffron, fenugreek seed, cloves, mustard seed, salt, pepper, and garlic before being smoked or salt-dried for ten days, and then stored away in wooden kegs until it loses its bright red color and turns firm. In the earliest times, it was pounded to a powder and reformed into sausages, hash, or pressed slices; today's pastirma is cured in whole pieces and sliced very thinly as it is served. The result is a palate-teasing cross between the air-dried Swiss *bündnerfleisch* (see page 330) and the fattier, juicier New York–style pastrami we know and love. The Turkish version, now also made in California, is chewy, pungent, and tingling with salt and spices, a perfect accompaniment to aperitifs, especially the iced, milky, and licorice-flavored Turkish raki.

Where: *In Los Angeles*, Sahag's Basturma Sandwich Shop, tel 323-661-5311; *in Glendale, CA*, Phoenicia, tel 818-956-7800, phoeniciala .com. **Mail order:** Marky's, tel 800-522-8427, markys.com (search basturma); littlearmenia .com (click on Stores, then Basturma). **Further information and recipes:** *Treasured Armenian Recipes* edited by Mrs. Alex Manoogian (1949); kalofagas.ca (search pastourma takes patience); youtube.com (search basturma step by step).

"FIGS ARE RESTORATIVE, AND THE BEST FOOD THAT CAN BE TAKEN BY THOSE WHO ARE BROUGHT LOW BY LONG ILLNESS."—PLINY THE ELDER

Pulled Smyrna Figs

Turkish

The Turkish town of Smyrna is now known as İzmir, but the region's legendary figs still bear its ancient name—though these days, the Smyrna fig (the variety that becomes the world's most exquisite dried fig) is cultivated in many parts of the world. Most commonly grown in Europe and in California, it is also known as the Calimyrna fig.

Delicious as its offspring may be, none rivals the figs grown in their native soil. Fresh Smyrna figs are delectably honey-sweet, soft, and chewy, and cannot be sampled anywhere but in Turkey; for the best, you must travel to İzmir and its surroundings during harvest, between mid-August and mid-September. Soon after, most of the crop is sun-dried.

In the best tradition, the silver-brown, cushiony figs are "pulled" onto rush strands and tied into a garland. This way, the fruit is not compressed and so remains pillowy; as it dries its surface develops a sugary crystal veneer, the figs' centers retaining a velvety softness that is offset by the needling crackle of its tiny seeds.

Vintage ad for Camel figs

But to prevent them from drying too much during export or long storage, Smyrna figs can be layered and packaged in paper or baskets.

Any that do become too dry and hard to chew still have delicious possibilities. Dried figs can be steamed until malleable and then stuffed with a toasted almond and a clove or a mix of creamy cheese and honey, and baked with a dousing of port wine until the fruit is glazed and the wine is syrupy. It's a dessert best served warm with a splash of cold sweet cream.

MAIL ORDER: amazon.com (search indus organic turkish dried figs; turkish figs sun dried); igourmet.com (search smyrna figs). **FURTHER INFORMATION AND RECIPES:** *The Glorious Foods of Greece* by Diane Kochilas (2001); food52.com (search roasted stuffed figs); lidiasitaly.com (search stuffed figs sibari-style). **SPECIAL EVENT:** Fig Fest, San Diego, September, figfestsd.com. **SEE ALSO:** Fichi Ripieni al Forno, page 188.

A SWEET OF NARNIAN FAME

Rahat Lokum

Turkish

To many an acquired taste, *rahat lokum,* or Turkish delight, is a seriously sweet, compressed jelly known for both its gummy texture and its generous coating of confectioners' sugar. Colored pink when flavored with rosewater or

strawberries, green when mint-flavored, this candy is dredged in the powdered sugar that both sweetens and preserves it, and often in a coating of crushed pistachios. Citrus juices are alternative flavorings, while chopped dried apricots can add a sunny dimension.

The soft, chewy candy is cut into many different forms to create a pretty pastel rainbow of shapes and colors on serving trays and in confectionery showcases. They are front and center in the pristine cases of Hacı Bekir, the famous Istanbul shop that has been in existence since 1777, when it was founded by the confectioner who invented Turkish delight.

The candy itself has been an important export since 1936, when each year Turkey reportedly shipped off 750 tons. As with halvah (see page 483), that other famous Turkish sweet, "delight" is best experienced when accompanied by unsweetened hot tea or strong coffee. It also is best purchased in Middle Eastern food stores, where rapid turnover promises it will be fresh and cut into portions as ordered.

RETAIL AND MAIL ORDER: *In Istanbul,* Hacı Bekir, tel 90/216-336-1519, hacibekir.com (search

A "delight" invented during the eighteenth century

turkish delight); *in New York,* Kalustyan's, tel 800-352-3451, kalustyans.com (search turkish delight). **FURTHER INFORMATION AND RECIPES:** *The Oxford Companion to Food* by Alan Davidson (2006); *The Balkan Cookbook* by Vladimir Mirodan (1989); *A Mediterranean Feast* by Clifford A. Wright (1999); epicurious.com (search pistachio rosewater turkish delight); candy.about.com (search turkish delight).

⊢||||||||||||||||||||||||||||||||⊣

AN EDIBLE BRACELET

Simit

Turkish, Balkan, Middle Eastern, Arabic

J ewelry or bagel-like baked treat? This may be the first question that comes to mind when you spot this big, sesame-veneered, spiraled bread ring sold mornings on street corners in cities such as Istanbul, Athens, and Tunis. One whiff

should provide the answer, for the aroma of these toasty rolls is hard to resist. Traditionally eaten with either yogurt or jam, they'd be excellent vehicles for lox and cream cheese as well.

In addition to their satisfying texture and flavor, *similer* (in plural form) provide

entertainment as their vendors vie for attention, some with the most alluring cries. Others carry baskets of the breads on their heads, stacking the similer in ever more creative arrangements that may suggest the tower of Pisa, complete with the lean.

Spiral-shaped, crusty, and often compared to the pretzel

WHERE: *In New York and Cliffside, NJ,* Simit and Smith at multiple locations, simitandsmith.com. **MAIL ORDER:** Istanbul Food Bazaar, tel 973-955-2989, istanbulfoodbazaar.com (search simit). **FURTHER INFORMATION AND RECIPES:** *The Food and Wine of Greece* by Diane Kochilas (1993); mideastfood.about .com (search simit); turkishcookbook .com (click Pastries, then Turkish Bagel with Sesame Seeds). **SEE ALSO:** Bagels, page 427; Bialys, page 429; Soft Pretzels, page 620.

⊢||||||||||||||||||||||||||||||||⊣

THE HEART OF THE ARTICHOKE

Tsetov Gangar

Artichokes in Olive Oil

Turkish, Armenian

U nctuously oily and lemony tender, artichoke bottoms steamed with chunks of potato and onion make a sublime appetizer. Redolent of dill, onion, and lemon, they need only some thin, toasted pita to absorb any leftover dressing.

It is a preparation akin to artichokes *à la Greque,* or what in Greece is called *aginares me lemoni*

ke skordo, both sunny, hearty salads that make the most of their ingredients.

Tsetov Gangar

Serves 6 as an appetizer

2 lemons
6 very large artichokes, about 4" across top
4 medium onions, peeled and quartered
    lengthwise
4 medium waxy potatoes such as
    Yukon Gold, peeled and sliced
    ¼ to ½ inch thick
Salt and freshly ground white pepper
1 tablespoon sugar
1 tablespoon minced fresh dill
1 cup olive oil

1. Fill a large mixing bowl with cold water and add the juice of 1 lemon. Using a stainless-steel knife, remove all of the leaves from the artichokes but do not cut off the stems. (You can discard the leaves or, if you like, boil them and eat them.) Trim just the outer coating of the stems and scrape away the fuzzy choke from the base of each artichoke. Trim a small slice from the bottom of each artichoke stem. Cut each artichoke in half vertically, through the stem, and put the artichoke halves in the lemon water to keep them from turning brown.

2. Choose a large, nonreactive saucepan or skillet, preferably of enameled cast iron, in which the artichokes can fit in a single layer. Place the artichokes in the pan or skillet, cut side down. Fit the onion and the potato pieces around the artichokes, also in a single layer. Lightly sprinkle salt, white pepper, and sugar on top, followed by the dill. Add ½ cup of the olive oil.

3. Cover the artichoke mixture with an inverted heatproof dinner plate that fits very snugly within the rim of the pan or skillet. Pour 2½ cups of water over the plate and cover the pan.

4. Cook the artichoke mixture over medium heat until tender, about 45 minutes. If the water evaporates, lift plate and trickle in a small amount of water as needed to maintain the simmer. Then remove the lid and plate and add the remaining ½ cup of olive oil. Continue cooking until the artichokes are tender but not mushy when pierced with a skewer or knife blade, about 10 minutes longer.

5. Transfer the artichokes, onions, and potatoes with the remaining cooking liquid to a dish and let cool to room temperature if you are serving them the same day. Otherwise, refrigerate the artichokes, covered; they will keep for 2 days. Let the artichokes stand at room temperature for about 30 minutes before serving.

6. The artichokes look best served in individual portions, 2 halves standing together with the cut sides facing, stems up. Surround them with onions and potatoes and spoon a little of the cooking liquid over all. Cut the remaining lemon into wedges and serve them with the artichokes.

MAIL ORDER: For fresh artichokes in season, Melissa's Produce, tel 800-588-0151, melissas.com. **FURTHER INFORMATION AND ADDITIONAL RECIPES:** *The Cuisine of Armenia* by Sonia Uvezian (2004); for the Greek version, *The Foods of the Greek Islands* by Aglaia Kremezi (2000); epicurious.com (search lemon mint braised artichokes); saveur .com (search braised artichokes).

POLITICALLY CORRECT JAVA

Turkish Coffee

Turkish, Middle Eastern

Ask for Turkish coffee in a Greek or an Armenian restaurant and be prepared to be snubbed, if not openly insulted—and for the very same treatment to be yours should you request Greek coffee at meal's end in a Turkish restaurant.

Rarely has a beverage been so loaded with political history as the darkly hot and sweetly bracing brew. Originating in Ethiopia (see page 732), the brew was carried by the Turks to the lands they occupied in the days of the Ottoman Empire.

Based on the high-quality Arabica beans introduced from Yemen to the Turks in the middle of the sixteenth century, the coffee became popular almost instantly, sparking a network of roasting shops and coffee houses that were models for those that later flourished in Vienna. Poured into espresso-size cups from long-handled, pitcherlike brewing pots made of brass or copper, the velvety brew is a steamy, bracing elixir, usually sweet enough to be almost a dessert in itself. Because Turkish coffee is served with its pulverized grounds, it should never be stirred in the cup but should instead be allowed to rest several minutes after the pour so the grounds can settle.

Even today in Istanbul, you'll find strong opinions regarding the type of beans, their degree of roasting, and which point along the Bosphorus has the best water for the brew. Although cooking with sugar in varying amounts is now the standard method, originally Turks took their coffee without any sweetener and nibbled on their intricate, honeyed pastries to counteract the bitterness. Now they—and probably you—will take both the sugared coffee and the pastries.

To prepare authentic Turkish coffee, it is necessary to have the right pot, or *cezve*. This can be large enough to make several cups, or smaller, for individual portions. It's also crucial to have authentic Turkish coffee that is ground to a very fine powder. The coffee is stirred into cold water in the pot, along with sugar, then heated very slowly to a boil (preferably, although rarely now, over a charcoal fire). Once boiling, half of the coffee is poured into cups, the balance brought back to a boil for a second time before being poured. An alternative method holds that the coffee should boil and subside three times. Either way, resist the temptation to stir, lest you end up with a mouthful of soggy powder.

When the liquid is drained from the cup, the grounds form patterns that can be read to tell your fortune, just as tea leaves can. Some cafés and restaurants in Turkey have the readers on hand. Ask for a reading if you dare.

MAIL ORDER: Istanbul Food Bazaar, tel 973-955-2989, istanbulfoodbazaar.com (search mehmet efendi turkish coffee; cube sugar); world market.com (search turkish coffee maker); for equipment, recipe, and coffee, Turkish Coffee World, tel 800-649-7438, turkishcoffeeworld.com. **FURTHER INFORMATION AND RECIPES:** *Arabesque* by Claudia Roden (2005); *A Mediterranean Feast* by Clifford A. Wright (1999); *Spice* by Ana Sortun (2006); mideastfood.about.com (search turkish coffee); npr.org (search turkish coffee); turkish-coffee.org.

IF LASAGNA WERE TURKISH

Water Börek

Turkish

Börek usually denotes a crisp and flaky phyllo-based Greek or Middle Eastern pastry that can be both sweet and savory. But this magical and dazzling Turkish main course begins with a surprise: uncooked phyllo dough that is very

briefly boiled or steamed to a noodlelike consistency. The silky, sheer-cooked sheets of dough are then layered with crumbles of feta cheese, sprinklings of dill, and a final glossing of melted butter, and baked lasagna-style into a sumptuously creamy indulgence. Although ground lamb with a touch of tomato and feta cheese is sometimes used for the filling, the pure, sunny flavors of the dairy version make for a more memorable dish.

Given the presence of dough in this main course, fitting first courses would be appetizer mezes such as the famed Turkish mussels (page 488) or vegetable dolmas stuffed with currant-studded rice pilaf (page 482); the cold stewed eggplant dish *İmam bayıldı;* the pastrami-like,

cured, spiced beef that is *pastirma* (page 489); or a tomato, cucumber, and green pepper salad. In the place of phyllo-based pastries for dessert, fruit or slices of Turkish halvah (page 483) make for lovely finales.

FURTHER INFORMATION AND RECIPES: *The Balkan Cookbook* edited by Snezana Pejakovic and Jelka Venisnik-Eror (1987); *The Sultan's Kitchen* by Ozcan Ozan (2001); *Binnur's Turkish Cookbook* by Binnur Tomay (2007); epicurious .com (search water borek); turkishcookbook .com (click Pastries, then Water Borek).

|||||||||||||||||||||||||||||||||||

WHERE THERE'S SMOKE, THERE'S EGGPLANT

Baba Ghanoush

Middle Eastern

If eggplant is the first essential ingredient in this silky, gray-green dip, smoke is certainly the second. Strikingly similar to the dish known in Romania as eggplant caviar, baba ghanoush is based on eggplant that has been slowly smoke-cooked:

either held and turned on a long fork over a gas flame, placed under a broiler, or most authentically, set on the grate of a wood-fired grill.

This last method is the one used on the streets outside of small restaurants in the Middle East, where, along with vegetables like peppers and onions, the eggplants are grilled on small charcoal braziers—tempting passers-by with mouth-watering aromas that invite them to come inside and feast. For the best results the ripely black-purple eggplant should be roasted whole, slowly and patiently for about thirty minutes, depending on its size, so it absorbs the smoke flavor as its pale green flesh becomes voluptuously satiny. Scooped out of the skin, the flesh is whipped or blended with the nut-sweet sesame paste tahini and a few shots of fresh lemon juice for tart, sunny

A famous eggplant dip

contrast. Garlic crushed to a paste with coarse salt is stirred in, and all is slightly chilled for about one hour.

Served in glass dishes, the baba ghanoush is anointed with a final, fine golden stream of olive oil, ruby red pomegranate seeds (when in season), and coarsely chopped or whole leaves of flat Italian parsley.

An accompaniment of pita is nonnegotiable.

WHERE: *In New York,* Mémé, tel 646-692-8450, memeonhudson.com; Ilili Restaurant, tel 212-683-2929, ililinyc.com. **FURTHER INFORMATION AND RECIPES:** *Arabesque* by Claudia Roden (2005); *Secrets of Cooking: Armenian, Lebanese, Persian* by Linda Chirinian (1986); epicurious .com (search baba ghanouj); cookstr.com (search baba ghanouj).

||||||||||||||||||||||||||||||||||

A UBIQUITOUS SPREAD THAT *CAN* BE SUBLIME

Hummus bi Tahini

Middle Eastern

One of the three essentials, along with tabbouleh and baba ghanoush, of the Middle Eastern appetizer array known as mezes, hummus is basically poor man's food, a nurturing, velvety bean puree enhanced with garlic and salt and luxuriously folded into the thick, mellow–sweet sesame paste that is tahini. Its economical nature partially explains its mind-boggling rags-to-riches rise to international fame, with the average big-city supermarket now offering a dizzying choice of packaged varieties, between the different brands and varied seasonings. But the answer also lies in its healthfulness, its appeal to vegetarians and those on low-fat diets, and its usefulness to hosts looking for a ready-made dip to offer with potato chips, crudités, or pieces of pita bread.

Unfortunately, popularity does not ensure a first-rate product. When practical, the most authentic hummus is made with freshly cooked (not canned) chickpeas that are worked with a stone mortar and pestle to leave behind a slight, appealing grittiness. Garlic is crushed in the mortar along with salt, and the tahini and fresh lemon juice are incorporated as a finishing touch. A slim stream of oil (preferably sesame, but olive oil is a fair alternative) drizzled over the top and a sprinkling of jewel-like pomegranate seeds lend touches of elegance.

The difference between mortar-and-pestle hummus and the blended stuff is very easy to discern. In Israel, hummus mavens can guide novices to the places that do it the old-fashioned and most delicious way.

Although primarily served for mezes, hummus slightly thinned with oil also makes a lush sauce for grilled lamb or baked fish.

Where: *In Jerusalem,* Abu Shukri, tel 972/2-627-1538; *in Houston,* Mary'z Lebanese Cuisine, tel 832-251-1955, maryzcuisine.com; *in New York,* Mémé, tel 646-692-8450, memeonhudson .com; Taim at two locations, taimfalafel.com; *in Chicago,* Athena Restaurant, tel 312-655-0000, athenarestaurantchicago.com. **Further information and recipes:** *Arabesque* by Claudia Roden (2005); *Secrets of Cooking: Armenian, Lebanese, Persian* by Linda Chirinian (1986); epicurious .com (search hummus); foodnetwork.com (search hummus for real).

||||||||||||||||||||||||||||||||||

A CHEESE THAT BEGINS AS YOGURT

Labneh

Middle Eastern

Slathered onto toasted pita bread. Seasoned with dill or garlic as a fragrant dip for raw vegetables or toasted chips. Ladled onto a gyro sandwich of sizzling hot and juicy lamb or beef. Flavored with dill or mint, garlic or minced scallions, and spread on pita that is rolled tightly, cigar-style, into a sandwich known as *arus* or *aroose*. In its many guises, labneh, the piquant fresh cheese made of yogurt, is a ubiquitous presence throughout the Middle East.

Thick, creamy, and tangy, like quark and kefir, it is made from lightly salted yogurt strained through muslin or cheesecloth. As the whey in the yogurt drains off, the cheese's flavor and texture are concentrated. Its consistency depends on how long it drains—in other words, on how much whey it loses. When labneh is drained for two or more days, it is formed into firm bite-size rounds known as *tabat labneh*, perfect for preserving in olive oil.

Historically speaking, it's this ability to be preserved that has allowed for labneh's survival since biblical days. In those times, fresh yogurt, which was made in abundance during summer months, could be transformed into labneh, then rolled into balls, preserved in oil, and set aside for winter. In any form, and no matter its precise texture, labneh is a singularly creamy palate teaser.

WHERE: *In New York,* Ilili Restaurant, tel 212-683-2929, ililinyc.com; *in Houston,* Mary'z Lebanese Cuisine, tel 832-251-1955, maryzcuisine .com; *across the U.S.,* Whole Foods Markets, wholefoodsmarket.com. **MAIL ORDER:** amazon .com (search karoun labne kefir yogurt cheese). **FURTHER INFORMATION AND RECIPES:** *Modern Flavors of Arabia* by Suzanne Husseini (2012); *Jerusalem: A Cookbook* by Yotam Ottolenghi and Sami Tamimi (2012); *Secrets of Cooking: Armenian, Lebanese, Persian* by Linda Chirinian (1986); bonappetit.com (search greek yogurt labneh); food52.com (search homemade labneh).

‖‖‖‖‖‖‖‖‖‖‖‖‖‖‖‖‖‖‖‖‖‖‖‖‖‖‖‖

SMALLER, EARTHIER, SILKIER

Lamb's Liver

Middle Eastern, Greek

Highly prized throughout the Middle East and the Balkans, lamb's liver is generally overlooked in other cuisines—and that may be just as well, considering how difficult it is to get. As a main course, at least three of the small livers would be required to adequately feed a party of four, and because each lamb is accorded only one liver, the supply is limited. What is available usually goes to butchers in Greek and Middle Eastern communities.

Far more subtle, tender, and silky than our cherished calf's liver, the lamb's liver bears the meat's same earthy, edgy meatiness. Often grilled over charcoal or wood along with lamb meat, the cubed liver is run onto skewers, alternating with bits of ivory fat and plenty of salt and pepper, to char lightly while remaining deliciously rose-pink within.

The Lebanese serve cubed lamb's liver raw, sprinkled with only a bit of lemon juice, salt, and olive oil, as part of the awesome meze appetizer spread. Or they prepare it as *mi'laaq mashwi bi toum,* in which cubes of liver are spread with a paste of crushed garlic, salt, black pepper, olive oil, and dried mint and either run onto skewers and broiled or lightly sautéed in unsalted butter. Served with fresh lemon, this dazzling and simple appetizer can also be a garnish for roasted lamb.

Not to be outdone, the Turks and Albanians have their own tempting way with lamb's liver. In *arnavut ciğeri,* the mildly anise-flavored liquor raki is the secret ingredient—used here as an astringent seasoning and marinade for the cubed meat. Drained and lightly dredged in flour, the aromatic liver is given a two-minute toss in hot olive oil and served on platters ringed with slivers of salt-wilted onions and medium-hot red chile peppers, the latter offering a sprightly, crunchy contrast to the silky meat.

MAIL ORDER: grassfedlamb.net (when available). **FURTHER INFORMATION AND RECIPES:** *The Food and Wine of Greece* by Diane Kochilas

(1993); *The Glorious Foods of Greece* by Diane Kochilas (2001); *Secrets of Cooking: Armenian, Lebanese, Persian* by Linda Chirinian (1986); saveur.com (search lamb's liver with whiskey and cream); epicurious.com (search easter lamb soup). **TIP:** If you can find lamb's liver and wish to prepare it simply at home, the rare treat shines when sliced and sautéed in butter with lemon juice, chopped parsley, and a good sprinkling of pungent capers. Lamb's liver can also be substituted for calf's liver in all recipes.

||||||||||||||||||||||||||||||||||

FOR THOSE WHO LOVE BEGINNINGS

Meze

Middle Eastern, Balkan, North African

What constitutes *mazzat* for the Lebanese, mezes for the Greeks, and *mezze* for the Turks (as well as *qimiyya* in Algeria and *ādū* in Tunisia, for the completists) is an often extensive collection of the small temptations we have

come to think of as appetizers. Yet their traditional function is as nibbles that accompany drinks and wind up standing in for dinner, in the manner of Spanish tapas or American bar food. In all of these cultures, the mezes are served communally, with guests dipping into serving bowls with pieces of bread, most often pita or the thin, crisp *lavash*. (It is said that this communal dipping implies mutual trust between guests and hosts, assuring that none need fear being poisoned—and thus the spread fulfills its role as a comforting ice-breaker and mood builder.)

The array of mezes can be almost stupefying, at its most extensive veering upward of forty small plates per outing. Such a large assortment will include varieties of olives, chunks or slices of ripe tomatoes flecked with parsley, several legume salads, snowy white cubes of earthy goat feta tossed with oily black olives and thyme, and fresh, seasonal vegetables simply presented with a bit of oil and lemon. And then

there are the meats, ranging from the usual suspects like *kibbeh* (see facing page) and various sausages to more unique offerings like boiled sheeps' feet or diced raw lamb's liver.

While each region has meze specialties of its own, some dishes are virtually universal, albeit with slight differences in seasoning. The following are a few of the most recognizable members of the array.

Tabbouleh. Foremost among mezes is the sprightly, phenomenally healthful salad most closely associated with Lebanon but with a verdant appeal that has made it an international favorite. Best in its most classic form, it should involve lots of coarsely chopped Italian parsley leaves tossed with nutlike grains of the soaked, whole wheat kernels known as bulgur, all given perky flavors and textural contrast with minced new white onions or scallions, fresh mint leaves, and sunny glossings of lemon juice and olive oil. (See page 503.)

An array of mezze adorns a table fit for a feast.

Hummus. Formally known as *hummus bi tahini,* this healthful puree of cooked chickpeas mixed with fragrantly sweet tahini (an oily sesame cream) and seasoned with hints of garlic and lemon juice is now virtually a worldwide staple. (See page 496.)

Tahini. The pure, creamy sesame paste, thinned with lemon juice and just enough water to make a mayonnaise-like consistency, may be enhanced with crushed garlic and salt to become a seductive dip on its own. It is also served as a sauce for grilled fish or for falafel in pita sandwiches.

Baba ghanoush. This satiny, celadon-colored puree gets its distinctive character from smoked eggplants that are preferably cooked over a wood-fired grill or open flame. Grilled whole until their insides collapse, the eggplants are peeled and their flesh is whipped into light cloudlets with salt, lemon juice, olive oil, garlic, and an enrichment of tahini. (See page 495.)

Cacık. Slivers of icy cucumber enfolded in a cool, creamy mix of yogurt, a little bit of water, and a heady pinch of crushed garlic and dried mint, *cacık* appears in various thicknesses—serving as salad, dip, or even soup.

Börek. Tiny, flaky phyllo turnovers filled with meat, cheese, or spinach are crunchy regulars on meze platters.

Kibbeh. A Lebanese specialty that has become a standard meze throughout the Middle East, *kibbeh* takes many forms. A soft, pasty blend of oniony lamb and whole wheat bulgur, it is made as authentically and as silkily as possible when tender raw lamb loin is pounded with coarse salt in a stone mortar with a wooden pestle.

Fritters and other fried foods. A range of fritters, from cheese and zucchini to even calves' or lambs' brains, are significant parts of the meze. (In cultures where alcohol is permitted, the meze is traditionally served alongside copious amounts of alcohol, and so heavier foods tend to reign.)

Fish. From fresh sardines and stuffed or fried mussels to fish smoked or marinated and grilled, the ocean lends a pungent depth to the meze (see Midye Dolmasi and Midye Tava, page 488).

To further compound the profusion of choices among such gastronomic riches, Iranian entries in the meze canon include *nan-o panir-o-gerdu,* a savory feta cheese and walnut dip made fragrant with basil, tarragon, mint, and garlic; the lentil dip called *adasi,* scented with orange and lime juices and angelica powder; and *kuku sabzi,* an aromatic, emerald-green herb frittata.

Other meze offerings may include slices of cold spicy sausages and pastirma (see page 489), glistening meat aspics, vegetables such as string beans or okra stewed with tomatoes, and miniature dolmas (see page 482), most especially those made with grape leaves.

The drink to pair with all of these enticements is an anise-flavored spirit that turns translucently milky when diluted with ice water—

ouzo to the Greeks, raki to the Turks, and arak in Lebanon and its environs. For observant Muslims, spring water, soft drinks, or fresh juices are the beverages of choice.

WHERE: *In Beirut,* for kibbeh, Al-Halabi, tel 961/452-3555; *in Brooklyn,* Tanoreen, tel 718-748-5600, tanoreen.com; *in Chicago,* The Parthenon, tel 312-546-3751, theparthenon.reachlocal.net; *in Houston,* Yia Yia Mary's, tel 713-840-8665, yiayiamarys.com; Mary'z

Lebanese Cuisine, tel 832-251-1955, maryz cuisine.com; *in Glendale, CA,* Phoenicia, tel 818-956-7800, phoeniciala.com; *in Montreal,* Barbounya, tel 514-439-8858, barbounya.com. **FURTHER INFORMATION AND RECIPES:** *A Mediterranean Feast* by Clifford A. Wright (1999); *A Taste of Persia* by Najmieh Batmanglij; *Arabesque* by Claudia Roden (2005); *The Glorious Foods of Greece* by Diane Kochilas (2001); *The Cuisine of Armenia* by Sonia Uvezian (2004).

THE AMAZING SPICE WORLD OF ANA SORTUN

Oleana Restaurant and Sofra Bakery and Café

Middle Eastern

Cambridge, Massachusetts, is rightly known as a place of learning—but for those with an adventurous palate and a taste for the exotic, its most valuable lessons may be those taught by Ana Sortun. Whether in her glowingly

romantic but informal restaurant Oleana, or in Sofra, her bustling bakery-café, she puts together an entrancing curriculum based on the spices that have been her passion ever since her first experiences of Turkey and its cuisine.

Just about all of the Middle Eastern and Mediterranean herbs and spices are featured in her dishes—sometimes flavoring the fresh produce she and her husband grow on their farm—to captivating results. At Oleana, that might mean fried mussels graced with the Turkish *tarator* sauce that blends almonds and garlic, or spring's first wild green nettles laced with Armenian halloumi string cheese and the sorrel-zapped yogurt cheese called *labneh* (see page

Ana Sortun, Oleana's chef

496). Escargots are enfolded in the same shredded-wheat-like pastry used for the dessert *kadayıf,* and served with smoked hummus and tabbouleh based on nicely peppery watercress instead of the usual parsley.

Whether you try lamb with Turkish spices, fried, flattened lemon chicken enlivened by the spice mix *za'atar,* or a frothy lamb and eggplant moussaka, you will be plagued with regret when you see all the many other enticing dishes alighting around you.

Solution: Keep going back until you have tried them all, and take friends along for shared tastings.

No matter when you go to the small, lively bakery-café that is Sofra, be prepared to wait your turn, most especially for weekend brunch. Homey, traditional dishes are the thing here, among them many soft, engaging mezes (see page 498) and egg numbers—a wonderful version of the egg-green-pepper-onion-tomato mix that is *chakchouka* (see page 697) stands out. With your cup of Turkish coffee, you can munch on a sesame-covered bagel-shaped *simit* (see page 492), an array of lusciously stuffed flatbreads, or cakes whose spices would seduce a sultan.

Where: *In Cambridge, MA,* Oleana, 134 Hampshire St., tel 617-661-0505, oleanarestaurant .com; Sofra Bakery and Café, 1 Belmont St., tel 617-661-3161, sofrabakery.com. **Further information and recipes:** *Spice: Flavors of the Eastern Mediterranean* by Ana Sortun (2006).

|||||||||||||||||||||||||||||||||||||||||||||||||||||||||||||||||||||||||||||||||||||||||||||||||||||||||||||||||||

"THE OLIVE TREE IS SURELY THE RICHEST GIFT OF HEAVEN."—THOMAS JEFFERSON

Olive Oil

What is left to say about olive oil? Since Old Testament times and even before, the sunny bronze, deliciously earthy and complex substance has been celebrated in contexts ranging from poetry to cosmetology (sometimes to the point of tiresome hype). Praised as much for its health-inducing qualities as for its contributions to gourmandise, the oil—prized perhaps more than the olives themselves—is the product of a beautifully gnarled, silver-leafed tree that can flourish for centuries.

Native to the Middle East, the *Olea europaea* is deeply rooted (literally, as its roots sometimes plunge 20 feet down into the ground) around the Mediterranean Sea, where it has long been cherished for the golden, green-tinged oil distilled from its bitter oval fruits. Greek athletes prized the oil as a coating for the skin, using it during competitions to create a barrier against dust. But early gastronomes also recognized the earthen oil's unrivaled potential in the kitchen, using it as a simple dip for salads and vegetables—history's first salad dressing—or as an aid in cooking.

Obtained by extraction, the oil is drawn from a paste of crushed olives, pit and all. Differences in pressing technique result in varying levels of quality, which trickle down according to labeling regulations meted out by the International Olive Council, headquartered in Madrid, and by various regional certification groups. While heated or repeated extractions draw the largest quantity of oil, single cold pressings produce some of the highest-quality oils, full-flavored and ranging from fruity and flowery to grassy and intensely sour-bitter, often with a peppery aftertaste. "Extra virgin" refers to oils that have been simply milled, pressed, and centrifuged, using no chemicals or heat. To receive this demarcation, the oil must also pass a tasting panel and tests measuring free fatty acids (extra virgin oils consist of less than 1 percent fatty acids, while virgin oils contain less than 2 percent).

Olives are grown and pressed throughout the Mediterranean and in places with similarly warm climates, including California and New Zealand, but the most delicate and nuanced oil derives from olives grown in France. There, small, ripe, black olives create sweet oils with an earthy patina that hints of the Provence sun. Italy, no slouch in this department either, harvests taggiasca olives around Liguria and Tuscany to create crisp, fruity oils that provide the perfect light dressing for any salad. And in Spain, one of the world's largest oil-producing countries, picual olives are pressed into peppery oils that are excellent for cooking. But that's only the beginning of the story. There are dozens of olive varieties, and

the fruits produce hundreds of differently textured and flavored oils—their nuances inspire a
connoisseurship that rivals that of oenophiles.
(Right down to the notion of tastings.)

Mail order: Zingerman's, tel 888-636-8162,
zingermans.com; olio2go.com, tel 866-654-6246.
Further information: *A Mediterranean Feast* by
Clifford A. Wright (1999); oliveoilsource.com;
Italian olive oil, olio2go.com; Spanish olive oil,
oliveoilfromspain.com; Greek olive oil, greek

oliveoils.com; French olive oil, creme-de-
languedoc.com (search olive oil). **Special events:**
New York International Olive Oil Competition,
New York City, April, nyoliveoil.com; Olive Tree
and Olive Oil Festival, Brisighella, Italy,
November, brisighella.org (click Events). **Tip:**
Olive oil should be stored in dark-colored glass
bottles kept in cool, dark places. The chlorophyll
that is responsible for the oil's bronze-green hue
also makes it sensitive to light.

—||||||||||||||||||||||||||||||||||||—

SEEDED FOR CRUNCH

Semsemiyeh

Sesame Seed Brittle

Middle Eastern, Arabic

Aconfection that we might take for granted, owing to its wide presence in health
food stores and at some of the most ordinary candy counters and shops,
sesame seed brittle can be a tantalizing and exotic treat—and it's a sweet fix

one can feel nobly healthy about.

Relatively inexpensive because of the simplicity of its ingredients, *semsemiyeh* (pronounced sin-see-MEE-yah) owes its magical
reputation to those tiny, crackling golden sesame
seeds. The crunchy, usually honey-sweetened
candy provides a between-meals lift to children
and adults alike. Sugar sometimes stands in, and
flavorings like rose- or orange blossom water or
even vanilla extract may be added to the mix. If
preparing this candy at home, taste the sesame
seeds to be sure they are not rancid.

An elemental candy made of sesame and honey

Sesame Seed Brittle

Makes about 12 servings

Sesame, peanut, or canola oil,
    for oiling the work surface
1¼ cups golden honey
1 scant teaspoon rosewater or orange
    blossom water, or ½ teaspoon pure
    vanilla extract
1¼ cups sesame seeds

1. Prepare a baking sheet or marble slab by
brushing the surface lightly with sesame, peanut, or canola oil, and oil the surface of a
wooden rolling pin.
2. Bring the honey to a boil in a heavy 2-quart
saucepan over low heat. Watch it very carefully,
as honey can boil over all at once, making a terrific and dangerous mess. Turn off the heat as
soon as honey begins to boil and add the rosewater, orange blossom water, or vanilla.
3. Quickly stir in the sesame seeds and beat the

mixture vigorously with a wooden spoon until it becomes thick and opaque, about 7 minutes. Pour the sesame seed mixture onto the prepared work surface and, using the prepared rolling pin and a light pressure, roll it flat to a thickness of about ¼ inch. Using a wide blade knife, quickly cut the sesame brittle into roughly 1- by 2-inch lozenge shapes before the candy has hardened. Let the brittle harden in a cool room overnight.

4. When thoroughly hardened, the sesame brittle pieces should be individually wrapped in plastic wrap and stored in a cool, dry place.

RETAIL AND MAIL ORDER: *In New York,* for seeds and flower waters, Kalustyan's, tel 800-352-3451, kalustyans.com; Sahadi's, tel 718-624-4550, sahadis.com. **MAIL ORDER:** candy.com (search joyva sesame honey crunch); amazon.com (search joyva sesame bars; kevala organic toasted sesame seeds; kay white rosewater; nielsen-massey orange blossom water). **FURTHER INFORMATION AND ADDITIONAL RECIPE:** *The Arabian Delights Cookbook* by Anne Marie Weiss-Armush (1993). **TIP:** Try this treat with hot mint tea, as they do in the Middle East.

WHERE FRESHNESS IS A KEY INGREDIENT

Tabbouleh

Middle Eastern, especially Lebanese

There's a lot of good cooking done throughout the Middle East, but some would argue that the most elegant versions of many of the region's dishes can be found in Lebanon. Nowhere is this argument borne out more noticeably than in the country's dazzling array of meze appetizers, with some Beirut cafés and restaurants offering assortments that contain between twenty and thirty exquisitely laid-out little dishes. Always among those (along with *hummus bi tahini,* baba ghanoush, and diced feta cheese with black olives and thyme) is tabbouleh, the bulgur, parsley, and mint salad whose popularity has resulted in many unfortunate incidents of mass-production.

In the real deal, toasty, nutty, bulgur wheat lends heft and intrigue to an onion-and-lemon-scented mix. The addition of tomato is optional—preferably as a side, so that its juices do not water down the verdant, leafy mix.

Tabbouleh

Serves about 8 as part of mixed mezes

*1 cup medium-grain bulgur
(use unprocessed, not precooked bulgur)*
1 cup finely chopped new, sweet onion
1 teaspoon salt
¼ teaspoon freshly ground black pepper
*1½ cups finely chopped flat-leaf parsley
leaves*
½ cup finely chopped spearmint leaves
*½ cup finely chopped, drained tomatoes
(optional), plus sliced tomatoes,
for garnish*
About ¾ cup olive oil
Juice of ½ large lemon
*Pita bread or sturdy lettuce leaves,
for serving*

1. Rinse the bulgur under cold running water several times until the water is clear. Soak the bulgur in cold water to cover for about 2 hours. Drain the bulgur, pressing out the excess water.

2. Place the bulgur in a mixing bowl and stir in the onion, salt, and pepper until well distributed. Add the parsley, spearmint, chopped tomatoes, if using, and just enough olive oil to make a moist mix without any excess unabsorbed oil.

3. Gradually add lemon juice to taste; the flavor should be pleasantly but not overwhelmingly tart. Taste for seasoning, adding more salt and/or pepper as necessary.

4. Serve the tabbouleh on a platter garnished with the tomato wedges and offer plenty of pita bread or loose lettuce leaves for scooping.

Where: *In New York,* Ali Baba at two

A classic among salads

locations, tel 212-683-9209, aliba baturkishcuisine.com. **Retail and mail order:** *In New York,* for bulgur, Kalustyan's, tel 800-352-3451, kalustyans.com (search bulghar); *in Brooklyn,* Sahadi's, tel 718-624-4550, sahadis.com (search bulgur). **Tip:** The essence of tabbouleh is freshness, with all ingredients chopped together no more than two hours before they are served. However, flavor improves during the first half hour, when the tabbouleh should be held, loosely covered, in the refrigerator.

|||||||||||||||||||||||||||||||||||||||||||||||||||||||||||||||||||||||||||||||||||||||||||||||||||||||||||||||||||||

PLEASE *DO* EAT THE GARNISH . . .

Parsley

So certain are some chefs that no guest actually eats the clumps of parsley garnishing their plates, they may not bother to wash it—an unfortunate reality for anyone biting into an unpleasant dose of grit, and an injustice to boot. Believed to whet the appetite and, due to its chlorophyll content, to sweeten the breath, delicious fresh parsley *should* be considered a green vegetable. As a bonus, it has virtually no calories and is high in Vitamin C and minerals such as iron, potassium, and sulfur salts, and also in antioxidants and fiber.

The herb is a member of the *Umbelliferea* botanical family, as is celery, and in fact the two are so closely related that ancient Greeks called them both *selinum;* the ancient Romans called parsley *Petroselinum,* hence its botanical name, *Petroselinum crispum.* Difficult to grow though hardy once propagated, in Medieval times it was thought to be the plant for the devil, one that could be planted successfully only on Good Friday, and only if the moon was rising.

Though an old English country saying warned that "Only the wicked can grow parsley," the plant has also been considered a harbinger of spring, figuring in the celebrations of both Passover and Easter.

The wicked herb comes in two varieties, flat-leaf Italian parsley and the curly kind known as curled parsley and common parsley. (The herb sometimes referred to as "Chinese parsley" is not actually parsley but rather cilantro, or coriander.) Of the two kinds of parsley, the flat variety is the superior flavoring, added to long-cooking dishes for its more robust, bright accent. Curly parsley, although also used as a slightly milder seasoning, is preferable as a garnish and in salads. Its leaves can be chopped to a finer texture for sprinkling, and overall its looks are more appealing.

Valued for the lift it gives to meat, fish and vegetable dishes, whether sprinkled over the cooked food or worked into its preparation, parsley also adds interest when stirred into cream or green olive oil sauces or mashed into compound butters, perhaps with garlic or shallots. But finding ways to present the herb on its own may be less obvious. Foremost among the tempting traditional recipes that feature it is the lively Middle Eastern salad, tabbouleh (see page 503). London chef Fergus Henderson used it to advantage in a salad of bone marrow with parsley and onions that was made famous at his St. John Bar & Restaurant (see page 26). But there's no need for parsley's reign to stop there.

Consider making it the star of a parsley cream soup, the main flavoring of a green risotto, or frying its leaves to a crisp emerald glow as a garnish for meat, fish, and poultry.

Mail order: For seeds, amazon.com (search parsley triple curled; herb parsley giant of italy). **Further information and recipes:** *The Whole Beast* by Fergus Henderson (2004); saveur.com (search parsley onion salad; cream of parsley soup; fried curly parsley); epicurious .com (search green herb risotto).

WHERE THE FLAVOR IS

Za'atar

Middle Eastern

A Middle Eastern herb with a pleasantly musty, dry and earthy essence that's vaguely reminiscent of oregano, thyme, and sage, *za'atar* (*Origanum syriacum*) grows wild most profusely in the Judean hills of Israel. Considered a cure for

everything from tooth decay to chronic cough to fatigue (when made into a stimulating tea), it's also known as the biblical hyssop. Za'atar can be combined as a blend with ground thyme, oregano, sumac, toasted sesame seeds, salt, and sometimes marjoram, a mix that is also known as za'atar and whose exact formula varies among countries. (Sometimes it doesn't actually include the herb za'atar; Jordanians opt for sumac, while in Lebanon the combination is sparked by dried orange peel.)

An herb beloved for its savory flavor

The za'atar herb itself has been overharvested to such an extent that the Haganat Hatevah, the Society for the Protection of Nature in Israel, now regulates the crop—but thankfully it is still widely available, and widely used.

Za'atar is a favorite at breakfast, added into croissants or atop pitas. For lunch it can be blended with olive oil or yogurt as a dip for pita. At dinner, it works its magic as an aromatic rub for meats, especially lamb.

Mail order: The Spice House, tel 847-328-3711, thespice house.com (search za'atar); amazon.com (search lebanon za'atar); Penzeys Spices, tel 800-741-7787, penzeys.com; Zamouri Spices, tel 913-829-5988, zamouri spices.com. **Further information and recipes:** *Planet Barbecue* by Steven Raichlen (2010); *Spice* by Ana Sortun (2006); *Jerusalem: A Cookbook* by Yotam Ottolenghi and Sami Tamimi (2012); mideastfoodabout.com (search za'atar recipe); cookstr.com (search za'atar; roasted chicken).

————————|||||||||||||||||||||||||||||||||————————

An Afghanistan Dinner

Afghani

At first glance, both the dishes and their names might seem to be Indian or Pakistani, Iranian or Mongolian, or, quite possibly, Middle Eastern. But a closer look and a few intriguing bites reveal an altogether different cuisine: the food of Afghanistan, similar in many ways to those cuisines it echoes, but with a hand-crafted look and a rustic, exotic flavor paradigm all its own. Yes, you'll find rice, kebabs, stuffed vegetables, and lots of lamb, beef, spinach, eggplant, pumpkin, cilantro, yogurt, mint, cardamom, cinnamon, and hot chiles here, but they are employed in tantalizing ways, with sweet and sour or hot and cool qualities often mingling together in one dish.

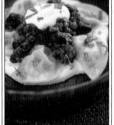

Afghani food first came onto the world stage in the 1970s, when Russia's invasion of that ancient land along the Silk Road drove refugees to the U.S. Some started small kebab houses in a few large cities, eventually graduating to more formal restaurants serving a wide range of dishes.

Aushak pasta with leek filling

These restaurants' menus, daunting at first glance, can be deliciously deciphered in the space of a couple of meals. Two of the country's most traditional soups usually start things off: *aush,* with its spicy ground beef, chewy handmade noodles, vegetables, and yogurt; or *mashawa,* a lighter, clearer mix of the same ingredients. Other tantalizing appetizers include *aushak,* leek dumplings that can be filled with beans or with ground beef, garnished in either case with minted yogurt; *bulanee gandana,* crisp, yogurt-topped pancakes stuffed with slivered scallions; and the crunchy pastry half-moons called *sambossas,* plumped with ground beef and mashed chickpeas and offset by a spicy yogurt sauce. Not to be overlooked are two tempting eggplant dishes: *borani,* in which the nightshade is cooked in tomato sauce, or *bharta,* a spread of roasted eggplant enlivened with garlicky yogurt and fiery chile peppers.

As a gratifyingly hearty main course, there's the famous *quabili palaw* (or *pilau*), an Afghani favorite. A rice-based dish made with chicken or lamb, it is enriched with caramelized carrots and onions, raisins, toasted almonds, and a rainbow of spices. Okra, a favored vegetable, lends its seductive viscosity to *chalous,* or rice dishes, along with lamb, onions, sweet green peppers, and tomatoes. *Samaaruq o rawaasg* is a seasonal offering of springtime rhubarb simmered with mushrooms and lamb in a piquant onion and tomato sauce. Currylike kormas include the lovely *korma-e-sabzi,* lamb braised with spinach and leeks, or *korma-e-daal,* in which the meat is served with onion- and garlic-flavored yellow lentils. And then, of course, there are the kebabs, most deliciously, the *kebab-e-murgh* and *kebab-e-gosfand.* The first serves up bits of boneless, skewer-grilled chicken with a cilantro-accented chutney on basmati rice, and the second is a lamb version skewered with tomatoes and onions.

Alongside come stingingly refreshing chutneys sparked with vinegar, chiles, the pickled fruits or vegetables known as *torshi,* and the

yeasty, ridged naan, a version of the flat Mughlai bread of the same name, but crackling under toppings of pungent, oniony black nigella seeds.

That describes just a sampling of the rich and complex Afghani menu. Although an Afghani dinner can include dessert, given its breadth, it is probably best finished off with a cup of hot cardamom-scented tea.

WHERE: *In Boston,* The Helmand, tel 617-492-4646, helmandrestaurant.com; *in St. Paul, MN,* Khyber Pass Café, tel 651-690-0505, khyberpass cafe.com; *in Skokie, Il,* Kabul House, tel 847-674-3830, kabulhouse.com; *in New York,* at three locations, Afghan Kebab House; *in Seattle,* Kabul Afghan Cuisine, tel 206-545-9000, kabul restaurant.com; *in Danville, CA,* Aryana Afghan Cuisine, tel 925-736-7781; *in Gardena, CA,* Afghan Express Restaurant, tel 310-920-7732, afghanexpressrestaurant.com. **FURTHER INFORMATION AND RECIPES:** *Flatbreads and Flavors* by Jeffrey Alford and Naomi Duguid (2008); *Afghan Food & Cookery* by Helen Saberi (2000); *Classic Afghan Cookbook* by Mousa M. Amiri (2002); afghankitchenrecipes.com; afghancooking.net.

A SWEET "SOUP" AT CHRISTMAS

Anoush Aboor

Golden Wheat and Apricot Pudding

Armenian, Turkish

Although it literally translates as sweet soup, *anoush aboor* is a sumptuous cold pudding and a traditional Armenian dessert served from Christmas to New Year's. Toothsome whole wheat berries (*gorgod* in Armenian) sweetened with honey and rosewater and studded with nuts and jewels of coral dried apricots and ruby pomegranate seeds, it's a mix that could be rebranded as a high-fiber health food treat. But seductive pleasure is enough of a reason to try what's actually quite an elegant dessert.

As in so many cultures, throughout Turkey and Armenia wheat grains symbolize prosperity. In Lebanon, the similar wheat berry dessert *kamhié* is laced with diced candied fruits. In Poland and Ukraine, the wheat berries go into the Christmas Eve pudding called *kutya*, cooked with honey and stirred through with nuts and ground poppy seeds, minus the dried fruits (see page 401).

Anoush Aboor

Serves 8 to 10

*3 cups hulled whole wheat berries
   (gorgod—or see Note below)*

1 teaspoon salt
1 cup golden raisins
12 dried apricots, quartered
½ cup pine nuts
½ cup chopped walnuts
½ cup blanched almonds
½ cup sugar, plus additional for garnish
½ cup honey
3 or 4 drops rose water
Ground cinnamon, for garnish
*Chopped nuts, for garnish (any or all of
   the nuts above will do nicely)*
*Pomegranate seeds (optional),
   for garnish*

1. Bring 8 cups of water to a boil in a large saucepan.

2. Meanwhile, rinse the wheat berries in a bowl in several changes of cold water until the water is clear and no dust remains on the berries.

Drain the wheat berries well and add them to the boiling water. Cover the pan tightly and let the wheat berries simmer slowly over low heat until the berries are completely tender. This will take between 3 and 5 hours, depending on the quality of the wheat berries. When the wheat berries are almost tender, add the teaspoon of salt and continue cooking until the wheat berries reach the consistency of porridge.

3. Drain off remaining water, if there is any. Place the pan over low heat and add the raisins, apricots, pine nuts, walnuts, almonds, sugar, and honey, stirring until the sugar has dissolved and the mixture is well blended, thick, and moist. Taste for sweetness, adding more sugar or honey as desired, and salt if needed. Turn off the heat and stir in the rosewater.

4. Spoon the pudding into a large bowl or individual serving bowls and chill until serving time. Just before serving, stir the pudding gently and top it with cinnamon, sugar, chopped nuts, and pomegranate seeds, if desired.

Note: The Italian whole-kernel wheat farro can be substituted for gorgod.

Mail order: amazon.com (search whole wheat berries; pearled farro). **Further information and other recipes:** *Secrets of Cooking: Armenian, Lebanese, Persian* by Linda Chirinian (1986); *The Cuisine of Armenia* by Sonia Uvezian (2004).

—||||||||||||||||||||||||||||||||||||—

A JEWEL OF A SOUP

Ash-e Anar

Pomegranate Soup

Iranian

With its jewel-like colors and beguiling aromas, few cuisines can match Iran's in terms of sheer sensory seduction. Think ruby glints of pomegranate seed, golden washes of saffron, the emerald sparkle of fresh coriander and mint leaves.

Or orangey turmeric, hot and sweet red chile peppers, earthy cumin, the pungent juice of limes or of bittersweet Seville oranges, crunches of jade pistachios or ivory almonds . . . The myriad herbs and seasonings that waft up from the country's luxurious hot dishes delight the nose as well as the eye, and of course, the palate.

That's certainly true of a soup no food lover should go without trying, and which begins and ends with pomegranates, the symbol of fertility and plenty. Good-luck pomegranates are worked into the soup first as paste and juice, combined with a base of pungently seasoned amber-yellow split peas. Fresh herbs and the ever-present turmeric are joined by plenty of black pepper and a hint of the airy, elusive angelica. A little lean ground beef or lamb and rice are added for extra body, along with one finely chopped beet cooked in the soup until it virtually disappears, leaving only its color behind.

The flavors are as vivid as the colors here, the final soup emerging with the sweet, sour, and winey overtones of the pomegranates, a combination that achieves extra depth if the soup is allowed to mellow and ripen in the refrigerator for twenty-four hours. For good measure, individual portions of the hot soup are garnished with a green-gold sauce of parsley sautéed with garlic and turmeric, and a final sprinkling of shiny pomegranate seeds.

Where: *In Houston,* Saffron Persian Café, tel 713-780-7474; Café Caspian, tel 281-493-4000, cafecaspian.com; **Mail order:** For whole pomegranates, November–January, pomstoyou

.com; for whole pomegranates and seeds, Melissa's Produce, tel 800-588-0151, melissas .com; for pomegranate juice, amazon.com. **FURTHER INFORMATION AND RECIPES:** *A Taste of Persia* by Najmieh Batmanglij (2004); *Secrets of*

Cooking: Armenian, Lebanese, Persian by Linda Chirinian (1986); *Pomegranates: 70 Celebratory Recipes* by Ann Kleinberg (2004); foodandwine. com (search persian pomegranate soup with meatballs).

IRAN'S NATIONAL DISH

Chelo Kebab

Iranian

Perhaps the most sublime of all Middle Eastern grills, this Iranian specialty begins with the savory *kubideh* (meaning squashed) *kebab* of ground lamb (and sometimes beef) and grated onion and saffron, marinated in yogurt and garlic.

What makes it a *chelo kebab* is the way the smoky charcoal-grilled meat is slid off its skewers and onto a bed of mellow basmati rice. A Tehran tradition sold in many of the pita shops that dot the city, it is made at home for holidays and special occasions like Norooz, or "New Day," the two-week observance of the Persian New Year that begins in mid-March.

The rice, cooked slowly until it forms a marvelously crunchy crust, is no slouch. Glossed with melted butter, it is enriched by a raw egg yolk broken and stirred into the mix along with the bright spice of sumac. Grilled tomatoes and warm pita bread provide the finishing touches to a feast

that is at once elegant and reassuringly rustic.

WHERE: *In Chicago*, Noon-O-Kabab, tel 773-279-9309, noonokabab.co; *in Sunnyvale, CA*, Chelokababi Restaurant, tel 408-737-1222, chelo kababi.com; *in Los Angeles*, Attari Sandwich Shop and Grill, tel 310-446-4660, attarisandwiches. com; *in Vienna, VA*, Shamshiry, tel 703-448-8883, shamshiry.com. **FURTHER INFORMATION AND RECIPES:** *New Persian Cooking* by Jila Dana-Haeri, Shahrzad Ghorashian, and Jason Lowe (2011); *A Taste of Persia* by Najmieh K. Batmanglij (2007); *Secrets of Cooking: Armenian, Lebanese, Persian* by Linda Chirinian (1986); saveur.com (search persian kebabs).

A NUT IN A LEAGUE OF ITS OWN

Pistachios

Iranian, Turkish

Sweet and tender, but with just enough crunch to entice, the small green pistachio (*Pistacia vera*) is one of the world's most prized nuts, an ancient pleasure beloved for its exotic flavor and its naturally salty essence. When it's not being compulsively eaten out of its shell, the pistachio is most often served roasted and salted. Its flavor, distilled to a gorgeously perfumy essence, is a famous enhancer of ice cream, candies, cakes, cookies, and on the savory side, of Middle Eastern stews.

A native of Turkey and Afghanistan, the low and bushy pistachio tree was introduced to Europe in the first century A.D. and today flourishes throughout the Middle East, the Mediterranean, and parts of North Africa. It is also widely cultivated in California, in whose climate it thrives. The best, biggest, and most intensely flavorful pistachios grow in Iran, the world's largest producer, but global sanctions currently prevent the importation of its sublime product.

The edible pistachio nut is the kernel inside the stone of a small, olivelike, and otherwise inedible fruit called a drupe. When the pistachio is ripe, the fruit turns red and the stone inside (the nut shell) parts slightly to expose the nut, making it easy to open—a stage often described as "laughing," which is what the shell looks like it's doing. But the joke's not on you. Pistachios are not only addictively delicious but are also high in antioxidants, amino acids, and the monounsaturated fats said to promote cardiovascular health.

Have you spied a red-shelled pistachio? It's not green pistachio's cousin or an effect related to the ripening of the fruit, but rather a now-uncommon marketing trick achieved via food coloring.

MAIL ORDER: Zenobia, tel 866- 936-6242, nuts onthenet.com. **FURTHER INFORMATION AND RECIPES:** *Arabesque* by Claudia Roden (2005); *The Foods of the Greek Islands* by Aglaia Kremezi (2000); *Nuts: More than 75 Delicious & Healthy Recipes* by Avner Laskin (2008); *A Taste of Persia* by Najmieh Batmanglij (2007); *Jerusalem: A Cookbook* by Yotam Ottolenghi and Sami Tamimi (2012); americanpistachios.org; cookstr .com (search pistachios); bonappetit.com (search spiced pistachios). **TIP:** Look for Zenobia brand pistachios. **SPECIAL EVENT:** Aegina Fistiki Fest (Aegina Pistachio Festival), Aegina, Greece, September, aeginafistikifest.gr.

---||||||||||||||||||||||||||||||||---

FOR GOOD FORTUNE AND FECUNDITY

Pomegranates

Iranian, Middle Eastern

If rubies could be liquified, the result might taste like the vibrant juice of the pomegranate—and in fact, liquifying rubies might well prove easier than trying to eat a pomegranate while maintaining a modicum of dignity.

Covered in leathery crimson skin, the pomegranate's globe encloses a matrix of tightly packed slippery, juicy, red arils surrounding white seeds. The arils are the edible part, so the pomegranates must be split open, a task best performed over a sink and in an outfit composed of disposable rags. The sink is also the best place to take mouthfuls of the seeds, chew out and swallow the luscious juices, and expectorate the seeds, edible but fibrous.

The pomegranate (*Punica granatum*) is native to Iran, but the fruit has charmed its way around the world, in its most ancient days distributed by the birds that dropped its seeds in distant gardens. The venerable fruits are even mentioned in the Bible—in Deuteronomy,

Moses promises to bring his people to "a land of wheat and barley, and vines and fig-trees and pomegranates."

Because of its many seeds, the pomegranate has long been a symbol of fertility and good fortune in Iran. The ruby-red fruit has also had a symbolic presence in Greek mythology. When Persephone, the daughter of Demeter (goddess of agriculture), is kidnapped to the underworld by Hades, he persuades her to eat six pomegranate seeds, dooming her to spend six months of each year in the underworld—during which time her mother's sadness on earth above would result in the gray, cold months of fall and winter.

Often called the "jewel of autumn"

Today, more than 760 varieties of the fruit are grown, and for centuries they have been cultivated all over the Middle East, in Egypt, Azerbaijan, and Israel in particular. By the eighteenth century, pomegranates had reached California by way of the American South, and there they flourished.

Good, ripe pomegranates have a perfumey, sweet-tart flavor prized in Middle Eastern cooking in seed form, or in jams and syrups, the former often used as a piquant garnish for hummus and baba ghanoush. But in the United States they've become something of a one-note wonder. In about the year 2000, the California-based company POM Wonderful, producers of fresh pomegranate juice, released studies touting the nutritional benefits of the antioxidant-packed, inflammation-fighting so-called "superfruit" the company used in its juices, and a pomegranate fever took hold.

Indeed, pomegranates are quite healthful—but the best way to get their benefits is to dig into the real thing. Back to the sink.

WHERE: Pomegranates can be found in upscale greengrocers, usually from October to February, and especially around Thanksgiving and Christmas. **MAIL ORDER:** Melissa's Produce, tel 800-588-0151, melissas .com; for pomegranate juices and teas, pom wonderful.com. **FURTHER INFORMATION AND RECIPES:** *Pomegranates: 70 Celebratory Recipes* by Ann Kleinberg (2004); *A Taste of Persia* by Najmieh Batmanglij (2007); *Arabesque* by Claudia Roden (2005); *The Foods of the Greek Islands* by Aglaia Kremezi (2000); cookstr.com (search pomegranate ice cream; warm lamb salad with pomegranate and walnuts); pome granates.org; pomwonderful.com. **SPECIAL EVENT:** Madera's Annual Pomegranate Festival, Madera, CA, November, pomegranatefestival.com.

----------||||||||||||||||||||||||||||||----------

YOU GOTTA HAVE HEART

Meorav Yerushalmi

Jerusalem Mixed Grill

Israeli

Among the world's popular street foods, it is doubtful that any could seem as improbable as a Jerusalem mixed grill (*meorav Yerushalmi*), an exuberant mixture of finely chopped, griddle-seared chicken hearts, necks, kidneys, livers, spleens, and other poultry offal—also known as "spare parts"—perfumed with onion, garlic, and a cloud of aromatic Middle Eastern spices, including turmeric, coriander, cloves, cardamom, and sumac. These spices account for the magic of this potent, deeply fragrant dish in which meat is flash-fried on a hot griddle and served hot off the grill top, either strewn on a platter or spooned into a pocket of soft, warm pita bread.

Wildly flavorful, enticingly chewy, and luxuriously greasy, this tumble of spare parts is the epitome of soul food. But you won't find it in full-fledged restaurants, or even at Grandma's. Meorav, as it's commonly called, is served almost exclusively in fast-food joints—it's a staple throughout Jerusalem and especially within the Mahane Yehuda, the city's venerable (100-plus-year-old) and massive outdoor marketplace. You can get a meorav there almost any time of day, but it's an especially popular treat at night among the young and hungry carousers who know a good thing when they taste it.

WHERE: *In Jerusalem,* Mahane Yehuda market, machne.co.il/en; Sima's, 82 Agrippas Street; *in Brooklyn,* Jerusalem Steakhouses II, tel 718-376-0680, jerusalemsteakhouse.com; *in Houston,* Al Aseel Grill & Café, tel 713-787-0400, alaseel grill.com. **FURTHER INFORMATION AND RECIPES:** *Jerusalem: A Cookbook* by Yotam Ottolenghi and Sami Tamimi (2012); *The Foods of Israel* by Sherry Ansky (2000); saveur.com (search jerusalem mixed grill).

||||||||||||||||||||||||||||||||||||||||||||||||||||||||||||||||||||||||||||||||||||||||||||||||||||||||||||||||||||||||

HOW GREEN ARE YOUR ALMONDS?

Green Almonds

Delicately crunchy and sweetly mellow, the mature almond has its share of fans. But a far more transporting taste sensation can be had when the elegant nut is consumed *before* it has fully ripened, when it is still a delicate springtime green. With its fuzzy, suedelike celadon covering peeled off, the moist kernel, gently firm against the teeth, reveals a fruity flavor that seems to match its ivory-green color.

Like the gorgeous snowy pink blossoms that grace almond trees, the green nuts are welcome harbingers of spring, cherished nibblers wherever almonds are grown. In areas such as California's Central Valley,

Tart, crisp, fuzzy, and young

the Mediterranean, and Iran, shoppers in local markets anxiously await the arrival of the first green almonds much as we do rhubarb, strawberries, and ramps. But while some upscale restaurants with a seasonal bent present green almonds as an exotic dessert fruit, as has been the delightful custom at L'Ami Louis in Paris, they are virtually unknown in many regions of the world. Growers prefer to harvest the larger, ripe crop as it fetches higher prices.

In Israel, according to the local food historian Dalia Lamdani, an even earlier unripe almond is valued: "The almonds that are picked at the earliest stage are babies—small and soft all over, when the shell has not hardened. At this stage, they are delicious eaten whole, cut up in salads or pickled." And generally, no other country makes more of the green charmers, which might be considered fitting since almonds, along with pistachios, are the only nuts mentioned in the Old Testament. A member of the *Rosaceae* botanical family, *Prunus amygdalus* is celebrated among a list of "choice products" in Genesis 43:11: "Take of the best fruits in the land in your vessels, and carry down the man a present, a little balm, and a little honey, spices, and myrrh, nuts, and almonds."

Let us hope they were young almonds, presented quite simply as a delicious snack to be eaten out of hand.

WHERE: *In San Francisco,* Alemany Farmers' Market between 101 and 280 junction; Ferry Plaza Market; *in Paris,* L'Ami Louis, tel 33/1-48-87-77-4. **MAIL ORDER:** Melissa's Produce, tel 800-588-0151, melissas.com. **FURTHER INFORMATION:** aglaiakremezi.com (search fresh fava and green almonds).

⊢||||||||||||||||||||||||||||⊣

LAMB TAKES A GOOD POUNDING

Kibbeh

Lebanese

O ther Middle Eastern countries may take pride in this combination of ground lamb and the nutty bulgur wheat grain, but nowhere does it get so much patient care and subtle seasoning as in Lebanon—indeed, the Lebanese regard

kibbeh as their national dish. There, in order to be taken seriously, the kibbeh must be made in the lengthy, exhausting, traditional way.

What this means is that the raw meat will be pounded, pounded, and pounded again in a *jorn* (a heavy stone mortar) with a *modakka* (a wooden pestle or mallet). Thus the soft, lean lamb loin is worked to a satiny paste before it gives way in the mortar to onions, salt, and pepper, which are also mashed before being repounded with the meat. Only then does the well-washed, drained, and kneaded golden bulgur join the party, this time with ice water to achieve a mixture so smooth it seems almost like fabric.

It's said that everyone in the neighborhood knows when the kibbeh is being made, by the rhythmic sound of a modakka thumping against jorn. Everyone gets ready for a treat, too, in whichever of the half-dozen or so forms the kibbeh takes.

Bulgur meets lamb in the national dish of Lebanon.

By far, the favored iteration is raw kibbeh, a seductive lamb tartare that lets the aromas of onions and pepper come through clearly, along with the fresh, meaty flavor of the lamb. But equally alluring is *kibbeh 'qrass mashwieh,* in which the pounded raw lamb is formed into small sausage rolls, each with a tiny dice of lard within, to be grilled over charcoal or fried in oil. For complexity, a stuffing of coarsely ground lamb, onions, pine nuts, salt, pepper, and cinnamon can be prepared to fill walnut-size balls of kibbeh; in Lebanon they will be quickly fried in olive oil, whereas in Syria the little stuffed croquettes are broiled. As *kibbeh bi laban,* the stuffed kibbeh balls are garnished with yogurt enlivened with salt-crushed garlic and dried mint.

That's just the tip of the kibbeh iceberg. For a more substantial version—*kibbeh bi sanieh,* or kibbeh in a tray—alternating layers of raw kibbeh and stuffing are patted into a rectangular baking pan. Doused with melted butter, the loaf is baked and served hot or at room temperature.

WHERE: *In Beirut,* Al-Halabi, tel 961/452-3555; *in New York,* Ilili Restaurant, tel 212-683-2929, ililinyc.com; *in Houston,* Mary'z Lebanese Cuisine, tel 832-251-1955, maryzcuisine.com; Abdallah's Lebanese Restaurant and Bakery, tel 713-952-4747, abdallahs.com; *in Glendale, CA,* Phoenicia, tel 818-956-7800, phoeniciala.com. **RETAIL AND MAIL ORDER:** *In New York,* for bulgur, Kalustyan's, tel 800-352-3451, kalustyans.com (search bulghar); *in Brooklyn,* Sahadi's, tel 718-624-4550, sahadis.com (search bulgur). **FURTHER INFORMATION AND RECIPES:** *Secrets of Cooking: Armenian, Lebanese, Persian* by Linda Chirinian (1986); *Arabesque* by Claudia Roden (2005); foodandwine.com (search kibbe jenkins); epicurious.com (search baked kibbeh); npr.org (search lebanese kibbe recipes).

⊢|||||||||||||||||||||||||||||||||⊣

A SWEET DATE WITH A HONEY

Murabba El Balah

Dates in Clove Syrup

Lebanese

D ates are grown and loved throughout the Middle East, but in Lebanon they are particularly well turned out in this seductive confection. The region formerly known as the Levant when it included Syria starts with an advantage, as it's the

place where the world's best, largest, and most flavorful dates are grown. Once peeled—an arduous task—the fresh dates are boiled to tenderness, then drained and dried until they're still soft but no longer watery. Pitting used to be done with a knitting needle, poked vertically through the date to dislodge the pit; these days several more specific metal instruments can be put to use.

Packed in a large saucepan alternating with layers of sugar, the dates stand overnight before being removed, brushed free of sugar, and stuffed with single whole blanched almonds. The sugar remains in the pan, to be cooked with water and a handful of whole cloves until a

syrup forms. Packed into the syrup, the dates sit and gather up clovey flavor for at least four days (and up to a month or so) in a cool dark place.

They emerge delicately spiced, chewy, and syrupy, with a satisfying inner crunch from the almond. Served on their own as addictive treats, perhaps with a cup of tea, they can also be used as a garnish for elegant rice puddings and ice creams.

MAIL ORDER: For dates, igourmet.com (search organic medjool dates); imperialdate gardens.com, tel 800-301-9349. **FURTHER INFORMATION AND RECIPE:** *Food from the Arab World* by Marie Karam Khayat and Margaret Clark Keatinge (1970).

A ZESTIER CONDIMENT

Hilbeh

Fenugreek Relish

Yemeni

The reddish-orange, spicy, and aromatic Middle Eastern condiment *hilbeh* is a somewhat foamy, pleasantly bitter regular on Yemeni tables. Also beloved in Israel, hilbeh finds a place at almost all meals as a dip, chutney, jelly, or flavor enhancer in one form or another.

Created from the tiny, hard fenugreek seeds (*Trigonella Foenum-graecum*) whose exotic taste is faintly reminiscent of cardamom, hilbeh, also known as fenugreek relish, is light and somewhat frothy. Its unique texture develops as the ground yellow-brown seeds are soaked in hot water for hours, turning into a thick, gelatinous paste when residual water is drained off; whisked quickly while more water is slowly added, the mixture achieves a foamy consistency. Lemon juice, garlic, tomato paste, salt, and cardamom, caraway, or cayenne pepper are blended in, resulting in a sour, tangy flavor that may seem unusual at first. Try slathering a dollop onto warm pita bread, or spooning some into soups or stews, and you may soon become a convert.

RETAIL AND MAIL ORDER: *In New York,* Kalustyan's, tel 800-352-3451, kalustyans.com; **MAIL ORDER:** Penzeys Spices, tel 800-741-7787, penzeys.com; Zamouri Spices, tel 913-829-5988, zamourispices.com. **FURTHER INFORMATION AND RECIPES:** *The New Book of Middle Eastern Food* by Claudia Roden (2000); *The Complete Middle East Cookbook* by Tess Mallos (2007); *Jerusalem: A Cookbook* by Yotam Ottolenghi and Sami Tamimi (2012); *Spice* by Ana Sortun (2006); cookstr.com (search spiced lamb chops with fenugreek sauce); food.com (search hilbeh) **TIP:** When ordering fenugreek, preground seeds are preferable, as the tough seeds are difficult to grind; if they aren't available, toasting the seeds for 20 minutes in a 325° oven makes the task easier. **SEE ALSO:** Chermoula, page 698; Tkemali, page 390.

HOT AND HOTTER

Zhoug

Yemeni

An intense, engagingly gritty chile paste that has been described as "Yemenite Tabasco," zhoug (pronounced ZUH-chug) is a revered condiment in the Middle East, most especially in Israel and of course Yemen. Its complex heat is de rigeur on the region's beloved pita sandwiches, and also supposedly plays a part in warding off sickness. The latter may be easy to believe once you experience its throat-blistering powers—zhoug really does seem hot enough to destroy a host of germs, so it's not surprising that Yemenites believe a daily dose wards off colds and heart disease.

Zhoug comes in two types: fiery red and emerald green.

Gastronomes risk the burn for the flavor boost zhoug adds to gyros, falafels, and shawarma wraps, as well as to indigenous breads, salads, yogurt dips, and grilled meat specialties. Of the two main versions of zhoug, the fiery red variety is especially hot and is made entirely of chile peppers; the emerald green paste infuses the peppers with parsley, cilantro, garlic, coriander leaves, cumin, and cardamom, for a more complex flavor. Both styles are eaten in much the same way: Thinned with either chopped fresh tomatoes or *hilbeh* (see page 515), the paste is transformed into the sauce that makes the Middle Eastern sandwich sing.

Retail and mail order: *In New York*, for ingredients, Kalustyan's, tel 800-352-3451, kalustyans.com. **Further information and recipes:** *Flatbreads & Flavors* by Jeffrey Alford and Naomi Duguid (2008); *Jerusalem: A Cookbook* by Yotam Ottolenghi and Sami Tamimi (2012); foodandwine.com (search spicy zhoug); food .com (search zhoug yemeni chili sauce).

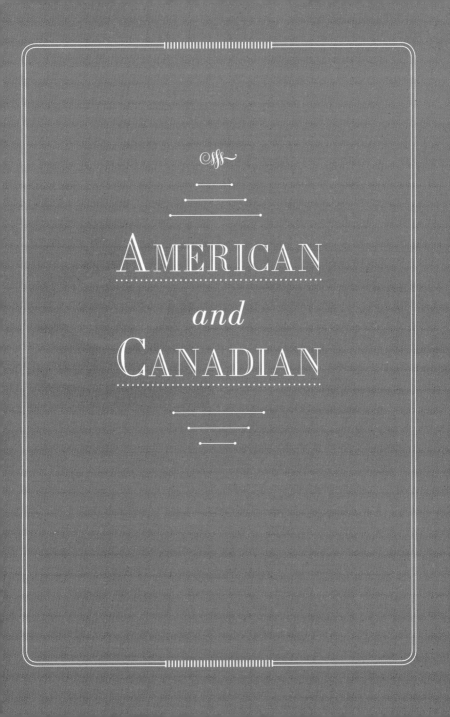

AMERICAN
and
CANADIAN

TASTE THE FUTURE, TODAY

Alinea

American

S pain has Ferran Adrià, that molecular wizard whose culinary feats stunned and delighted foodies around the world (see page 258). And Chicago has Grant Achatz, whose similarly innovative cuisine can be enjoyed in a spacious, peaceful restaurant called Alinea.

There, Achatz works his flavor miracles on dishes that look and sound improbable—until the first bite dispels all traces of doubt. These are dishes that force diners to reevaluate their ideas about food and flavor, dishes that anyone claiming the title of knowledgeable gourmand must experience firsthand.

They are creations that fall into the category dubbed molecular gastronomy, which perhaps would be better described as reduction cooking—a modern twist on a long tradition of classic French techniques such as simmering down broth repeatedly to achieve maximum flavor concentration, or scraping browned drippings from a roasting pan for the most intensely rich sauce base, a demi-glace. A similar idea guides the notion of espresso, in which coffee beans are dark-roasted and ground to a fine powder to allow intense, complete extraction of flavor.

With all sorts of technical innovations at their disposal, a cadre of well-educated, science-savvy chefs have been taking these notions even further: reducing ingredients to their most essential, concentrated flavors and presenting them in minimalistic forms such as foams or sheer, glassy gels. (In the best case scenarios, these will be combined with bits of solid food.)

"Ingredients plus manipulation equals finished dish," Achatz writes in his book *Alinea*. And what finished dishes they are, consistently presented in the most original ways and created not to shock, but to enhance the inherent qualities of the ingredients themselves.

At Alinea, visual surprises and puns abound.

In one dish, that might mean a silk-sheer strip of translucent bacon that is dried under low heat rather than fried to crispness, and suspended from a delicate wire "swing." (Hanging the bacon not only shows it off to advantage but also keeps it from crumbling or becoming soggy, as it might if lying on a plate.) And the tricks don't stop there. To round out the flavor profile with a touch of aromatic, candied sweetness, light lacings of dried apple and fresh thyme leaves are "glued" to the bacon with beadlike pipings of butterscotch.

A blast of flavor is an Achatz goal, and one he certainly achieves in his signature black truffle explosion—sliced black truffle and gelled black truffle juice topped with a gentle roll of silky romaine and a crunchy wafer of Parmesan cheese. One can find similarly subtle eruptions of taste and texture with ingredients as lofty as caviar or as earthy as beets. An ethereal combination of gelled cucumber and green almonds looks like a modern glass paperweight but tastes a whole lot better—cool, both sweet and bitter, and teasingly salty. On the rustic side, Achatz serves what is essentially a Japanese *donburi* casserole: pork, vegetables, and tofu steamed in heady broth. Where's the hitch? The ingredients are steamed in a sealed plaster globe. Broken open with a big wooden mallet at the table (by the diner, no less), it emits clouds of mouthwatering aromas.

When a thick, celadon-green plastic sheet is thrown across the table and Achatz himself appears armed with all manner of sweet ingredients—fruit (some fresh and some in syrup or jam form), nuts, and chocolate (variously in bits, syrup, and cream)—it's time for dessert. This lot comes in tubes and bottles, with which Achatz proceeds to do a Jackson Pollock of sweet dribbles, to be combined and eaten with fingers or spoons.

These creations and many more may appear on a menu that changes with the seasons and with Achatz's latest inspiration. It may not be a dinner for every night, but then no one goes to Alinea simply because he or she is hungry.

WHERE: 1723 N. Halsted St., Chicago, tel 312-867-0110, alinearestaurant.com. **FURTHER INFORMATION AND RECIPES:** *Alinea* by Grant Achatz (2008).

FOOD OF THE GODS

Ambrosia

American (Southern)

What do gods eat for breakfast, lunch, and dinner? According to the ancient Greeks, ambrosia was the food of choice on Mount Olympus. The word itself comes from the term for immortality, a quality the amorphous but presumably

delicious substance—whose exact components have never been specified in any text—was said to bestow upon anyone who ate it.

Enterprising Southerners were clearly inspired by that tantalizing promise when they conceived of what would become one of the region's most iconic and time-honored desserts, which began to appear in cookbooks toward the end of the nineteenth century. At its most basic, ambrosia is a layered salad of thinly sliced seedless oranges (preferably navels) topped with freshly grated coconut and a little confectioners' sugar, chilled well and then piled high in a punch bowl and neatly ladled out into bowls. Juicy, sweet, and cold, the dish was originally intended as a light, easy dessert to enjoy after a heavy meal—say, Thanksgiving or

Christmas dinner. And, presented in this way, ambrosia is indeed a treat, one that's both refreshing and surprisingly satisfying, especially if a generous sprinkling of sherry is added to the fruit.

Many, many variations on the theme have grown up along with the dish. Some Southern cooks add layers of sliced bananas or cubed pineapple, and sometimes both. Some substitute the easier-to-find sweetened coconut. Many prepare a mixture of fresh orange juice, honey, and a little Cointreau or rum and pour it over the top of the fruit-and-coconut layers before chilling the dish. All are appropriate and pleasing tweaks that don't deviate too far from the original. But a version of ambrosia that seems to have first appeared in the late 1950s, involving canned mandarin oranges, canned pineapple, marshmallows, maraschino cherries, and mayonnaise . . . this, as its chilling list of ingredients makes clear, is something to avoid at all costs.

WHERE: *In Savannah, GA,* Mrs. Wilkes' Dining Room, tel 912-232-5997, mrswilkes.com. **MAIL ORDER:** For seedless navel oranges, Hale Groves, tel 800-562-4502, halegroves.com. **FURTHER INFORMATION AND RECIPES:** *Southern Food* by John Edgerton (1993); *The Lee Bros. Simple Fresh Southern* by Matt Lee and Ted Lee (2009); *Mastering the Art of Southern Cooking* by Nathalie Dupree and Cynthia Graubart (2012); saveur.com (search ambrosia).

TWO HOME-EC CLASSICS

Apple Brown Betty and Apple Pandowdy

American

The much-loved apple has played a starring role in countless pies, crisps, crumbles, cobblers, pandowdies, slumps, grunts, betties, and more. A baked pudding, the betty consists of alternating layers of sugared and spiced fruit and golden-brown, buttered bread crumbs, combining into a delectable mix of meltingly soft aromatic apple and crunchy crumbs. It's a classic dessert that likely derives from the English pie-making tradition. First referred to in print in 1864 (although no one has ever been able to identify exactly who Betty was), the sweet treat achieved mass popularity in the United States after World War II—probably because it was easy to prepare on increasingly busy weeknights—then went on to become a mainstay of 1950s high school home-economics classes. All marriageable girls were expected to be able to make it—and why not? Its preparation is straightforward and the result is aromatic, homey, juicy perfection.

Abigail Adams, apple pandowdy fan

Pandowdy is another fine stage for apples, differing from apple brown betty in its use of a pastry crust (rather than layers of bread crumbs) that is pressed down slightly into the mixture; it also often contains maple syrup or brown sugar. The "dowdy" in the name isn't meant to be disparaging. Traditionally, dowdies were dishes of cooked fruit baked under a crust. In colonial days, "dowdying" meant slashing a pastry so as to submerge the crust into the dish's succulent filling—which probably explains how the dish got its name.

Eighteenth-century Americans baked this fragrant dessert in a skillet overnight, setting it in the embers of the hearth and then serving it in the morning for breakfast. Said to have been beloved by former first lady Abigail Adams, it is considered a precursor to the modern cobbler, crisp, or crumble.

The first step for both of these desserts is to choose the right apples, which is to say, those with a balance of sweet and tart flavors and a flesh that doesn't break down in the oven; good options include Cortland, Northern Spy, or a combination thereof. These should be peeled, cored, and cut into chunks or slices, then tossed with sugar, cinnamon, nutmeg, and cloves.

The best way to serve these treats is gently warm. Although vanilla ice cream seems an obvious accompaniment, better to copy the old English tradition of setting out a pitcher of cold heavy sweet cream to be poured over each serving.

Where: *In Boston,* Durgin-Park, tel 617-227-2039, durgin-park.com; *in Bethel, ME,* The Bethel Inn Resort, tel 800-654-0125, bethelinn .com. **Further information and recipes:** *Politics and Pot Roast* by Sarah Hood Salomon (2006); *The American Heritage Cookbook* by the editors of American Heritage Publ. Co. (1964); *The Fannie Farmer Cookbook,* 13th edition, by Marion Cunningham (1996); epicurious.com (search maple apple pandowdy; apple brown betty lewis); foodnetwork.com (search apple pandowdy lagasse). **See also:** Tarte Tatin, page 138, Apple Pie, below.

THE MOST AMERICAN DESSERT

Apple Pie

American

Not even such iconic American foods as hot dogs and hamburgers enjoy the status conferred on apple pie, the dessert that seems synonymous with all things homespun, simple, and true. Odd, considering that apple pies of all sorts are produced in virtually every European country, and that England's centuries-long history of meat and fruit pies is undoubtedly the inspiration behind this most American passion.

These days, apple pie can get short shrift as a mass-produced dessert, in coffee shops and chain restaurants where crusts approximate wet cardboard and canned apple fillings are mawkishly gooey. For the most part, that leaves home bakers to preserve the reputation of this national culinary treasure, a golden-brown, double-crust pie filled with juicy cinnamon- and sugar-enriched apples. And protect it they do, with great pride and many strongly held opinions.

One of the most common sources of argument among apple pie mavens is the type of apple best suited to the task. Some swear by greenings or Granny Smiths, their critics contending that these very sour fruits require too much sugar, resulting in a filling that is wet and syrupy, in an unpardonably soggy crust. Those whose chief concern is the possibility of a hot, sweet liquid oozing all over the oven choose the Golden Delicious, the least flavorful option but the driest. True cognoscenti opt for the snow-white, sweet/tart Cortland and/or the firm, full-flavored Northern Spy, both at their best between September and November. (Whichever the apple in your pie, it's wise to place a piece of aluminum foil under the pie pan in the oven, lest even the most reliable varieties result in a dripping, sticky mess.)

The discussion will then move on to the subject of the crust. Should it be a short crust (that is, flaky, butter-enriched, Continental-style pastry), or the very thin, crisp, Anglo-American version based on lard? Bakers will forever debate the definitive answer. Meanwhile the rest of us eat.

For a savory, decadent choice that harkens to the tradition of serving a slice of apple pie with a slice of Cheddar, half of the butter can be replaced by Cheddar, as it is in the following recipe.

Apple Pie
with Cheddar Cheese Crust

Makes one double-crust, 9-inch pie;
serves 6

For the pastry:

4 ounces sharp, aged Cheddar cheese,
*   preferably white*
8 tablespoons (1 stick) cold,
*   unsalted butter*
1¾ cups sifted all-purpose flour,
*   as needed*
½ teaspoon salt
¼ teaspoon mace
5 to 6 tablespoons ice water

For the filling:

5 large apples (about 2 pounds),
*   preferably Cortland or Northern Spy*
2 to 3 tablespoons lemon juice
⅔ cup sugar
Pinch of salt
½ teaspoon cinnamon
¼ teaspoon freshly grated nutmeg
About 1 tablespoon butter,
*   cut into tiny pieces*
1 large egg yolk
2 tablespoons milk

1. Make the pastry: Place the cheese in a food processor, and grate it to a fine meal; you should have about 1 cup loosely packed cheese. Cut the butter into small pieces.

2. Measure out 1⅔ cups of sifted flour and resift it with the salt and mace into the food processor. Add the grated cheese and butter and process until the mixture has the texture of fine meal.

3. Slowly trickle in the ice water, 2 tablespoons at a time, processing between each addition, until the dough leaves the sides of the bowl and forms a ball. If the dough seems too sticky, add more flour 1 tablespoon at a time; if it is too dry and crumbly, add more water 1 tablespoon at a time.

4. Place the dough on a lightly floured pastry board and divide it in half. Form each half into a ball and lightly knead each once or twice with the palm of your hand, to firm up the dough. Reshape each half into a ball and flatten them slightly into thick disks. Wrap each with plastic wrap or wax paper and chill for at least 1 hour, but preferably for 3 or 4 hours, or even overnight.

5. About 10 minutes before rolling out the dough, remove it from the refrigerator and let it warm up a bit. Roll out each disk of dough on a lightly floured surface to a thickness of ¼ inch. One round of rolled dough should be fitted into the bottom of an ungreased 9-inch pie pan, leaving extra hanging over. Roll out the second sheet of dough and drape it, untrimmed, over the lined pie pan. Cover the dough snugly with wax paper or plastic wrap and refrigerate the pie pan and dough while you prepare the apples.

6. Preheat the oven to 425°F.

7. Make the filling: Peel and core the apples and slice them vertically to ⅛- to-¼-inch thickness. Place them in a large bowl. Sprinkle the apples with a little lemon juice as you slice, to prevent discoloration.

8. Toss the apples with the sugar, salt, cinnamon, and nutmeg.

9. Remove the pie pan from the refrigerator and gently lift the top crust from the pan. Arrange a flat layer of apples that completely covers the bottom pie crust. Then heap the remaining apple slices on top and level them. Dot the apples evenly with the pieces of butter.

10. Fit the top pie crust over the apples, trimming the edges to just cover the rim of the pie pan and crimping them to the bottom crust with the tines of a fork dipped in cold water.

11. Bake the pie for 15 minutes, then reduce the heat to 350°F. Bake until the top crust begins to turn a light golden brown, another 25 minutes.

12. Beat the egg yolk with the milk in a small bowl. Remove the pie from the oven and brush the mixture all over the top crust. Sprinkle the crust liberally with sugar and return the pie to the oven until the edges of the pie are deep golden brown, another 10 to 15 minutes. Serve warm or cold.

Note: If you must serve this pie à la mode, the best flavors of ice cream to pair with the cheese crust would be vanilla or cinnamon. For purists, however, the pie needs no enhancement.

Where: *In San Francisco* (for a great apple pie made without Cheddar), Zuni Café, tel 415-552-2522, zunicafe.com. **Special events:** Applefest, Warwick, NY, October, warwick applefest.com; Bucktown Apple Pie Contest, Chicago, IL, October, bucktownapplepie contest.com; Dummerston Apple Pie Festival, Dummerston, VT, October, dummerston.com.

TEX-MEX IN THE HILL COUNTRY

Austin's Triple Threat

American (Texan)

As the Texas state capital, home to the state university and to lively arts, music, and tech scenes spurred by world-famous festivals, Austin is by all accounts the state's liveliest and most unfettered city. And among its wide range of young-spirited diversions, food is not the least.

While Austin boasts its share of inventive haute fare, the real treasures for visitors are the time-honored food styles that reflect the history of both city and state: Hill Country barbecue, Tex-Mex, and Texas-Country Southern.

For the truest, juiciest, and smokiest example of the Hill Country style, the ultimate destination is Kreuz Market, about a forty-minute drive from Austin, in Lockhart. Pronounced "Kritze" by many and "Kroitz" by just as many others, it follows a barbecue style created by the German butchers who settled in this area in the early 1900s, smoke-curing their meats as they had back home. Thus did one Charles Kreuz begin his meat market in Lockhart in 1900, although not in its current location.

Beef is the dominant choice here, with pork and Kreuz's hefty homemade sausages tied for second. When lines form in the parking lot at the busiest times, appetites are stoked by the sweet, burnished aroma of hickory wood in the smoke-pits. Meat here is sold by the pound, rustically sliced down onto pink butcher's paper and priced according to cut: brisket, shoulder, prime rib, chops, ribs, and so on. The only things that accompany the meat are slices of white bread and plastic knives and forks. Although sauce is available, it's regarded as heresy by purists, who prefer the other garnishes on display: sliced avocado, tomato, and

A former "seed and feed" store serves up Texas-style tacos.

jalapeños among them. Only the cooked meats, however, can be ordered online for shipping around the country.

At Austin's lively Güero's Taco Bar, hand-shaken margaritas, straight-up and ice cold, are the right accompaniments for warm hand-made corn tortillas, cheese-filled *tamales queso*, or lushly filled tacos with black beans and red chiles. As the wall posters in this informal diner setting attest, Güero's occupies a former "seed and feed" store that operated on the site from the late 1800s through the early 1990s. The tacos have been holding down the fort since 1995.

The same historic credentials apply to the teeming, busted-out barn of a restaurant that is the original Threadgill's, a musical landmark located in a former gas station and known as the place where Janis Joplin got her start. The menu reads like the index of a Texas cookbook, featuring such Lone Star classics as country-fried steak, fried chicken and gizzards with cream gravy, meat loaf, crispy fried oysters, syrupy-sweet baked desserts, and lots more (with several international options perhaps best bypassed in favor of local treats). There is still live music on certain nights, and if not, the juke-box never disappoints.

WHERE: *In Austin, TX,* Güero's Taco Bar, tel 512-447-7688, guerostacobar.com; Threadgill's, tel 512-451-5440, threadgills.com; *in Lockhart, TX,* Kreuz Market, tel 512-398-2361, kreuzmarket .com. **MAIL ORDER:** Kreutzmarket. com. **SEE ALSO:** Barbecue, page 526.

‖‖‖‖‖‖‖‖‖‖‖‖‖‖‖‖‖‖‖‖‖‖‖‖‖‖‖‖

BELLY UP

Bacon

American

One of the quintessential, defining aromas of the American breakfast, in recent years bacon has become so fashionable (almost ridiculously so) that it's been used as a flavoring for everything from ice cream to vodka. But the

homey pork cut's continuing position of honor in the world of gourmandise speaks to its lasting appeal. Pigs were domesticated around 5000 B.C. in Southeast Asia and the eastern Mediterranean, their meat cured in China by at least 200 B.C. and being salted, air-dried, and smoked by the first century A.D. in Rome, in a process not unlike what we use for pig belly today. The word *bacon* comes from the Germanic *bakkon*, meaning smoked pork, and was first used around the early twelfth century; the English quickly picked up both the term and the foodstuff, which made its way to America with the Pilgrims in 1620.

Slices of meat-striped fat cut from the pig's belly right below the ribs become magical when cured with salt, smoked, and finally sizzled in a skillet. Bacon is an otherworldly pleasure—crunchy, salty, woodsy, earthy, and addictive as a feel-good drug at a far lower street value. The stuff beguiles when eaten all by itself, but pair it with eggs, whether creamy and softly scrambled or runny and fried, and it becomes a foil worthy of an ode. It improves almost any sandwich it is layered into, and brings interest and energy when sprinkled on top of everything from salads and baked potatoes to pasta, soups, and maybe even ice cream.

Nowadays, artisanal bacon producers are busy developing unique cures featuring ingredients like maple syrup, molasses, demerara sugar, cinnamon-sugar, garlic, juniper, pepper, and more. Their creations can be full of character and deep, enticing flavors, but only a few choice supermarket bacons offer deliciously toothsome results that even the snootiest gourmand might cotton to.

And that's good news, for nothing evokes Sunday mornings in America—more than church bells ringing, and even in these fat-fearing times—than the salty-smoky-fatty perfume of frying bacon accompanied by the scents of toasting bread and freshly made coffee.

Where: *In New York,* Swine, tel 212-255-7675, swinenyc.com; Bar Bacon, tel 646-362-0622, barbacon.com. **Mail order:** store .nimanranch.com (search bacon); applegate .com (search bacon); shop.bentonscountry ham.com (click Products, then search bacon). **Further information and recipes:** *The Bacon Cookbook* by James Villas (2007); *Pig: King of the Southern Table* by James Villas (2010); *Beyond Nose to Tail* by Fergus Henderson and Justin Piers Gellatly (2007); epicurious.com (search bacon twists; bacon baklava; smoky bacon mac; spicy bacon and egg). **Tip:** Look for brands such as Niman Ranch for nitrate- and preservative-free "natural" bacon. When choosing the latter, note that the color is paler and browner than bacon with preservatives, which keep the meat more brightly red.

ONE HOT POTATO

Baked Idaho Russet Potatoes

American

For those who value simple pleasures, little compares to the delights of a big, oval Idaho russet potato oven-baked to perfection. High in starch, its cells separate when cooked, which renders it fluffy when baked. Once upon a time,

baked Idaho russets were standard DIY fare for kids, who would roast the spuds "mickey" style by burying them in hot coals. Cooked kitchen style, their crackling brown skins are split open at the top so globs of sweet butter can melt into their soft white interiors, along with coarse salt and grindings of black pepper. Wherever they are prepared, baking them au naturel is essential—potatoes baked in foil wrappings will wind up with soggy skin.

Some dollop on sour cream, but the dash of cold will temper what should preferably be a steaming-hot potato. Uncontroversial garnishes include butter, chives, parsley, crumbles of hot, crisp bacon, minced hot chiles, or a dash of Tabasco, or, more elegantly, a spoonful of caviar—red or black, as budget permits.

What makes the classic steak house favorite so delicious alongside a well-executed steak? Science doesn't have the answer, but the elemental combination of pure protein and starch seems to satisfy our deepest hungers, possibly because starch has enzymes that tenderize meat. Go ahead and throw in that glass of red wine for good measure—it's been shown to mitigate the buildup of cholesterol from red meat.

Mail order: Sun Valley Potato Growers, tel 208-438-2605, idaho-potatoes.com (see gift pack of potatoes); amazon.com (search famous idaho russet potatoes). **Further information and recipes:** *The Fannie Farmer Cookbook,* 13th edition, by Marion Cunningham (1996); all recipes.com (search perfect baked potato; baked potato salad; twice baked potatoes); idahopotatoes.com.

┤||||||||||||||||||||||||||||||├

ON TWAIN'S BUCKET LIST

Baked Rome Beauty Apples

American (New England)

In *A Tramp Abroad,* Mark Twain complains of the food he ate while traveling in Europe. "It has been many months, at the present writing, since I have had a nourishing meal," he writes in 1873, listing all of the foods he hopes will be ready

for him on his return. High on that list are baked apples with cream—a simple and most excellent request.

Best when prepared with the dark red, round, firm, and pungent Rome beauty variety, the apples exude the aromas of hot butter, cinnamon, caramelizing sugar, marmalade, or honey as they bake, with perhaps a few drops of dark rum for good measure. Then comes the warmth of their luxuriously soft interiors, with the edge of tartness Rome beauties are prized for, contrasted with cold, heavy sweet cream or a dab of softened vanilla ice cream. (The beauties began as a botanical accident in Rome, Ohio, but they are stunners only when slowly baked or steamed, moisture being necessary to enhance a flesh that is somewhat dry and fibrous when uncooked.)

Although the utter lack of adornment of the baked apple is part of the miracle of its transformation, an elegant German riff can be found in *äpfel im schlafrock,* or apple in a nightgown—the "gown" being a wrap of thin, rich pie-crust dough in which the raisin- and nut-filled apple bakes.

Mail order: Honeycrisp, tel 518-695-4517, honeycrisp.com (click Rome Apples). **Further information and recipes:** *From My Mother's Kitchen* by Mimi Sheraton (1979); *The Joy of Cooking* by Irma S. Rombauer, Marion Rombauer Becker, and Ethan Becker (2006); *The James Beard Cookbook* by James Beard (2002); saveur.com (search baked apples with calvados); epicurious.com (search brown sugar baked apples).

┤||||||||||||||||||||||||||||||├

RAKING IT OVER THE CHARCOAL

Barbecue

American (Southern, Southwestern)

Man has smoke-cooked meat over fire since ancient times—and Caribbean natives of the "new world" were certainly doing likewise, calling it *barbacoa* long before the colonists got in on the act. The modern idea of American

barbecue grew directly out of the barbacoa tradition, and smoking whole hogs over pits is a technique now common in both North Carolina and Virginia.

Since then, barbecue has been strongly associated with the southeastern United States. But the specialty, once relegated to wide-open rural spaces, has moved to the big city in a renaissance that is easily understandable, given the lusty appeal of these succulent meats. With some contingents swearing off meat and meat by-products entirely, or just lowering their meat consumption and upping their vegetable quotas, still others have only deepened their devotion to richly glazed, fragrant barbecue, elevating its mouthwatering bites of crisp fat and tender, juicy flesh to something approaching cult status.

"I think about barbecue like some people think about wine. The good stuff? You know it when you taste it." So says Keith Allen, pitmaster at Allen & Son, one of North Carolina's most important barbecue joints. But in truth, things aren't so simple, and depending on where you are, your definition of "the good stuff," and even of the very word *barbecue*, may vary. The variety inherent to the barbecue landscape is strongly linked to geography, which gives barbecue lovers that much more reason to travel.

Pulled pork on a soft bun

In North Carolina, it's all about hog. Along the eastern and coastal part of the state, pork shoulder (Allen & Son's specialty) is slow-cooked over hardwood coals; drenched in a hot, tangy sauce of vinegar and red pepper flakes, the meat is tucked into a soft white bun and topped with cool, sweet, mayonnaise-based coleslaw. Head west, where the Piedmont plateau's sand gives way to clay, and it's not just the soil that turns red—it's the barbecue, too. Western Carolina barbecue, also known as Lexington-style, means a slow-cooked pork shoulder seasoned with a vinegar-and-pepper sauce and sweetened by ketchup. In Texas, barbecue means smoky, pit-cooked beef brisket. Like Texans, Kentuckians also eschew pork for their barbecue, but they slow-cook mutton doused in a sauce of vinegar and Worcestershire.

In most regions, however, barbecue is synonymous with pork. In Louisiana, barbecue is *cochon de lait*: pulled meat from a suckling pig

that has been split, spatchcocked, and suspended on a frame or pit-roasted over hardwood coals, served in a split sub roll with slaw in the manner of a po'boy. In central South Carolina, pulled pork is dressed in a mustard-and-vinegar sauce and served in a bun or as a plate lunch, while in Kansas City, Missouri, the meat is placed atop slices of white bread with generous amounts of thick, sweet sauce that combines acidy tomatoes with sticky sweet molasses. In Memphis, Tennessee, a pungent dry-rub seasoning lends a spicy crust to the meltingly tender smoked pork ribs; no sauce need apply.

WHERE: *In New York,* Hill Country, tel 212-255-4544, hill countryny.com; Mighty Quinn's barbecue at multiple locations, mightyquinns bbq.com; *in Chapel Hill, NC,* Allen & Son Barbecue, tel 919-942-7576; *in Raleigh, NC,* Clyde Cooper's Barbeque, tel 919-832-7614, clydecoopersbbq.com; *in Charleston, SC,* Bessingers Barbeque, tel 843-556-1354, bessingers bbq.com; *in Memphis,* A&R Bar-B-Que, tel 901-774-7444, aandrbbq.com; Charlie Vergos' Rendezvous, tel 901-523-2746, hogsfly.com; *in Chicago,* Carson's, tel 312-280-9200, ribs.com; *in Kansas City, MO,* Arthur Bryant's, tel 816-231-1123, arthurbryantsbbq.com; *in Lockhart, TX,* Kreuz Market, tel 512-398-2361, kreuzmarket .com; *in Pearland, TX,* Killen's Texas Barbecue, tel 281-485-2272, killensbbq.com. **MAIL ORDER:** For state of the art grills, Grillworks, tel 855-434-3473, grillery.com; for barbecue sauce, clydecoopersbbq.com. **FURTHER INFORMATION AND RECIPES:** *The Barbecue! Bible* by Steven Raichlen (2008); southernbbqtrail.com (includes barbecue-based films, oral histories, and directions); cookstr.com (search memphis magic; barbecued spare ribs; neely's barbecue sauce). **SPECIAL EVENTS:** World Championship Barbecue Cooking Contest, Memphis, TN, May, memphis inmay.org; Big Apple Barbecue Block Party, New York, June, bigapplebbq.org.

—||||||||||||||||||||||||||||||—

A HISTORIC SOUTH CAROLINA SNACK

Benne Wafers

American (Southern)

Ultra-thin, crunchy, and both salty and sweet, the light brown benne wafer is the traditional sesame seed cookie of the lowlands of South Carolina. A standard item in the Southern pantry since the antebellum era, the cookie has a complex

past: *Benne* is the Bantu word for sesame, and both the term and the ingredient arrived in South Carolina in the seventeenth century, brought there by slaves from the Niger-Congo region of sub-Saharan Africa. Its influence on South Carolina is similar to the influence that okra, brought by West African slaves, has had on Louisiana cooking.

Long cultivated throughout the Middle East and Africa, and a key ingredient in many Asian cuisines, sesame seeds are one of the world's most ancient foods. The Bantu believe that eating benne seeds brings luck (a good thing since it's almost impossible to eat just one wafer).

A natural source of protein, the seeds bear a nutty, sweet aroma and, especially when toasted, a creamy, buttery flavor. Freed from their usual role as a crunch-adding condiment, in these flat, crackling cookies the seeds—mouthfuls of them—are the whole story.

Mail order: Byrd's, tel 800-291-2973, byrd cookiecompany.com (search benne wafers). **Further information and recipes:** *Mastering the Art of Southern Cooking* by Nathalie Dupree and Cynthia Graubart (2012); *The Lee Bros. Charleston Kitchen* by Matt Lee and Ted Lee (2013); saveur.com (search sweet benne wafers).

—||||||||||||||||||||||||||||||—

SOUTHERN HOSPITALITY ON A PLATE

Biscuits

American (Southern)

Biscuit. The word alone summons up images of cozy, tender, and snowy puffs dripping with melted butter and perhaps a droplet of honey, a meal- or snacktime bread that seems to symbolize Southern hospitality at its best. Served

hot, they are a welcome indulgence in settings of all sorts, whether they are split apart and liberally buttered at the family table or sandwiched with good, salty country ham and passed at cocktail parties.

The humble, raised-dough quick breads raise a few questions of their own, the first of

which concerns what exactly is meant by *biscuit*. Strictly speaking, the word itself comes from the Latin words *bis* and *coctus,* meaning twice baked: the method for making the hard, breadlike rusks that sustained seafarers on long voyages during the Middle Ages. The term *twice baked* means *biscotti* in Italian and *zweiback* in

German and also refers to those similarly treated cookies. Oddly enough, the traditional Southern biscuit is not twice baked, but carries the name nonetheless.

In the days before commercialized yeast and baking soda were on hand to add the air that would expand in oven heat and so enable the biscuit to rise, there is evidence that another type of biscuit was made. Beaten biscuits, which have all but disappeared now save for those made by a few tradition-minded home cooks, were small, dry, and smooth, made of a flour, lard, and milk dough that was literally beaten (with a pestle, a heavy skillet, or, legend has it, actual fists) repeatedly in order to incorporate air. By the 1850s, leavening agents were commercialized to take on much of that chore, and the labor-intensive biscuit gradually disappeared.

The laborer is still an important piece of the equation, as a great biscuit is rarely a standardized product. It is the provenance of the baker, in the case of the South usually a grandmother, to define her own biscuit using her own special formula. In general, a truly excellent Southern-style biscuit should be about one inch tall, golden on the outside, and white, light, and fluffy on the inside, with a slightly ridged top. It should taste pleasantly, appealingly floury, with slightly buttery overtones often achieved by using old-fashioned buttermilk instead of usual milk—buttermilk being the ingredient many a Southern cook swears by, along with the White Lily brand of flour. The classic shortening is lard, but on this subject debate is rife; some cooks prefer to use Crisco, and some even swear by margarine.

Whatever their particularities, hot home-made biscuits are integral and irreplaceable components of traditional Southern breakfasts, church socials, Fourth-of-July picnics, and countless other occasions, rituals, and celebrations. And of course, as biscuits and gravy, they're the centerpiece of a decadently soppy side dish best accompanied by a few equally decadent pieces of fried chicken.

WHERE: *In Nashville, TN,* Loveless Café, tel 615-646-9700, lovelesscafe.com; *in Chapel Hill, NC,* Crook's Corner, tel 919-929-7643, crooks corner.com; *in Asheville, NC,* Biscuit Head, tel 828-333-5145, biscuitheads.com; *in New York,* Waverly Inn, tel 917-828-1154, waverlynyc.com; *throughout the South,* at multiple locations, Biscuitville, biscuitville.com. **MAIL ORDER:** Sister Schubert's, tel 800-999-1835, sisterschuberts .com; Callie's Charleston Biscuits, tel 843-577-1198, calliesbiscuits.com. **FURTHER INFORMATION AND RECIPES:** *The Gift of Southern Cooking* by Edna Lewis with Scott Peacock (2003); *Biscuit Bliss* by James Villas (2003); *Callie's Biscuits and Southern Traditions* by Carrie Morey (2013); saveur.com (search liz smith's biscuits; honey buttermilk biscuits).

A HARD NUT TO CRACK

Black Walnuts

American

Native mainly to the eastern half of the United States (and then brought to Europe for cultivation in the early part of the seventeenth century), *Juglans nigra,* the black walnut, is just as much of a taste treasure shelled and eaten out of

hand as it is when used in various kinds of cookery. Far less subtle and soigné than the better- known English or Persian walnut, this darker member of the hickory, or *Juglandaceae,* family has a somewhat brazen, quintessentially nutty flavor, at once earthy, fruity, and teasingly fresh. It retains that flavor and its firm, slightly crackling texture when frozen in ice creams or baked in coffee cakes, cookies, and brownies, and nicely grainy carrot cakes. Pressed, the black walnut makes a fragrant salad oil.

A very hard shell makes black walnuts difficult to crack without breaking the kernels, which is why the shelled nuts are expensive and not as widely available as the English walnut. (The shell is so hard, in fact, that it is ground down to become an abrasive used in polishing machinery.)

Black walnut trees yield sought-after nuts, syrup, and wood.

The trees themselves are highly prized not only for their nuts but also for their sap (which is processed into syrup and sugar) and for the dark, strong wood that is crafted into beautiful and expensive furniture.

In addition to all of their other delicious, desirable attributes, black walnuts are high in protein and unsaturated fat, as well as in magnesium, manganese, phosphorus, Vitamin B6, pantothenic acid, and zinc, among other nutritional goodies. They won't make for a guilt-free brownie, of course, but where's the fun in that?

Mail order: Hammons Products Company, tel 800-872-6879, hammonsproducts.com; nuts .com, tel 800-558-6887. **Further information and recipes:** For Black Walnut Cranberry Pound Cake, *Jasper White's Cooking from New England* by Jasper White (1998); for Black Walnut Bread, *The American Heritage Cookbook* by the editors of American Heritage Publ. Co. (1964); saveur .com (search black walnut pumpkin pie; black walnut sauce); epicurious.com (search black walnut cake); blackwalnutrecipes.com.

DON'T HOLD THE MAYO

BLT Sandwich

American

A properly executed bacon, lettuce, and tomato sandwich isn't haute cuisine, but it may be diner food's best chance at approaching the sublime. The lunch-counter classic is defined by its simple combination of crisp, salty meat, acidic tomato, cool lettuce, creamy mayonnaise, and crunchy toast. Which means that with so little margin for error, the BLT's success is measured not only by the quality, but also by the precise state of its ingredients.

The bacon must be freshly fried and hot, and to such a crispness as to be just short of burned. The tomato must be juicily ripe and sliced razor thin. The lettuce should have both bite and flavor; Boston, romaine, and even peppery watercress are well suited, while iceberg is disqualified for having crunch but little else. One should be able to bite easily through the toasted bread, so if good-quality French-style *pain de mie* is not available, Pepperidge Farm's "Original" white will do nicely when toasted to a pale golden brown. Finally, if not homemade, the mayonnaise must be Hellmann's, or Best Foods as it is known in the West.

The exact origin of this feast-on-bread is hard to pin down, but it's a likely cousin of the bacon sandwiches that were traditionally served at teatime in the English countryside as early as the Victorian era; the first references to the BLT in print occur in British cookbooks published in the late 1920s. The sandwich became extremely popular in America after World War II, probably due to a confluence of events: lettuce and tomatoes were steadily available in supermarkets for the first time; women were beginning to work outside the home in greater numbers; and diner culture was dawning. It is the diner, in fact, that we most likely have to thank for creating the "BLT" short-order lingo, a charming example of how American slang has occasionally been shaped by lunch-counter jargon. Now, we even celebrate National BLT Month in April.

Where: *In New York* (for a simple classic), Eisenberg's Sandwich Shop, tel 212-675-5096, eisenbergsnyc.com; *in Los Angeles* (for an elegant version), Lucques, tel 323-655-6277, lucques.com. **Further information and recipes:** whatscookingamerica.net (search blt sandwich); republicofbacon.com (search perfect blt). **Tip:** It is important that the bacon be crisp and hot, so have all other ingredients at the ready before frying it.

"AND THIS IS GOOD OLD BOSTON, THE HOME OF THE BEAN AND THE COD."
—JOHN COLLINS BOSSIDY, FROM A 1910 SPEECH AT HOLY CROSS COLLEGE

Boston Baked Beans

American (New England)

Probably because of their somewhat plebian flavor and starchy texture, baked beans seem to cry for enriching molasses-like syrups to soften and sweeten them with a caramelized essence. This is the case with Swedish *bruna bönor*

(see page 366) as with Boston's own legendary favorite—so iconic that the city is known as Beantown.

Historians believe that Boston's bean fever began in the seventeenth century, when Native Americans taught early colonial settlers how to bake beans with bear fat in pits dug into the ground. Later, Puritans were said to fill pots with dry navy beans on Saturday and leave them to slowly simmer until Sunday, when they'd enjoy a dish of meltingly tender, delectably falling-apart beans without having to spoil the Sabbath with work.

It's not clear who first added what has become baked beans' characteristic ingredient, molasses, the touch that makes the familiar concoction so darkly rich and sweet—but in New England the timing probably coincided with the eighteenth- and nineteenth-century burgeoning of the molasses industry as part of the triangle trade between the eastern U.S. coast, Africa, and the West Indies. It wasn't until 1853 that the city's name appeared beside a recipe for the beans, in A. L. Webster's home cooking manual *The Improved Housewife.* (In addition to molasses, Webster's recipe calls for salt pork and saleratus—baking soda—both of which are now standard.)

By the 1930s, the bean dish had become so closely associated with Boston that the Ferrara Pan Candy Company of Chicago began marketing its reddish-brown, sugar-coated peanuts as Original Boston Baked Beans. Candy aside, the sweet beans—for some too sweet and thus doctored by souring dashes of vinegar—may be served as a meal or side dish and can be found in diners and any place hot dogs are served, in and out of Beantown.

WHERE: *In Boston,* Union Oyster House, tel 617-227-2750, unionoysterhouse.com; *in Boston and environs,* Jasper White's Summer Shack at four locations, summershackrestaurant.com. **MAIL ORDER:** store.oysterhousestore.com. **FURTHER INFORMATION AND RECIPES:** *The Fannie Farmer Cookbook,* 13th edition, by Marion Cunningham (1996); *Jasper White's Cooking From New England* by Jasper White (1998); cookstr.com (search boston baked beans).

THERE'S JOY IN BEING CANNED

Boston Brown Bread

American (New England)

A t first blush, canned bread sounds like a gimmick straight out of the 1950s' make-it-faster revolution of boxed cake mixes and powdered sauces, the kind of thing that might be marketed to schoolchildren or stocked on 7-Eleven gas station shelves. But there is nothing lowbrow or absurd about Boston brown bread, that bastion of regional American cooking: a dense, chewy, spongy loaf made of rye, cornmeal, and whole wheat flour, sweetened with molasses, and often steam-baked in, yes, an aluminum "tin" can. Boston's nineteenth-century food guru Fannie Farmer was an early popularizer of the sweet bread, advising the students at her cooking school: "A melon-mould or one-pound baking-powder boxes make the most attractive-shaped loaves, but a five-pound lard pail answers the purpose."

The hearty brown bread is indeed a useful answer to hearty appetites, but in colonial New England it met a range of needs. For one thing, the recipe made ready use of the region's steady crop of rye, introduced to the Northeast by the British and Dutch, and a suitable fit for the cool eastern climate. It also incorporated molasses, an imported product of the dark triangle trade in rum and slaves that took place between the eastern coast, Africa, and the West Indies. But the bread's principal purpose was to help keep the Sabbath in Puritan colonial kitchens. Before sundown on Saturday evening, Sunday's meal was set to cook, slowly, over warm coals. This included Boston's now legendary beans baking in a pot of molasses (see previous entry), and a partially covered tin of brown bread steaming in a hot kettle. Today, the same meal is still a Sunday staple in some northern kitchens—along with pot roast and potatoes—and you can find it in traditional New England–style restaurants, too. It's one of those treats that fills a kitchen with an especially warm, sweet aroma and is truly best homemade, so it's well worth trying out.

WHERE: *In Boston and environs,* Jasper White's Summer Shack, summershackrestaurant.com. **FURTHER INFORMATION AND RECIPES:** *The Fannie Farmer Cookbook,* 13th edition, by Marion Cunningham (1996); *Jasper White's Cooking from New England* by Jasper White (1998); epicurious.com (search boston brown bread jasper white). **TIP:** Dried raisins, cherries, and currants all are excellent additions to Boston brown bread recipes.

—||||||||||||||||||||||||||||||||||—

THE HAUTE-CUISINE HAMBURGER

Boulud Burger

American, Franco-American

Daniel Boulud, the justly celebrated French chef whose U.S. restaurants have earned the highest of marks, created a spectacular hamburger for DB Bistro Moderne, his urbane bistro in Manhattan's Theater District. Looking for all the world like a conventional large, nicely seared hamburger, its true elegance is revealed only on first bite.

It begins with pure, juicy, ground prime rib of beef. The quality of the ground meat is noteworthy in and of itself, but there are additional succulent surprises lurking within: meltingly tender shards of braised beef short rib, a luscious glob of silky foie gras, and aromatic shreds of black truffles—more than enough to seduce even the most jaded palates.

The luxurious burger is presented on a home-baked bun sprinkled with grated Parmesan, to be slathered to taste with a homemade tomato

Chef Boulud enjoys his masterpiece.

ketchup and lemony house-whipped mayonnaise. With the slimmest of crisp fries, its cost is north of $30, but aficionados claim it is worth every cent. At that price, one might do well to tuck a diamond ring into the foie gras as one high-rolling romantic did. No surprise, she said yes.

WHERE: *In New York, Miami, and Singapore,* DB Bistro Moderne, dbbistro.com. **FURTHER INFORMATION AND RECIPE:** For a video of Boulud making the burger, youtube.com (search db bistro moderne burger); for braised short ribs and whipped mayonnaise recipes, *Daniel: My French Cuisine* by Daniel Boulud (2013).

|||||||||||||||||||||||||||||||||||||||||||||||||||||||||||||||||||||||||||||||||||||||||||||||||||||||||||||||||||||||||||||

"THE HISTORY OF THE WORLD IS THE RECORD OF MAN IN QUEST
FOR HIS DAILY BREAD AND BUTTER." —HENDRIK WILLEM VAN LOON

Bread and Butter

Bread and butter is a food so basic it stands as a metaphor for all of our needs and concerns. We talk of earning our bread and butter, and remind ourselves of which side our bread is buttered on. But what kind of bread and which butter will do the trick? The bread must be firm-textured enough to remain intact as butter is spread over it. Besides lacking in character, overly soft commercial white breads will tear at this stage. Piping hot, freshly baked loaves may be too soft right out of the oven, and should be left to cool for a couple of hours; those that have been refrigerated should be held at room temperature for at least ten minutes.

If available from a bakery or your own kitchen, the firm-textured French sandwich bread *pain de mie* may take the bread-and-butter prize in the mild category. On the more flavorful end of the spectrum lie the German and eastern European sourdough or corned rye breads, with their pungent yeastiness and crisp crusts. Thin, square slices of chocolate-dark, malty, north European pumpernickel are delightfully chewy and hold the butter well, and the mild and buttery-tasting Jewish braided challah (see page 431) is rich enough to make the result seem almost like a dessert. (Challah should be cut into thicker, one-inch slices.)

As for the butter, it should be soft enough to spread easily but in no way runny. If it's too cold and firm, cut off the amount you need and mash it with a fork or knife blade until it is spreadable. Salted or sweet is the bread eater's choice; sweet butter can always be sprinkled with a pinch of coarse sea or kosher salt and, just maybe, a grinding or two of black pepper.

Where: *In New York,* Sullivan Street Bakery at two locations, sullivanstreetbakery.com; Breads Bakery, tel 212-633-2253, breadsbakery .com; Hot Bread Kitchen, tel 212-369-3331, hot breadkitchen.org; *in Long Island City, NY,* Tom Cat Bakery, tel 718-786-4224, tomcatbakery .com; *in Hoboken, NJ,* Marie's Bakery, tel 201-963-4281, rmariebreads.com; *in Philadelphia,* Faragalli's Bakery, tel 215-468-5197; *in Asheville, NC,* Farm & Sparrow, tel 828-633-0584, farmand sparrow.com; *in Los Angeles,* La Brea Bakery, tel 323-939-6813, labreabakery.com; in San Francisco, Tartine Bakery & Café, tel 415-487-2600, tartinebakery.com. **Further information and recipes:** *Bernard Clayton's New Complete Book of Breads* by Bernard Clayton (2006); saveur.com (search 20 great american bread bakeries); kingarthurflour.com.

A SWEET ENDING FOR STALE BREAD

Bread Pudding with Whiskey Sauce

American/Cajun

Hot butter and sweet, oozy lacings of bourbon whiskey bathing spongy bread that beckons with a crisply golden top crust . . . This is the enduring magic of an epic Cajun dessert. Pudding, the kind we eat for dessert, is one of those loosely defined, age-old dishes indigenous to many cultures around the world. But the origin of the term is much meatier, most likely tracing back to the Old French–inspired Cajun word for sausage, *boudin.* In the Middle Ages, the word referred to black and white savory sausage "puddings," and over the course of time evolved into the more common idea of a sweet, generally baked, generally milk-based dessert.

As always, frugal and inventive cooks realized that something delicious could be made from the stale bread with which they were continually confronted, and the bread pudding was born: slices or chunks of bread baked with eggs, milk, sugar, and various sweet and fragrant fixings into a sweet, chewy dessert. It took the Cajuns, those French-speaking Acadian exiles to Louisiana from maritime Canada, to spice up the formula with a creamy, bourbon-spiked sauce, poured over the pudding when it's fresh out of the oven. Long a staple of New Orleans restaurants, the Cajun pudding is lusciously thick and mouthwateringly sticky, made with porous, dry French bread that's excellent at soaking up plenty of sugar, freshly ground cinnamon, and vanilla complemented by the chewy sweetness of raisins or currants—which is not to say that executive chefs like Emeril Lagasse have not come up with delectable riffs, such as praline, and lemon-blueberry bread puddings. The pudding is

generally served as dessert, but a nice big, thick chunk along with a cup of bracing, chicory-laced, Creole coffee makes a decadent breakfast.

WHERE: *In New Orleans,* The Bon Ton Café, tel 504-524-3386, thebontoncafe.com; K-Paul's Louisiana Kitchen, tel 504-596-2530, chefpaul.com/kpaul; Emeril's Delmonico, tel 504-525-4937, emerilsrestaurants.com. **FURTHER INFORMATION AND RECIPES:** *New Orleans Classic Desserts* by Kit Wohl (2007); *The Dooky Chase Cookbook* by Leah Chase (1990); *Chef Paul Prudhomme's Louisiana Kitchen* by Paul Prudhomme (1984); epicurious.com (search favorite bread and butter pudding; bread pudding souffle).

⊢||||||||||||||||||||||||||||||⊣

IT'S ALL ABOUT CHOCOLATE

Brownies

America

To whom do we owe the intense pleasure of the dense chocolate brownie? One theory holds that Bertha Palmer, wife of the owner of Chicago's Palmer House Hotel, asked the chef to create a dainty chocolate dessert to serve at the

1893 Colombian Exposition—and thus the not-so-dainty brownie was born. Or was it the result of a happy accident, when a Maine librarian named Brownie Schrumpf omitted baking powder from a chocolate cake and ended up with a dense, flat bar? The list of possible inventors

A dense, fudgy delight and a classic American dessert

goes on, but the brownie's ascension to classic American dessert is due in no small part to the work of Duncan Hines and Betty Crocker, brands whose boxed mixes rose to popularity during the 1950s.

The brownie's commercial success should come as no surprise. The chocolaty dessert is portable, easy to make, and deeply satisfying to eat (especially with a glass of cold milk). But of course, brownie excellence does not come from a box. Cookie dough enthusiasts maintain that the best brownie is an underbaked brownie, damp and fudgy on the inside; for others, the best brownie is the one that is thoroughly baked to a more maturely spongy texture. When it comes to flavor, the most intense, richest chocolate taste is a goal commonly achieved through the use of very good quality dark, bittersweet chocolate. More timid palates prefer the milder milk chocolate, and some swear it's not a brownie without walnuts. Some demand pecans, while others stand for chocolate chips and these days, some welcome the lively touch of chile powder. (For Alice B. Toklas, the treat was wasted without a spiking of marijuana.) But the most texture-obsessed want all cake and refuse any possible distractions.

Tantalizingly chewy and luxuriously fudgy, with a deeply satisfying chocolate flavor, the beloved brownie speaks of simple childhood pleasures. To ensure that its reputation goes unmarred, a word of caution to parents: Forget the diabolical suggestion that you hide spinach in your children's brownie dough, a move guaranteed to breed a distrust more harmful than an iron deficiency.

Where: *In New York and Long Island,* Citarella at multiple locations, tel 212-874-0383,

citarella.com. **Retail and mail order:** *In New York,* Fat Witch at Chelsea Market, tel 888-419-4824, fatwitch.com (click Witches, then Fat Witch original; Java Witch; Fat Witch Walnut); Sarabeth's Bakery at Chelsea Market, tel 800-773-7378, sarabeth.com (search no nut brownies). **Further information and recipes:** For a classic recipe, see the back of packages of Baker's semisweet baking chocolate, *Sarabeth's Bakery* by Sarabeth Levine (2010); *The Art of Fine Baking* by Paula Peck (1961); *Chewy Gooey Crispy Crunchy Melt-in-Your-Mouth Cookies* by Alice Medrich (2010); epicurious.com (search brownies epicurious 2001; cocoa brownies bon appetit; chile brownies). **Tip:** A proper brownie should have a shiny, glistening top. To achieve that result, dip a knife blade into cold water and spread it over the top of the unbaked brownies in the pan before setting them in the oven.

"BRUNSWICK STEW IS WHAT HAPPENS WHEN SMALL MAMMALS CARRYING EARS OF CORN FALL INTO BARBECUE PITS." —ROY BLOUNT JR.

Brunswick Stew

American (Southern)

Care for some squirrel meat in your dinner? Although the origins of Brunswick stew are hotly debated, everyone seems to agree that squirrel was originally a feature of the distinctly Southern dish. Now replaced by rabbit, or more commonly

chicken, the meat is joined by potatoes, tomatoes, lima beans, corn, okra, and either fatback, salt pork, or bacon. The stew is distinguished by its trademark smokiness, the result of smoking the meats before they are added into the stew pot, along with a generous dose of smoky barbecue sauce.

A complete meal in which protein is mixed right in with the sides, the barbecue-in-a-bowl has

A backcountry smoked meat stew

its purported roots in Brunswick County, Virginia; Brunswick County, North Carolina; and Brunswick, Georgia—all of which were founded around the same time in the late 1700s. Virginians have the most elaborate legend, in which the dish they call "Virginia ambrosia" was created in 1828 by an African American chef named Jimmy Matthews, hired to cook for a squirrel-hunting party in the tobacco-growing community of Brunswick.

With an extra measure of pride, Georgia has gone so far as to create a monument to the dish: a twenty-five-gallon iron pot standing outside its coastal town of Brunswick, near Savannah, supposedly the vessel in which the first batch was cooked in 1898. North Carolina's claim seems to rest solely on the shoulders of the town name, combined with the state's significant barbecue tradition.

Whatever its origins, Brunswick stew has become a staple at barbecue joints and Fourth of July picnics throughout the South—whether its rich and complex juices are sopped up with tender biscuits, buttery wedges of cornbread, or crunchy fried cornmeal hushpuppies.

Where: *In New York, Westchester, New Jersey,* *and Florida,* Brother Jimmy's BBQ, brother jimmys.com; *in Charleston, SC,* Home Team BBQ, tel 843-225-7427, hometeambbq.com; *in Atlanta,* Swallow at the Hollow, tel 770-992-5383, swallowatthehollow.com; *in Newnan, GA,* Sprayberry's Barbecue, tel 770-253-4421, spray berrysbbq.com. **Further information and recipes:** *Bill Neal's Southern Cooking* by Bill Neal (1989); *A Gracious Plenty* by John T. Edge and Ellen Rolfes (1999); saveur.com, (search brunswick stew); epicurious.com (search brunswick stew; brunswick chicken); thedailymeal.com (search 25 best brunswick stews). **Special events:** Brunswick Stew Festival, Richmond, VA, November, richmond.com (search brunswick stew); for other stew-related events in Virginia from October through March, tel 866-STEWPOT.

ROMAN SALAD DAYS

Caesar Salad

American, Mexican-Italian

Cool, crisp romaine lettuce torn into fork-size pieces and tossed with golden croutons and a rich dressing of olive oil, fresh lemon juice, and egg yolk, with hints of zippy garlic, anchovies, and Parmesan, the elegant Caesar salad is easily satisfying enough to be a main course.

Popular as it is in Italian American eateries, you might assume that this dish was invented by Cornelia or Pompeia, the first and second wives of Julius Caesar, as a way of delighting the emperor. Its provenance is, in fact, much closer to home, dating back to a period during Prohibition when many southern Californians crossed the Mexican border to Tijuana, where they could drink their nights away without risking arrest.

One especially popular destination was Hotel Caesar's, run by an Italian American restaurateur named Caesar Cardini. According to culinary legend, one busy evening in 1924, Hotel Caesar's was running short of food, so the chef was compelled to make the most of what he had on hand: romaine lettuce, garlic, eggs, lemons, olive oil, Parmesan, and bread. A born showman, Cardini himself tossed these ingredients together tableside, reportedly with great flourish. Los Angelenos came home bragging about what they had eaten, and soon it became trendy to travel to Tijuana for the salad alone, never mind the cocktails and beer. None other than California native Julia Child made the trip as a young girl. In *From Julia Child's Kitchen,* she wrote, "One of my early remembrances of restaurant life was going to Tijuana in 1925 or 1926 with my parents, who were wildly excited that they should finally lunch at Caesar's Restaurant." Soon enough, the salad crossed the border, launching an American restaurant trend that has lasted more than eighty years—as well as a similarly long-lasting controversy over its legitimate ingredients. Attempting to approximate the salad based on their diners' descriptions, L.A. cooks added what has since become the dish's signature ingredient: anchovies. Cardini never used those briny little fish fillets, but he did employ Worcestershire sauce, which is made with anchovies and imparted that distinctive saltiness. (He also didn't use raw eggs, but rather broke lightly cooked eggs atop the salad as part of the presentation.)

Eventually, Cardini moved from Tijuana to Los Angeles to be closer to his core patrons, and when people began bringing bottles for Caesar to fill with his salad dressing, a cottage industry was born. (By 1990, sales of various brands of bottled Caesar dressing would reach $15.2 million.) The salad itself, meanwhile, spread across America, and by the 1950s it was a favorite in dining rooms from New York City's Rainbow Room to Cincinnati's Terrace-Hilton Hotel. Today, the Caesar is still a mainstay on menus everywhere, from white-tablecloth trattorias to corner pizzerias. Variations on the classic are legion, including additions of grilled chicken or tuna, and bottled Caesar dressings can be found in every supermarket. But nothing comes close to the delicious simplicity of the original, with fresh ingredients mixed directly in the salad bowl.

WHERE: *In Tijuana, Mexico,* Caesar's Restaurant, tel 52/664-685-1927, caesarstijuana .com; *in Santa Monica,* Vito Restaurant Santa Monica, tel 310-450-4999, vitorestaurant.com; *in Chicago,* David Burke's Primehouse, tel 312-660-6000, davidburkesprimehouse.com; *in Toronto,* Oyster Boy, tel 416-534-3432, oysterboy.ca; *throughout the U.S.,* The Palm Restaurant, the palm.com. **FURTHER INFORMATION AND RECIPES:** *The '21' Cookbook* by Michael Lomonaco (1995); *New American Table* by Marcus Samuelsson (2009); *The Fannie Farmer Cookbook,* 13th edition, by Marion Cunningham (1996); bonappetit .com (search classic caesar salad); cookstr.com (search original caesar salad). **SPECIAL EVENTS:** Caesar Salad Competition, Houston, TX, October, caesarsaladcompetitionhouston.com. **TIP:** To have the proper mix of lettuce to dressing, sheaves of romaine should be cut in approximately two-inch-long pieces.

"BELLE CALAS, TOUT CHAUD!"

Calas

American (Creole)

Now a mouthwatering brunch treat or snack with accents of winey yeast, the hot, sweet, and puffy fried rice dumplings of New Orleans were once a street food. *"Belle calas, tout chaud!"* was the call of the *calas* vendors,

then West African slave women who hawked the hot, spongy rounds from their carts on Sundays. Under French rule in the mid eighteenhundreds, Louisiana observed France's Code Noir. Among other punishing measures, the code mandated that Sunday be the only day off for slaves. But some of the slaves used those days to sell the sugar-dusted calas—one of their native foods—and according to several historians, bought their way to freedom with the proceeds.

After the Louisiana Purchase ended French rule, the calas remained in New Orleans, particularly embraced by Italian immigrants accustomed to *arancini*, the similar fried Sicilian rice balls. Originally derived from West African rice and pea fritters variously called *kárá, akara, kala,* or *calas,* the New Orleans version was adapted for whatever ingredients the slaves could get. Notable for the slightly tingling, fermented overtones of its yeast, the fritter's crisp, golden crust encases a gently yielding center

A fried-rice dessert with West African origins

combining sugar, flour, the yeast, eggs, and days-old, mildly fermented rice. Served searingly hot and dusted with powdered sugar, it is a specialty on Mardi Gras.

In recent years, the fritter has found a promoter in Poppy Tooker, a leader in New Orleans's Slow Food movement who has helped set a place for the pastry alongside beignets on several of the city's menus. After demonstrating her calas at a cooking class, Tooker was approached by a tearful man for whom the pastry evoked memories of his mother's New Orleans kitchen. The rest is brand-new history.

WHERE: *In New Orleans,* Elizabeth's, tel 504-944-9272, elizabethsrestaurantnola.com; The Old Coffeepot Restaurant, tel 504-524-3500, the oldcoffeepot.com. **FURTHER INFORMATION AND RECIPES:** *Crescent City Cooking* by Susan Spicer (2007); *Bill Neal's Southern Cooking* by Bill Neal (1989); *DamGoodSweet* by David Guas and Raquel Pelzel (2009); saveur.com (search calas fried rice fritters).

NOT QUITE WHAT THE DOCTOR ORDERED

Candied Apples

American

No country fair or fall festival is complete without the shining exemplar of simple pleasures that is the candied apple, shiny, red, crisp, and sweet. Key to the treat is a really good coating, thin and glassy, and the perfect crunchy-sugary

compliment to nature's more mellow confection within.

Surprisingly, the candied apple, also known as a jelly apple (and not to be confused with the caramel candied apple, with its brown toffee-flavored coating), has an actual provenance—and it's New Jersey. In 1908, Newark candy maker William Kolb was experimenting with a Christmas window display in his shop on Orange Street. He concocted a syrup out of melted sugar, red food coloring, and cinnamon

flavoring and dipped some apples into it, then placed the near-glowing orbs on his sills. Priced at a nickel each, they created an instant demand. Candied apples quickly spread to the Jersey Shore, and the crunchy sensation went on to be adopted by traveling circuses and candy shops across the country.

Not all candied apples are alike: A really excellent one pairs the sweetness of the shell with a suitably tart, very crisp apple, Granny Smith, Gala, and McIntosh being the best choices. Speared on a sturdy wooden stick, the apple is swirled in a cinnamon-flavored simple syrup heated nearly to the "hard crack" stage (about 300 degrees on a candy thermometer), then left to cool—and sometimes to hang around for far too long. The trick to buying premade candied apples is to get one that's fresh, and then to figure out how to eat it on the stick without dropping it or breaking your front teeth. (One technique involves turning the apple upside down, so the stick is underneath the apple in the manner of a very top-heavy ice-cream cone, giving the eater some much-needed leverage.)

Also known as a jelly apple, and highly compatible with country fairs

Synonymous with Halloween, the treats also have international and year-round appeal. Oddly, they've become a popular street food in China, where they are sold by bicycle vendors; in England, they are the traditional snack on Guy Fawkes Day, which commemorates the thwarting of an attempt to bomb Parliament in 1605. As a color, "candy apple–red" is applied to everything from sports cars to nail polish, and indeed the foodstuff does leave a semipermanent rosy tint. If there's a downside to candied apples, it's getting the sticky coating off your face. A tip: Baby oil works every time.

Where: *In Staten Island, NY,* Philip's Candy, tel 718-981-0062, philipscandy.com. **Mail order:** For ingredients and utensils, popcornsupply.com. **Further information and recipes:** *The Joy of Cooking* by Irma S. Rombauer, Marion Rombauer Becker, and Ethan Becker (2006); *The Fannie Farmer Cookbook:,* 13th edition, by Marion Cunningham (1996); candy.about.com (search candy apples); food52.com (search riff on caramel apples). **Special event:** National Apple Harvest Festival, near Gettysburg, PA, October, appleharvest.com. The Festival includes a booth devoted to candied apples.

—||||||||||||||||||||||||||||||||||||||—

EAT THE FRUIT, CANDY THE PEEL

Candied Citrus Peel

American, Continental

Just like canning and drying, candying can be a means of preservation—coating and infusing fruit with sugar is another curing method that helps it survive past its season. But beyond the practical, slim strips of sunset-gold orange rind and burnished, brassy ribbons of grapefruit peel magically turn the simplest desserts into sophisticated confections.

Somewhere along the line, a savvy and frugal confectioner figured out that candying the peels of citrus fruits amounted to a lovely treat—the marvelously aromatic strips become tender and sweet while retaining a pleasing astringency and a subtle bite, and they're relatively easy to make. To rid them of most of their bitter oils, the stripped peels, trimmed of white pith, are boiled in three changes of water. Poached in sugar syrup and then rolled in granulated sugar, they are then spread on an oiled or wax paper–covered surface or a marble surface to dry slowly. That's all there is to this fragrant magic.

Real candied citrus peels—the handmade kind, as opposed to the dried-out version usually found in supermarkets—are a wonderful and fragrant addition to holiday fruit cake, but they are especially valued as after-meal refreshers, nibbled with coffee, tea, or ice cream.

MAIL ORDER: amazon.com (search candied orange peel france; candied lemon peel france). **FURTHER INFORMATION AND RECIPES:** *From My Mother's Kitchen* by Mimi Sheraton (1979); *Chocolates and Confections* by Peter Greweling (2007); *The Joy of Cooking* by Irma S. Rombauer, Marion Rombauer Becker, and Ethan Becker (2006); *The Fannie Farmer Cookbook*, 13th edition, by Marion Cunningham (1996); cookstr .com (search candied citrus peel medrich; candied lemon or lime slices). **TIP:** When candying peels, it's best to use slightly underripe fruit and to gently parboil the peel; if the water boils too rapidly, the peel may toughen instead of softening.

⊦||||||||||||||||||||||||||||||⊦

AN ARISTOCRATIC TREAT IN A CUP

Charlotte Russe, American-Style

American

F ew desserts are so formal and elegant as an authentic French *charlotte russe,* supposedly created by the legendary pastry chef Marie-Antoine Carême, the most famous of the nineteenth-century French cooks and a purveyor of sugary

delights to Czar Alexander I. In the original and still most elegant version, a fez-shaped metal mold known as a charlotte is lined with liqueur-moistened, spongy ladyfingers and a frothy filling of whipped-cream-bolstered egg custard. Chilled until the custard is set, the dessert is topped with a layer of whipped cream.

So much for the French way. There's a democratized American version that is equally worthy of praise, a simpler sweet that became a customary street treat for children during the first half of the twentieth century. Its special container is essential to its existence: a small, stiff white paper cuff with scalloped edges and, for a bottom, a paper disc that can be gently pushed up. A tiny round of yellow sponge cake goes into the cuff as a base, followed by swirling cloudlets of sweetened whipped cream topped

with a bright red maraschino cherry—that last being beautiful to behold, but awful to taste. As children (or lucky grown-ups) walked along the street licking at the whipped cream and pushing up the disc, the contents rising to eating level with the moist cake treat left for last, it was not uncommon for the whole dessert to pop up and out onto the sidewalk, good for a laugh if it didn't prompt tears.

One charlotte russe tradition that seems to have persisted unnecessarily: It is generally available only in winter, a holdover from times when summer refrigeration was so chancy that any whipped cream in pastries sometimes soured in the heat.

WHERE: *In Staten Island, NY,* Holtermann's Bakery, tel 718-984-7095, holtermannsbakery .webs.com; Philip's Candy, tel 718-981-0062, philipscandy.com. **Further information and recipes:** *Desserts by the Yard* by Sherry Yard (2007); *All-American Desserts* by Judith M. Fertig

(2003); *The Brooklyn Cookbook* by Lyn Stallworth and Rod Kennedy Jr. (1991); capital newyork.com (search charlotte russe).

——————————————|||||||||||||||||||||||||||||||||||||——————————————

EASY-DOES-IT CHICKEN FOR COMPANY

Chicken Marbella

American

The secret of this beloved recipe's success may well lie in its ability to coax an air of refinement and even complexity out of the simplest ingredients and techniques. That, along with the intriguing appeal of contrasting but complementary flavors, goes a long way to explaining the enduring popularity of chicken Marbella with home cooks who love entertaining in an effortlessly flashy way.

The homey and economical slow-roasted chicken is marinated overnight, taking on the sweet and pungent overtones of olives, prunes, and capers before being baked with white wine and brown sugar. Simple from a technical point of view, chicken Marbella is even more convenient for its ability to be assembled up to three days prior to baking, although it can alternatively be prepared entirely the night before it's to be served. It is also one of those softly stewed dishes that ripens and mellows to taste even better the next day. Versatile enough to be served over couscous, steamed rice, mashed potatoes, egg noodles, or by itself with crusty bread and a green salad, and to be eaten hot or at room temperature, it also travels well to potluck parties.

The epitome of 1980s cooking and entertaining, the dish was devised by Sheila Lukins and Julee Rosso, partners in the New York catering shop The Silver Palate. Opened on the Upper West Side in 1977, the store sold a then quirky combination of multiethnic, vaguely sophisticated dishes that lent themselves to dinners for busy family weeknights but were also good enough for company. That philosophy

and doability is fully realized in chicken Marbella—a succulent, juicy, and deeply flavorful dinner that is easy enough to be made by even a novice cook, assuming the following recipe adapted from *The Silver Palate Cookbook* is carefully followed.

Chicken Marbella

Serves 6

½ cup olive oil
½ cup red wine vinegar
1 cup pitted prunes
½ cup pitted Spanish green olives
½ cup capers, with a bit of juice
6 bay leaves
1 head of garlic, peeled and pureed
½ cup fresh oregano, chopped,
    or ¼ cup dried oregano
Coarse salt and freshly ground black pepper
    to taste
2 chickens, 3½ to 4 pounds each, quartered
1 cup dry white wine
1 cup brown sugar
2 tablespoons finely chopped flat-leaf
    parsley

1. In a large bowl, combine the olive oil, vinegar, prunes, olives, capers and juice, bay leaves, garlic, and oregano, and season with salt and pepper. Add the chicken pieces and turn to coat. Cover and refrigerate overnight or up to 3 days.

2. Preheat the oven to 350°F. Arrange the chicken in a single layer in a shallow roasting pan; spoon the marinade over it evenly. Pour in the wine and sprinkle the chicken with the brown sugar.

3. Bake until the thigh pieces yield clear yellow juice when pricked with a fork, 50 to 60 minutes, basting two or three times with the pan juices once the chicken begins to brown. (When basting, do not brush off the sugar. If the chicken browns too quickly, cover the pan lightly with foil.)

4. Transfer the chicken pieces to a warm serving platter and top them with the prunes, olives, and capers; keep the platter warm. Place the roasting pan over medium heat and bring the pan juices to a boil. Reduce the juices to about ½ cup. Strain the juices into a heatproof bowl, add the parsley, and pour over the chicken. Chicken Marbella will keep, covered and refrigerated, for about 5 days.

FURTHER INFORMATION AND RECIPE: *The Silver Palate Cookbook* by Sheila Lukins and Julee Rosso (2007). **TIP:** When prepared with small drumsticks and wings, chicken Marbella makes a delicious appetizer.

WHAT THE EARL OF SANDWICH HATH WROUGHT

Chicken Sandwich

American

There comes a time when what every man or woman hungers for most is a simple chicken sandwich. To make that chicken sandwich a perfect one, the first thing you need is two slices of either *pain de mie*—that yeasty,

dense, square French sandwich loaf—sour rye, or a seed-crunched whole grain bread; the choice depends upon personal taste. Spread with softened sweet butter, or a combination of lemony mayonnaise and a bit of Dijon mustard, the bread should be layered with moist, freshly roasted or poached chicken breast, sliced tissue thin and sprinkled with a few crystals of coarse sea salt and grindings of black pepper. Any greens should be nonintrusive and kept to a minimum, if included at all, the best being tender Bibb or Boston lettuce or, for a sprightlier effect, watercress leaves (minus the tough stems). Tomato need not apply, lest it drown out other flavors. Equally unwelcome are the impostor turkey and low-quality commercial white bread that tears apart as it is bitten into.

Within these parameters, there is room for innovation. One that has become a classic is the triple-decker chicken, bacon, and tomato club sandwich. Another was the so-called chicken sandwich made famous in 1959 by one Albert Stockli, master chef at the then-new Four Seasons restaurant in Manhattan. His "sandwich" for four was a huge white china platter lined with crackling, parchment-thin slices of homemade rye melba toast; lightly brushed with butter, they were topped with boned chunks of hot roasted chicken complete with golden skin.

WHERE: *In New York,* Elephant & Castle, tel 212-243-1400, elephantandcastle.com; *in Savannah, GA,* Zunzi's, tel 912-443-9555, zunzis.com; *in Oakland, CA,* Bakesale Betty, tel 510-985-1213, bakesalebetty.com. **FURTHER INFORMATION AND**

RECIPES: *Gene Hovis's Uptown Down Home Cookbook* by Gene Hovis with Sylvia Rosenthal (1993); *The Joy of Cooking* by Irma S. Rombauer, Marion Rombauer Becker, and Ethan Becker (2006); *The Fannie Farmer Cookbook,* 13th edition, by Marion Cunningham (1996); saveur .com (search chicken and egg club sandwich); epicurious.com (search chicken sandwiches with chive butter; broiled chicken and roasted pepper sandwiches).

‖‖‖‖‖‖‖‖‖‖‖‖‖‖‖‖‖‖‖‖‖‖‖

THE PIE-THROWER'S FAVORITE

Chocolate Cream Pie

American

I n this wholly American dessert, the pleasure of a crisp pie crust is a foil for the decadence of a rich, silky chocolate pudding filling. No need to ask for whipped cream on the side, as the sweet and snowy topping is standard.

Because chocolate cream pie belongs to the American tradition of "icebox pies"—pies that aren't oven baked but are instead chilled to finished, firm perfection in the refrigerator—it is not only a crowd-pleaser but also incredibly easy to prepare. Called a "cream pie," although it really is a pudding pie, its filling is a custard made with milk, chocolate, sugar, and eggs, bound by cornstarch so its slices hold their shape. The custard ingredients are heated together and poured into a good, thick pre-baked crust that stands up to the filling without becoming soggy (such as a crumb crust made of graham crackers or cookies) and the pie is then chilled to our everlasting pleasure.

What's not to love about a pie filled with cream-topped chocolate pudding?

You'll find delicious icebox pies flavored with the likes of butterscotch, coconut cream, banana cream, and Key lime, but none packs quite so luxurious a punch as the chocolate. It's not quite as pleasant, perhaps, when tossed in your face, but it's a favorite for that purpose as it creates a mess yet is soft enough not to do much harm.

FURTHER INFORMATION AND RECIPES: *The Dessert Bible* by Christopher Kimball (2000); *Sinfully Easy Delicious Desserts* by Alice Medrich (2012); *The Joy of Cooking* by Irma S. Rombauer, Marion Rombauer Becker, and Ethan Becker (2006); *The Fannie Farmer Cookbook,* 13th edition, by Marion Cunningham (1996); epicu rious.com (search chocolate cream pie 2004). **TIP:** For a quick filling, try packaged chocolate pudding mix; Jell-O is the standard brand.

—||||||||||||||||||||||||||||||||—

YOU'RE NEVER TOO OLD

Cinnamon Toast

American

Crunchy, buttery, cinnamon-sugar-glazed toast is comfort food nonpareil, the balm applied by mothers of sniffling children since time immemorial. Most of the credit for its calming effect goes to the musky, earthy sweetness of cinnamon, the dried inner bark of the evergreen *Cinnamomum verum* tree. The tree is native to Sri Lanka, formerly Ceylon, and was introduced to the Seychelles Islands by the French in the early 1800s. (Both regions lead the world in cinnamon production today.)

Cinnamon has a subtle yet distinctive flavor. Even ground, it's a deeply concentrated, aromatic spice, embraced by a host of cuisines and used as a flavoring agent in everything from Mexican hot chocolate drinks to Moroccan lamb tagines. But the best way to appreciate the spice is atop some hot, lavishly buttered toast.

Warm and crunchy, slightly softened by rich butter and glazed with sprinklings of cinnamon and sugar, the kitchen-cupboard creation is a childhood pleasure whose aroma alone is well worth occasionally revisiting. The most ordinary white bread does the job beautifully, and the only trick is to allow the toasted slice to rest under the broiler until the sugar caramelizes, to achieve maximum candy-crunch. (No toasters need apply.)

Mail order: For sticks or powdered cinnamon, Penzeys Spices, tel 800-741-7787, penzeys.com. **Further information and recipes:** *The Joy of Cooking* by Irma S. Rombauer, Marion Rombauer Becker, and Ethan Becker (2006); *The Fannie Farmer Cookbook,* 13th edition, by Marion Cunningham (1996); epicurious.com (search cinnamon toast ice cream); food52.com (search maple cinnamon toast; homemade cinnamon toast crunch; cinnamon toast breakfast pudding).

—||||||||||||||||||||||||||||||||—

A FISHY SOUP, IN MORE WAYS THAN ONE

Cioppino

American (San Franciscan), Italian

The world over, a bowl of fish soup often presents a mystery and a discussion— what seafood swirls in its pungent broth, and how, exactly, should it be prepared? Pose these questions of San Francisco's thick, tomato-based, vegetable-rich cioppino, and be prepared for a multitude of options. Much like a minestrone laden with plenty of the seafood the city is famous for, it is said to be a descendant of the Genoan fish soup known as *ciuppin* (pronounced chee-o-PEEN). Introduced to San Francisco by Ligurian immigrants in the early nineteenth century, the soup was taken up by fishermen's wives in the North

Beach section that became the local little Italy. These days, the richest version to be found in that enchanting, hilly town is at the Tadich Grill (see page 629), a fixture since 1854.

Whatever orthodoxy dictates as to its correct contents—some say yes to shellfish (and then the question is which), others no—the Tadich soup is chock-full of fresh white-fleshed fish, shrimp, scallops, clams, and crabmeat. It doesn't skimp on the vegetables, either, its tomato-laden stock enhanced by dicings of carrots, green peppers, leeks, fennel, and celery.

Splashes of white wine join onion and garlic and spicings of basil, oregano, thyme, bay leaves, cayenne, and black pepper in a deeply flavorful mix. Served steaming hot, and even richer when reheated after a day in the refrigerator, the fragrant cioppino is best enjoyed with a chunk of San Francisco's famous, crusty sourdough bread.

Where: *In San Francisco,* Tadich Grill, tel 415-391-1849, tadichgrill.com. **Further information and recipes:** *Tadich Grill* by John Briscoe (2002); recipelink.com (search tadich cioppino).

A REAL SHELL GAME

Clams Casino

American, Italian

B riny cherrystone clams, fresh from the sea, garnished with strips or bits of lean bacon and flecks of sweet red and green peppers, topped with a slather of butter and sizzled under the broiler, offer a double dose of saltiness from

their surf-and-turf components. A dash of paprika contributes a bright glow to this old-fashioned Italian American appetizer.

Credit for its invention goes to Julius Keller, a former maître d'hôtel at the Narragansett Pier Casino, on the coast of Rhode Island. In his 1939 autobiography, he says he developed the dish in 1917 for a Mrs. Paran Stevens, a local (and expectedly demanding) social butterfly who hosted a luncheon at the restaurant.

Keller's version probably wasn't original in anything but the name (after the restaurant), as concoctions with clams and bacon are documented in cookbooks as early as the 1880s. But he put his particular clam treatment on the map, and ever since it has been associated with Rhode

A seaside tradition since 1917

Island, as well as with the old-fashioned northern Italian restaurants that seem to have adopted clams casino as their own. It's even traveled to the stage, by way of a modern burlesque performer who calls herself Clams Casino—an homage, she says, to Coney Island's boardwalk fare.

Where: *In Baltimore,* Mama's on the Half Shell, tel 410-276-3160, mamasmd.com; *in New York,* Patsy's, tel 212-247-3491, patsys.com; *throughout the U.S.,* Palm restaurants, thepalm .com. **Further information and recipes:** *Lidia's Italian-American Kitchen* by Lidia Matticchio Bastianich (2001); *Molto Italiano: 327 Simple Italian Recipes to Cook at Home* by Mario Batali (2005); saveur.com (search clams casino); cookstr.com (search clams casino mariani).

COBBLING A SALAD FOR THE LADIES WHO LUNCH

Cobb Salad

American

Although much in keeping with the French tradition of the *salade composée*, Cobb salad speaks to nothing so much as good old-fashioned American ingenuity. Invented in the 1930s at the Los Angeles restaurant The Brown Derby,

during the heyday of the Hollywood studio system, it was allegedly composed of a host of leftovers that owner Robert Cobb found hanging around in the kitchen—Roquefort cheese, chopped bacon, hard-cooked eggs, tomatoes, boneless skinless chicken breast, and avocado among them. Cubing and dicing the solids, Cobb tossed them with salt, black pepper, and a vinaigrette of olive oil, red wine vinegar, Worcestershire sauce, lemon juice, and garlic.

Cobb may have been starting with leftovers, but the success of this salad rests on the thoughtful preparation of each separate ingredient, and on varied and distinct textures ranging from tender to crunchy to creamy. The salad's distinctly American aspect probably comes from its resemblance to a chopped-up BLT sandwich, minus the bread; but thanks to the Brown Derby's history as a storied movie-star hangout where the likes of Ronald Reagan, Vivien Leigh, Clark Gable, and Lucille Ball lunched, the dish took on a life of its own, becoming an early and

enduring symbol of the power lunch and of California cuisine.

The original Brown Derby closed in 1985 and the landmark building that housed it was destroyed in an earthquake, but the tradition of Cobb salad continues just about anywhere "American food" is served, and today it's possible to find it bedecked with all manner of diced things. The salad comes up routinely in popular culture, memorably so on an episode of HBO series *Curb Your Enthusiasm* called "Trick or Treat." (A character named Cliff Cob tries to convince main character Larry David that his grandfather invented the Cobb salad at Chicago's Drake Hotel. Larry eventually proves him wrong.)

WHERE: *In New York and Santa Monica,* Michael's, michaelsnewyork.com, michaels santamonica.com;. *in Toronto,* Oyster Boy, tel 416-534-3432, oysterboy.ca. **TIP:** Ladies who lunch should take note: The not-so-diet-friendly Cobb packs a wallop in calories.

THE ORIGINAL AMERICAN PANCAKES

Corn Fritters

American

For some, the true flavor of summer can be found in a juicy red tomato, fresh off the vine. For others, nothing quite captures the innocent farm-fresh taste of the summer months like good old-fashioned corn fritters, the best of which are light in texture, creamy on the inside, and crisp on the outside—and most importantly, loaded with fresh sweet corn flavor.

Native Americans had been roasting corn and grinding it into meal to make cakes, breads, and porridges long before settlers adopted the practice and expanded the corn crop, along with the burgeoning nation's repertoire of corn dishes, throughout the colonies. (Cornbread, for one, is the obvious legacy of the Indian corn pone, from the Algonquin word *appone,* for a dish made of cornmeal, salt, and water.) But in colonial America, wheat was prized and corn was lowly. Corn pone, hoecakes, johnnycakes, spoon bread, and other corn-based "breads" were lesser foods, with the corn fritter born of a desire to stretch summer's bounty by mixing kernels of corn into a fairly standard batter—flour, egg, baking powder, a little milk, sometimes beer for extra leavening—just before frying it.

The summery fritters can skew savory or sweet.

In many coastal Southern communities, corn fritters are dubbed "corn oysters" for their resemblance to the fried bivalves, and the South in general is eternally associated with the fritters. Emblems of the region's fried-food culture, they are beloved side dishes alongside fowl, traditional fare at Thanksgiving dinners, and a great way to use up that stash of summer corn in the freezer. But the fritters are hardly restricted to the area below the Mason-Dixon Line—

they're also a Yankee favorite, a standard offering with a bowl of corn chowder or as part of a breakfast repast, served with maple syrup. (Reports of harvest breakfasts in the Connecticut Shaker colony, founded in 1792 in Enfield, show that autumnal breakfasts included hot apple cereal and corn fritters.)

Similar golden-fried, starchy puffs can be found around the globe. In Umbria, they are made with a batter that includes the famed local lentils; throughout India their batter incorporates freshly ground cumin seed. In Indonesia, corn fritters are a popular street food sold on carts throughout the day and into the night.

The standard American recipe is so forgiving as to be almost impossible to mess up—you can use the corn kernels whole or grated or incorporate some of each (which gives the fritters more textural variety). They are best when made with sweet fresh corn, but both leftover grilled or roasted corn and frozen corn are acceptable substitutes. The batter may be spiked with any number of ingredients, from a confetti of colorful peppers to fresh herbs to Parmesan; although they're often fried in vegetable oil, cooking them in rendered bacon fat, lard, or butter will work beautifully, too.

Corn Fritters

Makes 20 fritters

> 1 cup all-purpose flour
> 1 teaspoon kosher salt
> 1½ teaspoons baking powder
> 1 extra-large egg, lightly beaten
> 2 tablespoons milk
> 8 ounces corn kernels, fresh or frozen and thawed
> ¼ cup beer (optional)
> Canola oil or shortening, for frying

1. In a bowl, mix together the flour, salt, and baking powder.

2. Make a well in the center of the dry ingredients and add the egg, milk, corn, and beer, if using. Gradually combine the liquid into the flour mixture, mixing just until the batter is no longer lumpy. Cover and chill in the refrigerator for at least 30 minutes, or up to 1 hour.

3. In a heavy saucepan, heat 1 to 2 inches of oil over medium-high heat; it's hot enough when it quickly browns a small drop of batter. Drop the batter by the tablespoonful into the oil and fry, turning once, until the fritters are puffed and golden on both sides, about 3 minutes. Drain on paper towels and serve immediately, or place the fritters on a pan lined with paper towels and hold them at room temperature for up to 15 minutes. Remove paper towels and reheat them in a 200°F oven for 10 minutes before serving.

WHERE: *In Chester, VA,* Brock's Bar-B-Que, tel 804-796-7539, brocksbbq.com; *in Pigeon Forge, TN,* The Old Mill Restaurant, tel 865-429-3463, old-mill.com. **FURTHER INFORMATION AND ADDITIONAL RECIPES:** *Spice* by Ana Sortun (2006); *The Joy of Cooking* by Irma S. Rombauer, Marion Rombauer Becker, and Ethan Becker (2006); *Hoppin' John's Low Country Cooking* by John Martin Taylor (1992); *Jasper White's Cooking from New England* by Jasper White (1998); epicurious.com (search corn-jalapeno fritters); latinfood.about.com (search frituras de maiz); epicurious.com (search corn fritters with salsa; corn fritters with arugula and warm tomato salad). **TIP:** Chilling the batter for 30 minutes to 1 hour before frying helps the fritter hold together as it cooks.

⊢||||||||||||||||||||||||||||||||⊣

SUMMER'S BOUNTY, UNADULTERATED

Corn on the Cob

American

Among the many delicious gifts of the American summer, none seems quite so symbolic or so worthy of celebration as corn on the cob—nor has the year-round availability of corn from far-off places dimmed the excitement of serious eaters when local corn makes its first appearance. Because of the speed at which the corn's sweet sugars turn to tasteless starch after it is picked (especially in heat), the sooner corn is eaten after being harvested, the better. Boiled for three to five minutes in salted water, then slathered, steaming hot, with softened (but not melted) sweet butter and sprinkled with coarse salt to add a nicely gritty texture to the soft sweetness of the kernels, truly good corn on the cob is a fleeting pleasure that should never be taken for granted.

Not to be confused with the field corn used as grain and feed, sweet eating corn is grown commercially in several main varieties. Golden Cross Bantam is a deep yellow-gold and tends toward a heavy sweetness. Silver Queen generally has small white kernels and a mild sugar content that doesn't overwhelm its essential corn flavor, while the too-easy-to-like Honey and Cream or Sugar and Butter varieties with their combinations of gold and white kernels, overdo it with candy-sweet overtones. One of the best of the old-time corn varieties is Country Gentleman, with pearly-white kernels whose irregular rows suggest the gentleman might be in serious need of orthodontia. It is the most sophisticated and delicate of all corns, rich in flavor with a mildly sweet milk emanating from the kernels. Unfortunately, Country Gentleman isn't widely available—if you can't find it at a farmers' market near you, you may have to consider growing your own from seed.

When buying corn on the cob, the two things to look for are ripeness and freshness. The corn is ripe when the silk tassels poking out of its husks are a deep golden brown—pale tassels indicate the corn was picked too soon—and the tip of its ear is as fully covered with full-grown kernels as the body. To evaluate freshness, look for plump kernels. Stale, dry kernels will look a bit caved in. If in doubt, puncture one with a fingernail; a milky liquid should ooze out.

To store corn, keep it well wrapped in the vegetable compartment of your refrigerator; if you plan on keeping it for more than a day, wrap it in a wad of wet newspaper first. Wait to husk the corn until a few minutes before you're ready to cook it.

While whole corn cobs are most often boiled or steamed in a pot, a superior method is to cook them on an outdoor grill. To do that, pull the husks back without tearing them off, and remove all of the silk. Wet the palms of your hands and brush them over the kernels before folding the husks back in place. This protects the kernels from burning and traps moisture so that they steam and roast at the same time, emerging both tender and pleasantly smoky. Place the ears on a grill over white-hot coals and turn the ears every couple of minutes. The corn should be finished

(depending on the heat of the fire) in ten to fifteen minutes.

Where: For seeds, burpee.com (search country gentleman). **Further information and recipes:** *I Love Corn* by Lisa Skye (2012); *Mastering the Art of Southern Cooking* by Nathalie Dupree and Cynthia Graubart (2012); *Jasper White's Cooking from New England* by Jasper White (1998); epicurious.com (search corn on the cob with lime-chive butter); foodandwine.com (search grilled corn on the cob with roasted garlic and herbs). **Tip:** For an alternative to simple toppings of butter, salt, and pepper, take a hint from Mexico and sprinkle each buttered ear with lime juice and spicy chile powder.

Summer's bounty, best eaten right off the cob and directly after harvest, here served Mexican-style.

THE NATIONAL QUICK BREAD

Cornbread

American

Golden as the sun and hearty with a salt-sweet grit, cornbread is an equal sustainer of body and psyche—especially so when served hot and fragrant with butter or bacon drippings, with a cold glass of buttermilk on the side.

Grown all over the United States (particularly in the Midwest), corn remains closely identified with the Southern states, where cornbread has always been made with white—not yellow—cornmeal. Initially, it was slaves' food, made of meal mixed with water and baked in the hot sun on the hoes the slaves used in the fields (hence the name "hoecake," a synonym for cornbread). But the history of corn and cornbread goes back even further: Throughout the Americas, from Canada to Mexico, when European settlers arrived, Native Americans were adeptly roasting kernels of corn, then grinding them into a cornmeal that was cooked into a variety of breads, two of which we still know as tortillas and arepas.

Gradually, several key ingredients were added to create the basic formula of what is now known as American cornbread: salt, bacon grease, eggs, buttermilk, baking powder, baking soda, sugar, and flour. The most traditional way to make good cornbread is the way Southern cooks have been doing it since antebellum days. A batter of medium thickness, neither runny nor stiff, is made of coarsely ground white cornmeal and the aforementioned ingredients, minus the sugar. Ideally, just before it is poured out into a cast-iron skillet and baked in a hot oven, a couple of tablespoons of chopped-up bacon are stirred in. The resulting bread is a singularly spectacular affair: crisp on the outside, moist and soft on the inside, the corn lending a mineral flavor and the bacon a smoky richness.

WHERE: *In Roswell, GA,* Greenwood's, tel 770-992-5383, greenwoodsongreenstreet.com; *in Atlanta,* Watershed on Peachtree, tel 404-809-3561, watershedrestaurant.com; *in Savannah, GA,* Mrs. Wilkes' Dining Room, tel 912-232-5997, mrswilkes.com; *in Houston,* Goode Co. at multiple locations, goodecompany.com. **MAIL ORDER:** For stone-ground cornmeal, ansonmills.com. **FURTHER INFORMATION AND RECIPES:** *Bill Neal's Southern Cooking* by Bill Neal (1989); *Harvest to Heat* by Darryl Estrine and Kelly Kochendorfer (2010); *New American Table* by Marcus Samuelsson (2009); *Artisan Baking Across America* by Maggie Glezer (2000); epicurious .com (search real skillet cornbread; zucchini cornbread; cornbread for dressing); cookstr .com (search corn sticks; cranberry and sage cornbread). **SPECIAL EVENT:** National Cornbread Festival, South Pittsburg, TN, April, nationalcornbread.com. **SEE ALSO:** Arepas, page 659; Tortillas, page 657; Corn Fritters, page 547.

ALL PLAY AND NO WORK

Crab Cakes

American

It's easy to find bad crab cakes. Crabmeat is expensive, especially the jumbo lump meat, and fillers and binders are cheap—but nothing is worse than a bulge of something that used to be a glorious piece of crabmeat surrounded by a heap of starchy, mushy ingredients dragging it from glory.

A crab cake, at its essence, is made of four things: crabmeat (prime crab cakes are made with the solid white chunks of blue crab, labeled "jumbo lump"), binding (usually egg or mayonnaise), seasonings (various herbs, spices, and vegetables, including diced onions, green or red peppers, and scallions), and filler (bread crumbs, cracker crumbs, and so on). A good crab cake will contain just enough of these other ingredients to enhance the crabmeat itself, but no more.

The other secret to crab cake excellence is known far and wide by all Baltimore fishermen's wives: After the cakes are formed, they should be chilled for two or three hours in order to firm up, so that when they're eventually fried or broiled (both are acceptable, but lightly, delicately fried is better), they remain intact instead of falling apart.

There are more than 4,400 species of crab, most of them in North American waters, but it is the blue crab (*Callinectes sapidus*) of the Chesapeake Bay, along the mid-Atlantic coast, that is most sought after and that makes the very best crab cakes. Thus it was that the cakes sprang up in and around Baltimore in the 1820s, when the harvesting of the tidal waters of the eastern seaboard became the driving force of that town's prosperity. By 1939, crab cakes were so well known that they were served at the World's Fair in New York.

Golden brown, puffy pillows showcasing snowy, gently saline crabmeat, they offer easy, luxurious sustenance as an appetizer or main course—and as you can buy the meat already picked over, usually they do not require the tedious, messy task of working through the hard shells of the saltwater crustaceans to extricate their rich, sweet white meat. Be willing to make an exception, however, for crabmeat purchased on docks and from outdoor markets.

WHERE: *In Linthicum Heights, MD* (also mail order), G&M Restaurant, tel 877-554-3723, gand mcrabcakes.com; *in Savannah, GA,* Mrs. Wilkes' Dining Room, tel 912-232-5997, mrswilkes.com; *in Houston,* Danton's Seafood, tel 713-807-8889, dantonsseafood.com. **RETAIL AND MAIL ORDER:** *In Baltimore, MD,* Faidley Seafood in the Lexington Market, tel 410-727-4898, faidleyscrabcakes.com. **FURTHER INFORMATION AND RECIPES:** *Eating: A Memoir* by Jason Epstein (2009); *Mrs. Wilkes' Boardinghouse Cookbook* by Sema Wilkes (2001); *Jasper White's Cooking from New England* by Jasper White (1998); *New American Table* by Marcus Samuelsson (2009); cookstr .com (search crab cakes ponzek; thai crab cakes; jumbo crab cakes with spicy mayonnaise).

WHEN THE MUDBUGS ARE RUNNING

Crawfish

American (Louisianan)

Most of the English-speaking world knows these tiny, scarlet, freshwater crustaceans as crayfish, or in francophile circles as *écrevisses*. In Sweden, where they are wonderfully prepared, they are known as *kräfter* (see page 369).

But in Louisiana, where they grow both wild and farmed (and are devoured in abundance), *Procambarus clarkii* are called crawfish, mudbugs, or, pretentiously, miniature freshwater lobsters.

Time was when they could be enjoyed only between May and July, but farming has greatly lengthened their season without dampening the enthusiasm for the treats. In crawfish-loving territories, children are taught at an early age how to hold each tiny, spiky mudbug between thumb and forefinger in order to crack them open and efficiently make the most of their succulent meat before sucking the savory juices out of their heads. They are most sublime when simply steamed with the spice combination known as crab boil, which imparts aromas of bay leaf, chile pepper, black pepper, nutmeg, cloves, coriander seed, thyme, and more. Ideally they are eaten out of doors, on newspaper-covered tables, with plenty of paper towels and beer at hand.

More elaborate preparations include the famed Creole étouffée, a peppery, rose-colored crawfish stew with a rich sauce rewardingly sopped up by steamed rice. The crimson tails may also be crisply fried, or simmered with rice, tomatoes, and diced ham for a sumptuous jambalaya (see page 587). More ambitious cooks dig the meat from the shells and turn it into salads, or chop and mix it with finely diced scallions (aka green onions) and eggs before frying them into delicious patties. Those with even more time and patience may choose to stuff the crawfish heads with seasoned bread crumbs and crawfish meat before baking them. Crawfish pie is another favorite in Cajun country, with its flaky crust and

Halved ears of corn join the merry crawfish boil.

intimations of scallions, celery, parsley, garlic, and a nice dash or two of the native Tabasco sauce for fiery good measure.

Cooks far beyond Louisiana's borders can try their hands at crawfish recipes using frozen, uncooked specimens widely available in upscale fish markets; even some of the distant markets carry them fresh, usually by special order.

WHERE: *In New Orleans,* Deanie's Seafood, tel 504-581-1316, deanies.com; *in Lafayette, LA,* Prejean's, tel 337-896-3247, prejeans.com; *in Atlanta,* Big Easy Grille, tel 404-352-2777, bigeasygrille.com; *in Houston,* Ragin' Cajun at multiple locations, ragin-cajun.com; Danton's, tel 713-807-8883, dantonsseafood.com; *in New York,* Great Jones Cafe, tel 212-674-9304, greatjones.com; Aquavit (in August), tel 212-307-7311, aquavit.org. **MAIL ORDER:** lacrawfish.com, tel 800-221-8060; cajuncrawfish.com, tel 888-254-8626. **FURTHER INFORMATION AND RECIPES:** *Hoppin' John's Low Country Cooking* by John Martin Taylor (1992); *The Dooky Chase Cookbook* by Leah Chase (1990); bonappetit.com (search boiled crawfish with horseradish sauce); saveur.com (search crawfish boil). **SPECIAL EVENTS:** Louisiana Crawfish Festival, Chalmette, LA, March, louisianacrawfishfestival.com; Crawfish Eating Contest, New Orleans, April, deanies.com.

A SIDE DISH FOR POPEYE

Creamed Spinach

American

"I'm strong to the finich, 'cause I eats my spinach," sang the cartoon character Popeye as he downed the vegetable straight from a can. It must have been a cold, mushy, and acridly bitter sort of medicine. . . . How much happier he might

have been with a nice, warm bowl of creamed spinach, surely one of the most comforting preparations any vegetable has inspired. Though it's popular in many European countries, creamed

spinach has taken on an especially American character, thanks to the steak houses where it has become a menu fixture as a gentling foil to seared and bloody beef.

Sprightly, pine-green spinach leaves can be delicious when simply steamed and buttered, but a light and flavorful cream sauce neutralizes the needly bitterness of the vegetable's high oxalic acid content and mellows the texture of the chopped leaves.

To be at its best, the spinach must be fresh, never frozen or canned (a downright travesty), ideally young, tender, unbruised leaves that show an even Christmas-green right down to the tips of their stems. It must be thoroughly washed in at least two changes of water to ensure that all sand is removed before being cooked for about five minutes in rapidly boiling, well-salted water, preferably with a few paper-thin slices of onion or garlic to counteract its acidity.

Drained and cooled along with the cooked onion or garlic, the spinach should be picked up in small handfuls and squeezed as dry as possible prior to being finely chopped. Then it's stirred into a hot and freshly prepared cream sauce based on butter, flour, and either half-and-half or a mix of heavy sweet cream and a little whole milk seasoned with salt, pepper, and nutmeg, or a more fiery hint of mace, and given a gentle heating. To hold it for up to thirty minutes before serving, set it aside in the uncovered pot and spoon a thin layer of cream over the top, to be stirred in upon reheating.

Where: *Throughout the U.S.,* Palm Restaurant, thepalm.com; *in New York,* Porter House, tel 212-823-9500, porterhousenewyork .com. **Further information and recipes:** *The Joy of Cooking* by Irma S. Rombauer, Marion Rombauer Becker, and Ethan Becker (2006); *The Fannie Farmer Cookbook,* 13th Edition, by Marion Cunningham (1996); saveur.com (search creamed spinach locke-ober); epi curious.com (search creamed spinach 2004). **See also:** Ong choy, page 777.

⊢||||||||||||||||||||||||||||||⊣

A SWEETHEART OF A CHEESE

Creole Cream Cheese

American (Louisianan)

Although the term *Creole* may denote spiciness, in this case it refers to Louisiana's soft-as-silk, unctuously rich and creamy cheese, with its teasingly piquant and complex flavor. Essentially a farmer-style cheese—only slightly ripe—

it is made by adding bacterial starter and rennet to milk, so that it acidifies and coagulates into curds, then pressing out some of the curds' moisture to create a dryly malleable, gently crumbling spread. Buttermilk and sometimes cream or half-and-half are added to this soft, fresh cheese, an ultra-rich, creamy creation that calls to mind a French Fontainebleau.

Often incorporated into sweets, molded into hearts

New Orleans's romantic dessert

and served with strawberries for a delectable Valentine *coeur à la crème,* or sprinkled with sugar and slathered with cream and fresh fruit as a breakfast treat, the French-inspired cheese has a long history in New Orleans. An entry in *The Picayune's Creole Cook Book* of 1901 describes it being sold by a "cream cheese woman" who roamed the streets of the French Quarter with a covered basket holding a number of small, perforated tins.

The cheese almost went the way of the cream cheese woman herself. For many years, local dairies such as Gold Seal and Borden supplied it to the city, but today it is very difficult to find outside of traditional Creole restaurants. Many devotees make their own when they can't get to the few specialty shops or local dairies that stock it.

Where: *In New Orleans,* Commander's Palace, tel 504-899-8221, commanderspalace .com; *in Metairie, LA,* Dorignac's, tel 504-834-8216, dorignacs.com. **Mail order:** For cheese-cake made with Creole cream cheese, store .jfolse.com (search cheesecake). **Further information and recipes:** *The Picayune's Creole Cook Book* by The Times-Picayune Publishing Company (2014); nolacuisine.com (search creole cream cheese recipe); saveur.com (search coeur a la creme with strawberries); foodnet work.com (search homemade creole cream cheese). **Tip:** Blue Bell Creameries makes Creole Cream Cheese Ice Cream as a seasonal flavor. For information on where to purchase it, or to splurge on mail order, visit bluebell.com or call 979-836-7977.

‖‖‖‖‖‖‖‖‖‖‖‖‖‖‖‖‖‖‖‖‖‖‖‖‖

A TREAT STRAIGHT FROM HADES

Deviled Eggs

American

Luscious stuffed eggs can be found in various parts of Europe, especially France, but nowhere are the finger foods more frequently served than in the United States. Rich, flavorfully snackable favorites at Fourth of July picnics and summer

cocktail parties alike, the peeled, cooked eggs are halved, their yolks removed and mixed with mayonnaise, hot mustard, and an herb or spice or two, then piped or spooned back into the whites. It's a dish whose simplicity leaves little margin for error, particularly when it comes to the eggs themselves.

To ensure an appealing-looking finale, they must emerge from their shells in immaculate condition—a result best achieved by using eggs that are neither too old nor freshly laid. The fresher the egg, the fuller it will be in the shell and so the more difficult to peel; so it's wise to buy the eggs a week ahead and keep them refrigerated, allowing some of their water to evaporate and leaving them looser in the shell.

To prevent them from bursting while cooking, bring the refrigerated eggs to room temperature and pierce the wide bottom of each raw egg with an egg-piercer or a needle to let some air escape. Place them in a pot of cold water, bring it to a boil, and then reduce the heat and leave the eggs to barely simmer, half-covered, for eight to ten minutes, depending on their size. Immediately drain off the cooking water and run cold water into the pot to cool the eggs as rapidly as possible.

Then comes the critical peeling step, during which many a potential deviled egg has been lost. Proceed with care, tapping each egg gently on all sides until the shell is well crackled, then rolling them gently between your palms to loosen the shell before you peel. If the shell is stubborn, run a stream of cold water under a cracked edge to lift it off.

Let the eggs cool before cutting them in half lengthwise, then remove the yolks and place them in a bowl. Set the whites aside. Let the yolks cool slightly before mashing them with a stainless steel fork. If they are warm when mashed, they tend to turn wet and pasty; and they can be turned gray by a silver fork, or overly smooth and liquid by a food processor or blender.

Stir in salt, freshly ground pepper, mayonnaise, and hot Dijon-style mustard, and then the rest is up to you. For a spicier result, try a pinch of cayenne or a few drops of Tabasco, and if you want to add sophistication, stir in a dab or two of anchovy paste, foie gras, finely minced black truffles, chives, tarragon, or elegant chervil. Then refill the whites, by either spooning or piping the mashed yolks back in to form a raised mound. Place the filled eggs in a fairly deep glass or ceramic dish and cover it with plastic wrap or aluminum foil, making sure that the cover does

not crush the mounded yolks, and refrigerate. Remove the filled eggs from the refrigerator about fifteen minutes before serving.

For a reddish glow, sprinkle a bit of hot, sweet, or smoky paprika on top just before serving—a classically devilish finish.

Where: *In New York,* Foragers City Table, tel 212-243-8888, foragerscitygrocer.com. **Further information and recipes:** *The Joy of Cooking* by Irma S. Rombauer, Marion Rombauer Becker, and Ethan Becker (2006); *Deviled Eggs* by Debbie Moose (2004); *Mastering the Art of Southern Cooking* by Nathalie Dupree and Cynthia Graubart (2012); nytimes.com (search all-american deviled eggs); saveur.com (search deviled egg recipes).

A TASTE OF THE OLD WEST

Dinner at the Fort

American (Western)

Sometimes the tried, true, and rustic can offer the most delectable surprises, and nowhere is that better illustrated than at the outpost of Western kitsch that is the Fort, an awe-inspiring restaurant in Morrison, Colorado, about a thirty-minute drive southwest of Denver.

A great venue for fans of the old Wild West, be they grown-ups or children, the Fort was the creation of the late Sam Arnold, a student of all things western, who bought a piece of Colorado land and on it built an adobe-brick home as a reproduction of the historic trading post, Bent's Fort. With its fortress towers, high guard walls, and southwestern décor, the unusual architecture of what eventually became the restaurant is matched by hearty and equally unusual food.

Farm-raised local game is the specialty. The snake in that rattlesnake cake—with a pleasantly mild flavor not unlike chicken, served in a preparation similar to a crab cake—did indeed come from a farm, and ditto for those tender elk chops that taste like a cross between beef and

veal. Same goes for the venison, for the lean and flavorful buffalo and bison meat in its many forms, and for the tender quail.

Special offal dinners featuring assorted innards can be ordered in advance, and the tender, savory bison liver is a sure winner. Popular items on the standard menu include the delectable, buttery roast bison marrow bones favored by Julia Child, and a Historian's Platter that serves up guacamole with sides of the juicy bison sausage called boudies, bison tongue, and none other than the famed (or infamous) regional specialty known as Rocky Mountain oysters—fried buffalo testicles, with a flavor and texture much like that of sweetbreads. There also are smokehouse buffalo ribs, big and crunchy, a 20-ounce buffalo rib-eye steak, and "bison eggs" (pickled quail eggs wrapped with bison sausage meat and accented with sweet-hot raspberry-jalapeño jam).

Capping off the menu are the spectacular desserts, including the negrita, a whip of dark chocolate and Myers's rum heaped in a chocolate tulip cup; and the sweet, hot, and heady chocolate chile bourbon cake.

Where: 19192 Highway 8, Morrison, CO, tel 303-697-4771, thefort.com. **Further information and recipes:** *The Fort Cookbook* by Samuel P. Arnold (1997); *Shinin' Times at the Fort* by Holly Arnold Kinney (2010). **See also:** Carnivore, page 735.

||||||||||||||||||||||||||||||||

BRING BACK PUDDING

Double Chocolate Pudding

American

Whether it's spooned up with cloudlets of whipped cream or dipped into rivulets of heavy sweet cream, this rich, dark, velvety, quintessentially chocolaty confection has been the font of pleasant childhood memories for generations. If chocolate pudding has not achieved gourmand renown, that's probably because it is almost always made with packaged mixes. The proper devotion just might raise it to the level of the chocolate mousse or *pots de crème* (see pages 102 and 117) and it's up to home chefs to lead the charge.

The recipe below combines two chocolates—solid bittersweet and unsweetened cocoa powder—for double intensity. Supermarket bittersweet baking chocolate and brands of cocoa will do, but for the most exquisitely delicious results, use either Callebaut from Belgium (see page 144) or Valrhona from France. And be sure to top off each luscious serving with sweet cream, whipped or not.

Double Chocolate Pudding

Serves 4 to 6

2 ounces (2 squares) unsweetened baking chocolate, chopped or grated
1 scant cup sugar
2 cups cold whole milk
Pinch of salt
3 tablespoons cornstarch
3 tablespoons unsweetened cocoa powder
2 tablespoons (¼ stick) cold unsalted butter, cut in small pieces
½ teaspoon to 1 teaspoon pure vanilla extract
Lightly sweetened whipped cream or unwhipped heavy cream, for serving

1. Melt the chocolate in the top of a double boiler set over gently simmering water, stirring frequently.

2. Slowly stir in the sugar, 1⅔ cups of the milk, and the pinch of salt. Continue stirring until the mixture is completely integrated. Leave the milk and chocolate mixture over the gently simmering water.

3. Sift the cornstarch and cocoa together in a small bowl. Stir the remaining ⅓ cup of milk into the cocoa mixture, then slowly pour it into the hot milk and chocolate. Stir the chocolate mixture slowly but constantly until the pudding thickens and almost forms mounds when stirred gently, 7 to 8 minutes.

4. Cover the double boiler and continue cooking the chocolate mixture over very low heat without stirring for about 10 minutes.

5. Remove the top pan of the double boiler from the heat and slowly stir in the pieces of cold butter until they are melted and well incorporated.

6. Let the pudding cool for about 5 minutes, then stir in the vanilla, to taste. Pour the pudding into individual cups or a single large bowl. Cover the cups or bowl with plastic wrap to prevent a heavy skin from forming. Let the pudding cool at room temperature for about 10 minutes, then place it in the refrigerator for at least 7 hours or overnight. It will keep for about 2 days. Just before serving, top each portion with 1 to 2 tablespoons of lightly sweetened whipped cream or pour a little heavy cream on top.

MAIL ORDER: For chocolate, gourmetfood store.com (search belgian dark chocolate baking block; valrhona cocoa powder). **TIP:** Chocolate pudding, made from scratch or even from a package mix, is an excellent filling for Chocolate Cream Pie (see page 544). **SEE ALSO:** Pots de Crème, page 117.

CHOPS WITH A SIDE OF FLAME

Double-Rib Lamb Chops

American

If lamb chops are not a wholly American pleasure, the ultra-simple presentation is. Simply broiled, they are usually unadorned, save for a sprinkling of salt, and perhaps a dash of pepper and a quick smear of butter. The English can have their mint, and the French tend to cook their chops in racks. The very best lamb chop in the U.S. begins with Colorado lamb that has never seen a freezer, and with double chops cut from two adjoining ribs, their long bones only lightly Frenched, meaning that they were trimmed of the lumpiest fat and cartilage.

This is the time to shun charcoal and iron griddles in favor of the hot overhead flames of a preheated broiler—the only reliable way to render the teasingly gamey meat a deep rose at its center, while the edges of fat turn a crisply seductive golden brown.

An alternate triumph of the American steak house, double-rib lamb chops offer just the right meaty texture. They are to the silkier center-cut loin chops (also known as baby lamb chops) as the sirloin steak is to the all-too-tender filet mignon. The former assures a quintessentially meaty experience—and the long bones of the rib chops offer yet another bonus in that they can be picked up and gnawed upon after the meaty portions are gone.

The chops should be at room temperature before the cooking begins, and must be watched carefully while they broil, lest the fat catch fire and develop an unpleasantly acrid flavor. Should one salt before broiling or after? For maximum juiciness, it's best to sprinkle the chops with coarse salt immediately *after* they emerge from the broiler, but a light sprinkling of coarse salt before cooking does impart a sprightly essence as the salt caramelizes.

Although a somewhat Mediterranean touch can be added by brushing the broiled chops with a sprig of rosemary dipped in olive oil, no flavorings or condiments other than salt are needed. (Thankfully the days when rib chops were served with mint jelly are but a faint, unpleasant memory.)

WHERE: *Throughout the U.S.,* Palm restaurants, thepalm.com; *in San Francisco,* Tadich

Grill, tel 415-391-1849, tadichgrill.com. **Mail order:** For grass-fed lamb chops, lavalakelamb .com. **Further information and recipes:** *The Palm Restaurant Cookbook* by Brigit Legere Binns (2003); *The Fannie Farmer Cookbook*, 13th edition, by Marion Cunningham (1996); *The Joy of Cooking* by Irma S. Rombauer, Marion Rombauer Becker, and Ethan Becker (2006); cooks.com (search broiled lamb chops). **See also:** Agneau de Pré-Salé, page 50.

HOLD THE CREAM, AND THE EGGS

Egg Cream

American (New York)

S oda water from a seltzer bottle, Fox's U-Bet chocolate syrup, and whole milk—these and only these are the ingredients in a real chocolate egg cream, which authentically contains neither eggs nor cream. This New York original

was a standard street treat of yore, dispensed through the open fronts of newspaper and magazine stores throughout the city, but also made at home. The explanation as to how the drink got its name is lost to the archives of history, but thankfully the recipe survives intact.

There's no arguing the fact that the somewhat acidic, thick golden-brown syrup bears a taste one can only describe as deliciously . . . cheap. But there's a thrill in its sweet, chocolaty plainness, so happily modified by the rich taste of milk. Which comes first, syrup, seltzer, or milk? Ideally, syrup is first in the glass, followed by a little shot of seltzer and a quick stir. Then a trickle of milk, and a vigorous stirring as vibrant shots of soda are blasted in. The result is magically frothy and creamy and cool, reassuringly chocolaty and decep-

"Put a little syrup in it."

tively thick, with the seltzer's air bubbles adding an illusion of heft. (Who needs eggs and cream when you've got seltzer?)

During the Great Depression, soda fountains also dispensed small glasses of plain seltzer, known in New York as "two-cents plain" because of their price. "Put a little syrup in it, it shouldn't be too plain" was the classic New York comeback from savvy customers.

Where: *In New York,* Sammy's Roumanian Steakhouse, tel 212-673-0330, sammysromainan .com; Eisenberg's Sandwich Shop, tel 212-675-5096, eisen bergsnyc.com; *in Brooklyn and New York,* Junior's, juniors cheesecake.com; *in Saint Paul, MN,* Lynden's Soda Fountain, tel 651-330-7632, lyndens.com; *in South Pasadena, CA,* Fair Oaks Pharmacy and Soda Fountain, tel 626-799-1414, fairoakspharmacy.net. **Mail order:** webstaurantstore.com (search fox's u-bet chocolate syrup). **Further information and recipes:** *New York Cookbook* by Molly O'Neill (1992); *The Brooklyn Cookbook* by Lyn Stallworth and Rod Kennedy Jr. (1991); allrecipes.com (search chef john's chocolate egg cream; for a video, search how to make chocolate egg creams).

—|||||||||||||||||||||||||||||||||||||||—

Eggs Sardou

American (New Orleanian)

Riffs on eggs Benedict abound, most especially in New Orleans, where the idea of the festive weekend brunch probably began. Over a lightly toasted English muffin, the runny yolks of gently poached eggs might mingle with nicely firm and salty ham, smoked salmon, or savory creamed spinach. Eggs Sardou takes the eggy inventions several steps further, with credit for its invention going to Angelo (Antoine) Alciatore, chef at the eponymous restaurant Antoine's.

Born and raised in Marseille, Alciatore opened his French Quarter restaurant in 1840. Sometime during his tenure, the French playwright Victorien Sardou came for a visit, and the chef took to the kitchen in search of a way to honor him. He began by sliding poached eggs into "cups" composed of artichoke bottoms, topping them with slivers of anchovy and ham, and then napping them with a sunny, lemony hollandaise sauce. The result, a distinctly savory, salty delight, is still a classic New Orleans brunch dish at Antoine's, and also at Brennan's, where the anchovy and ham are replaced by creamed spinach, but the name of the dish remains the same.

WHERE: *In New Orleans*, Antoine's, tel 504-581-4422, antoines.com; The Old Coffee Pot Restaurant, tel 504-524-3500, theoldcoffeepot.com; *in Houston*, Brennan's, tel 713-522-9711, brennanshouston.com. **FURTHER INFORMATION AND RECIPES:** *Antoine's Restaurant Cookbook Since 1840* by Roy F. Guste Jr. (1979); *The Glory of Southern Cooking* by James Villas (2007); nolacuisine.com (search eggs sardou); saveur.com (search eggs sardou).

—|||||||||||||||||||||||||||||||||||||||—

Enstrom's Almond Toffee

American (Coloradan)

Great even when middling, almond toffee, alternatively known as butter crunch, simply doesn't get any better than that turned out by Enstrom's, the Grand Junction, Colorado, confectionery that's been at it for over sixty years. Founded by Chet Enstrom and his wife, Vernie, the shop is now run by the family's third generation. Enstrom's turns out many chocolaty sweets, but undoubtedly its most sublime offering is the almond toffee, a confection in which almond-dusted chocolate covers a slim inner crackling of crisp, buttery caramel and fresh almonds. You can opt for milk chocolate, but why would you? Go for the dark.

Enstrom's toffee lends itself to freezing, making it possible to lay in a large supply against stormy weather and bad times. When the craving hits, crack off frozen pieces and let them gently thaw on your tongue so the flavor combination of chocolate, nuts, and caramel slowly develops.

A few small pieces with a cup of coffee or espresso make for a light but still luxuriously decadent dessert after a large dinner. Following lighter fare, the toffee is unsurprisingly excellent when crumbled over scoops of vanilla, chocolate, or coffee ice cream.

Where: 701 Colorado Ave., Grand Junction, CO, tel 800-367-8766, enstrom.com.

⊣||||||||||||||||||||||||||||||||⊢

DINNER IN AN IGLOO

Eskimo Cook Book

American (Alaskan)

L ooking for a recipe for Eskimo ice cream made with reindeer tallow, seal oil, and berries, and maybe also enriched with the snowy white flakes of cooked lingcod, a favorite local fish? Or for information on how to prepare dried salmon

eggs and berries? Want to know how to freeze whole flounders so they can be eaten without being thawed? You'll find what you seek in a tiny paper pamphlet bearing the title *Eskimo Cook Book*, an endearing collectors' treasure still available through antiquarian bookdealers. (It also includes recipes for seal liver, loon, owl, oogruk flippers, bear feet, ptarmigan intestines, eskimo potatoes, and countless roots, branches, berries, and herbs, all handily defined in a little glossary.)

Salmon hangs to dry in the Alaskan island town of Shishmaref.

Written in 1952 by the students of the Shishmaref Day School in Shishmaref, Alaska, to raise funds for disabled children, the cookbook is filled with charming sketches accompanying many of the brief recipes—each signed by its youthful contributor. Recording the dishes their parents and grandparents traditionally prepared, the children unknowingly preserved a valuable slice of culinary history at a time of rapid change and modernization.

The fund-raising cookbook is an American invention developed in the South during the Civil War, when books of "receipts," as recipes were called then, were compiled and sold at Sanitary Fairs to aid wounded soldiers and their families. With the apparatus still in place after the war, various women's groups continued the practice, donating the income to needy hospitals, schools, churches, and local families. Although often amateurish, their recipes accurately reflected the cooking fashions of various periods, as they continue to do today.

Further information: *Eskimo Cook Book* by the children of the Shishmaref Day School is available at amazon.com and antiquarian sources. You can see an online version at archive.org/details/EskimoCookbook.

||||||||||||||||||||||||||||||||||||

"TRY OUR GIZZARD SOUP. IT'S REALLY HOT AND GARLICKY AND IT'S MADE WITH LOVE."
—FROM *DINNER AT THE HOMESICK RESTAURANT* BY ANNE TYLER

Ezra Tull's Gizzard Soup

American

The main character of Anne Tyler's charming novel, Ezra Tull, operates a restaurant in which guests cook their own food. The fictional restaurant's specialty may have a real Hungarian ancestor in *bechinalt*. It is also a bargain, what with the price of chicken gizzards. Keep any squeamish prospective diners in the dark and they may never suspect the origins of the soup's savory, well-trimmed, meaty bits.

Ezra Tull's Gizzard Soup
Serves 2

1 pound fresh chicken gizzards, halved
1 teaspoon salt
½ teaspoon freshly ground black pepper
3 tablespoons unsalted butter
3 cloves garlic, peeled and lightly crushed
    with the side of a chef's knife
2 tablespoons all-purpose flour

1. Place the gizzards, 4 cups water, and the salt and pepper in a large pot and bring it to a boil. Cover the pot, reduce the heat, and simmer until the gizzards are fully cooked, 1 hour.

2. Remove the gizzards and reserve the broth. Carefully trim all fat and cartilage from the gizzards. Chop the trimmed meat into small pieces and return them to the broth.

3. Melt the butter over low heat in a small saucepan. Add the garlic and sauté for a few seconds. Stir in the flour and cook over low heat until it becomes a smooth paste, a few seconds more.

4. Remove the pan from the heat and carefully pour in 1 cup of the hot broth, stirring constantly until smooth. Pour the smooth sauce base back into the simmering broth, and beat with a whisk until all the lumps disappear. Simmer the soup, partially covered, for 15 minutes, adding a little water if the mixture becomes too thick.

5. Taste, and add more salt and/or pepper, as desired. Serve at once in warm bowls, with crusty bread on the side.

FURTHER INFORMATION: *Dinner at the Homesick Restaurant* by Anne Tyler (1982). For the original *bechinalt* recipe that inspired Anne Tyler, see *The Impoverished Students' Book of Cookery, Drinkery, & Housekeepery* by Jay F. Rosenberg (1967).

||||||||||||||||||||||||||||||||||||

A WINE COUNTRY DREAM OF PARADISE

The French Laundry

American (Californian)

Thomas Keller, the impeccable chef-owner of the French Laundry in the eucalyptus-scented Napa Valley, is doubtlessly the most elegantly low-key member of the American "celebrity chefs." He has no buzzwords to hurl, no slogans to espouse, no signature plastic shoes. What he has instead is a legendary, almost spiritual quest for perfection, which manifests itself in his exquisite French-inspired, American-informed cooking. In the space of what was once actually a laundry, Keller opened his restaurant in 1994, after cooking in France (Taillevent, Guy Savoy), New York (Rakel), and Los Angeles (Checkers). And ever since, his ethereal food has won the kind of accolades that keep his fans booking reservations exactly two months in advance of their hoped-for dining dates.

A world-famous, Michelin-starred Napa delight

Set in an utterly serene, peaceful wine country landscape, the old stone house filled with the glow of many candles bears an instant, low-key mystique. But the food, of course, trumps the atmosphere. From the beginning, Keller's cooking has never been about convenience or shortcuts. His menu has always been built around many teasingly small courses, sublime and often whimsical, "tastes" meant to tease the palate and haunt it, simultaneously leaving you wanting more of what you had but eager and able to experience the next sensation. This was considered a revolutionary way to eat when Keller began, and diners took to it with abandon. Dining at the French Laundry became a symbol of food connoisseurship, and Keller was among the first chefs to take charge of

exactly where his ingredients came from—often growing his herbs and vegetables in the gardens adjoining his restaurant, or importing from as far away as necessary to get what he considered the best.

Keller was also an early innovator in the realm of food puns that surprised and delighted the palate as they amused the mind. There was "tongue in cheek" (braised beef cheek and veal tongue served with horseradish cream, baby leeks, and garden greens), "oysters and pearls" (sabayon of pearl tapioca with poached Malpeque oysters and caviar), "coffee and doughnuts" (cappuccino semifreddo with fried dough topped with cinnamon and sugar), "macaroni and cheese" (butter-poached Maine lobster with mascarpone-enriched orzo) and "salmon tartare ice-cream cone" (smoked salmon and crème fraîche in a cornet of house-made crackers).

After winning every imaginable award for both his restaurant (his was the first in America to receive three stars from the Michelin guide) and his own wizardry (James Beard Foundation Chef of the Year), what's a tireless perfectionist to do? Keller decided to take on New York City. In 2004, he opened Per Se in the Time Warner Center on Columbus Circle. To be sure of excellence in two places at once, he even linked the kitchens of both restaurants by live camera.

Per Se is an ethereal experience and an example of truly modern dining, with just sixteen tables overlooking the fountains of Columbus Circle and Central Park; it's an oasis for calm, adult meals in a bustling town full of food-lust. Keller's customers' favorites can be found on the menu, all turned out beautifully. Still, the rarified ambience of the original stone house in Napa cannot be duplicated amid the hurly-burly of Gotham, so there can be only one French Laundry.

WHERE: 6640 Washington St., Yountville, CA, tel 707-944-2380, frenchlaundry.com; Per Se, 10 Columbus Circle, New York, NY, tel 212-823-9335, perseny.com. **FURTHER INFORMATION AND RECIPES:** *The French Laundry Cookbook* by Thomas Keller (1999).

‖‖‖‖‖‖‖‖‖‖‖‖‖‖‖‖‖‖‖‖‖‖‖‖

A SHORELINE SUMMER FAVORITE

Fried Clam Roll

American (New England)

The New England staple of crunchy, golden strips of fried clams piled high on a buttery, soft roll and sparked with a dab of tartar sauce or lemon juice (or both) is an icon of the American summer, but it's a relatively recent addition to the food canon. Although fried clams can be seen on the 1865 menu of Boston's famed Parker House hotel, local legend tells a different tale.

Lawrence "Chubby" Woodman, the owner of a roadside clam stand in Essex, Massachusetts, north of Boston on the Atlantic Coast, claimed that one day in 1916, he dipped some of the fresh soft-shell clams from the Essex River in a batter and deep-fried them as a lark, just to see what would happen. The rest is gastronomic history—Woodman's has been an institution since that day, and the fried clam has become a classic. (Clearly the Parker House hotel didn't stake its claim loudly enough.)

A taste of the New England seaside

A few years later, one Thomas Soffron, a clam digger and businessman from Ipswich, Massachusetts, took Ipswich hard-shell clams and stretched their so-called "feet" (the longish muscular appendage outside the clam shell that is used for digging) and the soft inside "belly" to fry up the first batch of what he called clam strips. Soffron and his brothers went into business in 1932, marketing fried clam strips to folks who had never eaten fried clams before.

By chance, Howard Johnson, busily opening roadside restaurants in New England in the 1940s, was among the early fans of the new fried clams. He bought the clam strips, and the rights to them, from the Soffrons, and went on to create an empire of more than a thousand hotels and restaurants across the country, each one of them serving up fried clam "rolls"—the fried clam strips sandwiched in the sort of toasted hotdog buns known as "slices," with tartar sauce and lemon wedges on the side.

Where: *In Essex, MA,* Woodman's of Essex, tel 800-649-1773, woodmans.com; *in Ipswich, MA,* Clam Box, tel 978-356-9707, ipswichma.com/clambox; *in Boston and environs,* Jasper White's Summer Shack, summershackrestaurant.com; *in Wellfleet, MA,* Mac's Seafood, tel 800-214-0477, macsseafood.com; *in New York and Brooklyn,* Mary's Fish Camp, marysfishcamp.com; *in Nassawadox, VA,* The Great Machipongo Clam Shack, tel 757-442-3800, thegreatmachipongoclamshack.com; *in Santa Barbara and Ventura, CA,* Brophy Bros. Restaurant and Clam Bar, brophybros.com. **Mail order:** SeaPak Shrimp & Seafood Co., tel 888-732-7251, seapak.com (search clam strips). **Further information and recipes:** *Jasper White's Cooking from New England* by Jasper White (1998); *The New England Clam Shack Cookbook* by Brooke Dojny (2008); lobsters-online.com/lobsterfly (search ipswich fried clam roll recipe); seapak.com/recipes/new-england-clam-rolls; epicurious.com (search fried clams). **Tip:** The authentic "slices" are not readily available to consumers. The best substitute is a Pepperidge Farm hot dog bun, lightly toasted and buttered.

IT'S ALWAYS FIESTA TIME IN THE WINDY CITY

Frontera Grill and Topolobampo

American, Mexican

The best thing to have happened to Mexican food in the U.S. over the past few decades may be a native of Oklahoma City named Rick Bayless, whose parents ran a barbecue restaurant and whose great-grandparents opened Oklahoma's first grocery store. Bayless studied Spanish and Latin American studies and was working toward a PhD in anthropology when he was bitten by the (very serious, often incurable) Mexican food bug. Bayless and his wife Deann, who has long been his partner in life and food, spent the next few years in Mexico writing a cookbook they called *Authentic Mexican,* which was published to wide acclaim in 1987—and so a career was launched.

Upon their return to the U.S., the Baylesses settled in Chicago and opened Frontera Grill, a restaurant specializing in regional Mexican food. At the time it was unlike the general idea of a Mexican restaurant. The food wasn't Tex-Mex and wasn't covered in melted cheese, and the décor and ambience were colorful, bright, warm, and lively—but also classy and urbane. There were familiar dishes on the menu: possibly the most ethereal guacamole ever to be served in a restaurant north of the border, chunky and mouthwatering and always accompanied by homemade, freshly-fried tortilla chips; quesadillas filled with artisanal jack cheese and duck *carnitas*; and less familiar but still unintimidating offerings like yellowtail and cactus ceviche, or the Mexican casseroles known as *cazuelas,* filled with things like lamb shoulder in cascabel chile sauce and house-made fresh cheese.

The restaurant's conviviality and novel yet authentic approach to presenting real Mexican food to Americans was so well received that the Baylesses opened an adjoining second: Topolobampo, a more upscale, more expensive and serious restaurant aimed at the fine-dining crowd. It serves some of those same now-cherished flavors, but dresses them up in unusual and innovative designs. The *carne asada* is made with wagyu rib eye and organic slow-roasted lamb, drenched in a mole of dark chiles, almonds, raisins, tomato, garlic, and avocado leaf and served with a chayote, green bean, and guero chile salad on the side. It's no wonder that "Frontera for lunch, Topolo for dinner," is the mantra of Chicago's Mexican food buffs—natives and visitors alike.

The newest incarnation of the Baylesses' growing empire is Xoco, a street food–inspired café that specializes in sandwiches, salads, and authentic Mexican hot chocolate. The sleek, modern-looking newcomer is physically connected to its two big sisters, and its *torta* made with wood-fired pork carnitas, pickled onions and black beans is an excellent way to sample Bayless for just ten dollars—without a reservation.

Frontera Grill—style, pizzazz, great food

Where: Frontera Grill and Topolobampo, 445 North Clark St., Chicago, tel 312-661-1434; Xoco, 449 North Clark St. and 1471 North Milwaukee Ave, Chicago. **Further information:** rickbayless.com. **Tip:** Although most of the seating at Frontera Grill is on a first come–first served basis, the restaurant takes a limited number of reservations. At Topolobampo, reservations are necessary, and ought to be made six to eight weeks in advance.

ICE-COLD AS THE GALAXY

Frozen Milky Way

American

A New York childhood may not be necessary to foster a longing for this ultracold, chewy, and chocolaty treat, but let the record show that the frozen confection is a local creation. The beauty of the frozen Milky Way is twofold.

First, the freezing process mitigates some of the bar's overly soft texture and over-the-top sweetness. Then,

firmed up to an irresistible denseness, the layered candy provides an ecstatic rush of contrasts—the velvety tinge of chocolate, the brassiness of cooked sugar caramel, the soothing neutrality of cocoa nougat . . .

There's no real science to the freezing process. Each Milky Way candy bar, with its chocolate covering and nougat and caramel layers, brown-green-and-white wrapper intact, is placed in the freezer, where it stays until frozen solid—at least twenty-four hours. Then the wrapper is peeled off (hopefully it won't stick), and teeth cautiously wiggle into the firm, cold layers, the eater hoping not to mire fillings or dental crowns in the sublimely melting mass. It's a pleasure best enjoyed outdoors, with a napkin or two on hand.

Where: The candy is available at almost any supermarket and packaged candy counter in the U.S. **Tip:** For finicky teeth, unwrap and preslice your Milky Way, then firmly rewrap and freeze it. This allows the bites to be snapped off easily.

THE QUINTESSENTIAL CARNIVAL TREAT

Funnel Cakes

American

T here really is a funnel involved in funnel cakes: sweet, foamy, and eggy batter poured through a funnel directly into a vat of simmering hot oil, trickling in to form the lacy web of fried dough beloved by children of all ages. Looking like a giant, squiggly spiderweb of a doughnut, the cake is a treat with Pennsylvania Dutch roots. The recipe, for what is basically a cruller, most likely originated in northern Europe and emigrated to America with the first Mennonite settlers from southwestern Germany. They settled in the farmlands of Pennsylvania, where the funnel cakes were initially fried in lard and served as a snack to field workers. Today, they are a standard at food festivals and state fairs around the country—and are almost always fried in vegetable oil. And they remain part of Finland's May Day celebration, where a touch of grated lemon zest adds a bright note. While still hot, they are lavishly powdered with confectioners'

sugar, and they must be consumed immediately. Once cooled, they lose much of their crunchy, sugary appeal.

Where: *In Philadelphia*, Reading Terminal Market (on Saturdays), tel 215-922-2317, read ingterminalmarket.org; *in Ephrata, PA,* Green Dragon Market (on Fridays), tel 717-738-1117, greendragonmarket.com. **Further information and recipes:** *Classic Pennsylvania Dutch Cooking* edited by Betty Groff (2007); saveur.com (search lacy funnel cakes; finnish tippaleipa). **Special events:** Kutztown Folk Festival, Kutztown, PA, June–July, kutztownfestival.com; Iowa State Fair, Des Moines, IA, August, iowastatefair.org.

WHAT IT DOESN'T LOOK LIKE IS A DUCK

Geoduck Clam

American (Pacific Northwestern)

Without a doubt one of the world's strangest and most phallic-looking foods, the geoduck clam is a species of saltwater bivalve mollusk native to the Pacific Northwest. Its name comes from a Native American term for "dig deep"

(poor transcription forever has it pronounced as gooey-DUCK, whatever the original may have been). And indeed, these clams do burrow deep into the sandy bottom of Pacific Northwest waters. Especially common in the Puget Sound,

A diver sorts and crates harvested geoducks.

they are also found in the Strait of Juan de Fuca, off Vancouver Island, and in Northern California's Humboldt Bay.

Though geoducks have long been a food source in the northwest—smoke-dried by northwest Indian tribes and stored for winter consumption—for centuries they were relatively unknown elsewhere. The giant clams were largely unseen in the United States until 1960, when a U.S. Navy diver trying to recover a torpedo happened upon them on the bottom of Puget Sound. What a sight the clamshell must have been, with its large, protruding, hoselike siphon, so fleshy, wrinkled, and dark.

Although some geoducks weigh up to 15 pounds, the average weight is 1½ to 3 pounds with a siphon that's 5 to 15 inches long. Both the siphon and the meat inside the shell are eaten—and this is where the delicious geoduck proves itself to be more than a curiosity, with its chewy texture and a sweet, refreshing, clean, and briny flavor that bears a hint of cucumber.

In China, the imported clams are a prized delicacy, in no small part because of their physical appearance—for obvious reasons, eating *xiàng bá bàng* (or "elephant trunk," as the geoducks are called there) is said to be an aphrodisiac and to promote virility. There they are an important if relatively new ingredient in one of the country's numerous hot-pot preparations. In Japan, they are popularly served raw, pounded to tenderness, then thinly sliced as sashimi or sushi with a soy-spiked dipping or ponzu sauce.

As it became more popular around the world, geoduck's prices soared, and eventually in Asia a sort of black market grew up around

the prized clams. The Washington State Department of Fish and Wildlife now tightly regulates geoduck fishery, limiting it to a handful of companies that bid on the right to harvest from state or American Indian tidelands. How the tides have turned.

WHERE: *In Seattle,* The Walrus and the Carpenter Oyster Bar, tel 206-395-9227, thewalrus bar.com; *in Washington and Oregon,* Uwajimaya at four market locations, uwajimaya.com. **MAIL ORDER:** amazon.com (search fresh sashimi grade geoduck). **FURTHER INFORMATION AND RECIPES:** *The Fishmonger's Apprentice* by Aliza Green (2011); *50 Chowders* by Jasper White (2000); *Field Guide to the Geoduck* by David George Gordon (2003); *Northwest Bounty* by Schuyler Ingle and Sharon Kramis (1999); food52.com (search geoduck with sea beans and porcini).

A BIG STAR IN SALAD LAND

Giant Syrian Tomatoes

American

Although the hard-ripe travesties of mass agribusiness are infamously lacking in color, texture, and flavor, many countries have tomatoes to be proud of. The U.S. is no exception, and you don't have to look to the idiosyncratic heirloom

varieties now popular in farmers' markets (often more interesting in appearance than in taste) to find great American tomatoes. Several long-time varieties, the New Jersey beefsteak and Louisiana's creole among them, are cherished for their juiciness and their deep and winey essences.

But of all native tomatoes, none is so breathtaking as the Giant Syrian still custom-grown to strict organic standards for the innovative upscale restaurants of Napa and Sonoma by Forni Brown Welsh Gardens in Calistoga. The huge, meaty, orange-red fruit nurtured there fairly quivers with succulence and an almost bloody, beefy richness—its flavor so complete, even salt may be unnecessary. If you can resist

the temptation to eat the tomato as you would an apple, enjoy it thickly sliced, either on its own or as a garnish for steak; thinly sliced, it makes for the ultimate BLT.

For now, the only way to sample Giant Syrians is either to preorder them from Forni Brown and go to Calistoga to pick them up, or to order the seeds and grow your own. (Just beware of the squirrels and rabbits who'll be raring to get their paws on the red-ripened beauties.)

WHERE: Forni Brown Welsh, Calistoga, CA, tel 707-942-6123; **MAIL ORDER:** for Giant Syrian seeds and plants, localharvest.com (click Shop, then search giant syrian). **SEE ALSO:** San Marzano Tomatoes, page 235.

┤||||||||||||||||||||||||||||||├

UNDER THE SIDEWALKS OF NEW YORK

Grand Central Oyster Bar & Restaurant

American (New York City)

When it opened in 1913 in New York City's Grand Central Terminal, the restaurant now known as the Grand Central Oyster Bar didn't specialize in seafood. If it had an identity beyond its marvelous architecture—a cavernous subterranean space designed with the great Valencian architect Rafael Guastavino's celebrated arches of interlocking terra-cotta tiles—it was as a coffee shop. Only after the place was relaunched in 1974, having been closed for several years, did the new owners decide to parlay what was allegedly the old restaurant's best dish, oyster stew, into the cornerstone of a menu dominated entirely by the treasures of the sea.

Today, a couple dozen varieties of fresh fish are offered daily—almost all in your choice of simply broiled, steamed, grilled, or fried—as are oyster stews and pan roasts, chowders, seafood salads, and a selection of favorite seafood dishes from around the world. Here are coquilles St. Jacques, the Maine lobster roll, a bouillabaisse, and the English fish 'n' chips.

The famed oyster stew (oysters poached in cream and butter) is a thin, milky, slurp-worthy delight. The oyster pan roast is thicker, the aforementioned ingredients spiked with hot paprika and chile sauce and lovingly ladled, usually by a hassled yet generous waiter, over a slice of good toast. They're dishes that work thanks to the juxtaposition of the oysters' sharp sea saltiness with the milk's neutrality, and both are worth the price of admission—as is the quintessentially New York experience of eating oysters underground in a train station. (There's now a Brooklyn location as well.) Take your pick of a table covered in a red-and-white-checked cloth, the long, U-shaped counters in the wood-paneled salon, or the oyster bar itself.

Best of all, of course, are the impeccably fresh bivalves for which the place is named: thirty kinds, from the usual suspects—Belons and Wellfleets—to the Beaver Tails (Rhode Island), Duckabushes (Washington State), and Lady Chatterleys (Nova Scotia) of the world's waters. The list of beers—stout and oysters being an excellent and overlooked combo—and wines is impossibly long, and is part of why the place remains the best reason in the world to miss a train.

WHERE: Grand Central Terminal, 89 East 42nd St., New York, NY, tel 212-490-6650, oysterbarny.com; 256 5th Ave., Brooklyn, NY, tel 347-294-0596, oysterbar brooklyn.com. **FURTHER INFORMATION AND RECIPES:** *The Grand Central Oyster Bar & Restaurant Complete Seafood Cookbook* by Sandy Ingber and Ray Finamore (2013).

The stunning seafood restaurant at the heart of New York's Grand Central Station

Green Dragon Farmer's Market & Auction

American (Pennsylvanian)

A true American classic, the Green Dragon Farmer's Market & Auction is a dazzling Pennsylvania Dutch country set piece. Amid neat red barns with colorful painted "hex signs" and verdant farmlands traveled with horse and buggy by the Amish and Mennonites, every Friday the wares of more than four hundred farmers, craftsmen, merchants, cookware sellers, bakers, butchers, and candlestick makers are spread out across thirty acres.

It's a setup that dazzles the palate as much as the eye. Here you'll find very local, German-descended specialties such as pickled hard-cooked eggs, marbled red from their beet-juice bath; garlands of sausages and slabs of darkly smoked meats; gray blocks of the fatty breakfast pork mush scrapple, meant to be fried alongside eggs; and brilliant, locally grown vegetables that, depending on the season, might include tomatoes, melons, corn, and the extraordinary Mennonite celery—small, ivory, and so tender it manages to raise the mundane salad vegetable to new gastronomic heights.

Open for business since 1932

On the sweeter side, there are kaleidoscopic arrays of cookies that make one feel as though Christmas is around the corner, festive funnel cakes fried up and sugared on the spot (see page 566), and pies stacked up to dizzying heights—the golden-brown, molasses-filled shoofly (see page 618), crumbly apple pandowdy (see page 520), and pies with names like Love, Sunday, Monday, Wet Bottom, and Snitz, the latter made with dried apples.

Fruity jams are represented, of course, along with golden floral honey, quilts, second-hand books, and kitchen utensils that may be brand-new, antique, or just plain old. In between are small, open cafeterias and stands where copious, rib-sticking nourishment, such as hot dogs, Philadelphia cheesesteaks, and home-churned ice cream, are dished up.

Most stands are managed by the plainly dressed locals, the bearded men in blue work-shirts, black vests and pants, and wide-brimmed, yellow straw hats, the women in long black dresses and aprons, with kerchiefs or sheer organdy caps on their heads.

All congregate around what may be the market's most intriguing feature: the weekly feed auction. In a huge parking lot, trucks jam-packed with bales of timothy hay, alfalfa, grass, and clover form a ring around a central clearing where taciturn livestock owners bid for the batches with which they feed their animals. Led by an auctioneer in Amish dress, each bid rapidly progresses in a mystical jargon much like that of tobacco auctioneers. It's an entertaining and instructive event; a novice might learn that horses prefer timothy hay, while cattle love grass that is bright green, or clover if the blossoms are mauve pink.

WHERE: 955 North State St., Ephrata, PA, tel 717-738-1117, greendragonmarket.com.

⊦||||||||||||||||||||||||||||||||||⊦

EATING DR. SEUSS'S WORDS

Green Eggs and Ham

American

It's a dish with which anyone who has read and reread Dr. Seuss's bestselling children's classic will be familiar. As held aloft by that mischievous agent provocateur, Sam-I-Am, it appears as fried eggs with green yolks, plus a whole,

vibrantly green ham—a dish so embedded in the American psyche that it is offered on the brunch menus of restaurants all over the country.

Thankfully, interpretations generally eschew dyed ham or yolks, instead leaning to scrambled eggs or omelets verdant with chopped parsley or fines herbes, such as chives, tarragon, and chervil. Alternatively and more substantially, beaten eggs might enfold asparagus, spinach, Swiss chard, scallions, zucchini, or green peppers; or the eggs may be poached and served with a green herb cream sauce. Deviled, their mashed-up yolks do indeed wind up a spring-bright green when minced herbs are added. The ham is left as nature intended, rosy pink and simply sliced, or frizzled to a golden hue.

Not a fan no matter how they're prepared? In the words of Sam-I-Am, "You do not like them. So you say. Try them! Try them! And you may."

Where: *In New York*, Mehtaphor, tel 212-542-9440, mehtaphornyc.com; *in Nashville*, The Crow's Nest Restaurant, tel 615-783-0720, crowsnestnashville.com; *in Orlando, FL*, Green Eggs and Ham Café at Universal's Islands of Adventure, tel 407-224-4012, universalorlando .com (search green eggs); *in Ferndale, MI*, The Fly Trap, tel 248-399-5150, theflytrapferndale .com; *in Yountville, CA,* Bottega, tel 707-945-1050, botteganapavalley.com. **Further information and recipes:** *Green Eggs and Ham* by Dr. Seuss (1960); *Green Eggs and Ham Cookbook* by Georgeanne Brennan (2006); all recipes.com (search green eggs and ham quiche); epicurious.com (search devilish green eggs and ham); food52.com (search green eggs and ham for grownups; green eggs and ham kerstin; green eggs and ham shanley); abcnews .go.com (search green eggs and ham chiarello).

||||||||||||||||||||||||||||||||||||||||||||||||||||||||||||||||||||||||||||||||||||||||||||||||||||||||||||

THE SUNNY SIDE OF BREAKFAST

Fried Eggs

The French call them *oeufs au plat*—eggs on a plate—while the Italian *uovi fritti* and the Spanish *huevos fritos* simply mean fried eggs, something the Spanish love as an appetizer, broken open over mounds of fried potatoes (see page 260). The Germans order the more imaginative *spiegeleiern,* meaning "mirror eggs," which may be fried in butter with a hint of bacon grease. Whatever the name, all the world loves the instant, warm comfort of a fried egg.

To be at their best, they should be gently fried in unsalted butter and served cheerfully as golden suns, sunny-side up. Eggs fried in olive oil may have more sophisticated appeal and perhaps even win kudos from the cholesterol-conscious, but if you are eating egg yolks, why worry about the butter?

Breakfast cooks should seek out the freshest eggs possible, a condition that is sadly most obviously recognizable only at the moment the egg is broken into the pan: The fresher it is, the higher the yolk and white will stand, and the latter won't run out into a watery film. A nonstick pan is acceptable, even if it will not produce as tender a white as an uncoated pan—but coated or uncoated, you'll need that generous pat of butter. Heated until bubbling but not brown, it adds flavor and a haze of pale golden color, and when spooned over white and yolk will help the egg white set.

What constitutes doneness? There are two legitimate schools of thought on the question. One says the egg should show absolutely no brown edges, while the other demands a rim of lacy, golden fringe. Coarse salt should be sprinkled on as soon as the egg is in the pan, but freshly ground black pepper should not be added until the egg is on a warm plate, as it breaks down when heated. For extra zip, dot the yolk with a drop or two of green Tabasco sauce. To waste none of the yolk as it bursts, serve the eggs on lightly buttered toast or English muffins—or as a fried egg sandwich, in which case the egg should be fried over-easy, until the yolk becomes half-runny.

WHERE: *In New York,* at brunch, Blaue Gans, tel 212-571-8880, kg-ny.com/blaue-gans; at breakfast, Café Sabarsky, tel 212-288-0665, kg-ny.com/cafe-sabarsky. **FURTHER INFORMATION AND RECIPES:** *The Joy of Cooking* by Irma S. Rombauer, Marion Rombauer Becker, and Ethan Becker (2006); epicurious.com (search smoky olive oil fried eggs); saveur.com (search fried egg cunningham). **TIPS:** Because the egg is everything, try to get organic eggs from chickens that ate natural food. For the best fried egg sandwich, use a decent version of good old American white bread, preferably Pepperidge Farm's Original. No need to butter it. **SEE ALSO:** Huevos Rancheros, page 650; Huevos Estrellados, page 260; Chakchouka, page 697.

HISTORY IN A POT

Gumbo

American (Louisianan)

A rich and merrily sustaining mumbo-jumbo of a soup, gumbo includes ingredients as complex and diverse as the cultures represented in each big and welcoming, black-iron potful. It may be a delicately fragrant seafood-and-okra stew blushed with tomatoes, or it may be based on chicken or turkey, strengthened with diced ham or slices of spicy andouille sausage and a finishing flourish of barely poached oysters. Sometimes a wild duck, rabbit, or squirrel will be the featured player, highlighted perhaps by fiery tasso ham. No matter what, the gumbo will always be richly aromatic with thyme, bay leaf, garlic, and onions (and probably celery and tomatoes), its liquid backdrop almost stew-thick. And it will always be ladled into bowls along with mounds of steamed white rice.

A look at the evolution of gumbo makes it easy to understand why the soup is so frequently invoked as a synonym for the international melting pot. To the French pot-au-feu, thickened with its toasty flour-and-fat roux, West African slaves introduced further thickening via the viscous power of okra, the silky pod they called "gumbo." When okra was not in season, filé powder, made from crushed dried sassafras leaves and used by native Choctaw Indians, lent viscosity and a burnished outdoorsy flavor.

An okra-laced prawn gumbo over steamed rice

Whatever its multitude of ingredients, the gumbo must include a roux, and must be further thickened by either okra or filé powder, but never both. Generally, filé is used in more robust gumbos with chicken and sausage, and okra is used in a lighter, more delicate gumbo made with local seafood such as shrimp, crab, and oysters, but excluding finfish or the non-native lobster, clams, or scallops. Okra might also appear in one of the Lenten vegetable gumbos, such as a gumbo z'herbes, whose symbolic seven greens may include green leafy vegetables and herbs such as dill, tarragon, chives, thyme, parsley, and dandelion. Originally introduced to Louisiana by slaves brought from the Congo, like other gumbos it was altered by native Choctaws and Cherokees.

Whether it's an okra or a filé gumbo, the roux will always be there: a mix of fat and browned flour that adjusts the thickness and modifies the flavor, depending upon the kind of fat it contains. (Once asked if he used butter, bacon, vegetable oil, or rendered poultry fat for his roux, Jan Birnbaum, a Louisiana-born chef known for his monumental gumbos, answered, "All of them together.") The critical element in producing a fine roux is timing. For a layered complexity that hints of roasted nuts, caramel, and toasted bread, toast the flour slowly over very low heat or in the oven. Depending on the quantity of flour (gumbo chefs always keep a well-browned batch on hand), this step can take an hour or more.

It is fashionable these days to prefer vegetables and other solids, such as shrimp or poultry, firm and almost crunchy. Yet soft-cooked food is a distinctive feature of Southern cooking, probably initially in deference to health safety. Which brings us to yet another commonality in the great wide world of gumbo: All gumbos taste best when held for a day or two and reheated, giving the ingredients a chance to meld into a complex, unctuously flavorful whole.

WHERE: *In New Orleans,* Gumbo Shop, tel 504-525-1486, gumboshop.com; NOLA, tel 504-522-6652, emerilsrestaurants.com/nola-restaurant; Delmonico, tel 504-525-4937, emerilsrestaurants .com/emerils-delmonico; Emeril's, tel 504-528-9393, emerilsrestaurants.com/emerils-new-orleans; *in New Orleans and San Antonio,* Lüke, lukeneworleans.com, lukesanantonio.com; *in Baton Rouge, LA,* Tony's Seafood Market & Deli, tel 225-357-9669, tonyseafood.com; *in Lafayette LA,* Prejean's, tel 337-896-3247, prejeans.com; *in Houston,* Brennan's, tel 713-522-9711, brennans houston.com; *in Atlanta,* McKinnon's Louisiana Restaurant, tel 404-237-1313, mckinnons.com; *in New York, New Jersey, Connecticut, and Texas,* The Original Soupman, tel 212-956-0900, original soupman.com; *in Queens, NY,* Sugar Freak, tel

718-726-5850, sugarfreak.com. **FURTHER INFORMA-TION AND RECIPES:** *Chef Paul Prudhomme's Louisiana Cooking* by Paul Prudhomme (1984); *The Picayune's Creole Cookbook* by the New Orleans Times-Picayune (1987); *Lafcadio Hearn's Creole Cookbook* by Lafcadio Hearn (1990); *The Picayune's Creole Cook Book* by The Times-Picayune Publishing Company (2014); *The*

American Heritage Cookbook by the editors of American Heritage Publ. Co. (1964); epicurious .com (search gumbo z'herbes; gumbo filé; shrimp and andouille gumbo); saveur.com (search mr. b's gumbo ya-ya; alabama seafood gumbo; a southern gumbo supper). **SPECIAL EVENT:** Treme Creole Gumbo Festival, New Orleans, November, jazzandheritage.org/treme-gumbo.

TRUE COUNTRY HAM

Country Ham with Coca-Cola Red-Eye Gravy

American (Southern)

Never mind the stereotype of a thick-sliced country ham. True, cured country ham—with a velvety green-white coating of mold developed after a year or two of hanging—offers mahogany-brown meat so bitingly salty it should be sliced razor thin for edibility's sake, even after soaking. An American specialty far saltier and more ripely potent than the air- and salt-cured *jambón* and prosciutto of Europe, its salt-and-sugar cure gives it a flavor closer to that of China's Yunnan ham (see page 795). The most famous of American country hams is produced by Smithfield in Virginia, where hogs are fed local peanuts that impart a nuttiness to the smoke-and-salt overtones.

Either boiled or baked with frequent bastings, the ham is most delectably finished with the "red-eye pan gravy" that mitigates its saltiness with bitter black coffee and sometimes sugar. After boiling or baking, slices are simmered in an iron skillet with the coffee and plenty of the meat's own rich fat, the meat becoming succulently, meltingly tender. Buttered biscuits make the perfect mellowing accompaniment. As for the name: If the pan gravy is poured off into a bowl, the water-based coffee (reddened by the ham) sinks to the bottom, and the fat rises to the top, to form what looks like a giant red eye.

A delectable riff on the gravy is a specialty of the Colonnade Restaurant in Atlanta, Georgia, in which the sugar and coffee are replaced by Coca-Cola, that city's proudest contribution to mankind. The result is an enticingly warm and malty, caramelized savor that adds extra dimensions of richness to be sopped up with biscuits and grits. Sides of hotcakes or scrambled eggs are optional but advised.

WHERE: *In Atlanta, GA,* The Colonnade Restaurant, tel 404-874-5642, colonnadeatl.com; The Silver Skillet, tel 404-874-1388, thesilver skillet.com; *in Nashville,* Loveless Cafe, tel 615-646-9700, lovelesscafe.com. **MAIL ORDER:** Smithfield Hams, tel 800-926-8448, smithfield hams.com. **FURTHER INFORMATION AND RECIPES:** *Mastering the Art of Southern Cooking* by Nathalie Dupree and Cynthia Graubart (2012); cookstr.com (search fried country ham steaks with red-eye gravy); food52.com (search goat cheese grits with red eye gravy country ham and a fried egg). **SEE ALSO:** York Ham, page 33; Jabugo Ham, page 262.

—|||||||||||||||||||||||||||||||||—

ORIGINS OF A CLASSIC

Hamburger

American

Impatient, on-the-run Americans love the convenience of hand-held food. Fittingly, two quintessential American foods are German émigrés becoming U.S. citizens only after being stuffed into rolls. Named for the city of Frankfurt,

the frankfurter turned into the hot dog (see page 582), while the classic Deutsches beefsteak evolved into the hamburger, so named because so many German immigrants hailed from the rainy North Sea port of Hamburg. (Truth be told, sausages with buns have long been popular in Frankfurt, but it took an overseas trip for them to be commoditized as the classic food of streets and sports venues.)

The original Deutsches beefsteak is exactly what old-time menus in the U.S. listed as chopped or Salisbury steak: a knife-and-fork main course of pan-grilled ground sirloin topped with sautéed onions and pan drippings that created a mild, soft sauce. Just who first sandwiched the meat cake into a bun is open to question. Food historian Giovanni Ballarini offers the prevailing version of the story: Toward the end of the nineteenth century, soon-to-be American immigrants aboard ships were handed grilled meat patties between two slices of bread. (No plates, no water wasted in washing.) But in her famous 1747 English recipe book *The Art of Cookery, Made Plain and Easy*, Hannah Glasse refers to Hamburg "sausage," a chopped combination of beef, suet, and spices that she suggested be served with toast.

Or was the first really Charlie Nagreen, a fifteen-year-old who sold meatballs at a country fair in Seymour, Wisconsin, in 1885? Legend has it that he decided he could sell more meatballs if he put them between bread so customers could eat them out of hand while taking in the fair's attractions. And how about Louis Lassen, who in 1900 had a lunch wagon in New Haven,

Connecticut, where he sandwiched cooked scraps of beef between slices of bread? The wagon eventually became a shop, and Louis' Lunch sells hamburgers to this day.

In truth, history is beside the point when one bites into a richly beefy, succulently juicy burger, dripping from chin to napkin if not to shirtfront. Perfectly seared to a thin, savory crust (never charred to bitterness), and ideally cooked medium-rare—blood-crimson and a bit warm in the center—the burger is best encased in a fresh, lightly toasted and yeasty bun, sturdy enough to stay intact after absorbing drippings yet soft enough to be bitten into easily. The current fashion for hard-crusted rolls such as ciabatta and sourdough is a thoroughly nonfunctional design.

What goes between beef and bread? For purists that would be a paper-thin slice of sweet, raw onion (see Vidalia and Maui Onions, page 635) and a light smear of Heinz ketchup. Dijon mustard is a permissible alternative, but mayonnaise, Russian dressing, ranch-style dressing, sweet pickle relish, and so on, need not apply— nor should a frilly garden of salad greens and tomatoes that turn the meat cold. Cheese and bacon? Maybe, but not for those who value beef for its own sake. If there is to be cheese, it should be the subtly melting, mildly pungent type—real Cheddar, mozzarella, or Gruyère, not waxy, processed American cheese. Moldy or musty cheeses—the blues and those made with goat's or sheep's milk—lend a spoiled, fetid flavor.

The best hamburgers come from cuts of beef with some fat and texture, with chuck being an all-around good choice. For more flavor and body and slightly less fat, a half-and-half combination of chuck and sirloin, ground together so they are thoroughly blended, is the best choice. A small amount of brisket or some ground beef kidneys can be added to chuck, but round steak is to be avoided, as it tends to cook dry and tough. The late James Beard, the grand pooh-bah of American cuisine, liked to mix a touch of heavy sweet cream or diced bone marrow into the meat for extra richness, while the master of hamburger magic, Daniel Boulud, fills the center of his burger with scrumptious scraps of gently braised short rib, and, for good measure, a nice fat hunk of foie gras—a sublime (if pricey) treat (see page 89).

In truth, good beef needs very little seasoning. Just a dash of salt and pepper does the trick, although some add a bit of grated onion or crushed garlic and a sprinkling of a favorite herb, such as thyme, oregano, or chopped chives. The mixing should be done lightly, with a fork. Charcoal broiling will always be a favorite cooking method in the U.S., but for a more subtle result, sprinkle a heavy, black, cast-iron skillet with coarse salt, heat it up, and place the hamburgers in it, allowing at least an inch and a

The quintessential American meal

half of space between them so they do not steam. When the first side is seared and is easily loosened from the pan (after seven to eight minutes), add a touch of coarse salt to the raw side, flip it over, and fry for another six or seven minutes, or until blood rises to the surface when you press gently on the top of the burger with your finger. The salt will caramelize and burnish the beef's flavor.

Do not pat burgers down while they are frying, and try not to turn them more than once. For extra deliciousness, smear a dot of sweet butter on top just as you remove the burgers from the pan. Because it creates enormous clouds of smoke, this kind of pan-grilling should be done only in a well-ventilated cooking area.

WHERE: *In New York,* Corner Bistro, tel 212-242-9502, cornerbistrony.com; The Little Owl, tel 212-741-4695, thelittleowlnyc.com; *in New Haven,* Louis' Lunch, tel 203-562-5507, louislunch.com; *in Philadelphia,* Rouge, tel 215-732-6622, rouge98.com; *in Boston,* Mr. Bartley's Gourmet Burgers, tel 617-354-6559, mrbartley.com; *in Charleston and Nashville,* Husk, huskrestaurant.com; *in Atlanta,* Farm Burger at four locations, farmburger.com; Yeah! Burger at two locations, yeahburger.com; *in New Orleans,* Port of Call, tel 504-523-0120, portofcallnola.com; *in Chicago,* David Burke's Primehouse, tel 312-660-6000, davidburkesprimehouse.com; Ralph Lauren Restaurant, tel 312-475-1100, rlrestaurant.com; Owen & Engine, tel 773-235-2930, owenandengine.com; Kuma's Corner, tel 773-604-8769, kumascorner.com; *in Los Angeles,* Original Tommy's Hamburger, tel 213-389-9060, originaltommys.com; The Bowery Bar & Bistro, tel 323-465-3400, theboweryhollywood.com; *in San Francisco,* Zuni Café, tel 415-552-2522, zunicafe.com; *in Toronto,* Bymark restaurant, tel 416-777-1144, bymark.mcewangroup.ca; The Harbord Room, tel 416-962-8989, theharbordroom.com; *in Montreal,* Mister Steer, tel 514-866-3233, mistersteer.com; m:brgr, tel 514-906-0408, mbrgr.com; *in London,* Meat Mission, tel 44/20-7739-8212, meatmission.com; *in Paris,* Ralph's Restaurant, tel 33/1-44-77-76-00, ralphlaurenstgermain.com; *in Prague,* Peter's Burger Pub, tel 420/222-312-091, burgerpub.cz. **Further information and recipes:** *The James Beard Cookbook* by James Beard (2002); *The '21' Cookbook* by Michael Lomonaco (1995); saveur.com (search classic hamburger; cuban hamburger; japanese hamburger; favorite hamburger recipes; guide to hamburger meat); hamburgeramerica.com. **Special events:** Taste of Hamburg-er Festival, Hamburg, PA, tel 610-562-3106, tasteofhamburger.com; National Hamburger Festival, Akron, OH, August, hamburgerfestival.com. **Tip:** For a burger with a more sophisticated appeal, try the lamb burger: finely ground shoulder and leg meat, half and half, lightly mixed with a bit of grated onion or crushed garlic, salt, pepper, and some fresh thyme, and pan- or charcoal-grilled.

"FRIENDS ARE LIKE MELONS. / SHALL I TELL YOU WHY? /
TO FIND A GOOD ONE YOU MUST A HUNDRED TRY." —CLAUDE MERMET

Hand Melons

American (New York State)

G iven the appearance of the rose-tan Hand melon, with those fingerlike ridges around its rind, one might conclude that its name derives from its shape—it looks much like a hand holding a cantaloupe. In fact, the coral-fleshed, succulent muskmelon is grown on the farm of one John Hand, in upstate New York's Washington County.

The melons, actually a sort of cantaloupe, are available only in August, when they reach their juiciest, sweetest best. For years they have been the standard summertime dessert in the clubhouse restaurant of the neighboring Saratoga Race Track, where they are served au naturel. Only those grown on the Hand farm have a right to that name, but other similarly ridged and lavishly moist muskmelons from New York and New Jersey are available from late July through August, best when purchased at farmers' markets in the city and at stands along country roads. Hand melons are rarely found at conventional greengrocers, because their seductively moist, glowing coral flesh contains a great deal of water, making them highly perishable.

To avoid a disappointing melon selection, learn how to read the rind. As with most muskmelons (those with netted patterns on their rinds, including cantaloupe, crenshaw, and casaba), one can judge ripeness and quality by heft and texture. The ideal is a well-formed oval with no bruises or damp, moldy spots. The more textured the netting, the better the flavor of the fruit within. The melon should feel heavy in the hand for its volume, indicating juiciness. Sniffing can help but is less definitive, as is pressing the end of the melon to see if it gives. Melons ripen only when whole and uncut, so buying a cut, unripe portion is pointless. For like a cut cheese, a cut melon rots but never ripens.

Chill a melon in the refrigerator for at least two hours before serving, and allow it to stand at room temperature for about fifteen minutes after cutting so the flavor will rise to its fullest. As for serving, muskmelons in general make a wonderful accompaniment to sliced prosciutto. When eaten plain, a dash of lime or lemon juice adds a hint of sophistication.

Retail and mail order: *In Greenwich, NY,* Hand Melon Farm, tel 518-692-2376, handmelonfarm.com. **Further information and recipes:** saveur.com (search melon au porto); epicurious.com (search cantaloupe granita).

Hanger Steak, Flank Steak, and Skirt Steak

American, Continental

Beef mavens will tell you to order these flat, muscular, flavorful steaks rare, and no other way. Long the favorite of butchers, and dubbed "the kindest cuts" since they provide maximum flavor at minimum cost, they are at their beefiest and most toothsome when cooked rare, beyond which they become dry, tough, and stringy— a travesty easily avoided.

The hanger steak is the thick strip of meat, part of the steer's diaphragm, that "hangs" between the rib and the loin. Sometimes referred to as "the butcher's tenderloin," it is a favorite of the meat cutters who know that there's only one of these per animal, and that its flavor rivals that of a rib-eye steak. The French, who call it *onglet*, often choose it for bargain renditions of the bistro classic steak-frites, more traditionally prepared with a rib steak. So long as the hanger's tough center vein is removed by the butcher, resulting in two long steaks of almost equal size, both may be easily grilled or broiled for a pungently juicy outcome.

Flank steak—best enjoyed rare

The skirt steak is the diaphragm muscle itself—a long, flat piece of meat that lies between the steer's abdomen and chest cavity. It takes only a few minutes to sear this steak in a cast-iron skillet, broiler, or grill so that it forms a nice brown crust but remains juicy. Sadly, the skirt has become scarce, and more expensive, because of its popularity for use in fajitas and other Latino favorites.

The flank steak—*bavette de flanchet* to the French—is the authentic cut for London broil and also for Latino *matambre* (see page 668). A long, wide, and thin muscle from the steer's flank, or lower hindquarters, its fibrous, striated meat is sheathed in fat that is too often trimmed off in butcher shops, so that the meat tends to dryness when grilled; some butcher shops will order untrimmed flank steak from their suppliers if it's requested a few days ahead. Barring that, the best way to tenderize a flank is to marinate it.

Whether broiled or grilled, all of these steaks should be sliced thinly against the grain, with the knife held almost parallel to the cutting surface, as when slicing smoked salmon.

Mail order: De Bragga and Spitler, tel 646-873-6555, debragga.com. **Further information and recipes:** *The Steak Lover's Cookbook* by William Rice (1997); *The Butcher's Guide to Well-Raised Meat* by Joshua and Jessica Applestone, with Alexandra Zissu (2011); *The Barbecue! Bible* by Steven Raichlen (2008); epicurious.com (search grilled skirt steak; chile-marinated flank steak); saveur.com (search vegetable-stuffed rolled flank steak).

||||||||||||||||||||||||||||||||

EDIBLE GOLD

Hangtown Fry

American (Californian)

The California Gold Rush produced a great deal of wealth, but one of its richest legacies may be edible: the pancake- or frittata-style omelet studded with fried oysters and topped with crisp bacon that is known as Hangtown fry, a legend that has survived those rough-and-ready days.

The time: mid-1800s. The place: the lawless Hangtown, so called for its numerous hangings. (Before that nickname, it was called simply "Blood and Guts"; since 1854 it's been known as Placerville.) The origin story: An enthusiastic wildcatter strikes it rich in the Sierra foothills and walks into the El Dorado Hotel, demanding the costliest dish on the menu. The cook hastily assembles his most luxurious ingredients: eggs (which had to be transported delicately and cost about a dollar each), bacon (shipped all the way from the East Coast), and oysters (conveyed on ice from San Francisco, more than a hundred miles away).

The combination of flavors—sweet egg, salty oysters, smoky bacon—worked as enticingly then as it does now, most notably at San Francisco's Tadich Grill (see page 629). A few other places in San Francisco sometimes feature Hangtown fry, but Tadich's version is definitive for its mastery of textures: tender, fluffy eggs ever so lightly browned on the surface; crisp, meaty bacon; fresh, moist oysters, lightly breaded and pan-fried before joining the egg mixture. The heaping main dish is served with a unique, piquant, house-made tartar sauce, a sort of mayonnaise bound and thickened with mashed potatoes in a style close to that of the Balkan *scordolea*.

Where: *In San Francisco,* Tadich Grill, tel 415-391-1849, tadichgrill.com. **Further information and recipe:** *Tadich Grill* by John Briscoe (2002); saveur.com (search hangtown fry); epicurious.com (search fried oyster omelet).

||||||||||||||||||||||||||||||||

THE LEGAL KIND

Hash

American

From the French *haché,* meaning to chop, hash may be the world's most delicious way to use up what are often leftover bits of cooked meat and poultry. Easily prepared and equally easily consumed, the economical dish seems to have first surfaced in seventeenth-century England, but is now far more common in the U.S. Plain or topped with a fried or poached egg, it makes for a classic stick-to-your-ribs breakfast or brunch, but is also wonderfully handy as a last-minute dinner concoction.

The most popular hashes are those made with rosy, mildly salty corned beef or roast beef, gently tossed with finely chopped onion melted to softness in butter or bacon fat, and mixed with cooked, finely diced potatoes, salt, pepper, sometimes eggs, a few droplets of Worcestershire sauce, and sweet or hot paprika. Although fish is sometimes used for hash, it's not a great candidate for a lengthy pan-fry, often too soft and moist to attain the desired crispness and golden-brown hue. Pork other than ham tends to be too densely textured to work well as hash, but the much overlooked roasted or stewed lamb deserves more attention than it gets, mixed perhaps with cooked rice instead of potatoes, along with diced green peppers and some lamb-centric herbs, such as thyme or oregano.

The mass is usually slowly skillet-fried, piping hot, then flipped so the top and bottom both develop a thin, crackly veneer. Some cooks fry it in thick, individual oval cakes; others bake it with a topping of bread crumbs and perhaps grated cheese.

Long considered quick, cheap food, beef hash gave rise to the term *hash houses,* for cheap and unadorned restaurants. By contrast, chicken hashes have a more elegant reputation. Lighter and more sophisticated than other meat hashes, those based on breast of chicken (or perhaps of turkey, if it has been basted and kept moist during roasting) usually involve some sort of cream

sauce and are gratinéed with grated Gruyère or Parmesan. When it opened in 1910, the Ritz-Carlton Hotel restaurant in New York featured a creamy rendition devised by chef Louis Diat, and three versions of chicken hash used to be standard on the "21" menu: the house classic, still on the menu and served with wild rice and often scrambled eggs as a late supper; Chicken Hash St. Germaine, which was garnished with a jade-green puree of green peas and a cheese topping; and Chicken Hash Beyers, which was served with nice, grainy wild rice and the silky pea puree.

The Ritz-Carlton chicken hash, long favored by lunching ladies at the original Madison Avenue site, was graced with a sherry- and egg-yolk-enhanced cream sauce, making it the richest indulgence of all.

WHERE: *In New York,* The '21' Club, tel 212-582-7200, 21club.com; Keens Steakhouse, tel 212-947-3636, keens.com; *in Portland, ME,* Bintliff's American Cafe, tel 207-774-0005, bintliffscafe.com; *in Los Angeles,* The Grill, tel 323-856-5530, thegrill.com. **FURTHER INFORMATION AND RECIPES:** *The '21' Cookbook* by Michael Lomonaco (1995); *Simple Cooking* by John Thorne (1996); *The Gift of Southern Cooking* by Edna Lewis and Scott Peacock (2003); *The Fannie Farmer Cookbook,* 13th edition, by Marion Cunningham (1996); saveur.com (search keens steakhouse prime rib hash; chicken hash; corned beef hash).

RING IN THE NEW YEAR WITH CHAMPAGNE AND BEANS

Hoppin' John

American (Southern)

To the uninitiated, it probably looks like a simple plate of rice and legumes. But any southerner can tell you that the concoction of cheerily winking black-eyed peas, simply stewed with savory, meaty hog jowls and served atop a nurturing bed

of snowy short-grain rice—the dish known as hoppin' John—is a symbol of the comforts of

home, as well as a totem of good luck.

The dish began as a variation on the

nutritious rice-and-beans combination eaten throughout the Caribbean, most probably brought to the American South by West-African slaves. Legends abound as to the origin of its name, but there are references to "Hopping John" (somewhere along the line, the *g* was dropped) in both the prominent abolitionist Frederick Law Olmsted's book *A Journey in the Seaboard Slave States,* first published in 1856, and *The Carolina Housewife,* a collection of recipes by Sarah Rutledge, published in 1847.

As in so many other cultures, in the South sustaining staples such as beans symbolize good luck and renewal, and so are traditionally eaten on New Year's Day. For good measure they are garnished with cooked greens and cornbread, ensuring that the year ahead will be full of coins (the black-eyed peas), cash (the greens), and gold (the cornbread). Some throw in tomatoes, too, thought to symbolize health, if not a cache of rubies.

WHERE: *In Chapel Hill, NC,* Crook's Corner, tel 919-929-7643, crookscorner.com. **MAIL ORDER:** For dried peas, nuts.com (search blackeyed peas); amazon.com (search spicy world black eye

A New Year's tradition since the 1800s

peas). **FURTHER INFORMATION AND RECIPES:** Hoppin' John's *Lowcountry Cooking* by John Martin Taylor (2012); *Mastering the Art of Southern Cooking* by Nathalie Dupree and Cynthia Graubart (2012); *The Welcome Table* by Jessica B. Harris (1996); foodnetwork.com (search hoppin john lagasse); epicurious.com (hoppin john welcome table). **SPECIAL EVENT:** Hoppin' John Festival, Shakori Hills, Silk Hope, NC, September, with lots of music and a hoppin' John cook-off, hoppinjohn.org (click Be a Part).

MORE OF A PEA THAN A NUT

Peanuts

Where would the humble peanut be without the work of George Washington Carver, the noted horticulturist and chemist who began his groundbreaking research at the Tuskegee Institute in Alabama in 1903? The great popularizer certainly made his mark, introducing the mysterious creature and its many uses to the world stage. But despite its familiarity, the peanut (*Arachis hypogaea*) still remains ambiguous to many. Its name notwithstanding, it's not a nut, and it doesn't grow on trees. It's a legume, an

edible seed enclosed within a pod, just like beans, peas, and lentils.

Iconic American symbols nearly from day one, peanuts are thought to be indigenous to Peru, where evidence of them exists in tombs dating back to 750 B.C. New World explorers transported them to Europe, along with tomatoes, cacao beans, and potatoes, and they made their way to Africa as a consequence of the slave trade. (The term *goober,* the common nickname for the peanut, comes from its Congolese name, *nguba.*)

The peanut plant thrived in the American South, especially in Georgia, where just about half of all American peanuts are grown today; the peanut soup and peanut cake featured in cookbooks like Sarah Rutledge's *The Carolina Housewife,* published in 1847, are still traditional favorites throughout the region, where the peanut harvest is still a marker of seasons. Beyond the South, peanuts really took off when peanut butter was introduced at the World's Fair in St. Louis in 1904. Around the same time, Carver was beginning the work that would result in the introduction of more than three hundred peanut products, including an emulsion to beat bronchitis and a base for cosmetics. In 1906, an Italian immigrant named Amedeo Obici perfected a system for blanching whole roasted peanuts, which effectively removed the reddish jackets from the kernels; along with his partner, Mario Peruzzi, he went on to found Planters, the first company to market and package roasted, shelled peanuts. The "nuts" entered the political fray in the late 1970s, when Jimmy Carter rode his brand of just-folks politics from his peanut farm in Plains, Georgia, all the way to the Oval Office.

Today, China and India are the world's top peanut producers. Peanuts are beloved ingredients in many Asian dishes, and can be found in curry garnishes, Mexican moles, and sauces for satays (see page 848). But the nutty legume can

George Washington Carver

also be enjoyed all by itself, whether "wet" (boiled in briny water until meltingly tender, for a result referred to as "goober peas" since the days of the Civil War), roasted, or split out of the shell at baseball games. And of course, let us not forget the all-American snack spread, peanut butter (see page 607).

MAIL ORDER: The Peanut Shoppe of Williamsburg, tel 800-637-3268, thepeanutshop.com (search handcooked virginia peanuts; savannah peanuts; chipotle peanut crunch); amazon.com (search hampton farms no salt roasted in shell peanuts). **RETAIL AND MAIL ORDER:** *In Charlottesville, VA,* The Virginia Shop, tel 434-977-0080, thevashop.net (click Virginia Peanuts). **FURTHER INFORMATION AND RECIPES:** *Peanuts: The Illustrious History of the Goober Pea* by Andrew F. Smith (2006); *Hoppin' John's Lowcountry Cooking* by John Martin Taylor (2012); *Rick Bayless's Mexican Kitchen* by Rick Bayless (1996); *The Thousand Recipe Chinese Cookbook* by Gloria Bley Miller (1984); epicurious.com (search boiled peanuts; spiced peanuts; chinese chicken breast with peanuts; lemon rice with peanuts; asian slaw with peanuts). **TIP:** Peanut cream is an especially salty-and-sweet, decadent treat, an excellent recipe for which can be found in *The Silver Palate Good Times Cookbook* by Sheila Lukins and Julee Rosso (1985).

TO WALK THE DOG

Hot Dog

American

For the lover of hot dogs, to walk the streets of New York is to be constant prey to the tempting scents of a variety of wursts. Whether boiled, steamed, or grilled, these sputteringly hot and juicy "tube steaks," ideally in crackling natural casings, will be slipped into soft rolls. Smeared with cheap, brassy mustard or ketchup, they will be crowned with a rainbow of toppings like sauerkraut; soft onions in spicy tomato-based sauces; or raw onions, chili, and cheese, the type of wurst and topping varying from one locale to another. The experience will be enriched by the swirl of big-city street life, whether one stands and juggles food and drink or eats on the go, perhaps musing on a centuries-old comestible that exhibits the most modern concepts of package design—well-preserved, waste-free (only a napkin is necessary), and wholly sustaining of body and soul.

A smoked wiener of beef, pork, or both, sandwiched into a long, soft bun, the hot dog is a strictly American invention, and a native of Brooklyn, at that. Its frankfurter precursor emigrated from Frankfurt, Germany, with Antoine Feuchtwanger, who sold the steaming wurst at the turn of the twentieth century in St. Louis. If customers burned their fingers on the hot tubes of meat, their complaints do not survive. Enter Charles Feltman, another Frankfurt immigrant and the first to put these wursts in long rolls. He sold them from a rolling cart in Coney Island in about 1869, an enterprise so successful it led to his opening the tony Feltman's Restaurant in the

A New York City food cart tradition

same seaside neighborhood. One of his waiters, the young Nathan Handwerker, went out on his own in about 1905, moving just a few blocks away and conjuring up a spice recipe to add to the meat mix that remains a secret to this day—and is still in copious use at Nathan's Famous. Nathan's hot dogs are now sold packaged in supermarkets, with token Nathan's Famous outposts operating around the country, but the Coney Island original is the only place to get these snapping, grilled dogs in crisp natural casings. The popcorn-scented salt-sea air of the Atlantic Ocean, just across the famed boardwalk, and the screams and cries of roller coaster revelers add as much seasoning to the Nathan's dog as the mustard does.

Outside of Brooklyn, Katz's Delicatessen dishes up Manhattan's best, juiciest, and most pungent grilled hot dog. Wrapped in natural casing and served with sauerkraut or whatever else devotees favor, the dogs can be eaten at tables or carried away to be munched as one tours the historic and colorful Lower East Side. In the same neighborhood and beyond, no one can claim the title of true New Yorker without having succumbed to the lure of the blue-and-yellow umbrellas that are the defining characteristic of the Sabrett hot dog carts seen on street corners throughout the city. Though often overboiled, these gentle, beefy wursts gain interest through their toppings; many of the Sabrett vendors hail from the Greek island of Cyprus, and add a heady dash of their much-loved cumin to onions simmered in tomato sauce.

The hot dog has trotted out far beyond the Big Apple, too. Although street food stands aren't permitted in Chicago, it's another great hot dog town, hailed for the slim, all-beef, flame-broiled Vienna wieners known as red hots for the fieriest of reasons. That, and the coarser, garlic-laden Polnischer can be eaten in or carried out at the shabby but popular Wieners Circle in the Lincoln Park section of town. You can choose from dazzling toppings: sauerkraut, raw onions, sweet relish, dill pickles, tomatoes, hot peppers, celery salt, and more. Make sure to try the fabled hot and crunchy fries and chilled homemade lemonade as well.

Ballparks are prime real estate for hot dogs, but few can match the Brewers' stadium, Miller Park, in Milwaukee, where a strong German heritage inspires not only beer brewers but a wurst-savvy audience. Silvery German pork brat-wurst, paprika-bright Polnischers, and slim Chicago-style wieners, mild or red hot, comprise the dazzling array.

For hot-dogging it at home, Niman Ranch hot dogs offer more of a high-toned pleasure. Made of beef from grass-fed, hormone-free cat-tle, and packed into natural casings, they bring a purity of essence to the wiener enterprise.

Where: *In New York,* Katz's Delicatessen, tel 212-254-2246, katzsdelicatessen.com; *in Brooklyn,* Nathan's Famous, tel 718-946-2202, nathansfamous.com; *in Chicago,* The Wieners Circle, tel 773-477-7444, wienercircle.net; Hot

Doug's, tel 773-279-9550, hotdougs.com; *in Milwaukee, WI,* Miller Park, milwaukee.brewers .mlb.com; *in St. Louis,* Steve's on the Hill, tel 314-762-9899, steveshotdogsstl.com; *in Philadelphia,* Frankford Hall, tel 215-634-3338, frankfordhall .com; *in Marietta, GA,* Barkers Red Hots, tel 404-756-1542, barkershotdogs.com; *in New Orleans,* Lucky Dogs, food carts in the French Quarter, mainly on Bourbon Street and around Jackson Square Park, starting in mid-afternoon, lucky dogs.us; *in Austin, TX,* Frank, tel 512-494-6916, hotdogscoldbeer.com; *in Los Angeles,* The Short Stop, tel 213-482-4942; Skooby's, tel 323-468-3647, skoobys.com; *in North Hollywood, CA,* Vicious Dogs, tel 818-985-3647, viciousdogshot dogs.com. **Mail order:** Niman Ranch, niman ranch.com (search fearless franks); amazon .com (search nathan's hot dogs; nathan's coney island mustard).

FRIDAY, SATURDAY, SUNDAE

Hot Fudge or Butterscotch Sundae

American

The ultimate treat for children of all ages is a frosty tulip-shaped parfait glass filled with vanilla ice cream and smothered with a decadent pour of hot fudge or golden butterscotch, that tantalizing combination of butter and caramelized brown sugar. Next comes a crunchy topping of chopped walnuts or toasted almonds, a lush cloudlet of whipped cream, and a crowning rose-red cherry—an example of only too much being enough.

It's the all-American sundae, one of the best examples of the pleasures of contrasting temper-atures, and true heaven in a glass. Little can beat the thrill of dipping through its layers of melting ice cream, velvety sauce, and crunchy nuts.

There are many claims as to the origins of the beloved sundae, most of them incredibly hard to pin down. Of its alleged birthplaces, the most likely are Ithaca, New York; Two Rivers, Wisconsin;

and Evanston, Illinois. But the California Milk Advisory Board would have you believe that Hollywood deserves the credit, what with all those stories of starlets being discovered at drugstore soda fountains. And in truth, the sundae is a throw-back to those drugstore soda fountain days.

Geography aside, legend has it that the sun-dae was the result of the nineteenth-century blue laws that forbade the selling of sodas (among other temptations) on Sundays. Canny soda jerks substituted syrup for the soda in their ice-cream treats and called the new creation "sundae," adjusting the spelling so as not to offend religious leaders by taking the Lord's day in vain. Thus a star was born. Now the sundae is an American icon, made in almost endless variations, with myriad ice-cream flavors in combination with any number of acceptable toppings, from fruits and compotes to brownie bites and bits of candy. As might be expected, California claims the world record for the largest sundae, a dessert tower constructed in Anaheim in 1985—a 120-foot-tall indulgence made up of 4,667 gallons of ice cream. And how many spoons?

Where: *In New York,* Elephant & Castle, tel 212-243-1400, elephantandcastle.com; Serendipity, tel 212-838-3531, serendipity3.com; *in Forest Hills, NY,* Eddie's Sweet Shop, tel 718-520-8514; *in St. Louis,* Crown Candy Kitchen, tel 314-621-9650, crowncandykitchen.net. **Further information and recipes:** *Soda Fountain Classics* by Elsa Petersen-Schepelern (2001); *Jeni's Splendid Ice Cream Desserts* by Jeni Britton Bauer (2014); epicurious.com (search mint hot fudge sundaes; mexican hot fudge sundaes; southern peanut butterscotch sundaes; butterscotch sauce).

THE BERRY FOR WINE LOVERS

Huckleberries

American

Most of us identify the term *huckleberry* with Mark Twain's irascible Mississippi River hero, Huck Finn, but the succulent, ink-dark, purple berry gives the literary Huck a run for his money as a local folk favorite. Indigenous to the western mountainous regions of North America, huckleberries were used for barter before the settlers arrived. Though they are relatives of the blueberry genus *Vaccinium,* they have a far more intense, winey tang, and a pungent aroma that provides extra appeal.

Attempts to cultivate huckleberries are still in their infancy—like many wild things, they are tricky to grow and gather. Their slender shrubs don't grow well below 3,500 feet in elevation, taking up to fifteen years to mature and produce within the brief ripening season of July and August. Yet, to those who cherish their elusive flavor, they are worth the trouble and extra cost.

Oregon, Washington, Michigan, and Idaho lay claim to the largest crops, though Hungry Horse, Montana, nine miles west of the entrance to Glacier National Park, bills itself "the wild huckleberry capital of the West." Some parts of the Pacific Northwest appear to make a living out of canning and jamming the fruit, but that practice seems a wasteful use. Better to serve the berries fresh, under a mantle of sweet cream, or lightly crushed over vanilla ice cream, or baked into unctuously silken pies that leave red-purple traces of what resembles indelible ink on the tongue and teeth, much to the delight of young huckleberry eaters far and wide.

Mail order: Oregon Mushrooms, tel 800-682-0036, oregonmushrooms.com; Northwest Wild Foods, tel 866-945-3232, nwwildfoods.com; for huckleberry bushes, hartmannsplantcompany.com. **Further information and recipes:** The International Wild Huckleberry Association, wildhuckleberry.com (click Recipes, then Wild Huckleberry Cream Pie; Huckleberry Jam; Swedish Pancakes and Huckleberry Sauce); saveur.com (search huckleberry crisps); epicurious.com (search no-bake fresh fruit pie; huckleberry mostarda). **Tip:** Blueberries, especially if small, can be substituted in most recipes calling for huckleberries, but it will result in some loss of intensity.

‖‖‖‖‖‖‖‖‖‖‖‖‖‖‖‖‖‖‖‖‖

ICE CREAM, THROUGH A STRAW

Ice-Cream Sodas and Beyond

American

A favorite among women that was hailed as an "American drink" in an 1891 issue of *Harper's Weekly*, carbonated water (soda) was due for a new incarnation in the second half of the nineteenth century. It took a French émigré to think of adding syrup and, in 1874, an ingenious dessert maven of debatable identity to plop in a scoop of ice cream. To the genius who thought of adding creamy milk, the world remains thankful. Thus was the ice-cream soda born: a sparklingly refreshing, richly creamy drink with its frothy bubble head, its sweetly tingling liquid, and the final reward of lusciously softened ice cream to be spooned up between sips.

Once a ubiquitous treat dispensed at the soda fountains of local pharmacies, ice-cream sodas are now harder to find. But in the cafés, diners, and sweet shops where they are featured, a couple of time-honored favorites tend to persist: the "black and white," made with vanilla ice cream in a chocolate soda, or the "white and black," vanilla soda with chocolate ice cream. More sophisticated sippers opt for an all-coffee blend of ice cream and syrup, or for a pale blond, purely vanilla drink, or for a mochalike Broadway (chocolate ice cream with coffee syrup). In summer, flavored syrups may be replaced with fresh fruit—strawberry or peach ice-cream sodas are garnished with mashed strawberries or peaches.

At home, in the absence of an array of flavored syrups, the traditional ice-cream soda starts with flavored carbonated drinks: root beer, Coca-Cola, vanilla-scented cream soda, and ginger ale, with or without a trickle of milk, but always, of course, with a generous scoop of ice cream lowered in, and finished with a drizzle of soda. The classic root beer float, also known as a Black Cow, is best made with vanilla ice cream. Avoid the temptation to add a final flourish of whipped cream, which might weigh down the drink's light bubbliness.

Authenticity demands that the soda overflow as it is poured over the ice cream. Drink first, clean up later.

WHERE: *In New York,* for floats, Serendipity, tel 212-838-3531, serendipity3.com; *in Forest Hills, NY,* Eddie's Sweet Shop, tel 718-520-8514; *in St. Louis,* Fizzy's Soda Fountain & Grill, tel 314-395-4550, fizzyssoda fountain.com; Crown Candy Kitchen, tel 314-621-9650, crowncandykitchen .net; *in St. Paul, MN,* Lynden's Soda Fountain, tel 651-330-7632, lyndens.com; *in South Pasadena, CA,* Fair Oaks Pharmacy and Soda Fountain, tel 626-799-1414, fairoakspharmacy.net. **FURTHER INFORMATION AND RECIPES:** *Soda Fountain Classics* by Elsa Petersen-Schepelern (2001); cookstr.com (search root beer ice cream; orange ice cream soda); food.com (search fantastic ice cream soda); foodnetwork.com (search ice cream sodas garten).

⊢||||||||||||||||||||||||||||||||⊣

AN AFTER-MASS SUNDAY SNACK IN ARIZONA

Indian Fry Bread

American (Native American)

One of the nation's oldest Catholic churches, Mission San Xavier del Bac on the Tohono O'odham reservation near Tucson, Arizona, is worth a visit. The stark-white adobe building, erected in 1783, boasts renowned examples of Mission,

Moorish, Byzantine, *and* Mexican Renaissance design and an impressive collection of murals and statues. And then there's the matter of its Indian fry bread.

In a parking lot of the desert church, members of the tribe deep-fry irresistible slabs of the simple, knobby, thick bread as they have for hundreds of years. Drizzled with honey or filled with an array of toppings (it's sometimes sold elsewhere as a Navajo or Indian taco), it is an achingly simple food with a homey, stick-to-your-ribs appeal. But as the bread's few ingredients attest—water, flour, baking powder, and salt—fry bread isn't an indigenous food to native communities. Rather, it came about in the nineteenth century, when tribes on the Great Plains were forced to resettle and given government rations, including wheat flour and lard.

The bread has long since taken on a life of its own as an iconic symbol of both repression and independence. Today, it is served at an array of pan-tribal ceremonies and is a great source of pride among groups that persevered through unjust events like the Long Walk. As Indian rock musician Keith Secola sings in his song "Frybread," "But they couldn't keep the people down because born to the people was a Frybread Messiah, who said 'You can't do much with sugar, flour, lard, and salt. But you can add one fundamental ingredient: love.'"

WHERE: *Near Tucson, AZ,* Mission San Xavier del Bac, Sunday mornings, tel 520-294-2624, sanxaviermission.org; *in Phoenix, AZ,* The Fry Bread House, tel 602-351-2345; *in Denver,* Tocabe, tel 720-524-8282, tocabe.com. **FURTHER INFORMATION AND RECIPES:** *Southwest Indian Cookbook* by Marcia Keegan (1987); food network.com (search indian fry bread).

⊢||||||||||||||||||||||||||||||||⊣

A LOVE LETTER FROM HUNGRY OIL RIGGERS

Jambalaya

American (Louisianan)

A savory plateful of history, jambalaya may well be one of the very first examples of American fusion cooking. A classic example of some of our very best regional cuisine—that of Creole-Cajun Louisiana—it is a soul-satisfying rice dish in

the manner of pilaf, risotto, or paella. Based on short-grain rice, shrimp or crabmeat, spicy andouille sausage, and the even spicier smoked tasso ham, it is aromatic with diced green bell

The perfect dish for feeding a large and hungry crowd

pepper, onion, celery, garlic, perhaps a touch of tomato, and always a heady boost of thyme and bay leaves. Chicken in some form may also be added, whether as meat or cut-up giblets. All simmer together in a flavorful chicken or seafood stock, exchanging juices and flavors for a heady, difficult-to-set-aside result.

Now considered a Cajun dish, jambalaya is credited to several origins. Some say it was derived from the paella of the region's first Spanish colonists, who included their beloved *jamón* (ham) in what might be a linguistic derivation of jamón-paella. Another theory has the name coming from the Provençal word *jambalaia,* meaning a mishmash. The Cajuns wisely adopted the dish and made it their own, recognizing the appeal of this robust, throw-everything-in-the-pot, crowd-pleasing meal.

Whatever its beginnings, jambalaya is a favorite dish on oil rigs operating in the Gulf of Mexico, where workers share a similar food culture—including a preference for the unusual addition of black-eyed peas, as in the following recipe.

Black-Eyed Pea Jambalaya
Serves 10 to 12

1 tablespoon olive oil or unsalted butter
4 slices bacon, diced
3 medium-size onions, peeled and chopped
4 stalks of celery, coarsely diced
1 large green bell pepper, seeded and coarsely chopped
3 cloves of garlic, peeled and chopped
½ cup chopped Italian parsley leaves
2 teaspoons dried thyme
1 large bay leaf, finely crumbled
2 teaspoons salt
½ teaspoon black pepper
1½ pounds cooked ham, cut into 1-inch cubes
1½ pounds smoked sausage, such as spicy andouille or mild beef knockwurst, peeled and cut into bite-size chunks
2 cups dried black-eyed peas
2 cups white rice
Dash of Tabasco or pinch of dried red pepper flakes

1. Heat the olive oil or melt the butter in a large, heavy soup pot over moderate heat. Add the bacon and cook until the edges begin to turn brown, about 7 minutes.

2. Stir in the onions, celery, bell pepper, garlic, parsley, thyme, and bay leaf and cook over low heat, stirring, until the vegetables wilt and soften but do not turn brown, about 5 minutes. Stir in the salt and black pepper.

3. Add the ham, sausage, black-eyed peas, rice, and Tabasco sauce or red pepper flakes. Then, add enough water to cover, about 6 cups.

4. Cover the pot and cook the jambalaya over low heat until thickened and all ingredients are soft, 45 minutes to 1 hour, stirring often and adding more water, if necessary, to prevent scorching. Taste for seasoning, adding more salt, black pepper, and Tabasco or red pepper flakes as necessary. Serve the jambalaya very hot. If made in advance and refrigerated, you may need to add more water when reheating. It will keep in the refrigerator for about 5 days.

WHERE: *In Lafayette, LA,* Randol's, tel 337-981-7080, randols.com; Prejean's, tel 337-896-3247, prejeans.com; *in New Orleans,* K-Paul's Louisiana Kitchen, tel 504-596-2530, chefpaul .com/kpaul. **FURTHER INFORMATION AND RECIPES:** *Chef Paul Prudhomme's Louisiana Kitchen* by Paul Prudhomme (1984); *Bill Neal's Southern Cooking* by Bill Neal (1989); cookstr. com (search jambalaya; seafood jambalaya; creole-cajun jambalaya; chicken turkey kielbasa jambalaya).

|||||||||||||||||||||||||||||||||

SEASIDE EATING AWAY FROM THE SHORE

Jasper White's Summer Shack

American (New England)

New England's oceanfront towns have a reputation for superb Atlantic seafood and iconic chowders, fries, lobster rolls, and clam bakes. But visitors to big-city Boston can find such fare without leaving town—thanks to Jasper White,

whose Summer Shack restaurants bring Cape Cod to the home of the Cabots and the Lowells.

It's not often that a chef trades in white tablecloths for brown butcher paper, or scales down from a high-end, intimate restaurant favored by critics, and even by Julia Child, to a three-hundred-seat glorified clam shack, but that's exactly what Jasper White did in 2000. The New Jersey Shore native settled in Boston in 1979 and, with chef Lydia Shire, went on to run the dining rooms of the city's top three historic hotels. White opened his own high-end restaurant, Jasper's, on the Boston waterfront in 1983, and it quickly became a must-stop for local and visiting connoisseurs hoping to feast on caviar, oysters, and delicate lobster pan roasts. But when the infamous "Big Dig" construction project threatened White's business, he abruptly shut his doors in 1995 and regrouped. The result was the Summer Shack, a bright, pastel-hued restaurant stuffed with giant lobster tanks and old-fashioned steam kettles, where White

switched from caviar and oysters to corn dogs and (yes) oysters. A large, raucous, buzzing, and open-plan restaurant that evokes the outdoor clam joints lining New England's shores, Summer Shack is a place where diners can almost smell the sea breeze as they enjoy New England seafood classics like chowders, steamers and broth, clam bakes, fish fries, lobsters (steamed and in rolls), baked beans, and all the standbys of such beloved low-tech, sandy-floored places. Joining the seafood is the always outstanding fried chicken—sparklingly crisp, moist within, and almost devoid of grease.

WHERE: 50 Dalton St., Boston, tel 617-867-9955; 149 Alewife Brook Parkway, Cambridge, MA, tel 617-520-9500; 850 Providence Highway, Dedham, MA, tel 781-407-9955; Mohegan Sun Resort & Casino, Uncasville, CT, tel 860-862-9500; for all, summershackrestaurant.com. **FURTHER INFORMATION AND RECIPES:** *The Summer Shack Cookbook* by Jasper White (2011); *50 Chowders* by Jasper White (2000).

|||||||||||||||||||||||||||||||||

THE COOL GREEN ONE

Key Lime Pie

American (Floridian)

As its name suggests, the shimmering glass-green dessert is native to the Florida Keys, the home (in a manner of speaking) of the teasingly sweet-sour Key lime that inspires this enticingly cool treat. The pie is a deceptively simple affair based on pungent Key lime juice, sweetened condensed milk, and enriching egg, all combined to make a custard that is poured into a crushed graham cracker crust and topped with whipped cream. Complexity comes via the spicy and sunny flavor of the lime itself, in contrast to the sugar and the gentle sweet cream.

The golf-ball-size fruit botanically known as *Citrus aurantifolia* also travels under the monikers of Mexican lime and West Indian lime, after the two areas where it is actually most commonly grown. Small, yellowish, highly acidic, and nose-twitchingly aromatic, the fruit is originally indigenous to Malaysia, from where it made its way around the world, courtesy of Arab traders and the Crusaders, and was introduced to the Caribbean by the Spanish.

The fruit's association with Florida dates back to the early 1830s, when the prominent botanist Henry Perrine (then U.S. Consul in Campeche, Mexico) fortuitously planted limes from the Yucatán on Florida's Indian Key. In 1906, the pineapples that were the area's cottage industry were wiped out by a hurricane, and the limes presented an opportunity. Sadly, it was to be a short-lived success, as by 1926, severe hurricanes had also wiped out commercial Key lime production in southern Florida. These days, the larger, greener, hardier, seedless Persian limes are the prime crop grown in the Florida Keys, but a few locals do still grow the Key limes.

Where: *In Key West, FL,* Pepe's Café and Steak House, tel 305-294-7192, pepeskeywest .com; Kermit's Key West Key Lime Shoppe at two locations, tel 800-376-0806, keylimeshop .com; *in Miami Beach,* Joe's Stone Crab, tel 305-673-0365, joesstonecrab.com; *in Brooklyn,* Steve's Authentic Key Lime Pies, tel 718-858-5333, stevesauthentic.com. **Mail order:** Key West Key Lime Pie Co., tel 877-882-7437, key westkeylimepieco.com; for bottled Key lime juice, Nellie & Joe's Famous Lime Juice, tel 800-546-3743, keylimejuice.com; for whole fresh Key limes, except during summer months, Melissa's Produce, tel 800-588-0151, melissas.com; for dwarf Key lime trees, keylimepietree.com. **Further information and recipes:** *My Key West Kitchen* by Norman Van Aken and Justin Van Aken (2012); saveur.com (search key lime pie miami; frozen key lime pie on a stick). **Tip:** Some chefs dress up the pie by using true, baked pastry, but natives believe that this classic icebox pie turns soggy when anything but graham cracker (sometimes cinnamon-spiked) is used. Likewise, purists scoff at the practice of replacing the topping of whipped cream with meringue.

MARYLAND, BY WAY OF SOUTH CAROLINA

Lady Baltimore Cake

American

With three cloudlike layers of airy white cake alternating with a filling featuring dried fruits and a crunch of chopped pecans, and enveloped in an elegant satiny-white frosting, the Lady Baltimore cake stands tall as a symbol of the pastry kitchen of the American South.

One of many tearoom treats favored by ladies throughout the South toward the end of the nineteenth century, the cake was named for Joan Calvert, wife of the first Lord Baltimore. (The English colonizer who settled Baltimore is recognized by his own cake, the Lord Baltimore, but his—made with egg yolks and a filling of macaroon crumbs, toasted almonds, and maraschino cherries—never really took off.)

Although the city of Baltimore gets credit for the cake's name, recognition for its popularization belongs to the city of Charleston. When the baker Alicia Rhett Mayberry, who owned a café there, served Lady Baltimore cake to the visiting writer Owen Wistler at the turn of the twentieth century, he liked it so much that he used the name as the title of his next book. Published in 1906 and set in a fictionalized Charleston, its plot turns on a pivotal scene in which the narrator falls in love with a baker while ordering his own wedding cake—a Lady Baltimore. "Oh my goodness," the character effuses. "Did you ever taste it? It's all soft, and it's in layers, and it has nuts—but I can't write any more about it, my mouth waters too much." The book was well received, but the cake became the real star. For a while, it was the most-requested wedding cake at the café.

It's difficult to find a Lady Baltimore cake in

A light and luscious layer cake

a restaurant these days, but recipes abound in good Southern cookbooks. Technically, it is what's known in baking terminology as a silver cake—one made with egg whites only, no yolks. The resulting lightness is offset by the sweet, toothsome filling of raisins, nuts, and diced dried fruits like figs and dates moistened with a splash of sherry or brandy. The cake's beautiful snowdrift of icing is made by gradually pouring hot sugar syrup over stiffly beaten egg whites and whisking the mixture until it's utterly smooth and glossy.

Where: *In Baltimore,* Gertrude's restaurant in the Baltimore Museum of Fine Arts, tel 410-889-3399, gertrudes baltimore.com; *in Palo Alto, CA and environs,* The Prolific Oven Bakery & Café, prolificoven.com. **Further information and recipes:** *Southern Foods* by John Egerton (1993); *Mastering the Art of Southern Cooking* by Nathalie Dupree and Cynthia Graubart (2012); epicurious.com (search lady baltimore cake); marthastewart.com (search lady baltimore cake). **See also:** Irish Whiskey Cheesecake, page 47; Schwärzwalder Kirschtorte, page 311.

CLOUDS OF LEMON, SUNNY SKIES

Lemon Meringue Pie

American

Finding ways to prepare food the quick and easy way seems an especially American pursuit, one that came into full flower between the 1920s and 1950s as kitchens became more convenient and women grew busier outside

of the home. So it was with lemon meringue pie, a classic dessert that came in for its share of conveniencing with a shortcut that does not detract from the cool, sunny tartness of its custardy

lemon filling or the showy cloud of golden-brown meringue that crowns it.

In the place of a cooked egg custard, the filling gets its gentle sweetness and satiny texture from condensed milk flavored with freshly squeezed lemon juice and a generous amount of grated rind. A store-bought, ready-baked pie shell doesn't hurt either.

Easy Lemon Meringue Pie
6 to 8 servings

One 14-ounce can sweetened condensed milk
⅓ cup freshly squeezed lemon juice, strained
Grated zest of 1 small lemon
3 extra-large eggs, at room temperature, separated
1 empty, baked, 9-inch pie shell, in the pie pan
Pinch of salt
½ teaspoon cream of tartar
⅓ cup sugar

1. Combine the condensed milk, lemon juice, and grated zest with the egg yolks in a medium-size bowl and stir until smoothly blended. Do not whisk. Chill for 30 minutes. Pour the chilled mixture into the baked pie shell.
2. Preheat the oven to 350ºF.
3. Beat the egg whites with the salt in a large bowl

until the whites become frothy. Beat in the cream of tartar and, as the whites begin to form soft peaks, beat in the sugar 2 teaspoons at a time, until the whites are stiff but still shiny, about 4 minutes.
4. Heap the whites onto the lemon filling in the pie shell and, with the back of a metal spoon, spread and fluff the whites into peaks until the filling is completely covered, being sure that the whites are spread to the very edges of the pie crust.
5. Bake in the upper third of the preheated oven for about 15 minutes, or until the meringue peaks are golden brown. Cool at room temperature for at least 2 hours and up to 4 hours before serving. It is best not to chill the pie in the refrigerator, as that may cause the meringue to leak or wilt. Store loosely covered at room temperature.

WHERE: *In New York,* Bubby's, tel 212-219-0666, bubbys.com; Grand Central Oyster Bar, tel 212-490-6650, oysterbarny.com; *in Brooklyn,* Grand Central Oyster Bar Brooklyn, tel 347-294-0596, oysterbarbrooklyn.com; *in Highland, IL,* Blue Springs Café, tel 618-654-5788, foothipies.com. **FURTHER INFORMATION AND ADDITIONAL RECIPE:** *Hallelujah! The Welcome Table* by Maya Angelou (2007).

"IF THERE'S ANYTHING THAT A MAN LIKES BETTER THAN LIEDERKRANZ CHEESE, IT'S A SECOND HELPING OF LIEDERKRANZ CHEESE!"
—ADVERTISEMENT IN *LIFE* MAGAZINE, 1945

Liederkranz Cheese

American, German

A wonderful and nearly bygone accompaniment to beer, Leiderkranz is a descendant of the odoriferous German cheeses Limburger and Bismarck schlosskäse, with a meltingly soft, golden crust and a runny, ripe, and creamy interior. The cheese was developed by Adolphe Tode, owner of both a Manhattan delicatessen and the Monroe Cheese Company in Monroe, New York, in response to requests for old-country cheeses from his immigrant German clientele. He challenged his employees to come up with replicas, and in 1882, Emil Frey, one of Tode's cheesemakers, came through. As a test of its appeal, the cheese was served to New York's German American singing group, the Liederkranz Society, where it received high praise and was christened with the group's name, which means "wreath of song."

Some forty years later, few Americans know their Liederkranz from their Limburger—a shame, as the spreadable ivory cheese is spectacular atop thin, dark pumpernickel rye toast or any of the crackling Scandinavian crispbreads, especially when sprinkled with minced onion or chives. But there may be reason to sing again. Although the cheese nearly disappeared when it was discontinued by the Monroe Cheese Company in the mid-1980s,

in 2010 Wisconsin's DCI Cheese Company launched a line of Liederkranz, and it is once again being sold in blocks, fittingly staging its comeback in the American capital of cheese.

RETAIL AND MAIL ORDER: *In Milwaukee, WI,* West Allis Cheese & Sausage Shoppe, tel 414-543-4230, wacheese-gifts.com. MAIL ORDER: Hefti Creek Specialties, tel 608-237-1992, hefticreek .com. FURTHER INFORMATION AND RECIPE: *The German Cookbook* by Mimi Sheraton (2014) dcicheeseco.com/liederkranz. TIP: Broadly speaking, Liederkranz is classified as one of Germany's handcheeses (*handkäse*); see page 298.

||||||||||||||||||||||||||||||

LOBSTER GETS THE PRESIDENTIAL TREATMENT

Lobster Savannah

American (New England)

Although its name suggests the lowlands of the American South, lobster Savannah is actually a Boston original, an opulent dish of snowy boiled lobster meat blushed with rosy paprika and adorned with sherry, mushrooms, green peppers, pimientos, and a froth of béchamel sauce—all spooned back into the shell for a final baking under a sunny sprinkling of grated Parmesan. The result is a colorful, quintessentially rich, and aromatically complex blend of briny, buttery seafood, heady wine, and pungently sweet peppers.

The dish is strongly associated with Locke-Ober, once a stalwart on the Boston restaurant scene. First opened in 1875, it was an upscale hangout for politicians both local and national, as well as for affluent Harvard students and alums. (Former habitués of the clubby dining room included Theodore Roosevelt, Franklin Delano Roosevelt, and John F. Kennedy Jr.) Alas, it closed in 2012.

Lobster Savannah first appeared on the menu in the late 1930s, relatively expensive then as now and bearing more than a passing resemblance to the already-classic baked dish, lobster Thermidor; the latter is made of cooked, chopped lobster meat mixed with a béchamel sauce flavored with white wine and shallots. In those days lobster was plentiful and cheap, and adding butter, sherry, and other luxurious ingredients was a way of fancying it up to justify high prices. These days, the lobsters pack their own price punch, and although they're exquisite accompanied by nothing more than sizzling-hot melted butter and lemon, this elegantly stuffed presentation is entirely worth "shelling out" for.

WHERE: *In Boston,* Abe and Louie's, tel 617-536-6300, abeandlouies.com. FURTHER INFORMATION AND RECIPES: *Boston's Locke-Ober Café* by Ned and Pam Bradford (1978); for lobster Thermidor, *The Fannie Farmer Cookbook,* 13th edition, by Marion Cunningham (1996); food network.com (search lobster savannah).

‖‖‖‖‖‖‖‖‖‖‖‖‖‖‖‖‖‖‖‖‖‖‖‖‖‖‖‖‖

THE GREAT *HOMARUS AMERICANUS*

Maine Lobster

American (New England)

Shellfish lovers in other parts of the world may celebrate lobsters that are hairy, spiny, hunchbacked, shovel-headed, or even clawless, but Americans take pride in the specimen native to Maine—the one that famously offers the

pearliest meat, crimson-tinged and most succulent when extracted from the large, plump claws. Only slightly less moist are the substantial pieces from the tail, the knuckles, and even the thinnest legs of this magnificent crustacean offer fine picking for those diligent enough to crack them open and gnaw out the sublime shreds of meat. The gifts don't stop there, as there is still serious gustatory pleasure to be found in the gray-green tomalley, or liver, or in the jewel-like chunks of coral roe in females, both with a quintessential deep-sea flavor.

"Nowhere in the world . . . is the seafloor as densely populated with lobsters as in the Gulf of Maine," writes Trevor Corson in his book *The Secret Life of Lobsters.* Thanks to the strictly observed conservation he describes, that felicitous fact should remain true for a long time. And that's very welcome news, as the highly prized Maine lobster is exported to luxury restaurants almost everywhere in the world.

Although much is made of soft-shell lobsters caught in early summer, when they are molting, full-grown hard-shells are firmer and more pungently saline. And despite the popular belief that small specimens taste best and larger ones are tough, Mainers consider the most flavorful to be those weighing at least two pounds. Toughness results from overcooking, which is usually the result of fear that a very large lobster will emerge half-raw. Gentle boiling, or better yet, steaming, nets a silky-soft reward, one best enhanced by rivulets of hot melted butter and a dash or two of lemon juice—nothing more.

Broiling is another favorite cooking method, but it requires gentle heat and lavish, frequent bastings of butter—otherwise it's too harsh a process for the delicate taste, aroma, and texture of the meat.

In addition to being the base for elegant chowders and bisques, salads and boils, lobster meat triumphs in that other Maine specialty: the lobster roll, a tradition prepared in either of two ways, and most delightful when enjoyed at casual shacks set on the water's edge. The cooked meat, still warm, may be glossed with melted butter, or it may be chilled and dressed with mayonnaise as a salad. Either way, it's spooned into long, toasted "slices," top-cut hot dog rolls, for a treat that is sublimely soft and succulent—and ultimately much debated.

It may seem strange that such a simple preparation could inspire so much rating and counter-rating of lobster shacks, but the rolls do vary. There is the amount and freshness of the meat to consider, as well as the inclusion or exclusion of celery, the toastiness of the roll, and the kind and quantity of mayonnaise used. (For the lobster's sake, make it Hellmann's.) At Mabel's Lobster Claw in Kennebunkport—a joint said to be favored by the Bush family, whose summer compound is nearby—the salad is based only on the delectably plump knuckles of meat, extracted from the joints that link the claws to the body.

WHERE: *In Kennebunkport, ME,* Mabel's Lobster Claw, tel 207-967-2562, mabelslobster .com; *in Wiscasset, ME,* Red's Eats, tel 207-882-6128; *in Belfast, ME,* Young's Lobster Pound, tel

207-338-1160, youngslobsterpound.webs.com; *in Boston and environs,* Jasper White's Summer Shack, summershackrestaurant.com; *in New York,* Pearl Oyster Bar, tel 212-691-8211, pearl oysterbar.com; The Lobster Place at Chelsea Market, tel 212-255-5672, lobsterplace.com; Grand Central Oyster Bar, 212-490-6650, oyster barny.com; *in Brooklyn,* Grand Central Oyster Bar Brooklyn, tel 347-294-0596, oysterbarbrooklyn .com; *in Minneapolis,* Smack Shack, tel 612-259-7288, smack-shack.com; *in Austin, TX,* Perla's Seafood and Oyster Bar, tel 512-291-7300, perlas austin.com; *in Toronto,* Oyster Boy, tel 416-534-3432, oysterboy.ca. **MAIL ORDER:** Young's Lobster Pound, tel 207-338-1160, youngslobsterpound .webs.com. **FURTHER INFORMATION AND RECIPES:** *Lobster Rolls & Blueberry Pie* by Rebecca Charles and Deborah DiClementi (2003); *Jasper White's Cooking from New England* by Jasper White (1998); epicurious.com (search maine lobster bake; lobster blt; lobster rolls; corn and lobster chowder). **TIP:** Although Maine's gift to gourmandise is unsurpassed, it seems only fair to point out that the next-best lobsters are harvested in Long Island, New York, in waters around Montauk Point; these have slightly smaller, rounder claws, but lend themselves to similar delights.

FOR GOTHAM CHOWDERHEADS

Manhattan Clam Chowder

American (New York)

As succulent as the creamy salt pork, potato, onion, and mollusk combination known as New England clam chowder can be, New Yorkers tend to vote in favor of their own Manhattan version, with a light tomato broth that allows the essence of clams to come through clear and briny. Best when not thickened by starch, it's a minestrone-like soup, bright with carrots, onions, celery, potatoes, and plenty of chopped, giant chowder clams, accented by the defining flavor of thyme; unfortunately, a cornstarch-laden version from a can tends to be ubiquitous in the Greek coffee shops of New York City, especially on Fridays, a holdover from the time when Catholics could not eat meat on that day. These days, the local chowder tends to reach its summit at Aquagrill in Soho, and (usually) at the Oyster Bar in Grand Central Terminal, if it has not thickened down as the day wears on.

Outside of Manhattan, the best results may be ensured by home preparation. The flavor improves after twenty-four hours, so it's best to prepare the chowder a day ahead and reheat it before serving.

Manhattan Clam Chowder

Serves 6 as an appetizer

20 to 24 large chowder clams, or 40 to
    48 cherrystone clams, opened, with
    their liquor
2 medium-size carrots, peeled and diced
1 large onion, peeled and diced
2 ribs celery, diced
3 tablespoons unsalted butter
1 can (about 28 ounces) whole tomatoes
    with their liquid
2 to 3 cups boiling water, as needed
1 to 2 teaspoons salt
1 large boiling potato, peeled and diced
1 to 2 teaspoons dried thyme leaves
Freshly ground black pepper

1. Trim the hard portions of the clams from the soft parts and reserve them separately, as well as their liquor. Let the liquor stand so the sand will settle.

2. In a 2½-quart stainless steel or enameled soup pot or saucepan over medium-low heat, slowly sauté the carrots, onions, and celery in the butter until the vegetables begin to soften and become bright, about 5 minutes; do not brown them.

3. Remove the tomatoes from their liquid, crush them, and add them to the pot. Measure the tomato liquid and add to it enough boiling water to make 4 cups. Add the tomato water to the pot, along with the hard portions of the clams and 1 teaspoon salt. Simmer gently for about 20 minutes, until the clam pieces begin to soften.

4. Add the potato, the soft clam meat, the clam liquor, and 1 teaspoon thyme. Simmer until all the ingredients are tender, about 30 minutes. Taste for seasoning and add pepper to taste, and more salt and/or thyme, as needed. Simmer

briefly, then serve, or bring to room temperature, cover, and refrigerate. The chowder will keep, covered and refrigerated, for up to 5 days. To reheat the chowder, bring to room temperature for 30 minutes, then simmer over low heat until thoroughly hot. Do not allow to boil.

WHERE: *In New York,* Aquagrill, tel 212-274-0505, aquagrill.com; Grand Central Oyster Bar & Restaurant, tel 212-490-6650, oysterbarny.com; The Lobster Place at Chelsea Market, tel 212-255-5672, lobsterplace.com; *in Brooklyn,* Grand Central Oyster Bar Brooklyn, tel 347-294-0596, oysterbarbrooklyn.com; *in New York and Long Island,* Citarella at multiple locations, citarella .com. **TIP:** Using larger clams such as quahogs yields a more flavorful result, and they can usually be ordered a few days in advance from a fishmonger. **SEE ALSO:** Cioppino, page 545; Brodetto Vastese, page 170; Halászlé, page 393.

SUCCOTASH, CAJUN STYLE

Maque Choux

American (Louisianan)

Pronounced "mock shoe," Louisiana's succotash-like vegetable stew is one of summer's most cherished and colorful dishes, bright with flashes of red, green, and gold. Speculations as to the origin of its name range from a riff on an Afro–Native

Indian or Afro-French phrase to pure Cajun.

Richly flavorful and aromatically complex, with hints of bacon and butter, garlic, thyme, and bay leaf anointing its corn kernels, green peppers, onions, and tomatoes, it's a dish that withstands any number of variations. Some cooks add diced celery along with the green peppers to create the standard Louisiana culinary trinity (peppers, onion, celery), while others include okra whenever young and tender pods are available.

There are those who make the mistake of adding sugar, but grown-ups opt for several shots of Tabasco or hot chile peppers. The most significant variation lies in the choice of whether

to add cream. Doing so may lend a touch of French refinement, but at the expense of a more characteristic, zingy sprightliness.

Maque Choux
Serves 6 as a side dish

3 slices lean bacon, coarsely chopped (optional)

3 tablespoons unsalted butter or 1½ tablespoons butter and 1½ tablespoons olive oil, or more if needed

1 large green bell pepper, stemmed, seeded, and diced

1 medium-size onion, peeled and diced

1 teaspoon coarse salt

1 large or 2 small cloves of garlic, peeled
and thinly sliced
8 ounces small young okra pods, trimmed
and sliced (optional)
2 teaspoons dried thyme, crushed
1 large bay leaf
1 can (14 to 16 ounces) American-style
whole peeled tomatoes (without basil
or Italian seasonings)
Few drops of Tabasco sauce or 1 small hot
chile, seeded and diced (optional)
Freshly ground black pepper
4 medium-size ears of corn, husked

1. Slowly fry the bacon pieces, if using, in a heavy 2-quart casserole or saucepan (preferably of enameled cast iron), over moderate heat, until the fat is completely rendered and they are beginning to turn golden brown.

2. Add the butter and/or oil and heat for about 2 minutes before stirring in the green pepper and onion. Add more butter or oil if it's too dry for sautéing. Sprinkle with the salt and sauté over low heat, stirring frequently, until the vegetables are soft but have not taken on color.

3. Add the garlic, okra (if using), thyme, and bay leaf. Sauté slowly, stirring gently but almost constantly, until the okra stops "stringing" (extruding slimy strings), 7 to 8 minutes. If you aren't using okra, sauté until the garlic softens, about 2 minutes.

4. Crush the tomatoes and strain and reserve their liquid. Add the crushed tomatoes to the vegetables, along with the Tabasco sauce or

chile and several grindings of black pepper, and simmer slowly until the okra and other vegetables are thoroughly cooked and the tomatoes have broken down into a light sauce. Add some of the reserved tomato liquid as needed to keep the mixture from scorching.

5. Cut the kernels off the ears of corn. If you are serving immediately, add the corn to the vegetables and cook over moderate heat, stirring frequently for 10 to 15 minutes. Adjust the seasonings and remove the bay leaf before serving. If you are going to wait several hours before serving, do not add the corn. Turn off the heat, cover the pot, and set it aside at room temperature for up to 4 hours. When you are ready to serve, add the corn and cook gently over low heat. Reheated leftover maque choux is also delicious, as the softness of the corn and other vegetables lends an extra, soothing richness. Covered and refrigerated, it will keep for 4 to 5 days.

WHERE: *In Houston*, Brennan's, tel 713-522-9711, brennanshouston.com; *in New Orleans*, K-Paul's Louisiana Kitchen, tel 504-596-2530, chef paul.com/kpaul; *in Colorado Springs, CO*, Culpepper's Cajun Kitchen, tel 719-282-8479, cul peppers.net. **FURTHER INFORMATION AND OTHER RECI-PES:** *Chef Paul Prudhomme's Louisiana Kitchen* by Paul Prudhomme (1984); saveur.com (search maque choux and shrimp); epicurious.com (search corn and tasso maque choux). **TIP:** To serve maque choux as a main course, add 1 pound of small peeled, deveined shrimp to the vegetable mixture with the corn kernels, and simmer for 7 to 8 minutes until the shrimp are cooked.

AN ICONIC CAMPFIRE TREAT

Toasted Marshmallows

American

What exactly is a marshmallow? Really very little besides sugar and egg whites. But simplicity does not obviate the possibility of gastronomic triumph—in this case, that of a chewy, milk-white confection so airy it feels as though one is eating a small, sweet, and gentle cloud.

Beguiling even plain, marsh-mallows reach their apotheosis roasted over an open fire. Ideally they are speared onto young, green branches (dryer branches will burn) and held over a camp-fire (or, in a pinch, over a burner on a kitchen range), until brown and bubbling with hot, caramelizing sugar. That sizzling glaze creates the tantalizing contrast between the crisp, gently burnished outside and its creamy, molten center. If you sandwich them with a square of chocolate between graham crackers, you get the treat known to American children everywhere as the s'more. It's been a favorite since 1927, when the recipe was printed in the official Girl Scout Handbook, its magic lying in the way the marshmallow becomes a heat source that melts the chocolate to gooey, oozy perfection.

The candy's original confectioners took inspiration by way of the marshmallow plant (*Althaea officinalis*). Native to Europe and Asia, this member of the hollyhock family grows in salt marshes, its roots extruding a gummy substance that has been eaten in various forms since ancient times.

The traditional campfire treat

By the mid-nineteenth century, French confectioners were whipping marshmallow sap with sugar and egg whites to achieve a mushy froth that set to a gentle firmness; then, much like our molecular chefs of today, the early confectioners began to experiment, eventually learning to create marshmallows without relying on the plant itself.

To make their marshmallow-less marshmallow, they heated sugar to a syrup and then to the "hard ball stage"—when it reaches at least 121°C (250°F) on a candy thermometer and becomes quite sticky, yet firm enough to hold a shape. Combined with either gelatin or gum arabic, the mixture was whisked into beaten egg whites, dusted with additional sugar, and left to set, and then cut into cubes or rounds. Another one of Mother Nature's triumphs.

FURTHER INFORMATION AND RECIPES: foodnetwork.com (search homemade marshmallows); marthastewart.com (search homemade marshmallow recipe); allrecipes.com (search s'mores). **TIP:** Homemade marshmallows are usually softer and more delicate than commercial versions.

WAKE UP AND SMELL THE ICE CREAM

McConnell's Turkish Coffee Ice Cream

American (Californian)

There are many good coffee ice creams scooped up around the world, but for the lushest socko experience, none can vie with the Turkish coffee ice cream at the cool, sweet California temptation that is McConnell's.

An alluring, deep black-brown with a refreshing jolt of aroma, the creamy base gets a nicely gritty texture and an extra-rich essence from the fine grounds of Turkish-style, dark-roasted coffee stirred through it, just as such grounds remain in cups of the traditional hot brew (see page 493). Exactly the right amount of sugar balances the burnished, caffeine-zapped bitterness, rendering this a most addictive and stimulating frozen treat.

If you can get past the addiction, once you've had McConnell's Turkish coffee ice cream a few times, you might try three of its other delectable flavors: Brazilian coffee, tamer and silkier than the Turkish; island coconut, with flaky chips of sweet white coconut meat; and sherry-scented egg nog, tasting like Christmas all year round.

All of the ice creams offered in McConnell's sparkling, inviting shops are all-natural, based on hormone-free sweet cream, with egg yolks as the only stabilizers; their 15-percent overrun (the

percentage of air beaten into the cream) is low enough to assure a luxuriously thick ice cream. Historically, many Americans have preferred a high overrun, resulting in a light and airy ice cream they can eat more of by volume—the way ice cream is sold in the States. Selling by weight—the practice in Europe—gives a more accurate measure of actual content.

WHERE: *In Santa Barbara and Ventura, CA,* at three locations, McConnell's Fine Ice Creams, mcconnells.com. Also available in prepacked pints at California supermarkets: Ralphs, Vons, Albertsons, Bristol Farms, Gelson's, and Whole Foods.

FRIED CATFISH ON A MARSH

Middendorf's Thinfish

American (Louisianan)

There are more than 2,000 varieties of mud-loving, bottom-dwelling catfish in the world, living in inland and coastal waters on every continent except Antarctica. In Indonesia, they are grilled and sold from street carts. In India,

they are considered a special food to be eaten during monsoons. In Hungary, they are cooked in paprika sauce and served with tiny dumplings and homemade cheese curds. But in the American South, the words *fish fry* mean one thing and one thing only: catfish, and indeed, here the catfish is almost always fried.

Catfish farming has been big business in the South ever since the late 1970s, when farmers in the Mississippi Delta, facing a recession, traded in their soybean and cotton fields and instead dug ponds on their properties. And, as it turned out, catfish were the rare instance in which a farmed product tastes better than its wild cousin. The farmed fish is known for its sweetness, which the farmers attribute to the fact that the scavenging fish are continually exposed to controlled resources like clean water and pure food (corn and soy pellets,

naturally). Wild catfish, on the other hand, swim in often muddy waters, feeding at the bottom, and so can have a characteristically earthy flavor.

The single best place to eat Southern-fried catfish is at a rollicking joint called Middendorf's in Akers, Louisiana, about 40 miles north of New Orleans. Open since 1934, and only recently under new management—the original owners, who operated the place for three generations, sold in the aftermath of Hurricane Katrina—the place is a kind of compound, with an enormous dining room and waterside decks from which patrons can spy egrets and cranes in the marshes of Lake Maurepas.

This is bayou country, but its considerable charms are still trumped by the fish. You can get it fried in the usual way (called "thick" at Middendorf's), or opt for the house specialty of "thinfish," in which an already thin catfish fillet is sliced horizontally into delicately thin halves, much like scallopines. Dredged in fine cornmeal batter (known as fish fry), sprinkled liberally with black pepper, and then deep-fried in hot fat, the result is an utterly crisp affair. Some excellent, tiny, onion-flavored hushpuppies on the side round out the experience.

The city of New Orleans has its share of good eating, but for a down-home experience of the thinnest, crunchiest fish fry around, Middendorf's is worth the trip.

WHERE: 75 Manchac Way, Akers, LA, tel 985-386-6666, middendorfsrestaurant.com. **FURTHER INFORMATION AND RECIPES:** *Chef Paul Prudhomme's Louisiana Kitchen* by Paul Prudhomme (1984); *Eula Mae's Cajun Kitchen* by Eula Mae Dore and Marcelle Bienvenu; epicurious.com (search southern fried catfish; beer-battered catfish on vinegar slaw); uscatfish.com (click Recipes). **SPECIAL EVENTS:** World Catfish Festival, Belzoni, MS, April, belzonims.com/catfishfest .htm; "World's Biggest Fish Fry," Paris, TN, April, worldsbiggestfishfry.com.

A THOUSAND-LAYERED TREAT

Mille Crêpes at Lady M

American, French

In truth, they number fewer than a thousand, but nevertheless, the pile-up of twenty or so silken, golden-edged crêpes reaches true perfection at the café and patisserie Lady M, on Manhattan's Upper East Side (as well as several other locations). The artistry with which this dessert is made obviously appeals to the art gallery crowd in this tony neighborhood. Layered with a lusciously airy crème St-Honoré—vanilla custard pastry cream aerated with whipped cream—they make for a cool and towering enticement.

In France, the delicate treat is dubbed *gâteau de crêpes* and is traditionally enjoyed on February 2, for the holiday of La Chandeleur, or Candlemas. Superstition has it that if the cook flips a test crêpe successfully without it falling to the floor, hitting the ceiling, tearing, or developing a crease, he or she will have a very good year. At the least, a very good day is guaranteed to those who sample this lush dessert.

After the test run, the crêpes (made much like those for blintzes, see page 433, or palatschinken, see page 328) are turned out of the pan gilded on both sides. Kept moist as they cool, they are then spread with the pastry cream and stacked into layers. The top crêpe gets a lacy glaze of golden-brown caramelized sugar, and the cake is chilled to firmness, later to be sliced downward in towering wedges that reveal the thin, scrumptious layers of crêpe and filling.

Then it's time for the eating, which itself provides a many-layered thrill. First comes the gentle nudging of fork tines down through the soft, yielding layers, then the sweet aroma of cream, sugar, and vanilla, and finally the slightly chilly, creamy, and gently soft contrast of crêpe and cream. A couple of ripe strawberries or raspberries might be in order as a garnish, as would a glass of Champagne or chilled Château d'Yquem, or even a thin porcelain cup of Ethiopia's best Harar coffee. (A cappuccino, however, would be overkill.)

DINE IN, RETAIL, AND MAIL ORDER:, 41 East 78th St., New York, NY, tel 212-452-2222; The Plaza Food Hall, 1 West 59th St., New York, NY, tel

212-986-9260; Bryant Park Cake Boutique, 36 West 40th St., New York, NY, tel 212-452-2222; Los Angeles Cake Boutique, 8718 West 3rd St., Los Angeles, CA, tel 424-279-9495; Marina Square Shopping Mall, 6 Raffles Boulevard, Singapore, tel 65/6820-0830, ladym.com.

———————————————|||||||||||||||||||||||||||||||||———————————————

MOONPIES MAKING WHOOPIE

MoonPies

American

A chocolate-covered-marshmallow-and-graham-cracker sandwich seems like a treat any home kitchen dabbler might have come up with on a rainy day, but the classic cookie was actually the invention of the workers of the Chattanooga Baking Company of Chattanooga, Tennessee, founded in 1902.

In its early days, the company produced as many as 150 different types of soda crackers, animal crackers, cheese wafers, and other baked goods. But around 1917, a company salesman named Earl Mitchell noticed workers dipping graham crackers into melted marshmallow and letting them dry on the windowsill. His inspired tweak was to then dip the cookies in chocolate, and thus the MoonPie was born—tempting future generations with the contrast of crisp cracker, creamy marshmallow, and rich, enveloping chocolate. An alternative story has Mitchell coming up with the cookie by getting a Kentucky coal miner to describe his ideal snack, its shape and size (and ultimately, name) springing from the moment the miner looked up at the night sky and framed the full moon with his hands.

The response to the hybrid cookie-candy, a mess of sweetness akin to a hardened but still delicious s'more, was immediate, intense, and enduring. During the 1930s, MoonPies were a staple for hungry laborers, and by 1941, as World War II broke out, the Chattanooga Baking Company was sending hundreds of thousands of MoonPies to GIs stationed abroad, in what was both a generous move and a stroke of

branding genius. When NASCAR was officially founded in 1947, the MoonPie was there, too—the pies were a classic snack that fans packed into their sack lunches on race day, and they would forever be associated with the Daytona 500, first raced in 1957. Nowadays, nearly a million MoonPies are produced every day.

New England has its own take on the cookie "pie"—the Whoopie Pie, generally thought to be a creation of the Amish as a way to use leftover cake batter. Its soft, cakelike cookies—usually chocolate—encase a frosting or marshmallow filling. Legend has it that Amish women put the treats in farmers' lunch pails; when the farmers found them, they'd exclaim "whoopee!"

RETAIL AND MAIL ORDER: *In Chattanooga, Lynchburg, and Pigeon Forge, TN, and Charleston, SC,* Chattanooga Bakery, tel 423-877-0592, moonpie.com. MAIL ORDER: For whoopie pies, Wicked Whoopies, tel 877-447-2629, wickedwhoopies.com. FURTHER INFORMATION AND RECIPES: For recipes using MoonPies, moonpie.com; for homemade, allrecipes.com (search southern moon pies; whoopie pies); epicurious.com (search chocolate-oatmeal moon pies; whoopie pies).

||||||||||||||||||||||||||||||||

A HERO IN THE ROUND

Muffaletta

American (New Orleanian), Italian

Italo–New Orleanian cuisine is the special gift of the Italian immigrants, mainly from Sicily, who developed a Southern American culinary repertoire all their own, and one of its most lavish examples is this delectable riff on the hero, po'boy,

and submarine sandwich. Brought to true and epic magnificence at the Central Grocery, and to almost equal glory at the bar-tavern that is the old Napoleon House, both in the French Quarter, the muffaletta begins with a lightly golden, soft-crusted, round, Italian-style bread—really a giant roll, about ten inches in diameter.

The cut inner white surfaces of the bread are lightly brushed with olive oil, and then the sandwich construction begins. Layerings of firm, fatty, pungently peppered and garlicked Italian salami and rose-pink slabs of cooked ham alternate with sharp provolone cheese and, unless declined, abundant minced garlic. The real magic is supplied by slathers of olive oil and layers of finely chopped vegetable salads—green Sicilian olives and red pimientos, and a rainbow of vinegar-and-olive-oil-dressed pickled

vegetables such as cauliflower, red and green peppers, carrots, and white onions, all seasoned with oregano, more garlic, and a verdant toss of parsley. The oil will deliciously seep into the bread as the sandwich is firmly pressed together, somewhat in the manner of Provence's *pan bagnat* (see page 109).

Cut into quarters, the muffaletta—or "little muff"—is a lusciously leaky indulgence, and a meal best eaten with a bib of paper napkins.

WHERE: *In New Orleans,* Central Grocery, tel 504-523-1620, centralgroceryneworleans.com; Napoleon House, tel 504-524-9752, napoleon house.com. **FURTHER INFORMATION AND RECIPES:** *Cooking Up a Storm* by Marcelle Bienvenu and Judy Walker (2008); allrecipes.com (search muffaletta sandwich; olive salad for muffalettas; real n'awlins muffaletta).

||||||||||||||||||||||||||||||||

A SWEET FORM OF DIPLOMACY

Nesselrode Pie

American

Cool and airy and fragrant with rum, sherry, or brandy (alone or in any combination), Nesselrode pie is a deliciously frothy example of culinary influence. Essentially a cloud-light Bavarian cream mounded into a pie shell,

the dessert is named after one Karl Vasilyevich, aka Count Nesselrode, a Russian diplomat who was the son of a German count of the Holy

Roman Empire. The highlight of his distinguished nineteenth-century career, spent furthering Russia's interests in Europe, was negotiating the Treaty of Paris after the Crimean War.

In all, Nesselrode was a highly unlikely source for culinary inspiration, and credit doubtless belongs to his head chef, a man named Mouy. Nevertheless, Nesselrode will forever be associated with a genre of chestnut-flavored sweets, ethereally beguiling and, though now rare, once virtually ubiquitous. Arguably, the best of these is the Nesselrode pie: a chestnut custard cream mixed with candied fruits, currants, golden raisins, and whipped cream. The pudding became popular in the sweet shops of France and England, eventually making its way across the ocean and gaining fame in the 1920s as a Christmas dessert in New York restaurants. By the 1950s, it had somehow become a particular favorite in seafood restaurants, although it was still a hit in many of the era's other upscale restaurants, including Lindy's and Longchamps.

The Nesselrode and a variety of other soufflèd "chiffon" pies were also the specialty of one Mrs. Hortense Spier, of Hortense Spier Pies, on the Upper West Side of New York City. She sold desserts to restaurants all over Manhattan in the 1940s and '50s, but her biggest triumph was her Nesselrode filling—an especially voluptuous creation of Bavarian cream spiked with chestnuts and lots of candied fruits, chocolate shavings, and rum, all inflated to sublimity with beaten egg whites and clouds of whipped cream. Spier's children took over her bakery after her death in 1934, but by 1968 even her descendants were gone—and, sadly, the pies along with them. A sentimental favorite of home bakers with a taste for nostalgia, it only occasionally appears on restaurant menus.

WHERE: *In Orangeburg, NY,* at Christmastime, Le Gateau Suisse, tel 845-365-2194, legateau suisse.com. **FURTHER INFORMATION AND RECIPES:** *The New York Times Cookbook* edited by Craig Claiborne (1990); *New York Cookbook* by Molly O'Neill (1992); thefoodmaven.com (search nesselrode); savour-fare.com (search nesselrode); nytimes.com (search de gustibus nesselrode).

HOLD THE TOMATOES, BUT NOT THE CRACKERS

New England Clam Chowder

American

It wasn't too long after the Pilgrims landed near Plymouth Rock, in the winter of 1620, that they looked around for something hot to eat. And it was probably not too long after that that they encountered, either on their own or with help from the

Native Americans, the delicious bivalves common to New England's shores. The clams were cooked in covered pots of water over an open flame—the pot being key, as some claim the word *chowder* comes from the French term *chaudière,* meaning an iron cooking vessel.

Whatever the origins of its name, clam chowder is one of the earliest and most iconic of American dishes. The New England style, first referred to in print around 1730, was based on a water broth, but the creamy concoction we now think of as New England clam chowder was already favored at the beginning of the nineteenth century. Since then, its basic formula remains largely unchanged: a stew enriched with diced salt pork, tender flecks of sweet onions, and nicely substantial chunks of potato, all offsetting briny clams gentled with milk.

By the end of the century, a few regional variations had sprung up. Some cooks added chopped fish or crushed crackers or (quite wisely) butter; a thinner, milkier version can be found in Rhode Island's chowder, still strong and delicious. The creamy, aromatic soup is still sacred in New England, celebrated with chowder societies, competitions, festivals, and boat races.

For the fullest flavor, the majestic quahog (pronounced CWAH-hog), a hard-shell clam larger than three inches in diameter, is hard to beat. Too tough to be eaten raw, it cooks slowly and long, adding a delicious zest to chowders. (Quahogs measuring less than two inches in diameter are considered littlenecks; between two and three inches, they're called cherrystones. Both are tender and best eaten raw.)

Where: *In Plymouth, MA,* Wood's Seafood, tel 508-746-0261, woodsseafoods.com; *in Boston and environs,* Jasper White's Summer Shack, summershackrestaurant.com; *in Lincolnville, ME,* The Lobster Pound, tel 207-789-5550, lobster poundmaine.com; *in New York,* Pearl Oyster Bar, tel 212-691-8211, pearloysterbar.com; The Clam, tel 212-242-7420, theclamnyc.com; Adler, tel 212-539-1900, adlernyc.com; Grand Central Oyster Bar, 212-490-6650, oysterbarny.com; *in Brooklyn,* Grand Central Oyster Bar Brooklyn, tel 347-294-0596, oysterbarbrooklyn.com; *in Seattle,* The Walrus and the Carpenter Oyster Bar, tel 206-395-9227, thewalrusbar.com; *in Toronto,* Oyster Boy, tel 416-534-3432, oysterboy.ca. **Further information and recipes:** *Jasper White's Cooking from New England* by Jasper White (1998); *The Oyster Bar Cookbook* by Raymond Schilcher (1989); foodnetwork.com (search new england clam chowder lagasse). **Special event:** Great Chowder Cook-Off, Newport, RI, June, newportwaterfrontevents.com.

THE TREASURE OF THE SANDS

North Atlantic Clams on the Half-Shell

American (New England, Mid-Atlantic)

Describing clams as "the treasure hid in the sand," Elder William Brewster thanked God for the food that saw the Pilgrims through that first difficult winter in the Massachusetts Bay Colony—but even those fortunates who don't have to rely solely on the sea-breezy bivalves for nourishment may well thank the heavens for their existence.

Although there are clams of many types in various parts of the United States and the world, none are so brazenly bracing as those dug out of muddy shorelines along the North Atlantic Ocean, from Maine to New Jersey. The very essence of an East Coast summer lies in these salty, oozily silky *Mercenaria mercenaria*; farther south, clams seem to lose their diamond sparkle and intense flavor, and shellfish lovers are better off switching to crabs.

The clams are best eaten icily cold and raw, slurped right off the half-shell without interference from jazzed-up cocktail sauces or anything more than a trickle of fresh lemon juice and, intermittently, a few little round oyster crackers to help refresh the palate. The deepest pleasure seems to come from eating them outdoors, as close as possible to the ocean. Never mind about that table service—in contrast to the more serious, elegant oyster, these mollusks just seem to invite informality.

With their high content of protein and zinc, both the petite littlenecks (450 to a bushel) and the slightly larger cherrystones (300 to 325 to a bushel) can be cooked up into many tempting dishes, from clams casino (see page 546) to *spaghetti alle vongole*. Technically, all hard-shells fall into the general category of quahogs, but that name is generally reserved for the largest (125 to a bushel) hard-shell clams, so tough they are relegated to New England and Manhattan chowder pots (see pages 603 and 595). These

The tempting spoils of a successful clam dig

are delicious options, but none compares with the raw, unadorned treatment that requires careful work with a clam knife or oyster knife; the clams' white to stone-gray shells can shut tightly, hence the expression "to clam up."

WHERE: *In Essex, MA,* Woodman's of Essex, tel 800-649-1773, woodmans.com; *in Ipswich, MA,* Clam Box, tel 978-356-9707, ipswichma .com/clambox; *in Boston and environs,* Jasper White's Summer Shack, summershackrestaurant .com; *in Wellfleet, MA,* Mac's Seafood, tel 800-214-0477, macsseafood.com; *in New York,* The Lobster Place at Chelsea Market, tel 212-255-5672, lobsterplace.com; The John Dory Oyster Bar, tel 212-792-9000, thejohndory.com; Grand Central Oyster Bar, tel 212-490-6650, oyster barny.com; Mary's Fish Camp, marysfishcamp .com; *in Brooklyn,* Grand Central Oyster Bar Brooklyn, tel 347-294-0596, oysterbarbrooklyn .com; *in Greenport, NY,* Claudio's Clam Bar, tel 631-477-1889, claudios.com; *in Nassawadox, VA,* The Great Machipongo Clam Shack, tel 757-442-3800, thegreatmachipongoclamshack.com; *in Santa Barbara and Ventura, CA,* Brophy Bros. Restaurant and Clam Bar at two locations, brophybros.com. **RETAIL AND MAIL ORDER:** *In Belfast, ME,* Young's Lobster Pound, tel 207-338-1160, youngslobsterpound.webs.com. **FURTHER INFORMATION AND RECIPES:** *North Atlantic Seafood* by Alan Davidson (2012); **SPECIAL EVENTS:** Yarmouth Clam Festival, July, clamfestival.com; for other events in the U.S. and Canada, we loveclams.com (click Festivals).

―――――|||||||||||||||||||||||||||||―――――

A HUNDRED-YEAR-OLD CLASSIC

Oreos

American

As ageless as Cleopatra, and perhaps a bit more beloved, America's favorite chocolate cookie celebrated its centennial birthday on March 6, 2012. One hundred years after its initial release, this triumph of the Nabisco division of Kraft Foods still brings double-decker pleasure to children and grown-up cookie lovers, who famously enjoy the treat in a variety of ways.

All cherish the crackling crispness and toasty chocolate flavor of its cookie parts, fun to bite into when the sandwich is eaten intact, with the creamy, soft, and sugary white filling gentling the cookies' flavor and texture. Some, in an effort to prolong the pleasure, take the sandwich apart, the better to enjoy the filling as an intensely sugary treat. Some treat the cookies to a dip in a glass of cold milk—quick enough so that they don't dissolve and drown, but still effective in softening the cookies and imparting that delicious Oreo quality to the milk itself.

Not content with simply nibbling Oreos out of hand, fans are also incorporating them into recipes for piecrusts, cookies, and more. Crushed to fine crumbs with a rolling pin, the Oreo can lend crunchiness to a scoop of ice cream or a full-fledged sundae. (Indeed, the cookie has inspired its very own ice-cream flavor in cookies 'n cream, seen in innumerable ice-cream shops and freezer aisles the world over.)

The cookie was invented in New York's Chelsea neighborhood in 1912, in the building that now houses the Chelsea Market, and the name Oreo seems most likely to have come from the Greek *oreo,* meaning beautiful or nicely done. Although the lacy embossing on the cookie's surface has been redesigned several times, it still follows the original concept: a wreath centered around the word *Oreo.* But the cookie's name has been altered through the years, from the original Oreo Biscuit to the Oreo Sandwich, to the Oreo Creme Sandwich and, since 1976, to the Oreo Chocolate Sandwich Cookie. By any name, it seems likely to retain its "lick and dunk" mystique for at least one hundred years more.

WHERE: Any supermarket or grocery store. **FURTHER INFORMATION AND RECIPES:** *Oreo with a Twist* by Oreo and Jennifer Darling (1999); oreo .com (click Recipes); epicurious.com (search oreo overkill pie); cookstr.com (search chocolate cream sandwiches; mississippi mud pie).

NEVER PITY A PO'BOY

Oyster Po'boy

American (New Orleanian)

The signature sandwich of the city of New Orleans, the po'boy belongs to the general class of handheld super-sandwiches like heroes, subs, gyros, and grinders—this one a Depression-era staple first created around 1929,

when the coffee shop owners and onetime streetcar workers Bennie and Clovis Martin were trying to find a cheap and easy way to feed their former colleagues, who were on strike for higher pay. "Whenever we saw one of the striking men coming," Bennie Martin recalled, "one of us would say, 'Here comes another poor boy.'" The Martins enlisted a baker named John Gendusa (whose eponymous bakery is still in operation in New Orleans, with his great-grandson at the helm) to create loaves wide enough to hold substantial fillings that were cheap then, and a sandwich classic was born.

New Orleans–style French bread was already well suited to the sandwiching task: unusually crumbly on the outside, but very soft and airy inside. Its texture partially results from the city's high ambient humidity, which causes the yeast to become more active. One notable variation is the homemade pan bread, more of a Sicilian loaf, used on the epic oyster po'boys at the venerable Casamento's.

Several po'boy versions around town are considered authentic, with fillings ranging from roast beef and gravy to fried shrimp, and they're happily joined by newfangled contrivances like the cheeseburger po'boy. But the most cherished of all is the po'boy plumped with local, cornmeal-coated, fried Gulf Coast oysters. The juicy, crisp golden oysters are the filling that makes the sandwich truly sing, and the ingredient that truly established its fame.

A po'boy may be dressed, meaning it will be slathered with mayo or rémoulade and piled with shredded lettuce, tomatoes, pickles, and onions. But the fewer trappings the better, to allow the full flavor of oysters accented by lemon and a dressing to truly speak for itself.

WHERE: *In New Orleans,* Acme Oyster House, tel 504-522-5973, acmeoyster.com; Casamento's, tel 504-895-9761, casamentos restaurant.com; *in Akers, LA,* Middendorf's, tel 985-386-6666, middendorfsrestaurant .com; *in Baton Rouge, LA,* Tony's Seafood Market & Deli, tel 225-357-9669, tonyseafood .com; *in Asheville, NC,* The Oyster House Brewing Co., tel 828-575-9370, oysterhousebeers .com; *in New York,* The Lobster Place at Chelsea Market, tel 212-255-5672, lobsterplace.com; Pearl Oyster Bar, tel 212-691-8211, pearloyster bar.com; *in Toronto,* for fried oysters, Oyster Boy, tel 416-534-3432, oysterboy.ca. **FURTHER INFORMATION AND RECIPES:** *The Hog Island Oyster Lover's Cookbook* by Jairemarie Pomo (2007); for fried oysters, *Chef Paul Prudhomme's Louisiana Kitchen* by Paul Prudhomme (1984); saveur.com (search crabby jack's oyster po'boy). **SPECIAL EVENT:** Oak Street Po-Boy Festival, New Orleans, November, poboyfest.com.

Cornmeal-fried oysters in NOLA's signature sandwich

AN ALL-AMERICAN CLASSIC

Peanut Butter

American

Not even hot dogs and burgers are more thoroughly American than peanut butter, the mainstay of many a juvenile diet and a pleasure—if a secret one—for cupboard raiders of any age. The peanut, *Arachis hypogaea,* is in fact not really a nut at all, belonging instead to the bean family, Leguminosae. The indigenous plant with a winding green stalk was already well known to the Native Americans by the time Columbus reached the New World; in the sixteenth century, it found its way to Europe by way of the Portuguese, who prized it for its oil, which they used in cooking.

But peanut butter lovers owe the greatest thanks to Dr. George Washington Carver, who, in the early twentieth century, encouraged the cultivation of the peanut as a source of nourishment, especially for the poor. He may not have envisioned peanut butter as the primary outcome of his efforts, but the thick, creamy, intensely nutty spread has become one of America's favorite snacks, especially spread on bread, toast, crackers, matzo, or even celery—and best enjoyed with a glass of cold milk to prevent the peanut butter panic that ensues when large clumps stick to the roof of the mouth or the back of the tongue.

As a sandwich spread, peanut butter is classically combined with grape jelly, which carries a high "ick" factor for those who prefer less cloying accompaniments like raspberry jam or apple butter. Another alternative, Elvis's famous addition of banana slices and bacon strips, has rightfully achieved peanut-butter-sandwich infamy. Minus the banana, that bacon can join a splash of Tabasco sauce to create a delectable peanut butter sandwich with a hint of fire. And outside of the sandwich realm, in Southeast Asia and beyond, the spread is the basis of many sauces and dips.

Although it's widely available from producers far and wide—whether creamy or complete with crunchy pieces of peanut, pure or blended with various flavors of nonpeanut oils—peanut butter is easily made at home, the main requirement besides the nuts being a food processor and seasonings of choice. A slight tingle of salt and a minimal amount of sugar (if any) keep the taste from becoming insipid, and the nuts must be purchased roasted—roasting adds the spread's characteristic burnished depth and helps to keep it fresher longer, despite a slight loss of valuable nutrients such as protein, vitamin B, and niacin.

Peanut Butter

Yield: 1 pound

*1 pound shelled, roasted peanuts,
    with or without skins (see Note)*

1 teaspoon salt
*1 to 2 tablespoons unhydrogenated peanut
    oil, if needed*
Pinch of sugar (optional)

1. Divide the nuts into 4 equal parts. Put 1 batch in a food processor and process until the nuts are very coarsely cracked, to about the size of capers. Remove and reserve.

2. Process the second batch of nuts finer; they should have a fairly thick texture but still have some small distinct pieces. Remove and add to the reserved first batch.

3. Process the remaining 2 batches together to a very fine, butterlike puree, until the oil begins to ooze out of the mass. Remove and add this batch to the coarser 2 batches.

4. Sprinkle the peanut butter with the salt and, using a wooden spoon, gently but thoroughly blend all of the batches together. If the mixture is too dry to be spreadable, add a little peanut oil gradually until you have a spreadable consistency.

5. Taste and blend in additional salt and/or a pinch of sugar, if needed. Pack the peanut butter into a jar or crock, cover tightly, and store in a cool place (the refrigerator on a hot day) for at least 8 hours before serving. Stored in the refrigerator, the peanut butter will keep for about 2 months, although you may have to stir the oil back in if any rises to the surface.

Note: Peanut skins add flavor and fiber, so are best left on. However, for those who prefer the creamiest texture, the skins can be rubbed off by placing the nuts between two clean kitchen towels and gently rubbing back and forth.

RETAIL AND MAIL ORDER: *In New York,* Peanut Butter & Co., tel 212-677-3995, ilovepeanut butter.com; The Peanut Shoppe of Williamsburg, tel 800-637-3268, thepeanutshop.com. **FURTHER INFORMATION AND RECIPES:** *Creamy and Crunchy: An Informal History of Peanut Butter, the All-American Food* by Jon Krampner (2012); creamyandcrunchy.com.

Pecan Pie

American

Beneath a smooth, tan oval shell, its twin nutmeats look like elongated, withered, and darkened walnuts, but their flavor is deeper and woodsier, their texture softer and juicier. The pecan is North America's gift to a nutty world; as *Carya illinoensis,* it is a member of the hickory family whose English name derives from the Algonquin Indians, who called it *paccan.* Though it's been cultivated in Israel, South Africa, and Australia, its primary growing regions remain the American South and Mexico.

Justifiably popular in sugary Louisiana praline candies, roasted in spicy butter or in a sugar glaze as cocktail nibblers, or adding a nice chomp to ice cream, brownies, and cookies, the nut's real excuse for being is in the crunchy, opulently silky, sweet pie most famously baked from Georgia to Texas, where the best pecans are harvested.

An open piecrust, buttery and flaky, holds the thick mosaic of toasted pecan halves nestled against a soft corn-syrup gel seasoned with sugar, vanilla, and a good dash of rum or brandy. Whispers of cinnamon or nutmeg may join the fray, and the baked pie may be served with a spoonful of unsweetened whipped cream or a scoop of vanilla ice cream. But to best preserve maximum crunch and the contrast between crisp nuts and crust and soft filling, savor it on its own.

A rich staple of the Thanksgiving table, the pie offsets its calorie content with a healthy portion of the nineteen vitamins and minerals pecans are said to provide, plus antioxidant, cholesterol-lowering, and brain-protecting properties.

WHERE: *In Somerville, MA,* Petsi Pies, tel 617-661-7437, petsipies.com; *in Lecompte, LA,* Lea's Lunchroom, tel 318-776-5178, leaslunchroom.com; *in Houston,* Goode Co. at multiple locations, goodecompany.com. **MAIL ORDER:** For pecan pie in a wooden gift box, goodecompany.com (search brazos). **FURTHER INFORMATION AND RECIPES:** *Mastering the Art of Southern Cooking* by Nathalie Dupree and Cynthia Graubart (2012); *Sarabeth's Bakery* by Sarabeth Levine with Rick Rogers (2010); epicurious.com (search old-fashioned pecan pie).

Persimmon

American

The fiery orange-red, honey-ripe persimmon may be one of nature's most alluring gifts, requiring only a silvery spoon to dip into its satiny, jamlike center. With a sweet-tart flavor and a teasingly silky pulp, it's a fruit with serious seductive appeal, and just as much mystique. Various parts of the world claim some of the many, many types of persimmons as their own, and in his engrossing 1911 food guide, *The Grocer's Encyclopedia,* Artemas Ward describes it as "a fruit concerning which there is much confusion of information—and misinformation—even in works otherwise generally reliable."

A close relative of the date plum, the American persimmon (*Diospyros virginiana*) was called *putchamin* by the Algonquin Indians, who ate the fruit fresh off the tree, in the fall, and then dried any surplus to enjoy through winter. This type of persimmon still grows on the East Coast from Pennsylvania to Florida and as far west as Illinois, and has a distinctive taste that's described as a cross between an apricot and a date. Ripeness means everything here, as this fruit can be overly astringent and almost inedible when unripe—sharply tart, with a grainy texture that leaves the inside of the mouth dryly puckered long after the unfortunate tasting. (For the richest flavor, ambitious eaters are well advised to try hanging around a persimmon tree and catching the ultraripe fruit as it drops to the ground.)

The kaki persimmon (*Diospyros kaki*), also known as the Japanese persimmon (although originally from China and grown throughout Asia as well as in Italy, Israel, and California), is a broad category of persimmon that is larger than the American variety, and harder and flatter, too. There are two main varieties of kaki, and because they keep more easily than the American fruits, they are the ones most commonly seen in U.S. supermarkets: the pointed, deep red-orange *hachiya* (which makes up as much as 90 percent of the persimmons sold in the world) and the flatter, firmer, brightly orange *fuyu*. The first is more astringent than the American variety, while the second is a comparatively nonastringent persimmon and can be eaten in a less-than-ripe state.

Despite its finickiness, the genuine American article is far superior in flavor and texture, best enjoyed peeled at the top and served with a slim spoon for extracting the flesh, although it is also excellent doused with cream or baked into a cakelike pudding.

MAIL ORDER: Local Harvest, ships American persimmons in September and October, local harvest.org; Melissa's Produce, ships from September to December, tel 800-588-0151, melissas.com. **FURTHER INFORMATION AND RECIPES:** *Uncommon Fruits and Vegetables* by Elizabeth Schneider (2010); epicurious.com (search persimmon bread; persimmon fool; fuyu persimmon relish); cookstr.com (search persimmon gelato; persimmons grand marnier). **SPECIAL EVENT:** Annual Mitchell Persimmon Festival, Mitchell, IN, September, tel 800-580-1985, persimmonfestival.org.

THE COZIEST WIENERS

Pigs in a Blanket

American

Finger food doesn't get more addictive than pigs in a blanket, the diminutive "cocktail" wieners (beef or pork) snugly enfolded in miniature pastry wraps. After dipping them into a pungent mustard, we pop them into our mouths with grateful abandon, whether they come on a woven wicker platter or a silver tray.

Wrapping meat in pastry is an old-timey practice, but the pig in a blanket itself is probably a descendant of the canapés and sausage rolls that were popular during the Victorian era. Pigs in a blanket began appearing in American cookbooks in the early twentieth century, although the term was then used to refer to all manner of proteins, from chicken livers to oysters, wrapped in anything from biscuit dough to bacon. By the 1950s, the pastry-encased hot dog was universally understood as a pig in a blanket, and it grew to be a standard at backyard barbecues and bridge club dinners.

The piglets' appeal is easy to understand. Convenient, cute, and salty, they are an ideal foil for just about any preprandial drink, from a can of Budweiser to a flute of vintage Taittinger. Although they wax and wane in popularity, whenever they do appear they are always quickly consumed. And they will forever remain a bar mitzvah classic—the beef hot dogs used for kosher celebrants are sometimes called "franks in jackets," a term said to have originated at Katz's Delicatessen in lower Manhattan.

MAIL ORDER: For ready-to-bake, frozen kosher beef pigs in a blanket, hebrewnational .com; for high-end organic "pigs" (called Greatest Little Organic Smokey Pork Cocktail Franks), applegatefarms.com.

┤||||||||||||||||||||||||||||||├

THE HAWAIIAN WAY WITH CEVICHE

Poke

American (Hawaiian)

Cool, silky, and steeped in a pungent marinade, poke is inspired by Tahitian *poisson cru* (see page 912). It is also Hawaii's answer to ceviche, and is just one of the many dishes that testify to the extent of Hawaii's culinary melting pot,

deriving influences from immigrants from China, Japan, Korea, the Philippines, Puerto Rico, and Portugal. Rosy ahi tuna is the preferred fish, but yellowtail, fluke, bass, and snapper are well-regarded stand-ins, especially with tuna becoming scarce and endangered.

(Freshwater fish are to be avoided in raw dishes, as they can carry parasites, which are killed by cooking.)

Poke—pronounced POH-key—literally means to slice or cut into pieces, a simple description for a bright, piquant, vibrantly-flavored marinated fish salad. Though there is no one exact formula for the dish, and some say there are as many as two dozen "authentic" variations, the most common version contains cubes of raw fish, usually ahi tuna, mixed with seaweed, sea salt, chiles, sweet Maui onion, and light sesame oil. The ruby-red dice shimmers, each piece of fish slickly coated with sweet and tart flavors that hit the palate all at once. It's a pastel rainbow of a dish that can be served either raw or, less wonderfully, flash-fried.

An annual island contest celebrates poke's diversity.

Poke's delights are well known on all the islands, and versions of it are served at the most high-end restaurants. Celebrity chef Alan Wong has a signature version called Poki Pines: ahi balls encased in wonton wrappers, deep-fried, and served on avocado slices with wasabi sauce.

WHERE: *In Honolulu,* Ono Hawaiian Foods, tel 808-737-2275, onohawaiianfoods.com; Sam Choy's Seafood Grille, tel 808-422-3002, samchoys seafoodgrille.com; *in Honolulu and Seattle,* Sam Choy's Poke to the Max truck, samchoyspoke .com. **FURTHER INFORMATION AND RECIPES:** *Sam Choy's Poke* by Sam Choy (1999); *Sam Choy's Little Hawaiian Poke Cookbook* by Elizabeth Meahl (2004); *Poke* by Sam Choy (2009); saveur .com (search poke); allrecipes.com (search ahi poke salad; ahi poke basic). **TIP:** In Hawaii, decent poke can be found in the refrigerator section of some takeout food stores, and even gas stations and hardware stores.

⊢||||||||||||||||||||||||||||||⊣

"THE FINEST OF FISH"

Pompano

American (Southern)

As proof positive that the great questions are eternal, a *New York Times* domestic advice column from October 17, 1880, asks, "How Should Pompano Be Cooked?" The story on the proper way of cooking "the finest of fish" goes on:

"Should a pompano be broiled or boiled? Grave question full of delicate subtleties." (Spoiler alert: Both are great. Pompano is so delicious as to be impervious to minor details of preparation.)

For a great many years, the pompano (*Trachinotus carolinus*) has been considered one of the most luxurious fish available on the North American continent—with a generally high price that reflects its desirability. A slim, beautiful fish with edible silvery skin, a forked tail, and plump, smooth, pearly-white, and slightly oily flesh, it represents the best of both worlds: the seemingly contradictory appeal of a lean white fish and of a darker, more oily specimen, all in one fish. Harvested from about April to September in the Gulf of Mexico and along the Atlantic, from Florida to Virginia, it is found in densest concentration on

An elusive and luxurious fish

the west coast of Florida. Still, it is elusive and rare, a southern fish that's often found in northern markets. Like many a wily yachtsman, pompano goes where the money is.

Because the fish are relatively small—the largest pompanos can be three pounds, but average size is about half that—they're often served whole. One of the most beloved preparations comes from the classic French Quarter restaurants of New Orleans: *pompano en papillote,* said to have been created at Antoine's restaurant in honor of the Brazilian aviation balloonist Alberto Santos-Dumont. The fish is baked in parchment paper (to recall a balloon) with shrimp and lump crabmeat in a white wine sauce. Also in New Orleans, at Galatoire's, pompano almondine is sautéed and mantled with melted butter and slivers of toasted almonds. Both preparations are aromatic, toothsome delicacies—but when it comes to pompano, you really can't go wrong.

Where: *In New Orleans,* Antoine's, tel 504-581-4422, antoines.com; Galatoire's, tel 504-525-2021, galatoires.com. **Further information and recipes:** For pompano en papillote, *Chef Paul Prudhomme's Louisiana Cooking* by Paul Prudhomme (1984); kpauls.com (search fish en papillote); cookstr.com (search grilled pompano with lime and olive oil); saveur.com (search tommy's pompano en papillote); fishingdestinyguide.com (click Pompano under Local Fish). **Tip:** At first blush, pompano looks like a lot of other, cheaper, less delicately flavored members of the jack family, such as amberjack. Check for a slim, tapered tail and sharply defined fins, along with gleaming silver-blue scales and pale-gold undermarkings.

WHAT'S SO BAD ABOUT BEING FULL OF HOT AIR?

Popcorn

American

Salty, buttery, and crunchy may well be America's three favorite gustatory adjectives—and when they are used in combination to describe airy popped corn kernels, they result in nothing less than a national addiction. What would movies be without it? There is something seriously satisfying about the mouthfeel, texture, shape, and size of the savory confection, as pleasing to handle as it is to chew.

Long before there were movie theaters dotting American strip malls, several types of corn grew in the country's fields: sweet corn, dent corn (also called field corn), flint corn (or Indian corn), and popcorn. The last differs from its brethren in that each kernel contains a small drop of water surrounded by a hard outer surface and a hull of just the right thickness. Although some Native Americans attributed the corn's magical popping abilities to the work of a spirit living inside its kernels, it is the crucial water content that allows popcorn to pop as cheerily as it has for over 5,600 years. Archaeologists have found evidence of ancient corn popping in the caves of New Mexico, and Native Americans not only ate the corn but also incorporated it into ceremonial rituals, like the sixteenth-century Aztec festivals in which garlands of popcorn were placed on young girls' heads.

Corn was first popped *near* American movie theaters around 1912, when street vendors set up their carts outside to catch the hungry throngs. Soon, savvy theater owners realized they could reap additional profits by selling the snack themselves, and a winning combination was born—later to morph into the more elaborate, boxed popcorn known as Cracker Jack that was caramelized and tossed with roasted peanuts (and included a toy prize).

No one did more to modernize the popcorn concept than Orville Redenbacher, a Purdue University agricultural scientist from Brazil, Indiana, who burst onto the scene in 1965 with a variety of popping corn he cultivated and called "snowflake." Redenbacher's corn expanded twice as much as other popcorn kernels to produce a fluffier product, and on the advice of marketing consultants, he branded the product in his own image, using his picture and name on the label. Orville Redenbacher's Gourmet Popping Corn was introduced in Chicago at Marshall Field's in 1970, and the rest is history.

Although the Redenbacher's brand is strongly associated with microwaveable popcorn, before he died in 1995 Redenbacher himself insisted that the method of choice for popping corn was the old-fashioned one: in a kettle, with hot oil.

Hot-air poppers and electric poppers (now including kettle roasters) and all manner of popping gadgetry aside, the timeless and most delicious way to enjoy popcorn is fresh out of the kettle. It dazzles when drizzled with plenty of melted butter (not the oily, tasteless pseudo-butters slathered on in many movie theaters) and sprinkled with salt, but may be garnished with an endless variety of more interesting toppings, the best of which include freshly grated Parmesan and sweet or hot paprika, or freshly ground black pepper.

MAIL ORDER: For Orville Redenbacher's Gourmet Popping Corn, orville.com; for home poppers, vintage cartons, tubs, and other popcorn kitsch, epopcorn.com. **FURTHER INFORMATION AND RECIPES:** *The Fannie Farmer Cookbook,* 13th edition, by Marion Cunningham (1996); epicurious.com (search plain popcorn; chili popcorn; togarashi popcorn; parmesan pepper popcorn; popcorn crunch sundae); The Popcorn Board, popcorn.org.

‖|||||||||||||||||||||||||||‖

THE CRISPIEST CRACKLINGS

Pork Rinds

American (Southern)

True pork rinds, prized in the South from North Carolina to Texas and many places in between, are referred to by natives as "cracklings." They are special treats wherever seasonal hog butchering is the custom, and represent a frugal attempt to utilize everything but the oink.

The uninitiated believe cracklings to be fried pig skins, and at times that's accurate; but generally, cracklings result from the rendering of the pig's fat, with the exact skin-to-fat ratio earnestly debated among aficionados. Cut into pieces and placed in a lard pot, the trimmed fat (sometimes with a little skin attached) is gently fried until the rinds float to the top. Skimmed from the lard and spread out on a counter or platter lined with several layers of paper towels to drain, the cracklings may be seasoned with salt, black pepper, and chile pepper.

For those lucky enough to attend a hog killing, the most immediate spoils are the hot, salty-smoky cracklings, marvelously crisp and greaseless. As pork and its by-products become ever more fashionable, many quality restaurants are featuring homemade cracklings, which are also easily made in a home kitchen. (The crisp bits can be added to salads, mashed potatoes, polenta (and grits, cornbread, or classic Southern cracklin' bread.)

A far inferior substitute can be found in the potato chip aisle of supermarkets. These commercial pork rinds are made by cooking small pieces of pigskin in fat heated to 400 degrees until they pop up like popcorn, tasting mainly of salt and grease. As a favorite snack food of the forty-first American president, George H. W. Bush, they experienced a surge in sales in the early 1990s—and because they contain no carbohydrates, for a time they were also briefly embraced by protein-only dieters who ignored their high fat and sodium content.

WHERE: *In New York,* The Breslin, tel 212-679-1939, thebreslin.com; *in San Francisco,* the Ferry Plaza Farmers Market, tel 415-983-8030, ferrybuildingmarketplace.com; *in Los Angeles,* Animal, tel 323-782-9225, animalrestaurant.com; *in London,* St. John Smithfield Bar & Restaurant, tel 44/20-7251-0848, stjohngroup.uk.com. **MAIL ORDER:** amazon.com (search lowrey's microwave pork rinds; el sabroso pork cracklins). **FURTHER**

INFORMATION AND RECIPES: *Cast-Iron Cooking: From Johnnycakes to Blackened Redfish* by A. D. Livingston (2010); *Hoppin' John's Low Country Cooking* by John Martin Taylor (1992); epicurious.com (search pork cracklings; crackling corn bread). **SEE ALSO:** Schmaltz, page 464.

CREOLE SOUL FOOD

Red Beans and Rice

American (Louisianan)

With a large ham bone adding smoky overtones to this savory, garlic-zapped dish, the hearty, richly satisfying meal of red beans and rice deserves top billing in the annals of the world's most delectable peasant foods. A staple of all Louisiana cooks, like the hoppin' John of the Carolinas and Georgia (see page 580), it is considered a good-luck dish, to be consumed on New Year's Eve and New Year's Day.

Far more complex in flavor than its humble ingredients suggest, red beans and rice came to New Orleans via the city's French, Spanish, and African settlers and the Creole culture they developed. Indeed a poor man's food, sold inexpensively in diners and luncheonettes in the French Quarter, the dish was a customary Monday special—it takes a long time to prepare, and many family cooks got started on Sundays. Incidentally or not, it's also considered a great hangover cure, and by mid-morning on Monday, the red-beans-and-rice aroma permeates entire blocks of this party-minded city.

The most noteworthy of all red-beans-and-rice joints was called Buster Holmes, after its chef and owner. For nearly fifty years, it stood watch on the corner of Orleans and Burgundy Streets, a down-and-dirty joint with crowded tables and a counter, big pitchers of Dixie beer, and the world's most delicious red beans and rice. "Smoked ham and hot sausage are nice, and I like a little garlic," Buster Holmes told *The New York Times.* The real secret of his dish, however, was its texture. The beans were cooked until they were just tender enough to be falling apart and yet still maintained their shape, resulting in a velvety smoothness that a diner could nonetheless sink his teeth into. Buster Holmes retired in the early 1980s and passed away in 1994, but there are still plenty of New Orleans outposts, plain and fancy, where diners can find quality examples of red beans and rice. One of the best is Mother's, where the dish is a staple at breakfast, lunch, and dinner.

So reassuring is this dish that after Hurricane Katrina, in 2006, chefs took to the streets and ladled it out to rescue workers and displaced victims as the city was being rebuilt.

WHERE: *In New Orleans,* Mother's, tel 504-523-9656, mothersrestaurant.net; *in Asheville, NC,* The Oyster House Brewing Co., tel 828-575-9370, oysterhousebeers.com. **MAIL ORDER:** amazon .com (search zatarain's new orleans style red bean seasoning mix; bootsie's Louisiana Cajun red beans; organic kidney beans). **FURTHER INFORMATION AND RECIPES:** *The Buster Holmes Restaurant Cookbook* by Buster Holmes (2010); *The Dooky Chase Cookbook* by Leah Chase (1990); nytimes.com (search new orleans buster holmes sheraton).

┤||||||||||||||||||||||||||├

Saltwater Taffy

American

Forget Snooki and her band of "guidos and guidettes." Nothing says Jersey Shore like the wax-paper-wrapped, pastel-hued knobs of smooth, chewy candy known as saltwater taffy. The charmingly retro sweet actually has British origins,

its name an Americanized version of "toffee," the elastic confection of melted sugar and butter that was classically cooked over an open fire. Cooled on marble slabs, it was thrown onto large, wall-mounted hooks and repeatedly pulled by hand until it grew soft.

The seaside phenomenon started in the late nineteenth century, when a glassblower named Joseph Fralinger set up a taffy stand on the newly opened Atlantic City Boardwalk in 1885. Five years earlier, a confectioner named Enoch James, who would turn out to be Fralinger's lifelong competitor, had opened a brick-and-mortar candy shop in which he, too, sold taffy. The candy was an ideal beach treat; mostly made of flavored sugar, it was relatively easy for seaside vendors to make, and extremely pleasant for beachgoers to eat.

Contrary to its name, while it does traditionally contain a pinch of salt, it does not contain saltwater. How it came to be known as saltwater taffy is the stuff of legends. Several theories circulate, the most oft-repeated claiming that a Boardwalk candy maker had his stock of candies soaked by either an ambitious ocean wave or a nor'easter, and, having no other inventory, tried to sell the candies the following day. When a little girl came by and tasted a piece of the candy, she asked, "Is this saltwater taffy?"

Atlantic City confectioners, canny marketers long before branding was a science, knew that sea air and water were considered prescriptive cure-alls for a host of illnesses, and sought to capitalize on the term with their wares. Soon, both James and Fralinger were packaging their

The Jersey Shore's trademark souvenir

"saltwater taffy" in nifty, colorful metal tins decorated with scenes of the seascape, and in small and neat white paper sampler boxes. By the turn of the century, few tourists left Atlantic City without one of these assortments. And by then, the flavors and colors were part of the thrill, too. Historians say that molasses was the candy's first flavor, followed by the perennial favorites vanilla and chocolate. Nowadays there are upwards of twenty, including peanut butter (a big seller) and wintergreen (one of the least requested, according to candy makers).

As the world has gotten bigger, and saltwater taffy has spread down the Eastern seaboard, the taffy world has shrunk in some ways. Fralinger's and James' merged in 1990, but the parent company, a fifth-generation business run by the Glaser family, still keeps the brands separate, each with their respective recipes (which the family swears are different), flavors, box decorations, and store locations.

The gold standard of saltwater taffy is its texture and softness, and saltwater taffy sometimes gets a bad name from the old, hard pieces that lurk in candy stores and counters far from the Shore. But freshly made, it is singularly tender and chewy, a junky food that's easy to love and, once you're hooked, difficult to forget.

RETAIL AND MAIL ORDER: *In Atlantic City and on the Jersey Shore,* Fralinger's and James' Candy at various locations, tel 800-441-1404, jamescandy.com; *in Virginia Beach, VA, and the Outerbanks, NC,* Forbes Candies at various locations, tel 800-626-5898, forbescandies.com.

THE REAL WINNER AT SARATOGA

Saratoga (Potato) Chips

American

I deally composed of nothing more than earthy potato, salt, and oil, the intensely crispy potato chip is a fairly humble creation. But the irresistible combination of delicate, light-as-air texture and starchily addictive delectability make the thin, fried slice of potato an inspired innovation.

Although sliced deep-fried potatoes had existed in France since the late eighteenth century, Americans got the credit for inventing the potato chip. Regardless of its origin, the United States is definitely the place where the chip made its name—a case in point being March 14, National Potato Chip Day.

The king of all American snack foods was born (or improved) in the swanky horse-racing spa town of Saratoga Springs, New York, in 1853. A persnickety, well-to-do diner at Moon's Lake House sent his fried potatoes back to the kitchen for being cut too thick. The irritated cook, George Crum, sliced a new batch of potatoes into paper-thin disks, fried them, and liberally sprinkled them with salt, undoubtedly thinking he had sent a somewhat insulting message— *"These too thick for you, buddy?"* But the crunchy chips, light as air and tinglingly salty, were an instant hit. Crum became so famous for his chips that he opened his own restaurant in 1860, with a clientele that included the likes of the Hiltons and the Vanderbilts. Atop every table, Crum placed his signature "Saratoga chips" in baskets, and also sold boxes of them for takeout.

Sadly for him, he never patented or otherwise protected his invention, and soon the addictively crisp snacks had made their way to New York and then all around the country, becoming known simply as potato chips. In 2009, two entrepreneurs, Dan Jameson and Paul Tator, visited the Saratoga Springs History Museum and discovered an original box of Crum's chips. Upon further discovering that they had never been trademarked, they wisely bought the brand and now market their wares (actually made in Saratoga) as "The Original Saratoga Chips." One improvement has been the dark russets: chips cooked longer than usual to achieve an even toastier, more burnished finish.

With such an embarrassment of multiflavored chip choices lining our supermarket aisles, the original remains a reminder of how a good one ought to taste: fresh, crunchy, homemade, not greasy or full of preservatives, and generously salted. Salt is the true magic of the potato chip's appeal, in Saratoga and everywhere else.

FURTHER INFORMATION AND RECIPES: *One Potato, Two Potato* by Roy Finamore and Molly Stevens (2001); *The American Heritage Cookbook* by the editors of American Heritage

Publ. Co. (1964); originalsaratogachips.com. **TIP:** Other good brands on supermarket and grocery store shelves include Kettle Chips and Cape Cod Potato Chips.

PENNSYLVANIA DUTCH TREAT

Shoofly Pie

American

A dark and mysterious treat, shoofly pie is a blessedly enticing conglomeration of crust; a rich filling of dark, malty molasses, brown sugar, and butter; and a crackly crumb topping. The nicely gooey pie is a specialty of the Pennsylvania

Dutch country, that fifteen-county swath of southeastern Pennsylvania populated by Amish, Mennonites, and Moravians. Once upon a time it was served at the Sun Inn, the Moravian-style colonial hotel where George and Martha Washington were believed to have stayed. Built

A woman prepares a pie, Pennsylvania Dutch-style.

in Bethlehem, Pennsylvania, in 1758, the hotel is still open for tours today.

The most popular theory as to how the pie got its name is that its filling was so sweet, flies had to be shooed away as it cooled. A more probable conjecture has it inspired by Shoofly Molasses, a Philadelphia product that was popular in the late 1800s, when pies by that name first appeared. Whatever its American origins, the pie bears more than a passing resemblance to the toothachingly sweet British treacle tart that has been baked since medieval days in Europe (see page 31). For the Pennsylvania Dutch, it was a staple wintertime dessert—for that time of the year when the fruit supplies had dwindled down to nothing, and the very expensive eggs in the cupboard had been designated for more important uses. In those days, it was strictly eaten for breakfast, the kind of stick-to-your-ribs food that gave you energy to last until lunchtime. Today, it's almost exclusively a dessert, a delicious oddity and a terrific example of regional American food.

WHERE: *In Ephrata, PA,* on Fridays, The Green Dragon Farmer's Market & Auction, tel 717-738-1117, greendragonmarket.com. **RETAIL AND MAIL ORDER:** *In Intercourse, PA,* Kitchen Kettle Village, tel 800-732-3538, kitchenkettle.com. **FURTHER INFORMATION AND RECIPES:** *Pennsylvania*

Dutch Country Cooking by William Woys Weaver (1997); *Classic Pennsylvania Dutch Cooking* edited by Betty Groff (2007); foodnetwork.com (search shoo-fly pie alton brown); bonappetit .com (search shoofly pie lancaster central market).

SURF AND TURF, SOUTHERN STYLE

Shrimp 'n Grits

American (Southern)

Although a favorite throughout the South, shrimp 'n grits (using "and" to join these two luscious ingredients marks you as being someone "from away") is a particular specialty of South Carolina. Sweet, fresh shrimp, preferably local,

A Southern favorite

sprightly with black pepper and a generous dash of cayenne or Tabasco, are sautéed in butter, then nested on a soft and wavy bed of snowy stone-ground grits that have been whipped with butter and black pepper.

As tempting as that classic dish is, it is merely the jumping-off point for Robert Stehling, who, at his delectable restaurant, the Hominy Grill in Charleston, raises this simple soul food standard to the celestial with the triumph he bills as Pan-Fried Shrimp and Cheese Grits.

He cooks stone-ground grits from the local Anson mill in well-salted water, then gently tosses in a creamy combination of grated sharp white Vermont cheddar and Parmesan cheeses, butter, black pepper, and Tabasco. Next, he crowns each portion with tender shrimp that were pan-fried with crisp bits of smoky bacon, sliced mushrooms, chopped garlic, scallions, yet another dose of Tabasco, and a tingling shot of lemon juice. The rose-gold, spicy, pungent result, with its tantalizing textural contrasts, makes an ecstatically bracing breakfast, brunch, or lunch, especially when paired with hot biscuits or cornbread—again, lavishly buttered.

As the Hominy Grill only accepts reservations for parties of six or more, the dish, along with at least a dozen others that are equally good, makes for a very long wait in line, especially for weekend brunches.

WHERE: *In Charleston, SC,* Hominy Grill, tel 843-937-0930, hominygrill.com; *in New Orleans,* Atchafalaya restaurant, tel 504-891-9626, atchafalayarestaurant.com; *in Houston,* Zelko Bistro, tel 713-880-8691, zelkobistro.com; *in Chapel Hill, NC,* Crook's Corner, tel 919-929-7643, crookscorner.com; *in New York,* Red Rooster, tel 212-792-9001, redroosterharlem.com. **MAIL ORDER:** For grits, ansonmills.com. **FURTHER INFORMATION AND RECIPES:** *Nathalie Dupree's Shrimp and Grits Cookbook* by Nathalie Dupree and Marion Sullivan (2006); *The Gift of Southern Cooking* by Edna Lewis and Scott Peacock (2003); saveur .com (search shrimp and grits crooks corner). **SPECIAL EVENT:** Shrimp & Grits: The Wild Georgia Shrimp Festival, Jekyll Island, GA, September, jekyllisland.com/shrimp-and-grits.com.

━┤||||||||||||||||||||||||||||||├━

THE BENDY, TWISTY, KNOTTY ROLL

Soft Pretzels

American

Pretzels are among the world's oldest snacks—historians have evidence of the Roman armies eating them for sustenance, and their name is believed to have come either from the Latin *bracchium,* meaning arm, or the German word for small bread, *brötchen.* Wherever they began, they rose to popularity in German bakeries, and in many northern European countries they remain the symbol of a bread baker's shop. The brötchen traveled to America via the Palatine German immigrants to Pennsylvania, now known as the Pennsylvania Dutch, with the first commercial pretzel bakery in the U.S. opening in Lititz, Pennsylvania, in 1861; named for its owner, Julius Sturgis, it still turns out delicious, teasingly chewy pretzels.

The soft pretzel's charms are obvious. Yeasty, crisply firm on the outside but softly yielding inside, it is salty, chewy, neatly handheld, and brimming with toothsome, sink-your-teeth-in appeal. Crisp pretzels have their own snackable allure, certainly, but the soft versions are difficult to resist and seem like more-serious food, especially when they are fresh and still warm.

Prepared much like bagels (briefly boiled before being salted and baked), soft pretzels have long been a popular street food in American cities. Since the 1820s, street vendors in Philadelphia have made such brisk traffic with them that the city itself is sometimes referred to by locals as The Big Pretzel. There, and in other cities, the soft pretzels with flat, wide arms are customarily topped by a squiggle of yellow mustard. Satisfying as that might be, it lacks the sophistication of the German way, which is to split the pretzels and spread the insides with plenty of sweet butter, then to close the top and bottom, sandwich-style.

WHERE: *In Philadelphia,* Miller's Twist in the Reading Terminal Market, millerstwist.com. **RETAIL AND MAIL ORDER:** *In Lititz, PA,* Julius Sturgis Pretzel Bakery, tel 717-626-4354, juliussturgis .com. **FURTHER INFORMATION AND RECIPES:** *Classic Pennsylvania Dutch Cooking* edited by Betty Groff (2007); *The Artisan Jewish Deli at Home* by Nick Zukin and Michael Zusman (2013); epi curious.com (search hot soft pretzels; new york pretzels).

━┤||||||||||||||||||||||||||||||├━

BUSTERS, PEELERS, AND SHEDDERS

Soft-Shell Crabs

American

Honored for its sumptuous, quintessentially crabby crabmeat, *Callinectes sapidus* is the famed blue crab that flourishes along the eastern seaboard of the U.S. and around the coast of Florida, to the Gulf of Mexico. The best, most elegant crab in the world, its satiny lump meat is delectable in crab cakes or just out of its shell at a spicy Southern crab boil. But blue crabs reach their true apotheosis as youngsters, when they outgrow their shells. Bursting out to develop larger quarters for themselves, they become, for a brief span, the celestial treats known as soft-shell crabs, an American specialty only occasionally encountered in parts of Europe.

Prime season for these silky, gentle crustaceans is mid-spring, when the soft-shell squirmers are small enough to fit in the palm of your hand. A light sautéing in butter turned a golden nut-brown (known in French as *beurre noisette*) and a dash of lemon juice is all that's needed to add a warm and sunny sprightliness to the gently meaty, deep-sea essence of the tiny crabs, although a showering of toasted, thinly shaved almonds cannot go amiss. With great prudence and restraint, they can also be lightly fried after being tossed in salted and peppered flour, a method that adds an enticing edge of crispness to the tender meat.

Because there is just a matter of minutes, at most an hour, between the crab's bursting its shell and forming a new one—a period when it is considered a "peeler" or a "shedder"—crabmen look for a telltale red crack that develops close to the crab's back legs just before it molts. Gathered into "floats" or tanks and left in the water, the crabs are then picked up the second they lose their shells, before new ones begin to develop. In Louisiana, crabmen don't wait for the crabs to molt but actually "bust" the shells by hand; the delectable results are featured on upscale menus as "busters," each a tiny, quivering, translucent dream of a crab that gets only about a five-minute gilding in butter, then a light showering of minced parsley and lemon juice.

As the season wears on, the so-called soft-shell crabs become much larger, and have begun to develop the thin new shells that classify them as "buckrams." These lend themselves satisfactorily to heavier breading and a quick deep-frying in a light vegetable oil, and are ideally served as sandwiches on toasted soft buns with plenty of tartar sauce and coleslaw to keep things moist.

Where: *In Boston,* B&G Oysters, tel 617-423-0550, bandgoysters.com; *in Halethorpe, MD,* Cravin' Crabs, tel 410-636-2722, cravincrabs.com; *in New York and Santa Monica,* Michael's, michaelsnewyork.com, michaelssantamonica .com; *in New York,* Barchetta, tel 212-255-7400, barchettanyc.com; The Clam, tel 212-242-7420, theclamnyc.com; *in New Orleans,* Clancy's, tel 504-895-1111, clancysneworleans.com; Bayona, tel 504-525-4455, bayona.com; *in Houston,* Ninfa's, tel 713-228-1175, ninfas.com; *in Yountville, CA,* The French Laundry, tel 707-944-2380, frenchlaundry.com. **Further information and recipes:** *North Atlantic Seafood* by Alan Davidson (2012); *The French Laundry Cookbook* by Thomas Keller (1999); saveur.com (search panfried softshell crabs with garlic-herb butter); nytimes.com (search crunchy soft-shell crab recipe).

PILLOWY FRIED DOUGH

Sopaipillas

American (Southwestern)

G olden fried pillows of crisp yeast dough drizzled with honey, sopaipillas are the stuff of sweet dreams. Versions appear throughout Latin America (in Argentina a sopaipilla is actually a deep-fried tortilla), and Texas takes pride in these

puffy treats, too; for a time the Texas House of Representatives designated sopaipillas the state's official pastry. The airiest and lushest of the lot can be found in Albuquerque and other parts of New Mexico, where they are thought to have been developed a few hundred years ago. And they are a fitting example of New Mexico's melting-pot cuisine, an amalgam of foods and flavors informed by Native Americans, Hispanics, and a mix of early travelers on the Santa Fe Trail.

Whether in Texas or New Mexico, proper sopaipillas are based on bread dough that is rolled extra-thin and cut into small squares before being fried in boiling lard. It instantly balloons in the hot fat, creating an irresistibly light and airy result, a sort of popover that is crunchy on the outside and very tenderly yeasty within.

The treats are served as both desserts and breads, in the small baskets found on the tables of nearly every restaurant that features New Mexico's colorful cuisine. Some places now offer savory versions in which the sopaipillas are stuffed with delectably spiced fillings such as beef, pork, chicken, or refried beans. Diners are advised to try to resist overdoing it, lest they forfeit the rest of their meal.

Where: *In Albuquerque*, Casa de Benevidez, tel 505-898-3311, casadebenavidez.com; *in Santa Fe*, Plaza Cafe, tel 505-982-1664, thefamous plazacafe.com; *in Chimayó, NM*, Rancho de Chimayó, tel 505-351-4444, ranchodechimayo .com. **Further information and recipes:** *The Border Cookbook* by Cheryl Alters Jamison and Bill Jamison (1995); *Best of the Best from New Mexico Cookbook* edited by Gwen McKee and Barbara Mosley (2003); cookstr.com (search sopaipillas idone; sopaipillas jamison). **See also:** Indian Fry Bread, page 587; Bhel Puri, page 867.

WINGING IT

Southern Fried Chicken

American

The most beloved triumph of the Southern kitchen, fried chicken engenders arguments almost every time two or more devotees meet. Everyone seems to have a favorite trick or turn, some going back to what their mothers used to make, others to a bygone shack or restaurant. Perhaps their discussions are merely lovers' quarrels. What all agree on is that the meat should be dewily moist, succulently flavorful, with the quintessential sunny, rich chicken essence, and that it all be coated with a golden crunchy crust. For many, lots of salt and pepper are the only acceptable seasonings, while others demand the hot chile sting that distinguishes fried chicken around Nashville. And to most, pieces of fried chicken should be edible by hand, forks and knives obviating the sensuous pleasure of biting in and getting a big mouthful of crust and meat all at once.

Every expert knows just how chicken should be prepared, of course, starting with the freshest possible bird weighing no more than 2½ pounds. Not only will it be more tender than a larger bird, but it will also ensure the right proportion of crust to meat. Real purists might buy only dark meat in parts that have the most flavor and moisture; as they know, the best cuts for frying are thighs, drumsticks, and the third joint of the wing, which is white meat but much like a mini drumstick.

Among such culinary debates, a prime question is to brine or not to brine, and if so, in what sort of liquid. Brining is supposed to ensure juiciness and a teasing saltiness, but can that be better realized with salted water or buttermilk? (Opt for the latter: The milk enzymes tend to tenderize the meat.) Anti-briners think this step makes crispness more difficult to achieve because the higher moisture in the meat might cause steaming through the crust during frying. (They are right.)

And how to develop that maximum crispness in the crust? By dipping pieces into an egg-and-flour batter; or taking a triple run through flour, then beaten eggs, and finally, bread crumbs; or the best and favorite method, a simple tossing in seasoned flour.

How to fry, and in what vehicle? Most traditional Southern home cooks wisely opt for a deep, black iron skillet, and though all might acknowledge that lard is the frying vehicle that adds the most flavor and crispness, more now are combining it with vegetable oils or using the oils alone for health reasons. (Midway between the two are those using solid vegetable shortening, namely Crisco, that produces lard's crispness while being at least a little easier on arteries; but if fried chicken is only a sometime pleasure, why compromise?)

Now that the chicken is hot, crisp, and ready, what foods enhance it most? Biscuits, for sure (see page 528), buttered and perhaps dripping honey, and slightly vinegary Southern potato salad (see page 624), which is a better choice than French fries. In truly old-style fried-chicken outposts, you should also be able to have an appetizer of Southern fried-chicken gizzards, hearts, and livers, as on the menu at Stroud's in Kansas City. But there, as elsewhere, if cream gravy is offered, order it on the side, if at all. It is hard to understand why, having spent so much effort on achieving crispness, one would douse the chicken with a thick sauce that turns the crust to mush.

If you think Americans are inexplicably quirky about this gastronomic treat, take heart. Austrians can carry on just about as much as to the right way to turn out their *Wiener Backhendl* (see page 329), and Koreans debate the correct amounts of ginger, garlic, soy, and vinegar that make up the marinade for their version of fried chicken (see page 835).

WHERE: *In Kansas City, MO, and Fairway, KS,* Stroud's, stroudsrestaurant.com; *in Houston,* Barbecue Inn, tel 713-695-8112, thebarbecueinn .com; *in Charleston, SC,* Hominy Grill, tel 843-937-0930, hominygrill.com; *in Nashville,* Prince's Hot Chicken Shack, tel 615-226-9442; Hattie B's Hot Chicken, tel 615-678-4794, hattieb.com; *in New Orleans,* Willie Mae's Scotch House, tel 504-822-9503; *in New York,* Blue Ribbon Fried Chicken, tel 212-228-0404, blueribbonfried chicken.com; Bar and Library at NoMad, tel 347-472-5660, thenomadhotel.com; Charles' Country Pan Fried Chicken, tel 212-281-1800; *in Brooklyn,* Peaches HotHouse, tel 718-483-9111, bcrestaurantgroup.com/hothouse; *in Chicago,* Table Fifty-Two, tel 312-573-4000, tablefifty-two .com; *in San Francisco,* Frisco Fried, tel 415-822-1517, friscofried.biz; *in Yountville, CA,* Ad Hoc, tel 707-944-2487, adhocrestaurant.com; *in Ottawa, Canada,* Union 613, tel 613-231-1010, union613.ca; *in Montreal,* Dinette Triple Crown, tel 514-272-2617. For more restaurants serving good fried chicken, thedailymeal.com (search great american fried chicken roadmap). **FURTHER INFORMATION AND RECIPES:** *Mastering the Art of Southern Cooking* by Nathalie Dupree and Cynthia Graubart (2012); *New American Table* by Marcus Samuelsson (2009); *The Taste of Country Cooking* by Edna Lewis (1976); *Gene Hovis's Uptown Down Home Cookbook* by Gene Hovis with Sylvia Rosenthal (1993); *Fried & True* by Lee Brian Schrager and Adeena Sussman (2014); vogue.com (click Videos, then search david chang's fried chicken with caviar); saveur.com (search southern fried chicken dinner; extra-crispy fried chicken); cooking channeltv.com (search coca-cola brined fried chicken).

—||||||||||||||||||||||||||||||—

Southern Potato Salad

American

The French like their potato salad dressed in a light, tarragon-scented vinaigrette and served cold. Germans prefer theirs warm, glossed with a dressing of vinegar, mustard, and the bacon that adds some of its luxuriously golden grease.

American versions, always served cold, are generally coated with a silken veil of mayonnaise. But in the South, the church supper classic harkens to the German tradition. Made with cubed boiled potatoes, chopped hard-cooked eggs, crunchy celery, spicy mustard, a sprinkling of sweet pickle relish, and plenty of salt, it is simultaneously sweet and sour.

A staple for any summertime picnic or party

Distinctively yellow, tart, and bracing, it is the ideal foil for lusty fried chicken and meaty country ham. And, these days, it may come dressed up with untraditional garnishes such as Jerusalem artichoke relish, pimiento peppers, olives, and sometimes even mayonnaise.

Deliciously correct Southern-style potato salad demands waxy potatoes with a low starch content that won't break down as they boil, such as Yukon Golds, Kennebecs, fingerlings, Red Bliss, or other red-skinned potatoes. Starting the unpeeled potatoes in cold water and bringing them up to a boil will ensure that the inside cooks at the same time as the outside, preventing the potato from disintegrating. And letting the cooked potatoes cool before peeling and cutting them into cubes or slices provides further insurance against mealiness.

Prepared this way, potato salad will convert even those who scoff at the inclusion of sweet-sour, improbably green pickle relish.

Where: *In Savannah, GA,* Mrs. Wilkes' Dining Room, tel 912-232-5997, mrswilkes.com. **Further information and recipes:** *Mrs. Wilkes' Boardinghouse Cookbook* by Sema Wilkes (2001); *Bill Neal's Southern Cooking* by Bill Neal (1989); cookstr.com (search tangy buttermilk potato salad); epicurious.com (search potato salad dooky chase).

—||||||||||||||||||||||||||||||—

Steamer Clams and Broth

American (New England, Mid-Atlantic)

In contrast to the hard-shelled *Merceneria mercenaria*, the tiny, soft-shelled *Mya arenaria* clams are never eaten raw. With their thin and fragile, salt-white shells and protruding black-tipped necks, they are almost strictly an East Coast treat, popularly known as steamers. Because they never close tightly shut, the bivalves are considered by purists not to be true clams, a quibble of little import to steamer addicts.

Carefully purged of sand, the tiny clams are steamed briefly, with only a film of water as a starter at the bottom of the pot to get the process going. Having popped wide open after eight to ten minutes, they are served piping hot in big individual bowls. Proper accompaniments are generous pools of sweet and sunny melted butter and maybe—just maybe—a wedge of lemon. The real prize is the cupful of the steaming broth ladled out with each portion. All of the dish's seductive magic lies in that broth, the distillation of a languid North Atlantic summer in a single cup. Practically speaking, the broth is used for dipping cooked clams if they are sandy, and is then allowed to settle so it can be sipped without interference from grit.

Where: *In New York,* The Clam, tel 212-242-7420, theclamnyc.com; *in Boston and environs,* Jasper White's Summer Shack, summershack restaurant.com; *in Wellfleet, MA,* Mac's Seafood, tel 800-214-0477, macsseafood.com; *in Toronto,* Oyster Boy, tel 416-534-3432, oysterboy.ca. **Further information and recipes:** *Jasper White's Cooking from New England* by Jasper White (1998); *The New England Clam Shack Cookbook* by Brooke Dojny (2008). **See also:** Fried Clam Roll, page 564; North Atlantic Clams on the Half-Shell, page 604.

THE WISECRACKING CRABS. GET THEM WHILE YOU CAN!

Stone Crabs

American, Caribbean

Delicious stone crabs (*Menippe mercenaria*) are among the most rarified delicacies of the sea, in no small part because nearly everything about them is limited. Their season is short, running from October through May, and their only edible parts are their claws—unlike other crabs, stone crabs have no backfin meat. They can be found along Florida's Gulf Coast and up the Atlantic coast to North Carolina, but the mercurial and elusive creatures move around a lot, and it's not uncommon for fishermen to go for days without seeing them and then to hit a mother lode.

The good news? When claws are removed from the crab, the crab naturally regenerates them within eighteen months. In order for it to do so properly, the claw must be cleanly snapped off—a feat that requires supreme precision and experience, not to mention knowledge of the law: The state of Florida dictates the length of claw that may be taken, and also requires that any egg-bearing female be thrown back entirely unharmed. Every stone crab must be immediately returned to the water after its claw is removed, or held in a shaded place and wet down every half hour before being thrown back.

Though a few large-scale fishermen catch many thousands of pounds of stone crab per season, the crabs are mostly brought in by a small coterie of fishermen who own their own boats. There might be easier ways to get at the stone crab, but so far, attempts to farm-raise them have failed.

Decidedly within the rights of the consumer are the ways in which stone crab is prepared. Canny cooks long ago figured out how to boil and quickly chill the claw, enabling the meat to effortlessly slip from the shell instead of sticking, and also ensuring the finest, cleanest flavor, the meat so firm and toothsome that it bears resemblance to a lobster tail. Dipping the cold meat into melted butter is a rare pleasure, but better still is the claw's traditional dipping sauce, said to have been invented at the Hotel Nacional de Cuba, in Havana, Cuba (where the same stone crab is called the morro crab), in the 1930s: a mustard-based affair spiked with mayonnaise, vinegar, and sometimes a little horseradish that does much to enliven what's already a pristine and luxurious experience.

Regenerating stone crabs are only available from October to May.

Perhaps the most famous stone crab restaurant, Joe's Stone Crab in Miami Beach, began its life in 1913 as a lunch counter owned by Jewish immigrant Joe Weiss; to this day, the restaurant remains open from October to May each year, with guaranteed lines out the door. Stone crabs may be the main draw, but the sweet potato fries and Key lime pie have legions of fans, too. They're worth the wait.

Where: *In Miami and Washington, DC,* Joe's Stone Crab, tel 800-780-2722, joesstonecrab.com; *in Longboat Key, FL,* Moore's Stone Crab Restaurant, tel 941-383-1748, stonecrab.cc; *in Florida, Texas, and California,* Truluck's Seafood, Steak & Crab House, trulucks.com; *in New York,* Grand Central Oyster Bar, tel 212-490-6650, oysterbarny.com; *in Brooklyn,* Grand Central Oyster Bar Brooklyn, tel 347-294-0596, oysterbarbrooklyn.com. **Mail order:** Joe's Stone Crab, tel 800-780-2722, joesstonecrab.com. **Further information and recipes:** *Eat at Joe's: The Joe's Stone Crab Restaurant Cookbook* by Jo Ann Bass and Richard Sax (2000); saveur.com (search chilled stone crab with mustard sauce; joe's stone crab pot pie; baby spinach and stone crab salad). **Tip:** A frozen crab is a ruined crab, so spring for a plane ticket or the delivery fee for fresh crab, or skip it entirely.

BAGELS AND LOX ARE ONLY THE BEGINNING

Sunday Breakfast in New York

American, Jewish

The annals of the American menu hold countless iconic meals. There are peanut butter and jelly sandwiches for childhood lunches, steak and potatoes for grown-up dinners, roast turkey and pumpkin pie on Thanksgiving, cheeseburgers and fries any time at all, and many more. With stacks of syrup-drenched pancakes, piles of crunchy fried bacon, miles of hash browns, and eggs any which way, the country particularly shines in the breakfast category.

But not all American breakfasts commandeer the griddle. For New Yorkers, the morning meal of champions is a treasured Sunday ritual involving lox, cream cheese, and bagels—a simplified description of a complex spread that may include dark bread and bialys (see page 429), as well as creamy whitefish salad, eggs scrambled with lox, and blintzes (see page 433) or slices of authentic Russian coffee cake.

It's a menu made up of delicacies traditional to the Ashkenazic Jews of Eastern Europe. They came from cold places and hard times, so their favored foods were filling and preserved for ready availability in winter. These days, high rollers may opt to replace the lox with sturgeon, those caviar spawners that have a gorgeously salty, toothsome bite when smoked; with the silvery, fatty whitefish (see page 467); or even with the buttery, pink smoked salmon known as nova (and sometimes mistaken for lox) which is cured in brine and then cold-smoked. The lone inedible but essential accessory is the Sunday edition of *The New York Times*.

WHERE: *In New York*, Barney Greengrass, tel 212-724-4707, barneygreengrass.com. **DINE-IN, RETAIL, AND MAIL ORDER:** *In New York*, Russ & Daughters, tel 212-475-4880, russanddaughters .com; E.A.T., tel 212-772-0022, elizabar.com; Zabar's, tel 212-787-2000, zabars.com; *in Ann Arbor, MI*, Zingerman's, tel 734-663-3354, zinger mansdeli.com. **TIP:** For locations of kosher and kosher-style delis in more than fifty countries, see shamash.org/kosher.

GEORGIA NAMED THEM, GEORGIA CLAIMED THEM

Sweet Georgia Peaches

American (Southern)

The lyrical Sweet Georgia Brown may have inspired many devotees, but so did the state's equally sweet and seductive peach. With yellow-gold flesh and a sweet, floral fragrance that almost recalls freesias, the large, tender fruit is free-

stone, meaning it can easily be split by hand and comes away clean from the pit, to reveal a red-speckled center.

Ripe Georgia peaches lend themselves to the most luscious shortcakes and cobblers, and they make wonderful flavorings for ice creams and sorbets. Poached and napped with pureed raspberries and ice cream, they become the dish known as Peach Melba (see page 902). Split in half and topped with crushed macaroons and grated dark chocolate, they can be baked with a little red wine and served warm under a splash of cold, heavy sweet cream. But the peaches may be best appreciated on their own, whether eaten out of hand or more gracefully consumed with knife and fork. (Either way, be prepared with a bib or napkin to catch their delicious, honeyed juices.)

Peaches came to the New World as seeds, with Columbus, but they originated in China, where they are still highly prized as gifts and for special celebrations. The European seeds Columbus brought did especially well in the rich red soil of Georgia, after being introduced along the coast by Franciscan monks in the mid-sixteenth century. In the nineteenth century, a farmer named Raphael Moses began shipping Georgia peaches to other parts of the country, primarily along the East Coast.

Although the once celebrated Elberta peach is no longer commercially grown because of its relatively short shelf life, several of the forty or so Georgia-grown varieties come to upscale East Coast markets from June to early July. Georgia now ranks third in peach production after California and South Carolina. Both Georgia and South Carolina are excellent peach terrain, and have few competitors—save only perhaps Fredericksburg, Texas, where practically all of the superb limited early-summer crop is consumed within its big and hungry home state.

Mail order: Pearson Farm, tel 478-827-0750, pearsonfarm.com; Hale Groves, tel 800-562-4502, halegroves.com. **Further information and recipes:** *Mastering the Art of Southern Cooking* by Nathalie Dupree and Cynthia Graubart (2012); *Peaches* by Kelly Alexander (2013); cookstr .com (search peach cobbler venable; poached peaches in red wine; fresh peach dessert sauce). **Special event:** Georgia Peach Festival, Fort Valley, GA, mid-June, gapeachfestival.com. **Tip:** Peaches are ripe when their skin shows a slight blush and they give slightly to light pressure. Overripe, they become spotted or mushy. To ripen unripe peaches, leave them on a kitchen counter away from sunlight for a day or two. Avoid stacking ripe peaches to prevent bruising.

Peach seeds came to the New World with Columbus.

THE TATER WITH BENEFITS

Sweet Potatoes

American

Once upon a time in big cities, sweet potatoes were a standard type of street food, baked by vendors in makeshift ovens stoked with hot coals, then wrapped in newspaper. The intensely moist and sweet root vegetable

(*Ipomoea batatas*)—often mistakenly referred to as a yam—is one of the defining ingredients of the American South, where the vast majority of those harvested in the U.S. are grown. A member of the morning glory family, it is native to Central America, where it has existed since prehistoric times.

The root vegetable was initially brought to North America with the first settlers, prized because it fared well in the South's warm, arid soil, could be stored for months at a time in a simple mound of dirt, was thick-skinned and thus easy to bake directly on a heat source, and came packed with nutrients. (The sweet potato boasts large amounts of vitamins A, C,

and E, in addition to iron, calcium, copper, and fiber.) Early cultivated sweet potatoes were white or yellow inside—it wasn't until the mid-twentieth century that the now ubiquitous orange-fleshed sweet potato, high in beta-carotene, was introduced to southern U.S. soil. To differentiate the new variety from popular yellow or white versions, the orange potato was referred to by farmers and marketers as a yam (from the African *nyami,* a fibrous, tubular root vegetable of the *Dioscorea* genus that tastes very much like a sweeter version of the sweet potato, but is rarely grown in the U.S.).

Now synonymous with Thanksgiving, the sweet potato is festively baked into pies, or mashed and dressed as a casserole topped with a layer of marshmallows drizzled with melted butter and brown sugar—the latter sickeningly sweet to some, wildly addictive to others. But in recent years, cut and fried as an alternative to the traditional French fry (a favorite at Joe's Stone Crab in Miami Beach) or baked and served plain, it shows up more and more on restaurant menus as a side dish. Plainly roasted, drizzled with a little butter, and sprinkled with salt and pepper, the sweet potato is a distinctively earthy, homey, naturally sweet delight that's enough to make anyone homesick for the South.

WHERE: *In Miami and Washington, DC,* Joe's Stone Crab, tel 800-780-2722, joesstonecrab.com; *in Chapel Hill, NC,* Mama Dip's, tel 919-942-5837, mamadips.com. **FURTHER INFORMATION AND RECIPES:** *Eat at Joe's: The Joe's Stone Crab Restaurant Cookbook* by Jo Ann Bass and Richard Sax (2000); *Hoppin' John's Low Country Cookbook* by John Martin Taylor (2012); *The Sweet Potato Lover's Cookbook* by Lyniece North Talmadge (2010); epicurious.com (search sweet potato and yam galette; candied yams; mashed potatoes and yams garlic parmesan); saveur.com (search sweet potato french fries). **SPECIAL EVENTS:** Ham & Yam Festival, Smithfield, NC, April or May, hamandyam.com; Vardaman Sweet Potato Festival, Vardaman, MS, November, vardamansweetpotatofestival.org.

STILL MINING GOLD

Tadich Grill

American (Californian)

San Francisco has long been at the forefront of inventive California cuisine, but food-loving visitors to the stunning City by the Bay are missing something if they bypass a sampling of its historic culinary past. The very best place to do so is the century-old Tadich Grill, a sprawling, masculine spot in the heart of the city's financial district. It stands close to its original home, but a long way from its beginnings in 1849, as a coffee stand for forty-niners mining for gold.

In the old city tradition of men's clubs, the handsome wood-paneled eatery boasts several half-private alcoves that are especially suited to small lunch or dinner meetings. From any of the available vantage points, whether you're seated at the huge bar, at one of the wide tables, or in a coveted alcove, you can sample superb versions of San Francisco classics like the tomato-based seafood soup-stew called cioppino (see page 545). Also memorable are the delicately slim fillets of flounderlike sand dabs and the silky rex sole—both best pan-grilled—and the local oysters and crabs. Seafood is the specialty, but for non–fish eaters Tadich has always excelled at grilled lamb chops. The restaurant's most historical offering is the delicious hangtown fry (see page 579), said to have been invented by cooks in gold-mining camps—an omelet with thick strips of bacon folded around crunchy fried oysters.

Be sure to try the tartar sauce, a creamy, pungent blend with mashed boiled potatoes as its velvety base; its resemblance to Balkan *scordolea* (see page 381) may result from the Croatian origins of the Buich family, who bought the restaurant from John Tadich in 1928 and have been running it ever since.

WHERE: 240 California Street, San Francisco, tel 415-391-1849, tadichgrill.com. **FURTHER INFORMATION AND RECIPES:** *Tadich Grill* by John Briscoe (2002).

—|||||||||||||||||||||||||||||—

A TASTE OF SUNSHINE IN WINTER

Tangerines

American

"Almost every person has something secret he likes to eat," wrote M.F.K. Fisher in her essay "Borderland," describing the guilty pleasure she once found during a winter in a depressing quarter of Strasbourg. To amuse herself in her fancy hotel room, she froze sections of peeled tangerines out on her frosty window ledge, then quickly thawed them on a radiator: "It was then that I discovered how to eat little dried sections of tangerine. My pleasure in them is subtle and voluptuous and quite inexplicable. Perhaps it is that little shell, thin as one layer of enamel on a Chinese bowl, that crackles so tinily, so ultimately under your teeth. Or the rush of cold pulp just after it. Or the perfume. I cannot tell."

Secret habits aside, there's no need to attach guilt to the palate-tingling curiosity that is the tangerine (*Citrus reticulata*). A type of mandarin, the small, loose-skinned citrus fruit is notable for its unusual, tangy-sweet flavor, its lavish juiciness, and the ease with which it is peeled.

Mandarins originated in Asia and have been cultivated for more than three thousand years, but tangerines acquired their nickname near the end of the nineteenth century, when they were first imported to the United States from Tangier, Morocco. Other easy-to-peel mandarins include the tiny, seedless clementines, sometimes referred to as seedless tangerines, and the Satsumas developed in sixteenth-century Japan, but true tangerines are the most pungent in flavor.

Within the tangerine category, there are a number of hybrids, including the murcott, or honey tangerine, which is not nearly as delicious as the Ojai pixie (in season March to May) or the increasingly difficult-to-find Dancy. The fruits are widely grown in Florida and California, during a short season that runs from November to January—a good time to enjoy their wallop of vitamins A and C. This is all a lot to sing about, which is probably why there have been at least five bands called Tangerine.

MAIL ORDER: Melissa's Produce, tel 800-588-0151, melissas.com; Hale Groves, tel 800-562-4502, halegroves.com. **FURTHER INFORMATION AND RECIPES:** *Uncommon Fruits & Vegetables* by Elizabeth Schneider (2010); epicurious.com (search tangerine granita; tangerine chutney; tangerine bavarian).

—|||||||||||||||||||||||||||||—

WHAT COOKS COVET

Thanksgiving Turkey Broth

American

For most guests gathered around the Thanksgiving table, the priority is properly pacing the carnage in order to fully enjoy the holiday's spoils (while still leaving room for multiple slices of pie). But invariably, there will be a dedicated cook in the party who slyly, quietly waits for it all to end so that the state of the turkey carcass can be assessed and the real fun can begin. To such a canny person, the best part of the bird is that flavorful frame of bones that can be the basis for myriad great soups—imparting a roasty richness to a heady broth that can morph into mush-

Broth is a canvas for many soups.

room and barley soup (see page 450), Louisiana gumbo (see page 572), eastern European-style cabbage or beet borshch (see page 406), Middle Eastern lentil soup, and Italian minestrone (see page 206), to name only a few.

The bigger the turkey the better the bones, and a bird (preferably a tom) that weighs between 20 and 22 pounds before cooking should result in about 6 quarts of bracing stock—enough for three separate instances of soup making.

If soup is the real goal, a little foresight in prepping the turkey for roasting will serve you well. Avoid rubbing the inside of the turkey with a fine, powdery spice like turkey seasoning, as the flavor will stick to the bones and limit the broth's potential. Better to place whole, easily removed sprigs of herb inside the turkey, or, if using a finely ground spice, to season over or under the skin.

Once cooked, the carcass will probably have to be broken up to fit into a conventional

soup pot. Before doing so, it's a good idea to remove most of the meat so that it doesn't overcook as the stock reduces. (It can be added to the finished soup later.) Discard all skin, which will make the broth greasy. Bits of meat firmly stuck to the carcass should be left there to simmer away until they are finally removed along with the bones and any pot vegetables (such as celery, carrots, parsnips, turnips, and onions) added to the broth.

Usually, an hour and a half of slow, steady simmering is enough to produce a lusty broth. Once all bones, vegetables, and solids are strained out, the real soup making can begin. The supremely well-prepared Thanksgiving cook will begin at once, while the rest of us will chill or freeze our broth in 2-quart portions, keeping options open for the future.

Whatever the eventual soup pot holds, the deep, roasty flavor at its base should be treasured as one of the gifts of the kitchen, something wonderful made from something that at least *feels* like it's free.

FURTHER INFORMATION AND RECIPES: *Mastering the Art of French Cooking, Volume Two* by Julia Child, Simone Beck, and Louisette Bertholle (1970); *The Joy of Cooking* by Irma S. Rombauer, Marion Rombauer Becker, and Ethan Becker (2013); saveur.com (search turkey stock).

NOOKS AND CRANNIES GALORE

Thomas' English Muffins

American

The muffins Americans dub English derive from the crumpets of old England, baked on a griddle to achieve their characteristic flat, golden-brown top and bottom and their light, spongy, and airy open-crumb interior.

It's a process dating back to at least 1747, when the English home economist Hannah Glasse provided a recipe for them in her then groundbreaking book *The Art of Cookery Made Plain and Easy*. The crumpets' chief appeal, then as now, is what Glasse described as their inner "honeycomb" texture, which seems designed just to hold pools of melting butter and islands of marmalade.

English "muffins" made a spectacular debut in America thanks to Samuel Bath Thomas, a humble baker who left his native England in 1874, bound for America with little to his name but his family's recipe for a muffin baked on a hot stone griddle. After a few years working in a New York City bakery, in 1880 Thomas had saved up enough money to open his own, at 163 Ninth Avenue in today's Chelsea neighborhood.

Thomas' bakery sold all the usual breads—white and rye and the like—but also a curiosity called English muffins. Thomas advised his inquisitive customers that these were to be hand- or fork-split, not sliced, and toasted prior to serving. Word spread fast, and Thomas was soon opening other bakeries throughout the five boroughs and delivering his English muffins by horse and wagon. He died in 1919, long before his brand became the supermarket classic that it is today, and didn't get to see his muffins adopted as the standard base for eggs Benedict, quick home-made pizza snacks, or deluxe burgers.

TIP: To protect their airy texture, split English muffins with your fingers or a fork, working all the way around to ease the halves apart; avoid cutting them with a knife, which flattens and so ruins the inner crags.

A TOLL MOST HAPPILY PAID

Toll House Chocolate Chip Cookies

American

Salty-sweet, softly chewy, and studded with tiny melting pyramids of chocolate, Toll House chocolate chip cookies offer the kind of wholesome, homey pleasure that seems to catapult us straight back to childhood, when the essential accompaniment was a glass of cold milk—nowadays temptingly swappable for a cup of coffee or tea.

Among the pantheon of American food personalities and institutions, some are real (Chef Boyardee, Hidden Valley Ranch) and some are corporate (Betty Crocker, Aunt Jemima), brand names personified by various front men and women through the years. Nestlé Toll House stands proudly as a member of the "real" team, and it's also arguably the brand with the best culinary legacy.

The Toll House Inn was a historic bed-and-breakfast catering to travelers in Whitman, Massachusetts, about twenty-five miles south of Boston. In 1930, it was bought by a woman named Ruth Graves Wakefield—ironically, a dietician—and her husband. Wakefield was responsible for cooking and serving all the food, and the inn quickly gained a local reputation for excellence. One visitor who helped popularize her skills was the very real Duncan Hines, another notable on the list of American food names. A traveling salesman from Kentucky, in 1935 Hines began publishing a list of the best restaurants he found on the road. In it he included the Toll House Inn, and did much to publicize Wakefield's cooking and her home-made Indian pudding. But it was later in the decade that Wakefield would make her legendary mark, with what was allegedly one of the happiest accidents in culinary history.

Presumably, she was preparing to bake chocolate cookies when she discovered that she'd run out of baker's chocolate. What she had on hand was a bar of semisweet chocolate that her friend, the chocolate company owner Andrew Nestlé, had given her. She broke it into tiny pieces and put those pieces into her favorite batter for buttery sugar cookies. She thought the chocolate would thoroughly melt, but alas (or rather, fortunately) it did not.

The result, which she originally called the Toll House chocolate crunch cookie, was an immediate hit.

Soon after the cookie's debut, the Boston press trumpeted its excellence and published Wakefield's recipe. The cookie's popularity rose, and so

Pairs best with a glass of milk

too did sales of Nestlé's semisweet chocolate bars. Andrew Nestlé and Ruth Wakefield struck a deal. Nestlé would print the Toll House cookie recipe on its package, and Wakefield would receive a lifetime supply of Nestlé chocolate. Whether there was any additional compensation, we don't know, but in 1939 Nestlé introduced semisweet chocolate morsels, and today the package still carries the Toll House chocolate chip cookie recipe, which really remains the best.

WHERE: *In New York*, City Bakery, tel 212-366-1414, the citybakery.com. **MAIL ORDER:** Sarabeth's Bakery, tel 800-773-7378, sarabeth.com. **FURTHER INFORMATION AND RECIPES:** *Toll House Cook Book* by Ruth Wakefield (1953); cookstr.com (search chocolate chip cookies rosemary black; all-american chocolate chip cookies).

──────────||||||||||||||||||||||||||||||──────────

INSIDE EVERY GOOD LUNCH BOX

Tuna Salad Sandwich

American

Is there any American over the age of ten who hasn't experienced the cozy, satisfying lunchtime appeal of the classically mayonnaise-y tuna salad sandwich, perhaps crunched with celery and a sprightly green lettuce leaf?

Yet it's a pleasure well worth rediscovering. Although *fresh* is a justifiably lauded term where food is concerned, certain preserved ingredients (herring, anchovies, caviar, pickles, and dried fruits among them) have a character all their own. Canned tuna is just such an ingredient—the outcome of a long Mediterranean tradition of cooking and preserving various foods in olive oil, combined with a dose of American ingenuity.

The first American cannery was established in 1812 in New York, to preserve oysters, first in glass and then in tin. By the twentieth century, fish canning was an established industry, a particularly large segment of which was based in Monterey, California, and devoted to Pacific sardines. But in 1903, the annual sardine run was short, so canneries packed tuna instead—and a multimillion dollar business was born. Today U.S. canners pack more than 32 billion cans of tuna annually, either as large, solid pieces or as chunks packed in water, vegetable oil, or olive oil.

For first-rate tuna salad, the best choice is solid albacore, packed in light oil that won't fight with the mild flavor of mayonnaise. Well drained on paper towels before being gently broken up with a fork, the tuna should be mixed with finely diced celery, and possibly minced parsley, dill, chives, or tarragon for an airy hint of freshness. It gets a light fork tossing with a dash of lemon juice, a sprinkle of salt and pepper, and a healthy dab of mayonnaise, perhaps with a dab of Dijon mustard. Mixing it gently will avoid the matted-down effect that mars the salad in cheap coffee shops, where tuna is ground to oblivion in food processors.

Mayonnaise, by the way, means Hellmann's (or Best Foods in the West), and the salad should be piled onto good-quality American-style bread, like Pepperidge Farm Original White, or onto thinly sliced light multigrain bread, lightly toasted and spread with a little extra mayo. Add a leaf of a soft lettuce like Boston, or a more sophisticated sprig of peppery watercress if you like, but skip the tomato as its juices mess up the works in most instances.

Two New York classics that offer different but equally delicious versions are Eisenberg's Sandwich Shop, where a counter seat allows viewing of the sandwich's preparation, and Elephant & Castle, where a spread of guacamole adds luster.

WHERE: *In New York,* Eisenberg's Sandwich Shop, tel 212-675-5096, eisenbergsnyc.com; Elephant & Castle, 212-243-1400, elephantandcastle.com. **FURTHER INFORMATION AND RECIPES:** *The Fannie Farmer Cookbook,* 13th edition, by Marion Cunningham (1996); hellmanns.com (click Recipes, then search extra special tuna); epicurious.com (for alternatives to classic tuna salad sandwiches, search albacore tuna sliders; tuna sandwich provencal; happy fish salad sandwiches).

NOT JUST FOR THE DAY AFTER THANKSGIVING

The Perfect Turkey Sandwich

American (New York)

Once upon a time on Manhattan's food-obsessed Upper West Side, there was a revered restaurant-delicatessen known as the Tip Toe Inn, an invitation the locals followed in droves. Along with sublime examples of New York Jewish deli nosh—matzo ball soup, pastrami, corned beef, salamis, and the like—it sold a masterpiece of a turkey sandwich that will be well remembered by anyone fortunate enough to have tried it.

The Tip Toe is long closed, but the sandwich its deft countermen put together can be satisfactorily re-created at home (or ordered fairly convincingly at New York's Eisenberg's Sandwich Shop). It began with wide, thin slices of the best caraway-flecked, crisp-crusted Jewish rye bread. On the bottom slice were piled hand-pulled chunks of moist, freshly roasted dark turkey meat, capped off with paper-thin slices of white breast meat. Then came a padding of cold and crunchy carrot-and-cabbage coleslaw, topped off with a slathering of Russian dressing, that pink-blushed mixture of mayonnaise and Heinz's chili sauce. The sandwich halves were meant to be held in place by long, frilled toothpicks, but with one bite, the whole lascivious mess came undone—part of its charm, and a marvelous excuse for tucking a sizeable napkin under one's chin.

New Yorkers being famous for their complicated customized food orders, there had to be a few options available to those in the know. The classic sandwich could be ordered with white or dark meat only, or the combination could be had as a club sandwich, necessitating the addition of crisp bacon, ripe tomato, and an extra slice of bread. To each diner, his own order; it's still New York, after all.

WHERE: *In New York,* Eisenberg's Sandwich Shop, tel 212-675-5096, eisenbergsnyc.com. **SEE ALSO:** Chicken Sandwich, page 543.

SHED NO TEARS FOR THESE ONIONS

Vidalia and Maui Onions

American

Of all of the many guises and varieties, both wild and cultivated, of *Allium,* the botanical name for the onion family, the two sweetest are the Vidalia of Georgia and its Hawaiian cousin, the Maui. Both hybrids of the yellow granex onion, they are known for their large, semi-flat shape and their yellow skin and white flesh.

These are eating onions, which is to say they are suitable for eating raw, tossed into salads or onto sandwiches (most especially hamburgers), or chopped up and used as condiments for dishes like chili. But their high water content and gentle flavor also make them great candidates for sautéing. Because of their moisture, they turn out pale golden and rarely blacken. Simmered, they create an earthy, sweet sauce for sautéed meats and fish, or even something as plebeian as boiled potatoes. They are equally good baked whole as a side dish, peeled and topped with a little butter and sprinklings of sea salt.

Geography has played its part in the success of these particular bulbs. The Maui onions flourish in the deep-red volcanic earth on the upper slopes of Mount Haleakalā, Maui's dormant volcano. Vidalias, on the other hand, thrive in southeastern Georgia. They took hold there in the 1930s, when farmers searching for a new cash crop tried yellow granex bulbs. These turned out unexpectedly sweet and quickly became beloved. By the 1940s, onions from the region were known for their mild flavor, which scientists later discovered was due to the lack of sulfur in the local soil. In 1986, the legislature of Georgia passed the Vidalia Onion Act, confining the term *Vidalia* to onions from specific counties only.

Sweet onions in general tend to have a spring season. Mauis are

Onions have the utmost flavor and moisture when they're in season.

ready to be harvested as early as April, with a season that runs to about August, and Vidalias are harvested from late April through mid-June. Thanks to the innovation known in the produce industry as "controlled atmosphere storage," both onions are generally available until December (although they have more flavor and moisture and are generally less expensive when purchased in season).

MAIL ORDER: Take Home Maui, tel 800-545-6284, takehomemaui.com (click Maui Products, then Maui Onions); for Vidalia onions, Morris Farms, tel 800-447-9338, sweetonion.com. **FURTHER INFORMATION AND RECIPES:** *The Hali'maile General Store Cookbook* by Beverly Gannon and Bonnie Friedman (2000); epicurious.com (search vidalia onion pie; vidalia fritters); cook str.com (search onion soubise). **SPECIAL EVENTS:** Maui Onion Festival, first weekend in May, whalersvillage.com (click Events & Activities); Vidalia Onion Festival, Vidalia, GA, early spring, vidaliaonionfestival.com. **TIP:** Vidalia and Maui onions are essentially interchangeable served raw or cooked.

"WHEN ONE HAS TASTED IT, HE KNOWS WHAT THE ANGELS EAT."—MARK TWAIN

Watermelon

American

S lurpingly juicy, jolly, and red-fleshed, iced to a thrilling coolness, it's a happy sort of treat that instantly calls to mind summer festivities like Fourth of July picnics and lazy afternoons on the porch. Although iconically American,

watermelon has a long and international history, owing some of its significance on the world food stage to its ability to travel, well encased in its thick, dark-green protective packing of sturdy rind. It's also not quite a melon, but actually a member of the botanical family Cucurbitaceae, and hence a cousin to the more plebeian cucumber, pumpkin, and squash.

Originating in the subtropical African Kalahari desert thousands of years

A ripe melon is 92 percent water.

ago, the fruit is depicted in ancient Egyptian hieroglyphics dating back to well before 2000 B.C., when it appears to have been placed in the tombs of the dead in hopes of nourishing their spirits in the afterlife. By the tenth century, watermelon had traveled to Asia, and today China is its largest producer. Although the fruit is harvested in forty-four American states and in Mexico, the best examples come from the Southern states with which it is so heavily associated, Florida and Georgia in particular. Of the three hundred or so varieties grown, two to seek out are the Sugar Baby, a dark green, early variety, and the Charleston Gray, a huge, elongated, oval-shaped fruit with pale green marbled skin.

Many passionate watermelon eaters swear that their fruit is best enjoyed sprinkled with a bit of salt, which theoretically draws out some of the water while imparting a sweet-salty savor to the flesh. Although ambitious chefs have tinkered with refining what is essentially a messy eating process—transforming the brilliant red flesh into balls, cubes, sorbets, and granitas to adorn haute-cuisine menus—the best way to enjoy it is to take a big bite out of a half-moon slice and spit out the seeds—preferably while outdoors or leaning over a sink.

When selecting a watermelon during its prime, April-to-October season, follow three steps: First, look for a firm, symmetrical shape free of bruises and dents; second, lift it to feel if it seems heavy for its volume—it should, as a ripe watermelon will be 92 percent water; third, check to see if the underside has a creamy yellow spot marking where the fruit sat on the ground as it ripened in the sun.

Further information and recipes: *Mastering the Art of Southern Cooking* by Nathalie Dupree and Cynthia Graubart (2012); watermelon.org; cookstr.com (search watermelon cooler; watermelon gazpacho; watermelon and red onion salad). **See also:** A Basket of Summer Fruit, page 165; Hand Melons, page 577.

───┤||||||||||||||||||||||||||||||├───

POPEYE'S OTHER SUPPLEMENT

Wheatena

American

Among hot cereal devotees, cornmeal, oatmeal, and the ghostly white semolina known as Cream of Wheat may seem like worthy starts to a frigid winter morning, but none have the bracing, rustic texture, aroma, and flavor of old-school Wheatena. Ripe for rediscovery, the king of hot breakfast cereals is a beige-brown, cracked whole-wheat grain meal with a pleasantly nutty taste and a markedly gritty texture. As it simmers away in lightly salted water, it sends forth a hearty perfume—"Wake up and smell the Wheatena" could be as much of an inducement as the lure of brewing coffee, and the cereal has indeed had its share of jingles. Although Popeye memorably relied on spinach for his strength, between 1935 and 1937 the well-muscled sailor admonished young radio listeners, "Wheatena's me diet, I ax ya to try it, I'm Popeye the Sailor man! Toot. Toot."

High in iron, calcium, potassium, and fiber, among other nutrients, the down-home cereal was a New York invention, first ground and named on Manhattan's Mulberry Street, in 1879, by one George H. Hoyt, and now produced in Ohio by Homestat Farm Ltd., along with other old cereal favorites, Maltex and the maple oatmeal, Maypo.

Served in a heated bowl with a generous topping of butter to gloss its grittiness, Wheatena's stiff porridgey texture is its own humble reward. Some might add milk or cream, although they detract from its heat and chewiness, or sugar or syrup, even though salt and pepper make for more harmonious accents. One decidedly delicious way to eat Wheatena is fried. (This is also a great way to use any leftovers.) The cooked cereal should be spread out in a baking pan to a depth of about one and a half inches and chilled overnight; cut into about two-inch squares, it is then slowly fried golden brown on both sides in hot butter. Crisp bacon slices make the perfect garnish to a dish so good you might want it for lunch.

Mail order: amazon.com. **See also:** Oatmeal, page 18; Polenta, page 226; Mamaliga, page 385.

⊣||||||||||||||||||||||||||||||||||⊢

OTHERWISE KNOWN AS *CITRUS PARADISI*

White Grapefruit

American

I n the 1931 film *The Public Enemy*, James Cagney made cinematic history by angrily smashing a half-grapefruit into Mae Clark's face while they were seated at the breakfast table. The characters would have had a much better start to their day had they *eaten* the refreshingly sunny and tart, bittersweet citrus fruit—but then they would have robbed generations of film buffs of a disturbing, innovative, and much-discussed scene.

Introduced to Florida via seeds brought from Barbados in 1823 by one Count Odet Philippe, the fruit originally descended from the Jamaican sweet orange and the pomelo. That citrus fruit, the largest known, sailed from the East Indies to the Caribbean in 1696 with the seafaring Captain Shaddock, and may account for grapefruit's French name, *pamplemousse* and the Italian name, *pompelo*. The English name is a reminder that the fruit tends to grow in grapelike clusters.

Grapefruit's American story began in Florida along the Indian River, where the salt-infused soil is ideal for citrus trees. That state still grows the best grapefruit in the country and perhaps in the world, easily besting California and Texas, Spain, Cuba, China, Mexico, Brazil, India, South Africa, and Israel. The fruit comes in two distinct color families: the lean, elegant, pale yellow to diamond white, and the pink to ruby red. To a high content of Vitamins A and C, rosy grapefruit adds the antioxidant lycopene (the redder the fruit, the higher the lycopene)—though purists favor the yellow-white grapefruit for being zestier. The elegantly sunny, so-called white grapefruit has a sharper, clearer flavor than the sweeter red, but, perversely, is more difficult to find at greengrocers, perhaps because rose red has greater eye appeal. Interestingly, nature presents a dilemma with this fruit: While it is low in calories and offers beneficial vitamins, it also works against the effects of a certain category of medications, most notably including statins.

Grapefruit can be round or ovoid in shape, the latter awkward to serve, as the top, or pointed half, is difficult to nest in a bowl. Whatever the variety, look for bright and unbruised thin skin, a regular shape, and many tiny pinpoints of rust that indicate ripeness and the development of sugar, ensuring that the fruit will not be too sour. A seedless grapefruit (such as a Marsh) will have less flavor than one with large seeds (such as a Duncan), and the fruits should always be stored in the refrigerator.

Cut your grapefruit as close to serving time as possible, and remember that the bottom half will always be the juicier, a fact that might help you decide who gets which. Cut the fruit in half horizontally, then loosen each section with the small, curved, serrated blade of a grapefruit knife. Very sour grapefruit may need a light sprinkling of sugar, but there is no excuse for the travesty that is hot grapefruit, coated with white or brown sugar or honey, and perhaps cinnamon or sherry, then glazed under the broiler.

If you're feeling ambitious, save leftover grapefruit shells in the refrigerator until you have enough to make a sublime bitter marmalade, or to candy as you would orange peel.

Mail order: For Indian River grapefruit, Hale Groves, tel 800-562-4502, halegroves.com. **Further information and recipes:** *Heart of the Artichoke and Other Kitchen Journeys* by David Tanis (2010); *The Fannie Farmer Cookbook,* 13th edition, by Marion Cunningham (1996); *The Joy of Cooking* by Irma S. Rombauer,

Marion Rombauer Becker, and Ethan Becker (2006); epicurious.com (search grapefruit ambrosia; grapefruit tart; avocado and grapefruit salad; grapefruit campari sorbetto). **Tip:** The prime season for Florida grapefruit is from November through March. **See also:** Candied Citrus Peel, page 540.

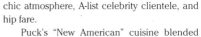

THE ORIGINAL CALIFORNIA PIZZA

Wolfgang Puck's Smoked Salmon Pizza

American (Californian)

The early life of the boyishly charming and wildly charismatic chef Wolfgang Puck hardly suggests a candidate for "guy who'd help invent California cuisine." The son of a hotel resort chef and a coal miner from Sankt Veit an der Glan, Austria, Puck was shipped off to work in a restaurant at the age of fourteen. It was tough-going by all reports, but he worked his way through kitchens of distinction in France and landed in America—to cook in Indianapolis. "I knew about the race so I figured, oh boy, this place must be like Monte Carlo," he told *The New York Times* in 1992.

Eventually some canny Los Angeles businessmen discovered Puck, and by 1982 he managed to open his own restaurant, Spago ("string" in Italian, and slang for spaghetti), on Sunset Boulevard in West Hollywood. With the décor of a modern, airy beach house, the whitewashed room had a huge open kitchen and an in-the-know vibe, and almost immediately became famous for its

Chef Puck adding final touches

chic atmosphere, A-list celebrity clientele, and hip fare.

Puck's "New American" cuisine blended Italian, French, and German influences and was especially beloved for its inventive salads and pizzas—none more than the smoked salmon version, a favorite of Joan Collins, Oprah, and Brad Pitt. "We got in some great smoked salmon and we didn't have time to bake bread so we made pizza," Mr. Puck has said of his creation. "Sometimes you make the best food when you are under pressure and have to improvise. You just have to have great ingredients to work with." Perhaps that's modest: You also have to have the ability to craft perfect pizza dough that manages to be both chewy and crisp, and the fortuitous insight to predict how, if you layer the smoked salmon on top of the pizza only *after* it comes out of the brick oven, it will become even more velvety and smooth.

Brushed with good-quality extra virgin olive oil and scattered with red onion slivers, the dough was cooked for three minutes in an impossibly hot wood-fired pizza oven. Taken out crisp and brown, it was slathered in dill crème, and then piled with extra-thin slices of house-smoked salmon, fresh chives, and several generous dollops of caviar.

Since those early days of improvisation, Puck has had an exceedingly well-choreographed career, complete with many more restaurants, brand extensions, and cookbooks. The original Spago was relocated to a new, highly glamorous dining room in Beverly Hills, where it remains something of a mecca for glitzy housewives, agents, and all manner of movie stars. The smoked salmon pizza, which was off the menu for a number of years and available only to regulars and special guests, is now back in rotation—for lunch only.

Where: *In Los Angeles, Las Vegas, Maui, Beaver Creek, CO,* Spago, wolfgangpuck.com; some of Puck's other restaurants, (of which there are more than sixty) including the Wolfgang Puck Bistro in Tulsa, OK, serve the pizza as well (albeit without the caviar). **Further information and recipes:** *Wolfgang Puck's Pizza, Pasta, and More!* by Wolfgang Puck (2004); *The Wolfgang Puck Cookbook* by Wolfgang Puck (1996); nytimes.com (search wolfgang puck's smoked salmon pizza); yumsugar.com (search pizza smoked salmon).

A MECCA FOR MEAT EATERS

Au Pied de Cochon

Canadian, French

B right, busy, loud, and joyful, Au Pied de Cochon is an essential stop for visitors to Montreal who like their meat luscious, fatty, and abundant—or in short, delicious. That is true whether one opts for anything made with foie gras (most

especially the tart) or the bison tongue heady with tarragon. There are nose-to-tail pork cuts, such as a half or a whole head (roasted for two), chops, and feet, or you can opt for the meat in tarts, terrines, and the pigs' blood sausage, boudin.

To no one's surprise, the operatic chef-owner, Martin Picard, a TV personality who has shared the screen with Anthony Bourdain, turns out a mean hamburger, but why would you settle for that when more enticing choices, such as tartares and ribs of bison or venison and a rosy carpaccio of duck breast, beckon? Duck and guinea hen are all you will find under the heading "Volaille"; mere chickens need not apply. And along with three versions of poutine (see page 642), there are sides, including crisp, savory *frites* infused with duck fat.

An open kitchen lends excitement here, as does theatrical tableside service. Don't miss a signature dish of duck for which the savory bird is steamed along with foie gras and garlic-infused cabbage, all within a tin can set in boiling water for just under half an hour: Picard's own version of *sous vide* cookery.

Lemon tart, crème brûlée, chocolate fondant, or sugar tart for dessert? Maybe you should have thought of that earlier.

Where: 536 Avenue Duluth East, Montreal, tel 514-281-1114, restaurantaupieddecochon.ca. **Further information and recipes:** *Au Pied de Cochon* by Martin Picard (2006).

—||||||||||||||||||||||||||||||—

Canada's Best Cheeses

Canadian

Given cheese's key place in both English and French food traditions, it's surprising that Canada does not have a more vibrant assortment of locally made cheeses. Still, a few deserve the attention of cheese lovers, whether they consider themselves turophiles (from the Greek *tyros*, meaning cheese) or caseophiles (from the Latin *caseus*). Fortunately, all travel well south of the Canadian border.

Oka is the first of these, an all-around snacking cheese that was created by Trappist monks who emigrated to Canada in the mid-nineteenth century and settled in the town of Oka, close to Montreal. They brought with them the method of producing Port Salut, a creamy, ripening, raw cow's milk cheese from their native province of Brittany. Their version has become a mildly tangy, satisfying, and gently chewy accompaniment to apples, pears, or crackling Scandinavian crisp breads, considered by some fans to be a plausible substitute for the richer, more complex, Burgundian Abbaye de Cîteaux. Although today's Oka is made of pasteurized cow's milk by the agricultural cooperative Agropur, the brown-crusted, four-pound wheels of cheese are still aged in the monastery cellars.

Not too surprisingly, Canada turns out a few noteworthy Cheddars, a legacy of the country's British origins. The best comes from the Forfar Dairy in Ontario, where the cheese matures for as long as nine years. But even younger Forfar cheeses provide the needling bite and slight granular crunch of calcium lactate crystals that delight Cheddar lovers and are usually characteristic of only long-aged cheese. Less distinguished perhaps, but more widely available and affordable, the buttery, smooth Black Diamond Cheddar is among the best of the mass-produced varieties. The older it is, the sharper and firmer, of course, and most of the black-wax-covered pieces in upscale food stores are marked with their age. Like most cheeses, Black Diamond is best cut to order from a large block or wheel. Because it is high in butterfat and only gently sharp, Black Diamond works well as part of the shortening in an apple pie crust (see page 521).

That English flair for Cheddars meets the French fondness for goat's milk in providing the inspiration for a series of black-wax-covered Québécois goat's milk Cheddars. They combine the funky patina and teasing saltiness of goat's milk cheeses with the firmness and slight chewiness of nicely crumbly Cheddars. The most distinguished is snowy Le Chèvre Noir, aged for a minimum of nine months and produced by Fromagerie Tournevent in the Quebec-province city of Chesterville.

WHERE: *In New York and environs,* Fairway Markets at multiple locations, fairwaymarket .com; Zabar's, tel 212-787-2000, zabars.com. **MAIL ORDER:** For Black Diamond Cheddar and Tournevent Chèvre Noir, amazon.com; for Oka, igourmet.com; for Forfar Cheddar, Forfar Dairy, tel 613-272-2107, forfar.com.

Canada puts its own twist on French cheesemaking.

———————————|||||||||||||||||||||||||||||||||———————————

Crispy Crunch

Canadian

American loyalty may belong to Nestlé's novelty candy bar Butterfinger, but objective and discerning palates would surely hand the laurels to Crispy Crunch, the treat Cadbury produces only in Canada. It was invented in 1912 by Harold Oswin, a Canadian confectioner who longed to combine chocolate and peanut butter. After several owners, Crispy Crunch was purchased by the British firm Cadbury in 1996, and somewhere along the way this sweet and crunchy teaser's original, plump log shape was redesigned.

Once out of their bright wrappers, Butterfinger and Crispy Crunch look very much alike; both are flat, slim, chocolate-covered five-and-half-inch strips with a center of peanuts in one of two textures. But the Cadbury bar is made of a more appealing, slightly darker chocolate and reveals a finer layered texture within—a firmer, crackling sort of taffy around a velvety fluff of peanuts. Where the flavor of Butterfinger is somewhat bland and simplistically sweet, Crispy Crunch provides an intriguing blend of saltiness, comforting sweetness, and the merest hint of bitterness, all of which add up to a superior candy.

Ingredients lists on both wrappers indicate that we are talking about junk food here, the kind of guilty pleasures that recall childhood indulgences. Some junk, however, is better than the rest, and Cadbury also earns points for vernacular—because everything on its wrapper appears in both French and English, as proscribed by law throughout the French-speaking provinces of Canada. And, to be sure, it all sounds better in French, what with "candy" as *friandise,* "nutrition facts" as *valeur nutritive,* "fat" as *lipids,* and carbohydrates as *glucides.* Alas, calories remain calories: 240 for the Crispy Crunch, 270 for Butterfinger.

MAIL ORDER: amazon.com (search cadbury crispy crunch). **TIP:** Freezing Crispy Crunch bars adds a lively textural crackle. No need to defrost before eating, but break off pieces or cut the bar with a knife if you fear for your teeth. Lightly crushed, frozen Crispy Crunch makes an indecently beguiling topping on scoops of vanilla or chocolate ice cream. **SEE ALSO:** Frozen Milky Way, page 566; Fried Mars Bar, page 38.

———————————|||||||||||||||||||||||||||||||||———————————

Poutine

Canadian (Québécois)

If someone offered you a heaping plateful of French fries drowned to sogginess in brown gravy and dotted with pale clumps of soft, barely creamy cheese, what would you do? Although some high-minded gastronomes might push it all away, the eater who digs in will be rewarded with a decadent mess of comfort foods. Happily the hoi polloi seem to be outnumbering the hoity-toity, and Quebec's increasingly popular poutine (poo-TEEN) is showing up not only all over Canada but in many parts of the U.S., in food trucks, market stands, and restaurants both casual and fancy.

This soppy treat is said to have originated in Quebec in the early 1950s, taking its name from the French *boudin*, referring to the puddinglike meat-and-blood fillings of sausages. And pudding is what poutine gets close to becoming, as the brown gravy soaks into fried potatoes. A further softening accent comes from the fresh, snowy cheese curds that melt slightly and lend a measure of gooey squeaky-ness to the stringy proceedings.

Elegant variations do turn up. In Montreal, the restaurant Au Pied de Cochon (see page

Poutine is even served at Canadian McDonald's.

640) has a version that includes foie gras, and also a Japanese-style sushi *temaki* roll enfolding the standard ingredients. In that same city, La Banquise offers twenty-eight variations on the poutine theme, including additions of hot dogs, bacon, and ethnic variations like the Italian (meat sauce), the Sichuan (highly spiced dandan noodles), the French La Danse (chicken, bacon, onions, and pepper sauce), and the Latino La Taquise (guacamole, sour cream, and tomatoes).

Pay your money and take your choice, but don't write off poutine until you've tried it.

WHERE: *In Montreal,* Au Pied de Cochon, tel 514-281-1114, restaurantaupieddecochon.ca; La Banquise, tel 514-525-2415, labanquise.com; *in Quebec,* Aux Anciens Canadiens, tel 418-692-1627, auxancienscanadiens.qc.ca; *in New York,* Shopsin's, tel 212-924-5160, shopsins.com; *in New York and Brooklyn,* Mile End Deli, mileend deli.com; *in Boston,* The Beehive, tel 617-423-0069, beehiveboston.com; *in Portland, ME,* Duckfat, tel 207-774-8080, duckfat.com; *in Chicago,* The Bad Apple, tel 773-360-8406, badapplebar.com; *in Austin, TX,* Banger's, tel 512-386-1656, bangersaustin.com; *in Los Angeles,* Animal, tel 323-782-9225, animalrestaurant .com. **FURTHER INFORMATION AND RECIPES:** *From Pemmican to Poutine* by Suman Roy and Brooke Ali (2010); saveur.com (search poutine); food .com (search real canadian poutine).

BLUEBERRY TIME IN TORONTO

Shritzlach

Canadian (Toronto), Jewish (Ashkenazic)

A pastry treat that should appeal to just about everyone who loves blueberries, *shritzlach* oddly remains a very local Jewish specialty in the lively and entertaining city of Toronto. (Perhaps the bun's none-too-mellifluous name has

something to do with its relative obscurity.) Barely known even in other parts of Canada, a

shritzlach looks for all the world like a puffy half-football. Crisp-crusted, yeasty pastry enfolds a luscious squoosh of juicy, glistening, tart-sweet blueberries. Enjoying them without dribbling the sparkling purple-blue juices onto ties or shirt fronts requires a certain amount of skill.

Although proper shritzlach can be made with frozen or canned blueberries, the best examples are available in summer when the fresh, winey Canadian blueberries are in season. Briefly simmered to silken softness with sugar and cornstarch, they are delicious when scented with cinnamon and a refreshing splash of lemon juice. Rolled-out yeast dough is cut into five-inch lengths, then blueberry filling is spooned onto each and the dough is folded over before being crimped and baked. Best served cozily warm from the oven and doused with heavy sweet cream or topped with vanilla ice cream, the shritzlach makes for an elegant fork-and-plate dessert. But it is almost as good at room temperature, eaten—carefully—out of hand with coffee, tea, or a glass of milk.

Locating culinary origins can be hazardous guesswork, but shritzlach may be related to the Polish dessert *czarna jagoda* (blueberries) *tort,* also known as *joagodzianki,* possibly brought to Canada by Jewish immigrants from Poland. The original dish consists of cooked and sweetened fruit spooned into a deep dish lined with a thick, baking-powder-leavened batter. As the dessert bakes, the batter rises and wraps over the berries to form a sort of cobbler.

WHERE: *In Toronto,* Eglinton Café & Bakery, tel 416-782-2891; Kiva's Bagels, tel 416-663-9933, kivasbagels.ca; Harbord Bakery, tel 416-922-5767, harbordbakery.ca. **FURTHER INFORMATION AND RECIPES:** *The World of Jewish Cooking* by Gil Marks (1996); *Jewish Food* by Matthew Goodman (2005); *Inside the Jewish Bakery* by Stanley Ginsberg and Norman Berg (2011); mymommashands.com (search toronto blueberry buns); jewishfood-list.com (click Recipes, then Breads, then Buns, Blueberry).

JUST DON'T CALL IT PASTRAMI

Smoked Meat

Canadian, Jewish, Romanian

Pastrami is generally acknowledged to be a Romanian invention, a beef cure achieved by first pickling and then smoking fat and juicy cuts of brisket and finishing them off with a heady coating of peppercorns and spices (see page 459). Done in the New York Jewish deli style, it's a softly grainy, juicy, peppery, and garlic-scented favorite. But up in Montreal in 1928, Reuben Schwartz, an immigrant from Romania, prepared something that, in his recollection, was closer to the native product. Schwartz's, the deli that he opened, still operates in its original location, and there the word *pastrami* is never used, except perhaps by untutored tourists. Rather it is designated smoked meat—*viande fumé* in French, the required language of Quebec province—and categorized as *Charcuterie Hébraïque,* or Hebrew characuterie.

Unlike New York pastrami, smoked meat is a firmer product that manages to emit some dewy moisture, but has a far more intense smoke flavor. Although smoked meat is produced elsewhere in Canada and now in New York, the super-casual Schwartz's, with its menu of lusty meat sandwiches and dishes, should be the maiden stop on the smoked meat tour, simply to establish standards. There it is prepared as it always has been, with prime beef brisket marinated for ten days in an herb and spice mixture, then freshly smoked daily. What results is meat that falls somewhere between what the Swiss call *bündnerfleisch* (see page 330), what the Italians call *bresaola,* and, just barely, what New Yorkers recognize as "real" pastrami.

Perhaps they always will remain skeptical, but smoked meat certainly deserves a chance.

Where: *In Montreal,* Schwartz's, tel 514-842-4813, schwartzsdeli.com; *in New York and Brooklyn,* Mile End Deli, mileenddeli.com; *in Oakland, CA,* Augie's Montreal Smoke Meat pop-up in Beauty's Bagel Shop, tel 510-776-7049. **Mail order:** amazon.com (search smoked montreal beef brisket). **Further information and recipes:** meatwave.com (search montreal smoked meat). **Tip:** Sliced and packaged smoked meat should be gently steamed back to life, following the instructions on the package; it is not meant to be eaten cold.

—|||||||||||||||||||||||||||||||||—

TORONTO'S MASTER CHINESE CHEF

The Cuisine of Susur Lee

Canadian, Chinese

Innovative chefs are inspired by various influences. Some long to imitate current culinary trends; others start from a grasp of science and technology; and more, one hopes, begin by drawing upon the cuisine or cuisines that they have been rooted in, whether during childhood or as grown-ups who have spent time in some foreign place. No matter how far such anchored chefs deviate from their backgrounds, they always seem to have a better framework for creating something that might be called new. No chef working today exemplifies that more than Susur Lee, born in China and trained in Hong Kong, where he became the chef at the legendary Peninsula Hotel on Kowloon.

From there he emigrated to Toronto, eventually winning acclaim for the Chinese-informed dishes he created at his first restaurant, Lotus. He went on to New York's Lower East Side and Washington, DC, where he turned out brightly festive, silken rainbow vegetable salads, such as the slivered cucumber with lotus root, avocado, and persimmons; crispy lobster deep-fried under a veneer of panko crumbs; juicy shrimp and pork dumplings in flower shapes never imagined by nature; and savory pork specialties, all at his restaurants Shang and Zentan. Although those last two closed much too soon, Lee still has TungLok Heen in Singapore, and the restaurants Lee and Bent are flourishing in his adopted city of Toronto. He is also planning a new complex in New York's One World Trade Center.

Lean, energetic, and charismatic, Susur Lee has starred on *Iron Chef America,* which has no doubt lured a wider array of diners to his tables. There they will find,

Chef Susur Lee is affiliated with over twenty restaurants.

among other enticements, dishes such as his duck confit rolled around crunchy nuts and bittersweet dried pineapple in the style of sushi, and silky black cod caramelized with Chinese fruit jams for a burnished sweet flavor, a winner similar to his New York dish of crisp-skinned chicken enhanced with mellow onion preserves. Cool fruit sorbets, mango and passion fruit *panna cotta,* and the French/Chinese Tong Yuen, a cross between sweet rice dumplings and chocolate nougat, are all well worth leaving room for.

WHERE: *In Toronto,* Lee, tel 416-504-7867, susur.com/lee; Bent, tel 647-352-0092, bent restaurant.com; *in Singapore,* TungLok Heen, tel 65/6884-7888, tunglokheen.com. **FURTHER INFORMATION AND RECIPES:** *Susur: A Culinary Life* by Susur Lee (2005).

―――――――|||||||||||||||||||||||||||||||||||||||||―――――――

A SAVORY MEAT CLASSIC FOR CHRISTMAS

Tourtière

Canadian (Québécois)

Although this French-Canadian classic spiced meat pie is a traditional treat during the days between Christmas and New Year's, it is much too fragrant and soul-satisfying to be relegated to that short of a stay on menus. Most traditionally prepared with only pork, the pie sometimes includes beef for contrasting flavor and texture. Whatever the meats, they are enhanced with plenty of onions, potatoes (cubed or mashed), a heady, Christmas-y sprinkling of cinnamon and cloves, and often nutmeg and allspice, plus the cook's choice of herbs. No wonder this lusty, savory stew under a flaky lid of pastry is an enduring favorite not only in Canada, but also across the border in several parts of New England, where each region has its own special spicing formulas and types of pastry.

As with so many dishes, there are conflicting opinions about its origins. Some claim the idea of meat pies came to Canada by way of early immigrants from France as far back as the mid-seventeenth century. The more assertively nationalistic insist that the *tourtière's* spicing and combination of ingredients is strictly Québécois, but that early forms were filled with the meat of game birds and animals, a version that still exists in areas where hunting is popular. Along with dishes known as *tians,* cassoulets, and casseroles, tourtière takes its name from the round pie tin in which sweet and savory *tourtes* are baked.

However it began, tourtière is evidence that a homey stew can take on special-occasion elegance when baked under a golden lid of pastry that, once broken open, allows for the escape of mouthwatering aromas.

WHERE: *In Quebec,* Aux Anciens Canadiens, tel 418-692-1627, auxancienscanadiens.qc.ca; *in Dover, NH,* Harvey's Bakery & Coffee Shop, tel 603-749-3564, harveysbakery.com; *in Attleboro, MA,* Morin's Hometown Bar & Grille, tel 508-222-9875, morins1911.com. **FURTHER INFORMATION AND RECIPES:** *A Taste of Quebec* by Julian Armstrong (2001); *Canada's Favourite Recipes* by Elizabeth Baird and Rose Murray (2012); canadianliving .com (search classic tourtière); allrecipes.com (search traditional french canadian tourtiere).

Mexican
and
Latin American

Argentine, Brazilian, Colombian,
Cuban, Peruvian, Venezuelan

⊢|||||||||||||||||||||||||||||||⊣

THE WHOLE YOU-KNOW-WHAT

Enchiladas

Mexican

It might not look like much at first—just a saucy red casserole topped with melted cheese. But dive into a piping-hot pan of plump and juicy enchiladas, and you will be rewarded with one of Mexico's great comfort foods.

Enchiladas is shorthand for *tortillas enchiladas,* meaning corn tortillas that have been "dipped" in a chile-based sauce. And indeed, food historians conjecture that the original enchiladas were probably the Mayan dish *papadzules:* corn tortillas dipped into a pumpkin-seed puree and filled with chopped boiled eggs. From these humble beginnings, countless variations developed throughout Mexico and beyond. Never mind the nineteenth-century travel guide *Through the Land of the Aztecs,* which called enchiladas "greasy tortilla sandwiches . . . sold everywhere . . . perfuming the air with a pungent, nauseous smell." That unfavorable review, penned in 1883 by an author who called himself "A gringo," clearly betrayed the prejudices of the time.

Gringo's taste notwithstanding, the dish has remained enormously popular and can be found in endless permutations, filled with anything from ground beef to shredded chicken to seafood, swimming in generous quantities of red or green chile sauce. There are the open-faced fried masa cakes topped with red chile sauce and black olives that they make in northern Mexico's Sonora, and the ever-popular New Mexican enchiladas, made by layering tortillas in a tall stack with cheese and onions in between and sauce over all. The kind most familiar to Americans is the belt-loosening Tex-Mex variation with a shredded cheese filling (usually Monterey jack) and a tomato-fortified red chile sauce, served with a scattering of raw onions and rice and beans alongside. In whatever combination of sauce and filling,

enchiladas are a rich, spicy, rustic pleasure.

WHERE: *In Mexico City,* La Casa de las Enchiladas at four locations, lacasadelas enchiladas.com; *in California,* Taquerias El Farolito at multiple locations, elfarolitoinc.com; *in Houston,* Pico's, tel 832-831-9940, picos.net; *in Dallas,* Fearings, tel 214-922-4848, fearingsrestau rant.com; *in New York,* Benny's Burritos, tel 212-633-9210, orderbennysburritos.com. **FURTHER INFORMATION AND RECIPES:** *The Cuisines of Mexico* by Diana Kennedy (1986); *Rick Bayless's Mexican Kitchen* by Rick Bayless (1996); saveur .com (search enchiladas). **SPECIAL EVENTS:** The Whole Enchilada Fiesta, Las Cruces, NM, September, enchiladafiesta.com.

A sauce-covered, exuberant mess of a dish

—|||||||||||||||||||||||||||||||||—

WHEN THE CHIPS ARE DOWN

Guacamole

Mexican

We have the ancient Aztecs to thank for the luscious, buttery, spicy dip that they called *ahuaca-mulli* (avocado sauce), and that we know as guacamole. These days, guacamole is still a simple affair, a bright-green mash of avocados sparked with onions, hot green chiles, garlic, cilantro, salt, and a generous squeeze of lemon or lime juice. The addition of tomatoes is controversial. However delicious those juicy, rosy fruits may be, they can dilute the rich texture and flavor of the mix, and make it more perishable to boot. Mexican cooks aren't all in agreement on this point, however, and ingredients vary from region to region. In the Jeréz market in Zacatecas, in north-central Mexico, for exam-

The world's most addictive dip

ple, guacamole is made with both tomatillo and sour cream. In the state of Guanajuato, in central Mexico, guacamole might contain small amounts of chopped peaches, grapes, or pomegranate seeds. And in New York, one Anna Falcone stirs in cooked corn kernels, while ABC Cocina adds green peas, and at élan, uni joins the luscious fray. Regardless of embellishments, though, everyone agrees that guacamole is best prepared and served in its authentic vessel, the *molcajete*, a black volcanic stone mortar. A wooden or ceramic bowl and a sturdy fork do almost as well.

Because of its simplicity, guacamole is only as tasty as the avocados it is made with, and the best variety for the occasion is the nutty, creamy Hass, a small avocado with rough skin that turns from green to purplish-black as it ripens. The Fuerte, with smooth green skin, is a good second choice—similar in flavor to the Hass and somewhat larger.

As anyone who has made guacamole knows, the single biggest pitfall is the avocados' rapid oxidation, which can turn the beautiful, sunny dip an unappetizing-looking brown. This is, to some degree, preventable, at least for an hour or two. Avoid reactive metal dishes and utensils when making your guacamole, and store it in a deep bowl, refrigerated and covered tightly with plastic wrap, with an avocado pit nested in the middle to forestall darkening. If you still get discoloration, just scrape off the top layer—what's left underneath should still be a vivid green.

Where: *In ten U.S. cities; San Juan, Puerto Rico; Panama City; and Dubai,* Rosa Mexicano, rosamexicano.com; *in Houston,* Irma's Southwest Grill, tel 713-222-0767, irmassouthwest.com; *in Austin, TX,* Güero's Taco Bar, tel 512-447-7688, guerostacobar.com; *in New York,* Coppelia, tel 212-858-5001, coppelianyc.com; élan, tel 646-682-7105, elannyc.com; ABC Cocina, tel 212-677-2233, abccocinanyc.com. **Mail order:** For Hass avocados, tel 760-749-4568, californiaavocados direct.com. **Further information and recipes:** *The Essential Cuisines of Mexico* by Diana Kennedy (2009); *Rick Bayless's Mexican Kitchen* by Rick Bayless (1996); bonappetit.com (search guacamole). **Special event:** Avocado Festival, Carpinteria, CA, October, avofest.com.

⊣||||||||||||||||||||||||||||||⊢

Huachinango a la Veracruzana

Mexican

Huachinango a la veracruzana is a pungent rainbow of a dish, with an enticing herbaceous fragrance and a jalapeño-heightened flavor enveloping filets of red snapper and small jewel-like cuts of vegetables. Native to Veracruz, it is made by marinating the fish in lime juice, then baking it under a tomato sauce that includes olives, capers, a variety of fresh herbs, and emerald glints of the jalapeños that give the dish heat and depth. Warm corn tortillas, served alongside, sop up fish and sauce. All manner of firm, white-fleshed fish can be used in place of the snapper, as it is the piquant and flavorful *veracruzana* sauce that is the true centerpiece of this beloved dish.

WHERE: *In Xalapa, Mexico,* Café y Restaurante La Parróquia, 52/228-817-7401; *in Veracruz City,* *Mexico,* Restaurante La Choza (no phone); *in Dallas,* Veracruz Café Dallas, at two locations, veracruzcafedallas.com; *in Houston,* Pico's, tel 832-831-9940, picos.net; *in New York,* Pampano, tel 212-751-4545, richardsandoval.com/pampano. **FURTHER INFORMATION AND RECIPES:** *Zarela's Veracruz* by Zarela Martinez with Anne Mendelson (2001); *New World Kitchen* by Norman Van Aken (2003); epicurious.com (search pescado a la veracruzana); cooking channeltv.com (search veracruz red snapper).

⊣||||||||||||||||||||||||||||⊢

Huevos Rancheros

Mexican

As their name suggests, huevos rancheros ("ranch eggs") were originally a hearty breakfast served to farmhands in rural Mexico, a simple, filling affair of eggs and spicy tomato salsa spooned over warm corn tortillas. The dish found its way north (probably along the Camino Real, the Spanish royal road linking Mexico City and western Louisiana that's now called the Old San Antonio Road). Eventually it made its way to San Antonio, just 150 miles from the Mexican border and the birthplace of Tex-Mex cuisine. From there, huevos rancheros became a diner staple across North America, served in innumerable variations, often including refried pinto or, better yet, black beans, slices of avocado, melted cheese, and garlic chile sauce. The eggs might be scrambled, poached, or omelet-style, but the best by far are fried, with their bursting yolks smothering the whole saucy, spicy mix. It's an exquisite mess, understandably considered by many to be ideal hangover fare, and inarguably a breakfast classic.

WHERE: *In San Antonio, TX,* El Mirador, tel 210-225-9444, elmiradorrestaurant.com; Mi Tierra Café, tel 210-225-1262, mitierracafe.com;

in Santa Barbara, CA, D'Angelo's Bakery, tel 805-962-5466; *in Montecito, CA,* San Ysidro Ranch, tel 805-565-1700, sanysidroranch.com; *in Chicago,* Frontera Grill, tel 312-661-1434, rickbayless.com; Xoco, tel 312-334-3688, rick bayless.com; *in New York,* ABC Cocina, tel 212-677-2233, abccocinanyc.com; La Esquina, tel 646-613-7100, esquinanyc.com; *in Brooklyn,* La Esquina, tel 718-393-5500, esquinabk.com. **FURTHER INFORMATION AND RECIPES:** *Rick Bayless's Mexican Kitchen* by Rick Bayless (1996); saveur .com (search huevos rancheros); epicurious .com (search huevos rancheros). **SEE ALSO:** Eggs Sardou, page 560; Migas, page 653.

A MARKET IN THE HEART OF MEXICO CITY

Mercado de La Merced

Mexican

With a history that dates back to the Spanish colonization of Mexico, La Merced has endured through the centuries as one of the world's largest and most spectacularly colorful and festive markets. Named for the La Merced monastery, which was built in 1594 and on whose grounds the market is now located, it is just east of Mexico City's famed Zócalo plaza and is a must-visit for anyone wanting to experience the many delectable specialties of the Mexican kitchen.

Since the mid-1980s, La Merced has been housed in several enormous, lofty buildings, each focusing on specific types of food or wares. To stand in any one of these vast halls is to be dazzled by the variety and abundance, but is also an opportunity to be educated and enticed by the fruits, vegetables, spices, meats, fish, and more that make up this country's diverse and tantalizing cuisine. To be sure, you'll need more than a single visit to take it all in.

In the largest hall, you'll find an immense array of fruits and vegetables—nopales (cactus pads), nimbly plucked of their spiny needles; a rainbow of chiles, dried and fresh; corn in hues from yellow to purple; jade-green tomatillos; banana leaves to be wrapped around rice and beans and steamed; and brilliant tropical fruits galore. Among the breathtaking sights of the meat hall are the enormous whole pigs' hides, flattened out and fried in one piece to be broken up into *chicharrones,* hanging aloft like great golden sails. Another hall is dedicated to fish and shellfish, both familiar and exotic, and still another is brimming with vivid and aromatic mounds of Mexican spices.

Among the Mercado de La Merced's offerings are authentic mole pastes and powders.

There is action, too, as *antojitos,* or street snacks, are prepared and sold on-site: Fresh tortillas are patted out and grilled; tacos and quesadillas stuffed to order with beef *picadillo,* roasted pork, beans, or cheeses; tamales wrapped and steamed; and corn kernels ground into fine yellow masa (meal). And of course, there are seriously sweet sweets, such as the eggy *natilla* custard, honeyed almond pastries, and cinnamon-spiced Mexican chocolate to be eaten or drunk hot—a reminder that we owe thanks to the Mayans and the Aztecs for this particular treat.

Traditional Mexican cookware and kitchen accessories fill another hall, with the bright textile mats, towels, and aprons and gleaming cut tinware and earthy pottery making for attractive, and useful, souvenirs. A crowded whirl of color, flavors, and aromas, La Merced is a sight to behold, and a highlight of any visit to Mexico City.

Where: East of the Zócalo, Mexico City. **When:** Daily, 8 a.m. to 7 p.m. **Tip:** To be sure your nosh does not have an unhappy ending, avoid all raw fruits and vegetables that cannot be peeled and drink only bottled beverages opened before your eyes.

FOOD OF THE GODS

Mexican Hot Chocolate

Mexican

E ven when the rich and satiny wonders of France and Belgium are taken into account, Mexico just might have the edge when it comes to hot chocolate— mainly due to the addition of the richly flavored, almost brandylike Mexican vanilla

and (most importantly) of cinnamon, added either by stirring the potion with a cinnamon stick or by flavoring it with a cinnamon-sugar mix. That exotic dash of cinnamon, and the way it combines with the sweet, boozy hint of vanilla extract seems to lend sophistication and depth to a drink that becomes decidedly grown-up.

Chocolate, of course, is a treat the world owes to the Aztecs and the Mayans. It is made from cacao, the fruit of a small tree native to the tropical forests of Central and South America that well deserves its botanical name, *Theobroma cacao,* "food of the gods." The Olmecs were the first to discover the delicious wonders of the cacao bean some three thousand years ago, but it was the Mayans and later the Aztecs who advanced its use and especially revered the bean. By the year 1400, the Aztecs were trading it as a form of currency and enjoying a variety of chocolate drinks, sometimes as a part of rituals, and sometimes just for pleasure. They combined

their treasured cacao with honey, nuts, seeds, and various spices, and developed chocolate-based drinks that are enjoyed in Mexico to this day.

Mexico's answer to coffee and doughnuts

Champurrado, which combines chocolate with *atole,* a creamy, warm, Mexican and Central American drink made with masa (cornmeal) or cornstarch, is especially popular at Christmas and New Year's and is generally served alongside churros (crisp, cinnamon-dusted strips of fried dough, see page 257) or *pan dulce* (sweet bread). *Tejate* is a Oaxacan specialty, a restorative cold drink made of chocolate, masa, and the aromatic tropical flowers known as *flor de cacao.* But the most delicious of all is the sweet, foamy Mexican hot chocolate, made from solid circular or hexagonal tablets of spiced chocolate (preferably Ibarra brand, from the Chocolatera de Jalisco in Guadalajara) that are dissolved into hot milk or cream, and then blended, using a utensil called a *molinillo,* a turned wooden whisk that is twirled between the palms. It whips the ingredients together, folding in just enough air to produce a silky texture and a heady froth. Regional variations might include anise or cayenne, but it is the essential trio of sweet chocolate, fragrant vanilla, and aromatic cinnamon that makes this such an enduring favorite.

Where: *In Oaxaca City, Mexico,* Chocolate Mayordomo, tel 52/951-512-0066, chocolate mayordomo.com.mx; *in Chicago,* Xoco at two locations, rickbayless.com/restaurants/xoco; Xocoatl at multiple locations, churrofactory.com. **Mail order:** For Ibarra chocolate, hot chocolate kits, and *molinillo* utensils, mex grocer.com. **Tip:** If you don't have a *molinillo,* a whisk or blender will produce appropriately frothy results. **See also:** Callebaut Chocolate, page 144.

EGGS WITH EVERYTHING

Migas

Mexican (Tex-Mex)

A big, lusciously messy scrambled egg dish with just the right amount of crunch and heat, *migas* is a much-loved breakfast throughout Mexico and the American southwest, especially in Texas. The Tex-Mex diner staple takes its name from the Spanish word for crumbs, as it is a New World take on a Spanish dish of day-old bread fried in olive oil with garlic and chorizo sausage.

Migas traveled to Texas with Mexican immigrants, and (because "everything is bigger in Texas") grew into a showstopping combination of crisp tortilla chips mixed into beaten eggs, along with diced onions, fresh chiles, tomato, and chewy, spicy flecks of chorizo. Crowned with a mellowing heap of shredded jack cheese and properly prepared, migas is an addictive mélange of salty and savory flavors and complementing textures—the crunch of the tortilla chips, the softness of the egg, the sting of chiles, and the neutralizing creaminess of the cheese. It should be crusty and golden brown, like a good omelet, and garnished with fiery hot sauce, refried beans (preferably black), warm tortillas, *café con leche,* and plenty of napkins.

Where: *In San Antonio, TX,* Ácenar, tel 210-222-2362, acenar.com; *in Austin, TX,* Güero's Taco Bar, tel 512-447-7688, guerostacobar.com; *in Kansas City, MO,* Classic Cup Café, tel 816-753-1840, classiccup.com. **Further information and recipes:** *Simple Fresh Southern* by Matt Lee and Ted Lee (2009); food.com (search tex-mex migas); epicurious.com (search migas). **Tip:** Migas is a wonderful use for tortilla chips gone stale.

—|||||||||||||||||||||||||||||||—

A SAUCE WITH SECRETS

Mole

Mexican

The intensely dark, rich, and flavorful family of sauces known as mole is one of the most subtle and sophisticated culinary gifts handed down to us from the Aztecs, who called it *mōlli* in their Nahuatl language, meaning mixture or concoction.

At its base, the mixture contains any number of indigenous Mexican chile peppers, fresh or dried, traditionally combined in the stone mortar and pestle called a *molcajete*. Other ingredients include fruits, vegetables, herbs and spices, and thickeners such as seeds, nuts, bread, and masa (cornmeal). The big surprise to novices is the inclusion in most moles of unsweetened chocolate, a finisher that adds a deep burnish and earthy undertones to the spicier seasonings.

The city of Puebla is usually acknowledged as the birthplace of mole as we know it today. Popular legend has it that in the sixteenth century the superior of the Santa Rosa convent there created a version of the traditional Aztec sauce to honor a visiting archbishop. Another story has the visit of a European viceroy to Puebla causing a stir among the royal chefs; and the head chef, Fray Pascual, becoming annoyed and ordering that all the ingredients lying around be gathered onto a single tray. Just then a mighty wind swept the ingredients into a pot where turkeys were stewing and thus was the first mole born.

Whatever its origins, the best-known version remains Puebla's mole poblano. It calls for at least twenty ingredients, including aromatics such as cinnamon, cloves, anise seed, and black pepper, along with poblano chiles and chocolate. Oaxaca is famously "the land of the seven moles," which include bright-green, cilantro-infused *moles verdes*; orangey-red moles made with plantain; *mole negro*, or black mole, made with nuts, chiles, dried fruits, and chocolate;

mole rojo (also called *mole colorado*), a dense, red concoction rich with tomatoes, sesame seeds, and sweet spices; and *manchamantel* ("tablecloth stainer"), a mixture of tomatoes, banana, pineapple, cinnamon, and ancho chiles. Other regional interpretations include peanut-buttery *cacahuate* moles and *mole almendrado*, a rich, dark-brown, almond-based version.

No matter the precise formula, the components are always pounded, blended, and then simmered together. Traditionally, mole is served over poultry, although many other proteins are routinely substituted. Besides patience and an arsenal of ingredients, Mexican cooks claim that the secret to a delicious mole has to do with the proper preparation of the chiles—specifically, the painstaking roasting of their seeds, which become charred bits that act like flavor bombs when mixed into the sauce.

WHERE: *In Puebla, Mexico,* Fonda la Mexicana, tel 52/222-232-6747; El Mural de los Poblanas, tel 52/222-242-0503, elmuraldelos poblanos.com; *in Houston,* Pico's, tel 832-831-9940, picos.net; *in Chicago,* Frontera Grill, tel 312-661-1434, rickbayless.com; *in Salt Lake City,* Red Iguana at multiple locations, rediguana .com; *in New York,* La Esquina, tel 646-613-7100, esquinanyc.com; *in Brooklyn,* La Esquina, tel 718-393-5500, esquinabk.com. **FURTHER INFORMATION AND RECIPES:** *The Essential Cuisines of Mexico* by Diana Kennedy (2000); rickbayless.com (search mole); saveur.com (search mole). **SPECIAL EVENT:** National Mole Festival, San Pedro Atocpan, Mexico, October, ferianacionaldel mole.com.

THE SUNNY ESSENCE OF THE TROPICS

Pineapple

I n 1493, when Christopher Columbus and his crew first laid eyes on *Ananas comosus* in Guadeloupe, they christened it "pine-apple" because its craggy, bronze, and prickly cylindrical form resembled a pinecone. Ever since, its juicy, sweet-and-sour, sun-gold flesh has been cultivated wherever nature permits.

In much of the world, it is known as *ananas*, derived from the name used by the Tupi Indians of South America (*nanas* meaning "wonderful fruit"), who cultivated the pineapple after it was brought to the continent by Brazilian sailors. In northern Europe, it became a symbol of exotic luxury, and was favored as a pricey garnish for steak and fish. The pineapple's artful form also inspired European furniture designers and architects throughout the eighteenth and early nineteenth centuries, when it commonly appeared as finials and other decorative elements in wood, iron, and stone.

Eventually, Hawaii emerged as one of the fruit's largest producers (and the place where pineapple canning was perfected in the late nineteenth century). And the fruit became so closely identified with those islands that, during the "tiki" craze of the late 1940s through the 1960s, it was the star ingredient in everything from cocktails to noodle dishes at so-called Hawaiian or Polynesian restaurants, such as Don the Beachcomber and Trader Vic's, throughout the U.S.

Today, the delectable fruit is still grown in Hawaii and beloved around the world, but it is a particular favorite in Latin American countries, enjoyed as *agua fresca* (fresh juice) in Mexico, in empanadas in Argentina, and grilled alongside meats in Cuba.

With its stately crown of gray-green, sword-like leaves, the pineapple is in fact a collection of tightly compressed individual berries, which accounts for the husk's three-dimensional mosaic of rosettes. The varieties of pineapples now most available in U.S. markets are the tapered Red Spanish, grown in Latin America, and the sturdy, cylindrical Smooth Cayenne, which was first cultivated in Hawaii, though it is now grown worldwide.

To check for ripeness, see if one of the top leaves can be easily pulled out (they should offer only a bit of resistance), and examine the husk's color. If it is entirely green under the buds, it will probably not ripen before it rots; there should at the very least be a yellow-pink blush around the bottom quarter of the fruit. If the husk is deep golden all over and the buds are withered and dry, it is past its prime.

Once you get it home, the pineapple should be stored upside down (or as close as you can manage while leaving the top intact) so its sweet juices permeate the entire length of the fruit.

Mail order: Melissa's Produce, tel 800-588-0151, melissas.com; Maui Gold Pineapple Company, tel 808-877-3805, pineapplemaui .com; Kaua'i Sugarloaf Pineapple, tel 808-635-0061, kauaisugarloaf.com. **Further information and recipes:** *The Hali'imaile General Store Cookbook* by Beverly Gannon (2000); *Cracking the Coconut* by Su-Mei Yu (2000); *New World Kitchen* by Norman Van Aken (2003). **Special event:** Lana'i Pineapple Festival, Lana'i, HI, July, lanaipineapplefestival.com. **Tip:** The pineapple husk provides an attractive and tidy container for serving. Simply quarter the fruit vertically, trim out the woody inner core, and undercut the flesh from the rind as you would with a slice of cantaloupe. Then slice the flesh into ½- to 1-inch-thick slices. The sliced sections can be eaten directly from their boat-shaped shells.

—|IIIIIIIIIIIIIIIIIIIIIIIIIIIIIII|—

A VEGGIE TO GET STUCK ON

Nopales

Mexican

If the thought of eating cactus seems unduly hazardous, you have probably not tried the gently sweet and enticingly pulpy pads known as nopales. The term refers to a large group of thorny plants (genus *Opuntia*) native to Mexico that were favorites of the Aztecs and Incas, who prized their thick, juicy young leaves. The flesh of these leaves, or pads, has a delicious and refreshing flavor that's a cross between that of artichoke, zucchini, and string bean, with a pleasantly chewy texture. But to get to it, cooks must first strip the pads of their spines, peel off the tough skin, and then cut the flesh into strips, an ordeal often better left to professionals with sturdy gloves and sharp knives. The results are well worth the effort, however. Briefly simmered and topped with the traditional squeeze of fresh lime juice, nopales are a fantastic addition to everything from salads to tacos, sandwiches, and omelets. (If you're not up to the task of preparing the nopales, you can buy the strips bottled, usually preserved in brine or vinegar, at Latin food shops.)

Where: *In Tijuana, Mexico,* La Fogata, tel 52/664-684-2250, restaurantlafogata.com; *in Chicago,* Los Nopales, tel 773-334-3149, losnopalesrestaurant.com. **Mail order:** Melissa's Produce, tel 800-588-0151, melissas.com; mexgrocer.com. **Further information and recipes:** *The Cuisines of Mexico* by Diana Kennedy (1986); rickbayless.com (search nopales). **Special event:** Festival del Nopal, Santa Cruz, CA, July, festivaldelnopal.com.

Beneath their spines, nopales reveal a luscious, juicy flesh.

—|IIIIIIIIIIIIIIIIIIIIIIIIIIIIIII|—

MOVE OVER, MATZO BALLS

Sopa de Tortilla

Mexican

Among the many delicious ways to enjoy tortillas, one of the very best is in a fragrant and bracing broth. A specialty of Mexico City, tortilla soup at its simplest and most authentic is a heady, golden chicken broth enriched with sautéed onions and roasted tomatoes, ancho chiles, epazote (a popular Mexican herb whose flavor suggests tarragon), and fried strips of tortillas to bolster the mix. Thick, rich, and altogether satisfying, it's a mix that benefits from the contrasting flavors and textures that characterize Mexican soul food at its best.

Tortilla soup started popping up on California menus and in American cookbooks in the mid-twentieth century, and its popularity stateside has never ebbed. Expectedly, it has sprouted countless variations and can now commonly be found made with beans (both pinto and black) and loaded with garnishes such as sour cream, avocado, diced fresh tomatoes, and various Mexican cheeses. Although perhaps not "authentic," these embellishments enhance the soup's complexity and flavor, whether in a version as elegant as Dean Fearing

created in Dallas for his own Fearing's restaurant or as rustic as the one devotees line up for on Saturdays at lunchtime at the San Antonio café, El Mirador.

WHERE: *In San Antonio, TX*, El Mirador, tel 210-225-9444, elmiradorrestaurant.com; *in Dallas*, Fearing's Restaurant, tel 214-922-4848, fearings restaurant.com; *in Los Angeles*, Loteria Grill at multiple locations, loteriagrill.com; *in CA and Las Vegas*, Border Grill at multiple locations, border grill.com; *in Chicago*, Frontera Grill, tel 312-661-1434, rickbayless.com. **FURTHER INFORMATION AND RECIPES:** *The Whole World Loves Chicken Soup* by Mimi Sheraton (1995); *Rick Bayless's Mexican Kitchen* by Rick Bayless (1996); *The Texas Food Bible* by Dean Fearing (2014); fearingsrestaurant .com (click Dean Fearing, then Recipes, then Dean's Tortilla Soup with South of the Border Flavors); epicurious.com (search tortilla soup).

⊣||||||||||||||||||||||||||||||⊢

MEXICO'S DAILY BREAD

Tortillas

Mexican

Warm and embracing, with just enough chew to be convincing, tortillas are the hallmark of Mexican cuisine, whether eaten alone as a snack, served alongside a bowl of soup, or used as the wrappers for tacos, enchiladas, burritos,

and quesadillas. Though often made with wheat flour, which offers a softer texture and milder flavor, they are best when made of the traditional masa (cornmeal), which imparts a subtle, rustic corn flavor and a rough-and-chewy texture that contrasts nicely with soft fillings. Cut into triangles and deep-fried, they become the ubiquitous and addictively snackable tortilla chips, best when freshly made, and indispensable as vehicles for salsas and guacamoles.

The method and ingredients used to make this round, thin, unleavened bread have changed little since they were first documented by the Spanish conquistadores who arrived in

Mexico in the late fifteenth century, and who bestowed upon them the name *tortilla*, meaning "little cake." In those times, tortillas (which the Aztecs called *tlaxcalli*) were created from native maize that was first parched in the hot sun, then rehydrated and softened in a combination of lime (calcium oxide), ash, and water. The kernels were then ground into dough called masa, shaped into cakes, and cooked on a stone griddle. Today, a premade maize-based flour called masa harina is sold commercially, and is simply mixed with water to make the traditional dough. Handmade tortillas are shaped, flattened (usually stamped down with a special tortilla press), and toasted on a hot griddle until speckled and golden but still soft and pliable, following a time-honored system.

The essential hallmark of Mexican cuisine

Although the basic method and ingredients have remained the same for centuries, there have always been regional differences in tortilla styles. Oaxaca's are known for their delicacy and thinness, while people of the mountainous towns of central Mexico prefer theirs made with blue corn. In northern Mexico, meanwhile, an entirely different kind of tortilla evolved, one made of wheat flour mixed with lard to form a rich, short dough that is rolled out into circles before being griddled. In whatever guise, tortillas offer comfort and sustenance. They are the very heart of any Mexican meal, and an ancient food grown ever more popular throughout the world.

WHERE: *In Culver City, CA,* Tito's Tacos, tel 310-391-5780, titostacos.com; *in CA and Las Vegas,* Border Grill at multiple locations, border grill.com; *in New York,* Taquitoria, tel 212-780-0121, taquitoria.com; Empellón Taqueria, tel 212-367-0999, empellon.com/taqueria. **MAIL ORDER:** For tortilla presses, mexgrocer.com. **FURTHER INFORMATION AND RECIPES:** *Authentic Mexican* by Rick Bayless with Deann Groen Bayless (2007); *My Mexico* by Diana Kennedy (1998); *New American Table* by Marcus Samuelsson (2009); saveur.com (search homemade tortillas). **SEE ALSO:** Frontera Grill and Topolobampo, page 565; Enchiladas, page 648; Huevos Rancheros, page 650; Migas, page 653; Sopa de Tortilla, page 656.

‐||||||||||||||||||||||||||||||‐

A FINE PICKLE

Verduras en Escabeche

Pickled Vegetables

Mexican

S imilar to the cool and lovely French appetizer of vegetables cooked *à la grecque,* Mexico's *verduras en escabeche,* often on the table as a premeal palate-tingler, adds a pungent bolt of chiles and a heady dose of garlic to the proceedings. The bowl may contain only one vegetable—green beans, say, or carrots—or it may hold a rainbow array, including tiny white onions, mushrooms, and whole jalapeño peppers, all of which have been simmered with lemon and herbs just until crisp-tender, and served cold. Garlic is a constant, whether in cloves or in whole heads, cooked to an inner softness so that the sting is gone but the buttery, aromatic flesh is ready to be spread on slivers of toasted tortillas or simply munched on its own.

Mexican Pickled Vegetables

Makes 1 pint

1 pound of a single vegetable or a mix: carrots, peeled and cut crosswise into ¼- to⅓-inch-thick slices; green beans, trimmed and cut into 1-inch lengths; small, peeled pearl onions; and/or small whole mushroom caps

1 head garlic, broken into unpeeled cloves (see Notes)

3 large jalapeño peppers, split lengthwise,
*   or 6 small whole (see Notes)*
1 cup vegetable oil, preferably corn oil,
*   but olive oil will do*
½ cup fresh lemon juice, or to taste
2 or 3 sprigs fresh cilantro, or 1 tablespoon
*   coriander seed*
1 small bay leaf
1 teaspoon dried Mexican oregano
6 to 8 crushed black peppercorns
Pinch of ground cumin

1. Place all of the vegetables in a deep, heavy saucepan. Add all the remaining ingredients and enough water to cover. Bring to a rapid boil over high heat, then reduce the heat to low and let simmer, partially covered, until all of the vegetables are almost tender, about 10 minutes.

2. Uncover the pan, let the liquid come to a rapid boil over high heat, and boil until all of the vegetables are tender but bright and still a bit firm, about 10 minutes. Using a slotted spoon, transfer the vegetables to a bowl and set it aside.

3. Boil the cooking liquid, uncovered, until it is reduced to a near syrupy state, about 10 minutes. Strain this sauce over the vegetables and stir to mix thoroughly.

4. Refrigerate the vegetables, covered, for at least one hour before serving, so they will be slightly cool. The pickled vegetables covered with their juices can be refrigerated for at least 1 week.

Notes: If you want to pickle just garlic, you will need 6 unpeeled heads in place of the vegetables here. The heads of garlic will need to cook a little longer than the vegetable mixture. Pierce each head of garlic with a needle in several places to shorten the cooking time.

You can also pickle just jalapeño peppers; you will need 24 jalapeños in place of the vegetables here.

FURTHER INFORMATION AND ADDITIONAL RECIPES: *Zarela's Veracruz* by Zarela Martinez with Anne Mendelson (2004); *Rick Bayless's Mexican Kitchen* by Rick Bayless (1996); bonappetit.com (search escabeche de verduras).

A rainbow, pickled and jarred

||||||||||||||||||||||||||||||||||

¡ARRIBA, AREPAS!

Arepas

Latin American

The rustic, pleasantly puffy, savory griddled corncakes enjoyed throughout Latin America have justifiably enjoyed a surge of popularity as a cheap and delicious street food in many parts of the U.S.—nowhere more so than in Queens,

N.Y., where Maria Piedad Cano, known as the "Sainted Arepa Lady," plies her savory trade.

A humble but addictive treat, they can be considered cuddly stand-ins for English muffins—

though they are a considerably heartier affair, the golden disks, craggy and rough-hewn, with a crisp, browned crust and warm, tender interior, are the perfect receptacles for melting pats of sweet butter and small amounts of more substantial fillings.

Considered among the basic breads of Latin America, in particular Colombia and Venezuela, arepas are believed to have originated in Colombia, where a variety of high-quality sweet corn flourishes in the mountainous terrain. Today, they are made from a special flour of precooked and finely ground corn, combined with hot water, salt, butter, and sometimes a mild cheese. The light cakes are a delicious foil for spicy stews and barbecued meats, and street vendors commonly offer them split and filled with beans and cheese (*arepa de dominó*) or shredded beef and cheese (*arepa de pelúa*). In Venezuela

Arepas con queso

especially, you'll find arepas served for all three meals, paired at breakfast with strong coffee and hot dipping chocolate.

WHERE: *In Caracas,* Arepa Factory, tel 58/212-285-1125; *in Humble, TX,* Arepas y Empanadas Doña Maria, tel 281-540-4449, aedonamaria.com; *in Las Vegas,* Viva Las Arepas, tel 702-366-9696, vivalasarepas.com; *in New York,* Caracas Arepa Bar at two locations, caracasarepabar.com; *in Queens,* The Arepa Lady, tel 347-730-6124, twitter.com/arepalady. **MAIL ORDER:** For Harina P.A.N., a brand of precooked cornmeal, amigofoods.com. **FURTHER INFORMATION AND RECIPES:** *The South American Table* by Maria Baez Kijac (2003); *Bobby Flay's Throwdown!* by Bobby Flay, Stephanie Banyas, and Miriam Garron (2010); epicurious (search reina pepiada arepas); saveur.com (search arepas de huevo).

||||||||||||||||||||||||||||||||||||||||||||||||||||||||||||||||||||||||||||||||||||||||||||||||||||

Bananas

Cheeringly sunny and bright, bananas are eaten just about everywhere on earth. Given their appetite-quelling density, nutritional benefits, low cost, and gentle, honeyed sweetness, their popularity is no surprise. They are equally enjoyable eaten out of hand, sliced into bowls of rich sweet cream or yogurt (with or without cereal), or as a flavoring for ice creams, pies, and custards. Fried or baked to a crisp and sparked with salt, they become snackable, chiplike nibblers. And they are often the

first solid food given to infants, so nourishing and comforting are these beloved fruits.

It may be hard to believe that something so ubiquitous could be in danger of extinction, but in fact scientists do worry about the fate of the Cavendish, the variety of banana we overwhelmingly consume (to the tune of more than 7 billion pounds a year in the U.S. alone). They worry with good reason, as there's historical precedent for the kind of species-eradicating blight that could put one of our favorite fruits at risk. The Cavendish has already succumbed in Asia and Australia. Could the plantations of Latin America, where the majority of America's bananas are grown, be next?

A case in point is the story of the Gros Michel banana, today an exotic and extremely difficult-to-find variety, but once the banana our grandparents sliced into their breakfast cereal. The first banana imported into the U.S., the Gros Michel is much more flavorful than the bananas we eat today. Rather large and almost evenly thick, less tapered than most types, the Gros Michel is sweeter and fruitier, with just a hint of verdant, leafy bitterness. During the 1950s, it was decimated by a fungus, and by the early '60s, the fruit industry had switched to the Cavendish.

Leave it to the celebrated chef Thomas Keller to attempt a small-scale resurrection. At the French Laundry, his restaurant in Napa Valley (see page 562), one of the occasional, seasonal menu items is an ice-cream dish garnished with a puree of Gros Michel. When he first added the dessert to the menu, the cognoscenti were abuzz. Where, they wondered, did he locate a supply of this legendary banana? Speculation had it that in Ecuador, there were survivors of the Gros Michel blight, and that Big Mikes, as they are affectionately known, were being secretly grown under the name Seda. But, supposedly, none were being exported. The theories multiplied. Were Gros Michels secretly being grown in California for this most prestigious chef? The likely truth: Gros Michels are reportedly being raised in very small quantities in the Congo, St. Lucia, and Jamaica, and they intermittently appear in the hands of certain dealers in the San Francisco and Los Angeles wholesale produce markets—which is how Keller most probably came by them.

The history of the coveted Gros Michel offers an important reminder for today's banana lovers: By mass-farming single varieties, we are providing vast tracts on which fungi can thrive. So do your part to encourage healthy banana diversity by seeking out rare breeds like the Gros Michel—and if you find some, please spread the word.

FURTHER INFORMATION: newyorker.com (search we have no bananas mike peed). **TIP:** Another banana worth trying is the celebrated Philippine lacatan variety, also grown in several places in the Caribbean.

HOT STUFF!

Chile Peppers

Latin American

A mong the traits characteristic of what psychologists classify as a risk-taking personality—alongside riding roller coasters, bungee jumping, and gambling—is the love of hotter-than-hot foods, generally in the form of chile

peppers or their enlivening extracts. Whatever mental state such a preference indicates, there is no doubt that a fiery tingle on the tongue keeps the palate from getting bored.

Not to be confused with black pepper, the product of a completely different plant, chiles are members of the nightshade family, along with potatoes, tomatoes, eggplant, and tobacco, all native to the Americas. It was, of course, Christopher Columbus who introduced these New World delicacies to Europe, and who is also the source of the misleading "pepper" moniker. On his voyage in search of a short sea route from Spain to the Spice Islands, he happened upon the hot, berrylike fruits we know as chiles, and mistook their heat for that of the black peppercorns that he sought in the East.

But chiles (of the *Capsicum* genus) are the only plants that contain capsaicin, a natural alkaloid compound that gives peppers their spark. Unlike black pepper, which burns on the back of the tongue, near the throat, heat from capsaicin is felt on the tip and sides of the tongue. The chile's unique type of heat is quantified on the so-called Scoville scale, which measures the piquancy based on the amount of capsaicin present. Invented in 1912 by the American pharmacist Wilbur Scoville, the scale goes from 0 (bell pepper) to upwards of 1.5 million (the Guinness-World-Record-holding Carolina Reaper).

Among the twenty-six known *Capsicum* species, only five are domesticated. Owing to its popularity and availability, the king of these is the short, stocky, thick-skinned jalapeño, most often picked when still green, although it turns red when fully ripe. Lending its kick to an array of dishes from salsas and stews to nachos, cornbread, and various cheeses (it is the pepper in pepper jack), the jalapeño ranges widely in heat (from about 2,500 to over 10,000 Scoville units) depending on its cultivation conditions and ripeness. Today, there are even jalapeño varieties specially bred for mildness, for those who enjoy the flavor but can't take the heat.

For more intrepid palates, the chiles of choice would be the squat, lanternlike, bright-orange habanero (*C. chinense*), the larger, hotter, red Savina habanero, which packs a wallop of 580,000 Scoville units, or the jolly little Scotch bonnet, astonishingly hot and particularly popular in the Caribbean. Easier-on-the-tongue varieties include the Anaheim (*C. annuum*), a green-to-red, long, flat pepper that ranges in heat from mild to medium, and the related but more pungent cascabels. They range from green to dark red and are generally dried, ground, and incorporated into Mexican sauces, meat dishes, and tamales.

Confusingly, many pepper varieties acquire new names after being dried or otherwise processed. Thus, medium-spiced poblanos (*C. annuum*)—triangular, dark-green peppers—become anchos or mulatos when dried, and jalapeños that have been smoked are labeled chipotle. One of the world's most popular dried peppers is paprika, a red powder that is actually comprised of an assortment of sweet to hot red peppers from the *C. annuum* cultivar, rather than one distinct pepper.

Whether your tastes run to sweet slices of mild bell pepper; mild, cheesy *chile rellenos* (stuffed peppers); pungent pickled jalapeños; or fiery hot chile sauces, consider the happy fact that chiles are a health food. A fresh green one is said to have as much vitamin C as six oranges, and one teaspoon of dried red chile powder should contain the recommended daily allowance of vitamin A. It's no wonder that this flavorful New World crop became a worldwide culinary staple.

MAIL ORDER: Specialty Produce, tel 619-295-3172, specialtyproduce.com (search chile pepper); MexGrocer.com, LLC, 858-270-0577, mexgrocer.com (search chile pepper). **FURTHER INFORMATION AND RECIPES:** *The Peppers Cookbook* by Jean Andrews (2005); *Vegetables from Amaranth to Zucchini* by Elizabeth Schneider (2001); chilepepperinstitute.org; for pepper growing guides, The Chile Man: thechileman.org/guide_home.php. **SPECIAL EVENTS:** Chile Pepper Festival, Brooklyn Botanical Gardens, Brooklyn, September, bbg.org (search chile pepper festival); Chile Pepper Festival, Bowers, PA, September, pepperfestival.com; Hatch Chile Festival, Hatch, NM, September, hatchchilefest.com. **TIP:** To extinguish the burning caused by chiles, some turn to dairy foods high in the milk protein casein. Another school of thought favors plain steamed rice or plain bread to perform a mopping-up action on the tongue. When handling chile peppers it is a good idea to wear rubber gloves or, if not, carefully wash your hands with hot water and soap to remove volatile oils. Be sure not to rub your eyes while working with chiles, and to carefully wash any work surfaces the peppers have touched. **SEE ALSO:** Pimentón, page 267; Paprika, page 395.

Dulce de Leche

Latin American

A mazing what a little milk, sugar, care, and patience can yield. For that is all you need to make *dulce de leche,* the simplest of treats. The milk and sugar simmer for an hour or more, allowing the flavors to meld and the sugar to caramelize and add a golden glow. By the time this happens, most of the water in the milk has evaporated. The result is a creamy, syrupy, solid-and-liquid hybrid that is a popular base for desserts all over Latin America. It is particularly well loved in Argentina, where it's essentially a national addiction and can be found in almost every neighborhood café or bakery.

Spanish and Portuguese colonists are generally credited with developing this sweet, originally as a way of preserving milk. Nowadays, it is spread on toast and eaten for breakfast, poured over cake, and used as a topping for flan and a filling for *panqueques* (sugar-dusted crêpes) and empanadas. Although long enjoyed in Latino communities in the United States, dulce de leche hit the mainstream in 1997, when Häagen-Dazs debuted its dulce de leche ice cream and Starbucks began mixing it into coffee drinks. Both were huge hits, and dulce de leche has been popular in American desserts ever since—it's even become a beloved flavor of Girl Scout cookies. It's hard to imagine any food going more mainstream than that.

MAIL ORDER: Amigofoods, tel 800-627-2544, amigofoods.com (search havanna dulce de leche). **FURTHER INFORMATION AND RECIPES:** *The South American Table* by Maria Baez Kijac (2003); *New World Kitchen* by Norman Van Aken (2003); saveur.com (search dulce de leche); epicurious.com (search dulce de leche ice cream; coconut dulce de leche). **SPECIAL EVENT:** Expo-Cañuelas & Dulce de Leche Festival, Cañuelas, Argentina, November, buenosaires .travel/Fiestas_Provinciales_Noviembre-en .aspx.

Empanadas

Latin American

A ll the world loves crisp pastry turnovers, plump with savory fillings, and among the most luscious of these is the empanada, an ingenious hand pie that is ubiquitous throughout Latin America. Easy to grab for a quick lunch and usually inexpensive, empanadas are a fast food par excellence—warmly aromatic crescents formed of flaky pastry dough filled with spiced meats and vegetables, which vary according to regional preferences, and baked or fried to golden perfection. (The word *empanada* means "that which is covered with bread" or, more simply, "embreaded.")

Favored throughout most of Latin America, and in a few regions of Spain as well, empanadas probably date back to the days of the conquistadors. In Veracruz, Mexico, they are often made with masa harina (cornmeal flour) and filled with *minilla*, a spicy, scintillating mixture of shark meat, chiles, olives, and capers. In Chile, empanadas may be stuffed with bits of clams, mussels, and sea scallops, while in Bolivia they make two kinds of meat fillings: *picante*, which is spicy, and *suave*, which is more gently seasoned. Potato and egg fill out both versions. Outside of Latin America, Galicia, Spain, is famous for the *empanada gallega*, filled with a stewlike blend of tuna or pork and peppers.

Argentina, though, is the mecca for empanada lovers. The puffy turnovers are one of that nation's most famous dishes, served as appetizers in the elegant restaurants, offered for takeout in neighborhood bakeries, and sold from street-food carts throughout the country. Regional specialties abound. In San Juan province, they are made with green olives, hard-cooked eggs, and a touch of tomato. In Tucumán province, empanadas are filled with diced, chile-spiced beef and sometimes scallions. *Zanahoria* (carrot) is a local favorite, and there is also a meatless empanada, enjoyed nationwide for Easter, stuffed with Swiss chard and chopped egg in a light béchamel sauce. For a sweet finish, dessert versions are filled with caramel-like dulce de leche (see page 663) as well as fresh pineapple or *membrillo* (quince paste).

Where: *In Buenos Aires,* La Cupertina, tel 54/11-4777-3711; *in Pucón, Chile,* Empanadas y Hamburguesas Lleu-Lleu; *in New York,* Buenos Aires Restaurant, tel 212-228-2775, buenosaires nyc.com; Chimichurri Grill, tel 212-586-8655, chimichurrigrill.com, Ruben's Empanadas, tel 212-962-5330, rubensempanadas.net; *in Miami,* Half Moon Empanadas at two locations, halfmoonempanadas.com; *in Los Angeles,* Empanada's Place, tel 310-391-0888, empana dasplace.com. **Further information and recipes:** *Food and Drink in Argentina* by Dereck Foster (2003); *The Art of South American Cooking* by Felipe Rojas-Lombardi (1991); saveur.com (search empanadas); foodandwine.com (search flaky beef empanadas). **Special event:** Latin American Empanada Festival, Tucumán province, Argentina, September, tucumanturismo .gov.ar (search empanada). **See also:** Knishes, page 443.

THE MOST BELOVED BEANS

Frijoles Negros, and a Soup of the Same

Latin American

Shiny black on the outside, smooth and creamy on the inside, black beans (*Phaseolus vulgaris*, sometimes called turtle beans) are the most popular bean variety in Latin America and a signature ingredient in dishes from Mexico to Chile;

they also appear in Cajun and Creole cuisine and in the foods of Latino communities in the United States and around the world.

Believed to have originated near Peru, they were brought to Europe by the Spanish in the late fifteenth century, along with other New

World discoveries such as tomatoes and chocolate. Like many foods, their history holds some darker moments—beans were cultivated in the southern United States as an inexpensive food source for slaves. Eventually they became a lasting culinary heritage itself in the region.

Earthy, smoky, sweet, and meaty in texture, black beans are high in protein, fiber, and antioxidants and low in fat. They are the foundation of everything from Brazilian feijoada to Tex-Mex huevos rancheros. Like their counterpart, the pinto bean, with which they frequently duel on Mexican restaurant menus, black beans are also excellent "refried": simmered in water until tender, then mashed and slowly cooked in oil over low heat with garlic and chiles. And, of course, because they are dense and hold up to long simmering, black beans make a seductive soup.

Many Latin American cuisines have their versions—Mexicans finish theirs with a garnish of *queso fresco* and fried tortilla strips—but Cuban black bean soup stands out for its surprisingly complex and wonderful mix of flavors and textures. The secret is the sautéed mixture of onions or scallions, garlic, and green peppers called *sofrito* (meaning browned in Spanish), which lends the dish its distinctive earthiness. As the finishing touch, pork trimmings or ham add saltiness and heft, and a little squeeze of fresh lemon or lime brightens the proceedings tremendously.

Traditionally served with a mound of snowy rice and chopped raw onions, the soup was reportedly a favorite of Ernest Hemingway during his Havana days, when he was a habitué of El Floridita restaurant—best known as the original home of the daiquiri. The bracing drink is an ideal accompaniment to the rich soup, so why not raise an icy glass before diving in, to toast Papa Hemingway and one of his favorite dishes.

WHERE: *In Miami,* Islas Canarias, tel 305-559-6666, islascanariasrestaurant.com; Versailles, tel 305-444-0204, versaillesrestaurant.com; *in Tampa, FL,* Columbia Restaurant, tel 813-248-4961, columbiarestaurant.com; *in Los Angeles,* El Floridita, tel 323-871-8612, elfloridita.com. **MAIL ORDER:** amazon.com (search cuban black bean mix; Iberia dried black beans). **FURTHER INFORMATION AND RECIPES:** *Coyote Café* by Mark Miller (2002); *Zarela's Veracruz* by Zarela Martinez with Anne Mendelson (2001); *In a Cuban Kitchen* by Alex Garcia (2004); cookstr .com (search cuban black bean soup); foodnet work.com (search cuban black bean soup). **TIP:** In supermarkets, look for Goya brand black beans, both dried (in bags) and cooked (in cans). **SEE ALSO:** Moros y Cristianos, page 677; Red Beans and Rice, page 615.

SOFT, SLOPPY, AND SOULFUL

Picadillo

Latin American

B elonging to the category of pungent, meaty comfort foods that make much out of little—and a first cousin of chili, *ropa vieja,* and sloppy joes—Latin America's *picadillo* is a full-flavored medley of tomatoes, sweet spices, and onions, combined

with finely chopped beef or pork. Derived from the word *picar,* "to chop," picadillo can be embellished with a variety of ingredients, although the foundation of simmered, chopped meat remains constant. In Mexico, raisins or pineapple sweeten the sauce, which is also spiked with peppers, enriched with potatoes, and scattered with almonds. In Cuba, green bell peppers are often added to the mix, their bitterness offset with warm spices like cinnamon, cloves, and cumin.

As diverse as the recipes for picadillo are, so is the manner in which it is presented. It may be tucked into the buttery shell of an empanada, poured over white rice or cornbread, sandwiched in a roll, baked with plantains, or stuffed into a taco or quesadilla along with luscious melted cheese. An inexpensive dish to make, picadillo is widely loved, a crowd pleaser whose complex spice and humble richness beat a sloppy joe any day.

Where: *In El Paso, TX,* H&H Car Wash and Coffee Shop, tel 915-533-1144; *in San Rafael, CA,* Sol Food Restaurant, tel 415-451-4765, sol foodrestaurant.com; *in New York,* Benny's Burritos, tel 212-254-2054, orderbennysburritos .com. **Further information and recipes:** *Rick Bayless's Mexican Kitchen* by Rick Bayless (1996); saveur.com (search picadillo).

A Latin-American cousin of chili, served over rice

POTATO CHIPS, MOVE OVER

Tostones

Latin American, Caribbean

Sweet and salty, crisp yet gently soft, warm and fragrant, fried plantain chips are to many Latin Americans and Caribbeans what potato chips are to us. Unlike spud chips, these salty discs have a short shelf life and taste best not more than thirty minutes out of the fryer, long before they chill to limpness. The basis for this delectable snack, the plantain (*Musa paradisiaca*), is a member of the banana family, but with a big difference: Unlike other peel-and-go bananas, plantains are rarely eaten raw, and then only in their near-rotting stage of purple-black ripeness. Bright green when immature, they ripen from yellow to red-gold until they blacken.

For the chips dubbed *tostones,* green plantains meant for frying are peeled, which is not so easy to do, as the unripe skins tend to cling. Then they are sliced about one inch thick, patted dry, and briefly deep-fried in vegetable oil to a pale golden color. The next step is to drain them on a paper towel or a similar absorbent surface and then sandwich them between two sheets of waxed paper or plastic wrap for flattening. Depending upon the skills of the cook, this may be done with the heel of a hand or with a small plate or a flat-bottomed glass. Anyone who loves specialized utensils or seeks mechanical perfection can resort to a *tostonera,* a hinged rectangular paddle made of wood or metal that clamps and spreads the plantain rounds to the correct ⅛-inch thickness. The fruit then receives another quick deep-frying and a liberal salting for a result that is most enticing as an accompaniment to rum or beer, whether served alone or alongside various dips or salsas.

A more substantial alternative to the simple flat tostone is the stuffed version, for which the correct tostonera has one flat side and one that is a convex half-dome. The dome presses a nest into the fried slice so it can be stuffed with a tomato-sauced seafood mix, seasoned ground meat, or cheese, plain or with olives. Once the stuffing is in place, a second flat tostone covers everything, for what becomes a serious, seductive mouthful.

Where: *In New York,* Victor's Cafe, tel 212-586-7714, victorscafe.com; Cuba, tel 212-420-7878, cubanyc.com; *in Miami,* Islas Canarias, tel 305-559-6666, islascanariasrestaurant.com; *in Houston,* Cafe Piquet, tel 713-664-1031, cafepiquet.net; *in Chicago,* Frontera Grill, tel 312-661-1434, rickbayless.com; *in Los Angeles,* Cuba de Oro, tel 323-661-5900, cubadeoro.com; *in ten U.S. cities; San Juan, Puerto Rico; Panama City; and Dubai,* Rosa Mexicano,

rosamexicano.com. **Mail order:** For plantains, Specialty Produce, tel 619-295-3172, specialty produce.com; for tostoneras, Cuban Food Market, tel 877-999-9945, cubanfoodmarket .com (search bamboo toston maker). **Further information and recipes:** *A Taste of Puerto Rico* by Yvonne Ortiz (1991); *Memories of a Cuban Kitchen* by Mary Urrutia Randelman and Joan Schwartz (1996); *New World Kitchen* by Norman Van Aken (2003); *Zarela's Veracruz* by Zarela Martinez with Anne Mendelson (2004); *The Sugar Reef Caribbean Cookbook* by Devra Dedeaux (1991); cookstr.com (search tostones with herbed salt raichlen; sweet fried plantains emmons).

Unlike bananas, plantains are rarely eaten raw.

⊢||||||||||||||||||||||||||||||⊣

HOW GREEN IS MY STEAK SAUCE

Chimichurri

Argentine

What ketchup is to burgers and mustard to hot dogs in the U.S., the supple, aromatic, bright-green *chimichurri* sauce is to grilled steak in Argentina. A heady blend of green herbs such as parsley and cilantro, along with garlic,

oregano, bay leaf, onion, and sometimes hot red pepper flakes, chimichurri looks like liquid emeralds and offers endless enticement to the palate. Although primarily served with beef in Argentina, the sauce does every bit as much for grilled or roasted lamb, pork, fish, chicken, and

especially (though surprisingly), duck, and it makes for a fragrant, tenderizing marinade as well. Red bell peppers are a common addition to the classic chimichurri mix, and some cooks like to add tomatoes, although they tend to sweeten and water down the result. Thyme is favored by those who prefer a certain earthy dimension, and cooks with fond memories of Italian *salsa verde* may be inspired to add a spoonful of minced capers.

As for that charming name, there are at least two theories of its origin. One is that the sauce was created by and named for a British meat dealer named Jimmy Curry. Another suggests it was derived from the phrase *che mi curry,* a misguided request for curry spoken by English soldiers who had been captured after unsuccessfully attempting to invade Argentina, a Spanish colony at the time.

Chimichurri
Makes about 1½ cups

½ cup olive oil
2 tablespoons red wine vinegar
2 tablespoons finely minced yellow onion
½ teaspoon dried hot chile flakes
1 clove garlic, finely minced
½ cup finely chopped fresh flat-leaf parsley
   leaves
¼ cup finely chopped fresh cilantro leaves
1 tablespoon finely minced sweet red bell
   pepper
½ teaspoon dried oregano, or 1 teaspoon
   minced fresh oregano leaves
1 small bay leaf, very finely crumbled

Combine all the ingredients in a bowl and stir vigorously, then let stand for at least 2 hours at room temperature, or for 7 to 8 hours, covered, in the refrigerator, to allow the flavor to develop. Serve it at room temperature. Chimichurri keeps very well and can be made in advance and stored in tightly closed glass jars in the refrigerator for up to 1 week.

Argentina's famously pungent, garlicky sauce

Where: *In New York,* Chimichurri Grill, tel 212-586-8655, chimichurrigrill.com. **Further information and additional recipes:** *New World Kitchen* by Norman Van Aken (2003); foodand wine.com (search traditional chimichurri); epicurious.com (search chimichurri); asado argentina.com (search chimichurri). **Tip:** For a supermarket fix, try Goya Chimichurri Sauce.

THE HUNGER KILLER

Matambre
Stuffed Flank Steak

Argentine

Its name a contraction of the Spanish words for kill and hunger, *matambre* is a classic Argentine dish of flank steak split, pounded, and rolled around an herb-flecked vegetable stuffing, and served at room temperature in colorful pinwheel slices. Although somewhat tricky to prepare, matambre is an ideal special-occasion entrée, elegant on the plate and needing no last-minute fussing in the kitchen. As a bonus, matambre improves upon standing, and its leftovers make a great sandwich filling.

To become matambre, the flank steak must first be butterflied, then generously seasoned with herbs and garlic. Topped with spinach, carrots, and hard-cooked eggs, it is rolled up and secured with kitchen twine, seared for a nice brown crust, braised in strong beef stock, then cooled and sliced. The colorful, confettilike filling and the tender, juicy meat make an enticing,

unforgettable combination of flavors and textures. The pride of the pampas, indeed.

WHERE: *In Buenos Aires,* Café Margot, tel 54/11-4957-0001; *in Pittsburgh, PA,* Gaucho Parrilla Argentina, tel 412-709-6622, eatgaucho .com; *in Los Angeles,* Gaucho Grill at two locations, tel 310-447-7898, gauchogrilldining.com. **FURTHER INFORMATION AND RECIPES:** *Braise* by Daniel Boulud (2006); *The Art of South American Cooking* by Felipe Rojas-Lombardi (1991); *New World Kitchen* by Norman Van Aken (2003); foodnetwork.com (search matambre); saveur .com (search matambre). **SEE ALSO:** Carpetbag Steak, page 895.

GOING NUTS IN THE AMAZON

Brazil Nuts

Brazilian

The largest and most eye-catching nuts in any mixed assortment, the tapered, mahogany-shelled Brazil nuts (*Bertholletia excelsa*) delight with their mellow, buttery overtones and their firm, meaty texture and toothsome snap, especially

when roasted and lightly salted.

The yellow-beige nuts are the products of the huge, majestic Brazil nut trees that grow wild in the Amazon River basin. (These are also known as monkey pot trees, because hungry primates often get their hands stuck inside the round, woody pods that house up to three dozen of the nuts, each in its own woody shell.) The trees are most plentiful in the country for which they are named, of course, but they also grow in Bolivia, Venezuela, Peru, and Ecuador. More tree facts: Because the Brazil nut tree is so tall—150 feet is not an unusual height—and grows in dense jungle, it's impossible for harvesters to climb. The nuts are therefore gathered only after the fruit ripens and falls to the ground.

In addition to being deliciously satisfying, Brazil nuts are rich in heart-healthy oils, protein, and very high in selenium, a mineral some doctors believe helps prevent prostate cancer. Just two nuts a day meets the daily requirement, which is handy, as they're also high in calories.

MAIL ORDER: nuts.com; superiornutstore .com. **FURTHER INFORMATION AND RECIPES:** *Tasting Brazil* by Jessica B. Harris (1992); epicurious .com (search roasted asparagus brazil nut; brazil nut banana parfait). **TIP:** Brazil nuts may be refrigerated or frozen for up to nine months. Informed consumers search out Brazil nuts from the cooperatives of indigenous Amazon farmers, looking for the "Fair Trade" mark, RONAP, which is the Spanish acronym for Organization of Organic Brazil Nut Gatherers of Peru.

---||||||||||||||||||||||||||||||||||||||||---

BET YOU CAN'T EAT JUST ONE

Cashews

Brazilian

The plump and cheery comma-shaped cashew nut, lightly roasted and salted, ranks high among foods that are difficult to stop eating once you have started. Less known is the cashew apple from which the cashew nut dangles, the latter

encased in an unlovely bulbous appendage of its own. The pulpy, sweet apples are edible, and in cashew-producing regions are frequently juiced or made into jams and chutneys. But the delicate fruits rot within twenty-four hours of dropping from the tree, and so aren't exportable in their fresh state. The nuts, however, with their sweet, irresistible flavor and their innumerable culinary uses, are well worth saving.

An important crop for their native Brazil, where the apple is especially prized and the nuts are commonly added to sauces and eaten as snacks, cashews also grow in parts of Africa and in India, where they add depth to stews like *shahi korma*. In the U.S., they have found favor

in part as a substitute for peanuts among those with allergies, although, alas, the cashew is not allergy-proof. To make them even easier to like, cashews have one of the lowest fat contents among nuts, and contain antioxidants and healthy oils. Although generally eaten on their own as a nutritious snack, chopped, toasted cashews are an elegant addition to stews, sauces, stir-frys, and salads.

Mail order: nuts.com; superiornutstore .com; bazzininuts.com. **Further information and recipes:** *Tasting Brazil* by Jessica B. Harris (1992); International Tree Nut Council, nut health.org/cashews; epicurious.com (search cashews).

---||||||||||||||||||||||||||||||||||||||||---

A BOWL OF PLENTY, AND THEN SOME

Feijoada

Brazilian

The very definition of homey and hearty, the smoky, salty Brazilian stew of meat and beans called *feijoada completa* is *completa*, and then some. An epic feast displayed on a lavish buffet, it is a huge and sustaining lunch meant to take

up the better part of an afternoon. Almost everyone in Brazil, from supermodels to farmers, takes pleasure in a regular feijoada—most traditionally as a special-occasion Saturday luncheon that most definitely needs to be followed by a lengthy nap.

To a basic black bean stew flavored with onions, tomatoes, cilantro, and garlic, all manner of pork and other meats are added, including *carne seca* (dried beef) and linguica (smoked pork sausage). Before the official eating begins, guests are offered *caldinho de feijão*, bean broth served in small ceramic cups or shot glasses, often garnished with fried pork rinds (*torresmos*). The actual feijoada is served informally, with hot beans usually in a tureen, and the meats alongside on clay platters. Traditional accompaniments include fluffy white rice, orange slices (meant to cut some of the dish's richness), sautéed collard greens, hotter-than-hot sauce made of habanero chiles, and fine, crunchy *farofa,* made of toasted manioc flour (also known as cassava flour), to be sprinkled over all.

Taking its name from the Portuguese word for bean (*feijão*), feijoada likely originated in the 1600s in Recife, on Brazil's northeastern coast, on the vast sugar plantations built by Portuguese colonists. It may be partly derived from the Portuguese meat and vegetable stew *cozido,* but was probably an invention of the African slaves brought over to work the fields, who added black beans to the cuts of meats that the plantation owners discarded (pigs' ears, feet, and tails and the like). Also perhaps harkening to the stew's sugar plantation roots, the traditional accompaniment to feijoada is cachaça, the potent sugarcane brandy that is

Brazil's most popular liquor. While mainly known abroad as an ingredient in caipirinha cocktails, in its native Brazil the clear and fresh-tasting spirit is often artisanally produced and sipped on its own. When enjoyed with feijoada, it serves as what the French call a *trou Normand,* there a traditional between-courses break during long meals to down shots of calvados, thereby burning a hole (*trou*) in already full stomachs to accommodate more food. With an hours-long feijoada feast before you, a few nips of cachaça are a most welcome, fortifying palate cleanser.

WHERE: *In Rio de Janeiro,* Caesar Park Hotel (for Saturday lunch only), tel 55/21-2525-2525, caesarpark-rio.com; Casa da Feijoada, tel 55/21-2247-2776; *in Miami,* Boteco, tel 305-757-7735, botecomiami.com; *in New York,* Ipanema, tel 212-730-5848, ipanemanyc.com; *in Cambridge, MA,* Muqueca Restaurant, tel 617-354-3296, muquecarestaurant.com. **FURTHER INFORMATION AND RECIPES:** *The Art of South American Cooking* by Felipe Rojas-Lombardi (1991); *The South American Table* by Maria Baez Kijac (2003); *Tasting Brazil* by Jessica B. Harris, (1992); foodandwine.com (search feijoada).

"WHO COULD HAVE IMAGINED THAT UNDER THE DIRTY RAGS THERE WERE HIDDEN SUCH GRACE AND BEAUTY, SO ARDENT A BODY, A FRAGRANCE OF CLOVE THAT MADE YOUR HEAD SPIN!"—FROM GABRIELA, CLOVE AND CINNAMON

Gabriela, Clove and Cinnamon by Jorge Amado

Brazilian

The sensuous food and languid climate of the cacao-trading town of Ilhéus in Brazil make for a seductive trip well worth taking. Fortunately, armchair travelers can get there by way of the late Brazilian author Jorge Amado, who used

his hometown as the setting of one of his most famous novels, *Gabriela, Clove and Cinnamon.*

The story follows the romance between

Nacib, a Syrian-born bar owner, and Gabriela, a cook and barmaid who prepares for her lover an enticing array of lushly spiced, tropical dishes typical of the Afro-Bahian region. Food buffs will be beguiled by the novel's descriptions of the dazzling markets, where vendors rush about and where Gabriela shops for tropical produce and fresh fish, like silvery snooks and dorados (mahi-mahi) so fresh they still flop on tables. Most of all, they will be seduced (just like Nacib) by Gabriela's cooking: luscious, crisply fried *bacalao* (cod) fritters; dainty shrimp pies; tiny balls of black bean paste, sprightly with onion and golden *dende* (palm oil); softly soothing porridges of manioc or *farofa*, cornmeal or rice, glossy with coconut milk; buttery chunks of corn on the

Author Jorge Amado

cob, yams, fried bananas, chicken stew, jerked beef, and pots of steaming coffee frothy with hot milk and served with crunchy little pastries, redolent of spices and honeyed sweetness. It is a wonder that since this delicious book was published in 1958, there has been no related cookbook. But surely somewhere in Brazil there must be—or should be—a restaurant named Gabriela.

FURTHER INFORMATION AND RECIPES: *Gabriela, Clove and Cinnamon* by Jorge Amado (1958); *Tasting Brazil* by Jessica B. Harris (1992); *The Art of South American Cooking* by Felipe Rojas-Lombardi (1991).

||||||||||||||||||||||||||||||||||

BAHIAN BLISS

Moqueca

Fish Stew

Brazilian

The two most common varieties of *moqueca* (moh-KAY-kah), the old-fashioned and deeply flavorful Brazilian fish stew, are *moqueca capixaba*, which comes from the state of Espirito Santo, and the moqueca of Bahia, in northeastern Brazil.

Due to the slave trade that brought Africans to the region to work the sugar, cacao, and coffee plantations, Bahia was heavily influenced by West African traditions and customs (notably by the African-Brazilian religion of Candomblé) and this dish—the most memorable of the two versions—is no exception.

Long considered peasant fare, moqueca began as a way to use up the plentiful, cheap local fish, such as mackerel and kingfish. Its fragrant base of garlic, onion, peppers, and fish broth (*caldo de peixe*), made from fish heads and scraps, takes on a brilliant red-orange glow thanks to the liberal inclusion of rich, sunny

palm oil (called *dende*). To the deep, oceanic flavor of that pungent broth, *moqueca baiana* adds shellfish marinated in lemon juice and then slowly simmered in tomato sauce. Cilantro is sprinkled into the pot for its herbaceous freshness, and coconut milk delivers the final creamy touch.

The finished moqueca is always served alongside *pirão*, a kind of porridge made from manioc flour (also known as cassava flour), or with plain white rice. Palm oil, a key ingredient in moqueca, has become controversial for its high saturated fat content—but it is a favorite ingredient in the Brazilian pantry, prized for its thick, velvety texture, complex flavor, and unique color. Olive oil is a suitable substitute for the health-conscious.

WHERE: In Salvador, Brazil, Casa das Portas Velhas, tel 55/71-3324-8400, acasadasportas velhas.com.br/english/servicos.php; in Oxnard, CA, Moqueca Brazilian Cuisine, tel 805-204- 0970, moquecarestaurant.com; in New York, Chicago, Miami, Coral Gables, Las Vegas, and London, SushiSamba, sushisamba.com. **FURTHER INFORMATION AND RECIPES:** The Brazilian Table by Yara Castro Roberts (2009); Tasting Brazil by Jessica B. Harris (1992); southamericanfood .about.com (search moqueca).

A MEATY PERFORMANCE

Rodízio

All-You-Can-Eat Skewered Grilled Meats

Brazilian

Succulent chunks, slices, steaks, and chops of grilled beef, veal, lamb, pork, and chicken are much-loved throughout South America, where barbecue is known as *churrasco* and *churrascarias* are the restaurants that feature wood-fired grills (much like our steak houses, with menus offering various cuts of meats cooked to order). But the Brazilian riff on this culinary custom is something else again—a dramatic and enticing floor show called *rodízio*, for which the churrasco meats are run onto giant skewers and theatrically paraded around the dining room. As they circulate among the tables, waiters display their juicy, fragrant wares. When diners choose their cut, the meat is sliced onto plates directly from the skewers and the waiters move on. The inexperienced can lose out by filling up on the first offerings, then regretting that decision when the juicy filets and rib eyes take center stage. "All you can eat" is the theme, and stomach capacity proves the only deterrent in the end.

Beef fares best in this type of cooking, and livers and hearts can be temptingly chewy and rich. In Brazil, the meat will almost always be from the zebu, a particularly lean breed of cattle—although pork or lamb chops, well edged with fat, retain enough moisture to remain succulent. Rodízio protocol calls for an opener of appetizers and salads from a dazzling, tiered buffet, something the experienced bypass in anticipation of the more solid delights to come. As the skewered meats are served, they are accompanied by some of the garnishes that also highlight the Brazilian feijoada meal (see page 670): the toasty, fluffy manioc or *farofa* grain, rice, crisp fried potatoes, steamed collard greens, black beans, refreshing onion and roseate pepper salads, fried bananas, and various habanero-chile-spiked dips and sauces. Slices of glazed, grilled pineapple are a typical palate cleanser and, given the proceedings, a sufficient dessert as well.

WHERE: In Rio de Janeiro, Churrascaria Porcão, porcao.com.br; in New York, Churrascaria Plataforma, tel 212-245-0505, churrascaria plataforma.com; Ipanema, tel 212-730-5848, ipanemanyc.com; in Houston, Churrascos at multiple locations, cordua.com/churrascos. **FURTHER INFORMATION AND RECIPES:** Seven Fires: Grilling the Argentine Way by Francis Mallman and Peter Kaminsky (2009); The Barbecue! Bible by Steven Raichlen (2008); bbq.about.com (search traditional churrascos); foodnetwork .com (search emeril's churrasco skewers).

Vatapá

Bahian Fish Stew

Brazilian

A rainbow of tropical flavors, dazzlingly rich and substantial, *vatapá* is not for the faint of heart. The stewlike main course, one of the most famous of all Brazilian dishes, is a combination of fish, shrimp, coconut milk, manioc flour (also known as cassava flour), *dende* (palm oil), and cashews, bolstered with white rice.

The bright-yellow dish is a specialty of Bahia, on the country's northeastern coast, established around 1500 by Brazil's first Portuguese settlers. The city's culture and cuisine was heavily influenced by the West Africans brought as slaves to work the sugar and coffee plantations. Reflecting this influence, vatapá is a typical filling for Bahia's *acarajé* fritters, black-bean-based cakes believed by practitioners of the local Afro-Brazilian religion Candomblé to be the ritual food of their goddess Yansa, ruler of the winds. Freshly fried by vendors lining the cobblestone streets of the Bahian capital of Salvador, rich and golden and brimming with vatapá, it seems like food for the gods indeed.

Where: *In Salvador, Brazil,* Museu da Gastronomia Baiana, tel 55/71-3324-4553, ba.senac.br/museu; *in Buenos Aires,* Me Leva Brasil, tel 54/11-4832-4290, melevabrasil.com.ar;

A sunny, fish-based stew from Bahia

in New York, Ipanema, tel 212-730-5848, ipanemanyc.com. **Further information and recipes:** *The Brazilian Kitchen* by Leticia Moreinos Schwartz (2012); *Tasting Brazil* by Jessica B. Harris (1992); foodnetwork.com (search vatapa).

Colombian Supremo Coffee

Colombian

With its mild, clean flavor, medium acidity, convincing body, and deep, rich, well-rounded aroma, Colombian coffee is considered by many connoisseurs to be the world's most "balanced" variety. That balance is characteristic of the beans of the *Coffea arabica* plant, and it is bolstered by Columbia's just-right mix of latitude (mountainous), climate (tropical), and rainfall (plentiful), enabling the beans to ripen properly and maintain their flavor. Colombians eventually found that growing the coffee plants in the shade improved the bean's growth and development, and a culture and industry grew up, slowly and painstakingly, around the crop.

"Supremo" designates the highest grade of beans, uniform in size, comparatively large, and producing an extra-smooth brew with delicate acidity. The high price of Colombian supremo beans reflects both quality control and method of production. Farmers still hand pick and hand wash the beans, which were originally transported from the mountainous communities by mule to the railroad stations, and then whisked to ports to be distributed worldwide. Long before it was trendy to describe foods by the region in which they're grown or produced, the Colombian Coffee Federation began to include regions of origin on its labeling, in the hopes of gaining a following among coffee drinkers.

In 1960, in a stroke of marketing genius, the Federation invented a fictional coffee grower named Juan Valdez, a friendly-looking farmer who transported his coffee beans through the Colombian mountains astride his mule. Marketing specialists report that five months after the campaign was launched, there was a 300 percent increase in consumer identification of Colombian supremo as the world's best beans; half a century later, it is still among the world's most sought-after coffee. Today, there are more than 500,000 coffee-growing families in Colombia, many of whom have been harvesting it since it first came to the country. The mules may be no more, but the status and quality of this centuries-old crop endures.

When shopping for supremo, look for the words "100% Colombian" on the label, and particularly for mention of the regions of Santander, Magdalena, and Nariño. Not all Colombian coffee is supremo, so if possible, look closely at the beans. Supremo beans should be round and uniform in size, and they are the only beans in which the characteristic center split remains light in color after roasting.

RETAIL AND MAIL ORDER: *In New York*, McNulty's Tea & Coffee Co., tel 212-242-5351, mcnultys.com. **FURTHER INFORMATION:** www.juan valdez.com. **SEE ALSO:** Ethiopian Coffee, page 732; Blue Mountain Coffee, page 691.

SWEET, TART, AND SALTY

Cascos de Guayaba con Queso

Guava Shells with Cream Cheese

Cuban

The simply prepared but addictive dessert of rosy stewed guava shells (*cascos de guayaba,* or "guava helmets") filled with cream cheese and served with crackers is an odd specialty of Latin America and the Spanish-speaking islands of

the West Indies, particularly Cuba. Some denizens of the Tampa, Florida, neighborhood of Ybor City insist that the dessert was developed there—a century ago, the town did have two guava processing plants and the local newspaper promoted the "A Guava a Day" recipe contest, which at one point featured a recipe for this unusual dish.

The ingredients certainly have their charms. Known for its sweet-tart flavor and decidedly aromatic nature, the guava (*Psidium guajava*) is a plum-size tropical fruit native to Peru. Guavas contain eugenol, one of the essential oils found in cloves, and when cooked, the fruit produces a honeylike syrup that contrasts nicely with the cool tanginess of cream cheese. Slightly salty crackers add just the right bit of crunch.

Cooked guava, with its honeylike syrup "con queso"

each "helmet" with a teaspoon of cream cheese. Drizzle the syrup over all and serve with saltine crackers alongside. The memorable result will be a comforting combination of sweet and salty, creamy and tart.

WHERE: *In Miami,* Islas Canarias, tel 305-559-6666, islas canariasrestaurant.com. **FURTHER INFORMATION AND RECIPES:** *Nuevo Latino* by Douglas Rodriguez (2002); *A Taste of Puerto Rico* by Yvonne Ortiz (1997); epicu rious.com (search guava cream cheese pastry). **TIP:** Canned guavas are surprisingly good and available in most supermarkets—look for the excellent Goya brand.

The dessert is rarely found in the U.S. but is easy to make at home—it may sound odd, but don't knock it until you've tried it. Simply strain canned guavas, reserving the syrup, and fill

—————————|||||||||||||||||||||||||||||||——————————

A TASTE OF HAVANA IN MIAMI

———————————

Islas Canarias

Cuban

It's difficult to decide which is the more incredible feature of these two Miami outposts of authentic Cuban cuisine—that such casual luncheonettes can turn out such delicious food, or that the prices are so amazingly low. Both locations of

Islas Canarias are huge, sprawling, noisily lively eateries catering to a Cuban and Cuban-informed population. There is usually a wait for tables at peak lunch and dinner hours, but the service is fast and the staff frenetically efficient. The specialties run to wonderfully savory, hearty dishes that reflect Cuba's blend of influences from Spain, Africa, and the island's indigenous Indian population.

A meal at Islas Canarias might start with black bean soup, dark and mysterious as midnight, accented with white rice, diced raw onions, and a shot of lemon juice (see page 665), or perhaps hot and crisp *frituras de bacalao,* codfish fritters. The main course might

be a juicy, grilled Creole steak with black beans and rice, or the similarly garnished, seductively tender *ropa vieja* ("old clothing," see page 678)—slow-cooked shredded beef—or the simmered ground beef *picadillo a la habanera,* named for the fiery chile pepper that ignites it. There is also softly sweet, golden-hued *arroz con pollo* (chicken and rice), the light, Catalan-style meatballs called *albondigas,* and crackling-skinned *lechón asado,* roast pig. Crisp on the outside and sweetly buttery within, fried plantains are not to be missed. For fish lovers, there are ceviches, the mixed shellfish stew called *cazuelita,* and gorgeously golden fried red snapper or kingfish, that large, silvery mackerel relative much favored in Cuba. Despite the quick casualness of these places, there is definitely time for cocktails, such as daiquiris, mojitos, and piña coladas, along with flavored rums and other standard Cuban imbibables. Anyone who can manage dessert has a fine choice between several featuring dulce de leche (see page 663), as well as flan, caramelized milk custard, and more, all dazzlingly sweet.

Where: 13695 SW 26th St., Miami, tel 305-559-6666; 285 NW 27th St., Miami, tel 305-649-0440, islascanariasrestaurant.com. **Tip:** The Islas Canarias Café, 3804 SW 137 Avenue, tel 305-559-0111, has an informal but still stylish setting, and a more limited menu of Cuban classics, many given a slightly modern spin. It's a lovely place to grab a bite, but it lacks the authenticity of the two luncheonettes.

HISTORY ON THE PLATE

Moros y Cristianos

Black Beans and Rice

Cuban

Moros y cristianos, "Moors and Christians," is the traditional name for the classic Cuban side dish of black beans and rice. A pared-down version of the black bean soup that Cubans so cherish, moros y cristianos is conjectured by historians to date back to the 1500s, when the Spanish Christians fought the North African Moors over the acquisition of the Spanish city of Grenada. Christian loyalists, well established in Cuba at the time, named the dish after the struggle going on back home, and its nickname stuck, although today it may not be considered politically correct.

The preparation is simple: dried black beans are soaked and slowly stewed with a ham hock, ham bone, or pork rind, then flavored with *sofrito* (a sauté of onions, green peppers, garlic, and various herbs). The fragrant, velvety soft beans are either mixed into or served atop steamed white

The classic Cuban side dish

rice, and eaten alongside grilled meats or fish with golden disks of fried plantain—or enjoyed alone as an inexpensive, nourishing main course. Humble though it is, the dish is also celebratory; no late-night Noche Buena (Christmas Eve) feast is complete without it. You can find moros y cristianos throughout the Caribbean and Latin America, and wherever the dish appears it is considered lucky, a symbol of plenty and fertility, and a harbinger of spiritual renewal.

Where: *In Viña del Mar, Chile*, Moros y Cristianos, tel 56/32-320-9971, morosycristianos.cl; *in Miami*, Islas Canarias at two locations, islascanariasrestaurant.com; *in Los Angeles*, El Floridita, tel 323-871-8612, elfloridita.com; *in New York*, Cuba Restaurant, tel 212-420-7878, cubanyc.com; *in Burtonsville, MD*, Cuba de Ayer Restaurant, tel 301-476-9622, cubadeayerrestaurant.net. **Further information and recipes:** *Tastes Like Cuba* by Eduardo Machado (2008); cookstr.com (search christians and moors). **See also:** Sopa de Frijoles Negros, page 664; Hoppin' John, page 580; Red Beans and Rice, page 615.

‖‖‖‖‖‖‖‖‖‖‖‖‖‖‖‖‖‖‖‖‖‖‖‖‖

RAGS TO CULINARY RICHES

Ropa Vieja

Cuban

"Old clothes" is the literal translation of this traditional beef stew, which is said to have been invented in the Canary Islands—a Spanish sailor's last stop on his voyage to the New World—and later adopted all over Latin America, with Cuba expressing particular devotion. The dish is a peasant-food staple featuring shredded flank steak, a juicy and flavorful but inexpensive cut, simmered for a long time with tomatoes and sometimes wine. Legends abound as to the origins of the name, but it seems fairly obvious: The shredded, stewed meat has a torn-up look suggesting wet rags. It may not be pretty, but its homely looks yield a comforting, stick-to-your-ribs main course.

There are, of course, many regional and local variations to the dish. In its native Canary Islands, it includes garbanzo beans, while in Argentina, it is made with lamb or goat instead of beef. In Brazil, they call it *roupa velha*, and often enjoy it on sandwiches; in Cuba, where it is most revered, it is enhanced with *sofrito*, a mellow sauté of onions, garlic, peppers, and tomatoes, scented with oregano. In many Tex-Mex joints across the U.S., meanwhile, it's not uncommon to find *ropa vieja* as a filling for burritos, tacos, and quesadillas. But it is best on its own, served Cuban-style, with rice and plantains—a comforting, restorative old friend.

WHERE: *In Miami,* Islas Canarias at two locations, islascanariasrestaurant.com; *in Los Angeles,* Versailles restaurants at multiple locations, versaillescuban.com; *in Bellaire, TX,* Café Piquet, tel 713-664-1031, cafepiquet.net; *in New York,* Cuba Restaurant, tel 212-420-7878, cubanyc.com; Coppelia, tel 212-858-5001, coppelianyc.com. **FURTHER INFORMATION AND RECIPES:** *Memories of a Cuban Kitchen* by Mary Urrutia Randelman and Joan Schwartz (1992); *The Sugar Reef Caribbean Cookbook* by Devra Dedeaux (1991); saveur.com (search ropa vieja); epicurious.com (search ropa vieja). **SEE ALSO:** Picadillo, page 665.

‖‖‖‖‖‖‖‖‖‖‖‖‖‖‖‖‖‖‖‖‖‖‖‖‖

HAVE A HEART

Anticuchos

Skewered Beef Heart

Peruvian

A favorite street snack in Peruvian cities, *anticuchos* are fragrant bite-size chunks of grilled beef heart on tiny bamboo skewers. In many European countries, beef, lamb, and calf hearts are stuffed and braised as main courses. But Peruvians serve up the specialty as casual fare, easily nibbled off of delicate skewers straight from the charcoal braziers of street vendors or, if homemade, sautéed with bacon in a heavy skillet.

Marinated overnight in a blend of red wine vinegar, cumin, fresh hot red chiles, dried green ancho chiles, and garlic, the hearts (and sometimes other organ meats) emerge savory and tender and ready for grilling.

Anticuchos were popularized in the U.S. in the 1960s by the lavish New York City restaurant La Fonda del Sol, formerly housed in the famed Time & Life Building. They featured it as an appetizer, prepared with beef heart as well as liver and kidneys, and marinated and grilled to perfection. Nowadays, it can be found in Peruvian and other South American restaurants across the country—often made out of nonorgan meats to suit American palates—but somehow it is most delicious hot off the coals, prepared by a vendor on an ancient side street in Lima.

Where: *In Houston,* Andes Café, tel 832-659-0063, andescafe.com; *in Los Angeles,* Picca, tel

Anticuchos—one of barbecue's more unique offerings

310-277-0133, piccaperu.com; *in San Francisco,* Piqueo's, tel 415-282-8812, piqueos.com. **Further information and recipes:** *The Art of South American Cooking* by Felipe Rojas-Lombardi (1991); food network.com (search anticuchos); epicurious .com (search anticuchos de lomo).

FAR FROM NIBLETS

Choclo
Incan Corn

Peruvian

One of the most interesting corns still grown today, the Incan *choclo* was first cultivated in the fields of Cuzco and the Sacred Valley and still grows only in Peru's coastal region. Often eaten boiled, alongside meat dishes, its pale yellow ears hold puffy, oversize kernels with a nutty, milky flavor and an encitingly chewy, hefty texture. It is also a key ingredient in Chile's *cazuela de vacuno,* a rustic, filling beef stew studded with pumpkin and potato, and *pastel de choclo,* a savory pie made with beef, cumin, and raisins. In Ecuador, it is served toasted and appears in a variety of ceviches; in Venezuela, it is featured in the specialty *arepas de choclo,* fried corn cakes topped with fresh cheese. And in Buenos Aires, empanadas are sometimes filled with the white corn stew known as *humitas,* which is fortified with fat kernels of choclo.

All of these preparations are flavorful, but the very best treatment of all is the simplest, available at roadside stands all over Peru, where it is known as *choclo y queso*—grilled ears of corn slathered in fresh cheese.

Where: *In San Francisco,* Piqueo's, tel 415-282-8812, piqueos.com; *in Provo, UT,* Pantruca's, tel 801-373-9712, pantrucas.com; *in Wilmington, DE,* Pochi Restaurant, tel 302-384-6654, pochi winebar.com. **Mail order:** amigofoods.com. **Further information and recipes:** *A Canon of Vegetables* by Raymond Sokolov (2007); *The Art of South American Cooking* by Felipe Rojas-Lombardi (1991); saveur.com (search beef chicken and corn pie).

—|||||||||||||||||||||||||||||||||—

Papa Morada

Peruvian

Y ou may never have seen a purple cow, but a purple potato sighting has become a more and more distinct possibility: The earthy, nutty Peruvian native called *papa morada* has been finding fans worldwide, and is now being cultivated far

from its homeland. Probably first grown about two thousand years ago, in the South American highlands of the Andes, the purple potato is one of the so-called heritage or heirloom varieties. Purple potatoes are generally small and dense, with dark-gray skin and flesh that has an amethyst glow when raw, and dulls slightly when cooked. Because they have a midrange starch content, they are equally suited to roasting, frying, or mashing, and with their mild, gentle flavor, they are ideal for combining with other potato varieties, adding a blush of glorious color. Now cultivated in the United States, purple potatoes are becoming easier to find, and are worth seeking out, especially at farmers' markets. Their striking appearance aside, they're better for you than regular

Purple heirloom potatoes

potatoes, as they contain antioxidants such as anthocyanins (also found in plums and in "superfoods" such as blueberries), which is responsible for their color.

MAIL ORDER: Specialty Produce, tel 619-295-3172, specialtyproduce.com (search purple potato); Melissa's Produce, tel 800-588-0151, melissas.com. **FURTHER INFORMATION AND RECIPES:** *One Potato, Two Potato* by Roy Finamore and Molly Stevens (2001); *Vegetables from Amaranth to Zucchini* by Elizabeth Schneider (2001); *Nuevo Latino* by Douglas Rodriguez (2002); *New World Kitchen* by Norman Van Aken (2003); *The Art of South American Cooking* by Felipe Rojas-Lombardi (1991); specialityproduce.com (scroll produce list to find "potatoes fingerling purple peruvian").

—|||||||||||||||||||||||||||||||||—

Pollo a la Brasa

Rotisserie-Grilled Chicken

Peruvian

J ust when the world thought it had seen every possible way a chicken could be cooked, along came the Peruvian rotisserie trend. With its juicy meat and pungent flavor, the chicken had such a broad appeal that it became the focus of restaurants all over the U.S., and with good reason.

As the plump bird spins on a rotisserie, the very aroma can start mouths watering. And when it emerges with crisp, gently golden-brown skin protecting succulently moist meat, all to be dipped into a hotly seasoned, green *ají verde* or the milder, creamy, golden *ají amarillo,* a kind of magic has taken place.

It takes some time for chicken to get that good. First, the whole, cleaned bird, trimmed of all visible fat, is marinated for twenty-four hours in a fragrant blend of lime juice, white wine, chiles, cilantro, garlic, ginger, cumin, and oregano. After a final slathering of the marinade and sprinklings of pepper and paprika, it begins its slow, closely watched spin on the grill. Cut into serving pieces, it is ready to be dipped into the fiery *ají verde* sauce, which combines cilantro, hot green ají chiles, garlic, and judicious zaps of cumin and pepper. Sour cream and fresh white cheese are whipped together to make the milder *ají amarillo,* flavored with ginger, the milder yellow ají pepper, and garlic and dosed with annatto powder to impart the sunny hue. Mashed or fried potatoes and crisp disks of softly sweet, fried plantain are the right foils, as is some ice-cold beer.

Peruvian rotisserie makes for excellent, way-above-average takeout. Fortunately, ambitious home cooks can achieve almost the same results without a rotisserie by simply roasting a similarly marinated chicken in the oven. For a memorable special-occasion dinner, the marinade can be applied to small, individual birds, such as cornish hens, each as a complete portion. Just don't forget the salsa—and the beer.

WHERE: *In NY, FL, and NC,* Pio Pio at multiple locations, mypiopio.com; *in Chicago,* D'Candela, tel 773-478-0819, dcandela.com; *in Centennial, CO,* La Polleria, tel 720-583-1051, lapolleria.com; *in CA and Miami,* El Pollo Inka at multiple locations, elpolloinka.com; *in Houston,* Andes Café, tel 832-659-0063, andescafe.com. **FURTHER INFORMATION AND RECIPES:** *The Everything Peruvian Cookbook* by Morena Cuadra and Morena Escardo (2013); *A Taste of Peru,* by Daniel McKay (2012); epicurious.com (search peruvian grilled chicken); southamericanfood .about.com (search pollo a la brasa). **SEE ALSO:** Salt-Roasted Chicken, page 780.

────────────│││││││││││││││││││││││││││││──────────────

WHEN IS A GRAIN NOT A GRAIN?

Quinoa

Peruvian

Quinoa (pronounced KEEN-wha) is an ancient plant with tremendously healthful properties. Although prepared like a grain, *Chenopodium quinoa,* grown in the Andes, is actually a relative of spinach and chard that produces great

quantities of edible seeds, which have been a staple food since the days of the Aztecs and the Incas. In fact, quinoa was a major commodity crop for the Incas, who referred to it as "the mother grain."

Like rice, the tiny, pearl-like seeds expand in volume when cooked, but they have an engagingly nutty flavor all their own. Though they are no longer hand harvested, their processing has remained relatively unchanged: threshing the seed heads to remove the seeds, winnowing the seeds to remove the husks, and washing them to remove the bitter compounds that coat the seed.

Quinoa used to be a hugely important ingredient only in South American cuisine, but it's now riding a wave of popularity in the United States, whole and ground into flour for gluten-free breads and pastas; typically served as a side dish or salad, quinoa can replace rice or couscous in almost any preparation. Nutritionists approve, as the seeds are loaded with protein and essential amino acids, and are also richer in nutrients, lower in carbohydrates, and higher in fiber than most grains.

Quinoa is a superfood with nine essential amino acids and a lot of protein.

Where: *In Houston,* Andes Café, tel 832-659-0063, andescafe.com; *in New York,* Forager's City Table, tel 212-243-8888, foragerscitygrocer.com; *in San Francisco,* Piqueo's, tel 415-282-8812, piqueos.com. **Retail and mail order:** *In New York and Brooklyn,* Foragers City Grocer, tel 212-243-8888, foragerscitygrocer.com. **Further information and recipes:** *The Art of South American Cooking* by Felipe Rojas-Lombardi (1991); *Ancient Grains for Modern Meals* by Maria Speck (2011); *Quinoa 365* by Patricia Green and Carolyn Hemming (2010); epicurious.com (search coconut quinoa; quinoa stuffing; quinoa salad); foodandwine.com (search herbed quinoa pilaf; quinoa oatmeal baked apples).

CARIBBEAN

Haitian, Jamaican

‖‖‖‖‖‖‖‖‖‖‖‖‖‖‖‖‖‖‖‖‖‖‖‖‖‖‖‖

A PUMPKIN WORTH SQUASHING

Calabaza

Caribbean, Latin American

The Caribbean calabaza (*Cucurbita moschata*), also known as the West Indian pumpkin, is unique among squashes. Its amber-and-olive-green exterior embodies a perfect autumn palette and its bright, burnt-orange flesh is smooth, unlike the stringy meat of most North American pumpkins, with a rich, nutty sweetness akin to that of butternut squash. The only hardship in preparing calabaza is common to almost all pumpkinlike squashes: It's a beast to peel and chop. The hefty calabaza, which can grow as large as a watermelon, is perhaps the most difficult of all, sometimes requiring both cleaver and hammer. No wonder, then, that in many markets, it is often sold precut, in ready-to-cook pieces. Popular in the Caribbean and Central and South America, where it is native, the calabaza is a staple in stews and soups (it's a marvelous thickener), but is also good simply roasted, fried, or baked. Like all pumpkins, its salted, toasted seeds (called *pepitas* in Spanish) are ideal for nibbling. A superb substitute in any pumpkin recipe, the calabaza is wholly worthy of a place at the holiday table—whether cooked or used as a lovely autumnal centerpiece.

MAIL ORDER: Melissa's Produce, tel 800-588-0151, melissas.com. **FURTHER INFORMATION AND RECIPES:** *Vegetables from Amaranth to Zucchini* by Elizabeth Schneider (2001); *The Sugar Reef Caribbean Cookbook* by Devra Dedeaux (1991); *New World Kitchen* by Norman Van Aken (2003); *Nuevo Latino* by Douglas Rodriguez (2002); nytimes.com (search jamaican pumpkin soup). **TIP:** If buying a whole calabaza, look for one with the stem intact and with the fewest bruises and blemishes. If purchasing it precut, avoid pale pieces with blemishes or wet spots.

‖‖‖‖‖‖‖‖‖‖‖‖‖‖‖‖‖‖‖‖‖‖‖‖‖‖‖‖

A STEW THAT SEDUCES

Callaloo

Caribbean

Honored in a classic calypso tune, this ubiquitous Caribbean stew came to the islands in the seventeenth century from Africa. According to the song, the spicy dish of stewed greens has the power to induce any man who eats it to propose to the woman who prepared it. Small wonder its appeal has been so enduring.

On the ground, callaloo is also often used as the name of the plants whose leaves provide the base for the dish; these differ from region to region, but are most often either of the spinach-like taro or amaranth variety. Cooked, they have a bright emerald color, a pleasingly silky texture, and a warm, sunny flavor reminiscent of collard greens, though more complex.

When used in the famously flavor-packed stew, the gently simmered greens are added to the pot at the last minute, so that they won't overcook and lose their deep-green color. An array of traditional ingredients and spices precedes them, most notably onion, okra, and garlic, as well as coconut milk, chiles, and yams or green bananas; depending on the region, these will be joined by a little salt pork, salt cod, beef, or crabmeat. Although it is usually served alongside meat dishes, callaloo served as a main course might be bolstered with sweet and sticky dumplings and served piping hot with rice and slices of avocado—and it might well be followed by an offer of marriage.

Callaloo is a bright-green stew with a complex mix of flavors.

WHERE: *In New York,* Miss Lily's at two locations, misslilysnyc.com; *in Miami,* Jamaica Kitchen, tel 305-596-2585, jamaicakitchen.com. **FURTHER INFORMATION AND RECIPES:** *Lucinda's Authentic Jamaican Cookbook* by Lucinda Scala Quinn and Quentin Bacon (2006); *The Sugar Reef Caribbean Cookbook* by Devra Dedeaux (1991); *New World Kitchen* by Norman Van Aken (2003); *Nuevo Latino* by Douglas Rodriguez (2002); *Authentic Recipes from Jamaica* by John DeMers and Eduardo Fuss (2005); epicurious.com (search callaloo stew); cookstr.com (search callaloo).

—————————||||||||||||||||||||||||||||||——————————

CONCH COMES OUT OF ITS SHELL

Conch Chowder

Caribbean

Besides being the delight of shell collectors, who like to hold it to an ear to hear the sea—most likely the result of the concentration of ambient sounds in its echo chamber—the oversized, pearly-pink conch (pronounced conk) holds within its shell a savory seafood morsel simmered by Caribbean cooks into a rich chowder. Once extracted from that swirled, horn-shaped shell, the conch, a variety of sea snail, must first be tenderized by being pounded or steamed, or both. Its intense, deep-sea, clamlike flavor, with a savory, meaty edge, is well worth the effort.

Delicious marinated as the prime ingredient in cold salads, or fried in crunchy fritters, it also appears in the chowder that is so beloved throughout the Caribbean; famously, in Key West, Florida, it is combined with aromatic vegetables, potatoes, and minced ham or salt pork, then simmered to supple softness with a blush of tomato and a sting or two of hot sauce or minced Scotch bonnet peppers. In the Bahamas, a shot of rum might provide the finishing touch. In other island kitchens, sliced green plantains may be added to the mix for their sweet and starchy richness, as might coconut milk, grated fresh coconut, a shot of sherry and allspice, plus a final sprinkling of chopped scallions. If you come across a completely stingless version of conch chowder, reach for the hot sauce. The fiery zest of chiles adds drama and lift, and is a must for this otherwise mild soup.

WHERE: *In Key West, FL,* Conch Republic Seafood Company, tel 305-294-4403, conchrepublicseafood.com; The Conch Shack, tel 305-295-9494, myconchshack.com; Schooner Wharf Bar, tel 305-292-3302, schooner

A fisherman diving for conch

wharf.com. **MAIL ORDER:** For conch, Charleston Seafood, tel 888-609-3474, charlestonseafood.com; Giovanni's Fish Market, tel 888-463-2056, giovannisfishmarket.com; for conch chowder, Islamorada Fish Company and Market, tel 800-258-2559, ifcstonecrab.com. **FURTHER INFORMATION AND RECIPES:** *Iron Pots and Wooden Spoons* by Jessica B. Harris (1989); *The Sugar Reef Caribbean Cookbook* by Devra Dedeaux (1991); *Zarela's Veracruz* by Zarela Martinez with Anne Mendelson (2004); foodnetwork.com (search bahamian conch chowder).

A SUNNY, CREAMY COOLER

Piña Colada

Caribbean

The piña coladas we most often encounter in the U.S. are watery, overly sweet concoctions based on canned or frozen pineapple and coconut concentrate. But made with fresh ingredients, as it is throughout the Caribbean, the piña colada

is an elegant, luxurious, and cooling mix of the tart sunniness of pineapple and the sweet creaminess of coconut, usually fortified with a generous dose of rum. As such, it is eminently worthy of summer-afternoon parties or island-themed brunches. In some of our own cities, especially New York, alcohol-free piña coladas have become the drink of choice with hot dogs.

Piña Colada
Serves 4 with ice cubes, 3 without

2½ cups grated fresh coconut
2½ cups boiling water
3 cups cored and chopped fresh pineapple
2½ tablespoons sugar, or more to taste
1 ounce dark rum per serving (optional)

Ice cubes (optional), for serving
Thin slices of peeled fresh ginger
*   (optional), for garnish*
Fresh mint sprigs (optional), for garnish
Thin lime wedges (optional), for garnish

1. Place the grated coconut in a heatproof bowl and add the boiling water. Let stand at room temperature for about 1 hour.
2. Line a strainer with a double thickness of cheesecloth and strain the coconut water into a bowl. Let the strainer stand over the bowl for about 10 minutes, then gather the cheesecloth together to form a sack and gradually squeeze all of the remaining liquid into the bowl. Discard the coconut solids. You should have about 2½

cups of coconut milk; refrigerate it, covered, until chilled, about 1 hour. (Coconut milk will last in the fridge for 3 days.)

3. Place the pineapple, sugar, and chilled coconut milk in a blender and puree until smooth, about 2 minutes, allowing perhaps just the finest flecks of pineapple to remain. Taste and add more sugar if necessary. Refrigerate the piña colada mixture for about 1 hour.

4. When ready to serve, stir before pouring. If you use rum, pour 1 ounce of dark rum into each of 3 tall 10-ounce tumblers (or 4 tumblers if using ice cubes). Add 3 or 4 ice cubes, if desired. Pour the chilled piña colada mixture into the tumblers and stir briefly. If desired, garnish each piña colada with a slice of ginger, a sprig of mint, or a lime wedge.

WHERE: *In Key West, FL,* Schooner Wharf Bar, tel 305-292-3302, schoonerwharf.com; *in New York,* Papaya King at multiple locations, papayaking.com. **MAIL ORDER:** For coconut, Melissa's Produce, tel 800-588-0151, melissas .com. **FURTHER INFORMATION AND RECIPES:** *A Taste of Puerto Rico* by Yvonne Ortiz (1997); cookstr .com (search piña colada). **TIP:** If the piña coladas are to be served with straws, it will be necessary to strain the blended drink to remove all of the pineapple solids, which is really too bad. Better to sip the piña coladas without straws and maintain the texture.

PUCKER UP

Soursop

Caribbean, Latin American

The big, green, oval soursop, bristling with spiny prickles, suggests a fruity grenade as it hangs from the branches of the tropical evergreen *Annona muricata,* which thrives throughout the Caribbean, Latin America, and parts of southeast Asia. A first cousin to the cherimoya and the custard apple, soursop (known in Latin American countries as *guanábana*) has crackly, papery skin that lightens from dark green to a yellowish citrine as it ripens, and mouth-puckeringly sour white flesh that suggests a mildly fermented blend of lemon and pineapple. It is always picked before fully ripe to avoid bruising, but once it's ready to eat, the juicy soursop can be enjoyed raw, spooned right out of its shell. (Its large, shiny black seeds are toxic but, fortunately, relatively few in number.)

On its own, soursop is said to have many valuable nutritional benefits, among them large amounts of vitamins B and

C and calcium. Mostly, though, the fruit is prized for the winey freshness it imparts to candy and desserts.

In Jamaica and the Bahamas, the pulverized pulp, strained of fibers, is blended with condensed milk and frozen into simple and pleasing ice creams and sherbets.

In Brazil and Puerto Rico, it figures in drinks such as *champola de guanábana,* for which the snowy fruit is whipped with milk and sugar, chilled, and served over ice cubes with a sprinkling of freshly grated nutmeg. It's a light and refreshing sort of a milkshake that is a traditional after-school snack for children. A generous addition of rum, also traditional, transforms it into a decidedly grown-up treat.

Mail order: amazon.com (search fresh soursop fruit; soursop exotic tropical juice); ali baba.com (search soursop). **Further information and recipes:** *A Taste of Puerto Rico* by Yvonne Ortiz (1997); *The Oxford Companion to Food* by Alan Davidson (1999); epicurious .com (search guanabana sherbet; guanabana sorbet).

SEEING STARS

Star Apple

Caribbean

A West Indies native, the plump, round, tropical star apple (*Chrysophyllum cainito*) is beguiling to behold, with an exterior hue that varies from bronzed purple to green, sometimes with a warm coppery tone. Cut in half, the fruit reveals

the colorful, star-shaped pattern for which it is named. That pattern is hidden beneath latex-rich skin and a tough rind, so peeling the fruit takes effort, and the eater must carefully separate the exterior from the pulp. But the star apple's flesh is worth getting at. Mild, custardy, and sweetly juicy, it's often described as tasting like a cross between an apple and a plum.

In the Caribbean, especially in Jamaica where the fruit thrives, the star apple finds its way into juices, desserts, and salads. "Matrimony," a Jamaican specialty, is an especially rich, sweet-tart medley of star apples, oranges, condensed milk, and nutmeg. But the star apple doesn't require an arranged marriage, as it is perfectly delicious on its own, well chilled and scooped out of its shell with a spoon.

Star apples can be found in Latin American, Caribbean, and South Asian markets from late winter to early spring. The lovely shade tree is not widely planted in the U.S.; consequently the fruit is hard to find.

Mail order: In season, Local Harvest, local harvest.com (click Shop and search star apple). **Tip:** When selecting star apples, look for fruit with slightly wrinkled skin that is soft to the touch. To show off the fruit's interior, cut into a star apple horizontally, never from the stem.

TWICE AS NICE

Diri ak Djon-Djon

Haitian

An everyday culinary staple the world over, rice can also take on elegant guises, and not only in the form of Italian risotto or Middle Eastern pilaf (see pages 233 and 481). One of the most interesting, and inexplicably overlooked, is Haiti's djon-djon rice—*riz djon-djon* in French and *diri ak djon-djon* in Haitian Creole.

Djon-djon refers to the tiny black mushrooms that are said to grow exclusively in Haiti, most plentifully in the north; they give riz djon-djon its burnished, silvery-brown color and its smoky, earthy flavor. Their caps are the only part added to the rice; the tough but full-flavored stems are simmered separately, and the strained cooking liquid is used to cook the rice, adding richness and a deeper patina.

The flavorful Haitian side dish

The dish begins with a flavoring base of diced salt pork, fried until crisp and then added to sautéed green peppers, scallions, and garlic. For an extra zap of flavor, many add tiny dicings of fiery Scotch bonnet peppers. Raw, long-grain white rice is then stirred in, along with the mushrooms and their cooking liquid, plus seasonings including thyme and mace. When the rice is tender, it is tossed with a fork and served steaming hot and fragrant, sometimes as a side dish, but more usually a main course, bolstered with bits of cooked poultry, meat, or fish.

As Haitian immigrants have settled in various cities of the United States, dried djon-djon mushrooms can now be found in some stateside groceries. If they cannot, dried European mushrooms such as porcinis are fair substitutes. But the smoky dicings of salt pork are nonnegotiable.

MAIL ORDER: For dried djon-djon mushrooms, Sam's Caribbean, tel 877-846-7267, sams247.com. **FURTHER INFORMATION AND RECIPES:** *Iron Pots and Wooden Spoons* by Jessica B. Harris (1989); *A Taste of Haiti* by Mirta Yurnet-Thomas and Jay H. Moscowitz (2004); haitiancooking.com (search black mushroom rice).

A SAILOR'S SONG

Ackee

Jamaican

W hen Harry Belafonte performed the song "Jamaica Farewell" in a legendary 1959 concert at Carnegie Hall, he told the audience that as a child in the West Indies, he often swam off the docks with the local boys and heard it being sung by sailors as they shipped out. One of its lines memorably mentions rice made with ackee, the West African tropical fruit *Blighia sapida,* introduced to Jamaica in the eighteenth century and now cultivated all over the island. The scientific name honors Captain William Bligh, who brought the fruit from Jamaica to England in 1793.

Looking rather like a smooth-skinned, reddish peach, the ackee belongs to the same family as the lychee. Inside the fruit are three shiny black seeds surrounded by a fleshy, creamy coat that is its only edible part. The ackee is best enjoyed at the height of ripeness, when it is succulent, pleasantly oily, and sweet, and it may be eaten raw, fried in oil, or roasted (when cooked, its texture resembles that of scrambled egg). It's also canned, and because ackee seeds are toxic if the fruit is under- or overripe, only the canned, cooked fruit can be imported to the United States.

In Jamaica, ackee refers not just to the fruit but also to the national dish, in which it features prominently along with salt-preserved fish, almost always cod or mackerel. Traditionally eaten for breakfast, the dish resembles a kind of egg scramble in which the salted fish is sautéed with boiled ackee, onions, hot Scotch bonnet chiles, tomatoes, and plenty of black pepper. Pimiento peppers, bacon, and fresh tomatoes are the usual garnishes. It is a delicious mishmash of contrasting flavors, colors, and textures, especially when served with rice and boiled plantains—a dish as restorative for homebodies as it must have been for sailors setting out to trade rum, in need of sustenance and the comforting flavors of home.

Where: *In Kingston, Jamaica,* Jamaica Inn, tel 876-974-2514, jamaicainn.com; *in Miami,* Jamaica

Kitchen, tel 305-596-2585, jamaicakitchen.com; *in New York,* Miss Lily's at two locations, misslilys.com. **Mail order:** amazon.com (search ackee). **Further information and recipes:** *Authentic Recipes from Jamaica* by John De Mers and Eduardo Fuss (2005); *Jamaican Recipes Cookbook* by K. Reynolds-James (2013); saveur .com (search ackee and saltfish).

In Jamaica, eating ackee can mean fruit and fish for breakfast.

FOR A RUMMY CHRISTMAS

Black Fruitcake

Jamaican

Although it's a Christmas classic throughout the Caribbean, so-called black fruitcake is especially celebrated in Jamaica, where it was likely developed. The spicy, fragrant, boozy fruitcake is steeped in both dark rum and tradition.

Dense, moist, and festively rich, the cake's gorgeous dark-brown color results from the combination of brown sugar, molasses, and rum—the very ingredients that drew British colonists to the islands.

The British plum pudding probably inspired this holiday dessert, but while British cakes are often made with brandy (originally as a way to preserve them), the Jamaican black fruitcake features local rum, sometimes combined with a

red Jamaican cooking wine called Red Label, and perfumed with almond essence and rosewater. Into that brew go raisins, prunes, dried cherries, and currants, left to soak for months at a time in cool cellars. When it's time to make the cake, the softened, tipsy fruits are ground into a paste, making for a smoother texture than that of other fruitcakes. The finished cake is encased in a satiny, hard white icing and served in thin slices as a celebratory finish to Christmas dinner. The process is time and labor intensive, but the sweetly rich reward is a highlight of the holiday season. And, if there are any leftovers, one need only douse the fruitcake with additional rum to restore the texture and keep it moist and delicious for days.

Where: *In Kingston, Jamaica,* Susie's Bakery and Café, tel 876-968-5030. **Retail and mail order:** Jamaican Black Cakes, tel 561-907-8150, jamaicanblackcakes.com; The Sweetest Thing Cupcake and Bakery Shoppe, tel 876-410-6576, thesweetestthingja.com. **Further information and recipes:** *Visions of Sugarplums* by Mimi Sheraton (1981); *Jamaican Recipes Cookbook* by K. Reynolds-James (2013); allrecipes.com (search jamaican fruitcake). **See also:** Bread Pudding with Whiskey Sauce, page 534; Irish Whiskey Cheesecake, page 47.

COFFEE AT THE PEAK

Blue Mountain Coffee

Jamaican

Nestled high in the Blue Mountains of Jamaica, at more than 3,000 feet above sea level, some 15,000 acres of coffee trees produce what many connoisseurs call the best beans in the world. They are certainly among the most expensive, retailing for $35 a pound or more, and very elusive. As much as 90 percent of Blue Mountain coffee is sold directly to Japan, and the remaining 10 or so percent is split up largely among American and European buyers. While some coffee drinkers find the acidity a bit overwhelming, to its devotees Jamaican Blue Mountain coffee has a perfect balance between acidity and body, a distinctive mellowness and sweetness, and an unforgettably rich, fruity aroma.

The drink, made from the roasted beans of the *Coffea arabica* plant, has been known and enjoyed since at least the thirteenth century and is thought to have originated in Ethiopia. But something about the terroir (the special combination of soil and climate) in the Blue Mountains of Jamaica produces an extraordinary product—in contrast to coffee beans from the lowlands of Jamaica, which are so ill-valued they're used only as filler in cheap blends. Part of the Blue Mountain bean's charm is its scarcity and unpredictable nature—when not produced at optimal conditions, or when improperly roasted, it can taste almost ropy. It has a passionate following, however, and true believers insist that no one can legitimately be called a coffee connoisseur without having tasted Blue Mountain beans.

Retail and mail order: *In New York,* McNulty's Tea and Coffee Co., tel 800-356-5200, mcnultys.com; Zabar's, tel 212-787-2000, zabars.com. **Further information:** *Are You Really Going to Eat That?* by Robb Walsh (2004). **See also:** Ethiopian Coffee, page 732; Colombian Supremo Coffee, page 674.

A famous high-altitude crop

——————————————|||||||||||||||||||||||||||||||||——————————————

Curried Goat

Jamaican

Though Zora Neale Hurston is best-known for her fiction, she was also an anthropologist, and in 1938, she published an ethnographic account of voodoo and related African rituals in Jamaica and Haiti. In it, she recounts an epic prewedding groom's feast of curried goat, served with banana dumplings and copious amounts of rum. It seemed remarkable to her because women were never allowed at such a feast—a feast so masculine, she wryly notes, that "chicken soup would not be allowed. It must be made from roosters."

If that custom has changed, the dish itself remains: a hearty, warming, spicy concoction of goat meat slowly stewed with wafts of curry powder and mellowing touches of onions, tomatoes, and potatoes, all to be ladled over steamed rice and peas. The recipe likely came to Jamaica by way of East Indian immigrants who moved to the island (then a British colony) after slavery was abolished there in the 1830s.

Traditionally, it's served alongside "mannish water," a very peppery soup (which supposedly acts as an aphrodisiac) made from a goat's head and innards boiled with yams, bananas, carrots, and turnips. No longer for men only, curried goat is now a mainstay throughout Jamaica and just about anyplace Jamaican dishes are served.

WHERE: *In Kingston, Jamaica,* Jamaica Inn, tel 876-974-2514, jamaicainn.com; Miss T's Kitchen, tel 876-795-0099, misstskitchen.com; *in New York,* Miss Lily's at two locations, misslilys.com; *in Bronx, NY,* Kingston Tropical Bakery Inc., tel 718-798-0076; *in Miami,* Jamaica Kitchen, tel 305-596-2585, jamaicakitchen.com; *in Honolulu,* Jawaiian Irie Jerk Restaurant, tel 808-388-2917, jawaiianiriejerk.com; *in London,* Chef Collin Brown, tel 44/20-7515-8177, chef collinbrown.co.uk. **FURTHER INFORMATION AND RECIPES:** *Authentic Recipes from Jamaica* by John De Mers and Eduardo Fuss (2005); *Jamaican Recipes Cookbook* by K. Reynolds-James (2013).

——————————————|||||||||||||||||||||||||||||||||——————————————

A PATTY THAT'S A PIE

Meat Patties

Jamaican

Meat-filled pastry turnovers are favored in many cultures as a delectable way to turn inexpensive cuts of meat into tantalizing and elegant morsels. In Jamaica, they take the form of pungent, juicy meat patties, derived from Spanish *pasteles* and English meat pies and enhanced with the signature Afro-Indian touches that add such zest to Jamaica cuisine. Meat patties have become famous, treasured as a street snack or quick and simple main course, and wherever Jamaicans are to be found, you will also be lucky enough to find vendors and shops dedicated to this island specialty.

A spicy, flavorful meal in a pocket

Their popularity is well-deserved. The flat, turmeric-gilded crescents of crisp piecrust reveal supple, fragrant fillings: ground beef, thyme, and breadcrumbs accented with onions, garlic, zaps of Jamaica's favorite Scotch bonnet chiles—and always with a curry powder that is redolent of cumin, turmeric, dried mustard, fenugreek, ginger, cardamom, and cinnamon, a reminder of the East Indian indentured servants who did much of the cooking in British colonial days. When baked, Jamaican meat patties are warmly satisfying and successfully stand up to reheating; fried, they are even more crackling and juicy, though they don't reheat as well and are, of course, less healthful.

Although usually filled with beef, curried goat (see facing page) is a festive and savory stand-in, as is callaloo (see page 684), fish, or vegetables. Sweet patties might be served for special occasions such as weddings, filled with meat, apples, and cinnamon—a nice patty if you can get it.

WHERE: *In Kingston, Jamaica,* Jamaica Inn, tel 876-974-2514, jamaicainn.com; *in New York,* Miss Lily's at two locations, misslilys.com. **MAIL ORDER:** Tower Isle's, tel 718-495-2626, towerisles patties.com. **FURTHER INFORMATION AND RECIPES:** *The Brooklyn Cookbook* by Lyn Stallworth and Rod Kennedy Jr. (1991); *The Sugar Reef Caribbean Cookbook* by Devra Dedeaux (1991); cookstr.com (search jamaica beef patties); islands.com (search jamaican meat patties); jamaicans.com (search meat patties).

A RUBY-RED BREW FOR CHRISTMAS CHEER

Sorrel Punch

Jamaican

To Europeans and the fans of their food, sorrel denotes a tart, spinachlike herb used in soups and sauces. But in the Caribbean and in parts of the Middle East, it refers to a tropical bushy shrub (*Hibiscus sabdariffa*), also known as hibiscus or

roselle (see Karkade, page 710). The plant came to the Caribbean from India via British colonists, and arrived in Jamaica in the eighteenth century. Its edible red petals taste like a cross between rhubarb and cranberry, a flavor that becomes the eye-opening, sweet-tart basis for the lively, garnet-colored Christmas drink of Jamaica.

To make it, the dried red blossoms (also enjoyed preserved in jams and chutneys) are covered with boiling water and steeped with sugar and sometimes a little ginger, until the liquid becomes syrupy. Served ice cold, the sorrel mixture is combined with dark rum and diluted with water for a drink that is fragrant, quenching, and intoxicating—a punch that looks like liquid rubies, garnished with vivid, cranberry-red sorrel buds.

WHERE: *In Kingston, Jamaica,* Jamaica Inn, tel 876-974-2514, jamaicainn.com; Miss T's Kitchen, tel 876-795-0099, misstskitchen.com; *in New York,* Miss Lily's, at two locations, misslilys .com. **MAIL ORDER:** For dried sorrel, West Indian Shop, tel 877-323-5582, westindianshop .com; amazon.com (search dried sorrel). **FURTHER INFORMATION AND RECIPES:** *Visions of Sugarplums* by Mimi Sheraton (1981); epicurious.com (search jamaican sorrel rum punch, then click All Recipes). **TIP:** For a livelier if less authentic refresher, substitute sparkling water for still water.

AFRICAN

NORTH AFRICAN
Egyptian, Moroccan, Tunisian

WEST AFRICAN
Nigerian, Senegalese

EAST AND SOUTHERN AFRICAN
Ethiopian, Kenyan,
Mozambican, South African

‖‖‖‖‖‖‖‖‖‖‖‖‖‖‖‖‖‖‖‖‖‖‖‖‖‖‖‖‖‖

A HEAVEN-SCENTED BREW

Cardamom Coffee

North African, Egyptian

With its mildly mentholated, sweetly warm overtones, cardamom is the seasoning of choice for coffee throughout North Africa and parts of the Middle East. Simmered along with sugar and finely ground dark-roasted beans, the crushed gray-white cardamom seeds lend an aromatic essence that makes for a bracing hot beverage. Served in tiny, espresso-style cups, the grounds-in coffee is taken pure and black by true aficionados, and with milk by the more timid. Although it would probably shock traditionalists, cardamom coffee is also delicious iced or made into a pleasantly perfumed cappuccino, and strained it can be used as the base for a refreshing sorbet or Italian-style granita.

Cardamom Coffee

Makes about 1 cup (see Note)

1 tablespoon espresso-style ground coffee, preferably dark-roasted Yemen mocha
Seeds of 1 cardamom pod, crushed, or ¼ teaspoon ground cardamom
½ to 1½ teaspoons sugar

1. Combine the coffee, cardamom, and ½ teaspoon sugar in a small saucepan (if you like it sweeter you can add more later). Add 1 cup of water and slowly heat over medium flame so that the coffee simmers for about 8 minutes.

2. Stir the coffee gently until it comes to a boil. Immediately remove the coffee from the heat and spoon the froth that has developed into a cup or cups, then add the coffee, including the grounds. Serve immediately, warning guests to allow the grounds to settle and then not to stir the coffee.

Note: If you are serving the coffee in traditional espresso-size cups, this amount will serve 3 or 4. In that case, divide the froth among the cups before pouring in the brewed coffee. This will work only if all guests have the same preference.

Where: *In Cairo,* El-Fishawi Café, tel 20/2-2590-6755; *in Montclair, NJ,* Mesob, tel 973-655-9000, mesobrestaurant.com. **Mail order:** For coffee, McNulty's Tea & Coffee Co., Inc., tel 212-242-5351, mcnultys.com; for cardamom, Penzeys Spices, tel 800-741-7787, penzeys.com. **Further information:** astray.com (search arabic coffee). **Tip:** Cardamom can be purchased already powdered, but retains a fresher flavor in its pods, which are easily broken open so the inner seeds can be crushed. **See also:** Turkish Coffee, page 493; Coffee in Vienna, page 320.

A dash of cardamom makes for a tasty cup of joe.

Chakchouka

North African, Israeli

One of the world's most colorful scrambles, *chakchouka* is a red (tomatoes), green (peppers), and yellow (eggs) favorite across North Africa and also in Israel, having arrived there with Jewish émigrés. Arabs taking this recipe across the

Mediterranean might have inspired the similar French and Spanish dish *piperade*, which was in turn transformed in the U.S. into that diner standard, the so-called Spanish omelet. On its home turf, chakchouka's essential combination of eggs and vegetables appears in several delectable versions, although it's hard to beat the simplicity and savoriness of the original.

Chakchouka (also known as *shakshouka* and *tchoutchouka*) begins with sweet green peppers and onions gently sautéed to softness in olive oil, sometimes with a dash of stinging-hot *harissa* chile paste, and then simmered with tomatoes until fairly thick. Cooled slightly, the sauce is stirred into beaten eggs and the mixture is either scrambled in a skillet or double boiler, or oven-baked in a deep dish. Alternatively, the cooked vegetable sauce might be poured into a baking pan and the eggs cracked into small hollows pressed into it, to bake until the whites are set but the yolks remain runny. Either way, the result is a succulent ooze of creamy eggs spiked with the tangy vegetables, sweet onions, and whispers of fresh herbs. In Alexandria, Egypt, they might add dill, while garlic appeals to chakchouka fans in Israel and Tunisia.

The Israeli headquarters for theatrically presented chakchouka is the restaurant Dr. Shakshuka, in Old Jaffa, outside of Tel Aviv. There, the garrulous owner, Bino Gabso, a native of Tripoli, specializes in a piquant, warming, baked version of this eponymous dish, along with shawarma, couscous, and more startling delicacies like stewed calf's intestines. As the restaurant's name suggests, spellings of this ubiquitous Mediterranean egg dish vary, with chakchouka being a Berber word for ragout.

Whether spelled with a C or an S or a T, baked or scrambled, this classic dish is well worth mastering at home.

This colorful scramble is the perfect light lunch.

WHERE: *In Tel Aviv-Jafo, Israel,* Dr. Shakshuka, tel 972/3-682-2842, shakshuka.rest.co.il; *in New York,* Mémé, tel 646-692-8450, memeonhudson .com; The Hummus Place at multiple locations, hummusplace.com; *in San Francisco,* Café Zitouna, tel 415-673-2622, sfcafezitouna.com. **FURTHER INFORMATION AND RECIPES:** *The Book of Jewish Food* by Claudia Roden (1996); *Jerusalem* by Yotam Ottolenghi and Sami Tamimi (2012); epicurious.com (search chakchouka); foodandwine.com (search tomato stew with poached eggs).

━━━━━━━━|||||||||||||||||||||||||||||||||||━━━━━━━━

A GREEN SAUCE THAT GOES WITH EVERYTHING

Chermoula

North African

L ushly green with a tangy bite, the sauce known as *chermoula* is used throughout North Africa as a seasoning, marinade, and garnish, akin to the Argentine *chimichurri* (see page 667) and the Italian *salsa verde*. The base is aromatic cilantro leaves, crushed in a mortar along with parsley, garlic, cumin, sweet paprika or dried chiles or the fiery Moroccan chile paste *harissa*, salt, black pepper, and vinegar or lemon juice. Depending upon the food it will be enhancing, the cook might also stir in olive oil, minced onion, cinnamon, saffron, or even honey and raisins.

North African spice blend

Traditionally favored as an accompaniment to grilled fish, chermoula makes a delicious marinade and topping for all manner of barbecued meats, most especially lamb and chicken. A truly all-purpose condiment, it would also make a statement as a zesty topping for American barbecue standbys like hot dogs, steaks, and hamburgers, and impart a spicy Mediterranean accent to sides like grilled corn on the cob and potato salad.

WHERE: *In New York,* Mémé, tel 646-692-8450, memeonhudson .com; *in Chicago,* Shokran, tel 773-427-9130, shokranchicago.com; *in San Francisco,* Café Zitouna, tel 415-673-2622, sfcafezitouna.com. **MAIL ORDER:** For prepared chermoula spice mix, amazon.com (search zamouri chermoula; henry langdon chermoula); for individual spices, Penzeys Spices, tel 800-741-7787, penzeys.com. **FURTHER INFORMATION AND RECIPES:** *Arabesque* by Claudia Roden (2006); *The Food of Morocco* by Paula Wolfert (2011); herbivoracious.com (search chermoula); splendidtable.org (search chermoula); foodnetwork.com (search chermoula).

━━━━━━━━|||||||||||||||||||||||||||||||||||━━━━━━━━

AN EPIC GRAIN-BASED ENTRÉE

Couscous

North African

A snowy mound of tender, toothsome, rice-sized bits of pasta, suffused with a robustly aromatic stew of vegetables, spoon-tender chunks of lamb, rabbit, chicken, squab, or fish, and toppings of softly boiled chickpeas, dried pumpkin, and raisins, each portion doused with a ladleful of lush broth, fired with spicy harissa sauce . . .

A must-have dish in any Moroccan restaurant, and in many French bistros as well, couscous is really an event, as much about the elaborate preparation as the serving and the eating. Its foundation is the tiny, granular pasta, couscous, which gives its name to the dish and to the metal steamer pots it's cooked in, dubbed *couscoussiers* by the French. Traditionally, the only utensils used to eat it are the fingers of the right hand, which squeeze together bite-size balls of couscous that soak up the stew. For those reluctant to dig in with their hands, fork and spoon are always available.

At first glance, the cooked couscous resembles coarse semolina grains, and in fact it begins as semolina flour, sprinkled with water and worked by hand until it clumps into tiny pellets, which are then pushed through a sieve or basket. It's a task that demands considerable skill; fortunately, pot-ready dried couscous is ubiquitous. It's not as good as homemade, of course, but it's a fair trade-off, considering the years of practice and hours of labor that go into hand-formed couscous.

Couscous lends itself well to a variety of dishes.

After it is formed, the slightly dampened couscous goes into the steamer basket of the couscoussier, while in the pot below, vegetables such as tomatoes, zucchini, turnips, carrots, eggplant, and cabbage simmer along with onions, garlic, meat (usually), and broth, seasoned with spices that might include coriander, cumin, thyme, cinnamon, saffron, and hot and sweet peppers. The stew sends up the fragrant steam that cooks and fluffs the grains of couscous and whets the appetite.

Variations abound, including a Moroccan dessert couscous flavored with cinnamon and sugar and served with butter. A delicate, saffron-bright chicken couscous made with tiny new artichokes and other vegetables in a creamy sauce is a beloved springtime lunch of the Berbers, an indigenous North African ethnic group that gave couscous its name. On home ground, a couscous feast is almost always served as an epic lunch, akin to the Brazilian *feijoada* (see page 670) and the Italian *bollito misto,* as it is considered much too heavy for the evening meal.

WHERE: *In Fez, Morocco,* Palais de Fes Dar Tazi, tel 212/661-147-268, palaisdefes.com; Restaurant Al Fassia (in the Sofitel Fes Palais Jamias), tel 212/535-634-331; *in Marrakesh, Morocco,* Al Fassia Gueliz, tel 212/524-434-060, alfassia.com; Al Fassia Aguedal, tel 212/524-381-138, alfassia.com; *in Paris,* Le Mansouria, tel 33/1-43-710016, mansouria.fr; Timgad, tel 33/1-45-74-23-70, timgad.fr; *in New York,* Mémé, tel 646-692-8450, memeonhudson.com; Barbès Restaurant, tel 212-684-0215, barbesrestaurant nyc.com; *in Washington, DC,* Marrakesh, tel 202-393-9393, marrakeshdc.com; *in Boston,* Kasbah, tel 617-539-4484, kasbahrestaurant.com. **MAIL ORDER:** For couscous, Marky's, tel 800-522-8427, markys.com; Zingerman's, tel 888-636-8162, zingermans.com; for couscoussier, Williams-Sonoma, williams-sonoma.com; for individual spices, Penzeys Spices, tel 800-741-7787, penzeys.com. **FURTHER INFORMATION AND RECIPES:** *Arabesque* by Claudia Roden (2006); *The Food of Morocco* by Paula Wolfert (2011); food.com (search traditional north african couscous); cookstr.com (search fluffy couscous); for classes in preparing couscous and other Moroccan dishes in Marrakesh, Souk Cuisine, tel 212/673-804-955. **TIP:** Some North African restaurants, both stateside and abroad, require couscous to be ordered twenty-four hours in advance and have a set minimum for group size.

⊣||||||||||||||||||||||||||||||⊢

Harira

North African

No *diffa,* or celebratory feast, would be complete without this richly complex soup, a leaner version of which is served to break the Ramadan fast each day at sundown. The flavorful broth, made from both chicken and lamb, is bolstered with giblets, lentils or chickpeas, onion, celery, and tomatoes, and spiced with cilantro, cinnamon, turmeric, saffron, and bracing shots of lemon and hot chiles in the form of Morocco's incendiary *harissa* paste. At its most lavish, *harira* is thickened with broken lengths of fine vermicelli pasta, simmered in the soup, and beaten egg yolks, which impart a satiny texture to the rose-red soup.

Harira

Serves about 8 as a first course;
serves 4 or 5 as a main course

⅔ *cup dried lentils or chickpeas*
2 pounds chicken legs or thighs,
  with skin and bones
1 pound chicken giblets trimmed and
  cleaned
1½ pounds lamb shoulder,
  trimmed and cut in ½-inch cubes
2 teaspoons salt
½ *teaspoon freshly ground black pepper*
3 tablespoons olive oil or unsalted butter
1 large onion, chopped
1 cup canned crushed tomatoes
  with their juices
2 ribs celery with their leaves
5 to 6 sprigs fresh flat-leaf parsley, plus
  chopped parsley for garnish (optional)
3 sprigs fresh cilantro, plus chopped
  cilantro for garnish (optional)
1 cinnamon stick (2 inches long)
1 teaspoon turmeric
Pinch of powdered saffron or saffron
  threads
½ *teaspoon harissa (Moroccan or North*
  African chile paste), or ½ teaspoon
  dried red pepper flakes, plus harissa
  for serving
1 cup broken uncooked vermicelli,
  in 1- to 1½-inch lengths
3 extra-large egg yolks
3 tablespoons freshly squeezed lemon juice

1. Soak the lentils or chickpeas in cold water to cover for about 6 hours. Rinse, drain, and set the lentils or chickpeas aside.

2. Place the chicken parts, giblets, and lamb in a 6-quart pot and add water to cover. Add the salt and pepper and bring to a boil over moderately high heat. Reduce the heat to moderate and let simmer for about 15 minutes, skimming off the foam as it rises to the surface.

3. Meanwhile, heat the olive oil or butter in a small skillet over low heat. Add the onion and cook until lightly browned, about 8 minutes. Add the browned onion to the pot with the chicken and lamb. Add the tomatoes with their juices and the celery, parsley and cilantro sprigs, cinnamon stick, turmeric, saffron, harissa or red pepper flakes, and the drained lentils or chickpeas.

4. Let the soup simmer gently but steadily, partially covered, until the chicken is falling from the bones and the lamb is tender, about 1 hour. As the soup cooks, add enough water to maintain the original level of liquid.

5. Using a slotted spoon, remove the chicken and lamb from the pot. Trim all of the skin and bones from the chicken and discard them, along with the cooked vegetables and the cinnamon stick.

Cut or shred the chicken and lamb into spoonable pieces and return them to the soup. The soup can be prepared up to this point and refrigerated, covered, for up to 24 hours. (Before resuming, if you prefer a lean final result, skim any congealed fat from the surface.) Let the soup come to a simmer before continuing with the recipe.

6. About 20 minutes before serving, add the vermicelli to the soup and let it simmer until soft, about 7 minutes.

7. To thicken the soup, beat the egg yolks with the lemon juice in a small bowl. Using a ladle, slowly trickle some hot soup into the egg yolk mixture, beating constantly with a wire whisk. When you have added about 2 cups of the soup to the yolk mixture, turn off the heat and slowly pour the yolk mixture into the soup, beating constantly with the wire whisk.

8. Taste for seasoning, adding more salt, pepper, and/or lemon juice as necessary. Let the soup heat for 5 minutes but do not let it come to a boil. Ladle the soup into bowls and sprinkle each portion with parsley or cilantro, if desired. Pass harissa at the table for those who want a fiery accent.

Variations: Canned lentils or chickpeas can be substituted for the dried. If you are using these, rinse them under cold running water and add them to the soup, about 10 minutes before the vermicelli. If you prefer, either the chicken or the lamb can be eliminated, in which case double the amount of whichever meat you use.

WHERE: *In Paris,* Timgad, tel 33/1-45-74-23-70, timgad.fr; *in New York,* Boulud Sud, tel 212-595-1313, bouludsud.com; *in Boston,* Kasbah, tel 617-539-4484, kasbahrestaurant.com; *in Chicago,* Shokran, tel 773-427-9130, shokran chicago.com; *in San Francisco,* Café Zitouna, tel 415-673-2622, sfcafezitouna.com. **MAIL ORDER:** For harissa, Zingerman's, tel 888-636-8162, zingermans.com; for individual spices, Penzeys Spices, tel 800-741-7787, penzeys.com. **FURTHER INFORMATION AND ADDITIONAL RECIPE:** moroccan food.about.com (search classic moroccan harira); for classes in preparing harira and other Moroccan dishes in Marrakesh, Souk Cuisine, tel 212-673-804-955, soukcuisine.com.

A RED HOT DIP FOR THE BRAVE

Matbucha

North African, Israeli

A welcome component of every course but dessert, the North African and Israeli relish *matbucha* is fiery in color, aroma, and flavor. It may appear as a sparkling meze appetizer, a dip for bread, a spread for pita sandwiches, or a

condiment for salads and grilled or roasted fish, chicken, or meat.

Based on softly cooked tomatoes slowly simmered in olive oil with grilled or sautéed green peppers, onions, and garlic, until the ingredients meld together, the lush puree gets final touches of pine nuts, cumin, and a heady sprinkling of crushed, hot red peppers or a dash of the hot sauce harissa. Ideally left to ripen for five to eight hours before being served, it is best appreciated at room temperature.

If prepared in large quantity, matbucha can also be used as the base for the baked egg dish *chakchouka* (see page 697), the spicy crimson sauce lending a pungent accent and mingling with the eggs' runny yolks.

Given the current taste for hot-flavored foods, it would not be surprising to see matbucha join the ranks of other international hot sauces as a fashionable garnish for hamburgers, hot dogs, pasta, various barbecued meats, and even pizzas. A little stirred into a lentil or bean soup would not go amiss either.

Where: *In New York,* Mémé, tel 646-692-8450, memeonhudson.com. **Further information and recipes:** *A Taste of Morocco* by Robert Carrier (1997); *The Food of Morocco* by Paula Wolfert (2011); gemsinisrael.com/matbucha; kosherfood.about.com (search matboucha); allrecipes.com (search matbucha).

⊢||||||||||||||||||||||||||||⊣

ON THE LAMB

Méchoui

Spit-Roasted Lamb

North African

In a recipe that dates to the mid-twentieth century, Madame Z. Guinaudeau, a French ophthalmologist who lived and worked in Morocco for many years, begins her instructions for *méchoui* with rather gory and specific directions for

slaughtering a young sheep (including "plunging a knife into the carotid") before roasting it on a spit. Nowadays, méchoui is just as likely to refer to a nicely spit-roasted leg of lamb, no elaborate butchery required. Essential to its flavor and succulence, however, are frequent bastings with butter spiced with both hot and sweet paprika, black pepper, coriander, salt, and sometimes ginger. Some cooks allow the meat to marinate in the butter mixture for several hours and then may insert slivers of garlic under a thin layer of fat, a seal to prevent loss of the delicious juices. As the meat turns slowly on a spit (cranked mechanically or by hand), it develops a pungent, crackling crust while the interior turns rosy red and absorbs the hot and sweet flavors of the seasonings. The challenge is to keep sneaky fingers from pulling off luscious chunks of the spiced meat as it roasts.

When a whole or half lamb is cooked, the choicest morsels are the kidneys and the plump,

Succulent lamb requires multiple butter bastings.

tender nugget of meat under each shoulder blade. At Berber feasts, the guest of honor is usually presented with such a treat by the host—

often a sheikh—who literally hands it over, the right hand being the utensil with which the meat is served and eaten. In some higher-end Moroccan restaurants, rosy slices of méchoui might be presented alongside a plate of couscous, sauced with vegetables and their gravy. And while méchoui is preferably roasted outdoors, over a wood or charcoal fire, practicality has its place, and the meat is often prepared in home ovens.

WHERE: *In Marrakesh, Morocco,* food stalls in Méchoui Alley; *in Paris,* Le Mansouria, tel 33/1-43-710016, mansouria.fr; Le Méchoui du Prince, tel 33/1-40-518848, lemechouiduprince.com; *in Los Angeles,* Moun of Tunis, tel 323-874-3333, mounoftunis.la. **MAIL ORDER:** For lamb cuts, Stemple Creek Ranch, tel 415-883-8253, stemple creek.com; D'Artagnan, tel 800-327-8246, dartag nan.com. **FURTHER INFORMATION AND RECIPES:** *A Taste of Morocco* by Robert Carrier (1997); *Couscous and Other Good Food from Morocco* by Paula Wolfert (1987); *Traditional Moroccan Cooking* by Madame Z. Guinaudeau (2004); jamieoliver.com (search mechoui lamb); nytimes.com (search lamb roasted moroccan); for classes in preparing méchoui and other Moroccan dishes in Marrakesh, Souk Cuisine, tel 212/673-804-955, soukcuisine.com.

ONE SPICY SAUSAGE

Merguez

North African

A Berber creation that dates back to at least the thirteenth century, merguez sausages are dense and chewy, fired with *harissa*, the hot North African chile paste, and aromatic with garlic. Usually made of fat-enriched ground veal, although lamb and beef are frequent alternatives, and eaten either fresh or dried (in the traditional, pre-refrigeration manner), the sausages are a burnished dark red and fragrant with a spice blend that might include fennel, coriander, cinnamon, and allspice.

The juicy, compact, fresh merguez are grilled over a wood fire, then slid into pita bread and topped with salad and perhaps the lemony sesame sauce, tahini; they are also fried and sliced into egg dishes, or served whole in mixed grills. The dried sausages serve as a hearty seasoning in substantial long-cooked dishes, such as couscous (see page 698) and *tagines* (see page 704).

Given North Africa's proximity to France and the Iberian peninsula, and these areas' interlocking histories, it is small wonder that merguez has become a standard item in French and Spanish markets. Going even further back, the merguez is likely to have inspired Spain's chorizo, which has similar seasonings and characteristics (although it is made with pork, a meat forbidden to Muslims). The two sausages can in fact be used interchangeably in many Iberian dishes, as in paella (see page 265) or the Portuguese clam and sausage specialty *cataplana.*

WHERE: *In New York,* Mémé Mediterranean, tel 646-692-8450, memeonhudson.com; Epicerie Boulud, tel 212-595-9606, epicerieboulud.com. **MAIL ORDER:** D'Artagnan, tel 800-327-8246, dartag nan.com; Marky's, tel 800-522-8427, markys .com. **FURTHER INFORMATION AND RECIPES:** *The Soul of a New Cuisine* by Marcus Samuelsson (2006); *The Food of Morocco* by Paula Wolfert (2011); *Sausage* by Nichola Fletcher (2012); serious eats.com (search homemade merguez); food52 .com (search merguez ragout).

━━━━━━━━━━━━━━┤||||||||||||||||||||||||||||├━━━━━━━━━━━━━━

A HOT TEA WITH A COOL TASTE

Mint Tea

North African

Technically, cool is not a taste, but that is the defining menthol-induced trait mint imparts to any dish or drink it seasons, whether served cold or hot. Cool is an especially marked characteristic of mint tea, a refreshing symbol of hospitality that is served (usually hot) throughout North Africa and in parts of the Middle East. The herb of choice for the brew is candy-sweet spearmint (*Mentha spicata*), with bouquets of the fresh green sprigs crammed into a prewarmed brewing pot along with boiling water, sugar, and tea leaves. In Morocco, mild green tea is preferred, and a few droplets of rosewater may be added for a romantic touch. Egyptians tend to prefer robust black teas with sugar, just a few leaves of mint, and sometimes, hints of cardamom or clove. Lemon and honey are also possibilities, and the tea is occasionally served iced, a fairly modern departure from tradition.

Typically, mint tea is brewed in a silvery pot with a long, graceful spout. To serve, the pot is held high and the tea is poured 12 to 20 inches down into tiny gold-embossed glasses set on a brass, silver, or copper tray, a high-wire act that gives the tea a nice foamy head and is a mark of showmanship at many restaurants and cafés. Mint tea is customarily offered to guests on arrival in homes, and when deals have been struck in old-fashioned shops and souks, it may be ordered in from a nearby café, as a symbol of goodwill. Favored between and after meals, it is often sipped along with nibbles of *rahat lokum*—the sugared, fruit-flavored jellies known as Turkish delight (see page 491).

WHERE: *In Washington, DC,* Marrakesh, tel 202-393-9393, marrakeshdc.com. **MAIL ORDER:** For dried mint, Penzeys Spices, tel 800-741-7787, penzeys.com; Mighty Leaf, tel 877-698-5323, mightyleaf.com; David's Tea, tel 888-873-0006, davidstea.com. **FURTHER INFORMATION AND RECIPES:** *The New Book of Middle Eastern Food* by Claudia Roden (2000); *The Food of Morocco* by Paula Wolfert (2011); *The Africa Cookbook* by Jessica B. Harris (2010); palaisdesthes.com (search moroccan hospitality).

━━━━━━━━━━━━━━┤||||||||||||||||||||||||||||├━━━━━━━━━━━━━━

ALL IN A STEW

Tagine

North African

Like the pans we call casseroles and the earthenware dishes the French call *tians,* a *tagine* is both a cooking vessel and the heady, substantial North African stew cooked in it. A combination of deep, wide terra-cotta bowl and high-peaked, conical cover that directs and concentrates heat, the tagine may hold myriad combinations of meats, poultry, or fish with various vegetables and seasonings. Slowly cooked over direct fire or on a bed of ashen charcoal, the ingredients in the covered tagine simmer to melting richness, absorbing aromatic spices such as saffron, cinnamon, and ginger, along with onions and garlic.

Nuts such as pistachios or almonds, along with raisins or dates, go into many tagines, as do baby artichokes, cardoons, fava beans, and spring peas in season. A much-favored Moroccan version is prepared with tender pieces of young chicken, chunks of salt-preserved lemons, crumbles of spicy merguez sausage, and briny, oily cracked green olives. Lamb or mutton is the most popular red meat for tagines, and either is especially delicious under a mantle of eggplant and tomatoes, or paired with black olives and soft-cooked string beans.

Once cooked and ready to serve, the still-covered and searingly hot tagine is fitted into a specially shaped basket that is colorfully woven in geometric patterns, the better to handle the dish and present it to guests, who ladle portions out onto individual

Traditional Moroccan tagines

plates and mix in dashes of *harissa* as desired. Served alongside are steamed rice, fluffy mounds of couscous, or fresh, hot bread to soak up the juices and mellow the spice.

WHERE: *In Paris,* Le Mansouria, tel 33/1-43-710016, mansouria.fr; Timgad, tel 33/1-45-74-23-70, timgad.fr; *in New York,* Mémé, tel 646-692-8450, memeonhudson.com; Boulud Sud, tel 212-595-1313, bouludsud.com; Barbes Restaurant, tel 212-684-0215, barbesrestaurant nyc.com; *in Washington, DC,* Marrakesh, tel 202-393-9393, marrakeshdc.com; *in Boston,* Kasbah, tel 617-539-4484, kasbahrestaurant.com; *in San Francisco,* Café Zitouna, tel 415-673-2622, sfcafezitouna.com. **MAIL ORDER:** Tagines by Riado, tel 305-888-1799, tagines .com; for harissa and couscous, Marky's, tel 800-522-8427, markys .com. **FURTHER INFORMATION AND RECIPES:** *The Food of Morocco* by Paula Wolfert (2011); *The Africa Cookbook* by Jessica B. Harris (2010); cookstr.com (search tunisian lamb); bonappetit.com (search moroccan beef meatball tagine); for classes in preparing tagines and other Moroccan dishes in Marrakesh, Souk Cuisine, tel 212/673-804-955, soukcuisine .com.

—||||||||||||||||||||||||||||||||||—

A DELICIOUS OASIS

Andrea Mariouteya

Egyptian

Great food is only one of the attractions at Andrea, a charming and entertaining outdoor farm-restaurant. Its oasis-like setting in Cairo, on the road to Giza and its pyramids, draws locals and visitors from all over Egypt, families crowding

around rustic tables under grapevines and wisteria-sheltered arbors. Andrea is a particularly special treat for a Friday lunch, as part of a

leisurely afternoon that starts the Muslim sabbath. This is the best time for people watching, as parents play with their children and everyone takes in the sunshine while eating their way through a bright, fresh meal.

Andrea's specialty is spit-roasted chicken and quail, simply seasoned with salt and pepper and cooked until lusciously well done, so the meat melts off the bones. Savory rice pilaf is the standard accompaniment. While you wait for the main course, an enticing array of mezes, or appetizers, may include olives, pickles, sautéed chicken livers, hummus (see page 496), baba ghanoush (smoky eggplant dip, see page 495), and *dolmas* plumped with ground lamb and rice (see page 482).

An attraction not to be missed is the sight of bread baking in an exact reproduction of an ancient Egyptian, beehive-shaped oven. Pressed against the oven's round walls, the bread dough curves into crisp, thin sheaves that are served at the restaurant, a reminder that it was the ancient Egyptians who first used yeast as leavening for bread, and eventually to make beer, a beverage also offered here, along with local wines. A charming, shaded retreat from the modern, ever-bustling metropolis of Cairo, and a short drive from the Great Pyramids, Andrea is the ideal spot to get an authentic taste of Egypt, old and new.

WHERE: 59-60 Mariouteya Canal Rd., Giza, Cairo, tel 20/2-3833-1133, andreamariouteya .com.

||||||||||||||||||||||||||||||||

CRÈME DE LA CRÈME

Biram Ruzz

Egyptian

The description "creamed chicken with rice" doesn't quite do justice to the molded, golden-crusted layer cake that is the Egyptian dish *biram ruzz*. An elegant special-occasion offering, it begins with chunks of chicken nestled between two layers of the long-grain rice Egyptians prefer, all arranged in a buttered three- to four-inch-deep casserole dish and topped with a simmering sauce of milk, sweet cream, rich chicken stock, and, for an aromatic touch, a dash of nutmeg. Baked and inverted onto a serving plate, the dish emerges as a crisp, gilded cake to be cut into wedges, revealing the fragrantly luscious interior.

Most authentically, the chicken is used in whole pieces, skin and bones and all, but nowadays, skinless and boneless meat is often substituted. Even if one forgoes the full flavor of the skin-and-bones version, dark meat is preferable, although again, white breast meat is often the choice these days.

As a time-saver and a way to use leftovers, a version of biram ruzz can be made with all manner of meat or fish, along with already-cooked rice, resulting in a somewhat looser, less-rich dish. For an even richer variation on the original, however, cheese replaces cream in the sauce to form a thicker, crunchier crust. A garnish of black olives adds a nice edge of saltiness. If you happen to find any of the deliciously flavored rice left over, it can then make a satisfying side dish.

WHERE: *In Cairo,* Abou Shakra, tel 20/2-2703-1444, aboushakra.net. **MAIL ORDER:** For Egyptian rice, al-salamimports.com. **FURTHER INFORMATION AND RECIPES:** *Egyptian Cuisine* by Nagwa E. Khalil (1980); *My Egyptian Grandmother's Kitchen* by Magda Mehdawy (2006); *Egyptian Cooking and Other Middle Eastern Recipes* by Samia Abdennour (2010); food.com (search egyptian rice casserole).

LOAVES AS LIGHT AS AIR

Eesh Baladi

Caraway Bread

Egyptian

In a city full of local color and an endlessly vibrant street life, one of Cairo's oldest and most folkloric sights is the *eesh baladi* vendor, most typically a woman in a flowery smock and headscarf carrying aloft a large wooden rack or basket

of what appear to be balloons of bread that flatten as they cool. In the passageways of the souks and in the busy, old downtown streets, the sudden whiff of yeast and toasty grain may tempt a hungry visitor with visions of reaching up and grabbing one of the airy loaves.

Prepared with nutty, brown whole wheat flour and flecked with fragrant caraway seeds, baladi is reminiscent of the puffy fried Indian bread called *poori,* but virtually greaseless because it is baked. Torn strips of the chewy, aromatic bread may be

A woman prepares baladi over a fire in Cairo, Egypt.

topped with snowy chunks of salty feta cheese and sprinkled with fresh dill or mint, and the bread is also used to scoop up classic meze dips and salads such as hummus, baba ghanoush, and tabbouleh. In its very simplest, and perhaps most delicious presentation, the warm caraway-scented bread is glossed with honey or spread with butter, either of which, along with a cup of thick, strong cardamom coffee (see page 696), makes for a fortifying breakfast.

In the unlikely event that any baladi is left over and dries out, not a crumb of the much-loved bread goes to waste. Rather, the loaves

are moistened with olive oil and vinegar or lemon juice and tossed with chunks of cucumber, tomatoes, sweet green peppers, scallions, and seasonings of fresh mint or the nicely sour spice sumac. The result is known as *fattoush,* a first cousin to the Italian *panzanella* (see page 215), both being refreshing Mediterranean summer salads that make good use of stale bread.

FURTHER INFORMATION AND RECIPES: *Egyptian Cooking and Other Middle Eastern Recipes* by Samia Abdennour (2010); *Authentic Egyptian Cooking* by Nehal Leheta (2013); cookingwith thebible.com (search eesh baladi).

——||||||||||||||||||||||||||||||——

A DELICATE ANSWER TO PIZZA

Feteer

Egyptian

In the world of North African and Middle Eastern cuisine—where minimalist doughs like the paper-thin phyllo reign supreme—*feteer* is a lesser-known triumph. A flaky, thin sort of Egyptian crêpe, feteer functions more or less like pizza—spread with toppings, it is then folded and eaten sans utensils. Usually served in casual, open-fronted cafés, the kneaded, buttery yeast dough is shaped into balls and rolled out like piecrust. Tossed and twirled high in the air, it expands and stretches until translucent. The baker, of course, makes quite a floor show of the twirling, similar to that of the boldest Neapolitan pizza-tosser.

Baked to glassy crispness, the feteer is topped with all manner of savories: cheeses, eggs, meats, fish, vegetables, and sauces with scallions, mint, and hot chiles, or sweeter choices such as raisins, nuts, cinnamon, and sugar, or dried dates, figs, and apricots. A modern version takes pizza head-on, and includes mozzarella, tomato sauce, and a grated Parmesan-like cheese. However it's filled, the feteer is a crunchy and succulently rich pastry that will surely challenge the Italian pie for your affections.

Where: *In Cairo,* Fatatri el-Hussein, tel 20/2-3709-4930. **Further information and recipes:** *Egyptian Cuisine* by Nagwa E. Khalil (1980); food.com (search feteer bel asaag); foodblend .wordpress.com (search feteer); youtube.com (search baked egyptian feteer).

——||||||||||||||||||||||||||||||——

THE PEOPLE'S BREAKFAST

Ful Medames

Egyptian

Essentially a fava bean porridge, *ful medames* is so basic to the Egyptian diet that the price of the broad, brown beans is often regulated by the government to ensure they're affordable to the poor. As so often occurs, though, this humble breakfast dish has become stylish, albeit gussied up with some costlier add-ons.

Sold at street stands, cafés, and restaurants throughout Egypt, the slowly simmered beans transform into a creamy, earthy stew. For the most modest version, plain flaxseed oil may be stirred in at the table. Pricier bowls are glossed with olive or sesame oil, or even butter. In addition, toppings might include pickled beets, parsley, cumin, green chiles, raw or fried onions, tomato and hot sauces, and lemon juice. Hard-cooked eggs are a typical accompaniment, sometimes boiled in the soup as it cooks; the reddish-brown color of the beans and their rich, smoky flavor seeps through the shell to the egg itself. Lighter trimmings often appear alongside, including raw salads, yogurt, pita bread, and crunchy pickled vegetables such as turnips, cucumbers, and radishes, cutting through some of the richness and rounding out this savory, super-substantial morning meal.

Where: *In Brooklyn,* Tanoreen, tel 718-748-5600, tanoreen.com; *in Ann Arbor, MI,* La Marsa, tel 734-622-0200, lamarsacuisine.com. **Further information and recipes:** egyptian-cuisine-recipes.com (search ful medames); epicurious.com (search ful medames).

||||||||||||||||||||||||||||||

THE OTHER DARK MEAT

Hamam Meshwi

Grilled Pigeon

Egyptian

L ook closely at the livestock represented on ancient Egyptian tomb paintings and you will spot pigeons along with the ducks, geese, and cattle. The moist, tender, flavorful dark meat of these small birds was probably as cherished in the days of King Tut and Cleopatra as it is by latter-day gourmands—leftovers of a funerary pigeon stew dating from the second dynasty were unearthed in a tomb at Saqqara. For those and other feasts, pigeons were probably grilled over wood-charcoal fires in much the same way as they are today.

All of which should make you feel a part of ancient history as you sit down to the succulent specimens prepared at one of Cairo's cafés, the best places in Egypt to enjoy grilled squab (as young pigeons are called). With any luck, the fire is kept properly bright as the chef works a big fan formed of long turkey tail feathers, whipping up heat to create pinwheels of swirling sparks while guests munch on bright vegetable appetizers until the birds are ready.

Traditionally, Egyptian pigeons are raised in towering, conical dovecotes, and are considered at their succulent best at about six weeks old, before they begin to fly and develop tough muscles. Stateside, farm-raised squab can

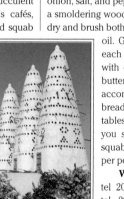

Pigeon dovecotes in Egypt

be special-ordered from many butcher shops or meat departments. While it's rare to find squab grilled in the simple, straightforward Egyptian manner in U.S. restaurants, it couldn't be easier to prepare at home. The cleaned, room-temperature birds should be patted dry and split in half along the backbone, then marinated for about an hour in a mixture of grated onion, salt, and pepper. Just before grilling over a smoldering wood-charcoal fire, pat each bird dry and brush both bird and grill with vegetable oil. Grill for 10 to 15 minutes on each side, basting once or twice with oil or, even better, clarified butter. The grilled squabs are best accompanied by rice pilaf, pita bread, and bowls of pickled vegetables. Depending on what else you serve, and the size of your squabs, allow at least two birds per person.

Where: *In Cairo,* Farahat, tel 20/2-2592-6595; El Mashrabia, tel 20/2-7348-3501. **Mail order:** D'Artagnan, tel 800-327-8246, dartagnan.com. **Further information**

AND RECIPES: *Authentic Egyptian Cooking* by Nehal Leheta (2013); *Egyptian Cooking and Other Middle Eastern Recipes* by Samia Abdennour (2010); *My Egyptian Grandmother's Kitchen* by Magda Mehdawy (2006). **TIP:** Fresh pigeons are preferable, but good quality frozen ones are fine; they should be thawed in the refrigerator before they are split.

A DRINK WITH THE GHOST OF NAGUIB MAHFOUZ

Karkade at El-Fishawi Café

Egyptian

A bracing, ruby-red beverage, *karkade* is a traditional refresher in Egypt, Eritrea, and Ethiopia. Made from dried red hibiscus flowers that are brewed and flavored with sugar and lemon juice, it is a sweet-tart restorative that suggests bright and sophisticated cranberry juice. Some prefer it hot, spiced with cinnamon and cloves, others find it more appealing ice cold, the better to appreciate its jewel-like clarity and clean flavor. Although karkade can be found in food shops and restaurants throughout Egypt, it is especially evocative at the lively El-Fishawi Café, a coffeehouse that has been a landmark meeting place for literati almost since it opened in 1773.

The café is one of Egypt's oldest landmarks.

It is set at the edge of Cairo's expansive Khan el-Khalili bazaar, with its seductive din, dizzying scents of spices, coffee, and grilling meats, and kaleidoscopic array of merchandise (pearl-inlaid wooden boxes, jewelry, fabrics, camel saddles, and much more). El-Fishawi is also known as the Café of Mirrors because of the looking glasses that hang, lean, and perch everywhere, reflecting the dazzling mishmash of chandeliers, artwork, and antique furniture that spills out into the market's slim passageway.

Crowds at tables include students, local pols, haggling merchants, and tourists writing postcards. Aside from perfectly brewed karkade, El-Fishawi offers sweet mint tea (see page 704), fragrant cardamom coffee (see page 696), *sahlab* (the thick, creamy, hot beverage favored in wintertime), as well as small snacks. More adventurous types will want to try another of its typical pleasures: *sheesha* (also known as narghiles or hookahs), the hubble-bubble water pipes that Egyptians love to dream by, just as the café's most famous literary habitué, the Nobel laureate Naguib Mahfouz, did.

WHERE: *In Cairo,* El-Fishawi Café, Muski St. in Khan el-Khalili bazaar, tel 20/2-2590-6755. **FURTHER INFORMATION AND RECIPES:** *Egyptian Cooking and Other Middle Eastern Recipes* by Samia Abdennour (2010); *My Egyptian Grandmother's Kitchen* by Magda Mehdawy (2006); egyptian-cuisine-recipes.com (search karkade). **TIP:** Dried hibiscus flowers can be found in Middle Eastern markets, and in shops catering to Jamaicans, who prepare a similar drink called sorrel punch (see page 693).

||||||||||||||||||||||||||||||||

Kosheri

Rice, Lentil, and Pasta Pilaf

Egyptian

Never mind those ancient wonders at Giza, the monumental pyramids built of sand-colored stone and granite. When hungry in Egypt, look for warm, edible pyramids of the rice and lentil dish *kosheri* (KOO-shery),

a satisfying street food presented in tall, tapering mounds on huge, shiny metal platters.

A savory one-dish meal, Cairo's version of kosheri is an irresistible medley of tiny yellow lentils and rice simmered in stock and accented with crunchy vermicelli fried to golden crispness and onions lightly browned in butter. In Alexandria, a short pasta such as orzo or elbow macaroni might be added to the mix, and for heartier versions all over Egypt, cooked ground lamb or beef is stirred in. As portions are served, they are doused with garlicky wine vinegar and fiery tomato and chile sauces, adding zest to what is essentially a hearty, protein-rich plate of beans and rice.

In all its variations, kosheri is seasoned with mastic, the exotic, musky, earthy plant resin (see page 476). It comes in the form of glassy white pebbles, the crystallized resin

of the *Pistacia lentiscus* tree, which is cultivated only on the Greek island of Chios in the Aegean Sea but grows in the wild around the Mediterranean. Crushed and added as a thickener, stabilizer, and flavoring to Greek and Egyptian breads and dishes both sweet and savory, the mastic imparts a distinctly piney, slightly bitter edge. Hot mint tea (see page 704) provides a fitting finish to the quick meal.

WHERE: *In Cairo,* Abou Sherif Kusheri, tel 20/2-2423-9788; Koshary El Tarir, at multiple locations, cairo360.com (search koshary el tarir); *in Ann Arbor, MI,* La Marsa, tel 734-622-0200, lamarsacuisine.com. **FURTHER INFORMATION AND RECIPES:** *Egyptian Cooking and Other Middle Eastern Recipes* by Samia Abdennour (2010); *My Egyptian Grandmother's Kitchen* by Magda Mehdawy (2006); egyptian-cuisine-recipes.com (search kosheri).

||||||||||||||||||||||||||||||||

Mahalabia and Aish-el-Saraya

Milk Pudding and Bread Pudding

Egyptian

Few desserts are sweeter than those whipped up in North African and Middle Eastern kitchens, and fewer still are more luxuriously sensual than *mahalabia* and *aish-el-saraya,* two seductive Egyptian specialties. Mahalabia is a boiled milk pudding, a description that doesn't nearly do justice to this ethereal, creamy-white, sweetly mellow dessert that holds its own against similar cool treats such as the creamy Italian *panna cotta* and the French blancmange. It owes its distinctive, pearly translucence to a cornstarchlike base of rice flour, stirred into cold milk along with sugar, and simmered until the mixture begins to thicken. Finely ground almonds are added for their texture and their bittersweet overtones, and, as a final fragrant touch, the mixture is perfumed with orange blossom water or rosewater. Chilled in pretty glass bowls, it sets into a light, lovely, and shivery pudding. Just before serving, each portion is decorated with chopped almonds and pistachios.

The second dessert, aish-el-saraya, or "bread of the palace," is so simple to prepare and requires such humble ingredients that it may seem to belie its lofty name. But dip into this sumptuous pudding, made from thick slices of white bread baked under a dousing of butter and caramelized sugar or honey, and you'll understand. Tooth-achingly sweet and fragrant with rosewater, each portion is given a sprinkling of chopped pistachios and an incredibly rich topping of *eishta*—the ivory-colored cream that gathers atop whole, non-homogenized milk and is so dense that it can be picked up with a fork. Served warm with a crown of this cold, velvety cream, aish-el-saraya is a royal treat indeed.

WHERE: *In Cairo,* El Mashrabia, tel 20/2-7348-3501; *in Brooklyn,* for mahalabia (called sahlab), Tanoreen, tel 718-748-5600, tanoreen .com. **FURTHER INFORMATION AND RECIPES:** *Egyptian Cuisine* by Nagwa E. Khalil (1980); *Egyptian Cooking and Other Middle Eastern Recipes* by Samia Abdennour (2010); *My Egyptian Grandmother's Kitchen* by Magda Mehdawy (2006); lifestylefood.com.au (search aish al saraya); taste.fourseasons.com (search mahalabia with orange). **TIP:** When making aish-el-saraya at home, crème fraîche or Devonshire cream can be substituted for *eishta.*

IT'S A SLIPPERY SOUP

Molokhia

Egyptian

With a flavor that combines hints of tart sorrel and spinach, mellowed by slightly toasty overtones, the long, green-leafed vegetable *molokhia* (mel-oo-HEE-ya) is the basis of the soup that bears its name, one of Egypt's best-loved

national dishes. Simmered in a broth made from chicken, duck or, preferably, rabbit, the leaves (from the *Corchorus olitorius* plant, whose tough fibers are made into jute) impart a mucilaginous texture, much as okra does. That is the characteristic most seductive to Egyptians, modern and ancient, the latter of whom believed the vegetable cured everything from freckles to mange.

Today, molokhia is appreciated for its distinctive flavor and texture, as well as its high nutrient content: It contains iron, calcium, and vitamins A and C, as well as antioxidants. Despite such valuable benefits, though, the slippery brew can be off-putting to novices, who pale at the stringy—read, slimy—spoonfuls, at least until they become hooked on the soup's savory silkiness.

The molokhia leaves not only impart the viscosity that enriches the broth and gives it substance, but also the almost antique, bronze-green color and distinctive vegetal flavor, which is accented with a final flourish of *taklia,* a condiment of crushed, sautéed garlic spiked with coriander, cayenne pepper, and other herbs and spices that vary from cook to cook. Steamed white rice is spooned into the soup as one eats, soaking up the rich broth and cutting through the slippery texture.

Although generally served as soup, the vegetable also appears as a side dish, most delightfully in *fattet molokhia,* where it is combined into a casserole with toasted pita, cooked rice or chopped chickpeas, garlic, and butter.

While fresh molokhia leaves are the best and most authentic choice for these dishes, they are nearly impossible to find in the U.S.; dried or frozen leaves provide an acceptable alternative and are available in many Greek and Middle Eastern food stores. The dried leaves are crushed and steeped, much like tea

leaves, until they double in bulk and can then be simmered in the meat stock—the frozen leaves maintain much more flavor, however, and thus are widely preferred.

Where: *In Cairo,* El Mashrabia, tel 20/2-7348-3501. **Further information and recipes:** *A Book of Middle Eastern Food* by Claudia Roden (1974); *My Egyptian Grandmother's Kitchen* by Magda Mehdawy (2006); *The Africa Cookbook* by Jessica B. Harris (2010); egyptian-cuisine-recipes.com (search molokhia).

SWEETER THAN MILK AND HONEY

Om Ali

Creamy Phyllo Pastry

Egyptian

For a dish with such ominous beginnings, *om ali* proves to be a remarkably felicitous dessert. As the story goes, the name, which means "Ali's mother," refers to the first wife of an Ayyubid dynasty (twelfth to thirteenth century) king.

Om ali is similar to bread pudding.

When he was murdered by his second wife, Om Ali retaliated by having her killed. No sooner was the dirty deed done than she created this dish as her glorified version of milk and honey—the food of the Promised Land. She served the luscious dessert to everyone in the palace in celebration.

And festive it is, with flaky, paper-thin leaves of phyllo pastry layered with a rich mixture of chopped pistachios, walnuts, pine nuts, raisins, butter, sugar, vanilla, and cinnamon and covered with heavy sweet cream. Baked into a fragrant pudding, om ali is firm but satiny, with the phyllo retaining some of its flaky crispness.

It is served gently warm with an extra splash of chilled cream and chopped nuts; adding a generous scoop of vanilla or cinnamon ice cream or some sliced strawberries on the side would not be considered amiss either, tradition notwithstanding.

Widely available in Cairo restaurants, om ali is the perfect finish to a multicourse meal of Egyptian specialties, like roasted pigeons plumped with rice pilaf (see page 709) or snowy, white-fleshed fish baked with onions, tomatoes, potatoes, and heady spices.

WHERE: *In Cairo* , El Mashrabia, tel 20/2-7348-3501; *in Ann Arbor, MI,* La Marsa, tel 734-622-0200, lamarsacuisine.com. **FURTHER INFORMATION AND RECIPES:** *The New Book of Middle Eastern Food* by Claudia Roden (2000); egyptian-cuisine-recipes .com (search om ali).

⊢||||||||||||||||||||||||||||||⊣

A FALAFEL BY ANY OTHER NAME

Tamia

Fava Bean Croquettes

Egyptian

Known elsewhere as falafel, these hot and crunchy deep-fried bean croquettes are called *tamia* in Egypt, based on the Arabic and Hebrew word *taam,* meaning flavor. There are differences between falafel and tamia, however, beyond their names. According to the Middle Eastern food scholar Claudia Roden, tamia are believed to have been created by Christian Copts in Egypt for religious feasts, most especially Lent, when meatless dishes take center stage. The Israeli falafel, most familiar to Americans, is based on ground chickpeas, which produce a somewhat heavier texture and more rustic flavor, while the Egyptian tamia is made of milder, fresher-tasting broad beans (also known as fava beans).

The dried beans are soaked, then ground with enlivening additions of scallions, garlic, fresh herbs, cumin, sesame seeds, hot paprika, eggs, and plenty of salt and pepper. Formed into small, hamburgerlike cakes, they are dropped into sizzling oil until they float to the surface as crisp, gold-and-green patties. Drained on paper and sprinkled with minced parsley, they are served instantly. Too hot to handle is just hot enough.

Tamia may be arranged on beds of chopped salad, or stuck with toothpicks and enjoyed as hors d'oeuvres. They are at their best, however, when layered into warm pita rounds along with sharp pickled vegetables, cool, garlicky yogurt sauce, and a thin blanket of the slightly sweet sesame sauce tahini. A favorite Egyptian street food, tamia is doled out by vendors across the country, but many tamia connoisseurs consider the gold standard to be those—deep-fried to order, served seething hot—at Cairo's El Tabei El Domyati, a chain of lively cafés that first opened its doors in 1926.

WHERE: *In Cairo,* El Tabei El Domyati at multiple locations, cairo360.com (search el tabei el domyati). **FURTHER INFORMATION AND RECIPES:** *The New Book of Middle Eastern Food* by Claudia Roden (2000); *My Egyptian Grandmother's Kitchen* by Magda Mehdawy (2006); foodrepublic .com (search fava bean falafel); epicurious.com (search egyptian falafel, then click Ta'miyya).

B'stilla

Moroccan

B'stilla (sometimes spelled *bisteeya* or *pastilla*) is among the most distinguished dishes of Morocco. This savory, decadent meat pie consists of wafer-thin, crisp leaves of phyllo pastry layered with moist, gamy braised squab, butter, chopped hard-cooked eggs, and almonds or pistachios, all perfumed with garlic, onion, cinnamon, saffron, orange blossom water, and more. The baked pie is generously glossed with melted butter and decorated with crisscross sprinklings of confectioners' sugar and cinnamon, for a combination of flavors that ranges tantalizingly from savory to sweet and back again.

Prepared with costly squab and a panoply of spices, b'stilla is a popular main course in elegant homes and restaurants, but, made with chicken and a humbler list of ingredients, it is also sold in wedges from souk stalls and street vendors. Prepared with chicken, it is also a favorite festive food of Moroccan Jews—with some proprietary pride, as they may have introduced the luscious pie to North Africa when they were expelled from Andalusia during the Spanish Inquisition.

Although at first glance the b'stilla's tissue-thin pastry suggests phyllo, the basis of many Arabic and Middle Eastern confections, the authentic pastry is in fact *warkha*. A culinary feat, warkha is made from small, kneaded balls of gossamer dough, which are tossed against a hot pan or griddle until they stick together in one overlapping sheet. Considering the difficulty of that step, many cooks rely on prepared warkha, which can be found in some Moroccan food markets in the U.S., although phyllo leaves are widely substituted as well. Time-intensive, extravagantly spiced, rich and buttery, it's no wonder b'stilla is the star of the Moroccan table.

WHERE: *In Paris,* Le Mansouria, tel 33/1-43-71-00-16, mansouria.fr; Timgad, tel 33/1-45-74-23-70, timgad.fr; *in New York,* Boulud Sud, tel 212-595-1313, bouludsud.com; Barbes Restaurant, tel 212-684-0215, barbesrestaurantnyc.com; Poseidon Bakery, tel 212-757-6173, poseidenbakery.com; *in Boston,* Kasbah, tel 617-539-4484, kasbah restaurant.com; *in Washington, DC,* Marrakesh, tel 202-393-9393, marrakeshdc.com; *in San Francisco,* Café Zitouna, tel 415-673-2622, sfcafe zitouna.com. **MAIL ORDER:** For phyllo, The Fillo Factory, fillofactory.com; for squab, D'Artagnan, tel 800-327-8246, dartagnan.com. **FURTHER INFORMATION AND RECIPES:** *The Book of Jewish Food* by Claudia Roden (1996); *The Food of Morocco* by Paula Wolfert (2011); epicurious.com (search squab b'stilla).

B'stilla is both sweet and savory.

┤||||||||||||||||||||||||||||||├

LOVELY TRIANGLES

Briks and Briouats

Filled Pastry Turnovers

Moroccan, Tunisian

I n an effort to make much out of little by enhancing leftover ingredients or stretching costly ones, many cultures wrap such foods in pastry that is then steamed or fried into nourishing dumplings and turnovers. In Morocco and Tunisia

that effort results in *briks* and *briouats,* thin, crackling triangles of crisp pastry enfolding a number of succulent fillings, spiced ground lamb or tuna being particular favorites. As with *b'stilla* (see previous page), *warkha,* the paper-thin, crêpe-like pastry cooked on a griddle, is the traditional wrap for briks and briouats, but the more readily available phyllo is often

A Marrakesh shopkeeper surveys the variety of sweets.

substituted. They make a tempting first course or between-meals snack, no utensils needed, and are widely sold at street and souk stands.

Though designed to be eaten out of hand, the almost diabolically irresistible Moroccan briks present a challenge. Lurking in the middle, perhaps nested in ground lamb or accompanied merely by spices and fresh cilantro, is an egg. Placed there raw, it lightly cooks as the turnover fries in vegetable oil; the white gently sets, but the yolk remains liquid, ready to spurt out if bitten into with abandon. A ready napkin is a wise precaution.

Smaller but with a greater variety of fillings, briouats are prepared with the same pastry as briks, but are often stuffed with spiced ground lamb or fish, brains or sweetbreads, chopped spicy merguez sausage, or any combination thereof. All are good accompaniments to cool white wine, icy beer, or the milky, anise-flavored spirit, arak. As sweet nibbles served with glasses of hot mint tea, briouats are filled with chopped peanuts or cooked rice, and scented with anise seed, cinnamon, sugar, and grated orange rind or orange blossom water.

Where: *In Fez,* Restaurant Al Fassia (in the Sofitel Fes Palais Jamias), tel 212/535-634-331; *in Paris,* Le Mansouria, tel 33/1-43-71-00-16, mansouria.fr; Timgad, tel 33/1-45-74-23-70, timgad.fr; *in New York,* Boulud Sud, tel 212-595-1313, bouludsud.com; Barbes Restaurant, tel 212-684-0215, barbesrestaurantnyc.com. **Further information and recipes:** moroccanfood.about .com (search briouats; khobz).

HORNS OF PLENTY

Kab el Ghzal

Gazelle Horn Cookies

Moroccan

Crunchy with freshly made almond paste and perfumed with orange blossom water or rosewater, the tapered, elongated cookies known as *kab el ghzal*, or gazelle horns, are a standard in the pastry shops of Morocco. Traditionally served

with mint tea (see page 704) or coffee, they also make for sophisticated accompaniments to dessert wine. With their pleasantly sandy texture, gently sweet almond essence, and generous dusting of confectioners' sugar, the tempting pastries are reminiscent of Mexican wedding cookies (*pastelitos de boda*) and Greek Christmas cookies (*kourambiedes*), also made with ground nuts and with a similar texture and pleasantly toasty richness.

The dessert with mint tea

Gazelle horns hold a place of particular honor on bakery shelves, along with the round and crunchy, almond-topped, butter-laden cookies called *ghoriba*, and the crisp *briwats*—

honey-soaked phyllo leaves folded around a delicate almond filling. These sweets, as well as the Tunisian date cookies called *makroud*, are the favored desserts when daytime fasting ends during the month-long holiday of Ramadan, served after the traditional dinner that begins with bowls of *harira* (see page 700), a lentil- or chickpea-based soup.

Where: *In Casablanca,* Patisserie Bennis Habous, 212/522/303/025. **Further information and recipes:** *Café Morocco* by Anissa Helou (1999); *The Food of Morocco* by Paula Wolfert (2011); moroccanfood.about.com (search gazelle horns); food.com (search moroccan gazelle horns); youtube.com (search gazelle horns).

┤||||||||||||||||||||||||||||├

NOSHING IN THE KASBAH

The Medina Menus of Fez and Marrakesh

Moroccan

Although Morocco's culinary specialties can be enjoyed throughout the country, at restaurants both humble and highbrow, there is no more exciting and entertaining place to sample them than within the medinas of Fez and

Marrakesh. Strictly speaking, medina means a city or a town, but as many urban centers were modernized, the term came to be reserved for the oldest non-European part of a city, where the market stalls or souks are grouped. Within the medina in Marrakesh, you will find the kasbah, an unused fortress whose antique walls enclose narrow streets and shops.

The medina menu is an awesome one, and food is usually available from midday on, though it takes on far more magic in the evening. At the famous square Jemaa El Fna in Marrakesh, visitors can work up an appetite watching storytellers, snake-charmers, fortune-tellers, jugglers, dancers, and more, all performing for tips amidst the swirl of activity. The atmosphere is that of an enormous, convivial house party, and the air is filled with scents of frying oil, lemon, mint, coffee, oranges, almond paste, and the caramelized sugar of hot sweets.

Lured by the mouthwatering aroma of meat grilling over wood fires, diners may choose to start with the tiny, tender kebabs or brochettes; usually of lamb but also made with chicken or beef or tender innards such as livers or kidneys, they are seasoned with onion, cumin, coriander, garlic, and perhaps a touch of lemon juice. Wedges of flaky *b'stilla* (squab pie, see page 715) or snails simmered in a broth redolent of grassy green herbs may be the next course. From there, one can move on to small, manageable bowls of *harira* soup (see page 700), a plate of couscous (see page 698), or a *tagine*, (see page 704). There

may be sticks of fried eggplant and a rainbow of salads made from beets, carrots, tomatoes, onions, green peppers, and cauliflower. Surely the most astonishing dish on offer is the boiled sheep's head, a shocker to the uninitiated but familiar to those who have encountered the *capozelle* (roasted whole sheep's head) of southern Italy. In Morocco, unlike Italy, the well-cooked head is not presented intact, but rather in tender bite-size pieces, so it can be savored easily, with bread as the only utensil. For a sweet finish, there are slivers of orange-, yellow-, and red-fleshed melons and chewy almond- or pistachio-studded nougat served on lollipop sticks. Fresh orange juice, almond milk, and the ubiquitous teas and coffees wash down petite honeyed pastries.

Of course, food is not the only thing to sample in the crowded, colorful, fragrant, clattering confines of the medinas. Save time and energy to shop for mother-of-pearl-inlaid wooden boxes, objects large and small made of gleaming brass, newly dyed wool, carpets, djellabahs (traditional North African robes), jewelry, leather goods, and more—all hawked and haggled over, providing a sense of accomplishment to buyers and sellers alike, and a sure way to work up an appetite.

Where: *In Marrakesh,* Jemaa El Fna, tel 212/661-350-878, jemaa-el-fna.com; *in Fez,* Fes el Bali. **Further information and recipes:** *Couscous and Other Good Food from Morocco* by Paula Wolfert (1987); *The Food of Morocco* by Paula Wolfert (2011); noteatingoutinny.com (search eating out in marrakesh).

⊣||||||||||||||||||||||||||||||⊢

SNAKE BITES

M'hanncha

Almond Coiled Pastry

Moroccan

At first glance one might think it's baklava, and although it bears a great resemblance to that sticky pastry, form is everything where *m'hanncha*—"the snake"—is concerned. As with so many Arabic and Middle Eastern pastries, this one starts with a stack of phyllo leaves brushed with melted butter. Spread with almond paste redolent of orange blossom water, sugar, and mastic, the sheets are tightly rolled and coiled into a single spiral, to achieve a tidy presentation and compactly toothsome texture. Once out of the oven, the crisp, flaky, and golden-brown pastry is dusted with confectioners' sugar and crisscrossed with cinnamon before being cut into slightly curved wedges. Sweet mint tea or the strong, heavily spiced Arabic coffee are the traditional accompaniments to the delicious little snake-cake, but it also pairs well with cold, dry white wine, for a nicely astringent note. Straying even farther from tradition, dabs of crème fraîche or thick yogurt neatly mitigate the chewy pastry's intense sweetness.

Where: *In New York,* Poseidon Bakery, tel 212-757-6173, poseidonbakery.com. **Mail order:** For phyllo, The Fillo Factory, fillofactory.com. **Further information and recipes:** *A Taste of Morocco* by Robert Carrier (1997); *The Food of Morocco* by Paula Wolfert (2011); mideastfood .about.com (search m'hanncha); epicurious .com (search snake cake); morocco.com (search m'hanncha).

||||||||||||||||||||||||||||||||

SUNSHINE BY THE JARFUL

Mssiyar

Salt-Preserved Lemons

Moroccan

The honey-gold salted lemons curing in tall glass jars are among the most dazzling sights in the conserve shops of the souks, part of a rainbow of fruit and vegetable pickles that suggest three-dimensional stained glass. Providing what is probably the most iconic and tantalizing flavor in Moroccan cookery, salted lemons, *mssiyar,* combine the sweet, the sour, and the salty with a faintly mysterious bitterness. Their meltingly tender rinds taste every bit as beautiful as they look, whether they grace salads or are cooked in chunks along with meats, poultry, or fish.

Cured lemons are quintessentially Moroccan.

Although sold prepared across North Africa, salted lemons are best homemade, and seasonings differ with the region. For purists, salt, lemon juice, and a judicious span of time make up the cure, although some cooks add peppercorns, cinnamon, bay leaves, cloves, or coriander, which enhance their flavor but limit the lemons' uses to certain dishes.

Most traditionally, the lemons are quartered vertically, cut to the base but not through it, so that all the sections remain attached. With coarse sea salt pressed between the sections, they are reshaped and then tightly layered into glass jars and covered with freshly squeezed lemon juice. Standing in a warm corner of the kitchen, or on a shelf in front of a sunny window for three to four weeks, the lemons gradually turn a rich gold and their rinds tenderize and take on a satiny sheen. Once pickled, they will keep without refrigeration for almost a year, and almost every part is usable, most especially the rind and the syrupy pickling juice, although the pulp is prized as well.

Preserved lemon is a key ingredient in many Moroccan *tagines* (see page 704), as well as an array of sauces and salads. But one of the simplest and most subtle uses is a relish of diced salted lemon rind tossed with pitted, brine-cured black olives and seasoned with a few drops of lemon juice, dried oregano, and flecks of dried hot chile peppers. The relish lends itself to American-style barbecued ribs and chicken as well as it does to Moroccan dishes, so it's the ideal way to incorporate preserved lemons into your own repertoire.

WHERE: Jars of preserved lemons are available in most markets devoted to North African and sometimes Middle Eastern foods. **MAIL ORDER:** Zingerman's, tel 888-636-8162, zingermans .com; Marky's, tel 800-522-8427, markys.com. **FURTHER INFORMATION AND RECIPES:** *Arabesque* by Claudia Roden (2005); *Mourad: New Moroccan* by Mourad Lahlou (2011); epicurious.com (search preserved lemons 2005); foodnetwork .com (search salted preserved lemons).

THE TASTE OF PURE GOLD

Orange Salads

Moroccan

M orocco boasts several justly celebrated varieties of oranges, including the sweet-tart navels and Valencias; tangy, vibrant blood oranges; and the sophisticated, bitter bigarades (Seville oranges), used for marmalade. Inspired

by their palate-tingling flavor and glowing, sunny color, which makes any dish look festive, Moroccans and other North Africans work the juice and dried or grated zest of oranges into fish, meat, and vegetable stews, as well as pastries and cakes. Not surprisingly, all taste best just-picked, and one of the purest ways to appreciate the essence of Moroccan oranges is as freshly squeezed juice, widely available in souk stalls and street stands around the country—a heady way to start the day, or a midday pick-me-up.

Most beautiful, however, are Morocco's exquisite, polychrome orange salads, each so simple that a description is practically a recipe. One of the most popular contrasts peeled and thickly sliced oranges with shiny black olives, diced garnet-red onion, and emerald parsley, dressed with lemon juice and olive oil and spiced with cumin and chiles or cayenne. For a salad that suggests pure gold, grated raw carrots top peeled orange sections tossed with orange blossom water, cinnamon, and a touch of lemon juice and sugar. Red radish finely grated over orange slices or segments evokes a sunset, and needs only the slightest drizzle of lemon juice and olive oil, and a sprinkling of sugar and orange blossom water. The same salad made with grated, seeded cucumber instead of radishes has a cooling, spring-morning appeal.

Simplest, and perhaps most refreshing, is a salad of several different types of oranges, in colors that range from pale yellow to deep orange to blood red, thinly sliced with a light dressing of orange juice and a touch of olive oil. For slightly sweeter salads that can be served as dessert, chopped dates, raisins, almonds, pistachios, or walnuts may be added to sliced oranges, with a dressing of olive oil, lemon juice, and orange blossom water and sprinklings of cinnamon and confectioners' sugar as the final touch.

WHERE: *In Paris,* Timgad, tel 33/1-45-74-23-70, timgad.fr. **MAIL ORDER:** For oranges, Hale Groves, tel 800-562-4502, halegroves.com; California Oranges, tel 559-539-2251, californiaoranges.com; Cross Creek Groves, tel 800-544-8767, crosscreek groves.com. **FURTHER INFORMATION AND RECIPES:** *A Taste of Morocco* by Robert Carrier (1997); *The Food of Morocco* by Paula Wolfert (2011); food.com (search north african orange salad); saveur.com (search orange and radish salad).

A DIFFERENT SCHOOL OF FISH

Sweet and Savory Roasted Fish

Moroccan

Although whole fish cooked with citrus-accented sweet sauces and dotted with fruit and nuts may sound strange to some, variations on that dish are much favored throughout the world, from China to eastern Europe. Nowhere is such a

dish so highly prized as along the North African coast. The preferred fish there is of the firm-fleshed, oily type—eel, shad, carp, mackerel, and bluefish, although swordfish and snapper, mullet and sea bass are also common.

Adventurous eaters who seek out these savory-sweet North African fish dishes, in restaurants or cookbooks devoted to the foods of this region, will be rewarded with a whirl of new flavors to experience. At their best, the dishes contrast the rich ocean flavor of the main ingredient with the exotic spicing of the sweet-sour garnish. Shad with stuffed dates is a specialty of Fez, in Morocco, and it takes considerable patience to prepare, starting with large, soft dates (ideally from Tafilalet in Morocco, though California-grown medjools work well, as do prunes) that are pitted and stuffed with cooked rice that has been seasoned with almonds, cinnamon, and ginger. The dates are placed in the whole, gutted fish, which is then baked with a crusty cinnamon topping.

Variation of cooked whole fish

For the Moroccan dish known as *hut ben-oua,* whole fish is stuffed and coated with almond paste flavored with cinnamon, ginger, saffron, and orange blossom water; the finished product is spicy-sweet, with distinctively toasty, nutty overtones. *Tasira,* also Moroccan, is made with sea eels in a sauce of soft-cooked onions and raisins or chopped dates, with aromatic spices and sprightly hints of orange and lemon juice. Food historians speculate that these dishes might be the forerunners of the famous sweet-sour fish dishes of the Jewish ghettos in Venice and Rome, still served throughout the diaspora, particularly on Rosh Hashanah.

WHERE: *In Fez,* Restaurant Al Fassia (in the Sofitel Fes Palais Jamias), tel 212/535-634-331; *in Tunis,* Dar El Jeld, tel 216/71-560-916, dareljeld.com. **FURTHER INFORMATION AND RECIPES:** *Traditional Moroccan Cooking* by Madame Z. Guinaudeau (2004); *The Food of Morocco* by Paula Wolfert (2011); epicurious.com (search sea bass moroccan salsa).

—||||||||||||||||||||||||||||||||||||—

A STEW OF GOLDEN APPLES

Maraqat al-Safarjal

Aromatic Ragout of Quince and Lamb

Tunisian

The softly simmered stew known as *tagine* in Morocco (see page 704) is called *maraqat* in Tunisia, and few recipes are more intriguing than the version called *maraqat al-safarjal,* a combination of tender chunks of lamb and tart

and winey quince. Resembling very hard, sour apples—they are never eaten raw—quince are thought by some to have been the divine

There is no combination like lamb and quince.

"golden apples" of Greek legend. Whether or not that is true, it's no myth that quinces lend a creamy, applesauce-like texture and a neatly astringent contrast to the rich, supple lamb in maraqat al-safarjal. Seasonings of rosewater or dried rose petals, coriander, onion, cayenne, and ginger only enhance the elegant result, just as they do to similar sweet-and-savory Moroccan and Algerian dishes made with lamb and prunes or pitted dates scented with cinnamon.

MAIL ORDER: For tagine cooking vessels, Tagines by Riado, tel 305-888-1799, tagines.com; for quince, Melissa's Produce, tel 800-588-0151, melissas.com. **FURTHER INFORMATION AND RECIPES:** *A Mediterranean Feast* by Clifford A. Wright (1999); *Arabesque* by Claudia Roden (2006); marthastewart.com (search lamb and quince tagine); saveur.com (search lamb quince and okra tagine); chow.com (search lamb and quince stew).

—||||||||||||||||||||||||||||||||||||—

EVERYONE LOVES A DOUGHNUT

Yo-Yo

Tunisian

The relationship between this irresistible, honeyed pastry and the child's toy on a string is a mystery—if, in fact, a relationship exists at all. What is clear, however, is the appeal throughout North Africa of these lusciously syrupy sweets.

As the puffy, ring-shaped crullers emerge from the deep-fryer, they are punctured and then drenched with a golden coat of honey scented with the zest and juice of oranges, for a rich and oozing texture. Despite the fact that they are too tender and gooey to actually dunk, the Tunisian yo-yos are delicacies Dunkin' Donuts might be well advised to adopt.

Doughnuts, of course, are internationally beloved, but the Tunisian yo-yo bears particular resemblance to the syrup-coated *koeksisters* of South Africa (see page 741) and *sfenj*—which are richer, yeastier rings, also honey-soaked, and are considered Hanukkah specialties by Moroccan

Doughnuts smothered in honey

and Israeli Jews. Some versions of yo-yo are merely dusted with confectioners' sugar after being fried, while others are glossed with a syrup perfumed with lemon juice and orange blossom water. Nontraditional though it may be, a nice scoop of vanilla ice cream or lemony sherbet set in the middle of a yo-yo turns the casual sweet into a stylish, tempting dessert.

FURTHER INFORMATION AND RECIPES: *A Quintet of Cuisines* by Michael and Frances Field (1970); *Couscous and Other Good Food from Morocco* by Paula Wolfert (1987); food geeks.com (search tunisian doughnuts); food.com (search orange doughnuts with honey).

—||||||||||||||||||||||||||||||||||—

A SPICY, STARCHY EGG SCRAMBLE

Gari Foto

West African

The appealingly starchy *gari*—cassava meal ground to the texture of grits—is the basis of the dish known as *gari foto*. For what could be considered a West African answer to fried rice, the gari is first steamed, then sautéed with onion, garlic, and tomatoes seasoned with ginger and salt, and fiery red chile peppers are stirred in. For a finish, beaten eggs are scrambled in, adding their sunny hue to the lightly golden gari. As with fried rice, and with the same economy, bits of leftover cooked fish, meat, or poultry may be added to the mixture to make it even more substantial.

Gari foto is a staple in West Africa, served at any time of day, but its palette of brilliant, contrasting colors makes it a particularly pretty candidate for a brunch or lunch buffet. Bright terra-cotta-colored kidney beans may be striped across the top or served as a side dish, and sprinklings of chopped parsley or cilantro would not be amiss.

WHERE: *In Bronx, NY,* Papaye, tel 718-676-0771, papayeny.com. **MAIL ORDER:** For cassava meal, Sundial Herbs, tel 718-798-3962, sundialherbs.com. **FURTHER INFORMATION AND RECIPES:** *African Cooking* by Laurens van der Post (1970); *A Good Soup Attracts Chairs* by Fran Osseo-Asare (2006); ghananation.com (search gari foto).

╟||||||||||||||||||||||||||||╢

A BEER WITH A PEPPERY BITE

Ginger Beer

West African

With a slight, tingling sparkle that the French describe as *pétillant,* African ginger beer takes on the mild alcoholic headiness usually associated with hard cider or the Russian drink *kvass.* A forerunner to ginger ale, this so-called beer is a lightly astringent palate awakener; with a slice of citrus fruit, and perhaps a pour of rum, it makes a refreshing beverage on hot days. Although authentic ginger beer can be purchased in African and Caribbean neighborhoods, it is easy to make at home, where its sweetness and spice can be adjusted to suit your taste.

Ginger Beer

Makes about 2 quarts

¼ pound fresh ginger
1 quart boiling water
½ cup floral honey
5 to 8 whole cloves
1 cinnamon stick (1 inch long)
Grated zest of ½ lime or lemon
¼ cup freshly squeezed lime or lemon juice
Ice, citrus fruit juice, and/or dark rum
    (optional), for serving

1. Peel the ginger and cut it into small pieces. Put the ginger in a food processor, adding just enough cold water to puree it.

2. Scrape the pureed ginger into a large, heat-proof glass or ceramic bowl or pitcher and add the boiling water, honey, cloves, cinnamon stick, and lime or lemon zest and juice. Stir the contents together. Cover loosely with a kitchen towel and keep the mixture in a warm place for about 4 hours, skimming off the foam as it accumulates on the surface.

3. Stir in 1 quart of cold water and taste for sweetness, adding more honey or lime or lemon juice as needed. Strain the ginger beer and pour it into glass or ceramic bottles. Cap the bottles tightly and store them in the refrigerator. Serve the ginger beer as soon as it is chilled, or wait 2 to 3 days for it to ferment and start to fizz slightly. In either case, it can be diluted with ice, more cold water, or fruit juice—or, for an extra jolt, dark rum. Chilled and covered, the ginger beer will keep for one week.

FURTHER INFORMATION AND RECIPES: *The Soul of a New Cuisine* by Marcus Samuelsson (2006); cookstr.com (search african ginger beer).

|||||||||||||||||||||||||||||||||||||||||||||||||||||||||||||||||||||||||||||||||||||||||||||||

ROOTED IN FLAVOR

Ginger

It is truly the world's spice, unparalleled in its warming flavor and nose-tingling aroma. Tan, knobby, and sold in contorted, fingerlike lengths, ginger enlivens almost all of the world's cuisines. Though often called a root, it is in fact the underground stem, or rhizome, of a fragrant, tropical flowering plant (*Zingiber officinale*). Ginger is perhaps most highly prized in Asia, where it works much as lemon does elsewhere, lending a spirited astringency especially to seafood and pork. Ginger is also the prime, defining warm seasoning in winter and Christmas desserts throughout the world, particularly in Europe; in West Africa and the Caribbean, it is fermented into sunny, bracing ginger beer (see facing page).

Although it is commonly dried and powdered, ginger is at its potent best when fresh, peeled, and chopped or grated as a pungent, peppery, and slightly citrusy flavoring for all sorts of dishes, savory and sweet. The parts of the rhizome closest to the stalk, known as stem ginger, are delicate and perishable and are therefore often preserved in syrup or candied in sugar, to be added to cakes and other desserts. The fresh green leaves of the ginger plant are valued as a flavoring and garnish, imparting a subtle ginger flavor, and may also be brewed into tea. Dried ginger has less power than fresh, but it is also commonly steeped in boiling water to make a palliative tea. Ginger might also be pickled or

preserved in jam, among a long list of other uses and preparations.

Probably originating in India long before historical records began, ginger was, along with pepper, the most traded commodity on the historic spice routes between Asia and Europe. By the sixteenth century, it was being cultivated in Africa and the Caribbean as well as all over Asia. Valued by the ancient Greeks and Romans primarily for its medicinal properties, it has also long been a part of traditional Chinese medicine and India's Ayurvedic practice, and even today it is used to alleviate or prevent nausea as well as respiratory infections.

MAIL ORDER: Melissa's Produce, tel 800-588-0151, melissas.com (search ginger root; organic ginger); Penzeys Spices, tel 800-741-7787, penzeys.com. **FURTHER INFORMATION AND RECIPES:** *The Soul of a New Cuisine* by Marcus Samuelsson (2006); *A Spoonful of Ginger* by Nina Simonds (2011); saveur.com (search ginger beer); epicurious.com (search ginger cookies; ginger syrup; ginger doughnuts; carrots with ginger). **TIP:** Avoid fresh ginger that looks dried out and woody, as it will have lost its flavor. Store in the crisper of the refrigerator and wrap the cut end in plastic wrap to minimize the loss of aroma. **SEE ALSO:** Steamed Fish with Ginger, page 789; Destrooper's Ginger Thins, page 146; Ginger Tea; page 835.

THE FIRST GUMBO

Soupe Gumbo

West African

The seeds of the petite, fluted okra pod came to the Americas with the slaves who carried them over from West Africa—and thus it is that the American "gumbo" comes from the Bantu word for okra. Among the vegetable's many other

uses, okra's viscous juices can be used to add flavor and texture to soups.

On the Ivory Coast, formerly a French colony, okra features in what's called a *soupe*

gumbo. An ancestor to Louisiana's famed, deep-red gumbo, soupe gumbo starts as a thin chicken broth. Into the pot go shredded chicken, mashed okra, onions, and a tomato sauce, all ignited with hot red chile peppers and plenty of black pepper for a fiery, multidimensional spiciness. Generous mounds of steamed white rice served in small bowls on the side ameliorate the heat—somewhat.

A similar okra soup, *nkruma-nkwan*, is a favorite in Ghana, where peeled and cubed small white eggplants, known as garden eggs, are added. Rice is

Also known as ladies' fingers

sometimes served alongside, but a common alternative in Ghana and other West African countries is *fufu*—a thick mash or dumplinglike balls made from any of the locally abundant

starches, such as yams, potatoes, cornmeal, or cassava.

MAIL ORDER: For okra, Melissa's Produce, tel 800-588-0151, melissas.com. **FURTHER INFORMATION AND RECIPES:** *The Whole World Loves Chicken Soup* by Mimi Sheraton (1995); *The Africa Cookbook* by Jessica B. Harris (2010); *Iron Pots and Wooden Spoons* by Jessica B. Harris (1999); *The African-American Kitchen* by Angela Shelf Medearis (1994); *Cooking the West African Way* by Bertha Vining Montgomery and Constance Nabwire (2001); pbs.org/food (search west african gumbo; for fufu, search pounded yam).

HAVING A DEEP-FRIED BALL

Akara

Black-Eyed Pea Fritters

Nigerian

The crunchy, spicy Nigerian fritters called *akara* and also known as *kosai* are similar to the Middle Eastern falafel, but with a lively dose of freshly ground black pepper and hot chile powder added in. Among West Africa's most

popular street foods, the crisp bean cakes start with dried black-eyed peas. Soaked, rubbed to remove the outer skins, and then ground to a paste, the beans are mixed with water, egg, chile powder, and onion, and the batter is then formed into balls or patties and deep-fried in peanut oil or the much richer palm oil.

Brought by slaves to the Americas centuries ago, the fritters became a specialty of Bahia, in Brazil, where they are known as *acarajé*. Around the Caribbean, they may be based on dried, salted cod or even pumpkin. Nigerian variations, meanwhile, include ground meat or mashed, lightly cooked okra.

At their simplest, akara are easy enough to make at home, perfect for passing around with

predinner drinks, or to accompany soups and salads. Garlic and chopped parsley or cilantro are untraditional but enhancing liberties. The fritters also benefit from generous dabs of fresh Mexican salsa, or a dipping sauce of garlic-infused yogurt.

MAIL ORDER: For dried black-eyed peas, igourmet, tel 877-446-8763, igourmet.com. **FURTHER INFORMATION AND RECIPES:** *The African-American Kitchen* by Angela Shelf Medearis (1994); *Iron Pots and Wooden Spoons* by Jessica B. Harris (1989); *The Africa Cookbook* by Jessica B. Harris (2010); *The Best of African Cuisine* by Karena Andrews (2014); foodnetwork.com (search akara); epicurious.com (search akara).

╫||||||||||||||||||||||||||╫

Efo Riro
Soup of Greens

Nigerian

A standard on Nigerian menus, *efo riro* is a velvety soup or stew that takes its name from a local green that combines elements of spinach and kale. Made from an intensely flavorful mixture of onion, tomatoes, thyme, ground hot chile peppers, and the local greens, it is often fortified with fresh or dried fish such as catfish, cod, or flounder, or with shrimp where it's available. The traditional accompaniment is some form of *fufu*, the starchy, substantial, and absorbent dumplings or mash that work much as bread does when served with soups and stews; *fufu* made with yams is called *iyan,* while that made of cassava is known as *eba.*

The slave trade brought efo to eastern Brazil, and a variation on the soup remains a favorite in the coastal state of Bahia, albeit with enriching additions of smoked shrimp, crabmeat, garlic, and cilantro. In both Brazil and Nigeria, efo is traditionally made with liberal doses of palm oil (*dende*); thick and strongly flavored, the oil is an acquired taste for the uninitiated, and milder vegetable oil can be substituted. The fish, chiles, and handfuls of fresh greens are flavorful enough on their own.

Further information and recipes: *Iron Pots and Wooden Spoons* by Jessica B. Harris (1989); *The African-American Kitchen* by Angela Shelf Medearis (1994); *The Africa Cookbook* by Jessica B. Harris (2010); *The Soul of a New Cuisine* by Marcus Samuelsson (2006); *A Taste of Africa* by Dorinda Hafner (2002); *Cooking the West African Way* by Bertha Vining Montgomery and Constance Nabwire (2001); food.com (search efo riro); allnigerianrecipes.com (search efo riro); foodnetwork.com (search efo).

╫||||||||||||||||||||||||||╫

Egusi Seeds

Nigerian

R esembling a cross between pumpkin and watermelon, the Nigerian melon known as *egusi* isn't cultivated for its dry, bland flesh, but rather for its seeds, which become beloved toasty, salty nibbles in the countries of West Africa.

Quickly roasted or sautéed in hot peanut or palm oil and then liberally sprinkled with salt, the seeds are a popular street snack (as salted nuts are the world over) and an excellent source of protein and healthy fats.

Skillful Nigerian cooks do much more with the seeds than snack on them, however, often pounding them to add flavor and thickness to slowly simmered dishes. Among the more delicious results are the stews made with egusi seeds, tomatoes, onions, cayenne, and black pepper, plus various kinds of fish and shellfish or chicken that have been sautéed until golden brown. Spinachlike greens are a standard addition as well, and *fufu* dumplings made with yam, cassava, or potatoes—or steamed white rice—are the expected accompaniments.

WHERE: *In Bronx, NY,* Papaye, tel 718-676-0771, papayeny.com. **MAIL ORDER:** For egusi seeds, amazon.com. **FURTHER INFORMATION AND RECIPES:** *Iron Pots and Wooden Spoons* by Jessica B. Harris (1989); *Cooking the West African Way* by Bertha Vining Montgomery and Constance Nabwire (2001); celtnet.org .uk/recipes (search egusi).

|||||||||||||||||||||||||||||||||||||

A MEAL WITH FLAIR

Dinner in Senegal

Senegalese

Style is at the heart of Senegalese cuisine, with its raffish dishes bold in color, flavor, and texture. And if the rapidly growing number of Senegalese restaurants throughout the United States is any indication, it's on its way to becoming the newest player in the culinary fusion game. Some Senegalese specialties may already seem vaguely familiar, probably because they inspired much of the cooking of the southern U.S., particularly Louisiana. Slaves from Senegal, which was later part of French West Africa, brought their culinary traditions with them, and even when preparing French and American dishes in plantation kitchens, they "seasoned to taste." The influence stuck, fortunately, and can still be detected in many southern dishes.

Jollof rice, for example, cooked in various forms throughout West Africa, suggests meat-enriched rice specialties like jambalaya. If West African rice isn't available, basmati rice (see page 867) has the perfect, gently perfumed aroma and silky texture for this dish, in which it is simmered in chicken stock and combined with crisply browned chicken, sausages, or smoked ham, along with tomatoes, hot chiles, cabbage or other green vegetables, and spices that might include cinnamon, coriander seeds, pepper, cumin, and more.

Another rice-based pride of the Senegalese kitchen is *thiebu djen* (pronounced chee-boo chen)—the country's national dish. Featuring smoked or dried and fresh fish, this stew combines tomatoes, garlic, onions, chiles, calabaza squash (see page 684), carrots, eggplant, turnip, cabbage, sweet potatoes, okra, and manioc or cassava root. At its most odiferously authentic, *thiebu djen* is made with the hyperfishy dried fish called *guedge,* which takes some getting used to. Heaped on a big mound of rice, it is served communal style, much in the manner of couscous (see page 698).

Tart lemon, sweet onion, and hot chiles make the sunny marinade for chicken *yassa.* For this easy-to-like dish, pieces of chicken browned on a grill or under a broiler are simmered in the marinade along with onions and chiles that have been lightly sautéed to add an extra burnish of flavor. Sometimes prepared with fish instead of chicken, it is simplicity itself, and easily adaptable to a home grill.

Peanuts, also called groundnuts, are the basis of many African stews, including the lamb *mafe* of Senegal. Creamy peanut butter, lightly sweetened, adds richness and body to the gravy, while seared lamb pieces are accompanied by an array of vegetables such as cauliflower, potato, okra, and carrots, and ignited by hot chiles. The antidote is a pile of steamed white rice, which always appears alongside.

One of West Africa's best-loved stews is the oddly named palaver sauce, an intensely flavored combination of soft-cooked meat or poultry and spinachlike greens, with an accent of chiles and smoked fish such as kippers, served over rice, red beans, or both. Why palaver? One theory links the name to guests chatting with each other while waiting to be served; another says it refers to quarrels that broke out over the stew pot, as diners crowded in for a bowlful and got splattered with the ropy, messy greens. Whatever the true origin, there is no arguing with this crowd favorite.

To accompany your Senegalese meal, try a quenching ginger beer (see page 724) or karkade, rose-red hibiscus petal juice (see page 710), or a light, crisp Senegalese beer such as Flag or Gazelle. And for dessert, rejoice if *thiakry* is on the menu, a cooling whip of couscous or millet and yogurt, studded with fresh fruits, raisins, and nuts and topped with grated nutmeg.

WHERE: *In Dakar, Senegal*, Chez Loutcha, tel 221/33-821-0302; *in New York*, Lenox Saphire, tel 212-866-9700, lenoxsaphire.com. **FURTHER INFORMATION AND RECIPES:** *The Africa Cookbook* by Jessica B. Harris (2010); *"My Cooking" West African Cookbook* by Dokpe L. Ogunsanya (1998); *Cooking the West African Way* by Bertha Vining Montgomery and Constance Nabwire (2001); foodandwine.com (senegalese okra stew); foodnetwork.com (search joloff rice); saveur.com (search thieboudienne); celtnet .org.uk (search senegal).

A sunny bowl of chicken yassa over white rice

FRUIT FROM THE TREE OF LIFE

Baobab

East African

Native to sub-Saharan Africa, the fuzzy, bronze, football-shaped baobab fruit (*Adansonia digitata*) grows on a tree that has many uses—so many, in fact, that the baobab tree is known as the Tree of Life. To be fully appreciated, the baobab must be tasted in all of its varied forms. Eaten fresh, the fruit's soft white flesh, popularly called monkey bread, has a sweet–tart, citrusy quality and a dryish, powdery texture. Rich in calcium and vitamin C, that flesh can be dried and ground and used in cooking to thicken sauces, or it can be whipped into creamy smoothies. The seeds are also dried and ground into a seasoning or soaked to make a drink; roasted and salted, they are a satisfying snack whose nutty flavor is somewhere between almond and pistachio. Baobab leaves are also edible, and are generally simmered to thicken soups or cooked on their own, much like spinach or sorrel.

The towering, weirdly tapering baobab tree—nicknamed the "upside down tree"—with its spongy bark, looks half animal, half plant, and almost ready to lope away. Considered by many Africans to be something of a panacea that supposedly alleviates mild and serious ailments alike, baobab-derived products might eventually find their way to pharmacies as well as gourmet food shops across the globe. (In recent years, the EU and the U.K. approved importation of baobab fruit, amid much controversy due to the tree's scarcity in its native lands.) Should you find yourself on the savannah, however, keep this legendary advice in mind: Drink the water in which baobab seeds

The baobab tree is known as the Tree of Life.

have soaked and crocodiles won't touch you. But pick a baobob flower and you're likely to become a lion's plat du jour.

Mail order: For baobab jelly, Zingerman's, tel 888-636-8162, zingermans.com; for fruit powder, Z Natural Foods, tel 888-963-6637, znatural foods.com; for seeds, Trade Winds Fruit, tradewindsfruit.com; for various baobab products, baobab.org. **Further information and recipes:** *The Africa Cookbook* by Jessica B. Harris (1998); *African Cooking* by Laurens van der Post (1970); baobab.org (click Baobab Recipes).

⊣|||||||||||||||||||||||||||||||⊢

ALL QUACKED UP

Zanzibar Duck

East African

The brilliant South African writer Laurens van der Post, in his text for the Time-Life volume *African Cooking,* from 1970, recalled the many clove-scented dishes he ate as a youth in his homeland. Among them was a slow-roasted leg of lamb studded with this exotically scented spice, and a braised, aromatic duck that he enjoyed many times along the East African coast. He dubbed it Zanzibar duck, honoring the Tanzanian island that (along with neighboring Pemba) produces what are arguably the world's best and most pungent cloves. ("Arguably" because many, particularly in Britain, consider cloves from Penang in Malaysia to be the best.)

Having originated in Indonesia, clove trees were introduced to Zanzibar and Pemba in the nineteenth century, and those areas rapidly became the world's leading sources of the thorny spice. Dried for safe storage, cloves are best purchased whole and fragrantly fresh, before the oils, and therefore the flavor, have evaporated. If powdered cloves are called for, grind them just before use in a spice mill or coffee grinder.

The following is adapted from van der Post's recipe for the savory, meltingly tender duck. Lemon, which also flourishes in this region, seasons the pungent sauce and brightens the unctuously rich duck meat. He recalls having had the dish with plain steamed rice, but a more festive if much heartier accompaniment would be Zanzibar rice *pilau*, enriched with bits of shrimp or poultry and redolent of cardamom, ginger, cumin, pepper, cinnamon, and of course, clove.

Zanzibar Duck

Serves 4

1 duck (about 5 pounds), preferably
a moulard
Duck giblets, trimmed and cleaned
15 to 18 whole cloves
1 hot red or green jalepeño chile pepper
(about 2 inches long), seeded and diced
About ½ cup peanut oil
2 cups beef or chicken stock,
or a combination of the two
1 tablespoon coarse salt
½ medium-size lemon
About ½ cup freshly squeezed strained
lemon juice
1 red bell pepper, seeded
and diced
3 cups plain steamed white
rice, for serving

1. Remove all of the pin feathers from the duck and trim off any excess fat around the cavities. Rinse the duck under cold running water and pat it dry with paper towels. Refrigerate the duck, uncovered, overnight. This will enable the skin to dry and become taut so the fat will drain off more easily during braising.

2. Chop the duck liver and place it in a small saucepan, along with the whole duck neck, gizzard, and heart, and half of the cloves and chile pepper. Add 2 tablespoons of peanut oil and cook over moderate heat until the meats lose their raw look, about 5 minutes. Add the stock and let simmer for about 15 minutes. Remove and discard all of the giblets except the chopped liver. Set the stock mixture aside.

3. Preheat the oven to 450°F.

4. Rub the inside of the duck with about 1 teaspoon of the coarse salt. Place the remaining cloves inside the duck, along with the lemon half. Using a skewer or slender knife point, prick the duck skin around the thighs and wings. Truss the duck, then rub it all over with a little of the peanut oil. Roast the duck, breast side up, in an uncovered casserole or roasting pan until it is a light golden brown, about 15 minutes.

5. Reduce the oven temperature to 350°F. Add the stock mixture to the casserole or roasting pan. Cover the casserole or roasting pan and let the duck braise for 1 hour, basting it every 15 minutes. If the holes pierced in the thighs and wings close, pierce them again so the fat can drain off.

6. Pour the lemon juice over the duck and sprinkle the remaining 2 teaspoons of salt and the red bell pepper over it. Cover the duck again and let it continue to braise until the juices run clear when a thigh is pierced with a knife, about 20 minutes.

7. Transfer the duck to a platter and let it rest for about 15 minutes before carving. Meanwhile, skim the fat from the pan juices. Let the pan juices come to a boil over high heat and let boil until reduced and slightly syrupy, about 5 to 8 minutes. Taste for seasoning, adding more salt as necessary. Strain the sauce and carve the duck. Serve it with the sauce spooned over it and rice on the side.

MAIL ORDER: For moulard duck, D'Artagnan, tel 800-327-8246, dartagnan.com; for Madagascar cloves, Penzeys Spices, tel 800-741-7787, penzeys .com. **FURTHER INFORMATION AND RECIPES:** *African Cooking* by Laurens van der Post (1970); for Zanzibar Rice Pilau recipe, zanzinet.org/recipes (click Zanzibar Dishes, then Zanzibar Pilau).

THE ORIGINAL BREW

Ethiopian Coffee

Ethiopian

Although high-quality coffee is grown in several parts of Africa, most notably Tanzania and Kenya, the world's premium Arabica bean is believed to have originated in Ethiopia, where the drink may have taken its name from the former

kingdom of Kaffa—although Ethiopians call their favorite drink *bunna* (pronounced boo-na). Some historians believe the wild Arabica beans were nibbled here as far back as the sixth century A.D. But, according to the colorful legend, they were not brewed until the ninth century, when a goat herder named Khaldi noticed his flock leaping about wildly after chewing on some red berries that were lying on the ground. He took the beans to a local imam, who threw them into a fire and said, "These berries are the devil's work, so back to the devil they go." Tantalized by the aroma of the roasting beans, the goat herder crumbled some and threw them in water to steep. Generations have been doing so ever since.

Cultivated mainly in the highland rainforests of the Djimma, Harrar, and Yirgacheffe regions, Ethiopian coffee is considered by many to be the best in the world. Roasted in what is known as the mocha *style* (distinct from true mocha *beans,* the best of which are from Yemen), the hard, relatively dry beans result in a refreshingly acidic, eye-opening brew. Djimma beans produce a rustic,

sharp-tasting beverage, while those from the higher slopes of Harrar lend a smoother, more winey flavor, with an engaging, unexpected wildness. Beans from Yirgacheffe, most famously those grown in the Gedeo Zone, have a uniquely floral, citrusy character, while maintaining that winey depth.

Traditionally flavored with butter, salt, and spices, coffee in Ethiopia reportedly wasn't sweetened with sugar until the arrival of the Italians, who occupied the country in 1935. Ethiopians prefer their coffee scented with cloves and cinnamon and sweetened with native wild mountain honey. Brewed in a specialized, long-necked clay vessel called a *jebena,* it is always served scalding hot. A succession of three cups per person is de rigueur in the formal Ethiopian coffee-drinking ritual, which usually takes place after a feast and may be accompanied by the burning of incense.

WHERE: *In Addis Ababa,* Habesha, tel 251/116-182-253/58; Tomoca, tel 251/111-111-781/83, tomocacoffee.com; *in New York,* Queen of Sheba, tel 212-397-0610, shebanyc.com; *in Montclair, NJ,*

A jebena is used for brewing.

Mesob, tel 973-655-9000, mesobrestaurant.com; *in Washington, DC,* Dukem, tel 202-667-8735, dukemrestaurant.com; Meskerem, tel 202-462-4100, meskeremethiopianrestaurantdc.com. **Mail order:** McNulty's Tea & Coffee Co., tel 212-242-5351, mcnultys.com; The Ethiopian Coffee Company, tel 44/0207-746-2969, theethiopian coffeecompany.co.uk; Buunni Coffee, tel 347-819-0705, buunnicoffee.com. **Further information and recipes:** ethiopianrestaurant.com (click Ethiopian Coffee); food.com (search ethiopian coffee). **Tip:** Look for names such as Harrar, Djimma, Yergacheffe Gedeo, and Ethiopian mocha or mocha-style.

DINNER FROM THE LAND OF SHEBA

A Traditional Ethiopian Feast

Ethiopian

We don't know for sure what wiles the Queen of Sheba worked to lure King Solomon in Old Testament days, but her arsenal may well have included a sampling of her native cuisine—for an Ethiopian dinner is a dramatically

seductive meal, ripe with bold, spice-burnished preparations and colorful, stylized customs and tableware.

These days, Ethiopian restaurants decorated with colorful fabrics, carpets, wall hangings, and handcrafts, their offerings loosely suggestive of the cuisines of the Middle East and India, are popular in urban areas of the United States—a phenomenon that dates back at least thirty-five years. Staff may be dressed in native tunics and robes, and some of the restaurants feature live music and traditional dancers. Typically, diners sit on low wooden stools in front of basket tables called *mesobs,* woven in brilliant, intricate geometric designs, and servers present pitchers and basins so guests can wash their hands before dining.

The first specialty to appear is invariably *injera,* a tangy, light, and spongy sort of crêpe that looks like a big ivory napkin and that serves as both bread and eating utensil. Made with a sourdough batter based on a flour of whole wheat, barley, millet or, most authentically, teff (the native grain also known as lovegrass), injera is

The basis of a true Ethiopian meal is the injera.

moist and pliable. It neatly enfolds mouthfuls of stews and other foods served in communal bowls, usually made of terra-cotta and set in basket holders. According to etiquette, diners tear off pieces of injera and eat with the right hand only—the left being considered unclean.

The meal might begin with *sambossas,* meat-filled pastry turnovers, and perhaps the clear ginger-and-garlic-scented chicken soup, *yedoro shorba. Kitfo,* a tartare of finely cubed raw beef brightened with onions, ginger, garlic, cardamom, and lemon juice, might also appear early on. Like many of the other dishes on offer, kitfo is glossed with spiced butter and spiked with *berbere,* the incendiary seasoning made with *mit'mita,* an Ethiopian spice mix based on bird's-eye chiles (*Capsicum frutescens*). What follows will almost surely include a *wett* or two, the Ethiopian stew that may be based on fish, beef, lamb, or chicken; the latter, called *doro wett,* is a great favorite in which the chicken is simmered to melting tenderness with exotic herbs and spices, and garnished with hard-cooked eggs. There should also be an herbed vegetable stew such as *yataklete kilkil,* served with *yekik alich'a,* a soothing sauce similar to Indian *dahl,* made from split peas or, tastier yet, lentils.

If all that richness and spice works up a thirst, quaff an Ethiopian beer or try the mead-like honey wine, *t'ej,* which may be flavored with ginger or fruit. The wine will have to satisfy your sweet tooth, too, as traditionally Ethiopian dinner feasts don't involve dessert, though a cup of dark-as-midnight coffee brewed from Ethiopian beans (see page 732) provides a delicious, and fitting, conclusion.

Where: *In Addis Ababa,* Habesha, tel 251/116-182-253/58; *in New York,* Queen of Sheba, tel 212-397-0610, shebanyc.com; *in Montclair, NJ,* Mesob, tel 973-655-9000, mesob restaurant.com; *in Washington, DC,* Dukem, tel 202-667-8735, dukemrestaurant.com; Meskerem, tel 202-462-4100, meskeremethiopianrestaurant dc.com. **Mail order:** For berbere spice blend, Zamouri Spices, tel 913-829-5988, zamourispices .com; for teff flour, bobsredmill.com. **Further information and recipes:** *Exotic Ethiopian Cooking* compiled and edited by Daniel J. Mesfin (2006); *The Soul of a New Cuisine* by Marcus Samuelsson (2006); *African Cookbook: Recipes from Ethiopia, Nigeria, and Kenya* by Rachel Pambrun (2012); saveur.com (search ethiopian flatbread; ethiopian lentil stew); cookingchanneltv.com (search kitfo; doro wat); howtocookgreatethiopian.com (click Recipes).

TO MARKET, TO MARKET

Merkato

Ethiopian

Anyone who appreciates the drama of sprawling, open-air markets might well consider spending a week discovering the alleys and byways of the Merkato in the Ethiopian capital, Addis Ababa. Said to be the largest of Africa's many epic

markets, it is virtually a town in itself, covering about four square miles, with a daily occupancy of more than twelve thousand people working in some seven thousand individual enterprises. Begun as a segregated European preserve by the Italians, who occupied Ethiopia in 1935 (*mercato* means market in Italian), by the 1960s it had developed into the primary market for local vendors and customers alike.

The seething, dusty whirl of activity and the din of hawking and bargaining begins as the market is being prepared, about three and a half hours before it opens to the public, at 8:30 a.m., and continues until early evening. Stalls display a variety of goods: household utensils, native crafts (of leather, metal, and textiles), clothing, electronics, auto parts, and livestock that might include donkeys and camels. All, however, are overshadowed by the kaleidoscopic, aromatic array of foods.

Huge, round baskets and wooden crates, carried by porters on their heads or backs, hold dazzling piles of fruits and vegetables both familiar and unknown to foreign visitors. Tomatoes, mangoes, pumpkin, spinach, collard and mustard greens, plantains, tough-looking orange corn, earthy roots such as cassava and

The Merkato employs over twelve thousand people.

taro, the native grain teff, football-shaped baobabs, and mounds of fresh and dried beans and seeds, all share space with a rainbow of spices. One section of the market is devoted to fish, another to dairy products, meats, and poultry, and still another to the largest and most important Ethiopian export, coffee (see page 732). Here you can see the huge variety of coffee beans the country is noted for, and then sample some for yourself, roasted in hot pans before your eyes, ground, brewed, and sweetened with sugar (in the Italian style). When you are ready for a break from the whirling chaos, retreat to one of the cafés on the Merkato's perimeter, where shoppers snack, gossip over coffee, and observe the bustling scene.

WHERE: In the Addis Ketema area of Addis Ababa. **WHEN:** Daily, except Sunday, from 6 a.m. to early evening. **FURTHER INFORMATION AND RECIPES:** *The Soul of a New Cuisine* by Marcus Samuelsson (2006); lonelyplanet.com (search addis ababa merkato).

A "BEAST OF A FEAST"

Carnivore

Kenyan

All globetrotting meat eaters should aspire to one day sit down to a meal at the celebrated Carnivore, arguably sub-Saharan Africa's most famous restaurant, though also one of its more touristic. Close to Wilson Airport in Nairobi, the capital

of Kenya, the casual, open-air Carnivore is modeled in part on Brazilian all-you-can-eat *rodízio* (see page 673) but features the traditional Maasai style of roasting meat (*nyama choma*) by running it onto spears that are lowered into a huge charcoal pit. As rhythmic music and the lively scene put them in a celebratory mood, guests are seated on zebra-striped chairs and served the soup of the day, their appetites already whetted by the tantalizing aroma of grilling meat.

And what meats they are! On any given day, the changing menu board might list ostrich meatballs, crocodile, and camel hump, alongside leg of lamb, various sausages, and ox heart; for the less intrepid diner, Carnivore also offers simple steaks and chicken yakitori among some other offerings. The meat-stacked Maasai spears are carried to the tables, where cuts chosen by guests sizzle onto red-hot cast-iron plates in the *churrasco* manner. The meat does not stop coming until diners set a white paper flag of surrender over their tray. Various sauces—garlic, mint, sweet-and-sour, and the Argentine green-herbed *chimichurri*—are on hand, along with surprisingly familiar side dishes like cole slaw and beans and rice, and homemade brown bread.

Desserts are similarly conventional (apple pie, cheesecake, ice cream), but a cup of world-class Kenyan coffee makes for a restorative finish. Fanciful tropical-fruit cocktails and international beers are among the other beverages on hand, as are an impressive number of South African wines. Not served, thankfully, is the cattle blood and milk cocktail that is a mainstay of the elegant, nomadic Maasai, famous for their speed and skill as hunters and warriors.

WHERE: *In Nairobi, Kenya,* Carnivore, tel 254/733-611-608, tamarind.co.ke/carnivore; *in Johannesburg, South Africa,* Carnivore Johannesburg, 27/11-950-6000, recreationafrica .co.za/carnivore.

|||||||||||||||||||||||||||||||||||||||||||||||||||||||||||||||||||||||||||||||||||||||||||||||||||||||||

GOOD THINGS IN TINY PACKAGES

Sesame Seeds

Conjuring up a flavor that is at once sunny and nutty, delicate yet satisfying, airy yet ripely rich, is a task worthy of the finest chefs—but that irresistible combination is one that occurs naturally in the tiny oval that is *Sesamum indicum,* the sesame seed. Native to Africa, sesame is an annual herb whose small seeds (which may be white, yellow, brown, or black, depending on variety) have a sweet, almondy flavor that deepens with roasting. The seeds are also pressed to produce the intensely flavorful, rich oil that is a key ingredient in various cuisines around the world.

Legend has it that the seeds wafted out of Africa when ripe sesame pods split and the almost weightless seeds were scattered by the four winds. The splitting of the sesame pod might also have inspired the magical phrase "Open Sesame," so well known from the story "Ali Baba and the Forty Thieves." The seed probably stopped first in Egypt on its way out of Africa, about four thousand years ago, where it was given the name *sesemt.*

Ancient Babylonians cultivated sesame seeds for their oil, which was a favorite in the palace of Nebuchadnezzar, and they have been central to the cuisines of the Middle East since the Biblical era. In Middle Eastern countries, sesame seeds are sprinkled on pita and other breads. They form the basis of halvah, a chewy and grainy confection made from ground sesame seeds and honey, sometimes with nuts or chocolate mixed in (see page 483). And they're ground into the sumptuous paste called tahini that, when combined with chickpeas and seasonings, makes the now ubiquitous dip, hummus (see page 496).

Sesame seeds also show up frequently in Asian cooking; the oil, whether pale (made from raw seeds) or a deep golden bronze, (made from toasted seeds) is a key ingredient in China's wide variety of stir-fries. And in Japan the seeds are a staple of the vegetarian menus of Buddhist monasteries.

They arrived in the Americas in the seventeenth century, brought over by West African slaves, and became a favorite ingredient in the American South, where they are called benne seeds, from an African word for seed. In New Orleans and Charleston, they are baked into a cookie called a benne wafer (see page 528), and made into benne brittle and benne balls, sesame seeds bound with corn syrup and brown sugar.

No matter where or how they are eaten, sesame seeds are a healthful addition to any diet—a complete protein, they provide the full complement of amino acids and are also an excellent source of minerals and cholesterol-lowering fiber. It's no wonder that, however they arrived, the humble little seeds are beloved in every corner of the globe.

MAIL ORDER: Penzeys Spices, tel 800-741-7787, penzeys.com. **FURTHER INFORMATION AND RECIPES:** *Vegetarian Cooking for Everyone* by Deborah Madison (2007); *The Complete Asian Cookbook* by Charmaine Solomon (1976); *Mastering the Art of Southern Cooking* by Nathalie Dupree and Cynthia Graubart (2012); *The Kimchi Chronicles* by Marja Vongerichten (2011); *Cracking the Coconut* by Su-Mei Yu (2000); *Sesame Seed Greats* by Jo Franks (2012); *Welcome Table* by Jessica B. Harris (1995); saveur.com (search soba noodles with sesame seeds; homemade sesame seed buns; hawaiian sesame cabbage).

||||||||||||||||||||||||||||||||

TAKING THE HEAT

Piri-Piri Shrimp

Mozambican

Piri-piri is the Swahili word for the red-hot bird's-eye chile peppers, the memorable sauce made from them, and any foods they fire up—although delectably tender and buttery, the gently cooked shrimp in this dish are merely an excuse for the searing piri-piri sauce itself. (Lemon juice stirred into hot melted butter is spooned over the finished dish to ease the chiles' sting, a task also attempted by an accompaniment of white rice, and lots of it.)

As part of what was once Portuguese-colonized Africa, Mozambique's cuisine wound up influencing that of other colonies in Brazil and the Caribbean. There, piri-piri sauce (also known as peri-peri, pil-pil, or pilli-pilli) appears in varied forms and may include additional aromatic spices. But in Mozambique, it is virtually the national dish. Used as a marinade or for basting grilled or sautéed shrimp, prawns, or chicken, the sauce begins with the chopped, super-hot chiles (seeds are included for the brave, or eliminated for the timid), simply pureed with lemon juice, garlic,

Sauce is the star of the dish.

oil or melted butter, and parsley. The most demanding cooks will want to prepare their own, but bottled piri-piri, such as the Nando's brand, holds its own among the hot sauces of the world.

WHERE: *In Atlanta,* 10 Degrees South, tel 404-705-8870, 10degreessouth.com; *in Brooklyn,* Madiba, tel 718-855-9190, madibarestaurant.com; *in Washington, DC, Maryland, and Virginia,* Nando's Peri-Peri, nandosperiperi.com. **MAIL ORDER:** For bottled Piri-Piri sauces, igourmet.com (search peri-peri); southafricanfoodshop.com (click Shopping, then The Taste of Peri-Peri). **FURTHER INFORMATION AND RECIPES:** *The Soul of a New Cuisine* by Marcus Samuelsson (2006); oprah.com (search shrimp piri piri); hotsauce.com (search african rhino peri peri); epicurious.com (search prawns peri peri).

—||||||||||||||||||||||||||||||||||—

Africa Café

South African

The adventurous palate is in for a treat at the colorful, casual Africa Café, set in a charming eighteenth-century Georgian house on a historic, rejuvenated street of shops and restaurants in Cape Town. Waitresses in brightly patterned skirts and turbans serve communal bowls of the ten to fifteen preparations available for sampling from a set menu that represents many different African cuisines, including those of Ethiopia, Mozambique, Malawi, and Kenya, as well as the South African cultures of the Zulu, the Ndebele, and the Xhosa.

The varying specialties might include cassava flatbread; Ethiopian *sik sik wat,* a tender beef fillet in a hot *berbere* chile sauce; East African *mchicha wa nazi* pies plumped with spinach, peanuts, and coconut cream; the spicy mixed vegetable dish that is Soweto *chakalaka*; Zanzibar bean stew; and Malawai *mbatata,* sweet potato, cheese, and *simsim* (sesame seed) balls. Ivory Coast mussels are gently simmered in a coconut sauce, and Mozambique's *piri-piri* shrimp (see page 737) is often available as well. From the Xhosa, who traditionally lived in the Transkei region south of Natal, come *imifino* patties, formed of spinach and the coarsely ground corn called mealie-meal. Tanzanian mango chicken and South African *ithanga*—crisp, cinnamon-scented pumpkin fritters—are among other savory-sweet choices.

Finish up with Kenyan coffee or the lightly perfumed rooibos tea brewed from the leaves of the "red bush" plant which is native to South Africa. There are also tempting fruity cocktails and a comprehensive list of much-respected South African wines. After the meal, be sure to browse the restaurant's gift shop, with its impressive selection of local, artisanal ceramic tableware. Bowls, plates, and mugs of terra-cotta handpainted in bright African colors and motifs are both traditional and strikingly modern—a fitting remembrance for your visit.

WHERE: Shortmarket St., Cape Town, tel 27/21-422-0221, africacafe.co.za. **TIP:** This pleasant café is geared toward tourists, so make the most of it as an easy introduction to a new cuisine.

—||||||||||||||||||||||||||||||||||—

Bobotie

South African

Whether made with ground beef or lamb, or in vegetarian versions based on lentils or beans, *bobotie* is a uniquely rich, flavorful, deep-dish casserole that takes on the heady charm of curry spices such as turmeric and cumin. These flavors are deepened and brightened by additions of lemon juice, dried lemon leaves, raisins, almonds, onions, and hints of brown sugar. Some cooks press hard-cooked egg halves into the mixture, while others add diced apples or pears, peanuts, or chopped dried apricots, for a mincemeatlike touch. Whatever the add-ons, the dish is finished with a lid of golden brown egg custard that may be scented with cinnamon or nutmeg, for a result reminiscent of Greek moussaka. Steamed white rice is the appropriate accompaniment, as it soaks up the rich, hot juices that spring forth as portions are cut.

As with so many South African dishes, the history of bobotie reflects the complicated, international history of the nation and its colonial past. The dish's name is Afrikaans, the language of white South Africans mostly of Dutch descent, and the spices recall Dutch colonial days in Indonesia and the Indonesian slaves the Dutch brought with them to South Africa to serve as cooks. The dish was a fixture in Afrikaner kitchens for centuries, with the first recipe appearing in print in 1609. Today, bobotie is the centerpiece of festive meals and a Sunday family favorite throughout the country, and is a standard on South African restaurant menus throughout the world.

WHERE: *In Cape Town,* Boschendal Le Café, tel 27/21-870-4282, boschendalrestaurants.co.za; *in New York,* Braai, tel 212-315-3315, braainyc .com; *in Brooklyn,* Madiba, tel 718-855-9190, madibarestaurant.com. **FURTHER INFORMATION AND RECIPES:** *African Cooking* by Laurens van der Post (1970); *Kwanzaa* by Eric V. Copage (1991); *The African-American Kitchen* by Angela Shelf Medearis (1991); epicurious.com (search bobotie); cookstr.com (search bobotie).

A FAR CRY FROM RABBIT FOOD

Bunny Chow

South African

I t's chow all right, of the quickest and most elemental kind, but it has nothing whatsoever to do with rabbits. Instead, bunny chow is deeply spicy and saucy curry—made most traditionally with lamb, but sometimes with fish, beef, or

Pair this comfort food with a pint of cold beer.

vegetables—spooned into a hollowed-out half-loaf of white bread. Especially popular around Durban, this warm, squishy sort-of sandwich is a reminder of the many cultures and ethnicities that fused in the South African kitchen. In the early twentieth century, descendants of Indian immigrants who came to South Africa to work on sugar plantations opened curry restaurants, which flourished as inexpensive eateries. Slices of white bread were served with the curries when patrons ate in the restaurant, but for takeout the loaf-sandwiches emerged as an alternative.

The term *bunny chow* is, in fact, used as a metaphor for South Africa's ethnically mixed population, similar to the American "melting pot," and also for any hectic mishmash of an event. It is conjectured by some that the name "bunny" might be derived from the names given to the South African Indians—they were called Banias or Banyas—who first served this concoction in Durban. An alternative theory suggests that the half-loaf resembles a bun. Either way, this delectably messy comfort food well may catch on in the U.S., now that some South African eateries are beginning to feature it.

Until then, though, you easily can make your own, first by stewing up your favorite curry, then cutting a loaf of unsliced white bread in half horizontally and gently pulling out the soft insides, careful to leave an intact shell of crust. Ladle in the curry, which should be hot in seasonings and temperature, drizzle in a tingling bit of zingy chutney, and enjoy. Cold beer is the most suitable accompaniment, but ginger beer (see page 724) or iced tea flavored with lemon or ginger would do almost as well.

WHERE: *In Durban, South Africa,* Moyo Ushaka, tel 27/31-332-0606, moyo.co.za; *in New York,* Xai Xai (pronounced shy shy), tel 212-541-9241, xaixaiwinebar.com; *in Brooklyn,* Madiba, tel 718-855-9190, madibarestaurant.com. **FURTHER INFORMATION AND RECIPES:** congocookbook.com (click Soup & Stew, then Bunny Chow); food .com (search bunny chow).

A FRUIT THAT GLOWS

Cape Gooseberry

South African

P icture a Chinese lantern and you'll get a sense of the *Physalis peruviana* plant. The papery green-and-purple husks of the lantern-shaped calyx hide a berry that gives up luscious juices when ripely golden, enhanced by tiny, edible seeds

that lend a crackling tingle. This is one of the prized fruits of South Africa, where it arrived from its native Peru (hence its botanical name) in the early nineteenth century. Also known as a

The berries are a welcome addition to a fruit salad.

ground cherry, the Cape gooseberry is not in fact a cherry or even a gooseberry, but a member of the ominous-sounding and generally delicious nightshade (*Solanaceae*) clan, which includes tomatoes, eggplants, peppers, potatoes, and, the black sheep, tobacco. It is closely related to the tomatillo (*Physalis ixocarpa*), which has a similar appearance and is used in many Mexican green sauces.

Much favored in South Africa in salads, candies, compotes, ice creams, sorbets, pies and, most notably, jams and syrups, Cape gooseberries are a particularly special treat when fresh and at the peak of their autumn season. Their intriguing flavor, vaguely reminiscent of kumquat, though gentler, combines the sour bite of pineapple with the cool sweetness of tomato. They are often available at farmers' markets in the U.S., and with their striking appearance and unusual taste, they make an elegant addition to fruit salads and dessert plates. Or, do as the South Africans do and simmer them with sugar and water into a thick compote, which can be put on everything from toast to grilled meats.

The so-called Chinese lantern, *Physalis alkekengi,* favored in bouquets for its bright orange husks, is similar to the Cape gooseberry—but few realize its berries are edible, so

it is often relegated to decorative uses. The Italians, however, have a special way with the fruit of *Physalis alkekengi,* covering them with chocolate icing, leaving a cheery sprig of leafy husks at the top.

Mail order: Melissa's Produce, tel 800-588-0151, melissas.com. **Further information and recipes:** *Uncommon Fruits and Vegetables* by Elizabeth Schneider (2010); foodandwine.com (search cape gooseberry compote); food network.com (search cape gooseberry relish); seedtosupper.com (click Tomatillos).

GOLDEN BRAIDS OF SWEETNESS

Koeksisters, or Koe'sisters

South African

To Dutch-descended South Africans, called Afrikaners, the name for crullers is either *koeksisters* or *koe'sisters.* Formed into long, exquisite braids, or molded into high and puffy rounds, they are yeast-based, spiced pastries deep-fried in

vegetable oil until golden brown. The difference between the two depends on the finishing touches. If they are dipped into a satiny sugar syrup, they emerge as koeksisters. But when the hot braids or rounds are dusted with an aromatic haze of powdered ginger, cinnamon, and cardamom they are koe'sisters.

Those wishing to circumvent the selection process can sample the koe'sisters made by the Indonesian-descended Cape Malay community, which handily combine both of these styles. The balls of richly spiced dough, which may contain ginger, cinnamon, anise, and citrus zest, are fried in oil, then simmered in sugar syrup, and finally, rolled in shredded coconut.

In any of these sweet variations, served hot and fresh, the fried confections are luscious accompaniments to coffee, and are extra-special weekend breakfast treats.

Where: *In Cape Town,* the Bo-Kaap, the bustling open-air market in the Malaysian quar-

Finished with sugar syrup or powdered spices

ter; *in New York,* Braai, tel 212-315-3315, braai nyc.com; *in Brooklyn,* Madiba, tel 718-855-9190, madibarestaurant.com. **Further information and recipes:** *The Soul of a New Cuisine* by Marcus Samuelsson (2006); food.com (search koeksisters); koeksister.us (click Koeksister Recipe).

—||||||||||||||||||||||||||||||||||—

ONE EGG FEEDS A DOZEN

Ostrich Egg Omelet

South African

I f the recipe reads, "One egg feeds twelve," it's probably referring to that of an ostrich, that subtle, creamy abundance of protein contained in a huge, beautifully mottled, ivory shell. Indeed, preserved ostrich shells have been objets d'art for

centuries—once holes are pierced at the top and bottom of the shell, its contents can be blown out into a bowl, much as Easter eggs are emptied before being decorated. During the Renaissance, the shells were formed into prized, fantastically expensive goblets and decanters, often fitted with spouts and stems of silver and gold.

These birds' eggs are becoming more readily available.

Also desirable for its stylish feathers and luxurious, durable leather, the ostrich was, for a time, in danger of extinction on its home ground, which ranges from the Cape of Good Hope to North Africa. But now that ostriches are bred on ranches—and their lean and tender meat is featured at many restaurants and

upscale butcher shops, both stateside and in parts of South Africa—their eggs are also more common. Visitors to ostrich ranches not only can observe these mythic, long-legged creatures up close, but often can sample that rare and almost comically oversized dish, the ostrich egg omelet.

An ostrich egg, the largest of any bird, weighs about three pounds. Practically speaking, it's only possible to prepare one as an omelet or scramble. (You would need an enormous pot—and quite a lot of time—to boil one, and dividing one gigantic fried egg among twelve people could get rather messy.) With a flavor somewhat milder than a chicken's egg, and a slightly more watery white, the frothy ostrich egg is best enjoyed when it is whisked and cooked gently in a large skillet, seasoned simply with salt and pepper, and perhaps topped with a few fiery dashes of hot chile sauce. Ostrich egg omelets are on the menu in many restaurants throughout Africa, particularly in the south, where the eggs are farmed; in the States, if you plan to be in Oklahoma City in May, make a reservation for the annual Ostrich Egg Breakfast sponsored by that city's zoo.

Where: *In Oudtshoorn, South Africa,* Highgate Ostrich Show Farm, highgate.co.za; *in New York,* Braai, tel 212-315-3315, braainyc .com; *in Oak Hills, CA,* The Summit Inn, tel 760-949-8688; *in Oro Grande, CA,* OK Corral Ostrich

Farm, tel 760-964-4233, highdesertinsider.com/ okcorral. **Mail order:** Floeck's Country Ranch, tel 575-461-1657, floeckscountry.com; Highland Farm, tel 518-537-6397, eat-better-meat.com; Roaming Acres, tel 973-202-9344, roamingacres .com. **Further information and recipes:** American Ostrich Association, ostriches.org;

African Cooking by Laurens van der Post (1970); indianpointranch.com (click Recipes, then Edible Ostrich Eggs); bonappetit.com (search ostrich egg frittata); youtube.com (search cooking an ostrich egg). **Special event:** Annual Ostrich Egg Breakfast, Oklahoma City, May, okc zoo.com (search ostrich egg breakfast).

—||||||||||||||||||||||||||||||||||—

A SPINY CATCH

Rock Lobster, or Crayfish

South African

The tough-shelled, spiny rock lobster (fittingly also known as a spiny lobster) developed a bad reputation among American foodies, similar to the declining status of Florida's rock lobsters. For years, it invariably arrived on our shores

frozen—rock hard, as it happened—resulting in meat that was tough and dry after preperation. To make matters worse, the lobsters were often oven broiled, which desiccated them even further. But in South African homes and restaurants, these shellfish—known generally as crayfish, a freshwater species they are related to—are always served fresh from the ocean and dewily moist, and justifiably count among the country's most prized treats.

Although sometimes gently grilled in the shell, the pearly meat is at its juiciest when the lobsters are boiled or steamed and then slathered with hot melted butter. They may also be found in fancier, delectable variations, including a Malaysian-informed curry stew that is redolent of chiles, turmeric, mustard seeds, pepper, and cumin. Some cooks extract the meat from the shell, mince it, and then combine it

Spiny lobster is a delicate treat.

with eggs, bread crumbs, or rice and spices. This mix might be pan-fried, much as crab-cakes are made, or packed back into the lobster shells and baked in the style of deviled crab.

A hugely popular catch in South Africa, the rock lobster is fished primarily off the coast of the Cape of Good Hope, where the crustaceans are now protected by a set of strict legal regulations. Fishing is prohibited during certain times within the season (which runs from April to mid-November), and all fishermen are subject to a bag limit; additionally, they must throw back any specimens measuring less than 80 millimeters (about 3 inches) from their wiggly head to the base of their fidgety tail.

Various resorts along South Africa's beaches, such as Table Bay and Lambert's Bay, feature lobster diving among their recreational activities. And, of course, specialties based on that gently saline crustacean make frequent appearances on local menus.

WHERE: *In Lambert's Bay, South Africa,* Waves Restaurant and Lobster Port Restaurant at Lambert's Bay Hotel, tel 27/27-432-1126, lambertsbayhotel.co.za. **FURTHER INFORMATION AND RECIPES:** *The Complete South African Cookbook* by Magdaleen van Wyk (2007); cookstr.com (search grilled rock lobster).

‖‖‖‖‖‖‖‖‖‖‖‖‖‖‖‖‖‖‖‖‖‖‖‖‖‖

FIGHTING FISH

Snoek

South African

A bony, oily fish, snoek (*Thyrsites atun*) may perhaps be an acquired taste, but judging by its native popularity, it deserves a try, something best accomplished on its home grounds. Long and silvery-blue-skinned, with sharp teeth to ward off predators, snoek has a strong, fishy flavor much like mackerel and will appeal most to novices when the firm flesh is smoked or worked into a well-seasoned spread or pâté. Another favored form of snoek is known by the Afrikaans name, *ingelegde vis,* and is prepared much in the style of an *escabeche.*

Originally developed as a preserved food for sailors at sea, floured fillets of the fish are lightly fried in vegetable oil, then pickled in a marinade of vinegar and vegetable oil seasoned with bay leaves, turmeric, cumin, powdered mustard, black pepper, and onions. Packed in jars, it is said to keep for months, but can also be eaten after marinating in the refrigerator for just a few days. Served chilled with hot, boiled potatoes or crisp toast and a glass of cold white wine, it makes a teasing appetizer or a light hot weather lunch.

WHERE: *In Lambert's Bay, South Africa,* Waves Restaurant at the Lambert's Bay Hotel, tel 27/27-432-1126, lambertsbay hotel.co.za. **FURTHER INFORMATION AND RECIPES:** *The Oxford Companion to Food* by Alan Davidson (1999); *The Complete South African Cookbook* by Magdaleen van Wyk (2007); "Dissed Fish" by Calvin Trillin, newyorker.com (search dissed fish); ejozi.co.za (search snoek); rsa-over seas.com (search ingelegde vis). **TIP:** Mackerel is a fair substitute for snoek, and especially suitable for pickling.

Fishermen popularized the fish among South Africans.

Springbok

South African

Even if they wouldn't think twice about ordering suckling pig, rabbit, or lamb, tender-hearted visitors to South Africa are a bit surprised when they spot springbok on local menus. Wasn't this the very same animal they just ogled through binoculars on the safari's preserve? Indeed, the gazelle-like member of the antelope family, with its fluffy white tail and distinctive horns, does exist in the wild—but it's also raised for meat on farms, and is in no danger of extinction. So if you have the chance, get a grip and sample one of South Africa's premier gourmet treats, a tender meat with a sweeter, less gamy flavor than venison and an incomparable rose-red color. Its delicate flavor and leanness are the result of the springbok's free-ranging diet as it grazes on the semiarid grasslands of southeastern Africa.

A roasted haunch is one of South Africa's best-loved special-occasion dishes, but other cuts are variously grilled or marinated and braised. The springbok is especially appreciated for its liver, which makes for what is considered the most savory biltong, dried strips of meat that resemble jerky. Cubes of tougher cuts might appear as *sosaties,* skewers of meat that have been marinated in a curry sauce made extra tart with tamarind juice.

WHERE: *In Johannesburg,* Melrose Arch, tel 27/11-684-1477, moyo.co.za; *in Cape Town,* Blouberg, tel 27/21-554-9671, moyo.co.za; *in Stellenbosch, South Africa,* 5 Ryneveld, tel 27/21-886-4842, 5ryneveld.com. **RETAIL AND MAIL ORDER:** *In New York,* Jonty Jacobs, tel 855-952-2627, jontyjacobs.com. **FURTHER INFORMATION:** *African Cooking* by Laurens van der Post (1970).

A roast saddle of springbok with fruit chutney

Wandie's Place

South African

In the heart of the historic Dube section of Soweto, a township in Johannesburg, sits Wandile Nadala's humble saloon, or *shebeen,* which opened in 1981. Over the years, Wandie's Place expanded and became a must-visit for local and visiting musicians, artists, pols, and celebrities, including the likes of Bill Clinton, Brad Pitt, Sir Richard Branson, and Evander Holyfield. Once a gathering place for anti-apartheid activists, most famously Nelson Mandela and Desmond Tutu, it is in the midst of a neighborhood now undergoing rapid gentrification. The walls are crammed with souvenir memorabilia, and a stunning, framed beaded sign with tribal motifs lets you know you've landed in the correct joint—you're at "Wandie's Place, Soweto."

Chef Wandile Ndala

The amiable Wandile, a member of South Africa's Xhosa tribe, greets guests with a big, generous smile as he advises on the menu, which includes rich and aromatically spiced native stews of oxtail, beef, and mutton, grilled meats, and the slightly sweet, tomato-sauced tripe dish that is *mogodu*. Along with these go cushioning starches, such as velvety pumpkin mash, steamed rice, or sticky white *fufu*

dumplings made from corn, taro, or potatoes. There is also the Xhosa favorite *umngqusho*, a heady porridge of beans simmered with samp, the dried, cracked, white corn kernels also traditional to Native Americans in New England, and in such southwestern states as New Mexico, albeit without the alluring scents of allspice, nutmeg, and cloves that perfume the South African dish. Here you can also find exotic specialties, such as the dried caterpillars known as *mopane*, and stewed cane rat, but for the most part, the menu offers easy-to-like dishes, which are laid out on a self-service buffet. South African wine or sprightly homemade ginger beer (see page 724) complete a meal well seasoned with local history.

WHERE: 618 Makhalemele St., Soweto, South Africa, tel 27/11-982-2796, wandies.co.za. **FURTHER INFORMATION AND RECIPES:** funkymunky .co.za/african.html.

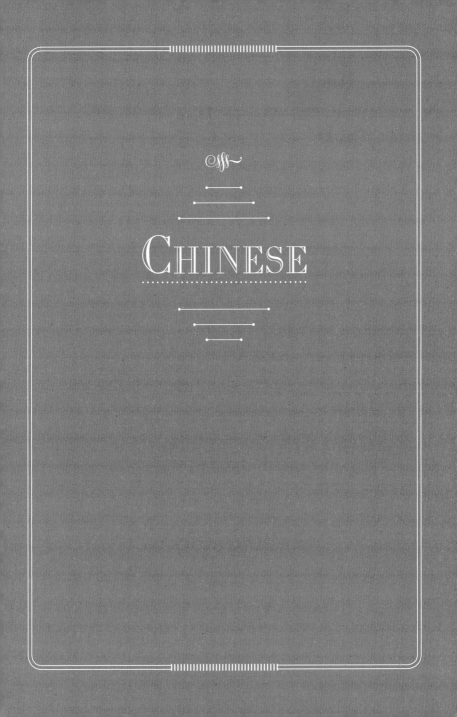

CHINESE

┤||||||||||||||||||||||||||||├

WHAT A PEAR!

Asian Pear

Chinese, Japanese, Korean

With its burnished, bronze peel and round shape, the Asian pear resembles a cross between an apple and a Bosc pear—hence its nickname, the "apple pear." *Pyrus pyrifolia,* however, is not a hybrid, but the native pear of China,

Japan, and Korea, prized for its mild, gently sweet, and refreshing flavor, snappily crisp flesh, and pleasantly chewy skin. Believed to have originated in China, the fruit was introduced to California by Chinese immigrants during the Gold Rush. Now cultivated all around the world, it grows in more than a thousand varieties; some twenty types are commonly available, mostly the varieties the Japanese call *nashi* or *nijisseiki* ("twentieth century").

The firm, crackling pears should be enjoyed raw, as cooking ruins their delicate texture and flavor. While they can be sliced or chomped into on their own, they also lend their crunch and mild sweetness to savory salads, relishes, and slaws.

This fruit is somewhat more labor-intensive to grow than European varieties, and must ripen completely on the tree and then be transported with a great deal of care—which is why Asian pears are generally more expensive than their European counterparts. Although they keep for months in the refrigerator, they are ready to eat when bought, and are best during their peak season, from midspring through midsummer.

MAIL ORDER: thefruitcompany.com (search asian pears). **FURTHER INFORMATION AND RECIPES:** *Uncommon Fruits and Vegetables* by Elizabeth Schneider (2010); *Asian Flavors of Jean-Georges* by Jean-Georges Vongerichten (2007); saveur .com (search pickled asian pears); epicurious .com (search green tea poached pear); produce oasis.com (search asian pears). **TIP:** Select the most fragrant fruit, with no soft spots, and store it for a week at room temperature, or up to three months in the refrigerator.

┤||||||||||||||||||||||||||||├

A PARAGON OF POULTRY

Beijing Kao Ya

Peking Duck

Chinese

The creator of Peking duck deserves a place in the history books for his or her seductively delicious invention. Panache and ingenuity were certainly required in dreaming up this tantalizing dish, in which the duck's skin is cooked to

a crisp, golden glassiness, and the meat is moist and sweetly earthy; both are enfolded in hot,

paper-thin crêpes or cushiony, snow-white steamed buns. The whole exudes a complex, almost smoky fragrance that is enhanced by a star anise–scented powder of six other peppery, aromatic spices.

The dish's preparation is as wondrous as its flavor. First, there is the duck itself, a well-fed, white-feathered, carefully raised bird known as the Imperial Peking duck, the ancestor of the Long Island duck. The first step in preparing the duck is treating the skin so that it will become taut and easily separate from the underlying fat during the slow roasting. To that end, the whole bird is hung in cool, open, circulating air for twenty-four hours; most authentically, air is first pumped into the carcass through a tiny hole punctured between breast and wing. Just before it is roasted, the duck is lacquered with a pungent combination of rice wine vinegar, honey, plummy hoisin sauce, ginger, oil, and perhaps hot chile peppers. Finally, the sauce-varnished bird is hung vertically or slid onto a rack and slowly roasted, its fat dripping off into a pan as it receives frequent additional bastings of sauce.

At table, the skin will usually be presented as a first course, with the meat to follow, always with scallions, cucumbers, and a sweet-spicy spread of fruity hoisin sauce, and freshly made, gently warm pancakes or buns. For a final course, the duck carcass, still with juicy bits of meat attached, can be made into a delicate, soothing soup, flavored with shredded cabbage and scallions.

One of the most traditional and intriguing presentations of this celestial dish can be found at the famed Da Dong Roast Duck restaurant in Beijing, where women are given little plates of coarse white sugar crystals to sprinkle onto the duck, because, it is explained, a bygone empress felt that women's palates were too delicate for strong and peppery flavors. Too bad for men, as the sugar adds a sweet crunch that plays well against the crisp, baconlike skin.

WHERE: *In Beijing,* Da Dong Roast Duck, tel 86/10-6582-2892; *in New York,* Peking Duck House at two locations, pekingduckhousenyc .com; *in Toronto,* Crown Princess Fine Dining, tel 416-923-8784, crown-princess.ca. **FURTHER INFORMATION AND RECIPES:** *The Chinese Cookbook* by Craig Claiborne and Virginia Lee (1972); *The Thousand Recipe Chinese Cookbook* by Gloria Bley Miller (1984); chineserecipes.com (search peking duck); marthastewart.com (search martha liao's peking duck).

A deeply traditional dish with a four-hundred-year history

TAKE THESE APPLES FOR A SPIN

Candied Apple Fritters

Chinese American

Long before the word *fusion* was permanently borrowed from the world of nuclear physics and grafted onto the food realm, the Chinese were busy adapting their food to suit American tastes. In need of a showy dessert, Chinese

American restaurants took a hint from the candied apple and introduced this sticky-sweet, hot-and-cold treat. Preparation usually takes place tableside, with slim, batter-coated apple slices caramelized in hot oil and sugar, and, while still sizzling hot, plunged into ice water so that the syrup instantly hardens into a candied glaze. The hiss of the hot apples going into the cold water invariably provokes oohs and aahs, not to mention a Pavlovian mouthwatering from

A tableside twist on candy apples

diners anticipating the crunchy, sweet treat. Dinner theater indeed.

Surprisingly, the dessert, which was first popularized in Cantonese restaurants in the U.S., has an actual provenance. Known alternatively as spun apples, Peking glazed apples, and Peking drawn-thread glazed apples, the original is a tradition of North China and appears in restaurants in Beijing, usually sprinkled with white or black sesame seeds. During the dire days of the Mao regime, when food shortages were commonplace, this favorite dessert was made with potatoes or yams in place of the more expensive apples. Fortunately, this treat is sometimes found on the menus of America's more old-timey Chinese restaurants—and of course it is not too difficult to prepare at home.

FURTHER INFORMATION AND RECIPES: *The Modern Art of Chinese Cooking* by Barbara Tropp (1996); *The Ultimate Chinese & Asian Cookbook,* edited by Linda Doeser (1998); *Chinese Pavilion* by Elisa Vergne (2003); recipe goldmine.com (search chinese candied apples); chinesefood.about.com (search candied banana fritters, use the apple variation).

THE JEWELS AMONG MEATBALLS

Chen-Chu-Jou-Wan

Pearl Balls

Chinese

A dim sum favorite that is a specialty of Suzhou, the picturesque, canal-laced city near Shanghai, these spiky meatballs are made from a mix of minced pork, dried mushrooms, pungent ginger, crunchy water chestnuts, scallions, soy sauce, and rice wine—much the same as other Chinese meatballs, but with a unique finishing touch. Once the tiny balls are shaped, they are rolled in short-grain glutinous rice that has been soaked and drained, the rice grains pressed firmly into the meatballs until they look like rough-edged snowballs. Carefully laid out in a single layer on an oiled, heatproof plate, they are placed in a bamboo steamer for about half an hour, until the meat is thoroughly cooked and the rice forms a sturdy, crunchy, crystalline crust. A dip of light soy sauce with rice wine vinegar and a dab of fiery Chinese mustard, mixed to the eater's taste, is the only enhancement needed.

Some Chinese cooks prefer a larger version of pearl balls, served as part of a main course, much like lion's heads (see page 784), but without cabbage.

WHERE: *In New York,* Joe's Shanghai at three locations, joe shanghairestaurants.com; *in San Francisco,* Yank Sing at multiple locations, yanksing.com; *in Daly City, CA,* Koi Palace, koipalace

A meat-filled trompe l'oeil

.com. **FURTHER INFORMATION AND RECIPES:** *The Thousand Recipe Chinese Cookbook* by Gloria Bley Miller (1984); *Chinese Gastronomy* by Hsiang Ju Lin and Tsuifeng Lin (1969); *Delicious Dim Sum* by Cooking Penguin (2013); *Cooking Classics: Dim Sum* by Ng Lip Kah (2014). **SEE ALSO:** Onigiri, page 812; Köttbullar, page 368.

+|||||||||||||||||||||||||||||||||+

THE BRAVE LIKE IT HOT

Chengdu Ji

Chengdu Chicken

Chinese (Sichuanese)

There are two things you have to like a lot to appreciate this specialty of the Sichuan city of Chengdu: chicken, naturally, but more important, red-hot dried chile peppers. One look at the dish, with its moist and tender sauce-glazed bits of chicken blanketed by myriad curled, vermillion chiles, and you might think those two ingredients were matched pound for pound in the recipe. But for those with a fireproof palate, and the knowledge that taking intermittent mouthfuls of plain steamed white rice will dampen the flames, *Chengdu ji* is an addictive treat.

The chicken itself—both light and dark meat, and preferably bone-in to maintain juiciness and enhance flavor—is cut into large chunks, then stir-fried in peanut oil along with slivers of fresh ginger, garlic, scallions, those incendiary whole peppers, and a bit of ground Sichuan pepper (see page 770). For a savory balance, rice wine or sherry and a pinch of sugar will join the mix, with some toasted peanuts often tossed in for crunch and a bit of creamy relief from the spicy sauce.

Of course, you aren't really expected to eat all, or even most, of the peppers. Rather, as you wend your way through the morsels of chicken and nuts, you pick up bits and pieces of crumbly chile flakes with your chopsticks. Invariably, that leaves most of the peppers on the plate, which is a painful sight for those disinclined to waste. If this describes you, consider taking the flavorful leftovers home in a doggy bag and using them to approximate this dish at home. The chiles will have lost a bit of their fire, a fact your family might well appreciate.

WHERE: *In New York,* Wu Liang Ye, tel 212-398-2308, wuliangyenyc.com; *in Chicago,* Yan Bang Cai, tel 312-842-7818, yanbangcaichicago .com; *in San Francisco,* Ton Kiang Restaurant, tel 415-752-4440, tonkiang.net. **FURTHER INFORMATION AND RECIPES:** *Mrs. Chiang's Szechwan Cookbook* by Jung-Feng Chiang with Ellen Schrecker and John Schrecker (1987); chinese food.about.com (search chengdu ji chicken); ifood.tv (search chengdu ji chicken). **SEE ALSO:** Sichuan Eggplant, page 785.

—||||||||||||||||||||||||||||||||||—

Chiu Chow Oyster Omelet

Chinese (Fukienese)

The food of Chiu Chow (also spelled Teochew, and situated in the northeast corner of China's Canton province) makes for a unique and memorable stop in a journey among China's seemingly endless regional cuisines, but it's

relatively unknown outside the country. Marked by the mild flavors typical of Canton, it also shows the influence of the neighboring Fujian region.

One of the most savory Chiu Chow dishes is the oyster omelet, a version of which is a particular favorite in the night markets of Taipei. The success of the richly filling street snack depends upon the freshest, tiniest raw oysters, a handful of which are stirred into beaten eggs, along with a small amount of a binder such as potato, rice, or cornstarch to create a pancake effect. Green onions are another possible addition.

Vendors cooking up after-hours treats at the Shilin Night Market

After being cooked in a hot iron pan greased with either rendered lard or vegetable oil, it is flipped once, frittata-style, so both sides take on a lightly golden laciness. The finishing touch is a pungent, winey aged soy sauce blended with spicy chile sauce and a tangy splash of lime juice, all to enhance the flavor of the silky, saline oysters.

The most fitting way to wash down an oyster omelet is with a tiny, espresso-size cup of Chiu Chow iron tea or Kung Fu tea, brewed from aged tea leaves native to Fujian. As strong in aroma and flavor as its name and gray-black color imply, iron tea has drily astringent overtones and is always taken as a sort of digestive before or after meals, in shot-size portions lest it prove too harsh for the stomach.

Given the similarity between the Chiu Chow oyster omelet and San Francisco's famed

Hangtown fry (see page 579), one cannot help wondering if a cook hailing from Chiu Chow and working in the gold-mining camps near Placerville, California (nicknamed Hangtown), did not first present this dish, never mind that the oysters in the Gold Rush version came to be fried, and that crisp bacon served as a garnish. We may never know for sure, but the long and influential history of Chinese cuisine in California, and in the American West in general, would certainly back up such a theory.

Where: *In Hong Kong,* Pak Loh Chiu Chow Restaurant, tel 852/2576-8886, pakloh.com; City Chiu Chow Restaurant, tel 852/2723-6226; *in Queens,* Main Street Imperial Taiwanese Gourmet, tel 718-886-8788. **Further information and recipes:** *The Best of Taiwanese Cuisine* by Karen Bartell (2002); food52.com (search taiwanese oyster omelet); seriouseats.com (search taiwanese oyster omelet).

—||||||||||||||||||||||||||||||—

LOBSTER, SAUCED WITH NOSTALGIA

Chow Lung Har
Lobster Cantonese

Chinese American (Cantonese)

Just as Italian American red-sauce cooking has been snootily denigrated by champions of "authentic" Italian food for decades, so too were Cantonese American dishes downgraded in the late 1960s and the 1970s, when Americans

were introduced to the so-called "real" cuisine of China. Oddly, these inexpensive Americanized Italian and Chinese dishes we first came to know and love represented the southern cooking of each country, and would be dismissed in turn, as the new-to-us northern chefs won the culinary high ground. Yet, many who grew up with the old favorites miss them still, partly out of nostalgia, but also because they were, in fact, very good, whatever their origins. No dish exemplifies this more than lobster Cantonese and its less-expensive spin-off, shrimp in lobster sauce.

Made with live lobsters pulled from bubbling tanks, lobster Cantonese was often one of the most expensive choices on what were generally modestly priced menus. It began with fresh chunks of moist, pearly lobster chopped into sections, shell and all, to protect the meat and add a distinctly oceanic flavor to the sauce. Bits of tender pork and lots of crushed garlic also went into the wok, along with shavings of fresh ginger, perhaps a little sherry or white wine, and sometimes fermented black beans. For a gossamer gravy, a little cornstarch was dissolved in chicken stock. And for the masterful finishing touch, half-beaten eggs were poured in to quickly set into cloudlets of whites and soft, custardy yolks. Topped with threads of scallion and nested on a hill of white rice to absorb the juices, it was—and is—as rich and engaging as any dish turned out for the Imperial Court of old.

Less expensive but equally delicious, shrimp in lobster sauce is so named because it

is prepared in the same sauce and with essentially the same ingredients, except that in place of whole lobster, it is made with freshly shelled, butterflied shrimp. Both dishes, fortunately, can still be found in what might be deemed old-fashioned Chinese restaurants in the U.S., although occasionally they do make appearances on some upscale menus as well.

Lobster Cantonese, a garlicky, gingery delight

WHERE: *In New York,* Congee Village at two locations, congeevillagerestaurants.com; *in Toronto,* Crown Princess Fine Dining, tel 416-923-8784, crown-princess.ca. **FURTHER INFORMATION AND RECIPES:** *The Thousand Recipe Chinese Cookbook* by Gloria Bley Miller (1984); *Quick and Easy* by Martin Yan (2004); nytimes.com (search lobster cantonese); epicurious.com (search lobster cantonese).

—|||||||||||||||||||||||||||||||||—

AMERICA'S FIRST TASTE OF CHINA

Chow Mein

Chinese American

A staple in the United States since the 1930s, a time when "Chinese food" meant egg foo yung and chop suey, chow mein has a unique social history. The words are an Americanized version of *chao mian,* Mandarin for "stir-fried noodles"—

an age-old and decidedly simple Chinese dish composed of boiled noodles quickly stir-fried in a wok with a sprinkling of meat and vegetables and a drizzle of cooking oil and soy sauce.

The foundation of the dish is the Chinese art of stir-frying, the point of which is to show off fresh ingredients by cooking them quickly over very high heat, so that they remain crisp and distinct. It's a technique that is fast and relatively simple, which is why one of the dish's American origin stories places it as a practice of Chinese immigrants working the railroads in the late nineteenth century. As they saw their fellow laborers preparing these quick lunches for themselves, American workers became interested and had a taste. The rest is history—or at least apocrypha.

As chow mein became popular, it evolved to be made with both soft and crisp noodles, bulked up with shrimp, chicken, or pork, and paired with a cornstarch-thickened, vaguely sweet brown sauce. In this and other iterations, it proved just

exotic enough to become wildly popular, in its time a late-night supper staple at swank eateries like the Stork Club in Manhattan and Trader Vic's in Los Angeles and a common counter specialty at big-city dime stores and roadside cafés, often sandwiched between slices of white bread.

When freshly and carefully prepared, chow mein is a truly comforting dish marked by delightfully contrasting textures: al dente vegetables and silky noodles in a soothingly simple sauce, topped with additional noodles fried to crispy threads. Fortunately, this time-honored crowd-pleaser of the American culinary canon is here to stay.

FURTHER INFORMATION AND RECIPES: *The Thousand Recipe Chinese Cookbook* by Gloria Bley Miller (1984); *The Fortune Cookie Chronicles* by Jennifer 8. Lee (2008); cookstr.com (search chicken chow mein); saveur.com (search two sides brown); for a discussion on the history and lore of chow mein, *Fashionable Food: Seven Decades of Food Fads* by Sylvia Lovegren (2005).

—|||||||||||||||||||||||||||||||||—

TREATS FOR PANDAS AND PEOPLE

Chuk Sun

Bamboo Shoots

Chinese, Japanese, Southeast Asian

When the world at large discovered the charms of Chinese food in the mid-twentieth century, a host of canned "exotic" ingredients appeared on supermarket shelves to help the trend along. Among these were bamboo shoots (*chuk sun* or *zhu sun*), the sprouts of a tall, woody grass that may belong to any of several genera—and to several hundred species within those, only a handful of which are edible.

Although canned foods can be convenient, fresh bamboo shoots are a far and fortunate cry from the limp and salty preserved substitutes. The fresh shoots have a distinctly clean, sweet, green flavor and a satisfyingly crunchy bite. The level of crispness varies depending on the amount of fiber in each species, but they all deliver a suitable snap. And that matters, as bamboo shoots are prized most of all for the texture they lend to a variety of Asian dishes—whether they are slivered and added to soups and vegetable dishes, diced and mixed into fillings for dumplings, pickled for use as garnish, or shredded atop salads and noodle dishes.

The shoots have been harvested since ancient times in China and Japan, particularly in the bamboo forests of Kyoto. They must be picked as soon as their tips appear above the ground, which occurs almost immediately after the rains in either winter or spring, depending

on the variety. Such is their pervasiveness in China, where fresh shoots can be found in grocery stores in large tubs of water, that anything that develops rapidly is likened to "bamboo shoots after the rain."

Wherever they are found, fresh shoots should be peeled and blanched before being consumed. Most species contain a small amount of the toxin cyanide, but it can be quickly boiled away, a process that also reduces the shoots' natural bitterness.

MAIL ORDER: Melissa's Produce, tel 800-588-0151, melissas.com; Specialty Produce, tel 619-295-3172, specialtyproduce.com. **FURTHER INFORMATION AND RECIPES:** *The Seventh Daughter: My Culinary Journey from Beijing to San Francisco* by Cecilia Chang (2007); *Beyond Bok Choy* by Rosa Lo San Ross (1996); saveur.com (search pork hocks with bamboo shoots). **TIP:** To store fresh bamboo shoots, wrap them in paper towels and keep them in the refrigerator for up to two weeks. If you must resort to the canned variety, just before using, rinse them well to remove saltiness and blanch for five minutes to get rid of any tinny taste.

A BIG BEEF WITH ZEST

Chun Pei Ngau Yuk

Orange Beef

Chinese (Hunanese)

Hailing from Hunan province, this aromatic, meaty stir-fry is a perennial favorite on Chinese restaurant menus the world over. The dish consists of strips of beef, generally flank steak, quickly cooked with garlic, fresh ginger, chiles, and

grated dried orange peel. It's the fragrant orange peel that accounts for the dish's name, in both English and Chinese, where *chun pei ngau yuk* literally means old beef—the *old* referring to the desiccated orange peel. Some chefs mistakenly reach for fresh citrus peel, because it has more juice and zing, but the dried version imparts a more sophisticated,

subtle polish. Either way, the orange acts as a foil to the rich beef and sauce, supplying hints of sweetness and, crucially, a little bitterness, too. Mostly, though, the rind lends its distinctive perfume, as do the other aromatic ingredients, to a dish whose powerful, mouthwatering fragrance should fill a dining room. Sadly, subpar versions of this simple classic abound, particularly those in which the beef is heavily breaded and deep-fried, or for which orange marmalade is used in the sauce. But authentic orange beef, properly prepared, is a light, bright, comfort-food classic.

Where: *In New York,* Shun Lee West, tel 212-595-8895, shunleewest.com; Shun Lee Palace, tel 212-371-8844; *in Houston,* Café Ginger, tel 713-528-4288, cafeginger.net; *in Toronto,* Crown Princess Fine Dining, tel 416-923-8784, crown-princess.ca. **Further information and recipes:** *Mastering the Art of Chinese Cooking* by Eileen Yin-Fei Lo (2009); *The Shun Lee Cookbook* by Michael Tong (2007); *The Art of Chinese Cooking* by Rebekah Lin Jewell

The classic orange beef is a marmalade-free affair.

(2009); cookstr.com (search orange beef); foodandwine.com (search orange beef).

SHANGHAIED BY FLAVOR

Chung Yau Bang

Scallion Pancakes

Chinese (Shanghainese)

Crisp yet moistly tender and redolent of that green-and-white onion, scallion pancakes were traditionally part of a Shanghai dim sum breakfast, but now make regular appearances at lunch and dinner as an appetizer on Chinese restaurant menus. Made from a wheat-based dough rather than a crêpe- or pancakelike batter, *chung yau bang* are basically fried flatbreads—in the same school as fried Indian *parathas* and the Korean *panjeon,* a heartier

China's addictively chewy and salty "pancakes"

interpretation that usually includes bits of various shellfish along with minced green onions, a combination also found in the Vietnamese crêpes *banh xeo* and the Japanese *okonomiyaki* pancakes.

For chung yau bang, finely chopped scallions are blended into a near paste with salt, a pinch of sugar, and either some lard or vegetable shortening. Flour and water are the sole ingredients used for the dough; mixed and kneaded to a smooth, pliable state, it is rolled out in circles before being filled with the scallion mixture and rerolled and twisted into tight coils. Fried in a vegetable oil (preferably peanut), the small cakes emerge crunchily brown on raised spots and silky in their crannies—a tantalizing contrast resulting from their coiled, uneven texture—the scallions' oniony bite accenting the mild, slightly oily dough. Delectable accompaniments to soup, the pancakes also benefit from a dip in soy sauce.

But a word to the wise: Although scallion pancakes appear on many Chinese restaurant menus, all too often they arrive soggy and greasy. They might be made in advance, then reheated to order, or fried in less-than-pristine cooking oil, short cuts that give the dish a bad name. One solution: Master the art of making them yourself at home. They require no hard-to-find ingredients or equipment—and a freshly fried scallion pancake is something your dinner guests will long remember.

WHERE: *In New York,* Congee Village, Allen Street location, tel 212-941-1818, congeevillage restaurants.com; *in San Francisco,* Yank Sing at multiple locations, yanksing.com; *in Vancouver,* Grand Dynasty Seafood Restaurant, tel 604-432-6002, granddynasty.ca. **FURTHER INFORMATION AND RECIPES:** *The Dim Sum Book* by Eileen Yin-Fei Lo (1982); cookstr.com (search flaky scallion pancake); bonappetit.com (search scallion pancakes); foodnetwork.com (search scallion pancakes ginger sauce).

A PORRIDGE THAT'S JUST RIGHT

Congee

Chinese, Korean

The Chinese believe in hearty, sustaining breakfasts, and congee, a creamy, steamy rice porridge, is the favorite solution, much as oatmeal (see page 18) is in many Western cultures. Variations on congee (known as *jook* in Korea and some regions of China) can be found throughout Asia—and it's sold everywhere from street stands to dim sum palaces to airport lounges.

The original began in southern China as both a simple, filling, warming way to start the day and an economical use of last night's leftover rice. Its preparation is as simple as cooking gets: Short-grain white rice is simmered in well-salted water until it approaches mush, then served with a variety of tasty and nutritious toppings. The toppings depend on where you are: In Beijing, congee is enlivened with spicy pickled vegetables, bits of sausage, dried fish, preserved "thousand-year-old" eggs, and cubes of tofu. In Guangdong province, rice porridge is usually served alongside another dish, such as stir-fried vegetables. Throughout China, congee is often enriched with chicken, snails, frogs, and various seafood (a costly version is topped with abalone), and sometimes long, crisp strips of crullerlike fried dough (*youtiao*) that add a pleasant oily crunch. In its plainer forms, or topped with therapeutic ingredients, it's considered a healing food for all manner of ailments—most common among them, hangovers.

WHERE: *In New York,* Congee Village at two locations, congeevillagerestaurants.com; *in Washington, DC,* New Big Wong, tel 202-628-0491; *in San Francisco,* Hing Lung, tel 415-398-8838; *in Toronto,* Congee Wong at two locations, congeewong.com. **FURTHER INFORMATION AND RECIPES:** *Mastering the Art of Chinese Cooking* by Eileen Yin-Fei Lo (2009); *Beyond the Great Wall* by Naomi Duguid and Jeffrey Alford (2008); *The Thousand Recipe Chinese Cookbook* by Gloria Bley Miller (1984); epicurious.com (search chinese chicken rice porridge); cookstr.com (search chinese rice soup). **SEE ALSO:** Biryani, page 868; Ochazuke, page 812; Ginger Fried Rice, page 838; Risotto, page 233.

—||||||||||||||||||||||||||||||||—

Da Shidai Meishi Food Court, Beijing

Chinese

Given the staggering breadth, depth, and variety of Chinese cuisine and its scope and complexity, it's a relief for food-minded visitors to Beijing to be able to take an easy shortcut. The Da Shidai Meishi food court, on the lower level of a sparkling modern building just off the city's main drag, East Chang'an Avenue, offers just that: a home for more than two dozen open-kitchen stands featuring the cuisines of almost all Chinese provinces. Cooks call out, carny style, to attract passersby, and the air vibrates with the sizzling sounds and aromas of frying onions, meats, and starchy-sweet steaming dumplings as hungry workers and tourists stand in line for bites.

With great flair, the vendors dish up specialties such as Shanghai's fat, juicy soup dumplings, thick noodles, and chewy twists of dried tofu, or the more delicate dim sum of Guangdong. The hotly spiced soups and cold noodle and vegetable dishes of Sichuan and Hunan are here. From Yunnan come satiny, white, rice-flour noodles floating in heady chicken broth adrift with leafy green vegetables, and an amazing quick-fix, a flavored sticky rice wrapped and steamed in a shiny, green lotus leaf packet that, when unwrapped, serves as a bowl.

Other Asian countries are also represented in Da Shidai Meishi: Korea is here with its hot pots, Japan with teppan grills and ramen, and India with thinly crisp and buttery *parathas* enfolding scrambled eggs with minced scallions, among other choices.

For those looking for the full meal experience, there are many desserts on offer, from fresh fruit salads to sticky-sweet confections and pastries, and a variety of beverages, most temptingly, freshly pressed watermelon juice. A moveable feast, Chinese-style.

WHERE: *In Beijing*, Da Shidai Meishi food court, Lower Level 1, Oriental Plaza (Dongfang Guangchang), Wangfujing Street at East Chang'an Avenue.

—||||||||||||||||||||||||||||||||—

Da Zha Xie

Shanghai Hairy Crab

Chinese

Easy to identify by the dense patches of scruffy dark hair on its claws, the sweetly moist, meaty Shanghai hairy crab has long legs and a body roughly the size of an adult's palm—or the size of a rice bowl, as they say in China. Its firm but satiny flesh (joined in female crabs by an especially delectable bright-orange roe) is so delicate that in China the crab is simply steamed whole, and is never seasoned during the cooking process. Only as it is being eaten is it dipped, bite by bite, into a ginger-scented blend of rice vinegar and soy sauce.

The highly prized crustacean is native to the coastal estuaries of eastern Asia, from Korea in the north to the Chinese province of Fujian in the south, with the most sought-after (and pricey) specimens coming from Yangcheng Lake, just west of Shanghai. Also known as the Chinese mitten crab (*Eriocheir sinensis*), it is perhaps the most delicious of the 4,500 known species of crab—although Chesapeake Bay blue crab enthusiasts might well take exception (see page 552).

In Chinese medicine, hairy crab is believed to have an intensely "cooling" (*yin*) effect on the body, so it must be paired with ample "warming" foods like ginger and cups of potent, amber-hued rice wine. It is generally served with little else, although the meat might appear atop custards at luxe banquets. Each year, a veritable frenzy erupts, especially in Shanghai, during the six-week crab season, from mid-September through October. Today, however, the crustacean is becoming available in China year-round, in part because this invasive species has made its way to North America and Europe, where it is viewed as a pest. The immigrant crabs are nowhere near as coveted as those

A simple treatment befits what might be the most delicate crab on earth.

succulent Yangcheng specimens, which can fetch upward of $100 per kilogram in tonier markets and restaurants.

WHERE: *In Shanghai,* Old Shanghai Moon Restaurant, tel 86/21-3218-9888, jinjianghotels.com; Jesse Restaurant, tel 86/21-6282-9260; Wang Bao He Restaurant, tel 86/21-6322-3673; *in Hong Kong,* Wu Kong Shanghai Restaurant, tel 86/852-2366-7244, wukong.com.hk; *in New York,* Oriental Garden, tel 212-619-0085, orientalgardenny.com. **FURTHER INFORMATION AND RECIPES:** *The Thousand Recipe Chinese Cookbook* by Gloria Bley Miller (1984); bamskitchen.com (search hairy crabs). **TIP:** Although importing and serving the hairy crab is prohibited in the United States, a similar preparation can be applied to other hard-shell crabs.

RED-HOT AND ADDICTIVE

Dan Dan Mian

Dan Dan Noodles

Chinese (Sichuanese)

The emblematic street food of Sichuan province and a favorite of night markets throughout China, red-hot dan dan noodles are named for the poles that street vendors in the city of Chengdu once used to cart their cooking pots and equipment. One of many *xiao chi* (little eats) sold at outdoor food stalls, *dan dan mian* are bowls of fresh wheat noodles and minced preserved vegetables flavored with an incendiary blend of chile oil, Sichuan peppercorns, dark and light soy sauces, rice and black vinegars, and fragrant, dark sesame paste. It's a challenging kind of heat, and one that can also be addictive—you don't know if you can manage another bite, but it's so achingly delicious you can't stop. There are countless variations on the sauce, in Sichuan and beyond, and it is said that no two cooks make it exactly the same way. Some prefer less or no sesame paste (in Taiwan, chopped peanuts are added instead), while others incorporate ginger or garlic or both. For a protein boost, the noodles may be topped with bits of minced beef or ground pork. In all its many forms, what remains constant are those pleasantly chewy noodles and that fiery, red-hot sauce.

Where: *In Chengdu,* Long Chao Shou, tel 86/28-8666-6947; *in New York,* Wu Liang Ye, tel 212-398-2308, wuliangyenyc.com; *in Chicago,* Lao Sze Chuan, tel 312-326-5040, tonygourmet group.com; *in San Francisco,* Z & Y, tel 415-981-8988, zandyrestaurant.com. **Further information and recipes:** *Land of Plenty: A Treasury of Authentic Sichuan Cooking* by Fuchsia Dunlop (2003); *The Shun Lee Cookbook* by Michael Tong (2010); bonappetit.com (seach dan-dan noodles); foodandwine.com (search dan-dan noodles); theguardian.com (search how to make a bowl of noodles).

AS SWEET AND GREEN AS SPRINGTIME

Dau Mui

Snow Pea Shoots

Chinese

The tiny, tendril tips of snow pea plants (*Pisum sativum* var. *saccharatum*) are among the most coveted of Chinese vegetables, beloved for their crisp delicacy and subtle, watercress-like flavor. These shoots have a relatively short season, because as the weather grows warmer, they mature and turn tough. They also have a relatively short shelf life, and to be at their best they must be sprightly and fresh, never wilted or dull. These factors combine to make the pea shoots, known as *dau mui* in Cantonese, a rarified and expensive delight. In classic Chinese cooking, *dau mui* are either quickly stir-fried in a little oil, often with a light but enriching touch of fermented tofu and garlic, or added right before serving to soups and noodle dishes as a light, crunchy, irresistible garnish. They make a worthy addition to non-Chinese dishes as well, such as salads or atop a classic Italian sweet-pea or shellfish risotto.

Where: *In New York,* Congee Village at two locations, congeevillagerestaurants.com; *in Toronto,* Crown Princess Fine Dining, tel 416-923-8784, crown-princess.ca. **Mail order:** For seeds, evergreenseeds.com; Kitazawa Seed Co., tel 510-595-1188, kitazawaseed.com. **Further information and recipes:** *Beyond Bok Choy* by Rosa Lo San Ross (1996); *The Wisdom of the Chinese Kitchen* by Grace Young (1999); foodandwine .com (search pea shoots and shiitakes with shrimp); saveur.com (search pea shoots bean curd). **Tip:** Store unwashed pea shoots in a plastic bag in the refrigerator for no more than a day, and wash them just before using so they don't get soggy.

Dim Sum

Chinese (Cantonese)

The custom is known as *yum cha*: drinking tea while nibbling on dim sum, the steamy, juicy dumplings that translate to "heart's delights." Plumped with gingery-garlicky pork, beef, chicken, shrimp, crabmeat, and vegetables, they not only stir the heart but beguile the palate and satisfy the stomach as well. With a variety of fillings, doughs (made from wheat, rice, or tapioca flours), shapes, dipping sauces, and cooking methods (steaming, boiling, frying), dim sum dumplings are a diverse, exotically flavored, and easily shared lot. To boot, the most typical way in which they are served—from carts circulated around sprawling, casual dining rooms so diners can take their pick after a look-see—adds up to a freewheeling, entertaining kind of meal. In some of the higher-end dim sum restaurants, diners order from menus; their compensation for not being able to have a look-see is the reward of cooked-to-order dumplings that arrive hot and fresh.

Although they are the star attraction, dumplings are not all there is to a dim sum meal. Other standards include spring rolls; stuffed and fried crab claws; grated turnip cakes spiked with pork and pungent Chinese sausage, best when grilled tableside, right on the cart; tiny slivers of ducks' tongues, sweet or spicy; chewy chicken or duck feet; pork-stuffed green peppers; braised tripe; various noodle dishes; stir-fried eggplant; and, to finish, the rice porridge congee (see page 757). Among the long, long list of options, the following are must-try dim sum favorites within the Cantonese school—Canton being China's most famous province for the dim sum ritual, followed by Sichuan:

The wide world of dim sum ranges from an infinite variety of dumplings to spring rolls and noodle dishes.

Shiu Mai (steamed pork dumplings). Looking like little fluted cups or open blossoms, these steamed dumplings (whose name translates to "cook and sell") are made with either a thin wheat flour dough or wonton skins and are always filled with pork, and sometimes scallions and mushrooms. Along with *har gow* (below), *shiu mai* are the most ubiquitous of Cantonese dumplings, and their quality is a good indicator of a dim sum restaurant's overall excellence.

Har Gow (shrimp dumplings). The dough for these dumplings is made with both wheat and tapioca flours, resulting in a slightly sticky translucence. Formed into little pleated pouches with ruffled tops, they are plumped with chopped shrimp, perhaps some pork fat, scallions, sesame oil, and bamboo shoots or water chestnuts, before being sent to the steamer.

Guotie (pot stickers). A Shanghai and Beijing favorite, these half-moon-shaped, pork-filled dumplings are fried on one side and steamed on the other for a crunchy-soft contrast in textures. Served with a tart, chile-spiked vinegar and soy dipping sauce, the garlicky treats are best eaten piping hot, still sizzling from the wok.

Gai See Guen (rice noodle rolls). Given the satiny texture and delicacy of their dough, these shiny, slippery bundles of wide rice noodles enfolding shredded chicken, pork, mushrooms, and bamboo shoots are as difficult to eat as they are to prepare. Both efforts are worthwhile, however—for, doused with a sweetened soy-and-sesame sauce, the silky, mellow noodles and rich, meaty filling make a delicious match.

Siu Loon Bau or Xiaolongbau (Shanghai soup dumplings). Great, pleated balls of wheat flour dough, pinched tightly at the top, hold hot—very hot—meat broth and a mix of spices, water chestnuts, pork, and sometimes crab and its coral (roe), for one of the most satisfying and filling offerings on the dim sum scene. The trick to popping them into your mouth without getting scorched is to first nip a small opening in the top and suck out just a bit of the soup. But the real skill lies in making them, which involves shaping the dumplings around a mixture of filling and diced gelled chicken and pork stock; once steamed, the stock melts into a hot soup. These dumplings also often appear outside of the dim sum feast, as an appetizer course arriving six or eight to a cabbage-leaf-lined steamer basket.

Guk Char Siu Bau (baked pork buns). For a scrumptious three or four bites, famously soft, snowy-white, yeast-raised buns enclose chopped roast pork flavored with scallions, garlic, sugar, sesame oil, and dark, salty oyster sauce. A moister, chewier result can be found in steamed versions of the bun (*jing char siu bau*).

WHERE: *Throughout Asia, as well as in Los Angeles, Seattle, and Sydney, Australia,* Din Tai Fung, dintaifungusa.com; *in Hong Kong,* Luk Yu Tea House, tel 86/852-2523-5464; *in New York,* Dim Sum Go Go, tel 212-732-0797, dimsumgogo .com; *in Richmond, VA,* Peter Chang's China Café, tel 804-364-1688, peterchangrva.com; *in San Francisco,* Yank Sing at multiple locations, yank sing.com. **MAIL ORDER:** For steamers and woks, Food Service Warehouse, tel 877-877-5655, food servicewarehouse.com (search dim sum steamers; asian serving utensils; wok); Mrs. Lin's Kitchen, tel 925-251-0158, mrslinskitchen.com (search 12" bamboo steamer). **FURTHER INFORMATION AND RECIPES:** *Dim Sum: The Art of Chinese Tea Lunch* by Ellen Leong Blonder (2002); *Delicious Dim Sum* by Cooking Penguin (2013); *Asian Dumplings: Mastering Gyoza, Spring Rolls, Samosas, and More* by Andrea Nguyen and Penny De Los Santos (2009); epicurious.com (search shrimp dumplings; pork pot stickers); saveur.com (search dim sum brunch at home); seriouseats.com (search dim sum inspired party). **TIP:** Busy weekend mornings are the best times for a dim sum feast, ensuring the greatest variety, the freshest dumplings, and the liveliest (and most crowded) dining room.

|||||||||||||||||||||||||||||||||||

THE BELLY OF THE BEAST

Dong Bo Rou

Glazed Pork Belly

Chinese

With its moist and silky texture and intense meatiness, rich pork belly glazed and cooked the Chinese way is an incomparably alluring dish. Combining garlic, ginger, rice wine, and a meltingly sweet patina of rock sugar, it represents the apotheosis of this now-gourmet poor man's cut. A most seductive version is one of the specialties of Dr. Martha Liao, the Manhattan-based retired geneticist who prepares spectacular Chinese feasts for friends whenever and wherever her husband, Hao Jiang Tian, sings a role in an opera or concert. While her Peking duck (see page 748) may be her most talked-about dish, the sleeper at her multicourse feasts is this delectable braised pork, served with stir-fried greens and steamed white rice or tender yeast-raised buns purchased from a Chinese bakery or restaurant. For those not lucky enough to be the guest at one of her incomparable dinners, she generously shares her recipe below.

Martha Liao's Glazed Pork Belly

Serves 6 to 8,
more if accompanied by other dishes

1 tablespoon peanut, corn,
or canola oil
4 thin slices peeled fresh ginger
6 cloves garlic, peeled and lightly
crushed with the side of a chef's knife
1 piece (3 pounds), 2 inches thick,
boneless pork belly with skin on
1 tablespoon rice wine or dry sherry
2 tablespoons dark soy sauce
1 tablespoon light soy sauce
1 large piece of Chinese rock sugar
(rock candy) or 1½ teaspoons
granulated sugar
2 scallions, both green and white portions,
cut into 2-inch lengths

Steamed white rice or store-bought Chinese
steamed yeast buns, for serving

1. Place the oil, ginger, and garlic in a heavy pot with a lid and cook over high heat until garlic begins to color, 1 to 2 minutes, watching carefully to prevent scorching.
2. Add the pork belly, skin side down, and cook, turning frequently, until all sides are seared to a light golden brown, about 10 minutes. Add the rice wine or sherry, cover the pot, and cook 1 to 2 minutes until the wine evaporates.
3. Reduce the heat to medium and add the dark and light soy sauces along with the rock sugar and scallions. Add 1 cup of water and, when the liquid is bubbling, cover the pot and reduce the heat to low. Let simmer slowly until the liquid is thick and syrupy and the pork belly is a rich, bronzed brown, about 1 hour and 30 minutes. If the liquid cooks down too quickly before the pork is done, add a little more water to prevent scorching. There should be 1½ to 2 cups of sauce remaining.
4. Cut the pork belly into 1½- to 2-inch-thick slices. Place it on a warm platter and pour the sauce, complete with the ginger, garlic, and scallions, over the meat. Serve immediately with steamed white rice or Chinese buns.

WHERE: *In New York,* Red Farm at two locations, redfarmnyc.com; *in Vancouver,* Sea Harbour Seafood Restaurant, tel 604-232-0816, seaharbour.com. **MAIL ORDER:** For rock sugar, amazon.com (search blooming lump candy; jansal valley rock sugar). **SEE ALSO:** Pork Rinds, page 614.

—|||||||||||||||||||||||||||||||—

Dong Qua Tang

Winter Melon Soup

Chinese (Cantonese)

Despite its name and watermelon-like appearance, the winter melon is actually a gourd, coveted for its smooth texture, subtly sweet taste, and ability to absorb strong flavors when cooked. In various Eastern medicine traditions, the melon is also considered a curative, a natural cleanser for the body that invigorates all the organs, the kidneys in particular.

Native to Southeast Asia and grown throughout southern China, where it is called *dong qua*, winter melon is made into a variety of soups in Chinese regional cuisines, some simply clear broths flavored with the mild, cucumber-like pulp. The Cantonese version is the most elaborate, a soup that is mostly seen in restaurants and that few home cooks attempt, except perhaps for feast days. The melon's flesh is

A lovely and ornate showcase for the winter melon

scooped out of its rind, and then the rind is carved into a tureen shape, with meaningful words or symbols like dragons, fish, or cherry blossoms chiseled into its surface. The flesh is cubed and combined with strong chicken stock, mushrooms, daylily bulbs, ginger, scallions, various spices, and roast duck (although more upscale versions might include crabmeat, scallops, or shark's fin), before being returned to the carved rind for serving, garnished with slivers of Yunnan ham (see page 795). Distinctively aromatic and tasty, it makes for a visually stunning, exotic delight.

WHERE: *In Shanghai*, Jesse Restaurant, tel 86/21-62822–9260; *in New York*, Congee Village, at two locations, congeevillagerestaurants.com; *in Chicago*, Yan Bang Cai, tel 312-842-7818, yanbangcaichicago.com; *in San Francisco*, Ton Kiang Restaurant, tel 415-752-4440, tonkiang.net; *in Daly City, CA*, Koi Palace, koipalace.com; *in Vancouver*, Sea Harbour Seafood Restaurant, tel 604-232-0816, seaharbour.com. Note that many restaurants require winter melon soup to be ordered ahead for a party of at least six. **MAIL ORDER:** Melissa's Produce, tel 800-588-0151, melissas.com. **FURTHER INFORMATION AND RECIPES:** *The Wisdom of the Chinese Kitchen* by Grace Young (1999); *The Thousand Recipe Chinese Cookbook* by Gloria Bley Miller (1984); epicurious.com (search winter melon soup). **TIP:** The season for winter melons generally runs from November to May. They are available in Chinese markets and some gourmet grocery stores. Look for melons with smooth rinds free of soft spots or mold.

Fish Market Restaurants

Chinese

A once common sight in China's sprawling, noisy seaside fish markets, now sadly fading from the urban scene, are the many small, informal cookshops where diners can have their fish cooked to order and served on the spot.

You can still find some in two of Hong Kong's most visited markets, the Sai Kung Seafood Market and the Lei Yue Mun Seafood Bazaar, both in former fishing villages. How the fish is prepared is generally left up to the cook, who might opt to steam rather than fry a specimen purchased live in order to show off the satiny freshness of meat and skin. Frying—to a crisp, greaseless, and golden state—is reserved for fish that, though bright-eyed and fresh, was purchased on ice, usually because it was too big or came from too far away to be kept alive in tanks.

The cookshops, which can also be found in Singapore, Taiwan, and Canton province, offer an education in Chinese fish and seafood preparation as well as an adventure that's just plain fun. Wandering the markets, shoppers will see colorful piles of unfamiliar, exotic fishes, along with more standard types such as silvery, squirming eels; clams in several varieties; stony, sea-green crabs; purplish octopus; ivory squid; gold-scaled carp; and silvery bass and flounder. After staking out his desired cookshop, the customer flags that shop for the fishmonger while making his purchase; the assortment of fish is delivered to its destination, usually arriving shortly before the customer. Then it is best to leave the rest up to the cook, biding time by sipping tea or beer and eagerly anticipating the six-, eight-, or ten-course fish feast that awaits.

WHERE: *In Hong Kong,* Sai Kung Seafood Market, discoverhongkong.com/eng (search sai kung seafood street); Lei Yue Mun Seafood Bazaar, Kowloon, tel 86/852-2727-2830, lei-yue-mun.com/seafood-bazaar.html. **TIP:** A less traditional but similar experience can be found in the many food malls of Singapore and Taiwan, where the big retail fish markets serve their wares in dining rooms. **SEE ALSO:** Billingsgate Fish Market, page 3; Tsukiji Fish Market, page 821.

Flavor & Fortune

Chinese

"Dedicated to the art and science of Chinese cooking," is the way this quarterly magazine's purpose is stated, to which one can only add, "and how!" The publication is a delightful and informative must-read for all who love the extraordinary cuisine of China, one of the world's oldest, most expansive, and most diverse in scope, no doubt a result of the size and age of the country and the awesome ingenuity of its cooks. It is said that the Chinese eat everything that flies except an airplane and anything with four legs except a table, and that, in short, is the subject of this refreshingly artisanal and idiosyncratic magazine.

Flavor & Fortune is scrupulously edited by Dr. Jacqueline M. Newman, a dietetics and nutrition professor emeritus at Queens College in New York. Living in Queens, with its burgeoning Chinese food scene, she became almost obsessive in an interest that prompted many visits to China and elsewhere in search of the best of the best interpretations of China's culinary traditions. To further research, she established the Institute for the Advancement of the Science and Art of Chinese Cuisine and publishes the magazine under that banner.

With a roster of contributors that includes the celebrated chef and author Ken Hom, *Flavor & Fortune* runs well-illustrated articles that highlight obscure and common ingredients and dishes from all regions of China, including recipes; reports on restaurants, food shops, and books; and interesting food lore, customs, and holidays.

The magazine maintains an impressively huge archive on its website, flavorandfortune .com, with more than 1,000 recipes. Just about any Chinese ingredient or dish mentioned in this book can be found on the site, and, for good measure, so can many Japanese, Korean, and Southeast Asian foods.

Anyone who just can't get enough of Chinese food will find that *Flavor & Fortune* at least in part fills in the gaps.

FURTHER INFORMATION: *Flavor & Fortune,* P.O. Box 91, Kings Park, NY, 11754, flavorand fortune.com.

⊢||||||||||||||||||||||||||||||⊣

THE FLOWERING OF FLAVOR

Gau Choy

Garlic Chives

Chinese

First cousins to the tender, slim chives (*Allium schoenoprasum*) that Europeans and Americans value for their gentle oniony flavor and bright color, the pungent, hard- and flat-stemmed *gau choy,* or garlic chives (*Allium tuberosum*) are

preferred in China—hence their other common name, Chinese chives. Their starry white blossoms lend fragrance and a potent garlicky taste to dishes, while the deep-green stems, which tend to be fibrous and papery, are cooked as a vegetable or a garnish to impart an onion-garlic savoriness accented by a hint of grassy freshness.

The white flower buds generally only appear on garlic chives in spring and summer, but the green stems are available all year round,

sold in clipped and bundled form. In Canton, they are considered a special home-cooked treat when stir-fried with peanuts, slivers of silky white tofu, and chopped pickled vegetables, all glossed with a briny combination of soy sauce and oyster sauce. The stems are also delicious gently steamed and served as a garnish for soups or, along with vegetables, shrimp, or pork, as a filling for steamed or fried dumplings. Western cooks, too, can find ample uses for garlic chives. Minced and gently sautéed

The pungent garlic chive is favored in China.

exotic sophistication and a boost of vitamins A and C. Although they're usually available at farmers' markets, they are also easy to grow from seed—well watered and given ample sunlight, they will survive temperate winters outdoors and provide tasty stalks all year.

MAIL ORDER: For garlic chives, Melissa's Produce, tel 800-588-0151, melissas.com; for seeds, Burpee, tel 800-888-1447, burpee.com (search garlic chives); for potted plants, The Growers Exchange, tel 888-829-6201, the growers-exchange.com. **FURTHER INFORMATION AND RECIPES:** *Beyond Bok Choy* by Rosa Lo San Ross (1996); *The Oxford Companion to Food* by Alan Davidson (1999).

until tender in hot butter, they can be beaten into scrambled eggs or omelets, or stirred into cream sauces to top poached fish, for a touch of

||||||||||||||||||||||||||||||||||||||||||||||||||||||||||||||||||||||||||||||||||||||||||||||||||||||||||

*"YOU CAN NEVER HAVE ENOUGH GARLIC. WITH ENOUGH GARLIC,
YOU CAN EAT THE NEW YORK TIMES."*—MORLEY SAFER, *60 MINUTES* CORRESPONDENT

Garlic, White and Black

It doesn't take the nose of an investigative journalist to discover that garlic intensifies the flavor of anything it touches. Whether it is an improvement or a violation depends upon your point of view. This is a love-it-or-hate-it bulb with a vibrant aroma that leaves its mark wherever it reaches—from the hands that prepare it to the breath of those who love to eat it, as well as the cutting boards and knife blades in between. It is by all odds the most pungent member of the *Allium* family, which is saying something considering its siblings are leeks and onions. Many are physically allergic to its powerful oils.

There are dozens of varieties of garlic, which can be divided into two main categories: soft-neck (*Allium sativum sativum,* large plants whose milder bulbs are commonly sold in groceries) and hard-neck (*Allium sativum ophioscorodon,* spicier varieties whose bulbs form around hard, central stalks, also known as garlic scapes, which can be used much like chives).

One bulb of garlic can contain anywhere from five to twenty separate cloves, each wrapped in a papery white skin. So-called elephant garlic, while containing the same number of cloves per bulb, does so in a gigantic way—but the appeal is more to the eye than to the palate, as the flavor is surprisingly mild. All varieties can be prepared in the same manner, whether eaten raw, roasted, sautéed, fried, or pickled.

Native to central Asia, garlic has been cultivated for at least 6,000 years; it's mentioned in both the Bible and the Qur'an, and clay artifacts representing garlic bulbs were found in an Egyptian tomb dated to 3750 B.C. The ancient Greeks and Romans dubbed garlic "the stinking rose," even though it is a member of the lily family, but perhaps they did so because roses are known for their perfume—and so, perversely, is garlic. These days, China harvests the vast majority of the world's garlic, but other major producers include India, South Korea, the

United States (primarily California), and Spain. More and more, in the spirit of the locavore movement, fresh artisan garlic is a favorite in farmers' markets. Crossing geographic and cultural boundaries, the fragrant bulb in its flaky white jacket improves and enriches the cuisine of many nations on earth. In Spain, garlic is chopped and fried in olive oil, then mixed with water, torn chunks of bread, and poached eggs to create the warming, healing soup *sopa de ajo* (see page 267). Italians incorporate it into many dishes, and it shines in *spaghetti aglio-olio*, that pasta tossed only with olive oil (*olio*) and lightly gilded flecks of garlic (*aglio*). In France, it flavors roasted meats and escargots and distinguishes the provençale sauce aioli (see page 93), so popular with seafood, and Eastern European Jewish deli meats and cooked dishes would have no place to go without it. Across Asia and India, garlic heightens stir-fries, curries, and chutneys, and in Morocco it appears in the fiery chile-based condiment harissa. Today's creative chefs have even been toying with it as an ingredient in the pastry kitchen, to say nothing of a seasoning in ice cream. Only in northern Europe does a little garlic go a long way.

Although non–garlic lovers often consider a devotee to be vulgar and lowbrow because of the reeking breath it causes, it is generally beloved for its savory essence and endearing bite. On a more practical note, garlic was probably first consumed for its medicinal properties. Full of antioxidants and vitamin C, it was long used in ancient health remedies, for everything from fatigue to smallpox. French gravediggers in the eighteenth century combined it with wine, believing the combination would prevent the spread of plague, and it was considered a deterrent to pre-vaccine polio, when children were thought to be protected from what was then known as infantile paralysis by wearing cloth-wrapped amulets of garlic around their necks. Soldiers in both World Wars were given garlic to eat as a guard against gangrene, and today, it's believed to fight heart disease, the common cold, and various forms of cancer. Garlic is even believed to have supernatural properties,

famously warding off the vampires who are said to be allergic to its curative elements. Garlic's real magic power, however, is how it can transform the humblest ingredients into many of the world's most delicious and beloved dishes.

Fashion and innovation being what they are, a new variation known as black garlic is currently on the flavor horizon, championed by creative chefs always on the prowl for something new. It is garlic that has been put through several stages of ripening or fermentation by being alternately dried and humidified until it "cooks" to a rich black color and develops overtones that are described as being sweet and somewhere between licorice and chocolate. In fact, many chefs like to call it "the new chocolate" and are using it for desserts. One advantage: no garlicky after-breath.

WHERE: *In San Francisco and Beverly Hills,* The Stinking Rose Garlic Restaurants, thestink ingrose.com. For black garlic, *in New York,* Aldea, tel 212-675-7223, aldearestaurant.com; *in Chicago,* Tru, tel 312-202-0001, trurestaurant .com. **MAIL ORDER:** Melissa's Produce, tel 800-588-0151, melissas.com. **FURTHER INFORMATION AND RECIPES:** *The Garlic Lovers' Cookbook* by Gilroy Garlic Festival Staff (1995); *The Stinking Cookbook* by Jerry Dal Bozzo (2004); food52 .com (search chicken with 40 cloves of garlic; leg of lamb with garlic sauce); cookstr.com (search roasted garlic oil van aken); saveur.com (search gai yahng; korean dipping sauce condiment); tastespotting.com (search madhur jaffrey's garlic ginger cranberry chutney); blackgarlic.com (search black garlic t-bone steak; mushroom and black garlic risotto); girli chef.com (search black garlic chocolate chunk ice cream). To learn how garlic is blackened, naturalhealthmag.com (search garlic but better). **SPECIAL EVENT:** The Gilroy Garlic festival, Gilroy, CA, July, tel 408-842-1625, gilroygarlicfes tival.com. **TIPS:** Although garlic is available peeled, chopped, and packed in oil, or dried and ground into a powder, its flavor is compromised through processing, so whole fresh garlic is by far preferable. To remove garlic's pungent scent from hands, rub them with lemon juice and salt. To clean up breath after indulging, chewing on chlorophyll-rich parsley leaves will do as much good as commercial breath sweeteners and adds valuable nutrients to your diet.

⊢||||||||||||||||||||||||||||||||⊣

BARBECUE'S SECRET INGREDIENT

Hai Xian Jiang

Hoisin Sauce

Chinese

H*ai xian jiang,* which the English-speaking world knows as hoisin sauce, may sound like a well-worn food cliché but is in fact a flavor base that lies at the very heart of the Chinese food tradition. Thick, richly dark, bittersweet, and plummy, it makes for a delicious, terrifically multipurpose ingredient. Although its name is the Chinese word for seafood (as pronounced in the Cantonese dialect), it is in fact neither made with nor generally served with fish. Its complex flavor is instead a result of ingredients that include winey, earthy fermented soybeans, sugar, garlic, black pepper, anise-accented five-spice powder, chile peppers, and vinegar.

A favorite in dishes all over the Chinese menu, most notably Peking duck (see page 748) and moo shu pork, hoisin sauce is perhaps most closely associated with Cantonese cuisine, especially barbecued spareribs (see page 771) and roast pork. Indeed, the sauce's mellow sweetness and versatility make it an excellent accompaniment to any meat that comes off the grill, perfect for including in marinades and bastes—which is why it has become a premier "secret ingredient" on the barbecue circuit in the U.S.

MAIL ORDER: amazon.com (search koon chun hoisin; lee kum kee hoisin, amoy hoi sin); asianfoodgrocer.com (search lee kum kee hoisin). **FURTHER INFORMATION AND RECIPES:** epicurious.com (search balsamic hoisin sauce; spicy hoisin chicken). **TIP:** Hoisin sauce can be kept for up to a year in a tightly covered jar in the refrigerator.

⊢||||||||||||||||||||||||||||||||⊣

ALL STEAMED UP OVER PORK AND EGGS

Hom Don Jing Gee Yok

Steamed Pork with Salted Duck Eggs

Chinese (Cantonese)

S o humble is this gentle, comforting dish—usually a home-cooked treat—that it is difficult to find on the menus of Chinese restaurants, even those specializing in the cuisine of Canton. Fortunately, it's easy to prepare. It begins, as so many

Chinese dishes do, with finely ground pork bolstered with chopped water chestnuts, rice wine, soy sauce, a little cornstarch, and the raw, salt-cured duck egg called *hom don* (see page 769). The lightly seasoned pork is patted into a thick pancake onto a heatproof, rimmed plate; the egg is separated and the white is glossed over the meat as the yolk slips into a well that has been pressed into the center of the pancake; and the whole is sprinkled with minced scallions. Placed in a bamboo steamer for about fifteen minutes, the meat emerges pale pink and moist, studded with nice crisp bits of water chestnut; the yolk remains a bit runny, just enough to create a rich, sunny sauce.

If this sounds like more than you can tackle at home, try asking for it by name (*hom don jing gee yok*) at an authentic Cantonese restaurant. Your servers just might be willing to convey the request to the kitchen, where it can almost surely be met. The dish may well be a nostalgic taste of home for many Cantonese, perhaps including your chef.

WHERE: *In New York*, Amazing 66, tel 212-334-0099, amazing66.com. **MAIL ORDER:** For salted duck eggs, amazon.com (search chinese century eggs). **FURTHER INFORMATION AND RECIPES:** *The Chinese Cookbook* by Craig Claiborne and Virginia Lee (1972); *The Thousand Recipe Chinese Cookbook* by Gloria Bley Miller (1984); atablefortwo.com.au (search steamed pork mince with salted duck egg). **TIP:** If you can't find salted duck eggs, use fresh chicken eggs sprinkled with salt.

A SPICE WITH A LOT OF BUZZ

Huajiao

Sichuan Peppercorns

Chinese (Sichuanese)

With their woodsy, aromatic earthiness and lip-tingling, addictive, slow-burn heat, Sichuan peppercorns (*Zanthoxylum simulans*) are among the world's most intriguing spices. The hallmark flavor of the cuisine of western China, where they are called *huajiao*, they are not true peppercorns, but rather the red-brown berries of a large, prickly shrub.

Native to Sichuan Province and cultivated there possibly as far back as the Neolithic period, the spice is used to fire up marinades, roasted meats, fish, poultry, and cooking oil for a number of classic regional dishes, including tea-smoked duck (see page 797), hot-and-sour cabbage, barbecued spareribs (see facing page), and dry-fried chicken. It's also essential to five-spice powder, a common Chinese seasoning blend that typically also includes cinnamon, cloves, fennel seed, and star anise.

Prized for their sensory effect as much as for their flavor, the peppercorns trigger a distinctive buzzing tingle on the lips (called *ma la* in Chinese) that surprises novices and thrills pepper's legions of devotees.

Further adding to the raffish allure of these wrinkled, mahogany-hued berries is the fact that, from 1968 to 2005, the United States banned their importation on the grounds that they could potentially carry a canker harmful to citrus crops. Although the ban was widely flouted—many vendors of Chinese medicine sold the peppercorns secretly and chefs found ways to get them—it did make the spice harder to come by, and that much more tantalizing for its rarity. To have the ban lifted, Chinese exporters agreed to heat-treat their peppercorns to kill any traces of the virus. Die-hard aficionados bemoan this treatment, which tempers the spice's potency, but it assures a steady supply for U.S. fans of authentic Sichuan cuisine and of the smoky, lemony heat that only huajiao can provide.

MAIL ORDER: amazon.com (search olive nation sichuan peppercorns). **FURTHER INFORMATION AND RECIPES:** *Mrs. Chiang's Szechwan Cookbook* by Jung-Feng Chiang with Ellen Schrecker and John Schrecker (1987); *Shark's Fin and Sichuan Pepper* by Fuchsia Dunlop (2009); saveur.com (search capital of heat). **TIP:** To experience the full effect of the peppercorns, toast them in a dry frying pan over moderate heat for 7 to 8 minutes. Store toasted peppercorns in a jar with a tight-fitting lid in a cool, dry place; they will keep for several months. Crush them just before using to release their aromatic oils.

—||||||||||||||||||||||||||||||||||||||||—

TEXAS, MOVE OVER

Kao-Pai-Ku

Barbecued Spareribs

Chinese

Long before regional barbecue became a nationwide obsession, Chinese restaurants were beguiling their clientele with their chewy but tender, sweet-and-sour spareribs. Succulently mellow, with a caramelized crust and crackling fat, the ribs are from the part of the pig adjacent to the belly—where bacon comes from—and thus are full of rich flavor.

Barbecued in the Cantonese *char siu* style, the ribs acquire their distinctive lacquered exterior and zesty taste from a marinade of honey and salty-sweet hoisin sauce (see page 769)—the dark, thick condiment made from fermented soybeans, vinegar, garlic, sugar, and spices, usually five-spice powder (anise, cinnamon, cloves, Sichuan pepper, and fennel or licorice root). The hoisin sauce tints the ribs their characteristic mahogany color and provides an intense savoriness, while the honey caramelizes to a crackling, sugary char. Unlike barbecued ribs from the American South, which are most often rubbed with spices and then smoked on a grill before being "mopped" with

Pork spareribs with rice and greens

tomato-and-vinegar-based sauces, Chinese-style ribs marinate in the hoisin mixture before being slowly roasted. Although delicious on their own, gnawed straight off the bone and perhaps paired with cold Chinese beer, they are occasionally garnished with a sprinkle of sesame seeds or a dab of hot Chinese mustard.

WHERE: *In New York,* Red Farm at two locations, redfarmnyc.com. **FURTHER INFORMATION AND RECIPES:** *Raichlen on Ribs, Ribs, Outrageous Ribs* by Steven Raichlen (2006); *Mastering the Art of Chinese Cooking* by Eileen Yin-Fei Lo (2009); saveur.com (search chinese barbecued spareribs); cookstr.com (search shun lee's bbq ribs); epicurious.com (search chinese bistro ribs; chinese hawaiian ribs). **SEE ALSO:** Bulgogi, page 829; Barbecue, page 526.

━━━━━━━━━━━━━━━━━━━━━━━━━━━━━━━━━━━━ ╢||||||||||||||||||||||||||||||||||╟ ━━━━━━━━━━━━━━━━━━

A SWEET OLD CHESTNUT

Li-Tzu-Tan-Kao

Peking Dust

Chinese

F avored in northern China since at least the third century B.C., Chinese chestnuts (*Castanea mollissima*) make up the simple but delicious Peking dust, one of the best festive desserts in the country's cuisine. Akin to the French-Italian chestnut

dessert Mont Blanc, and commonly served at the conclusion of elegant Chinese banquets, Peking dust is a pyramid of cooked, finely pureed chestnuts spread over a base of whipped cream, a most unusual ingredient in what is an almost entirely dairy-free cuisine. (The dessert was perhaps originally developed by European expats in Beijing, and named for the city's notorious dustiness.) The chestnuts here are unsweetened, enjoyed for their pure, wild, woodsy flavor, with sugar added only to the whipped cream. Although they are nontraditional additions, the puree isn't harmed by a sprinkling of cinnamon or a light moistening of

rum or vanilla. Once mounded on a serving platter, the dessert is decorated with glazed whole chestnuts, pecan halves, or the beloved candied walnuts (see page 792), for a nice bit of crunch.

MAIL ORDER: For fresh chestnuts, Washington Chestnut Company, tel 306-966-7158, washing tonchestnut.com; for frozen and canned chestnuts, Marky's, tel 800-522-8427, markys.com. **FURTHER INFORMATION AND RECIPES:** *Chinese Cooking* by Emily Hahn (1968); *The Thousand Recipe Chinese Cookbook* by Gloria Bley Miller (1984); food.com (search peking dust); chinese food.about.com (search peking dust).

━━━━━━━━━━━━━━━━━━━━━━━━━━━━━━━━━━━━ ╢||||||||||||||||||||||||||||||||||╟ ━━━━━━━━━━━━━━━━━━

A WELCOME STING

Liang Ban Hai Zhe

Sichuan Cold Jellyfish Salad

Chinese (Sichuanese)

A slippery, stinging menace to beachgoers around the world, jellyfish are the translucent, umbrella-shaped members of the invertebrate *phylum Cnidaria*, a collection of hundreds of species of beautiful and occasionally deadly coastal

water creatures that have been populating oceans for more than 500 million years. For at least the last thousand of those years, the Chinese have been cooking up the edible varieties they call *hai zhe,* prized for their cartilaginous crunch

and slight chewiness, along with a mild flavor that is easily enhanced by sauces.

Sichuan jellyfish salad is a cool, crackly delight, notable for the inclusion of the region's classic spices, including the signature Sichuan pepper (see page 770), plus ginger, garlic, top-quality soy sauce, and scallions. Depending on the cook, the hot chiles typical of Sichuan cuisine might also be added to the dish, for a sting that is very real, but far more benign than that of a live jellyfish.

Eaten straight from the sea, jellyfish would be impossibly tough, so their preparation is of prime importance. Most of the edible jellyfish belong to the order Rhizostomae and have relatively large and rigid bodies. (One prized variety is found along the coast of the state of Georgia—in 2013, three million pounds were exported to China.) Once harvested, they are thoroughly cleaned, then cut into thin strips and preserved or dried in salt. Then, only after they are soaked in water overnight and briefly boiled, are they tossed in their aromatic dressing.

WHERE: *In Shanghai,* Fortune Palace, Jin Jiang Hotel, tel 86/21-3218-9888, jinjiang hotels.com; *in New York,* Wu Liang Ye, tel 212-398-2308, wuliangyenyc.com; *in Washington, DC,* New Big Wong, tel 202-628-0491; *in Houston,* East Wall Restaurant, tel 713-981-8803; *in San Gabriel, CA,* Shanghai No. 1 Seafood Village, tel 626-282-1777; *in Toronto,* Crown Princess Fine Dining, tel 416-923-8784, crown-princess.ca. **FURTHER INFORMATION AND RECIPES:** *The Thousand Recipe Chinese Cookbook* by Gloria Bley Miller (1984); food.com (search sesame jellyfish; sesame jellyfish with chili sauce); thehongkong cookery.com (search jellyfish salad).

━┤||||||||||||||||||||||||||├━

A PEARL OF A FRUIT

Lychee

Chinese

The prickly-skinned lychee is China's most famous fruit, and for good reason. Inside its spiny, rosy skin lies a silken, milky-white sphere of intensely juicy pulp, with a flavor that is floral and subtly sweet, and hinting at dessert wine.

At the center of the strikingly refreshing fruit is a single, shiny dark-brown seed, inedible and easily discarded.

Grown on large evergreen trees that thrive in subtropical climates, lychees have been cultivated in South China since at least the first century B.C., and they've been the subject of legend and lore ever since. Lychee obsession was a hallmark of various dynasties, most especially during the later period of the Ming Dynasty, the late sixteenth and early seventeenth centuries, when the members of secret lychee clubs

Southern China's native berry

supposedly met in temples and ate hundreds of the fruits in a single sitting.

Today, lychees are still most extensively cultivated in China, but are also found in a narrow stretch of Southeast Asia that extends from Thailand to northern India, and in other warm, wet places such as Brazil, Hawaii, and Florida. The fruit travels well if it's picked just before it ripens, making it easy to find fresh lychees during their very short season, which generally lasts from May through June. The fruits may also be dried whole (thus known as "lychee nuts"), the pulp becoming raisinlike, or may be peeled, pitted, and canned.

In China, lychees might appear alongside pork in a stir-fry or be fermented into a sweet dessert wine. Nothing, however, matches the decadent elegance of a bowl of the fresh stuff, peeled and served chilled on a bed of crushed ice.

Mail order: For fresh lychees in season, lychee-based products, and general information, lycheesonline.com; Specialty Produce, tel 619-295-3172, specialtyproduce.com (search lychees). **Further information and recipes:** *Uncommon Fruits and Vegetables* by Elizabeth Schneider (2010); cookingchanneltv.com (search cucumber lychee salad); epicurious.com (search coconut and lychee sorbet). **Tip:** Fresh lychee nuts should be stored in the refrigerator and eaten within three days or they will lose flavor.

⊢||||||||||||||||||||||||||||||||||⊣

CRUNCHY, SUBTLY SWEET, COOLING

Matai

Water Chestnuts

Chinese

A singularly crunchy delight, the water chestnut, or *matai* in Chinese, has a refreshing, icy bite that adds textural interest to many Chinese dishes, particularly those made with finely ground meat. Not actually a chestnut, or any

other kind of nut, the water chestnut (*Eleocharis dulcis*) is the edible tuber of an aquatic plant, tasting much like the South American tuber jicama when eaten fresh and raw.

Native to China, water chestnuts grow along the muddy edges of ponds, lakes, and flood plains and are harvested for their corms—the fat, water-storing offshoots of their roots. Arriving on American shores with the first waves of Chinese immigrants, they quickly became a staple on restaurant menus, appearing in stir-fries, soups, salads, and meat and fish dishes. As a result of that popularity, they have long been peeled and canned for easy accessibility.

Because of their crispness and subtly sweet flavor, water chestnuts offer an especially welcome note of variety in many traditional, soft-textured, saucy regional Chinese dishes, and their mild flour is used as a thickener or to make jellylike sweets that are favorite dim sum treats. Originally prized for their medicinal qualities—very high in potassium and fiber, they are considered by the Chinese to be a "cooling" food that reduces fever and detoxifies the body—they have been cultivated for centuries in rice paddies, and are traditionally enjoyed fresh or quickly blanched, for maximum crunch. Although they maintain their texture even when canned, their flavor is far superior

Peeling a bounty of water chestnuts at a market in Asia

when fresh; for that reason they're worth tracking down at Asian markets, where they are usually available year-round.

WHERE: *In New York,* The Dumpling Man, tel 212-505-2121, dumplingman.com. **MAIL ORDER:** For fresh sliced water chestnuts, Melissa's Produce, tel 800-588-0151, melissas.com; for canned water chestnuts, amazon.com. **FURTHER INFORMATION AND RECIPES:** *Revolutionary Chinese Cookbook* by Fuchsia Dunlop (2007); *Beyond Bok Choy* by Rosa Lo San Ross (1996); chinese food.about.com (search water chestnuts); cookstr.com (search water chestnuts sugar snap peas and shiitakes); epicurious.com (search water chestnut cake). **TIP:** Fresh water chestnuts should look fat and glossy, with no soft spots. Thoroughly scrub and peel them before use, and blanch them if they won't be cooked before eating—they can transmit water-borne illnesses if improperly handled.

||||||||||||||||||||||||||||||||

THE MUSHROOM THAT'S ALL EARS

Mu Er

Tree Ear Mushrooms

Chinese

A rare case of truth in advertising, the tree ear mushroom (*Auricularia auricula* or *Auricularia polytricha*) is just what it sounds like: a floppy, ear-shaped, wrinkly and ruffled fungus that grows wild on fallen hardwood and coniferous trees in forests around the world. Known in Mandarin Chinese as wood ear (*mu er*) or cloud ear (*yun er*) and as *wan yee* in the Cantonese dialect, they are the star ingredient in popular Chinese dishes such as hot and sour soup (see page 781) and moo shu pork. Always sold dried, and rehydrated in warm water

The chewy, ear-shaped fungus

before being used, the mushrooms have a subtly earthy flavor, but it's the texture, at once chewy and slippery and crunchy, that really distinguishes them. Tree ears have the distinct ability to retain their texture during long cooking, and to absorb the flavors of surrounding ingredients.

Tree ears are also believed to have medicinal properties, most especially as a palliative to problems of the heart—physical problems, that is. A groundbreaking study released by researchers at the University of Minnesota in the early 1980s showed that tree ears may slow the tendency of the blood to clot, thus combating heart disease. As for other matters of the heart, who's to say that love couldn't bloom over a platter of sweet-and-savory moo shu pork, studded with crunchy tree ears?

MAIL ORDER: amazon.com (search mushroom house dried wood ear). **FURTHER INFORMATION AND RECIPES:** *The Thousand Recipe Chinese Cookbook* by Gloria Bley Miller (1984); *The Shun Lee Cookbook* by Michael Tong (2010); cookstr.com (search fortune noodle meatball soup); chinesefood.about.com (search cloud ears; wood ears). **TIP:** Dried tree ears will keep indefinitely if stored in a cool, dry place in an airtight container. Before using, soak them in warm water for 20 to 30 minutes.

—||||||||||||||||||||||||||||||||—

A SLURPY FEAST IN A BOWL

Niu Rou Mian

Taiwanese Beef Noodle Soup

Chinese (Taiwanese)

Redolent of anise, steaming bowls of long, soft noodles topped with tidbits of tender beef in an intensely spiced gravy are a much-favored street food in Taiwan, particularly in the capital city of Taipei. Something of a regional staple, this

heady soup, called *niu rou mian,* is dispensed from small stands and in noodle shops as an inexpensive and restorative one-dish meal. Part of the venerable Chinese noodle tradition, it was introduced to Taiwan by mainland Chinese soldiers in the late 1940s and immediately took hold. The original version showed fiery Sichuan influences, but in Taiwan, more temperate flavoring, such as mellow red-bean paste, ginger, and sweet spring onions, prevails.

Cilantro adorns an earthy, meaty noodle soup.

Because beef was not a traditional or plentiful ingredient in Taiwan when the dish took hold, the vendors in the cities' marketplaces improvised with cuts of offal, mainly stomach and heart, and, as with so many soul-food traditions, these humble parts have become beloved classic ingredients. The sweetly aromatic broth is garnished with pickled mustard greens and fresh cilantro, which are mixed into the seductively silky, piping-hot noodles for a fresh and tangy flavor contrast as they entwine in the bowl. Although they are enjoyed equally for breakfast or a midnight snack, Taiwanese beef noodles are most popular as a hearty and complete lunch. Usually purchased from street vendors, the noodles are generally negotiated in crowded spaces, requiring the eater to be quite adept at slurping, chewing, and deftly wielding chopsticks on slippery noodles—usually while standing. It's an inelegant business, but beef noodle devotees will tell you that the messy, communal aspect of the tradition actually adds zest to the flavor.

Where: *In Taipei,* Yong Kang Beef Noodles, tel 886/2-2351-1051; Old Zhang's Beef Noodles, tel 886/2-2396-0927; *in Queens,* Main Street Imperial Taiwanese Gourmet, tel 718-886-8788. **Further information and recipes:** *Chinese Cooking: Taiwanese Style* by Lee-Hwa Lin (1991); epicurious.com (search taiwanese beef noodle soup); thekitchn.com (search taiwanese beef noodle soup); youtube.com (search taiwanese beef noodle soup); for an instructional video, wokwithnana.tumblr.com (click Archive, then Taiwanese Beef Noodle Soup).

├IIIIIIIIIIIIIIIIIIIIIIIIIIIIIIIIIIIIIII┤

NOT THE POPEYE KIND

Ong Choy

Water Spinach

Chinese, Southeast Asian

Not really spinach at all, this verdant, slender-leafed green should be cause for celebration—particularly during late spring and early summer, when it is abundant. Known in Southeast Asia as *kangkong* and botanically as

Ipomoea aquatica, so-called water spinach has a less mineral, more peppery flavor than its namesake green, suggestive instead of watercress or young and tender dandelion greens. And it truly is more akin to watercress, in that they both grow in water. But, like spinach, *ong choy* has a high water content and cooks down very quickly, its firm stems and silky leaves creating an appealing textural contrast.

Whether of the pale green variety that the Chinese prefer or the darker leaves that appeal more to the Thais and Vietnamese, the plant's pungency lends itself to several preparations. Perhaps most delicious is a dish of ong choy quickly stir-fried with garlic and lusciously preserved bean curd, resulting in a flavor so rich it is hard to believe that no meat is involved. For a palate-tingling effect, salty shrimp paste is added in China; in Thailand and Vietnam, a similar effect comes from the fermented fish sauce *nam pla* or *nuoc mam* and flecks of pickled ginger. Either way, the plain steamed white rice served alongside provides an excellent foil for the flavor and texture of the greens.

WHERE: *In New York,* Congee Village at two locations, congeevillagerestaurants.com; *in Queens,* Main Street Imperial Taiwanese Gourmet, tel 718-886-8788. **MAIL ORDER:** For seeds, Ali Express, aliexpress.com (search ong choy). **FURTHER INFORMATION AND RECIPES:** *Beyond Bok Choy* by Rosa Lo San Ross (1996); *The Oxford Companion to Food* by Alan Davidson (1999); foodnetwork.com (search stir fried water spinach); saveur.com (search water spinach garlic fermented tofu). **TIP:** Like all dark-green, leafy vegetables, ong choy is high in both iron and antioxidants, nutritional benefits that are well preserved by the stir-fry method, which cooks the greens in their own healthful juices. **SEE ALSO:** Watercress, page 863.

├IIIIIIIIIIIIIIIIIIIIIIIIIIIIIIIIIIIIIII┤

BLACK DRAGON BREW

Oolong Tea

Chinese

An aromatic and full-bodied tea that is among the world's best-loved varieties and a darling of connoisseurs, oolong lies between fully oxidized black teas and unoxidized green teas. Known in China as *wu long*, which translates to "black dragon," oolong's leaves are picked primarily from *Camellia sinensis* bushes in the Fujian and Guangdong provinces, along China's southeastern coast. Brewed oolong can range from pale green to deep amber-gold, and the exact character of the tea varies based on where it was grown and how it was processed. In general, though, Chinese oolongs are bold and earthy, with toasty and sometimes fruity notes that add up to an eye-opening drink. During their oxidation, which begins in sunlight and is completed in a warm room, oolong leaves curl up into small twists. This means they require multiple steepings to fully release their essence. Some varieties, such

Tea is served in Hong Kong.

as Fujian's coveted *tieguanyin*, require up to twelve infusions to reach peak flavor (but you can enjoy all the steepings along the way).

But there's more to oolong than its complex taste. The inhabitants of China's oolong-growing regions have long known of the tea's healthful properties and, in traditional Chinese medicine, it is prescribed for spleen, stomach, and kidney disorders, among a host of other ailments. Modern science has confirmed the tea's health-giving properties, having found that it is high in polyphenols, a compound that scientists believe helps reduce fats such as triglycerides and remove toxins such as cell-damaging free radicals in our bodies. More whimsically, in Fujian, there is a well-known legend about an official of the Ming dynasty who was deathly ill but was saved by drinking oolong. To honor the plant, he is said to have had royal red robes draped around the tea bushes to protect them. The result: a prized tea called Da Hong Pao (Royal Red Robe)—one of the most coveted varieties of oolong.

WHERE: *In New York*, McNulty's Tea & Coffee, tel 800-356-5200, mcnultys.com; *in Northampton, MA*, Tea Trekker, tel 413-584-5116, teatrekker.com; *in Vancouver,* The Chinese Tea Shop, tel 604-633-1322, thechineseteashop.com. **FURTHER INFORMATION:** oolongteainfo.com. **TIP:** For prime flavor, before steeping oolong, rinse the leaves in a teapot with hot water. Strain off the water and add boiling water for steeping.

AN EGG THAT AGES WELL

Pidan

Preserved Duck Egg

Chinese

With their creamy texture and rich, faintly earthy flavor, big, yolky duck eggs are great favorites in Chinese cuisine, whether eaten alone or incorporated into other dishes. One of the most famous—or infamous—duck egg preparations is the so-called thousand-year-old egg, or *pidan,* a fresh duck egg nested in a mix of lime-rich clay, ashes, and salt for about three months. Dug up and served gelled, with a dip of soy sauce, rice wine, and minced ginger, or boiled and cut into quarters to show off a translucent, pearly gray exterior and a boldly jade-green yolk, the egg's flavor suggests sulphur,

An infamous Chinese delicacy

smoke, and a funky ripeness that is either loved or hated. Often appearing at banquets and rarely prepared at home, thousand-year-old eggs (sometimes called Ming Dynasty eggs) are sold ready-aged in Chinese markets.

Less daunting preparations include *hom don,* salt-preserved eggs, and *cha ye dan,* tea eggs; both can be prepared with chicken eggs, although duck are much preferred. For salt eggs, the raw eggs are soaked in brine for about a month and then boiled, shelled, and quartered or chopped into dishes like steamed pork with salted egg (see page 769). The firm saltiness of the whites and the deep red-orange of the yolks are a favorite way to enrich and enliven congee (see page 757), and the eggs are also baked whole into traditional mooncakes, pastries for celebrating the harvest festival.

Tea eggs are as pretty as they are tasty. While they may be simply flavored and colored with tea alone, they are far more intriguing when spiced. In such a preparation, hard-cooked eggs in their shells are gently crackled and resimmered for close to three hours in water dosed with tea leaves (preferably oolong, see previous entry), star anise, cinnamon, cloves, soy sauce, pinches of brown sugar, and perhaps a few drops of rice wine or vinegar. Drained, chilled, and peeled, they reveal lovely marbled patterns of ivory, pink, and golden brown. A favorite food at China's night markets and a few Japanese restaurants, they are also often made at home and kept on hand for a quick and flavorful snack.

WHERE: *In New York,* Amazing66, tel 212-334-0099, amazing66.com; Congee Village at two locations, congeevillagerestaurants.com. **MAIL ORDER:** amazon.com (search cooked salted duck eggs). **FURTHER INFORMATION AND RECIPES:** *The Thousand Recipe Chinese Cookbook* by Gloria Bley Miller (1984); *The Chinese Cookbook* by Craig Claiborne and Virginia Lee (1972); instructables.com (search century eggs); silk roadgourmet.com (search making 1000 year eggs).

BLACK MAGIC CHICKEN

Qi Guo Ji

Steamed Chicken Soup

Chinese (Yunnanese)

This magnificent cure-all will definitely ease a head cold, but it's not for the faint of heart: Spiked with fresh ginger, scallions, and rice wine, a bowl of the clear, savory elixir has a nose-tingling aroma and packs a powerful punch. The soup

is traditional in China's southern Yunnan province, where it is made in a special steamer—a

stout, lidded terra-cotta pot with a hollow chimney at its core (think Bundt pan). Placed atop a pot of boiling water, the chicken-and-spice-filled steamer slowly sweats a whole chicken in a bit of rich chicken stock, drawing out its savory juices for maximum flavor. Prior to serving, the soup is skimmed and strained. The ginger and scallions are scrapped, and the chicken is set aside to use in a separate dish (although some cooks gently pull off pieces of the meat and float it in the broth).

Any chicken will do, but traditional Chinese cooks favor the Silkie breed—*wu gu ji,* meaning black-boned, which describes its most striking characteristic, along with its dark-gray skin and meat. Hailed for their medicinal and energy-boosting properties since at least the eighth century, and revered for their distinctly gamy flavor, Silkies give the broth a silvery tint and add depth to the flavor. The black birds are hard to come by (you may be able to find them at a live poultry market in Chinatowns), but they are sure to supercharge the intensity—and, perhaps, the curative powers—of this excellent chicken soup.

WHERE: *In Singapore,* Seng Kee Black Herbal Chicken Soup, tel 65/9001-4000; Tian Tian Hainanese Chicken Rice at three locations, tiantianchickenrice.com. **MAIL ORDER:** For the traditional Yunnan Steamer, Little e Pottery, littleepottery.com (search yunnan). **FURTHER INFORMATION AND RECIPES:** *The Whole World Loves Chicken Soup* by Mimi Sheraton (2000); cookstr.com (search yunnan steamed chicken soup); nytimes.com (search yunnan steamed chicken soup); chinasichuanfood.com (click Archive, then Silkie Chicken Soup). **SEE ALSO:** Golden Yoich, page 439; Chawanmushi, page 801.

ONE SALTY BIRD

Salt-Roasted Chicken

Chinese (Cantonese, Hakka)

Despite its preparation, this Cantonese specialty emerges from the oven moist and flavorful, not the least bit salty beyond the pleasantly saline undertones of its parchment-crisp, golden skin. To make salt-roasted chicken, a cleaned, plucked

bird is hung or laid out on a rack for three or four hours in a cool, airy spot, or in the refrigerator overnight, thus allowing its skin to dry and become taut, similar to the preparation of Peking duck (see page 748). The roasting vessel is a cast-iron or enameled cast-iron casserole, into which go three to five pounds of coarse salt for a very slow heating on the stove. A quantity of the hot salt is scooped out and set aside to make room for the chicken, then is packed over the bird. The covered casserole is set in a very hot oven for one and a half to two hours; at the end of the cooking time, the salt will be compacted into a solid crust. Once the crust is broken open and the chicken lifted out, excess salt

A salt crust leaves behind crunchy skin and moist meat.

is brushed from its surface and the bird is ready to serve.

A centuries-old Chinese technique, the salt-roasting method is also favored in parts of Europe and has been adopted by some American chefs. The heavy blanket of salt allows for even heating and crispy skin, ensuring moistness without the need to baste or turn the chicken as it roasts. No surprise, then, that salt-roasting does as much for whole fish (a particular specialty of Spain) as for chicken. In the Cantonese tradition, the finished salt-roasted chicken is chopped with a cleaver into small nuggets—succulent meat, crunchy bones, crisp skin and all—to be dipped into ginger-zapped soy sauce.

WHERE: *In New York,* Congee Village at two locations, congeevillagerestaurants.com; *in San Francisco,* Ton Kiang Restaurant, tel 415-752-4440, tonkiang.net. **FURTHER INFORMATION AND RECIPES:** *The Thousand Recipe Chinese Cookbook* by Gloria Bley Miller (1984); foodandwine.com (search hakka salt baked chicken); splendid table.org (search salt roasted chicken).

CHICKEN SOUP'S MOST POTENT RIVAL

Seun Lot Tong

Hot and Sour Soup

Chinese (Sichuanese)

The palliative effects of chicken soup—the famous "Jewish penicillin"—pale beside the powers of this age-old Chinese brew, a culinary superstar that also happens to be one of the world's best remedies for a head cold. Hot and sour soup began its steamy, curative existence in the Sichuan province of western China. The two most important ingredients, and the source of its name, are pepper (usually white pepper, although chile oil or red pepper flakes are sometimes employed in its stead), which makes it hot, and *shaoxing jiu,* rice wine, which makes it sour. Because fresh vegetables are scarce in the region—then and even now—a couple of dried ingredients are included, such as tree ear mushrooms (see page 775) and daylily buds, to be revived by the steaming hot broth. To these are added soft, custardy tofu, crisp bamboo shoots, and a gloss of sesame oil. Pork and pork blood make up the classic protein components, although chicken is considered an acceptable, if nontraditional, substitute. The most important thing is that the soup be hot—in both temperature and taste. Not so hot as to scald the throat or the tongue, but enough to heat the mouth as it passes through, and generate lots of steam, which is seen as life-giving in Chinese culture. Almost as important is the texture. Hot and sour soup should be thick and slightly slippery, so that it goes down easily and is richly satisfying, with intermittent soft clumps to chew on. If all goes well, it is sure to cure whatever ails you, whether it's hunger pangs, sniffles, or your psyche.

WHERE: *In Shanghai,* Fortune Palace, Jin Jiang Hotel, tel 86/21-3218-9888, jinjianghotels .com; *in New York,* Wu Liang Ye, tel 212-398-2308, wuliangyenyc.com; *in Chicago,* Lao Sze Chuan, tel 312-326-5040, tonygourmetgroup .com; *in San Francisco,* Ton Kiang, tel 415-387-8273, tonkiang.net; *in Toronto,* Crown Princess Fine Dining, tel 416-923-8784, crown-princess .ca. **FURTHER INFORMATION AND RECIPES:** *The Shun Lee Cookbook* by Michael Tong (2007); *Sichuan Cooking* by Fuchsia Dunlop (2003); epicurious .com (search hot and sour soup).

—||||||||||||||||||||||||||||||||||||||—

Shellfish in Black Bean Sauce

Chinese

Although the familiar dark and earthy black bean sauce—made from fermented soybeans rather than the black beans common to Mexican cuisine—often adorns fish and crustaceans such as shrimp, lobster, and crab, it is perhaps most mouthwatering when simmered with mollusks: mussels, oysters, long amber-shelled razor clams or their small, sweet counterparts, the tiny sea snails called periwinkles, or some combination thereof. The shells themselves, left on during cooking and serving, catch and hold delectable little mouthfuls of the winey fermented beans, enhanced by soy sauce and thick, rich oyster sauce, sharp bits of ginger, scallions, and garlic, and in the Sichuan version (as opposed to the Cantonese), flecks of hot dried red chile peppers, all sprightly contrasts to the briny, buttery meat within. It's a good idea to eat the mollusks over small bowls of steamed white rice, so all of the drippings collect and make the rice sweetly saucy.

Shellfish in Black Bean Sauce

*Serves 4, accompanied by other dishes
in a typical Chinese meal*

4 tablespoons fermented black beans
1 tablespoon freshly squeezed lemon juice
⅓ cup dry sherry or rice wine
*6 tablespoons peanut oil, sesame oil,
    or a vegetable oil other than olive oil*
*1 tablespoon finely minced peeled
    fresh ginger*
2 cloves garlic, minced
*1 of the following: 3 pounds small clams
    or razor clams, alive in their shells;
    24 oysters, opened just before cooking
    but left on the half shell without severing
    the muscle that connects to the shell;
    3 pounds mussels, scrubbed and
    debearded; or 3 pounds periwinkles,*
*scrubbed, soaked for 24 hours in a bowl
    of water in the refrigerator, and drained*
2 tablespoons soy sauce
2 tablespoons oyster sauce
*2 tablespoons finely chopped scallions,
    both green and white portions*
Sugar, to taste
Salt, to taste
*2 tablespoons cornstarch diluted in
    ½ cup cold water*
Fresh cilantro sprigs, for serving
Unseasoned steamed white rice, for serving

1. Combine the fermented black beans, lemon juice, and sherry or rice wine in a small bowl and set aside.

2. Heat a wok or cast-iron skillet over high heat and add the oil, swirling it evenly over the pan. Add the ginger and garlic and cook until they lose their raw smell, 1 to 2 minutes, being careful not to let the garlic turn brown.

3. Add the shellfish, stirring to coat them with the ginger and garlic. If you are using oysters on the half shell, place them carefully in the wok or skillet, flesh side up, and continue with the other steps gently, trying not to let them flip over.

4. Pour in the black bean mixture and let simmer for 1 minute before adding the soy sauce, oyster sauce, and scallions. Cover the wok or skillet and let the shellfish cook until they open, or until the oyster flesh is cooked, 3 minutes at most. Season with sugar and salt.

5. Stir in the dissolved cornstarch and let the sauce simmer, uncovered, until it becomes slightly opaque and thickens to the consistency of thin cream, about 1 minute.

6. Serve the shellfish at once, garnished with cilantro sprigs and with lots of steamed white rice alongside.

WHERE: *In New York*, Oriental Garden, tel 212-619-0085, orientalgardenny.com; Congee Village at two locations, congeevillagerestaurants .com; *in Washington, DC,* New Big Wong, tel 202-628-0491; *in Richmond, VA,* Peter Chang's China Café, tel 804-364-16788, peterchangrva .com; *in Chicago,* Yan Bang Cai, tel 312-842-7818, yanbangcaichicago.com. **MAIL ORDER:** For fermented black beans, igourmet, tel 877-446-8763, igourmet.com.

‖‖‖‖‖‖‖‖‖‖‖‖‖‖‖‖‖‖‖‖‖‖‖‖‖‖‖‖

THAT ESSENTIAL WOODLAND FLAVOR

Dried Shiitake (Black) Mushrooms

Chinese, Japanese

Cooked simply, bok choy can be a disappointingly subtle vegetable—watery and largely unmemorable. But flavored with black mushrooms (which is what the Chinese call dried shiitake mushrooms), soy sauce, and garlic in the classic Chinese preparation, the cabbage is imbued with deep, foresty flavors that turn it into a succulent treat.

It's not the only dish that owes its savory depth to the mushrooms, a woodland fungus that grows on the bark of rotting wood and has been cultivated for centuries in China and Japan. Fresh, the flat-topped mushroom is known for a meaty texture and a rich, earthy, and almost equally meaty flavor. Dried, its woodsy flavor is concentrated to a pungency that frequently finds its way into soups and sauces.

The dried mushrooms add depth to a variety of dishes.

The dried mushrooms must soak in warm water to soften up before use, and during that time all of their attributes intensify—so that the mushrooms' essential flavor becomes even stronger, and the soaking liquid becomes a wonderful side project, an especially savory addition to whatever dish the mushrooms will enhance. The advantage of all dried mushrooms, and particularly of this one, is that a little goes a long way—and buying them dried means you can use them in any season, not just in mushroom-rich autumn.

MAIL ORDER: amazon.com (search dried sliced shiitake black mushrooms). **FURTHER INFORMATION AND RECIPES:** *My Grandmother's Chinese Kitchen* by Eileen Yin-Fei Lo (2006); *The Thousand Recipe Chinese Cookbook* by Gloria Bley Miller (1984); *The Shun Lee Cookbook* by Michael Tong (2010); saveur.com (search bok choy with black mushrooms); epicurious.com (search stir fried tofu and shiitake mushrooms). **TIP:** Dried shiitakes needn't be limited to use in Asian dishes; they are a marvelous addition to any soup, stew, or daube that calls for mushrooms.

—|||||||||||||||||||||||||||||—

THE MANE COURSE

Shi Zi Tou

Lion's Head Meatballs

Chinese (Shanghainese)

Said to have originated in the eastern Chinese city of Yangzhou, this luscious dish owes its name to its appearance. Giant golden pork meatballs (the lions' heads) are served with frilly slices of braised, bittersweet cabbage leaves that loosely suggest a mane. Enriched with supple pork belly, the juicy, palm-size meatballs are flavored with ginger, water chestnuts, scallions, sherry, and sometimes black mushrooms or bamboo shoots, and then fried or braised in oil. When the meat is cooked through, the cabbage leaves are added to the same pot or earthenware casserole, along with a little water, soy sauce, and perhaps a dash of sherry or sugar to deepen the flavor and create a rich, meaty broth.

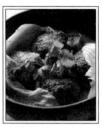

Pork meatballs and cabbage

In some versions, the meatballs are steamed in stock along with the cabbage instead of being fried, for a more delicate, if less savory, dish. In Shanghai, whole baby bok choy take the place of larger, round cabbage leaves and form cheerful cushions for the meaty "heads," and in still another variation, the meat and vegetables are "red-cooked," braised in a mixture of soy sauce, sugar, and spices for a deep flavor and dark mahogany hue. Served in soup bowls, the lions' heads and manes immersed in the fragrant and nourishing broth, the dish is as pleasing to the eye as it is to the palate.

Where: *In New York,* Joe's Shanghai, Chinatown location, tel 212-233-8888, joeshanghairestaurants .com; *in San Gabriel, CA,* Mei Long Village, tel 626-284-4769. **Further information and recipes:** *The Thousand Recipe Chinese Cookbook* by Gloria Bley Miller (1984); *The Chinese Cookbook* by Craig Claiborne and Virginia Lee (1972); cookstr.com (search lions head meatballs); food52.com (search lions head meatballs); cookingchanneltv.com (search lions head meatballs).

—|||||||||||||||||||||||||||||—

A WARMING FEAST FROM THE STEPPES

Shua Yang Jou

Mongolian Hot Pot

Chinese, Mongolian

It could be argued that all Asian hot pots are Mongolian, having been inspired by that northern country's frigid winters and the need to heat its great big yurts, those striking round dwellings erected by nomads. But although hot pots are served throughout China, where they've been popular for centuries, the best place to experience one in a classic Mongolian-style feast is in the colorful central Chinese city of Xi'an, the home of the famed terra-cotta soldiers and a large Muslim-Mongolian population.

Hot pots are almost always offered as a communal meal, even in restaurants. The group gathers at a round table and is outfitted with a single big ball of steamed, yeast-raised dough and medium-size, flared soup bowls. The central brazier is full of a heady broth generally made with lamb, and as it heats up, diners pinch off tiny rounds of the tender dough and drop them into their empty bowls. When they have pinched as much as they want, waiters carry the bowls to the kitchen, somehow remembering which belongs to whom. In the kitchen, the dough balls are dropped into boiling stock and soon swell into puffy, absorbent dumplings. They are then returned to the diners, who add hot pepper, minced garlic, a splash of vinegar and soy sauce, a little cilantro, and other seasonings to their bowls.

When the broth on their table is seethingly hot, diners wield long chopsticks to pluck thin slices of raw lamb—the much-preferred meat in this area—or beef, along with onions, cabbage, carrots, and mushrooms, from large platters and swish each morsel in the simmering broth to the desired degree of doneness. These are added to the individual bowls, alongside the delectably

A quick dip in hot broth, with dumplings on the side

squishy dumplings and spicy seasonings. Once the solids have been consumed, the hot broth is ladled into the bowls as a final feast.

Where: *In Xi'an*, Tong Sheng Xiang, tel 86/29-8721-8711; *in Arcadia, CA*, Hai Di Lao Hot Pot, tel 626-455-7232; *in the U.S., China, Japan, and Canada*, Little Sheep Mongolian Hot Pot at multiple locations, littlesheephotpot.com. **Further information and recipes:** *The Seventh Daughter: My Culinary Journey from Beijing to San Francisco* by Cecilia Chang (2007); *The Thousand Recipe Chinese Cookbook* by Gloria Bley Miller (1984); chinesefood.about.com (search mongolian lamb).

—————————————|||||||||||||||||||||||||||||||||||||—————————————

SPICY, SILKY, AND SWEET-SCENTED

Sichuan Eggplant

Chinese

G ently salty and silky eggplant prepared in the Sichuan style is justifiably one of the region's most famous dishes. Following the main principles of Sichuan cuisine, the preparation is distinguished by a generous dose of mouth-tingling,

addictive Sichuan pepper (see page 770), a "warming" ingredient that contrasts—in the yin-yang tradition of Chinese cooking—with the mild, thin, purple or white Asian eggplants, which are cooling, or *yin.* The eggplants are diced or slivered and then quickly stir-fried over blazingly high heat with a small amount of ground pork, plus the pepper, garlic, chiles, sesame oil, and ginger, all "hot" ingredients. The result is an especially fragrant, satiny concoction of contrasting flavors, balanced further by its traditional accompaniment of steamed rice (another "cool" food), and substantial enough to serve as a main course.

The Asian eggplant is loaded with vitamins, minerals, and antioxidants and has beneficial digestive properties, making Sichuan eggplant surprisingly healthful, given its richness and depth of flavor. The dish is a masterpiece easily realized at home, requiring only skills at wok cooking and knife use—and the patience to do a lot of chopping.

Where: *In Shanghai,* Fortune Palace, Jin Jiang Hotel, tel 86/21-3218-9888, jinjianghotels .com; *in New York,* Wu Liang Ye, tel 212-398-2308, wuliangyenyc.com; *in Washington, DC,* New Big Wong, tel 202-628-0491; *in Richmond,*

VA, Peter Chang's China Café, tel 804-364-1680, peterchangrva.com; *in Atlanta,* Little Szechuan, tel 770-451-0192, littleszechuanatlanta.com; *in Chicago,* Yan Bang Cai, tel 312-842-7818, yanbangcaichicago.com; *in Toronto,* Crown Princess Fine Dining, tel 416-923-8784, crownprincess.ca. **Mail order:** For Asian eggplant, Specialty Produce, tel 619-295-3172, specialty produce.com. **Further information and recipes:** *Sichuan Cooking* by Fuchsia Dunlop (2003); *Mrs. Chiang's Szechuan Cookbook* by Jung-Feng Chiang with Ellen Schrecker and John Schrecker (1987); *Henry Chung's Hunan Style Chinese Cookbook* by Henry Chung (1978); saveur.com (search sichuanese fried eggplant; sichuan eggplant essentials). **Tip:** Grown in California and in some southern U.S. states, Asian eggplants are readily found in specialty supermarkets and farmers' markets. When selecting your eggplants, look for fruits that feel heavy for their size, and are shiny purple or creamy white. Dull spots or brown stains indicate overripeness. **See also:** Aubergine en Caton, page 54, Nasu, page 809.

‖‖‖‖‖‖‖‖‖‖‖‖‖‖‖‖‖‖‖‖‖‖‖‖‖‖‖

BEANS BY THE YARD

Sijidou Chao Rousi

String Beans with Pork

Chinese (Sichuanese)

Y ou cannot claim to really appreciate green beans until you have tried the Chinese long bean (*Vigna unguiculata* subspecies *sesquipedalis*), also called a snake bean or yard-long bean and known in Chinese as *bak dau gok* or *tseng dau*

gak. With skin that appears tougher than it turns out to be, its long, slender pods (ranging from 18 to 30 inches in length), bulging slightly with seeds, become miraculously tender and flavorful when cooked in the Sichuan style. The mild beans are a perfect foil for Sichuan's traditional pungent spices, and

the flavorful dish that pairs them with pork is a favorite in Chinese restaurants the world over.

The beans are wok-fried until they're smoky and blistered, then flavored with zaps of garlic and ginger, soy sauce, and, for extra sustenance, ground pork. Like so many Sichuan specialties, it strikes many contrasting notes at once: tender and crunchy, sweet and tangy, robust and light.

WHERE: *In Shanghai,* Fortune Palace, Jin Jiang Hotel, tel 86/21-3218-9888, jinjianghotels.com; *in New York,* Wu Liang Ye, tel 212-398-2308, wuliangyenyc.com; *in Atlanta,* Little Szechuan, tel 770-451-0192, littleszechuan atlanta.com; *in Chicago,* Yan Bang Cai, tel 312-842-7818, yanbangcaichicago.com; *in San Francisco,* Betelnut Pejiu Wu, tel 415-929-8855, betelnutrestaurant.com; *in Vancouver,* Grand Dynasty Seafood Restaurant, tel 604-432-6002, granddynasty.ca. **FURTHER INFORMATION AND RECIPES:** *The Seventh Daughter: My Culinary Journey from Beijing to San Francisco* by Cecilia Chang (2007); *Beyond Bok Choy* by Rosa Lo San Ross (1996); foodandwine.com (search sichuan long beans). **TIP:** Long beans, sold in most Asian groceries, are characteristically bent, and should be somewhat flexible and free of dark spots.

BRIGHT YELLOW NOODLES, PROVENANCE UNCERTAIN

Singapore Mei Fun

Chinese, Singaporean

As Calvin Trillin wrote in a 2007 *New Yorker* article, "Singapore mei fun, a noodle dish often found in Chinatown restaurants, is, it almost goes without saying, unknown in Singapore." True though that may be, when it comes to good food, authenticity is a moving target, and flavor is concrete. And so it goes with the curious case of "Singapore mei fun," a creation that is ubiquitous on America's Chinese takeout menus, and reassuringly alike everywhere it is found. The name may not have anything to do with Singapore, but among its charms are very thin, vermicelli-like rice noodles bathed in a mildly hot, neon yellow curry sauce and topped with a combination of stir-fried egg, shredded vegetables, and your protein of choice.

The result is a succulent, slurpable bowl of fun spiced with nothing more complicated than yellow curry powder and chile peppers. The only true key to the dish's tastiness is to get it fresh and hot out of the wok. Depending on one's routine, Singapore mei fun is excellent either for dinner on a busy weeknight or for a snack at two in the morning, after a night of partying.

WHERE: *In New York*, Joe's Shanghai, Chinatown location, tel 212-233-8888, joeshang hairestaurants.com; *in Washington, DC,* New

A spicy bowl of Chinese American goodness

Big Wong, tel 202-628-0491; *in Toronto,* Crown Princess Fine Dining, tel 416-923-8784, crown-princess.ca; *in Vancouver,* Jade Seafood Restaurant, tel 604-249-0082, jadesrestaurant.ca. **FURTHER INFORMATION AND RECIPES:** *Florence Lin's Complete Book of Chinese Noodles, Dumplings and Bread* by Florence Lin (1993); rasamalaysia.com (search singapore fried rice noodles); epicurious.com (search singapore hawker rice noodles; singapore noodles).

—|||||||||||||||||||||||||||||||||—

Soy Sauce

Chinese, Japanese, Pan-Asian

Those ubiquitous red- or green-topped bottles lining tables at sushi bars and Chinese takeout joints around the world belie the sophistication of what can be one of the world's most interesting condiments—soy sauce, which has been

made in China from fermented soybeans for at least three thousand years and was once used primarily to preserve foods, especially meats and fish.

Soy sauce is made of ingredients that don't vary much from brand to brand: soybeans, yeast, water, salt, and sometimes wheat. But the quality of the original ingredients and the care with which they are treated can make the difference between a subtly delicious condiment and a boring salty brew.

Before mass production, making soy sauce required an extremely laborious process; the result was a

A soy sauce maker stirs soybeans and other ingredients.

brew with an astonishingly meaty, earthy flavor. Some of the descendants of soy sauce makers still do it the old-fashioned way: steaming fresh whole soybeans until they become soft, drying them out on flat, round straw mats, sprinkling them with yeast until they begin to form mold (either *Aspergillus oryzae* or *Aspergillus sojae*), then mixing them with a brine of water and salt in large crocks, and allowing them to ferment for six months to a year or longer. It is this fermentation process that lends soy sauce its umami—the so-called fifth flavor (after bitter, salty, sweet, and sour) that is often described as "savory."

About a thousand years ago, the sauce migrated to Japan along with Chinese Buddhist monks. It was quickly adopted there and became especially prevalent in the country's classic pickle preparations. Today Japan is

home to the Kikkoman corporation and to the largest soy sauce plant in the world—and soy sauce is the not-so-secret ingredient in a countless number of stir-fries, meat and fish dishes, savory snacks, and marinades throughout Asia. Like mustard, it's a condiment that can be used on its own but also forms the base for an infinite variety of sauces.

While in China most soy sauce is made from soybeans alone, or from a mixture of soybeans and a small amount of wheat, in Japan soy sauce (called shoyu) is made of a more equal combination of soybeans and wheat, the latter sometimes roasted or toasted for additional flavor. Such differences account for variations in flavor and saltiness as well as a wide range of colors—from caramel blonde–brown to the purplish inky black of the justly famous

Japanese soy sauce tamari. Made from miso soy (fermented soybean paste) and aged (preferably in a wood barrel) for a richer, smoother, more mellow flavor, tamari takes its name from the Japanese word *tamaru,* which means "accumulated" and is a good way to describe the sauce's essence. "White" or "clear" soy, which has long been used in Japan, is brewed mostly from wheat and is actually amber in color; because it does not darken the food it seasons, it's a good aesthetic match for white-fleshed fish. But generally, a darker sauce is considered more desirable; in upscale restaurants in Japan you may hear customers call soy sauce by the name *murasaki,* which means purple and refers to a royal reputation—and to the color of very fine and strong soy sauce.

MAIL ORDER: hoohing.com (search soy sauce); chefshop.com (search soy sauce); for small-batch soy sauce made with southern Kentucky wheat and aged in bourbon barrels, Zingerman's, tel 888-636-8162, zingermans.com (search bluegrass soy sauce). **FURTHER INFORMATION AND RECIPES:** *The Thousand Recipe Chinese Cookbook* by Gloria Bley Miller (1984); *Washoku: Recipes from the Japanese Home Kitchen* by Elizabeth Andoh (2005); *Cracking the Coconut* by Su-Mei Yu (2000); saveur.com (search soy sauce marinated ribs; soy chili sauce; sambal kecap).

A FRAGRANT, LIGHT TOUCH FOR TRULY FRESH FISH

Steamed Fish with Ginger and Scallions

Chinese (Cantonese)

I n the classic cooking style of the Canton province of southern China, where seafood is exalted, the freshness of fish is not just a point of pride, but actually a determinant of how a specimen will be prepared. Traditionally, a fish purchased

The freshest fish demands the simplest treatment.

alive would never be served fried, and an older or frozen specimen would never be steamed. Enhanced by the three most beloved flavorings in all of Chinese cooking—soy sauce, ginger, and scallions—gently steamed fresh fish is the signature dish of Canton, and a glorious example of the region's technique and philosophy.

The fish, usually rock cod (also known as rockfish, plentiful in the Pacific near California), although sometimes sea bass, snapper, and small striped bass are substituted, must be freshly caught. In China, especially in big cities like Hong Kong, fish markets sell shoppers live fresh fish that they may carry to one of many small nearby cookshops to have it steamed on the spot (see page 765). The fish is treated with a very light hand, sprinkled with a combination of garlic, ginger, scallions, and sometimes mushrooms and a little rice wine, and then steamed in either a wok or a traditional bamboo steamer. It cooks just until delicately flaking, and is then drizzled with soy sauce, sometimes mixed with sesame oil, combined with more fresh ginger, scallions, and sprays of cilantro. The preparation is basic, but it's the perfect way to treat a quality catch when it's exquisitely fresh—delicate, fragrant, and respectful of the fish's flavor and texture.

Where: *In New York,* Oriental Garden, tel 212-619-0085, orientalgardenny.com; *in Washington, DC,* New Big Wong, tel 202-628-0491; *in Rockville, MD,* Seven Seas Restaurant, tel 301-770-5020, sevenseasrestaurant.com; *in Chicago,* Yan Bang Cai, tel 312-842-7818, yanbangcaichicago.com; *in Vancouver,* Ginger & Soy, tel 778-279-8862, gingerandsoy.ca. **Further information and recipes:** *Cooking Without Borders* by Anita Lo and Charlotte Druckman (2011); *The Wisdom of the Chinese Kitchen* by Grace Young (1999); foodandwine.com (search steamed whole fish scallions); cookstr.com (search halibut steamed fresh ginger). **See also:** Golden Yoich, page 439.

HEADS UP, FISH LOVERS

Fish Cheeks

B eloved worldwide for their velvety softness and delicate flavor, delectably tender morsels of fish cheeks are a particular favorite in China, where the pieces (which lie just above the jaw) are the most prized bites of steamed or fried whole fish. At a Chinese dinner party, the fish's head is placed facing the guest of honor, giving that person the first chance to pluck out the sweet cheeks.

But fish cheeks have fans all over the world. In Spain, the Basques enjoy what they call the *kokotxas,* the cheeks of cod or hake; these are typically served with *pil-pil,* a silky green sauce made from olive oil, garlic, hot peppers, and the fish's cooking juices. The Portuguese, meanwhile, are fond of including cheeks in their thick, aromatic fish stews—it's considered good luck to find one in your bowl. In Iceland, cod cheeks (along with cod tongues) are salt-cured, smoked, or cooked in a cream sauce, and in Japan the cheeks of yellowtail and halibut are usually grilled, basted with sweet ponzu sauce. In New England, where cod is king, and in the Great

The cut reserved for the lucky guest of honor

Lakes region, where walleye and lake trout reign supreme, fish cheeks are a just reward for the fishermen; back at camp, they carefully excise the cheeks and fry them up in a cornmeal batter spiced with cayenne and garlic.

You will occasionally see fish cheeks sold on their own in fish markets, but since few fishmongers go through the unprofitable trouble of extracting the cheeks from small fish, the majority of those in markets are from larger fish such as cod, salmon, halibut, hake, striped bass, and northern pike. Canny fishmongers sometimes pluck them from whole fish to keep for themselves, so obtaining a pair requires special diligence—double checking to see that your whole fish has an intact head—the rewards of which are heavenly, tender bites that taste of the sea, only sweeter. As for how to prepare them, given their near universal appreciation in the world's seafood repertoire, you have innumerable recipes to choose from.

Where: *In Shanghai,* Jesse Restaurant, tel 86/21-6282-9260; *in New York,* Barchetta, tel 212-255-7400, barchettanyc.com; *in San Luis Obispo, CA,* Goshi Japanese Restaurant, tel 805-543-8942, goshis.com. **Further information and recipes:** *Complete Game and Fish Cookbook* by A. D. Livingston (1996); *Mrs. Chiang's Szechwan Cookbook* by Jung-Feng Chiang with Ellen Schrecker and John Schrecker (1987); *Nobu Miami: The Party Cookbook* by Nobu Matsuhisa (2008); saveur.com (search halibut cheeks with baby leeks); allrecipes.com (search halibut cheeks with ginger orange sauce).

A TINY MUSHROOM WITH A BIG FLAVOR

Straw Mushrooms

Chinese

Resembling a cartoon mushroom from a children's book, China's adorably diminutive, dark-capped straw mushroom (*Volvariella volvacea*) is charming to behold. Also called a paddy straw mushroom, as it grows best in the straw left over from the cultivation of rice, the versatile fungus bears an appealingly earthy flavor. Although mushrooms may be one of the world's earliest cultivated foods, mentioned in Chinese documents as far back as the later Chou dynasty (approximately 900 B.C.), the petite earthen straw mushroom is a latecomer, believed to have been farmed starting in the early nineteenth century.

Historians speculate that straw mushrooms were most likely cultivated first at the Nanhua Buddhist monastery in northern Canton, where monks are documented as having grown them on fermented rice straw. They must have caught on quickly because by 1875 boxes of the Nanhua mushrooms were presented as gifts to Chinese royalty. Widely cultivated today (mainly in southern China and Southeast Asia, where the mushrooms thrive in the hot, steamy climatic conditions) and grown on straw as well as on bales of wool, the mushrooms have retained their status as a delicacy. But because they are tricky to store, fresh straw mushrooms are very rare and are hard to find outside of China and Southeast Asia. They are mostly sold dried or canned, almost always in their "egg stage"—the period before the caps emerge from beneath a tissuelike covering. Mushrooms in this state are said to better absorb the juices of foods they are cooked with, providing an unrivaled burst of flavor to soups and stir-fries.

Mail order: amazon.com (search dynasty whole peeled straw mushrooms; dried paddy straw mushrooms). **Further information and recipes:** *The Chinese Kitchen* by Eileen Yin-Fei Lo (1999); *The Shun Lee Cookbook* by Michael Tong (2010). **Tip:** Canned straw mushrooms should be drained and rinsed before use, and dried mushrooms should be rinsed repeatedly in cool water before they are soaked for one hour. (Keep in mind that the flavor of the dried mushroom is far more intense than that of the canned.)

———————|||||||||||||||||||||||||||||||||||————————

Sung-Shu-Yu

Suzhou Squirrel Fish

Chinese (Suzhou)

Noted for mild and sweet flavors and intricately garnished gourmet dishes, the city of Suzhou, about sixty miles west of Shanghai in Jiangsu Province, claims a delectable, beautifully fried carp as its own. The golden fish, which represents good luck and abundance, is plump with fat and has richly meaty flesh encased in large, flaky bronze scales—attributes that lend themselves perfectly to this intricate preparation. The "squirrel" in the name of this dish (*sung-shu-yu*) comes from the furry look of the finished carp and the way its tail curls as it fries in hot oil. To attain that texture, the skin of the whole cleaned fish is scored all over in a diamond pattern. Dredged in cornstarch, it is then deep-fried in a wok, and turned as needed while the scored scales unfurl into a spiky furlike coat. Other freshwater fish, such as pike, whiting, and perch, can be prepared this way, but because they are generally smaller than carp, the result is less dramatic.

Fish scales turned into edible art

The finished dish is crunchy and mellow, flavored with scallions, salty ham, dried mushrooms, bamboo shoots, and garlic, all simmered in pan juices; as a tantalizing final touch, a garlic sauce or a zesty, sweet-and-sour blend of sugar, rice wine or sherry, and pungent minced fresh ginger seals the deal. In Suzhou kitchens, squirrel fish will be elaborately garnished with pink shrimp, green grapes, and bright-yellow squares of cooked, pressed egg yolk.

WHERE: *In Chicago,* Yan Bang Cai, tel 312-842-7818, yanbangcaichicago.com. **FURTHER INFORMATION AND RECIPES:** *The Chinese Cookbook* by Craig Claiborne and Virginia Lee (1972); ifood.tv (search squirrel fish).

———————|||||||||||||||||||||||||||||||||||————————

Tianzha Hetao

Candied Nuts

Chinese

While we recognize candied walnuts and pecans as a hallmark of the upscale composed salad, they are also a favorite appetizer in many Chinese restaurants. Particularly beloved in Beijing, they are a traditional offering at multicourse banquets as one of the little dishes that kicks off the meal, along with relishes and pickles. But chunky walnuts or pecans candied to a crunchy, sweet, and glossy dark golden brown may be added to main-course chicken, shrimp, and beef dishes to delicious effect as well.

Their preparation is simple. The shelled nutmeats are first quickly boiled, to remove any bitterness. While still hot, they're tossed with sugar and, finally, stir-fried in a wok. Beyond their applications in Chinese food, their welcome sweetness and texture make them great to have around to munch at cocktail hour, to garnish fancy salads, or to top ice cream and other enticing desserts.

FURTHER INFORMATION AND RECIPES: *The Breath*

A sweet treat usually offered as an appetizer

of a Wok by Grace Young (2004); nytimes.com (search chinese sugared walnuts); cookstr.com (search candied walnuts).

—||||||||||||||||||||||||||||||||||||||—

EGG-DROP SOUP GETS AN UPGRADE

West Lake Soup

Chinese (Hangzhounese)

With its gentle flavors and colorful dishes, the cuisine of the eastern Chinese city of Hangzhou resembles that of Shanghai, around 100 miles to its northeast. Hangzhou is well loved and much visited for its exquisite scenery, which

includes not only mountains but the celebrated, island-studded West Lake, historically of great value to local commercial fishermen; as a result, a number of dishes sprung up in Hangzhou with "West Lake" as inspiration.

The very best known of these is a frothy white soup that is both delicate and richly flavorful, with lovely, silky drifts of poached egg white floating amid a mix of diced black mushrooms, cushiony chunks of whitefish or carp or tender crumbles of ground beef, peas, and sometimes fresh herbs, all in a broth fragrant with soy sauce, rice wine, ginger, and onions. Light, nourishing, and wholesome, the dish is an inspired, sophisticated variation on traditional egg-drop soup.

WHERE: *In New York,* Congee Village at two locations, congeevillagerestaurants.com; *in Philadelphia,* Tai Lake Restaurant, tel 215-922-0698, tailakeseafoodrest.com; *in San Francisco,* Ton Kiang Restaurant, tel 415-752-4440, tonkiang .net; *in Daly City, CA,* Koi Palace, koipalace .com; *in Vancouver,* Western Lake Chinese Seafood Restaurant, tel 604-321-6862. **FURTHER INFORMATION AND RECIPES:** *How to Cook Everything* by Mark Bittman (2003); seriouseats.com (search chichi's west lake soup); nytimes.com (search minimalist hearty soup). **TIP:** Chinese chefs whisk the egg whites with long cooking chopsticks as they are drizzled into the soup, thereby aerating them to form pillows of silky froth, as opposed to strands of boiled egg.

—||||||||||||||||||||||||||||||||—

XO Sauce

Chinese

G iven the omnipresence of this spicy, pungently salty, carmine-red sauce on Chinese restaurant menus and in gourmet food shops, one might suppose it were an antique condiment in the manner of soy, oyster, and hoisin sauces. But in

fact, the pricey XO is a newcomer to the Chinese pantry. Most experts set its origins in the late 1970s or early '80s in Hong Kong, when, during a particularly flush period, it was common for guests in the city's upscale supper clubs to order XO-grade Cognac by the bottle. In a quest to emulate Cognac's luxuriousness, a Hong Kong chef concocted this dark and beguiling mixture, which would soon appear on the menu at several haute restaurants. Very little about the sauce is either exact or simple, and each restaurant has its own formula. A few "secret ingredients," however, are universal, including dried scallops, dried shrimp, bits of Yunnan ham (see page 795), soy sauce, and fish sauce. Other additions might include lemongrass, chile peppers, and lots of garlic. What it rarely, if ever, includes is Cognac.

The sauce lends an appealingly sharp, salty yet complex flavor to soups, casseroles, and stir-fries, as well as seafood, meat, poultry, vegetable, rice, and noodle dishes.

Because it is made with expensive ingredients and is very concentrated, restaurants in China sometimes add an extra charge for dollops of XO sauce, especially on humble dishes such as rice rolls or dim sum dumplings. Inventive chefs with fusion on their minds add it to all sorts of pan-Asian dishes, as well as to seafood salads, barbecue sauces, marinades, and seafood cocktail sauces. Most professional chefs and many ambitious home cooks simmer up their own XO at a wise savings over the bottled variety. It is wise to make small batches, as the intensely flavored sauce is generally used sparingly and loses its spunk after two months.

MAIL ORDER: amazon.com (search lee kum kee xo); for Chili XO sauce, Yank Sing, tel 415-957-9990, yanksing.com. **FURTHER INFORMATION AND RECIPES:** *Momofuku* by David Chang (2009); saveur.com (search xo sauce); marthastewart.com (search xo sauce); epicurious.com (search beef and snow peas xo sauce).

—||||||||||||||||||||||||||||||||—

Yan Wo Tang

Bird's Nest Soup

Chinese

S ometimes luxury and oddity go hand in hand. A savory case in point is bird's nest soup, an ancient Chinese delicacy that has been coveted for more than six hundred years. Since the days of the Ming dynasty, Chinese cooks have prized the nests of the tiny swiftlets who attach themselves high up on the walls in the Vietnamese and Thai bat caves along the coasts of the South China Sea. Also found in similar caves in Borneo and throughout Indonesia, the nest constructions are no ordinary feats: The swiftlets make them mostly out of strands of saliva that dry and harden when exposed to air, thus adhering to the cave walls.

The birds nest in the spring, and each summer small groups of harvesters, usually folks whose relatives have been in the business for many years, climb the cave walls on bamboo ladders and delicately carve out the teacup-size, whitish structures. It's a dangerous business, and one that doesn't scale, which is why birds' nests are so expensive, sometimes costing upward of thousands of dollars per pound, and why bird's nest soup itself can be so costly—upward of $40 or so per bowl, and into the hundreds of dollars. It is particularly renowned in the traditional Cantonese restaurant Man Wah, in the Mandarin Oriental Hotel in Hong Kong, where the different versions served range from about $120 per serving to close to $600.

Most bird's nest aficionados agree that the flavor of the nest itself is actually quite bland. For this reason the nests are never eaten on their own, but are instead carefully cleaned, soaked in water for several hours, and then simmered in chicken broth; usually a little ginger, an egg, and slivers of Yunnan ham are added to the soup for flavor. A less-common, sweet preparation involves cooking the nests with sugar into a sweet dessert soup. In both cases, it is the texture of the melted nests, a kind of gelatinous noodle that makes the whole mix quite viscous, that is the desired result.

The Chinese ascribe many medicinal benefits to the nests, including skin-saving and anti-aging properties, and as such their reputation as delicacies is only further enhanced. They are also said to be an aphrodisiac and a great source of virility, which does nothing to hurt their lore, either. Although the soup is invariably discussed alongside and compared to shark's fin soup, another ancient Chinese delicacy, bird's nest has the benefit of being prepared without attendant moral or ethical issues, yet another of its exotic charms.

WHERE: *In Hong Kong,* Man Wah, tel 852/2522-0111; mandarinoriental.com; *in New York,* Oriental Garden, tel 212-619-0085, oriental gardenny.com; *in Daly City, CA,* Koi Palace, koi palace.com. **FURTHER INFORMATION AND RECIPES:** *Extreme Cuisine: The Weird & Wonderful Foods That People Eat* by Jerry Hopkins (2004); *The Thousand Recipe Chinese Cookbook* by Gloria Bley Miller (1984); food.com (search bird's nest soup); youtube.com (search traditional bird's nest soup). **TIP:** Nests may be bought in Asian groceries and specialty Chinese markets; they are often stored under lock and key, but they aren't particularly hard to find.

CHINA'S OWN COUNTRY HAM

Yunnan Ham

Chinese (Yunnanese)

A southwestern region that borders Laos, Myanmar, Tibet, and Vietnam, the Yunnan province of China is home to a unique cuisine known for its pronounced spicy heat as well as the influence of its Southeast Asian neighbors and its large ethnic minority population. The region itself is prized for its natural resources, especially its tropical flora. But its most famous food is its ham, a dry-cured, dense, and salty treat revered the world over but, alas, not cleared for import to the United States.

That's too bad, as Yunnan ham, produced in the region for close to three hundred years, is considered a paragon of umami, the elusive fifth taste most often described as savory, and much talked about these days. The ham is often favorably compared with Spain's Jabugo ham (see page 262)—also banned in the U.S., until quite recently—and the salt-cured country hams produced in the southern U.S., especially the Smithfield brand. Like those specialty hams, Yunnan's are deeply flavorful haunches—very lean, mahogany red, smoky, and intense—that are produced following secret, closely guarded processes.

As with so many famous hams, the magic has a lot to do with the hog itself, a small, wild-foraging breed raised only in the Yunnan and neighboring Sichuan provinces and so far unable to thrive elsewhere. Curing the ham is a time-honored affair that requires an exacting procedure, with many months of salting and curing needed to create the exact right hue (brick red), texture (dry but not leathery), and aroma (pungent and meaty). The results are prized above all others in China, and are sold by top grocers there either whole (usually

Making the air-dried ham is an all-consuming enterprise.

complete with leg and hoof) or in paper-thin slices. Yunnan ham is considered a necessity for top-quality, rich stock, and it's featured in many classic Chinese special-occasion soups, including, bird's nest (see page 794), and winter melon (see page 764). It adds an extra savory layer to braised duck and chicken dishes, and the Chinese also eat it steamed with a honey glaze, much like an American honey-baked ham.

MAIL ORDER: For the closest U.S. substitute, Smithfield Marketplace, tel 888-741-2221, smithfieldmarketplace.com (search genuine smithfield ham). **FURTHER INFORMATION AND RECIPES:** *Hot Sour Salty Sweet* by Jeffrey Alford and Naomi Duguid (2000); *The Thousand Recipe Chinese Cookbook* by Gloria Bley Miller (1984); chinesefood.about.com (search yunnan ham). **SEE ALSO:** York Ham, page 33, Jabugo ham, page 262.

------------------------⊣||||||||||||||||||||||||||||||⊢------------------------

A KRAUT WITH KICK

Zha Cai

Sichuan Preserved Vegetable

Chinese

M ade from the fat, tuberous stems of the mustard green plant, *zha cai* is a cold dish with a hot flavor—a zesty addition to fried rice, soups, and tofu dishes, and a key component of classic Sichuan dan dan noodles (see page 759) that is prized for its sweet-tart tanginess. Salted, pressed, dried, rubbed with hot red chile paste, and fermented in earthenware jars, the pale, silky slivers enliven the palate and add crunchy texture to a range of spice-rich traditional Sichuan dishes. Like other fermented foods, including its cousins sauerkraut and kimchi (see pages 308 and 833), zha cai is claimed to be very healthful, with abundant vitamin C and probiotics, the so-called friendly bacteria that are major digestive aids and possibly even immune-system boosters. Regardless of its health benefits, it is one of the region's signature and most distinctive pleasures.

Making zha cai from scratch is very tricky under the best of circumstances—finding the right kind of mustard stem poses the first challenge—so even accomplished Chinese cooks prefer to buy it ready-made. Fortunately, that means it is widely sold in Asian grocery stores and can easily be found outside its home countries. Delicious with meats, it provides an easy way to enliven simple dishes and deserves to be seen on menus everywhere, even in places where it does not customarily belong.

Mail order: amazon.com (search zha cai). **Further information and recipes:** *The Thousand Recipe Chinese Cookbook* by Gloria Bley Miller (1984); *Susanna Foo Chinese Cuisine* by Susanna Foo (2002); foodandwine.com (search sichuan pickled cucumbers); epicurious.com (search pickled vegetables david chang). **Tip:** Look for it in Asian groceries, in cans or pouches marked "Sichuan Preserved Vegetable." Top brands include May Ling, Tang Meng, and Bright Pearl.

THIS DUCK IS NOT FOR SIPPING

Zhangcha Ya

Tea-Smoked Duck

Chinese (Sichuanese)

It almost seems as though one could sample a thousand different Chinese duck dishes, so numerous and delectable are recipes for that crisp-skinned poultry. Each province has its own version, with Beijing's ingenious Peking duck (see page 748) being perhaps the most famous. The southwestern Sichuan province, however, known for the fiery chiles and the unique Sichuan pepper that enflame its typical dishes, is capable of more complex pleasures. Among them is a duck that is smoked in a wok over camphor leaves and twigs along with dry tea leaves, resulting in a bird with golden-brown crackling skin, moist meat, and an aroma and flavor that are at once sweetly mellow, antique, and earthy.

Before it is smoked, the whole duck is marinated in a mix of ground star anise, citrusy Sichuan pepper, ginger, garlic, and rice wine or dry sherry, then hung to dry for several hours until the skin is thin and taut. But that is only step one: Then comes blanching the duck in boiling water or steaming it over a wok, smoking it, and finally, deep-frying it in vegetable oil. Chopped into succulent chunks—bones, skin, and all—the duck is dipped into a mix of vinegar and soy sauce as it is eaten.

Often tea-smoked duck is served with the same sort of tiny, puffy, scallion-flecked, yeast-raised buns—*hua juan,* or "flower buns"—that are used to sandwich slices of Peking duck. Because camphor is not always easy to come by, the duck is sometimes smoked over black tea leaves alone, which has a lovely and sweet, aromatic effect, although it lacks the wildly exotic contrast imparted by the faintly musty essence of camphor. (For some cooks, the tea-only version is preferable, as it produces none of the potent camphor fumes.)

A camphor- and tea-smoked delicacy

Subtle distractions aside, the dish, with its many steps and long list of ingredients, is generally reserved for banquets and celebrations—which means that if you see it on a menu, you should leap at the chance to try it.

WHERE: *In New York,* Wu Liang Ye, tel 212-398-2308, wuliangyenyc.com; *in Chicago,* Yan Bang Cai, tel 312-842-7818, yanbangcaichicago .com; *in Richmond, VA,* Peter Chang's China Café, tel 804-364-1688, peterchangsrva.com. **MAIL ORDER:** For rohan duck, D'Artagnan, tel 800-327-8246, dartagnan.com; for black tea, The Republic of Tea, tel 800-298-4832, republicoftea .com; The Chinese Tea Shop, tel 604-633-1322, thechineseteashop.com. **FURTHER INFORMATION AND RECIPES:** *Mrs. Chiang's Szechwan Cookbook* by Jung-Feng Chiang with Ellen Schrecker and John Schrecker (1987); *Henry Chung's Hunan Style Chinese Cookbook* by Henry Chung (1978); foodnetwork.com (search tea smoked duck); saveur.com (search tea smoked duck); nymag .com (search tea smoked duck).

JAPANESE
and
KOREAN

—||||||||||||||||||||||||||||||||||—

NOT YOUR AVERAGE LUNCH BOX

Bento

Japanese

A thoroughly modern concept that in fact dates back about four hundred years, to the Edo period, the Japanese *bento* box offers a perfectly balanced, delightful meal in a portable container. Although it may be eaten at a restaurant,

bento is meant as a sort of picnic, presented in wood or plastic or, at its most elegant, in gleaming lacquered boxes divided to hold an array of small bites. It may contain a few rice cakes bound with nori (dried seaweed), perhaps a small, pink slice of fish cake, a shrimp or steamed crayfish, a rainbow of pickled vegetables and plums, and perhaps a nugget of sweet glazed chicken. All are designed to keep and transport well and to be eaten at room temperature. When sold to go in Japan, whether in upscale shops or from carts on a train, each box (called *ekiben* if purchased on a train) is marked with the time it was packed, and may be sold for only up to four hours after preparation. Bento boxes are also sometimes prepared at home by those with the time and inclination to make a particularly delectable—if painstaking—lunch for themselves or their family.

Each region of Japan has its own style of bento, although all are planned with the seasons in mind. Even in inexpensive bento boxes, made of plastic or paper and dispensed from

street stands or fast food outlets, the respect for color, texture, freshness, and flavor is obvious. In Mie Prefecture, specifically at Matsusaka Station, the ekiben feature the local beef, which rivals Kobe in quality and rarity; in coastal regions, such as Toyama Prefecture or Hokkaido, bentos are sure to include sushi, crab, and salted fish; and in Gunma Prefecture, they come in a clay pot rather than a box, which keeps the contents (rice, chicken, egg, and vegetables) piping hot. Although closely associated with rail travel, bento boxes are also offered to travelers on some Japanese airlines. As it turns out, this centuries-old culinary tradition lends itself perfectly to dining in the clouds.

WHERE: *In Tokyo,* Matsuri, tel 81/033-212-1889; Nippon, tel 81/033-212-4088; Odori, tel 81/033-213-4352; *in New York,* BentOn Café, tel 212-608-8850, bentoncafe.com; Dainobu at two locations, dainobu.us; *in Washington, DC,* Sushi Taro, tel 202-462-8999, sushitaro.com; *in Chicago,* Slurping Turtle, tel 312-464-0466, slurpingturtle.com/chicago; *in Houston,* Kata Robata, tel 713-526-8858, katarobata.com; *in Seattle,* Fuji Sushi, tel 206-624-1201, fujisushi seattle.com; *in San Francisco,* Suika, tel 415-967-2636, suikasuikasuika.com; *in Brentwood, CA,* Takao Sushi, tel 310-207-8636, takaobrentwood .com. **MAIL ORDER:** For bento boxes, Happy Mall, tel 909-718-9999, happymall.com; Bento & Co, tel 81/757-082-164, bentoandco.com; Japan Centre, tel 44/020-3405-1151, japancentre.com. **FURTHER INFORMATION AND RECIPES:** *Practical Japanese Cooking* by Shizuo Tsuji (1991); *The Just Bento Cookbook* by Makiko Itoh (2011).

A five-course meal in a box

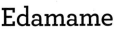

A WELL-BALANCED CUP

Chawanmushi

Steamed Custard-Soup

Japanese

S ome foods are so special as to defy categorization, and such is the case with the delicate custard-soup called *chawanmushi*, meaning "steamed in a tea cup." As its charming name implies, each portion is steamed and served in a tiny, specially made, lidded cup.

Beyond its base, a soupy mix of egg lightly beaten with stock, the exact contents of the chawanmushi vary. Sometimes the custard contains a hidden surprise—a perfect steamed shrimp, a thin and meltingly tender slice of tofu, an earthy exotic mushroom, or a chewy ginko nut or two.

The custard itself adheres to this basic ratio: one part egg to three parts dashi, the broth made of the kelp and shaved bonito that lends flavor to most Japanese soups and noodles, or chicken stock as a substitute. The warm dashi must be slowly poured into the beaten egg, lightly mixed, and strained into the little pots. So as not to curdle the egg, the chawanmushi cups are then steamed slowly over very low heat.

Chawanmushi may be eaten cold, as a refreshing start to a summertime meal, but it is much preferred hot. It may well be a rival to the famed "Jewish penicillin" style soup (see page 439) for rich flavor, and yet it is possessed of an ethereal texture, both pleasingly light and pleasantly substantial.

WHERE: *In New York,* EN Japanese Brasserie, tel 212-647-9196, enjb.com; Hatsuhana at two locations, hatsuhana.com; *in Brookline, MA,* Shiki, tel 617-738-0200, shikibrookline.com; *in Houston,* Kata Robata, tel 713-526-8858, katarobata.com; *in San Francisco,* Ame, tel 415-284-4040, amerestaurant.com; *in Los Angeles,* Shunji, tel 310-826-4739, shunji-ns.com; *in Seattle,* Miyabi 45th, tel 206-632-4545, miyabi45th.com. **FURTHER INFORMATION AND RECIPES:** *Japanese Cooking: A Simple Art* by Shizuo Tsuji (2012); for chef Ming Tsai's recipe for maitake chawanmushi, mingspantry.com/maitmuschawm.html; cookstr.com (search chawan mushi japanese savory steamed custard); foodandwine.com (search chawan mushi david chang). **SEE ALSO:** Tom Kha Gai, page 846; Qi Guo Ji (steamed chicken soup), page 779.

A SNACK FOR POD PEOPLE

Edamame

Japanese

S erved as a pre-sushi nibble, the small, familiar bowl of delicate, jade-colored pods is an addictive treat that happens to be among the most nutritionally significant foods in the world. For *edamame* is actually the Japanese term for fresh soy beans, the word literally translating to "beans on branches." With their bright green, tapered husks that pop open to reveal two or three delicious, round beans, they may look like peas in their pods, but the similarity ends there. Much firmer and richer, the well-salted, nutty-flavored beans are the stuff that, along with fish, supplies the Japanese with the majority of their protein: The beans are fully 35 percent protein, in addition to being loaded with essential amino acids, fiber, and phytonutrients.

Also used to make other mainstays of the Southeast Asian diet, including miso, tofu, and shoyu (soy sauce), the beans were first cultivated in China around the third millennium B.C. They soon spread into neighboring countries, and eventually became a cornerstone of the Japanese diet—part of the reason *Japanese Women Don't Get Old or Fat*, at least according to a 2006 book by Tokyo native Naomi Moriyama.

As edamame, though, the soybeans appear in their most elemental form—soaked in salt water while still in their pods to flavor and soften them, they are quickly boiled to tenderness, then served either cold or at room temperature. They're best when gently warm, topped with good crunchy sea salt, and sucked right out of the pod alongside a cold beer.

WHERE: *In Atlanta*, Taka Sushi, tel 404-869-2802, takasushiatlanta.com; *in Brentwood, CA*, Takao Sushi, tel 310-207-8636, takaobrentwood.com. **MAIL ORDER:** For precooked edamame, Melissa's Produce, tel 800-588-0151, melissas.com; for fresh stalks, edamameusa.com; for frozen edamame, Japan Centre, tel 44/020-3405-1151, japancentre.com; for seeds, Kitazawa Seed Company, tel 510-595-1188, kitazawaseed.com. **FURTHER INFORMATION AND RECIPES:** *Edamame: 60 Tempting Recipes Featuring America's Hottest New Vegetable* by Anne Egan (2003); *Washoku* by Elizabeth Andoh (2012); *Japanese Cooking: A Simple Art* by Shizuo Tsuji (2012); saveur.com (search edamame salad); bonappetit.com (search edamame hummus). **TIP:** Shelled edamame can be incorporated into spring salads, tossed with canned tuna or crab-meat alongside parsley or chervil, or added to risotto instead of peas.

├|||||||||||||||||||||||||||||||┤

RISKY FISHY BUSINESS

Fugu

Japanese

When the poison of the occasionally deadly blowfish or puffer fish is consumed, a slow and steady numbing of one's body begins. It starts with the mouth and tongue and spreads to the internal organs, so that the unlucky

eater is still conscious but completely paralyzed and unable to move, speak, and, eventually, to breathe. A gruesome way to go, no doubt about it, but what keeps the fugu culture going is the fact that that poison, tetrodotoxin, can also cause a coveted and pleasing numbing sensation when absorbed in trace amounts. Hence, everything is in the hands of the chef. Can he deliver the tiniest amount of numbing—keeping in mind that enough tetrodotoxin to kill a person could fit on the head of a pin—and the maximum amount of fresh flavor without killing his diners?

A big part of the appeal of the boundary-pushing delicacy, a specialty in Japan for millennia, is the idea that fugu might be delicious enough to be worth the risk. And indeed, it is. With its clean flavor, the lean fish is truly pristine, fresh, and evocative of the deep sea. "Deep" is key, as the tetrodotoxin is produced by the shellfish the notoriously bottom-feeding blowfish love to eat.

Not all fugu are deadly. Of the more than one hundred varieties, about a third can kill. But there's no coming back from the deadly ones, as tetrodotoxin has no known antidote—so in Japan, only licensed chefs are allowed to prepare and sell fugu. The famously rigorous licensing exam involves performing the following tasks before board-certified instructors: identifying the fish even when out of season, demonstrating the ability to differ-entiate poisonous fugu species from nonpoisonous ones, identify-ing which parts of the fugu are toxic, and proving an ability to clean the fish correctly.

A licensed chef at work

Of the fugu varieties, the *torafugu,* or tiger blowfish, caught in the waters off Miyazaki Prefecture in southern Japan, is considered the very best; it is also, naturally, the most poison-ous. Fugu innards can be extremely poisonous, so licensed restaurants are required to keep the entrails in a special container under lock and key, then deposit these remains at fish markets, where city authorities supervise their incineration. When the beloved Kabuki actor Mitsugoro Bando VIII died of fugu liver con-sumption at a Kyoto restaurant in 1975, the Japanese authorities prohibited the serving of the liver altogether.

To tempt fate, most fugu meals are served in courses. A typical meal might include fugu sashimi, fried fugu, smoked fugu, and fugu hot pot. The *shirako,* the sperm sac, is served separately, usually raw but sometimes grilled, its slices sometimes arranged to resemble a crane—a symbol of longevity in Japan.

WHERE: *In Tokyo,* Ajiman, tel 81/3-3408-2910; Tsukiji Yamamoto, tel 31/3-3541-7730; *in New York,* Masa, tel 212-823-9800, masanyc .com; *in Washington, DC,* Sushi Taro, tel 202-462-8999, sushi taro.com; *in Seattle,* Shiki at two locations, tel 206-281-1352, shiki japaneserestaurant.com. **FURTHER INFORMATION:** *The Year of Eating Dangerously* by Tom Parker Bowles (2007); nymag.com (search for die for adam platt); nytimes.com (search one man's fugu is another man's poison; if the fish liver can't kill is it really a delicacy?). **TIP:** Fugu's season runs from October to early spring; it's considered a winter food in Japan, and in sum-mer most of the fugu houses either close or serve the farm-raised versions that are consid-ered inferior.

SOY ON ICE

Hiyayakko

Chilled Tofu

Japanese

An understandable favorite during Japan's hot and humid summers, *hiyayakko* is so seductively delicious that it often sneaks onto menus throughout the year. It begins with the very freshest tofu (soybean curd) of the prime type known as silky, or *kinu*. Snow-white and quivery, it is custard-soft, with just enough body to be cut into delicate cubes, revealing a wobbly center that brings to mind Italian *panna cotta* or crème caramel.

The alabaster curd is served chilled, sometimes nested on ice cubes, and topped with finely minced scallions, fresh ginger, and—most flavorful of all—feathery, translucent shavings of *katsuobushi*: the salty, vaguely smoky, and ripe-tasting dried flakes of bonito, an oily fish of the mackerel family. Sold in thick, dry slabs and grated as needed, bonito is a nutritious garnish, popular on vegetable and rice dishes, which keeps almost indefinitely if stored properly. (It is also expensive, and therefore is traditionally a most welcome wedding gift.) The combination of the grassy, creamy tofu and the sharp accents of scallions and ginger, plus the savory salinity of the bonito, is further enhanced by a quick dip in the best aged soy sauce, for an addictive (and nutritious) appetizer or light lunch, in any weather. Picking the slippery tofu up with chopsticks is a learned and worthwhile skill.

WHERE: *In New York*, EN Japanese Brasserie, tel 212-647-9196, enjb.com; Yakitori Totto, tel 212-245-4555, tottonyc.com; *in Brookline, MA*, Shiki, tel 617-738-0200, shikibrookline.com; *in Atlanta*, Taka Sushi, tel 404-869-2802, takasushiatlanta.com; *in Chicago*, Oysy Sushi, tel 312-670-6750, oysysushi.com. **MAIL ORDER:** For bonito, marukaiestore.com; asianfoodgrocer.com. **FURTHER INFORMATION AND RECIPES:** *A Taste of Japan* by Donald Richie (1982); *Japanese Cooking: A Simple Art* by Shizuo Tsuji (2012); japanesefood.about.com (search hiyayakko); Japan Centre, tel 44/020-3405-1151, japancentre.com (choose Recipe, search hiyayakko chilled tofu).

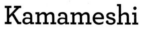

A POT OF COMFORT-FOOD GOLD

Kamameshi

Kettle-Steamed Rice

Japanese

Among the staples that afford the most nourishing comfort, rice has to rank foremost in any cuisine, whether in sweet puddings, savory risottos and pilafs, or in its myriad uses in Asian dishes—particularly when it acts as the meal's

A simple, homey dish that's full of nutrients

centerpiece, as it does in the classic dish *kamameshi*. Not widely known outside of Japan, the simple casserole of steamed rice with bits of vegetables, seafood, poultry, or meat is traditionally served at specialized restaurants, although it is now becoming available more widely in the U.S.

Wherever it is served, kamameshi is cooked to order in individual portions and presented to diners in the small metal pot in which it was simmered, set into rustic wood blocks. The non-glutinous short-grain rice (*uruchi mai*) will be gently infused with aged soy sauce and mirin, a sweet rice wine, along with bits of onion and perhaps ginkgo nuts and woodsy mushrooms, among other ingredients. The result is a soft, intricately melded combination of savory tastes and bequiling textures; although it's easily negotiated with chopsticks, one might long to dig in with a spoon.

Where: *In New York,* Robataya, tel 212-979-9674, robataya-ny.com; *in Daly City, CA,* Kamameshi House, tel 650-952-0444. **Mail order:** For rice, marukaiestore.com; for casserole pot, korin.com (search aluminum kamameshi pot); rakuten.com; Japan Centre, tel 44/020-3405-1151, japancentre.com. **Further information and recipes:** food.com (search chicken kamameshi); youtube.com (search kamameshi rice with chicken katsu). **See also:** Risotto, page 233; Paella, page 265; Kosheri, page 711; Biryani, page 868.

CAKE FOR TEATIME IN JAPAN

Kasutera

Japanese

Simplicity is one of the reigning qualities of Japanese cuisine—and although *kasutera* is a Portuguese import, it's no exception. Addictively light, airy, and sweet, the golden sponge cake is one of those basic and time-honored concoctions of eggs, sugar, flour, and corn or malt syrup or honey. At its most unadorned, it could pass for a loaf of bread. For many years it was served plain, but over time it's been doctored with favorite Japanese flavorings, like green tea, or elaborately decorated and garnished. The most famous kasutera in Nagasaki can be had at Fukusaya, a bakery that has been operating since 1624 and is thought to have been the first to introduce the cake to the general public. Its wares, with their caramel-hued crusts and bright-yellow centers, are said to get their color and richness from very high-quality egg yolks.

A sunny, spongy cake

Along with tobacco and gunpowder, the cake first came to the country with the Portuguese sailors who arrived in the port city of Nagasaki in the 1600s. The original was in fact much more of a bread—*pão de Castela,* meaning "bread from Castile"—and Castella is still a widely used name for the cake. The sailors, with some Spaniards among them, traveled with the sweet bread in part because it could be stored for long periods of time. It also contained no dairy, which appealed to the Japanese sensibility.

Although the Spanish withdrew from Japan in 1624 and the Portuguese were banished in 1639, the cake remained, adapted over time to fit the Japanese craving for what were then novel Western sweets. Today it remains a beloved treat, easily the most well-known Japanese dessert.

Where: *In Nagasaki,* Fukusaya, tel 81/95-821-2938, castella.co.jp; *in Tokyo, Shanghai, Singapore, London, San Francisco, and New York,* Minamoto Kitchoan, kitchoan.com. **Further information and recipes:** *The Sweet Spot: Asian-Inspired Desserts* by Pichet Ong and Genevieve Ko (2007); japanesefood.about.com (search kasutera recipe); justonecookbook .com (search castellan).

⊣||||||||||||||||||||||||||||⊢

THE CRUNCHIEST GOURD

Kyuri

Japanese Cucumber

Japanese

More than in any other variety, the essence of crunch can be found in the Japanese cucumber called *kyuri,* the slender, long, slightly curved, bumpy, dark green–skinned specimen that shows up in myriad Japanese dishes. You might

find kyuri thinly sliced in *sunomono* ("vinegared things"), a class of fresh, vinegar-dressed side-dish salads that make refreshingly tart accompaniments to all sorts of hot and spicy foods. Lightly pickled as *kyuri asa-zuke,* it's the perfect ending to a meal, and it's also ubiquitous as an ingredient and garnish in sushi and sashimi. Unlike most commercially grown cucumbers in the U.S., kyuri have thin, tender skins that can be eaten; no need to peel them. They are also said to be burp-free.

Like watermelons, cucumbers are surprisingly watery members of the gourd family. Among the most popular vegetables in Japan, they are believed to have originated in India and to have been cultivated in soils around the world for no fewer than three thousand years.

Kyuri in particular grow well and widely in California, and are therefore relatively easy to find in Asian markets throughout the U.S.

MAIL ORDER: Melissa's Produce, tel 800-588-0151, melissas.com; Mitsuwa Marketplace, mitsuwa.com; for seeds, Kitazawa Seed Company, tel 510-595-1188, kitazawaseed.com. **FURTHER INFORMATION AND RECIPES:** *Cooking* by James Peterson (2007); *Vegetables from Amaranth to Zucchini* by Elizabeth Schneider (2001); epicurious.com (search japanese cucumber salad with vinegar); saveur.com (search japanese pickled cucumbers kyuri zuke). **TIP:** Slice kyuri thin and float them in a glass of ice-cold water. Squeeze in some fresh lime juice, and you've got a five-star spa drink.

||||||||||||||||||||||||||||||||||||||||||||||||||||||||||||||||||||||||||||||||||||||||||

SUN-GOLD RITE OF SPRING

Loquat

Despite the similarity between their names, the loquat and the kumquat aren't related; the kumquat is essentially a miniature orange, and the loquat is a distant cousin of the apple and pear. It's shaped like a pear, and its apricot-hued exterior reveals a cream-colored, luscious flesh within—succulent, sweetly tangy, and delicately soft.

A member of the rose family, the small, evergreen loquat tree (*Eriobotrya japonica*) yields one of the world's oldest cultivated fruits. Grown in Japan—and sometimes referred to as "Japanese plums"—and in many other parts of the world including the Mediterranean, loquats mature quickly and are among the first delectable rites of spring. But unlike apricots and peaches, they spoil quickly after picking, which is why they've never become an important commercial crop.

Splendid treats when eaten fresh, loquats are also delicious poached and served in their own syrup or made into the jams, jellies, and chutneys that are popular throughout Southeast Asia.

If you're lucky enough to find a ripe one, gently peel off its thin skin and munch away, much as you would a perfectly ready pear. The

A spring ritual, the loquat is a rare and delicious fruit.

Chinese believe the fruit to have medicinal properties: the ability to soothe a sore throat, and, when eaten in quantity, to produce a mildly sedative effect. The same can be said of the sweet loquat wine found in parts of Southeast Asia, although it may produce a certain loquacity as well.

Mail order: Melissa's Produce, tel 800-588-0151, melissas.com; amazon.com (search instant loquat throat comforter; loquat tea leaves; loquat honey syrup; loquat chili grilling glaze). **Further information and recipes:** *Uncommon Fruits and Vegetables* by Elizabeth Schneider (2010); saveur.com (search lamb meatballs with loquats); specialtyproduce.com (search loquats). **Special event:** Loquat Festival, Suzhou, China, May/June, en.visitsz.com (search loquat festival).

THE WORLD'S MOST EXPENSIVE MUSHROOMS

Matsutake

Japanese

M usty and toasty, the scent of the matsutake is as strong and memorable as the mushroom is elusive. The woodsy Japanese fungi (*Tricholoma matsutake*) grow wild in the red pine forests where they pick up their heavy signature aroma.

Nature's trickster, they grow sparingly, and never in the same place twice. Their rarity and their pungent flavor, along with a satisfyingly thick, meaty texture that goes through their stems, make them a sought-after luxury. Depending on its size and condition, a single matsutake can cost $20 to $50, making it the most expensive mushroom variety in the world. (Its competition, the truffle, is technically a spore and not a true mushroom.)

In their home country, matsutakes are foraged intently during the fall, with a fervor appropriate to a national pastime. Finding them is considered a rare burst of good fortune, not only because of their aroma and price tag but also because mushrooms are revered in Japanese culture, shrouded in mysticism, folklore, and ceremony. Symbolizing fertility, good health, and happiness, the matsutake is the most prized of all, and after the autumnal forage, whole meals are often constructed around the mushroom. Such a meal may begin with the most popular preparation, a dish called *dobin mushi,* which involves steaming the mushroom in a special teapot in its own broth, a method thought to enhance both the fragrance and the flavor. That may be followed by grilled caps and later, small bits steamed with rice.

Matsutakes may be imported—nestled in sawdust in little pine boxes—but the cost is generally prohibitive. Commercial cultivation of the mushroom has so far been a failure, but the good news is that an American variety (*Tricholoma magnivelare*) grows wild in the Pacific Northwest: the so-called white matsutake, not as powerfully flavorful, but less expensive.

The musty matsutake

Both varieties are worth the price, for tasting the earthy matsutake is a transformative experience thought to be a perfect evocation of umami, the Japanese term for "savory."

Mail order: For high-quality American white matsutake, Oregon Mushrooms, tel 800-682-0036, oregonmushrooms.com. **Further information and recipes:** *Kaiseki* by Yoshihiro Murata (2006); *Japanese Cooking: A Simple Art* by Shizuo Tsuji (2012); latimes.com (search grilled matsutake); japanesefood .about.com (search matsutake gohan). **Special event:** Matsutake Festival, Bhutan, August, tourism .gov.bt (search matsutake festival). **See also:** Tartuti de Alba, page 243; Truffes Noires, page 140; Borovik Ceps, page 405.

⊢||||||||||||||||||||||||||||||⊣

FIT FOR A SAMURAI

Miso Soup

Japanese

Care to swap that breakfast cereal for a steaming cup of cloudy, salty miso broth? It's estimated that more than 70 percent of Japanese citizens begin their day with a bowl of the savory soy-based soup thought to alkalize blood and revive the nervous system. But the dish is a mainstay well beyond morning there, available almost anytime, anywhere, and in endless variations; in the U.S. it is almost always offered at the start of a meal in Japanese restaurants. Done correctly, miso soup is a deeply satisfying tonic, a staple of the samurai warriors who developed their strict strength-building diet of soup, grains, and vegetables some seven hundred years ago. Not recommended for breakfast is the very best, strongest version, featuring whole clams—the bivalves' briny hit of salt water adds an irresistible depth and richness to the broth.

Actual miso—a mix of fermented soybeans, rice, salt, and water that is formed into a protein-packed paste similar in texture to peanut butter—is centuries old. Its roots are in *chiang,* a fermented soybean paste that was developed in

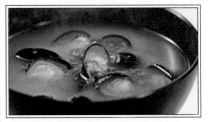

The savory broth can be bolstered with a few clams.

China more than 2,500 years ago by Buddhist priests. (The Chinese *chiang* character was pronounced hishio or misho.) Other components of the fortifying soup generally include dashi (a flavorful broth made of kelp and shaved bonito fish flakes that is a key component in most Japanese soups and noodle dishes), a protein such as tofu (or clams, if you're lucky), and a vegetable garnish such as scallions.

Unlike the chicken soups of the world, which take days of careful simmering and straining to prepare, miso's mix comes together relatively quickly. A good thing, considering the frequency with which it is consumed. Not fast enough? In Japan, you can help yourself to an instant cup of the stuff from miso-specific vending machines for a mere pittance.

Where: *In New York,* Nobu Fifty Seven, tel 212-757-3000, noburestaurants.com/fifty-seven; Yakitori Totto, tel 212-245-4555, tottonyc.com; *in Houston,* Uptown Sushi, tel 713-871-1200, uptown-sushi.com. **Mail order:** For dried miso mixes and miso paste, Mitsuwa Marketplace, mitsuwa.com. **Further information and recipes:** *Japanese Cooking: A Simple Art* by Shizuo Tsuji (2012); *The Miso Book* by John Belleme and Jan Belleme (2004); epicurious.com (search miso soup); cookstr.com (seach yellow miso soup).

SKINNY CHIC

Nasu

Japanese Eggplant

Japanese

Eggplants may have originated in India, making their way through China to Japan sometime in the eighth century. But the Japanese soil worked some kind of magic, producing a new cultivar that became integral to Japanese food and beloved around the world for its sweetness and relative versatility. Distinctively slender and small—only about four or five inches long at most—the Japanese eggplant, or *nasu,* has fewer seeds and less water than its larger, more bulbous American, or "globe," counterpart. It's also thinner skinned and a lot less bitter (no need to soak or salt it before cooking), with a flesh that becomes creamy and almost nutty in flavor when cooked.

Although it is treated like a vegetable, the glossy, purple-skinned eggplant is, like all eggplants, actually a fruit, a member of the nightshade (Solanaceae) family, along with the tomato, pepper, and potato. Luxurious treasures of the summer garden, in Japan eggplants are pickled (*nasu zuke*) and eaten alone or stuffed into sushi, deep-fried (as in tempura), grilled (as in *yaki nasu,* a favorite appetizer), and steamed with miso (*nasu dengaku*). They also lend themselves to the barbecue when lightly brushed with olive oil, sprinkled with sea salt, and tossed onto the grill.

Now grown in California and in various parts of the southern United States, Japanese eggplants are easy to find in specialty supermarkets and farmers' markets.

Where: *In Brentwood, CA,* Takao Sushi, tel 310-207-8636, takaobrentwood.com. **Mail order:** For fresh eggplants, marukaiestore.com; Mitsuwa Marketplace, mitsuwa.com; for seeds, Kitazawa Seed Company, tel 510-595-1188, kitazawaseed.com. **Further information and recipes:** *Washoku* by Elizabeth Andoh (2012); *Morimoto: The New Art of Japanese Cooking* by Masaharu Morimoto (2007); bonappetit.com (search ginger miso glazed eggplant); cookstr .com (search eggplant with yuzo miso sauce). **SPECIAL EVENT:** Northern California Soy and Tofu Festival, San Francisco, June, soyandtofufest .org. **TIP:** When selecting eggplants, look for those that are heavy for their size, and shiny and purple in appearance; dullness or brown stains indicate overripeness.

Nishiki Ichiba, Kyoto

Nishiki Market, Kyoto

Japanese

By default, any visit to the graceful antique city of Kyoto will include a tour of its many wondrous sights: the Ryoan-ji temple's Zen stone garden; the Gion geisha district with its old wooden teahouses; and Nijo Castle, where wooden

"nightingale floors" were designed to "chirp" if an intruder trod upon them to harm a sleeping shogun. . . . But to the food-obsessed, none seems as worthwhile as a day spent at Nishiki Ichiba, a slim, two-story, five-block stretch of more than a hundred shops and stalls selling dishes, utensils, and all manner of foods, herbs, spices, and teas. Scattered among the shops, food vendors sell inexpensive sweet and savory snacks—gently chewy rice and sweet bean paste confections, pickles, and bits of meats grilled on skewers—and hand out free samples. All inform the mind even as they delight the palate, and introduce novices to the essence of Japanese cuisine and its ingredients.

Known as "Kyoto's kitchen," Nishiki has in one form or another existed since the fourteenth century, first as a fish market before taking off and gradually expanding to its eclectic current configuration. Each vendor specializes in a single item, ingredient, or dish, and one stop for all should be Aritsugu, a knife shop that has operated since 1560 and is now run by the eighteenth generation of the namesake founding family. Once the official sword-maker to the Imperial House of Japan, during the seventeenth and eighteenth centuries, the Aritsugus wisely transitioned from swords to sushi knives and moved to Nishiki in 1981. Eventually they expanded to produce various kitchen knives and cooking pots, all of the most impeccable quality, with prices to match, and to hold cooking classes in the shop. And for those who take their knives very seriously, they also provide sharpening services, a skill they have certainly honed over the centuries.

WHERE: Nishiki-koji-dori, Nakagyo-ku, tel 81/75-211-3882, kyoto-nishiki.or.jp. **WHEN:** 9 a.m. to 6 p.m., stores closed Wednesday or Sunday. **FURTHER INFORMATION:** japan-guide.com (search nishiki market).

Many of the market's vendors specialize in a particular item.

Nuta, Horenso no Ohitashi, and Natto

Raw Fish Salad, Cold Spinach Salad, and Fermented Soybeans

Japanese

Among the enchantments of the Japanese kitchen are the tiny portions of intensely flavored palate-teasers called *izakaya*. Usually served with sake as premeal bites or at casual bars—much like mezes or tapas—these might include *sunomono,* meaning "vinegared things," and *aemono,* or "dressed things." Both can be made from vegetables or fish, among other ingredients, but sunomono have a lighter, vinegar-based dressing while aemono feature somewhat thicker, creamier blends of raw egg yolks and pureed tofu or the fermented soybean paste miso, to suggest a very thin mayonnaise.

Bonito-topped ohitashi

Three of the most intriguing of the lot are the aemono called *nuta,* the sunomono *horenso no ohitashi,* and the supremely pungent *natto,* which is in a category of its own. Nuta is a simple, ceviche-like salad of silky-thin slivers of raw fish such as tuna, yellowtail, or fluke; squid; or shellfish such as clams. The savory salinity of the dish is balanced by a gently tangy combination of mustard paste, rice vinegar, light soy sauce, and dashi, a briny stock made from the dried kelp kombu and bonito flakes.

Horenso no ohitashi (often simply ohitashi on Japanese menus) or "drunken spinach," is a softly appealing salad of that leafy vegetable, blanched to emerald brightness then chilled in a marinade of dashi, soy sauce, and the sweet rice wine, mirin. Served cold in its marinade, the spinach gets a finishing touch of crunchy, sea-salty flakes of dried bonito.

If the first two are easy to like, natto is the offering that separates the strong from the weak, the adventurous from the timid. Made from small, golden brown soybeans fermented with the *Bacillus subtilis* bacterium, it reaches a fragrant stage that rivals that of the Swedish *surströmming* (fermented herring, page 343) or the stinkiest of cheeses. The fermentation imparts a silvery sheen and a satiny viscosity to the beans, as well as a flavor considered rotten by some. But for others the experience is downright addictive—especially once natto's layers of sweet, sour, and pungent are gentled with a dressing of soy sauce, mustard, and the raw yolk of a quail or chicken egg. Natto is the basis of the vegetarian sushi *natto maki,* in which small clumps of the beans are packed with rice and wrapped in seaweed—but so substantial is its flavor that natto is usually enjoyed simply on a bed of plain rice.

WHERE: *In New York,* EN Japanese Brasserie, tel 212-647-9196, enjb.com; *in Houston,* Zushi, tel 832-243-6203, zushihouston.com; *in Gardena, CA,* Sanuki No Sato, tel 310-324-9184, sanukino sato.com. **FURTHER INFORMATION AND RECIPES:** *The Book of Sushi* by Kinjiro Omae and Yuzuru Tachibana (1988); *Japanese Cooking: A Simple Art* by Shizuo Tsuji (2012); japanesefood.about .com (search seasonal boiled spinach; nuta with negi and wakame); seriouseats.com (search natto).

———————|||||||||||||||||||||||||||||||||———————

AS PURE AS COMFORT GETS

Ochazuke

Rice in Green Tea

Japanese

I f you've ever wished you could douse your cereal in coffee in order to save a few steps, *ochazuke* is for you. Its base is a broth of the strong, rustic green tea called *bancha*, brewed from large, coarse, full-flavored leaves along with flecks

of aromatic stems and woodsy twigs; in it floats a comforting helping of cooked short-grain rice. The name of the dish derives from *cha*, or tea (preceded by the honorific "o"), and *zuke*, meaning moistened or submerged. With its palate-cleansing properties and abundant antioxidants, bancha gives a healthful boost to the dish's uplifting, restorative gifts.

It's the perfect choice for those looking for a light breakfast or a satisfying between-meals lift. That's certainly its appeal to busy students and office workers. When some elegant accents are added, it also makes a fashionable finish to a restaurant meal. In Kyoto, where it is known as *bubuzuke*, it might appear at dinner parties, where it is offered to guests as a signal that it's time to leave.

There are a few variations on the classic preparation, among them using rice that is shaped into a ball and toasted, resulting in a nice crackle and a rich, grainy aroma. Variety also comes by way of

toppings, which might include dried salmon or cod flakes; bits of cooked, salted, or raw fish; flecks of crisp nori (dried seaweed); zingy *tsukemono* (pickles); and the fiery jade-green condiment wasabi, akin to horseradish.

Although they are shunned by purists, and not nearly as healthy, packages of dehydrated "instant" seasonings for this dish are prevalent in Japan, resembling instant ramen mixes and similarly salty and preservative-laden. Simple and pure as ochazuke is, there is no reason to cut corners.

Where: *In Toyko,* Toricho, tel 81/3-3571-4650; *in New York,* Yakitori Totto, tel 212-245-4555, tottonyc.com. **Mail order:** for Japanese rice and green tea, marukaiestore.com; for green tea, hibiki-an.com. **Further information and recipes:** *Japanese Cooking: A Simple Art* by Shizuo Tsuji (2012); *Washoku* by Elizabeth Andoh (2005); saveur.com (search ochazuke); food52.com (search ochazuke).

———————|||||||||||||||||||||||||||||||||———————

A FISTFUL OF RICE

Onigiri, or Omusubi

Rice Balls

Japanese

E ngagingly chewy, moist, and hearty, the rice balls called *onigiri* or *omusubi* are the Japanese answer to lunch box sandwiches. A favorite picnic dish since the eleventh century, they were once known as *tonjiki* and were thus recorded in the diary of Lady Murasaki, author of what is considered the world's first novel, *The Tale of Genji.*

The filling and portable bites are made with cooked room-temperature white rice, lightly salted then pressed (*nigiri*) or gathered (*musubu*) into a firm but not crushed compact shape, with a surprise tucked inside—favorite stuffings, include the sweet-sour pickled *umeboshi* plum, considered beneficial for digestion; a bit of salt-glazed salmon; a grilled or pickled wild mushroom; or a vegetable relish. Made at home or purchased from convenience stores or upscale groceries, the palm-size bundles are generally shaped into cylinders, spheres, or triangles, but can occasionally take on even more fanciful forms. Most appealingly, onigiri can be wrapped in a sheet of bronze-green nori (dried, pressed seaweed) for a neatly intact bundle with a nice snap and a hint of the sea. Alternatively, for textural interest and a warmer

flavor, the shaped onigiri can be lightly toasted in a skillet.

One can only hope that one day onigiri might catch on and become as ubiquitous around the world as they are in Japan, where they are sold everywhere from parks and beaches to train stations—a healthy but utterly tasty answer to the hot dog or pizza slice.

WHERE: *In New York,* Café Zaiya at three locations, zaiyany.com; Yakitori Totto, tel 212-245-4555, tottonyc.com; *in Atlanta,* Taka Sushi, tel 404-869-2802, takasushiatlanta.com; *in Los Angeles and Santa Monica,* Sunny Blue, sunnyblueinc.com. **MAIL ORDER:** For Japanese rice and nori, marukaiestore.com. **FURTHER INFORMATION AND RECIPES:** *The Tale of Genji* by Lady Murasaki (Translated by Royall Tyler, 2007); *Washoku* by Elizabeth Andoh (2012); *Homestyle Japanese Cooking in Pictures* by Sadako Kohno (1991); foodnetwork.com (search onigiri); japanesefood.about.com (search rice balls).

SNACKS FOR ALL SEASONS

Senbei
Rice Crackers
Japanese

The term *confections* generally brings to mind sweets, be they candies, frozen creams, nut or bean pastes, or cakes and cookies. But in the Japanese lexicon, it covers all manner of treats served with green tea, including the tantalizing

senbei—bite-size rice crackers that are salty and tangy, with only the faintest hint of caramelized sweetness. Whether shaped into tiny squares, balls, or sticks, the snacks are seasoned with salt, soy sauce, miso, or mirin, and perhaps also with spicy chile, wasabi, or curry powder; and they are wrapped or flecked with nori, the bronzed dried seaweed that lends a savory, oceanic essence to the addictive nibblers.

A classic between-meals snack also favored with aperitifs and, more recently, as an accompaniment for cheeses, senbei are quite beautiful to

Rice crackers for well-rounded snacking

behold, with a golden-brown, lacquerlike glaze that suggests bits of ceramic tile and adds to their delightful crunch. Most traditionally, the crackers are served after being freshly grilled on metal grids over charcoal, which imparts a smoky patina, but they are much more commonly found in packages or scooped out of bulk bins.

Differing only in size and shape from senbei are *arare* (the aptly named "hailstones"). They come in innumerable bite-size shapes and flavors and are the smallest and crispest members of the family. When wrapped with seaweed, they are known as *norimaki arare.* Shaped into elongated crescents, they are *kaki-no-tane,* so-called because of their resemblance to persimmon, or *kaki,* seeds. The pastel-colored *hina*

arare, in small, fanciful forms such as tiny eggs, are featured from midwinter to spring as part of the March celebration of the Doll Festival, or Hinamatsuri. In Hawaii, arare are called *kakimochi*—brought there by Japanese farm workers who emigrated to the islands in the early twentieth century—and are mixed with popcorn for an addictively crunchy, salty treat; in Japan they will often appear tossed in with roasted nuts, Chex Mix style.

WHERE: *In Shizouka, Japan,* Aoi Senbei, tel 81/54-252-6260, aoisenbei.com; *in Washington and Oregon,* Uwajimaya, uwajimaya.com. **MAIL ORDER:** marukaiestore.com (search oishisahyak-kei arare and shirakiku arare); Mitsuwa Marketplace, mitsuwa.com.

DIP INTO A DIY DINNER

Shabu-Shabu

Japanese

Seething hot pots of savory broth in which sliced meats and vegetables are cooked right at the table are specialties throughout Asia, but they're especially common in the northern regions (see Shua Yang Jou, Mongolian hot pot, page 784).

There they act as warming communal traditions, fulfilling room-heating and ritualistic functions as well as culinary ones.

The pots themselves are typically made of a large metal bowl slipped over a chimney outfitted with a brazier that gives off an intense heat, and sometimes has an open flame. Of the latter, the most spectacular—and scary, if you sit too close—is the Chinese "chrysanthemum pot," named after the flames that leap around its base and suggest petals of the namesake flower.

Not surprisingly, given the attention Japan pays to the aesthetics of cuisine, that country is the source of the most elegantly refined hot pots, the *nabemono.* These include the *mizutaki* ("water-simmered") variety made with chicken, and *chirinabe,* made with fish, either of which

might be cooked in a big heatproof casserole called *donabe.* Of the nabemono, the most well known outside of Japan is the hot pot called shabu-shabu, meaning "swish swish," its name referring to the gentle swishing sound the thinly cut meat, tofu, and vegetables make as they are sloshed around in the simmering broth to cook.

The meal is usually a festive group event, in the manner of Swiss fondue, and begins by heating up a broth flavored with the briny giant kelp called kombu. Napa cabbage, onions, carrots, and a few earthy mushrooms might be added to the pot. Each diner is armed with long chopsticks or a fondue fork and a small dipping bowl, as well as condiments such as the citrusy, dark *ponzu* sauce, toasted sesame sauce, minced scallions, and finely grated daikon, the pungent giant

Hot pot ingredients await a dip in steaming broth.

platters are paper-thin slices of beef or lamb, or some of each, lacy with ivory fat, plus shiitake mushrooms, slivered scallions, and maybe also thin rounds of onion, small leaves of napa cabbage, dark and herbaceous chrysanthemum leaves, cubes of tofu, and perhaps sliced fresh bamboo shoots. The meat is best cooked rare, with the vegetables simmered to slightly firm tenderness; when done, each bite is dipped into the sauce bowl. After everything has been cooked and consumed, the broth, now intensely flavored, is ladled into the dipping bowl and the result is happily quaffed.

Where: *In Kyoto,* Junidanya, tel 81/75-561-1655,; *in Gardena, CA,* Sanuki No Sato, tel 310-324-9184, sanukinosato.com. **Mail order:** For hot pots, korin.com (search shabu-shabu hot pot; chopstick cooking long). **Further information and recipes:** *The Cooking of Japan* by Rafael Steinberg (1969); *Japanese Cooking: A Simple Art* by Shizuo Tsuji (2012); *Japanese Hot Pots* by Tadashi Ono and Harris Salat (2011); japanesefood.about.com (search beef shabu-shabu); epicurious.com (search shabu-shabu). **See also:** Waterzooi à la Gantoise (Belgian Chicken Stew), page 151.

white radish. Salt and the chile-hot seven-spice powder *shichimi* might also be on the table, for added sprightliness. All of these are mixed to taste in the dipping bowls, and the cooking begins.

Colorfully fanned out on huge serving

--------||||||||||||||||||||||||||||||||--------

SOME LIKE IT COLD

Soba
Buckwheat Noodles

Japanese

Among the world's cherished noodles, Japanese soba is one of the most unusual forms: a silky, toasty, spaghetti-like stick made from buckwheat flour. Once a food of the poor, it's now considered a subject worthy of devoted

connoisseurship, with the very best examples made from freshly harvested and milled buckwheat mixed with water and a bit of hard-wheat flour, the dough kneaded and cut by hand into slender strands with a chewy bite. Although in

soba restaurants, the noodles can be had hot in rich broths fleshed out with bits of chicken, duck, shrimp tempura, tofu, mushrooms, or other offerings, purists opt for *zaru soba*—"soba in a basket," which might really mean soba on a bamboo mat, with the noodles served cold. (Quite cold, in fact, especially when there's cracked ice under that bamboo mat.)

Nothing could be simpler than this briefly boiled noodle, chilled and dipped into a sauce that, according to the diner's preference, might include mirin (sweet rice wine), soy sauce, wasabi, raw egg yolk, finely minced scallions, dashi (kelp and fish broth), and daikon radish. Flecks of nori (dried seaweed) are the garnish preferred by soba mavens; at the end of the meal, some of the tasty cooking water might be warmed up and ladled into the sauce dish for a palate-cleansing finish.

Soba is always served as a main course, never a side dish or appetizer. Although it is popular throughout Japan, it is traditionally the noodle of Tokyo and of northern Japan. Udon, the thick, satisfyingly chewy, ivory wheat-flour noodle, is a specialty of southern Japan and Osaka. While they are interchangeable in many recipes, soba is more likely than udon to be served cold; udon is most pleasant in hot broth.

For a really unusual treat, try soba sushi, a specialty in some soba houses, and one that usually must be ordered in advance. For this, anywhere from twenty-five to thirty strands of the very fine, vermicelli-like noodles are rolled, tied together, and cooked in boiling water. When cool, they are wrapped in nori and sliced crosswise in the manner of maki sushi rolls. The chewy strands enfolded in the snappingly crisp seaweed with some sesame seeds, diced cucumber, and radish sprouts, all dipped into the pungent soba sauce, add up to a delicacy well worth seeking out.

Where: *In Toyko,* Toshian, tel 81/3-3444-1741; *in New York,* Soba Nippon, tel 212-489-2525, sobanippon.com; EN Japanese Brasserie, tel 212-647-9196, enjb.com; *in Washington, DC,* Sushi Taro, tel 202-462-8999, sushitaro.com; *in Los Angeles,* Soba Sojibo, tel 310-479-1200; *in Brentwood, CA,* Takao Sushi, tel 310-207-8636, takaobrentwood.com; *in Seattle,* Miyabi 45th, tel 206-632-4545, miyabi45th.com. **Mail order:** asiangrocer.com; marukaiestore.com; for buckwheat flour, bobsredmill.com. **Further information and recipes:** *Japanese Cooking: A Simple Art* by Shizuo Tsuji (2012); *Washoku* by Elizabeth Andoh (2005); saveur.com (search zaru soba; soba dipping sauce); epicurious.com (search mint and scallion soba noodles); thekitchn.com (search how to make buckwheat noodles from scratch).

THE ACTUAL LAND OF THE LOTUS EATERS

Subasu

Pickled Lotus Root

Japan

In this incomparably crunchy, fresh, pickled offering, thin, round disks of sliced lotus root—whose big, lacy openings are actually air chambers that keep the aquatic plant afloat—are gently simmered in a sweetened vinegar mixture. The result bears tantalizing counterpoints of texture and flavor, sparked by the salty-sweet, tangy vinaigrette, the lotus root, *renkon* in Japanese, retains its crispness while gaining an inner tenderness.

Lotus is a favorite food throughout Asia, harvested for its roots as well as its leaves and blossoms, and representing purity and enlightenment in the Buddhist tradition. The tan, sausage-shaped root can also be cooked with pork bones into a homey, curative Chinese soup, or simmered with a sticky-sweet soy glaze for a favorite Korean appetizer. In Japan, the root can be prepared tempura style, in thin, crackle-coated disks that complement other vegetables and seafood. But *subasu,* with its clean and pure flavor, may be the very best showcase for the lotus root's icy crunch and subtle taste.

WHERE: *In Chicago,* Oysy Sushi, tel 312-670-6750, oysysushi.com; Vora, tel 312-929-2035, vorachicago.com. **MAIL ORDER:** marxfoods.com (search fresh lotus root); Mitsuwa Marketplace, mitsuwa.com. **FURTHER INFORMATION AND RECIPES:** *Washoku* by Elizabeth Andoh (2005); *Asian Ingredients* by Bruce Cost (2000); *Japanese Farm Food* by Nancy Singleton Hachiso (2012);

starchefs.com (search pickled lotus root); cdkitchen.com (search marinated lotus root).

Lotus root's holes are actually air chambers.

ALL IN ONE BITE

Sushi

Japanese

When it comes to sushi, there is no margin for error: Everything has to be just right. The fish must be ocean fresh. It must be cut just thin enough, and perfectly against or with the grain, as dictated by its structure. It must feel nicely cool against the lips and, on a mixed platter, must contribute the right hue and texture to the rainbow array of fish. Serious connoisseurs always sit at the sushi bar, eating each offering as it is presented, so there is no chance for the temperature or texture to go wrong. The freshness of the fish is so important that a bona fide maven—a *tsujin*—would have sushi only for lunch, as the morning's catch ages as the day wears on.

Hard as it may be to believe, given those exacting conditions, sushi is really about the rice—or at least it was in the beginning, in the fourth century B.C. when, in Southeast Asia, salted rice was used to preserve fish. Around the eighth century A.D., the practice reached Japan, and along the way, the combination became a delicacy in its own right.

Nowadays, sushi rice must be prepared with the same exactitude as is the fish. It must be short-grain (called *uruchimai,* it's the kind used to make sake), seasoned only with salt, sugar, and rice vinegar, and tossed gently in a wooden bowl to cool to room temperature before serving. An exception is the so-called Nozawa style, pioneered by Los Angeles sushi chef Kazunori Nozawa, in which the rice is served very warm and softly falling apart, making the sushi a little more difficult to navigate with either chopsticks or fingers, the latter being the preferred way with all sushi. The other exception, of course, is sashimi: raw fish slices served without any rice at all, often as a sort of appetizer preceding a sushi meal.

Strict sushi orthodoxy also dictates that the sushi master, or *itamae,* must have closely clipped fingernails, short hair, a cap, and for the most strict, no eyeglasses. (Also for the most finicky, the itamae may not be a woman—women's hands are too warm, they say.) The cutting board should be of a hard, white wood, and the knives of the sharpest samurai steel, costing hundreds if not thousands of dollars, especially if custom-made. The protocol for dipping sushi mandates that it should be turned so the fish goes into the soy sauce, called *murasaki* in sushi terminology, with a dab of the fiery horseradish-like green wasabi added separately, never mushed into the sauce. And that wasabi root (never reconstituted powder, see page 825) should be grated to order on a piece of sharkskin stretched over a frame; a wooden grater is an acceptable substitute, but metal is not. Between the cost of fresh, sushi-grade fish, and this catalog of exacting rules and equipment, it's no wonder a sushi dinner can run to hundreds of dollars per person at the finest establishments.

There are four main styles of sushi. *Nigiri* ("hand-pressed") sushi appears as colorful fish slices atop oblongs of rice, formed in the palm of the *itamae*'s hand. Because these are so unadorned, they are generally made with the very best quality of fish. Fish that may be a bit less perfect in color or cut goes into *maki* sushi, bits of fish inside the rice in nori-wrapped rolls. These include bite-size as well as giant rolls, called *futomaki*, and the cone-shaped hand rolls, *temaki*, that might be filled with strips of grilled salmon skin, yellowtail, spicy tuna tartare, or glazed eel. *Chirashi* (or "scattered") sushi is an artful sort of rice bowl, with bits of various raw fish and shellfish, pickles, ginger, radish, and more, the lot painstakingly arranged, or sometimes just scattered loosely, over sushi rice. *Battera* sushi is an Osaka specialty, for which layers of mackerel and rice are gently pressed into a rectangular mold, before being cut out and served in ladyfinger-size portions.

Some of the most appealing and popular fish for sushi are tuna, the fatty belly (*toro*) being the prime choice; yellowtail, or *hamachi*; the chewy giant geoduck clam; silky globs of *uni*, the roe-producing gonads of the sea urchin; saltwater eel grilled with the sweet burnish of a teryaki-style sauce; and glassy, orange-red salmon roe, often topped with a raw quail egg yolk. In season, there may also be tiny, fried softshell spider crabs wrapped in rice for a succulent hand roll.

When all goes right, which is usually dictated to some degree by price, such a meal delivers the delectable and unparalleled experience of cool fish, sweet and tangy rice, salty soy sauce, and the spark of wasabi, all in one bite—which is the only way to eat a piece of sushi: No nibbling allowed. Sake or tea are the typical accompaniments, but a scotch and soda can lend a nicely astringent note.

WHERE: *In Tokyo,* Turuhachi, tel 81/3-3262-9665; Daiwa Sushi, tel 81/3-3547-6807; Sushi-Jiro, tel 81/3-3535-3600, sushi-jiro.jp; *in New York,* Masa and Bar Masa, tel 212-823-9800, masanyc.com; Hatsuhana at two locations, hatsuhana.com; Sushi Yasuda, tel 212-972-1001, sushiyasuda.com; *in New York, Los Angeles, and Honolulu,* Sushi Sasabune, sasabunenyc.com; *in Washington, DC,* Sushi Taro, tel 202-462-8999, sushitaro.com; *in Atlanta,* Taka Sushi, tel 404-869-2802, takasushiatlanta.com; *in Houston,* Kata Robata, tel 713-526-8858, katarobata.com; Uptown Sushi, tel 713-871-1200, uptown-sushi.com; *in Los Angeles,* Nozawa Bar, tel 424-216-6158, nozawabar.com. **MAIL ORDER:** for utensils, sushinow.com; asiangrocer.com. **FURTHER INFORMATION AND RECIPES:** *Sushi Secrets* by Kazuko Masui and Chihiro Masui (2004); *Japanese Cooking: A Simple Art* by Shizuo Tsuji (2012); *A Taste of Japan* by Donald Richie (1993); sushimaster.com; sushiencyclopedia.com; foodandwine.com (search how to make sushi with morimoto); foodnetwork.com (search master sushi rice); gourmet.com (search great tips for homemade sushi rolls). For sushi-making courses, *in New York and environs,* Sushi by Simon, tel 212-340-1339, sushibysimon.com; *in San Francisco,* Breakthrough Sushi, tel 415-533-1755, breakthroughsushi.com; Tokyo Sushi Academy, tel 81/3-2260-1755, sushischool.jp;

in Kamloops, Canada, Kamloops Japanese Canadian Association, tel 250-376-9629, kjca.ca. **Tip:** To get deep into the world of sushi at the hands of a master, watch the documentary *Jiro Dreams of Sushi,* directed by David Gelb (2012).

⊢|||||||||||||||||||||||||||||||||⊣

ROLLED, NOT FLIPPED

Tamagoyaki

Japanese Omelet

Japanese

Just as aspiring Western chefs are judged by the strength of their omelet making, sushi connoisseurs believe that you can tell how good the chef is by tasting his *tamagoyaki*—the moist and succulent strips of layered omelet served atop rice as *nigiri* (hand-pressed) sushi. What they're looking for is a delicately sweet flavor and a soft texture that is neither spongy nor wet, neither dry nor browned, but instead perfectly light, airy, and almost soufflélike, a bite-size morsel full of delightful nuance. If that sounds unfamiliar, you may never have experienced real, freshly made tamago. For nowadays, many restaurants, both in America and abroad, buy big blocks of frozen premade tamago from wholesale suppliers, with predictable results.

To achieve a proper tamagoyaki, a sushi chef must be nimble, quick, and painstaking as he follows a series of time-honored steps, using the special square pan called *tamagoyakinabe* to ensure that the finished product has even edges and a uniform thickness. First the eggs are beaten with dashi (the typical Japanese stock base), sake, or mirin (a sweet rice wine), a pinch of sugar, and a splash of soy sauce. The pan is ever so lightly slicked with oil and heated, and the egg mixture is poured in. As it pan-grills, the chef uses chopsticks to gently fold the omelet over onto itself until it becomes a long, rectangular block and the layers have completely melded together. After the omelet is cooked, but before it cools, it is gently pressed in a bamboo mat to set its dense texture and its shape. Cut into rectangles, it is ready to be placed atop the mounds of sushi rice.

The word *tamago* actually means "egg" in Japanese, and tamago comes in many forms: quail eggs are *uzura no tamago*; *onsen tamago* is literally "hot spring cooked egg" and refers to an egg poached slowly in low-temperature water; *yude tamago* is a hard-cooked egg; *hanjuku tamago* is soft-boiled. But it's only the tamagoyaki omelet that is the true test of a master's skill—so much so that legends abound about sushi masters who don't take phone calls or allow visitors into the kitchen while they're making tamago.

Where: *In New York, Sydney, and Toronto,* Momofuku restaurants, momofuku.com; *in New York,* Hatsuhana at two locations, hatsuhana .com. **Further information and recipes:** *Washoku* by Elizabeth Andoh (2005); momofukufor2.com (search tamago-yaki recipe); epicurious.com (search tamago sushi; egg sushi; omelet sushi).

—||||||||||||||||||||||||||||||||||—

INTO THE FRYING KETTLE

Tempura

Japanese

With its clean, unmarred flavors and minimalistic approach to ingredients, Japanese food tends toward simplicity and lightness. That's true even when it comes to the deep-fried specialty of tempura, the famously light-as-air seafood and vegetable bites that are common to practically every corner of Japan. To achieve what might be the world's perfect fry, tempura chefs pay particular attention to the kinds of cooking oils they choose. Most favor some combination of sesame oil, which lends a nutty flavor, and vegetable oil, although various exotic choices are employed sometimes, too, especially fragrant, light camellia oil. The chefs lean toward choice fillings with clean flavors. The strong inherent flavors of chicken, pork, and beef are generally believed to overwhelm the batter—more favorable are shrimp, the most common tempura ingredient; a range of fish and seafood such as scallops, squid, tiny crabs, *kisu* (a small white-fleshed fish), *anago* (saltwater eel); and vegetables including snow peas, shiitake mushrooms, asparagus, squash, onion, and Japanese eggplant.

But the batter is where tempura truly distinguishes itself, with the secret to its lightness lying not so much in the ingredients (an unsurprising mix of flour, egg, and water) as in their treatment. The water must be iced, and the batter must remain discernibly lumpy, folded together with a brief whisking of a fork or chopsticks. This last is what prevents gluten from forming and creating a heavy, bready coating. All that remains for the fillings is a dredging in flour, a dip in the batter, and a very brief plunge into the deep-fryer for tempura perfection to emerge, the succulent ingredients kept moist and flavorful by their protective coating and the quickness of the fry.

In direct contrast to the sheer, lacy quality of the cleanly fried foods, the dish itself has

The perfection of tempura is a form of art.

murky origins. A commonly held theory is that the Jesuit missionaries who came to Japan from Portugal in the sixteenth century were the inspiration. Evidence lies in the Latin term *quattuor tempora* (four times)—a reference to the four weeks in the traditional Catholic calendar containing "ember days," on which no meat was to be eaten. On these days, observant Portuguese generally ate vegetable and seafood fritters.

Some modern tempura chefs, however, contend that the technique of deep-frying batter-dipped foods was introduced to Japan by the Chinese less than three hundred years ago and was initially embraced by mountain-dwelling Zen monks who wished to make their vegetarian diet more palatable.

Regardless of when it first appeared, tempura flourished into an iconic dish that is presented a variety of ways: on its own; on top of a bowl of rice, along with a concentrated version of *tentsuyu* sauce made of kombu (dried sea kelp), *katsuobushi* (dried, smoked bonito flakes), mirin (sweet rice wine), and soy sauce; paired with soba and udon noodles; and even as a filler in sushi rolls.

Everyone agrees on the best way to eat it: right at the counter, one piece at a time, each fresh and hot from the fryer.

Where: *In Tokyo,* Ten-Ichi, tel 81/3-3571-1949, tenichi.co.jp; *in New York,* Morimoto, tel 212-989-8883, morimotonyc.com; *in Los Angeles,* Sawtelle Tempura House, tel 310-479-5989. **Further information and recipes:** *Japanese Cooking: A Simple Art* by Shizuo Tsuji (2012); cookstr.com (search vegetable tempura); foodandwine.com (search morimotos shrimp tempura with miso mayonnaise).

FISH CITY

Tsukiji Fish Market, Tokyo

Japanese

Time was when food- and adventure-loving tourists donned raincoats and rubber boots and slunk out of hotels at 4:30 in the morning to take in Tsukiji—fondly pronounced *skiji*—the world's most stupendous wholesale fish market and,

to many minds, Tokyo's most spectacular sight. Tourists are now barred until after 9:00 a.m., but what they enter is still truly Fish City, a series of enormous covered halls on the banks of the Sumida River (although the market is being relocated to its own island in advance of the 2020 Olympics), illuminated by bare lightbulbs and truck headlights in the morning mists. Everywhere you turn there are crates and dollies amid a pervasive wetness, hence the raincoats and rubber boots to protect against the constant spray of hoses. Market stalls crackle with activity and are stacked with every sort of sea creature you can imagine, and probably some you can't—spiny red crabs and spiny lobsters, grassy knobs of sea urchins, coral reefs of red salmon roe, tumbling mounds of ink-purple octopuses, black-and-white-striped tiger fish, silver-leafed whitebait, and gizzard shad covered in gilded silver scales.

The main event is the tuna hall and the auction that takes place there daily at about

5:00 a.m., for which special passes must be obtained. As much as 191 tons of tuna may be sold there daily, an especially astonishing sum when you realize that this occurs six days a week at Tsukiji alone. Enormous whole tuna, frosty white if frozen or silver-blue if fresh, are laid out in seemingly endless rows looking like fighter planes on an airstrip, their tails cut off so that the amount of prized fat can be ascertained. Buyers with flashlights closely examine the fish, deciding which to bid on, which they do with hand signals that make the process look like a big, crowded game of rock-paper-scissors.

It is nearly impossible not to start craving some sparkling fresh sushi after a visit to Tsukiji. Fortunately, it is a desire easily satisfied at one of the small sushi restaurants within the market, particularly Daiwa and Sushi Bun. Both dispense no-frills sushi to hungry market workers and tourists for about half the price of what the same items would cost in Tokyo's center. On particularly good days, the menu might include coral twists of *akagai* (ark clam), paper-thin slices of nicely chewy *awabi* (abalone), *torigai* (cockles), and the seductive morsel that is *shako*, which resembles a cross between a crab and a shrimp and is usually briefly boiled before serving. You can be sure that whatever is on the menu, however exotic or familiar,

A fish auction in Tokyo

will be surpassingly fresh—and a most memorable breakfast.

WHERE: 5-2-1 Tsukiji, Chuo, tel 81/3-3542-1111, tsukiji.or.jp/english; Daiwa Sushi, tel 81/3-3547-6807, and Sushi Bun restaurant, tel 81/3-3541-3860, are both on block 5-2-1 in the market. **WHEN:** Open every day except Sunday and holidays from 5 a.m. to 2 p.m., from 9 a.m. for visitors. **FURTHER INFORMATION:** japan-guide .com (search tsukiji).

A CHARMING URCHIN

Uni

Sea Urchin

Japanese

"It was a brave man who first ate an oyster," said Jonathan Swift. What then would he have said about the person who first ate a sea urchin? It would be hard to imagine less prepossessing candidates for gourmandise than these stiff, spiky balls that may range in color from black-green to emerald and even to tints of red and lavender. And should a swimmer step on one, a visit to a doctor to have the painful and sometimes poisonous quill extracted might put him off his feed for quite a while.

Yet, ever on the prowl for a new treat, some courageous and curious ancient gourmand spliced open the spine-covered shell and tasted one of the five small, quivery, bright orange-red lobes within, and the rest is gastronomic history. Apparently, the first taster was beguiled by the lusciously silky texture and the teasingly salty, slightly astringent flavor—somewhere between caviar and the coral roe of female lobsters, although the edible parts of the urchin, described as tongues, are not roe but the sex glands.

Known to have existed for 450 million years, the shellfish were dubbed "urchins" by

some, "sea hedgehogs" or "curls" by others, and there are between 700 and 800 varieties around the world. Two of the most highly prized for flavor and texture are *Strongylocentrotus droebachiensis*, which inhabits the North Atlantic, including the English Channel and the coasts of Norway and Maine, and *Paracentrotus lividus*, which lives in the Mediterranean. Oddly, the North Atlantic urchin is rarely eaten by locals. Rather, it is exported mostly to Japan and other parts of Asia, where local supplies cannot keep up with demand.

The Japanese mostly eat *uni* uncooked—its sunny hue and deep-sea essence make it a favorite atop sushi. In fact, it is doubtful that a conscientious Japanese chef or home cook would serve fresh sea urchins any way but raw. However, at the bygone Soto, once one of New York's finest sushi restaurants, chef-owner

Sotohiro Kosugi fried uni in a thin, delicate tempura batter that he finished with his homemade dehydrated uni powder for an extra belt of flavor. And bottled, lightly cooked sea urchins are sometimes blended with egg yolks, along with sake and mirin, for an intensely yellow mayonnaise. But Shizuo Tsuji, author of *Japanese Cooking* and former proprietor of Japan's foremost professional cooking school, advised, "As delicious as this dressing is, do not waste fresh sea urchin on it. Eat fresh sea urchin raw!"

The Mediterranean variety is a longtime favorite of the Spanish (who call them *erizo de mar*), the Italians (*riccio di mare*), and the French (*oursin*). Those who love them most like to eat them close to shore, split (with or without a special slim, curved opener), and rinsed with seawater and perhaps squirted with lemon juice. Italians also cook them up into pasta sauces, and the French sometimes lightly boil them like a coddled egg, or puree them into mayonnaise-type sauces.

Despite their long history as European delicacies, sea urchins really became well known in the U.S. as *uni,* and the Japanese name has prevailed.

WHERE: *In Tokyo,* Sushi-Jiro, tel 81/3-3535-3600, sushi-jiro.jp; Daiwa Sushi, 81/3-3547-6807; *in New York,* Sushi Nakazawa, tel 212-924-2212, sushinakazawa.com; for ravioli with sea urchin, Sandro's, tel 212-288-7374, sandrosnyc.com; élan, tel 646-682-7105, elannyc.com; *in Boston,* O Ya, tel 617-654-9909, oyarestaurantboston.com; *in Washington, DC,* Sushi Taro, tel 202-462-8999, sushitaro.com; *in Atlanta,* Taka Sushi, tel 404-869-2802, takasushiatlanta.com; *in Houston,* Uptown Sushi, tel 713-871-1200, uptown-sushi.com; *in San Francisco,* Izakaya Yuzuki, tel 415-556-9898, yuzukisf.com; *in Los Angeles,* Nozawa Bar, tel 424-216-6158, nozawabar.com. **MAIL ORDER:** For fresh uni packed in trays, Catalina Offshore Products, store.catalinaop.com. **FURTHER INFORMATION AND RECIPES:** *Sushi-Making at Home* by Hiro Sone and Lissa Doumani (2014); *Morimoto: The New Art of Japanese Cooking* by Masaharu Morimoto (2007); epicurious.com (search sea urchin mousse with ginger vinaigrette); food network.com (search uni risotto with seared japanese scallops); saveur.com (search chilled sea urchin and farro pasta). **SPECIAL EVENT:** Teuri Uni Matsuri, Teuri, Japan, August, seaurchinfacts. com (click Sea Urchin Facts Festivals).

THE LUCKIEST CATTLE

Wagyu

Japanese

There are two basic principles for a truly great steak: The fat must be white and sweet, and the meat must retain its juices. Finding both qualities in one piece of meat is a rare thing indeed, which is why Japanese beef, with its tender, fine-grained texture, soft juiciness, and sweet, almost graceful flavor, is so revered (and also so expensive). *Wagyu,* the term used to describe premium Japanese beef from a special breed of cattle, contains fully three times more fat than U.S. prime (the best grade of American beef), and its high quality is attributed to that incredible marbling. But the marbling itself results from a culture of animal husbandry with almost preposterously high standards.

The most famous wagyu may be Kobe, derived from a centuries-old strain of Japanese Black cattle from the Hyōgo Prefecture. These are the pampered cows rumored to be treated to daily massages as a way of distributing surface fat within their muscles and producing that classic marbling. It's been reported that the cattle are fed a steady diet of beer in order to fatten them up, and that is partially true: They are fed high-fiber foods like hay, wheat bran, corn, and soybean byproducts—sometimes with a weekly beer or two thrown in. (The rumor that the cows get to hear Mozart while they're eating and drinking, however, is false.)

Another, less-known type of premium Japanese beef, considered by some to be even fattier than Kobe (though that is a hotly disputed point), is Matsuzaka, from a town of the same name in the Mie Prefecture. Because Matsuzaka cows are in far shorter supply than Kobe, their meat has never been sold for export. Those lucky enough to have tried it—a feat currently impossible outside of Japan—say that it's like Kobe only more so, with even more tenderness and denser marbling.

The Japanese beef so revered for its marbling and purity

Over the years, a very small number of wagyu stock made their way to the U.S. for breeding. Inevitably, the presence of domestic cows has led to a predilection among some American chefs for mixing small amounts of wagyu into trendy comfort foods like burgers or meat loaf, largely for the purpose of cashing in on the high prices diners are willing to pay for the exotic, top-notch beef.

In Japan, however, they take their beef very seriously, and it's no surprise that they apply the same exacting, spare yet elegant aesthetic to its preparation as they do to that of raw fish. Like sashimi, wagyu may be enjoyed raw and thinly sliced. It may also, of course, be grilled on a *teppan* grill or *yaki* grill to make sukiyaki, or dipped into hot pot broths as in shabu-shabu (see page 814). Whatever the presentation, the point is not to obscure the meat's flavor behind spices, herbs, and sauces, but to make the most of its inherent beauty.

WHERE: *In Kyoto,* Kobemisono Kyototen, tel 81/75-255-2981; *in Osaka,* Matsusakagyu Yakiniku M, tel 81/6-6221-2917; *in multiple locations in the U.S. and Asia,* Gyu-kaku, gyu-kaku .com; *in New York,* EN Japanese Brasserie, tel 212-647-9196, enjb.com; Morimoto, tel 212-989-8883, morimotonyc.com; *in Washington, DC,* Bourbon Steak, tel 202-944-2026, bourbon steakdc.com; *in Houston,* Uptown Sushi, tel 713-871-1200, uptown-sushi.com; *in San Francisco,* 5A5 Steak Lounge, tel 415-989-2539, 5a5stk.com. **RETAIL AND MAIL ORDER:** For American wagyu, *in New York,* Lobel's Prime Meats, tel 877-783-4512, lobels.com; *in Chicago,* Allen Brothers, tel 800-852-2205, allenbrothers.com. **MAIL ORDER:** DeBragga, debragga.com; Japan Premium Beef, tel 212-260-2333, japanpremiambeef.jimdo.com. **FURTHER INFORMATION AND RECIPES:** *The Japanese Grill* by Tadashi Ono and Harris Salat (2009); American Wagyu Beef Association, wagyu.org. **TIP:** Remember that all American wagyu is not created equal—you could be talking about a steer that's 75 percent wagyu blood versus one that's 97 percent.

—||||||||||||||||||||||||||||||||||—

THE DEEP-SEA SOURCE OF UMAMI

Wakame, Kombu, and Agar

Japanese

Although seaweed has been eaten for thousands of years by everyone from the Irish to the Aborigines, it will forever be associated with Asian food, and specifically with Japan. What most Westerners are just beginning to appreciate is that beyond the dried nori used to wrap sushi lies a whole world of flavors, textures, and colors. Whatever its form, seaweed is rich in glutamate, the amino acid responsible for the mysterious and magical umami flavor that lovers of Japanese food forever tout.

There's wakame, the glittering green-silver seaweed that grows in shallow water near Japanese shorelines. Chewy and tangy, it's the kind often featured in seaweed salads. Kombu are the very chewy dark strips of kelp that grow in deep ocean waters and are the main ingredient in the traditional Japanese broth known as dashi. Agar is the intricately branched, thin, and wispy red sea vegetable that grows in deep, dark waters and is used as a gelling and congealing agent in a host of foods, including clear Asian noodles.

Today's scientists prefer to call seaweed a sea vegetable, and they're not wrong: Of the hundreds of types of marine algae found in our global waters, many are edible, nutritious, and delicious. High in vitamin B, magnesium, iron, calcium, and other minerals, they've been embraced by homeopaths as vital ingredients in "healing diets" good for cancer patients and people with extreme food allergies.

Where: *In New York,* Hatsuhana at two locations, hatsuhana.com; *in Atlanta,* Taka Sushi, tel 404-869-2802, takasushiatlanta.com; *in Houston,* Uptown Sushi, tel 713-871-1200, uptown-sushi .com; *in Seattle and environs,* Uwajimaya Asian Market at four locations, uwajimaya.com; *in Brentwood, CA,* Takao Sushi, tel 310-207-8636, takaobrentwood.com. **Mail order:** Mitsuwa Marketplace, mitsuwa.com; for kelp, edible seaweed.com; wholefoodsmarket.com (search eden organic sea vegetables). **Further information and recipes:** *Vegetables from the Sea* by Jill Gusman (2003); *The New Seaweed Cookbook* by Crystal June Madeira (2007); saveur.com (search pickled seaweed salad; crab wrapped in seaweed). **Special event:** Seaweed Festival, Tawi-Tawi, Philippines, September through October, localphilippines.com (search seaweed festival).

—||||||||||||||||||||||||||||||||||—

THE CLEANEST HEAT

Wasabi

Japanese

If the bright, neon-green, strongly flavored paste on your sushi platter looks almost unnaturally tinted, it may be—though the color won't actually be an indication of quality. As vibrantly green as its imitators, fresh wasabi is made from the root of mountain hollyhock, or *Eutrema wasabi*, a perennial herb that grows wild along the banks of cold mountain streams in Japan. Known for a strong, head-clearing heat that quickly fades into sweetness and leaves almost no aftertaste, wasabi's flavor is most often compared to that of horseradish and mustard.

Although the herb is commercially grown in Japan, and by a few boutique growers in the U.S., its cultivation is tricky. Wasabi requires an almost entirely consistent water temperature and takes years to mature, which explains why the fresh roots are difficult to find outside of Japan—where they are sold in grocery stores in pans of water—and quite expensive. And, perhaps, why the norm in most sushi restaurants has historically been a paste made of dried horseradish, dried mustard, and food coloring. It is a poor substitute for the vibrant, bracing, astringent, and yet addictive effects of the real thing.

Genuine wasabi can be found dried into a powder, which turns into the signature

paste when combined with water. When starting with a fresh root, simply peeling, trimming, and grating it produces the superfine paste. In Japan, there's a special grater just for this purpose, formed with a piece of sharkskin stretched tightly across a bamboo frame. Cooks run the root over the sharkskin, scraping together the finely ground paste that collects on the paddle.

Word to the wise: When first grated, the flavor of the fresh wasabi root is at its most powerful. Continued exposure to air weakens its heat.

WHERE: *In New York,* Masa, tel 212-823-9800, masanyc.com; *in New York, Los Angeles, and Honolulu,* Sushi Sasabune, trustmesushi.com and sasabunenyc.com. **MAIL ORDER:** For fresh wasabi root and wasabi powder, Real Wasabi, tel 877-492-7224, realwasabi.com; Pacific Coast Wasabi, tel 604-351-0969, wasabia.com; for sharkskin grater, korin.com. **FURTHER INFORMATION AND RECIPES:** *Washoku* by Elizabeth Andoh (2012); *Japanese Cooking: A Simple Art* by Shizuo Tsuji (2012); saveur.com (search scallops with wasabi ginger; soba noodles with wasabi and shiitake mushrooms; wasabi mint granite).

EVERYTHING YOU NEED TO KNOW TO COOK JAPANESE

Understanding Washoku

Japanese

Washoku is the Japanese term for an aesthetic concept of complete kitchen and table harmony—including individual dishes, meals, and the way they are presented—and is the subject and title of an extraordinary cookbook written by

Elizabeth Andoh. An American who in 1967 went to Japan as a student, she married a prominent Japanese businessman and made her life there, setting about studying the intricacies of the country's food and culture before becoming a teacher and writer. Her beautifully

illustrated, handsome book is graced with meticulously clear instructions on techniques, ingredients (including where to get them), and presentation, and should entice anyone seriously interested in understanding what Japanese food is all about. Making the recipes and studying the book will greatly enhance readers' experience and understanding of Japanese cuisine, whether at home or in restaurants. The recipes might even inspire inventive cooks to adapt Japanese methods and combinations to Western dishes.

As an introduction to the concept of washoku, Andoh presents its five basic principles. The first three concern the harmony of color (red, yellow, green, black, and white must be present for a dish to be considered balanced), flavor (salty, sour, sweet, bitter, spicy), and cooking method (simmering, broiling, frying, steaming). The fourth relates to the sensual nature of the food, meaning it must appeal to all five senses, not just taste and smell. The fifth principle is philosophical, with a basis in Buddhist teachings, and calls for proper appreciation of human labor and Mother Nature as joint providers of the meal.

More practically speaking, washoku will teach you how to cook perfect rice, find new types of noodles and vegetables to add to your repertoire, and prepare dishes—fragrant toasted rice in tea broth (*ocha-zuke*), red and white pickled radishes (*kohaku su-zuke*), citrus- and soy-glazed swordfish (*kajiki maguro no yuan yaki*), tangy seared chicken wings (*tori teba no su itame*), lemon-simmered kabocha squash (*kabocha no sawayaka ni*), and for dessert, poached peaches in lemon-ginger miso sauce (*hakuto no dengaku*), to name just a few—that are sure to become household favorites.

FURTHER INFORMATION: *Washoku* by Elizabeth Andoh (2005); *Kibo* by Elizabeth Andoh (2012); *Kansha* by Elizabeth Andoh (2010); *At Home with Japanese Cooking* by Elizabeth Andoh (1980); information on all aspects of Japanese cuisine is available at Andoh's website, tasteofculture.com.

A BIRD ON A STICK

Yakitori

Japanese

Yaki may mean grilled and *tori* may mean bird, but to describe yakitori simply as grilled chicken would be almost libelous. The tiny bamboo skewers of charcoal-broiled poultry, best savored at the counters of Japanese restaurants specializing in its preparation, are an apotheosis of the form. At its purest, yakitori is made with moistly succulent, dark leg and thigh meat, boneless and stripped of the skin. Marinated in a glaze of dark and light soy sauce, rock sugar, and the sweet cooking wine mirin, the chunks of chicken, sometimes along with gizzards, livers, and other organ meats, are threaded onto skewers alternating with snippets of scallions, tiny, whole sweet or hot green peppers, or asparagus tips, and cooked over hot coals until lightly charred and caramelized. The browned, salty-sweet morsels are eaten right off the skewers, sprinkled with a bit of aromatic *sansho* pepper powder or *shichimi*, a hot blend of seven spices, typically alongside a cold, crisp Japanese beer.

Deceptively simple, properly prepared yakitori can be a difficult treat to find, as all too often restaurants use white meat chicken to appeal to a broader clientele, sacrificing flavor in the process. Yakitori reaches total perfection, however, at the tiny, cramped Toricho in the Roppongi district in Tokyo. A fixture on the Ginza for seventy-three years, Toricho is now on its third generation of owner-cooks so devoted to their craft that they used to close during the summer months, believing that refrigeration kills the flavor of chicken. At the ten-seat counter, yakitori variations are served in courses and might include skewers of grilled quail eggs, ginkgo nuts, mushrooms, and eggplant, with a final treat of sublime cubes of duck with scallions and a palate-cleansing *ochazuke* soup of green tea and rice (see page 812).

WHERE: *In Tokyo,* Toricho, tel 81/3-3571-4650; *in New York,* Yakitori Totto, tel 212-245-4555,

The apotheosis of bird on a stick

tottonyc.com. **MAIL ORDER:** for yakitori skewers and hibachi grills, surlatable.com. **FURTHER INFORMATION AND RECIPES:** *The Japanese Grill* by Tadashi Ono and Harris Salat (2009); *The Essential New York Times Grilling Cookbook* (2014); saveur.com (search negima yakitori); cookstr.com (search chicken yakitori). **SPECIAL EVENT:** Kurume Yakitori Festival, Kurume, Japan, September, tel 81/9-4238-1811, kurumeyakitori .or.jp. **SEE ALSO:** Kebabs, page 484; Satay, page 848.

CITRUS WITH A TWIST

Yuzu

Japanese

Not too long ago, a mention of yuzu to Western diners might have gotten a puzzled look in return. But the mouth-puckeringly sour *Citrus junos,* long cherished in Japan and only slightly less so in the Himalayas and China,

now appears on many Western menus, prized as it is for the sunny tanginess and lemon-grapefruit aroma it imparts to soups, sauces, salad dressings, and desserts. Now also cultivated in California, where it was first grown by Japanese immigrants in the nineteenth century, the yuzu looks much like a little, bright-yellow mandarin orange—but it is most valued for its knobby rind, which is pared off and slivered or grated over the dishes it enhances. The pungent juice, strained of its many seeds, is made into marinades for meats and into sauces like the soy- and mirin-based ponzu, the favored condiment for sashimi, while the pulp is usually simmered into jam.

The yuzu's flavor is said to approximate a combination of lemon and lime juices, but that is only partially true, for it bears an extra punch

of aroma, and a burnished, complex acidity that also evokes orange and grapefruit.

Because this fruit has a long growing season, stretching from late summer to midwinter, yuzu juice and rind most often appear fresh, but the juice can be purchased bottled or, like the shaved rind, frozen, during the rest of the year. Like the lemon in the West, the uses for yuzu in Japanese cuisine are seemingly endless, but appreciation of the fruit doesn't end in the kitchen. In the Japanese custom honoring *toji,* the winter solstice, the ritual known as the *yuzu-buro* involves adding several whole yuzus to a tub of hot water, so the bather can squeeze the yuzu juice onto his or her body while inhaling its nose-twitchingly sharp perfume, thus relaxing the mind and keeping winter illnesses at bay.

WHERE: *In New York,* Cagen, tel 212-358-8800, cagenrestaurant.com. **MAIL ORDER:** Melissa's Produce, tel 800-588-0151, melissas.com. **FURTHER INFORMATION AND RECIPES:** *Japanese Cooking: A Simple Art* by Shizuo Tsuji (2012); *Washoku* by Elizabeth Andoh (2005); epicurious.com (search mushroom salad with yuzu dressing); bonappetit.com (search yuzu kosho); saveur.com (search grilled scallops with yuzu kosho vinaigrette; sencha sour). **TIP:** Look for firm fruit with no soft spots and a pronounced citrus aroma. Yuzu will keep up to two weeks at room temperature, and for a month in the refrigerator or freezer.

---||||||||||||||||||||||||||||||||---

THE TABLETOP BARBECUE

Bulgogi

Korean

Centuries before George Foreman introduced his "lean, mean grilling machine" to American shopping networks in the early 1990s, cooks across Korea were barbecuing thin, salty strips of beef to a gentle char on tabletop coals. Known as

bulgogi (or *bool kogi*), from the Korean words for "fire" and "meat," this Asian style of barbecue is cooked indoors as often as out, and derives the bulk of its flavor from a classic marinade of soy sauce, honey, sesame, scallions, and a generous quantity of garlic. Contrary to the "slow and low" American barbecue tradition, thinly sliced bulgogi is quick-cooked over searingly high heat atop a perforated, round piece of metal that covers the grill's coals. Beyond the succulent, famously flavorful beef, marinated chicken, pork, tofu, shrimp, and squid are possible alternatives.

As is characteristic of Korean food, the protein comes with a host of accoutrements. Rice will always be present, of course, but so may the

It's hard to know which is the real draw in the Korean barbecue tradition—the succulent meats or the spicy side dishes.

lettuce leaves or scallion pancakes that provide a wrapping for the meat, along with anywhere from five to twenty-five of the side dishes called *banchan.* These include the fiery chile paste *gochujang* for heat, the spicy fermented pickles or cabbage called kimchi (of which there are said to be more than two hundred variations) for sourness and crunch, *doenjang* (fermented soybean paste) for salt, and sliced fresh plum for a sweet, fruity tang.

Constructing plates with just the right balance is up to the diner—and in some barbecue joints, so is the actual cooking of the meat. Such is the case at Chicago's legendary Korean barbecue house San Soo Gab San. (Its name means "mountain water valley mountain," which is also the name of a mountain in North Korea beloved for its scenic views.) The restaurant keeps its coals lit until 5:00 a.m., making it a favorite of chefs just getting off work in the wee hours. In Los Angeles, home to a large and vibrant Korean community, it was only a matter of time before the passion for Korean barbecue merged with the food truck trend; and so it is that bulgogi trucks (called Kogi) now roam the city. As at all Korean grill restaurants, the beef, short ribs, and soowan galbi are also favorites.

WHERE: *In New York,* Hanjan, tel 212-206-7226, hanjan26.com; *in Chicago,* San Soo Gab San, tel 773-334-1589; *in Los Angeles,* Kogi bulgogi truck schedules, kogibbq.com; Sun Ha Jang, tel 323-634-9292; Soowan Galbi, tel 213-365-9292; *in Houston,* Bonga Garden Restaurant, tel 713-461-5265. **FURTHER INFORMATION AND RECIPES:** *One Big Table* by Molly O'Neill (2010); *The Korean Table* by Debra Samuels and Taekyung Chung (2008); *The Kimchi Chronicles* by Marja Vongerichten (2011); epicurious.com (search beef bulgogi); foodnetwork.com (search beef bulgogi).

THE NEXT BIG HOT SAUCE?

Gochujang

Hot Pepper Paste

Korean

W hat ketchup is to American burgers and hot dogs, *gochujang* is to the Korean *bulgogi* (see page 829)—gochujang just has a bit more kick. It does for those coal-cooked, salty, thin strips of beef and for Korean food in general what *harissa*

(see page 700) does for Moroccan cuisine and *berbere* does for Ethiopian, among other national tastes for heat. A fiery condiment consisting of dried chile peppers, rice powder, and soybean paste (*doenjang*) that is slowly fermented in large clay pots, the deep-red sauce lends a pungent bite to a variety of traditional Korean meat, rice, and lettuce-wrapped dishes.

Before *sriracha* (see page 844) and its brethren penetrated international markets, Korean immigrants spoke of smuggling in

The fiery fermented condiment is both marinade and hot sauce.

their gochujang by boat. Now no longer contraband, the sauce has come to serve as a base for other sauces and dips, combined with garlic, honey, and ginger, or thinned with soy sauce or sesame oil in Americanized brands like Annie Chun's. At one point, these spurred headlines in the *Korean Herald* such as, "Gochujang, the next big hot sauce?" It isn't yet, but its time will come—along with a certain future as a stylish substitute for American barbecue sauce.

RETAIL AND MAIL ORDER: Whole Foods Market, wholefoodsmarket.com (search annie chun's gochujang). **MAIL ORDER:** anniechun.com (search gochujang); koamart.com (search hot pepper paste); hmart.com (search hot pepper paste). **FURTHER INFORMATION AND RECIPE:** For gochujang-spiced chicken wings, *The Kimchi Chronicles* by Marja Vongerichten (2011); *The Korean Table* by Debra Samuels and Taekyung Chung (2008); foodnetwork.com (search chili paste ming tsai); seriouseats.com (search sweet and spicy chili sauce).

DISHING UP CONTEMPORARY KOREAN

Hanjan

Korean American

Given its hefty flavors, its crimson chili stings, and its invitingly large menus of barbecues, noodles, and satisfying vegetable dishes, it's no wonder that Korean cuisine is joining Chinese, Japanese, and Thai food as one of America's favorites. Popular in its traditional form, Korean food was bound to be updated as its more creative chefs became influenced by contemporary presentations of other Asian cuisines.

One of the most talented practitioners of what might be dubbed nouvelle Korean is Hooni Kim, chef-proprietor of two New York restaurants: Danji, where he first made his name on a menu that is half traditional and half modern,

Pig's trotters at Hanjan

and the welcoming, stylish Hanjan, which he opened in 2013. It was a winner from the start, with its casual but smart woodsy setting that affords a variety of seating possibilities—from barstools to benches to bona fide tables, a combination that appeals especially to the crowd that flows in for a late evening fix.

The real draw for all, however, is the food that reflects influences of Japan along with new and precise plating techniques. Many choices are presented as small plates with huge flavors, a case in point being the rainbow of kimchi (see page 833) based on cabbage, cucumbers, radishes, bean sprouts, or whatever other seasonal vegetable captures the chef's fancy. A traditional dish such as the scallion pancake (*haemul pajeon*) is neatly presented with a garnish of local squid, and the radish kimchi with beef-brisket-infused fried rice (*ggak-dugi bokkeum bap*) gets a topping of egg with a runny yolk to act as part of the sauce. The slim fillet of mackerel (*go-deung-uh gui*), done Japanese teriyaki style, gleams under its gently sweet soy glaze, and the skewered meats, such as the Galbi barbecued beef and the pork belly (*ssamjang*), are miniature in the style of Japanese yakitori (see page 827).

Other modern triumphs are what Kim bills as "freshly killed chicken wings," succulent after mellowing in a soy-sake marinade before being grilled to become tantalizingly juicy and savory. Crisp, crunchy, and golden are the adjectives that come to mind while nibbling on fried chicken with pickles, *tong-dak* style—boneless dark meat veneered with a thin, crackling coating. Even more modern perhaps are the silky, snowy chunks of fresh tofu in a pungent vinaigrette dressing and the spicy yet balanced tofu and fish stew.

Late-night diners pour in for the lusty, aromatic Korean-Japanese dish *ramyun*. A ramen that is served only after 9 p.m., it is based in a pork-, chicken-, and fish-bones broth that simmers for 12 hours before being ladled out to join thin slivers of pork, silky noodles, and vegetables. Although not billed as such, this may well be the nightcap that really assures sweet dreams.

WHERE: *In New York,* Hanjan, 36 West 26th St., tel 212-206-7226, hanjan26.com; Danji, 346 West 52nd St., tel 212-586-2880, danjinyc.com.

POSSIBLY THE WORLD'S SLIPPERIEST STIR-FRY

Japchae

Korean

Not all noodles are made exclusively of wheat. To Italy's potato-based gnocchi and China's mung bean pasta, add the clear and slippery "glass" noodles made from sweet potato starch that lend their unique texture to this classic Korean stir-fry. Tossed with beef, vegetables, and toasted sesame seeds, *dang myun* act as the centerpiece of a soft, welcoming mix that soothes body and mind, the kind of food that seems just right for a cold winter's night.

Strips of beef, thinly sliced carrots, onions, mushrooms (usually oyster and shiitake), garlic, and bok choy are generally present, but ingredients may vary—the dish provides an excellent way for home cooks to use up leftovers or small amounts of vegetables. Ideally, each ingredient will be julienned to noodlelike dimensions, then stir-fried separately to optimal texture before being tossed with the boiled or soaked noodles in the pan; the simple stir-fry sauce is made with sesame oil and soy sauce, and sometimes with brown sugar.

The result is comfort food at its finest, a great showcase for textures and flavors both delicate and bold. A mainstay at Korean restaurants and a favorite of Korean home cooks—the latter generally serve it at room temperature, in a large platter—*japchae* is also commonly associated with Korean holidays and celebrations. Although the dish is made with sweet-potato noodles, the thinner and less translucent Chinese mung bean noodles are sometimes substituted.

WHERE: *In New York,* New Wonjo, tel 212-695-5815, newwonjo.com; *in Houston,* Grandma Noodle, tel 713-973-0044; *in San Diego,* Friend's House, tel 858-292-0499. **FURTHER INFORMATION AND RECIPE:** *Dok Suni: Recipes from My Mother's Korean Kitchen* by Jenny Kwak (1998); *Cooking Korean Food with Maangchi* by Maangchi (2012); saveur.com (search chap chae); gourmet.com (search chap chae). **MAIL ORDER:** For the noodles, koamart.com (search nang-myun).

‡||||||||||||||||||||||||||||‡

Kimchi

Korean

Whatever other adjectives may be used to describe pickles, *incendiary* or *titillating* are rarely among them. Yet those are perfect descriptions of kimchi, the spicy-hot, salty, sweet-and-sour fermented vegetables that are the standard starters to any Korean meal.

The most basic preparation is *tong kimchi,* made with *baechu,* or napa cabbage, but that is only the beginning. Also represented in the standard assortment of kimchi placed on dining tables are diced white radishes (*kkakdugi*), scallions (*pa kimchi*), and cucumbers (*oi-kimchi*), among many others. (Seoul's Kimchi Museum has documented 187 varieties.) To make kimchi, the sliced vegetables are tied in bundles and marinated in brine, usually along with hot red peppers, in a paste or in threads, plus salty, pungent fish or shrimp paste, leeks, garlic, ginger, and sugar. The time for fermentation—which can range from days to weeks—depends on the vegetables, the season, and whether the kimchi is being prepared in barrels or crocks, indoors or out. Outdoors and buried is the traditional approach, as the cure is anything but odorless.

Kimchi doesn't look like much when it arrives in its little dishes—wet-looking vegetables with a fiery red patina. But once tasted, the contrast of the silky crunch of the vegetables with the spicy marinade, vinegary bite, and fermented ripeness delights all but the most timid palates. Although served as an appetizer, kimchi usually stays on the table throughout the meal to complement other classic Korean dishes, such as sliced meats grilled over hotplates at the table— typically beef (*bulgogi,* see page 829), short ribs (*kalbi*), beef tongue (*hyeomit gui*), and chicken (*dak gui*)—or ultra-crispy fried chicken (*yang-nyeom dak*) or dumpling soup (*mandu guk*), to name just a few. Cabbage kimchi is also fried into pancakes (*kimchijeon*) and simmered in various

A chef prepares kimchi with napa cabbage.

soups and stews, none more popular than the thick, brick-red *kimchi jjigae,* enriched with tender chunks of pork and ivory cubes of tofu.

Although it is a fairly new discovery in the West, kimchi is ancient fare, having been mentioned in documents dating back about two thousand years. Originally called *chimchae,* meaning "soaked vegetables" in Chinese, at its start kimchi was soaked only in brine or sometimes beef stock, although by the twelfth century other seasonings began to be added. (Chiles, a New World crop, wouldn't be added until the eighteenth century.) Kimchi in North Korea tends to be less salty and fiery than in the south, and there are other regional and seasonal preferences. In the spring and summer months, for example, you might be more likely to encounter cool, refreshing cucumber kimchi, while wintertime kimchis might include radish and mustard leaves.

Besides the fact that it is a near-obligatory staple at any meal, Koreans shout "kimchi!" when they get their picture taken—the way Americans say "cheese." At your next dinner party or barbecue, your guests will smile, too, if treated to a spicy-crisp array of kimchi alongside American classics like hot dogs, burgers, and grilled chicken.

WHERE: *In New York,* Hanjan, tel 212-206-7226, hanjan26.com; *in Houston,* Korean Noodle House, tel 718-225-8870; *in Los Angeles,* Kobawoo House, tel 213-389-7300; Pot, tel 213-368-3030, eatatpot.com; *in San Diego,* Friend's House, tel 858-292-0499. **MAIL ORDER:** For kimchi, DIY kimchi kit, and Korean red pepper powder, Mother in Law's Kimchi, tel 347-746-6161, milkimchi.com;

for Korean red pepper powder and cellophane noodles, koamart.com; for jarred Korean salted shrimp, hmart.com. **FURTHER INFORMATION AND RECIPES:** *The Kimchi Chronicles* by Marja Vongerichten (2011); *Quick and Easy Korean Cooking* by Cecilia Hae-Jin Lee (2009); foodand wine.com (search traditional kimchi); cookstr .com (search quick kimchi). **TIP:** To immerse yourself in the world of kimchi—its history, place in Korean culture, and many varieties—pay a visit to the Kimchi Field Museum in Seoul, tel 82/260-026-456, kimchimuseum.co.kr.

———————|||||||||||||||||||||||||||||||||||||—————————

A DRAMATIC CULINARY TV TOUR OF KOREA

Kimchi Chronicles

Korean, American

With its bright colors and flavors, fiery spice, and bold preparation methods, the cuisine of Korea reflects a combination of influences from China, Japan, and Mongolia, adapted over the centuries into new and original forms. To fully understand and appreciate these dishes, still generally represented only in their most casual form outside of their natural habitat, you have two options. One is to spend a year or so touring South Korea (the North being mostly off-limits since the 1950s), traveling to farms, markets, and fishing villages, spending time with cooks and various artisanal food producers, and eating—a lot—as you go. Or you could stay home and order the cookbook and DVD editions of the 2011 PBS series *Kimchi Chronicles.* In thirteen absorbing episodes, the charismatic narrator Marja Vongerichten leads the tour through her native country and then cooks Korean dishes with her husband, the renowned French-Alsatian chef Jean-Georges Vongerichten, in their country home kitchen.

With occasional traveling companions such as actor Hugh Jackman and his wife, Deb, and actress Heather Graham, Marja is a gracious, engaging host, whether visiting a tea plantation or an odoriferous kimchi storeroom, or at a harborside café downing a stunningly elaborate traditional breakfast soup, adrift with noodles, fish, and intensely hot chiles. During visits to a series of restaurants, each featuring a different Korean specialty, our guide dines her way through barbecue, grilled right on the table, and all manner of rice, meat, poultry, and fish dishes, augmented always with bountiful vegetables, plenty of garlic, chiles, and, of course, kimchi.

Your appetite thoroughly whetted, the Vongerichtens together provide a detailed and helpful lesson in re-creating these dishes at home. In the end, the lively and engaging *Kimchi Chronicles* is a history lesson, travel guide, and cooking class all rolled into one.

MAIL ORDER: For a DVD of *Kimchi Chronicles,* hmart.com, barnesandnoble.com. **FURTHER INFORMATION AND RECIPES:** *The Kimchi Chronicles* by Marja Vongerichten (2011); kimchichronicles.tv.

———————||||||||||||||||||||||||||||||————————

Saenggang Cha

Ginger Tea

Korean

G iven its ancient tea tradition, so shrouded in custom and ceremony, it's no surprise to find that many of Korea's brews are believed to offer both refreshment and folk medicine. The most delicious, warming, and comforting of all may be *saenggang cha,* the ginger tea that is also among the most curative. The rhizome—or thick underground root—of the flowering plant *Zingiber officinale,* ginger has been used medicinally in many cultures for thousands of years, and with good reason: The enzymes it contains counteract the inflammation responsible for a variety of ills. Many Koreans report that at the first sign of a cold, their grandmothers immediately head to the cupboard to brew the gingery concoction, also believed to settle the stomach and prevent motion sickness.

The tea itself is a deceptively simple brew: Slices of fresh ginger are boiled, sweetened with honey, and spiced with cinnamon. Sometimes a garnish of a few pine nuts is floated on top. In the restorative and deeply relaxing drink, the intrinsically peppery flavor of the ginger is tempered by the honey's sweetness and the cinnamon's musk. With its heady aroma and strong yet sweet flavor, it might even have the power to cure an oncoming bad mood.

WHERE: *In New York,* to experience traditional Korean tea house culture, Franchia, tel 212-213-1001, franchia.com. **MAIL ORDER:** koamart.com (search ginger tea package); for ginger crystals, amazon.com (search instant ginger honey crystals). **FURTHER INFORMATION AND RECIPE:** *Growing Up in a Korean Kitchen* by Hi Soo Shin Hepinstall (2001); *The Kimchi Chronicles* by Marja Vongerichten (2011); maangchi.com (search saenggangcha); food .com (search korean ginger tea). **TIP:** As a convincing shortcut, dried, sweet ginger crystals can be spooned into a cup of boiling water, or better yet, a cup of a favorite tea. **SEE ALSO:** Mint Tea, page 704; Oolong Tea, page 777.

———————||||||||||||||||||||||||||||||————————

Yangnyeom Dak

Korean Fried Chicken

Korean, Korean American

C hicken has long played a central role in Korean cooking, but it wasn't until about twenty years ago that the fried preparation, *yangnyeom dak,* became a staple dish in takeout shops all over Seoul. No one is quite certain what precipitated the rise of the distinctively Southern American food on the Korean table, although the global ubiquity of Kentucky Fried Chicken might be one indicator. In any case, Koreans have certainly found a way to make it their own.

Korea's spicy and garlicky take on fried chicken

The key to the Korean style is to fry the chicken whole (generally), and to fry the chicken twice (always). The small birds are lightly rolled in a flour batter, deep-fried at a low temperature for ten minutes, drained, and then refried for an additional ten minutes. Sparingly coated with a hot pepper and garlic sauce, they are cut up into parts and served with accompaniments of pickled radishes and cold beer. The result is addictive spicy, crunchy fare somewhat in the manner of America's buffalo chicken wings. No wonder, then, that Korean fried chicken shops have proliferated from New York to Los Angeles.

WHERE: *In multiple locations in the U.S. and Asia,* Bonchon, bonchon.com; *in New York and Los Angeles,* Kyochon, kyochonus.com; *in Tucker, GA,* Matthews Cafeteria, tel 770-939-2357, matthewscafeteria.com; *in Johns Creek, GA,* Joy Pizza and Chicken, tel 770-813-8882, johnscreekchicken.com. **FURTHER INFORMATION AND RECIPES:** *The Kimchi Chronicles* by Marja Vongerichten (2011); *Quick and Easy Korean Cooking* by Cecilia Hae-Jin Lee (2009); saveur.com (search korean fried chicken); nytimes.com (search koreans share their secret for chicken); seriouseats.com (search best korean fried chicken). **SEE ALSO:** Southern Fried Chicken, page 622.

THAI

and

SOUTHEAST ASIAN

Indonesian, Malaysian,
Singaporean, Vietnamese

———————|||||||||||||||||||||||||||||||||—————

ONE SERIOUSLY SPICY BIRD

Gai Yang

Thai, Laotian

Deceptively humble, this ubiquitous Thai chicken dish is said to have originated in Laos (where it is called *ping gai*) and ranks among the world's great chicken creations when it is carefully prepared and grilled to order. Its defining

flavor comes from a marinade that combines *nam pla*, the salty, pungent fish sauce, with crushed coriander seeds, woody stalks of lemongrass, grated ginger, slivers of hot green and red chiles, rice wine vinegar, palm sugar, garlic, and oyster and soy sauces; sometimes it also includes the dark, jamlike Chinese hoisin sauce (see page 769) for an added savory dimension. But the dish may be even more notable for the technique it employs in treating the small, tender chickens. Split along the backbone and then opened flat and pounded in a process known as butterflying, they are set to absorb the marinade before being grilled whole.

After a twenty-four-hour soak in the refrigerator, the chicken is patted dry and grilled over hot charcoal or roasted in a very hot oven. Wedges of lemon, sprigs of cilantro, and a variety of sweet and hot dipping sauces are the standard garnishes for the moistly tender, crisp, and pungent bird, which is chopped into large, manageable chunks and eaten out of hand. *Gai yang* is typically served alongside steamed sticky rice, pad thai noodles, green papaya salad, and crisp saltwater pickles—and, as with any barbecue, Thai beer completes the experience.

WHERE: *In New York*, Jaiya at two locations, jaiya.com; *in Brookline, MA*, Dok Bua Thai Kitchen, tel 617-232-2955, dokbua-thai.com. **MAIL ORDER:** For oyster sauce and lemongrass, Thai Supermarket Online, tel 888-618-8424, importfood .com, Grocery Thai, tel 818-469-9407, grocerythai .com. **FURTHER INFORMATION AND RECIPES:** *Southeast Asian Food* by Rosemary Brissenden (2012); *Crying Tiger: Thai Recipes from the Heart* by Supatra Johnson (2004); templeofthai.com (click Thai Recipes, search gai yang); epicurious.com (search gai yang); rasamalaysia.com (search gai yang).

———————|||||||||||||||||||||||||||||||||—————

"THE DISCOVERY OF A NEW DISH DOES MORE FOR HUMAN HAPPINESS THAN THE DISCOVERY OF A STAR."—JEAN ANTHELME BRILLAT-SAVARIN

Jean-Georges Vongerichten's Ginger Fried Rice

Thai-French American

When we think about fried rice, we typically summon up images of the Chinese standard, the satisfying accompaniment to many Cantonese dishes that is also a smart way to use up leftover bits of meat and vegetables. But that humble dish came in for a transcendent transformation at the hands of Jean-Georges Vongerichten, the French-Alsatian chef who worked in Thailand and developed a taste for Asian ingredients, eventually melding them with his suave French technique at his restaurants in New York and Las Vegas. Those who love Thai flavors will get particular joy from the ginger fried rice served at his Spice Market restaurants, one of the most delectable results of Vongerichten's particular brand of fusion.

He begins with flower-scented jasmine rice that is cooked and chilled the day before it is to be fried and served. The rice is quickly stir-fried with leeks in clarified chicken fat; for vegetarians or those without clarified chicken fat on hand, the chef recommends peanut oil as a fair if less flavorful substitute. Either way, the result

Signage welcomes patrons to Spice Market in London.

is an irresistibly crunchy, mellow-yet-flavorful mound of rice, which is then encrusted with golden crumbles of fried minced ginger and garlic. The dish is topped off with a fried egg, the runny yolk of which serves as a supple sauce for the rice.

Although ginger fried rice is listed as a side dish on Vongerichten's Spice Market menus in New York, London, and Doha, Qatar (as well as at Perry Street in New York, where his son, Cedric, is chef), it tends to steal the spotlight. In fact, a bowl of this rice with the almost equally delicious green papaya salad or a portion of peanut-and-chile-sauced chicken satay makes for a lovely and complete Thai lunch.

Where: Spice Market, 403 W. 14th St., New York, tel 212-675-2322, spicemarketnewyork .com; Leicester Square, 10 Wardour St., London, tel 44/20-7758-1088, spicemarketlondon.co.uk; W Hotel & Residences, West Bay Lagoon, Doha, Qatar, tel 974/44-535-000, spicemarketdoha .com. *In New York,* Perry Street, tel 212-352-1900, perrystrestaurant.com. **Further information and recipes:** *Asian Flavors of Jean-Georges* by Jean-Georges Vongerichten (2007); food52.com (search jean-georges ginger fried rice).

CURRYING FAVOR

Kaeng

Curries of All Kinds

Thai

Curry in Thailand is called *kaeng,* and it may be yellow, red, or green, which can be read as "hot," "hotter," and "Hurry! Pass the rice!" Anyone gasping after a mouthful of what are surely the world's most incendiary but deliciously rewarding

curries is ill advised to seek relief from a beverage, hot or cold. Liquids only spread the spice-carrying oils over the surface of the tongue, when what you want is the mopping-up action of plain rice. Thus forewarned, you can begin to explore the various kaengs of Thailand, all thinner and soupier than their saucier Indian relatives and quite spicy-hot, even at their mildest.

Yellow curries (*kaeng kari*) are a good starting point for novices, as they are the least palate-singeing of the bunch. Like all Thai curries, they have a base of coconut milk with a paste of toasted and powdered spices, which in this case includes turmeric (for the yellow hue), star anise, cinnamon, bay leaves, crushed dried chiles, fermented shrimp paste, ginger, coriander seeds, and cumin. They may be bolstered with beef, lamb, or chicken chunks and usually also include onions, potatoes, and pineapple chunks.

Blushing from liberal doses of red chile powder, red curries (*kaeng phet*) are made with white pepper, cumin, coriander seeds, nutmeg, cilantro roots, garlic, lemongrass, the grated rind of fragrant kaffir limes, and ginger or, preferably, the more potent Southeast Asian rhizome galangal. They also have coconut milk, of course, for a sauce well suited to roasted pork, duck, beef, shrimp, or eel. Bamboo shoots, sweet Thai basil, and pumpkin are sometimes tossed in as well.

Green curries (*kaeng keow wan*) get their color, and their heat, from plenty of deceptively sweet-looking hot green chiles, seeds and all. The spice paste is made by grinding together lemongrass, shallots, ginger, coriander (seeds and roots), cumin, white pepper, and kaffir lime zest, along with palm sugar, garlic, and holy basil, a powerfully flavored herb that is a particular favorite in Thailand. The paste is cooked in coconut milk, and beef or chicken and quartered small, round Thai eggplants are the standard additions to this hottest of hot curries.

A great favorite in Thailand, massaman curry (*kaeng musmun*) is one that is not designated by color. It is more Indian in style and is actually a legacy of Muslim spice traders, hence its name, which probably evolved from Arabic. Certainly it contains plenty of the spice trader's wares: cumin, caraway, cinnamon, cloves, star anise, cardamom, nutmeg, white pepper, and ginger. It also has cashews, limes, garlic, lemongrass, and tiny, super-hot red bird's-eye chiles. Although it is spicy, the overall effect is more aromatic than fiery, balanced by the tart juice of tamarind

or bitter oranges (such as Sevilles or calamondins, small fruits similar to tangerines), as well as chunks of potato, pineapple, and chicken or beef. It is rarely made with pork, likely due to the dish's Muslim roots. Massaman curry is typically served with sweet-tart pickled ginger or *achat*, a pickled cucumber relish, and, as with all Thai curries, bowls of steamed white rice—either fluffy, flowery jasmine, or the delightfully dense and chewy sticky rice.

WHERE: *In New York,* Jaiya at two locations, jaiya.com; *in Brookline, MA,* Dok Bua Thai Kitchen, tel 617-232-2955, dokbua-thai.com; *in Boston,* Brown Sugar Cafe, tel 617-787-4242, brownsugarcafe.com; *in Chicago,* Amarit Thai & Pan Asian Cuisine, tel 312-939-1179; *in New Orleans,* La Thai Uptown, tel 504-899-8886, lathaiuptown.com; *in Las Vegas,* Lotus of Siam, tel 702-735-3033, saipinchutima.com; *in Los*

Spices for yellow, red, and green curries, from mild to hot

Angeles, Night+Market at two locations, night marketla.com; Jitlada Restaurant, tel 323-667-9809, jitladala.wordpress.com. **MAIL ORDER:** For Thai ingredients, Thai Supermarket Online, tel 888-618-8424, importfood.com; Grocery Thai, tel 818-469-9407, grocerythai.com. **FURTHER**

INFORMATION AND RECIPES: *Cracking the Coconut: Classic Thai Home Cooking* by Su-Mei Yu (2000); *Simple Thai Food* by Leela Punyaratabandhu (2014); *Everyday Thai Cooking* by Katie Chin (2013); saveur.com (search the star of siam); seriouseats.com (search kaeng kari kai).

|||||||||||||||||||||||||||||||||||||||||||||||||||||||||||||||||||||||||||||||||||||||||||||||||||||||||||||||||||||||||||||||

"A MEAL FOR A MAN, BOTH MEAT AND DRINK."—MARCO POLO

Coconut

Agiant nut with roots in tropical Asia, the coconut was named by the sixteenth-century Portuguese explorers who saw *coco* faces—Portuguese for "monkey"—in the distinctive markings on the bottom of its thick husk. Ever since, its unique appearance and properties have been the object of fascination, both for humans and for the monkeys who love to climb the coconut palm.

Getting beyond the nut's thick, hard husk and its woody nutshell to its creamy, rich, white meat takes some doing. A hammer or machete is the instrument of choice, and the difficulty is part of what makes the coconut legendary. Split open, the nut reveals flesh that lends itself to a dazzling array of uses: In shredded, chipped, chunked, or pureed form, fresh or more typically toasted or dried, it adds an addictive tropical flavor and a lusciously rich texture to recipes ranging from candy to curry and from layer cakes to smoothies. Inside the coconut, the meat encases the coconut "water": a clear, slightly sweet, mineral-packed delight that has become a health trend for its high levels of rehydrating electrolytes.

Grated coconut adds sweetness and chewiness to some macaroons, and the Thai use its "milk" (the rich liquid squeezed from its grated, pressed meat) as a soothing, creamy ingredient in savory curries. Caribbean cooks include coconut cream or milk in succotash and soups.

And where would the world's beach bars be without the piña colada, that dangerously easy-to-drink concoction of coconut cream (coconut milk's even richer twin) blended with pineapple juice and rum (see page 686)?

Not to be overshadowed by its famous fruit, the coconut palm comes in handy in other ways. In some tropical cultures, its leaves are woven into baskets and roofs. Its trunk, as many a shipwreck fable has proven, can be hollowed out into a canoe, and the fibrous strings that entwine the coconut's husk can be made into ropes. The coconut shell itself may be carved into utensils or split in half and used as a cup from which to drink unadulterated, deliciously fresh coconut water straight from the source, a treat hawked along Rio de Janeiro's beaches.

Among its other attributes, the versatile fruit floats, and being carried away by ocean currents enabled it to propagate along the world's coastlines. It grows twenty degrees north and south of the equator and can now be found from Hawaii south to Madagascar, and even inland in tropic zones of places like India. Worldwide demand for the coconut and its by-products—including coconut oil, which is used in soaps, paints, baked goods, and homeopathic remedies—sustains major industries in the tropics, where workers climb to the tops of trees to remove the nuts. When fully mature, the coconut falls to the ground on its own, depositing an excellent source of food and water right at a lucky eater's feet. (Less-lucky passersby won't get a meal out of the bargain: Dropping from heights of up to 80 feet, the nut is the suspected cause of about 150 deaths a year.)

Mail order: Thai Supermarket Online, tel 888-618-8424, importfood.com; Rani's World Foods, tel 281-440-8080, ranisworldfoods.com (search coconut milk; coconut flakes). **Further information and recipes:** *Cracking the Coconut* by Su-mei Yu (2000); *Coconut Lover's Cookbook* by Bruce Fife (2010); *Rose's Heavenly Cakes* by Rose Levy Beranbaum (2009); *Bake!* by Nick Malgieri (2010); cookstr.com (search thai coconut chicken); foodandwine.com (search coconut desserts). **Tip:** To identify fresh coconuts, look for ones with firm husks. When shaken, the juice inside should make an audible sloshing sound, indicating that the nut hasn't dried out. To open the coconut, drill into the softest of the three eyes on the end of the husk and let the water drain out into a bowl. Use a hammer to smash open the nut. Then pry the meat from the shell with a sharp knife. **Special events:** Cape Coral Coconut Festival, Cape Coral, FL, November, capecoral.net; Coconut Festival, Kapaa, Kauai, HI, October, kbakauai.org.

⊢||||||||||||||||||||||||||||||⊣

SWEET, HOT, AND CRUNCHY

Mee Krob

Crisp Noodles

Thai

Given how many cultures love noodles, it would seem that if any cooks in the world were given some sort of starch-based flour—whether from wheat, rice, beans, buckwheat, or even potatoes—they would set about forming this comfort food. One of the most original and unusual noodle preparations is Thai *mee krob,* made with dried, thread-thin rice noodles.

The best way to describe a platter of mee krob, which simply means "crisp noodles," is as a nest of pure spun gold on a bed of fresh herbs and crunchy bean sprouts. Its gilded tangle contains a palate-tingling combination of sweetly glazed, crisply fried rice noodles, gently scrambled eggs, and diced onion, pork, and shrimp. Served as an appetizer or side dish, it is accented by the anchovy-based

An effective escort for curry

fermented fish sauce *nam pla,* as well as scallions, hot chiles, and just enough tamarind or lime juice to balance out the golden palm sugar glaze.

Mee krob serves as a foil for some of the spicier Thai curries by providing the textural contrast of its crackling lacy strands. It also soothes the palate with the bittersweet overtones of caramelized palm sugar, while the bits of vegetable, meat, or shellfish work as added seasonings to the curry itself. One might almost consider it what trendy menu planners call a palate refreshener.

Fortunately for Western cooks, all of the ingredients necessary for mee krob are available in Asian markets as well as by mail order. As with fried rice, it is possible to substitute just about any meat, poultry, or shellfish for the pork and shrimp, thereby making elegant and delicious use of leftovers.

WHERE: *In New York,* Jaiya at two locations, jaiya.com; *in Boston,* Brown Sugar Cafe, tel 617-787-4242, brownsugarcafe.com; *in Cambridge, MA,* The Similans, tel 617-491-6999, brownsugar cafe.com; *in Washington, DC,* Bua Thai, tel 202-265-0828, buathai.com; *in New Orleans,* La Thai Uptown, tel 504-899-8886, lathaiuptown.com; *in Houston,* Vieng Thai, tel 713-688-9910; *in Norwalk, CA,* Renu Nakorn, tel 562-921-2124. **MAIL ORDER:** For Thai rice vermicelli, palm sugar, rice vinegar, and fermented fish sauce, Thai Supermarket Online, tel 888-618-8424, import food.com. **FURTHER INFORMATION AND RECIPES:** *Cracking the Coconut* by Su-Mei Yu (2000); *Thai Food* by David Thompson (2002); thaitable.com (search mee grob); cookstr.com (search vegetarian mee krob). **SEE ALSO:** Dan Dan Noodles, page 759; Taiwanese Beef Noodles, page 776; Singapore Mei Fun, page 787; Pho Bo, page 862.

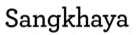

A DESSERT THAT'S READY FOR ITS CLOSE-UP

Sangkhaya

Coconut Custard

Thai

At a time when chefs vie to come up with the most enticing and creative presentations for dishes, desserts foremost among them, it's amazing that this Thai specialty has not caught on in the Western world and taken its rightful place alongside such international favorites as tiramisù (see page 245), profiteroles, and crème brûlée.

Sangkhaya is an addictive combination of coconut milk, eggs, and palm sugar, scented with rosewater or pandan leaves and sometimes vanilla, cinnamon, or nutmeg. Depending on the season, Thai cooks might steam the custard directly in a woody coconut shell, complete with a thin lining of its sweet white meat, or in a small pumpkin or squash, which is sliced into elegant, sugar-glazed wedges for serving. In this latter variation, the dessert makes a seductive mini-meal, with protein by way of the egg and vegetable by way of the pumpkin. Fashionable foodies would most certainly approve.

WHERE: *In New York,* Jaiya at two locations, jaiya.com; *in Brookline, MA,* Dok Bua Thai Kitchen, tel 617-232-2955, dokbua-thai.com. **MAIL ORDER:** For coconuts and palm sugar,

Squash filled with sweet coconut custard

Grocery Thai, tel 818-469-9407, grocerythai.com. **FURTHER INFORMATION AND RECIPES:** *Thai Food* by David Thompson (2002); *The Taste of Thailand* by Vatcharin Bhumichitr (1988); *Simple Thai Food* by Leela Punyaratabandhu (2014); amok cuisine.com (search sankya lapov); asian desserts.co (search sankya lapov).

———————————|IIIIIIIIIIIIIIIIIIIIIIIIIIIII|———————————

RED-HOT AND VERY COOL

Sriracha Sauce

Thai, Vietnamese

It's an American success story with a culinary twist: David Tran, born and raised in Vietnam but of Chinese descent, emigrated to the United States as a refugee in the late 1970s. He found much to his liking, save only a hot sauce that would satisfy him. Settling in Los Angeles, he started making various sauces of his own, including the chile- and garlic-based *sriracha* (pronounced SEE-rotch-ah), a Thai sauce popular in Vietnam and named after the coastal town of Sri Racha in Thailand. Tran began selling his hot sauces from a food truck in L.A.'s Chinatown, and today his company, Huy Fong Foods in the San Gabriel Valley, ships out some 20 million bottles of sriracha each year. Appearing on supermarket and home pantry shelves and restaurant tables all around the world, the American-made, Chinese-Vietnamese-Thai sauce can be considered a classic example of the global culinary melting pot.

Add this for a spicy kick.

It takes only a taste or two of the thick, firecracker-red sauce—identifiable by its clear plastic squeeze bottle, bright-green plastic top, and the cocky rooster adorning the label (the source of its other name, "rooster sauce")—to understand its success and iconic status. Fiery fresh, ripe red jalapeño peppers are its base, made aromatic with garlic and turned sweet-and-sour by way of vinegar and sugar. Thanks to its exploding popularity, these days you can find sriracha paired with everything from sushi to potato chips. It is an astoundingly versatile ingredient, blended into sauces, mayonnaise, sour cream, cheese spreads, pâtés, beans, and soups that range from classic tomato to Vietnam's *pho* to seafood chowders. Delightful atop scrambled, poached, or fried eggs, it also makes a perky dip for egg rolls and enlivens meatballs, meat loaf, and even vegetable stews such as ratatouille and the Cajun corn dish *maque choux* (see pages 124 and 596). Sriracha also gives a spicy edge to Italian pasta sauces such as marinara, Bolognese, and amatriciana (see page 219) and can easily replace hot chile flakes on pizza, for a slight hint of the exotic.

Although Tran's rooster sauce is the most visible sriracha on the American market, there are several other brands, mostly made in Southeast Asia with names like Shark (a thinner, sweeter, more traditional Thai version) and Dragonfly. Try them all if you like. They all have their devoted followers, but it's hard to beat the balanced complexity and charm—and worldwide popularity—of Tran's.

Mail order: Huy Fong Foods, huyfong.com; Asian Food Grocer, tel 888-482-2742, asian foodgrocer.com; Temple of Thai, templeofthai .com; iGourmet, igourmet.com. **Further information and recipes:** *The Sriracha Cookbook* by Randy Clemens (2011); seriouseats.com (search how to make sriracha); nydailynews.com (search make your own sriracha). **See also:** XO Sauce, page 794; Wasabi, page 825.

|||||||||||||||||||||||||||||||||||||

BISTRO-STYLE, WITH A TWIST

Thai Mussels

Thai

Although first popularized in America during World War II's food shortages as an inexpensive form of seafood, mussels have been eaten around the world for more than a thousand years. The most popular of the lot are common blue mussels (*Mytilus edulis*), Mediterranean mussels (*M. galloprovincialis*), Baltic mussels (*M. trossulus*), and the green-lipped mussels of New Zealand (*Perna canaliculus*), but there are more than a dozen edible species. And among the most memorable mussel preparations is the distinctly Thai-born version in which the shiny, dark, and thin-shelled mollusks are steamed in a wildly fragrant coconut milk broth laden with lemongrass stalks, kaffir lime leaves, purple basil, and red chile paste.

With their chewy texture and natural saltiness, mussels stand up beautifully to the slew of bold flavors, lending their own distinctive sea essence to the mix. The result is a dish that is beloved around the world for its aromatic charms and its comforting presentation.

Whether you consider this brothy dish laden with mussels a soup or stew is really your call—by any designation it is a satisfying combination. It would be a shame to concentrate only on the shiny, salty mollusks and not spoon up every drop of the heady broth that rivals that of the classic French *moules marinière* (steamed in an elixir of butter, shallots, thyme, bay leaf, and white wine) or the Italian *zuppa di cozze* (simmered in a garlicky marinara-style tomato broth). The more robust Thai version is rendered exotic by the funky acidity of the lemongrass, the edgy astringency of the kaffir limes, and the fire of the chile paste. Although bread might seem to be the best vehicle for sopping up this elixir, in true Thai fashion, spooning it up neatly would do it more justice.

Where: *In New York,* Jaiya at two locations, jaiya.com; *in Boston,* Brown Sugar Cafe, tel 617-787-4242, brownsugarcafe.com; *in Cambridge, MA,* The Similans, tel 617-491-6999, brownsugarcafe.com; *in New Orleans,* La Thai Uptown, tel 504-899-8886, lathaiuptown.com; *in Houston,* Vieng Thai, tel 713-688-9910; *in San Francisco,* Rin's Thai Restaurant, tel 415-821-4776, rinsthaisf.com; *in Norwalk, CA,* Renu Nakorn, tel 562-921-2124; *in Seattle,* Ray's Boathouse Café, tel 206-789-3770, rays.com. **Mail order:** For Thai ingredients, Thai Supermarket Online, tel 888-618-8424, importfoods.com. **Further information and recipes:** *Ray's Boathouse: Seafood Secrets of the Pacific Northwest* by Danyel Smith and Ken Gouldthorpe (2003); *The Taste of Thailand* by Vatcharin Bhumichitr (1988); *Simply Thai Cooking* by Wandee Young and Byron Ayanoglu (2011); *Asian Flavors of Jean-Georges* by Jean-Georges Vongerichten (2007); thaifood.about.com (search thai seafood soup); foodnetwork.com (search thai spiced mussel soup). **See also:** Green-Lipped Mussels, page 910.

The dish first became popular during World War II.

—||||||||||||||||||||||||||||||||||—

CHICKEN SOUP ON STEROIDS

Tom Kha Gai

Coconut-Chicken Soup

Thai

The whole world really does love chicken soup, and the golden, sustaining broth has been a symbol of affection, strength, and good health since the days of the ancient Romans, from Denmark to Ethiopia and from Italy to China. Among the many versions, the Thai rendition called *tom kha gai* or *dtom khaa gai* deserves to be celebrated.

Incredibly aromatic, the soup is distinguished by a complex blend of flavors. It begins as a savory broth enriched with creamy coconut milk seasoned with the pungent, slightly sour, and peppery Thai ginger called galangal. The broth profits from the sting of Thai bird's-eye chiles, the tang of lemongrass, the earthiness of shiitake mushrooms, and the brightness of fresh lime juice and cilantro. The resulting symphony is equal parts sour, creamy, earthy, and delicious. Like most chicken soups, a cup of it can soothe your soul—but this one packs a flavor wallop that will simultaneously bolster your spirits.

Although it's a homey standard on the menus of Thai restaurants the world over, its definitive haute-cuisine version is rightly credited to the skillful and innovative French-Alsatian chef Jean-Georges Vongerichten at Vong. The restaurant is no longer, but the recipe lives on online.

WHERE: *In New York*, Kittichai, tel 212-925-2991, kittichairestaurant.com; *in Brookline, MA*, Dok Bua Thai Kitchen, tel 617-232-2955, dokbua-thai.com; *in Chicago*, Amarit Thai & Pan Asian Cuisine, tel 312-939-1179; *in Houston*, Kanomwan, tel 713-923-4230; *in Las Vegas*, Lotus of Siam, tel 702-735-3033, saipinchutima .com. **MAIL ORDER:** For Thai ingredients, Thai Supermarket Online, tel 888-618-8424, import food.com. **FURTHER INFORMATION AND RECIPES:** *The Whole World Loves Chicken Soup* by Mimi Sheraton (1995); bonappetit.com (search tom kha gai); cookstr.com (search thai soup vongerichten). **SEE ALSO:** Golden Yoich, page 439; Qi Guo Ji (Steamed Chicken Soup), page 779.

—||||||||||||||||||||||||||||||||||—

"ITS TASTE CAN ONLY BE DESCRIBED AS . . . INDESCRIBABLE, SOMETHING YOU WILL EITHER LOVE OR DESPISE." —ANTHONY BOURDAIN

Durian

Southeast Asian

The legendary durian or *Durio zibethinus*—the so-called stinking melon— is said to have been on earth since the days of the dinosaurs, and frankly, it smells like it. The creatures must have had strong stomachs, as the tropical fruit is remarkable for its overwhelming, unforgettable smell. The nausea-inducing scent has been compared to everything from rotting onions to sewage, which is why durians are banned on public transport in Indonesia and in hospitals in Bangkok.

A sign prohibits durians in Penang, Malaysia.

The fruit is forbidding to look at, too: Football-shaped and -sized, it has a brownish-green, thorny shell (*duri* being the Malay word for spike) and can weigh up to ten pounds. Folks walking under a durian tree have been known to endure a concussion, or worse, if they are hit by the falling fruit. If they survive the passage and are willing to hold their noses long enough to split open the shell, they'll be rewarded with a distinctively buttery, almond-tinged, sweet-and-sour flavor and a smoothly custardlike texture. For an additional layer of durian experience, the sticky pulp coating the fruit's large seeds may be gnawed or sucked off.

Durian trees originated in Malaysia but have been cultivated throughout Southeast Asia, particularly in Indonesia. The fruit is generally harvested from mid-April until mid-June, and mostly eaten fresh and raw (in the food stalls and markets of those regions, vendors commonly let the customer who pays a premium choose a melon and then cut a small segment out for sampling; if the buyer doesn't like the fruit, he or she can choose another until satisfied). Durians are also sold in dried form and are used to flavor various sweets. They appear in pastry creams and milkshakes as well as in the Magnolia brand durian ice cream that is popular in the Davao region of the Philippines.

The Javanese believe that durians have detoxifying and aphrodisiacal properties, but they didn't do much for Charles Darwin, who famously said of the fruit, "May your worst enemies be forced to eat it." What would he have made of the multitude of YouTube videos depicting first-time durian experiences, a surprisingly popular social trend for new visitors to Southeast Asia?

FURTHER INFORMATION AND RECIPES: yearofthe durian.com; thaifood.about.com (search how to eat durian). **SPECIAL EVENT:** Penang Durian Festival, Balik Pulau, Penang, Malaysia, June/July, visit penang.gov.my (search durian balik pulau).

——————————|||||||||||||||||||||||||||||||||——————————

THE HIRSUTE FRUIT

Rambutan

Southeast Asia

R*ambut* is the Malaysian word for hair, and rambutan is known as the hairy fruit for the fine, long strands that dangle from its crimson exterior. When the rind is torn open and the fruit is simply pinched out, what emerges is a whitish, translucent-fleshed globe about the size of a golf ball. Tart and sweet, it is known for its fragrant scent and distinctly pleasant, rosy aroma.

A close botanical cousin of the lychee (see page 773), the tropical rambutan (*Nephelium lappaceum*) has its origins in Malaysia but is extremely popular throughout Southeast Asia and in India. You once had to travel to places like Borneo to enjoy it, as the very perishable fruit is quite rare outside of its stomping grounds. Now, however, it is also grown in small quantities in Hawaii, and it may be canned in its own syrup and sold for export.

MAIL ORDER: For fresh rambutans (which must be shipped overnight), with limited availability, Melissa's Produce, tel 800-588-0151, melissas.com; for fresh or canned rambutans, Thai Supermarket Online, tel 888-618-8424, importfood.com. **FURTHER INFORMATION AND RECIPES:** uktv.co.uk (click Goodfoodchannel logo, search soup of rambutan pork and crab). **SPECIAL EVENTS:** Rambutan Festival, San Pablo City, Laguna, Philippines, August, sitiodeamor.com (click Announcements); Rambutan Festival, Surat Thani Town, Thailand, July, ferrysamui.com/rambutan-fair.

--------------------||||||||||||||||||||||||||||||||||--------------------

THE TINIEST KEBABS

Satay

Southeast Asian

These quick-cooking, tender, and savory little barbecue brochettes are found all over Southeast Asia—particularly in Indonesia, Thailand, Malaysia, Singapore, and the Philippines, where they are the quintessential meat-on-a-stick.

Satay is generally made with chicken, beef, pork, or lamb, the meat first marinated in a tangy paste made of turmeric, garlic, shallots, pepper, coriander, and sometimes dried shrimp paste or (especially in Malaysia) palm sugar. (For chicken satay, most Asian cooks prefer dark meat, such as chicken thigh, as it better retains its tenderness when grilled.) Although you can find fish satay in some regions, delicate seafood doesn't usually stand a chance against a characteristically pungent marinade and a blast of charcoal heat.

Skewered on bamboo sticks and laid onto a long, narrow grill over white-hot wood charcoal, the meat is basted with additional paste or a mixture of palm sugar and oil as it cooks. In Southeast Asia, the basting instrument will often be a homemade brush made from a lemongrass stalk—a neat trick, and a clever way to impart a little extra tang to the meat (somewhat like the way Italian grill chefs brush meats with a swab of rosemary dipped in olive oil).

Served with a simple salad of cucumber and vinegar, along with a chile-spiked peanut dip, satay is generally enjoyed as a high-flavor, protein-packed appetizer. A popular snack at the Asian night markets, where it is sold by stall vendors, its salty, garlicky flavor makes it a wonderful match for sweet, strong tropical cocktails.

A favorite dish of the Philippines

Where: *In Singapore,* Tiong Bahru Market Food Center; *in New York,* Jaiya at two locations, jaiya.com; *in Chicago,* Amarit Thai & Pan Asian Cuisine, tel 312-939-1179, eatamaritthai .com; *in San Francisco and San Mateo, CA,* Thai Satay Restaurant & Bar, thaisatay.com; *in Las Vegas,* Lotus of Siam, tel 702-735-3033, saipin chutima.com. **Retail and mail order:** *In New York,* Bangkok Center Grocery, tel 212-349-1979, bangkokcentergrocery.com. **Mail order:** For ingredients, Thai Supermarket Online, tel 888-618-8424, importfood.com. **Further information and recipes:** *Simple Thai Food* by Leela Punyaratabandhu (2014); *Indonesian Cooking* by Dina Yuen (2012); *Asian Grilling* by Su-Mei Yu (2002); *Pok Pok* by Andy Ricker (2013); saveur.com (search satay udang; muu satay; lemongrass pork satay); foodnetwork.com (search chicken satay with spicy peanut sauce). **Tip:** The complex, fragrant, and flavorful satay marinade is excellent for other dishes, too: Try tossing shrimp or cubes of silken tofu with it, quickly sautéing them in a very hot pan, and then serving them over rice; it's also excellent for marinating pork tenderloin or leg of lamb before oven roasting.

MYSTERIOUSLY SOUR, SURPRISINGLY UBIQUITOUS

Tamarind

This sweet-sour fruit is complex, exotic, and tangy, and well worth tracking down. Native to Africa but grown in tropic zones around the world, the large and lovely tamarind tree produces clusters of slim, papery-thin, brown pods; inside are small beans surrounded by a rich, flavorful, mildly acidic pulp.

Across the equatorial band, different parts of the tamarind are prized and put to use in a variety of ways. In Indian and Southeast Asian cooking, the meaty pulp is turned into syrup or mashed before being used as a flavoring agent, contributing a pleasantly sour, citrusy zing to the region's distinctive soups, curries, and stews. In the West Indies, the fruit is sweetened with sugar and made into patties that are sold as a kind of natural candy in the marketplaces of Jamaica, Cuba, and the Dominican Republic. In Latin America, the syrup is used to flavor soft drinks and juices, most familiarly the popular brand of Mexican soda pop, Jarritos. In China and Indonesia, the seeds of the fruit are roasted as crisp, nutty snacks. And the fruit has been in frequent use in the West for many decades—as an ingredient in Worcestershire sauce, it's an essential component of the Bloody Mary you enjoy at Sunday morning brunch.

The easiest, most convenient way to employ tamarind is in its paste form, far better than the powdered or bottled versions. Thanks to that signature ripe, sour tang, even a small amount slipped into a stir-fry or sauce can revamp and enliven things exponentially.

The tree and its pods are also the objects of spiritual symbolism; certain African tribes consider it sacred, and some Burmese believe the tree to be home to a rain god. The fruit itself is revered across many cultures for its medicinal properties; its pulp is thought to be a powerful anti-inflammatory, a cure for sunstroke, and a tonic for swollen joints, and tamarind lotions and extracts are used in treating everything from conjunctivitis to dysentery to leprosy.

Mail order: For tamarind in various forms, Rani's World Foods, tel 281-440-8080, ranis worldfoods.com. **Further information and recipes:** *Cracking the Coconut* by Su-mei Yu (2000); *Classic Indian Cooking* by Julie Sahni (1980);

Indian Cooking Unfolded by Raghavan Iyer (2013); cookstr.com (search tamarind chutney suneeta); foodandwine.com (search tamarind shrimp soup); bonappetit.com (search grilled chicken with tamarind orange glaze). **Tip:** If you can't find tamarind, you may be able to substitute lemon—although aside from being sour the flavors aren't really related.

--||||||||||||||||||||||||||||||||||--

THIS LITTLE PIGGY WENT TO BALI

Babi Guling
Balinese Suckling Pig

Indonesian (Balinese)

In his 1937 book *Island of Bali,* artist and ethnographer Miguel Covarrubias describes in detail the preparation of a spit-roasted pig for a banquet, including its slaughter and cleaning with boiling water and a sharp piece of coconut shell.

"When it comes to preparing banquet food," he notes, "it is the men, as is universally the case, who [. . .] prepare the festival dishes of roast suckling pig (*bé guling,* in local dialect) . . . the cooking of which requires the art of famous specialists." The beast is stuffed, head to tail, with red chiles, garlic, red onions, turmeric, ginger, salt, black pepper, fish paste, and various aromatic leaves, before being sewn up and basted with turmeric-tinted water for flavor and color, and turned and roasted over a

A Balinese pig roast is usually reserved for special occasions.

low wood fire. "After a few hours of slow roasting, the juiciest and most tender pork is obtained, flavored by the fragrant spices, inside of a deliciously brittle skin covered with a golden-brown glaze. Few dishes in the world can be compared with a well made bé guling," the author concludes.

Balinese roast suckling pig, now called *babi guling,* is still a star of the island's cuisine, generally reserved for weddings and other feast days, although it is also available at restaurants that specialize in the dish. As in Covarrubias's day, side dishes and garnishes might include bean sprouts with crushed peanuts, pyramids of rice, grated coconut, salted duck eggs, and beverages such as *brem,* a sweet wine made from glutinous rice, or the heady palm wine *tuak.*

The Balinese town of Ubud became famous as an artist colony and tourist destination in the 1950s and 1960s, and visitors who were the fortunate guests of the local prince, or *tjokorda,* were served very similar, spice-stuffed pigs that were roasted in deep earthen pits lined with banana leaves. Ubud has been considered a mecca for suckling pig ever since, and its status was ensured when Anthony Bourdain visited the town for an episode of his television show *No Reservations* and declared the babi guling he found there the best he'd ever tasted. One has to wonder how many others he experienced for that comparison.

Where: *In Ubud, Bali,* Ibu Oka, tel 62/361-976345; *in New York,* Daisy May's BBQ, tel 212-977-1500, daisymaysbbq.com (minimum two days advance notice for half or full pig roasts); Rotisserie Georgette, tel 212-390-8060, rotisserieg.com (minimum three days advance notice for whole suckling pig). **Further information and recipe:** gourmet.com (search whole hog with balinese spices).

IT ALL BEGINS WITH RICE

Rijsttafel

Indonesian, Dutch

A lesson in the history of colonialism (along with one of its more benign consequences) can be found in the fact that recipes for Indonesian food are still considered essential in Dutch cookbooks. During the 350 years that the Dutch controlled Indonesia through the Dutch East India Company, planters and traders developed a taste for the spicy, tropical local fare that was in such sharp and colorful contrast to their own wintry soups and stews. With their palates beguiled by such delicacies as salted, curried duck eggs, satays of meat or chicken dipped into spicy peanut sauces, the rainbow of pickled vegetables that is *gado-gado,* and the sustaining spiced fried rice dish known as *nasi goreng,* they attempted meals based on all of those favorites, all at once. The repasts the Dutch named *rijsttafel,* or rice table feasts, centered on rice mounded on shiny green banana leaves, accompanied by a parade of dishes, sauces, and condiments called *sambals.*

Returning the compliment, Indonesians began to offer their own version of the meal, preparing more authentically seasoned versions of dishes that the Dutch liked, and calling the menu *nasi padang: nasi* for rice, *padang* for meal. To this day, no self-respecting food buff would go to any large Dutch city—most especially Amsterdam—without seeking out at least one restaurant featuring rijsttafel. Invariably, the meal would include some of these classic offerings:

Acar timun. Fresh and crunchy saltwater-pickled cucumbers with minced red chiles.

Ajam roedjak. Tender stewed chicken in a sauce of hot chiles and coconut cream.

Gado-gado. Cold, colorful mixed vegetables tossed together for a refreshing salad dressed with a vinegar- and garlic-accented peanut sauce.

Ikan pepesan. Silvery steamed mackerel in an incendiary chile sauce.

Kroepoek. Glassily crisp shrimp puffs that look like big, snowy potato chips.

Loempiah. Soft-skinned, Chinese-style egg rolls with fillings of chives, roast pork, and chicken.

Nasi goreng. Javanese fried rice tossed with bits of roast pork, garlic, and chile, all bound with eggs scrambled into the frying rice.

Oedang piendang koening. Charcoal-grilled jumbo shrimp in a lemongrass-scented sweet-and-sour sauce.

Otak-otak. Grilled fish cakes with chile-peanut sauce.

Pisang goreng. Sweet and meaty bananas baked in butter with salt and lemon or lime juice.

Redang. Beef stewed in a pungent curry sauce.

Sambal goreng. A hotly spiced side dish that may be based on shrimp, green beans, soy cakes, or cheese.

Satay. Pork, chicken, beef, or goat cubes charcoal-grilled on tiny bamboo skewers and dipped in a pungent chile-peanut sauce.

Seroendeng. A condiment of crisply fried coconut flakes tossed with roasted peanuts.

Soto ajam. A heady and slightly sour chicken soup enriched with coconut milk.

WHERE: *In Amsterdam,* Tempo Doeloe, tel 31/20-625-6718, tempodoeloerestaurant.nl; Restaurant Blauw, tel 31/206-755-000, restaurant blauw.nl; *in Jakarta,* Kunstkring Paleis, tel 62/21-390-0-899, tuguhotels.com (click Tugu Kunstkring Paleis, then Indonesia Cultural Dining); *in New York,* Bali Nusa Indah, tel 212-265-2200, balinusa indah.net; *in Brookline, MA,* Java Indonesian Restaurant, tel 718-832-4583; Selamat Pagi, tel 718-701-4333, selamatpagibrooklyn.com; *in Miami,* The Indomania Restaurant, tel 305-535-6332, indomaniarestaurant.com; *in Houston,* Rice Bowl Chinese and Indonesian Restaurant, tel 281-988-9912, ricebowlhouston.com; *in San Francisco,* Borobudur, tel 415-775-1512, borobudursf.com. **MAIL ORDER:** indofoodstore .com (search limes; kecap soy sauce; shrimp crackers; ibu sambal; sambal chili sauce; palm sugar). **FURTHER INFORMATION AND RECIPES:** *Authentic Recipes from Indonesia* by Heinz Von Holzen, Lother Arsana, and Wendy Hutton (2006); *The Art of Dutch Cooking* by C. Countess van Limburg Stirum (1962); foodandwine.com (search gado gado); epicurious.com (search indonesian fried rice); saveur.com (search rijstaffel; acar timun; gulai sayur); nytimes.com (search soto ayam); dutchcommunity.com (search how to prepare a typical indonesian rijsttafel).

TO NYONYA'S HOUSE WE GO

A Peranakan Dinner

Malaysian

Although fusion cuisine seems quintessentially modern, it is old news to the Peranakan population of Singapore and Malaysia. This group, made up of descendants of the Chinese who immigrated to the so-called British Straits Settlements (Malacca, Penang, and Singapore) centuries ago, has developed an array of warmly spiced, intriguing dishes that harmoniously meld influences from China, Indonesia, and

India into a style all their own. Peranakan is the formal name for this group, as well as their cuisine, but the women are generally known as Nyonya (meaning both grandmother and her home cooking) and the men as Baba (meaning grandfather, who probably does the eating).

Although many restaurants in the United States serve Nyonya food, it is at its best on home ground, most especially in Singapore and in Malaysia's Penang. As with many Asian meals, it is best if there are four to six adventurous diners so everyone can sample many dishes, beginning with *Nyonya rojak,* a rainbow-colored, sweet-tart fruit-and-seafood salad. Along with the salad, there might be tamarind-marinated pork or beef satay in a tongue-tingling chile-peanut sauce (see page 848), as well as the silky-soft spring rolls *poh piah,* formed of translucent crêpes rolled at the table to envelop shrimp or crabmeat, cucumber, eggs, and fried garlic, all adding up to a flavorful and filling first course. The follow-up might be *asam laksa,* a hot-and-sour soup made with shredded fish and thick, white rice noodles, flavored with tamarind, onion, fish sauce, Thai basil, and chunks of pineapple. A generous dash of hot chile paste in your bowl will not be amiss.

While you still have room, try chile crabs, the fieriest of the fiery. These hard-shell crabs are submerged whole in a velvety mix of red chiles, garlic, scallions, coriander, tomato ketchup, salted soybeans, malt vinegar, and soy sauce, all of which enhance the firm, ocean-fresh crabmeat that you pick and chew out of the shells. A messy business but worth it. After you have a hot towel to mop up your hands and face, proceed to *otak-otak,* a firm fish cake (preferably made from an oily variety, like Spanish mackerel or kingfish) wrapped in a banana leaf and grilled; or, if prepared Penang-style, it will be steamed and will exude the gentle aroma of coconut cream. As the meal goes along, refresh your palate with the bright pickled-vegetable relishes known as *acar.*

Although Chinese-Malaysian in origin, *nasi ayam,* Hainanese chicken rice (see page 854) always appears on the menu of Peranakan restaurants as well as being sold from street stalls and at night markets throughout Singapore. It is a cool, mellow combination of chicken steamed so gently that its flesh emerges silky and sweet, and rice cooked in the chicken's delicate, aromatic broth. Also not Nyonya in origin, but likely on the menu nonetheless, is the Indonesian spiced coconut milk stew that is beef *rendang,* slow-cooked for hours until the meat becomes tender and deeply flavorful. Bowls of *itek tim,* however, are a purely Peranakan main-course soup, studded with chunks of duck, pigs' trotters, cabbage, Chinese mushrooms, salted plums, and lime juice.

For a sweet finish, hope that *pulot hitam* is offered. Served hot or cold, it is a toothsome pudding of silvery-black glutinous rice sweetened with *gula melaka,* dark-brown palm sugar, to be eaten along with spoonfuls of coconut cream. Also delightful are *kuih,* or rice-based cakes and puddings that come in a variety of shapes and colors, but are generally flavored with coconut and the floral pandan leaf sweetened with palm sugar. Brightly tinted and achingly sweet, they bring the Nyonya feast to a suitably festive close.

Singapore's chile crab

WHERE: *In New York and Brooklyn,* Nyonya at three locations, ilovenyonya.com; *in Minneapolis,* Peninsula Malaysian Cuisine, tel 612-871-8282, peninsulamalaysiancuisine.com. **FURTHER INFORMATION AND RECIPES:** *Cradle of Flavor* by James Oseland (2006); *The New Mrs. Lee's Cuisine* by Lee Chin Koon (2004); *Peranakan Heritage Cooking* by Philip Chia (2001); *Traditional Nonya Cuisine* by Lucy Koh (2004); rasamalaysia.com (search laksa; otak; rojak); seriouseats.com (search curry laksa); saveur.com (search nyonya udang masak nanas).

╫||||||||||||||||||||||||||||╫

COOL COMFORT

Nasi Ayam

Hainanese Chicken Rice

Malaysian, Singaporean, Chinese

C hicken and rice come together to delicious effect in many cultures, but perhaps never so simply as in this version, brought to Singapore by Chinese immigrants from Hainan province and quickly assimilated. Now ubiquitous in that

food-centric island nation, chicken rice is as popular at casual street-market stalls as it is in the polished cafés of top hotels, and everywhere in between. It is the go-to dish for the convalescent and for all who need a quick bit of comfort during a stressful day. To be at its coolly fragrant, chickeny best, this rather minimalist dish has to be prepared with the best ingredients and careful, attentive restraint.

It begins with a fresh, plump whole chicken that is gently poached in a heady broth with fresh ginger, scallions, and garlic. Once cooked to moist, silky perfection, the bird is quickly rinsed in cold water to stop the cooking and tighten the skin, then receives a light polishing of oil to add sheen and help retain moisture. Chopped into chunks (bones and all) and served at room temperature, the chicken is bedded down on crisp, cold slices of cucumber under cilantro leaves and minced scallions. Bites are dipped into a salty-sweet sauce of hot chiles, scallions, ginger, soy sauce, and malt or rice vinegar. Beside that appealing platter, there is always a generous bowl of gently warm short-grain rice that has first been sautéed in vegetable oil or chicken fat, along with minced garlic and shallots; steamed in the reserved aromatic stock from the chicken, the rice takes on a mellow flavor that makes it a perfect foil for the chicken and spicy sauce. A cup of the warm, clear stock is usually served on the side, for a final, super-comforting touch.

WHERE: *In Singapore,* Chin Chin Eating House, tel 65/6337-4640; Tian Tian Hainanese Chicken Rice at three locations, tiantianchickenrice.com; *in New York,* Nyonya, tel 212-334-3669, ilovenyonya.com; *in San Francisco,* Penang Garden, tel 415-296-7878. **FURTHER INFORMATION AND RECIPES:** epicurious.com (search hainanese chicken rice); adorasbox.net (search nasi ayam hainanese chicken); saveur.com (search hainanese chicken rice).

╫||||||||||||||||||||||||||||╫

A FEAST FOR THE SENSES IN THE LION CITY

Tekka Centre, Singapore

Singaporean, Indian

W hen Sir Stamford Raffles claimed Singapore for the British Crown in 1819, he set about designating separate living areas for the varied ethnic groups, especially the large number of Indians he brought along as aides and troops. Their designated ghetto was around Serangoon Road, an area now known as Little India, a destination in itself for fine Indian crafts and food shops. The centerpiece of the enclave is Tekka Centre, a soaring market pavilion filled with wondrous scents and a cacophony of sounds, as sellers announce their wares to passersby and buyers haggle and chat.

Those wares include rainbows of gold, yellow, red, purple, gray-green, and black spices; lacy green herbs; burlap sacks of sweet-scented basmati rice (see page 867); prepared masala spice mixes and jewel-bright *sambal* relishes; fish and meat; tooth-achingly sweet confections; and unusual and delectable prepared treats no serious nosher should miss. There is *murtabak,* a sweet-savory pie with buttery layers of a phyllo-type pastry and nuts, spices, chicken, lamb, or pigeon, all topped with powdered sugar, much in the manner of the Moroccan *b'stilla* (see page 715). There are sumptuous, sunny rice *biryanis* (see page 868) flecked with chicken or lamb and gilded with spices, and *rojak,* a tart salad of marinated fruits and vegetables plus shrimp or squid.

The cool yogurt drink *lassi* (see page 879) whether scented with cardamom, fruit, or chiles, is the perfect foil for the spicy food, as is another specialty, a pineapple smoothie consisting only of the fresh fruit blended to a creamy froth before your eyes. Thus fortified, one has strength to head to the second floor of Tekka Centre and explore row after row of luminous brassware, colorful jewelry, and rainbows of marvelous fabrics.

Where: 665 01-201 Buffalo Road, at the corner of Bukit Timah Road and Serangood Road. **When:** Daily, 6:30 a.m. to 9:00 p.m. **Further information:** travelinsider.qantas.com.au (search serangoon).

⊢||||||||||||||||||||||||||||||⊣

TOP BANANAS

Banana Blossoms

Vietnamese, Southeast Asian

With an alluring flavor that suggests a subtle combination of bananas and onions, plus a hint of bitter almond, the so-called banana flower used in Southeast Asian cuisines actually comes from a species of plantain. Deep mauve

on the outside, paling to creamy pink as their petals coil toward the center, the dense blossoms, packed with tiny protobananas, can weigh more than a pound. Because they are bitter when raw, the blossoms are opened and peeled (somewhat like an artichoke) and blanched in boiling water and lemon juice before being added to salads, as in Vietnam; or cooked in coconut milk for curries, as in Indonesia and Malaysia; or fried with curry

Banana flowers, or hearts

spices, as in parts of India. Both the harvesting and the preparation are labor-intensive, so the blossoms are generally considered something of a delicacy.

The Vietnamese treatment, a salad called *goi bap chuoi,* is perhaps the most delicious, as it lets the blossom's unusual flavor shine. The prepared blossoms are tossed with fermented fish sauce (*nuoc mam*) along with peanuts and sometimes sesame seeds, orange and lime juices, and diced grilled meats such as chicken or pork. Bean sprouts, cilantro, garlic, and ginger may be added, along with grated green papaya or mango. Thanks to the banana blossom's complex and savory flavor, the salad can also be prepared without meat, as a classic Buddhist vegetarian specialty. Either way, it is typically served in the sturdy, purple-pink outer petals of the blossom, which look like little boats and make for a stunningly photogenic presentation.

Where: *In Hanoi,* La Verticale, tel 84/4-3944-6316, verticale-hanoi.com; *in San Gabriel, CA,* Phong Dinh Restaurant, tel 626-307-8868, phong dinh.com. **Mail order:** Grocery Thai, tel 818-469-9407, grocerythai.com. **Further information and recipes:** *The Oxford Companion to Food* by Alan Davidson (2006); *Cracking the Coconut* by Su-mei Yu (2000); *Into the Vietnamese Kitchen* by Andrea Nguyen (2006); theculinarychroni cles.com (search banana blossom salad); food network.com (search banana blossom salad); food.com (search banana blossom guinatan); heavytable.com (search cooking with banana flower).

SANDWICHING IN TWO CULTURES

Banh Mi

Vietnamese

A French-Vietnamese hybrid of a sandwich, the *banh mi* has become a fixture at gourmet sandwich shops, coffee counters, and strip-mall dive restaurants all over the world. Should it fade from the culinary limelight, the sandwich will still exist in the annals of language—it has scored a spot in the *Oxford English Dictionary* as "a Vietnamese snack consisting of a baguette (traditionally baked with both rice and wheat flour) filled with a variety of ingredients, typically including meat, pickled vegetables, and chili peppers."

Despite its ubiquity, the sandwich's exact ingredients are hard to pin down. A fresh, hearty, crusty baguette (one of the two ingredients that represents the French colonial influence) is a must, and many of the best banh mi makers go so far as to bake their own. Layered inside will be an array of vegetables and spreads, usually including a slaw of shredded carrots and daikon radish, chile peppers, garlic, fermented fish sauce, cucumber, cilantro, and a pork-infused aioli (French influence number two). The real variation occurs in the creation's combination of proteins, which may include all or some of the following: ham, headcheese, steamed pork roll sausage seasoned with fish sauce (*cha lua*), minced barbecued pork (*nem nuong*), fried tofu, Vietnamese salami (*thit nguoi*), pork liver pâté, and sardines. Banh mi is traditionally inexpensive street food, but these days it has become high style and so its prices rise accordingly.

Where: *In New York,* Nam Pang at multiple locations, nampangnyc.com; *in Washington, DC,* BonMi, tel 202-285-0012, eatbonmi.com; *in Atlanta,* Lee's Bakery, tel 404-728-1008; *in Houston,* Café TH, tel 713-225-4766, cafeth.com; *in Manhattan Beach, CA,* Little Sister, tel 310-545-2096, littlesistermb.com; *in Culver City and Costa Mesa, CA,* East Borough, east-borough .com. **Further information and recipes:** *Momofuku* by David Chang (2009); *The Banh Mi Handbook* by Andrea Nguyen (2014); bonappetit .com (search pork meatball banh mi); epicurious .com (search chicken sandwich banh mi); battleofthebanhmi.com.

MEAT ON "BUN"

Bun Cha Gio

Rice Noodle Roll with Pork

Vietnamese

The street food of Vietnam need not always be a grab-and-go affair. Like the elaborate *pho bo* (see page 862), *bun cha gio* is a nourishing meal-in-a-bowl that is eaten at open-front shops or stalls where customers sit at low counters on small stools or what look like overturned plastic mop buckets.

Communal serving bowls hold *bun,* the slim rice vermicelli, bright green herbs such as sawtooth coriander, cress, scallions, and cilantro, and varieties of fresh hot chiles. Individual bowls contain raw, crisp vegetables such as slivered cucumbers and grated carrots, as well as pork, typically in grilled slices or tiny, compact, and juicy meatballs. The bowl may also include chunks of golden, crisply fried spring rolls filled with pork and wrapped in flaky leaves of rice paper. (Served without the spring rolls, the dish is known simply as *bun cha.*) Diners add noodles and herbs to taste, and a light broth is spooned over all. For even more flavor, condiments are at hand, including soy sauce, *nuoc mam* (fermented fish sauce), hot sauce, rice vinegar, lime wedges, and for extra crunch and richness, crushed roasted peanuts. The idea is to add bits of this and dabs of that as you go to keep your palate interested, until you can eat no more. The result is delicious, light, and utterly satisfying.

Vietnamese cuisine includes a vast assortment of *bun*-based dishes, ranging from brothy soups to cool salads, topped with seafood, grilled beef, or tofu. A particularly restorative hot-weather variation on bun cha gio is *bun thit nuong,* a specialty of southern Vietnam, which consists of silky rice vermicelli served chilled and topped with a grilled pork chop, a leafy pile of fresh herbs, and filaments of grated carrots and the gently bitter Asian white radish, daikon. Like so many Vietnamese dishes, bun cha gio and its ilk feature intriguing contrasts of tastes and temperatures—sweet, sour, bitter, salty, cool and hot—and textures that range from silky soft to crackling crisp. Complete with meat or fish, noodles, and a variety of herbs and vegetables, they make for nutritious, balanced, and satisfying all-in-one meals, in Hanoi or right at home.

WHERE: *In Hanoi,* Dac Kim, tel 84/438-287-060, bunchahangmanh.vn; *in New York,* Le Colonial, tel 212-252-0808, lecolonialnyc.com; *in New Orleans,* Lilly's Café, tel 504-599-9999; *in Los Angeles,* Brodard Chateau, tel 714-899-8273, brodard.net/chateau; *in San Gabriel, CA,* Phong Dinh Restaurant, tel 626-307-8868, phongdinh .com. **FURTHER INFORMATION AND RECIPES:** *Into the Vietnamese Kitchen* by Andrea Nguyen (2006); *Authentic Vietnamese Cooking* by Corinne Trang (1999); vietnamesefood.com.vn (search bun cha gio); aspicyperspective.com (search bun cha gio).

A dish representative of Vietnam's street food

Cha Ca La Vong and Ca Chien

Turmeric Fish and Fried Catfish

Vietnamese

A specialty of Hanoi, *cha ca la vong* is a pungently glazed fish dish so beloved that it has a street named after it (Cha Ca Street, or Grilled Fish Street), along which you can find the restaurant, Cha Ca La Vong, that is credited with its invention. In the widely copied preparation, fillets of catfish (farmed in the Chau Doc river and thus sweeter and less "muddy" tasting than wild catfish) are marinated for up to twelve hours in a heady mixture of ground fresh galangal (the sharp-tasting ginger relative native to Southeast Asia), shrimp paste, golden turmeric, lemon juice, *nuoc mam* (fermented fish sauce), a hefty dose of crushed black peppercorns, and finely chopped hot green chiles. First grilled over charcoal along with sprigs of scallions, the charred fish is then quickly fried in hot peanut

Cha Ca La Vong features turmeric and catfish.

oil with more sliced scallions and, often, a generous handful of fresh dill. The fragrant fish, a cheery bright yellow from the turmeric, is served with roasted peanuts and a light sauce made from nuoc mam or shrimp paste blended with more black pepper and lime juice. For a mellow flavor contrast, it is accompanied by *bun* (thin rice vermicelli), flaky rice crackers, or warm jasmine rice.

To the south, Saigon has its own delectable way with catfish in the dish *ca chien* (fried fish). Unlike the rather delicate treatment of cha ca la vong, here the floured fish fillets are seasoned simply with garlic and black pepper and deep-fried in peanut oil. The crispy, golden fillets are then served with a zesty sauce of rice vinegar, nuoc mam, garlic, palm sugar, green chiles, and lemon or lime juice. Thin slices of cucumber, scallions, and cilantro provide color and crisp freshness, and it wouldn't be complete without a bowl of steamed white rice. Less elaborately spiced than its northern sibling, ca chien is a particularly delicious take on the globally adored concept of fried fish, with the characteristic touches of heat, crunch, and cool herbs that make it uniquely Vietnamese.

WHERE: *In Hanoi,* Cha Ca La Vong, tel 84/4-3825-3929; La Verticale, tel 84/4-3944-6316, verticale-hanoi.com; *in New York,* Le Colonial, tel 212-252-0808, lecolonialnyc.com; Wong, tel 212-989-3399, wongnewyork.com; *in Boston,* Pho Pasteur, tel 617-482-7467, phopasteurboston.net; *in Las Vegas,* Lotus of Siam, tel 702-735-3033, saipinchutima.com; *in San Gabriel, CA,*

Phong Dinh Restaurant, tel 626-307-8868, phong dinh.com. **Mail order:** Grocery Thai, tel 818-469-9407, grocerythai.com (search fish sauce; jasmine rice; shrimp paste). **Further information AND RECIPES:** *Into the Vietnamese Kitchen* by Andrea Nguyen (2006); nytimes.com (search cha ca la vong; ca chien sot ca); cookstr.com (search cha ca fish).

⊢||||||||||||||||||||||||||||||||⊣

STUCK ON SUGARCANE

Chao Tom

Grilled Shrimp on Sugarcane

Vietnamese

F̲ew dishes are more astonishing or pleasing to first-timers than *chao tom,* a charcoal-grilled kebab of pounded shrimp packed around a stick of fresh sugarcane, a concept as improbable as it is delectable. Although technically an

appetizer, it's so hard to say "when" to this delicious dish that it often winds up as a main course.

In this sweet-and-savory treat, tender shrimp—widely farmed in Vietnam—is ground and pounded with rich pork fat into a smooth pâté. Swirled with toasted rice powder, shallots, garlic, fish sauce (*nuoc mam*), golden rock sugar, and black pepper, the mixture is packed firmly around freshly peeled, juicy sugarcane and then grilled, preferably over wood charcoal for a smoky patina.

Sugarcane and shrimp come together at street markets.

The rather elaborate serving presentation for chao tom includes sheer, round sheets of tender, chewy rice paper, soft lettuce leaves, lacy shreds of scallions, carrots, and cucumber, and aromatic sprays of cilantro and basil. There might also be *bun* (slim rice vermicelli), a lusciously thick, chile-fired peanut sauce, and more fish sauce brightened into a lively dip with lime juice, rice vinegar, and hot green chiles. Coarsely crushed roasted peanuts are the final topping, sprinkled over all. Lucky diners build the dish by layering a sheet of rice paper, a lettuce leaf, vegetables and sauces, and finally the grilled shrimp, which is slid off the sugarcane. The pile is rolled

up as compactly as possible (and then eaten, without utensils, as deftly as possible). Chewing the sugarcane adds a sweet finishing touch, albeit one a dentist might disapprove of.

Where: *In New York,* Nha Trang, tel 212-233-5948, nhatrangone.com; *in Boston,* Pho Pasteur, tel 617-482-7467, phopasteurboston.net; *in Manhattan Beach, CA,* Little Sister, tel 310-545-2096, littlesistermb.com. **Further information AND RECIPES:** *The Best of Nicole Routhier* by Nicole Routhier (1996); foodnetwork.ca (search chao tom); vietworldkitchen.com (search grilled shrimp on sugarcane); rasamalaysia.com (search shrimp chao tom).

||||||||||||||||||||||||||||||||||||||||||||||||||||||||||||||||||||||||||||||||||||||||||||||||||||||||||||

RIPE FRUIT, GREEN SALAD

Papaya

The glowing golden-orange of the skin of the ripe papaya (*Carica papaya*), a pear-shaped fruit native to Central America and cultivated in tropical countries around the globe, reveals an opulent and juicy, honey-sweet flesh that eases across the palate and down the throat with an almost lascivious appeal. To be enjoyed at its luscious fullest, the papaya must be fresh and fully ripe, so tender and full-flavored that it needs no enhancement, save perhaps for the classic accompaniment of a squirt of fresh lime juice that nicely spikes the low-acid fruit.

The papaya tree, looking like a palm with even larger, fingerlike leaves, is something of a botanical curiosity, growing to its full height of twenty or so feet in less than two years. Nutritionally, papayas are a superfood, with digestive and stomach-soothing abilities; some even believe that they help treat ulcers. They contain the enzyme papain, which is useful in breaking down protein and thus is found in meat tenderizing products. This goes back to ancient times, when tropical cultures made a practice of wrapping papaya leaves around meat.

When choosing a papaya, pick one that is subtly soft and gives way to gentle pressure. Store papayas at room temperature (never in a refrigerator) until ripe, then cut them in half lengthwise and scrape out the seeds. Peel and cut the fruit into manageable pieces, sprinkle them with lime juice, and refrigerate for at least an hour before serving. Or do as they do in Southeast Asia, where unripe, green papayas are used as vegetables, shredded or thinly sliced and seasoned with peppers and lime in crisp, refreshing salads.

WHERE: *In New York,* for papaya smoothies, Papaya King at two locations, papayaking.com; Jaiya at multiple locations, jaiya.com; *in Skokie, IL,* Tub Tim Thai, tel 847-675-8424, tubtimthai skokie.com; *in Houston,* for salad, Thai Bistro, tel 713-669-9375, txthaibistro.com; *in San Francisco,* The Slanted Door, 416-861-8032, slanteddoor .com; *in Berkeley, CA,* for tropical fruit sherbet, Chez Panisse, tel 510-548-5525, chezpanisse .com. **MAIL ORDER:** Melissa's Produce, tel 800-588-0151, melissas.com. **FURTHER INFORMATION AND RECIPES:** *Chez Panisse Fruit* by Alice Waters (2002); *Cracking the Coconut* by Su-Mei Yu (2000); saveur.com (search fruta bomba); weheartfood.com (search papaya salad).

|||||||||||||||||||||||||||||||||

(UN)RIPE FOR DISCOVERY

Goi Du Du, or Som Tam

Green Papaya Salad

Vietnamese, Thai

Contrary to the usual advice about selecting fruit that is perfectly ripe, the papaya that does best in this tart, refreshing salad is one that is rock hard, immature, and very prettily lime green. The unripe fruit is refreshingly acidic and crunchy and, because of its firmness, can easily be grated for this slawlike dish.

Intriguing versions of this salad exist in both Thailand and Vietnam, where papayas are abundant thanks to those nations' tropical climates. In both, it is usually served as a first course that remains on the table throughout the meal to be dipped into as an occasional between-courses palate-cleanser.

In Vietnam, where the salad is called *goi du du*, it is a summery rainbow of shredded green papaya pulp tossed with sunny shreds of carrots, red peppers and, often, white daikon radish and scallions. In northern Vietnam, strips of spicy-sweet beef jerky are a most traditional ingredient, although paper-thin slices of grilled sirloin add a richer flavor and a desirable juiciness to the mix; in the south, the salad is more likely to include shrimp or pork. Finishing touches include cilantro and an extra-tangy dressing of rice vinegar, garlic, salt, sugar, black pepper, chile sauce, and lime or lemon juice.

The more elaborate Thai version, *som tam*, begins with the grated green fruit, enhanced with a range of flavorful and pungent additions, among which might be brined crab or fermented fish. At its most basic, though, the papaya is simply tossed with green beans or long beans (see page 786) and tomatoes. The secret to this mix is the rather incendiary dressing, which begins with a paste of garlic, hot chiles, roasted peanuts, dried shrimp, and palm sugar and is then thinned with splashes of the ever-present fermented fish sauce, *nam pla,* and lime juice. To be considered authentic, the dressing must be pounded with mortar and pestle (the *tam* in som tam means "to pound"), never mixed in a food processor or blender. It is both permissible and traditional, however, to substitute unripe mango for the papaya, for a slightly fruitier but still tart and crunchy salad.

Where: *In Hanoi,* La Verticale, tel 84/ 4-3944-6316, verticale-hanoi.com; *in New York,* Kittichai, tel 212-925-2991, kittichai restaurant.com; *in Chicago,* Amarit Thai &

Pan Asian Cuisine, tel 312-939-1179; *in Las Vegas,* Lotus of Siam, tel 702-735-3033, saipin chutima.com; *in San Gabriel, CA,* Phong Dinh Restaurant, tel 626-307-8868, phongdinh.com; *in Culver City and Costa Mesa, CA,* East Borough, east-borough.com; *in Manhattan Beach, CA,* Little Sister, tel 310-545-2096, little sistermb.com. **Mail order:** For green papayas, Thai Supermarket Online, tel 888-618-8424, importfood.com. **Further information and recipes:** For the Vietnamese salad, *The Best of Nicole Routhier* by Nicole Routhier (1996); for the Thai salad, *Thai Food* by David Thompson (2002); *Simple Thai Food* by Leela Punyaratabandhu (2014); *Cracking the Coconut* by Su-mei Yu (2000); *Into the Vietnamese Kitchen* by Andrea Nguyen (2006); thaitable .com (search green papaya salad); cookstr .com (search som tum); bonappetit.com (search thai green papaya salad). **See also:** Papaya, facing page.

Unripe papaya is necessary for this enticing salad.

╾||||||||||||||||||||||||||||╼

BEEF: IT'S WHAT'S FOR BREAKFAST

Pho Bo

Beef Noodle Soup

Vietnamese

For the very best reasons, Vietnamese *pho* (rice noodle soup) and the cafés that serve it are sweeping the globe. Given that the sweetly spicy, warming beef noodle soup makes for an amazingly sustaining, inexpensive, and complete one-

bowl meal (and that, apparently, the world can't get enough noodle soup), its dedicated following is no surprise.

Hot, fragrant *pho bo* (the original and most-loved *pho*) mainly consists of a broth that is simmered slowly for anywhere from five to twelve hours, depending on how finicky, and patient, the cook is, and should include both oxtail and beef marrowbones. To achieve a clear broth, as is most desirable, the bones are blanched and rinsed before going into the pot, along with *nuoc mam* (fermented fish sauce) and a hefty spice bag that might contain cinnamon, star anise, clove, peppercorns, and charred ginger, among many other aromatics. Once simmered, a thin layer of fat is left on top of the soup; to skim it all off would be to sacrifice its twinkling golden glimmer and a whole lot of flavor.

The broth is bolstered by thin, silky white rice noodles; bouquets of sprightly green herbs such as sawtooth coriander, basil, chives, and fernlike cresses; chunks of softly cooked oxtail and brisket; and finally, paper-thin slices of raw beef that cook in the hot broth as you eat. In Vietnam, the more authentic and less touristic pho cafés might offer a range of much more exotic beef parts, from udder to tendons to every imaginable organ.

Pho bo really is the Vietnamese national dish, served at street stands all over the country, primarily between six and ten in the morning and then again late at night, although a few places catering to tourists serve it for lunch, usually substituting chicken for beef in those off

hours. The correct pronunciation is something between "few" and "fuh," very much like the French word *feu* (fire), as in *pot au feu,* which, in fact, turns out to be the origin of this dish. In the late nineteenth century, when the French occupied the country that was then called Tonkin, they cooked their traditional beef dishes, including the stew they called pot au feu. Beef was barely known in the country then—the Vietnamese ate chicken and pork primarily, saving cattle for farm work—so it is believed that pho emerged when Vietnamese cooks took the leavings from the French colonial kitchens and created their own version of pot au feu.

Pho bo soup is being added to menus everywhere.

Hanoi, the Vietnamese capital, is the recognized birthplace of pho bo, but regional variations have cropped up around the country, most especially in Saigon, to the south, where bean sprouts and rock sugar are just two of the ingredients not usually found in the north. *Pho ga*, made from chicken and its broth, is a much lighter variation and is enriched with a raw egg yolk, which forms silky ribbons as it coddles in the hot broth. And as one might expect in this age of culinary inventiveness, there are haute phos to be found, made from salmon, duck, and even foie gras.

WHERE: *In Hanoi*, Pho Bat Dan; Spices Garden in Sofitel Metropole Hanoi Hotel, tel 84/4-3826-6919, sofitel-legend.com (click Hotel Metropol, then Bars and Restaurants); La Verticale, tel 84/4-3944-6316, verticale-hanoi .com; *in San Francisco*, The Slanted Door, tel 415-861-8032, slanteddoor.com; Turtle Tower at three locations, turtletowersf.com; *in San Gabriel, CA*, Phong Dinh Restaurant, tel 626-307-8868, phongdinh.com; *in Culver City, CA*, East Borough, tel 310-596-8266, east-borough.com; *in New York*, Nha Trang, tel 212-233-5948, nhatrangone.com; Le Colonial, tel 212-252-0808, lecolonialnyc.com; *in Boston*, Pho Pasteur, tel 617-482-7467, phopasteur boston.net; *in New Orleans*, Lilly's Café, tel 504-599-9999; *in Houston*, Pho Danh No 2, tel 281-879-9940. **MAIL ORDER:** For Thai basil, rice noodles, and fish sauce, Grocery Thai, tel 818-469-9407, grocerythai.com. **FURTHER INFORMATION AND RECIPES:** *Into the Vietnamese Kitchen* by Andrea Nguyen (2006); *Authentic Vietnamese Cooking* by Corinne Trang (1999); vietworld kitchen.com (search beef pho); cookingchannel tv.com (search beef pho, pho ga); cookstr.com (search pho bo); the splendidtable.com (search pho ga).

A TONGUE-TINGLING "NOSE-TWISTER"

Watercress

The tender, round-leafed watercress that thrives in running fresh water is said to flourish only if that water is clean and free of pollutants, making it dear to the hearts of those who eat for health as well as pleasure. Its botanical name—*Nasturtium officinale*—misleadingly suggests a relation to the edible nasturtium plant, but the only thing they share is the "nose-twisting" quality indicated by their Latin moniker. Although delicate in texture and appearance, watercress is delightfully bracing, with a peppery flavor and just enough bitter bite to remind us that it belongs also to the *Brassicaceae*, or mustard, family. As delicious as cultivated watercress can be, it pales beside the icy-sharp wild sprays pulled out of running mountain streams and brooks.

An elegant and multipurpose green, it is commonly stir-fried with garlic and tofu or cooked into a popular, restorative soup in China. In the West it is usually eaten raw, either incorporated into salads or used as a flavorful garnish nestled beside rare steak or broiled lamb chops, where it absorbs the meaty juices as its only dressing.

Trimmed of its toughest stems, watercress acts as a stylish replacement for lettuce in many sandwiches, most famously in Britain's dainty tea treats, and shines when part of fresh herb mixes for omelets, dressings, cheese spreads, and cream sauces. It is a refined flavor and texture enhancer in soups such as France's *potage cressonière* (watercress and potato soup) and the curative Chinese favorite made with pork bones and watercress. In Japan, it makes a beloved addition to soupy noodle hot pots, and in Vietnam, it is the preferred accompaniment to stir-fried beef.

Growing wild and cultivated in Asia and Europe for millennia, and in the United States since at least the eighteenth century, watercress was a particular favorite of the ancient Persians, who made a complete meal of it with bread. The ancient Greeks and Romans valued it more as medicine than as food, believing it could treat everything from baldness to toothaches, a belief that persisted for centuries. As the Victorian chef Alexis Soyer writes in *The Pantropheon*, his 1853 tome on ancient cookery, "Persons who made it their habitual food found their wits sharpened and their intelligence more active and ingenious." We may no longer turn to watercress to raise our IQs, but its hefty levels of vitamin A and C, and minerals such as iron and potassium, certainly make it a smart addition to your diet.

FURTHER INFORMATION AND RECIPES: *Beyond Bok Choy* by Rosa Lo San Ross (1996); *Vietnamese Home Cooking* by Charles Phan (2012); *Vegetables from Amaranth to Zucchini* by Elizabeth Schneider (2001); *Watercress Greats* by Jo Franks (2012). TIP: Watercress is a stylish and beguiling substitution for lettuce in America's classic BLT sandwich (see page 530).

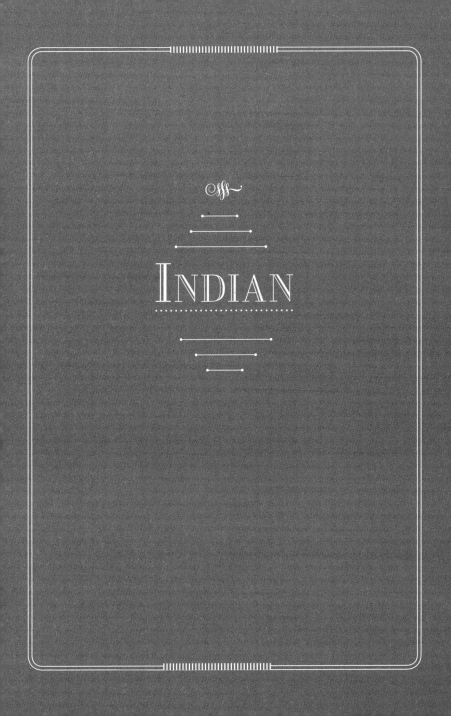

INDIAN

⊦||||||||||||||||||||||||||||||⊦

FRUIT FIT FOR A RAJAH

Alphonso Mango

Indian

What makes a food sensual? Generally, a combination of qualities that might involve a memorable and mysterious flavor, a vivid hue, a silky-smooth texture, and a beguiling if somehow unplaceable aroma. And in this, a perfectly ripe mango delivers. So luscious, so juicy, so sweet as sin is the fruit, with its overpoweringly lush flavor and sunny tropical scent, that one almost feels compelled to eat it in private.

If it's the right mango, that is. Despite the fact that there are hundreds of varieties in the world, mango pickings in the U.S. have been notoriously slim, usually limited to four varieties. Inviting though they may be, they pale beside the real thing— the mangoes of India, where the fruit is believed to have originated.

Much to the dismay of the fruit's vocal fans, India's mangoes were long embargoed in the U.S., as they can harbor a rare weevil unknown in American orchards and farms. After a great deal of negotiating, the ban was lifted in the landmark nuclear trade pact of 2006, following a plan to gently irradiate the produce to kill or sterilize the insects. Ever since, America's mango situation has vastly improved. "Whatever anyone else might say," wrote Indian food writer Madhur Jaffrey in *The New York Times*, "India gets nuclear fuel for its energy needs and America, doing far better in what might be called a stealth victory, finally gets mangoes."

To fans, the cultivar known as Alphonso, a relatively small, tennis-ball-size enticement considered by many to be "the king of mangoes," was well worth the wait. Specially fostered by farmers in prime coastal orchards near Mumbai, where it has grown for thousands of years, it has a smooth, fiberless texture and an intoxicatingly powerful aroma that is redolent of coconut.

But one act that should remain forbidden by a host of international laws would be introducing the fruit to a blender for the purpose of turning it into a smoothie— this mango's flavor is far too special not to be enjoyed on its own.

WHERE: *In New York,* Junoon, tel 212-490-2100, junoonnyc.com; *in Washington, DC,* Rasika, tel 202-637-1222, rasikarestaurant.com; *in Houston,* The Bombay Brasserie, tel 713-355-2000, thebombaybrasserie.com. **MAIL ORDER:** In season, Melissa's Produce, tel 800-588-0151, melissas.com; Exotic Fruit Market, tel 877-398-0141, exoticfruitmarket.net; Savani Farms, tel 855-696-2646, savanifarms.com. **FURTHER INFORMATION AND RECIPES:** *The Mongo Mango Cookbook* by Cynthia Thuma (2001); *Mangoes & Curry Leaves* by Jeffrey Alford and Naomi Duguid (2005); *Indian Cooking Unfolded* by Raghavan Iyer (2013); the guardian.com (search ottolenghi's mango recipes); vegrecipesofindia.com (search mango recipes). **SPECIAL EVENT:** International Mango Festival, Coral Gables, FL, July, fairchildgarden.org (click Events, then July).

||||||||||||||||||||||||||||||||

THE WORLD'S MOST DELICATE RICE

Basmati Rice

Indian

The long-grain basmati has been cultivated in the Indian Himalayan foothills—where some scholars believe all rice originated—for centuries. The foundation of many classic dishes in both Indian and Persian cuisine, it is an essential ingredient in *biryani*, the classic Mogul Empire dish consisting of layers of meat and rice spiked with saffron and garnished with gold or silver leaf (see page 868). But among the more than eight thousand varieties of rice grown across the globe, what is it that makes this particular grain so special?

Although there are several answers to the question, the best place to start may be with the grain's aroma. Basmati means "the fragrant one" in Sanskrit, and indeed the nutty, buttery scent that hangs heavily in the air is more than matched by its rich flavor, cozily reminiscent of popped corn. Then there's the rice's famously delicate texture, partly the result of its aging process. Customarily the best basmati is aged for six months to a year, always in burlap sacks stuffed with leaves from ancient East Indian Neem trees. The leaves function as a kind of insecticide, and keep the grains fresh and preserve their signature scent. Lastly, the rice is beloved for its fluffiness. Well rinsed in several changes of water to rid it of excess starch, basmati becomes one of the least sticky varieties of rice, a quality that makes it ideal for cooking.

WHERE: *In Delhi and environs,* Sagar Ratna, sagarratna.in; Karim's Hotel, tel 91/11-2326-9880, karimhoteldelhi.com; *in New York,* Tamarind, tel 212-775-9000, tamarind22.com; Dawat, tel 212-355-7555, dawatnewyork.com; *in Washington, DC,* Rasika, tel 202-637-1222, rasikarestaurant.com; Masala Art, tel 202-362-4441, masalaartdc.com; *in San Francisco,* Amber India, tel 415-777-0500, amber-india.com. **RETAIL AND MAIL ORDER:** *In New York,* Kalustyan's, tel 800-352-2451, kalustyans.com. **MAIL ORDER:** iShopIndian, tel 877-786-8876, ishopindian.com; tilda.com (click Products, then Where to Buy). **FURTHER INFORMATION AND RECIPES:** *Seductions of Rice* by Jeffrey Alford and Naomi Duguid (2003); *Madhur Jaffrey Indian Cooking* by Madhur Jaffrey (2003); epicurious.com (search coconut basmati rice; saffron steamed basmati); saveur.com (search pohp batalu jo pulao; middle eastern rice toasted almonds); foodnetwork.com (search ina garten basmati rice recipe).

||||||||||||||||||||||||||||||||

A SAVORY, CRISPY RICE SNACK

Bhel Puri

Indian (Gujarati)

Iconic, omnipresent, nostalgia-inducing, and loyalty-inspiring, the *chaats* of India are akin to American hot dogs, pretzels, and other beloved street snacks—and they are infinitely varied. The cold vegetarian salads are based on a crisp, starchy underpinning, such as puffed rice, fried chickpeas, or broken-up samosas or *papadums,* doused with cool yogurt and heightened with a mix of exotic spices into a bright and zesty mélange.

Among the chaats of Gujarat, especially along the avenues and alleys of its capital, Mumbai (formerly Bombay), *bhel puri* is an understandable favorite. An enticement of taste and textural contrasts, it provides an object lesson in flavor identification that begins with puffs and chips of rice, chickpea, and wheat flours deep-fried to nutty crispness. Tossed with peanuts, the mix is showered with hot, salty, and sweet condiments and spices like cayenne, cardamom, cumin, ginger, brown palm sugar, lemony tamarind, and fresh coriander, all flavors that light up the whole palate with

Bhel puri, India's popular street snack, for sale in Delhi

each bite. Addictively stimulating, bhel puri is one of those foods that cannot be relinquished until totally consumed. Leftovers are unlikely.

WHERE: *In New York,* Pongal, tel 212-696-9458, pongalnyc.com; Dawat, tel 212-355-7555, dawatnewyork.com; *in Boston,* Maharaja, tel 617-547-2757, maharajaboston .com; *in Washington, DC,* Masala Art, tel 202-362-4441, masalaartdc.com; *in Chicago,* Indian Garden, tel 312-280-4910, indiangardenchicago .com; *in Los Angeles,* Mayura, tel 310-559-9644, mayura-indian-restaurant.com; *in Toronto,* Udupi Palace, tel 416-405-8189, udupipalace.ca.

RETAIL AND MAIL ORDER: *In New York,* Kalustyan's, tel 800-352-2451, kalustyans.com. **MAIL ORDER:** For bhel puri, rice flour, chickpea flour, tamarind concentrate, and puffed rice, iShopIndian, tel 877-786-8876, ishopindian.com; for fresh tamarinds, Melissa's Produce, tel 800-588-0151, melissas.com. **FURTHER INFORMATION AND RECIPES:** *Chaat Cookbook* by Tarla Dalal (2000); *The Cooking of India* by Santha Rama Rau (1969); vegrecipesofindia.com (search bhel puri); indianfood.about.com (search bhel puri); sanjeevkapoor.com (search bhel puri). **SEE ALSO:** Kosheri, page 711.

⊣||||||||||||||||||||||||||||||⊢

A MAGNIFICENT CONSTRUCTION IN RICE

Biryani

Indian

India's flowery, aromatic basmati rice (see page 867) is the basis of many great dishes, foremost among them being *pulao,* a rice dish similar to pilaf and risotto. But for special occasions and discerning palates, *biryani* is the rice dish that becomes the main event, a specialty said to have been a favorite of the seventeenth-century Mogul ruler Shah Jahan—he who infamously blinded the architect of the Taj Mahal to ensure that his magnificent palace would never be replicated. (The despot may have deserved neither feast nor palace, but his taste was certainly irreproachable.)

Moist but still shapely grains of cooked rice form the base of the richly flavorful dish. Tossed with onions that are lightly seared in the clarified butter called ghee, the rice is enriched with golden raisins and a variety of crunchy nuts that might include almonds, pistachios, and cashews. The braised meat that adds substance and depth is almost always young lamb, flavored in a virtual raid on the Indian spice cupboard. Cumin, cinnamon, cardamom, cloves, pepper, turmeric, nutmeg, and cayenne might all make an appearance, and the aromatic results—rice and meat—are placed in alternating layers in a deep, heavy pot with a topping of saffron-tinted rice for a final golden glow. Baked slowly in the hermetically sealed pot, the rice absorbs the rich juices of the lamb and its spicy stock to emerge wet but not runny, with every grain temptingly separate.

If the top layer of saffron rice is not luxurious enough, tradition demands a topping of flakes of either gold or silver leaf just before the biryani is presented on its serving platter—a final touch that's certainly worthy of royalty.

WHERE: *In Delhi,* Karim's Hotel, tel 91/11-2326-9880, karimhoteldelhi.com; *in London,* Gymkhana, tel 44/020-3011-5900, gymkhana london.com; *in New York,* Dawat, tel 212-355-7555, dawatnewyork.com; Tamarind, tel 212-775-9000, tamarind22.com; *in Boston,* Maharaja, tel 617-547-2757, maharajaboston.com; *in Cambridge, MA,* Punjabi Dhaba, tel 617-547-8272, royalbharatinc.com; *in Chicago,* Sheesh Mahal Dhaba, tel 773-274-4444, sheeshmahal dhaba.com; Udupi Palace, tel 773-338-2152, udupipalacechicago.net; Jaipur, tel 312-526-3655, jaipurchicago.com; *in Houston,* The Bombay Brasserie, tel 713-355-2000, thebombaybrasserie .com; *in Los Angeles,* Mayura, tel 310-559-9644, mayura-indian-restaurant.com; *in San Francisco,* Amber India, tel 415-777-0500, amber-india .com. **FURTHER INFORMATION AND RECIPES:** *Mughlai Khana* by Tarla Dalal (2007); *Classic Indian Cooking* by Julie Sahni (1980); saveur.com (search pakistani lamb biryani; how to make chicken biryani). **SEE ALSO:** Risotto, page 233; Kosheri, page 711.

IT'S A FRUIT! IT'S A VEGETABLE! IT'S A BABY CROCODILE!

Bitter Melon

Indian, Asian

Botanically a fruit but prepared as a vegetable, the bitter melon lends its tart, quininelike flavor and a green pepper's crispness to numerous soups, stews, and stir-fries indigenous to various Asian cuisines. The bumpy green gourd may be powdered, pickled, juiced, and eaten raw or cooked—but for most of us, this member of the squash–cucumber (Cucurbitaceae) family may be easiest to find as a supplement at the local health food store. Bitter melon is renowned worldwide for its medicinal properties, thought to be effective in the treatment of such disparate conditions as acne, the common cold, and diabetes.

This so-called melon (*Momordica charantia*), also known as a balsam apple (the name given to it by the American painter James Peale in a still life now at the Metropolitan Museum of Art), bitter gourd, or bitter cucumber, is between five and ten inches long. (The larger it grows, the weaker its flavor.) If it is being used for cooking, a bitter melon will be cut open, its seeds and fibrous core discarded, and its dense flesh typically softened by blanching or parboiling before being put to use. It is when it is split that its appearance suggests a crocodilian animal.

A farmers' market find

An acquired taste, the gourd is most effective as an earthy seasoning in a large-scale production, such as a complex curry.

Mail order: For the fruit, Melissa's Produce, tel 800-588-0151, melissas.com; for seeds, Evergreen Y.H. Enterprises, evergreenseeds.com

(search bitter gourd). **Further information and recipes:** *My Grandmother's Chinese Kitchen* by Eileen Yin-Fei Lo (2006); *Mangoes & Curry Leaves* by Jeffrey Alford and Naomi Duguid (2005); *660 Curries* by Raghavan Iyer (2008); *Beyond Bok Choy* by Rosa Lo San Ross and Martin Jacobs (1996); *Vegetables from Amaranth to Zucchini* by Elizabeth Schneider (2001); saveur.com (search stir fried bitter melon with chicken wings; bitter melon with pork and black bean sauce; mighty melon); for numerous tips and recipes, the National Bitter Melon Council, bittermelon.org. For an extraordinary artist's view of bitter melon, met museum.com (search still life with balsam apple).

THE TANG TO PAIR WITH SPICE

Chatni

Indian

India's national condiment is unquestionably chutney, the relish made of pickled or stewed fruits and vegetables. The word is an Anglicized version of the Sanskrit *chatni,* which means "licking good," and it generally lives up to its name. But when it comes to exactly *which* chutney, debate never ends, for India boasts an incredible array of the intensely flavorful condiment, varying not only according to geography and region, but also within individual families. As an Indian adage aptly puts it, no two chutneys are alike, and the condiment's span stretches from the coconut chutney popular in South India and generally eaten with *idlis* (dumplings, see page 875) and *dosas* (similar to crêpes, see page 874) to the sour cherry chutney of Kashmir, and from the mint chutney also typically eaten with samosas to fresh

coriander-peanut chutney from the state of Gujarat in western India.

Despite these many variations, all chutneys have some qualities in common. They are always eaten in small quantities to complement the flavors of other foods. They are always pungent, and often acidic, providing an excellent counterbalance to the sometimes unremitting spice of dishes like curries. And they are always vegetarian. Within those parameters, they range from the simplest varieties, made of uncooked mixtures of herbs and spices, to the chunky, jamlike iterations Westerners are most familiar with—slow-cooked concoctions of fruit stewed with sugar and vinegar, and spiced with the familiar Indian flavors of cumin, cardamom, tamarind, ginger, and turmeric.

In traditional Indian households, chutneys are usually made fresh for each meal, by a home cook who grinds herbs and spices together into a paste. The most popular chutney in the world is the mango chutney ubiquitous throughout northwestern India and in Indian restaurants abroad. Its prevalence is due in part to the British, who first encountered mango chutney in their colonial days—the enormously popular jarred brand of mango chutney, Major Grey's, being one direct result. (The company that produces it, Crosse & Blackwell, was founded in 1706 and has long claimed that Major Grey was an actual person, an officer in the Bengal Lancers and a foodie.) Other notable brands include SWAD and Patak.

Where: *In New York,* Dawat, tel 212-355-7555, dawatnewyork.com; *in Boston,* Maharaja, tel 617-547-2757, maharajaboston.com; *in Washington, DC,* Rasika, tel 202-637-1222, rasika restaurant.com; Masala Art, tel 202-362-4441, masalaartdc.com; *in Chicago,* Udupi Palace, tel 773-338-2152, udupipalacechicago.net; *in Los Angeles,* Mayura, tel 310-559-9644, mayura-indian-restaurant.com; *in Toronto,* Udupi Palace, tel 416-405-8189, udupipalace.ca. **Retail and mail order:** *In New York,* Kalustyan's, tel 800-352-3451, kalustyans.com; *at multiple locations across the U.S.,* Patel Brothers, patelbros.com (search mint, garlic, tamarind, and mango chutneys). **Further information and recipes:** *Indian Regional Classics* by Julie Sahni (2001); *Indian Cooking Unfolded* by Raghavan Iyer (2013); cookstr.com (search tamarind chutney); epicurious.com (search cilantro chutney).

||||||||||||||||||||||||||||||||||||||||||||||||||||||||||||||||||||||||||||||||||||||||||||||||||||||||||||||

THE EVERYTHING-NICE SPICE

Cinnamon

A long with vanilla and chocolate, cinnamon is one of the most essential flavors of the baking world. But this exotic, sweetly aromatic spice is good for much more than a gooey breakfast roll or a refined coffee cake or a delightful topping for a sugar-crunched piece of toast (see page 545). The ancient, fragrant spice adds its warm, sweet, deeply rich and satisfying essence to savory foods the world over, providing a kick to Mediterranean spit-fired and grilled meats, adding depth to African stews and *tagines,* and acting as the secret ingredient in Cincinnati's famed chili and Mexico's hot chocolate (see page 652).

Careful cooks are well advised to read their spice labels carefully, as a cinnamon ringer called cassia—a member of the extended *Cinnamomum* genus—is often labeled as cinnamon but has a flavor that is harsher, hotter, and more bitter. The real thing, *C. verum* or *zeylanicum,* is a delicate golden spice derived from the inner bark of evergreen trees in Madagascar, India, the Seychelles, Latin America, and their native home, Sri Lanka.

With their fragrant green leaves and bark, the trees can grow upward of 50 feet tall, but are generally pruned and cultivated when they reach a more manageable 7 or 8 feet. Once the outer bark is removed, the trees' inner layer of bark is cut and dried into brittle, coiled sticks known as quills—these, in their unadulterated state, are the cinnamon sticks we love to swirl in our hot chocolate.

As a flavoring, cinnamon has been enjoyed for centuries; it is mentioned numerous times in the Old Testament and was used by the ancient Greeks and Romans both as a cooking ingredient and to perfume their bodies in religious rituals. The Roman emperor Nero is said to have burned a year's supply to honor his wife at her funeral. Pharmacists, bakers, and confectioners favor oil extracted from cinnamon, which gives them the flavor without the dusty flecks.

Any way you roll the bark, it's a powerful flavoring. Cinnamon is also heralded for its health benefits, believed to increase glucose metabolism levels, stimulate memory, relieve congestion, and reduce the inflammation associated with arthritis, and because it contains high levels of chromium, it wards off or tempers diabetes, too.

RETAIL AND MAIL ORDER: *In New York,* Kalustyan's, tel 800-352-2451, kalustyans.com. **FURTHER INFORMATION AND RECIPES:** For cinnamon rolls, *The Bread Baker's Apprentice* by Peter Reinhart (2001); *I Love Cinnamon Rolls!* by Judith Fertig (2012); *Spice* by Ana Sortun (2006); foodnetwork.com (search cincinnati chili). **TIP:** For true cinnamon, look for Sri Lanka or Ceylon on the label. **SEE ALSO:** Cinnamon Granita, page 184; Cannoli, page 173.

THE GO-WITH-EVERYTHING BEAN PUREE

Dal

Indian

Indians don't often serve a dinner without a dal, the spicy, nutty dish of pureed dried beans that is poured over rice or eaten with the tandoori bread, naan. Easy to cook in comparison to some of the more elaborate creations of the Indian kitchen, it's a delicious and highly nutritious dish that is frequently based on yellow or black lentils. That's no surprise, as much of the world's stock of the tiny, disk-shaped legume comes from India. Lentils are among the country's most consumed and produced commodities, and of them, yellow lentils (*toovar dal,* also referred to as *toor dal* or *arhar dal*) are the most common, while the black are more highly prized for dal.

To be turned into this mainstay of the Indian diet, the mildly nutty, split and hulled yellow lentils from the *Cajanus cajan* plant are gently, slowly cooked with a variety of spices until they completely fall apart, and are then mashed into a silky, flavorful puree. Black gram beans (*urad dal* when split, and *sabat urad* or *kali dal* when whole) from the *Phaseolus mungo* plant are also popular choices for dals, particularly in the northern Punjab region. There, the whole kali dal beans are slowly cooked with onions, tomatoes, ghee, yogurt, and spices. The result is an unforgettably rich, aromatic, flavorful dish. But red kidney beans may also be used as the basis for a dal, as well as yellow split peas, red lentils, and more. Each dal has a personality, color, and spice of its own, and there are many variations on the theme.

If tucking into the high-protein bean dish as a side to an already heavy meal of meat, rice, bread, and various sauces seems like overkill, remember that many Indians are vegetarian and so consider the dal as a main dish in its own right. Indeed, this might be how it was initially consumed: Food historians speculate that the pea-, bean-, or lentil-based dish was ideal working-class food, inexpensive and easy-to-prepare fuel for a day of manual labor.

WHERE: *In Delhi,* Karim's Hotel, tel 91/11-2326-9880, karimhoteldelhi.com; *in Boston,*

Maharaja, tel 617-547-2757, maharajaboston .com. **RETAIL AND MAIL ORDER:** *At multiple locations across the U.S.*, Patel Brothers, patelbros .com; *in New York*, Kalustyan's, tel 800-352-2451, kalustyans.com. **MAIL ORDER:** For dried lentils, beans, and prepared dal, iShopIndian, tel 877-786-8876, ishopindian.com. **FURTHER INFORMATION AND RECIPES:** *Classic Indian Cooking* by Julie Sahni (1980); *Know Your Dals and Pulses* by Tarla Dalal (2008); *Indian Cooking Unfolded* by Raghavan Iyer (2013); nytimes.com (search new york dals); foodandwine.com (search buttery pigeon pea dal); cookstr.com (search dhaabay di dal; rajasthan mixed dal); sbs.com.au (search black lentils kaali dal).

THE COFFEE-LOVER'S TEA

Darjeeling Tea

Indian

The steep Himalayan slopes in West Bengal don't make handpicking tea leaves easy, but the effort is worthwhile. From the arid, semi-acidic soil on these peaked ridges comes Darjeeling, India's—if not the world's—choicest tea.

Tea pickers handpick leaves for the "Champagne of Teas."

amber liquor tinged with the sweetness of peaches—a flavor that varies in strength with each flush during the region's short growing season.

First-flush Darjeelings are picked in early spring—February to April—and are prized for their bright flavor and floral aroma. Second flushes, for which Darjeeling is perhaps best known, give off flavors similar to muscatel and currants. In the summer, when heavy rains roll in for monsoon season, Darjeeling's least-favored leaves are plucked; although their flavor is the most intense, it's the least complex and is usually the filling for tea bags. Between October and November, the autumnal flush is harvested, known for its warm, woody, copper-colored brew. Darjeeling tea leaves can be stored for up to six months, a good thing when shipping to markets becomes difficult during the harsh Himalayan winter months.

With its bracing flavor and deep amber glow, it is known as the coffee drinker's tea.

It was Dr. A. Campbell, an English military official stationed in Darjeeling, who gave root to the industry there in the 1830s. When Campbell's attempt to plant an English flower garden failed, he turned to tea, planting Chinese and Indian bush varieties of *Camellia sinensis* (the tea plant is a member of the flowering *Camellia* genus) to see how they'd fare. What grew, very slowly, were long, golden-tipped leaves that produced a floral

WHERE: *In Darjeeling*, Nathmulls Tea Room 91/354-225-6437, nathmulltea.com; *in Paris*, Mariage Frères, tel 33/1-43-47-18-54, mariage freres.com; *in New York*, McNulty's Tea & Coffee Co., Inc.; tel 212-242-5351, mcnultys.com. **Further information and recipes:** *Chai: The Experience of Indian Tea* by Rekha Sarin and Rajan Kapoor (2014); darjeelingtealovers.com. **Tip:** Brew Darjeelings for three to five minutes, perhaps less for first-flush leaves. **See also:** Georgian Black Tea, page 388.

|||||||||||||||||||||||||||||||

THE WORLD'S THINNEST GRIDDLE CAKE

Dosa

Indian

A non-initiate entering a South Indian vegetarian restaurant for the first time would be excused for wondering about the great rolled sheets of golden brown wrapping paper at almost every table, to say nothing of the diners tearing off bits and actually eating the thing in scraps. For a big round scroll of parcel-wrapping paper is exactly what a delectable *dosa* looks like—although it's actually a paper-thin crêpe or pancake, usually based on rice and/or split black lentils (*urad dal*), nicely earthy fenugreek seeds, and a small amount of the clarified butter, ghee.

The dosa's earthy batter is generally allowed to ferment and rise for eight to ten hours to develop a bubbly texture and a ripe, complex flavor of toasted grain and butter. Then comes the fun part: a process well worth witnessing if you can talk your way into a dosa kitchen to see it. Poured onto a huge, round, greased dosa stone or iron griddle, the batter is instantly spread into a silky, thin round. As its underside takes on a polished, sun-browned glaze, the top remains ever so slightly moist and spongy. At a certain point—and only real dosa craftsmen know when the time is just right—the pancake is gently lifted off the griddle and immediately rolled up while still warm and soft.

This plain-paper dosa is, to many aficionados, the best of all, its torn-off pieces offering the most exemplary textural interest. Cracklingly crisp on the outside and dewily spongy within, the plain dosa is perfect for dipping into vegetable curries, chutneys, and sauces such as the yogurt *raita* and the black or yellow lentil dal. Some dosas have seasonings and spices mixed into the batter, the best of these combining onions, chiles, and minced fresh gingerroot. And as *masala* dosas, the pancakes can be rolled around soft, steamy, and sustaining stuffings of cheese or various combinations of mashed potatoes, peas, and onion (with or without hot spicing).

Using pieces of dosa to make a wrap is an appealing idea, not least because it fits

The hours-long rising period is worth every minute for the first bite.

in with current anti-gluten trends, but it's one that can compromise the pancake's ideal texture. Still, stuffed dosas make for delicious handheld fast food, whether they are enjoyed at restaurants or the eat-in/take-out shops that make a specialty of them.

Where: *In Delhi and environs,* Sagar Ratna, sagarratna.in; *in New York,* Pongal, tel 212-696-9458, pongalnyc.com; *in Cambridge, MA,* Dosa Factory, tel 617-868-3672, dosa-factory .com; *in Chicago,* Udupi Palace, tel 773-338-2152, udupipalacechicago.net; *in Los Angeles,* Mayura, tel 310-559-9644, mayura-indian-restaurant.com; *in Toronto,* Udupi Palace, tel 416-405-8189, udupipalace.ca. **Retail and mail order:** For dosa mix, *at multiple locations across the U.S.,* Patel Brothers, patelbros.com; *in New York,* Kalustyan's, tel 800-352-2451, kalustyans.com. **Mail order:** For dosa mix and griddles, iShopIndian, tel 877-786-8876, ishop indian.com. **Further information and recipes:** *Madhur Jaffrey's World-of-the-East Vegetarian Cooking* by Madhur Jaffrey (1981); cookstr.com (search dosa); epicurious.com (search rava dosa with potato chickpea masala); lifestyle food.com.au (search southern savory pancakes). **See also:** Roti, and Other Breads, page 884; Injera, page 733.

―――――――――||||||||||||||||||||||||||||||||||――――――――――

NIBBLES, STEAMED AND FRIED

Idli and Vada

Indian (Tamil)

Traditional breakfast favorites in the Indian provinces of Tamil Nadu and Gujarat, these paired dishes also appear as appetizer options on the menus of restaurants inspired by those regions, especially those specializing in vegetarian

food. They may be ordered separately, but together they offer an alluring contrast between light, steamed dumpling and cruller-like, savory deep-fry.

At their simplest and most traditional, the ivory, soufflé-light *idlis* are based on a dough made of a combination of rice and split black lentils; the dough ripens for about twelve hours, the lentils acting as a mild leavening, before it is poured into palm-size molds and steamed. Less common but far more complex are the richer idlis that combine semolina-like wheat flour, grated coconut, flecks of fiery green chiles, and the touch of yogurt that renders them moist and satiny. Either version must be served steaming hot and accompanied by

South Indian breakfast

dipping sauces such as the yellow lentil dal, a nicely acidic tamarind sauce, or an aromatic and verdant cilantro chutney.

Alongside the steamed starter, the *vada* provides a crisp contrast as a sort of doughnut, albeit one made of lentils. It begins as a thick, white *urad dal* that is mixed with chopped coconut, cilantro, green chiles, and grated fresh gingerroot. Shaped into doughnutlike rounds, complete with center holes or indentations, the dumplings are lightly deep-fried in neutral vegetable oil. As soon as they turn a toasty golden brown, they are briefly drained and served red-hot. They, too, can be dipped into the sauces that enliven idlis, as well as in a version of *raita* that is pungent with cilantro, coconut, chiles, and cumin. Alternating bites of each is highly recommended.

Where: *In Delhi and environs,* Sagar Ratna, sagarratna.in; *in New York,* Pongal, tel 212-696-9458, pongalnyc.com; Tulsi, tel 212-888-0820, tulsinyc.com; *in Cambridge, MA,* Punjabi Dhaba, tel 617-547-8272, royalbharatinc.com; *in Chicago,* Udupi Palace, tel 773-338-2152, udupi palacechicago.net; *in Los Angeles,* Mayura, tel 310-559-9644, mayura-indian-restaurant.com; *in Artesia, CA,* Woodlands, tel 562-860-4000, wood landsartesia.net; *in Toronto,* Udupi Palace,

tel 416-405-8189, udupipalace.ca. **Retail and mail order:** For vada mix and rice flour, *at multiple locations across the U.S.,* Patel Brothers, patelbros.com; *in New York,* Kalustyan's, tel 800-352-2451, kalustyans.com. **Mail order:** For vada mix, idli cooker, and rice flour, Indian Blend, tel 888-753-4299, indianblend.com. **Further information and recipes:** *Madhur Jaffrey's World-of-the-East Vegetarian Cooking* by Madhur Jaffrey (1981); *The Cooking of India* by Santha Rama Rau (1969); indianfood.about.com (search medu vada; idli) food.com (search medu vada); seriouseats.com (search idli).

──────┤||||||||||||||||||||||||||||||||||├──────

AN ANCIENT GLAZED CRULLER

Jalebi

Indian

The varietal world of doughnuts does not begin and end with the powdered sugar, chocolate, cream fillings, and jam of Dunkin' Donuts and Krispy Kreme. In the *jalebi,* India's exquisitely sweet fried dough, that spectrum encompasses the flavors of rosewater and saffron. With a form reminiscent of funnel cakes, it's a classic Indian dessert that could be described in Western terms as "squiggly fried crullers in thick, flavored syrup." But such a description does little justice to an appealingly slippery treat that is elevated by its exotic perfume.

The basic jalebi dough is made with flour, baking powder, and water, although some cooks add yogurt and semolina as well. Allowed to rest for a short time in order to ferment slightly, the dough is formed into loops as it is poured through a nozzle over a pan of hot ghee. As soon as the dough sets in the pan, it's scooped out and dropped into the fragrant syrup.

Singularly delicious, the treat also has a real provenance. Scholars believe the recipe has Persian origins, and that it was adapted by

Indian cooks as long ago as 1450. Fittingly, similar confections appear throughout the Middle East, particularly in Afghanistan, Lebanon, and Iran, where glazed and sticky hot dough pieces are made for special occasions as well as given to the less fortunate at Ramadan.

Where: *In Dehli,* Old Famous Jalebi Wala in the bustling old market, Chandni Chowk; *in Washington, DC,* Rasika, tel 202-637-1222, rasika restaurant.com; *in Chicago,* Indian Garden, tel 312-280-4910, indiangardenchicago.com. **Further information and recipes:** *Sanjeev Kapoor's Khana Khazana* by Sanjeev Kapoor and Alyona Kapoor (2002); *Indian Cooking Unfolded* by Raghavan Iyer (2013); *Street Food of India* by Stephi Bergenson (2010); epicurious.com (search jalebi); indianfood.about.com (search jalebi); food.com (search instant jalebis).

||||||||||||||||||||||||||||||||

ICE CREAM, WITHOUT THE CHURN

Kulfi

Indian

A delectable frozen dessert is an extra blessing in a country with such sweltering summers and generally spicy food. This Indian delight is an unchurned milk-based dessert, making it more akin to the layered "semifrozen"

wonder that is the Italian *semifreddo* than to your typical ice cream.

Requiring little in the way of special equipment, the creamily dense and usually intensely sweet *kulfi* is made by simmering fresh milk—often mixed with sweetened condensed milk—over low heat for a long time. No eggs, no cream. Once reduced and thickened, the resultant cream is typically flavored with gently aromatic spices like cardamom, rosewater, or saffron, although it can also be combined with mango puree, pistachios, dark chocolate, or almonds. Poured into aluminum or stainless-steel conical molds and frozen, it emerges as a cold and creamy affair, one whose distinctively granular texture makes a virtue of the ice crystals that form when the ice cream mixture isn't kept moving as it freezes.

The convenient technique is actually an ancient one, dating back to the days of the Mogul Empire, when ice was carried down from the mountains to the emperors' homes by slaves. There, it was used to fuel a form of early air conditioning, and at the same time to create tempting desserts in which the ice was simply mixed with flavored milk or cream and poured into metal molds to set.

Ubiquitous in Indian restaurants today, the treat is also very easy to replicate at home, using Popsicle trays. The look may not quite duplicate what you'd see at a traditional Mogul banquet, but the taste will be equally luxurious.

Where: *In Delhi and environs,* Sagar Ratna, sagarratna.in; Karim's Hotel, tel 91/11-2326-9880, karimhoteldelhi.com; *in New York,*

There are no eggs or cream in this cool treat.

Tamarind, tel 212-775-9000, tamarind22.com; *in Washington, DC,* Rasika, tel 202-637-1222, rasikarestaurant.com; *in Chicago,* Jaipur, tel 312-526-3655, jaipurchicago.com; *in Houston,* Kiran's, tel 713-960-8472, kiranshouston.com; *in San Francisco,* Amber India, tel 415-777-0500, amber-india.com. **Further information and recipes:** *Mangoes & Curry Leaves* by Jeffrey Alford and Naomi Duguid (2005); *New Indian Home Cooking* by Madhu Gadia (2000); *Indian Cooking Unfolded* by Raghavan Iyer (2013); cookstr.com (search saffron kulfi; pistachio ice cream); foodnetwork.com (search pista kulfi).

‖‖‖‖‖‖‖‖‖‖‖‖‖‖‖‖‖‖‖‖‖‖‖‖‖

OF WINE AND CURRY

Lamb Vindaloo

Indian

D espite its preparation at many a standard-issue Indian restaurant, there's more to vindaloo than mere heat. The dish originated more than four hundred years ago in the Indian colony of Goa, on India's southwestern coast, a region heavily influenced by Portuguese culture ever since Vasco de Gama first set foot there in 1498—and the word *vindaloo* likely derives from the Portuguese terms for the dish's two most important ingredients: wine vinegar (*vinho*) and garlic (*alhos*).

While a vindaloo should indeed be hot, what's paramount is its combination of the spices that de Gama came looking for in the first place. In addition to the wine vinegar and garlic, the sauce is based on an aromatic paste made of cayenne, black pepper, cardamom, mustard seed, fenugreek, ginger, coriander, and turmeric. The paste itself can be used to coat any number of proteins—the pork that is beloved by the large Catholic population in Goa, or chicken for the region's Muslims and Hindus. Of all meats, however, lamb is the best foil for vindaloo's powerfully fragrant, warming spices, the meat's distinctive softness making it ideal for absorbing the sauce's rich, dark essence.

A Goa colony specialty

Boneless and cubed, the lamb is tenderized by marinating in the wine vinegar for several hours, after which the meat is tossed with the paste, very lightly seared so as to seal the spices but not burn them, and cooked over moderate heat. Then water or stock is added and the meat is allowed to simmer for nearly an hour. The final result is an agreeably unctuous, stewlike dish that excites the palate with its needling interplay of spice, sourness, and slightly gamy meat. Welcome relief from the hot flavors comes from the traditional accompaniment of fluffy basmati rice.

An excellent introduction to vindaloo comes by way of Madhur Jaffrey, the Indian actress and cookbook author who is known for her special love of the preparation. You can sample her lamb vindaloo at Dawat, the Indian restaurant in New York City for which she is the chief consultant, or try your hand at one of her recipes in your own kitchen.

WHERE: *In New York,* Dawat, tel 212-355-7555, dawatnewyork.com; Tamarind, tel 212-775-9000, tamarind22.com; *in Boston,* Maharaja, tel 617-547-2757, maharajaboston.com; *in Cambridge, MA,* Punjabi Dhaba, tel 617-547-8272, royalbharatinc.com; *in Washington, DC,* Masala Art, tel 202-362-4441, masalaartdc.com; *in Chicago,* Jaipur, tel 312-526-3655, jaipurchicago.com; *in Houston,* The Bombay Brasserie, tel 713-355-2000, thebombaybrasserie.com; Kiran's, tel 713-960-8472, kiranshouston.com; *in Los Angeles,* Mayura, tel 310-559-9644, mayura-indian-restaurant.com; *in San Francisco,* Amber India, tel 415-777-0500, amber-india.com. **RETAIL AND MAIL ORDER:** *In New York,* for spices, Kalustyan's, tel 800-352-2451, kalustyans.com. **FURTHER INFORMATION AND RECIPES:** *Madhur Jaffrey's Quick & Easy Indian Cooking* by Madhur Jaffrey (1996); *Indian Cooking* by Madhur Jaffrey (2003); *100 Essential Curries* by Madhur Jaffrey (2013); saveur.com (search chicken vindaloo).

Lassi

Indian

Milk shakes are delicious, but beyond providing pleasure, the sweet treats can't be said to accomplish much. *Lassis,* on the other hand, are distinctive both for their flavors and for their important purpose in India's spicy food culture—that of refreshing a diner's palate and adding protein to the meal. Although particularly associated with the Punjab region, in northwest India, lassis are a popular street food throughout the Indian subcontinent and a mainstay at Indian restaurants around the world.

The base of a lassi is yogurt, the higher in quality and richer in fat the better, and its essence lies in that yogurt's sweet-tart flavor. Diluted with very cold water and flavored with various combinations of fruit, herbs, spices, and floral essences, the resulting drink is blended with plenty of ice and served alongside hot-spiced dishes.

The most familiar version, the sweet and creamy mango lassi, doesn't represent the lassi's full spectrum—for lassis may be either salty or sweet. *Namkeen lassi* is the name for the salty version, a drink that generally contains roasted cumin seeds, freshly ground black pepper, and garlic. *Metha lassi,* the sweet kind, is often made with flavorings like ginger, mint, or cardamom, and rosewater. Or indeed, with mango.

Like milk shakes, lassis are beloved by kids of all ages—which means that wise parents who wish to expand their offsprings' palates might introduce them to Indian cuisine by way of the cool, soothing shake. (Preferably the sweet kind.)

WHERE: *In Delhi,* Karim's Hotel, tel 91/11-2326-9880, karimhoteldelhi.com; *in Chicago,* Udupi Palace, tel 773-338-2152, udupipalace chicago.net; *in Los Angeles,* Mayura, tel 310-559-9644, mayura-indian-restaurant.com; *in Toronto,* Udupi Palace, tel 416-405-8189, udupipalace.ca. **FURTHER INFORMATION AND RECIPES:** *Indian Cooking Unfolded* by Raghavan Iyer (2013); *Madhur Jaffrey's World-of-the-East Vegetarian Cooking* by Madhur Jaffrey (1981); cookstr.com (search sweet lassi; mango lassi); indianfoodforever.com (search jeera lassi; mango lassi). **TIP:** For the most satisfying results, use unflavored whole Greek-style yogurt as a base. Also, sweet lassi can be overly filling when served before or during a meal; salty or spicy versions seem more suited to food, with the others sipped afterward as desserts.

Mulligatawny Soup

Indian, Anglo-Indian

A British-Indian hybrid, the simple yet beguilingly delicious soup called mulligatawny takes its name from the Tamil words *millagu-tanni,* meaning pepper water. Originating in southern India in the eighteenth century, during the period of the British Raj, it was a dish Indian servants devised for their English masters. At first, the soup resembled a *rasam*, a curry-spiced broth with lentils, but over time it bulked up to include carrots, onions, or leeks, and sometimes either tomato or cubes of peeled apple (for tartness), its stock enriched with lamb or chicken bones and sometimes a little meat. Gradually its colonial origins were forgotten.

Some modern cooks may add a final step to the mulligatawny tradition by stirring in a little coconut milk or cream, for a result that's more delicate than the bold, peppery curry-spiked blend. Either way, it's a deeply fragrant soup, wonderful for a cold or flu, soothing on a snowy day, and always marvelously restorative. In India, mulligatawny is often served with rice on the side, but elsewhere in the world, it is simply served up by the bowlful—just as it was on the famous *Seinfeld* episode in which Kramer tries to convince Elaine to brave New York's famed "Soup Nazi" for a bowlful. Al Yeganeh, the cook with the Hell's Kitchen soup stand who inspired the soup episode, still simmers mulligatawny in his various Original SoupMan franchises.

WHERE: *In New York, New Jersey, Connecticut, and Texas,* Original Soupman restaurants, originalsoupman.com; *in New York,* Tamarind, tel 212-775-9000, tamarind22.com; *in Boston,* Maharaja, tel 617-547-2757, maharaja boston.com; *in Chicago,* Udupi Palace, tel 773-338-2152, udupipalacechicago.net. **FURTHER INFORMATION AND RECIPES:** *100 Weeknight Curries* by Madhur Jaffrey (2011); *Ango-Indian Cuisine* by Bridget White (2013); saveur.com (search mulligatawny); epicurious.com (search mulligatawny) indianfoodforever.com (search mulligatawny).

OUT OF THE INDIAN FRYING PAN

Pakora and Bhajia

Indian

Although the U.S. has a reputation as the land of fried food, such preparations have worldwide appeal—the draw has to do with the crunchy coatings and strong flavors heightened by quick heat. When accomplished quickly and with

fresh, light vegetable oils, frying need not be as hazardous as the health food army has claimed.

Thus it is that we can easily enjoy two delights of the Indian kitchen: *pakoras* and *bhajias*. The lustier of the two is the delectably hot and sizzling pakora, a puffy fritter made with a variety of vegetables or sometimes with shrimp. Its savory magic is highly

India's version of fried food

dependent upon a quality batter, with golden chickpea flour and sometimes rice flour assuring a crackling crisp finish, and a small sprinkle of baking soda that provides its airy lightness. Powdered turmeric, mustard, cumin, crushed hot red pepper flakes, and ground black peppercorns lift that golden coating with a tantalizing spiciness that highlights the cuts of fresh raw vegetables it coats. The most seductive are the thinly sliced onion rings that make *piaz pakoras,* with other appealing possibilities including eggplant rounds, chopped chile-enhanced potatoes, florets of cauliflower, and the white cheese that is *paneer.* When tiny shrimp—garlic-, ginger-, and chile-zapped—make up the fritters, the pakoras are known as *jheenga pakoras.*

After the ingredients of choice are dipped into the velvety batter and quickly deep-fried in light vegetable oil (canola being a preferred choice for modern-day cookery), the pakoras are drained and eaten while still hot and crisp. Served with flavorful yogurt sauces or herbaceous chutneys, they are much loved as appetizers or simply as snacks to complement drinks or tea.

The sesame-oil-fried bhajia is a far more delicate sort of fritter, made of a creamy batter of chickpea flour, salt, and water and the thinly sliced vegetables it features. Especially delicate when made with the firm, dark green leaves of New Zealand–type spinach, they are also a delicious treatment for paper-thin slices of potato, onion, zucchini, eggplant, and even whole tiny okra. Pakoras and bhajias are often ordered together for variety in textures and flavors.

Where: *In New York,* Dawat, tel 212-355-7555, dawatnewyork.com; *in Chicago,* Indian Garden, tel 312-280-4910, indiangardenchicago .com; *in Houston,* Kiran's, tel 713-960-8472, kiranshouston.com; *in Artesia, CA,* Woodlands, tel 562-860-4000, woodlandsartesia.net; *in Toronto,* Udupi Palace, tel 416-405-8189, udupi palace.ca. **Retail and mail order:** *In New York,* for chickpea and rice flours, Kalustyan's, tel 800-352-2451, kalustyans.com. **Further information and recipes:** *100 Weeknight Curries* by Madhur Jaffrey (2011); *The Indian Cookbook* by Blake Roman (2014); indianfoodforever.com (search vegetable pakora; bhajias); cookstr.com (search batter dipped vegetable fritters).

||||||||||||||||||||||||||||||||

THUS ATE ZARATHUSTRA

The Parsi Kitchen

Indian, Persian

It is not possible to claim thorough knowledge of the many diverse cuisines represented within India if one is not at least a little familiar with the colorfully supple, warmly savory specialties of the Parsis. The fire-worshipping Parsi sect,

dedicated to the prophet Zoroaster and the god Ahura Mazda (creator of all things light and good), originated in ancient Persia. But more than twelve centuries ago, persecution forced the Parsis to flee. Some settled in Afghanistan. Most went to the Indian state of Gujarat and also to the city of Bombay, the present-day Mumbai. (Parsi legend is said to have inspired Mozart's *The Magic Flute.*) Thus, an intriguing Indian-Persian cuisine was born, replete with the subtle perfumes and colors of rose petals and rosewater, jade-green pistachios, ivory almonds, ruby-red pomegranates, bright cilantro and mint, and snowy coconut—and with needling-hot Indian spices such as fresh ginger, red and green chiles, cumin, cardamom, mustard, turmeric, and more.

Lovers of rice, poultry and goat, and other meats, the Parsis have a particular passion for eggs. Mostly scrambled, a preparation known as *ekuri,* eggs appear in Parsi cooking in a mind-boggling slew of variations, scrambled with or cooked over any number of ingredients, including bananas, eggplant, dried fruits and nuts, cubes of bread, and even brains. *Tamatar per eeda* is a combination that echoes the spicy egg-and-tomato dish of Italy (*uove en purgatorio*), North Africa's chakchouka (see page 697), and the Basque *piperade*. For the fragrant Parsi interpretation, a satiny sauce of stewed tomatoes, ginger, garlic, chiles, onions, and cilantro is poured into a skillet or individual baking dish. Raw eggs are poured into depressions in the sauce, and the dish is either oven-baked or covered and cooked on the stove. When perfectly cooked, the yolks are still runny enough to mingle with the sauce.

Another defining Parsi meal is *patra ni machi*, based on pomfret, a silvery, flounderlike fish from waters around India's west coast. Filleted and spread with an aromatic coconut chutney, the fish is wrapped in shiny green banana leaves and steamed (preferably) or sometimes baked. Opened at the table, the packet sends forth perfumes of ginger, mint, cilantro, garlic, and fresh lime, all enhancing the fish's delicately moist white flesh.

And then there's the famous Bombay duck, which is neither made from duck nor invented in that regional capital. Actually, it's a rather odoriferous dried fish used primarily as a seasoning and based on the local *boomla*, a member of the bony lamprey family that is also eaten fresh. But dried, as *sookha boomla*, and flaked or cut into pieces and fried, it lends a teasingly salty, crisp accent as a garnish in many dishes,

Steamed fish with coriander served in a banana leaf

including curries. (How sookha boomla became "Bombay duck" is a mystery lost to time—it's connected either to a train called the Bombay Daak or to a miscommunication with an Englishman.) Because it is dried in the open air, the food has been banned for import by the European Union, but is available in Canada and some Indian restaurants in the U.S.

Dhansak, a complex and intricately prepared stew of meats and vegetables, has many variations but is best when it includes young lamb and tripe, long-simmered with several kinds of beans and vegetables such as pumpkin, tomatoes, onions, and eggplant. Seasoned with ginger, cloves, pepper, cinnamon, cumin, and mint, the results are crowned with a layer of crisp, golden onion slivers.

Similar to risotto (see page 233), but with a more exotic flavor, is the dish known as *vagharela chawal ne murghi:* chicken and spices simmered to velvety richness with sweet-scented basmati rice. Spices are prodigiously represented throughout Parsi cooking, appearing in the rainbow of *sambals* (chile sauces) that complement breads and main courses. Persian-inspired sorbets or baked rice custards delicately seasoned with rosewater provide the gently sweet finale.

With its wide array of flavors, the Parsi kitchen offers more than enough pleasures to keep a restaurant in booming business. Sadly, few such eateries can be found outside Gujarat and its environs—which means your best bet may be finding a gifted Parsi home cook near you, and keeping her close.

WHERE: *In Mumbai,* Ideal Corner, tel 91/222-262-1930; Café Britannia, tel 91/222-261-5264; *in Artesia, CA,* Woodlands, tel 562-860-4000, woodlandsartesia.net. **MAIL ORDER:** For food-grade rose petals and rosewater, amazon.com. **FURTHER INFORMATION AND RECIPES:** *Parsi Food and Customs* by Bhicoo J. Manekshaw (1996); *The Cooking of India* by Santha Rama Rau (1969); for Parsi recipes, parsicuisine.com; sanjeevkapoor.com (search parsi); saveur.com (search parsi style scrambled eggs); food.com (search ekuri).

||||||||||||||||||||||||||||||||||

HOW TO TURN RICE INTO COOL VELVET

Phirni

Indian

Smooth, rich, and creamy, the classic Indian dessert *phirni* (sometimes spelled *firni*) is a delicate pudding made with rice flour and milk and flavored with that warm and sweet Indian spice, cardamom. A specialty of Muslims, with origins in

the sweets of ancient Persia and the Middle East, phirni is also a Punjabi favorite, particularly well represented at wedding banquets and during the festival holiday Diwali.

The Indian version of rice pudding, velvety phirni is made with rice flour instead of rice grains, or occasionally with almond flour. Comparatively subtle, phirni isn't nearly as sweet as some of the other traditional Indian desserts—namely *kulfi* and *jalebi* (see pages 877 and 876)—which often seem cloying to uninitiated palates. If the phirni is not flavored with the classic cardamom, it may be perfumed by the gentle aromas of rosewater or saffron.

In India, phirni is almost always served in small earthenware or terra-cotta pots called *shakoras* (sometimes spelled *shikoras*) that are virtually impossible to find outside of the country. The vessels are believed to imbue the pudding with a special, earthy flavor. Ceramic ramekins or what Americans call custard cups are equally suitable.

FURTHER INFORMATION AND RECIPES: Madhur Jaffrey includes the recipe for her mother's phirni in her memoir *Climbing the Mango Trees* (2007); *Sanjeev Kapoor's Khana Khazana* by Sanjeev Kapoor and Alyona Kapoor (2002); *Classic Indian Cooking* by Julie Sahni (1980); seriouseats.com (search phirni rice pudding); indianfood.about.com (search phirni). **SEE ALSO:** Anoush Aboor, page 507; Rizogalo, page 478.

A favorite for weddings and Diwali

||||||||||||||||||||||||||||||||||

SEEING ORANGE, TASTING GREEN

Rangpur Lime

Indian

With its bright orange rind, the Rangpur lime looks a lot more like a tangerine, and it's commonly mistaken for one, too. But the fruit's botanical name, *Citrus* x *limonia* Osbeck, as well as another commonly used moniker, kona lime, provide a better indicator of its flavor. Prized for its sour, orange-colored juice and floral aroma, the Rangpur is actually part lemon, part mandarin, but its tart juice may be substituted in any recipe that calls for limes, particularly pies and cocktails, for a flavor that is more complex, pure, and agreeably astringent. These qualities make it well suited to glazes for roasted meats.

Native to India, the rangpur grows on tall, slender trees. The fruits are also cultivated in California and Florida, and are harvested from November through the end of winter. Rangpurs don't come cheap—they cost about $10 per pound, yielding approximately seven limes.

Even so, with one in hand you will be in for a decidedly enticing treat. As an exotic replacement for conventional lime, try Tanqueray's Rangpur Gin; with its powerful bite, the spirit makes for an exhilirating gin and tonic.

Where: *In New York and Chicago,* in season, Eataly, eatalyny.com; Dean & Deluca, tel 800-221-7714, deananddeluca.com.; *in New York, Washington, DC, and Boston,* Baldor, baldorfood.com. **Mail order:** For dwarf trees, Four Winds Growers, tel 877-449-4637, fourwindsgrowers.com. **Further information and recipes:** fruitsinfo.com (search rangpur); specialtyproduce.com (search rangpur).

Roti, and Other Breads

Indian

For many of us, the word *bread* conjures up loaves that are rectangular or round, but such shapes have nothing to do with the ingenious hot and grainy marvels turned out quickly in India. All are closer to what might be considered crêpes, wafers, or pancakes, and get their nutty fragrances and flavors from wheat flours, fine or coarse. A few require yeast for leavening, but most are made of dough that is allowed to ferment to ensure a light finish and a complex flavor. Ideally suited to dipping into *sambals*, chutneys, and curries, these breads—roti—are almost always made to order. And whether prepared in a tandoor oven, on a griddle, or in the deep-fryer, they are best eaten fresh and hot.

Roti, also known as chapati, is an unleavened pancakelike whole wheat bread, that is cooked on an iron griddle

Puris use the same dough as roti, but are fried.

known as a *tava.* One of the most basic of all Indian breads, it resembles a cross between a tortilla and a pita, and is often buttered on one side.

Another well-known Indian bread is naan, a flat and chewy white bread reminiscent of pizza crust. It has a pleasingly pully texture and a nicely charred patina, a result of being baked on the stone walls of a tandoor oven. The richest of Indian breads, naan is made with white flour, yeast or other leavening, eggs, milk, salt, and sugar. A variation on naan can be stuffed with fillings of potatoes, onions, or nuts and raisins, in which case it is called *kulcha.*

Phulka, a puffed-up round made with whole wheat flour on an iron griddle, is a nicely bready accompaniment to main courses. *Puri,* or *poori,* differs from chapati only in that the rounds are deep-fried, so that the resultant puffs have a deep, rich brown, and shiny surface.

The snackable *kachori* takes a trip back into the deep-fryer as well, for small, crisp rounds of bread stuffed with a pungent combination of black lentil dal, hot chile flakes or powder, and cumin seeds. (A similar dough, deep-fried into chewy rounds, results in what are called *bhatura.*) *Paratha* is another member of the fried bread family, forming golden-brown, flaky, layered rounds, although this one gleams after being fried in ghee on a tava griddle.

WHERE: *In Delhi and environs,* Sagar Ratna, sagarratna.in; *in Delhi,* Karim's Hotel, tel 91/11-2326-9880, karimhoteldelhi.com; *in New York,* Tamarind Tribeca, tel 212-775-9000, tamarind restaurantsnyc.com; *in Boston,* Maharaja, tel 617-547-2757, maharajaboston.com; *in Cambridge, MA,* Punjabi Dhaba, tel 617-547-8272, royal bharatinc.com; *in Washington, DC,* Masala Art,

tel 202-362-4441, masalaartdc.com; *in Chicago,* Jaipur, tel 312-526-3655, jaipurchicago.com; *in Houston,* Kiran's, tel 713-960-8472, kirans houston.com; *in Los Angeles,* Mayura, tel 310-559-9644, mayura-indian-restaurant.com; *in San Francisco,* Amber India, tel 415-777-0500, amber-india.com; *in Toronto,* Udupi Palace, tel 416-405-8189, udupipalace.ca. **RETAIL AND MAIL ORDER:** *At multiple locations across the U.S.,* for lentil and rice flour, Patel Brothers, patelbros .com; *in New York,* for rice, chickpea, and wheat flours, Kalustyan's, tel 800-352-2451, kalustyans.com. **FURTHER INFORMATION AND RECIPES:** *Classic Indian Cooking* by Julie Sahni (1980); *An Invitation to Indian Cooking* by Madhur Jaffrey (1973); *Indian Cooking Unfolded* by Raghavan Iyer (2013); *More Indian Breads* by Kanchan Kabra (2010); *Easy Roti Recipes* by Ajala Sing (2014); cookstr.com (search chapatis, naan); indianfood.about.com (search kulcha; paratha; poori). **TIP:** When they come with an order of Indian takeout, these breads suffer a bit from being wrapped while hot and often wilt, losing some of their appealing texture.

LAMB, GREEN AND EASY

Saag Gosht

Indian, Pakistani

Comforting, restrained, and marvelously aromatic, this soft stew of slowly simmered lamb cooked with a melting, satiny spinach sauce gets its palate-whetting aroma and subtle heat from generous quantities of ginger and garlic,

hints of coriander and turmeric, and a mass of tender, well-sweated onions. As is traditional in many of India and Pakistan's deeply flavorful specialties, before being incorporated with the other ingredients the spices are gently fried in plenty of oil to coax out the full breadth of their flavor.

Saag gosht dates back to the days of the seventeenth-century Mogul Empire, when Muslims ruled the country. This explains why a

very similar preparation is popular in both Pakistani and Persian cuisines. The word *saag* in Hindi technically means any sort of greens, but most especially spinach, and back in those days the vegetables might include mustard greens, which have been cooked in clay pots in parts of India since 2000 B.C. Today the greens are almost always spinach. The protein varies—chicken, beef, and shrimp are frequent favorites—but lamb is the meat of choice and for good reason, as its texture and gamy overtones highlight the spinach's silkiness.

The seductive stew is generally served with plain rice pilaf and a good Indian bread such as a roti (see page 884), which provides a foil for its richness and a vehicle for sopping up its soothing sauce.

WHERE: *In Boston,* Maharaja, tel 617-547-2757, maharajaboston.com; *in Cambridge, MA,* Punjabi Dhaba, tel 617-547-8272, royalbharatinc.com; *in Chicago,* Jaipur, tel 312-526-3655, jaipurchicago.com; *in Houston,* The Bombay Brasserie, tel 713-355-2000, thebombaybrasserie.com; Kiran's, tel 713-960-8472, kiranshouston.com; *in Los Angeles,* Mayura, tel 310-559-9644, mayura-indian-restaurant.com. **FURTHER INFORMATION AND RECIPES:** *Classic Indian Cooking* by Julie Sahni (1980); *An Invitation to Indian Cooking* by Madhur Jaffrey (1973).

RED-HOT IN COLOR AND FLAVOR

Tandoori Murgh

Indian

Tandoori *murgh* (chicken) gets its name from its cooking vessel, the tandoor oven, but the succulent red-stained specialty owes its fame and ubiquity at least partially to its hue. What gives the meat that trademark blush? It might just as easily be paprika, red chile powder, or food coloring, the last being the colorizer recommended by the actress and grande dame of Indian cuisine, Madhur Jaffrey.

Although other meats, such as lamb, and seafood, like shrimp and lobster, are roasted in tandoors, chicken is a favorite choice. Its juiciness and distinctive flavor starts with a tenderizing, sour marinade of yogurt, lemon juice, garlic, and ginger, along with a spice blend variously consisting of coriander, cumin, cloves, cardamom, black pepper, and chile—and it ends, of course, with roasting in the tandoor. Although the etymological link isn't readily apparent to the untrained ear, historians believe that the word *tandoor* derives from *nâr*, the Semitic word for fire, and place the clay oven's origins in Babylonian times. Especially associated with the Mogul emperors who held sway over India from the sixteenth century to the early eighteenth century, it is basically an oversize jar, with a distinctive beehive shape and an opening at the bottom for adding and removing fuel.

Chicken, usually cubed and skewered on long sticks, takes especially well to the tandoor treatment, its mildness an ideal foil for the roasty flavor the oven imparts; another technique involves placing halves or pieces of the bird in a casserole and setting that in the bottom of the tandoor, for delectable, fork-tender results. But the tandoor is also often employed to make bread, a dramatic process in which the dough is slapped onto its vertical walls and quickly bakes into disks thanks to a combination of radiant heat and convection.

Tandoori chicken can become the basis of other dishes as well. In chicken *tikka masala,* it is sauced with a rich stew of tomatoes, cream or coconut milk, turmeric, paprika, and other spices. As chicken *makhani,* it is coated in a spice-laden sauce of butter, cashew paste, and tomato puree. But it is as the original, unsauced tandoori chicken, thrillingly red and tangy, although milder than it looks, that it provides one of the most elemental pleasures of the Indian kitchen.

WHERE: *In New Delhi, Dubai, Abu Dhabi,*

London, New York, and other locations, Moti Mahal, motimahalindia.com; *in Delhi,* Karim's Hotel, tel 91/11-2326-9880, karimhoteldelhi.com; *in New York,* Tamarind Tribeca, tel 212-775-9000, tamarindrestaurantsnyc.com; Dawat, tel 212-355-7555, dawatnewyork.com; *in Boston,* Maharaja, tel 617-547-2757, maharajaboston.com; *in Cambridge, MA,* Punjabi Dhaba, tel 617-547-8272, royalbharatinc.com; *in Washington, DC,* Rasika, tel 202-637-1222, rasikarestaurant.com; *in Chicago,* Jaipur, tel 312-526-3655, jaipurchicago.com; *in Houston,* The Bombay Brasserie, tel 713-355-2000, thebombaybrasserie.com; Kiran's, tel 713-960-8472, kiranshouston.com; *in Los Angeles,* Mayura, tel 310-559-9644, mayura-indian-restaurant.com; Al-Noor, tel 310-675-4700, alnoor-restaurant.net; *in San Francisco and environs,* Shalimar at two locations, shalimarsf.com; Amber India, tel 415-777-0500, amber-india.com. **Mail order:** For Indian-made residential clay tandoor ovens, tandoors.com. **Further information and recipes:** *Classic Indian Cooking* by Julie Sahni (1980); *Indian Cooking Unfolded* by Raghavan Iyer (2013); cookstr.com (search tandoori chicken); foodandwine.com (search grilled tandoori chicken).

HOT OFF THE VEGETARIAN GRIDDLE

Uthappam

Indian

The practice of vegetarianism has extremely ancient roots in India—and particularly in the South Indian kitchen, which produces this intriguingly bubbly, soufflélike, egg-free pancake. Often the centerpiece of a South Indian

meal, the *uthappam* is usually eaten with a cucumber- or chile-brightened yogurt *raita,* curried vegetables, rice, and bread stand-ins such as *dosa* (see page 874). Magically, its batter contains neither eggs nor dairy products but is instead based on ground rice and the fragrantly flavorful black lentils known as *urad dal.*

Seasoned with earthy fenugreek seeds, the dal and soaked rice are allowed to ferment for about ten hours at room temperature, a process that helps the batter puff up and gives the finished pancake its appealingly light texture. Additions, such as green, white, and red bits of chiles, potatoes, peas, cabbage, grated fresh coconut, and sometimes ruby flecks of tomato, are optional, and the final uthappam may be mildly or very hotly seasoned. Preferably fried in ghee, India's clarified butter, on a hot stone griddle or an iron pan, the pancake is slowly cooked on one side only, until its top begins to

bubble. To retain its airiness, it must be served immediately after being garnished with lacy green sprays of cilantro.

In an amusing variation, a dozen or so uthappams can be stacked up in layers, each spread with a pungent, savory chutney of the

Uthappam is a much-loved vegetarian dish.

relatively dry school—think onion, mint, coconut, or peanuts. For serving, the stack is sliced layer-cake style, or vertically, to reveal a rainbow of colors and flavors.

Where: *In Delhi and environs,* Sagar Ratna, sagarratna; *in New York,* Pongal, tel 212-696-9458, pongalnyc.com; *in Cambridge, MA,* Punjabi Dhaba, tel 617-547-8272, royalbharat inc.com; *in Washington, DC,* Rasika, tel 202-637-1222, rasikarestaurant.com; *in Chicago,* Udupi Palace, tel 773-338-2152, udupipalace chicago.net; *in Los Angeles,* Mayura, tel 310-559-9644, mayura-indian-restaurant.com; *in Toronto,* Udupi Palace, tel 416-405-8189, udupipalace.ca. **Retail and mail order:** *In New York,* for rice flour, Kalustyan's, tel 800-352-2451, kalustyans .com. **Further information and recipes:** indian foodforever.com (search vegetable uthappam; rava uthappam); vegrecipesofindia.com (search uthappam).

Vegetarian Thali

Indian

Dazzled by the embarrassment of choices on an Indian vegetarian menu? Then take the easy and delicious way out by ordering the tasting menu, or *thali.* In this traditional Indian feast, a multitude of dishes are presented all at once in a colorful array of textures, temperatures, aromas, and flavors. Either placed together at the center of a table or compartmentalized on a metal-rimmed platter called, like the meal itself, a thali, the spread is a sight to behold. The thali is typically served without utensils, the bread and rice providing all the vehicle that's needed for scooping up the treasures its bowls have to offer.

Although, in the U.S., the multifaceted meal often shows up as a vegetarian offering in South Indian restaurants, in India a thali is for carnivores, too. Either way, it is no random assortment—the dishes are carefully paired to complement one another in terms of flavor and texture.

Small metal bowls called *katooris* hold a variety of chutneys and dips. A cool yogurt *raita* will be in evidence, as will fresh salads, dals (see page 872), and *sabzi*—a category of vegetable dishes cooked in sauce that includes *dum aloo,* whole potatoes dressed in spicy yogurt. Other staples include rice and breads, such as whole wheat roti (see page 884), which are placed at the center of the thali, and pickles, which sit toward the platter's edge.

The rest is up to the cook's discretion, but will most certainly involve a curry or two. And on the all-encompassing plate, dessert is frequently a feature, too. You can even eat it first, if you like—in some parts of India the sweet porridges are eaten along with the rest of the dishes in the thali. It's all part of that legendarily sweet-fiery-salty-cool-bitter balance that Indian cuisine so often strives for and achieves.

Where: *In Delhi and environs,* Sagar Ratna, sagarratna.in; *in New York,* Vatan, tel 212-689-5666, vatanny.com; Pongal, tel 212-696-9458, pongalnyc.com; *in Chicago,* Udupi Palace, tel 773-338-2152, udupipalacechicago .net; *in Los Angeles,* Mayura, tel 310-559-9644, mayura-indian-restaurant.com; *in Toronto,* Udupi Palace, tel 416-405-8189, udupipalace .ca. **Mail order:** For traditional thali plates, amazon.com (search thali stainless steel plate; puja thali; meenakari floral peacock puja thali). **Further information and recipes:** *Madhur Jaffrey's World-of-the-East Vegetarian Cooking* by Madhur Jaffrey (1981); indianfoodforever .com (search indian vegetarian recipes). **Tip:** If you choose to eat this the Indian way, foregoing utensils and using your hands with bread or rice, remember to rely only on your right hand, which is considered good etiquette.

||||||||||||||||||||||||||||||||||||||||||||||||||||||||||||||||||||||||||||||||||||||||||||||||||

SPICES WORTH FIGHTING FOR

Nutmeg and Mace

"**C**onvicts and sailors sometimes have recourse to nutmeg. About a teaspoon is swallowed with water. Results are vaguely similar to marijuana with side effects of headache and nausea." In his novel *Naked Lunch,* the counterculture prophet William S. Burroughs was referring, of course, to the supposed hallucinogenic properties of the Indonesian spice, which are said to exist only when it's taken in large quantities. He could say similar things about mace, which is derived from the same seed. But what's most special about both spices are their warm, aromatic essence and peppery-sweet, deeply rich flavors.

The *Myristica fragrans* tree (literally, "musty scent") is the only plant that's the source of two spices. Its seed, which closely resembles a walnut in both size and shape, was once upon a time a zealously protected commodity. During the sixteenth and seventeenth centuries it was an object of war between the Dutch and British, who vied for its native Molucca Islands (also known as the Spice Islands). Those islands were the sole place the tree grew, so nutmeg and mace were enormously rare and consequently expensive. Nutmeg's cost soared even higher in the seventeenth century, when doctors prescribed the spice as a preventative for the Black Plague, and Dutch entrepreneurs reportedly sold it at a 60,000 percent markup. Dutch law prohibited exporting the nutmeg tree from the Spice Islands, but in the 1740s, the adventurous one-armed French botanist Pierre Poivre managed to smuggle the tree to Mauritius, where it flourishes to this day.

Nutmeg was so expensive and prized in colonial America that skilled craftsmen turned wood into false nutmegs, a practice so prevalent in Connecticut that it has been known as the Nutmeg State ever since. A warning to the naive was, "Don't take any wooden nutmegs."

The evergreen *Myristica fragrans* has now spread throughout the tropics, particularly in Grenada, where its large yellow fruits fall to the ground when ripe, then crack open to reveal the spindly, fire-red aril, which makes mace, literally gripping the nutmeg seed within its yellow-gold, apricotlike fruit. Both nutmeg and mace are exported and used in dishes worldwide.

Sometimes it seems as though hints of nutmeg appear everywhere. It is an ingredient in the expected host of cookies, cakes, and pies (and no cup of eggnog would be complete without it), but it's also a prevalent flavor in

Coca-Cola, pickles, and savory dishes such as quiche Lorraine (see page 123) and tortellini. It also does wonders for cooked spinach, plain or creamed (see page 553).

Male and female nutmegs reveal mace-wrapped nuts inside.

Sold whole, in dried, lacy pieces called blades, as well as ground, mace is interchangeable with nutmeg in recipes, although mace is decidedly sharper in flavor and a bit sweeter, with hints of citrus and coriander. Its subtlety is most prized in French béchamels and India's spice mix garam masala, and it is a traditional flavoring in all-American hot dogs and doughnuts. Incidentally, unlike pepper spray—which is made from capsaicin, the compound that gives peppers their fire—the spray called Mace has no relation to the spice. It is a much more benign seasoning, and far from weapons-grade.

MAIL ORDER: For top-quality whole Indonesian nutmeg, chefshop.com, tel 800-596-0885; for nutmeg and mace, Kalustyan's, tel 800-352-3451, kalustyans.com; Penzeys Spices, tel 800-741-7787, penzeys.com; for a nutmeg grater, fantes.com; Sur La Table, tel 800-243-0852, surlatable.com. **FURTHER INFORMATION AND RECIPES:** *Caribbean Pot Luck* by Suzanne Rousseau and Michele Rousseau (2014); *Indian Cooking Unfolded* by Raghavan Iyer (2013); *Visions of Sugarplums* by Mimi Sheraton (1968); for quiche Lorraine, *Mastering the Art of French Cooking, Volume 1* by Julia Child, Louisette Bertholle, and Simone Beck (1961); epicurious.com (search wilted spinach with nutmeg butter; spice cookies; mace cake; ras el hanout); saveur.com (search nutmeg infused eggnog; nutmeg ice cream; nutmeg doughnuts; she-crab soup); jovinacooksitalian.com (search tortellini en brodo). **TIP:** Once you've grated fresh nutmeg over a dish, you'll never again be satisfied with the preground type, whose flavor fades fast. Invest in a good small grater.

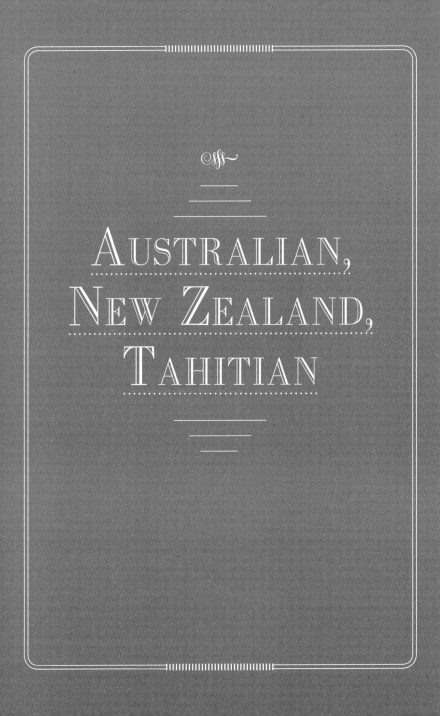

AUSTRALIAN, NEW ZEALAND, TAHITIAN

|||||||||||||||||||||||||||||||||||||

A COOKIE FOR REMEMBRANCE

ANZAC Biscuits

Australian and New Zealand

The golden syrup called treacle is the magic ingredient that imparts sweetly burnished overtones to this crunchy, round oatmeal-and-coconut biscuit (or "cookie" to Americans), a beloved treat in Australia and New Zealand whether freshly baked or purchased in packages. Devised by Australian women in search of delicious but durable biscuits to bake and send to their serviceman husbands, far off in battle during World War I, ANZAC biscuits have become an icon of national pride— especially on April 25,

a day of commemoration for the Australian and New Zealand Army Corps (ANZAC). Conceived to recognize those who fought courageously in 1915 during the ill-fated battle of Gallipoli, perhaps one of the worst military defeats in Australia's history, ANZAC Day now honors servicemen killed in all of the country's wars.

ANZAC Biscuits

Makes about 30 cookies

½ cup (1 stick) unsalted butter, plus
   butter for greasing the baking sheet
¾ cup sugar
2 tablespoons treacle (golden syrup)
1 teaspoon baking soda
2 to 3 tablespoons boiling water
¾ cup sifted all-purpose flour
1 cup uncooked rolled oats or
   old-fashioned oats
¾ cup dried flaked unsweetened
   coconut
Pinch of salt

1. Preheat the oven to 300°F. Butter a large baking sheet.

2. Combine the butter, sugar, treacle, and baking soda in a small, heavy saucepan over low heat. Add just enough boiling water to form a smooth mixture. Increase heat to moderate and let it come to a boil, then remove it from the heat.

3. Stir in the flour, oats, coconut, and salt. Mix thoroughly. Form large cookies by dropping 1 tablespoon of dough at a time onto the prepared baking sheet, spacing the cookies about 2½ inches apart. Bake the cookies until they are golden brown and crisp, 20 to 30 minutes.

4. Transfer the cookies to a wire rack to cool. The cookies can be stored for up to three weeks in an airtight container in a cool place, but not in the refrigerator.

WHERE: *In Wellington, New Zealand,* Logan Brown, tel 64/480-151-14, loganbrown.co.nz; *in New York,* The Musket Room, tel 212-219-0764, musketroom.com; *in Brooklyn,* Kiwiana, tel 718-230-3682, kiwiana-nyc.com; *in Los Angeles,* Bronzed Aussie, tel 213-243-0770, bronzedaussie .us; *in Marietta, GA,* Australian Bakery Café, tel 678-797-6222, australianbakerycafe.com; *in Vancouver,* Moose's Down Under Bar and Grill, tel 604-683-3300, moosesdownunder.com. **MAIL ORDER:** aussiefoodmart.com (search anzac); for treacle, britishfooddepot.com.

‖‖‖‖‖‖‖‖‖‖‖‖‖‖‖‖‖‖‖‖‖‖‖‖‖

GONE FISHIN'

Barramundi

Australian

As the silvery-bronze, red-eyed barramundi feed on small fish and crustaceans, their firm, white flesh develops a complex, pan-oceanic flavor. That is what makes *Lates calcarifer* one of Australia's most highly prized and most expensive eating fish, especially when they are caught in moving estuary waters, which impart a clean, delicate flavor to the fish. (The spirited fighters are also favorite game fish around northern Australia; they are suckers for live bait, especially crabs and shrimp.)

Named by Australian aborigines, and also known as giant sea perch, barramundi like to hang around rocky ledges and assorted brambles in brackish waters where sea and freshwater meet. Older specimens caught in the muddier waters, especially in winter, sometimes acquire the same sort of musty, earthy overtones common to bottom-feeding catfish and carp, a flavor some connoisseurs value and others loathe.

Barramundi is now imported, fresh and frozen, into the U.S., along with other excellent if slightly less lauded Australian fish, such as Tasmanian ocean trout (a rainbow trout with delicate salmon-pink flesh, farmed in saltwater) and hiramasa kingfish (richly oily fish with pearl-gray flesh that is high in Omega-3s). In some cases, barramundi is raised in Australia from tiny live specimens sent over from Chinese hatcheries in sealed sacks of water.

Barramundi's flavor is far too subtle to survive breading and frying; the light, smooth flesh is best appreciated by broiling and baking—although even that requires a good deal of basting with melted butter. For an authentic touch, there's also the cooking method favored by Australian aborigines and described by Alan Davidson in *Seafood: A Connoisseur's Guide and Cookbook:* wrapping a whole barramundi in fresh ginger leaves and baking it outdoors under white-hot coals.

WHERE: *In Sydney and environs,* Doyles on the Beach, tel 61/2-9337-2007, doyles.com.au; *in Cairns, Australia,* Ochre Restaurant, tel 64/7-4051-0100, ochrerestaurant.com.au; *in New York,* The Australian, tel 212-869-8601, theaustralian nyc.com. **MAIL ORDER:** For frozen barramundi, Anderson Seafoods, tel 855-654-3474, shop andersonseafoods.com. **FURTHER INFORMATION AND RECIPES:** *A Multitude of Fishes* by Ann Creber (1987); *Seafood: A Connoisseur's Guide and Cookbook* by Alan Davidson (1989); *Sydney Seafood School* by Roberta Muir (2014); good housekeeping.com (search barramundi); the betterfish.com; epicurious.com (search roasted barramundi); www.nativefish.asn.au (search barramundi); finecooking.com (search charmoula barramundi).

Barramundi is a sweet and buttery fish with a delicate texture.

||||||||||||||||||||||||||||||||||||||||||||||||||||||||||||||||||||||||||||||||||||||||||||||||||

A SUCKER THAT TAKES A POUNDING

Abalone

If you have any doubts that the snowy, saline, gently chewy meat of the abalone is altogether delicious, consider the hardships gone through to harvest and prepare it and the sky-high prices it commands. A tough mollusk of the *Haliotis* family and really a giant sea snail, it clings to rocks with a long abductor muscle that's known as a foot and is its edible part. The foot must be pried off the rocks with a special metal tool wielded by deep-sea divers, a dangerous endeavor that results in fatalities each year.

Nonetheless, the world's varieties of abalone are so in demand that they all are protected from overfishing to some degree or another. Many are now being farmed in various regions, especially in the icy Pacific waters off

Freshly sliced abalone

Australia, New Zealand, and Northern California. The two most favored varieties are the blackfoot abalone (*Haliotis iris*), found mostly in New Zealand, where it is known by its Maori name, *paua*, and the red abalone (*Haliotis rufescens*), the largest of all and the one preferred along the Pacific coast of the U.S.

Not only is the abalone difficult to wrest from the rocks, but it's also a challenge to extricate from its shell, and once out, the flesh must be pounded to edibility. The result is a texture and flavor that suggests a combination of calamari and conch. Even the mollusk's shells, once emptied, are prized. Their shimmering nacreous lining is the basis of mother-of-pearl, which is inlaid into many decorative objects such as boxes, small dishes, and dressing-table accessories. Considering all this, it is no wonder whole live abalones go for about one hundred dollars apiece and thus are subject to the black market and bootlegging.

Although harvesting abalone is illegal in Oregon and Washington, it is permitted for licensed sport around Monterey Bay in California from April to November, excluding July. Commercial fishing for wild abalone is illegal, but the state is home to abalone farms, including one in Cayucos, where much of the "catch" goes to local restaurants and fish markets. In New Zealand, paua is gathered recreationally and commercially, with strict catch limits set for each, and it is also farmed.

In addition to fresh, abalone is available canned and dried (the latter look like large, round, dried mushrooms). Both are usually less expensive than when they are fresh and better suited to cooking, the dried being preferable to the canned. It is also much favored by the Chinese for medicinal purposes.

How does the world eat abalone? The Japanese favorite is raw abalone as sashimi, but some chefs simmer the slim steaks in sake and serve it warm. The Chinese like dried abalone braised with sea cucumber or stir-fried with hot chiles and vegetables. Koreans favor abalone in *jeonbokjuk*, their version of the Chinese rice porridge congee (see page 757). In France's Brittany, pounded slices are sautéed in butter, then topped with a sauce of muscadet, garlic, parsley, and pepper, and baked in a hot oven for about five minutes to emerge as *ormeaux au beurre Breton*. In Spain, where abalone is called *oreja de mar* (ear of the sea), it is served raw or lightly fried for tapas sometimes topped with an egg. In New Zealand, it's often minced, combined with onions and chiles, and fried as fritters.

No matter where you eat it, it's a delicacy—among the world's greatest, costliest comestibles.

WHERE: *In Wellington, New Zealand,* Logan Brown, tel 64/4-801-5114, loganbrown.co.nz; *in Shanghai and Abu Dhabi,* Hakkasan, hakkasan .com; *in Honolulu,* Chef Mavro, tel 808-944-4714, chefmavro.com; *in Los Angeles,* Bon Juk, tel 213-380-2248, bonjuk.co.kr; Zo, tel 213-935-8409; *in Cayucos, CA,* Hoppe's Garden Bistro & Wine Shop, tel 805-995-1006, hoppesbistro.com; *in San Francisco,* Boulevard, tel 415-543-6084, boulevard restaurant.com; North Beach Restaurant, tel 415-392-1700, northbeachrestaurant.com; *in Bow, WA,* The Oyster Bar, tel 360-766-6185, theoyster bar.net; *in New York,* Amazing 66, tel 212-334-0099; Toro, tel 212-691-2360, toro-nyc.com. **RETAIL AND MAIL ORDER:** *In Morro Bay, CA,* Giovanni's Fish Market, tel 888-463-2056, giovannisfishmarket .com; *in Vancouver,* Sea Harbour Seafood Restaurant, tel 604-232-0816, seaharbour.com. **FURTHER INFORMATION AND RECIPES:** *The Abalone Book* by Peter Howorth (1978); *The Thousand Recipe Chinese Cookbook* by Gloria Bley Miller (1984); *Japanese Cooking* by Shizuo Tsuji (2012); *North Atlantic Seafood* by Alan Davidson (2012); sbs.com.au (search paua tapas recipe); bbc.com (search why abalone is new zealand's catch of the day); montereyabalone.com (click Recipes).

||||||||||||||||||||||||||||||

A STEAK WITH DEEP POCKETS

Carpetbag Steak

Australian

A ustralia's carpetbag steak combines two of the country's most celebrated products: fresh, sea-bright oysters and (ideally) free-range, grass-fed beef. The name of this specialty derives from the shape of the finished dish. Although many recipes call for broiling the steaks or grilling them over charcoal, those methods tend to dry out the meat and prevent its beefy juices from mingling into the oozy lushness of the salty oysters. Better to sauté the steaks for a moistly tender result with maximum flavor contrast.

Carpetbag Steaks

Serves 4

Necessary equipment: Kitchen string and a trussing needle or small satay-type skewers

4 filet mignon steaks, each about 2 inches thick or 7 to 8 ounces
Salt and freshly ground black pepper
8 medium-size oysters, as freshly shucked as possible

6 tablespoons (¾ stick) unsalted butter
2 tablespoons finely chopped fresh flat-leaf parsley
2 to 3 anchovy fillets (optional), finely mashed

1. Using a very sharp knife with a thin blade, cut a 2-inch-long horizontal slit on the edge of each steak to make a pocket about 2 inches deep.

2. Sprinkle salt and pepper onto both sides of each oyster. Slip 2 oysters, side by side, into the pocket of each steak.

3. Close the opening of each pocket, either by sewing it shut using kitchen string and a trussing needle, or by fastening it with a small skewer. Pat the steaks dry on both sides with paper towels.

4. Heat 3 tablespoons of the butter in a large, heavy skillet, preferably cast-iron or copper, over moderate heat. When the bubbling subsides, arrange the oyster-stuffed steaks in the skillet, making sure that they do not touch one another.

5. Cook the steaks on one side until lightly browned, 3 to 4 minutes, then turn them over and lightly brown them on the second side, about 3 to 4 minutes time. Reduce the heat to low and cook the steaks, turning them frequently, 7 minutes longer for very rare steak, or 9 to 10 minutes for medium-rare. Anything more cooked than that will hardly be worth eating.

Transfer the steaks to individual serving plates.

6. Melt the remaining 3 tablespoons of butter in the skillet and stir in the parsley. Spoon some of the parsley butter over each steak before serving. If you like the edgy sophistication that anchovies can impart, stir the mashed fillets into the parsley butter before spooning it over the steaks.

WHERE: *In Woodvale, Western Australia,* Paul Conti Wines, tel 61/894-099-160, paulconti wines.com.au; *in Hobart, Tasmania,* Ball & Chain Grill, tel 61/362-232-655, ballandchain .com.au; *in New York,* The Musket Room, tel 212-219-0764, musketroom.com.

┤||||||||||||||||||||||||||||||├

BREAD WITH A TWIST

Damper

Australian

A specialty of the outback bush country, damper is an elemental bread with a wood-fire-etched crust and a gentle, sconelike flavor. The perfect foil for heavy barbecues and thick stews, when glossed with butter and a generous drizzling of wild honey or golden syrup it becomes a popular accompaniment to "billy tea," the strong black tea cooked in the outback in a metal jug over a wood fire.

The authentic, simple, stiff dough involves only flour, water, and a little salt—and a preparation one can easily imagine becoming the next big trend among experimentally minded outdoor cooks.

Kneaded until it blisters, the dough must rest for an hour before being rolled into a thick, snakey rope that is then twisted, serpent-style, around a long, freshly cut, green tree branch. Holding that branch over a red-hot charcoal fire and turning it frequently for about an hour isn't the most comfortable of endeavors, but it's the most authentic. As an alternative, the dough can be patted into a pan and baked in a cast-iron camp oven. Baker's choice, but the less labor-intensive task does lead to a somewhat less delectable result.

These days, the dough might include cheese, herbs, nuts, raisins, or crushed wattle-seeds (see page 907) as a stylish touch. Whatever the contents, the finished, crusty results should be served piping hot.

WHERE: *In Cairns, Australia,* Ochre Restaurant, tel 61/7-4051-0100, ochrerestaurant .com.au; *in Inverell, Australia,* Royal Restaurant on Byron, tel 61/267-210-351, royalinverell.com/ restaurant. **FURTHER INFORMATION AND RECIPE:** *The Down Under Cookbook* by Graeme Newman (1987); *Cooking the Australian Way* by Elizabeth Germaine (2013); *Australian Damper Recipes* by Loreena Walsh (2014); food.com (search australian damper); bbc.co.uk (aussie olive damper bread); lifestylefood.com.au (search aussie olive damper bread).

┤||||||||||||||||||||||||||||||├

BY THE BEAUTIFUL SEA

Doyles on the Beach

Australian

A rite of passage not to be missed by any first-time, food-loving visitor to Australia, Doyles on the Beach has been a delightful venue for local seafood since 1885. Run by the fifth generation of its founding family, the restaurant now has several outposts in Sydney—but the original spot in Watsons Bay is the only one that offers the pleasurable experience of sitting outdoors right on the beach in the convivial café, overlooking the water after a short and lovely ferry ride from Sydney.

The most felicitous time for a visit would be a sunny weekday, when weekend crowds aren't lined up for tables and the staff has more time to explain the qualities of each denizen of the local deep. Not to be overlooked are the house-classic prawn cocktail, the elegant Queensland tin can scallops, the creamy froth of a seafood chowder, Sydney rock oysters (see page 904), fish and chips fried in a crackling beer batter, briny blue swimmer crabs, snowy white flathead fillets, delicate sand whiting, barramundi (see page 893), ocean trout and hiramasa kingfish, meaty tiger prawns barbecued or fried in cakes, green-lipped New Zealand mussels (see page 910), and whatever the seasonal day's catch may be.

The menu also features many international seafood dishes, but the simplest preparations are best for those really interested in appreciating the unique qualities of each variety of fish.

Other Doyles locations vary more in style than in substance, with much the same menu choices more simply prepared—as at the Sydney Fish Market and on the Watsons Bay wharf, where taking away has as many devotees as eating in.

WHERE: Doyles on the Beach, 11 Marine Parade, Watsons Bay, Sydney, tel 61/2-9337-2007, doyles.com.au; Doyles at Sydney Fish Markets, Gipps St., Pyrmont, tel 61/2-9552-4339; Doyles on the Wharf, Fishermans Wharf, Watsons Bay, Sydney, tel 61/2-9337-1572. **TIP:** The Doyle kitchens' advice on all manner of basic fish preparations is generously shared, along with recipes, on the website (doyles.com.au).

┤||||||||||||||||||||||||||||||├

AN OLD BIRD UP TO NEW TRICKS

Emu

Australian

S maller than its African near-cousin the ostrich, and with three toes instead of two, the emu (*Dromaius novaehollandiae*) is another one of those strangely flightless runners. It is also the world's second-largest living bird, growing up to five or six feet in height. Much prized as a food source by Australia's aborigines, the giant bird is farmed in the U.S. as well as in its native land.

Thought to have been in existence for 80 million years, the emu has amazingly delicate and silky rose-pink meat, with a texture and a mild, fresh taste that suggests very soft veal. Low in fat and cholesterol and high in iron, emu can be substituted for beef or veal in recipes, but the lean and fragile meat is best just lightly cooked— or, even better, marinated in olive oil with fresh green herbs and served near-raw in gossamer carpaccio slices. Ground and seasoned, emu meat can also be turned into fresh or smoked sausages.

Although, like the ostrich's, the huge egg of the emu is edible, its thick shell and large size make it heavy to handle. That shell, however, dark teal or blue in color, is often carved and sold for its decorative appeal. More practically, the oil of the emu is valued as a cosmetic moisturizer and as a palliative for skin burns.

WHERE: *In Cairns, Australia,* Ochre Restaurant, tel 61/7-4051-0100, ochrerestaurant .com.au. **FURTHER INFORMATION AND RECIPES:** *Australian Greats* by Jo Franks (2012); uniquely emu.com (search emu meat); food.com (search barbequed emu).

The only birds larger than emus are ostriches.

AT HOME WITH AN ORIGINAL

Granny Smith Apples

Australian

The lightly speckled, spring-green apples are regulars in U.S. markets, but nothing compares with the experience of biting into the firm, tart specimens in their native land, especially in late October to early November, when they are

freshly picked. Spectacularly crunchy and sour-sweet, the cheerful apples are celebrated each year in late October at the Granny Smith Festival in the Sydney suburb of Eastwood.

What's wrong with an American Granny Smith? Nothing much, but Granny Smiths available in the U.S. are either imported or grown

on the West Coast. Although the sturdy apples store well and retain their crispness, the imported ones tend to be milder in flavor than they are when freshly picked; the U.S.-grown version lacks the intense sour edge and the almost glassy texture of the Australian originals.

A hybrid, born of the parents *Malus domestica* and *M. sylvestris*, the apple was first propagated around 1868 by Australia's Maria Ann Sherwood Smith (the "Granny" honored by its name). Although Granny Smiths have so saturated the American market as to seem almost indigenous, they were not introduced into the States until the 1970s.

Considered as good for cooking as they are for eating out of hand, the apples are not the best choice for pies, where crisp crusts are desirable; like so many sour apples, they exude a lot of juice and require much sugar, which melts into a syrup. But their clean, astringent tones make them the perfect foil for strong, blue-veined cheeses and lusty aged Cheddars. A word of caution: Because of their firm texture, Granny Smith apples have been known to scratch gums and occasionally even crack dentures if bitten into too vehemently.

MAIL ORDER: For apples, The Fruit Company, tel 800-387-3100, thefruitcompany.com; boxed greens.com; for a list of orchards and markets by state, orangepippin.com. **FURTHER INFORMATION AND RECIPES:** *Apples: From Harvest to Table* by Amy Pennington (2013); *The Apple Lover's Cookbook* by Amy Traverso (2011); foodandwine .com (search granny smith apple crisp); cookstr .com (search green apple sherbet; caramel apple tart); epicurious.com (search crab meat and beet puree on granny smith apple). **SPECIAL EVENT:** Granny Smith Festival, Eastwood, New South Wales, Australia, late October, ryde.nsw.gov.au/ grannysmithfestival. **TIP:** If picked at the perfect degree of ripeness, the green peel of the Granny Smith will be illuminated by a slight yellow glow.

"KANGAROO FLESH, NOT BREAD, WAS THE STAFF OF LIFE."
—FROM *THE FATAL SHORE,* BY ROBERT HUGHES

Kangaroo

Australian

Small wonder that the logo for Qantas Airlines is a kangaroo, the hip-hopping animal that most of us associate with Australia. With its charmingly maternal front pocket for a baby kangaroo, the prancing marsupial deceptively suggests a very large pet and is frequently called into service as a model for children's stuffed animals— although in fact it's quite pugnacious.

Given the kangaroo's sentimental appeal, it might be hard to come around to the idea of eating its meat; but the once-endangered animal, low on the food chain and thus an ecologically efficient feeder, is now being farmed in the U.S. as well as in its native land. Low in fat and cholesterol, the mildly flavored meat is beeflike in texture. Marinated in thick chunks and grilled on skewers, it makes a succulent appetizer, especially if it is doused with a spicy sauce; larger cuts are equally good stewed or grilled like steaks. Kangaroo is best eaten rare; like beef cuts such as hanger and skirt steak, it dries out and becomes discouragingly chewy when well done.

Perhaps the most widely known and oldest Australian dish based on kangaroo is the soup made with the animal's muscular and gelatinous tail; like oxtail, it imparts an unctuous smoothness to the broth. Many years ago, canned kangaroo tail soup imported from Australia was a must-have on the shelves of any American food shop with hopes of being considered "gourmet." The idea of the soup must have held more allure than the actual product, whose extremely metallic, salty flavor did not exactly gain favor among serious eaters. Yet, cut into joints and simmered with carrots, onions, turnips, celery, and barley, the meat becomes spoon-tender. Seasoned with bay leaves, nutmeg, and cayenne, the soup develops into a sustaining brew, further heightened by a final shot of red wine and a sprinkling of chopped parsley.

Where: *In Cairns, Australia,* Ochre Restaurant, tel 61/7-4051-0100, ochrerestaurant.com.au; *in New York,* The Australian, tel 212-869-8601, theaustraliannyc.com; Burke & Wills, tel 646-823-9251, burkeandwillsny.com; *in Vancouver,* Moose's Down Under Bar and Grill, tel 604-683-3300, moosesdownunder.com. **Mail order:** For kangaroo meat, Marx Foods, tel 866-588-6279, marxfoods.com. **Further information and recipes:** *The Exotic Meats Cookbook* by Jeanette Edgar (2009); *Australian Greats* by Jo Franks (2012); bbcgoodfood.com (search kangaroo steaks); taste.com.au (search seared kangaroo with raspberry glaze); australian.food.com (search kangaroo burgers).

—||||||||||||||||||||||||||||||||||||||—

SPONGING OFF THE LAMINGTONS

Lamingtons

Australian

I n the beginning, there was stale pound cake, an economical pastry cook, and a eureka moment. The pastry cook in question was trying to come up with something in honor of Baron Lamington, the British governor of Queensland who

The cake celebrates a bygone governor of Queensland.

held forth in Government House from 1895 to 1901, and the cook's invention was both simple and inspired. He cut the simple vanilla-flavored cake into 3-inch squares, about ¾ inch thick, and covered each with a thick, slick coating of rich chocolate icing. To gild the lily, he dredged the squares in dried, slightly sweetened flaked coconut and topped them with whipped cream.

This is how Lamingtons are still served at teatime today, although they may instead be baked as full-size cakes. Let's hope that nowadays the treats will be made with fresh pound cake. Possible further enrichments include stacking multiple squares or cake layers with jam and/or pastry cream spread in between.

A word to the wise: Buying packaged Lamingtons, which are much in the style of Twinkies or Ring Dings, is not advisable.

Where: *In Brooklyn,* Kiwiana, tel 718-230-3682, kiwiana-nyc.com; *in Los Angeles,* Bronzed Aussie, tel 213-243-0770, bronzedaussie

.us; *in Marietta, GA,* Australian Bakery Café, tel 678-797-6222, australianbakerycafe.com; *in Vancouver,* Moose's Down Under Bar and Grill, tel 604-683-3300, moosesdownunder.com.

FURTHER INFORMATION AND RECIPES: *Cooking the Australian Way* by Elizabeth Germaine (2013); saveur.com (search lamingtons); davidlebovitz .com (search lamingtons).

--------||||||||||||||||||||||||||||||--------

A TOUGH NUT TO CRACK

Macadamia Nut

Australian

With the mouth-pleasing texture of giant hazelnuts and a sophisticated, toasty sweetness, macadamias, or *Macadamia ternifolia,* are considered by many to be the best eating nuts of all. Although they are widely grown and

celebrated in Hawaii, they are actually native to Australia, where they are also known as Queensland nuts.

Most alluring when roasted to an ivory-gold patina and lightly sea-salted, the nuts are now regarded as healthful, but got a bad rap in years past as being high in unhealthy fat. This perception was due in part to the custom of glossing them with coconut oil before roasting, which both preserved the nuts and added a delicious flavor of its own. Alas, savory coconut oil contains a lot of saturated fat, so it was replaced with lighter vegetable oils that only slightly compromise the nuts' still-tantalizing flavor.

The commercial cultivation of the macadamia nut—which is named for a Dr. John Macadam, a friend of one of the botanists, Ferdinand von Mueller, who studied and identified the tree—began in the mid-nineteenth century, around Brisbane in Queensland. Although easily harvested on the ground after they drop in clusters from the trees, macadamias have very hard shells under their velvety green husks. Careful handwork is required to crack them without breaking the kernel (which is most valuable when intact), and that shelling process is what accounts for the price of macadamias, the

most expensive of all nuts. Prized as they are for their fragrant oil and their softly spreading butter, the whole nut fetches the highest price. But crumbled macadamias are delectable additions to vegetable and fruit salads, ice creams (think hot fudge sundaes), chocolates, brittles, and other candies. In the hands of creative chefs, they've recently also become a golden, crunchy breading on fish, chicken, and pork.

Like all nuts, macadamias are susceptible to rancidity, and should be stored in a cool place to avoid it. They are best obtained fresh from a reliable store where they can be sampled before purchase. Canned macadamias are often stale, so look carefully for an expiration date and hope that the container was kept cool.

MAIL ORDER: nuts.com, tel 800-558-6887.
FURTHER INFORMATION AND RECIPES: *The Mauna Loa Macadamia Cookbook* by Leslie Mansfield (1998); *The Hali'imaile General Store Cookbook* by Beverly Gannon and Bonnie Friedman (2000); *Best of the Best from Hawaii Cookbook* by Gwen McKee (2004); cookstr.com (search banana macadamia coconut coffee cake; macadamia nut chicken breasts); epicurious.com (search banana macadamia nut muffins); australian-macadamias.org.

—||||||||||||||||||||||||||||||||||—

AS SWEET AS A PRIMA BALLERINA

Pavlova

Australian, New Zealand

A somewhat recent addition to menus in the U.S., the stylish Pavlova is a dessert claimed by both Australia and New Zealand. It was inspired, of course, by Anna Pavlova, the Russian ballerina who performed in both those countries in 1926. Was it first created in 1934 (New Zealand), or in 1935 (Australia)? Take your pick, and count yourself part of a long-running controversy.

Light and frothy, the confection is based on a particular kind of meringue that is crunchy on the outside but slightly soft and creamy, marshmallow-like, within—an effect achieved by the addition of cream of tartar or cornstarch, plus a touch of vinegar or lemon juice beaten into the mounting egg whites. The meringue, which can be formed and baked a few hours in advance, actually becomes a bowl: Just before being served, it is filled with whipped cream topped by one or more seasonal fresh fruits, such as berries, kiwis, passion fruit, and pineapple.

The meringue itself may be flavored with coffee, wattleseeds (see page 907), cocoa, or vanilla. And who would complain if its filling were ice cream, topped with whipped cream and fruit? Not a ballerina's first choice, perhaps, but a tempting thought for the rest of us.

WHERE: *In Cairns, Australia,* Ochre Restaurant, tel 64/7-4051-0100, ochrerestaurant .com.au; *in New York,* The Musket Room, tel 212-219-0764, musketroom.com; Le Bernardin, tel 212-554-1515, le-bernardin.com; *in Brooklyn,* Kiwiana, tel 718-230-3682, kiwiana-nyc.com; *in Montreal,* Ta Pies, tel 514-277-7437, ta-pies.com; *in Vancouver,* Moose's Down Under Bar and Grill, tel 604-683-3300, moosesdownunder.com. **FURTHER INFORMATION AND RECIPES:** *The Down Under Cookbook* by Graeme Newman (1987); *Cooking the Australian Way* by Elizabeth Germaine (2013); *Australian Greats* by Jo Franks (2012); *The Gourmet Cookbook* by Ruth Reichl (2006); foodnetwork.com (search mixed berry pavlova); cookstr.com (search pavlova); australianfood.about.com (search pavlova).

—||||||||||||||||||||||||||||||||||—

FIRST DESSERT, THEN DIET TOAST

Peach Melba, Melba Toast

Australian (with a French touch)

A perfect sun-gold peach, peeled and poached in vanilla syrup. A crimson puree of fresh, uncooked raspberries. A scoop of vanilla ice cream. Created by a French chef working in a London hotel, in celebration of an Australian diva, the luscious summer dessert that is Peach Melba could be considered a tricountry triumph.

Nellie Melba was the name of the celebrated opera star. Born Helen Porter Mitchell in

Melbourne in 1861, she adopted her chosen name to honor her birthplace, long before she became famous. The generally accepted story is that Auguste Escoffier, then the chef at the Savoy Hotel, heard her sing at Covent Garden in London, and was inspired to create the dessert for a party she attended in 1892. Whether the hotel manager—a man named César Ritz, who would soon open a hotel or two of his own—asked him to do so is still open to question. Whatever the case, the result is an irresistible combination of sweet-tart peach and soft, fruity raspberries complementing the smooth ice cream—a dessert well worth singing for.

Apparently the dessert proved too tempting to the luxury-loving diva. Perhaps because she ate too much of her namesake peach dessert, over time Dame Nellie Melba became seriously overweight and ill. In 1897, Escoffier was apparently moved to provide an antidote. For her diet, the great chef invented melba toast. Ever since, the world has been subjected to hideously stale or limp packaged examples of what was at first a very good creation.

Strange as it may sound, at the height of its fame, from the 1950s to the 1970s, the '21' Club in New York was as renowned for its housemade rye melba toast as it was for its hamburger. Today, similar melba toast perfection can be attained at home. Place a single layer of very thin white or rye bread slices on a baking sheet and slide it into a 200°F to 250°F oven, turning the slices several times until they are a medium golden brown on both sides, about 25 minutes.

Once cool, the slices will become crisp and can be stored for about two weeks in an airtight container.

MAIL ORDER: For fresh Georgia peaches in season, Hale Groves, tel 800-562-4502, hale groves.com. **FURTHER INFORMATION AND RECIPES:** For peach Melba, *Escoffier: Le Guide Culinaire* by Auguste Escoffier (2011); *The New York Times Dessert Cookbook* by Florence Fabricant (2006); *Joy of Cooking* by Irma Rombauer (2006); *The Perfect Peach* by David Mas Masumoto (2013); *Peaches* by Kelly Alexander (2013); saveur.com (search peach melba); pbs.org (search peach melba); mpeckcooks.com (search peach melba) epicuri ous.com (search herbed melba toasts); exam iner.com (search homemade melba toast); parade.com (search homemade melba toast). **TIP:** Without ice cream, the raspberry-topped poached peach is known as peach (*pêche*) cardinale. For a perfect recipe, see *Mastering the Art of French Cooking, Volume 1* by Julia Child, Simone Beck, and Louisette Bertholle (1961).

THERE'S A PIE IN YOUR SOUP

Pie Floater

Australian

If the name doesn't get you, perhaps the dish itself will. A specialty of the city of Adelaide, a pie floater is exactly that—an upside-down beef-, onion-, carrot-, and gravy-filled meat pie topped with tomato sauce and set adrift in a bowl of nicely thick green pea soup. Perhaps the oddest part of the awkward-to-handle invention—should one use a fork? a knife? a spoon?—is not its admittedly offbeat components but the fact that it was once popular as a street food, sold from carts.

Dating back to the 1870s, the floater was dubbed a South Australian Heritage Icon by the National Trust of Australia in 2003. Although it's native to Adelaide, one of the most popular places to have it is Harry's Café de Wheels, a cart near the Woolloomooloo Bay Finger Wharf in Sydney. Its succulent floaters with their green, red, and golden-brown color scheme have drawn visitors such as Marlene Dietrich, Frank Sinatra, Anthony Bourdain, Elton John, and many others.

Pie floaters are still dished up at several restaurants in Adelaide today. And rumors continually swirl regarding the forthcoming resurrection of this or that pie cart. No wonder—with its offbeat sensibility and cold-weather appeal, the floater is due for a street-food revival.

Where: *In Adelaide,* Bakery on O'Connell, tel 61/8-8361-7377, bakeryonoconnell.com.au; for an upscale version, The Kings, tel 61/8-8212-6657, thekingsbardining.com; *in Sydney,* Harry's

Café de Wheels, tel 61/2-9357-3074, harryscafe dewheels.com.au; *in Boston,* KO Catering and Pies at two locations, kocateringandpies.com. **Further information and recipes:** food.com (search pea soup floater); lifestylefood.com.au (meat pie floater); homegrown.org (search australian pie floater).

An offbeat delicacy from the city of Adelaide

—|||||||||||||||||||||||||||||||||||—

BEST BY THE TRIPLE DOZEN

Sydney Rock Oysters

Australian, New Zealand

No raw seafood fan should miss the chance to sample the tiny, rose-silver gem that is the Sydney rock oyster, or *Saccostrea commercialis,* the most highly prized of the many oysters that spawn in the bays and inlets of Australia, from Queensland to Victoria and around New Zealand. Inside their ridged, charcoal-gray shells, the meat is succulently silky, with a palate-tingling salinity that grows stronger in oysters harvested in the northernmost waters of that eastern coast.

Sliding down easily, an order of a dozen of these petite briny beauties should be considered a bare minimum. Two to three dozen as an appetizer is more like it, and if true hunger is a factor, who knows? For purists, the only permissible flavoring is a quick squirt of lemon juice.

Although Sydney rock oysters are regulars on upscale menus in Hong Kong and other nearby ports, they are rarely sent farther from their native waters—with the exception of the occasional showy special event for which they are heavily packed in ice and shipped by air.

Sydney rocks aren't the only Australian and New Zealand oysters worth trying. Other local specimens include rock oysters from Albany, Camden Haven, the Nambucca River, Pambula Lake, Wallis Lake, and several spots along the coasts of New South Wales and New Zealand.

Among the many places in New South Wales where one may try the greatest variety of local oysters, two favorites are the Boathouse on Blackwattle Bay, where they are served with an optional Champagne-and-shallot mignonette dip; and the no-frills stands and stalls of the sprawling Sydney Fish Market, where they can be slurped informally and at fairly reasonable prices. Between those luscious indulgences, one can wander through the operatic fish market, established in 1945, and take in the working port, the colorful daily auctions, and the school of fish cookery. The market claims to have more species of seafood than any other in the world, except for Tokyo's famed Tsukiji (see page 821).

Where: *In Sydney,* The Boathouse on Blackwattle Bay, tel 61/2-9518-9011, boathouse .net.au; Sydney Fish Market, sydneyfishmarket .com.au; Doyles on the Beach, tel 61/2-9337-2007, doyles.com.au; *in Wellington, New Zealand,* Logan Brown, tel 64/480-151-14, logan brown.co.nz. **Further information and recipes:** *A Multitude of Fishes* by Ann Creber (1987); foodnetwork.com (search sydney rock oyster pasty); lifestylefood.com.au (search sydney rock oyster with chili dressing); taste.com.au (search oysters with champagne sauce).

THE DEVIL IN THE HONEY POT

Tasmanian Leatherwood Honey

Australian

The color of molten gold, this headily perfumed and elegant honey is derived from the nectar of the starry white blossoms of 350-year-old leatherwood trees. Canny bees gather the nectar in the humid rainforests of Tasmania, the only place on earth where the *Eucryphia lucida* tree grows. The unblended honey that results has a unique, smoked candy flavor with a hint of spicy bitterness and a slightly overripe aroma like that of some aged cheeses. Just as with those cheeses, it may take a little getting used to, but any acclimation period will be well worth the effort. Sampled by the spoonful, drizzled onto yogurt or vanilla ice cream, stirred into tea or warm milk, or spread over hot buttered English muffins, scones, or flaky croissants, leatherwood honey is all sweetness and engaging complexity.

Most attractive in tall, tapering glass bottles, the honey is also sold in cans. Because it is neither filtered nor heated, it tends to become very thick; setting the closed bottle or can in warm water will help make the honey more fluid and spreadable.

After you fall in love with this sophisticated honey, you'll want to get behind the effort to protect the endangered leatherwood trees. Along with neighboring eucalyptus trees, they are the frequent victims of the lumber industry. Saving the leatherwood forest has important benefits beyond the obvious pleasure of continuing to enjoy its honey. Also at stake is the livelihood of the beekeepers whose hives are already declining in number, and the local farmers who depend on busy bees to cross-pollinate their crops.

MAIL ORDER: markethallfoods.com (search leatherwood); deandeluca.com (search leatherwood); igourmet.com (search leatherwood). **FURTHER INFORMATION AND RECIPES:** *Australian Greats* by Jo Franks (2012); feastmagazine.com (search rustic fig tart with tasmanian leatherwood); sbs.com.au/food (search blue cheese and leatherwood); marthastewart.com (search honey and pine nut tart); saveyourleather woodhoney.com; tasmanianhoney.com. **TIP:** As with all honeys, remember the old rule for safest storage: Honey keeps where salt stays dry.

SLIP ANOTHER SHRIMP ON THE BARBIE

Tiger Prawn

Australian

With so many of these large, sumptuously meaty crustaceans shipped off for export, it may be easier to spot their yellow-striped gray shells in Japan, Hong Kong, Southeast Asia, and the U.S. than in their native Australia. Wherever it is that they are enjoyed, though, the large tails of *Penaeus esculentus* are where the good eating lies. Whether grilled or steamed, they are almost always cooked in the shell to protect the delicate meat they contain and keep it succulently tender.

Fresh tiger prawns in their native Queensland

A particular favorite around the South Pacific, tiger prawns make appearances in foods as diverse as spicy Southeast Asian barbecues, Indian curries, and Japanese tempura and sushi dishes (see pages 820 and 817), as well as in Chinese black-bean-and-ginger stir-fries. In the spirit of globalization, they also adapt to Italian scampi recipes (see page 238), and their raw meat is firm enough to be treated American crab-cake-style, removed from the shell and chopped and mixed with egg and seasonings for fried croquettes.

As delectable as those fairly complex preparations can be, the prawn's subtle essence is best perceived in the simple prawn cocktail that's a popular standard in upscale seafood restaurants of Australia. Skip the cocktail sauce and instead use just a drizzle of lemon juice as a dressing, if you must.

WHERE: *In Sydney,* Sydney Fish Market, tel 61/2-9004-1100, sydneyfishmarket.com.au; Doyles on the Beach, tel 61/2-9337-2007, doyles .com.au; *in Cairns, Australia,* Ochre Restaurant, tel 64/7-4051-0100, ochrerestaurant.com.au; *in Vancouver,* Moose's Down Under Bar and Grill, tel 604-683-3300, moosesdownunder.com. **MAIL ORDER:** Seattle Fish Company, tel 303-329-9595, seattlefish.com; Sea-Ex, sea-ex.com. **FURTHER INFORMATION AND RECIPES:** *A Multitude of Fishes* by Ann Creber (1987); *Australian Greats* by Jo Franks (2012); *Australia the Beautiful Cookbook* by Elise Pascoe (1995); sbs.com.au/food (search salt and pepper tiger prawns); cookstr .com (search tiger shrimp and onions); austral ianprawns.com.au (search tiger prawns).

||||||||||||||||||||||||||||||||

JUST FOLLOW YOUR NOSE

Vegemite

Australian

The only foods that can prepare a novice palate for Vegemite, Australia's favorite relish and spread, are rotted anchovies, English Marmite, or Gentleman's Relish, all of which are yeasty, fetid, dense brown pastes said to build strength and overall well-being, to say nothing of character. Given its acrid stench and gluey texture, one might wonder why Vegemite should be tasted at all—even if does live up to its touted health benefits. The reason should be obvious to those who take their eating seriously, for this is one of the world's most iconic and memorable national flavors and so deserves understanding.

Now owned by Kraft, Vegemite was created in Australia in 1922 by an entrepreneur named Fred Walker and a chemist named Dr. Cyril Callister. Despite the stinky overtones of the caramelized all-vegetable mix, Australian children cry for it as American tots do for peanut butter and jelly. Their parents spread it on buttered toast or bread as a snack or a sandwich, or on biscuits as a special treat at teatime. Vegemite has recently become a featured menu item at Melbourne-style cafés now opening around the U.S. It's even said to be habit-forming.

Brewer's yeast, a by-product of beer brewing in this suds-happy land, is the ingredient that adds a generous belt of Vitamin B and provides the product's defining flavor as well as its seriously pungent aroma. As one drives toward the Melbourne factory, its smell begins to fill the air from some twenty minutes away.

New Zealanders are said to prefer the slightly sweeter English Marmite, so for the sake of experience, try both.

WHERE: *In New York,* Little Collins, tel 212-308-1969, littlecollinsnyc.com; *in Seattle,* Kangaroo and Kiwi, tel 206-297-0507, kangaroo andkiwi.com. **MAIL ORDER:** World Market, tel 877-967-5362, worldmarket.com; iGourmet, tel 877-446-8763, igourmet.com. **FURTHER INFORMATION AND RECIPES:** *Cooking the Australian Way* by Elizabeth Germaine (2013); thekitchn.com (search 7 recipes with marmite); grubstreet.com (search harness the putrid power of vegemite); vegemite.com.au. **SEE ALSO:** Gentleman's Relish, page 13.

||||||||||||||||||||||||||||||||

THE CHOCOLATE-LIKE SEED

Wattleseed

Australian

Produced by the sunny yellow–blossomed Australian acacia tree—a type that includes more than a hundred species—the wattleseed (aka acacia seed) should primarily be valued for its savory, rich flavor, a sort of gianduja-plus that combines hints of chocolate, coffee, and hazelnuts. But its health properties are inevitably taken into account, as that rich taste comes from a high-fiber, protein-filled seed whose low glycemic index is a boon to diabetics. Roasted and crushed to a powder suggestive of coffee grounds or cocoa powder, wattleseeds are frequently added as a seasoning to cakes, breads, ice creams, pastries, and other desserts. These days some inventive chefs work them into sauces for meats and poultry as well, for a bit of crunch in addition to flavor.

Until fairly recently, they were known mostly to aborigines in the dry outback regions of Australia. There, they are still among the many intriguing spices and edibles that make up what is known as "bush tucker," the Australian slang for food made from ingredients procured from the wilderness. In 1984, Vic Cherikoff, an experimental chef doing research on bush tucker, began to study wattleseeds and their culinary possibilities, thereby taking the first step toward making them a widespread seasoning.

Other bush tucker specialties include native seasonings such as the spicy Tasmanian pepperleaf, aromatic lemon myrtle leaves, and pungent red quandong berries, in addition to a number of wild birds, insects, and animals like the wallaby and the kangaroo (see page 899), and the bread known as damper (see page 896). Having taken a fashionable turn as of late, bush tucker is being reconceived as restaurant fare on Australian menus both at home and abroad.

WHERE: *In Cairns, Australia,* Ochre Restaurant, tel 64/7-4051-0100, ochrerestaurant .com.au. **MAIL ORDER:** The Spicery, thespicery .com (search wattleseed). **FURTHER INFORMATION AND RECIPES:** starchefs.com (search wattleseed); foodnetwork.com (search wattleseed ice cream).

A CHOCOLATE COOKIE FOR TEATIME

Afghan Biscuits

New Zealand, Australian

How this crunchy chocolate cookie got its name remains a mystery, but its nicely sandy texture and rich cocoa flavor obviate the need for a backstory. Whether Afghans were initially made by Afghani immigrants or, as some say, named for their resemblance to the rocky mountains of Afghanistan, they're just right for tea and coffee, or with glasses of cold milk for the kids. Equally popular in Australia and New Zealand, Afghans also have a special place on the dessert table during the Christmas holidays.

Improbably enough, the crunch in these cookies comes from the addition of crushed cornflakes, which are folded into the dough along with generous amounts of cocoa and vanilla. Once baked and cooled, the thick, round cookie (or biscuit, as it is known on native ground) is further enhanced by a thin wash of dark chocolate icing and a single toasted walnut half.

WHERE: *In Wellington, New Zealand,* Logan Brown, tel 64/480-151-14, loganbrown.co.nz; *in New York,* The Musket Room, tel 212-219-0764, musketroom.com; *in Montreal,* Ta Pies, tel 514-277-7437, ta-pies.com. **MAIL ORDER:** sanza.co.uk (search afghan biscuits). **FURTHER INFORMATION AND RECIPES:** *The Down Under Cookbook* by Graeme Newman (1987); *The Australian Blue Ribbon Cookbook* by Liz Harfull (2014); kiwibaking.com (search afghan biscuits); saveur.com (search afghans).

Colonial Goose

New Zealand, Australian

The British settlers who arrived in New Zealand in the early nineteenth century created an inimitable dish that has come to be known as "colonial goose": a boned leg of mutton stuffed and roasted to imitate the much-missed English goose at Christmas. Both New Zealand and Australia now claim the so-called goose as one of their national dishes, although it's becoming more and more difficult to find. When you do run across it, it is likely to be made with the delicate Australian and New Zealand lamb we love to import, and is a far cry from the way the dish used to taste in the days when lambs were allowed to grow into sheep. Fully raised sheep, by the way, provided meatier, fattier meat for the table, and made the animals more profitable for ranchers.

Meat from fully raised sheep was once commonly used in the dish.

Colonial Goose

Serves 8 to 10

Necessary equipment: Skewers, or kitchen string, and a trussing needle

½ cup (1 stick) butter, melted, or
    ½ cup light vegetable oil or rendered
    lamb fat
1 small onion, grated
⅔ cup fresh white bread crumbs
1 extra-large egg, lightly beaten
3 tablespoons finely minced fresh flat-leaf
    parsley
2 teaspoons minced fresh thyme leaves, or
    ½ teaspoon crushed dried thyme leaves
    (see Variations)
Grated zest of 1 lemon
Salt and freshly ground black pepper
1 leg of lamb, or 1 half-leg of mutton
    (6 to 7 pounds; see Note)

1. Preheat the oven to 425°F.

2. Heat ¼ cup of the butter, oil, or fat in a small skillet over very low heat and stir in the onion. Cook the onion until it loses its raw smell, about 1 minute. Stir in the bread crumbs and cook slowly, stirring, until the bread crumbs turn light golden, 3 to 4 minutes.

3. Remove the skillet from the heat and mix in the egg, parsley, thyme, lemon zest, and a pinch each of salt and pepper. Let the stuffing cool.

4. Rub salt and pepper inside the pocket in the leg. Spoon the cooled stuffing into the pocket in the meat. Close the pocket tightly, either by fastening it with skewers or by sewing it shut using kitchen string and a trussing needle. Brush the top of the meat with the remaining ¼ cup of butter, oil, or rendered fat, and sprinkle it with salt and pepper.

5. Set the leg on a rack in a large roasting pan

and insert a meat thermometer halfway into the thickest part of the leg, but not touching the bone. Roast the meat until the membrane on top of the roast begins to stiffen and turn golden, about 20 minutes. Reduce the heat to 350°F and continue roasting the leg, basting it with the drippings about every 15 minutes, until the meat thermometer registers 135°F for rare or 145°F for medium, about 1 hour. If you like your meat more well done than that, do not make this dish; longer cooking will render the meat and the stuffing dry and tasteless.

6. Transfer the leg to a cutting board, place it in a warm spot in the kitchen, and let it rest for 15 minutes before carving.

Note: Have a butcher bone the leg of lamb or mutton, leaving only the shank bone intact. This will form a large pocket in the leg. The top membrane, the fell, should not be trimmed off the lamb.

Variations: If you prefer the taste of sage, substitute 3 minced fresh sage leaves or ½ teaspoon powdered dried sage for the thyme.

In New Zealand, 1 tablespoon of honey is sometimes stirred into the cooked bread crumb mixture, along with about ½ cup finely chopped dried apricots. If you like garlic, feel free to add a finely minced, medium-size clove to the cooked bread crumb mixture; by the same token, you might throw in ⅓ cup chopped macadamia or pistachio nuts. Such additions are delicious if not authentic.

Further information and recipes: *Cooking the Australian Way* by Elizabeth Germaine (2013); foodnetwork.com (search colonial goose); bite.co.nz (search colonial goose).

FLEXING MUSSELS

Green-Lipped Mussels

New Zealand

Known to many as the world's premium mussel, the large, thin-shelled, "green-lipped" or "green-shell" variety is as likely to be found in upscale fish markets and restaurants in the States as it is around its native waters. Farmed near

New Zealand is the biggest exporter of the mussel.

the shores of Korea, Japan, China, Southeast Asia, and New Zealand, the last being the world's largest exporter, *Perna canaliculu* boasts an alluring, deep sea–emerald color that yellows when exposed to sunlight.

Bivalves from the North Atlantic might be the mollusks of choice for those who prefer them salty, small, and very firm. But because the green-lipped mussel is plumper and can grow to eight inches in length, it can be grilled or baked without shriveling or drying. Of course, its greatest appeal lies in its flavor, which carries the sophisticated overtones of salt and copper and the soupçon of sweet sea air that make the green-lipped mussel so prized in Mediterranean and Asian dishes. (The flavor of the ivory-colored male mussel meat tends to be sharper and saltier than the lusher, milder orange meat of the female, and Mr. Mussel is more appealing simply steamed and served cold; his lady friend is better suited to more complex soups and stews.)

True mollusk lovers may cringe at the use of extracts from green-lipped mussels as anti-inflammatories, prescribed to treat various types of arthritis and damaged joints (as Gertrude Stein would say, "very interesting if true"). But anyone suffering from such pains will undoubtedly find eating the mussels to be the most felicitous prescription of all.

WHERE: *In New York*, The Musket Room, tel 212-219-0764, musketroom.com; Citarella, tel 212-874-0383, citarella.com; *in Brooklyn*, Kiwiana, tel 718-230-3682, kiwiana-nyc.com; *in Cayucos, CA*, Hoppe's Garden Bistro, tel 805-995-1006, hoppesbistro.com. **FURTHER INFORMATION AND RECIPES:** *A Multitude of Fishes* by Ann Creber (1987); *The New Zealand Seafood Cookbook* by Auckland Seafood School (2010); *The Great Mussel and Clam Cookbook* by Whitecap Books (2004); foodnetwork.com (search green-lip mussels); kiwiwise.co.nz (garlic and white wine mussels); seafood.co.nz (click Types of Fish, then Greenshell Mussel). **SEE ALSO:** Thai mussels (page 845).

MOVE OVER, ROCKY ROAD

Hokey Pokey Ice Cream

New Zealand

Take some of the coolest, creamiest vanilla ice cream on earth, add the smoky-sweet crackle of honeycomb toffee known as hokey pokey, and you have the seductive textural and flavor contrast that makes this New Zealand dessert magical.

The name, also used at one time in England and in the United States for ice cream mixed with other ingredients, is thought to have been derived from the Italian ice-cream street vendors who would call out *Ecco un poco,* meaning "Here's a little," or *O'che poco,* meaning "Oh, how little!" Fortunately for us, there's no need to keep the portions small.

Anxious to get started on a little hokey pokey of your own? It's easy enough to make at home. All that's required for honeycomb toffee is golden syrup, superfine sugar, and baking soda (see recipe references below). Simply allow ready-made vanilla ice

Full of honeycomb's crackle

cream to soften so that the toffee (or nut brittle, if you like) can be folded in, then refreeze the ice cream. That's all the hocus-pocus required to produce a delicious batch of hokey pokey.

WHERE: *In Brooklyn*, Kiwiana, tel 718-230-3682, kiwiana-nyc.com; *in Corning, NY*, Hokey Pokey's Ice Creamery and Yogurt Haus, tel 607-962-4720. **FURTHER INFORMATION AND RECIPES:** nigella.com (search hokey pokey); australianfood.about.com (search hokey pokey ice cream); sbs.com.au/food (search anzac biscuit hokey pokey sandwich); goodtoknow.co.uk (search honeycomb toffee).

BIRD, FRUIT, NATIONAL IDENTITY

Kiwi Fruit

New Zealand

With the kiwi bird as their national symbol and the fuzzy, bronze-green kiwi fruit as one of their most epicurean exports, it's no wonder New Zealanders fondly refer to themselves as Kiwis. (Whether they prefer to align themselves with the flightless, tailless bird or with the plump, juicy fruit—*Actinidia deliciosa,* also known as a Chinese gooseberry—may be a matter of personal preference.)

As valued for its stunning, glassy-green interior as it is for its unique flavor, the kiwi fruit suggests a combination of banana, citrus, and pineapple. Peeled and sliced horizontally, it reveals a sort of stained-glass star pinpointed with tiny black seeds.

That appearance is part of the reason the kiwi has had such success on the international stage. First exported to the United States in the 1950s, and then made fashionable by French chefs with a nouvelle cuisine bent, the fruit is now widely grown in California.

Unfortunately, as with so much mass-produced produce, the domestic kiwi is often bred for shelf life. Picked unripe, it is rarely noteworthy for more than its unusual appearance and a vague sourness. Far better varieties arrive from New Zealand or even Italy, currently the world's largest producer, or from any boutique orchard or family tree where they are allowed to ripen in the sunshine and turn a deep bronze. The best kind of kiwi remains green on the inside; the gold kiwi, or Hinabelle, developed for its cheerful orangey hue and lower acidity, is a blander and less interesting fruit.

MAIL ORDER: Melissa's Produce, tel 800-588-0151, melissas.com; Pittman & Davis, tel 800-289-7829, pittmandavis.com. **FURTHER INFORMATION AND RECIPES:** *Uncommon Fruits and Vegetables* by Elizabeth Schneider (2010); *The Purple Kiwi Cookbook* by Karen Caplan (2000); *Cooking the Australian Way* by Elizabeth Germaine (2013); epicurious.com (search kiwi sorbet, kiwi pomegranate angel pies); kiwifruit.org/recipes. **TIP:** Kiwis are not only delicious, they're also good for you—they are high in vitamin C, potassium, and actinidin, a protein-tenderizing enzyme similar to the papain in papaya (see page 860).

LET THE CITRUS DO THE COOKING

Poisson Cru

Tahitian

Cool and piquant, the colorful raw fish salad *poisson cru* is an enticing appetizer or lunch from the French Polynesian island of Tahiti. "Raw" is not the real story with this sparkling salad, for the fish marinates in acidic citrus juices that lend a firmness and opacity to its flesh—"cooking" it, in a sense, much as similar marinades do for ceviche or Hawaiian poke. Favorite *poissons* tend to be white-fleshed saltwater swimmers such as snapper, halibut, flounder, and fluke, but sliced sea scallops are also de rigueur, along with tuna and salmon.

With fresh catch in hand, few dishes could be simpler to prepare. The Tahitian method

Prepared for motu—*the traditional beachside meal*

calls for about 1½ pounds of fillets of fish, sliced into small, thin ribbons or squares, about ¼ inch thick and 2 inches long or square. Placed in a glass or ceramic bowl and covered with about ¾ cup strained fresh lime juice and ½ cup chopped mild young onions, the fish marinates in the refrigerator for about 6 hours. After marinating, the flesh will be firm, looking as though it had been cooked.

To tie it all together, the salad is well drained and the fish is tossed with diced tomatoes, scallions, and green pepper. A dressing of creamy coconut milk (known as lolo sauce in Fiji) is the finishing touch, and the dish is most traditionally and prettily served in a large scallop or clam shell.

FURTHER INFORMATION AND RECIPES: *Foods of the World* by Rafael Steinberg (1970); epicurious .com (search poisson cru); foodnetwork.com (search poisson cru coconut lime; halibut poisson cru); gohawaii.about.com (search tahitian poisson cru). **SEE ALSO:** Poke, page 611.

THE FLAVOR OF INNOCENCE

Tahitian Vanilla

Tahitian

So pervasive is vanilla as a flavoring in our ice creams, puddings, cookies, and cakes that we may forget what it actually is. With a delicate, flowery flavor, Tahitian vanilla reminds us that the vanilla bean comes from a member of the

orchid family, in this case *Vanilla tahitensis*. It is one of the most prized iterations of this innocently sweet seasoning (with the Mexico and Madagascar beans as runners-up), but the high-quality bean is very expensive no matter which sunny, orchid-friendly region it comes from. The flowers need to be hand-pollinated when they are grown in nonnative regions that lack the insects to do the job, and the pods themselves must be painstakingly dried and cured by hand. All of this amounts to a labor-intensive process,

hence the prevalence of synthetic vanilla flavorings, generally a poor substitute for the real thing. Using vanilla beans for flavoring requires splitting the slender dried pod and scraping out the pasty seed mass within. Although more complicated than resorting to pure vanilla extract, there are extra rewards in flavor. Additionally, empty pods can be stored in sugar to impart their flavor and aroma—useful for making desserts and confections.

Prized by cooks and bakers all over the

world, on home ground Tahitian vanilla is worked into beverages, puddings, fruit salads, and desserts, as well as the base flavor for a rich coconut cream sauce that graces shellfish and chicken dishes. Vanilla is also used as a scent, as well as a flavoring, and is believed to calm

The extract is used in aromatherapy and desserts.

nerves and impart a sense of ease. In Victorian times it was a common and non-scandalous perfume for women to wear, with a bit dabbed on wrists and necks, the sweeter to smell.

WHERE: *In New York,* for Tahitian vanilla ice cream, Le Bernardin, tel 212-554-1515, le-bernardin.com. **MAIL ORDER:** For beans, Marky's, tel 800-522-8427, markys.com (search tahitian vanilla); for extract, iGourmet, tel 877-446-8763, igourmet.com; Sur la Table, tel 800-243-0852, surlatable.com. **FURTHER INFORMATION AND RECIPES:** *Vanilla 101 Cookbook* by Amy Bugbee (2012); foodnetwork.com (search tahitian vanilla creme brulee); cookstr.com (search pears poached tahitian vanilla); jamesbeard.org (search tahitian vanilla roasted pineapple); nielsenmassey.com (click Consumer, then Recipes).

INDEXES

Special Indexes

General Index

Special Indexes

Ⓢ§§~

Recipes

Featured Restaurants

World-Class Markets

Holiday Foods

CHRISTMAS

General Index

~⟨∬∬~

X

Photo Credits

FRONT COVER (center graphic)

LiliGraphic/fotolia.

FRONT COVER (clockwise from top right)

Gareth Morgans/age fotostock, Andrew Walters/Alamy Images, alekseyk100/fotolia, dream79/fotolia, Caggiano Photography/age fotostock, Nigel Dickinson/Alamy Images, Bergfee/fotolia, Ivan Floriani/fotolia, Katherine Welles/iStock/Thinkstock Images, Brian Jannsen/Alamy Images, Mira/Alamy Images, James Baigrie/The Image Bank/Getty Images, Medioimages/Photodisc/Getty Images, Jag_cz/iStock/Thinkstock Images, Giovanni Mereghetti/age fotostock, Maria Brzostowska/iStock/Thinkstock Images, Jean Cazals/age fotostock, Philip Lewis/Alamy Images.

BACK COVER (clockwise from top right)

Lianxun Zhang/fotolia, Adrian Rosu Savinoiu/iStock/Thinkstock Images, stu99/iStock Editorial/Thinkstock Images, aruba200/iStock/Thinkstock Images, Andrew Furlong Photography/iStock/Thinkstock Images, Kristina Rutten/fotolia, Angel Simon/fotolia, Lauri Patterson/E+/Getty Images, teleginatania/fotolia, Alexcrab/iStock/Thinkstock Images, Guiziou Franck/hemis.fr/Getty Images, Carnet/age fotostock, Luca Tettoni/age fotostock, Dave Stamboulis/Alamy Images, Comugnero Silvana/fotolia, Jules Kitano/iStock/Thinkstock, Vertmedia/Martin R./fotolia, nosonjai/iStock/Thinkstock Images, DAJ/Thinkstock Images, author photo: Eric Ethridge.

TABLE OF CONTENTS

p. xi (top) Jeffrey Banke/fotolia, p. xi (bottom) Sergii Figurnyi/fotolia, p. xii (top) uckyo/fotolia, p. xii (middle) heinteh/fotolia, p. xii (bottom) vainillaychile/fotolia.

INTRODUCTION

p. xiv Jupiterimages/Stockbyte/Thinkstock Images, p. xv maratr/iStock/Thinkstock Images, p. xvi Brian Jannsen/Alamy Images.

BRITISH AND IRISH

age fotostock: p. 10 (top) Stuart MacGregor, p. 19 Gareth Morgans, p. 22 Dorota i Bogda Bialy, p. 30 foodanddrinkphotos co, p. 35 Dorling Kindersley/UI, p. 42 David Lyons, p. 43 Monkey Business-LBR, p. 47 FoodCollection; **Alamy Images:** p. 14 Marc Tielemans, p. 15 Nigel Dickinson, pp. 29, 45 Bon Appetit, p. 33 Lordprice Collection; **fotolia:** pp. 3, 27 Joe Gough, p. 8 (top) nadger, p. 8 (bottom) Martin Turzak, p. 10 (bottom) Jeffrey Banke, p. 11 Marco Mayer, p. 12 M. Studio, p. 23 Viktorija, p. 25 SunnyS, p. 34 TwilightArtPictures, p. 39 Monkey Business, p. 41 teressa, p. 46 Scruggelgreen; **Getty Images:** p. 6 Peter Macdiarmid/Getty Image News, p. 16 VisitBritain/Pawel Libera/Britain On View, p. 17 Gary Jones/Moment, p. 20 Steve Lupton/Photolibrary, p. 31 Steve Brown Photography/Photolibrary, p. 32 James Baigrie/Photodisc.

FRENCH

age fotostock: p. 64 FOTOSEARCH RM, p. 72 Radvaner, p. 82 Chris Dave, p. 85 Danny Culbert, p. 87 Rauzier-Riviere, p. 89 Amiel, p. 94 Bono, p. 104 F. Teigler, p. 105 Chris Alack, p. 106 Bernhard Winkelmann, p. 110 Element Photo, p. 116 Stocksign, p. 118 Fleurent, p. 119 Studio DHS, p. 136 Michael Marquand, p. 139 Hall, p. 141 Teubner Foodfoto; **Alamy Images:** pp. 51, 79, 97, 137 Bon Appetit, pp. 56, 91 Hemis, p. 58 Paris Pierce, p. 69 Philip H. Coblentz, p. 70 Martin Turzak, p. 88 Jacek Nowak, pp. 109, 134 Photocuisine, p. 114 es-cuisine/PhotoAlto, p. 115 Food and Drink Photos, p. 123 funkyfood London/Paul Williams, p. 124 Karen Appleyard, p. 131 (bottom) Tim E. White, p. 132 MBI; **fotolia:** p. 53 Printemps, p. 61 sarsmis, p. 73 daughter, p. 77 Giuseppe Porzani, p. 83 Volodymyr Krasyuk, p. 93 daffodilred, p. 128 (top) Frederic Prochasson, p. 128 (bottom) Brad Pict, p. 131 (top) Shawn Hempel, p. 140 Dani Vincek; **Getty Images:** p. 50 Nancy Brown/The Image Bank, p. 52

Edouard Boubat/Gamma-Photo, p. 55 Howard Kingsnorth/Taxi, p. 63 Pierre Verdy/AFP, p. 67 Ian O'Leary/Dorling Kindersley, p. 75 Image Source, p. 80 Charity Burggraaf, p. 98 Photo Marylise Doctrinal, p. 100 Matthew O'Shea/Photographer's Choice, p. 102 Crackphotos/age fotostock, p. 112 Steve Brown Photography/Photolibrary, p. 121 Peter Williams/Photolibrary, p. 127 Medioimages/Photodisc, p. 133 Kathryn Russell Studios/Photolibrary, p. 138 James Baigrie/The Image Bank, p. 135 Maurice Rougemont/Gamma-Rapho.

BELGIAN AND DUTCH

age fotostock: p. 145 EKA, p. 148 Elisabeth Coelfen, p. 151 Wolfgang Schardt; **Alamy Images:** p. 153 Profimedia.CZ a.s, pp. 154, 158 Frans Lemmens; **fotolia:** p. 152 Sandra van der Steen; **Getty Images:** p. 147 Philippe Desnerck/Photolibrary, p. 149 Dorling Kindersley, p. 155 Frans Lemmens/Lonely Planet Images, p. 160 Lehner/E+; **Superstock:** p. 156 Album/Joseph Martin.

ITALIAN

age fotostock: p. 167 Marina Horvat, p. 169 Keller & Keller Photo, p. 170 Valerie Janssen, p. 182 Nico Tondini, p. 183 Imagerie, p. 190 (bottom) Imagerie, p. 190 (top) Stefano Scata, p. 195 Ken Field Photography, p. 199 Dorota i Bogda Bialy, p. 200 Adriano Bacchella, p. 201 Jorg Lehmann, p. 207 Alessandro Canova, p. 209 K. Arras, p. 211 FOTOSEARCH RM, p. 231 Picture Partners, p. 239 Juanma Aparicio, p. 244 STOCKFOOD LBRF, p. 251 Eising Studio-Food; **Alamy Images:** p. 172 Tim Hill, p. 178 CuboImages srl, pp. 188, 197 Bon Appetit, p. 208 Eye Ubiquitous, p. 213 StudioSource, p. 230 Elio Lombardo; **fotolia:** p. 164 evgenyb, p. 171 Comugnero Silvana, p. 174 Carlo de Santis, p. 193 Ivan Floriani, p. 196 Saratm, p. 202 Printemps, p. 204 photocrew, p. 205 Angel Simon, p. 214 Luiz, p. 235 Uros Petrovic, p. 237 S.E. shooting, p. 240 David Smith, p. 241 Giuseppe Porzani, p. 245 M. Studio, p. 246 travelbook, p. 247 margo555, p. 248 Giuseppe Parisi; **Getty Images:** p. 165 Fototeca Gilardi, p. 186 Edoardo Fornaciari/Gamma-Rapho, p. 194 Sabine Lubenow/LOOK, p. 203 Guiziou Franck/hemis.fr, p. 210 Fabio Bianchini/Photodisc, p. 216 Nicole Branan/E+, p. 223 Floortje/E+, p. 224 Peter Adams/The Image Bank, p. 226 Slow Images/Photographer's Choice, p. 228 Chris Alack/Stockfood Creative, p. 242 Brian Hagiwara/FoodPix, p. 252 Joff Lee/Photolibrary; **Thinkstock Images:** p. 180 Malgorzata Slusarczyk/Hemera, p. 218 foodandstyle/iStock, p. 222 Tatiana Fuentes/iStock.

SPANISH AND PORTUGUESE

age fotostock: p. 254 Lawton, p. 261 Ildi Papp; **Alamy Images:** p. 266 imagebroker, p. 270 Mira; **fotolia:** p. 256 eldorado, p. 263 joserpizarro, p. 267 bit24; **Getty Images:** p. 259 El Bulli Restaurant, p. 274 Ron Dahlquist/Perspectives; **Thinkstock Images:** p. 258 Lew Robertson/iStock, p. 268 HurleySB/iStock.

GERMAN, AUSTRIAN, AND SWISS

age fotostock: p. 278 Jorg Lehmann, p. 281 Chromorange, p. 282 Ernst Wrba, pp. 292, 294 FoodPhotogr. Eising, p. 303 Zoonar/Karl Allgaeue, p. 306 Karl Newedel, p. 312 Martin Siepmann, p. 315 Bildagentur Waldhaeus, p. 322 Marie Jose Jarry, p. 335 Bagros; **Alamy Images:** p. 300 Helmut Corneli, p. 319 nagelestock.com, p. 326 Martin Thomas Photography, p. 327 Witold Skrypczak, p. 330 Bon Appetit; **fotolia:** p. 279 Andreas F., p. 285 Photocrew, p. 286 davis, p. 289 Stefanie B., p. 297 Bergfee, p. 301 manla, p. 304 fieryphoenix, p. 308 Doris Heinrichs, p. 310 Georgios Kollidas, p. 316 Vertmedia/Martin R., p. 323 Dusan Zidar, p. 324 martensn, pp. 332, 336 sumnersgraphicsinc; **Getty Images:** p. 277 Leonard McCombe/Time & Life Pictures, p. 299 Holger Leue/Lonely Planet Images; **Thinkstock Images:** p. 321 Zoonar RF.

SCANDINAVIAN

age fotostock: p. 338 Ingvar Bjork, p. 342 Joris Luyten, p. 345 C. Fleurent, p. 348 Jean Cazals, p. 353 Bianca Brandon-Cox, p. 355 Christer Tvedt, p. 361 Susie M. Eising, p. 369 Plattform, p. 372 Winfried Heinze, p. 374 Lars Paulsson; **Alamy Images:** p. 347 K. Iden, p. 368 Mircea Costina, p. 371 David Sanger Photography, p. 373 Chad Ehlers; **fotolia:** p. 340 scis65, p. 341 alekseyk100, p. 344 mallivan, p. 358 Victoria P., p. 365 York, p. 375 steamroller; **Getty Images:** p. 356 Lauri Patterson/E+, p. 362 Yadid Levi/Photolibrary; **Thinkstock Images:** p. 351 marinakhlybova/iStock.

EASTERN EUROPEAN

age fotostock: p. 398 Funkystock, p. 414 Vladimir Shulevsky; **Alamy Images:** pp. 378, 387, 394 Simon Reddy, p. 392 blickwinkel, p. 405 Food Centrale Hamburg GmbH, p. 411 Bon Appetit, p. 413 RIA Novosti, p. 423 foodfolio; **fotolia:** p. 379 Gordan Jankulov, p. 380 tycoon101, p. 383 Taratorki, p. 390 Oleksiy Drachenko, p. 396 Massimiliano Gallo, p. 399 dobri71, p. 400 nickola_che, p. 402 Maria

Brzostowska, p. 407 teleginatania, p. 416 timolina, p. 421 Liliya Sayfeeva, p. 422 Sergii Figurnyi; **Thinkstock Images:** p. 385 kalozzolak/iStock, p. 388 pilipphoto/iStock, p. 408 AlexPro9500/iStock, p. 412 Svetlana Kolpakova/Hemera, p. 419 minadezhda/iStock.

JEWISH

age fotostock: p. 433 Martin Jacobs, pp. 447, 448 PhotoStock-Israel, p. 458 Maximilian Stock LTD, p. 466 Sudres; **Alamy Images:** p. 438 Simon Reddy, p. 443 ZUMA Press, Inc., p. 456 WORLDWIDE photo, p. 457 Evan Spiler, p. 467 PhotoStock-Israel; **fotolia:** p. 464 kostrez; **Getty Images:** p. 426 Andrew Pini/Photolibrary, p. 428 Gordana Jovanovic/E+, p. 432 Brian Hagiwara/Photolibrary, p. 437 Ulrich Kerth/Stockfood Creative, p. 462 SABAH ARAR/AFP, p. 471 Armstrong Studios/Photodisc, p. 472 David Bishop Inc./Photolibrary; **Thinkstock Images:** p. 431 Jupiterimages/Stockbyte, p. 435 Fuse, p. 440 Zoryanchik/iStock, p. 451 AndreySt/iStock, p. 452 Adrian Rosu Savinoiu/iStock, p. 454 Tetra Images, p. 463 Ivan Kmit/iStock.

GREEK, TURKISH, AND MIDDLE EASTERN

age fotostock: p. 476 Funkystock, p. 482 Frederic Vasseur, p. 495 Nico Tondini, p. 499 Bernhard Winkelmann, p. 504 Descordes, p. 506 Studio Adna; **Alamy Images:** p. 474 Art of Food, p. 477 Food Centrale Hamburg GmbH, p. 490 Chronicle, p. 516 Bon Appetit; **fotolia:** p. 480 Teodora_D, p. 487 dimakp, p. 491 dream79, p. 492 Kristina Rutten, p. 505 Ekaterina Lin, p. 509 Laurentiu Iordache, p. 512 nito; **Getty Images:** p. 475 George Tsafos/Lonely Planet Images, p. 479 Shelley Dennis/E+, p. 500 Wendy Maeela/Boston Globe; **Thinkstock Images:** p. 483 MaestroBooks/iStock, p. 486 laperla_foto/iStock, p. 489 vschlichting/iStock, p. 502 Jiri Hera/iStock, p. 511 Ls9907/iStock, p. 513 Paul Brighton/iStock.

AMERICAN AND CANADIAN

age fotostock: p. 520 JT Vintage, p. 536 Michael Cogliantry, p. 557 Elisabeth Calfen, p. 578 Food Image Source, p. 607 Douglas Johns, p. 611 Stockfood LBRF, p. 618 Jeff Greenberg; **Alamy Images:** p. 518 LOOK Die Bildagentur der Fotografen GmbH, p. 523 Kim Karpeles, p. 559 ClassicStock, p. 561 Global Warming Images, p. 563 Cephas Picture Library, p. 565 National Geographic Image Collection, p. 566 Stanley Marquardt, p. 567 Aurora Photos, p. 569 AA World Travel Library, p. 570 George Sheldon, pp. 581, 612 Bon Appetit, p. 641 PureStock; **fotolia:** p. 548 sky_dream, p. 550 azurita, p. 564 Bill, p. 601 Bert Folsom, p. 631 teleginatania, p. 633 Brent Hofacker; **Getty Images:** p. 527 The Power of Forever Photography/E+, p. 533 Stan Honda/AFP, p. 539 Philippe Desnerck/Photolibrary, p. 546 Universal Images Group, p. 554 Brian Hagiwara/Photodisc, p. 576 Ray Kachatorian, p. 582 Hulton Archive/Stringer/Archive Photos, p. 586 Tetra Images, p. 591 Spencer Jones/Stockfood Creative, p. 616 Jamie Grill, p. 645 Illya S. Savenok/Stringer/Getty Images Entertainment; **Thinkstock Images:** p. 530 Maria Brzostowska/iStock, p. 535 ly-ly/iStock, p. 540 Charles Taylor/iStock, p. 544 Jack Puccio/iStock, p. 553 David Lee/iStock, p. 573 ITStock Free/Polka Dot, p. 583 stu99/iStock Editorial, pp. 588, 605 Jupiterimages/Stockbyte, pp. 598, 622 bhofack2/iStock, p. 608 Bozidar Jokanovic/iStock, p. 609 Zoonar RF, p. 614 joephotographer/iStock, p. 619 ginauf/iStock, p. 624 Andrea Skjold/iStock, p. 626 Alexcrab/iStock, p. 628 aruba200/iStock, p. 635 Katherine Welles/iStock, p. 636 Diana Taliun/iStock, p. 638 maratr/iStock, p. 639 Bill Pugliano/Getty Images News, p. 643 Fudio/iStock, p. 646 martiapunts/iStock.

MEXICAN AND LATIN AMERICAN

age fotostock: p. 648 Caggiano Photography, p. 666 Kurt Wilson, p. 668 Matilda Lindeblad, p. 672 DEA/G DAGLI ORTI; **Alamy Images:** p. 651 David R. Frazier Photolibrary, Inc., p. 652 Blend Images, p. 659 Philip Lewis, p. 660 dbimages, p. 676 Gastromedia, p. 677 Mariano Montero, p. 682 Pierre Kapsalis; **fotolia:** p. 649 cobraphoto, p. 658 bit24, p. 674 Paul Brighton; **Getty Images:** p. 679 Hoberman Collection/UIG, p. 680 Noemi Hauser; **Thinkstock Images:** p. 655 atoss/iStock, p. 656 Alexcrab/iStock, p. 661 Wavebreakmedia Ltd/Wavebreak Media, p. 663 Anaja Creatif/iStock, p. 667 John Rodriguez/iStock, p. 669 only_fabrizio/iStock.

CARIBBEAN

age fotostock: p. 689 Bagros; **Alamy Images:** p. 685 Tim Hill, p. 691 Robert Harding World Imagery; **Getty Images:** p. 686 Brian J. Skerry/National Geographic, p. 688 Nigel Noyes/Photographer's Choice, pp. 690, 693 Gusto Images/Photolibrary; **Thinkstock Images:** p. 687 Noppharat05081977/iStock, p. 694 amnachphoto/iStock.

AFRICAN

Adobe Stock: p. 725; **age fotostock:** p. 697 Sarka Babicka, p. 698 Rynio, p. 702 H Bischof, p. 709 Sylvain Grandadam, p. 717 Akiko Ida, p. 721 Jacqui Blanchard Phot, p. 722 Ginet-Drin, p. 728 Dorling Kindersley/UI, p. 731 Tim Hill/UIG, p. 743 Gerard Lacz; **Alamy Images:** p. 707 John Rocha Photo/Egypt, p. 710 Gary Cook, p. 713 (bottom) Bon Appetit, p. 716 Anne-Marie Palmer, p. 723 Image Source, p. 729 Photocuisine, p. 733 Horizons WWP, p. 735 Grant Rooney, p. 737 Food Centrale Hamburg GmbH, p. 744 Geof Kirby; **fotolia:** p. 699 fahrwasser, p. 713 (top) uckyo, p. 726 vanillaechoes; **Getty Images:** p. 715 Gina Sabatella/Photodisc, p. 739 GO!/Sam Reinders/Gallo Images, pp. 741,745 Images of Africa, p. 746 Ray Tamarra/Getty Images Entertainment; **Thinkstock Images:** p. 696 tashka2000/iStock, p. 701 PicturePartners/iStock, p. 705 J ules Kitano/iStock, p. 719 Lesyy/iStock, p. 730 Nono07/iStock, p. 732 Dereje Belachew/iStock, p. 740 Marina Lohrbach/iStock, p. 742 Martynasfoto/iStock.

CHINESE

age fotostock: p. 750 K. Arras, p. 756 (top) Corbis, p. 771 Robyn Mackenzie, p. 775 R. Koenig, p. 779 Oleg Blazhyievskyi, p. 780 Andrew Young, p. 790 Sudres, pp. 793, 797 FoodCollection; **Alamy Images:** p. 752 Horizon Images/Motion, p. 769 Mediablitzimages, p. 784 Laurie Strachan, pp. 785, 796 Bon Appetit, p. 788 EPA European Pressphoto Agency b.v., p. 792 Michael Snell; **fotolia:** p. 751 dreambigphotos, p. 756 (bottom) azurita, p. 773 anankkml, p. 787 Martin Turzak; **Getty Images:** p. 764 Keith Beaty/Toronto Star, p. 778 Graham Day/Photolibrary, p. 789 Brian Hagiwara/Photolibrary; **Thinkstock Images:** p. 748 morningarage/iStock, p. 749 Andrew Furlong Photography/iStock, p. 753 Jupiterimages/Stockbyte, p. 754 sommail/iStock, p. 759 Peng Wu/iStock, p. 761 nosonjai/iStock, p. 767 artpritsadee/iStock, p. 774 sugar0607/iStock, p. 776 Nina Lao/iStock, p. 783 natashamam/iStock, p. 786 Chengyu Zheng/iStock.

JAPANESE AND KOREAN

age fotostock: p. 804 JTB Photo, p. 808 (bottom) Tohru Minowa/a collec, p. 810 Giovanni Mereghetti, p. 813 JTB Photo, p. 822 Jochen Tack/imageBROKER, p. 824 MIXA, p. 830 Topic Photo Agency; **Alamy Images:** p. 801 (top) Amana Images Inc.; **fotolia:** p. 808 (top) TAGSTOCK3, p. 817 fkruger, p. 829 Lianxun Zhang; **Getty Images:** p. 800 whitewish/E+, p. 803 Jerry Driendl/The Image Bank, p. 805 artparadigm/Photodisc, p. 811 MIXA, p. 831 Philip Lewis/Bloomberg; **Thinkstock Images:** p. 801 (bottom) Irfan Nurdiansyah/iStock, p. 807 PinkBadger/iStock, p. 815 ronniechua/iStock, pp. 818–819 sashahaltam/iStock, p. 820 Okea/iStock, p. 826 morningarage/iStock, p. 828 Monkey Business Images, p. 832 Paul Brighton/iStock, p. 833 DAJ, p. 836 Sirichai Thaveesakvilai/iStock.

THAI AND SOUTHEAST ASIAN

age fotostock: p. 842 (bottom) Tim Hill, p. 845 Carnet, p. 857 Philippe Body, p. 859 Grant Rooney; **Alamy Images:** p. 838 Bon Appetit, p. 839 Mim Friday, p. 847 Jack Sullivan, p. 850 Robert Harding World Imagery, pp. 853, 858 Simon Reddy; **fotolia:** p. 843 kungverylucky, p. 852 heinteh; **Getty Images:** p. 844 Robyn Beck/AFP, p. 861 MIXA, p. 862 Brett Stevens/Cultura; **Thinkstock Images:** p. 840 Jag_cz/iStock, p. 842 (top) iSailorr/iStock, p. 848 (top) sripfoto/iStock, p. 848 (bottom) danekalbo/iStock, p. 855 nayneung1/iStock, p. 864 DAJ.

INDIAN

age fotostock: p. 878 Melina Hammer, p. 882 Joerg Lehmann, p. 887 Hemant Mehta; **Alamy Images:** p. 868 David Pearson, p. 874 LENS AND LIGHT/Balan Madhavan, p. 875 Simon Reddy, p. 883 IndiaPicture; **fotolia:** p. 866 vainillaychile, p. 873 tracingtea, p. 888 Arvind Balaraman; **Getty Images:** p. 890 Annie Owen/Robert Harding World Imagery; **Thinkstock Images:** p. 867 Ivenks/iStock, p. 870 SemiSweetStock/iStock, p. 876 zkruger/iStock, p. 877 bonchan/iStock, p. 880 Jultud/iStock, p. 884 graphia76/iStock.

AUSTRALIAN, NEW ZEALAND, AND TAHITIAN

age fotostock: p. 910 Sarka Babicka, p. 911 Peter Cassidy; **Alamy Images:** p. 904 Neil Setchfield, p. 906 Bruce Miller, p. 914 Christine Osborne Pictures; **fotolia:** p. 893 sutsaiy, p. 903 unpict, p. 909 Dmitry Pichugin; **Getty Images:** p. 892 Brendon Thorne/Bloomberg, p. 894 DAJ, p. 913 Sarah Bossert/E+; **Thinkstock Images:** p. 896 Janet Hastings/iStock, p. 898 John Carnemolla/iStock, p. 900 Joey1106/iStock, p. 901 faengsrikum/iStock.